RAPID REVIEW

Kimmel, Weygandt, Kieso
Principles of Accounting

FINANCIAL STATEMENTS

Order of Preparation	Date
1. Income statement	For the period ended
2. Retained earnings statement	For the period ended
3. Balance sheet	As of the end of the period
4. Statement of cash flows	For the period ended

Income Statement (perpetual inventory system)

Name of Company Income Statement For the Period Ended		
Sales revenues		
Sales	$X	
Less: Sales returns and allowances	X	
Sales discounts	X	
Net sales		$X
Cost of goods sold		X
Gross profit		X
Operating expenses		
(Examples: store salaries, advertising, delivery, rent,		
depreciation, utilities, insurance)		X
Income from operations		X
Other revenues and gains		
(Examples: interest, gains)	X	
Other expenses and losses		
(Examples: interest, losses)	X	X
Income before income taxes		X
Income tax expense		X
Net income		$X

Income Statement (periodic inventory system)

Name of Company Income Statement For the Period Ended			
Sales revenues			
Sales		$X	
Less: Sales returns and allowances		X	
Sales discounts		X	
Net sales			$X
Cost of goods sold			
Beginning inventory		X	
Purchases	$X		
Less: Purchase returns and allowances	X		
Net purchases	X		
Add: Freight in	X		
Cost of goods purchased		X	
Cost of goods available for sale		X	
Less: Ending inventory		X	
Cost of goods sold			X
Gross profit			X
Operating expenses			
(Examples: store salaries, advertising, delivery, rent,			
depreciation, utilities, insurance)			X
Income from operations			X
Other revenues and gains			
(Examples: interest, gains)		X	
Other expenses and losses			
(Examples: interest, losses)		X	X
Income before income taxes			X
Income tax expense			X
Net income			$X

Retained Earnings Statement

Name of Company Retained Earnings Statement For the Period Ended	
Retained earnings, beginning of period	$X
Add: Net income (or deduct net loss)	X
	X
Deduct: Dividends	X
Retained earnings, end of period	$X

STOP AND CHECK: Net income (loss) presented on the retained earnings statement must equal the net income (loss) presented on the income statement.

Balance Sheet

Name of Company Balance Sheet As of the End of the Period			
Assets			
Current assets			
(Examples: cash, short-term investments, accounts			
receivable, merchandise inventory, prepaids)			$X
Long-term investments			
(Examples: investments in bonds, investments in stocks)			X
Property, plant, and equipment			
Land		$X	
Buildings and equipment	$X		
Less: Accumulated depreciation	X	X	X
Intangible assets			X
Total assets			$X
Liabilities and Stockholders' Equity			
Liabilities			
Current liabilities			
(Examples: notes payable, accounts payable, accruals,			
unearned revenues, current portion of notes payable)			$X
Long-term liabilities			
(Examples: notes payable, bonds payable)			X
Total liabilities			X
Stockholders' equity			
Common stock			X
Retained earnings			X
Total liabilities and stockholders' equity			$X

STOP AND CHECK: Total assets on the balance sheet must equal total liabilities and stockholders' equity; and, ending retained earnings on the balance sheet must equal ending retained earnings on the retained earnings statement.

Statement of Cash Flows

Name of Company Statement of Cash Flows For the Period Ended	
Cash flows from operating activities	
Note: May be prepared using the direct or indirect method	
Cash provided (used) by operating activities	$X
Cash flows from investing activities	
(Examples: purchase / sale of long-term assets)	
Cash provided (used) by investing activities	X
Cash flows from financing activities	
(Examples: issue / repayment of long-term liabilities,	
issue of stock, payment of dividends)	
Cash provided (used) by financing activities	X
Net increase (decrease) in cash	X
Cash, beginning of the period	X
Cash, end of the period	$X

STOP AND CHECK: Cash, end of the period, on the statement of cash flows must equal cash presented on the balance sheet.

(continued on next page)

RAPID REVIEW

ACCOUNTING CONCEPTS (Chapters 1–4)

Characteristics	Assumptions	Principles	Constraints
Relevance	Monetary unit	Revenue recognition	Materiality
Reliability	Economic entity	Matching	Conservatism
Comparability	Time period	Full disclosure	
Consistency	Going concern	Cost	

BASIC ACCOUNTING EQUATION (Chapter 3)

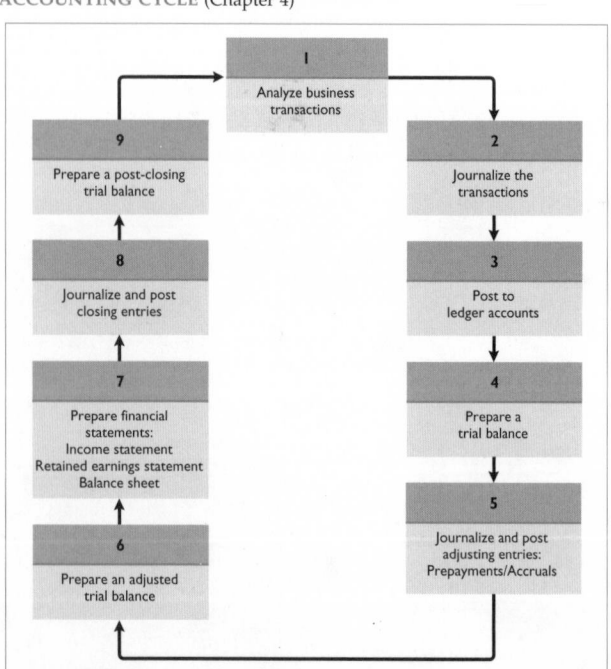

Basic Equation	Assets = Liabilities +	Stockholders' Equity
Expanded Basic Equation	Assets = Liabilities + Common Stock + Retained Earnings − Dividends + Revenues − Expenses	
Debit / Credit Rules		

ADJUSTING ENTRIES (Chapter 4)

	Type		Adjusting Entry	
Prepayments	1. Prepaid expenses		Dr. Expenses	Cr. Assets
	2. Unearned revenues		Dr. Liabilities	Cr. Revenues
Accruals	1. Accrued revenues		Dr. Assets	Cr. Revenues
	2. Accrued expenses		Dr. Expenses	Cr. Liabilities

Note: Each adjusting entry will affect one or more income statement accounts and one or more balance sheet accounts.

Interest Computation

Interest = Face value of note $\times$ Annual interest rate $\times$ Time in terms of one year

CLOSING ENTRIES (Chapter 4)

Purpose

1. Update the Retained Earnings account in the ledger by transferring net income (loss) and dividends to retained earnings.
2. Prepare the temporary accounts (revenue, expense, dividends) for the next period's postings by reducing their balances to zero.

ACCOUNTING CYCLE (Chapter 4)

1 Analyze business transactions

2 Journalize the transactions

3 Post to ledger accounts

4 Prepare a trial balance

5 Journalize and post adjusting entries: Prepayments/Accruals

6 Prepare an adjusted trial balance

7 Prepare financial statements: Income statement Retained earnings statement Balance sheet

8 Journalize and post closing entries

9 Prepare a post-closing trial balance

INVENTORY (Chapters 5 and 6)

Ownership

Freight Terms	Ownership of goods on public carrier resides with:
FOB Shipping point	Buyer
FOB Destination	Seller

Perpetual vs. Periodic Journal Entries

Event	Perpetual	Periodic

Purchase of goods	Inventory
	  Cash (A/P)
		Purchases
		  Cash (A/P)

Freight (shipping point)	Inventory
	  Cash
		Freight In
		  Cash

Return of goods	Cash (or A/P)
	  Inventory
		Cash (or A/P)
		  Purchase Returns and Allowances

Sale of goods	Cash (or A/R)
	  Sales
	Cost of Goods Sold
	  Inventory
		Cash (or A/R)
		  Sales
		No entry

End of period	No entry	Closing or adjusting entry required

CASH (Chapter 7)

Principles of Internal Control

Establishment of responsibility
Segregation of duties
Documentation procedures
Physical, mechanical, and electronic controls
Independent internal verification
Other controls

Bank Reconciliation

Bank	Books
Balance per bank statement	Balance per books
Add: Deposits in transit	Add: Unrecorded credit memoranda from bank statement
Deduct: Outstanding checks	Deduct: Unrecorded debit memoranda from bank statement
Adjusted cash balance	Adjusted cash balance

Note: 1. Errors should be offset (added or deducted) on the side that made the error.
2. Adjusting journal entries should only be made on the books.

STOP AND CHECK: Does the adjusted cash balance in the Cash account equal the reconciled balance?

(continued at back of book)

eGrade Plus
with EduGen
www.wiley.com/college/kimmel
Based on the Activities You Do Every Day

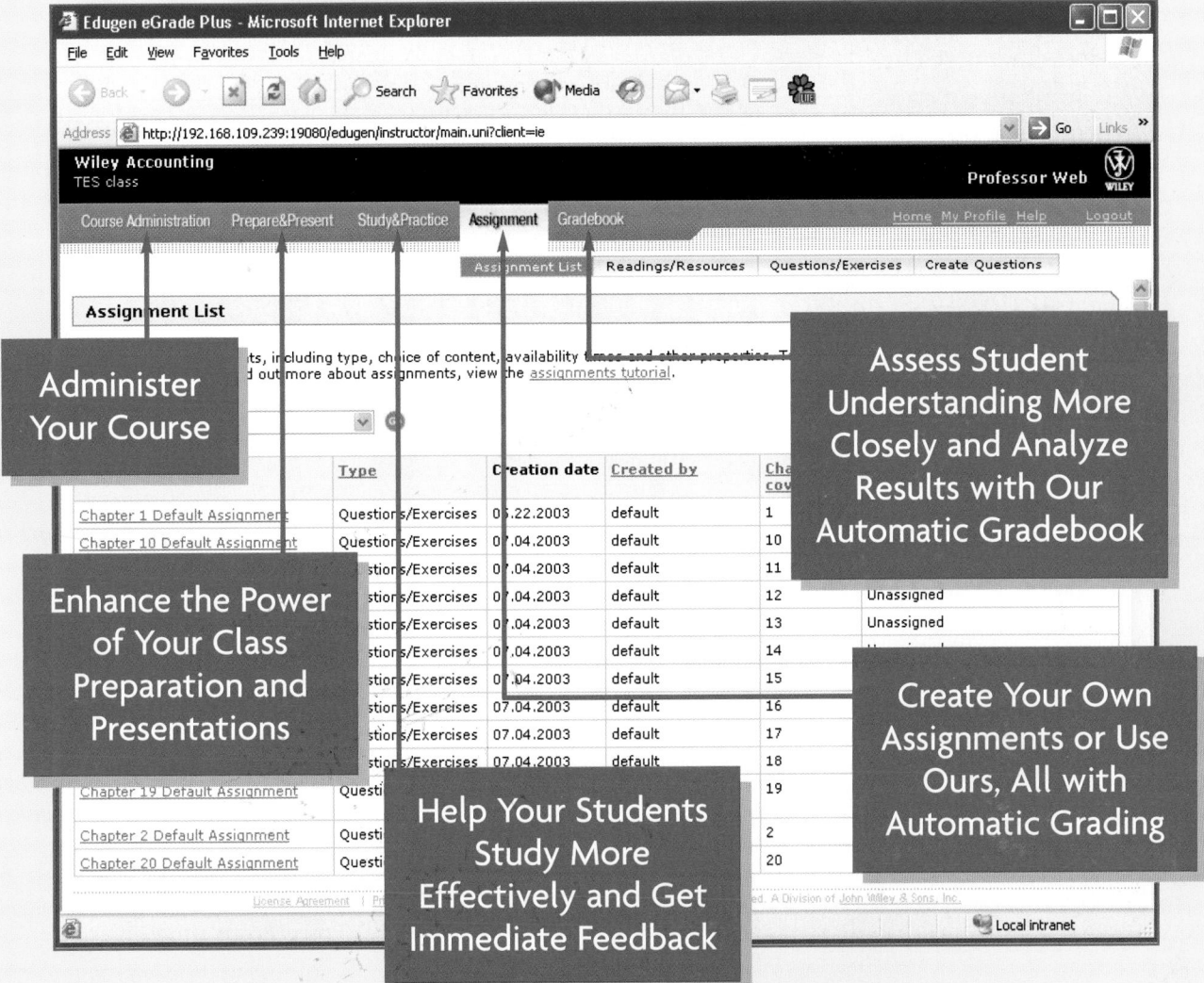

Administer Your Course

Enhance the Power of Your Class Preparation and Presentations

Help Your Students Study More Effectively and Get Immediate Feedback

Assess Student Understanding More Closely and Analyze Results with Our Automatic Gradebook

Create Your Own Assignments or Use Ours, All with Automatic Grading

All the content and tools you need, all in one location, in an easy-to-use browser format.
Choose the resources you need, or rely on the arrangement supplied by us.

Now, many of Wiley's Book Companion Sites are available with EduGen, allowing you to create your own teaching and learning environment. Upon adoption of EduGen, you can begin to customize your course with the resources shown here. eGrade Plus with EduGen integrates text and media and keeps all of a book's online resources in one easily accessible location. eGrade Plus integrates two resources: homework problems for students and a multimedia version of this Wiley text. With eGrade Plus, each problem is linked to the relevant section of the multimedia book.

Administer Your Course

Course Administration tools allow you to manage your class and integrate your Wiley website resources with most Course Management Systems, allowing you to keep all of your class materials in one location.

Enhance the Power of Your Class Preparation and Presentations

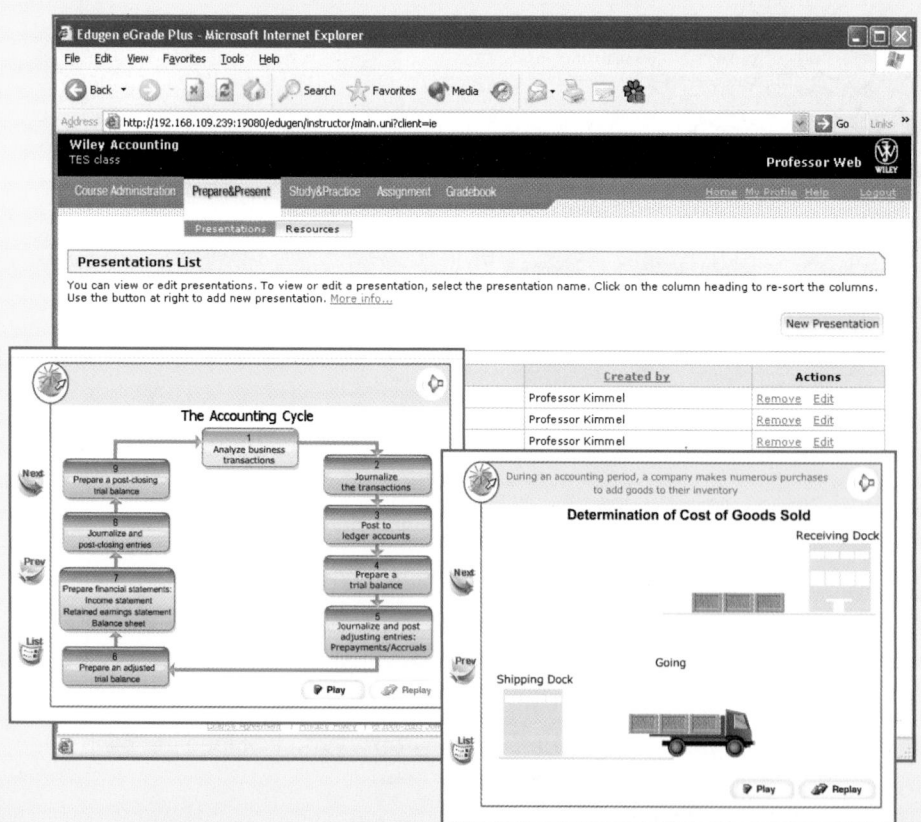

A **"Prepare and Present" tool** contains all of the Wiley-provided resources, such as **a multimedia version of the text, interactive chapter reviews, web-based tutorials, videos,** and **PowerPoint slides,** making your preparation time more efficient. You may easily adapt, customize, and add to Wiley content to meet the needs of your course.

Create Your Own Assignments or Use Ours, All with Automatic Grading

An **"Assignment"** area allows you to create **student homework** and **quizzes** that utilize **Wiley-provided question banks,** and an **electronic version of the text.** One of the most powerful features of Wiley's premium websites is that student assignments will be automatically graded and recorded in your gradebook. This will not only save you time but will provide your students with immediate feedback on their work.

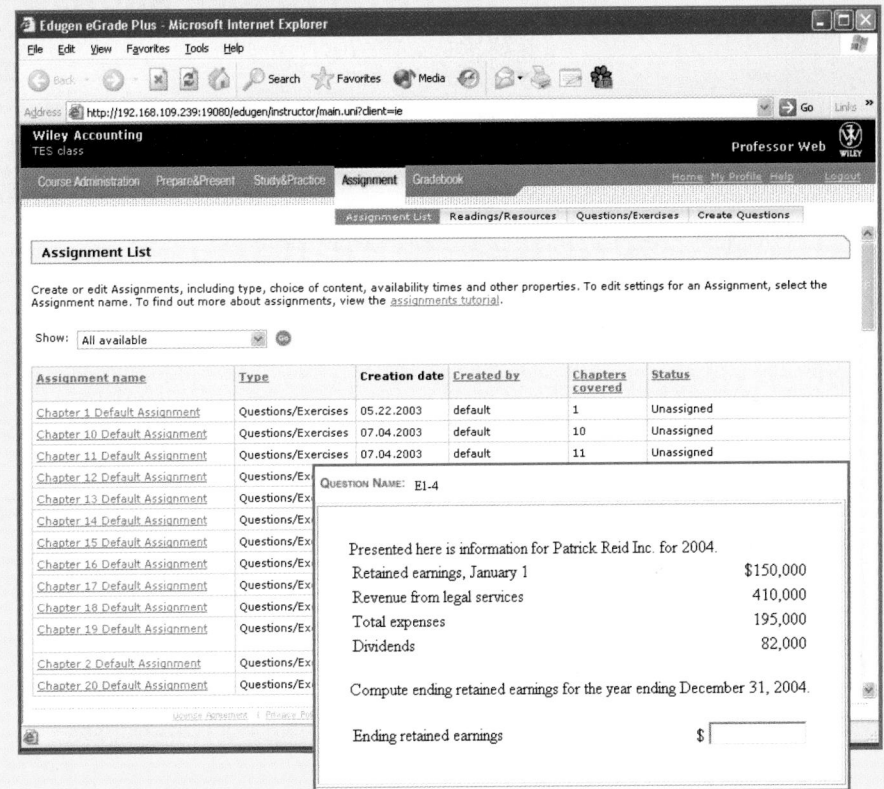

Assess Student Understanding More Closely

An **Instructor's Gradebook** will keep track of your students' progress and allow you to analyze individual and overall class results to determine their progress and level of understanding.

Students,
eGrade Plus with EduGen Allows You to:

Study More Effectively

Get Immediate Feedback When You Practice on Your Own

Our website links directly to **electronic book content,** so that you can review the text while you study and complete homework online. Additional resources include **interactive chapter reviews, web-based tutorials,** and **self-assessment quizzing.**

Complete Assignments / Get Help with Problem Solving

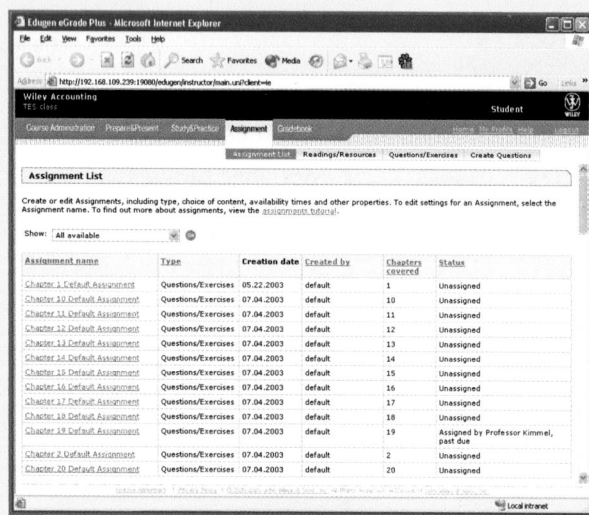

An **"Assignment"** area keeps all your assigned work in one location, making it easy for you to stay on task. In addition, many homework problems contain a **link** to the relevant section of the **electronic book,** providing you with a text explanation to help you conquer problem-solving obstacles as they arise.

Keep Track of How You're Doing

A **Personal Gradebook** allows you to view your results from past assignments at any time.

Principles of Accounting

Tools for Business Decision Making

PAUL D. KIMMEL, PHD, CPA
Associate Professor of Accounting
University of Wisconsin—Milwaukee

JERRY J. WEYGANDT, PHD, CPA
Arthur Andersen Professor of Accounting
University of Wisconsin

DONALD E. KIESO, PHD, CPA
KPMG Emeritus Professor of Accountancy
Northern Illinois University

JOHN WILEY & SONS, INC.
WILEY

Dedicated to
our parents and our in-laws,
and to our families,
most especially our spouses,
Merlynn
Enid
Donna

PUBLISHER: Susan Elbe
EXECUTIVE EDITOR: Jay O'Callaghan
SENIOR DEVELOPMENT EDITOR: Nancy Perry
MARKETING MANAGER: Steven Herdegen
OUTSIDE DEVELOPMENT EDITOR: Ann Torbert
ASSOCIATE EDITOR: Ed Brislin
MEDIA EDITOR: Allison Keim
PRODUCTION SERVICES MANAGER: Jeanine Furino
SENIOR PRODUCTION EDITOR: Norine Pigliucci
TEXT DESIGNER: Dawn L. Stanley
ILLUSTRATION EDITOR: Sandra Rigby
PRODUCTION MANAGEMENT SERVICES: Ingrao Associates
PHOTO EDITOR: Sara Wight
COVER PHOTO: ©Dave Schiefelbein/The Image Bank/Getty Images

This book was set in New Aster by TECHBOOKS and printed and bound by Von Hoffmann. The cover was printed by Von Hoffmann.

This book is printed on acid-free paper. ∞

Library of Congress Cataloging-in-Publication Data

Kimmel, Paul D.
   Principles of accounting: tools for business decision making/Paul D. Kimmel, Jerry J. Weygandt, Donald E. Kieso.
      p. cm.
   Various multi-media instructional aids are available to supplement the text.
   Includes index.
   ISBN 0-471-40133-1 (cloth)
   1. Accounting. I. Kieso, Donald E. II. Kimmel, Paul D. III. Title.
   HF5635.W5243 2003
   657—dc22

                                                                    2003057076

The specimen financial statements in Appendix A are reprinted with permission from the Tootsie Roll Industries, Inc. 2002 Annual Report. © Tootsie Roll Industries, Inc. The specimen financial statements in Appendix B are reprinted with permission from the Hershey Foods Corporation 2002 Consolidated Financial Statements and Management's Discussion and Analysis. © Hershey Foods Corporation.

ISBN 0-471-40133-1
WIE ISBN 0-471-45185-1
Printed in the United States of America

10 9 8 7 6 5 4 3 2 1

Paul D. Kimmel, PhD, CPA, received his bachelor's degree from the University of Minnesota and his doctorate in accounting from the University of Wisconsin. He is an Associate Professor at the University of Wisconsin—Milwaukee, and has public accounting experience with Deloitte & Touche (Minneapolis). He was the recipient of the UWM School of Business Advisory Council Teaching Award and the Reggie Taite Excellence in Teaching Award, and is a three-time winner of the Outstanding Teaching Assistant Award at the University of Wisconsin. He is also a recipient of the Elijah Watts Sells Award for Honorary Distinction for his results on the CPA exam. He is a member of the American Accounting Association and has published articles in *Accounting Review, Accounting Horizons, Advances in Management Accounting, Managerial Finance, Issues in Accounting Education, Journal of Accounting Education,* as well as other journals. His research interests include accounting for financial instruments and innovation in accounting education. He has published papers and given numerous talks on incorporating critical thinking into accounting education, and helped prepare a catalog of critical thinking resources for the Federated Schools of Accountancy.

Jerry J. Weygandt, PhD, CPA, is Arthur Andersen Alumni Professor of Accounting at the University of Wisconsin-Madison. He holds a Ph.D. in accounting from the University of Illinois. Articles by Professor Weygandt have appeared in the *Accounting Review, Journal of Accounting Research, Accounting Horizons, Journal of Accountancy,* and other academic and professional journals. These articles have examined such financial reporting issues as accounting for price-level adjustments, pensions, convertible securities, stock option contracts, and interim reports. Professor Weygandt is author of other accounting and financial reporting books and is a member of the American Accounting Association, the American Institute of Certified Public Accountants, and the Wisconsin Society of Certified Public Accountants. He has served on numerous committees of the American Accounting Association and as a member of the editorial board of the *Accounting Review;* he also has served as President and Secretary-Treasurer of the American Accounting Association. In addition, he has been actively involved with the American Institute of Certified Public Accountants and has been a member of the Accounting Standards Executive Committee (AcSEC) of that organization. He has served on the FASB task force that examined the reporting issues related to accounting for income taxes and is presently a trustee of the Financial Accounting Foundation. Professor Weygandt has received the Chancellor's Award for Excellence in Teaching and the Beta Gamma Sigma Dean's Teaching Award. He is on the board of directors of M & I Bank of Southern Wisconsin and the Dean Foundation. He is the recipient of the Wisconsin Institute of CPA's Outstanding Educator's Award and the Lifetime Achievement Award. In 2001 he received the American Accounting Association's Outstanding Accounting Educator Award.

Donald E. Kieso, PhD, CPA, received his bachelor's degree from Aurora University and his doctorate in accounting from the University of Illinois. He has served as chairman of the Department of Accountancy and is currently KPMG Emeritus Professor of Accountancy at Northern Illinois University. He has public accounting experience with Price Waterhouse & Co. (San Francisco and Chicago) and Arthur Andersen & Co. (Chicago) and research experience with the Research Division of the American Institute of Certified Public Accountants (New York). He has done postdoctorate work as a Visiting Scholar at the University of California at Berkeley and is a recipient of NIU's Teaching Excellence Award and four Golden Apple Teaching Awards. Professor Kieso is the author of numerous other accounting and business books and is a member of the American Accounting Association, the American Institute of Certified Public Accountants, and the Illinois CPA Society. He has served as a member of the Board of Directors of the Illinois CPA Society, the AACSB's Accounting Accreditation Committees, the State of Illinois Comptroller's Commission, as Secretary-Treasurer of the Federation of Schools of Accountancy, as Secretary-Treasurer of the American Accounting Association and on several corporate boards. Professor Kieso is currently serving on the Board of Trustees and Executive Committee of Aurora University, and as a member of the Boards of Directors of Kishwaukee Community Hospital and Valley West Community Hospital. He served as a charter member of the national Accounting Education Change Commission. He is the recipient of the Outstanding Accounting Educator Award from the Illinois CPA Society, the FSA's Joseph A. Silvoso Award of Merit, and the NIU Foundation's Humanitarian Award for Service to Higher Education.

The goal of this text is to introduce students to accounting in a way that demonstrates the importance of accounting to society and the relevance of accounting to their future careers. We strive to teach students those things that they really need to know and to do it in a way that maximizes their opportunities for successful completion of the course. To accomplish these goals, the foundation of this text relies on a few key beliefs.

"It really matters." The failures of Enron, WorldCom, Arthur Andersen, and others has had devastating consequences. Our Business Insight—Ethics Perspective boxes, Ethics cases, video clips on the CD, and a number of our Feature Stories and Research Cases are designed to reveal accounting's critical role to society. In short, it has never been more clear that accounting really matters.

"Less is More." Our instructional objective is to provide students with an understanding of those core concepts that are fundamental to the use of accounting. Most students will forget procedural details within a short period of time. On the other hand, concepts, if well taught, should be remembered for a lifetime. Concepts are especially important in a world where the details are constantly changing.

Decision Checkpoints

"Don't just sit there—do something." The overriding pedagogical objective of this book is to provide students with continual opportunities for active learning. One of the best tools for active learning is strategically placed questions. Our discussions are framed by questions, often beginning with rhetorical questions and ending with review questions. Even our selection of analytical devices, called Decision Toolkits, uses key questions to demonstrate the purpose of each.

"I'll believe it when I see it." This text employs a "macro" approach in its first two chapters. That is, rather than start by showing how to record transactions, we instead use the first two chapters to teach students how to understand and use the real financial statements of **Tootsie Roll**, **Hershey**, and **Best Buy**. Many students determine their opinion of a course during the initial weeks. Students will be most willing to commit time and energy to a topic when they believe that it is relevant to their future career. By employing this macro approach, we clearly demonstrate the relevance of accounting during the period that students are forming their impression of the course.

"You need to make a decision." All business people must make decisions. Decision making involves critical evaluation and analysis of the information at hand, and this takes practice. We have integrated important analytical tools throughout the book. After each new decision tool is presented, we summarize the key features of that tool in a Decision Toolkit. At the end of each chapter, we provide a comprehensive demonstration of an analysis of a real company using the decision tools presented in the chapter.

"It's a small world." The Internet has made it possible for even small businesses to sell their products virtually anywhere in the world. Few business decisions can be made without consideration of international factors. To heighten student awareness of international issues, we have many references to international companies and issues and provide A Global Focus exercise in each of the financial accounting chapters.

TOOLS FOR STUDENT SUCCESS

Principles of Accounting provides many proven pedagogical tools to help students learn accounting concepts and apply them to decision making in the business world. This pedagogical framework emphasizes the *processes* students undergo as they learn. Turn to the **Student Owner's Manual** on page xx to see all the learning tools of the book in detail. Here are a few key features.

Learning How to Use the Text

- The **Student Owner's Manual**, p. xx, and notes in red in Chapter 1, explain to students how to take advantage of the text's learning tools to help achieve success in the course.

- A **Learning Styles Quiz**, p. xxix, includes tips on in-class and at-home learning strategies.

- **The Navigator** guides students through each chapter by pulling all the learning tools together into a learning system. Throughout the chapter, **The Navigator** prompts students to use the learning aids and to set priorities as they study.

Understanding the Context

- **Study Objectives**, listed at the beginning of each chapter, reappear in the margins and again in the **Summary of Study Objectives**.

- A **Feature Story** helps students picture how the chapter topic relates to the real world of accounting and business and serves as a recurrent example.

- A **Chapter Preview** links the Feature Story to the major topics of the chapter and provides a road map to the chapter.

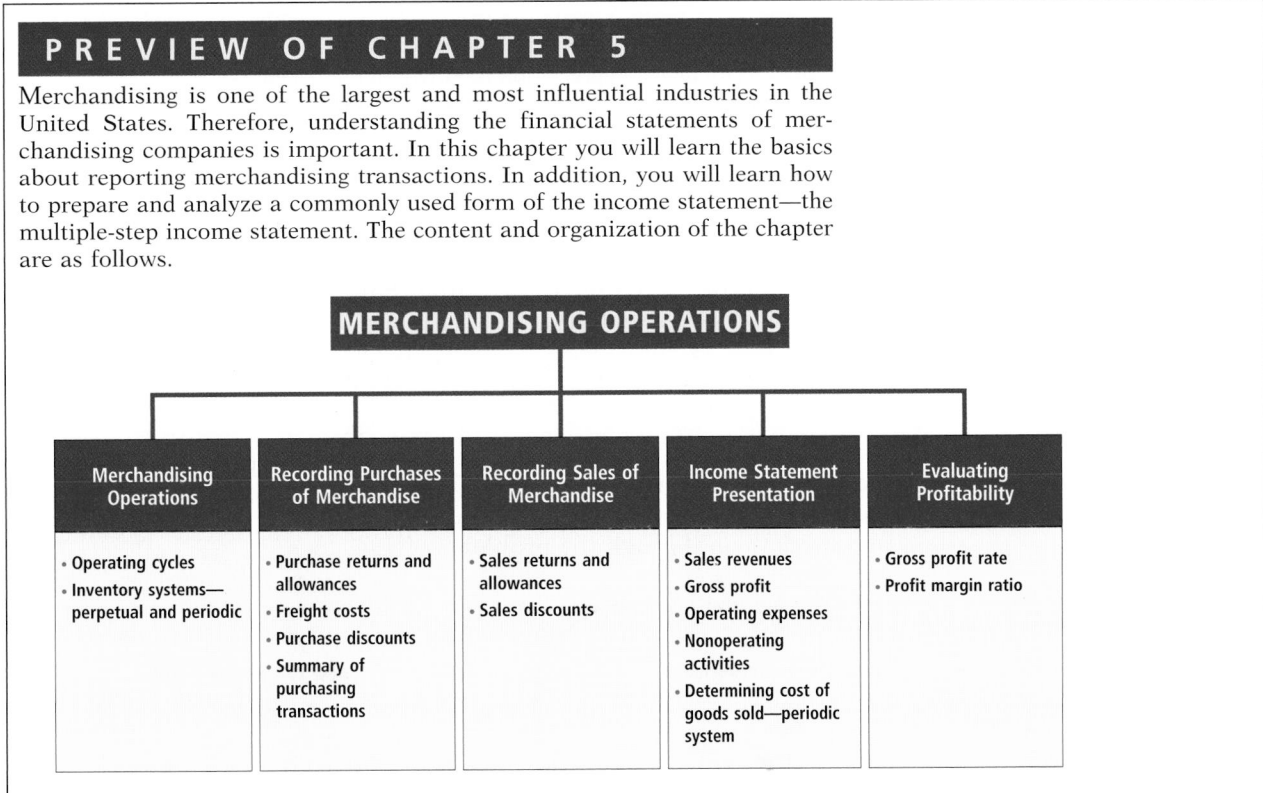

PREVIEW OF CHAPTER 5

Merchandising is one of the largest and most influential industries in the United States. Therefore, understanding the financial statements of merchandising companies is important. In this chapter you will learn the basics about reporting merchandising transactions. In addition, you will learn how to prepare and analyze a commonly used form of the income statement—the multiple-step income statement. The content and organization of the chapter are as follows.

MERCHANDISING OPERATIONS

Merchandising Operations	Recording Purchases of Merchandise	Recording Sales of Merchandise	Income Statement Presentation	Evaluating Profitability
• Operating cycles • Inventory systems—perpetual and periodic	• Purchase returns and allowances • Freight costs • Purchase discounts • Summary of purchasing transactions	• Sales returns and allowances • Sales discounts	• Sales revenues • Gross profit • Operating expenses • Nonoperating activities • Determining cost of goods sold—periodic system	• Gross profit rate • Profit margin ratio

TOOLS FOR STUDENT SUCCESS

Learning the Material

- Emphasis on accounting experiences of **real companies and business situations throughout**.

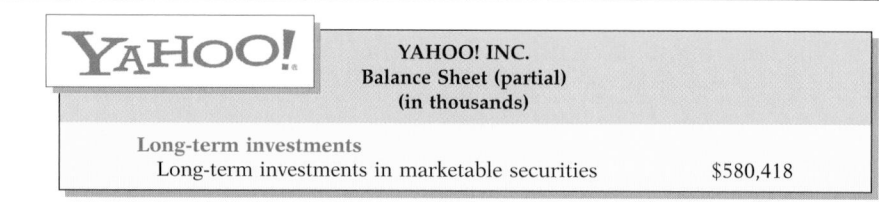

YAHOO! INC. Balance Sheet (partial) (in thousands)	
Long-term investments	
Long-term investments in marketable securities	$580,418

- Four types of **Business Insight** boxes give students glimpses into how real companies make decisions using accounting information.
- **Color illustrations**, including **Infographics**, help students visualize and apply accounting concepts to the real world.
- **Before You Go On** sections provide learning checks (**Review It**) and mini demonstration problems (**Do It**). Questions marked with the **Tootsie Roll** send students to find information in Tootsie Roll's 2002 annual report that is both printed in and packaged with the book.

BEFORE YOU GO ON . . .

 Review It

1. What are the major sections in a classified balance sheet?
2. What is the primary determining factor to distinguish current assets from long-term assets?
3. What was Tootsie Roll's largest current asset at December 31, 2002? The answer to this question is provided on page 100.
4. Where is accumulated depreciation reported on the balance sheet?

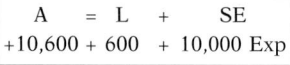

A	=	L	+	SE
+10,600		+ 600		+ 10,000 Exp

Cash Flows

- **Accounting Equation analyses** in the margin next to key journal entries reinforce understanding of the impact of an accounting transaction on the financial statements. They report the **cash effect** of each transaction to reinforce understanding of the difference between cash effects and accrual accounting.
- **Helpful Hints, Alternative Terminology**, and highlighted **Key terms and concepts** help focus students on key concepts as they study the material.
- **International Notes** provide a convenient way to expose students to international issues.
- **Decision tools** useful for analyzing and solving business problems are presented and then summarized in **Decision Toolkits**. A **Using the Decision Toolkit** exercise asks students to use the decision tools presented in the chapter and takes them through the problem-solving steps.

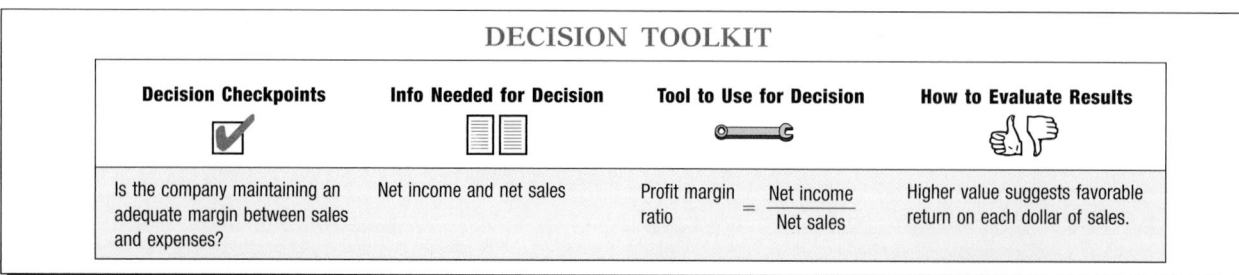

DECISION TOOLKIT

Decision Checkpoints	Info Needed for Decision	Tool to Use for Decision	How to Evaluate Results
Is the company maintaining an adequate margin between sales and expenses?	Net income and net sales	Profit margin ratio $=$ $\dfrac{\text{Net income}}{\text{Net sales}}$	Higher value suggests favorable return on each dollar of sales.

TOOLS FOR STUDENT SUCCESS

Putting It Together

At the end of each chapter are several features useful for review and reference.

- A **Summary of Study Objectives** reviews the main points of the chapter.
- The **Decision Toolkit—A Summary** presents in one place the decision tools used throughout the chapter.
- A **Glossary** of key terms gives definitions with page references to the text.
- A **Demonstration Problem** with an **Action Plan** gives students another opportunity to refer to a detailed solution to a representative problem before they do homework assignments.

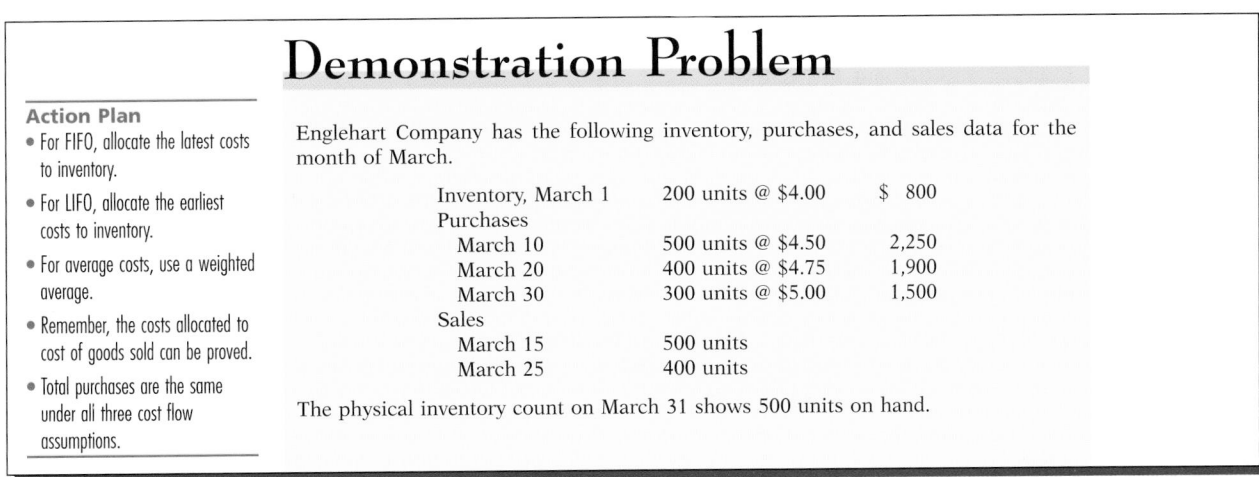

Action Plan
- For FIFO, allocate the latest costs to inventory.
- For LIFO, allocate the earliest costs to inventory.
- For average costs, use a weighted average.
- Remember, the costs allocated to cost of goods sold can be proved.
- Total purchases are the same under all three cost flow assumptions.

Demonstration Problem

Englehart Company has the following inventory, purchases, and sales data for the month of March.

Inventory, March 1	200 units @ $4.00	$ 800
Purchases		
March 10	500 units @ $4.50	2,250
March 20	400 units @ $4.75	1,900
March 30	300 units @ $5.00	1,500
Sales		
March 15	500 units	
March 25	400 units	

The physical inventory count on March 31 shows 500 units on hand.

Developing Skills Through Practice

Each chapter is supported by a full complement of homework material. **Self-Study Questions**, **Questions**, **Brief Exercises**, **Exercises**, and two sets of **Problems** are all keyed to the Study Objectives. In addition,

- Certain Questions, Exercises and Problems make use of the decision tools presented in the chapter. These are marked with the ⚲ icon.
- Certain Exercises and Problems can be solved using the **Excel** and **Peachtree** supplements that are available to accompany the text and are identified by these icons.
- Others can be solved with the **General Ledger Software** available with the text and are marked with this icon.

TOOLS FOR STUDENT SUCCESS

Expanding and Applying Knowledge

Broadening Your Perspective is a unique section at the end of each chapter that offers a wealth of resources for those instructors who want to broaden the learning experience by bringing in more real-world decision making, analysis, and critical-thinking activities.

▶ **BROADENING YOUR PERSPECTIVE**

Financial Reporting and Analysis

FINANCIAL REPORTING PROBLEM: *Tootsie Roll Industries, Inc.*

BYP1-1   Simplified 2002 financial statements of **Tootsie Roll Industries, Inc.** are given in Illustrations 1-11 through 1-14.

Instructions
Refer to Tootsie Roll's financial statements to answer the following questions.
   (a) What were Tootsie Roll's total assets at December 31, 2002? At December 31, 2001?

In the Financial Accounting chapters—

- A **Financial Reporting Problem** directs students to study various aspects of the financial statements of **Tootsie Roll Industries, Inc.**, which are printed in Chapter 1 (in simplified form) and in Appendix A (in full).

- A **Comparative Analysis Problem** offers the opportunity to compare and contrast the financial reporting of **Tootsie Roll Industries, Inc.**, with a competitor **Hershey Foods Corporation.**

- **Interpreting Financial Statements** problems offer minicases that ask students to read parts of financial statements of actual companies and use the decision tools of the chapter to interpret them.

- A **Global Focus** problem asks students to apply concepts presented in the chapter to specific situations faced by actual international companies.

In the Managerial Accounting chapters—

- **Managerial Analysis** assignments build analytical and decision-making skills in situations encountered by managers.

- **Real-World Focus** problems ask students to apply techniques and concepts presented in the chapter to specific situations faced by actual companies.

Throughout the book—

- **Research Cases** direct students to the *Wall Street Journal* and other business periodicals for further study and analysis of key topics.

- **Group Decision Cases** help promote group collaboration and build decision-making and business communication skills by requiring teams of students to evaluate a manager's decision.

- **Financial Analysis on the Web** problems guide students to Web sites from which they can mine and analyze information related to the chapter topic.

- **Communication Activities** provide practice in written communication, a skill much in demand among employers.

- **Ethics Cases** ask students to analyze situations, identify the ethical issues involved, and decide on an appropriate course of action.

Key Features of Each Chapter

CHAPTER 1, Introduction to Financial Statements

- Explains the purpose of each financial statement.
- Uses financial statements of a hypothetical company (to keep it simple), followed by those for a real company, Tootsie Roll Industries (to make it relevant).
- Presents accounting assumptions and principles.

CHAPTER 2, A Further Look at Financial Statements

- Discusses revenues, expenses, assets, and liabilities.
- Presents the classified balance sheet.
- Applies ratio analysis to real companies—Best Buy and Circuit City (current ratio, debt to total assets, earnings per share, price-earnings ratio, current cash debt coverage, and cash debt coverage).

CHAPTER 3, The Accounting Information System

- Covers transaction analysis—emphasizes fundamentals while avoiding unnecessary detail.

CHAPTER 4, Accrual Accounting Concepts

- Emphasizes difference between cash and accrual accounting.
- Discusses how some companies manage earnings through accrual practices.
- Presents minimal discussion of closing and work sheets; provides additional detail in an appendix.

CHAPTER 5, Merchandising Operations and the Multiple-Step Income Statement

- Introduces merchandising concepts using perpetual inventory approach.
- Presents the multiple-step income statement.
- Applies ratio analysis to real companies—Target and Wal-Mart (gross profit rate and profit margin ratio).
- In an appendix, introduces the periodic inventory approach and compares it to perpetual.

CHAPTER 6, Reporting and Analyzing Inventory

- Covers cost flow assumptions and their implications for financial reporting. For simplification, emphasizes the periodic approach. Cost flow assumptions under perpetual inventory systems covered in an appendix.
- Applies ratio analysis to real companies—Target and Wal-Mart (inventory turnover).
- Discusses implications of LIFO reserve for real company—Caterpillar Inc.

CHAPTER 7, Internal Control and Cash

- Covers internal control concepts and implications of control failures.
- Presents bank reconciliation as a control device.
- Discusses cash management, including operating cycle and cash budgeting.

CHAPTER 8, Reporting and Analyzing Receivables

- Presents the basics of accounts and notes receivable, bad debt estimation, and interest calculations.
- Discusses receivables management, including determining to whom to extend credit; establishing payment period; monitoring collections; evaluating the receivables balance; and accelerating receipts.
- Applies ratio analysis to a real company—McKesson (receivables turnover).

CHAPTER 9, Reporting and Analyzing Long-Lived Assets

- Covers the basics of plant assets and intangible assets.
- Discusses basics of buy or lease decision.
- Covers the implications of depreciation method choice; shows details of accelerated methods in appendix.
- Applies ratio analysis to real companies—Southwest Airlines and AirTran (asset turnover and return on assets).
- Demonstrates implications of estimated useful life for intangible amortization.
- Includes a discussion of statement of cash flows presentation of fixed-asset transactions.

CHAPTER 10, Reporting and Analyzing Liabilities

- Covers current liabilities: notes payable, sales taxes, payroll, unearned revenues, and current maturities of long-term debt.
- Covers long-term liabilities, bond pricing, and various types of bonds.
- Straight-line amortization and effective interest method covered in an appendix.
- Includes present value discussion in an appendix at the back of the book.
- Discusses basics of contingent liabilities, lease obligations, and off-balance-sheet financing.
- Applies ratio analysis to real companies—Ford and General Motors (current ratio, debt to total assets ratio, and times interest earned).
- Includes a discussion of statement of cash flows presentation of debt transactions.

CHAPTER 11, Reporting and Analyzing Stockholders' Equity

- Presents pros and cons of corporate form of organization.
- Covers issues related to common and preferred stock, and reasons companies purchase treasury stock.
- Explains reasons for cash dividends, stock dividends, and stock splits and implications for analysis.
- Discusses debt versus equity choice.
- Applies ratio analysis to real companies—Nike and Reebok (return on common stockholders' equity, payout ratio).

- Includes a discussion of statement of cash flows presentation of equity transactions.

CHAPTER 12, Reporting and Analyzing Investments

- Explains why companies purchase investments.
- Presents alternative methods of accounting for investments.
- Discusses consolidation accounting at conceptual level.
- Analyzes implications of unrealized gains and losses of real company—**KeyCorp.**

CHAPTER 13, Statement of Cash Flows

- Explains purpose and usefulness of statement of cash flows.
- Splits chapter into two sections, allowing instructor to use either the indirect approach, the direct approach, or both.
- Applies ratio analysis to real companies—**Microsoft**, **Oracle**, **AMD**, and **Intel** (free cash flow, current cash debt coverage ratio and cash debt coverage ratio).

CHAPTER 14, Financial Statement Analysis

- Capstone chapter—reinforces previous analytical tools and demonstrates their interrelationships, as well as presents new tools.
- Discusses "sustainable income" and implications of discontinued operations, extraordinary items, accounting changes, nonrecurring charges, and comprehensive earnings.
- Demonstrates horizontal and vertical analysis of **Kellogg**.
- Discusses factors that affect the quality of earnings.
- In an appendix, applies comprehensive ratio analysis to real companies—**Kellogg** and **General Mills.**

CHAPTER 15, Managerial Accounting

- Compares and contrasts managerial accounting with financial accounting.
- Identifies three broad functions of management.
- Defines three classes of manufacturing costs.
- Distinguishes between product costs and period costs.
- Presents costs of goods manufactured section of income statement.
- Presents overview of trends in managerial accounting including shift toward service industries, value chain management, enterprise resource planning, just-in-time inventory, and activity-based costing.

CHAPTER 16, Job Order Cost Accounting

- Provides overview of cost accounting systems.
- Illustrates flow of costs in a job order cost system.
- Presents use of job cost sheet.
- Demonstrates use of predetermined overhead rate.

- Illustrates basic entries for job order cost system.
- Provides simple presentation of overapplied and underapplied overhead.

CHAPTER 17, Process Cost Accounting

- Explains the difference between job order and process costing systems.
- Illustrates the flow of costs and end-of-period accounting procedures for process costing.
- Demonstrates computation of physical units of production, equivalent units of production, and unit costs.
- Shows how to assign costs to units of output and prepare a production cost report.
- Contrasts activity-based costing (ABC) to traditional costing systems.
- Identifies numerous activities, activity cost pools, and cost drivers.
- Discusses implications of value-added and non-value added activities.
- Illustrates use of ABC in service industries.
- Reviews the benefits and limitations of ABC.
- Illustrates use of just-in-time inventory systems.
- Appendix illustrates application of ABC.

CHAPTER 18, Cost-Volume-Profit Relationships

- Distinguishes between variable and fixed costs, and explains relevant range and mixed costs.
- Identifies components and assumptions of CVP analysis.
- Discusses concept of contribution margin.
- Illustrates calculation of break-even point.
- Discusses margin of safety and target net income.
- Illustrates CVP income statement.
- Appendix presents variable and absorption costing.

CHAPTER 19, Budgetary Planning

- Discusses benefits of budgeting.
- Illustrates the process of assembling information for a master budget.
- Prepares budgeted income statement, balance sheet, and cash budget.
- Discusses use of budgets in merchandising, service, and not-for-profit enterprises.

CHAPTER 20, Budgetary Control and Responsibility Accounting

- Explains how budgets are used to control costs and operations.
- Contrasts static budgets and flexible budgets.
- Uses a case study to illustrate usefulness of flexible budgets.
- Illustrates responsibility reporting systems.
- Defines cost centers, profit centers, and investment centers.

- Illustrates the computation and use of return on investment and (in a chapter appendix) residual income.

CHAPTER 21, Performance Evaluation Through Standard Costs

- Differentiates between a standard and a budget.
- Discusses advantages of standard costs and methods of computing.
- Illustrates computation of direct materials variance, direct labor variance, and manufacturing overhead variance.
- Demonstrates analysis through comparison of actual with standard.
- Appendix illustrates the journal entries for a standard cost system.

CHAPTER 22, Incremental Analysis and Capital Budgeting

- Explains the concepts of relevant cost, opportunity cost, and sunk cost.
- Applies incremental analysis in the following decision settings:
  - Accepts an order at a special price
  - Make or buy
  - Sell or process further, including discussion of joint costs
  - Retain or replace equipment
  - Eliminate an unprofitable segment
- Describes and illustrates four methods of evaluating capital expenditures:
  - Cash payback technique
  - Net present value method
  - Internal rate of return method
  - Annual rate of return technique

Active Teaching and Learning Supplementary Material

Principles of Accounting *features a full line of teaching and learning resources. Driven by the same basic beliefs as the textbook, these supplements provide a consistent and well-integrated learning system. This hands-on, real-world package guides* **instructors** *through the process of active learning and gives them the tools to create an interactive learning environment. With its emphasis on activities, exercises, and the Internet, the package encourages* **students** *to take an active role in the course and prepares them for decision making in a real-world context.*

 # Wiley's Integrated Technology Solutions

Helping Teachers Teach and Students Learn
www.wiley.com/college/kimmel

The *Principles of Accounting* companion website provides a seamless integration of text and media and keeps all of the book's online resources in one easily accessible location.

For Instructors

On this website instructors will find electronic versions of the Solutions Manual, Test Bank, Instructor's Manual, Computerized Test Bank, and other resources.

In addition, portions of the *Principles of Accounting* Instructor website are available in a premium version, allowing instructors to create their own teaching and learning environment. These premium websites, powered by Wiley's EduGen technology platform, provide many additional tools and resources for instructors and students. Upon adoption of a premium content, Wiley will create a unique course instance that instructors can begin to customize by employing the following helpful tools:.

- **Course Administration** tools help instructors manage their course and integrate Wiley website resources with

Course Management Systems, thereby helping instructors keep all class materials in one location.

- A **"Prepare and Present"** tool contains all of the Wiley-provided resources, such as PowerPoint slides, Interactive Chapter Reviews, and Lecture Outlines, making your preparation time more efficient. You may easily adapt, customize, and add to Wiley content to meet the needs of your course.

- An **"Assignment"** area is one of the most powerful features of Wiley's premium websites. This area of the website allows professors to assign homework and quizzes comprised of text Exercises and Problems. Instructors save time as results are automatically graded and recorded in an instructor gradebook. Students benefit by the option to receive immediate feedback on their work, allowing them to determine right away how well they understand the course material.

- An **Instructor's Gradebook** will keep track of student progress and allow instructors to analyze individual and overall class results to determine their progress and level of understanding.

For Students

The *Principles of Accounting* Student website provides a wealth of support materials that will help students develop their conceptual understanding of class material and increase their ability to solve problems. On this website students will find PowerPoint Presentations, Web Quizzing, and other resources. In addition, portions of the student website are available in a premium version powered by Wiley's EduGen technology platform. On the premium sites, students will find the following resources:

- **"Study and Practice"** resources that can include select interactive, end-of-chapter problems linked directly to text content, allowing students to review the text while they study. Additional resources can include Interactive Chapter Reviews and other problem-solving resources.

- An **"Assignment"** area that helps students stay "on task" by containing all homework assignments in one location. Many homework problems contain a link to the relevant sections of the ebook, providing students with context-sensitive help that allows them to conquer problem-solving obstacles.

- A **Personal Gradebook** for each student that will allow students to view their results from past assignments at any time.

Instructor's Active Teaching Aids

Instructor's Resource CD-ROM. The Instructor's Resource CD (IR CD) provides all instructor support material in an electronic format that is easy to navigate and use. The IR CD contains an electronic version of instructor print supplements that can be used in the classroom, for printing out material, for uploading to your own website, or for downloading and modifying. The IR CD gives you the flexibility to access and prepare instructional material based on your individual needs.

Solutions Manual. The Solutions Manual contains detailed solutions to all exercises and problems in the textbook and suggested answers to the questions and cases. Each chapter includes *an assignment classification table*, an *assignment characteristics table*, and a *Bloom's taxonomy table*. Print is large and bold for easy readability in lecture settings, and instructors may duplicate portions of the manual without paying a permissions fee. The Solutions Manual has been carefully verified by a team of independent accuracy checkers. *(Also available at* http://www.wiley.com/college/kimmel *and on the IR CD.)*

Solutions Transparencies. Packaged in an organizer box with chapter file folders, these transparencies feature detailed solutions to all exercises and problems in the textbook as well as suggested answers to the Broadening Your Perspectives activities. They feature large, bold type for better projection and easy readability in large classroom settings.

Instructor's Manual. The Instructor's Manual is a comprehensive set of resources for preparing and presenting an active learning course. The manual discusses how to incorporate all the supplements, includes information on group and active learning, and has sample syllabi for use of the textbook. The Instructor's Manual also includes a series of discussions on how to incorporate ethics material and communication activities in the classroom.

In addition to *comprehension checks* and *short vocabulary and multiple-choice quizzes*, each chapter also includes a number of activities and exercises designed to engage students in the learning process. Some of these activities include *Research and Communication exercises*, *International and Social Responsibility exercises*, and *Ethics exercises*. *(Also available at* http://www.wiley.com/college/kimmel *and on the IR CD.)*

PowerPoint Presentation Material. This PowerPoint lecture aid contains a combination of key concepts, images, and problems from the textbook for use in the classroom. Designed according to the organization of the material in the textbook, this series of electronic transparencies can be used to visually reinforce accounting principles. *(Available at* http://www.wiley.com/college/kimmel *and on the IR CD.)*

Test Bank. The Test Bank is a comprehensive testing package that allows instructors to tailor examinations according to study objectives, learning skills, and content. Examination questions focus on concepts, decision making, and the real-world environment. Actual financial statements are used throughout to provide a relevant context for questions.

In addition to a *final exam*, the Test Bank provides an *achievement test for every two chapters* in the textbook and a *comprehensive exam for every four chapters* of the text. The tests, easy to photocopy and distribute to students, consist of problems and exercises as well as multiple-choice, matching, and true/false questions. *(Also available at* http://www.wiley.com/college/kimmel *and on the IR CD.)*

Computerized Test Bank. This software allows instructors to create and print multiple versions of the same test by scrambling the order of all questions found in the print Test Bank. The computerized test bank also allows users to customize exams by altering or adding new problems. *(Available at* http://www.wiley.com/college/kimmel *and on the IR CD.)*

WebCT and Blackboard. WebCT or Blackboard offers an integrated set of course management tools that enable instructors to easily design, develop, and manage Web-based and Web-enhanced courses.

The Wiley *Principles of Accounting* WebCT and Blackboard courses contain the basic course management shell with all on-line resources for students. It allows the professor to present all or part of a course on-line and helps the student organize the course material, understand key concepts, and access additional tools. Your Wiley WebCT and Blackboard course can be customized to fit individual, professor needs. Contact your Wiley representative for more information.

Business Extra Select. Wiley's Business Extra Select program contains copyright-cleared content from XanEdu's premier databases of leading business resources such as INSEAD, Ivey, and Harvard Business School Cases, *Fortune, The Economist*, the *Wall Street Journal*, and more.

Creating a Business Extra Select CoursePack is easy. Combine the content from this title with your Business Extra Select choices in a single custom-published CoursePack in just a few simple steps. No other custom publishing program is this seamless and easy to use! For more information about Business Extra Select, please contact your Wiley representative or go to www.wiley.com/college/bxs.

Students' Active Learning Aids

The *Principles of Accounting* website. As described earlier, the book's student website at www.wiley.com/college/kimmel provides a wealth of support materials that will help students develop their conceptual understanding of course concepts and increase their ability to solve problems. On this website students will find PowerPoint Presentations, Web Quizzing, and other resources. In addition, portions of the student website are available in a premium version containing interactive study aids powered by Wiley's EduGen technology platform.

 Take Action! CD-ROM. Available as a supplement to accompany the main text, this dynamic CD contains study tools such as interactive chapter reviews and self-tests for *every* chapter of the textbook. This CD is an excellent resource for class preparation and review.

Student Workbook. The Student Workbook is a comprehensive review of accounting and is a powerful tool when used in the classroom and in preparation for exams. The workbook guides students through chapter content while focusing on study objectives and the decision-making process.

Each chapter contains objectives, chapter reviews, multiple-choice exercises, problems, and matching questions. Solutions are written with detail in order to effectively provide immediate feedback.

Working Papers. Working Papers are accounting forms for all end-of-chapter exercises, problems, and cases. A convenient resource for organizing and completing homework assignments, they demonstrate how to correctly set up solution formats and are directly tied to textbook assignments.

Annual Report Project. This practice set is designed to provide students the opportunity to analyze a corporate annual report. The practice set provides hands-on exposure to financial statements of actual companies, emphasizes the importance of the notes to financial statements, and provides an opportunity to examine the application of procedures and methods discussed in the main text.

Beacon Lumber Practice Set. This practice set introduces students to many of the most common business events and shows how to record them in standard accounting format through a series of classroom discussions, role playing, and homework assignments. By getting involved in the ongoing activity of a typical small company, students begin to draw connections between the everyday work of ordinary business and the rules of accounting.

Excel Working Papers. Available on CD-ROM, these Excel-formatted forms can be used for end-of-chapter exercises, problems, and cases. The Excel Working Papers provide students with the option of printing forms and completing them manually, or entering data electronically and then printing out a completed form. By entering data electronically, students can paste homework to a new file and e-mail the worksheet to the instructor.

General Ledger Software. The General Ledger Software program allows students to solve select end-of-chapter text problems or customized problems using a computerized accounting system. Easy to use, GLS demonstrates the immediate effects of each transaction and enables students to enter and post journal entries, and to generate trial balances, and income statements. This software contains a voice-guided tour of GLS and allows students to create their own data diskette.

Peachtree Complete® Accounting Software, Problems & Workbook. This workbook teaches students how to effectively use Peachtree Complete® Accounting Software, a valuable accounting tool, and also reviews basic accounting concepts. The Peachtree Software and templates provided on a CD attached to the workbook allow students to see the effects of journal entries on balance sheets, income statements, and other accounting forms. Many of the problems in the workbook are derived from select problems found in the main text.

Solving Principles of Accounting Problems Using *Excel for Windows*. This workbook and accompanying Excel templates allow students to complete select end-of-chapter exercises and problems identified by a spreadsheet icon in the margin of the main text. A useful introduction to computers, these electronic spreadsheets also enhance students' accounting skills.

Financial Accounting Tutor (FacT) CD. FacT is a self-paced **CD-ROM** designed to review financial accounting concepts. It uses simple examples that introduce concepts gradually and reveal the logic underlying the accounting process. Discussions and examples are followed by brief, interactive problems that provide immediate feedback.

Acknowledgments

During the course of development of *Principles of Accounting*, the authors benefited greatly from the input of focus group participants, manuscript reviewers, ancillary authors, and proofers. The constructive suggestions and innovative ideas of the reviewers and the creativity and accuracy of the ancillary authors and checkers are greatly appreciated.

Reviewers and Focus Group Participants
for *Principles of Accounting*

John Babich, *Kankakee Community College*

Richard Barnhart, *Grand Rapids Community College*

Charles Birnberg, *Bergen Community College*

Ken Bohn, *Tarrant County College*

Lisa Bostick, *University of Tampa*

Anna Boulware, *St. Charles Community College*

Gary Bridges, *University of Texas, San Antonio*

Janet Cassagio, *Nassau Community College*

Jack Cathey, *Univ. North Carolina, Charlotte*

Michael Cathey, *George Washington University*

Mike Chatham, *University of Akron*

Shifei Chung, *Rowan University*

Ginger Clark, *University of Cincinnati*

Sandra Cohen, *Columbia College (IL)*

Susan Cordes, *Johnson County Community College*

Kenneth P. Couvillion, *San Joaquin Delta College*

Thomas L. Davies, *University of South Dakota*

Susan Davis, *Green River Community College*

Peggy DeJong, *Kirkwood Community College*

Laura Denton, *Maysville Community College*

Kevin Dooley, *Kapi'olani Community College*

Carol Dutton, *South Florida Community College*

Randy Edwards, *Appalachian State University*

Richard Ellison, *Middlesex County College*

Denise English, *Boise State University*

Patricia A. Fedje, *Minot State University*

Richard H. Ghio, *San Joaquin Delta Community College*

Ward Harder, *Motlow State*

William Harvey, *Henry Ford Community College*

Michael Haynes, *Mississippi Gulf Coast Comm. College*

Lyle Hicks, *Danville Area Community College*

Charles Holley, *Virginia Commonwealth University*

Michele Johnson, *George Fox University*

George Joseph, *Savannah State University*

Sanford Kahn, *University of Cincinnati*

Phil Kintzele, *Central Michigan University*

Jo Koehn, *Central Missouri State University*

Michael Krause, *Lemoyne College*

Robert Laycock, *Montgomery College*

Rosemarie LeFebvre, *Mohave Community College*

Lynn Mazzola, *Nassau Community College*

Maureen McBeth, *College of DuPage*

Deirdre McRoy, *Florida A&M University*

Pamela A. Meyer, *University of Louisiana, Lafayette*

Richard Milani, *Hibbing Community College*

Karen Murray, *Framingham State College*

Allan O'Bryan, *Rochester Community & Tech. College*

Emeka Ofobike, *University of Akron*

Bruce Oliver, *Rochester Institute of Technology*

Obeua S. Persons, *Rider University*

Douglas Pfister, *Lansing Community College*
Tamara Phelan, *Northern Illinois University*
Charles Pineno, *Clarion University*
Kathy S. Pollock, *Indiana University-Purdue University, Fort Wayne*
Donald Raux, *Siena College*
Tom Ribb, *Dickinson State University*
John Ribezzo, *Community College of Rhode Island*
Renee Rigoni, *Monroe Community College*
Sharon L. Robinson, *Frostburg State University*
Mohd A. RuJoub, *Eastern Connecticut State University*
Jeff Slater, *North Shore Community College*

Jeff Spoelman, *Grand Rapids Community College*
Geoff Turck, *Highline Community College*
Ingrid Ulstad, *University of Wisconsin, Eau Claire*
Sue Van Boven, *Paradise Valley Community College*
Sonja Villaire, *Florida Institute of Technology*
David Weiner, *University of San Francisco*
Anne Wessely, *St. Louis Community College*
Karen Wisniewski, *County College of Morris*
Rahnl Wood, *Northwest Missouri State University*
Robert Wyatt, *Drury University*
Mary Zenner, *College of Lake County (IL)*

Ancillary Authors, Contributers and Proofers

Lee Cannell, *El Paso Community College:*
  Test Bank author and Solutions Manual proofer
Sandra Cohen, *Columbia College:* eGrade proofer
Mel Coe, *DeVrie Institute of Technology–Atlanta*:
  Peachtree Workbook
Denise M. English, *Boise State University*:
  Excel Workbook author
Larry R. Falcetto, *Emporia State University:*
  Instructor's Manual II, Check Figures, and Test Bank author, Solutions Manual and eGrade proofer
Cecelia M. Fewox, *College of Charleston:*
  Student Workbook I author
Jessica Frazier, *Eastern Kentucky University:*
  Instructor's Manual author
Sarah Frank, *University of West Florida:*
  WebCT and Blackboard author
Clyde Galbraith, *West Chester University:*
  eGrade proofer
Carol Hartley, *Providence College:* PowerPoint Presentation author
Nancy A. Herring: Annual Report Project author
Wayne Higley, *Buena Vista University*:
  Content proofer and technical advisor
Harry Howe, *SUNY-Geneseo:*
  Beacon Lumber Practice Set author

Douglas W. Kieso, *University of California-Irvine:*
  Student Workbook II author
David Koeppen, *Boise State University:*
  Excel Workbook author
Gary Lubin: General Ledger Software developer
Laura McNally: eGrade author and programmer
Patricia Mounce, *Mississippi College:* Instructor's Manual author
Sally Nelson, *Northeast Iowa Community College:*
  GLS User's Guide author and eGrade proofer
Rex Schildhouse, *University of Phoenix:*
  eGrade proofer, Peachtree Workbook author
Alice Sineath, *Forsyth Technical Community College:*
  Solutions Manual proofer
Teresa Speck, *St. Mary's University:*
  Text and Solutions Manual proofer
Diane Tanner, *University of North Florida:*
  Test Bank II author
Sheila Viel, *University of Wisconsin-Milwaukee:*
  Problem material contributor and text proofer
Dick D. Wasson, *Southwestern College:*
  Excel Working Papers and Working Papers author, Solutions Manual proofer

We appreciate the exemplary support and professional commitment given us by our publisher Susan Elbe, executive editor Jay O'Callaghan, development editors Nancy Perry and Ann Torbert, associate editor Ed Brislin, senior editorial assistant Brian Kamins, program assistant Kristen Babroski, media editor Allie Keim, vice-president of higher education production and manufacturing Ann Berlin, designer Dawn Stanley, illustration editor Sandra Rigby, photo editor Sara Wight, production manager Jeanine Furino, production editor Norine Pigliucci, product manager at TECHBOOKS Carole Kuhn, and project editor Suzanne Ingrao at Ingrao Associates.

We thank Tootsie Roll Industries and Hershey Foods Corporation for permitting us the use of their 2002 Annual Reports for our specimen financial statements and accompanying notes.

Suggestions and comments from users are encouraged and appreciated. Please feel free to email any one of us at account@wiley.com.

PAUL D. KIMMEL
Milwaukee, Wisconsin

JERRY J. WEYGANDT
Madison, Wisconsin

DONALD E. KIESO
DeKalb, Illinois

HOW TO USE THE STUDY AIDS IN THIS BOOK

CHAPTER **1**

Introduction to Financial Statements

Study Objectives at the beginning of each chapter give you a framework for learning the specific concepts covered in the chapter. Each study objective reappears in the margin where the concept is discussed. Finally, you can review the study objectives in the **Summary** at the end of the chapter text.

The Navigator is a learning system designed to guide you through each chapter and help you succeed in learning the material. It consists of (1) a checklist at the beginning of the chapter, which outlines text features and study aids you will need, and (2) a series of check boxes that prompt you to use the learning aids in the chapter and set priorities as you study.

STUDY OBJECTIVES

After studying this chapter,
you should be able to:

1 Describe the primary forms of business organization.
2 Identify the users and uses of accounting information.
3 Explain the three principal types of business activity.
4 Describe the content and purpose of each of the financial statements.
5 Explain the meaning of assets, liabilities, and stockholders' equity, and state the basic accounting equation.
6 Describe the components that supplement the financial statements in an annual report.
7 Explain the basic assumptions and principles underlying financial statements.

THE NAVIGATOR ✔

▶ Scan *Study Objectives*   ☐
▶ Read *Feature Story*   ☐
▶ Read *Preview*   ☐
▶ Read text and answer *Before You Go On*
    p. 10 ☐   p. 15 ☐   p. 26 ☐
▶ Work Using the *Decision Toolkit*   ☐
▶ Review Summary of *Study Objectives* ☐
▶ Work *Demonstration Problem*   ☐
▶ Answer *Self-Study Questions*
▶ Complete *Assignments*

FEATURE STORY

Financial
Reporting:
A Matter of Trust

In 2002 the financial press was full of articles about financial scandals and accounting misdeeds. It started with **Enron**, but then spread to **Xerox**, **Qwest**, **Global Crossing**, and **WorldCom**, among others. Many of the articles expressed concern that as an increasing number of misdeeds came to public attention, a mistrust of financial reporting in general was developing. These articles made clear just how important accounting and financial reporting are to the U.S. and world financial markets and to society as a whole. Without financial reports, managers would not be able to evaluate how well their company is doing or to make decisions about the best way to make their company grow in the future. Without financial reports, investors and lenders could not make informed decisions about how to allocate their funds. There is no doubt that a sound, well-functioning economy depends on accurate and dependable financial reporting.

The Feature Story helps you picture how the chapter topic relates to the real world of accounting and business. References to the Feature Story throughout the chapter will help you put new ideas in context, organize them, and remember them. Most end with the Internet addresses of the companies cited in the story.

PREVIEW OF CHAPTER 1

How do you start a business? How do you make it grow into a widely recognized brand name like **Tootsie Roll**? How do you determine whether your business is making or losing money? When you need to expand your operations, where do you get money to finance expansion—should you borrow, should you issue stock, should you use your own funds? How do you convince lenders to lend you money or investors to buy your stock? Success in business requires making countless decisions, and decisions require financial information.

The purpose of this chapter is to show you what role accounting plays in providing financial information. The content and organization of the chapter are as follows.

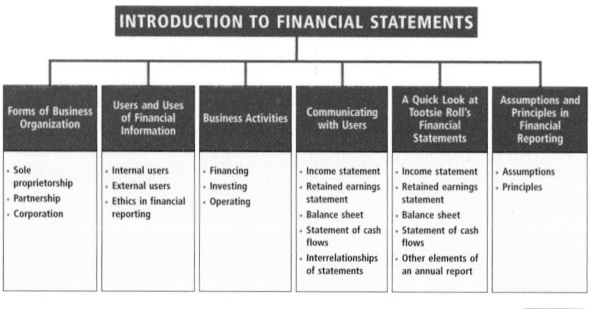

INTRODUCTION TO FINANCIAL STATEMENTS

Forms of Business Organization	Users and Uses of Financial Information	Business Activities	Communicating with Users	A Quick Look at Tootsie Roll's Financial Statements	Assumptions and Principles in Financial Reporting
• Sole proprietorship • Partnership • Corporation	• Internal users • External users • Ethics in financial reporting	• Financing • Investing • Operating	• Income statement • Retained earnings statement • Balance sheet • Statement of cash flows • Interrelationships of statements	• Income statement • Retained earnings statement • Balance sheet • Statement of cash flows • Other elements of an annual report	• Assumptions • Principles

THE NAVIGATOR

The Preview links the Feature Story with the major topics of the chapter and describes the purpose of the chapter. It then outlines the topics that are discussed. This narrative and visual preview helps you organize the information you are learning.

6   CHAPTER 1   Introduction to Financial Statements

the risks of granting credit or lending money. Some questions that may be asked by investors and creditors about a company are shown in Illustration 1-3.

Illustration 1-3

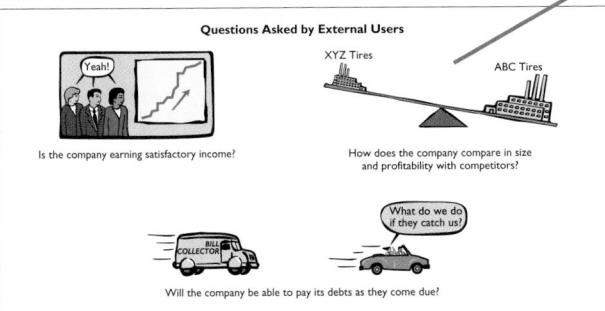

Questions Asked by External Users

Is the company earning satisfactory income?

How does the company compare in size and profitability with competitors?

Will the company be able to pay its debts as they come due?

> **Color Illustrations** such as this **info-graphic**, help you visualize and apply information as you study. They reinforce important concepts and therefore often contain material that may appear on exams.

The information needs and questions of other external users vary considerably. **Taxing authorities**, such as the Internal Revenue Service, want to know whether the company complies with the tax laws. **Regulatory agencies**, such as the Securities and Exchange Commission or the Federal Trade Commission, want to know whether the company is operating within prescribed rules. **Customers** are interested in whether a company will continue to honor product warranties and otherwise support its product lines. **Labor unions** want to know whether the owners have the ability to pay increased wages and benefits. **Economic planners** use accounting information to analyze and forecast economic activity.

 Business Insight
ETHICS PERSPECTIVE

Enron, Dynegy, Duke Energy, and other big energy-trading companies reported record profits at the same time as California was paying extremely high prices for energy and suffering from blackouts. This disparity caused regulators to investigate the energy traders to make sure that the profits were earned by legitimate and fair practices.

> **Business Insight** examples give you more glimpses into how actual companies make decisions using accounting information. These high interest boxes are classified by four different points of view—ethics, investor, international, and management.

ETHICS IN FINANCIAL REPORTING

Imagine trying to carry on a business or invest money if you could not depend on the financial statements to be honestly prepared. Effective communication and economic activity would be impossible. Information would have no credibility. Effective financial reporting depends on sound ethical behavior.

> **Key Terms** and concepts are printed in blue where they are first explained in the text. They are listed and defined again in the end-of-chapter **Glossary**.

The **retained earnings statement** shows the amounts and causes of changes in retained earnings during the period. The time period is the same as that covered by the income statement. The beginning retained earnings amount is shown on the first line of the statement. Then net income is added and dividends are deducted to calculate the retained earnings at the end of the period. If a company has a net loss, it is deducted (rather than added) in the retained earnings statement.

By monitoring the retained earnings statement, financial statement users can evaluate dividend payment practices. Some investors seek companies that pay high dividends. Other investors seek companies that instead of paying dividends reinvest earnings to increase the company's growth. Lenders monitor their corporate customers' dividend payments because any money paid in dividends reduces a company's ability to repay its debts. Illustration 1-6 presents Sierra Corporation's retained earnings statement.

Illustration 1-6 Sierra Corporation's retained earnings statement

Helpful Hint The heading of this statement identifies the company, the type of statement, and the time period covered by the statement.

SIERRA CORPORATION Retained Earnings Statement For the Month Ended October 31, 2005	
Retained earnings, October 1	$ 0
Add: Net income	2,860
	2,860
Less: Dividends	500
Retained earnings, October 31	$2,360

> Each chapter presents **decision tools** that help decision makers analyze and solve business problems. At the conclusion of the text discussion, a **Decision Toolkit** summarizes the key features of a decision tool and reviews why and how you would use it.

DECISION TOOLKIT

Decision Checkpoints	Info Needed for Decision	Tool to Use for Decision	How to Evaluate Results
What is the company's policy toward dividends and growth?	Retained earnings statement	How much of this year's income did the company pay out in dividends to shareholders?	A company striving for rapid growth will pay a low (or no) dividend.

> **Study Objectives** reappear in the margins where the related topic is discussed. End-of-chapter assignments are keyed to study objectives.

STUDY OBJECTIVE
5
Explain the meaning of assets, liabilities, and stockholders' equity, and state the basic accounting equation.

BALANCE SHEET

The **balance sheet** reports assets and claims to those assets at a specific **point** in time. These claims are subdivided into two categories: claims of creditors and claims of owners. As noted earlier, claims of creditors are called **liabilities**. Claims of owners are called **stockholders' equity**. This relationship is shown in equation form in Illustration 1-7. This equation is referred to as the basic accounting equation.

The Coca-Cola Company

THE COCA-COLA COMPANY Balance Sheet (partial) (in millions)	
Current assets	
Cash and cash equivalents	$1,866
Short-term investments	68
Trade accounts receivable	1,882
Inventories	1,055
Prepaid expenses and other assets	2,300
Total current assets	$7,171

Illustration 2-5 Current assets section

Financial statements appear regularly throughout the book. Those from actual companies are identified by a logo or photo. Often, numbers or categories are highlighted in red to draw your attention to key information.

A company's current assets are important in assessing its short-term debt-paying ability, as explained later in the chapter.

LONG-TERM INVESTMENTS

Long-term investments are generally investments in stocks and bonds of other corporations that are normally held for many years. It also includes investments in long-term assets such as land or buildings that are not currently being used in the company's operating activities. In Illustration 2-4 Franklin Corporation reported total long-term investments of $7,200 on its balance sheet. **Yahoo! Inc.** reported long-term investments in its balance sheet as shown in Illustration 2-6.

Alternative Terminology Long-term investments are often referred to simply as **investments**.

Alternative Terminology notes present synonymous terms that you may come across in practice.

Accounting Equation Analyses appear in the margin next to key journal entries. They will help you understand the impact of an accounting transaction on the financial statements and on the company's cash flows.

Freight Costs Incurred by Seller

In contrast, **freight costs incurred by the seller on outgoing merchandise are an operating expense to the seller**. These costs increase an expense account titled Freight-out or Delivery Expense. For example, if the freight terms on the invoice in Illustration 5-4 had required that PW Audio Supply (the seller) pay the $150 freight charges, the entry by PW Audio would be:

May	4	Freight-out	150	
		Cash		150
		(To record payment of freight on goods sold)		

$$A = L + SE$$
$$-150 \qquad -150 \text{ Exp}$$
Cash Flows
-150

When the freight charges are paid by the seller, the seller will usually establish a higher invoice price for the goods, to cover the expense of shipping.

PURCHASE DISCOUNTS

The credit terms of a purchase on account may permit the buyer to claim a cash discount for prompt payment. The buyer calls this cash discount a purchase discount. This incentive offers advantages to both parties: The purchaser saves money, and the seller is able to shorten the operating cycle by converting the accounts receivable into cash earlier.

The **credit terms** specify the amount of the cash discount and time period during which it is offered. They also indicate the length of time in which the purchaser is expected to pay the full invoice price. In the sales invoice in Illustration 5-4, credit terms are 2/10, n/30, which is read "two-ten, net thirty." This means that a 2% cash discount may be taken on the invoice price, less ("net of") any returns or allowances, if payment is made within 10 days of the invoice date (the **discount period**); otherwise, the invoice price, less any returns or allowances, is due 30 days from the invoice date. Alternatively, the discount period may extend to a specified number of days following the month in which the sale occurs. For example, 1/10 EOM (end of month) means that a 1% discount is available if the invoice is paid within the first 10 days of the next month.

Helpful Hints in the margins are like having an instructor with you as you read. They further clarify concepts being discussed.

Helpful Hint The term *net* in "net 30" means the remaining amount due after subtracting any sales returns and allowances and partial payments.

BEFORE YOU GO ON . . .

▶ **Review It**

1. What are the major sections in a classified balance sheet?
2. What is the primary determining factor to distinguish current assets from long-term assets?
3. What was **Tootsie Roll's** largest current asset at December 31, 2002? The answer to this question is provided on page 100.
4. Where is accumulated depreciation reported on the balance sheet?

▶ **Do It**

Baxter Hoffman recently received the following information related to Hoffman Corporation's December 31, 2005, balance sheet.

Prepaid expenses	$ 2,300	Inventory	$3,400
Cash	800	Accumulated depreciation	2,700
Property, plant, and equipment	10,700	Accounts receivable	1,100

Prepare the assets section of Hoffman Corporation's balance sheet.

Action Plan

• Present current assets first. Current assets are cash and other resources that are reasonably expected to be consumed in one year.
• Subtract accumulated depreciation from property, plant, and equipment to determine net property, plant, and equipment.

Solution

HOFFMAN CORPORATION Balance Sheet (partial) December 31, 2005		
Assets		
Current assets		
Cash	$ 800	
Accounts receivable	1,100	
Inventory	3,400	
Prepaid expenses	2,300	
Total current assets		$ 7,600
Property, plant, and equipment	10,700	
Less: Accumulated depreciation	2,700	8,000
Total assets		$15,600

Before You Go On sections follow each key topic. *Review It* questions prompt you to stop and review the key points that you have just studied. If you cannot answer these questions, you should go back and read the section again.

Review It questions marked with the Tootsie Roll icon direct you to find information in Tootsie Roll Industries' 2002 Annual Report, packaged with new copies of the book and printed in Appendix A (near the back of the book). Answers appear at the end of the chapter.

Brief *Do It* exercises ask you to put to work your newly acquired knowledge. They outline an **Action Plan** necessary to complete the exercise and show a **Solution**.

THE NAVIGATOR

A **Using the Decision Toolkit** exercise follows the final set of *Review It* questions in the chapter. It asks you to use business information and the decision tools presented in the chapter. You should think through the questions related to the decision before you study the **Solution** provided.

Using the Decision Toolkit

Hershey Foods Corporation, located in Hershey, Pennsylvania, is the leading North American manufacturer of chocolate—for example, Hershey's Kisses, Reese's Peanut Butter Cups, and Kit Kat bars. Imagine that you are considering the purchase of shares of Hershey's common stock.

Instructions

Answer these questions related to your decision whether to invest.

(a) What financial statements should you request from the company?
(b) What should these financial statements tell you?
(c) Should you request audited financial statements? Explain.
(d) Will the financial statements show the market value of Hershey Foods' assets? Explain.
(e) Simplified financial statements for Hershey Foods are shown in Illustrations 1-20 through 1-23. What comparisons can you make between Tootsie Roll and Hershey in terms of their respective results from operations and financial position?

Summary of Study Objectives

1 *Describe the primary forms of business organization.* A sole proprietorship is a business owned by one person. A partnership is a business owned by two or more people. A corporation is a separate legal entity for which evidence of ownership is provided by shares of stock.

2 *Identify the users and uses of accounting information.* Internal users are managers who need accounting information in planning, controlling, and evaluating business operations. The primary external users are investors and creditors. Investors (stockholders) use accounting information to help them decide whether to buy, hold, or sell shares of a company's stock. Creditors (suppliers and bankers) use accounting information to assess the risk of granting credit or loaning money to a business. Other groups who have an indirect interest in a business are taxing authorities, regulatory agencies, customers, labor unions, and economic planners.

3 *Explain the three principal types of business activity.* Financing activities involve collecting the necessary funds to support the business. Investing activities involve acquiring the resources necessary to run the business. Operating activities involve putting the resources of the business into action to generate a profit.

4 *Describe the content and purpose of each of the financial statements.* An income statement presents the revenues and expenses of a company for a specific period of time. A retained earnings statement summarizes the changes in retained earnings that have occurred for a specific period of time. A balance sheet reports the assets, liabilities, and stockholders' equity of a business at a specific date. A statement of cash flows summarizes information

ing equation. Assets are resources owned by a business. Liabilities are the debts and obligations of the business. Liabilities represent claims of creditors on the assets of the business. Stockholders' equity represents the claims of owners on the assets of the business. Stockholders' equity is composed of two parts: common stock and retained earnings. The basic accounting equation is: Assets = Liabilities + Stockholders' Equity.

6 *Describe the components that supplement the financial statements in an annual report.* The management discussion and analysis provides management's interpretation of the company's results and financial position as well as a discussion of plans for the future. Notes to the financial statements provide additional explanation or detail to make the financial statements more informative. The auditor's report expresses an opinion as to whether the financial statements present fairly the company's results of operations and financial position.

7 *Explain the basic assumptions and principles underlying financial statements.* The monetary unit assumption requires that only transaction data capable of being expressed in terms of money be included in the accounting records of the economic entity. The economic entity assumption states that economic events can be identified with a particular unit of accountability. The time period assumption states that the e[...] divided into arti[...] ingful accounting[...] period. The going[...] enterprise will co[...] carry out its exis[...] The cost princi[...]

The **Summary of Study Objectives** reviews the main points related to the Study Objectives. It provides you with another opportunity to review what you have learned as well as to see how the key topics within the chapter fit together.

30 **CHAPTER 1** Introduction to Financial Statements

DECISION TOOLKIT—A SUMMARY

Decision Checkpoints	Info Needed for Decision	Tool to Use for Decision	How to Evaluate Results
Are the company's operations profitable?	Income statement	The income statement reports on the success or failure of the company's operations by reporting its revenues and expenses.	If the company's revenue exceeds its expenses, it will report net income; otherwise it will report a net loss.
What is the company's policy toward dividends and growth?	Retained earnings statement	How much of this year's income did the company pay out in dividends to shareholders?	A company striving for rapid growth will pay a low dividend.
Does the company rely primarily on debt or stockholders' equity to finance its assets?	Balance sheet	The balance sheet reports the company's resources and claims to those resources. There are two types of claims: liabilities and stockholders' equity.	Compare the amount of debt versus the amount of stockholders' equity to determine whether the company relies more on creditors or owners for its financing.
Does the company generate sufficient cash from operations to fund its investing activities?	Statement of cash flows	The statement of cash flows shows the amount of cash provided or used by operating activities, investing activities, and financing activities.	Compare the amount of cash provided by operating activities with the amount of cash used by investing activities. Any deficiency in cash from operating activities must be made up with cash from financing activities.

At the end of each chapter; the **Decision Toolkit—A Summary** reviews the techniques for decision making that were covered in the chapter.

The **Glossary** defines all the **key terms** and **concepts** introduced in the chapter. Page references help you find any terms you need to study further. **CD** and **Web Icons** tell you that you can review these terms interactively either on the CD or the website.

Glossary

Accounting The process of identifying, recording, and communicating the economic events of a business to interested users of the information. (p. 5)

Annual report A report prepared by corporate management that presents financial information including financial statements, notes, and the management discussion and analysis. (p. 20)

Assets Resources owned by a business. (p. 9)

Auditor's report A report prepared by an independent outside auditor stating the auditor's opinion as to the fairness of the presentation of the financial position and results of operations and their conformance with accepted accounting standards. (p. 22)

Balance sheet A financial statement that reports the assets, liabilities, and stockholders' equity at a specific date. (p. 12)

Basic accounting equation Assets = Liabilities + Stockholders' Equity. (pp. 12–13)

Certified Public Accountant (CPA) An individual who has met certain criteria and is thus allowed to perform audits of corporations. (p. 22)

Common stock Stock representing the primary ownership interest in a corporation. In the balance sheet it represents the amount paid in by stockholders. (p. 8)

Comparative statements A presentation of the financial statements of a company for multiple years. (p. 18)

Corporation A business organized as a separate legal entity having ownership divided into transferable shares of stock. (p. 3)

Cost principle An accounting principle that states that assets should be recorded at their cost. (p. 25)

Dividends Distributions of cash or other assets from a corporation to its stockholders. (p. 8)

Economic entity assumption An assumption that economic events can be identified with a particular unit of accountability. (p. 23)

Demonstration Problem

Jeff Andringa, a former college hockey player, quit his job and started Ice Camp, a hockey camp for kids ages 8 to 18. Eventually he would like to open hockey camps nationwide. Jeff has asked you to help him prepare financial statements at the end of his first year of operations. He relates the following facts about his business activities.

In order to get the business off the ground, he decided to incorporate. He sold shares of common stock to a few close friends, as well as buying some of the shares himself. He initially raised $25,000 through the sale of these shares. In addition, the company took out a $10,000 loan at a local bank. A bus for transporting kids was purchased for $12,000 cash. Hockey goals and other miscellaneous equipment were purchased with $1,500 cash. The company earned camp tuition during the year of $100,000 but had collected only $80,000 of this amount. Thus, at the end of the year it was still owed $20,000. The company rents time at a local rink for $50 per hour. Total rink rental costs during the year were $8,000, insurance was $10,000, salary expense was $20,000, and administrative expenses totaled $9,000, all of which were paid in cash. The company incurred $800 in interest expense on the bank loan, which it still owed at the end of the year.

The company paid dividends during the year of $5,000 cash. The balance in the corporate bank account at December 31, 2005, was $49,500.

Instructions

Using the format of the Sierra Corporation statements in this chapter, prepare an income statement, retained ea[...] flows. (*Hint*: Prepare the sta[...] of information from one sta[...]

A **Demonstration Problem** is the final step before you begin homework. These sample problems provide you with an **Action Plan** in the margin that lists the strategies needed to approach and solve the problem. The **Solution** demonstrates both the form and content of complete answers.

Solution to Demonstration Problem

Action Plan
- On the income statement: Show revenues and expenses for a period of time.
- On the retained earnings statement: Show the changes in retained earnings for a period of time.
- On the balance sheet: Report assets, liabilities, and stockholders' equity at a specific date.
- On the statement of cash flows: Report sources and uses of cash from operating, investing, and financing activities for a period of time.

ICE CAMP
Income Statement
For the Year Ended December 31, 2005

Revenues		
Camp tuition revenue		$100,000
Expenses		
Salaries expense	$20,000	
Insurance expense	10,000	
Administrative expense	9,000	
Rink rental expense	8,000	
Interest expense	800	
Total expenses		47,800
Net income		$ 52,200

ICE CAMP
Retained Earnings Statement
For the Year Ended December 31, 2005

Retained earnings, January 1, 2005		$ 0
Add: Net income		52,200
		52,200
Less: Dividends		5,000
Retained earnings, December 31, 2005		$47,200

Self-Study Questions

Self-Study/Self-Test

Answers are at the end of the chapter.

(SO 1) 1. Which is *not* one of the three forms of business organization?
  (a) Sole proprietorship. (c) Partnership.
  (b) Creditorship. (d) Corporation.

(SO 1) 2. Which is an advantage of corporations relative to partnerships and sole proprietorships?
  (a) Lower taxes.
  (b) Harder to transfer ownership.
  (c) Reduced legal liability for investors.
  (d) Most common form of organization.

(SO 3) 3. Which is *not* one of the three primary business activities?
  (a) Financing. (c) Advertising.
  (b) Operating. (d) Investing.

(SO 4) 4. Which statement about users of accounting information is *incorrect*?
  (a) Management is considered an internal user.
  (b) Taxing authorities are considered external users.
  (c) Present creditors are considered external users.

  (d) Regulatory authorities are considered internal users.

(SO 4) 5. Net income will result during a time period when:
  (a) assets exceed liabilities.
  (b) assets exceed revenues.
  (c) expenses exceed revenues.
  (d) revenues exceed expenses.

(SO 4) 6. What section of a cash flow statement indicates the cash spent on new equipment during the past accounting period?
  (a) The investing section.
  (b) The operating section.
  (c) The financing section.
  (d) The cash flow statement does not give this information.

(SO 4) 7. Which financial statement reports assets, liabilities, and stockholders' equity?
  (a) Income statement.
  (b) Retained earnings statement.
  (c) Balance sheet.
  (d) Statement of cash flows.

(SO 5) 8. As of December 31, 2005, Stoneland Corporation has assets of $3,500 and stockholders' eq-

Self-Study Questions provide a practice test, keyed to Study Objectives, that gives you an opportunity to check your knowledge of important topics. Answers appear at the end of the chapter. **CD** and **Web icons** tell you that you can answer these **Self-Study Questions** interactively on either the CD or the website. There is an additional **Self-Test** at the website that can further help you master the material.

Questions

1. What are the three basic forms of business organizations?

2. What are the advantages to a business of being formed as a corporation? What are the disadvantages?

3. What are the advantages to a business of being formed as a partnership or sole proprietorship? What are the disadvantages?

4. "Accounting is ingrained in our society and is vital to our economic system." Do you agree? Explain.

5. Who are the internal users of accounting data? How does accounting provide relevant data to the internal users?

6. Who are the external users of accounting data? Give examples.

7. What are the three main types of business activity? Give examples of each activity.

8. Listed here are some items found in the financial statements of Ruth Weber, Inc. Indicate in which financial statement(s) each item would appear.
  (a) Service revenue. (d) Accounts receivable.
  (b) Equipment. (e) Common stock.
  (c) Advertising expense. (f) Wages payable.

9. Why would a bank want to monitor the dividend payment practices of the corporations it lends money to?

13. What is retained earnings? What items increase the balance in retained earnings? What items decrease the balance in retained earnings?

14. What is the basic accounting equation?

15. (a) Define the terms *assets*, *liabilities*, and *stockholders' equity*.
  (b) What items affect stockholders' equity?

16. Which of these items are liabilities of Kool-Jewelry Stores?
  (a) Cash. (f) Equipment.
  (b) Accounts payable. (g) Salaries payable.
  (c) Dividends. (h) Service revenue.
  (d) Accounts receivable. (i) Rent expense.
  (e) Supplies.

17. How are each of the following financial statements interrelated? (a) Retained earnings statement and income statement. (b) Retained earnings statement and balance sheet. (c) Balance sheet and statement of cash flows.

18. What is the purpose of the management discussion and analysis section (MD&A)?

19. Why is it important for financial statements to receive an unqualified auditor's opinion?

20. What types of information are presented in the notes to the financial statements?

Questions allow you to explain your understanding of concepts and relationships from the chapter. Use them to help prepare for class discussion and tests.

A special icon indicates review and homework material that asks you to use the **decision tools** presented in the chapter.

Brief Exercises help you focus on one Study Objective at a time and thus help you build confidence in your basic skills and knowledge.

Brief Exercises

BE1-1 Match each of the following forms of business organization with a set of characteristics: sole proprietorship (SP), partnership (P), corporation (C).

(a) _____ Shared control, tax advantages, increased skills and resources.
(b) _____ Simple to set up and maintains control with founder.
(c) _____ Easier to transfer ownership and raise funds, no personal liability.

Describe forms of business organization.
(SO 1)

BE1-2 Match each of the following types of evaluation with one of the listed users of accounting information.

1. Trying to determine whether the company complied with tax laws.
2. Trying to determine whether the company can pay its obligations.
3. Trying to determine whether a marketing proposal will be cost effective.
4. Trying to determine whether the company's net income will result in a stock price increase.
5. Trying to determine whether the company should employ debt or equity financing.

(a) _____ Investors in common stock.   (d) _____ Chief Financial Officer.
(b) _____ Marketing managers.   (e) _____ Internal Revenue Service.
(c) _____ Creditors.

Identify users of accounting information.
(SO 2)

BE1-3 Indicate in which part of the statement of cash flows each item would appear: operating activities (O), investing activities (I), or financing activities (F).

(a) _____ Cash received from customers.
(b) _____ Cash paid to stockholders (dividends).
(c) _____ Cash received from issuing new common stock.
(d) _____ Cash paid to suppliers.
(e) _____ Cash paid to purchase a new office building.

Classify items by activity.
(SO 3, 4, 5)

BE1-4 Presented below are a number of transactions. Determine whether each transaction affects common stock (C), dividends (D), revenue (R), expense (E), or does not affect stockholders' equity (NSE). Provide titles for the revenues and expenses.

(a) Costs incurred for advertising.
(b) Assets received for services performed.
(c) Costs incurred for insurance.

Determine effect of transactions on stockholders' equity.
(SO 4)

...es.
...holders.
...ge for allowing the use of the company's building.
...s used.
...quipment.

Exercises

Match items with descriptions.
(SO 1, 2, 4, 6)

E1-1 Here is a list of words or phrases discussed in this chapter:

1. Corporation   4. Partnership   7. Accounts payable
2. Creditor   5. Stockholder   8. Auditor's opinion
3. Accounts receivable   6. Common stock

Instructions
Match each word or phrase with the best description of it.

_____ (a) An expression about whether financial statements are presented in a reasonable fashion.
_____ (b) A business enterprise that raises money by issuing shares of stock.
_____ (c) The portion of stockholders' equity that results from receiving cash from investors.

Exercises, which are more difficult than Brief Exercises, help you continue to build confidence in your ability to use the material learned in the chapter.

Problems: Set A

P1-1A Presented below are five independent situations.

(a) Ann Cunningham, a college student looking for summer employment, opened a vegetable stand along a busy local highway. Each morning she buys produce from local farmers, then sells it in the afternoon as people return home from work.
(b) Robert Steven and Phillip Cantor each owned separate swing-set manufacturing businesses. They have decided to combine their businesses and try to expand their reach beyond their local market. They expect that within the coming year they will need significant funds to expand their operations.
(c) Three chemistry professors at FIU have formed a business to employ bacteria to clean up toxic waste sites. Each has contributed an equal amount of cash and knowledge to the venture. The use of bacteria in this situation is experimental, and legal obligations could result.
(d) Michelle Beal has run a successful, but small cooperative health food store for over 20 years. The increased sales of her store have made her believe that the time is right to open a national chain of health food stores across the country. Of course, this will require a substantial investment in stores, inventory, and employees in each store. Michelle has no savings or personal assets. She wants to maintain control over the business.
(e) Mary Emery and Richard Goedde recently graduated with graduate degrees in economics. They have decided to start a consulting business focused on teaching the basics of international economics to small business owners interested in international trade.

Determine forms of business organization.
(SO 1)

Instructions
In each case explain what form of organization the business is likely to take—sole proprietorship, partnership, or corporation. Give reasons for your choice.

P1-2A Financial decisions often place heavier emphasis on one type of financial statement over the others. Consider each of the following hypothetical situations independently.

Identify users and uses of financial statements.
(SO 2, 4, 5)

Each **Problem** helps you pull together and apply several concepts from the chapter. Two sets of **Problems—A** and **B**—are keyed to the same Study Objectives and provide additional opportunities for practice.

Problems: Set B

P1-1B Presented below are five independent situations.

(a) Three physics professors at MIT have formed a business to improve the speed of information transfer over the Internet for stock exchange transactions. Each has contributed an equal amount of cash and knowledge to the venture. Although their approach looks promising, they are concerned about the legal liabilities that their business might confront.
(b) Geoff Jackson, a college student looking for summer employment, opened a bait shop in a small shed at a local marina.
(c) Peter Bates and Jerry Fine each owned separate shoe manufacturing businesses. They have decided to combine their businesses. They expect that within the coming year they will need significant funds to expand their operations.
(d) Mary Browne, Carol Lampe, and Bonnie Kurt recently graduated with marketing degrees. They have been friends since childhood. They have decided to start a consulting business focused on marketing sporting goods over the Internet.
(e) Mark Mozena wants to rent CD players and CDs in airports across the country. His idea is that customers will be able to rent equipment and CDs at one airport, listen to the CDs on their flights, and return the equipment and CDs at their destination airport. Of course, this will require a substantial investment in equipment and CDs, as well as employees and locations in each airport. Mark has no savings or personal assets. He wants to maintain control over the business.

Instructions
In each case explain what form of organization the business is likely to take—sole proprietorship, partnership, or corporation. Give reasons for your choice.

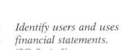

P1-2B Financial decisions often place heavier emphasis on one type of financial statement over the others. Consider each of the following hypothetical situations independently.

Identify users and uses of financial statements.
(SO 2, 4, 5)

Certain Exercises and Problems, marked with a pencil icon help you practice **business writing skills**, which are much in demand among employers.

P3-6A   The trial balance of Valet Dry Cleaners on June 30 is given here.

VALET DRY CLEANERS
Trial Balance
June 30, 2005

	Debit	Credit
Cash	$12,532	
Accounts Receivable	10,536	
Supplies	4,844	
Equipment	25,950	
Accounts Payable		$15,878
Unearned Revenue		1,730
Common Stock		36,254
	$53,862	$53,862

The July transactions were as follows.

July	8	Received $5,189 in cash on June 30 accounts receivable.
	9	Paid employee salaries $2,100.
	11	Received $4,925 in cash for services provided.
	14	Paid creditors $10,750 of accounts payable.
	17	Purchased supplies on account $618.
	22	Billed customers for services provided $4,700.
	30	Paid employee salaries $3,114, utilities $1,467, and repairs $492.
	31	Paid $700 cash dividend.

Instructions
(a) Prepare a general ledger using T accounts. Enter the opening balances in the ledger accounts as of July 1. Provision should be made for the following additional accounts: Dividends, Dry Cleaning Revenue, Repair Expense, Salaries Expense, and Utilities Expense.
(b) Journalize the transactions.
(c) Post to the ledger accounts.
(d) Prepare a trial balance on July 31, 2005.

P3-7A   This trial balance of Dubuque Company does not balance.

DUBUQUE COMPANY
Trial Balance
May 31, 2005

	Debit	Credit
Cash	$ 5,650	
Accounts Receivable		$ 2,750
Prepaid Insurance	700	
Equipment	8,000	
Accounts Payable		4,500
Property Taxes Payable	560	
Common Stock		5,700
Retained Earnings		6,000
Service Revenue	6,690	
Salaries Expense	4,200	
Advertising Expense		1,100
Property Tax Expense	800	
	$26,600	$20,050

Your review of the ledger reveals that each account has a normal balance. You also discover the following errors.

Problems: Set A   145

Journalize transactions, post, and prepare a trial balance.
(SO 3, 5, 6, 7, 8)

Peachtree

General Ledger Problems, identified by an icon, are selected problems that can be solved using the *General Ledger Software* package.

Problems marked with the **Peachtree** icon can be worked using *Peachtree Complete Accounting® to Accompany Principles of Accounting.* A separate student workbook that includes the software is available for purchase.

(d) Cash $ 4,023
Tot. trial
balance $53,355

Prepare a correct trial balance.
(SO 8)

Check figures in the margin provide key numbers to let you know you're on the right track.

Spreadsheet Exercises and Problems, identified by an icon, are selected problems that can be solved using the spreadsheet software *Solving Principles of Accounting Problems Using Excel.*

The **Broadening Your Perspective** section helps you pull together various concepts from the chapter and apply them to real-world business situations.

In the **Financial Reporting Problem** you study various aspects of the financial statements of Tootsie Roll Industries, which are printed in Chapter 1 (in simplified form) and in Appendix A (in full).

BROADENING YOUR PERSPECTIVE

Financial Reporting and Analysis

FINANCIAL REPORTING PROBLEM: *Tootsie Roll Industries, Inc.*

BYP1-1   Simplified 2002 financial statements of Tootsie Roll Industries, Inc. are given in Illustrations 1-11 through 1-14.

Instructions
Refer to Tootsie Roll's financial statements to answer the following questions.
(a) What were Tootsie Roll's total assets at December 31, 2002? At December 31, 2001?
(b) How much cash did Tootsie Roll have on December 31, 2002?
(c) What amount of accounts payable did Tootsie Roll report on December 31, 2002? On December 31, 2001?
(d) What were Tootsie Roll's sales revenue in 2002? In 2001?
(e) What is the amount of the change in Tootsie Roll's net income from 2001 to 2002?
(f) The accounting equation is: Assets = Liabilities + Stockholders' Equity. Replacing the words in that equation with dollar amounts, give Tootsie Roll's accounting equation at December 31, 2002.

A **Comparative Analysis Problem** offers the opportunity to compare and contrast the financial reporting of Tootsie Roll with a competitor, Hershey Foods.

Research Cases direct you to the *Wall Street Journal* and other business periodicals and references for further study and analysis of key topics.

Interpreting Financial Statements offers minicases that ask you to read parts of financial statements of actual companies and use the decision tools from the chapter to interpret this information.

---

46 CHAPTER 1 Introduction to Financial Statements

COMPARATIVE ANALYSIS PROBLEM: *Tootsie Roll vs. Hershey Foods*

BYP1-2 Simplified financial statements of Hershey Foods Corporation are presented in Illustrations 1-20 through 1-23, and Tootsie Roll's simplified financial statements are presented in Illustrations 1-11 through 1-14.

Instructions
(a) Based on the information in these financial statements, determine the following for each company.
  (1) Total assets at December 31, 2002.
  (2) Accounts receivable at December 31, 2002.
  (3) Net sales for 2002.
  (4) Net income for 2002.
(b) What conclusions concerning the two companies can you draw from these data?

RESEARCH CASE

BYP1-3 The February 6, 2002, issue of the *Wall Street Journal* includes an article by Steve Liesman, Jonathan Weil, and Michael Schroeder entitled "Accounting Debacles Spark Calls for Change: Here's the Rundown."

Instructions
Read the article and answer the following questions.
(a) What concern is raised by the fact that some audit firms receive significant payments from their audit clients for non-audit work, such as consulting? What solutions have been proposed in response to this potential problem?
(b) At the time of this article, who policed the accounting profession? What alternative has been proposed by the Securities and Exchange Commission (SEC)?
(c) What criticisms have been made of the primary accounting standards-setting group, the Financial Accounting Standards Board (FASB)?
(d) In what ways, and from what groups, is the SEC demanding more disclosure?

INTERPRETING FINANCIAL STATEMENTS

BYP1-4 The year 2000 was not a particularly pleasant year for the managers of Xerox Corporation, or its shareholders. The company's stock price had already fallen in the previous year from $60 per share to $30. Just when it seemed things couldn't get worse, Xerox's stock fell to $4 per share. The data below were taken from the December 31, 2000, statement of cash flows of Xerox. All dollars are in millions.

Cash used in operating activities		$ (663)
Cash used in investing activities		(644)
Financing activities		
Dividends paid	$ (587)	
Net cash received from issuing debt	3,498	
Cash provided by financing activities		2,911

Instructions
Analyze the information above, and then answer the following questions.
(a) If you were a creditor of Xerox, what reaction might you have to the above information?
(b) If you were an investor in Xerox, what reaction might you have to the above information?
(c) If you were evaluating the company as either a creditor or a stockholder, what other information would you be interested in seeing?
(d) Xerox decided to pay a cash dividend in 2000. This dividend was approximately equal to the amount paid in 1999. Discuss the issues that were probably considered in making this decision.

A GLOBAL FOCUS

BYP1-5 Today companies must compete in a global economy. Both Tootsie Roll and Hershey must compete with Nestlé. Nestlé, a Swiss company, is the largest food company in the world. If you were interested in broadening your investment portfolio, you

---

Fina...

might consider investing in Nestlé. However, investing in international compa... pose some additional challenges. Consider the following excerpts from the notes t... financial statements.

NESTLÉ
Notes to the Financial Statements (partial)

(a) The Group accounts comply with International Accounting Standards (IAS) issued by the International Accounting Standards Committee (IASC) and with the Standards Interpretations issued by the Standards Interpretation Committee of the IASC (SIC).
(b) The accounts have been prepared under the historical cost convention and on an accrual basis. All significant consolidated companies have a 31st December accounting year end. All disclosures required by the 4th and 7th European Union company law directives are provided.
(c) On consolidation, assets and liabilities of Group companies denominated in foreign currencies are translated into Swiss francs at year-end rates. Income and expense items are translated into Swiss francs at the annual average rates of exchange or, where known or determinable, at the rate on the date of the transaction for significant items.

Instructions
Discuss the implications of each of these items in terms of the effect it might have (positive or negative) on your ability to compare Nestlé to Tootsie Roll and Hershey Foods. (*Hint:* In preparing your answer, review the discussion of principles and assumptions in financial reporting.)

FINANCIAL ANALYSIS ON THE WEB

BYP1-6 *Purpose:* Identify summary information about companies. This information includes basic descriptions of the company's location, activities, industry, financial health, and financial performance.

Address: http://biz.yahoo.com/i (or go to **www.wiley.com/college/kimmel**)

Steps
1. Type in a company name, or use the index to find company name.
2. Choose **Profile**. Perform instructions (a)–(c) below.
3. Click on the name of the company's industry to identify others in this industry. Perform instructions (d)–(e) below.

Instructions
Answer the following questions.
(a) What was the company's net income? Over what period was this measured?
(b) What was the company's total sales? Over what period was this measured?
(c) What is the company's industry?
(d) What are the names of four companies in this industry?
(e) Choose one of the competitors. What is this competitor's name? What were its sales? What was its net income?

BYP1-7 *Purpose:* This exercise is an introduction to the major international accounting firms.

Addresses: Deloitte & Touche www.deloitte.com/
 Ernst & Young www.ey.com/
 KPMG www.us.kpmg.com/
 PricewaterhouseCoopers www.pwcglobal.com/

A Global Focus asks you to apply concepts from the chapter to specific situations faced by actual foreign companies.

Financial Analysis on the Web exercises guide you to Web sites where you can find and analyze information related to the chapter.

Critical Thinking

GROUP DECISION CASE

BYP1-8 This activity provides a survey of the Tootsie Roll financial statements to increase your familiarity with their contents.
  (a) What CPA firm performed the audit of Tootsie Roll's financial statements?
  (b) What was the amount of Tootsie Roll's earnings per share in 2002?
  (c) What are the company's total assets in Mexico and Canada?
  (d) What did management suggest as the causes of the increases in the sales and profits of the Canadian subsidiary in 2002?
  (e) What were net sales in 1998?
  (f) How many shares of Class B common stock have been authorized?
  (g) How much cash was spent on capital expenditures in 2002?
  (h) Over what life does the company depreciate its buildings?
  (i) What is the URL for the company's Web site?
  (j) What was the value of raw material inventories in 2001?

BYP1-9 Kelly Services, Inc. is a service company that provides personnel for temporary positions, primarily nontechnical. When a company requests assistance, Kelly matches the qualifications of its standby personnel with the requirements of the position. The companies pay Kelly Services; Kelly Services, in turn, pays the employees.
  In a recent annual report, Kelly Services chronicled its contributions to community services over the past 30 years, or so. The following excerpts illustrate the variety of services provided.

  1. KellyWeek, a Saint Patrick's Day customer appreciation event, originated in California. Kelly Services made donations of stationery, office decorations, and decals containing the company's name.
  2. In support of Lady Bird Johnson's "Keep America Beautiful" campaign in the 1960s, the company donated, and its employees planted, gladiola gardens in cities across the United States.
  3. The company initiated a holiday drawing in which thousands of customers throughout the United States and Canada nominate their favorite children's charities. Winning charities in the drawing receive a monetary donation from Kelly Services in the name of the customer.
  4. KellyWeek was expanded by making donations of temporary help.
  5. Kelly executives regularly volunteer their time and resources to serve as role models and mentors to youth in the Detroit area.

Instructions
With the class divided into groups, answer the following.
  (a) The economic entity assumption requires that a co
      penses of its employees separate from business exp

> The **Group Decision Case** helps you build decision-making skills by analyzing accounting information in a less structured situation. These cases require teams of students to evaluate a manager's decision or lead to a decision among alternative courses of action. They also give practice in building business communication skills.

> **Communication Activities** help you build business communication skills by asking you to engage in real-world business situations using writing, speaking, or presentation skills.

> Through the **Ethics Cases**, you will reflect on typical ethical dilemmas, analyze the issues involved, and decide on an appropriate course of action.

COMMUNICATION ACTIVITY

BYP1-10 Karen Lloyd is the bookkeeper for James Company, Inc. Karen has been trying to get the company's balance sheet to balance. She finally got it to balance, but she still isn't sure that it is correct.

JAMES COMPANY, INC.
Balance Sheet
For the Month Ended December 31, 2005

Assets		Liabilities and Stockholders' Equity	
Equipment	$20,500	Common stock	$11,000
Cash	10,500	Accounts receivable	(3,000)
Supplies	2,000	Dividends	(2,000)
Accounts payable	(5,000)	Notes payable	12,000
Total assets	$28,000	Retained earnings	10,000
		Total liabilities and stockholders' equity	$28,000

Instructions
Explain to Karen Lloyd in a memo (a) the purpose of a balance sheet, and (b) why this balance sheet is incorrect and what she should do to correct it.

ETHICS CASE

BYP1-11 Rules governing the investment practices of individual certified public accountants disallow them from investing in the stock of a company that is audited by their firm. Recently the Securities and Exchange Commission has become concerned that some accountants are violating this rule. In response to an SEC investigation of its firm, PricewaterhouseCoopers fired 10 people and spent $25 million educating its employees regarding the investment rules and installing an investment tracking system. A discussion of these issues is provided in a June 8, 2000, *Wall Street Journal* article by Michael Schroeder, "SEC, Accounting Firms Reach Pact on Conflicts."

Instructions
Read the article and answer the following questions.
  (a) Why do you think rules exist that restrict auditors from investing in companies that are audited by their firms?
  (b) Some accountants argue that they should be allowed to invest in a company's stock as long as they themselves aren't involved in working on the company's audit or consulting. What do you think of this idea?
  (c) Today a very high percentage of publicly traded companies are audited by only four very large public accounting firms. These firms also do a high percentage of the one for publicly traded companies. How does this fact comrding whether CPAs should be allowed to invest in compa
      n?

Answers to Self-Study Questions
1. b   2. c   3. c   4. d   5. d   6. a   7. c   8. a   9. a   10. c   11. c

Answer to Tootsie Roll Review It Question 3, p. 15
Using dollar amounts, Tootsie Roll's accounting equation is:

	Assets	=	Liabilities	+	Stockholders' Equity
	$646,080,000	=	$119,340,000	+	$526,740,000

> Remember to go back to the Navigator box on the chapter-opening page and check off your completed work.

> **Answers to Self-Study Questions** provide feedback on your understanding of concepts.

> **Answers to *Review It* Questions** based on the Tootsie Roll financial statements appear here.

> After you complete your homework assignments, it's a good idea to go back to **The Navigator** checklist to see if you have used all the chapter's study aids.

This questionnaire aims to find out something about your preferences for the way you work with information. You will have a preferred learning style and one part of that learning style is your preference for the intake and the output of ideas and information.

Circle the letter of the answer that best explains your preference. Circle more than one if a single answer does not match your perception. Leave blank any question that does not apply:

1. You are about to give directions to a person who is standing with you. She is staying in a hotel in town and wants to visit your house later. She has a rental car. Would you
   a. draw a map on paper?
   b. tell her the directions?
   c. write down the directions (without a map)?
   d. pick her up at the hotel in your car?

2. You are not sure whether a word should be spelled "dependent" or "dependant." Do you
   c. look it up in the dictionary?
   a. see the word in your mind and choose by the way it looks?
   b. sound it out in your mind?
   d. write both versions down on paper and choose one?

3. You have just received a copy of your itinerary for a world trip. This is of interest to a friend. Would you
   b. call her immediately and tell her about it?
   c. send her a copy of the printed itinerary?
   a. show her on a map of the world?
   d. share what you plan to do at each place you visit?

4. You are going to cook something as a special treat for your family. Do you
   d. cook something familiar without the need for instructions?
   a. thumb through the cookbook looking for ideas from the pictures?
   c. refer to a specific cookbook where there is a good recipe?

5. A group of tourists has been assigned to you to find out about wildlife reserves or parks. Would you
   d. drive them to a wildlife reserve or park?
   a. show them slides and photographs?
   c. give them pamphlets or a book on wildlife reserves or parks?
   b. give them a talk on wildlife reserves or parks?

6. You are about to purchase a new CD player. Other than price, what would most influence your decision?
   b. The salesperson telling you what you want to know.
   c. Reading the details about it.
   d. Playing with the controls and listening to it.
   a. Its fashionable and upscale appearance.

7. Recall a time in your life when you learned how to do something like playing a new board game. Try to avoid choosing a very physical skill, e.g. riding a bike. How did you learn best? By
   a. visual clues—pictures, diagrams, charts?
   c. written instructions?
   b. listening to somebody explaining it?
   d. doing it or trying it?

8. You have an eye problem. Would you prefer that the doctor
   b. tell you what is wrong?
   a. show you a diagram of what is wrong?
   d. use a model to show what is wrong?

9. You are about to learn to use a new program on a computer. Would you
   d. sit down at the keyboard and begin to experiment with the program's features?
   c. read the manual that comes with the program?
   b. call a friend and ask questions about it?

10. You are staying in a hotel and have a rental. You would like to visit friends whose address/location you do not know. Would you like them to
   a. draw you a map on paper?
   b. tell you the directions?
   c. write down the directions (without a map)?
   d. pick you up at the hotel in their car?

11. Apart from price, what would most influence your decision to buy a particular book?
   d. You have used a copy before.
   b. A friend talking about it.
   c. Quickly reading parts of it.
   a. The appealing way it looks.

12. A new movie has arrived in town. What would most influence your decision to go (or not go)?
   b. You heard a radio review about it.
   c. You read a review about it.
   a. You saw a preview of it.

13. Do you prefer a lecturer or teacher who likes to use
   c. a textbook, handouts, readings?
   a. flow diagrams, charts, graphs.
   d. field trips, labs, practical sessions?
   b. discussion, guest speakers?

	a.	b.	c.	d.
Count your choices:	❏	❏	❏	❏
	V	A	R	K

Now match the letter or letters you have recorded most to the same letter or letters in the Learning Styles Chart. You may have more than one learning style preference—many people do. Next to each letter in the Chart are suggestions that will refer you to different learning aids throughout this text.

LEARNING STYLES CHART

VISUAL

INTAKE: TO TAKE IN THE INFORMATION	TO MAKE A STUDY PACKAGE	TEXT FEATURES THAT MAY HELP YOU THE MOST	OUTPUT: TO DO WELL ON EXAMS
• Pay close attention to charts, drawings, and handouts your instructor uses • Underline. • Use different colors. • Use symbols, flow. charts, graphs, different arrangements on the page, white space.	• Convert your lecture notes into "page pictures." To do this: • Use the "Intake" strategies. • Reconstruct images in different ways. • Redraw pages from memory. • Replace words with symbols and initials • Look at your pages.	**The Navigator** **Feature Story** **Preview** **Infographics/Illustrations/ Photos** **Accounting Equation/ Cash Flow Analysis** **Business Insights** **Decision Toolkits** **Key Terms in blue** **Words in bold** **Using the Decision Toolkit** **Demonstration Problem/ Action Plan** **Questions/Exercises Problems** **Financial Analysis on the Web** **Exploring the Web**	• Recall your "page pictures." • Draw diagrams where appropriate. • Practice turning your visuals back into words.

AURAL

INTAKE: TO TAKE IN THE INFORMATION	TO MAKE A STUDY PACKAGE	TEXT FEATURES THAT MAY HELP YOU THE MOST	OUTPUT: TO DO WELL ON EXAMS
• Attend lectures and tutorials. • Discuss topics with students and instructors. • Explain new ideas to other people. • Use a tape recorder. • Leave spaces in your lecture notes for later recall. • Describe overheads, pictures, and visuals to somebody who was not in class.	You may take poor notes because you prefer to listen. Therefore: • Expand your notes by talking with others and with information from your textbook. • Tape record summarized notes and listen. • Read summarized notes out loud. • Explain your notes to another "aural" person.	**Infographics/Illustrations** **Business Insights** **Review It/Do It/Action Plan** **Using the Decision Toolkit** **Summary of Study Objectives** **Glossary** **Demonstration Problem/ Action Plan** **Self-Study Questions** **Questions/Exercises/Problems** **Financial Analysis on the Web** **Group Decision Case** **Communication Activity** **Ethics Case**	• Talk with the instructor. • Spend time in quiet places recalling the ideas. • Practice writing answers to old exam questions • Say your answers out loud.

SOURCE: Adapted from VARK pack. Copyright Version 4.1 (2002) held by Neil D. Fleming, Christchurch, New Zealand and Charles C. Bonwell, Green Mountain Falls, Colorado 80819, U.S.A. The VARK website is at www.vark-learn.com.

READING/WRITING

INTAKE: TO TAKE IN THE INFORMATION	TO MAKE A STUDY PACKAGE	TEXT FEATURES THAT MAY HELP YOU THE MOST	OUTPUT: TO DO WELL ON EXAMS
• Use lists and headings. • Use dictionaries, glossaries, and definitions. • Read handouts, textbooks, and supplementary library readings. • Use lecture notes.	• Write out words again and again. • Reread notes silently. • Rewrite ideas and principles into other words. • Turn charts, diagrams, and other illustrations into statements.	**The Navigator** **Feature Story** **Study Objectives** **Preview** **Review It/Do It/Action Plan** **Using the Decision Toolkit** **Summary of Study Objectives** **Glossary** **Self-Study Questions** **Questions/Exercises/Problems** **Writing Problems** **Research Case** **Interpreting Financial Statements** **Group Decision Case** **Communication Activity** **Ethics Case**	• Write exam answers. • Practice with multiple-choice questions. • Write paragraphs, beginnings and endings. • Write your lists in outline form. • Arrange your words into hierarchies and points.

KINESTHETIC

INTAKE: TO TAKE IN THE INFORMATION	TO MAKE A STUDY PACKAGE	TEXT FEATURES THAT MAY HELP YOU THE MOST	OUTPUT: TO DO WELL ON EXAMS
• Use all your senses. • Go to labs, take field trips. • Listen to real-life examples • Pay attention to applications. • Use hands-on approaches. • Use trial-and-error methods.	You may take poor notes because topics do not seem concrete or relevant. Therefore: • Put examples in your summaries. • Use case studies and applications to help with principles abstract concepts. • Talk about your notes with another "kinesthetic" person. • Use pictures and photographs that illustrate an idea.	**The Navigator** **Feature Story** **Preview** **Infographics/Illustrations/ Photos** **Accounting Equation/ Cash Flow Analysis** **Decision Toolkits** **Review It/Do It/Action Plan** **Using the Decision Toolkit** **Summary of Study Objectives** **Demonstration Problem/ Action Plan** **Self-Study Questions** **Questions/Exercises/Problems** **Financial Reporting Problem** **Comparative Analysis Problem** **Research Case** **Group Decision Case**	• Write practice answers. • Role-play the exam situation.

For all learning styles: Be sure to use the CD-ROM and Web site to enhance your understanding of the concepts and procedures of the text. In particular, use the **Interactive Self-Study** and **Self-Tests**, **Key Term Matching Activities**, **Interactive Chapter Reviews**, and **Web-based Tutorials**.

BRIEF CONTENTS

CONTENTS

CHAPTER 8

Reporting and Analyzing Receivables, *365*

CHAPTER 9

Reporting and Analyzing Long-Lived Assets, *411*

CHAPTER 10

Reporting and Analyzing Liabilities, *463*

CHAPTER 21

Performance Evaluation Through Standard Costs, *995*

CHAPTER 22

Incremental Analysis and Capital Budgeting, *1037*

APPENDIX A

Specimen Financial Statements: Tootsie Roll Industries, Inc., *A-1*

APPENDIX B

Specimen Financial Statements: Hershey Foods Corporation, *B-1*

APPENDIX C

Time Value of Money, *C-1*

APPENDIX D

Payroll Accounting, *D-1*

Introduction to Financial Statements

The Feature Story helps you picture how the chapter topic relates to the real world of accounting and business. You will find references to the story throughout the chapter.

Study Objectives give you a framework for learning the specific concepts covered in the chapter.

STUDY OBJECTIVES

After studying this chapter, you should be able to:

1 Describe the primary forms of business organization.

2 Identify the users and uses of accounting information.

3 Explain the three principal types of business activity.

4 Describe the content and purpose of each of the financial statements.

5 Explain the meaning of assets, liabilities, and stockholders' equity, and state the basic accounting equation.

6 Describe the components that supplement the financial statements in an annual report.

7 Explain the basic assumptions and principles underlying financial statements.

THE NAVIGATOR ✔

▶ Scan *Study Objectives* ☐

▶ Read *Feature Story* ☐

▶ Read *Preview* ☐

▶ Read text and answer *Before You Go On*
   p. 10 ☐   p. 15 ☐   p. 26 ☐

▶ Work Using the *Decision Toolkit* ☐

▶ Review Summary of *Study Objectives* ☐

▶ Work *Demonstration Problem* ☐

▶ Answer *Self-Study Questions* ☐

▶ Complete *Assignments* ☐

FEATURE STORY

Financial Reporting: A Matter of Trust

In 2002 the financial press was full of articles about financial scandals and accounting misdeeds. It started with **Enron**, but then spread to **Xerox**, **Qwest**, **Global Crossing**, and **WorldCom**, among others. Many of the articles expressed concern that as an increasing number of misdeeds came to public attention, a mistrust of financial reporting in general was developing. These articles made clear just how important accounting and financial reporting are to the U.S. and world financial markets and to society as a whole. Without financial reports, managers would not be able to evaluate how well their company is doing or to make decisions about the best way to make their company grow in the future. Without financial reports, investors and lenders could not make informed decisions about how to allocate their funds. There is no doubt that a sound, well-functioning economy depends on accurate and dependable financial reporting.

The Navigator is a learning system designed to prompt you to use the learning aids in the chapter and to set priorities as you study.

In order to make financial decisions as either an investor or a manager, you need to know how to read financial reports. In this book you will learn about financial reporting and some basic tools used to evaluate financial reports. In the first chapter we introduce you to the real financial statements of a company whose products most of you probably are familiar with—**Tootsie Roll**. We have chosen the financial statements of Tootsie Roll because they are a good example from the real world. Tootsie Roll's presentation of its financial results is complete, yet also relatively easy to understand. Chapter 1 presents these financial statements in a simplified fashion, while an appendix to this textbook contains the statements in their entirety.

Tootsie Roll started off humbly in 1896 in a small New York City candy shop owned by Austrian immigrant Leo Hirshfield. The candy's name came from his five-year-old daughter's nickname—"Tootsie." Today, the Chicago-based company produces more than 49 million Tootsie Rolls and 16 million Tootsie Pops *each day*. In fact, Tootsie Pops are at the center of one of science's most challenging questions: How many licks does it take to get to the Tootsie Roll center of a Tootsie Pop? The answer varies: Licking machines created at Purdue University and the University of Michigan report an average of 364 and 411 licks, respectively. In studies using human lickers, the answer ranges from 144 to 252. We recommend that you take a few minutes today away from your studies to determine your own results.

Source: Tootsie Roll information adapted from www.tootsie.com.

Every **chapter-opening Feature Story** ends with the **Internet addresses** of the companies cited in the story to help you connect with these real businesses and explore them further.

On the World Wide Web
Tootsie Roll Industries:
www.tootsie.com

How do you start a business? How do you make it grow into a widely recognized brand name like **Tootsie Roll**? How do you determine whether your business is making or losing money? When you need to expand your operations, where do you get money to finance expansion—should you borrow, should you issue stock, should you use your own funds? How do you convince lenders to lend you money or investors to buy your stock? Success in business requires making countless decisions, and decisions require financial information.

The purpose of this chapter is to show you what role accounting plays in providing financial information. The content and organization of the chapter are as follows.

The **Preview** describes the purpose of the chapter and outlines the major topics and subtopics you will find in it.

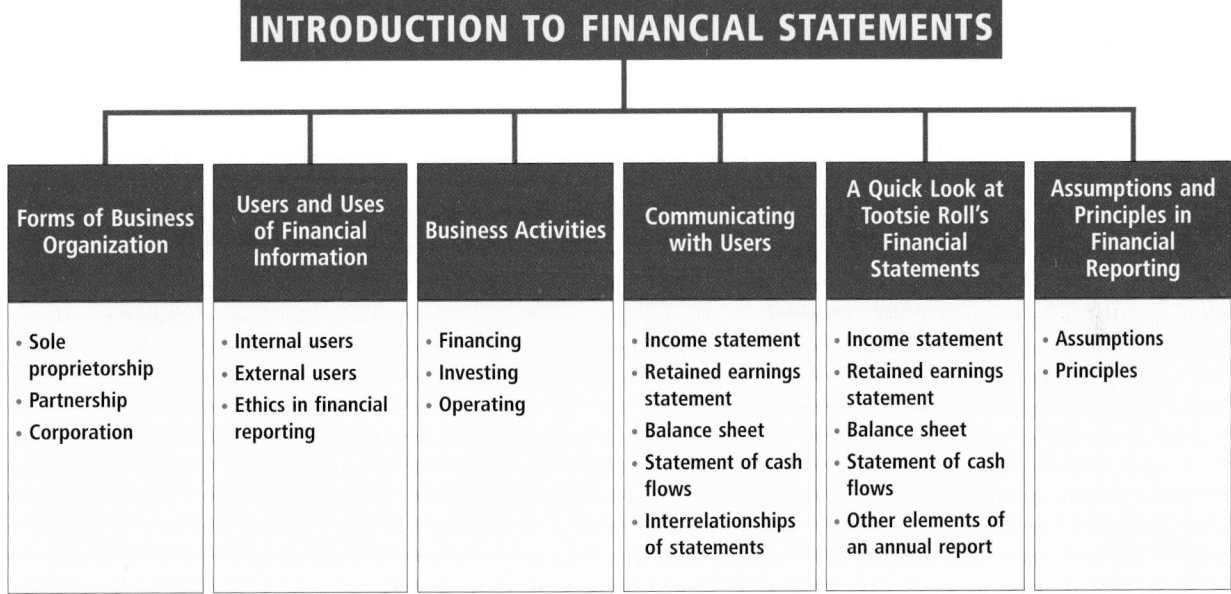

Forms of Business Organization

Suppose you graduate with a marketing degree and open your own marketing agency. One of your initial decisions is what organizational form your business will have. You have three choices—sole proprietorship, partnership, or corporation. A business owned by one person is a **sole proprietorship**. A business owned by more than one person is a **partnership**. A business organized as a separate legal entity owned by stockholders is a **corporation**.

You will probably choose the sole proprietorship form for your marketing agency. It is **simple to set up** and **gives you control** over the business. Small owner-operated businesses such as barber shops, law offices, and auto repair shops are often sole proprietorships, as are farms and small retail stores.

Another possibility is for you to join forces with other individuals to form a partnership. Partnerships often are formed because one individual does not have **enough economic resources** to initiate or expand the business, or because **partners bring unique skills or resources** to the partnership. You and your partners should formalize your duties and contributions in a written partnership

STUDY OBJECTIVE
1
Describe the primary forms of business organization.

Terms that represent essential concepts of the chapter topic are printed in blue where they are first explained in the text. They are listed and defined again in the **glossary** at the end of the chapter.

3

agreement. Partnerships are often used to organize retail and service-type businesses, including professional practices (lawyers, doctors, architects, and certified public accountants).

As a third alternative, you might organize as a corporation. As an investor in a corporation you receive shares of stock to indicate your ownership claim. Buying stock in a corporation is often more attractive than investing in a partnership because shares of stock are **easy to sell** (transfer ownership). Selling a proprietorship or partnership interest is much more involved. Also, individuals can become **stockholders** by investing relatively small amounts of money. Therefore, it is **easier for corporations to raise funds**. Successful corporations often have thousands of stockholders, and their stock is traded on organized stock exchanges like the New York Stock Exchange. Many businesses start as sole proprietorships or partnerships and eventually incorporate. For example, in 1896 Tootsie Roll was started as a sole proprietorship, and by 1919 it had incorporated.

Other factors to consider in deciding which organizational form to choose are **taxes and legal liability**. If you choose a sole proprietorship or partnership, you generally receive more favorable tax treatment than a corporation. However, a disadvantage of proprietorships and partnerships is that proprietors and partners are personally liable for all debts of the business; corporate stockholders are not. In other words, corporate stockholders generally pay higher taxes but have no personal liability. We will discuss these issues in more depth in a later chapter. Illustration 1-1 highlights the three types of organizations and the advantages of each.

Illustration 1-1 Forms of business organization

Illustrations like this one convey information in pictorial form to help you visualize and apply the ideas as you study.

Sole Proprietorship
-Simple to establish
-Owner controlled
-Tax advantages

Partnership
-Simple to establish
-Shared control
-Broader skills and resources
-Tax advantages

Corporation
-Easier to transfer ownership
-Easier to raise funds
-No personal liability

Although the combined number of proprietorships and partnerships in the United States is more than five times the number of corporations, the revenue produced by corporations is eight times greater. Most of the largest enterprises in the United States—for example, Coca-Cola, ExxonMobil, General Motors, Citigroup, and Microsoft—are corporations. Because the majority of U.S. business is transacted by corporations, the emphasis in this book is on the corporate form of organization.

Users and Uses of Financial Information

The purpose of financial information is to provide inputs for decision making. **Accounting** is the information system that identifies, records, and communicates the economic events of an organization to interested users. Many people have an interest in knowing about the ongoing activities of the business. These people are **users** of accounting information. Users can be divided broadly into two groups: internal users and external users.

STUDY OBJECTIVE
2
Identify the users and uses
of accounting information.

INTERNAL USERS

Internal users of accounting information are managers who plan, organize, and run a business. These include **marketing managers**, **production supervisors**, **finance directors**, **and company officers**. In running a business, managers must answer many important questions, as shown in Illustration 1-2.

Illustration 1-2

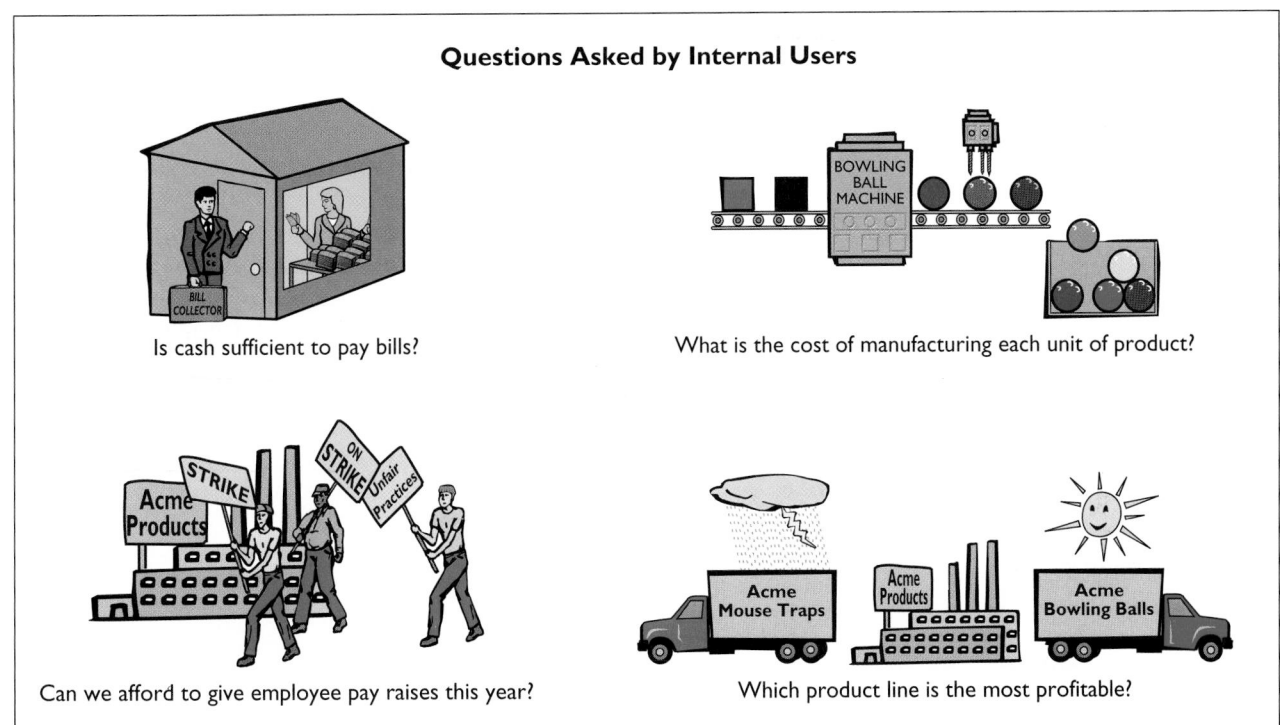

Questions Asked by Internal Users

Is cash sufficient to pay bills?

What is the cost of manufacturing each unit of product?

Can we afford to give employee pay raises this year?

Which product line is the most profitable?

To answer these and other questions, you need detailed information on a timely basis. For internal users, accounting provides internal reports, such as financial comparisons of operating alternatives, projections of income from new sales campaigns, and forecasts of cash needs for the next year. In addition, summarized financial information is presented in the form of financial statements.

EXTERNAL USERS

There are several types of **external users** of accounting information. **Investors** (owners) use accounting information to make decisions to buy, hold, or sell stock. **Creditors** such as suppliers and bankers use accounting information to evaluate the risks of granting credit or lending money. Some questions that may be asked by investors and creditors about a company are shown in Illustration 1-3.

Illustration 1-3

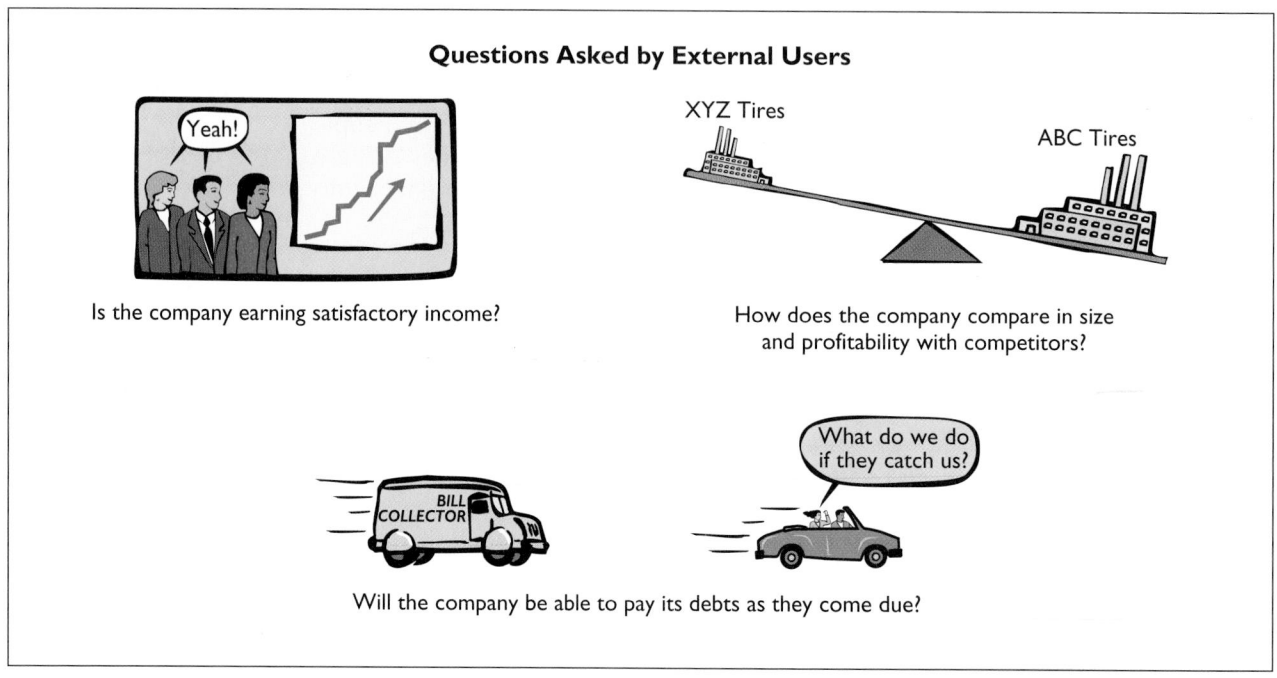

Questions Asked by External Users

Is the company earning satisfactory income?

How does the company compare in size and profitability with competitors?

Will the company be able to pay its debts as they come due?

The information needs and questions of other external users vary considerably. **Taxing authorities**, such as the Internal Revenue Service, want to know whether the company complies with the tax laws. **Regulatory agencies**, such as the Securities and Exchange Commission or the Federal Trade Commission, want to know whether the company is operating within prescribed rules. **Customers** are interested in whether a company will continue to honor product warranties and otherwise support its product lines. **Labor unions** want to know whether the owners have the ability to pay increased wages and benefits. **Economic planners** use accounting information to analyze and forecast economic activity.

Business Insights provide examples of business situations from various perspectives—ethics, investor, international, and management.

Business Insight
ETHICS PERSPECTIVE

Enron, Dynegy, Duke Energy, and other big energy-trading companies reported record profits at the same time as California was paying extremely high prices for energy and suffering from blackouts. This disparity caused regulators to investigate the energy traders to make sure that the profits were earned by legitimate and fair practices.

ETHICS IN FINANCIAL REPORTING

Imagine trying to carry on a business or invest money if you could not depend on the financial statements to be honestly prepared. Effective communication and economic activity would be impossible. Information would have no credibility. Effective financial reporting depends on sound ethical behavior.

To sensitize you to ethical situations and to give you practice at solving ethical dilemmas, we address ethics in a number of ways in this book: (1) A number of the Feature Stories as well as other parts of the text discuss the central importance of ethical behavior to financial reporting. (2) Business Insight boxes with an ethics perspective highlight ethics situations and issues in actual business settings. (3) At the end of the chapter, an Ethics Case simulates a business situation and asks you to put yourself in the position of a decision maker in that case. (4) The CD that accompanies this book has video segments on critical accounting issues. In the process of analyzing these various ethics cases and your own ethical experiences, you should apply the three steps outlined in Illustration 1-4.

Illustration 1-4 Steps in analyzing ethics cases

Solving an Ethical Dilemma

1. Recognize an ethical situation and the ethical issues involved.

Use your personal ethics to identify ethical situations and issues. Some businesses and professional organizations provide written codes of ethics for guidance in some business situations.

2. Identify and analyze the principal elements in the situation.

Identify the *stakeholders*—persons or groups who may be harmed or benefited. Ask the question: What are the responsibilities and obligations of the parties involved?

3. Identify the alternatives, and weigh the impact of each alternative on various stakeholders.

Select the most ethical alternative, considering all the consequences. Sometimes there will be one right answer. Other situations involve more than one right solution; these situations require an evaluation of each and a selection of the best alternative.

Business Activities

All businesses are involved in three types of activity—financing, investing, and operating. For example, the founder of Tootsie Roll needed financing to start and grow his business. Some of this **financing** came from personal savings, and some likely came from outside sources like banks. The cash obtained was then **invested** in the equipment necessary to run the business, such as mixing equipment and delivery vehicles. Once this equipment was in place, the founder could begin the **operating** activities of making and selling candy.

The **accounting information system** keeps track of the results of each of the various business activities—financing, investing, and operating. Let's look in more detail at each type of business activity.

STUDY OBJECTIVE
3
Explain the three principal types of business activity.

FINANCING ACTIVITIES

It takes money to make money. The two primary sources of outside funds for corporations are borrowing money and issuing shares of stock in exchange for cash.

For example, Tootsie Roll Industries may borrow money in a variety of ways. It can take out a loan at a bank, borrow directly from investors by issuing debt securities called bonds, or borrow money from its suppliers by purchasing goods on credit. Persons or entities to whom Tootsie Roll owes money are its **creditors**. Amounts owed to creditors—in the form of debt and other obligations—are called liabilities.

Financing

Specific names are given to different types of liabilities, depending on their source. Tootsie Roll, for instance, might purchase chocolate and corn syrup on credit from suppliers; the obligations to pay for these supplies are called **accounts payable**. Additionally, Tootsie Roll may have a **note payable** to a bank for the money borrowed to purchase delivery trucks. It may also have **wages payable** to employees, and **sales and real estate taxes payable** to the local government. Debt securities sold to investors that must be repaid at a particular date some years in the future are called **bonds payable**.

A corporation may also obtain funds by selling shares of stock to investors. When Tootsie Roll initially became a corporation, the shares were probably issued to a small group of individuals who had an interest in starting the business. However, as the business grew, it became necessary to sell shares more broadly to obtain additional financing. **Common stock** is the term used to describe the total amount paid in by stockholders for the shares they purchase.

The claims of creditors differ from those of stockholders. If you loan money to a company, you are one of its creditors. In lending money, you specify a payment schedule (for example, payment at the end of three months). As a creditor, you have a legal right to be paid at the agreed time. In the event of nonpayment, you may legally force the company to sell its property to pay its debts. The law requires that creditor claims be paid before stockholders' claims.

Stockholders, on the other hand, have no claim to corporate resources until the claims of creditors are satisfied. If you buy a company's stock instead of loaning it money, you have no legal right to expect any payments until all of its creditors are paid. However, many corporations make payments to stockholders on a regular basis as long as there is sufficient cash to cover required payments to creditors. These payments to stockholders are called **dividends**.

Business Insight
ETHICS PERSPECTIVE

All U.S. states that allow gambling have also set up "gaming commissions" to protect gamblers from casinos that might try to cheat them. The creation of gaming commissions is generally supported by casino owners because they know that people won't play a game if they think it is "rigged." Similarly, people won't "play" the stock market if they think it is rigged.

After the stock market crash of 1929, many investors lost faith in both the stock market and companies' financial statements. Ever since then, the U.S. government has tried to ensure that the stock market is fair and that corporate financial statements present an accurate depiction of a company's finances. That is why the collapse of **Enron**, and with it the collapse of the auditing firm **Arthur Andersen**, is so important. In the months that followed the Enron scandal, countless articles in the financial press read like the following one from the February 21, 2002, *Wall Street Journal*:

> **U.S. Share Prices Slump**—Accounting concerns dragged down **IBM, J.P. Morgan**, and **Disney** on Tuesday.

A telling quote from that article explained the importance of accounting for the companies involved, for investors, and for the economy as a whole: "Analysts say repeated disclosures about questionable accounting practices have bruised investors' faith in the reliability of earnings reports, which in turn has sent stock prices tumbling."

INVESTING ACTIVITIES

Once the company has raised money through financing activities, it will then use that money in investing activities. Investing activities involve the purchase of those resources a company needs in order to operate. During the early stages of the company's life it must purchase many resources. For example, computers, delivery trucks, furniture, and buildings are resources obtained from investing activities. Resources owned by a business are called **assets**. Different types of assets are given different names. Tootsie Roll's mixing equipment is an asset referred to as **property, plant, and equipment**. One of a company's most important assets is its **cash**.

Investing

Many of the company's assets are purchased through investing activities. Others, however, result from operating activities. For example, if Tootsie Roll sells goods to a customer and does not receive cash immediately, then Tootsie Roll has a right to expect payment from that customer in the future. This right to receive money in the future is an asset called an **account receivable**.

Alternative Terminology
Property, plant, and equipment is sometimes called **fixed assets**.

OPERATING ACTIVITIES

Once a business has the assets it needs to get started, it can begin its operations. Tootsie Roll is in the business of selling all things that smell, look, or taste like candy. It sells Tootsie Rolls, Tootsie Pops, Blow Pops, Caramel Apple Pops, Mason Dots, Mason Crows, Sugar Daddy, and Sugar Babies. In short, if it has anything to do with candy, Tootsie Roll sells it. We call the sale of these products revenues. In accounting language, **revenues** are the increase in assets resulting from the sale of a product or service in the normal course of business. For example, Tootsie Roll records revenue when it sells a candy product.

Operating

Revenues arise from different sources and are identified by various names depending on the nature of the business. For instance, Tootsie Roll's primary source of revenue is the sale of candy products. However, it also generates interest revenue on debt securities held as investments. Sources of revenue common to many businesses are **sales revenue**, **service revenue**, and **interest revenue**.

Before Tootsie Roll can sell a single Tootsie Roll, Tootsie Pop, or Blow Pop, it must purchase sugar, corn syrup, and other ingredients, mix these ingredients, process the mix, and wrap and ship the finished product. It also incurs costs like salaries, rents, and utilities. All of these costs, referred to as expenses, are necessary to produce and sell the product. In accounting language, **expenses** are the cost of assets consumed or services used in the process of generating revenues.

Expenses take many forms and are identified by various names depending on the type of asset consumed or service used. For example, Tootsie Roll keeps track of these types of expenses: **cost of goods sold** (such as the cost of ingredients), **selling expenses** (such as the cost of salespersons' salaries), **marketing expenses** (such as the cost of advertising), **administrative expenses** (such as the salaries of administrative staff, and telephone and heat costs incurred at the corporate office), and **interest expense** (amounts of interest paid on various debts).

Tootsie Roll compares the revenues of a period with the expenses of that period to determine whether it earned a profit. When revenues exceed expenses, **net income** results. When expenses exceed revenues, a **net loss** results.

BEFORE YOU GO ON . . .

▶ Review It

1. What are the three forms of business organization and the advantages of each?
2. What are the two primary categories of users of financial information? Give examples of each.
3. What are the three types of business activity?
4. What are assets, liabilities, common stock, revenues, expenses, and net income?

▶ Do It

Classify each item as an asset, liability, common stock, revenue, or expense.

Cost of using property   Issuance of ownership shares
Truck purchased   Amount earned from providing service
Notes payable   Amounts owed to suppliers

Action Plan

- Classify each item based on its economic characteristics. Proper classification of items is critical if accounting is to provide useful information.

Solution

Cost of using property is classified as expense.
Truck purchased is classified as an asset.
Notes payable are classified as liabilities.
Issuance of ownership shares is classified as common stock.
Amount earned from providing service is classified as revenue.
Amounts owed to suppliers are classified as liabilities.

Communicating with Users

Assets, liabilities, expenses, and revenues are of interest to users of accounting information. For business purposes, it is customary to arrange this information in the format of four different **financial statements**, which form the backbone of financial accounting:

- To present a picture at a point in time of what your business owns (its assets) and what it owes (its liabilities), you would present a **balance sheet**.

- To show how successfully your business performed during a period of time, you would report its revenues and expenses in the **income statement**.

- To indicate how much of previous income was distributed to you and the other owners of your business in the form of dividends, and how much was retained in the business to allow for future growth, you would present a **retained earnings statement**.

- And finally, of particular interest to your bankers and other creditors, you would present a **statement of cash flows** to show from what sources your business obtained cash during a period of time and how that cash was used.

To introduce you to these statements, we have prepared the financial statements for a marketing agency, Sierra Corporation.

INCOME STATEMENT

The purpose of the **income statement** is to report the success or failure of the company's operations for a period of time. To indicate that Sierra's income statement reports the results of operations for a **period of time**, the income statement is dated "For the Month Ended October 31, 2005." The income statement lists the company's revenues followed by its expenses. Finally, the net income (or net loss) is determined by deducting expenses from revenues.

Why are financial statement users interested in net income? Investors are interested in a company's past net income because it provides some information about future net income. Investors buy and sell stock based on their beliefs about the future performance of a company. If you believe that Sierra will be even more successful in the future and that this success will translate into a higher stock price, you should buy Sierra's stock. Creditors also use the income statement to predict the future. When a bank loans money to a company, it does so with the belief that it will be repaid in the future. If it didn't think it was going to be repaid, it wouldn't loan the money. Therefore, prior to making the loan the bank loan officer will use the income statement as a source of information to predict whether the company will be profitable enough to repay its loan.

Amounts received from issuing stock or paid out as dividends are not used in determining net income. Amounts received from or paid to shareholders are not revenues or expenses. For example, $10,000 of cash received from issuing new stock was not treated as revenue by Sierra Corporation, and dividends paid of $500 were not regarded as a business expense. Sierra Corporation's income statement is shown in Illustration 1-5.

SIERRA CORPORATION Income Statement For the Month Ended October 31, 2005		
Revenues		
Service revenue		$10,600
Expenses		
Salaries expense	$5,200	
Supplies expense	1,500	
Rent expense	900	
Insurance expense	50	
Interest expense	50	
Depreciation expense	40	
Total expenses		7,740
Net income		$ 2,860

Illustration 1-5 Sierra Corporation's income statement

Helpful Hint The heading identifies the company, the type of statement, and the time period covered. Sometimes another line indicates the unit of measure—e.g., "in thousands" or "in millions."

Helpful Hints help clarify concepts being discussed.

DECISION TOOLKIT

Decision Toolkits summarize the financial decision-making process.

Decision Checkpoints	Info Needed for Decision	Tool to Use for Decision	How to Evaluate Results
Are the company's operations profitable?	Income statement	The income statement reports on the success or failure of the company's operations by reporting its revenues and expenses.	If the company's revenue exceeds its expenses, it will report net income; otherwise it will report a net loss.

RETAINED EARNINGS STATEMENT

If Sierra is profitable, at the end of each period it must decide what portion of profits to pay to shareholders in dividends. In theory it could pay all of its current-period profits, but few companies choose to do this. Why? Because they want to retain part of the profits to allow for further expansion. High-growth companies, such as **Microsoft**, **Amazon.com**, and **Cisco Systems**, often choose to pay no dividends. **Retained earnings** is the net income retained in the corporation.

The **retained earnings statement** shows the amounts and causes of changes in retained earnings during the period. The time period is the same as that covered by the income statement. The beginning retained earnings amount is shown on the first line of the statement. Then net income is added and dividends are deducted to calculate the retained earnings at the end of the period. If a company has a net loss, it is deducted (rather than added) in the retained earnings statement.

By monitoring the retained earnings statement, financial statement users can evaluate dividend payment practices. Some investors seek companies that pay high dividends. Other investors seek companies that instead of paying dividends reinvest earnings to increase the company's growth. Lenders monitor their corporate customers' dividend payments because any money paid in dividends reduces a company's ability to repay its debts. Illustration 1-6 presents Sierra Corporation's retained earnings statement.

Illustration 1-6 Sierra Corporation's retained earnings statement

Helpful Hint The heading of this statement identifies the company, the type of statement, and the time period covered by the statement.

SIERRA CORPORATION Retained Earnings Statement For the Month Ended October 31, 2005	
Retained earnings, October 1	$ 0
Add: Net income	2,860
	2,860
Less: Dividends	500
Retained earnings, October 31	$2,360

DECISION TOOLKIT

Decision Checkpoints	Info Needed for Decision	Tool to Use for Decision	How to Evaluate Results
What is the company's policy toward dividends and growth?	Retained earnings statement	How much of this year's income did the company pay out in dividends to shareholders?	A company striving for rapid growth will pay a low (or no) dividend.

BALANCE SHEET

The **balance sheet** reports assets and claims to those assets at a specific **point** in time. These claims are subdivided into two categories: claims of creditors and claims of owners. As noted earlier, claims of creditors are called **liabilities**. Claims of owners are called **stockholders' equity**. This relationship is shown in equation form in Illustration 1-7. This equation is referred to as the **basic accounting equation**.

Illustration 1-7 Basic accounting equation

Assets = Liabilities + Stockholders' Equity

This relationship is where the name "balance sheet" comes from. Assets must be in balance with the claims to the assets.

As you can see from looking at Sierra's balance sheet in Illustration 1-8, assets are listed first, followed by liabilities and stockholders' equity. Stockholders' equity is comprised of two parts: (1) common stock and (2) retained earnings. As noted earlier, common stock results when the company sells new shares of stock. Retained earnings is the net income retained in the corporation. Sierra has common stock of $10,000 and retained earnings of $2,360, for total stockholders' equity of $12,360.

Illustration 1-8 Sierra Corporation's balance sheet

SIERRA CORPORATION
Balance Sheet
October 31, 2005

Assets

Cash	$15,200
Accounts receivable	200
Advertising supplies	1,000
Prepaid insurance	550
Office equipment, net	4,960
Total assets	$21,910

Liabilities and Stockholders' Equity

Liabilities		
Notes payable	$ 5,000	
Accounts payable	2,500	
Interest payable	50	
Unearned revenue	800	
Salaries payable	1,200	
Total liabilities		$ 9,550
Stockholders' equity		
Common stock	10,000	
Retained earnings	2,360	
Total stockholders' equity		12,360
Total liabilities and stockholders' equity		$21,910

Creditors analyze a company's balance sheet to determine the likelihood that they will be repaid. They carefully evaluate the nature of the company's assets and liabilities. For example, does the company have assets that could be easily sold to repay its debts? Managers use the balance sheet to determine whether inventory is adequate to support future sales and whether cash on hand is sufficient for immediate cash needs. Managers also look at the relationship between debt and stockholders' equity to determine whether they have the best proportion of debt and common stock financing.

DECISION TOOLKIT

Decision Checkpoints	Info Needed for Decision	Tool to Use for Decision	How to Evaluate Results
Does the company rely primarily on debt or stock-holders' equity to finance its assets?	Balance sheet	The balance sheet reports the company's resources and claims to those resources. There are two types of claims: liabilities and stockholders' equity.	Compare the amount of debt versus the amount of stock-holders' equity to determine whether the company relies more on creditors or owners for its financing.

STATEMENT OF CASH FLOWS

The primary purpose of a **statement of cash flows** is to provide financial information about the cash receipts and cash payments of a business for a specific period of time. To help investors, creditors, and others in their analysis of a company's cash position, the statement of cash flows reports the cash effects of a company's: (1) operating activities, (2) investing activities, and (3) financing activities. In addition, the statement shows the net increase or decrease in cash during the period, and the amount of cash at the end of the period.

Users are interested in the statement of cash flows because they want to know what is happening to a company's most important resource. The statement of cash flows provides answers to these simple but important questions:

Where did cash come from during the period?
How was cash used during the period?
What was the change in the cash balance during the period?

The statement of cash flows for Sierra, in Illustration 1-9, shows that cash increased $15,200 during the year. This increase resulted because operating activities (services to clients) increased cash $5,700, and financing activities increased cash $14,500. Investing activities used $5,000 of cash for the purchase of equipment.

Illustration 1-9 Sierra Corporation's statement of cash flows

SIERRA CORPORATION
Statement of Cash Flows
For the Month Ended October 31, 2005

Cash flows from operating activities		
Cash receipts from operating activities	$11,200	
Cash payments for operating activities	(5,500)	
Net cash provided by operating activities		$ 5,700
Cash flows from investing activities		
Purchased office equipment	(5,000)	
Net cash used by investing activities		(5,000)
Cash flows from financing activities		
Issuance of common stock	10,000	
Issued note payable	5,000	
Payment of dividend	(500)	
Net cash provided by financing activities		14,500
Net increase in cash		15,200
Cash at beginning of period		0
Cash at end of period		$15,200

Helpful Hint The heading of this statement identifies the company, the type of statement, and the time period covered by the statement.

DECISION TOOLKIT

Decision Checkpoints	Info Needed for Decision	Tool to Use for Decision	How to Evaluate Results
✔			
Does the company generate sufficient cash from operations to fund its investing activities?	Statement of cash flows	The statement of cash flows shows the amount of cash provided or used by operating activities, investing activities, and financing activities.	Compare the amount of cash provided by operating activities with the amount of cash used by investing activities. Any deficiency in cash from operating activities must be made up with cash from financing activities.

INTERRELATIONSHIPS OF STATEMENTS

Because the results on some statements are used as inputs to other statements, the statements are interrelated. These interrelationships are evident in Sierra's statements in Illustration 1-10 (on page 16).

1. The retained earnings statement is dependent on the results of the income statement. Sierra reported net income of $2,860 for the period. This amount is added to the beginning amount of retained earnings as part of the process of determining ending retained earnings.

2. The balance sheet and retained earnings statement are interrelated because the ending amount of $2,360 on the retained earnings statement is reported as the retained earnings amount on the balance sheet.

3. The statement of cash flows and the balance sheet are also interrelated. The statement of cash flows shows how the cash account changed during the period by showing the amount of cash at the beginning of the period, the sources and uses of cash during the period, and the $15,200 of cash at the end of the period. The ending amount of cash shown on the statement of cash flows must agree with the amount of cash on the balance sheet.

Study these interrelationships carefully. To prepare financial statements you must understand the sequence in which these amounts are determined, and how each statement impacts the next.

BEFORE YOU GO ON . . .

▶ Review It

1. What questions might each of the following decision makers ask that could be answered by financial information: bank loan officer, stock investor, labor union president, and federal bank regulator?

2. What are the content and purpose of each statement: income statement, balance sheet, retained earnings statement, and statement of cash flows?

3. The accounting equation is: Assets = Liabilities + Stockholders' Equity. **Tootsie Roll**'s financial statements are provided in Appendix A at the end of this book. Replacing words in the equation with dollar amounts, what is Tootsie Roll's accounting equation at December 31, 2002? The answer to this question is provided on page 50.

Review It questions marked with this **Tootsie Roll icon** require that you use Tootsie Roll's 2002 Annual Report in Appendix A at the back of the book.

Illustration 1-10 Sierra
Corporation's financial
statements

SIERRA CORPORATION
Income Statement
For the Month Ended October 31, 2005

Revenues		
Service revenue		$10,600
Expenses		
Salaries expense	$5,200	
Supplies expense	1,500	
Rent expense	900	
Insurance expense	50	
Interest expense	50	
Depreciation expense	40	
Total expenses		7,740
Net income		$ 2,860

Helpful Hint Note that final
sums are double-underlined,
and negative amounts (in the
statement of cash flows) are
presented in parentheses.

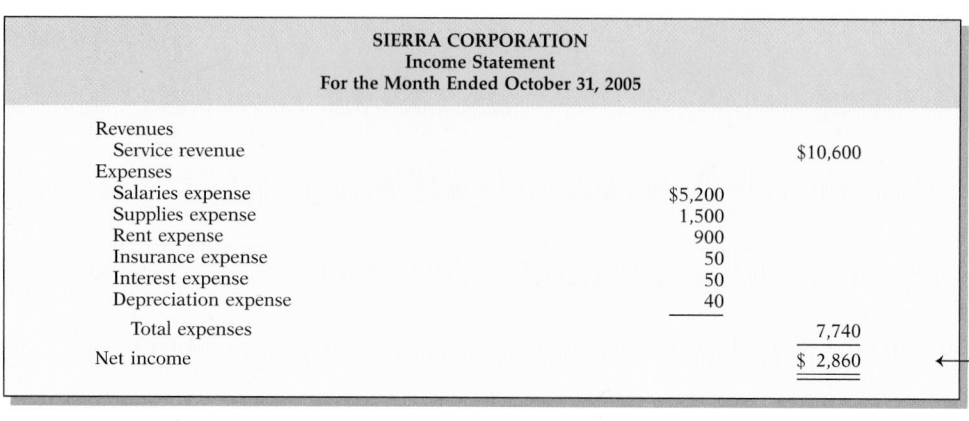

SIERRA CORPORATION
Retained Earnings Statement
For the Month Ended October 31, 2005

Retained earnings, October 1		$ 0
Add: Net income		2,860
		2,860
Less: Dividends		500
Retained earnings, October 31		$ 2,360

Helpful Hint The arrows in this
illustration show interrelationships of the four financial
statements.

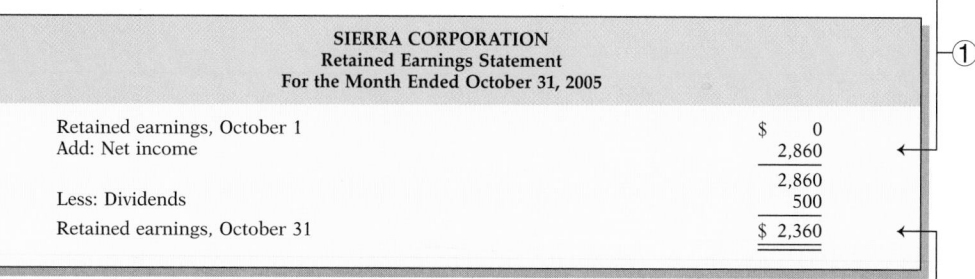

SIERRA CORPORATION
Balance Sheet
October 31, 2005

Assets

Cash		$15,200
Accounts receivable		200
Advertising supplies		1,000
Prepaid insurance		550
Office equipment, net		4,960
Total assets		$21,910

Liabilities and Stockholders' Equity

Liabilities		
Notes payable	$5,000	
Accounts payable	2,500	
Interest payable	50	
Unearned revenue	800	
Salaries payable	1,200	
Total liabilities		$ 9,550
Stockholders' equity		
Common stock	10,000	
Retained earnings	2,360	
Total stockholders' equity		12,360
Total liabilities and stockholders' equity		$21,910

SIERRA CORPORATION
Statement of Cash Flows
For the Month Ended October 31, 2005

Cash flows from operating activities		
Cash receipts from operating activities	$11,200	
Cash payments for operating activities	(5,500)	
Net cash provided by operating activities		$ 5,700
Cash flows from investing activities		
Purchased office equipment	(5,000)	
Net cash used by investing activities		(5,000)
Cash flows from financing activities		
Issuance of common stock	10,000	
Issued note payable	5,000	
Payment of dividend	(500)	
Net cash provided by financing activities		14,500
Net increase in cash		15,200
Cash at beginning of period		0
Cash at end of period		$15,200

▶ Do It

CSU Corporation began operations on January 1, 2005. The following information is available for CSU Corporation on December 31, 2005: service revenue $17,000; accounts receivable $4,000; accounts payable $2,000; building rental expense $9,000; notes payable $5,000; common stock $10,000; retained earnings $?; equipment $16,000; insurance expense $1,000; supplies $1,800; supplies expense $200; cash $1,400; dividends $600. Prepare an income statement, a retained earnings statement, and a balance sheet using this information.

Action Plan

• Report the revenues and expenses for a period of time in an income statement.
• Show the amounts and causes (net income and dividends) of changes in retained earnings during the period in the retained earnings statement.
• Present the assets and claims to those assets at a specific point in time in the balance sheet.

Solution

CSU CORPORATION
Income Statement
For the Year Ended December 31, 2005

Revenues		
Service revenue		$17,000
Expenses		
Rent expense	$9,000	
Insurance expense	1,000	
Supplies expense	200	
Total expenses		10,200
Net income		$ 6,800

CSU CORPORATION
Retained Earnings Statement
For the Year Ended December 31, 2005

Retained earnings, January 1	$ 0
Add: Net income	6,800
	6,800
Less: Dividends	600
Retained earnings, December 31	$6,200

CSU CORPORATION
Balance Sheet
December 31, 2005

Assets

Cash		$ 1,400
Accounts receivable		4,000
Supplies		1,800
Equipment		16,000
Total assets		$23,200

Liabilities and Stockholders' Equity

Liabilities		
Notes payable	$ 5,000	
Accounts payable	2,000	
Total liabilities		$ 7,000
Stockholders' equity		
Common stock	10,000	
Retained earnings	6,200	
Total stockholders' equity		16,200
Total liabilities and stockholders' equity		$23,200

☑ THE NAVIGATOR

A Quick Look at Tootsie Roll's Financial Statements

The same relationships that you observed among the financial statements of Sierra Corporation are evident in the 2002 financial statements of **Tootsie Roll Industries, Inc.**, which are presented in Illustrations 1-11 through 1-14. We have simplified the financial statements to assist your learning—but they may look complicated to you anyway. Do not be alarmed by their seeming complexity. (If you could already read and understand them, there would be little reason to take this course, except possibly to add a high grade to your transcript—which we hope you'll do anyway.) By the end of the book, you'll have a great deal of experience in reading and understanding financial statements such as these. **Tootsie Roll's actual financial statements are presented in Appendix A at the end of the book**.

Before we dive in, we need to explain two points:

1. Note that numbers are reported in thousands on Tootsie Roll's financial statements—that is, the last three 000s are omitted. Thus, Tootsie Roll's net income in 2002 is $66,388,000, not $66,388.

2. Tootsie Roll, like most companies, presents its financial statements for more than one year. Financial statements that report information for more than one period are called comparative statements. Comparative statements allow users to compare the financial position of the business at the end of an accounting period with that of previous periods.

Helpful Hint The percentage change in any amount from one year to the next is calculated as follows:

$$\frac{\text{Change during period}}{\text{Previous value}}$$

Thus, the percentage change in income is:

$$\frac{\text{Change in income}}{\text{Previous year's income}}$$

INCOME STATEMENT

Tootsie Roll's income statement is presented in Illustration 1-11. It reports total revenues in 2002 of $397,204,000. It then subtracts four types of expenses—cost of goods sold; selling, marketing, and administrative expenses; amortization expense; and income tax expense—to arrive at net income of $66,388,000. This is a 1.1% increase from income for the previous year.

Illustration 1-11
Tootsie Roll's income statement

Financial statements of real companies, like these, are accompanied by either a company logo or an associated photograph.

TOOTSIE ROLL INDUSTRIES, INC.
Income Statements
For the Years Ended December 31, 2002, and December 31, 2001
(in thousands)

	2002	2001
Revenues		
Sales revenue	$393,185	$391,755
Other revenues	4,019	6,843
Total revenues	397,204	398,598
Expenses		
Cost of goods sold	220,765	216,657
Selling, marketing, and administrative expenses	75,751	77,376
Amortization expense	—	3,778
Income tax expense	34,300	35,100
Total expenses	330,816	332,911
Net income	$ 66,388	$ 65,687

RETAINED EARNINGS STATEMENT

Tootsie Roll presents information about its retained earnings in the retained earnings statement in Illustration 1-12. (Many companies present changes in retained earnings in a broader report called the Statement of Stockholders' Equity.) Find the line "Retained earnings, December 31, 2001." This number, $149,440,000, agrees with the retained earnings balance from the December 31, 2001, balance sheet.

Illustration 1-12 Tootsie Roll's retained earnings statement

TOOTSIE ROLL INDUSTRIES, INC.
Retained Earnings Statements
For the Years Ended December 31, 2002, and December 31, 2001
(in thousands)

Retained earnings, December 31, 2000	$167,941
Add: Net income	65,687
Other adjustments	277
	233,905
Less: Dividends	84,465
Retained earnings,* December 31, 2001	149,440
Add: Net income	66,388
	215,828
Less: Dividends	79,028
Other adjustments	1,139
Retained earnings,* December 31, 2002	$135,661

*Includes adjustments for other items.

As we proceed down the retained earnings statement, the next figure is net income of $66,388,000. Tootsie Roll distributed dividends of $79,028,000. The ending balance of retained earnings is $135,661,000 on December 31, 2002. Find this amount of retained earnings near the bottom of Tootsie Roll's balance sheet for December 31, 2002 (Illustration 1-13 on page 20).

BALANCE SHEET

As shown in its balance sheet in Illustration 1-13 (page 20), Tootsie Roll's assets include the kinds previously mentioned in our discussion of Sierra Corporation, such as cash, inventories, and property, plant, and equipment, plus other types of assets that we will discuss in later chapters, such as prepaid expenses. Tootsie Roll's total assets increased from $618,676,000 on December 31, 2001, to $646,080,000 on December 31, 2002. Its liabilities include accounts payable as well as items not yet discussed, such as postretirement health care and life insurance benefits payable.

You can see that Tootsie Roll relies far more on equity financing than on debt—it has over four times as much stockholders' equity as it has liabilities. As you learn more about financial statements we will discuss how to interpret the relationships and changes in financial statement items.

STATEMENT OF CASH FLOWS

Tootsie Roll's cash decreased $1,025,000 during 2002. Tootsie Roll's balance sheet shows that cash was $106,532,000 at December 31, 2001, and $105,507,000 at December 31, 2002. The reasons for this decrease can be determined by exam-

Illustration 1-13
Tootsie Roll's balance
sheet

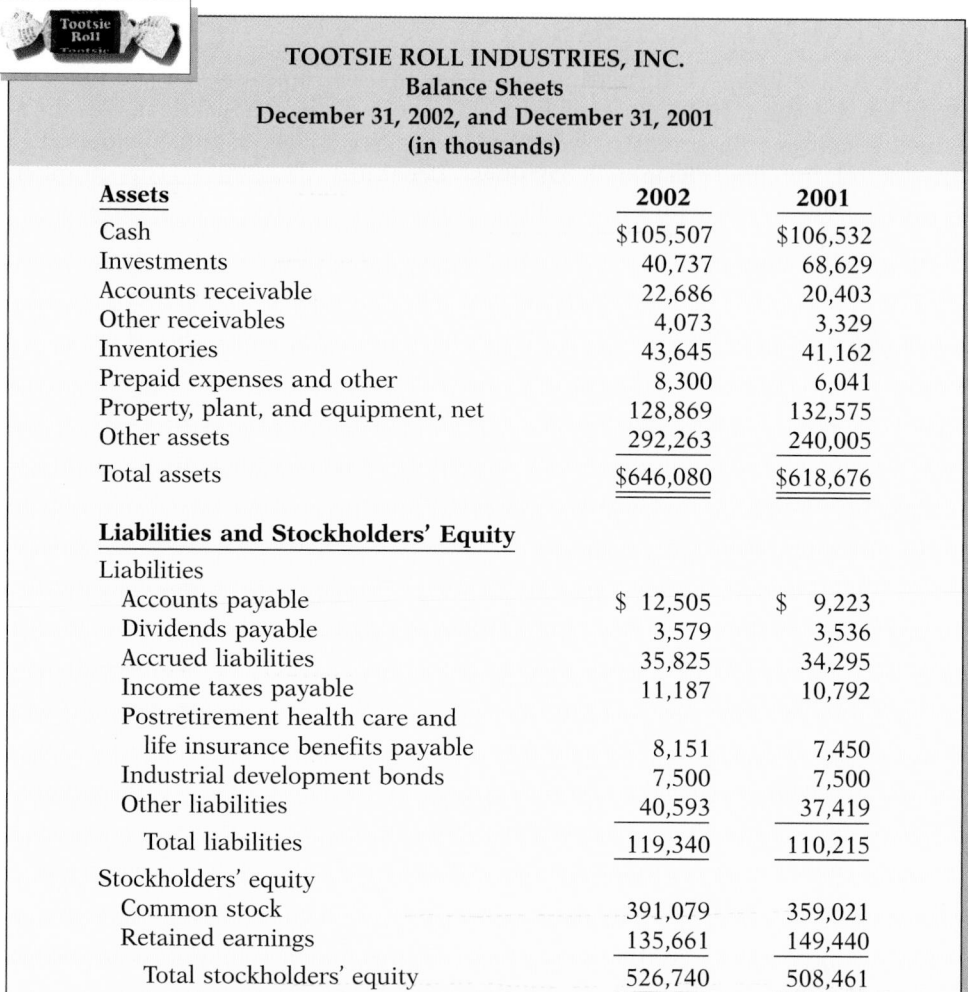

TOOTSIE ROLL INDUSTRIES, INC.
Balance Sheets
December 31, 2002, and December 31, 2001
(in thousands)

Assets	2002	2001
Cash	$105,507	$106,532
Investments	40,737	68,629
Accounts receivable	22,686	20,403
Other receivables	4,073	3,329
Inventories	43,645	41,162
Prepaid expenses and other	8,300	6,041
Property, plant, and equipment, net	128,869	132,575
Other assets	292,263	240,005
Total assets	$646,080	$618,676

Liabilities and Stockholders' Equity	2002	2001
Liabilities		
Accounts payable	$ 12,505	$ 9,223
Dividends payable	3,579	3,536
Accrued liabilities	35,825	34,295
Income taxes payable	11,187	10,792
Postretirement health care and life insurance benefits payable	8,151	7,450
Industrial development bonds	7,500	7,500
Other liabilities	40,593	37,419
Total liabilities	119,340	110,215
Stockholders' equity		
Common stock	391,079	359,021
Retained earnings	135,661	149,440
Total stockholders' equity	526,740	508,461
Total liabilities and stockholders' equity	$646,080	$618,676

ining the statement of cash flows in Illustration 1-14. Tootsie Roll generated $71,203,000 from its operating activities during 2002. Its investing activities included capital expenditures (purchases of property, plant, and equipment) as well as purchases and sales of investment securities. The net effect of its investment activities was an outflow of cash of $25,304,000. Its financing activities involved the repurchase of its own common stock and the payment of cash dividends. In all, the net effect of the cash generated from its operating activities, less the cash used in its investing and financing activities, was a decrease in cash of $1,025,000.

OTHER ELEMENTS
OF AN ANNUAL REPORT

STUDY OBJECTIVE
6

Describe the components
that supplement the
financial statements in an
annual report.

U.S. companies that are publicly traded must provide their shareholders with an **annual report** each year. The annual report always includes the financial statements introduced in this chapter. In addition, the annual report includes other important information such as a management discussion and analysis section, notes to the financial statements, and an independent auditor's report. No analysis of a company's financial situation and prospects is complete without a review of each of these items.

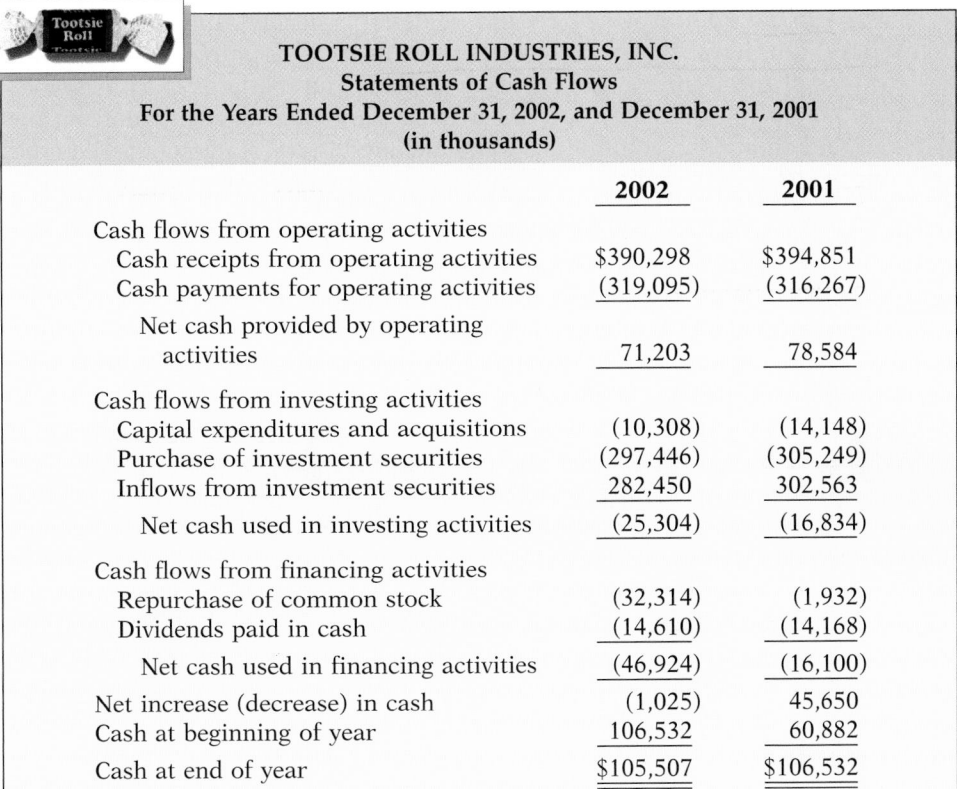

TOOTSIE ROLL INDUSTRIES, INC.
Statements of Cash Flows
For the Years Ended December 31, 2002, and December 31, 2001
(in thousands)

	2002	2001
Cash flows from operating activities		
Cash receipts from operating activities	$390,298	$394,851
Cash payments for operating activities	(319,095)	(316,267)
Net cash provided by operating activities	71,203	78,584
Cash flows from investing activities		
Capital expenditures and acquisitions	(10,308)	(14,148)
Purchase of investment securities	(297,446)	(305,249)
Inflows from investment securities	282,450	302,563
Net cash used in investing activities	(25,304)	(16,834)
Cash flows from financing activities		
Repurchase of common stock	(32,314)	(1,932)
Dividends paid in cash	(14,610)	(14,168)
Net cash used in financing activities	(46,924)	(16,100)
Net increase (decrease) in cash	(1,025)	45,650
Cash at beginning of year	106,532	60,882
Cash at end of year	$105,507	$106,532

Illustration 1-14
Tootsie Roll's statement of cash flows

Management Discussion and Analysis

The **management discussion and analysis (MD&A)** section covers three financial aspects of a company: **its ability to pay near-term obligations, its ability to fund operations and expansion, and its results of operations**. Management must highlight favorable or unfavorable trends and identify significant events and uncertainties that affect these three factors. This discussion obviously involves a number of subjective estimates and opinions. A brief excerpt from the MD&A section of Tootsie Roll's annual report is presented in Illustration 1-15.

TOOTSIE ROLL INDUSTRIES, INC.
Management's Discussion and Analysis of
Financial Condition and Results of Operations

The company continues to maintain a conservative financial posture. Aside from an immaterial amount of operating leases, the company has no off-balance sheet financing arrangements, and our simple financial structure does not utilize any "special purpose entities" or other obscure financing arrangements.

Illustration 1-15
Tootsie Roll's management discussion and analysis

Notes to the Financial Statements

Every set of financial statements is accompanied by explanatory notes and supporting schedules that are an integral part of the statements. The **notes to the financial statements** clarify information presented in the financial statements, as well as expand upon it where additional detail is needed. Information in the notes does not have to be quantifiable (numeric). Examples of notes are descriptions of the significant accounting policies and methods used in preparing the statements, explanations of uncertainties and contingencies, and various statistics and details too voluminous to be included in the statements. The notes are essential to understanding a company's operating performance and financial position.

Illustration 1-16 is an excerpt from the notes to Tootsie Roll's financial statements. It describes the methods that Tootsie Roll uses to account for revenues.

Illustration 1-16 Notes to Tootsie Roll's financial statements

TOOTSIE ROLL INDUSTRIES, INC.
Notes to Financial Statements

Revenue recognition
Revenues are recognized when products are shipped and delivered to customers.

Auditor's Report

Another important source of information is the **auditor's report**. An **auditor** is an accounting professional who conducts an independent examination of a company's financial statements. Only accountants who meet certain criteria and thereby attain the designation **Certified Public Accountant (CPA)** may perform audits. If the auditor is satisfied that the financial statements provide a fair representation of the company's financial position, results of operations, and cash flows in accordance with generally accepted accounting principles, then an **unqualified opinion** is expressed. If the auditor expresses anything other than an unqualified opinion, then the financial statements should be used only with caution. That is, without an unqualified opinion, we cannot have complete confidence that the financial statements give an accurate picture of the company's financial health.

Illustration 1-17 is an excerpt from the auditor's report from Tootsie Roll's 2002 annual report. Tootsie Roll received an unqualified opinion from its auditor, PricewaterhouseCoopers.

Illustration 1-17 Excerpt from auditor's report on Tootsie Roll's financial statements

TOOTSIE ROLL INDUSTRIES, INC.
Excerpt from Auditor's Report

To the Board of Directors and Shareholders of Tootsie Roll Industries, Inc.

In our opinion, the accompanying consolidated statement of financial position and the related consolidated statement of earnings, comprehensive earnings and retained earnings and of cash flows present fairly, in all material respects, the financial position of Tootsie Roll Industries, Inc. and its subsidiaries at December 31, 2002 and 2001, and the results of their operations and their cash flows for each of the three years in the period ended December 31, 2002, in conformity with accounting principles generally accepted in the United States of America.

Business Insight
INTERNATIONAL PERSPECTIVE

Concern over the quality and integrity of financial reporting is not limited to the United States. Recently the Chinese Ministry of Finance reprimanded a large accounting firm for preparing fraudulent financial reports for a number of its publicly traded companies. Afterward, the state-run news agency noted that investors and analysts actually felt that the punishment of the firm was not adequate. In fact, a 2001 survey of investors in China found that less than 10% had full confidence in companies' annual reports. As a result of these concerns the Chinese Institute of Certified Public Accountants vowed to strengthen its policing of its members.

Assumptions and Principles in Financial Reporting

The Financial Accounting Standards Board (FASB) is the primary accounting standards body in the United States. To develop accounting standards, the FASB relies on some key assumptions and principles. These assumptions and principles form a foundation for financial reporting that we will refer to throughout the book.

STUDY OBJECTIVE
7
Explain the basic assumptions and principles underlying financial statements.

ASSUMPTIONS

Monetary Unit Assumption

First let's talk about the assumptions. In looking at Tootsie Roll's financial statements you will notice that everything is stated in terms of dollars. The **monetary unit assumption** requires that only those things that can be expressed in money are included in the accounting records.

   This assumption has important implications for financial reporting. Because the exchange of money is fundamental to business transactions, it makes sense that we measure a business in terms of money. However, it also means that certain important information needed by investors, creditors, and managers is not reported in the financial statements. For example, customer satisfaction is important to every business, but it is not easily quantified in dollar terms; thus it is not reported in the financial statements.

Economic Entity Assumption

The **economic entity assumption** states that every economic entity can be separately identified and accounted for. For example, suppose you are a stockholder in Tootsie Roll. The amount of cash you have in your personal bank account and the balance owed on your personal car loan are not reported in Tootsie Roll's balance sheet. The reason is that, for accounting purposes, you and Tootsie Roll are separate accounting entities. In order to accurately assess Tootsie Roll's performance and financial position, it is important that we not blur it with your personal transactions, or the transactions of any other person (especially its managers) or company.

Time Period Assumption

Next, notice that Tootsie Roll's income statement, retained earnings statement, and statement of cash flows all cover periods of one year, and the balance sheet is prepared at the end of each year. The **time period assumption** states that the life of a business can be divided into artificial time periods and that useful reports covering those periods can be prepared for the business. All companies report financial results at least annually. Many also report at least every three months (quarterly) to stockholders, and many prepare monthly statements for internal purposes.

Going Concern Assumption

The **going concern assumption** states that the business will remain in operation for the foreseeable future. Of course many businesses do fail, but in general, it is reasonable to assume that the business will continue operating. The going concern assumption underlies much of what we do in accounting. To give you just one example, if going concern is not assumed, then plant assets should be stated at their liquidation value (selling price less cost of disposal), not at their cost. Only when liquidation of the business appears likely is the going concern assumption inappropriate.

These four accounting assumptions are shown graphically in Illustration 1-18.

Illustration 1-18
Accounting assumptions

Monetary Unit

Measure of employee satisfaction | Salaries paid
Total number of employees | Percent of international employees

$ Acct. Records -Salaries paid

Only those things that can be expressed in terms of money should be included in the accounting records.

Economic Entity

Ford
DaimlerChrysler
GM

Every economic entity can be separately identified and accounted for.

Time Period

1998 — 2008
2000 2002 2004 2006
Start of business — QTR 1 QTR 2 QTR 3 QTR 4 — End of business
J F M A M J J A S O N D

The economic life of a business can be divided into artificial time periods.

Going Concern

Now — Future

The enterprise will continue in operation long enough to carry out its existing objectives.

PRINCIPLES

Cost Principle

All of the assets on Tootsie Roll's financial statements are recorded at the amount paid for them. The **cost principle** dictates that assets are recorded at their cost. This is true not only at the time the asset is purchased, but also over the time the asset is held. For example, if Tootsie Roll were to purchase some land for $30,000, it would initially be reported on the balance sheet at $30,000. But what would Tootsie Roll do if, by the end of the next year, the land had increased in value to $40,000? The answer is that under the cost principle the land would continue to be reported at $30,000.

The cost principle is often criticized as being irrelevant. Critics contend that market value would be more useful to financial decision makers. Proponents of the cost principle counter that cost is the best measure because it can be easily verified from transactions between two parties, whereas market value is often subjective.

> **Helpful Hint** Recently, some accounting rules have been changed, requiring that certain investment securities be recorded at their market value.

Full Disclosure Principle

Some important financial information is not easily reported on the face of the statements. For example, Tootsie Roll has debt outstanding. Investors and creditors would like to know the terms of the debt; that is, when does it mature, what is its interest rate, and is it renewable? Or Tootsie Roll might be sued by one of its customers. Investors and creditors might not know about this lawsuit. The **full disclosure principle** requires that all circumstances and events that would make a difference to financial statement users should be disclosed. If an important item cannot reasonably be reported directly in one of the four types of financial statements, then it should be discussed in notes that accompany the statements. Some investors who lost money in **Enron**, **WorldCom**, and **Global Crossing** have complained that the lack of full disclosure regarding some of the companies' transactions caused the financial statements to be misleading.

These two accounting principles are shown graphically in Illustration 1-19.

Illustration 1-19
Accounting principles

BEFORE YOU GO ON . . .

▶ **Review It**

1. What is the intent of the management discussion and analysis section in the annual report?
2. Why are notes to the financial statements necessary? What kinds of items are included in these notes?
3. What is the purpose of the auditor's report?
4. Describe the assumptions and principles of accounting addressed in this chapter.

✔ THE NAVIGATOR

Using the Decision Toolkit

Using the Decision Toolkit exercises ask you to use information from financial statements to make financial decisions. We encourage you to think through the questions related to the decision before you study the solution.

Hershey Foods Corporation, located in Hershey, Pennsylvania, is the leading North American manufacturer of chocolate—for example, Hershey's Kisses, Reese's Peanut Butter Cups, and Kit Kat bars. Imagine that you are considering the purchase of shares of Hershey's common stock.

Instructions

Answer these questions related to your decision whether to invest.

(a) What financial statements should you request from the company?
(b) What should these financial statements tell you?
(c) Should you request audited financial statements? Explain.
(d) Will the financial statements show the market value of Hershey Foods' assets? Explain.
(e) Simplified financial statements for Hershey Foods are shown in Illustrations 1-20 through 1-23. What comparisons can you make between Tootsie Roll and Hershey in terms of their respective results from operations and financial position?

Illustration 1-20 Hershey Foods' income statement

HERSHEY FOODS CORPORATION **Income Statements** **For the Years Ended December 31, 2002, and** **December 31, 2001 (in thousands)**		
	2002	**2001**
Revenues		
Sales revenue	$4,120,317	$4,137,217
Expenses		
Cost of goods sold	2,561,052	2,668,530
Selling, marketing, and administrative expenses	860,978	1,056,053
Interest expense	60,722	69,093
Income tax expense	233,987	136,385
Total expenses	3,716,739	3,930,061
Net income	$ 403,578	$ 207,156

HERSHEY FOODS CORPORATION	
Retained Earnings Statements	
For the Years Ended December 31, 2002, and	
December 31, 2001 (in thousands)	
Retained earnings December 31, 2000	$ 981,962
Add: Net income	207,156
	1,189,118
Less: Dividends	154,750
Other adjustments	70,377
Retained earnings December 31, 2001	963,991
Add: Net income	403,578
	1,367,569
Less: Dividends	167,821
Other adjustments	8,588
Retained earnings December 31, 2002	$1,191,160

Illustration 1-21 Hershey Foods' retained earnings statement

HERSHEY FOODS CORPORATION		
Balance Sheets		
December 31, 2002, and December 31, 2001		
(in thousands)		
Assets	**2002**	**2001**
Cash	$ 297,743	$ 134,147
Accounts receivable	370,976	361,726
Inventories	503,291	512,134
Prepaid expenses and other	91,608	159,534
Property, plant, and equipment, net	1,486,055	1,534,901
Other assets	730,878	544,988
Total assets	$3,480,551	$3,247,430
Liabilities and Stockholders' Equity		
Liabilities		
Accounts payable	$ 124,507	$ 133,049
Accrued liabilities	356,716	462,901
Income taxes payable	37,499	2,568
Short-term debt and other	28,124	7,926
Long-term debt and liabilities	1,213,962	1,238,013
Other liabilities	348,040	255,769
Total liabilities	2,108,848	2,100,226
Stockholders' equity		
Common stock	180,543	183,213
Retained earnings	1,191,160	963,991
Total stockholders' equity	1,371,703	1,147,204
Total liabilities and stockholders' equity	$3,480,551	$3,247,430

Illustration 1-22 Hershey Foods' balance sheet

Illustration 1-23 Hershey Foods' statement of cash flows

HERSHEY FOODS CORPORATION
Statements of Cash Flows
For the Years Ended December 31, 2002, and
December 31, 2001 (in thousands)

	2002	2001
Cash flows from operating activities		
Cash receipts from operating activities	$4,111,067	$ 4,155,171
Cash payments for operating activities	(3,485,724)	(3,448,766)
Net cash provided by operating activities	625,343	706,405
Cash flows from investing activities		
Capital expenditures	(132,736)	(160,105)
Other, net	164	36,118
Net cash used in investing activities	(132,572)	(123,987)
Cash flows from financing activities		
Issuance of long-term debt	304	379
Repayment of long-term debt	(9,578)	(826)
Dividends paid in cash	(167,821)	(154,750)
Issuance of common stock	86,491	30,210
Repurchase of common stock	(84,194)	(40,322)
Other, net	(154,377)	(314,931)
Net cash used in financing activities	(329,175)	(480,240)
Net increase (decrease) in cash	163,596	102,178
Cash at beginning of year	134,147	31,969
Cash at end of year	$ 297,743	$ 134,147

Solution

(a) Before you invest, you should investigate the income statement, retained earnings statement, statement of cash flows, and balance sheet.

(b) You would probably be most interested in the income statement because it tells about past performance and thus gives an indication of future performance. The retained earnings statement provides a record of the company's dividend history. The statement of cash flows reveals where the company is getting and spending its cash. This is especially important for a company that wants to grow. Finally, the balance sheet reveals the relationship between assets and liabilities.

(c) You would want audited financial statements—statements that a CPA (certified public accountant) has examined and expressed an opinion that the statements present fairly the financial position and results of operations of the company. Investors and creditors should not make decisions without studying audited financial statements.

(d) The financial statements will not show the market value of the company. As indicated, one important principle of accounting is the cost principle, which states that assets should be recorded at cost. Cost has an important advantage over other valuations: It is objective and reliable.

(e) Many interesting comparisons can be made between the two companies. Tootsie Roll is smaller, with total assets of $646,080,000 versus $3,480,551,000 for Hershey, and it has lower revenue—$397,204,000 versus $4,120,317,000 for Hershey. In addition, Tootsie Roll's cash provided by operating activities of $71,203,000 is less than Hershey's $625,343,000. While useful, these basic measures are not enough to determine whether one company is a better investment than the other. In later chapters you will learn tools that will allow you to compare the relative profitability and financial health of these and other companies.

Summary of Study Objectives

1 *Describe the primary forms of business organization.* A sole proprietorship is a business owned by one person. A partnership is a business owned by two or more people. A corporation is a separate legal entity for which evidence of ownership is provided by shares of stock.

2 *Identify the users and uses of accounting information.* Internal users are managers who need accounting information in planning, controlling, and evaluating business operations. The primary external users are investors and creditors. Investors (stockholders) use accounting information to help them decide whether to buy, hold, or sell shares of a company's stock. Creditors (suppliers and bankers) use accounting information to assess the risk of granting credit or loaning money to a business. Other groups who have an indirect interest in a business are taxing authorities, regulatory agencies, customers, labor unions, and economic planners.

3 *Explain the three principal types of business activity.* Financing activities involve collecting the necessary funds to support the business. Investing activities involve acquiring the resources necessary to run the business. Operating activities involve putting the resources of the business into action to generate a profit.

4 *Describe the content and purpose of each of the financial statements.* An income statement presents the revenues and expenses of a company for a specific period of time. A retained earnings statement summarizes the changes in retained earnings that have occurred for a specific period of time. A balance sheet reports the assets, liabilities, and stockholders' equity of a business at a specific date. A statement of cash flows summarizes information concerning the cash inflows (receipts) and outflows (payments) for a specific period of time.

5 *Explain the meaning of assets, liabilities, and stockholders' equity, and state the basic accounting equation.* Assets are resources owned by a business. Liabilities are the debts and obligations of the business. Liabilities represent claims of creditors on the assets of the business. Stockholders' equity represents the claims of owners on the assets of the business. Stockholders' equity is composed of two parts: common stock and retained earnings. The basic accounting equation is: Assets = Liabilities + Stockholders' Equity.

6 *Describe the components that supplement the financial statements in an annual report.* The management discussion and analysis provides management's interpretation of the company's results and financial position as well as a discussion of plans for the future. Notes to the financial statements provide additional explanation or detail to make the financial statements more informative. The auditor's report expresses an opinion as to whether the financial statements present fairly the company's results of operations and financial position.

7 *Explain the basic assumptions and principles underlying financial statements.* The monetary unit assumption requires that only transaction data capable of being expressed in terms of money be included in the accounting records of the economic entity. The economic entity assumption states that economic events can be identified with a particular unit of accountability. The time period assumption states that the economic life of a business can be divided into artificial time periods and that meaningful accounting reports can be prepared for each period. The going concern assumption states that the enterprise will continue in operation long enough to carry out its existing objectives and commitments. The cost principle states that assets should be recorded at their cost. The full disclosure principle dictates that circumstances and events that matter to financial statement users must be disclosed.

DECISION TOOLKIT—A SUMMARY

Decision Checkpoints	Info Needed for Decision	Tool to Use for Decision	How to Evaluate Results
Are the company's operations profitable?	Income statement	The income statement reports on the success or failure of the company's operations by reporting its revenues and expenses.	If the company's revenue exceeds its expenses, it will report net income; otherwise it will report a net loss.
What is the company's policy toward dividends and growth?	Retained earnings statement	How much of this year's income did the company pay out in dividends to shareholders?	A company striving for rapid growth will pay a low dividend.
Does the company rely primarily on debt or stockholders' equity to finance its assets?	Balance sheet	The balance sheet reports the company's resources and claims to those resources. There are two types of claims: liabilities and stockholders' equity.	Compare the amount of debt versus the amount of stockholders' equity to determine whether the company relies more on creditors or owners for its financing.
Does the company generate sufficient cash from operations to fund its investing activities?	Statement of cash flows	The statement of cash flows shows the amount of cash provided or used by operating activities, investing activities, and financing activities.	Compare the amount of cash provided by operating activities with the amount of cash used by investing activities. Any deficiency in cash from operating activities must be made up with cash from financing activities.

Glossary

Accounting The process of identifying, recording, and communicating the economic events of a business to interested users of the information. (p. 5)

Annual report A report prepared by corporate management that presents financial information including financial statements, notes, and the management discussion and analysis. (p. 20)

Assets Resources owned by a business. (p. 9)

Auditor's report A report prepared by an independent outside auditor stating the auditor's opinion as to the fairness of the presentation of the financial position and results of operations and their conformance with accepted accounting standards. (p. 22)

Balance sheet A financial statement that reports the assets, liabilities, and stockholders' equity at a specific date. (p. 12)

Basic accounting equation Assets = Liabilities + Stockholders' Equity. (pp. 12–13)

Certified Public Accountant (CPA) An individual who has met certain criteria and is thus allowed to perform audits of corporations. (p. 22)

Common stock Stock representing the primary ownership interest in a corporation. In the balance sheet it represents the amount paid in by stockholders. (p. 8)

Comparative statements A presentation of the financial statements of a company for multiple years. (p. 18)

Corporation A business organized as a separate legal entity having ownership divided into transferable shares of stock. (p. 3)

Cost principle An accounting principle that states that assets should be recorded at their cost. (p. 25)

Dividends Distributions of cash or other assets from a corporation to its stockholders. (p. 8)

Economic entity assumption An assumption that economic events can be identified with a particular unit of accountability. (p. 23)

Expenses   The cost of assets consumed or services used in ongoing operations to generate revenues. (p. 9)

Full disclosure principle   Accounting principle that dictates that circumstances and events that make a difference to financial statement users should be disclosed. (p. 25)

Going concern assumption   The assumption that the enterprise will continue in operation long enough to carry out its existing objectives and commitments. (p. 24)

Income statement   A financial statement that presents the revenues and expenses and resulting net income or net loss of a company for a specific period of time. (p. 11)

Liabilities   The debts and obligations of a business. Liabilities represent claims of creditors on the assets of a business. (p. 7)

Management discussion and analysis (MD&A)   A section of the annual report that presents management's views on the company's short-term debt paying ability, expansion, financing, and results. (p. 21)

Monetary unit assumption   An assumption stating that only transaction data that can be expressed in terms of money be included in the accounting records of the economic entity. (p. 23)

Net income   The amount by which revenues exceed expenses. (p. 9)

Net loss   The amount by which expenses exceed revenues. (p. 9)

Notes to the financial statements   Notes that clarify information presented in the financial statements, as well as expand upon it where additional detail is needed. (p. 21)

Partnership   A business owned by more than one person. (p. 3)

Retained earnings   The amount of net income kept in the corporation for future use, not distributed to stockholders as dividends. (p. 12)

Retained earnings statement   A financial statement that summarizes the changes in retained earnings for a specific period of time. (p. 12)

Revenues   The assets that result from the sale of a product or service. (p. 9)

Sole proprietorship   A business owned by one person. (p. 3)

Statement of cash flows   A financial statement that provides information about the cash inflows (receipts) and cash outflows (payments) for a specific period of time. (p. 14)

Stockholders' equity   The stockholders' claim on total assets. (p. 12)

Time period assumption   An accounting assumption that the economic life of a business can be divided into artificial time periods. (p. 24)

Demonstration Problem

Jeff Andringa, a former college hockey player, quit his job and started Ice Camp, a hockey camp for kids ages 8 to 18. Eventually he would like to open hockey camps nationwide. Jeff has asked you to help him prepare financial statements at the end of his first year of operations. He relates the following facts about his business activities.

   In order to get the business off the ground, he decided to incorporate. He sold shares of common stock to a few close friends, as well as buying some of the shares himself. He initially raised $25,000 through the sale of these shares. In addition, the company took out a $10,000 loan at a local bank. A bus for transporting kids was purchased for $12,000 cash. Hockey goals and other miscellaneous equipment were purchased with $1,500 cash. The company earned camp tuition during the year of $100,000 but had collected only $80,000 of this amount. Thus, at the end of the year it was still owed $20,000. The company rents time at a local rink for $50 per hour. Total rink rental costs during the year were $8,000, insurance was $10,000, salary expense was $20,000, and administrative expenses totaled $9,000, all of which were paid in cash. The company incurred $800 in interest expense on the bank loan, which it still owed at the end of the year.

   The company paid dividends during the year of $5,000 cash. The balance in the corporate bank account at December 31, 2005, was $49,500.

Instructions

Using the format of the Sierra Corporation statements in this chapter, prepare an income statement, retained earnings statement, balance sheet, and statement of cash flows. (*Hint:* Prepare the statements in the order stated to take advantage of the flow of information from one statement to the next, as shown in Illustration 1-10.)

Demonstration Problems are a final review before you begin homework. **Action Plans** that appear in the margins (see next page) give you tips about how to approach the problem. The **Solution** provided illustrates both the form and content of complete answers.

Solution to Demonstration Problem

Action Plan

- On the income statement:
  Show revenues and expenses for a period of time.

- On the retained earnings statement:
  Show the changes in retained earnings for a period of time.

- On the balance sheet:
  Report assets, liabilities, and stockholders' equity at a specific date.

- On the statement of cash flows:
  Report sources and uses of cash from operating, investing, and financing activities for a period of time.

ICE CAMP
Income Statement
For the Year Ended December 31, 2005

Revenues		
Camp tuition revenue		$100,000
Expenses		
Salaries expense	$20,000	
Insurance expense	10,000	
Administrative expense	9,000	
Rink rental expense	8,000	
Interest expense	800	
Total expenses		47,800
Net income		$ 52,200

ICE CAMP
Retained Earnings Statement
For the Year Ended December 31, 2005

Retained earnings, January 1, 2005	$ 0
Add: Net income	52,200
	52,200
Less: Dividends	5,000
Retained earnings, December 31, 2005	$47,200

ICE CAMP
Balance Sheet
December 31, 2005

Assets

Cash	$49,500
Accounts receivable	20,000
Bus	12,000
Equipment	1,500
Total assets	$83,000

Liabilities and Stockholders' Equity

Liabilities		
Bank loan payable	$10,000	
Interest payable	800	
Total liabilities		$10,800
Stockholders' equity		
Common stock	25,000	
Retained earnings	47,200	
Total stockholders' equity		72,200
Total liabilities and stockholders' equity		$83,000

ICE CAMP
Statement of Cash Flows
For the Year Ended December 31, 2005

Cash flows from operating activities	
Cash receipts from operating activities	$80,000
Cash payments for operating activities	(47,000)
Net cash provided by operating activities	33,000
Cash flows from investing activities	
Purchase of bus	(12,000)
Purchase of equipment	(1,500)
Net cash used by investing activities	(13,500)
Cash flows from financing activities	
Issuance of bank loan payable	10,000
Issuance of common stock	25,000
Dividends paid	(5,000)
Net cash provided by financing activities	30,000
Net increase in cash	49,500
Cash at beginning of period	0
Cash at end of period	$49,500

☑ THE NAVIGATOR

This would be a good time to return to the **Student Owner's Manual** at the beginning of the book (or look at it for the first time if you skipped it before) to read about the types of homework materials that appear at the ends of chapters. Knowing the purpose of the different assignments will help you appreciate what each contributes to your accounting skills and competencies.

The tool icon indicates that an instructional activity employs one of the decision tools presented in the chapter. The pencil icon ▭▭▭▷ indicates that an instructional activity requires written communication.

Self-Study Questions

Self-Study/Self-Test

Answers are at the end of the chapter.

(SO 1)   **1.** Which is *not* one of the three forms of business organization?
    (a) Sole proprietorship.   (c) Partnership.
    (b) Creditorship.   (d) Corporation.

(SO 1)   **2.** Which is an advantage of corporations relative to partnerships and sole proprietorships?
    (a) Lower taxes.
    (b) Harder to transfer ownership.
    (c) Reduced legal liability for investors.
    (d) Most common form of organization.

(SO 3)   **3.** Which is *not* one of the three primary business activities?
    (a) Financing.   (c) Advertising.
    (b) Operating.   (d) Investing.

(SO 4)   **4.** Which statement about users of accounting information is *incorrect*?
    (a) Management is considered an internal user.
    (b) Taxing authorities are considered external users.
    (c) Present creditors are considered external users.

    (d) Regulatory authorities are considered internal users.

5. Net income will result during a time period when: (SO 4)
    (a) assets exceed liabilities.
    (b) assets exceed revenues.
    (c) expenses exceed revenues.
    (d) revenues exceed expenses.

6. ▭▭▭ What section of a cash flow state-   (SO 4)
ment indicates the cash spent on new equipment during the past accounting period?
    (a) The investing section.
    (b) The operating section.   *p20*
    (c) The financing section.   *capital expend.*
    (d) The cash flow statement does not give this information.

7. Which financial statement reports assets, liabil-   (SO 4)
ities, and stockholders' equity?
    (a) Income statement.
    (b) Retained earnings statement.
    (c) Balance sheet.
    (d) Statement of cash flows.

8. As of December 31, 2005, Stoneland Corpora-   (SO 5)
tion has assets of $3,500 and stockholders' eq-

uity of $2,000. What are the liabilities for Stoneland Corporation as of December 31, 2005?

(a) $1,500. (c) $2,500.
(b) $1,000. (d) $2,000.

(SO 6) 9. The segment of a corporation's annual report that describes the corporation's accounting methods is the:

(a) notes to the financial statements.
(b) management discussion and analysis.
(c) auditor's report.
(d) income statement.

(SO 7) 10. The cost principle states that:

(a) assets should be recorded at cost and adjusted when the market value changes.

(b) activities of an entity should be kept separate and distinct from its owner.
(c) assets should be recorded at their cost.
(d) only transaction data capable of being expressed in terms of money should be included in the accounting records.

11. Valuing assets at their market value rather than at their cost is inconsistent with the: (SO 7)

(a) time period assumption.
(b) economic entity assumption.
(c) cost principle.
(d) All of the above.

THE NAVIGATOR

Questions

1. What are the three basic forms of business organizations?

2. What are the advantages to a business of being formed as a corporation? What are the disadvantages?

3. What are the advantages to a business of being formed as a partnership or sole proprietorship? What are the disadvantages?

4. "Accounting is ingrained in our society and is vital to our economic system." Do you agree? Explain.

5. Who are the internal users of accounting data? How does accounting provide relevant data to the internal users?

6. Who are the external users of accounting data? Give examples.

7. What are the three main types of business activity? Give examples of each activity.

8. Listed here are some items found in the financial statements of Ruth Weber, Inc. Indicate in which financial statement(s) each item would appear.

(a) Service revenue.   (d) Accounts receivable.
(b) Equipment.   (e) Common stock.
(c) Advertising expense. (f) Wages payable.

9. Why would a bank want to monitor the dividend payment practices of the corporations it lends money to?

10. "A company's net income appears directly on the income statement and the retained earnings statement, and it is included indirectly in the company's balance sheet." Do you agree? Explain.

11. What is the primary purpose of the statement of cash flows?

12. What are the three main categories of the statement of cash flows? Why do you think these categories were chosen?

13. What is retained earnings? What items increase the balance in retained earnings? What items decrease the balance in retained earnings?

14. What is the basic accounting equation?

15. (a) Define the terms *assets*, *liabilities*, and *stockholders' equity*.
    (b) What items affect stockholders' equity?

16. Which of these items are liabilities of Kool-Jewelry Stores?

(a) Cash.   (f) Equipment.
(b) Accounts payable.   (g) Salaries payable.
(c) Dividends.   (h) Service revenue.
(d) Accounts receivable.   (i) Rent expense.
(e) Supplies.

17. How are each of the following financial statements interrelated? (a) Retained earnings statement and income statement. (b) Retained earnings statement and balance sheet. (c) Balance sheet and statement of cash flows.

18. What is the purpose of the management discussion and analysis section (MD&A)?

19. Why is it important for financial statements to receive an unqualified auditor's opinion?

20. What types of information are presented in the notes to the financial statements?

21. What purpose does the going concern assumption serve?

22. Sue Leonard is president of Better Books. She has no accounting background. Leonard cannot understand why market value is not used as the basis for accounting measurement and reporting. Explain what basis is used and why.

23. What is the importance of the economic entity assumption? Give an example of its violation.

Brief Exercises

BE1-1 Match each of the following forms of business organization with a set of characteristics: sole proprietorship (SP), partnership (P), corporation (C).

(a) _____ Shared control, tax advantages, increased skills and resources.
(b) _____ Simple to set up and maintains control with founder.
(c) _____ Easier to transfer ownership and raise funds, no personal liability.

Describe forms of business organization.
(SO 1)

BE1-2 Match each of the following types of evaluation with one of the listed users of accounting information.

1. Trying to determine whether the company complied with tax laws.
2. Trying to determine whether the company can pay its obligations.
3. Trying to determine whether a marketing proposal will be cost effective.
4. Trying to determine whether the company's net income will result in a stock price increase.
5. Trying to determine whether the company should employ debt or equity financing.

(a) _____ Investors in common stock.   *(d)* _____ Chief Financial Officer.
(b) _____ Marketing managers.   *(e)* _____ Internal Revenue Service.
(c) _____ Creditors.

Identify users of accounting information.
(SO 2)

BE1-3 Indicate in which part of the statement of cash flows each item would appear: operating activities (O), investing activities (I), or financing activities (F).

(a) _____ Cash received from customers.
(b) _____ Cash paid to stockholders (dividends).
(c) _____ Cash received from issuing new common stock.
(d) _____ Cash paid to suppliers.
(e) _____ Cash paid to purchase a new office building.

Classify items by activity.
(SO 3, 4, 5)

BE1-4 Presented below are a number of transactions. Determine whether each transaction affects common stock (C), dividends (D), revenue (R), expense (E), or does not affect stockholders' equity (NSE). Provide titles for the revenues and expenses.

(a) Costs incurred for advertising.
(b) Assets received for services performed.
(c) Costs incurred for insurance.
(d) Amounts paid to employees.
(e) Cash distributed to stockholders.
(f) Assets received in exchange for allowing the use of the company's building.
(g) Costs incurred for utilities used.
(h) Paid cash to purchase equipment.
(i) Received cash from investors in exchange for common stock.

Determine effect of transactions on stockholders' equity.
(SO 4)

BE1-5 In alphabetical order below are balance sheet items for Herbert Company at December 31, 2005. Prepare a balance sheet following the format of Illustration 1-8.

Accounts payable	$85,000
Accounts receivable	81,000
Cash	35,500
Common stock	31,500

Prepare a balance sheet.
(SO 4, 5)

BE1-6 **Eskimo Pie Corporation** markets a broad range of frozen treats, including its famous Eskimo Pie ice cream bars. The following items were taken from a recent income statement and balance sheet. In each case identify whether the item would appear on the balance sheet (BS) or income statement (IS).

(a) _____ Income tax expense.   *(f)* _____ Net sales.
(b) _____ Inventories.   *(g)* _____ Cost of goods sold.
(c) _____ Accounts payable.   *(h)* _____ Common stock.
(d) _____ Retained earnings.   *(i)* _____ Receivables.
(e) _____ Property, plant, and equipment.   *(j)* _____ Interest expense.

Determine where items appear on financial statements.
(SO 4, 5)

BE1-7 Indicate which statement you would examine to find each of the following items: income statement (I), balance sheet (B), retained earnings statement (R), or statement of cash flows (C).

Determine proper financial statement.
(SO 4)

(a) Revenue during the period.
(b) Supplies on hand at the end of the year.
(c) Cash received from issuing new bonds during the period.
(d) Total debts outstanding at the end of the period.

Use basic accounting equation.
(SO 5)

BE1-8   Use the basic accounting equation to answer these questions.
(a) The liabilities of Schweitz Company are $90,000 and the stockholders' equity is $300,000. What is the amount of Schweitz Company's total assets?
(b) The total assets of Donovan Company are $170,000 and its stockholders' equity is $90,000. What is the amount of its total liabilities?
(c) The total assets of Snyder Co. are $700,000 and its liabilities are equal to half of its total assets. What is the amount of Snyder Co.'s stockholders' equity?

Use basic accounting equation.
(SO 5)

BE1-9   At the beginning of the year, Simonis Company had total assets of $800,000 and total liabilities of $500,000.
(a) If total assets increased $150,000 during the year and total liabilities decreased $80,000, what is the amount of stockholders' equity at the end of the year?
(b) During the year, total liabilities increased $100,000 and stockholders' equity decreased $70,000. What is the amount of total assets at the end of the year?
(c) If total assets decreased $90,000 and stockholders' equity increased $110,000 during the year, what is the amount of total liabilities at the end of the year?

Identify assets, liabilities, and stockholders' equity.
(SO 5)

BE1-10   Indicate whether each of these items is an asset (A), a liability (L), or part of stockholders' equity (SE).
(a) Accounts receivable.   (d) Office supplies.
(b) Salaries payable.   (e) Common stock.
(c) Equipment.   (f) Notes payable.

Determine required parts of annual report.
(SO 6)

BE1-11   Which is *not* a required part of an annual report of a publicly traded company?
(a) Statement of cash flows.
(b) Notes to the financial statements.
(c) Management discussion and analysis.
(d) All of these are required.

Define full disclosure principle.
(SO 7)

BE1-12   The full disclosure principle dictates that:
(a) financial statements should disclose all assets at their cost.
(b) financial statements should disclose only those events that can be measured in dollars.
(c) financial statements should disclose all events and circumstances that would matter to users of financial statements.
(d) financial statements should not be relied on unless an auditor has expressed an unqualified opinion on them.

Exercises

Match items with descriptions.
(SO 1, 2, 4, 6)

E1-1   Here is a list of words or phrases discussed in this chapter:

1. Corporation   4. Partnership   7. Accounts payable
2. Creditor   5. Stockholder   8. Auditor's opinion
3. Accounts receivable 6. Common stock

Instructions
Match each word or phrase with the best description of it.

_____ (a) An expression about whether financial statements are presented in a reasonable fashion.
_____ (b) A business enterprise that raises money by issuing shares of stock.
_____ (c) The portion of stockholders' equity that results from receiving cash from investors.

_____ **(d)** Obligations to suppliers of goods.

_____ **(e)** Amounts due from customers.

_____ **(f)** A party to whom a business owes money.

_____ **(g)** A party that invests in common stock.

_____ **(h)** A business that is owned jointly by two or more individuals but that does not issue stock.

E1-2 This information relates to Rose Co. for the year 2005.

Retained earnings, January 1, 2005	$64,000
Advertising expense	1,800
Dividends paid during 2005	7,000
Rent expense	10,400
Service revenue	58,000
Utilities expense	2,400
Salaries expense	28,000

Prepare income statement and retained earnings statement.
(SO 4)

Instructions

After analyzing the data, prepare an income statement and a retained earnings statement for the year ending December 31, 2005.

E1-3 The following information was taken from the 2001 financial statements of pharmaceutical giant **Merck and Co.** All dollar amounts are in millions.

Retained earnings, January 1, 2001	$31,489.6
Materials and production expense	28,976.5
Marketing and administrative expense	6,224.4
Dividends	2,905.7
Sales revenue	47,715.7
Research and development expense	2,456.4
Tax expense	3,120.8
Other revenue	685.9
Other expense	341.7

Prepare income statement and retained earnings statement.
(SO 4)

Instructions

After analyzing the data, prepare an income statement and a retained earnings statement for the year ending December 31, 2001.

E1-4 Presented here is information for Patrick Reid Inc. for 2005.

Retained earnings, January 1	$150,000
Revenue from legal services	410,000
Total expenses	195,000
Dividends	82,000

Prepare a retained earnings statement.
(SO 4)

Instructions

Prepare the 2005 retained earnings statement for Patrick Reid Inc.

E1-5 Consider each of the following independent situations.

(a) The retained earnings statement of Stasik Corporation shows dividends of $68,000, while net income for the year was $75,000.

(b) The statement of cash flows for Royal Cruise Corporation shows that cash provided by operating activities was $10,000, cash used in investing activities was $110,000, and cash provided by financing activities was $130,000.

Interpret financial facts.
(SO 4)

Instructions

For each company provide a brief discussion interpreting these financial facts. For example, you might discuss the company's financial health or its apparent growth philosophy.

E1-6 This information is for Kiltie Corporation for the year ended December 31, 2005.

Cash received from lenders	$20,000
Cash received from customers	65,000
Cash paid for new equipment	50,000
Cash dividends paid	6,000
Cash paid to suppliers	20,000
Cash balance 1/1/05	12,000

Prepare a statement of cash flows.
(SO 5)

Instructions

Prepare the 2005 statement of cash flows for Kiltie Corporation.

Calculate missing amounts.
(SO 4, 5)

E1-7   Here are incomplete financial statements for Jackson, Inc.

JACKSON, INC.
Balance Sheet

Assets		Liabilities and Stockholders' Equity	
Cash	$ 5,000	Liabilities	
Inventory	10,000	Accounts payable	$ 5,000
Building	50,000	Stockholders' equity	
Total assets	$65,000	Common stock	(a)
		Retained earnings	(b)
		Total liabilities and stockholders' equity	$65,000

Income Statement

Revenues	$80,000
Cost of goods sold	(c)
Administrative expenses	10,000
Net income	$ (d)

Retained Earnings Statement

Beginning retained earnings	$10,000
Net income	(e)
Dividends	5,000
Ending retained earnings	$33,000

Instructions

Calculate the missing amounts.

Prepare a statement
of cash flows.
(SO 5)

E1-8   The following data are derived from the 2002 financial statements of mail order and online direct merchant **Lands' End**. All dollars are in thousands. Lands' End has a year-end of February 1, 2002, for its 2002 financial statements.

Cash paid for repayment of debt	$ 771
Cash received from issuance of common stock	14,520
Cash balance at January 27, 2001	75,351
Cash paid for goods and services	1,502,068
Cash paid for new buildings and equipment	40,514
Cash received from customers	1,575,573

Instructions

After analyzing the data, prepare a statement of cash flows for Lands' End for the year ended February 1, 2002.

Correct an incorrectly
prepared balance sheet.
(SO 5)

E1-9   Drew Maher is the bookkeeper for Swann Company. Drew has been trying to get the balance sheet of Swann Company to balance. It finally balanced, but now he's not sure it is correct.

SWANN COMPANY
Balance Sheet
December 31, 2005

Assets		Liabilities and Stockholders' Equity	
Cash	$18,500	Accounts payable	$16,000
Supplies	8,000	Accounts receivable	(10,000)
Equipment	40,000	Common stock	40,000
Dividends	7,000	Retained earnings	27,500
Total assets	$73,500	Total liabilities and stockholders' equity	$73,500

Instructions
Prepare a correct balance sheet.

E1-10   Erik Park Inc. is a public camping ground near the Lathom Peak Recreation Area. It has compiled the following financial information as of December 31, 2005.

Compute net income and prepare a balance sheet.
(SO 4, 5)

Revenues during 2005: camping fees	$137,000	Dividends	$ 4,000
Revenues during 2005: general store	25,000	Notes payable	50,000
Accounts payable	11,000	Expenses during 2005	138,000
Cash	10,500	Supplies	2,500
Equipment	119,000	Common stock	40,000
		Retained earnings (1/1/2005)	11,000

Instructions
(a) Determine net income from Erik Park Inc. for 2005.
(b) Prepare a retained earnings statement and a balance sheet for Erik Park Inc. as of December 31, 2005.

E1-11   Kellogg Company is the world's leading producer of ready-to-eat cereal and a leading producer of grain-based convenience foods such as frozen waffles and cereal bars. The following items were taken from its 2001 income statement and balance sheet. All dollars are in millions.

Identify financial statement components and prepare an income statement.
(SO 4, 5)

____ Retained earnings	$1,564.7	____ Long-term debt	$5,619.0
____ Cost of goods sold	4,128.5	____ Inventories	574.5
____ Selling and		____ Net sales	8,853.3
administrative expenses	3,523.6	____ Accounts payable	577.5
____ Cash	231.8	____ Common stock	103.8
____ Notes payable	513.3	____ Income tax expense	322.1
____ Interest expense	351.5		
____ Other expense	54.0		

Instructions
Perform each of the following.
(a) In each case identify whether the item is an asset (A), liability (L), stockholders' equity (SE), revenue (R), or expense (E).
(b) Prepare an income statement for Kellogg Company for the year ended December 31, 2001.

E1-12   The following items were taken from the balance sheet of **Nike, Inc.**

Classify items as assets, liabilities, and stockholders' equity and prepare accounting equation.
(SO 5)

1. Cash	$ 304.0	7. Inventories	$1,424.1
2. Accounts receivable	1,621.4	8. Income taxes payable	21.9
3. Common stock	300.2	9. Property, plant, and equipment	1,618.8
4. Notes payable	860.7	10. Retained earnings	3,194.3
5. Other assets	851.3	11. Accounts payable	432.0
6. Other liabilities	1,010.5		

Instructions
Perform each of the following.
(a) Classify each of these items as an asset, liability, or stockholders' equity. (All dollars are in millions.)
(b) Determine Nike's accounting equation by calculating the value of total assets, total liabilities, and total stockholders' equity.

E1-13   The summaries of data from the balance sheet, income statement, and retained earnings statement for two corporations, Chiasson Corporation and Maxim Enterprises, Ltd., are presented below for 2005.

Use financial statement relationships to determine missing amounts.
(SO 5)

	Chiasson Corporation	Maxim Enterprises, Ltd.
Beginning of year		
Total assets	$ 90,000	$130,000
Total liabilities	80,000	(d)
Total stockholders' equity	(a)	95,000
End of year		
Total assets	(b)	180,000
Total liabilities	120,000	55,000
Total stockholders' equity	40,000	(e)
Changes during year in retained earnings		
Dividends	(c)	5,000
Total revenues	215,000	(f)
Total expenses	165,000	80,000

Instructions

Determine the missing amounts. Assume all changes in stockholders' equity are due to changes in retained earnings.

Classify various items in an annual report.
(SO 6)

E1-14 The annual report provides financial information in a variety of formats including the following.

> Management discussion and analysis (MD&A)
> Financial statements
> Notes to the financial statements
> Auditor's opinion

Instructions

For each of the following, state in what area of the annual report the item would be presented. If the item would probably not be found in an annual report, state "Not disclosed."

(a) The total cumulative amount received from stockholders in exchange for common stock.

(b) An independent assessment concerning whether the financial statements present a fair depiction of the company's results and financial position.

(c) The interest rate that the company is being charged on all outstanding debts.

(d) Total revenue from operating activities.

(e) Management's assessment of the company's results.

(f) The names and positions of all employees hired in the last year.

Identify accounting assumptions and principles.
(SO 7)

E1-15 Presented below are the assumptions and principles discussed in this chapter.

1. Full disclosure principle.   4. Time period assumption.
2. Going concern assumption.   5. Cost principle.
3. Monetary unit assumption.   6. Economic entity assumption.

Instructions

Identify by number the accounting assumption or principle that is described below. Do not use a number more than once.

____ (a) Is the rationale for why plant assets are not reported at liquidation value. (*Note:* Do not use the cost principle.)

____ (b) Indicates that personal and business record-keeping should be separately maintained.

____ (c) Assumes that the dollar is the "measuring stick" used to report on financial performance.

____ (d) Separates financial information into time periods for reporting purpose.

____ (e) Indicates that market value changes subsequent to purchase are not recorded in the accounts.

____ (f) Dictates that all circumstances and events that make a difference to financial statement users should be disclosed.

Identify the assumption or principle that has been violated.
(SO 7)

E1-16 Mere Co. had three major business transactions during 2005.

(a) Merchandise inventory with a cost of $208,000 is reported at its market value of $260,000.

(b) The president of Mere Co., Issam Mere, purchased a truck for personal use and charged it to his expense account.

(c) Mere Co. wanted to make its 2005 income look better, so it added 2 more weeks to the year (a 54-week year). Previous years were 52 weeks.

Instructions
In each situation, identify the assumption or principle that has been violated, if any, and discuss what should have been done.

Problems: Set A

P1-1A   Presented below are five independent situations.

Determine forms of business organization.
(SO 1)

(a) Ann Cunningham, a college student looking for summer employment, opened a vegetable stand along a busy local highway. Each morning she buys produce from local farmers, then sells it in the afternoon as people return home from work.

(b) Robert Steven and Phillip Cantor each owned separate swing-set manufacturing businesses. They have decided to combine their businesses and try to expand their reach beyond their local market. They expect that within the coming year they will need significant funds to expand their operations.

(c) Three chemistry professors at FIU have formed a business to employ bacteria to clean up toxic waste sites. Each has contributed an equal amount of cash and knowledge to the venture. The use of bacteria in this situation is experimental, and legal obligations could result.

(d) Michelle Beal has run a successful, but small cooperative health food store for over 20 years. The increased sales of her store have made her believe that the time is right to open a national chain of health food stores across the country. Of course, this will require a substantial investment in stores, inventory, and employees in each store. Michelle has no savings or personal assets. She wants to maintain control over the business.

(e) Mary Emery and Richard Goedde recently graduated with graduate degrees in economics. They have decided to start a consulting business focused on teaching the basics of international economics to small business owners interested in international trade.

Instructions
In each case explain what form of organization the business is likely to take—sole proprietorship, partnership, or corporation. Give reasons for your choice.

P1-2A   Financial decisions often place heavier emphasis on one type of financial statement over the others. Consider each of the following hypothetical situations independently.

Identify users and uses of financial statements.
(SO 2, 4, 5)

(a) An investor is considering purchasing commmon stock of the **Bally Total Fitness** company. The investor plans to hold the investment for at least 3 years.

(b) **Boeing** is considering extending credit to a new customer. The terms of the credit would require the customer to pay within 60 days of receipt of goods.

(c) The president of **Northwest Airlines** is trying to determine whether the company is generating enough cash to increase the amount of dividends paid to investors in this and future years, and still have enough cash to buy new flight equipment as it is needed.

(d) **Bank of America** is considering extending a loan to a small company. The company would be required to make interest payments at the end of each year for 5 years, and to repay the loan at the end of the fifth year.

Instructions
In each of the situations above, state whether the decision maker would be most likely to place primary emphasis on information provided by the income statement, balance sheet, or statement of cash flows. In each case provide a brief justification for your choice. Choose only one financial statement in each case.

Prepare an income statement, retained earnings statement, and balance sheet.
(SO 4, 5)

1. what sheet

Marginal **check figures** provide a key number to let you know you're on the right track.

Net income	$ 3,000
Ret. earnings	$ 1,300
Tot. assets	$78,700

Determine items included in a statement of cash flows and prepare the statement.
(SO 4, 5)

Net increase $46,000

Comment on proper accounting treatment and prepare a corrected income statement.
(SO 4, 7)

P1-3A Next Day Delivery was started on May 1 with an investment of $45,000 cash. Following are the assets and liabilities of the company on May 31, 2005, and the revenues and expenses for the month of May, its first month of operations.

Accounts receivable	$11,200	Notes payable	$30,000
Service revenue	9,600	Rent expense	1,200
Advertising expense	900	Equipment	60,300
Accounts payable	2,400	Repair expense	700
Cash	7,200	Fuel expense	3,400
		Insurance expense	400

No additional common stock was issued in May, but a dividend of $1,700 in cash was paid.

Instructions

Prepare an income statement and a retained earnings statement for the month of May and a balance sheet at May 31, 2005.

P1-4A Presented below are selected financial statement items for Johnson Corporation for December 31, 2005.

Inventory	$ 55,000
Cash paid to suppliers	89,000
Building	400,000
Common stock	20,000
Cash dividends paid	7,000
Cash paid to purchase equipment	26,000
Equipment	40,000
Revenues	200,000
Cash received from customers	168,000

Instructions

Determine which items should be included in a statement of cash flows, and then prepare the statement for Johnson Corporation.

P1-5A Montana Corporation was formed during 2004 by Nancy Hoeff. Nancy is the president and sole stockholder. At December 31, 2005, Nancy prepared an income statement for Montana Corporation. Nancy is not an accountant, but she thinks she did a reasonable job preparing the income statement by looking at the financial statements of other companies. She has asked you for advice. Nancy's income statement appears as follows.

MONTANA CORPORATION
Income Statement
For the Year Ended December 31, 2005

Accounts receivable	$12,000
Revenue	60,000
Rent expense	18,000
Insurance expense	5,000
Vacation expense	2,000
Net income	48,000

Nancy has also provided you with these facts.

1. Included in the revenue account is $7,000 of revenue that the company earned and received payment for in 2004. She forgot to include it in the 2004 income statement, so she put it in this year's statement.
2. Nancy operates her business out of the basement of her parents' home. They do not charge her anything, but she thinks that if she paid rent it would cost her about $18,000 per year. She therefore included $18,000 of rent expense in the statement.
3. To reward herself for a year of hard work, Nancy went to Greece. She did not use company funds to pay for the trip, but she reported it as an expense on the income statement since it was her job that made her need the vacation.

Instructions

(a) Comment on the proper accounting treatment of the three items above.

(b) Prepare a corrected income statement for Montana Corporation.

Net income $48,000

P1-6A A number of accounting reporting situations are described below.

(a) In preparing its financial statements, Seco Corporation omitted information about an ongoing lawsuit which its lawyers advised the company could very well lose when it gets to court.

(b) Dot.com Corporation believes its people are its most significant assets. It estimates and records their value on its balance sheet.

(c) Barton, Inc. is carrying inventory at its current market value of $100,000. The inventory had an original cost of $75,000.

(d) Bonilla Corp. is in its fifth year of operations and has yet to issue financial statements.

(e) Steph Wolfson, president of Classic CD Company Ltd., bought a computer for her personal use. She paid for the computer with company funds and recorded it in the "Computers" account. *sole prop.*

Identify the assumption or principle violated.
(SO 7)

Instructions

For each of the above situations, list the assumption or principle that has been violated, and explain why the situation described violates this assumption or principle.

Problems: Set B

P1-1B Presented below are five independent situations.

(a) Three physics professors at MIT have formed a business to improve the speed of information transfer over the Internet for stock exchange transactions. Each has contributed an equal amount of cash and knowledge to the venture. Although their approach looks promising, they are concerned about the legal liabilities that their business might confront.

(b) Geoff Jackson, a college student looking for summer employment, opened a bait shop in a small shed at a local marina.

(c) Peter Bates and Jerry Fine each owned separate shoe manufacturing businesses. They have decided to combine their businesses. They expect that within the coming year they will need significant funds to expand their operations.

(d) Mary Browne, Carol Lampe, and Bonnie Kurt recently graduated with marketing degrees. They have been friends since childhood. They have decided to start a consulting business focused on marketing sporting goods over the Internet.

(e) Mark Mozena wants to rent CD players and CDs in airports across the country. His idea is that customers will be able to rent equipment and CDs at one airport, listen to the CDs on their flights, and return the equipment and CDs at their destination airport. Of course, this will require a substantial investment in equipment and CDs, as well as employees and locations in each airport. Mark has no savings or personal assets. He wants to maintain control over the business.

Determine forms of business organization.
(SO 1)

Instructions

In each case explain what form of organization the business is likely to take—sole proprietorship, partnership, or corporation. Give reasons for your choice.

P1-2B Financial decisions often place heavier emphasis on one type of financial statement over the others. Consider each of the following hypothetical situations independently.

(a) **The North Face, Inc.** is considering extending credit to a new customer. The terms of the credit would require the customer to pay within 30 days of receipt of goods.

(b) An investor is considering purchasing common stock of **Amazon.com**. The investor plans to hold the investment for at least 5 years.

(c) **Chase Manhattan** is considering extending a loan to a small company. The company would be required to make interest payments at the end of each year for 5 years, and to repay the loan at the end of the fifth year.

Identify users and uses of financial statements.
(SO 2, 4, 5)

(d) The president of **Campbell Soup** is trying to determine whether the company is generating enough cash to increase the amount of dividends paid to investors in this and future years, and still have enough cash to buy equipment as it is needed.

Instructions

In each situation, state whether the decision maker would be most likely to place primary emphasis on information provided by the income statement, balance sheet, or statement of cash flows. In each case provide a brief justification for your choice. Choose only one financial statement in each case.

Prepare an income statement, retained earnings statement, and balance sheet. (SO 4, 5)

P1-3B On June 1 Mediocre Service Co. was started with an initial investment in the company of $26,200 cash. Here are the assets and liabilities of the company at June 30, and the revenues and expenses for the month of June, its first month of operations:

Cash	$ 6,000	Notes payable	$14,000
Accounts receivable	4,000	Accounts payable	1,300
Revenue	8,000	Supplies expense	1,200
Supplies	2,400	Gas and oil expense	900
Advertising expense	500	Utilities expense	300
Equipment	32,000		

The company issued no additional stock during June, but dividends of $2,200 were paid during the month.

Net income $5,100
Ret. earnings $2,900
Tot. assets $44,400

Instructions

Prepare an income statement and a retained earnings statement for the month of June and a balance sheet at June 30, 2005.

Determine items included in a statement of cash flows and prepare the statement. (SO 4, 5)

P1-4B Presented below is selected financial information for Beverly Corporation for December 31, 2005.

Inventory	$ 25,000
Cash paid to suppliers	100,000
Building	200,000
Common stock	50,000
Cash dividends paid	13,000
Cash paid to purchase equipment	15,000
Equipment	40,000
Revenues	100,000
Cash received from customers	137,000

Instructions

Net increase $9,000

Determine which items should be included in a statement of cash flows and then prepare the statement for Beverly Corporation.

Comment on proper accounting treatment and prepare a corrected balance sheet. (SO 4, 5, 7)

P1-5B Kohlenberg Corporation was formed on January 1, 2005. At December 31, 2005, Ed Murphy, the president and sole stockholder, decided to prepare a balance sheet, which appeared as follows.

KOHLENBERG CORPORATION
Balance Sheet
December 31, 2005

Assets		Liabilities and Stockholders' Equity	
Cash	$20,000	Accounts payable	$40,000
Accounts receivable	55,000	Notes payable	15,000
Inventory	30,000	Boat loan	13,000
Boat	18,000	Stockholders' equity	55,000

Ed willingly admits that he is not an accountant by training. He is concerned that his balance sheet might not be correct. He has provided you with the following additional information.

1. The boat actually belongs to Murphy, not to Kohlenberg Corporation. However, because he thinks he might take customers out on the boat occasionally, he decided to list it as an asset of the company. To be consistent he also listed as a liability of the corporation his personal loan that he took out at the bank to buy the boat.

2. The inventory was originally purchased for $15,000, but due to a surge in demand Ed now thinks he could sell it for $30,000. He thought it would be best to record it at $30,000.

3. Included in the accounts receivable balance is $10,000 that Ed loaned to his brother 5 years ago. Ed included this in the receivables of Kohlenberg Corporation so he wouldn't forget that his brother owes him money.

Instructions

(a) Comment on the proper accounting treatment of the three items above.

(b) Provide a corrected balance sheet for Kohlenberg Corporation. (*Hint:* To get the balance sheet to balance, adjust stockholders' equity.)

Tot. assets $80,000

P1-6B A number of accounting reporting situations are described below.

Identify the assumption or principle violated.
(SO 7)

(a) In preparing its financial statements, Karim Corporation tried to estimate and record the impact of the recent death of its president.

(b) The Saint John Shipbuilding Co. Ltd. takes a very long time to build ships—sometimes up to 5 years. It is wondering if it would be appropriate to report its financial results once every 2 years.

(c) Paradis Inc. recently purchased a power boat. It plans on inviting clients for outings occasionally, so the boat was paid for by the company and recorded in its records. Marc Paradis's family will use the boat whenever it is not being used to entertain clients. They estimate that the boat will be used by the family about 75% of the time.

(d) Because of a "flood sale," equipment that is worth $300,000 was purchased for only $200,000. The equipment was recorded for $300,000 on Bourque Corporation's books.

Instructions

For each of the above situations, list the assumption or principle that has been violated. Explain why the situation described violates this assumption or principle.

BROADENING YOUR PERSPECTIVE

Financial Reporting and Analysis

FINANCIAL REPORTING PROBLEM: *Tootsie Roll Industries, Inc.*

BYP1-1 Simplified 2002 financial statements of **Tootsie Roll Industries, Inc.** are given in Illustrations 1-11 through 1-14.

Instructions

Refer to Tootsie Roll's financial statements to answer the following questions.

(a) What were Tootsie Roll's total assets at December 31, 2002? At December 31, 2001?

(b) How much cash did Tootsie Roll have on December 31, 2002?

(c) What amount of accounts payable did Tootsie Roll report on December 31, 2002? On December 31, 2001?

(d) What were Tootsie Roll's sales revenue in 2002? In 2001?

(e) What is the amount of the change in Tootsie Roll's net income from 2001 to 2002?

(f) The accounting equation is: Assets = Liabilities + Stockholders' Equity. Replacing the words in that equation with dollar amounts, give Tootsie Roll's accounting equation at December 31, 2002.

COMPARATIVE ANALYSIS PROBLEM: *Tootsie Roll vs. Hershey Foods*

BYP1-2 Simplified financial statements of **Hershey Foods Corporation** are presented in Illustrations 1-20 through 1-23, and **Tootsie Roll**'s simplified financial statements are presented in Illustrations 1-11 through 1-14.

Instructions
(a) Based on the information in these financial statements, determine the following for each company.
   (1) Total assets at December 31, 2002.
   (2) Accounts receivable at December 31, 2002.
   (3) Net sales for 2002.
   (4) Net income for 2002.

(b) What conclusions concerning the two companies can you draw from these data?

RESEARCH CASE

BYP1-3 The February 6, 2002, issue of the *Wall Street Journal* includes an article by Steve Liesman, Jonathan Weil, and Michael Schroeder entitled "Accounting Debacles Spark Calls for Change: Here's the Rundown."

Instructions
Read the article and answer the following questions.
(a) What concern is raised by the fact that some audit firms receive significant payments from their audit clients for non-audit work, such as consulting? What solutions have been proposed in response to this potential problem?
(b) At the time of this article, who policed the accounting profession? What alternative has been proposed by the Securities and Exchange Commission (SEC)?
(c) What criticisms have been made of the primary accounting standards-setting group, the Financial Accounting Standards Board (FASB)?
(d) In what ways, and from what groups, is the SEC demanding more disclosure?

INTERPRETING FINANCIAL STATEMENTS

BYP1-4 The year 2000 was not a particularly pleasant year for the managers of **Xerox Corporation**, or its shareholders. The company's stock price had already fallen in the previous year from $60 per share to $30. Just when it seemed things couldn't get worse, Xerox's stock fell to $4 per share. The data below were taken from the December 31, 2000, statement of cash flows of Xerox. All dollars are in millions.

Cash used in operating activities		$ (663)
Cash used in investing activities		(644)
Financing activities		
Dividends paid	$ (587)	
Net cash received from issuing debt	3,498	
Cash provided by financing activities		2,911

Instructions
Analyze the information above, and then answer the following questions.
(a) If you were a creditor of Xerox, what reaction might you have to the above information?
(b) If you were an investor in Xerox, what reaction might you have to the above information?
(c) If you were evaluating the company as either a creditor or a stockholder, what other information would you be interested in seeing?
(d) Xerox decided to pay a cash dividend in 2000. This dividend was approximately equal to the amount paid in 1999. Discuss the issues that were probably considered in making this decision.

A GLOBAL FOCUS

BYP1-5 Today companies must compete in a global economy. Both Tootsie Roll and Hershey must compete with **Nestlé**. Nestlé, a Swiss company, is the largest food company in the world. If you were interested in broadening your investment portfolio, you might consider investing in Nestlé. However, investing in international companies can pose some additional challenges. Consider the following excerpts from the notes to Nestlé's financial statements.

NESTLÉ
Notes to the Financial Statements (partial)

(a) The Group accounts comply with International Accounting Standards (IAS) issued by the International Accounting Standards Committee (IASC) and with the Standards Interpretations issued by the Standards Interpretation Committee of the IASC (SIC).

(b) The accounts have been prepared under the historical cost convention and on an accrual basis. All significant consolidated companies have a 31st December accounting year end. All disclosures required by the 4th and 7th European Union company law directives are provided.

(c) On consolidation, assets and liabilities of Group companies denominated in foreign currencies are translated into Swiss francs at year-end rates. Income and expense items are translated into Swiss francs at the annual average rates of exchange or, where known or determinable, at the rate on the date of the transaction for significant items.

Instructions

Discuss the implications of each of these items in terms of the effect it might have (positive or negative) on your ability to compare Nestlé to Tootsie Roll and Hershey Foods. (*Hint:* In preparing your answer, review the discussion of principles and assumptions in financial reporting.)

FINANCIAL ANALYSIS ON THE WEB

BYP1-6 *Purpose:* Identify summary information about companies. This information includes basic descriptions of the company's location, activities, industry, financial health, and financial performance.

Address: http://biz.yahoo.com/i (or go to **www.wiley.com/college/kimmel**)

Steps
1. Type in a company name, or use the index to find company name.
2. Choose **Profile**. Perform instructions (a)–(c) below.
3. Click on the name of the company's industry to identify others in this industry. Perform instructions (d)–(e) below.

Instructions

Answer the following questions.
   (a) What was the company's net income? Over what period was this measured?
   (b) What was the company's total sales? Over what period was this measured?
   (c) What is the company's industry?
   (d) What are the names of four companies in this industry?
   (e) Choose one of the competitors. What is this competitor's name? What were its sales? What was its net income?

BYP1-7 *Purpose:* This exercise is an introduction to the major international accounting firms.

Addresses: **Deloitte & Touche** www.deloitte.com/
   Ernst & Young www.ey.com/
   KPMG www.us.kpmg.com/
   PricewaterhouseCoopers www.pwcglobal.com/

Steps

Go to the homepage of a firm that is of interest to you.

Instructions

Answer the following questions. (You can answer for either the U.S. or the global firm.)

(a) Name two services provided by the firm.

(b) What is the firm's total annual revenue?

(c) How many people are employed by the firm?

Critical Thinking

GROUP DECISION CASE

BYP1-8   This activity provides a survey of the **Tootsie Roll** financial statements to increase your familiarity with their contents.

(a) What CPA firm performed the audit of Tootsie Roll's financial statements?

(b) What was the amount of Tootsie Roll's earnings per share in 2002?

(c) What are the company's total assets in Mexico and Canada?

(d) What did management suggest as the causes of the increases in the sales and profits of the Canadian subsidiary in 2002?

(e) What were net sales in 1998?

(f) How many shares of Class B common stock have been authorized?

(g) How much cash was spent on capital expenditures in 2002?

(h) Over what life does the company depreciate its buildings?

(i) What is the URL for the company's Web site?

(j) What was the value of raw material inventories in 2001?

BYP1-9   Kelly Services, Inc. is a service company that provides personnel for temporary positions, primarily nontechnical. When a company requests assistance, Kelly matches the qualifications of its standby personnel with the requirements of the position. The companies pay Kelly Services; Kelly Services, in turn, pays the employees.

In a recent annual report, Kelly Services chronicled its contributions to community services over the past 30 years, or so. The following excerpts illustrate the variety of services provided.

1. KellyWeek, a Saint Patrick's Day customer appreciation event, originated in California. Kelly Services made donations of stationery, office decorations, and decals containing the company's name.

2. In support of Lady Bird Johnson's "Keep America Beautiful" campaign in the 1960s, the company donated, and its employees planted, gladiola gardens in cities across the United States.

3. The company initiated a holiday drawing in which thousands of customers throughout the United States and Canada nominate their favorite children's charities. Winning charities in the drawing receive a monetary donation from Kelly Services in the name of the customer.

4. KellyWeek was expanded by making donations of temporary help.

5. Kelly executives regularly volunteer their time and resources to serve as role models and mentors to youth in the Detroit area.

Instructions

With the class divided into groups, answer the following.

(a) The economic entity assumption requires that a company keep the personal expenses of its employees separate from business expenses. Which of the activities listed above were expenses of the business, and which were personal expenses of the employees? Be specific. If part of the donation is business and part is personal, note which part is each.

(b) For those items that were company expenses, tell whether the expense was probably categorized as an advertising expense, employee wages expense, grounds maintenance expense, or charitable contribution expense. You may use any or all of the categories. Explain your answer.

COMMUNICATION ACTIVITY

BYP1-10 Karen Lloyd is the bookkeeper for James Company, Inc. Karen has been trying to get the company's balance sheet to balance. She finally got it to balance, but she still isn't sure that it is correct.

JAMES COMPANY, INC.
Balance Sheet
For the Month Ended December 31, 2005

Assets		Liabilities and Stockholders' Equity	
Equipment	$20,500	Common stock	$11,000
Cash	10,500	Accounts receivable	(3,000)
Supplies	2,000	Dividends	(2,000)
Accounts payable	(5,000)	Notes payable	12,000
Total assets	$28,000	Retained earnings	10,000
		Total liabilities and stockholders' equity	$28,000

Instructions
Explain to Karen Lloyd in a memo (a) the purpose of a balance sheet, and (b) why this balance sheet is incorrect and what she should do to correct it.

ETHICS CASE

BYP1-11 Rules governing the investment practices of individual certified public accountants disallow them from investing in the stock of a company that is audited by their firm. Recently the Securities and Exchange Commission has become concerned that some accountants are violating this rule. In response to an SEC investigation of its firm, **PricewaterhouseCoopers** fired 10 people and spent $25 million educating its employees regarding the investment rules and installing an investment tracking system. A discussion of these issues is provided in a June 8, 2000, *Wall Street Journal* article by Michael Schroeder, "SEC, Accounting Firms Reach Pact on Conflicts."

Instructions
Read the article and answer the following questions.
   (a) Why do you think rules exist that restrict auditors from investing in companies that are audited by their firms?
   (b) Some accountants argue that they should be allowed to invest in a company's stock as long as they themselves aren't involved in working on the company's audit or consulting. What do you think of this idea?
   (c) Today a very high percentage of publicly traded companies are audited by only four very large public accounting firms. These firms also do a high percentage of the consulting work that is done for publicly traded companies. How does this fact complicate the decision regarding whether CPAs should be allowed to invest in companies audited by their firm?
   (d) Suppose you were a CPA and you had invested in **IBM** when IBM was not one of your firm's clients. Then two years later, after IBM's stock price had fallen considerably, your firm won the IBM audit contract. You will not in any way be involved in working with the IBM audit, which will be done by one of your firm's other offices in a different state. You know that your firm's rules, as well as U.S. law, require that you sell your shares immediately. If you do sell your shares immediately you will sustain a large loss. Do you think this is fair? What would you do?
   (e) Why do you think PricewaterhouseCoopers took such extreme steps in response to the SEC investigation?

Answers to Self-Study Questions

1. b 2. c 3. c 4. d 5. d 6. a 7. c 8. a 9. a 10. c 11. c

Answer to Tootsie Roll Review It Question 3, p. 15

Using dollar amounts, **Tootsie Roll**'s accounting equation is:

Assets	=	Liabilities	+	Stockholders' Equity
$646,080,000	=	$119,340,000	+	$526,740,000

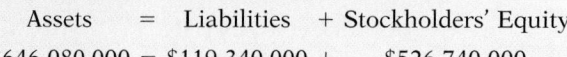

Remember to go back to the Navigator box on the chapter-opening page and check off your completed work.

A Further Look at Financial Statements

STUDY OBJECTIVES

After studying this chapter,
you should be able to:

1 Explain the meaning of generally accepted accounting principles and describe the basic objective of financial reporting.

2 Discuss the qualitative characteristics of accounting information.

3 Identify two constraints in accounting.

4 Identify the sections of a classified balance sheet.

5 Identify and compute ratios for analyzing a company's profitability.

6 Explain the relationship between a retained earnings statement and a statement of stockholders' equity.

7 Identify and compute ratios for analyzing a company's liquidity and solvency using a balance sheet.

8 Identify and compute ratios for analyz- ing a company's liquidity and solvency using a statement of cash flows.

 THE NAVIGATOR

THE NAVIGATOR ✔

▶ Scan *Study Objectives* ☐

▶ Read *Feature Story* ☐

▶ Read *Preview* ☐

▶ Read text and answer *Before You Go On*
   p. 57 ☐   *p. 62* ☐   *p. 68* ☐
   p. 71 ☐   *p. 74* ☐

▶ Work Using the *Decision Toolkit* ☐

▶ Review Summary of *Study Objectives* ☐

▶ Work *Demonstration Problem* ☐

▶ Answer *Self-Study Questions* ☐

▶ Complete *Assignments* ☐

FEATURE STORY

Just Fooling Around?

Few people could have predicted how dramatically the Internet would change the investment world. One of the most interesting results is how it has changed the way ordinary people invest their savings. More and more people are spurning investment professionals and instead are striking out on their own, making their own investment decisions.

Two early pioneers in providing investment information to the masses were Tom and David Gardner, brothers who created an online investor bulletin board called the **Motley Fool**. The name comes from Shakespeare's *As You Like It*. The fool in Shakespeare's plays was the only one who could speak unpleasant truths to kings and queens without being killed. Tom and David view themselves as 20th-century "fools," revealing the "truths" of Wall Street to the small investor, who they feel has been taken advantage of by Wall Street insiders. Their online bulletin board enables investors to exchange information and insights about companies.

Critics of these bulletin boards contend that they are high-tech rumor mills. They suggest that because of the fervor created by bulletin board chatter, stock prices get bid up to unreasonable levels. Bulletin board participants rarely give their real identities, instead using aliases. Consequently, there is little to stop people from putting misinformation on the board to influence a stock's price in the direction they desire. For example, the stock of **PairGain Technologies** jumped 32 percent in a single day as a result of a bogus takeover rumor started on an investment bulletin board. Some observers are concerned that small investors—ironically, the very people the Gardner brothers are trying to help—will be hurt the most by misinformation and intentional scams.

To show how these bulletin boards work, suppose that in July 1997 you had $10,000 to invest. You were considering **Best Buy Company**, the largest seller of electronics equipment in the United States. You scanned the Internet investment bulletin boards and found messages posted by two different investors. Here are excerpts from actual postings during the same week in 1997:

From: "TMPVenus," June 14, 1997: "Where are the prospects for positive movement for this company? Poor margins, poor management, astronomical P/E!"

From "broachman," June 18, 1997: "I believe that this is a LONG TERM winner, and presently at a good price."

One says sell, and one says buy. Whom should you believe? If you had taken "broachman's" advice and purchased the stock in July 1997, by the spring of 2002 the $10,000 you invested would have been worth over $270,000. Best Buy was one of America's best-performing stocks during that period of time.

Deciding what information to rely on is becoming increasingly complex. For example, shortly before its share price completely collapsed, nearly every professional analyst who followed **Enron** was recommending its stock as a "buy."

Rather than getting swept away by rumors, investors must sort out the good information from the bad. One thing is certain—as information services such as the Motley Fool increase in number, gathering information will become even easier. Evaluating it will be the harder task.

☑ THE NAVIGATOR

On the World Wide Web
Motley Fool: www.fool.com.
Best Buy Company: www.bestbuy.com

If you are thinking of purchasing Best Buy stock, or any stock, how can you decide what the stock is worth? If you own a stock, how can you determine whether it is time to buy more stock—or time to bail out? Your decision will be influenced by a variety of considerations; one should be your careful analysis of a company's financial statements. The reason: Financial statements offer relevant and reliable information, which will help you in your stock purchase decisions.

In this chapter we begin by looking at the objectives of financial reporting. We then take a closer look at the balance sheet and introduce some useful ways for evaluating the information provided by the statements.

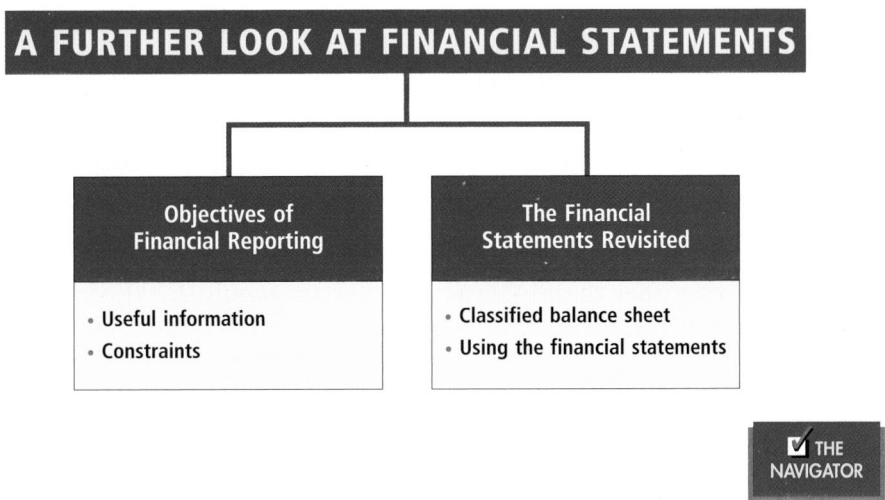

A FURTHER LOOK AT FINANCIAL STATEMENTS

Objectives of Financial Reporting
- Useful information
- Constraints

The Financial Statements Revisited
- Classified balance sheet
- Using the financial statements

☑ THE NAVIGATOR

SECTION ONE
OBJECTIVES OF FINANCIAL REPORTING

Financial reporting is the term used to describe all of the financial information presented by a company—both in its financial statements and in additional disclosures provided in the annual report. For example, if you are deciding whether to invest in Best Buy stock, you need financial information to help make your decision. Such information should help you understand Best Buy's past financial performance and its current financial picture, and give you some idea of its future prospects. Although information found on electronic bulletin boards like the Motley Fool is useful, it is no substitute for careful study of financial reports. The primary objective of financial reports is to provide information that is useful for decision making.

Characteristics of Useful Information

How does a company like Best Buy decide on the amount and type of financial information to disclose? What format should it use? How should assets, liabilities, revenues, and expenses be measured? The answers to these questions are found in accounting rules that have substantial authoritative support and are recognized as a general guide for financial reporting purposes. These rules are referred to as **generally accepted accounting principles (GAAP)**. They are

STUDY OBJECTIVE
─── 1 ───
Explain the meaning of GAAP and describe the basic objective of financial reporting.

determined by standard-setting bodies in consultation with the accounting profession and the business community.

The **Securities and Exchange Commission (SEC)** is the agency of the U.S. government that oversees U.S. financial markets and accounting standard-setting bodies. The primary accounting standard-setting body in the United States is the **Financial Accounting Standards Board (FASB)**. The FASB's overriding criterion is that the accounting rules should generate the most **useful** financial information for making business decisions. To be useful, information should possess these qualitative characteristics: relevance, reliability, comparability, and consistency.

Business Insight
INVESTOR PERSPECTIVE

In the aftermath of **Enron**, much attention has turned toward the Securities and Exchange Commission (SEC). In 2000, companies filed 98,000 reports with the SEC, 14,000 of which were annual reports. But budget shortfalls and staffing limitations meant that the SEC was able to review only 2,280 of these annual reports. As a result of SEC reviews, companies are often required to improve the disclosures in their annual report. Enron's report had not been reviewed since 1997.

STUDY OBJECTIVE
2
Discuss the qualitative
characteristics of
accounting information.

RELEVANCE

Information of any sort is relevant if it would influence a decision. Accounting information is **relevant** if it would make a difference in a business decision. For example, when **Best Buy** issues financial statements, the information in the statements is considered relevant because it provides a basis for forecasting Best Buy's future earnings. Accounting information is also relevant to business decisions because it confirms or corrects prior expectations. Thus, Best Buy's financial statements help **predict** future events and **provide feedback** about prior expectations for the financial health of the company.

In addition, for accounting information to be relevant it must be **timely**. That is, it must be available to decision makers before it loses its capacity to influence decisions. In order to increase the timeliness of financial reports, the SEC recently required that companies provide their annual report to investors within 60 days of their year-end. They had previously been allowed up to 90 days.

RELIABILITY

Reliability of information means that the information can be depended on. To be reliable, accounting information must be **verifiable**—we must be able to prove that it is free of error. Also, the information must be a **faithful representation** of what it purports to be—it must be factual. If Best Buy's income statement reports sales of $20 billion when it actually had sales of $10 billion, then the statement is not a faithful representation of Best Buy's financial performance. Finally, accounting information must be **neutral**—it cannot be selected, prepared, or presented to favor one set of interested users over another. As noted in Chapter 1, to ensure reliability, certified public accountants audit financial statements.

COMPARABILITY

Let's say that you and a friend kept track of your height each year as you were growing up. If you measured your height in feet and your friend measured hers in meters, it would be difficult to compare your heights. A conversion would be necessary. In accounting, comparability results when different companies use the same accounting principles.

At one level, U.S. accounting standards are fairly comparable because they are based on certain basic principles and assumptions. These principles and assumptions allow for some variation in methods, however. For example, there are a variety of ways to report inventory. Often these different methods result in different amounts of net income. To make comparison across companies easier, each company **must disclose** the accounting methods used. From the disclosures, the external user can determine whether the financial information is comparable and try to make adjustments. Unfortunately, converting the accounting numbers of companies that use different methods is not as easy as converting your height from feet to meters.

One factor that can affect the ability to compare two companies is their choice of accounting or fiscal year-end. Most companies choose December 31 as their fiscal year-end, although an increasing number of companies are choosing dates other than December 31. In the notes to its financial statements, **Best Buy** states that its accounting year-end is the Saturday nearest the end of February. This can create two problems for analysis. First, if Best Buy's competitors use a different year-end, then when you compare them, you are not comparing performance over the same period of time or financial position at the same point in time. Also, by not picking a particular date, the number of weeks in Best Buy's fiscal year will change. For example, its fiscal years 2000 and 1999 had 52 weeks, but fiscal year 2001 had 53 weeks.

 International Note

Accounting standards vary from country to country. Most countries have their own standards-setting body. This can complicate comparison of companies from different countries, such as German corporation Adidas and U.S. corporation Nike. One group, the International Accounting Standards Board (IASB), has been organized to try to reduce the differences in accounting practices and standards across countries.

Helpful Hint An accounting time period that is one year long is called a **fiscal year**.

 Business Insight
MANAGEMENT PERSPECTIVE

Why do companies choose the particular year-ends that they do? For example, why doesn't every company use December 31 as the accounting year-end? Many companies choose to end their accounting year when inventory or operations are at a low. This is advantageous because compiling accounting information requires much time and effort by managers, so they would rather do it when they aren't as busy operating the business. Also, inventory is easier and less costly to count when it is low. Some companies whose year-ends differ from December 31 are **Delta Air Lines**, June 30; **Walt Disney Productions**, September 30; **Kmart Corp.**, January 31; and **Dunkin' Donuts, Inc.**, October 31.

CONSISTENCY

Users of accounting information often track a company's financial results over a series of years. To compare Best Buy's net income over several years, you'd need to know that it used the same accounting principles from year to year; otherwise, you might be "comparing apples to oranges." Consistency means that a company uses the same accounting principles and methods from year to year. Thus, if a company selects one inventory accounting method in the first year of operations, it is expected to continue to use that same method in succeeding years. When financial information has been reported on a consistent basis, the financial statements permit meaningful analysis of trends within a company.

A company *can* change to a new method of accounting if management can justify that the new method produces more useful financial information. In the year in which the change occurs, the change must be disclosed in the notes to the financial statements so that users of the statements are aware of the lack of consistency.

The characteristics that make accounting information useful are summarized in Illustration 2-1.

Illustration 2-1
Characteristics of useful information

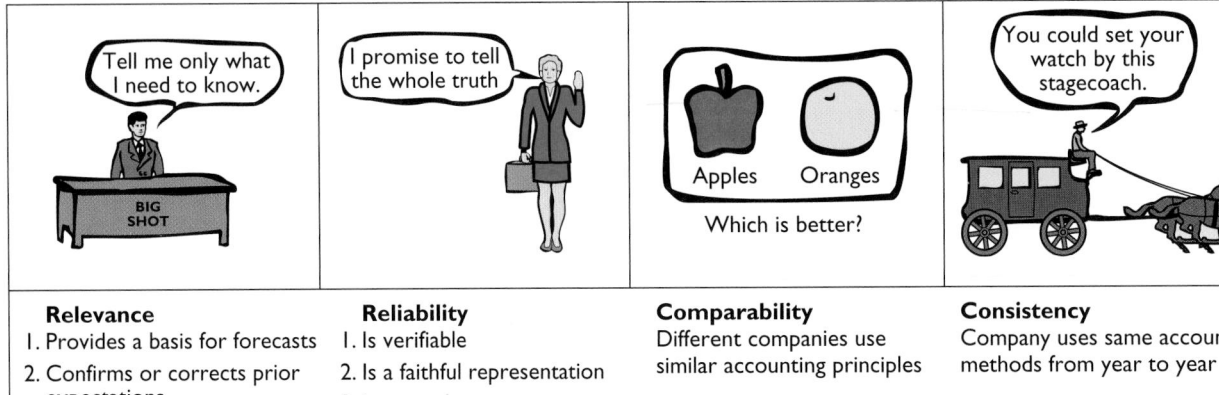

Relevance
1. Provides a basis for forecasts
2. Confirms or corrects prior expectations
3. Is timely

Reliability
1. Is verifiable
2. Is a faithful representation
3. Is neutral

Comparability
Different companies use similar accounting principles

Consistency
Company uses same accounting methods from year to year

Constraints in Accounting

STUDY OBJECTIVE
3
Identify two constraints in accounting.

The characteristics we have discussed are intended to provide users of financial statements with the most useful information. Taken to the extreme, however, efforts to provide useful financial information could be far too costly to the company. Therefore, constraints have been agreed upon to ensure that accounting rules are applied in a reasonable fashion, from the perspectives of both the company and the user. **Constraints** permit a company to apply generally accepted accounting principles without jeopardizing the usefulness of the reported information. The constraints are materiality and conservatism.

MATERIALITY

Materiality relates to a financial statement item's impact on a company's overall financial condition and operations. An item is **material** when its size makes it likely to influence the decision of an investor or creditor. It is **immaterial** if it is too small to impact a decision maker. In short, if the item does not make a difference, GAAP does not have to be followed. To determine the materiality of an amount—that is, to determine its financial significance—the item is compared with such items as total assets, sales revenue, and net income.

To illustrate how the constraint of materiality is applied, assume that Best Buy made a $100 error in recording revenue. Best Buy's total revenue is $10 billion; thus a $100 error is not material.

Helpful Hint In late 1999, the SEC issued stricter rules on materiality because it felt that too often companies were using materiality as an excuse not to report certain losses.

CONSERVATISM

Conservatism in accounting means that when preparing financial statements, a company should choose the accounting method that will be least likely to overstate assets and income. It **does not mean**, however, **that one should intentionally understate assets or income.**

A common application of the conservatism constraint is in valuing inventories. Inventories are normally recorded at their cost. Conservatism, however, requires that inventories are written down to market value if market value is below cost. Conservatism also requires that when the market value of inventory exceeds cost, the value of the inventory is not increased on the books, but instead remains at cost. This practice results in lower net income on the income statement and a lower amount reported for inventory on the balance sheet.

The two constraints are graphically depicted in Illustration 2-2.

Illustration 2-2
Accounting constraints

Materiality

For small amounts, GAAP does not have to be followed.

Conservatism

When in doubt, choose the solution that will be least likely to overstate assets and income.

BEFORE YOU GO ON . . .

▶ **Review It**

1. What are generally accepted accounting principles?
2. What is the basic objective of financial information?
3. What qualitative characteristics make accounting information useful?
4. What are the materiality constraint and the conservatism constraint?

☑ THE NAVIGATOR

SECTION TWO
THE FINANCIAL STATEMENTS REVISITED

In Chapter 1 we introduced the four financial statements. In this section we review the financial statements and present tools that are useful for evaluating them. We begin by introducing the classified balance sheet.

The Classified Balance Sheet

The balance sheet presents a snapshot of a company's financial position at a point in time. To improve users' understanding of a company's financial position, companies often group similar assets and similar liabilities together. This is useful because it tells you that items within a group have similar economic characteristics. A **classified balance sheet** generally contains the standard classifications listed in Illustration 2-3.

STUDY OBJECTIVE
4
Identify the sections of a classified balance sheet.

Illustration 2-3
Standard balance sheet
classifications

Assets	Liabilities and Stockholders' Equity
Current assets	Current liabilities
Long-term investments	Long-term liabilities
Property, plant, and equipment	Stockholders' equity
Intangible assets	

These groupings help readers determine such things as (1) whether the company has enough assets to pay its debts as they come due, and (2) the claims of short- and long-term creditors on the company's total assets. Many of these groupings can be seen in the balance sheet of Franklin Corporation shown in Illustration 2-4. Each of the groupings is explained next.

Illustration 2-4 Classified
balance sheet

FRANKLIN CORPORATION
Balance Sheet
October 31, 2005

Assets

Current assets			
Cash		$ 6,600	
Short-term investments		2,000	
Accounts receivable		7,000	
Inventories		4,000	
Supplies		2,100	
Prepaid insurance		400	
Total current assets			$22,100
Long-term investments			
Investment in stock of Walters Corp.		5,200	
Investment in real estate		2,000	7,200
Property, plant, and equipment			
Land		10,000	
Office equipment	$24,000		
Less: Accumulated depreciation	5,000	19,000	29,000
Intangible assets			
Patents			3,100
Total assets			$61,400

Liabilities and Stockholders' Equity

Current liabilities			
Notes payable		$11,000	
Accounts payable		2,100	
Salaries payable		1,600	
Unearned revenue		900	
Interest payable		450	
Total current liabilities			$16,050
Long-term liabilities			
Mortgage payable		10,000	
Notes payable		1,300	
Total long-term liabilities			11,300
Total liabilities			27,350
Stockholders' equity			
Common stock		14,000	
Retained earnings		20,050	
Total stockholders' equity			34,050
Total liabilities and stockholders' equity			$61,400

CURRENT ASSETS

Current assets are assets that are expected to be converted to cash or used up by the business within one year. In Illustration 2-4 Franklin Corporation had current assets of $22,100. For most businesses the cutoff for classification as current assets is one year from the balance sheet date. For example, accounts receivable are included in current assets because they will be converted to cash through collection within one year. Supplies is a current asset because we expect that it will be used up by the business within one year.

Some companies use a period longer than one year to classify assets and liabilities as current because they have an operating cycle longer than one year. The **operating cycle** of a company is the average time that it takes to purchase inventory, sell it on account, and then collect cash from customers. For most businesses this cycle takes less than a year, so they use a one-year cutoff. But, for some businesses, such as vineyards or airplane manufacturers, this period may be longer than a year. **Except where noted, we will assume that one year is used to determine whether an asset or liability is current or long-term.**

Common types of current assets are (1) cash, (2) short-term investments, such as short-term U.S. government securities, (3) receivables (notes receivable, accounts receivable, and interest receivable), (4) inventories, and (5) prepaid expenses (insurance and supplies). On the balance sheet, these items are listed in the order in which they are expected to be converted into cash. Illustration 2-5 presents the current assets of **The Coca-Cola Company**.

The Coca-Cola Company

THE COCA-COLA COMPANY
Balance Sheet (partial)
(in millions)

Current assets	
Cash and cash equivalents	$1,866
Short-term investments	68
Trade accounts receivable	1,882
Inventories	1,055
Prepaid expenses and other assets	2,300
Total current assets	$7,171

Illustration 2-5 Current assets section

A company's current assets are important in assessing its short-term debt-paying ability, as explained later in the chapter.

LONG-TERM INVESTMENTS

Long-term investments are generally investments in stocks and bonds of other corporations that are normally held for many years. It also includes investments in long-term assets such as land or buildings that are not currently being used in the company's operating activities. In Illustration 2-4 Franklin Corporation reported total long-term investments of $7,200 on its balance sheet. **Yahoo! Inc.** reported long-term investments in its balance sheet as shown in Illustration 2-6.

Alternative Terminology
Long-term investments are often referred to simply as **investments**.

Illustration 2-6
Long-term investments
section

YAHOO! INC. Balance Sheet (partial) (in thousands)	
Long-term investments	
Long-term investments in marketable securities	$580,418

PROPERTY, PLANT, AND EQUIPMENT

Alternative Terminology
Property, plant, and equipment
is sometimes called **fixed assets**.

Property, plant, and equipment are assets with relatively long useful lives that are currently being used in operating the business. This category includes land, buildings, machinery and equipment, delivery equipment, and furniture. In Illustration 2-4 Franklin Corporation reported office equipment of $24,000.

Depreciation is the practice of allocating the cost of assets to a number of years, rather than simply expensing the full purchase price of the asset in the year of purchase. Assets that the company depreciates should be reported on the balance sheet at cost less accumulated depreciation. The accumulated depreciation account shows the total amount of depreciation that has been expensed thus far in the asset's life. In Illustration 2-4 Franklin Corporation reported accumulated depreciation of $5,000. Illustration 2-7 presents the property, plant, and equipment of ski and sporting goods manufacturer **K2, Inc.**

Illustration 2-7
Property, plant, and
equipment section

K2, INC. Balance Sheet (partial) (in thousands)		
Property, plant, and equipment		
Land and land improvements	$ 1,641	
Buildings and leasehold improvements	30,241	
Machinery and equipment	134,831	
Construction in process	3,462	$170,175
Less: Accumulated depreciation		101,771
		$ 68,404

INTANGIBLE ASSETS

Helpful Hint Sometimes
intangible assets are reported
under a broader heading called
Other assets.

Many companies have assets that do not have physical substance yet often are very valuable. These assets are referred to as **intangible assets**. They include patents, copyrights, and trademarks or trade names that give the company **exclusive right** of use for a specified period of time. Franklin Corporation reported intangible assets of $3,100. Illustration 2-8 shows how media giant **AOL Time Warner, Inc.** reported its intangible assets.

Illustration 2-8
Intangible assets
section

AOL TIME WARNER, INC. Balance Sheet (partial) (in millions)	
Intangible assets	
Music catalogues and copyrights	$ 2,935
Cable television and sports franchises	27,371
Brands and trademarks	10,650
Goodwill and other intangible assets	126,942

CURRENT LIABILITIES

In the liabilities and stockholders' equity section of the balance sheet, the first grouping is current liabilities. **Current liabilities** are obligations that are to be paid within the coming year. Common examples are accounts payable, wages payable, bank loans payable, interest payable, taxes payable, and current maturities of long-term obligations (payments to be made within the next year on long-term obligations). In Illustration 2-4 Franklin Corporation reported five different types of current liabilities, for a total of $16,050.

Within the current liabilities section, notes payable is usually listed first, followed by accounts payable. Other items are then listed in any order. The current liabilities section adapted from the balance sheet of **Gap Inc.** is shown in Illustration 2-9.

Illustration 2-9 Current liabilities section

GAP INC. Balance Sheet (partial) (in thousands)	
Current liabilities	
Notes payable	$ 41,889
Accounts payable	1,105,117
Accrued expenses and other current liabilities	909,227
Total current liabilities	$2,056,233

LONG-TERM LIABILITIES

Obligations expected to be paid after one year are classified as **long-term liabilities**. Liabilities in this category include bonds payable, mortgages payable, long-term notes payable, lease liabilities, and pension liabilities. Many companies report long-term debt maturing after one year as a single amount in the balance sheet and show the details of the debt in notes that accompany the financial statements. Others list the various types of long-term liabilities. In Illustration 2-4 Franklin Corporation reported long-term liabilities of $11,300. In its balance sheet, **Northwest Airlines Corporation** reported long-term liabilities as shown in Illustration 2-10.

Illustration 2-10 Long-term liabilities section

NORTHWEST AIRLINES CORPORATION Balance Sheet (partial) (in millions)	
Long-term liabilities	
Long-term debt	$4,828
Long-term obligations under capital leases	393
Deferred credits and other liabilities	3,300
Total long-term liabilities	$8,521

STOCKHOLDERS' EQUITY

Alternative Terminology
Common stock is sometimes called **capital stock**.

Stockholders' equity is divided into two parts: common stock and retained earnings. Investments of assets into the business by the stockholders are recorded as common stock. Income retained for use in the business is recorded as retained earnings. These two parts are combined and reported as **stockholders' equity** on the balance sheet. In Illustration 2-4 Franklin reported common stock of $14,000 and retained earnings of $20,050.

BEFORE YOU GO ON . . .

▶ Review It

1. What are the major sections in a classified balance sheet?
2. What is the primary determining factor to distinguish current assets from long-term assets?

3. What was **Tootsie Roll**'s largest current asset at December 31, 2002? The answer to this question is provided on page 100.
4. Where is accumulated depreciation reported on the balance sheet?

▶ Do It

Baxter Hoffman recently received the following information related to Hoffman Corporation's December 31, 2005, balance sheet.

Prepaid expenses	$ 2,300	Inventory	$3,400
Cash	800	Accumulated depreciation	2,700
Property, plant, and equipment	10,700	Accounts receivable	1,100

Prepare the assets section of Hoffman Corporation's balance sheet.

Action Plan

• Present current assets first. Current assets are cash and other resources that are reasonably expected to be consumed in one year.
• Subtract accumulated depreciation from property, plant, and equipment to determine net property, plant, and equipment.

Solution

HOFFMAN CORPORATION Balance Sheet (partial) December 31, 2005		
Assets		
Current assets		
Cash	$ 800	
Accounts receivable	1,100	
Inventory	3,400	
Prepaid expenses	2,300	
Total current assets		$ 7,600
Property, plant, and equipment	10,700	
Less: Accumulated depreciation	2,700	8,000
Total assets		$15,600

Using the Financial Statements

In Chapter 1 we introduced the four financial statements. We discussed how these statements provide information about a company's performance and financial position. In this chapter we extend this discussion by showing you specific tools that can be used to analyze financial statements to make a more meaningful evaluation of a company.

RATIO ANALYSIS

Ratio analysis expresses the relationship among selected items of financial statement data. A **ratio** expresses the mathematical relationship between one quantity and another. The relationship is expressed in terms of either a percentage, a rate, or a simple proportion. To illustrate, **Best Buy** has current assets of $2,929 million and current liabilities of $2,715 million. The relationship between these accounts is determined by dividing current assets by current liabilities, to get 1.08. The alternative means of expression are:

Percentage: Current assets are 108% of current liabilities.

Rate: Current assets are 1.08 times as great as current liabilities.

Proportion: The relationship of current assets to liabilities is 1.08:1.

For analysis of the primary financial statements, ratios can be classified as follows.

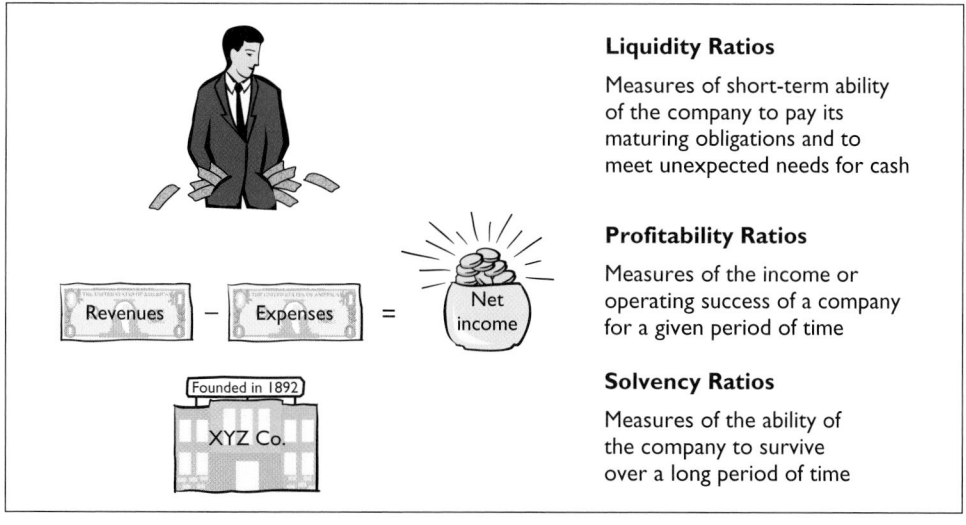

Liquidity Ratios

Measures of short-term ability of the company to pay its maturing obligations and to meet unexpected needs for cash

Profitability Ratios

Measures of the income or operating success of a company for a given period of time

Solvency Ratios

Measures of the ability of the company to survive over a long period of time

Illustration 2-11 Financial ratio classifications

Ratios can provide clues to underlying conditions that may not be apparent from inspection of the individual components of a particular ratio. However, a single ratio by itself is not very meaningful. Accordingly, in this and the following chapters we will use:

1. **Intracompany comparisons** covering two years for the same company.

2. **Industry average comparisons** based on average ratios for particular industries.

3. **Intercompany comparisons** based on comparisons with a competitor in the same industry.

USING THE INCOME STATEMENT

Best Buy Company tries to generate a profit for its shareholders by selling electronics goods. The income statement reports how successful it is at generating a profit from its sales. The income statement reports the amount earned during the period—revenues—and the costs incurred during the period—expenses. An income statement for Best Buy is provided in Illustration 2-12.

Illustration 2-12
Best Buy's income
statement

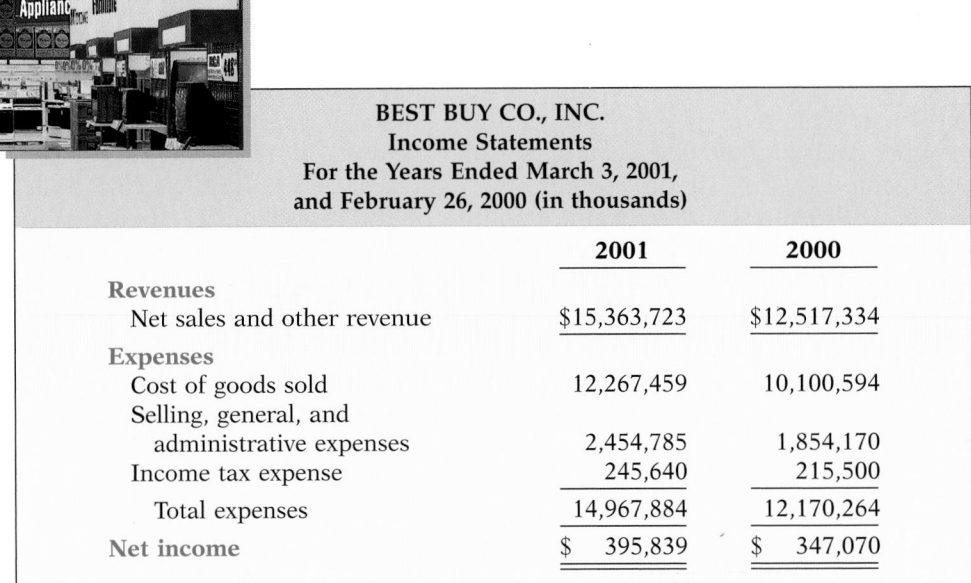

BEST BUY CO., INC. Income Statements For the Years Ended March 3, 2001, and February 26, 2000 (in thousands)		
	2001	**2000**
Revenues		
Net sales and other revenue	$15,363,723	$12,517,334
Expenses		
Cost of goods sold	12,267,459	10,100,594
Selling, general, and administrative expenses	2,454,785	1,854,170
Income tax expense	245,640	215,500
Total expenses	14,967,884	12,170,264
Net income	$ 395,839	$ 347,070

From this income statement we can see that Best Buy's sales and net income both increased during the year. Net income increased from $347,070,000 to $395,839,000. In order to increase net income, the company needs its sales to increase more than its expenses. While this was the case for Best Buy during this period, this is not as easy as it sounds. The consumer electronics business is very competitive. New models are constantly arising, making old models obsolete. Buyers are fickle, and sales are very susceptible to economic swings. Best Buy's primary competitor is **Circuit City**. Circuit City reported net income of $160,802,000 for the year ended February 28, 2001.

To evaluate the profitability of Best Buy, we will use ratio analysis. **Profitability ratios** measure the operating success of a company for a given period of time. We will look at two examples of profitability ratios: earnings per share and the price-earnings ratio.

Business Insight
INVESTOR PERSPECTIVE

Profitability matters. Recently, when the warehouse store chain **Costco** missed its estimated earnings per share figure by 1 cent (earning 26 cents instead of a projected 27 cents), its stock price fell by 25%. Although it isn't unusual for a company's share price to react to earnings announcements, a move of this magnitude is unusual. In addition, the share price of many other companies' stocks fell as a result of the news. In this case investors reacted so dramatically because Costco's financial health is viewed as a good indicator of the strength of the economy as a whole. Investors feared that the economy was "headed south."

EARNINGS PER SHARE. Earnings per share (EPS) measures the net income earned on each share of common stock. It is computed by dividing **net income** by the **average number of common shares outstanding during the year**. Stockholders usually think in terms of the number of shares they own or plan to buy or sell, so reducing net income earned to a per share amount provides a useful perspective for determining the investment return. Advanced accounting courses present more refined techniques for calculating earnings per share. For now, a basic approach is to divide earnings available to common stockholders by average common shares outstanding during the year. Earnings available to common stockholders is calculated as net income less dividends paid on another type of stock, called preferred stock (Net income − Preferred stock dividends). By comparing earnings per share of a single company over time, one can evaluate its relative earnings performance from the perspective of a shareholder—that is, on a per share basis.

PRICE-EARNINGS RATIO. It is very important to note that comparisons of earnings per share across companies are **not meaningful** because of the wide variations in the numbers of shares of outstanding stock among companies and in the stock prices. Instead, in order to make a meaningful comparison of earnings across firms, we calculate the price-earnings ratio. The price-earnings ratio is an oft-quoted statistic that measures **the ratio of the market price of each share of common stock to the earnings per share**. It is computed by dividing the market price per share of stock by earnings per share.

The price-earnings (P-E) ratio reflects the investors' assessment of a company's future earnings. The ratio of price to earnings will be higher if investors think that current earnings levels will persist or increase than it will be if investors think that earnings will decline. A high price-earnings ratio might also indicate that a stock is priced too high and is likely to come down. From the information presented below, the earnings per share and price-earnings ratios for **Best Buy** in 2001 and 2000 are calculated in Illustration 2-13. (Note that to simplify our calculations, we assumed that any change in shares for Best Buy occurred in the middle of the year.)

(in thousands)	2001	2000
Net income	$395,839	$347,070
Preferred stock dividends	–0–	–0–
Shares outstanding at beginning of year	200,379	203,620
Shares outstanding at end of year	208,138	200,379
Market price of stock at end of year	$40.10	$48.00

Illustration 2-13 Best Buy earnings per share and price-earnings ratio

From 2000 to 2001, Best Buy's earnings per share increased. Its price-earnings ratio decreased. This decrease might reflect a belief that Best Buy's profitability and growth will not continue.

As noted, earnings per share cannot be meaningfully compared across companies. Price-earnings ratios, however, can be compared. Illustration 2-14 lists five companies and their earnings per share and price-earnings ratios for 2001 (calculated at the end of each company's fiscal year). Note the difference in price-earnings ratios between **Sears** and **Intel**.

Illustration 2-14
Variability of earnings performance ratios among companies

Company	Earnings Per Share	Price-Earnings Ratio
Intel	$0.19	169.7
Microsoft	1.45	47.8
General Motors	1.79	27.5
Kellogg	1.19	25.4
Sears, Roebuck	2.25	21.3

Business Insight
INTERNATIONAL PERSPECTIVE

The French know a lot about food and wine—but stocks are another matter. One observer went so far as to state, "Indeed, until recently the French widely derided people who invested in stocks as Anglo-Saxon speculators, greedy capitalists who deviously manipulated financial markets to line their pockets." But when stock markets (or as the French say, *les Bourses*) around the world hit record highs, many French began taking classes to learn more about how to invest. Many have a lot to learn. For example, Jacques Giraudou decided to take a class after he sustained a huge investment loss. He had purchased an investment in the Eurotunnel, which proceeded to lose 70% of its value over a two-year period. Only after two years did he realize that he had purchased stocks rather than bonds.

SOURCE: Suzanne McGee, "The French Try to Demystify Investing," *Wall Street Journal* (May 27, 1999), p. C1.

DECISION TOOLKIT

Decision Checkpoints	Info Needed for Decision	Tool to Use for Decision	How to Evaluate Results
How does the company's earnings performance compare with that of previous years?	Net income available to common shareholders and average common shares outstanding	$\text{Earnings per share} = \dfrac{\text{Net income} - \text{Preferred stock dividends}}{\text{Average common shares outstanding}}$	A higher measure suggests improved performance, although the number is subject to manipulation. Values should not be compared across companies.
How does the market perceive the company's prospects for future earnings?	Earnings per share and market price per share	$\text{Price-earnings ratio} = \dfrac{\text{Stock price per share}}{\text{Earnings per share}}$	A high ratio suggests the market has favorable expectations, although it also may suggest stock is overpriced.

USING THE STATEMENT OF STOCKHOLDERS' EQUITY

As discussed in Chapter 1, the retained earnings statement describes the changes in retained earnings during the year. This statement adds net income and then subtracts dividends from the beginning retained earnings to arrive at ending retained earnings.

Recall, however, that stockholders' equity is comprised of two parts: retained earnings and common stock. Therefore, the stockholders' equity of most companies is affected by factors other than just changes in retained earnings. For example, the company may issue or retire shares of common stock. Most companies, therefore, use what is called a **statement of stockholders' equity**, rather than a retained earnings statement, so that they can report **all changes** in stockholders' equity accounts. Illustration 2-15 is a simplified statement of stockholders' equity for **Best Buy**.

BEST BUY CO., INC. Statement of Stockholders' Equity (in thousands)	Common Stock	Retained Earnings
Balances at March 2, 1998	$270,607	$ 265,105
Issuance of common stock	281,951	
Net income		216,282
Balances at February 27, 1999	552,558	481,387
Repurchase of common stock	(285,030)	
Net income		347,070
Balances at February 26, 2000	267,528	828,457
Issuance of common stock	330,104	
Net income		395,839
Balances at March 3, 2001	$597,632	$1,224,296

Illustration 2-15
Best Buy's statement of stockholders' equity

One observation that can be made from this financial statement is that Best Buy's common stock increased as the result of transactions in the company's own stock during this three-year period. Another observation from this financial statement is that Best Buy paid no dividends during the last three years. You might wonder why Best Buy paid no dividends during years when it was profitable. In fact, recently two Best Buy shareholders discussed this question about Best Buy's dividend policy on an investor bulletin board. Here are excerpts:

From "Katwoman": "Best Buy has a nice price increase. Earnings are on the way up. But why no dividends?"

From "AngryCandy": "I guess they feel they can make better use of the money by investing back in the business. They still view Best Buy as a rapidly growing company and would prefer to invest in expanding the infrastructure (building new stores, advertising, etc.) than in paying out dividends. . . . If Best Buy gets to the stage of 'stable, big company' with little room for expansion, then I'm sure you'll see them elect to pay out a dividend."

AngryCandy's response is an excellent explanation of the thought process that management goes through in deciding whether to pay a dividend. Management must evaluate what its cash needs are. If it has uses for cash that will increase the value of the company (for example, building a new, centralized warehouse), then it should retain cash in the company. However, if it has more cash than it has valuable opportunities, then it should distribute its excess cash as a dividend.

BEFORE YOU GO ON . . .

▶ Review It

1. What are the three ways that ratios can be expressed?
2. What is the purpose of profitability ratios? Explain earnings per share and the price-earnings ratio.
3. What does a statement of stockholders' equity show?

☑ THE NAVIGATOR

USING A CLASSIFIED BALANCE SHEET

Illustration 2-16
Best Buy's balance sheet

You can learn a lot about a company's financial health by also evaluating the relationship between its various assets and liabilities. A simplified balance sheet for **Best Buy** is provided in Illustration 2-16.

BEST BUY CO., INC. Balance Sheets (in thousands)		
Assets	**March 3, 2001**	**February 26, 2000**
Current assets		
Cash and cash equivalents	$ 746,879	$ 750,723
Receivables	209,031	189,301
Merchandise inventories	1,766,934	1,183,681
Other current assets	205,819	114,755
Total current assets	2,928,663	2,238,460
Property and equipment	1,987,392	1,093,471
Less: Accumulated depreciation	543,220	395,387
Net property and equipment	1,444,172	698,084
Other assets	466,752	58,798
Total assets	$4,839,587	$2,995,342
Liabilities and Stockholders' Equity		
Current liabilities		
Accounts payable	$1,772,722	$1,313,940
Accrued compensation payable	154,159	102,065
Accrued liabilities	545,590	287,888
Accrued income taxes	127,287	65,366
Current portion of long-term debt	114,940	15,790
Total current liabilities	2,714,698	1,785,049
Long-term liabilities		
Long-term debt	121,952	99,448
Other long-term liabilities	181,009	14,860
Total long-term liabilities	302,961	114,308
Total liabilities	3,017,659	1,899,357
Stockholders' equity		
Common stock	597,632	267,528
Retained earnings	1,224,296	828,457
Total stockholders' equity	1,821,928	1,095,985
Total liabilities and stockholders' equity	$4,839,587	$2,995,342

Liquidity

Suppose you are a banker considering lending money to Best Buy, or you are a computer manufacturer interested in selling it computers. You would be concerned about Best Buy's **liquidity**—its ability to pay obligations that are expected to become due within the next year or operating cycle. You would look closely at the relationship of its current assets to current liabilities.

STUDY OBJECTIVE

7

Identify and compute ratios for analyzing a company's liquidity and solvency using a balance sheet.

WORKING CAPITAL. One measure of liquidity is **working capital**, which is the difference between the amounts of current assets and current liabilities:

$$\text{Working Capital} = \text{Current Assets} - \text{Current Liabilities}$$

When working capital is positive, there is greater likelihood that the company will pay its liabilities. When working capital is negative, short-term creditors might not be paid, and the company might ultimately be forced into bankruptcy. Best Buy had working capital in 2001 of \$213,965,000 (\$2,928,663,000 − \$2,714,698,000).

CURRENT RATIO. **Liquidity ratios** measure the short-term ability of the enterprise to pay its maturing obligations and to meet unexpected needs for cash. One liquidity ratio is the **current ratio**, which is computed by dividing current assets by current liabilities.

The current ratio is a more dependable indicator of liquidity than working capital. Two companies with the same amount of working capital may have significantly different current ratios. The 2001 and 2000 current ratios for Best Buy, for **Circuit City**, and industry averages are shown in Illustration 2-17.

Illustration 2-17 Current ratio

$$\text{Current Ratio} = \frac{\text{Current Assets}}{\text{Current Liabilities}}$$

	2001	2000
Best Buy ($ in millions)	$\frac{\$2,929}{\$2,715} = 1.08:1$	$\frac{\$2,238}{\$1,785} = 1.25:1$
Circuit City	2.20:1	2.09:1
Industry average	1.49:1	

What does the ratio actually mean? Best Buy's 2001 current ratio of 1.08:1 means that for every dollar of current liabilities, Best Buy has \$1.08 of current assets. Best Buy's current ratio decreased in 2001. When compared to the industry average of 1.49:1, and Circuit City's 2.20:1 current ratio, Best Buy's liquidity should be investigated further.

The current ratio is only one measure of liquidity. It does not take into account the **composition** of the current assets. For example, a satisfactory current ratio does not disclose whether a portion of the current assets is tied up in slow-moving inventory. The composition of the assets matters because a dollar of cash is more readily available to pay the bills than is a dollar of inventory. For example, suppose a company's cash balance declined while its merchandise inventory increased substantially. If inventory increased because the company is having difficulty selling its products, then the current ratio might not fully reflect the reduction in the company's liquidity.

Solvency

Now suppose that instead of being a short-term creditor, you are interested in either buying Best Buy's stock or extending the company a long-term loan. Long-term creditors and stockholders are interested in a company's long-run **solvency**—its ability to pay interest as it comes due and to repay the balance of a debt due at its maturity. **Solvency ratios** measure the ability of the enterprise to survive over a long period of time. The debt to total assets ratio is one source of information about long-term debt-paying ability.

DEBT TO TOTAL ASSETS RATIO. The **debt to total assets ratio** measures the percentage of assets financed by creditors rather than stockholders. Debt financing is more risky than equity financing because debt must be repaid at specific points in time, whether the company is performing well or not. Thus, the higher the percentage of debt financing, the riskier the company.

The debt to total assets ratio is computed by dividing total debt (both current and long-term liabilities) by total assets. The higher the percentage of total liabilities (debt) to total assets, the greater the risk that the company may be unable to pay its debts as they come due. The ratios of debt to total assets for Best Buy, for Circuit City, and industry averages are presented in Illustration 2-18.

Helpful Hint Some users evaluate solvency using a ratio of liabilities divided by stockholders' equity. The higher this "debt to equity" ratio, the lower is a company's solvency.

Illustration 2-18 Debt to total assets ratio

$$\text{Debt to Total Assets Ratio} = \frac{\text{Total Liabilities}}{\text{Total Assets}}$$

	2001	2000
Best Buy ($ in millions)	$\frac{\$3,018}{\$4,840} = 62\%$	$\frac{\$1,899}{\$2,995} = 63\%$
Circuit City	39%	46%
Industry average	26%	

The 2001 ratio of 62% means that $0.62 of every dollar invested in assets by Best Buy has been provided by Best Buy's creditors. Best Buy's ratio exceeds the industry average of 26% and Circuit City's ratio of 39%. The higher the ratio, the lower the equity "buffer" available to creditors if the company becomes insolvent. Thus, from the creditors' point of view, a high ratio of debt to total assets is undesirable. Best Buy's solvency appears lower than that of Circuit City and lower than the average company in the industry.

The adequacy of this ratio is often judged in the light of the company's earnings. Generally, companies with relatively stable earnings, such as public utilities, can support higher debt to total assets ratios than can cyclical companies with widely fluctuating earnings, such as many high-tech companies. In later chapters you will learn additional ways to evaluate solvency.

Business Insight
INVESTOR PERSPECTIVE

Debt financing differs greatly across industries and companies. Here are some debt to total assets ratios for selected companies:

	Debt to Total Assets Ratio
Callaway Golf Company	21%
Advanced Micro Devices	37%
American Pharmaceutical Partners	46%
Eastman Kodak Company	78%
Sears, Roebuck & Company	86%
General Motors Corporation	94%

DECISION TOOLKIT

Decision Checkpoints	Info Needed for Decision	Tool to Use for Decision	How to Evaluate Results
Can the company meet its near-term obligations?	Current assets and current liabilities	$\text{Current ratio} = \dfrac{\text{Current assets}}{\text{Current liabilities}}$	Higher ratio suggests favorable liquidity.
Can the company meet its long-term obligations?	Total debt and total assets	$\text{Debt to total assets ratio} = \dfrac{\text{Total liabilities}}{\text{Total assets}}$	Lower value suggests favorable solvency.

BEFORE YOU GO ON . . .

▶ Review It

1. What is liquidity? How can it be measured using a classified balance sheet?
2. What is solvency? How can it be measured using a classified balance sheet?

▶ Do It

Selected financial data for Drummond Company at December 31, 2005, are as follows: cash $60,000; receivables (net) $80,000; inventory $70,000; total assets $540,000; current liabilities $140,000; and total liabilities $270,000. Compute the current ratio and debt to total assets ratio.

Action Plan

• Use the formula for the current ratio: Current assets ÷ Current liabilities.
• Use the formula for the debt to total assets ratio: Total liabilities ÷ Total assets.

Solution

The current ratio is 1.5:1 ($210,000 ÷ $140,000). The debt to total assets ratio is 50% ($270,000 ÷ $540,000).

 THE NAVIGATOR

USING THE STATEMENT OF CASH FLOWS

As you learned in Chapter 1, the statement of cash flows provides financial information about the sources and uses of a company's cash. Investors, creditors, and others want to know what is happening to a company's most liquid resource— its cash. In fact, it is often said that "cash is king" because if a company can't

STUDY OBJECTIVE
8
Identify and compute ratios for analyzing a company's liquidity and solvency using a statement of cash flows.

generate cash, it won't survive. To aid in the analysis of cash, the statement of cash flows reports the cash effects of (1) a company's **operating activities**, (2) its **investing activities**, and (3) its **financing activities**.

Sources of cash matter. For example, you would feel much better about a company's health if you knew that its cash was generated from the operations of the business rather than borrowed. A cash flow statement provides this information. Similarly, net income does not tell you *how much* cash the company generated from operations. The statement of cash flows can tell you that. In summary, neither the income statement nor the balance sheet can directly answer most of the important questions about cash, but the statement of cash flows does. A simplified statement of cash flows for **Best Buy** is provided in Illustration 2-19.

Illustration 2-19
Best Buy's statement of cash flows

BEST BUY CO., INC.
Statement of Cash Flows
(in thousands)

	For fiscal year ending	
	March 3, 2001	**February 26, 2000**
Cash flows provided by operating activities		
Cash receipts from operating activities	$15,319,118	$12,437,123
Cash payments for operating activities	(14,510,914)	(11,660,675)
Net cash provided (used) by operations	808,204	776,448
Cash flows provided by investing activities		
(Increase) decrease in property and plant	(657,706)	(361,024)
Other cash inflow (outflow)	(372,096)	(55,310)
Net cash provided (used) by investing	(1,029,802)	(416,334)
Cash flows provided by financing activities		
Issue of equity securities	235,379	32,229
Increase (decrease) in borrowing	(17,625)	(29,946)
Dividends, other distributions	0	(397,451)
Net cash provided (used) by financing	217,754	(395,168)
Net increase (decrease) in cash and equivalents	(3,844)	(35,054)
Cash and equivalents at start of year	750,723	785,777
Cash and equivalents at year-end	$ 746,879	$ 750,723

Different users have different reasons for being interested in the statement of cash flows. If you were a creditor of Best Buy (either short term or long term), you would be interested to know the source of its cash in recent years. This information would give you some indication of where it might get cash to pay you. If you have a long-term interest in Best Buy as a stockholder, you would look to the statement of cash flows for information regarding the company's ability to generate cash over the long run to meet its cash needs for growth.

Companies get cash from two sources: operating activities and financing activities. In the early years of a company's life it typically won't generate enough cash from operating activities to meet its investing needs, so it will have to issue stock or borrow money. An established company, however, will often be able to meet most of its cash needs with cash from operations. Best Buy's cash provided by operating activities in the previous three years was sufficient to meet its needs for acquisitions of property, plant, and equipment. For example, in 2001 cash provided by operating activities was $808,204,000, whereas cash spent on property, plant, and equipment was $657,706,000. However, in 2001 Best Buy also purchased other businesses to expand its business lines. In order to finance these investing activities, Best Buy had to supplement its internally generated cash with cash from outside sources, by issuing new stock.

— **CURRENT CASH DEBT COVERAGE.** Earlier we introduced you to measures of liquidity and solvency. The statement of cash flows can also be used to calculate additional measures of liquidity and solvency. The **current cash debt coverage ratio** is a measure of liquidity that is calculated as cash provided by operating activities divided by average current liabilities. It indicates the company's ability to generate sufficient cash to meet its short-term needs. In general, a value below .40 times is considered cause for additional investigation of a company's liquidity.

— **CURRENT CASH COVERAGE.** The **cash debt coverage ratio** is a measure of solvency that is calculated as cash provided by operating activities divided by average total liabilities. It indicates the company's ability to generate sufficient cash to meet its long-term needs. Illustration 2-20 presents each of these measures for Best Buy and Circuit City. Industry measures are not available for these ratios. A general rule of thumb is that a ratio below .20 times is considered cause for additional investigation.

Illustration 2-20 Current cash debt coverage ratio and cash debt coverage ratio

$$\text{Current Cash Debt Coverage Ratio} = \frac{\text{Cash Provided by Operations}}{\text{Average Current Liabilities}}$$

	2001	2000
Best Buy ($ in millions)	$\frac{\$808}{(\$2,715 + \$1,785)/2^*} = .36$ times	$\frac{\$776}{(\$1,785 + \$1,410)/2^*} = .49$ times
Circuit City	.12 times	.53 times

$$\text{Cash Debt Coverage Ratio} = \frac{\text{Cash Provided by Operations}}{\text{Average Total Liabilities}}$$

	2001	2000
Best Buy ($ in millions)	$\frac{\$808}{(\$3,018 + \$1,899)/2^*} = .33$ times	$\frac{\$776}{(\$1,899 + \$1,498)/2^*} = .46$ times
Circuit City	.09 times	.37 times

*Amounts used to calculate average current liabilities and average total liabilities are taken from Best Buy's balance sheet (Illustration 2-16). Current liabilities at year-end 1999 were $1,410 million, and total liabilities at year-end 1999 were $1,498 million. Also note that amounts in the ratio calculations have been rounded.

We can use these measures to supplement the current ratio and debt to total assets ratio, to evaluate Best Buy's liquidity and solvency. Best Buy's current cash debt coverage ratio of .36 is slightly less than the recommended minimum level of .40, suggesting that its liquidity is adequate. On the other hand, Circuit City's value of .12 is less than the recommended level. Recall, however, that Circuit City's current ratio was quite high. The conflicting results of these two measures suggest that further evaluation of Circuit City's liquidity is warranted. For example, it is possible that Circuit City's current ratio was so high because it had accumulated obsolete inventory. This would result in a high current ratio, even though the inventory was not very liquid.

Best Buy's cash debt coverage ratio of .33 is well in excess of the recommended minimum level of .2, suggesting that its solvency is acceptable. Again, Circuit City's value falls short of the recommended level, leaving its solvency in doubt. We will investigate other measures of liquidity and solvency in later chapters.

DECISION TOOLKIT

Decision Checkpoints	Info Needed for Decision	Tool to Use for Decision	How to Evaluate Results
Can the company meet its near-term obligations?	Current liabilities and cash provided by operating activities	Current cash debt coverage ratio $= \dfrac{\text{Cash provided by operations}}{\text{Average current liabilities}}$	A higher ratio indicates liquidity, that the company is generating cash sufficient to meet its near-term needs.
Can the company meet its long-term obligations?	Total liabilities and cash provided by operating activities	Cash debt coverage ratio $= \dfrac{\text{Cash provided by operations}}{\text{Average total liabilities}}$	A higher ratio indicates solvency, that the company is generating cash sufficient to meet its long-term needs.

BEFORE YOU GO ON . . .

▶ Review It

1. What information does the statement of cash flows provide that is not available in an income statement or a balance sheet?
2. What does the current cash debt coverage ratio measure?
   What does the cash debt coverage ratio measure?

☑ THE NAVIGATOR

Using the Decision Toolkit

In this chapter we have evaluated a home electronics gaint, **Best Buy. Tweeter Home Entertainment** sells consumer electronics products from 154 stores on the East Coast under various names. It specializes in products with high-end features. A simplified balance sheet and income statement for Tweeter Home Entertainment are presented in Illustrations 2-21 and 2-22. Additional information: Tweeter's cash provided by

**TWEETER HOME
ENTERTAINMENT GROUP**
Balance Sheets
(in millions)

	September 30	
	2001	**2000**
Assets		
Current assets		
Cash and cash equivalents	$ 3.3	$ 34.3
Receivables	31.3	14.7
Inventories	129.2	86.0
Other current assets	7.5	3.9
Total current assets	171.3	138.9
Property, plant, and equipment, net	109.1	51.9
Other assets	200.0	44.2
Total assets	$480.4	$235.0
Liabilities and Stockholders' Equity		
Current liabilities		
Accounts payable	$ 38.6	$ 21.5
Accrued expenses	38.9	19.5
Other current liabilities	23.3	14.4
Total current liabilities	100.8	55.4
Long-term debt	36.7	0
Other liabilities	10.5	4.7
Total liabilities	148.0	60.1
Stockholders' equity	332.4	174.9
Total liabilities and stockholders' equity	$480.4	$235.1

Illustration 2-21 Tweeter Home Entertainment's balance sheet

**TWEETER HOME
ENTERTAINMENT GROUP**
Income Statements
(in millions)

	Years ended September 30	
	2001	**2000**
Sales	$540.1	$399.9
Cost of sales	343.3	251.6
Operating expenses	169.1	122.5
Interest expense/(income)	0.7	(1.1)
Other expense/(income)	(1.2)	(0.5)
Income tax expense	11.3	11.0
Total expenses	523.2	383.5
Net income	$ 16.9	$ 16.4

Illustration 2-22 Tweeter Home Entertainment's income statement

operating activities was $34,900,000 in 2001 and $1,700,000 in 2000. Assume that average shares outstanding during all of fiscal 2001 were 22.9 million and were 18.4 million during all of fiscal 2000. There was no preferred stock outstanding.

The stock price was $13.64 on September 30, 2001, and $36.31 on September 30, 2000.

Instructions

Using these statements, answer the following questions:

1. Calculate the current ratio for Tweeter for 2001 and 2000 and the current cash debt coverage ratio for 2001, and discuss its liquidity position.
2. Calculate the debt to total assets ratio for Tweeter for 2001 and 2000 and the cash debt coverage ratio for 2001, and discuss its solvency.
3. Calculate the earnings per share and price-earnings ratio for Tweeter for 2001 and 2000, and discuss its change in profitability.
4. Best Buy's accounting year-end was March 3, 2001, whereas Tweeter's was September 30, 2001. How does this difference affect your ability to compare their profitability?

Solution

1. Current ratio:

$$2001\ (\$171.3/\$100.8) = 1.70 \qquad 2000\ (\$138.9/\$55.4) = 2.51$$

Tweeter's liquidity declined from 2000 to 2001. In 2000 there was $2.51 of current assets available for every dollar of current liabilities. In 2001 there was $1.70. Tweeter's 2001 current ratio would probably be considered acceptable, but not strong. It is higher than that of Best Buy, but it is a much smaller company than Best Buy. Often, larger companies can get by with a lower current ratio.

Current cash debt coverage ratio:

$$2001 \quad \frac{\$34.9}{(\$100.8 + \$55.4)/2} = .45 \text{ times}$$

A value above .40 times for this ratio is generally considered acceptable. This measure of .45 times reduces our concern about Tweeter's marginal current ratio.

2. Debt to total assets ratio:

$$2001\ (\$148.0/\$480.4) = 31\% \qquad 2000\ (\$60.1/\$235.0) = 26\%$$

Based on the change in its ratio of debt to total assets, Tweeter's reliance on debt financing increased from 2000 to 2001. The increase in the value of this ratio suggests the company's solvency declined.

Cash debt coverage ratio:

$$2001 \quad \frac{\$34.9}{(\$148.0 + \$60.1)/2} = .34 \text{ times}$$

Tweeter's value of .34 times is higher than the generally acceptable level of .20 times. This would suggest that the company's solvency appears good.

3. Earnings per share:

$$2001\ (\$16.9/22.9) = \$0.74 \text{ per share} \qquad 2000\ (\$16.4/18.4) = \$0.89 \text{ per share}$$

Price-earnings ratio:

$$2001\ (\$13.64/\$0.74) = 18.4 \qquad 2000\ (\$36.31/\$0.89) = 40.8$$

Tweeter's earnings per share declined from $0.89 to $0.74, even though its net income increased. This happened because the number of shares increased. Its price-earnings ratio declined sharply. This decline mirrored a decline in P-E ratios in the stock market as a whole at that time.

4. Tweeter's income statement covers seven months not covered by Best Buy's. Suppose that the economy changed dramatically during this seven-month period, either improving or declining. This change in the economy would be reflected in Tweeter's income statement but would not be reflected in Best Buy's income statement until the following March, thus reducing the usefulness of a comparison of the income statements of the two companies.

Summary of Study Objectives

1 *Explain the meaning of generally accepted accounting principles and describe the basic objective of financial reporting.* Generally accepted accounting principles are a set of rules and practices recognized as a general guide for financial reporting purposes. The basic objective of financial reporting is to provide information that is useful for decision making.

2 *Discuss the qualitative characteristics of accounting information.* To be judged useful, information should possess these qualitative characteristics: relevance, reliability, comparability, and consistency.

3 *Identify two constraints in accounting.* The major constraints are materiality and conservatism.

4 *Identify the sections of a classified balance sheet.* In a classified balance sheet, assets are classified as current assets; long-term investments; property, plant, and equipment; or intangibles. Liabilities are classified as either current or long-term. There is also a stockholders' equity section, which shows common stock and retained earnings.

5 *Identify and compute ratios for analyzing a company's profitability.* Profitability ratios, such as earnings per share (EPS) and the price-earnings

(P-E), ratio, measure aspects of the operating success of a company for a given period of time.

6 *Explain the relationship between a retained earnings statement and a statement of stockholders' equity.* The retained earnings statement presents the factors that changed the retained earnings balance during the period. A statement of stockholders' equity presents the factors that changed stockholders' equity during the period, including those that changed retained earnings. Thus, a statement of stockholders' equity is more inclusive.

7 *Identify and compute ratios for analyzing a company's liquidity and solvency using a balance sheet.* Liquidity ratios, such as the current ratio, measure the short-term ability of a company to pay its maturing obligations and to meet unexpected needs for cash. Solvency ratios, such as the debt to total assets ratio, measure the ability of an enterprise to survive over a long period.

8 *Identify and compute ratios for analyzing a company's liquidity and solvency using a statement of cash flows.* The current cash debt coverage ratio measures a company's liquidity. The cash debt coverage ratio measures a company's solvency.

DECISION TOOLKIT—A SUMMARY

Decision Checkpoints ✔	Info Needed for Decision	Tool to Use for Decision	How to Evaluate Results
How does the company's earnings performance compare with that of previous years?	Net income available to common shareholders and average common shares outstanding	$\text{Earnings per share} = \dfrac{\text{Net income} - \text{Preferred stock dividends}}{\text{Average common shares outstanding}}$	A higher measure suggests improved performance, although the number is subject to manipulation. Values should not be compared across companies.
How does the market perceive the company's prospects for future earnings?	Earnings per share and market price per share	$\text{Price-earnings ratio} = \dfrac{\text{Stock price per share}}{\text{Earnings per share}}$	A high ratio suggests the market has favorable expectations, although it also may suggest stock is overpriced.
Can the company meet its near-term obligations?	Current assets and current liabilities	$\text{Current ratio} = \dfrac{\text{Current assets}}{\text{Current liabilities}}$	Higher ratio suggests favorable liquidity.
Can the company meet its long-term obligations?	Total debt and total assets	$\text{Debt to total assets ratio} = \dfrac{\text{Total liabilities}}{\text{Total assets}}$	Lower value suggests favorable solvency.
Can the company meet its near-term obligations?	Current liabilities and cash provided by operating activities	$\text{Current cash debt coverage ratio} = \dfrac{\text{Cash provided by operations}}{\text{Average current liabilities}}$	A higher ratio indicates liquidity, that the company is generating cash sufficient to meet its near-term needs.
Can the company meet its long-term obligations?	Total liabilities and cash provided by operating activities	$\text{Cash debt coverage ratio} = \dfrac{\text{Cash provided by operations}}{\text{Average total liabilities}}$	A higher ratio indicates solvency, that the company is generating cash sufficient to meet its long-term needs.

Glossary

Cash debt coverage ratio A measure of solvency that is calculated as cash provided by operating activities divided by average total liabilities. (p. 73)

Classified balance sheet A balance sheet that contains a number of standard classifications or sections. (p. 57)

Comparability Ability to compare the accounting information of different companies because they use the same accounting principles. (p. 55)

Conservatism The approach of choosing an accounting method, when in doubt, that will least likely overstate assets and net income. (p. 56)

Consistency Use of the same accounting principles and methods from year to year within a company. (p. 55)

Current assets Cash and other resources that are reasonably expected to be converted to cash or used up by the business within one year or the operating cycle, whichever is longer. (p. 59)

Current cash debt coverage ratio A measure of liquidity that is calculated as cash provided by operating activities divided by average current liabilities. (p. 73)

Current liabilities Obligations reasonably expected to be paid within the next year or operating cycle, whichever is longer. (p. 61)

Current ratio A measure used to evaluate a company's liquidity and short-term debt-paying ability, computed by dividing current assets by current liabilities. (p. 69)

Debt to total assets ratio Measures the percentage of total financing provided by creditors; computed by dividing total debt by total assets. (p. 70)

Earnings per share (EPS) A measure of the net income earned on each share of common stock; computed by dividing net income minus preferred stock dividends by the average number of common shares outstanding during the year. (p. 65)

Financial Accounting Standards Board (FASB) A private organization that establishes generally accepted accounting principles. (p. 54)

Generally accepted accounting principles (GAAP) A set of rules and practices, having substantial authoritative support, that are recognized as a general guide for financial reporting purposes. (p. 53)

Intangible assets Assets that do not have physical substance. (p. 60)

Liquidity The ability of a company to pay obligations that are expected to become due within the next year or operating cycle. (p. 69)

Liquidity ratios Measures of the short-term ability of the company to pay its maturing obligations and to meet unexpected needs for cash. (p. 69)

Long-term investments Generally, investments in stocks and bonds of other companies that are normally held for many years. Also includes long-term assets, such as land and buildings, not currently being used in the company's operations. (p. 59)

Long-term liabilities (Long-term debt) Obligations not expected to be paid within one year or the operating cycle. (p. 61)

Materiality The constraint of determining whether an item is large enough to likely influence the decision of an investor or creditor. (p. 56)

Operating cycle The average time required to go from cash to cash in producing revenues. (p. 59)

Price-earnings (P-E) ratio A measure of the ratio of the market price of each share of common stock to the earnings per share; it reflects the stock market's belief about a company's future earnings potential. (p. 65)

Profitability ratios Measures of the income or operating success of a company for a given period of time. (p. 64)

Property, plant, and equipment Assets of a relatively permanent nature that are being used in the business and are not intended for resale. (p. 60)

Ratio An expression of the mathematical relationship between one quantity and another; may be expressed as a percentage, a rate, or a proportion. (p. 63)

Ratio analysis A technique for evaluating financial statements that expresses the relationship among selected financial statement data. (p. 63)

Relevance The quality of information that indicates the information makes a difference in a decision. (p. 54)

Reliability The quality of information that gives assurance that it is free of error and bias. (p. 54)

Securities and Exchange Commission (SEC) The agency of the U.S. government that oversees U.S. financial markets and accounting standards-setting bodies. (p. 54)

Solvency The ability of a company to pay interest as it comes due and to repay the face value of debt at maturity. (p. 70)

Solvency ratios Measures of the ability of the company to survive over a long period of time. (p. 70)

Statement of stockholders' equity A financial statement that presents the factors that caused stockholders' equity to change during the period, including those that caused retained earnings to change. (p. 67)

Working capital The difference between the amounts of current assets and current liabilities. (p. 69)

Demonstration Problem

Listed here are items taken from the income statement and balance sheet of **Circuit City Stores, Inc.** for the year ended February 28, 2001. Certain items have been combined for simplification. Amounts are given in thousands.

Long-term debt, excluding current installments	$ 116,137
Cash and cash equivalents	446,131
Selling, general, and administrative expenses	2,516,582
Common stock	759,168
Accounts payable	902,560
Prepaid expenses and other current assets	57,623
Property and equipment, net	988,947
Cost of goods sold	10,163,706
Current portion of long-term debt	132,388
Income taxes payable	92,479
Interest expense	19,383
Deferred revenue and other long-term liabilities	107,114
Retained earnings	1,597,315
Merchandise inventory	1,757,664
Net sales and operating revenues	12,959,028
Accounts and notes receivable, net	585,761
Income tax expense	98,555
Other assets	35,207
Accrued expenses and other current liabilities	162,972
Notes payable	1,200

Instructions

Prepare an income statement and a classified balance sheet using the items listed. No item should be used more than once.

Action Plan

• In preparing the income statement, list revenues, then expenses.

• In preparing a classified balance sheet, list items in order of magnitude.

Solution to Demonstration Problem

CIRCUIT CITY STORES, INC.
Income Statement
For the Year Ended February 28, 2001
(in thousands)

Net sales and operating revenues		$12,959,028
Cost of goods sold	$10,163,706	
Selling, general, and administrative expenses	2,516,582	
Interest expense	19,383	
Income tax expense	98,555	
Total expenses		12,798,226
Net income		$ 160,802

CIRCUIT CITY STORES, INC.
Balance Sheet
February 28, 2001
(in thousands)

Assets

Current assets		
Cash and cash equivalents	$ 446,131	
Accounts and notes receivable, net	585,761	
Merchandise inventory	1,757,664	
Prepaid expenses and other current assets	57,623	
Total current assets		$2,847,179
Property and equipment, net		988,947
Other assets		35,207
Total assets		$3,871,333

Liabilities and Stockholders' Equity

Current liabilities		
Notes payable	$ 1,200	
Current portion of long-term debt	132,388	
Accounts payable	902,560	
Accrued expenses and other current liabilities	162,972	
Income taxes payable	92,479	
Total current liabilities		$1,291,599
Long-term liabilities		
Long-term debt, excluding current installments	116,137	
Deferred revenue and other long-term liabilities	107,114	223,251
Total liabilities		1,514,850
Stockholders' equity		
Common stock	759,168	
Retained earnings	1,597,315	
Total stockholders' equity		2,356,483
Total liabilities and stockholders' equity		$3,871,333

☑ THE NAVIGATOR

Self-Study Questions

Answers are at the end of the chapter.

(SO 1)   **1.** Generally accepted accounting principles are:
   (a) a set of standards and rules that are recognized as a general guide for financial reporting.
   (b) usually established by the Internal Revenue Service.
   (c) the guidelines used to resolve ethical dilemmas.
   (d) fundamental truths that can be derived from the laws of nature.

(SO 1)   **2.** What organization issues U.S. accounting standards?
   (a) Financial Accounting Standards Board.
   (b) International Accounting Standards Committee.
   (c) International Auditing Standards Committee.
   (d) None of the above.

(SO 2)   **3.** What is the primary criterion by which accounting information can be judged?
   (a) Consistency.
   (b) Predictive value.
   (c) Usefulness for decision making.
   (d) Comparability.

(SO 2)   **4.** Verifiability is an ingredient of:

	Reliability	Relevance
(a)	Yes	Yes
(b)	No	No
(c)	Yes	No
(d)	No	Yes

(SO 3)   **5.** What accounting constraint refers to the tendency of accountants to resolve uncertainty in a way least likely to overstate assets and revenues?
   (a) Comparability.   (c) Conservatism.
   (b) Materiality.   (d) Consistency.

(SO 4)   **6.** In a classified balance sheet, assets are usually classified as:
   (a) current assets; long-term assets; property, plant, and equipment; and intangible assets.
   (b) current assets; long-term investments; property, plant, and equipment; and common stock.
   (c) current assets; long-term investments; tangible assets; and intangible assets.
   (d) current assets; long-term investments; property, plant, and equipment; and intangible assets.

(SO 4)   **7.** Current assets are listed:
   (a) by liquidity.
   (b) by importance.
   (c) by longevity.
   (d) alphabetically.

(SO 5)   **8.** Which is *not* an indicator of profitability?
   (a) Current ratio.
   (b) Earnings per share.
   (c) Net income.
   (d) Price-earnings ratio.

(SO 5)   **9.** For 2005 Stoneland Corporation reported net income $24,000; net sales $400,000; and average shares outstanding 6,000. There were no preferred stock dividends. What was the 2005 earnings per share?
   (a) $4.00   (c) $16.67
   (b) $0.06   (d) $66.67

(SO 6)   **10.** The balance in retained earnings is not affected by:
   (a) net income.
   (b) net loss.
   (c) issuance of common stock.
   (d) dividends.

(SO 7)   **11.** Which of these measures is an evaluation of a company's ability to pay current liabilities?
   (a) Price-earnings ratio.
   (b) Current ratio.
   (c) Both (a) and (b).
   (d) None of the above.

THE NAVIGATOR

Questions

1. (a) What are generally accepted accounting principles (GAAP)?
   (b) What body provides authoritative support for GAAP?

2. (a) What is the basic objective of financial reporting?
   (b) Identify the qualitative characteristics of accounting information.

3. Sue Leonard, the president of Leon Company, is pleased. Leon substantially increased its net income in 2005 while keeping its unit inventory relatively the same. Dan Noonan, chief accountant, cautions Sue, however. Noonan says that since Leon changed its method of inventory valuation, there is a consistency problem and it is difficult to determine whether Leon is better off. Is Noonan correct? Why or why not?

4. What is the distinction between comparability and consistency?

5. Describe the two constraints inherent in the presentation of accounting information.

6. Your roommate believes that international accounting standards are uniform throughout the world. Is your roommate correct? Explain.

7. What is meant by the term *operating cycle?*

8. Define current assets. What basis is used for ordering individual items within the current assets section?

9. Distinguish between long-term investments and property, plant, and equipment.

10. How do current liabilities differ from long-term liabilities?

11. Identify the two parts of stockholders' equity in a corporation and indicate the purpose of each.

12.
    (a) Ruth Weber believes that the analysis of financial statements is directed at two characteristics of a company: liquidity and profitability. Is Ruth correct? Explain.
    (b) Are short-term creditors, long-term creditors, and stockholders primarily interested in the same characteristics of a company? Explain.

13. Name ratios useful in assessing (a) liquidity, (b) solvency, and (c) profitability.

14. David Rose is puzzled. His company had a price-earnings ratio of 25 in 2005. He feels that this is an indication that the company is doing well. Julie Bast, his accountant, says that more information is needed to determine the firm's financial well-being. Who is correct? Why?

15. What do these classes of ratios measure?
    (a) Liquidity ratios.
    (b) Profitability ratios.
    (c) Solvency ratios.

16. Holding all other factors constant, indicate whether each of the following signals generally good or bad news about a company.
    (a) Increase in earnings per share.
    (b) Increase in the current ratio.
    (c) Increase in the debt to total assets ratio.
    (d) Decrease in the cash debt coverage ratio.

17. Which ratio or ratios from this chapter do you think should be of greatest interest to:
    (a) a pension fund considering investing in a corporation's 20-year bonds?
    (b) a bank contemplating a short-term loan?
    (c) an investor in common stock?

Brief Exercises

Recognize generally accepted accounting principles.
(SO 1)

BE2-1 Indicate whether each statement is *true* or *false*.
(a) GAAP is a set of rules and practices established by accounting standard-setting bodies to serve as a general guide for financial reporting purposes.
(b) Substantial authoritative support for GAAP usually comes from two standards-setting bodies: the FASB and the IRS.

Identify qualitative characteristics.
(SO 2)

BE2-2 The accompanying chart shows the qualitative characteristics of accounting information. Fill in the blanks.

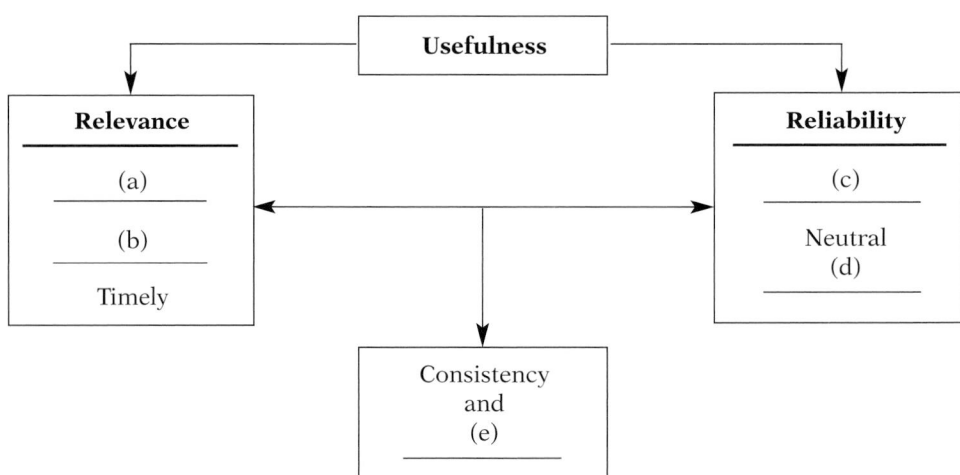

BE2-3 Given the *qualitative characteristics* of accounting established by the FASB's conceptual framework, complete each of the following statements.

(a) For information to be _____, it should have predictive or feedback value, and it must be presented on a timely basis.

(b) _____ is the quality of information that gives assurance that it is free of error and bias; it can be depended on.

(c) _____ means using the same accounting principles and methods from year to year within a company.

BE2-4 Here are some qualitative characteristics of accounting information:

1. Predictive value   3. Verifiable
2. Neutral   4. Timely

Match each qualitative characteristic to one of the following statements.

_____ (a) Accounting information should help users make predictions about the outcome of past, present, and future events.

_____ (b) Accounting information cannot be selected, prepared, or presented to favor one set of interested users over another.

_____ (c) Accounting information must be proved to be free of error.

_____ (d) Accounting information must be available to decision makers before it loses its capacity to influence their decisions.

BE2-5 Gidget Company uses these accounting practices:

(a) Inventory is reported at cost when market value is lower.
(b) Small tools are recorded as plant assets and depreciated.
(c) The income statement shows paper clips expense of $10.

Indicate the accounting constraint, if any, that has been violated by each practice.

BE2-6 A list of financial statement items for Bergmann Company includes the following: accounts receivable $14,000; prepaid insurance $3,600; cash $18,400; supplies $3,800, and short-term investments $8,200. Prepare the current assets section of the balance sheet listing the items in the proper sequence.

BE2-7 The following information (in millions of dollars) is available for **The Limited** for 2001: Sales revenue $9,363; net income $519; stock price $18.45 per share; preferred stock dividend $0; average shares outstanding 427.5 million. Compute the earnings per share and price-earnings ratio for The Limited for 2001.

BE2-8 For each of the following events affecting the stockholders' equity of BetterBooks, indicate whether the event would: increase retained earnings (IRE), decrease retained earnings (DRE), increase common stock (ICS), or decrease common stock (DCS).

_____ (a) Issued new shares of common stock.
_____ (b) Paid a cash dividend.
_____ (c) Reported net income of $75,000.
_____ (d) Reported a net loss of $20,000.

BE2-9 These selected condensed data are taken from a recent balance sheet of **Bob Evans Farms** (in millions of dollars).

Cash	$ 1.8
Accounts receivable	13.6
Inventories	17.0
Other current assets	11.3
Total current assets	$ 43.7
Total current liabilities	$158.1

Additional information: Current liabilities at the beginning of the year were $175.7 million, and cash provided by operations for the current year was $111.4 million.

What are (a) the working capital, (b) the current ratio, and (c) the current cash debt coverage ratio?

Exercises

Classify items as current or noncurrent, and prepare assets section of balance sheet.
(SO 4)

E2-1   The following items were taken from the December 31, 2001, assets section of the **Boeing Company** balance sheet. (All dollars are in millions.)

Inventories	$ 6,920	Other current assets	$ 2,444
Notes receivable—due after		Property, plant, and	
December 31, 2002	9,345	equipment	20,828
Notes receivable—due before		Cash and cash equivalents	633
December 31, 2002	1,053	Accounts receivable	5,156
Accumulated depreciation	12,369	Other noncurrent assets	7,890
Intangible assets	6,443		

Instructions
Prepare the assets section of a classified balance sheet, listing the current assets in order of their liquidity.

Prepare assets section of a classified balance sheet.
(SO 4)

E2-2   The following information (in thousands of dollars) is available for **H.J. Heinz Company**—famous for ketchup and other fine food products—for the year ended May 2, 2001.

Prepaid expenses	$ 157,801	Short-term investments	$ 5,371
Land	54,774	Buildings and equipment	3,826,006
Other current assets	23,282	Cash and cash equivalents	138,849
Intangible assets	2,765,892	Receivables	1,383,550
Other noncurrent assets	984,064	Accumulated depreciation	1,712,400

Instructions
Prepare the assets section of a classified balance sheet, listing the items in proper sequence and including a statement heading.

Prepare a classified balance sheet.
(SO 4)

E2-3   These items are taken from the financial statements of Megan Co. at December 31, 2005.

Building	$105,800
Accounts receivable	12,600
Prepaid insurance	4,680
Cash	20,840
Equipment	82,400
Land	61,200
Insurance expense	780
Depreciation expense	6,300
Interest expense	2,600
Common stock	66,000
Retained earnings (January 1, 2005)	40,000
Accumulated depreciation—building	45,600
Accounts payable	11,500
Mortgage payable	93,600
Accumulated depreciation—equipment	18,720
Interest payable	3,600
Bowling revenues	18,180

Instructions
Prepare a classified balance sheet; assume that $13,600 of the mortgage payable will be paid in 2006.

E2-4 The following items were taken from the 2001 financial statements of **Texas Instruments, Inc.** (All dollars are in millions.)

Prepare a classified balance sheet.
(SO 4)

Long-term debt	$1,211	Cash	$ 431
Common stock	2,904	Accumulated depreciation	4,094
Prepaid expenses	328	Accounts payable	1,205
Property, plant, and equipment	9,683	Other noncurrent assets	1,794
Other current assets	554	Other noncurrent liabilities	1,109
Other current liabilities	337	Retained earnings	8,975
Long-term investments	2,621	Accounts receivable	1,198
Short-term investments	2,513	Inventories	751
Loans payable in 2002	38		

Instructions
Prepare a classified balance sheet in good form as of December 31, 2001.

E2-5 These financial statement items are for Conner Corporation at year-end, July 31, 2005.

Prepare financial statements.
(SO 4, 6)

Salaries payable	$ 1,960
Salaries expense	54,700
Utilities expense	22,600
Equipment	15,900
Accounts payable	4,220
Commission revenue	61,100
Rent revenue	8,500
Long-term note payable	1,800
Common stock	16,000
Cash	24,200
Accounts receivable	8,780
Accumulated depreciation	5,400
Dividends	4,000
Depreciation expense	4,000
Retained earnings (beginning of the year)	35,200

Instructions
(a) Prepare an income statement and a retained earnings statement for the year. Conner Corporation did not issue any new stock during the year.
(b) Prepare a classified balance sheet at July 31.

E2-6 The following information is available for **Callaway Golf Company** for the years 2001 and 2000 (dollars in thousands, except share information).

Compute profitability ratios.
(SO 5)

	2001	2000
Net sales	$816,163	$837,627
Net income	58,375	80,999
Total assets	647,602	630,934
Share information		
Shares outstanding at year-end	66,990,484	68,843,722
Year-end stock price per share	$19.15	$18.63
Preferred dividends	–0–	–0–

There were 71,002,196 shares outstanding at the end of 1999.

Instructions
(a) What was the company's earnings per share for each year?
(b) What was the company's price-earnings ratio for each year?
(c) Based on your findings above, how did the company's profitability change from 2000 to 2001?

Compute liquidity ratios and compare results.
(SO 7)

E2-7   **Nordstrom, Inc.** operates department stores in numerous states. Selected financial statement data (in millions of dollars) for the year ended January 31, 2002, are as follows.

	End of Year	Beginning of Year
Cash and cash equivalents	$ 331	$ 25
Receivables (net)	698	722
Merchandise inventory	888	946
Other current assets	137	120
Total current assets	$2,054	$1,813
Total current liabilities	$ 948	$ 951

For the year, net sales were $5,634,000 and cost of goods sold was $3,766,000.

Instructions
  (a) Compute the working capital and current ratio at the beginning of the year and at the end of the current year.
  (b) Did Nordstrom's liquidity improve or worsen during the year?
  (c) Using the data in the chapter, compare Nordstrom's liquidity with **Best Buy's**.

Compute and interpret solvency ratios.
(SO 7, 8)

E2-8   The following data were taken from the 2002 and 2001 financial statements of **Lands' End, Inc.** (All dollars in thousands.)

	2002	2001
Current assets	$402,584	$319,073
Total assets	599,120	507,629
Current liabilities	185,564	178,874
Total liabilities	198,402	193,441
Total stockholders' equity	400,718	314,188
Cash provided by operating activities	73,505	60,564
Cash used in investing activities	40,514	44,553

Instructions
Perform each of the following.
  (a) Calculate the debt to total assets ratio for each year.
  (b) Calculate the cash debt coverage ratio for each year. (Total liabilities at year-end 2000 were $160,000,000.)
  (c) Discuss Lands' End, Inc.'s solvency in 2002 versus 2001.
  (d) Discuss Lands' End, Inc.'s ability to finance its investment activities with cash provided by operating activities, and how any deficiency would be met.

Problems: Set A

Comment on the objectives and qualitative characteristics of accounting information.
(SO 1, 2)

P2-1A   **Net Nanny Software International Inc.**, headquartered in Vancouver, specializes in Internet safety and computer security products for both the home and enterprise markets. Its balance sheet, as at June 30, 1999, reported a deficit (negative retained earnings) of US $5,678,288. It has reported only net losses since inception, June 30, 1996. In spite of these losses, Net Nanny's common shares have traded anywhere from a high of $3.70 to a low of $0.32 on the Canadian Venture Exchange.

Net Nanny's financial statements of the company have historically been prepared in Canadian dollars. As of June 30, 1998, the company adopted the U.S. dollar as its reporting currency.

Instructions
  (a) What is the objective of financial reporting? How does this objective meet or not meet Net Nanny's investor's needs?
  (b) Why would investors want to buy Net Nanny's shares if the company has consistently reported losses over the last few years? Include in your answer an assessment of the relevance of the information reported on Net Nanny's financial statements.

expected earning developing

(c) Comment on how the change in reporting information from Canadian dollars to U.S. dollars likely affected the readers of Net Nanny's financial statements. Include in your answer an assessment of the comparability of the information.   *US rules?*

P2-2A The following items are taken from the 2001 balance sheet of **Kellogg Company** (in millions).

Prepare a classified balance sheet.
(SO 4)

Common stock	$ 195.3
Other assets	5,513.8
Notes payable—current	513.3
Other current assets	333.4
Current maturities of long-term debt	82.3
Cash and cash equivalents	231.8
Other long-term liabilities	1,670.5
Retained earnings	676.2
Accounts payable	577.5
Other current liabilities	1,034.5
Accounts receivable	762.3
Property, net	2,952.8
Inventories	574.5
Long-term debt	5,619.0

Instructions
Prepare a classified balance sheet for Kellogg Company as of December 31, 2001.

Tot. current assets $ 1,902
Tot. assets $10,368.6

P2-3A These items are taken from the financial statements of Motzek, Inc.

Prepare financial statements.
(SO 4, 6)

Prepaid insurance	$ 1,800
Equipment	31,000
Salaries expense	36,000
Utilities expense	2,100
Accumulated depreciation	8,600
Accounts payable	10,200
Cash	4,300
Accounts receivable	7,500
Salaries payable	3,000
Common stock	5,900
Depreciation expense	5,700
Retained earnings (beginning)	14,000
Dividends	7,600
Service revenue	58,000
Repair expense	2,500
Insurance expense	1,200

Instructions
Prepare an income statement, a retained earnings statement, and a classified balance sheet as of December 31, 2005.

Net income $10,500
Tot. assets $36,000

P2-4A You are provided with the following information for Cheung Corporation, effective as of its April 30, 2005, year-end.

Prepare financial statements.
(SO 4, 6)

Accounts payable	$ 5,972
Accounts receivable	7,840
Accumulated depreciation	4,921
Depreciation expense	671
Cash	18,052
Common stock	20,000
Dividends	3,650
Equipment	$23,050
Sales revenue	12,590

Income tax expense	1,135
Income taxes payable	1,135
Interest expense	57
Interest payable	57
Long-term notes payable	5,700
Prepaid rent	2,280
Rent expense	760
Retained earnings, beginning	13,960
Salaries expense	6,840

Net income	$ 3,127
Tot. current assets	$28,172
Tot. assets	$46,301

Instructions

(a) Prepare an income statement and a retained earnings statement for Cheung Corporation for the year ended April 30, 2005.
(b) Prepare a classified balance sheet for Cheung as of April 30, 2005.
(c) Explain how each financial statement interrelates with the others.

Compute ratios; comment on relative profitability, liquidity, and solvency.
(SO 5, 7, 8)

P2-5A Comparative statement data for Campo Company and Gabelli Company, two competitors, are presented here. All balance sheet data are as of December 31, 2005, and December 31, 2004.

	Campo Company		Gabelli Company	
	2005	**2004**	**2005**	**2004**
Net sales	$450,000		$920,000	
Cost of goods sold	260,000		620,000	
Operating expenses	140,000		52,000	
Interest expense	3,000		10,000	
Income tax expense	11,000		65,000	
Current assets	180,000	$110,000	700,000	$550,000
Plant assets (net)	705,000	470,000	800,000	750,000
Current liabilities	60,000	52,000	250,000	275,000
Long-term liabilities	215,000	68,000	200,000	160,000

Additional information: Cash provided by operations for 2005 was $20,000 for Campo and $185,000 for Gabelli. The average number of shares outstanding was 200,000 for Campo and 400,000 for Gabelli. The stock price at December 31, 2005, was $2.50 for Campo and $7 for Gabelli.

Instructions

(a) Comment on the relative profitability of the companies by computing the net income, earnings per share, and price-earnings ratios for both companies for 2005.
(b) Comment on the relative liquidity of the companies by computing working capital, the current ratios, and the current cash debt coverage ratios for both companies for 2005.
(c) Comment on the relative solvency of the companies by computing the debt to total assets ratio and the cash debt coverage ratio for each company for 2005.

Compute liquidity, solvency, and profitability ratios.
(SO 5, 7, 8)

P2-6A The comparative statements of Brandon Company are presented here.

BRANDON COMPANY
Income Statements
For the Years Ended December 31

	2005	**2004**
Net sales	$712,000	$574,000
Cost of goods sold	420,000	335,600
Selling and administrative expense	143,880	149,760
Interest expense	7,920	7,200
Income tax expense	32,000	24,000
Net income	$108,200	$ 57,440

BRANDON COMPANY
Balance Sheets
December 31

Assets	2005	2004
Current assets		
Cash	$ 23,100	$ 21,600
Short-term investments	34,800	33,000
Accounts receivable (net)	106,200	93,800
Inventory	155,000	64,000
Total current assets	319,100	212,400
Plant assets (net)	465,300	459,600
Total assets	$784,400	$672,000

Liabilities and Stockholders' Equity	2005	2004
Current liabilities		
Accounts payable	$134,200	$132,000
Income taxes payable	24,000	24,000
Total current liabilities	158,200	156,000
Bonds payable	132,000	120,000
Total liabilities	290,200	276,000
Stockholders' equity		
Common stock	140,000	150,000
Retained earnings	354,200	246,000
Total stockholders' equity	494,200	396,000
Total liabilities and stockholders' equity	$784,400	$672,000

Additional information: Cash provided by operating activities was $82,300 for 2005. The average number of shares outstanding was 70,000 for 2005. The stock price at December 31, 2005, was $34.

Instructions
Compute these values and ratios for 2005.
- **(a)** Current ratio.
- **(b)** Working capital.
- **(c)** Current cash debt coverage ratio.
- **(d)** Debt to total assets ratio.
- **(e)** Cash debt coverage ratio.
- **(f)** Earnings per share.
- **(g)** Price-earnings ratio.

CASH provided by op=?
what is Avrg?

P2-7A Condensed balance sheet and income statement data for Von Mises Corporation are presented below.

Compute and interpret liquidity, solvency, and profitability ratios.
(SO 5, 7)

VON MISES CORPORATION
Balance Sheets
December 31

Assets	2005	2004	2003
Cash	$ 50,000	$ 24,000	$ 20,000
Receivables (net)	90,000	65,000	32,000
Other current assets	80,000	75,000	62,000
Long-term investments	90,000	70,000	50,000
Plant and equipment (net)	534,000	415,000	310,000
Total assets	$844,000	$649,000	$474,000

Liabilities and Stockholders' Equity	2005	2004	2003
Current liabilities	$ 98,000	$ 75,000	$ 70,000
Long-term debt	97,000	70,000	65,000
Common stock	400,000	340,000	300,000
Retained earnings	249,000	164,000	39,000
Total liabilities and stockholders' equity	$844,000	$649,000	$474,000

VON MISES CORPORATION
Income Statements
For the Years Ended December 31

	2005	2004
Sales	$705,000	$800,000
Cost of goods sold	420,000	400,000
Operating expenses (including income taxes)	200,000	237,000
Net income	$ 85,000	$163,000

Additional information: The average number of shares outstanding was 370,000 in 2005 and 320,000 in 2004. The stock price at December 31, 2005, was $4 and at December 31, 2004, was $10.

Instructions
Compute these values and ratios for 2004 and 2005.
  (a) Earnings per share.
  (b) Price-earnings ratio.
  (c) Working capital.
  (d) Current ratio.
  (e) Debt to total assets ratio.
  (f) Based on the ratios calculated, discuss briefly the improvement or lack thereof in the financial position and operating results of Von Mises from 2004 to 2005.

P2-8A Selected financial data (in millions) of two competitors, **Bethlehem Steel** and **United States Steel**, in 2001 are presented here.

Compute ratios and compare liquidity, solvency, and profitability for two companies.
(SO 5, 7)

	Bethlehem Steel Corporation	United States Steel Corporation
	Income Statement Data for Year	
Net sales	$ 3,334	$6,375
Cost of goods sold	3,469	6,091
Selling and administrative expense	360	436
Interest expense	91	141
Other income (loss)	380	253
Income tax expense (refund)	984	(328)
Net income	$(1,950)	$ (218)

	Bethlehem Steel Corporation	United States Steel Corporation
	Balance Sheet Data (End of Year)	
Current assets	$ 1,203	$2,073
Property, plant, and equipment (net)	2,687	3,084
Other assets	354	3,180
Total assets	$ 4,244	$8,337
Current liabilities	$ 272	$1,259
Long-term debt	5,653	4,572
Total stockholders' equity	(1,681)	2,506
Total liabilities and stockholders' equity	$ 4,244	$8,337
Average shares outstanding	130.33	88.99
Year-end share price	$ 0.45	$18.11
Preferred stock dividends paid	$ 40.5	–0–

Instructions

For each company, compute these values and ratios.
  (a) Working capital.
  (b) Current ratio.
  (c) Debt to total assets ratio.
  (d) Earnings per share.
  (e) Price-earnings ratio.
  (f) Compare the liquidity, profitability, and solvency of the two companies.

Problems: Set B

P2-1B A friend of yours, Emily Collis, recently completed an undergraduate degree in science and has just started working with a biotechnology company. Emily tells you that the owners of the business are trying to secure new sources of financing which are needed in order for the company to proceed with development of a new health care product. Emily said that her boss told her that the company must put together a report to present to potential investors.

Comment on the objective and qualitative characteristics of financial reporting. (SO 1, 2)

Emily thought that the company should include in this package the detailed scientific findings related to the Phase I clinical trials for this product. She said, "I know that the biotech industry sometimes has only a 10% success rate with new products, but if we report all the scientific findings, everyone will see what a sure success this is going to be! The president was talking about the importance of following some set of accounting principles. Why do we need to look at some accounting rules? What they need to realize is that we have scientific results that are quite encouraging, some of the most talented employees around, and the start of some really great customer relationships. We haven't made any sales yet, but we will. We just need the funds to get through all the clinical testing and get government approval for our product. Then these investors will be quite happy that they bought in to our company early!"

Instructions

  (a) What is financial reporting? Explain to Emily what is meant by generally accepted accounting principles.
  (b) Comment on how Emily's suggestions for what should be reported to prospective investors conforms to the qualitative characteristics of accounting information. Do you think that the things that Emily wants to include in the information for investors will conform to financial reporting guidelines?

*Prepare a classified balance
sheet.*
(SO 4)

P2-2B The following items are taken from the 2001 balance sheet of **Yahoo!, Inc.** (in thousands).

Common stock	$2,008,003
Property and equipment, net	131,648
Accounts payable	13,218
Other assets	357,085
Long-term investments	839,080
Accounts receivable	68,648
Prepaid expenses and other current assets	56,458
Short-term investments	553,795
Retained earnings (deficit)	(40,986)
Cash and cash equivalents	372,632
Long-term liabilities	53,812
Accrued expenses and other current liabilities	235,897
Unearned revenue—current	109,402

Instructions

Tot. current assets $1,051,533
Tot. assets $2,379,346

Prepare a classified balance sheet for Yahoo! Inc. as of December 31, 2001. (Note: Because Yahoo!'s cumulative losses exceeded its cumulative earnings, its balance sheet reports a retained earnings deficit.)

Prepare financial statements.
(SO 4, 6)

P2-3B These items are taken from the financial statements of Karr Corporation for 2005.

Retained earnings (beginning of year)	$26,000
Utilities expense	2,000
Equipment	66,000
Accounts payable	13,300
Cash	13,600
Salaries payable	3,000
Common stock	13,000
Dividends	12,000
Service revenue	82,000
Prepaid insurance	3,500
Repair expense	1,800
Depreciation expense	2,600
Accounts receivable	14,200
Insurance expense	2,200
Salaries expense	37,000
Accumulated depreciation	17,600

Net income $36,400
Tot. assets $79,700

Instructions

Prepare an income statement, a retained earnings statement, and a classified balance sheet as of December 31, 2005.

Prepare financial statements.
(SO 4, 6)

P2-4B You are provided with the following information for Commerce Crusaders, effective as of its April 30, 2005, year-end.

Accounts payable	$ 834
Accounts receivable	810
Building, net of accumulated depreciation	1,537
Cash	570
Common stock	900
Cost of goods sold	990
Current portion of long-term debt	450
Depreciation expense	335
Dividends paid during the year	325
Equipment, net of accumulated depreciation	1,220
Income tax expense	135
Income taxes payable	135

Interest expense	400
Inventories	967
Land	1,400
Long-term debt	3,500
Prepaid expenses	12
Retained earnings, beginning	1,600
Revenues	3,400
Selling expenses	440
Short-term investments	1,200
Wages expense	700
Wages payable	222

Instructions

(a) Prepare an income statement and a retained earnings statement for Commerce Crusaders for the year ended April 30, 2005.

(b) Prepare a classified balance sheet for Commerce Crusaders as of April 30, 2005.

Net income $400
Tot. current assets $3,559
Tot. assets $7,716

P2-5B Comparative financial statement data for Bates Corporation and Wilson Corporation, two competitors, appear below. All balance sheet data are as of December 31, 2005, and December 31, 2004.

Compute ratios; comment on relative profitability, liquidity, and solvency.
(SO 5, 7, 8)

	Bates Corporation		Wilson Corporation	
	2005	**2004**	**2005**	**2004**
Net sales	$1,949,035		$542,814	
Cost of goods sold	1,280,490		338,006	
Operating expenses	302,275		79,000	
Interest expense	6,800		1,252	
Income tax expense	47,840		7,740	
Current assets	427,200	$412,410	190,336	$160,467
Plant assets (net)	532,000	500,000	139,728	125,812
Current liabilities	66,325	75,815	35,348	30,281
Long-term liabilities	108,500	90,000	29,620	25,000

Additional information: Cash provided by operations for 2005 was $162,594 for Bates and $24,211 for Wilson. The average number of shares outstanding was 100,000 for Bates and 50,000 for Wilson. The stock price at December 31, 2005, was $25 for Bates and $14 for Wilson.

Instructions

(a) Comment on the relative profitability of the companies by computing the net income, earnings per share, and the price-earnings ratios for both companies for 2005.

(b) Comment on the relative liquidity of the companies by computing working capital, the current ratios, and the current cash debt coverage ratios for both companies for 2005.

(c) Comment on the relative solvency of the companies by computing the debt to total assets ratio and the cash debt coverage ratio for each company for 2005.

P2-6B Here are the comparative statements of Roger Petersen Company.

Compute liquidity, solvency, and profitability ratios.
(SO 5, 7, 8)

ROGER PETERSEN COMPANY
Income Statements
For the Years Ended December 31

	2005	2004
Net sales	$2,218,500	$2,100,500
Cost of goods sold	1,012,400	996,000
Selling and administrative expense	906,000	879,000
Interest expense	98,000	79,000
Income tax expense	84,000	77,000
Net income	$ 118,100	$ 69,500

ROGER PETERSEN COMPANY
Balance Sheets
December 31

Assets	2005	2004
Current assets		
Cash	$ 60,100	$ 64,200
Short-term investments	54,000	50,000
Accounts receivable (net)	207,800	102,800
Inventory	125,000	115,500
Total current assets	446,900	332,500
Plant assets (net)	625,300	432,000
Total assets	$1,072,200	$764,500
Liabilities and Stockholders' Equity		
Current liabilities		
Accounts payable	$ 200,000	$ 65,400
Income taxes payable	43,500	42,000
Total current liabilities	243,500	107,400
Bonds payable	210,000	200,000
Total liabilities	453,500	307,400
Stockholders' equity		
Common stock	330,000	286,500
Retained earnings	288,700	170,600
Total stockholders' equity	618,700	457,100
Total liabilities and stockholders' equity	$1,072,200	$764,500

Additional information: The cash provided by operating activities for 2005 was $190,800. The average number of shares outstanding during the year was 50,000. The stock price at December 31, 2005, was $30.

Instructions
Compute these values and ratios for 2005.

    (a) Working capital.

    (b) Current ratio.

    (c) Current cash debt coverage ratio.

    (d) Debt to total assets ratio.

    (e) Cash debt coverage ratio.

    (f) Earnings per share.

    (g) Price-earnings ratio.

P2-7B   Condensed balance sheet and income statement data for Gilles Corporation are presented here.

Compute and interpret liquidity, solvency, and profitability ratios.
(SO 5, 7)

GILLES CORPORATION
Balance Sheets
December 31

Assets	2005	2004	2003
Cash	$ 25,000	$ 20,000	$ 18,000
Receivables (net)	70,000	65,000	48,000
Other current assets	90,000	70,000	64,000
Long-term investments	75,000	60,000	45,000
Plant and equipment (net)	500,000	470,000	358,000
Total assets	$760,000	$685,000	$533,000

Liabilities and Stockholders' Equity	2005	2004	2003
Current liabilities	$ 75,000	$ 80,000	$ 70,000
Long-term debt	80,000	85,000	50,000
Common stock	340,000	300,000	300,000
Retained earnings	265,000	220,000	113,000
Total liabilities and stockholders' equity	$760,000	$685,000	$533,000

GILLES CORPORATION
Income Statements
For the Years Ended December 31

	2005	2004
Sales	$750,000	$670,000
Cost of goods sold	420,000	400,000
Operating expenses (including income taxes)	240,000	230,000
Net income	$ 90,000	$ 40,000

Additional information: The average number of shares outstanding was 32,000 in 2005 and 30,000 in 2004. The stock price at December 31, 2005, was $60, and it was $40 at the end of 2004.

Instructions
Compute these values and ratios for 2004 and 2005.
  (a) Earnings per share.
  (b) Price-earnings ratio.
  (c) Working capital.
  (d) Current ratio.
  (e) Debt to total assets ratio.
  (f) Based on the ratios calculated, discuss briefly the improvement or lack thereof in financial position and operating results from 2004 to 2005 of Gilles Corporation.

P2-8B Selected financial data (in millions) of two competitors, **Target** and **Wal-Mart**, are presented here.

Compute ratios and compare liquidity, solvency, and profitability for two companies.
(SO 5, 7)

	Target (2/3/01)	Wal-Mart (1/31/01)
	Income Statement Data for Year	
Net sales	$36,903	$191,329
Cost of goods sold	25,295	150,255
Selling and administrative expenses	8,840	31,550
Interest expense	425	1,374
Other income (loss)	(290)	1,837
Income taxes	789	3,692
Net income	$ 1,264	$ 6,295

	Target	Wal-Mart
	Balance Sheet Data (End of Year)	
Current assets	$ 7,304	$ 26,555
Noncurrent assets	12,186	51,575
Total assets	$19,490	$ 78,130
Current liabilities	$ 6,301	$ 28,949
Long-term debt	6,670	17,838
Total stockholders' equity	6,519	31,343
Total liabilities and stockholders' equity	$19,490	$ 78,130
Average shares outstanding	904	4,465
Year-end share price	$ 36.97	$ 56.80
Preferred stock dividends paid	–0–	–0–

Instructions

For each company, compute these values and ratios.
- **(a)** Working capital.
- **(b)** Current ratio.
- **(c)** Debt to total assets ratio.
- **(d)** Earnings per share.
- **(e)** Price-earnings ratio.
- **(f)** Compare the liquidity, solvency, and profitability of the two companies.

▶ BROADENING YOUR PERSPECTIVE

Financial Reporting and Analysis

FINANCIAL REPORTING PROBLEM: *Tootsie Roll Industries, Inc.*

BYP2-1   The financial statements of **Tootsie Roll Industries, Inc.**, are presented in Appendix A at the end of this book.

Instructions

Answer the following questions using the Consolidated Balance Sheet and the Notes to Consolidated Financial Statements section.
- **(a)** What were Tootsie Roll's total current assets at December 31, 2002, and December 31, 2001?
- **(b)** Are the assets included in current assets listed in the proper order? Explain.
- **(c)** How are Tootsie Roll's assets classified?
- **(d)** What were Tootsie Roll's current liabilities at December 31, 2002, and December 31, 2001?

COMPARATIVE ANALYSIS PROBLEM: *Tootsie Roll vs. Hershey Foods*

BYP2-2   The financial statements of **Hershey Foods** are presented in Appendix B, following the financial statements for **Tootsie Roll** in Appendix A. Hershey's year-end stock price was $67.44, Tootsie Roll's was $30.68. Hershey's average number of shares outstanding was 136,538,000, and Tootsie Roll's was 51,553,000.

Instructions

- **(a)** For each company calculate the following values for 2002.

(1) Working capital.	**(4)** Earnings per share.
(2) Current ratio.	**(5)** Price-earnings ratio.
(3) Debt to total assets ratio	

(b) Based on your findings above, discuss the relative liquidity, solvency, and profitability of the two companies.

RESEARCH CASE

BYP2-3 Several commonly available indexes enable individuals to locate articles from numerous business publications and periodicals. Articles can generally be searched for by company name or by subject matter. Four common indexes are the *Wall Street Journal Index*, *Business Abstracts* (formerly *Business Periodicals Index*), *Predicasts F&S Index*, and *ABI/Inform*.

Instructions
Use one of these resources to find a list of articles about **Best Buy**, **Circuit City**, or **Tweeter Home Entertainment**. Choose an article from this list that you believe would be of interest to an investor or creditor of this company. Read the article and answer the following questions. (*Note*: Your library may have either hard-copy or CD-ROM versions of these indexes.)
 (a) What is the article about?
 (b) What company-specific information is included in the article?
 (c) Is the article related to anything you read in this chapter?
 (d) Identify any accounting-related issues discussed in the article.

INTERPRETING FINANCIAL STATEMENTS

BYP2-4 The following information was reported by **Gap, Inc.** in its 2001 annual report.

	2001	2000	1999	1998	1997	1996	1995
Total assets (millions)	$7,591	$7,013	$5,189	$3,964	$3,338	$2,627	$2,343
Working capital (millions)	$ 988	$ (151)	$ 445	$ 319	$ 839	$ 554	$ 728
Current ratio	1.48	0.95	1.25	1.21	1.85	1.72	2.32
Debt to total assets ratio	0.63	0.58	0.57	0.60	0.53	0.37	0.30
Earnings per share	$ (0.01)	$ 1.03	$ 1.32	$ 0.95	$ 0.60	$ 0.48	$ 0.38

 (a) Determine the overall percentage increase in Gap's total assets from 1995 to 2001. What was the average increase per year? *% increase   37.3% per yr.*
 (b) Comment on the change in Gap's liquidity. Does working capital or the current ratio appear to provide a better indication of Gap's liquidity? What might explain the change in Gap's liquidity during this period?
 (c) Comment on the change in Gap's solvency during this period.
 (d) Comment on the change in Gap's profitability during this period. How might this affect your prediction about Gap's future profitability?

A GLOBAL FOCUS

BYP2-5 **Lign Multiwood** is a forest products company in Sweden. Its statements are presented in conformity with the standards issued by the Swedish Standards Board. Its financial statements are presented to be harmonized (that is, to have minimal difference in methods) with member countries of the European Union. The balance sheet presented on page 98 was taken from its 2000 annual report.

Instructions
List all differences that you notice between Lign Multiwood's balance sheet presentation (format and terminology) and the presentation of U.S. companies shown in the chapter. For differences in terminology, list the corresponding terminology used by U.S. companies.

FINANCIAL ANALYSIS ON THE WEB

BYP2-6 *Purpose:* Identify summary liquidity, solvency, and profitability information about companies, and compare this information across companies in the same industry.

Address: http://biz.yahoo.com/i (or go to **www.wiley.com/college/kimmel**)

LIGN MULTIWOOD
Balance Sheets
at December 31
(Swedish kronor)

ASSETS	2000	1999
Fixed assets		
Intangible fixed assets		
Balanced expenses for development work	28 407 064	12 056 864
Licence rights	1 200 000	600 000
	29 607 064	12 656 864
Material fixed assets		
Machinery and other technical plant	33 608 189	34 606 812
Fittings & fixtures, tools and installations	564 952	163 020
	34 173 141	34 769 832
Financial fixed assets		
Other long-term securities holdings	165 000	165 000
Deferred tax claim	3 042 000	1 129 000
	3 207 000	1 294 000
Total fixed assets	66 987 205	48 720 696
Current assets		
Stocks held etc.		
Stocks of test materials	554 000	116 924
	554 000	116 924
Short-term receivables		
Customer receivables	727 159	652 662
Other receivables	1 099 197	711 979
Prepaid costs and accrued income	2 479 411	1 620 467
	4 305 767	2 985 108
Cash in hand and on deposit	17 965 269	40 755 806
Total current assets	22 825 036	43 857 838
TOTAL ASSETS	89 812 241	92 578 534
EQUITY CAPITAL AND LIABILITIES		
Equity capital		
Tied equity capital		
Share capital	2 825 740	2 825 740
Tied reserves	56 745 410	56 745 410
	59 571 150	59 571 150
Accumulated loss		
Balanced loss	−2 801 000	− 598 000
Year's profit/loss	−4 933 000	−2 203 000
	−7 734 000	−2 801 000
	51 837 150	56 770 150
Minority interest	40 000	40 000
Long-term liabilities		
Other liabilities	33 619 451	34 162 457
	33 619 451	34 162 457
Short-term liabilities		
Accounts payable	2 151 435	1 232 505
Other liabilities	959 044	64 099
Accrued costs and prepaid income	1 205 161	309 323
	4 315 640	1 605 927
TOTAL EQUITY CAPITAL AND LIABILITIES	89 812 241	92 578 534

Steps
   1. Type in a company name, or use the index to find a company name. Choose **Profile**. Choose **Ratio Comparison**. Perform instructions (a) and (b) below.
   2. Go back to **Profile**. Click on the company's particular industry behind the heading "Industry." Perform instructions (c) and (d).

Instructions
Answer the following questions.
   (a) What was the company's current ratio, debt to equity ratio (a variation of the debt to total assets ratio), and price-earnings ratio?
   (b) What is the company's industry?
   (c) What is the name of a competitor? What is the competitor's current ratio, debt to equity ratio, and price-earnings ratio?
   (d) Based on these measures: Which company is more liquid? Which company is more solvent?

BYP2-7   The opening story described the dramatic effect that investment bulletin boards are having on the investment world. This exercise will allow you to evaluate a bulletin board discussing a company of your choice.

Address: http://biz.yahoo.com/i (or go to **www.wiley.com/college/kimmel**)

Steps
   1. Type in a company name, or use the index to find a company name.
   2. Choose **Msgs** (for messages).
   3. Read the ten most recent messages.

Instructions
Answer the following questions.
   (a) State the nature of each of these messages (e.g., offering advice, criticizing company, predicting future results, ridiculing other people who have posted messages).
   (b) For those messages that expressed an opinion about the company, was evidence provided to support the opinion?
   (c) What effect do you think it would have on bulletin board discussions if the participants provided their actual names? Do you think this would be a good policy?

Critical Thinking

GROUP DECISION CASE

BYP2-8   As the accountant for R. Soukup Industries, Inc., you have been requested to develop some key ratios from the comparative financial statements. This information is to be used to convince creditors that R. Soukup Industries, Inc. is liquid, solvent, and profitable, and that it deserves their continued support. Lenders are particularly concerned about the company's ability to continue as a going concern.

These are the data requested and the computations developed from the financial statements:

	2005	**2004**
Current ratio	3.1	2.1
Working capital	Up 22%	Down 7%
Debt to total assets ratio	0.60	0.70
Net income	Up 32%	Down 8%
Earnings per share	$2.40	$1.15
Price-earnings ratio	26.2	19.5

Instructions
R. Soukup Industries, Inc. asks you to prepare brief comments stating how each of these items supports the argument that its financial health is improving. The company wishes to use these comments to support presentation of data to its creditors. With the class divided into groups, prepare the comments as requested, giving the implications and the limitations of each item separately, and then the collective inference that may be drawn from them about R. Soukup's financial well-being.

COMMUNICATION ACTIVITY

BYP2-9   S.B. Barrett is the chief executive officer of Tomorrow's Products. Barrett is an expert engineer but a novice in accounting.

Instructions
Write a letter to S.B. Barrett that explains (a) the three main types of ratios; (b) examples of each, how they are calculated, and what they measure; and (c) the bases for comparison in analyzing Tomorrow's Products' financial statements.

ETHICS CASE

BYP2-10   A May 20, 2002, *Business Week* story by Stanley Holmes and Mike France entitled "Boeing's Secret" discusses issues surrounding the timing of the disclosure of information at the giant airplane manufacturer. To summarize, on December 11, 1996, **Boeing** closed a giant deal to acquire another manufacturer, **McDonnell Douglas**. Boeing paid for the acquisition by issuing shares of its own stock to the stockholders of McDonnell Douglas. In order for the deal not to be revoked, the value of Boeing's stock could not decline below a certain level for a number of months after the deal.

The article suggests that during the first half of 1997 Boeing suffered significant cost overruns because of severe inefficiencies in its production methods. Had these problems been disclosed in the quarterly financial statements during the first and second quarter of 1997, the company's stock most likely would have plummeted, and the deal would have been revoked. Company managers spent considerable time debating when the bad news should be disclosed. One public relations manager suggested that the company's problems be revealed on the date of either Princess Diana's or Mother Teresa's funeral, in the hope that it would be lost among those big stories that day. Instead, the company waited until October 22 of that year to announce a $2.6 billion write-off due to cost overruns. Within one week the company's stock price had fallen 20%, but by this time the McDonnell Douglas deal could not be reversed.

Instructions
Answer the following questions. Although it is not required in order to answer the questions, you may want to read the *Business Week* article.

   (a) Who are the stakeholders in this situation?
   (b) What are the ethical issues?
   (c) What assumptions or principles of accounting are relevant to this case?
   (d) Do you think it is ethical to try to "time" the release of a story so as to diminish its effect?
   (e) What would you have done if you were the chief executive officer of Boeing?
   (f) Boeing's top management maintains that it did not have an obligation to reveal its problems during the first half of 1997, and that it wouldn't do anything differently today. What implications does this have for investors and analysts who follow Boeing's stock?

Answers to Self-Study Questions
1. a   2. a   3. c   4. c   5. c   6. d   7. a   8. a   9. a   10. c   11. b

Answer to Tootsie Roll Review It Question 3, p. 62
Tootsie Roll's largest current asset at December 31, 2002, was cash and cash equivalents, at $105,507,000.

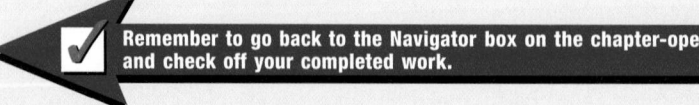

Remember to go back to the Navigator box on the chapter-opening page and check off your completed work.

The Accounting Information System

STUDY OBJECTIVES

After studying this chapter,
you should be able to:

1 Analyze the effect of business transactions on the basic accounting equation.

2 Explain what an account is and how it helps in the recording process.

3 Define debits and credits and explain how they are used to record business transactions.

4 Identify the basic steps in the recording process.

5 Explain what a journal is and how it helps in the recording process.

6 Explain what a ledger is and how it helps in the recording process.

7 Explain what posting is and how it helps in the recording process.

8 Explain the purposes of a trial balance.

 ☑ THE NAVIGATOR

THE NAVIGATOR ✔

▶ Scan *Study Objectives* ☐

▶ Read *Feature Story* ☐

▶ Read *Preview* ☐

▶ Read text and answer *Before You Go On*
   p. 116 ☐   p. 119 ☐   p. 128 ☐
   p. 130 ☐

▶ Work Using the *Decision Toolkit* ☐

▶ Review Summary of *Study Objectives* ☐

▶ Work *Demonstration Problem* ☐

▶ Answer *Self-Study Questions* ☐

▶ Complete *Assignments* ☐

FEATURE STORY

Accidents Happen

How organized are you financially? Take a short quiz. Answer *yes* or *no* to each question:

• Does your wallet contain so many cash machine receipts that you've been declared a walking fire hazard?

• Is your wallet such a mess that it is often faster to fish for money in the crack of your car seat than to dig around in your wallet?

• Was Michael Jordan playing high school basketball the last time you balanced your checkbook?

• Have you ever been tempted to burn down your house so you don't have to try to find all of the receipts and records that you need to fill out your tax returns?

If you think it is hard to keep track of the many transactions that make up *your* life, imagine what it is like for a major corporation like **Fidelity Investments**. Fidelity is the largest mutual fund management firm in the world, serving over 15 million investors. If you had your life savings invested at Fidelity Investments, you might be just slightly displeased if, when you called to find out your balance, the representative said, "You know, I kind of remember someone with a name like yours sending us some money—now what did we do with that?"

To ensure the accuracy of your balance and the security of your funds, Fidelity Investments, like all other companies large and small, relies on a sophisticated accounting information system. That's

not to say that Fidelity or anybody else is error-free. In fact, if you've ever really messed up your checkbook register, you may take some comfort from one accountant's mistake at Fidelity Investments. The accountant failed to include a minus sign while doing a calculation, making what was actually a $1.3 billion loss look like a $1.3 billion gain—yes, *billion!* Fortunately, like most accounting errors, it was detected before any real harm was done.

No one expects that kind of mistake at a company like Fidelity, which has sophisticated computer systems and top investment managers. In explaining the mistake to shareholders, a spokesperson wrote, "Some people have asked how, in this age of technology, such a mistake could be made. While many of our processes are computerized, accounting systems are complex and dictate that some steps must be handled manually by our managers and accountants, and people can make mistakes."

☑ THE NAVIGATOR

On the World Wide Web
Fidelity Investments: www.fidelity.com

As indicated in the Feature Story, a reliable information system is a necessity for any company. The purpose of this chapter is to explain and illustrate the features of an accounting information system. The organization and content of the chapter are as follows.

THE ACCOUNTING INFORMATION SYSTEM

Accounting Transactions	The Account	Steps in the Recording Process	The Recording Process Illustrated	The Trial Balance
• Analyzing transactions • Summary of transactions	• Debits and credits • Debit and credit procedures • Stockholders' equity relationships • Expansion of the basic equation	• The journal • The ledger • Chart of accounts • Posting	• Summary illustration of journalizing and posting	• Limitations of a trial balance

☑ THE NAVIGATOR

The Accounting Information System

The system of collecting and processing transaction data and communicating financial information to decision makers is known as the **accounting information system**. Accounting information systems vary widely. Factors that shape these systems include: the nature of the company's business, the types of transactions, the size of the company, the volume of data, and the information demands of management and others.

Most businesses of any size today use computerized accounting systems—sometimes referred to as electronic data processing (EDP) systems. These systems handle all the steps involved in the recording process, from initial data entry to preparation of the financial statements. In order to remain competitive, companies continually improve their accounting systems to provide accurate and timely data for decision making. For example, in its 2002 Annual Report, **Tootsie Roll** states, "We also invested in additional processing and data storage hardware during the year. We view information technology as a key strategic tool, and are committed to deploying leading edge technology in this area."

In this chapter we focus on a manual accounting system because the accounting concepts and principles do not change whether a system is computerized or manual, and manual systems are easier to illustrate. However, many of the problems in this and subsequent chapters can also be done using the computerized general ledger package that supplements this text.

Accounting Transactions

To use an accounting information system, you need to know which economic events to recognize (record). Not all events are recorded and reported in the financial statements. For example, suppose **General Motors** hired a new employee or purchased a new computer. Are these events entered in its accounting records? The first event would not be recorded, but the second event would. We call economic events that require recording in the financial statements **accounting transactions**.

An accounting transaction occurs when assets, liabilities, or stockholders' equity items change as a result of some economic event. The purchase of a computer by **General Motors**, the payment of rent by **Microsoft**, and the sale of advertising space by Sierra Corporation are examples of events that change a company's assets, liabilities, or stockholders' equity. Illustration 3-1 summarizes the decision process used to decide whether or not to record economic events.

Illustration 3-1
Transaction identification process

| Events | Purchase computer | Discuss product design with potential customer | Pay rent |

| Criterion | Is the financial position (assets, liabilities, or owner's equity) of the company changed? |

| | **Yes** | **No** | **Yes** |

| Record/ Don't Record | Record | Don't record | Record |

STUDY OBJECTIVE
—1—
Analyze the effect of business transactions on the basic accounting equation.

ANALYZING TRANSACTIONS

In Chapter 1 you learned the basic accounting equation:

$$\text{Assets} = \text{Liabilities} + \text{Stockholders' Equity}$$

In this chapter you will learn how to analyze transactions in terms of their effect on assets, liabilities, and stockholders' equity. **Transaction analysis** is the process of identifying the specific effects of economic events on the accounting equation.

The accounting equation must always balance. Each transaction has a dual (double-sided) effect on the equation. For example, if an individual asset is increased, there must be a corresponding:

Decrease in another asset, *or*

Increase in a specific liability, *or*

Increase in stockholders' equity.

It is quite possible that two or more items could be affected when an asset is increased. For example, if a company purchases a computer for $10,000 by paying $6,000 in cash and signing a note for $4,000, one asset (computer) increases $10,000, another asset (cash) decreases $6,000, and a liability (notes payable) increases $4,000. The result is that the accounting equation remains in balance—assets increased by a net $4,000 and liabilities increased by $4,000, as shown below.

Assets	=	Liabilities	+	Stockholders' Equity
+$10,000		+$4,000		
− 6,000				
$ 4,000	=	$4,000		

Chapter 1 presented the financial statements for Sierra Corporation for its first month. To illustrate how economic events affect the accounting equation, we will examine events affecting Sierra Corporation during its first month. If you are tempted to skip ahead after you've read a few of these, don't do it. Each has something unique to teach, something you'll need later. (We assure you that we've kept them to the minimum needed!)

EVENT (1). INVESTMENT OF CASH BY STOCKHOLDERS. On October 1 cash of $10,000 is invested in the business in exchange for $10,000 of common stock. This event is an accounting transaction because it results in an increase in both assets and stockholders' equity. There is an increase of $10,000 in the asset Cash and an increase of $10,000 in Common Stock on the books of Sierra Corporation. The effect of this transaction on the basic equation is:

	Assets	=	Liabilities	+	Stockholders' Equity
	Cash	=			Common Stock
(1)	+$10,000	=			+$10,000 Issued stock

The equation is in balance. **The source of each change to stockholders' equity is noted to the right of the transaction.** In this case it was an issuance of common stock. Keeping track of the source of each change in stockholders' equity is essential for later accounting activities—in particular, for the calculation of income.

EVENT (2). NOTE ISSUED IN EXCHANGE FOR CASH. On October 1 Sierra issued a 3-month, 12%, $5,000 note payable to Castle Bank. This transaction results in an equal increase in assets and liabilities: Cash (an asset) increases $5,000, and Notes Payable (a liability) increases $5,000. The specific effect of this transaction and the cumulative effect of the first two transactions are:

		Assets	**=**	**Liabilities**	**+**	**Stockholders' Equity**
		Cash	=	Notes Payable	+	Common Stock
	Old Balance	$10,000				$10,000
(2)		+5,000		+$5,000		
	New Balance	$15,000	=	$ 5,000	+	$10,000

$15,000

Total assets are now $15,000, and stockholders' equity plus the new liability also total $15,000.

EVENT (3). PURCHASE OF OFFICE EQUIPMENT FOR CASH.

On October 2 Sierra acquired office equipment by paying $5,000 cash to Superior Equipment Sales Co. This event is a transaction because an equal increase and decrease in Sierra's assets occur: Office Equipment (an asset) increases $5,000, and Cash (an asset) decreases $5,000.

		Assets			**=**	**Liabilities**	**+**	**Stockholders' Equity**
		Cash	+	Office Equipment	=	Notes Payable	+	Common Stock
	Old Balance	$15,000				$5,000		$10,000
(3)		−5,000		+$5,000				
	New Balance	$10,000	+	$ 5,000	=	$5,000	+	$10,000

$15,000 $15,000

The total assets are now $15,000, and stockholders' equity plus the liability also total $15,000.

EVENT (4). RECEIPT OF CASH IN ADVANCE FROM CUSTOMER.

On October 2 Sierra received a $1,200 cash advance from R. Knox, a client. This event is a transaction because cash (an asset) was received for advertising services that are expected to be completed by Sierra by December 31.

However, **revenue should not be recorded until the work has been performed**. In the magazine and airline industries, customers are expected to prepay. These companies have a liability to the customer until the magazines are delivered or the flight is provided. As soon as the product or service is provided, revenue can be recorded.

Since Sierra received cash prior to performance of the service, Sierra has a liability for the work due. Cash increases by $1,200, and a liability, Unearned Service Revenue (abbreviated as Unearned Revenue), increases by an equal amount.

		Assets			**=**	**Liabilities**			**+**	**Stockholders' Equity**
		Cash	+	Office Equipment	=	Notes Payable	+	Unearned Revenue	+	Common Stock
	Old Balance	$10,000		$5,000		$5,000				$10,000
(4)		+1,200						+$1,200		
	New Balance	$11,200	+	$5,000	=	$5,000	+	$ 1,200	+	$10,000

$16,200 $16,200

EVENT (5). SERVICES RENDERED FOR CASH. On October 3 Sierra received $10,000 in cash from Copa Company for advertising services performed. This event is a transaction because Sierra received an asset (cash) in exchange for services.

Advertising service is the principal revenue-producing activity of Sierra. **Revenue increases stockholders' equity.** Both assets and stockholders' equity are, then, increased by this transaction. Cash is increased $10,000, and Retained Earnings is increased $10,000. The new balances in the equation are:

		Cash	+	Office Equipment	=	Notes Payable	+	Unearned Revenue	+	Common Stock	+	Retained Earnings	
	Old Balance	$11,200		$5,000		$5,000		$1,200		$10,000			
(5)		+10,000										+$10,000	Service Revenue
	New Balance	$21,200	+	$5,000	=	$5,000	+	$1,200	+	$10,000	+	$ 10,000	

Assets = $26,200   Liabilities + Stockholders' Equity = $26,200

Often companies provide services "on account." That is, they provide service for which they are paid at a later date. Revenue, however, is earned when services are performed. Therefore, stockholders' equity would increase when services are performed, even though cash has not been received. Instead of receiving cash, the company receives a different type of asset, an **account receivable**. Accounts receivable represent the right to receive payment at a later date. Suppose that Sierra had provided these services on account rather than for cash. This event would be reported using the accounting equation as:

Assets	=	Liabilities	+	Stockholders' Equity	
Accounts Receivable	=			Retained Earnings	
+$10,000				+$10,000	Service Revenue

Later, when the $10,000 is collected from the customer, Accounts Receivable would decline by $10,000, and Cash would increase by $10,000.

Assets		=	Liabilities	+	Stockholders' Equity
Cash	Accounts Receivable	=			
+$10,000	−$10,000				

Note that in this case, stockholders' equity is not affected by the collection of cash. Instead we record an exchange of one asset (Accounts Receivable) for a different asset (Cash).

EVENT (6). PAYMENT OF RENT. On October 3 Sierra Corporation paid its office rent for the month of October in cash, $900. This rent payment is a transaction because it results in a decrease in cash.

Rent is an expense incurred by Sierra Corporation in its effort to generate revenues. **Expenses decrease stockholders' equity.** The rent payment is recorded by decreasing cash and decreasing stockholders' equity (specifically, Retained Earnings) to maintain the balance of the accounting equation. To record this transaction, Cash is decreased $900, and Retained Earnings is decreased $900. The effect of these payments on the accounting equation is:

		Assets		=	Liabilities		+	Stockholders' Equity	
		Cash +	Office Equipment	=	Notes Payable +	Unearned Revenue	+	Common Stock +	Retained Earnings
	Old Balance	$21,200	$5,000		$5,000	$1,200		$10,000	$10,000
(6)		−900							−900 **Rent Expense**
	New Balance	$20,300 +	$5,000	=	$5,000 +	$1,200	+	$10,000 +	$ 9,100

$25,300 = $25,300

EVENT (7). PURCHASE OF INSURANCE POLICY IN CASH.

On October 4 Sierra paid $600 for a one-year insurance policy that will expire next year on September 30. This event is a transaction because one asset was exchanged for another. The asset Cash is decreased $600. The asset Prepaid Insurance is increased $600 because the payment extends to more than the current month. Payments of expenses that will benefit more than one accounting period are identified as prepaid expenses or prepayments. The balance in total assets did not change; one asset account decreased by the same amount that another increased.

		Assets				=	Liabilities		+	Stockholders' Equity	
		Cash +	Prepaid Insurance +	Office Equipment		=	Notes Payable +	Unearned Revenue	+	Common Stock +	Retained Earnings
	Old Balance	$20,300		$5,000			$5,000	$1,200		$10,000	$9,100
(7)		−600	+$600								
	New Balance	$19,700 +	$ 600 +	$5,000		=	$5,000 +	$1,200	+	$10,000 +	$9,100

$25,300 = $25,300

EVENT (8). PURCHASE OF SUPPLIES ON CREDIT.

On October 5 Sierra purchased a three-month supply of advertising materials on account from Aero Supply for $2,500. Assets are increased by this transaction because supplies represent a resource that will be used in the process of providing services to customers. Liabilities are increased by the amount due Aero Supply. The asset Supplies is increased $2,500, and the liability Accounts Payable is increased by the same amount. The effect on the equation is:

		Assets				=	Liabilities			+	Stockholders' Equity	
		Cash + Supplies +	Prepaid Insurance +	Office Equipment		=	Notes Payable +	Accounts Payable +	Unearned Revenue +	Common Stock +	Retained Earnings
	Old Balance	$19,700	$600	$5,000			$5,000		$1,200	$10,000	$9,100
(8)		+$2,500						+$2,500			
	New Balance	$19,700+ $ 2,500 +	$600 +	$5,000		=	$5,000 +	$ 2,500 +	$1,200 +	$10,000 +	$9,100

$27,800 = $27,800

EVENT (9). HIRING OF NEW EMPLOYEES.

On October 9 Sierra hired four new employees to begin work on October 15. Each employee will receive a weekly salary of $500 for a five-day work week, payable every two weeks. Employees will receive their first paychecks on October 26. There is no effect on the accounting equation because the assets, liabilities, and stockholders' equity of the company have not changed. **An accounting transaction has not occurred.** At this point there is only an agreement that the employees will begin work on October 15. [See Event (11) for the first payment.]

EVENT (10). PAYMENT OF DIVIDEND.   On October 20 Sierra paid a $500 dividend. **Dividends** are a distribution of net income and not an expense. A dividend transaction affects assets and stockholders' equity: Cash and Retained Earnings are decreased $500.

		Assets			=	Liabilities			+	Stockholders' Equity		
	Cash	+ Supplies +	Prepaid Insurance	+ Office Equipment	=	Notes Payable	+ Accounts Payable	+ Unearned Revenue	+	Common Stock	+ Retained Earnings	
Old Balance	$19,700	$2,500	$600	$5,000		$5,000	$2,500	$1,200		$10,000	$9,100	
(10)	−500										−500	Dividends
New Balance	$19,200 +	$2,500 +	$600	+ $5,000	=	$5,000 +	$2,500 +	$1,200	+	$10,000 +	$8,600	
			$27,300					$27,300				

EVENT (11). PAYMENT OF CASH FOR EMPLOYEE SALARIES.   Employees have worked two weeks, earning $4,000 in salaries, which were paid on October 26. Like the costs that were incurred for rent, salaries are an expense. Because they are a cost of generating revenues, they decrease stockholders' equity. This event involving employees is a transaction because assets and stockholders' equity are affected, each by an equal amount. Thus, Cash and Retained Earnings are each decreased $4,000.

		Assets			=	Liabilities			+	Stockholders' Equity		
	Cash	+ Supplies +	Prepaid Insurance	+ Office Equipment	=	Notes Payable	+ Accounts Payable	+ Unearned Revenue	+	Common Stock	+ Retained Earnings	
Old Balance	$19,200	$2,500	$600	$5,000		$5,000	$2,500	$1,200		$10,000	$8,600	
(11)	−4,000										−4,000	Salaries
New Balance	$15,200 +	$2,500 +	$600	+ $5,000	=	$5,000 +	$2,500 +	$1,200	+	$10,000 +	$4,600	Expense
			$23,300					$23,300				

Business Insight
MANAGEMENT PERSPECTIVE

Many companies are finding that teaching their factory workers basic accounting skills can be a useful motivational tool. For example, **Rhino Foods** in Burlington, Vermont, uses a financial reporting game to motivate its production line employees. Employees are taught the costs of each element of the production process, from raw materials to machinery malfunctions, so that they will make decisions that will benefit the company. The employees' bonus checks (for managers as well as factory workers) are based on the results of the game. The owner, a former hockey coach, believes that his workers will work harder, and enjoy their work more, if they "know what the score is."

SUMMARY OF TRANSACTIONS

The transactions of Sierra Corporation are summarized in Illustration 3-2 to show their cumulative effect on the basic accounting equation. The transaction number and the specific effects of the transaction are indicated. Remember that

Event (9) did not result in a transaction, so no entry is included for that event. The illustration demonstrates three facts:

1. Each transaction is analyzed in terms of its effect on assets, liabilities, and stockholders' equity.
2. The two sides of the equation must always be equal.
3. The cause of each change in stockholders' equity must be indicated.

Illustration 3-2 Summary of transactions

	Assets				=	Liabilities			+	Stockholders' Equity		
	Cash	+ Supplies +	Prepaid Insurance +	Office Equipment	=	Notes Payable +	Accounts Payable +	Unearned Revenue	+	Common Stock +	Retained Earnings	
(1)	+$10,000				=					+$10,000		Issued stock
(2)	+5,000					+$5,000						
(3)	−5,000			+$5,000								
(4)	+1,200							+$1,200				
(5)	+10,000										+$10,000	Service Revenue
(6)	−900										−900	Rent Expense
(7)	−600		+$600									
(8)		+$2,500					+$2,500					
(10)	−500										−500	Dividends
(11)	−4,000										−4,000	Salaries Expense
	$15,200 +	$2,500 +	$600 +	$5,000	=	$5,000 +	$2,500 +	$1,200	+	$10,000 +	$ 4,600	
		$23,300						$23,300				

DECISION TOOLKIT

Decision Checkpoints	Info Needed for Decision	Tool to Use for Decision	How to Evaluate Results
Has an accounting transaction occurred?	Details of the event	Accounting equation	Determine the effect, if any, on assets, liabilities, and stockholders' equity.

The Account

Rather than using a tabular summary like the one in Illustration 3-2 for Sierra Corporation, an accounting information system uses accounts. An **account** is an individual accounting record of increases and decreases in a specific asset, liability, or stockholders' equity item. For example, Sierra Corporation has separate accounts for Cash, Accounts Receivable, Accounts Payable, Service Revenue, Salaries Expense, and so on. (Note that whenever we are referring to a specific account, we capitalize the name.)

In its simplest form, an account consists of three parts: (1) the title of the account, (2) a left or debit side, and (3) a right or credit side. Because the alignment of these parts of an account resembles the letter T, it is referred to as a **T account**. The basic form of an account is shown in Illustration 3-3.

Title of Account	
Left or debit side	Right or credit side
Debit balance	Credit balance

Illustration 3-3 Basic form of account

This form of account is used often throughout this book to explain basic accounting relationships.

DEBITS AND CREDITS

Today, the term **debit** indicates left, and **credit** indicates right. They are commonly abbreviated as **Dr.** for debit and **Cr.** for credit. These terms come from Latin words that originally meant "debtor" and "creditor." Today they are merely directional signals. They **do not** mean increase or decrease, as is commonly thought. The terms *debit* and *credit* are used repeatedly in the recording process to describe **where** entries are made in accounts. For example, the act of entering an amount on the left side of an account is called **debiting** the account. Making an entry on the right side is **crediting** the account.

When the totals of the two sides are compared, an account will have a **debit balance** if the total of the debit amounts exceeds the credits. Conversely, an account will have a **credit balance** if the credit amounts exceed the debits. Note the position of the debit or credit balances in Illustration 3-3.

The procedure of recording debits and credits in an account is shown in Illustration 3-4 for the transactions affecting the Cash account of Sierra Corporation. The data are taken from the Cash column of the tabular summary in Illustration 3-2.

STUDY OBJECTIVE

3

Define debits and credits and explain how they are used to record business transactions.

Tabular Summary	Account Form			
Cash	**Cash**			
$10,000	**(Debits)**	10,000	**(Credits)**	5,000
5,000		5,000		900
−5,000		1,200		600
1,200		10,000		500
10,000				4,000
−900				
−600	Balance	15,200		
−500	**(Debit)**			
−4,000				
$15,200				

Illustration 3-4 Tabular summary and account form for Sierra Corporation's Cash account

Every positive item in the tabular summary represents a receipt of cash; every negative amount represents a payment of cash. **Notice that in the account form the increases in cash are recorded as debits, and the decreases in cash are recorded as credits.** Having increases on one side and decreases on the other reduces recording errors and helps in determining the totals of each side of the account as well as the balance in the account. The account balance, a debit of $15,200, indicates that Sierra Corporation had $15,200 more increases than decreases in cash. That is, since it started with a balance of zero, it has $15,200 in its Cash account.

DEBIT AND CREDIT PROCEDURES

Each transaction must affect two or more accounts to keep the basic accounting equation in balance. In other words, for each transaction, debits must equal credits. The equality of debits and credits provides the basis for the double-entry accounting system.

Under the **double-entry system**, the dual (two-sided) effect of each transaction is recorded in appropriate accounts. This system provides a logical method for recording transactions. As was the case for the error in **Fidelity**'s accounts in the Feature Story, the double-entry system also offers a means of ensuring the accuracy of the recorded amounts. If every transaction is recorded with equal debits and credits, then the sum of all the debits to the accounts must equal the sum of all the credits. The double-entry system for determining the equality of the accounting equation is much more efficient than the plus/minus procedure used earlier. There, it was necessary after each transaction to compare total assets with total liabilities and stockholders' equity to determine the equality of the two sides of the accounting equation.

Dr./Cr. Procedures for Assets and Liabilities

In Illustration 3-4 for Sierra Corporation, increases in cash—an asset—were entered on the left side, and decreases in cash were entered on the right side. We know that both sides of the basic equation (Assets = Liabilities + Stockholders' Equity) must be equal. It therefore follows that increases and decreases in liabilities will have to be recorded *opposite from* increases and decreases in assets. Thus, increases in liabilities must be entered on the right or credit side, and decreases in liabilities must be entered on the left or debit side. The effects that debits and credits have on assets and liabilities are summarized in Illustration 3-5.

Illustration 3-5 Debit and credit effects—assets and liabilities

Debits	Credits
Increase assets	Decrease assets
Decrease liabilities	Increase liabilities

Asset accounts normally show debit balances. That is, debits to a specific asset account should exceed credits to that account. Likewise, **liability accounts normally show credit balances**. That is, credits to a liability account should exceed debits to that account. The normal balances may be diagrammed as in Illustration 3-6.

Illustration 3-6 Normal balances—assets and liabilities

Knowing which is the normal balance in an account may help when you are trying to identify errors. For example, a credit balance in an asset account such as Land or a debit balance in a liability account such as Wages Payable usually indicates errors in recording. Occasionally, however, an abnormal balance may be correct. The Cash account, for example, will have a credit balance when a company has overdrawn its bank balance (written a check that "bounced").

Business Insight
MANAGEMENT PERSPECTIVE

In automated accounting systems, the computer is programmed to flag violations of the normal balance and to print out error or exception reports. In manual systems, careful visual inspection of the accounts is required to detect normal balance problems.

Dr./Cr. Procedures for Stockholders' Equity

In Chapter 1 we said that stockholders' equity is comprised of two parts: common stock and retained earnings. In the transaction events earlier in this chapter, you saw that revenues, expenses, and the payment of dividends affect retained earnings. So we are now at the point where we can expand the subdivision of stockholders' equity to five. The five subdivisions of stockholders' equity are: common stock, retained earnings, dividends, revenues, and expenses. In a double-entry system, accounts are kept for each of these subdivisions.

COMMON STOCK.   Common stock is issued in exchange for the stockholders' investment. The Common Stock account is increased by credits and decreased by debits. For example, when cash is invested in the business, Cash is debited and Common Stock is credited. The effects of debits and credits on the Common Stock account are shown in Illustration 3-7.

Debits	Credits
Decrease Common Stock	Increase Common Stock

Illustration 3-7 Debit and credit effects—Common Stock

The normal balance in the Common Stock account may be diagrammed as in Illustration 3-8.

Illustration 3-8 Normal balance—Common Stock

RETAINED EARNINGS.   Retained earnings is net income that is retained in the business. It represents the portion of stockholders' equity that has been accumulated through the profitable operation of the company. Retained Earnings is increased by credits (for example, net income) and decreased by debits (for example, a net loss), as shown in Illustration 3-9.

Debits	Credits
Decrease Retained Earnings	Increase Retained Earnings

Illustration 3-9 Debit and credit effects—Retained Earnings

The normal balance for Retained Earnings may be diagrammed as in Illustration 3-10.

Illustration 3-10 Normal balance—Retained Earnings

DIVIDENDS. A dividend is a distribution by a corporation to its stockholders in an amount proportional to each investor's percentage ownership. The most common form of distribution is a cash dividend. Dividends result in a reduction of the stockholders' claims on retained earnings. Because dividends reduce stockholders' equity, increases in the Dividends account are recorded with debits. As shown in Illustration 3-11, the Dividends account normally has a debit balance.

Illustration 3-11 Normal balance—Dividends

REVENUES AND EXPENSES. When revenues are earned, stockholders' equity is increased. Accordingly, **the effect of debits and credits on revenue accounts is identical to their effect on stockholders' equity**. Revenue accounts are increased by credits and decreased by debits.

On the other hand, **expenses decrease stockholders' equity**. As a result, expenses are recorded by debits. Since expenses are the negative factor in the computation of net income and revenues are the positive factor, it is logical that the increase and decrease sides of expense accounts should be the reverse of revenue accounts. Thus, expense accounts are increased by debits and decreased by credits. The effects of debits and credits on revenues and expenses are shown in Illustration 3-12.

Illustration 3-12 Debit and credit effects—revenues and expenses

Debits	Credits
Decrease revenues	Increase revenues
Increase expenses	Decrease expenses

Credits to revenue accounts should exceed debits, and debits to expense accounts should exceed credits. Thus, **revenue accounts normally show credit balances, and expense accounts normally show debit balances**. The normal balances may be diagrammed as in Illustration 3-13.

Illustration 3-13 Normal balances—revenues and expenses

Business Insight
INVESTOR PERSPECTIVE

The **Chicago Cubs** baseball team has these major revenue and expense accounts:

Revenues	Expenses
Admissions (ticket sales)	Players' salaries
Concessions	Administrative salaries
Television and radio	Travel
Advertising	Ballpark maintenance

STOCKHOLDERS' EQUITY RELATIONSHIPS

As indicated in Chapters 1 and 2, common stock and retained earnings are reported in the stockholders' equity section of the balance sheet. Dividends are reported on the retained earnings statement. Revenues and expenses are reported on the income statement. Dividends, revenues, and expenses are eventually transferred to retained earnings at the end of the period. As a result, a change in any one of these three items affects stockholders' equity. The relationships of the accounts affecting stockholders' equity are shown in Illustration 3-14.

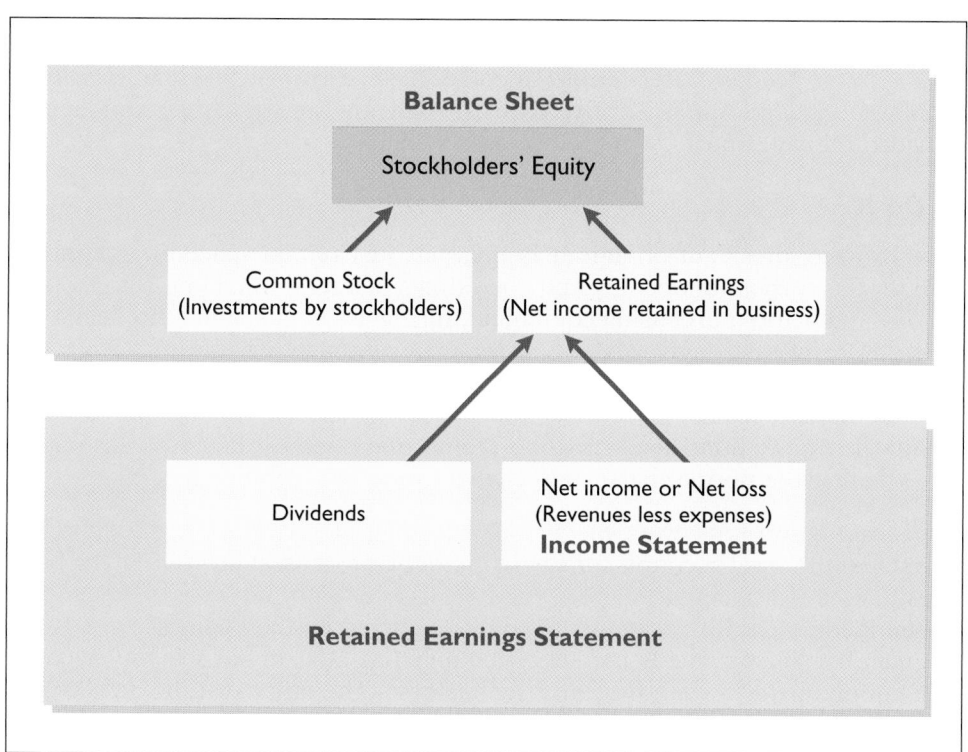

Illustration 3-14
Stockholders' equity relationships

EXPANSION OF THE BASIC EQUATION

You have already learned the basic accounting equation. Illustration 3-15 expands this equation to show the accounts that make up stockholders' equity. In addition, the debit/credit rules and effects on each type of account are illustrated. **Study this diagram carefully.** It will help you understand the fundamentals of the double-entry system. Like the basic equation, the expanded basic equation must be in balance; total debits must equal total credits.

Basic Equation	Assets	=	Liabilities	+					Stockholders' Equity						

Expanded Basic Equation	Assets	=	Liabilities	+	Common Stock	+	Retained Earnings	–	Dividends	+	Revenues	–	Expenses
Debit / Credit Rules	Dr. +	Cr. –		Dr. –	Cr. +		Dr. –	Cr. +		Dr. –	Cr. +		Dr. +	Cr. –		Dr. –	Cr. +		Dr. +	Cr. –

Illustration 3-15
Expansion of the basic
accounting equation

BEFORE YOU GO ON . . .

▶ **Review It**

1. What do the terms *debit* and *credit* indicate?
2. What are the debit and credit effects on assets, liabilities, and stockholders' equity?
3. What are the debit and credit effects on revenues, expenses, and dividends?
4. What are the normal balances for the following accounts of **Tootsie Roll Industries**: Accounts Receivable; Income Taxes Payable; Sales; and Selling, Marketing, and Administrative Expense? The answer to this question is provided on page 156.

▶ **Do It**

Kate Browne, president of Hair It Is Inc., has just rented space in a shopping mall for the purpose of opening and operating a beauty salon. Long before opening day and before purchasing equipment, hiring assistants, and remodeling the space, Kate was strongly advised to set up a double-entry set of accounting records in which to record all of her business transactions.

Identify the balance sheet accounts that Hair It Is Inc. will likely need to record the transactions necessary to establish and open for business. Also, indicate whether the normal balance of each account is a debit or a credit.

Action Plan

• First identify asset accounts for each different type of asset invested in the business.
• Then identify liability accounts for debts incurred by the business.
• Remember that Hair It Is Inc. will need only one stockholders' equity account for common stock when it begins the business. The other stockholders' equity accounts will be needed only after business has commenced.

Solution

Hair It Is Inc. would likely need the following accounts in which to record the transactions necessary to establish and ready the beauty salon for opening day: Cash (debit balance); Equipment (debit balance); Supplies (debit balance); Accounts Payable (credit balance); Notes Payable (credit balance), if the business borrows money; and Common Stock (credit balance).

☑ THE NAVIGATOR

Steps in the Recording Process

Although it is possible to enter transaction information directly into the accounts, few businesses do so. Practically every business uses these basic steps in the recording process:

STUDY OBJECTIVE
4
Identify the basic steps in the recording process.

1. Analyze each transaction in terms of its effect on the accounts.
2. Enter the transaction information in a journal.
3. Transfer the journal information to the appropriate accounts in the ledger (book of accounts).

The actual sequence of events begins with the transaction. Evidence of the transaction comes in the form of a **source document**, such as a sales slip, a check, a bill, or a cash register tape. This evidence is analyzed to determine the effect of the transaction on specific accounts. The transaction is then entered in the **journal**. Finally, the journal entry is transferred to the designated accounts in the **ledger**. The sequence of events in the recording process is shown in Illustration 3-16.

Illustration 3-16 The recording process

The Recording Process

| Analyze each transaction | Enter transaction in a journal | Transfer journal information to ledger accounts |

The basic steps in the recording process occur repeatedly in every business enterprise. The analysis of transactions has already been illustrated, and more examples of this step are given in this and later chapters. The other steps in the recording process are explained in the next sections.

THE JOURNAL

STUDY OBJECTIVE
5
Explain what a journal is and how it helps in the recording process.

Transactions are initially recorded in chronological order in **journals** before they are transferred to the accounts. For each transaction the journal shows the debit and credit effects on specific accounts. (In a computerized system, journals are now kept as files, and accounts are recorded in computer databases.)

Companies may use various kinds of journals, but every company has at least the most basic form of journal, a **general journal**. The journal makes three significant contributions to the recording process:

1. It discloses in one place the complete effect of a transaction.
2. It provides a chronological record of transactions.
3. It helps to prevent or locate errors because the debit and credit amounts for each entry can be readily compared.

Entering transaction data in the journal is known as **journalizing**. To illustrate the technique of journalizing, let's look at the first three transactions of Sierra Corporation. These transactions were: October 1, common stock was issued in exchange for $10,000 cash; October 1, $5,000 was borrowed by signing a note; October 2, office equipment was purchased for $5,000. In equation form, these transactions appeared in our earlier discussion as follows.

Assets	**= Liabilities +**	**Stockholders' Equity**
Cash	=	Common Stock
+$10,000		+$10,000 Issued stock

Assets	**= Liabilities +**	**Stockholders' Equity**
Cash	=	Notes Payable
+$5,000	+$5,000	

Assets		**= Liabilities +**	**Stockholders' Equity**
Cash	Office Equipment		
−$5,000	+$5,000		

Separate journal entries are made for each transaction. A complete entry consists of: (1) the date of the transaction, (2) the accounts and amounts to be debited and credited, and (3) a brief explanation of the transaction. These transactions are journalized in Illustration 3-17.

Illustration 3-17
Recording transactions in journal form

GENERAL JOURNAL

Date	Account Titles and Explanation	Debit	Credit
2005			
Oct. 1	Cash	10,000	
	Common Stock		10,000
	(Invested cash in business)		
1	Cash	5,000	
	Notes Payable		5,000
	(Issued 3-month, 12% note payable for cash)		
2	Office Equipment	5,000	
	Cash		5,000
	(Purchased office equipment for cash)		

Note the following features of the journal entries.

1. The date of the transaction is entered in the Date column.

2. The account to be debited is entered first at the left. The account to be credited is then entered on the next line, indented under the line above. The indentation differentiates debits from credits and decreases the possibility of switching the debit and credit amounts.

3. The amounts for the debits are recorded in the Debit (left) column, and the amounts for the credits are recorded in the Credit (right) column.

4. A brief explanation of the transaction is given.

It is important to use correct and specific account titles in journalizing. Since most accounts are used in the financial statements, erroneous account titles lead to incorrect financial statements. Some flexibility exists initially in selecting account titles. The main criterion is that each title must appropriately describe the content of the account. For example, a company could use any of these account titles for recording the cost of delivery trucks: Delivery Equipment, Delivery Trucks, or Trucks. Once the company chooses the specific title to use, however, all subsequent transactions involving the account should be recorded under that account title.

BEFORE YOU GO ON . . .

▶ **Review It**

1. What is the correct sequence of steps in the recording process?
2. What contribution does the journal make to the recording process?
3. What are the standard form and content of a journal entry made in the general journal?

▶ **Do It**

The following events occurred during the first month of business of Hair It Is Inc., Kate Browne's beauty salon:

1. Issued common stock to shareholders in exchange for $20,000 cash.
2. Purchased $4,800 of equipment on account (to be paid in 30 days).
3. Interviewed three people for the position of beautician.

In what form (type of record) should the company record these three activities? Prepare the entries to record the transactions.

Action Plan

• Record the transactions in a journal, which is a chronological record of the transactions.
• Make sure to provide a complete and accurate representation of the transactions' effects on the assets, liabilities, and stockholders' equity of the business.

Solution

Each transaction that is recorded is entered in the general journal. The three activities are recorded as follows.

1. Cash	20,000	
Common Stock		20,000
(Issued stock for cash)		
2. Equipment	4,800	
Accounts Payable		4,800
(Purchased equipment on account)		
3. No entry because no transaction occurred.		

☑ THE NAVIGATOR

STUDY OBJECTIVE
6
Explain what a ledger is and how it helps in the recording process.

THE LEDGER

The entire group of accounts maintained by a company is referred to collectively as the **ledger**. The ledger keeps in one place all the information about changes in specific account balances.

Companies may use various kinds of ledgers, but every company has a general ledger. A **general ledger** contains all the assets, liabilities, and stockholders' equity accounts, as shown in Illustration 3-18. A business can use a looseleaf binder or card file for the ledger, with each account kept on a separate sheet or card. Most businesses today, however, use a computerized accounting system. Whenever the term *ledger* is used in this textbook without additional specification, it will mean the general ledger.

Illustration 3-18 The general ledger

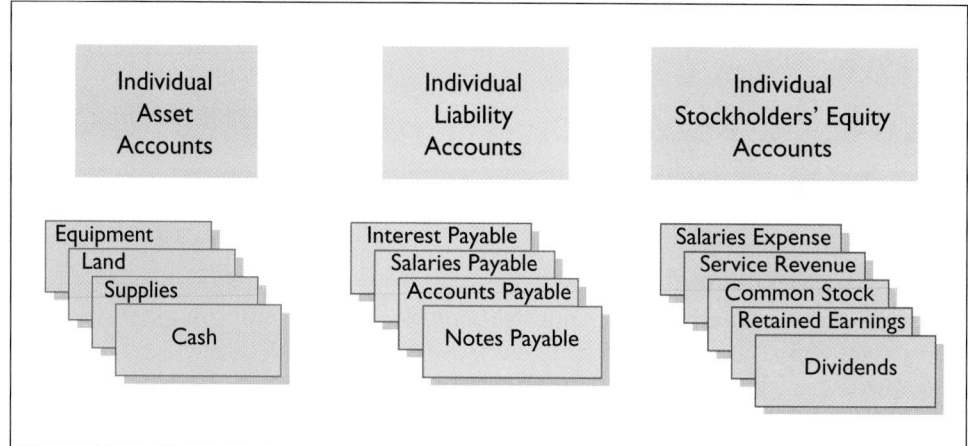

CHART OF ACCOUNTS

The number and type of accounts used differ for each company, depending on the size, complexity, and type of business. For example, the number of accounts depends on the amount of detail desired by management. The management of one company may want one single account for all types of utility expense. Another may keep separate expense accounts for each type of utility expenditure, such as gas, electricity, and water. Similarly, a small corporation like Sierra Corporation will not have many accounts compared with a corporate giant like **Ford Motor Company**. Sierra may be able to manage and report its activities in 20 to 30 accounts, whereas Ford requires thousands of accounts to keep track of its worldwide activities.

Most companies list the accounts in a **chart of accounts**. New accounts may be created as needed during the life of the business. The chart of accounts for Sierra Corporation is shown in Illustration 3-19. **Accounts shown in red are used in this chapter**; accounts shown in black are explained in later chapters.

Illustration 3-19 Chart of accounts for Sierra Corporation

SIERRA CORPORATION—Chart of Accounts

Assets	Liabilities	Stockholders' Equity	Revenues	Expenses
Cash	Notes Payable	Common Stock	Service Revenue	Salaries Expense
Accounts Receivable	Accounts Payable	Retained Earnings		Supplies Expense
Advertising Supplies	Interest Payable	Dividends		Rent Expense
Prepaid Insurance	Unearned	Income Summary		Insurance Expense
Office Equipment	Service Revenue			Interest Expense
Accumulated Depreciation—	Salaries Payable			Depreciation Expense
Office Equipment				

POSTING

The procedure of transferring journal entries to ledger accounts is called **posting**. **This phase of the recording process accumulates the effects of journalized transactions in the individual accounts.** Posting involves these steps:

1. In the ledger, enter in the appropriate columns of the debited account(s) the date and debit amount shown in the journal.

2. In the ledger, enter in the appropriate columns of the credited account(s) the date and credit amount shown in the journal.

The Recording Process Illustrated

Illustrations 3-20 through 3-30 show the basic steps in the recording process using the October transactions of Sierra Corporation. Its accounting period is a month. A basic analysis and a debit–credit analysis precede the journalizing and posting of each transaction. Study these transaction analyses carefully. **The purpose of transaction analysis is first to identify the type of account involved and then to determine whether a debit or a credit to the account is required.** You should always perform this type of analysis before preparing a journal entry. Doing so will help you understand the journal entries discussed in this chapter as well as more complex journal entries to be described in later chapters.

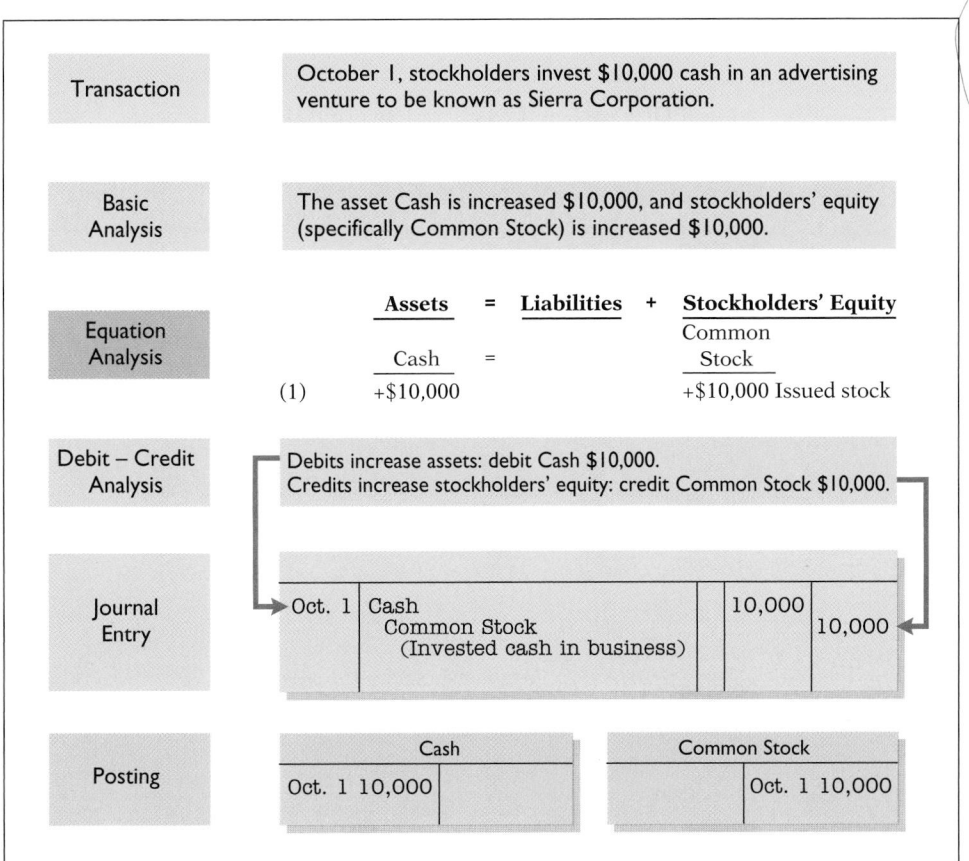

Illustration 3-20
Investment of cash by stockholders

Illustration 3-21 Issue of note payable

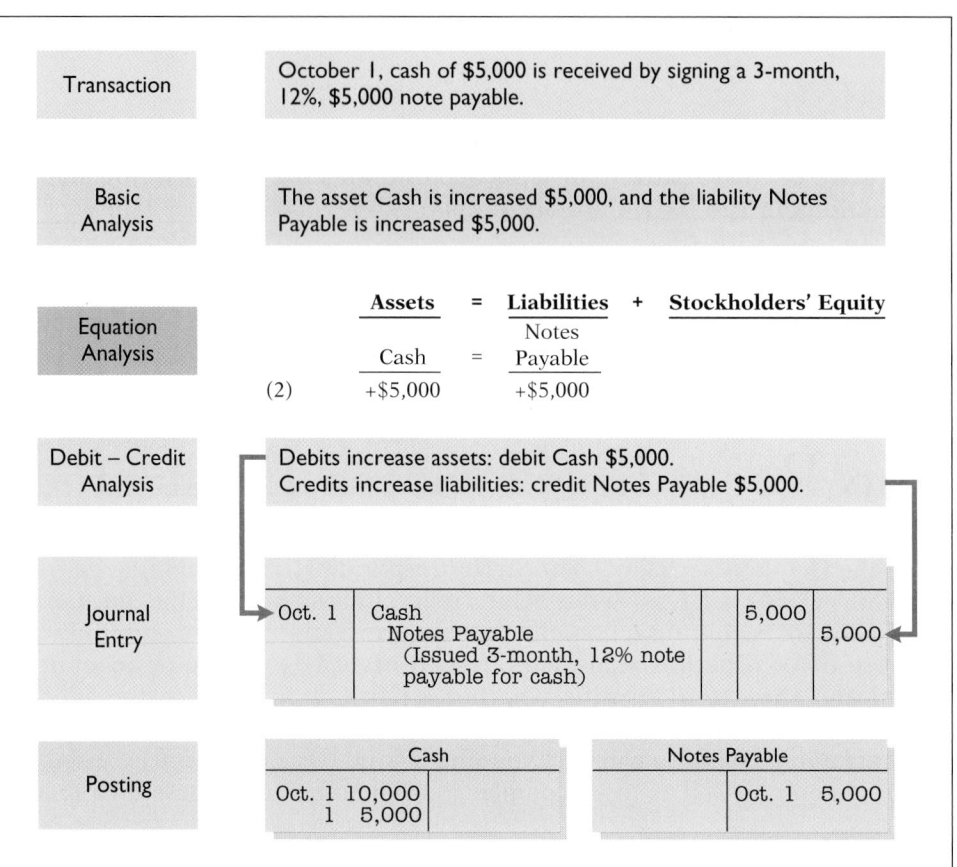

Transaction	October 1, cash of $5,000 is received by signing a 3-month, 12%, $5,000 note payable.
Basic Analysis	The asset Cash is increased $5,000, and the liability Notes Payable is increased $5,000.

Equation Analysis

	Assets	=	Liabilities	+	Stockholders' Equity
	Cash	=	Notes Payable		
(2)	+$5,000		+$5,000		

Debit – Credit Analysis

Debits increase assets: debit Cash $5,000.
Credits increase liabilities: credit Notes Payable $5,000.

Journal Entry

Oct. 1	Cash	5,000	
	Notes Payable		5,000
	(Issued 3-month, 12% note payable for cash)		

Posting

Cash		Notes Payable	
Oct. 1 10,000			Oct. 1 5,000
1 5,000			

Illustration 3-22 Purchase of office equipment

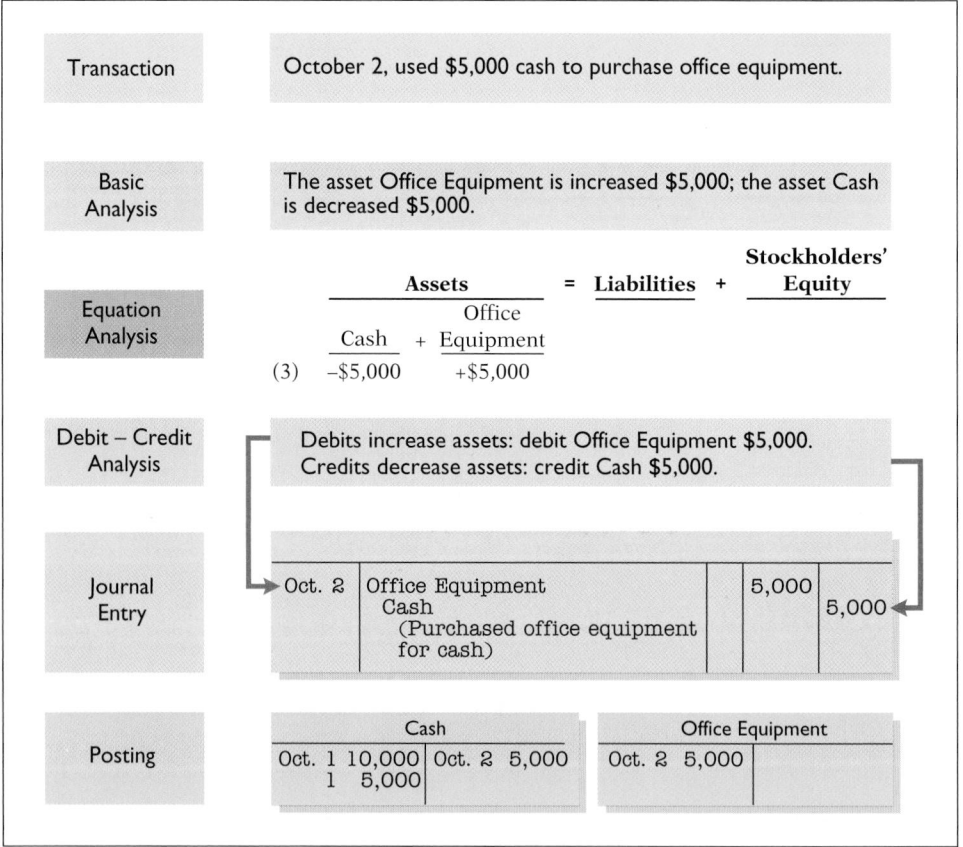

Transaction	October 2, used $5,000 cash to purchase office equipment.
Basic Analysis	The asset Office Equipment is increased $5,000; the asset Cash is decreased $5,000.

Equation Analysis

	Assets		=	Liabilities	+	Stockholders' Equity
	Cash	+ Office Equipment	=			
(3)	–$5,000	+$5,000				

Debit – Credit Analysis

Debits increase assets: debit Office Equipment $5,000.
Credits decrease assets: credit Cash $5,000.

Journal Entry

Oct. 2	Office Equipment	5,000	
	Cash		5,000
	(Purchased office equipment for cash)		

Posting

Cash		Office Equipment	
Oct. 1 10,000	Oct. 2 5,000	Oct. 2 5,000	
1 5,000			

Illustration 3-23 Receipt
of cash in advance from
customer

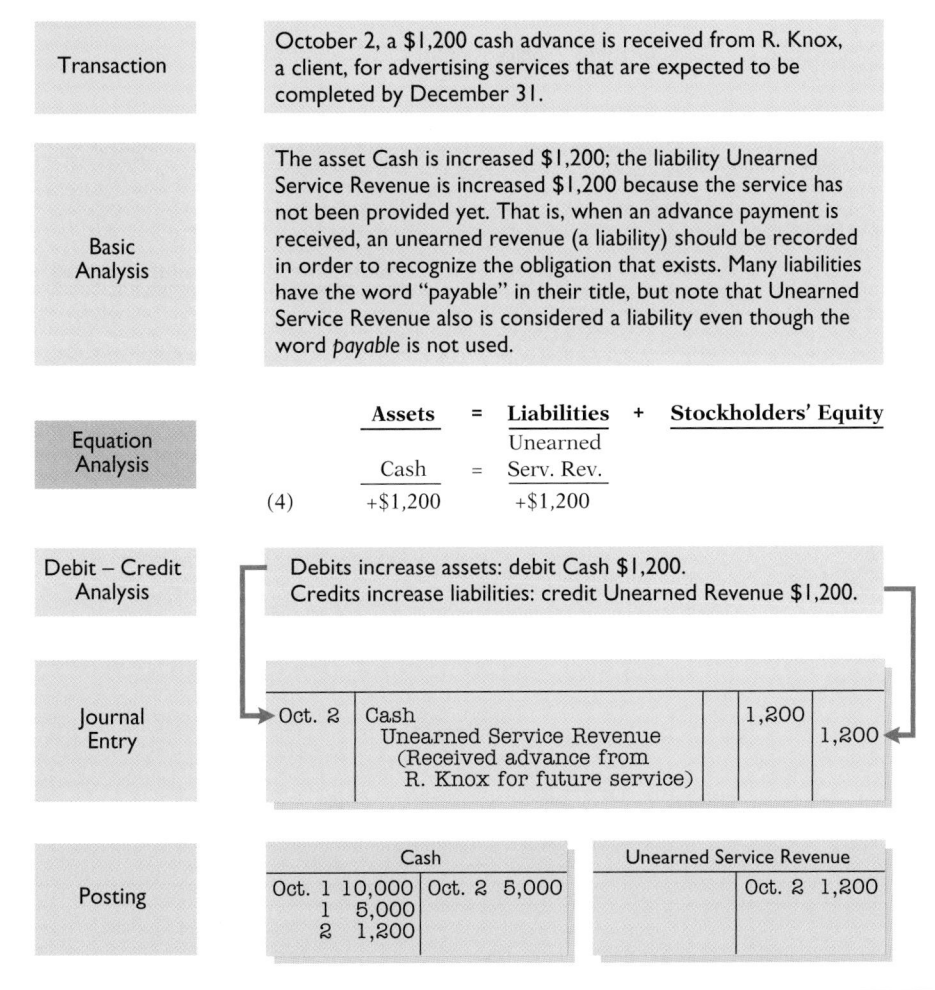

| Transaction | October 2, a $1,200 cash advance is received from R. Knox, a client, for advertising services that are expected to be completed by December 31. |

Basic Analysis

The asset Cash is increased $1,200; the liability Unearned Service Revenue is increased $1,200 because the service has not been provided yet. That is, when an advance payment is received, an unearned revenue (a liability) should be recorded in order to recognize the obligation that exists. Many liabilities have the word "payable" in their title, but note that Unearned Service Revenue also is considered a liability even though the word *payable* is not used.

Equation Analysis

	Assets	**=**	**Liabilities**	**+**	**Stockholders' Equity**
	Cash	=	Unearned Serv. Rev.		
(4)	+$1,200		+$1,200		

Debit – Credit Analysis

Debits increase assets: debit Cash $1,200.
Credits increase liabilities: credit Unearned Revenue $1,200.

Journal Entry

Oct. 2	Cash	1,200	
	Unearned Service Revenue		1,200
	(Received advance from R. Knox for future service)		

Posting

Cash		Unearned Service Revenue
Oct. 1 10,000	Oct. 2 5,000	Oct. 2 1,200
1 5,000		
2 1,200		

Illustration 3-24 Services
rendered for cash

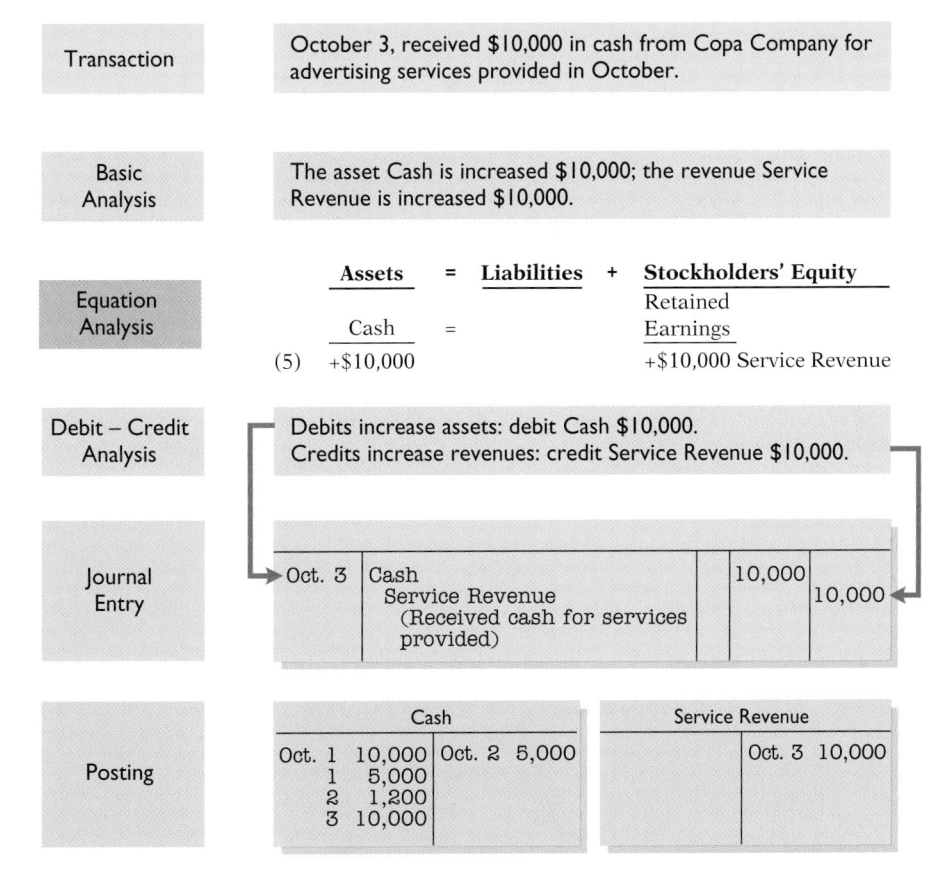

| Transaction | October 3, received $10,000 in cash from Copa Company for advertising services provided in October. |

Basic Analysis

The asset Cash is increased $10,000; the revenue Service Revenue is increased $10,000.

Equation Analysis

	Assets	**=**	**Liabilities**	**+**	**Stockholders' Equity**
	Cash	=			Retained Earnings
(5)	+$10,000				+$10,000 Service Revenue

Debit – Credit Analysis

Debits increase assets: debit Cash $10,000.
Credits increase revenues: credit Service Revenue $10,000.

Journal Entry

Oct. 3	Cash	10,000	
	Service Revenue		10,000
	(Received cash for services provided)		

Posting

Cash		Service Revenue
Oct. 1 10,000	Oct. 2 5,000	Oct. 3 10,000
1 5,000		
2 1,200		
3 10,000		

123

Illustration 3-25 Payment
of rent in cash

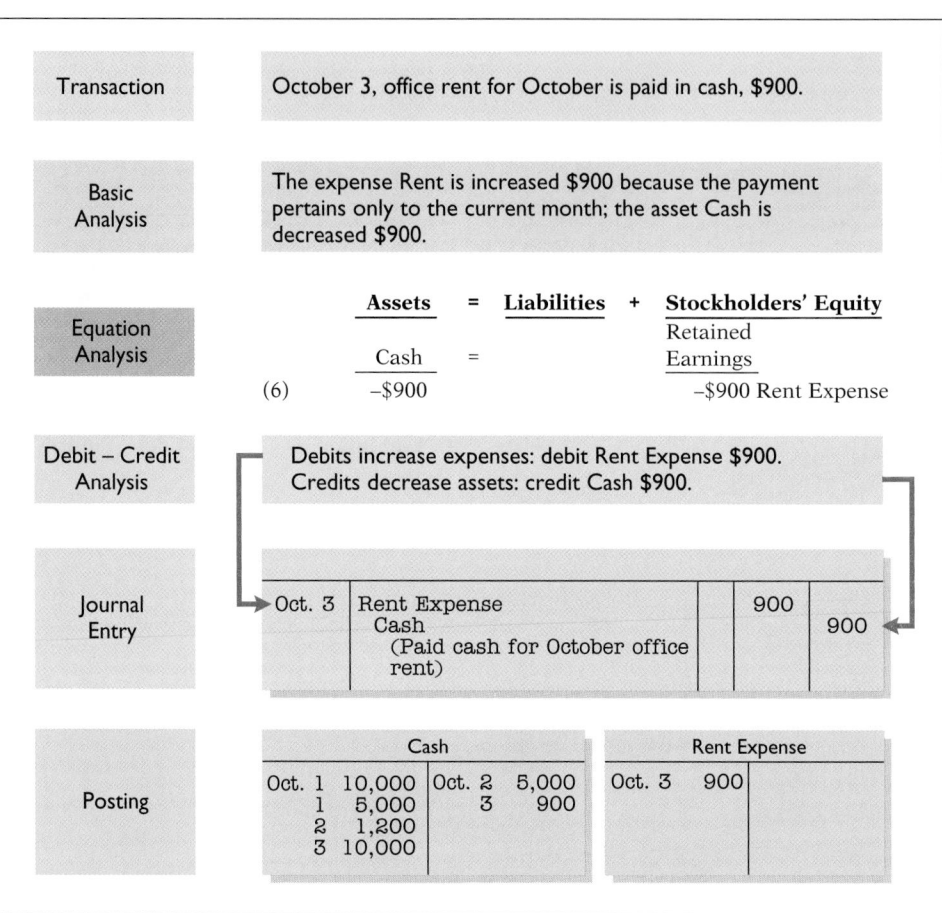

Illustration 3-26
Purchase of insurance
policy in cash

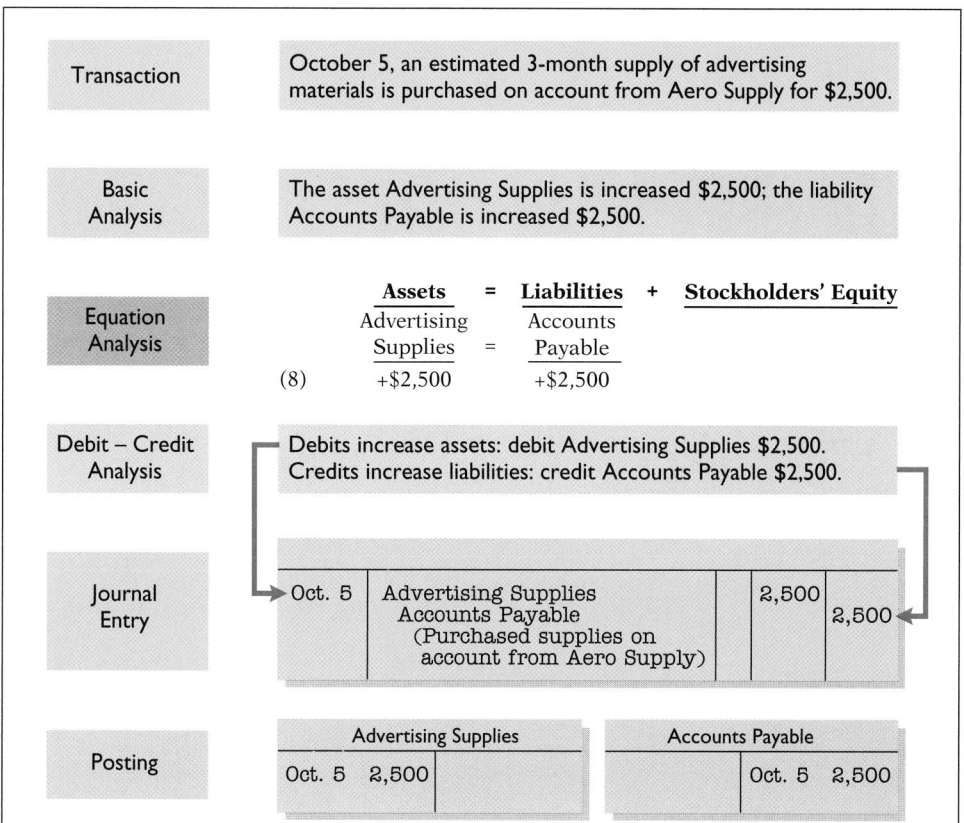

Illustration 3-27
Purchase of supplies on
credit

| Transaction | October 5, an estimated 3-month supply of advertising materials is purchased on account from Aero Supply for $2,500. |

| Basic Analysis | The asset Advertising Supplies is increased $2,500; the liability Accounts Payable is increased $2,500. |

Equation Analysis

	Assets	**=**	**Liabilities**	**+**	**Stockholders' Equity**
	Advertising Supplies	=	Accounts Payable		
(8)	+$2,500		+$2,500		

| Debit – Credit Analysis | Debits increase assets: debit Advertising Supplies $2,500. Credits increase liabilities: credit Accounts Payable $2,500. |

Journal Entry

Oct. 5	Advertising Supplies	2,500	
	Accounts Payable (Purchased supplies on account from Aero Supply)		2,500

Posting

Advertising Supplies			Accounts Payable	
Oct. 5 2,500				Oct. 5 2,500

Illustration 3-28 Hiring of
new employees

| Transaction | October 9, hired four employees to begin work on October 15. Each employee is to receive a weekly salary of $500 for a 5-day work week, payable every 2 weeks – – first payment made on October 26. |

| Basic Analysis | An accounting transaction has not occurred. There is only an agreement that the employees will begin work on October 15. Thus, a debit–credit analysis is not needed because there is no accounting entry. (See transaction of October 26 for first entry.) |

Illustration 3-29 Payment of dividend

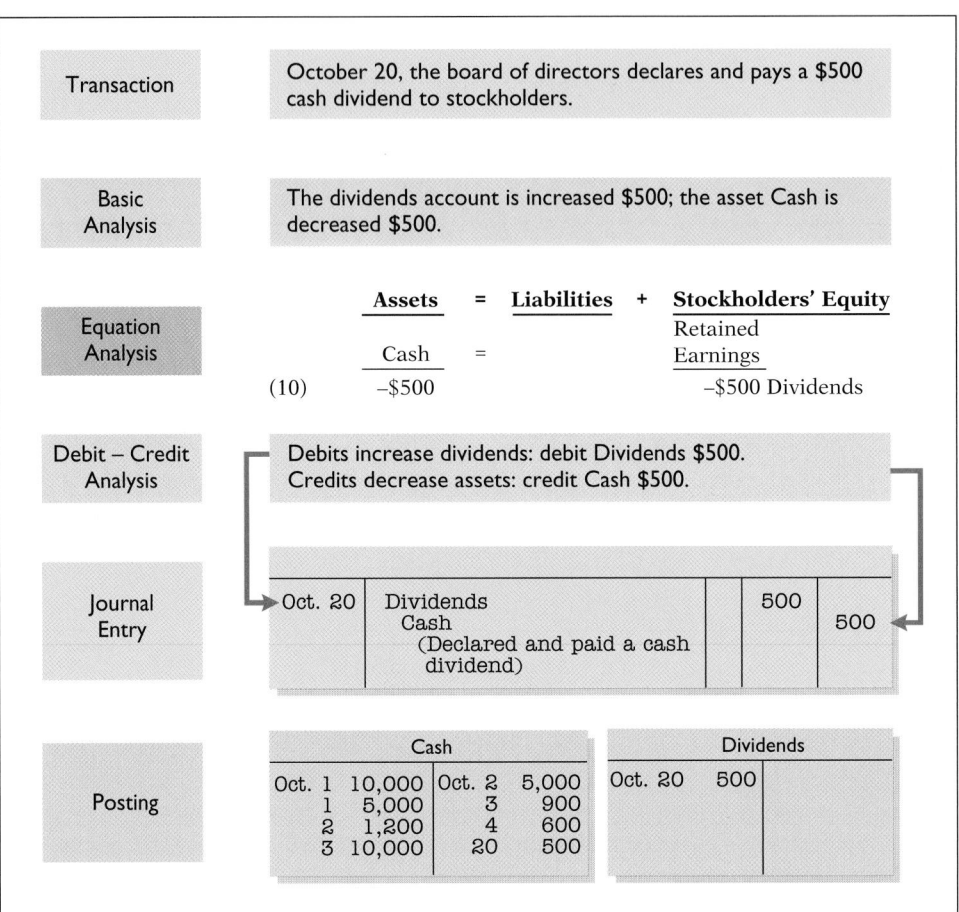

Illustration 3-30 Payment of cash for employee salaries

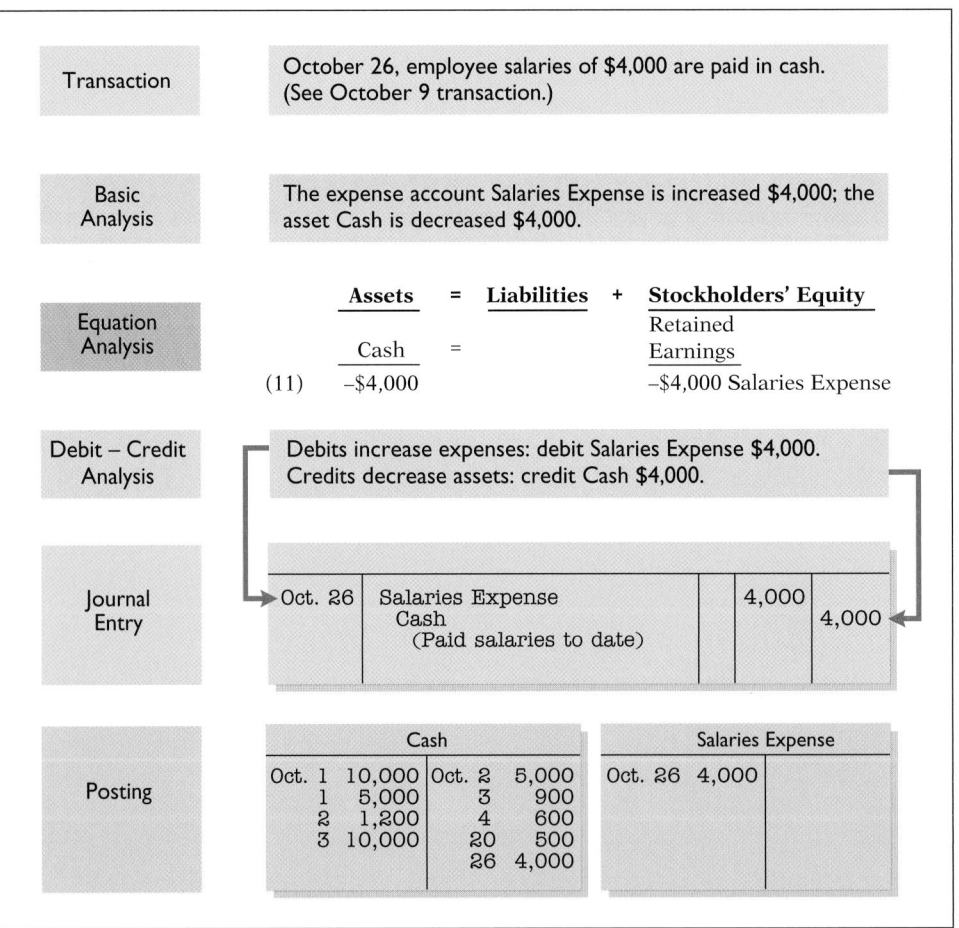

SUMMARY ILLUSTRATION OF JOURNALIZING AND POSTING

The journal for Sierra Corporation for the month of October is summarized in Illustration 3-31. The ledger is shown in Illustration 3-32 with all balances highlighted in red.

GENERAL JOURNAL

Date	Account Titles and Explanation	Debit	Credit
2005			
Oct. 1	Cash	10,000	
	Common Stock		10,000
	(Invested cash in business)		
1	Cash	5,000	
	Notes Payable		5,000
	(Issued 3-month, 12% note payable for cash)		
2	Office Equipment	5,000	
	Cash		5,000
	(Purchased office equipment for cash)		
2	Cash	1,200	
	Unearned Service Revenue		1,200
	(Received advance from R. Knox for future service)		
3	Cash	10,000	
	Service Revenue		10,000
	(Received cash for services rendered)		
3	Rent Expense	900	
	Cash		900
	(Paid cash for October office rent)		
4	Prepaid Insurance	600	
	Cash		600
	(Paid 1-year policy; effective date October 1)		
5	Advertising Supplies	2,500	
	Accounts Payable		2,500
	(Purchased supplies on account from Aero Supply)		
20	Dividends	500	
	Cash		500
	(Declared and paid a cash dividend)		
26	Salaries Expense	4,000	
	Cash		4,000
	(Paid salaries to date)		

Illustration 3-31 General journal for Sierra Corporation

GENERAL LEDGER

Illustration 3-32 General ledger for Sierra Corporation

Cash

Oct. 1	10,000	Oct. 2	5,000
1	5,000	3	900
2	1,200	4	600
3	10,000	20	500
		26	4,000
Bal.	**15,200**		

Unearned Service Revenue

		Oct. 2	1,200
		Bal.	**1,200**

Illustration 3-32 (continued) General ledger for Sierra Corporation

GENERAL LEDGER

Advertising Supplies				Common Stock	
Oct. 5	2,500			Oct. 1	10,000
Bal.	**2,500**			Bal.	**10,000**

Prepaid Insurance				Dividends	
Oct. 4	600		Oct. 20	500	
Bal.	**600**		Bal.	**500**	

Office Equipment				Service Revenue	
Oct. 2	5,000			Oct. 3	10,000
Bal.	**5,000**			Bal.	**10,000**

Notes Payable			Salaries Expense		
		Oct. 1	5,000	Oct. 26	4,000	
		Bal.	**5,000**	Bal.	**4,000**	

Accounts Payable			Rent Expense		
		Oct. 5	2,500	Oct. 3	900	
		Bal.	**2,500**	Bal.	**900**	

BEFORE YOU GO ON . . .

▶ **Review It**

1. How does journalizing differ from posting?
2. What is the purpose of (a) the ledger and (b) a chart of accounts?

▶ **Do It**

Selected transactions from the journal of Faital Inc. during its first month of operations are presented below. Post these transactions to T accounts.

Date		Account Titles	Debit	Credit
July	1	Cash	30,000	
		Common Stock		30,000
	9	Accounts Receivable	6,000	
		Service Revenue		6,000
	24	Cash	4,000	
		Accounts Receivable		4,000

Action Plan

• Journalize transactions to keep track of financial activities (receipts, payments, receivables, payables, etc.).
• To make entries useful, classify and summarize them by posting the entries to specific ledger accounts.

Solution

Cash				Accounts Receivable			
July 1	30,000			July 9	6,000	July 24	4,000
24	4,000						

Common Stock				Service Revenue		
		July 1	30,000			July 9	6,000

The Trial Balance

A trial balance is a list of accounts and their balances at a given time. Customarily, a trial balance is prepared at the end of an accounting period. The accounts are listed in the order in which they appear in the ledger. Debit balances are listed in the left column and credit balances in the right column. The totals of the two columns must be equal.

STUDY OBJECTIVE
8
Explain the purposes of a trial balance.

The primary purpose of a trial balance is to prove the mathematical equality of debits and credits after posting. Under the double-entry system this equality will occur when the sum of the debit account balances equals the sum of the credit account balances. **A trial balance may also uncover errors in journalizing and posting.** For example, a trial balance may well have allowed detection of the error at Fidelity Investments discussed in the Feature Story. **In addition, a trial balance is useful in the preparation of financial statements**, as explained in the next chapter.

These are the procedures for preparing a trial balance:

1. List the account titles and their balances.
2. Total the debit column and the credit column.
3. Verify the equality of the two columns.

The trial balance prepared from the ledger of Sierra Corporation is presented in Illustration 3-33. Note that the total debits, $28,700, equal the total credits, $28,700.

Illustration 3-33 Sierra Corporation trial balance

SIERRA CORPORATION Trial Balance October 31, 2005		
	Debit	**Credit**
Cash	$ 15,200	
Advertising Supplies	2,500	
Prepaid Insurance	600	
Office Equipment	5,000	
Notes Payable		$ 5,000
Accounts Payable		2,500
Unearned Service Revenue		1,200
Common Stock		10,000
Dividends	500	
Service Revenue		10,000
Salaries Expense	4,000	
Rent Expense	900	
	$28,700	$28,700

LIMITATIONS OF A TRIAL BALANCE

A trial balance does not prove that all transactions have been recorded or that the ledger is correct. Numerous errors may exist even though the trial balance columns agree. For example, the trial balance may balance even when any of the following occurs: (1) a transaction is not journalized, (2) a correct journal entry is not posted, (3) a journal entry is posted twice, (4) incorrect accounts are used in journalizing or posting, or (5) offsetting errors are made in recording the amount of a transaction. In other words, as long as equal debits and credits are posted, even to the wrong account or in the wrong amount, the total debits will equal the total credits. Nevertheless, despite its limitations, the trial balance is a useful screen for finding errors and is frequently used in practice.

BEFORE YOU GO ON . . .

▶ **Review It**

1. What is a trial balance, and how is it prepared?
2. What is the primary purpose of a trial balance?
3. What are the limitations of a trial balance?

☑ THE NAVIGATOR

DECISION TOOLKIT

Decision Checkpoints	Info Needed for Decision	Tool to Use for Decision	How to Evaluate Results
How do you determine that debits equal credits?	All account balances	Trial balance	List the account titles and their balances; total the debit and credit columns; verify equality.

Using the Decision Toolkit

The **Kansas Farmers' Vertically Integrated Cooperative, Inc. (K-VIC)**, was formed by over 200 northeast Kansas farmers in the late 1980s. Its purpose is to use raw materials, primarily grain and meat products grown by K-VIC's members, to process this material into end-user food products, and to distribute the products nationally. Profits not needed for expansion or investment are returned to the members annually, on a pro-rata basis, according to the market value of the grain and meat products received from each farmer.

Assume that the following information was prepared for K-VIC's trial balance.

KANSAS FARMERS' VERTICALLY INTEGRATED COOPERATIVE, INC.
Trial Balance
December 31, 2005
(in thousands)

	Debit	Credit
Accounts Receivable	$ 712,000	
Accounts Payable		$ 37,000
Advertising and Promotion Payable		141,000
Buildings	365,000	
Cash	32,000	
Cost of Goods Sold	2,384,000	
Current Maturity of Long-Term Debt		12,000
Inventories	1,291,000	
Land	110,000	
Long-Term Debt		873,000
Machinery and Equipment	63,000	
Notes Payable to Members		495,000
Retained Earnings		822,000
Sales Revenue		3,741,000
Salaries and Wages Payable		62,000
Selling and Administrative Expense	651,000	
Trucking Expense	500,000	
	$6,108,000	$6,183,000

Because the trial balance is not in balance, you have checked with various people responsible for entering accounting data and have discovered the following.

1. The purchase of thirty-five new trucks, costing $7 million and paid for with cash, was not recorded.

2. A data entry clerk accidentally deleted the account name for an account with a credit balance of $472 million, so the amount was added to the Long-Term Debt account in the trial balance.

3. December cash sales revenue of $75 million was credited to the Sales Revenue account, but the other half of the entry was not made.

4. $50 million of selling expenses were mistakenly charged to Trucking Expense.

Instructions

Answer these questions.
(a) Which mistake(s) have caused the trial balance to be out of balance?
(b) Should all of the items be corrected? Explain.
(c) What is the name of the account the data entry clerk deleted?
(d) Make the necessary corrections and balance the trial balance.
(e) On your trial balance, write BAL beside the accounts that go on the balance sheet and INC beside those that go on the income statement.

Solution

(a) Only mistake #3 has caused the trial balance to be out of balance.
(b) All of the items should be corrected. The misclassification error (mistake #4) on the selling expense would not affect bottom-line net income, but it does affect the amounts reported in the two expense accounts.
(c) There is no Common Stock account, so that must be the account that was deleted by the data entry clerk.
(d) and (e):

KANSAS FARMERS' VERTICALLY INTEGRATED COOPERATIVE, INC.
Trial Balance
December 31, 2005
(in thousands)

	Debit	Credit	
Accounts Receivable	$ 712,000		BAL
Accounts Payable		$ 37,000	BAL
Advertising and Promotion Payable		141,000	BAL
Buildings	365,000		BAL
Cash	100,000		BAL
Common Stock		472,000	BAL
Cost of Goods Sold	2,384,000		INC
Current Maturity of Long-Term Debt		12,000	BAL
Inventories	1,291,000		BAL
Land	110,000		BAL
Long-Term Debt		401,000	BAL
Machinery and Equipment	70,000		BAL
Notes Payable to Members		495,000	BAL
Retained Earnings		822,000	BAL
Sales Revenue		3,741,000	INC
Salaries and Wages Payable		62,000	BAL
Selling and Administrative Expense	701,000		INC
Trucking Expense	450,000		INC
	$6,183,000	$6,183,000	

THE NAVIGATOR

Summary of Study Objectives

1 *Analyze the effect of business transactions on the basic accounting equation.* Each business transaction must have a dual effect on the accounting equation. For example, if an individual asset is increased, there must be a corresponding (a) decrease in another asset, or (b) increase in a specific liability, or (c) increase in stockholders' equity.

2 *Explain what an account is and how it helps in the recording process.* An account is an individual accounting record of increases and decreases in specific asset, liability, and stockholders' equity items.

3 *Define debits and credits and explain how they are used to record business transactions.* The terms *debit* and *credit* are synonymous with *left* and *right*. Assets, dividends, and expenses are increased by debits and decreased by credits. Liabilities, common stock, retained earnings, and revenues are increased by credits and decreased by debits.

4 *Identify the basic steps in the recording process.* The basic steps in the recording process are: (a) analyze each transaction in terms of its effect on the accounts, (b) enter the transaction information in a journal, and (c) transfer the journal information to the appropriate accounts in the ledger.

5 *Explain what a journal is and how it helps in the recording process.* The initial accounting record of

a transaction is entered in a journal before the data are entered in the accounts. A journal (a) discloses in one place the complete effect of a transaction, (b) provides a chronological record of transactions, and (c) prevents or locates errors because the debit and credit amounts for each entry can be readily compared.

6 *Explain what a ledger is and how it helps in the recording process.* The entire group of accounts maintained by a company is referred to collectively as a ledger. The ledger keeps in one place all the information about changes in specific account balances.

7 *Explain what posting is and how it helps in the recording process.* Posting is the procedure of transferring journal entries to the ledger accounts. This phase of the recording process accumulates the effects of journalized transactions in the individual accounts.

8 *Explain the purposes of a trial balance.* A trial balance is a list of accounts and their balances at a given time. The primary purpose of the trial balance is to prove the mathematical equality of debits and credits after posting. A trial balance also uncovers errors in journalizing and posting and is useful in preparing financial statements.

DECISION TOOLKIT—A SUMMARY

Decision Checkpoints	Info Needed for Decision	Tool to Use for Decision	How to Evaluate Results
Has an accounting transaction occurred?	Details of the event	Accounting equation	Determine the effect, if any, on assets, liabilities, and stockholders' equity.
How do you determine that debits equal credits?	All account balances	Trial balance	List the account titles and their balances; total the debit and credit colums; verify equality.

Glossary

3A 6A BYP 3-4, 3-9

Account An individual accounting record of increases and decreases in specific asset, liability, or stockholders' equity items. (p. 110)

Accounting information system The system of collecting and processing transaction data and communicating financial information to interested parties. (p. 103)

Accounting transactions Events that require recording in the financial statements because they affect assets, liabilities, or stockholders' equity. (p. 104)

Chart of accounts A list of a company's accounts. (p. 120)

Credit The right side of an account. (p. 111)

Debit The left side of an account. (p. 111)

Double-entry system A system that records the dual effect of each transaction in appropriate accounts. (p. 112)

General journal The most basic form of journal. (p. 117)

General ledger A ledger that contains all asset, liability, and stockholders' equity accounts. (p. 120)

Journal An accounting record in which transactions are initially recorded in chronological order. (p. 117)

Journalizing The procedure of entering transaction data in the journal. (p. 118)

Ledger The group of accounts maintained by a company. (p. 119)

Posting The procedure of transferring journal entries to the ledger accounts. (p. 121)

T account The basic form of an account. (p. 111)

Trial balance A list of accounts and their balances at a given time. (p. 129)

Demonstration Problem

Bob Sample and other student investors opened Campus Carpet Cleaning, Inc. on September 1, 2005. During the first month of operations the following transactions occurred.

Peachtree

Sept. 1 Stockholders invested $20,000 cash in the business.
2 Paid $1,000 cash for store rent for the month of September.
3 Purchased industrial carpet-cleaning equipment for $25,000, paying $10,000 in cash and signing a $15,000 6-month, 12% note payable.
4 Paid $1,200 for 1-year accident insurance policy.
10 Received bill from the *Daily News* for advertising the opening of the cleaning service, $200.
15 Performed services on account for $6,200.
20 Declared and paid a $700 cash dividend to stockholders.
30 Received $5,000 from customers billed on September 15.

The chart of accounts for the company is the same as for Sierra Corporation except for the following additional accounts: Cleaning Equipment and Advertising Expense.

Instructions

(a) Journalize the September transactions.
(b) Open ledger accounts and post the September transactions.
(c) Prepare a trial balance at September 30, 2005.

Solution to Demonstration Problem

(a)

GENERAL JOURNAL

Date	Account Titles and Explanation	Debit	Credit
2005			
Sept. 1	Cash	20,000	
	Common Stock		20,000
	(Invested cash in business)		
2	Rent Expense	1,000	
	Cash		1,000
	(Paid September rent)		
3	Cleaning Equipment	25,000	
	Cash		10,000
	Notes Payable		15,000
	(Purchased cleaning equipment for cash		
	and 6-month, 12% note payable)		
4	Prepaid Insurance	1,200	
	Cash		1,200
	(Paid 1-year insurance policy)		
10	Advertising Expense	200	
	Accounts Payable		200
	(Received bill from *Daily News* for		
	advertising)		
15	Accounts Receivable	6,200	
	Service Revenue		6,200
	(To record services performed on account)		

Action Plan

• Proceed through the accounting cycle in the following sequence:

1. Make separate journal entries for each transaction.

2. Note that all debits precede all credit entries.

3. In journalizing, make sure debits equal credits.

4. In journalizing, use specific account titles taken from the chart of accounts.

5. Provide an appropriate explanation of each journal entry.

6. Arrange ledger in statement order, beginning with the balance sheet accounts.

7. Post in chronological order.

8. Prepare a trial balance, which lists accounts in the order in which they appear in the ledger.

9. List debit balances in the left column and credit balances in the right column.

				Debit	Credit
20	Dividends			700	
	Cash				700
	(Declared and paid a cash dividend)				
30	Cash			5,000	
	Accounts Receivable				5,000
	(To record collection of accounts receivable)				

(b) **GENERAL LEDGER**

Cash

Sept. 1	20,000	Sept. 2	1,000		
30	5,000	3	10,000		
		4	1,200		
		20	700		
Bal.	12,100				

Common Stock

		Sept. 1	20,000
		Bal.	20,000

Accounts Receivable

Sept. 15	6,200	Sept. 30	5,000
Bal.	1,200		

Dividends

Sept. 20	700	
Bal.	700	

Prepaid Insurance

Sept. 4	1,200	
Bal.	1,200	

Service Revenue

		Sept. 15	6,200
		Bal.	6,200

Cleaning Equipment

Sept. 3	25,000	
Bal.	25,000	

Advertising Expense

Sept. 10	200	
Bal.	200	

Notes Payable

		Sept. 3	15,000
		Bal.	15,000

Rent Expense

Sept. 2	1,000	
Bal.	1,000	

Accounts Payable

		Sept. 10	200
		Bal.	200

(c)

CAMPUS CARPET CLEANING, INC.
Trial Balance
September 30, 2005

	Debit	Credit
Cash	$12,100	
Accounts Receivable	1,200	
Prepaid Insurance	1,200	
Cleaning Equipment	25,000	
Notes Payable		$15,000
Accounts Payable		200
Common Stock		20,000
Dividends	700	
Service Revenue		6,200
Advertising Expense	200	
Rent Expense	1,000	
	$41,400	$41,400

Self-Study Questions

Self-Study/Self-Test

Answers are at the end of the chapter.

(SO 1) **1.** The effects on the basic accounting equation of performing services for cash are to:
   (a) increase assets and decrease stockholders' equity.
   (b) increase assets and increase stockholders' equity.
   (c) increase assets and increase liabilities.
   (d) increase liabilities and increase stockholders' equity.

(SO 1) **2.** Genesis Company buys a $900 machine on credit. This transaction will affect the:
   (a) income statement only.
   (b) balance sheet only.
   (c) income statement and retained earnings statement only.
   (d) income statement, retained earnings statement, and balance sheet.

(SO 2) **3.** Which statement about an account is *true?*
   (a) In its simplest form, an account consists of two parts.
   (b) An account is an individual accounting record of increases and decreases in specific asset, liability, and stockholders' equity items.
   (c) There are separate accounts for specific assets and liabilities but only one account for stockholders' equity items.
   (d) The left side of an account is the credit or decrease side.

(SO 3) **4.** Debits:
   (a) increase both assets and liabilities.
   (b) decrease both assets and liabilities.
   (c) increase assets and decrease liabilities.
   (d) decrease assets and increase liabilities.

(SO 3) **5.** A revenue account:
   (a) is increased by debits.
   (b) is decreased by credits.
   (c) has a normal balance of a debit.
   (d) is increased by credits.

(SO 3) **6.** Which accounts normally have debit balances?
   (a) Assets, expenses, and revenues.
   (b) Assets, expenses, and retained earnings.
   (c) Assets, liabilities, and dividends.
   (d) Assets, dividends, and expenses.

(SO 4) **7.** Which is *not* part of the recording process?
   (a) Analyzing transactions.
   (b) Preparing a trial balance.

   (c) Entering transactions in a journal.
   (d) Posting transactions.

8. Which of these statements about a journal is *false?*   (SO 5)
   (a) It contains only revenue and expense accounts.
   (b) It provides a chronological record of transactions.
   (c) It helps to locate errors because the debit and credit amounts for each entry can be readily compared.
   (d) It discloses in one place the complete effect of a transaction.

9. A ledger: (SO 6)
   (a) contains only asset and liability accounts.
   (b) should show accounts in alphabetical order.
   (c) is a collection of the entire group of accounts maintained by a company.
   (d) provides a chronological record of transactions.

10. Posting: (SO 7)
   (a) normally occurs before journalizing.
   (b) transfers ledger transaction data to the journal.
   (c) is an optional step in the recording process.
   (d) transfers journal entries to ledger accounts.

11. A trial balance: (SO 8)
   (a) is a list of accounts with their balances at a given time.
   (b) proves the mathematical accuracy of journalized transactions.
   (c) will not balance if a correct journal entry is posted twice.
   (d) proves that all transactions have been recorded.

12. A trial balance will not balance if: (SO 8)
   (a) a correct journal entry is posted twice.
   (b) the purchase of supplies on account is debited to Supplies and credited to Cash.
   (c) a $100 cash dividend is debited to Dividends for $1,000 and credited to Cash for $100.
   (d) a $450 payment on account is debited to Accounts Payable for $45 and credited to Cash for $45.

THE NAVIGATOR box appears near 12(d)

✓ THE NAVIGATOR

Questions

1. Describe the accounting information system and the steps in the recording process.

2. Can a business enter into a transaction that affects only the left side of the basic accounting equation? If so, give an example.

3. Are the following events recorded in the accounting records? Explain your answer in each case.
   (a) A major stockholder of the company dies.
   (b) Supplies are purchased on account.
   (c) An employee is fired.
   (d) The company pays a cash dividend to its stockholders.

4. Indicate how each business transaction affects the basic accounting equation.
   (a) Paid cash for janitorial services.
   (b) Purchased equipment for cash.
   (c) Issued common stock to investors in exchange for cash.
   (d) Paid an account payable in full.

5. Why is an account referred to as a T account?

6. The terms *debit* and *credit* mean "increase" and "decrease," respectively. Do you agree? Explain.

7. Tony Galego, a fellow student, contends that the double-entry system means each transaction must be recorded twice. Is Tony correct? Explain.

8. Colleen Mooney, a beginning accounting student, believes debit balances are favorable and credit balances are unfavorable. Is Colleen correct? Discuss.

9. State the rules of debit and credit as applied to (a) asset accounts, (b) liability accounts, and (c) the common stock account.

10. What is the normal balance for each of these accounts?
    (a) Accounts Receivable.
    (b) Cash.
    (c) Dividends.
    (d) Accounts Payable.
    (e) Service Revenue.
    (f) Salaries Expense.
    (g) Common Stock.

11. Indicate whether each account is an asset, a liability, or a stockholders' equity account, and whether it would have a normal debit or credit balance.
    (a) Accounts Receivable.
    (b) Accounts Payable.
    (c) Equipment.
    (d) Dividends.
    (e) Supplies.

12. For the following transactions, indicate the account debited and the account credited.
    (a) Supplies are purchased on account.
    (b) Cash is received on signing a note payable.
    (c) Employees are paid salaries in cash.

13. For each account listed here, indicate whether it generally will have debit entries only, credit entries only, or both debit and credit entries.
    (a) Cash.
    (b) Accounts Receivable.
    (c) Dividends.
    (d) Accounts Payable.
    (e) Salaries Expense.
    (f) Service Revenue.

14. What are the basic steps in the recording process?

15. (a) When entering a transaction in the journal, should the debit or credit be written first?
    (b) Which should be indented, the debit or the credit?

16. (a) Can accounting transaction debits and credits be recorded directly in the ledger accounts?
    (b) What are the advantages of first recording transactions in the journal and then posting to the ledger?

17. Journalize these accounting transactions.
    (a) Stockholders invested $9,000 in the business in exchange for common stock.
    (b) Insurance of $800 is paid for the year.
    (c) Supplies of $1,500 are purchased on account.
    (d) Cash of $7,500 is received for services rendered.

18. (a) What is a ledger?
    (b) Why is a chart of accounts important?

19. What is a trial balance and what are its purposes?

20. Tom Bars is confused about how accounting information flows through the accounting system. He believes information flows in this order:
    (a) Debits and credits are posted to the ledger.
    (b) Accounting transaction occurs.
    (c) Information is entered in the journal.
    (d) Financial statements are prepared.
    (e) Trial balance is prepared.
    Indicate to Tom the proper flow of the information.

21. Two students are discussing the use of a trial balance. They wonder whether the following errors, each considered separately, would prevent the trial balance from balancing. What would you tell them?
    (a) The bookkeeper debited Cash for $600 and credited Wages Expense for $600 for payment of wages.
    (b) Cash collected on account was debited to Cash for $900, and Service Revenue was credited for $90.

Brief Exercises

Determine effect of transaction on basic accounting equation.
(SO 1)

 BE3-1   Presented here are three economic events. On a sheet of paper, list the letters (a), (b), and (c) with columns for assets, liabilities, and stockholders' equity. In each column, indicate whether the event increased (+), decreased (−), or had no effect (NE) on assets, liabilities, and stockholders' equity.

(a) Purchased supplies on account.
(b) Received cash for providing a service.
(c) Expenses paid in cash.

BE3-2 Follow the same format as in BE3-1. Determine the effect on assets, liabilities, and stockholders' equity of the following three events.
(a) Issued common stock to investors in exchange for cash.
(b) Paid cash dividend to stockholders.
(c) Received cash from a customer who had previously been billed for services provided.

Determine effect of transaction on basic accounting equation.
(SO 1)

BE3-3 For each of the following accounts indicate the effect of a debit or a credit on the account and the normal balance.
(a) Accounts Payable.   (d) Accounts Receivable.
(b) Advertising Expense.   (e) Retained Earnings.
(c) Service Revenue.   (f) Dividends.

Indicate debit and credit effects.
(SO 3)

BE3-4 Transactions for Lena Company for the month of June are presented next. Identify the accounts to be debited and credited for each transaction.

June 1 Issues common stock to investors in exchange for $2,500 cash.
       2 Buys equipment on account for $900.
       3 Pays $500 to landlord for June rent.
      12 Bills J. Kronsnoble $700 for welding work done.

Identify accounts to be debited and credited.
(SO 3)

BE3-5 Use the data in BE3-4 and journalize the transactions. (You may omit explanations.)

Journalize transactions.
(SO 5)

BE3-6 Nish Adler, a fellow student, is unclear about the basic steps in the recording process. Identify and briefly explain the steps in the order in which they occur.

Identify steps in the recording process.
(SO 4)

BE3-7 Riko Corporation has the following transactions during August of the current year. Indicate (a) the basic analysis and (b) the debit–credit analysis illustrated on pages 121–126.

Aug. 1 Issues shares of common stock to investors in exchange for $5,000.
       4 Pays insurance in advance for 6 months, $2,100.
      16 Receives $900 from clients for services rendered.
      27 Pays secretary $500 salary.

Indicate basic debit–credit analysis.
(SO 4)

BE3-8 Use the data in BE3-7 and journalize the transactions. (You may omit explanations.)

Journalize transactions.
(SO 5)

BE3-9 Selected transactions for Cher Company are presented in journal form (without explanations). Post the transactions to T accounts.

Post journal entries to T accounts.
(SO 7)

Date	Account Title	Debit	Credit
May 5	Accounts Receivable	3,200	
	Service Revenue		3,200
12	Cash	1,900	
	Accounts Receivable		1,900
15	Cash	2,000	
	Service Revenue		2,000

BE3-10 From the ledger balances below, prepare a trial balance for Lumas Company at June 30, 2005. All account balances are normal.

Prepare a trial balance.
(SO 8)

Accounts Payable	$ 4,000	Service Revenue	$6,600
Cash	4,400	Accounts Receivable	3,000
Common Stock	20,000	Salaries Expense	4,000
Dividends	1,200	Rent Expense	1,000
Equipment	17,000		

BE3-11 An inexperienced bookkeeper prepared the following trial balance that does not balance. Prepare a correct trial balance, assuming all account balances are normal.

Prepare a corrected trial balance.
(SO 8)

ROSA COMPANY
Trial Balance
December 31, 2005

	Debit	Credit
Cash	$18,800	
Prepaid Insurance		$ 3,500
Accounts Payable		3,500
Unearned Revenue	2,200	
Common Stock		10,000
Retained Earnings		7,000
Dividends		5,000
Service Revenue		25,600
Salaries Expense	18,600	
Rent Expense		2,400
	$39,600	$57,000

Exercises

Analyze the effect of transactions.
(SO 1)

E3-1 Selected transactions for Sain Advertising Company, Inc., are listed here.

1. Issued common stock to investors in exchange for cash received from investors.
2. Paid monthly rent.
3. Received cash from customers when service was rendered.
4. Billed customers for services performed.
5. Paid dividend to stockholders.
6. Incurred advertising expense on account.
7. Received cash from customers billed in (4).
8. Purchased additional equipment for cash.
9. Purchased equipment on account.

Instructions
Describe the effect of each transaction on assets, liabilities, and stockholders' equity. For example, the first answer is: (1) Increase in assets and increase in stockholders' equity.

Analyze the effect of transactions on assets, liabilities, and stockholders' equity.
(SO 1)

E3-2 Shah Company entered into these transactions during May 2005.

1. Purchased computer terminals for $35,000 from Digital Equipment on account.
2. Paid $4,000 cash for May rent on storage space.
3. Received $15,000 cash from customers for contracts billed in April.
4. Provided computer services to Brieske Construction Company for $5,000 cash.
5. Paid Southern States Power Co. $11,000 cash for energy usage in May.
6. Stockholders invested an additional $22,000 in the business in exchange for common stock of the company.
7. Paid Digital Equipment for the terminals purchased in (1).
8. Incurred advertising expense for May of $1,000 on account.

Instructions
Indicate with the appropriate letter whether each of the transactions above results in:
(a) an increase in assets and a decrease in assets.
(b) an increase in assets and an increase in stockholders' equity.
(c) an increase in assets and an increase in liabilities.
(d) a decrease in assets and a decrease in stockholders' equity.
(e) a decrease in assets and a decrease in liabilities.
(f) an increase in liabilities and a decrease in stockholders' equity.
(g) an increase in stockholders' equity and a decrease in liabilities.

Analyze transactions and compute net income.
(SO 1)

E3-3 A tabular analysis of the transactions made during August 2005 by Bere Company during its first month of operations is shown on the next page. Each increase and decrease in stockholders' equity is explained.

	Cash	+	Accounts Receivable	+	Supplies	+	Office Equipment	=	Accounts Payable	+	Stockholders' Equity	
1.	+$15,000										+$15,000	Issued common stock
2.	−1,000 pd						+$5,000		+$4,000 we owe			
3.	−750				+$750 pd cash							
4.	+4,600		+$3,400								+8,000	Service Revenue done
5.	−1,500								−1,500			
6.	−2,000										−2,000	Dividends
7.	−800										−800	Rent Expense
8.	+450		−450									
9.	−2,900										−2,900	Salaries Expense
10.									+500		−500	Utilities Expense
												billed, not paid

Instructions

(a) Describe each transaction.

(b) Determine how much stockholders' equity increased for the month.

(c) Compute the net income for the month.

E3-4 The tabular analysis of transactions for Bere Company is presented in E3-3.

Prepare an income statement, retained earnings statement, and balance sheet.
(SO 1)

Instructions

Prepare an income statement and a retained earnings statement for August and a classified balance sheet at August 31, 2005.

NI 3800   RE 1400

E3-5 Selected transactions for Tastefully Yours, an interior decorator corporation, in its first month of business, are as follows.

Identify debits, credits, and normal balances.
(SO 3)

1. Issued stock to investors for $10,000 in cash.
2. Purchased used car for $8,000 cash for use in business.
3. Purchased supplies on account for $500.
4. Billed customers $2,600 for services performed.
5. Paid $200 cash for advertising start of the business.
6. Received $700 cash from customers billed in transaction (4).
7. Paid creditor $300 cash on account.
8. Paid dividends of $400 cash to stockholders.

Instructions

For each transaction indicate (a) the basic type of account debited and credited (asset, liability, stockholders' equity); (b) the specific account debited and credited (Cash, Rent Expense, Service Revenue, etc.); (c) whether the specific account is increased or decreased; and (d) the normal balance of the specific account. Use the following format, in which transaction 1 is given as an example.

	Account Debited				Account Credited			
Trans-action	(a) Basic Type	(b) Specific Account	(c) Effect	(d) Normal Balance	(a) Basic Type	(b) Specific Account	(c) Effect	(d) Normal Balance
1	Asset	Cash	Increase	Debit	Stock-holders' equity	Common Stock	Increase	Credit

E3-6 Data for Tastefully Yours, interior decorator, are presented in E3-5.

Journalize transactions.
(SO 5)

Instructions

Journalize the transactions. Do not provide explanations.

E3-7 This information relates to DeVoe Real Estate Agency Corporation.

Analyze transactions and determine their effect on accounts.
(SO 3)

Oct. 1   Stockholders invested $25,000 in exchange for common stock of the corporation.

      2   Hires an administrative assistant at an annual salary of $50,000.

3	Buys office furniture for $1,900, on account.
6	Sells a house and lot for B. Rollins; commissions due from Rollins, $6,200 (not paid by Rollins at this time).
10	Receives cash of $140 as commission for acting as rental agent renting an apartment.
27	Pays $700 on account for the office furniture purchased on October 3.
30	Pays the administrative assistant $1,200 in salary for October.

Instructions

Prepare the debit–credit analysis for each transaction as illustrated on pages 121–126.

Journalize transactions.
(SO 5)

E3-8   Transaction data for DeVoe Real Estate Agency are presented in E3-7.

Instructions

Journalize the transactions. Do not provide explanations.

Post journal entries and prepare a trial balance.
(SO 7, 8)

E3-9   The transaction data and journal entries for DeVoe Real Estate Agency are presented in E3-7 and E3-8.

Instructions

(a) Post the transactions to T accounts.
(b) Prepare a trial balance at October 31, 2005.

Analyze transactions, prepare journal entries, and post transactions to T accounts.
(SO 1, 5, 7)

E3-10   Selected transactions for Jay Leno Corporation during its first month in business are presented below.

Sept.	1	Issued common stock in exchange for $15,000 cash received from investors.
	5	Purchased equipment for $12,000, paying $5,000 in cash and the balance on account.
	25	Paid $3,000 cash on balance owed for equipment.
	30	Paid $500 cash dividend.

Leno's chart of accounts shows: Cash, Equipment, Accounts Payable, Common Stock, and Dividends.

Instructions

(a) Prepare a tabular analysis of the September transactions. The column headings should be: Cash + Equipment = Accounts Payable + Stockholders' Equity. For transactions affecting stockholders' equity, provide explanations in the right margin, as shown on page 110.
(b) Journalize the transactions. Do not provide explanations.
(c) Post the transactions to T accounts.

Journalize transactions from T accounts and prepare a trial balance.
(SO 5, 8)

E3-11   These T accounts summarize the ledger of Marla's Gardening Company Inc. at the end of the first month of operations.

Cash				Unearned Revenue	
Apr. 1	9,000	Apr. 15	600		Apr. 30	800
12	700	25	3,500		
29	400				
30	800				

Accounts Receivable				Common Stock	
Apr. 7	2,400	Apr. 29	400		Apr. 1	9,000

Supplies				Service Revenue	
Apr. 4	5,200				Apr. 7	2,400
					12	700

Accounts Payable				Salaries Expense	
Apr. 25	3,500	Apr. 4	5,200	Apr. 15	600	

Instructions
  (a) Prepare in the order they occurred the journal entries (including explanations) that resulted in the amounts posted to the accounts.
  (b) Prepare a trial balance at April 30, 2005.

E3-12 Selected transactions from the journal of Hoi Inc. during its first month of operations are presented here.

Post journal entries and prepare a trial balance.
(SO 7, 8)

Date	Account Titles	Debit	Credit
Aug. 1	Cash	1,600	
	Common Stock		1,600
10	Cash	2,900	
	Service Revenue		2,900
12	Office Equipment	6,000	
	Cash		1,000
	Notes Payable		5,000
25	Accounts Receivable	1,800	
	Service Revenue		1,800
31	Cash	600	
	Accounts Receivable		600

Instructions
  (a) Post the transactions to T accounts.
  (b) Prepare a trial balance at August 31, 2005.

E3-13 Here is the ledger for Khanna Co.

Journalize transactions from T accounts and prepare a trial balance.
(SO 5, 8)

Cash

Oct. 1	4,000	Oct. 4	400
10	750	12	1,500
10	8,000	15	250
20	800	30	300
25	2,000	31	500

Common Stock

		Oct. 1	4,000
		25	2,000

Accounts Receivable

Oct. 6	800	Oct. 20	800
20	740		

Dividends

Oct. 30	300		

Supplies

Oct. 4	400	Oct. 31	180

Service Revenue

		Oct. 6	800
		10	750
		20	740

Furniture

Oct. 3	3,000		

Store Wages Expense

Oct. 31	500		

Notes Payable

		Oct. 10	8,000

Supplies Expense

Oct. 31	180		

Accounts Payable

Oct. 12	1,500	Oct. 3	3,000

Rent Expense

Oct. 15	250		

Instructions
  (a) Reproduce the journal entries for only the transactions that **occurred on October 1, 10, and 20,** and provide explanations for each.
  (b) Prepare a trial balance at October 31, 2005.

Analyze errors and their effects on trial balance.
(SO 8)

E3-14 The bookkeeper for Convenient Repair Corporation made these errors in journalizing and posting.

1. A credit posting of $400 to Accounts Receivable was omitted.
2. A debit posting of $750 for Prepaid Insurance was debited to Insurance Expense.
3. A collection on account of $100 was journalized and posted as a debit to Cash $100 and a credit to Service Revenue $100.
4. A credit posting of $300 to Property Taxes Payable was made twice.
5. A cash purchase of supplies for $250 was journalized and posted as a debit to Supplies $25 and a credit to Cash $25.
6. A debit of $465 to Advertising Expense was posted as $456.

Instructions
For each error, indicate (a) whether the trial balance will balance; if the trial balance will not balance, indicate (b) the amount of the difference, and (c) the trial balance column that will have the larger total. Consider each error separately. Use the following form, in which error 1 is given as an example.

Error	(a) In Balance	(b) Difference	(c) Larger Column
1	No	$400	Debit

Prepare a trial balance.
(SO 8)

E3-15 The accounts in the ledger of SpeeDee Delivery Service contain the following balances on July 31, 2005.

Accounts Receivable	$13,642	Prepaid Insurance	$ 1,968
Accounts Payable	7,396	Repair Expense	1,200
Cash	?	Service Revenue	15,610
Delivery Equipment	59,360	Dividends	700
Gas and Oil Expense	758	Common Stock	40,000
Insurance Expense	523	Salaries Expense	4,428
Notes Payable, due 2008	28,450	Salaries Payable	900
		Retained Earnings	4,636

Instructions
(a) Prepare a trial balance with the accounts arranged as illustrated in the chapter, and fill in the missing amount for Cash.
(b) Prepare an income statement, statement of retained earnings, and a classified balance sheet.

Identify normal account balance and corresponding financial statement.
(SO 3)

E3-16 You are presented with the following list of accounts, in alphabetical order, selected from the 2001 financial statements of **Krispy Kreme Doughnuts, Inc.**

Accounts payable	Interest income
Accounts receivable	Inventories
Common stock	Prepaid expenses
Depreciation expense	Property and equipment
Interest expense	Revenues

Instructions
For each account, indicate (a) whether the normal balance is a debit or a credit, and (b) the financial statement—balance sheet or income statement—where the account should be presented.

Problems: Set A

Analyze transactions and compute net income.
(SO 1)

P3-1A Corellian Window Washing Inc. was started on May 1. Here is a summary of the May transactions.

1. Stockholders invested $16,000 cash in the company in exchange for common stock.
2. Purchased equipment for $5,000 cash.
3. Paid $700 cash for May office rent.
4. Paid $500 cash for supplies.
5. Purchased $550 of advertising in the *Beacon News* on account.
6. Received $5,200 in cash from customers for service.
7. Declared and paid a $500 cash dividend.
8. Paid part-time employee salaries $1,500.
9. Paid utility bills $140.
10. Provided service on account to customers $400.
11. Collected cash of $240 for services billed in transaction (10).

Instructions
(a) Prepare a tabular analysis of the transactions using these column headings: Cash, Accounts Receivable, Supplies, Equipment, Accounts Payable, Common Stock, and Retained Earnings. Revenue is called Service Revenue. Include margin explanations for any changes in Retained Earnings.
(b) From an analysis of the column Retained Earnings, compute the net income or net loss for May.

(b) Net income $2,710

P3-2A John Naboo started his own delivery service, Naboo Service Inc., on June 1, 2005. The following transactions occurred during the month of June.

Analyze transactions and prepare financial statements.
(SO 1)

June   1   Stockholders invested $18,000 cash in the business in exchange for common stock.
     2   Purchased a used van for deliveries for $10,000. John paid $2,000 cash and signed a note payable for the remaining balance.
     3   Paid $500 for office rent for the month.
     5   Performed $1,700 of services on account.
     9   Paid $200 in cash dividends.
    12   Purchased supplies for $150 on account.
    15   Received a cash payment of $750 for services provided on June 5.
    17   Purchased gasoline for $100 on account.
    20   Received a cash payment of $1,500 for services provided.
    23   Made a cash payment of $800 on the note payable.
    26   Paid $250 for utilities.
    29   Paid for the gasoline purchased on account on June 17.
    30   Paid $750 for employee salaries.

Instructions
(a) Show the effects of the previous transactions on the accounting equation using the following format. Assume the note payable is to be repaid within the year.

(a) Cash $15,650

		Assets		=	Liabilities		Stockholders' Equity	
Date	Cash +	Accounts Receivable +	Supplies +	Delivery Van =	Notes Payable +	Accounts Payable +	Common Stock +	Retained Earnings

Include margin explanations for any changes in Retained Earnings.
(b) Prepare an income statement for the month of June.
(c) Prepare a classified balance sheet at June 30, 2005.

(b) Net income $1,600

P3-3A Julie Molony opened Molony Company, a veterinary business in Hills, Iowa, on August 1, 2005. On August 31 the balance sheet showed: Cash $9,000; Accounts Receivable $1,700; Supplies $600; Office Equipment $6,000; Accounts Payable $3,600; Common Stock $13,000; and Retained Earnings $700. During September the following transactions occurred.

Analyze transactions and prepare an income statement, retained earnings statement, and balance sheet.
(SO 1)

1. Paid $3,100 cash for accounts payable due.
2. Received $1,600 from customers in payment of accounts receivable.
3. Purchased additional office equipment for $4,100, paying $1,000 in cash and the balance on account.

4. Earned revenue of $8,900, of which $2,300 is paid in cash and the balance is due in October.
5. Declared and paid a $600 cash dividend.
6. Paid salaries $700, rent for September $900, and advertising expense $250.
7. Incurred utility expenses for month on account $170.
8. Received $7,000 from Hilldale Bank; the money was borrowed on a 6-month note payable.

Instructions

(a) Cash $13,350
Ret. earnings $ 6,980

(a) Prepare a tabular analysis of the September transactions beginning with August 31 balances. The column headings should be: Cash + Accounts Receivable + Supplies + Office Equipment = Notes Payable + Accounts Payable + Common Stock + Retained Earnings. Include margin explanations for any changes in Retained Earnings.

(b) Prepare an income statement for September, a retained earnings statement for September, and a classified balance sheet at September 30, 2005.

Journalize a series of transactions.
(SO 3, 5)

Peachtree

P3-4A Alpine Valley was started on April 1 by Josh Stein. These selected events and transactions occurred during April.

Apr. 1   Stockholders invested $75,000 cash in the business in exchange for common stock.
      4   Purchased land costing $50,000 for cash.
      8   Purchased advertising in local newspaper for $1,800 on account.
      11 Paid salaries to employees $1,700.
      12 Hired park manager at a salary of $4,000 per month, effective May 1.
      13 Paid $3,000 for a 1-year insurance policy.
      17 Paid $600 cash dividends.
      20 Received $5,000 in cash from customers for admission fees.
      25 Sold 100 coupon books for $30 each. Each book contains ten coupons that entitle the holder to one admission to the park. (*Hint*: The revenue is not earned until the coupons are used.)
      30 Received $7,900 in cash from customers for admission fees.
      30 Paid $700 of the balance owed for the advertising purchased on account on April 8.

The company uses the following accounts: Cash, Prepaid Insurance, Land, Accounts Payable, Unearned Admissions, Common Stock, Dividends, Admission Revenue, Advertising Expense, and Salaries Expense.

Instructions
Journalize the April transactions, including explanations.

Journalize transactions, post, and prepare a trial balance.
(SO 3, 5, 6, 7, 8)

Peachtree

P3-5A Karen Brown incorporated Astromech Consulting, an accounting practice, on May 1, 2005. During the first month of operations, these events and transactions occurred.

May 1   Stockholders invested $52,000 cash in exchange for common stock of the corporation.
     2   Hired a secretary-receptionist at a salary of $1,000 per month.
     3   Purchased $800 of supplies on account from Read Supply Company.
     7   Paid office rent of $900 for the month.
     11 Completed a tax assignment and billed client $1,100 for services provided.
     12 Received $4,200 advance on a management consulting engagement.
     17 Received cash of $1,600 for services completed for H. Arnold Co.
     31 Paid secretary-receptionist $1,000 salary for the month.
     31 Paid 40% of balance due Read Supply Company.

The company uses the following chart of accounts: Cash, Accounts Receivable, Supplies, Accounts Payable, Unearned Revenue, Common Stock, Service Revenue, Salaries Expense, and Rent Expense.

Instructions

(c) Cash $55,580
Tot. trial
balance $59,380

(a) Journalize the transactions, including explanations.
(b) Post to the ledger T accounts.
(c) Prepare a trial balance on May 31, 2005.

P3-6A The trial balance of Valet Dry Cleaners on June 30 is given here.

Journalize transactions, post, and prepare a trial balance.
(SO 3, 5, 6, 7, 8)

Peachtree

VALET DRY CLEANERS
Trial Balance
June 30, 2005

	Debit	Credit
Cash	$12,532	
Accounts Receivable	10,536	
Supplies	4,844	
Equipment	25,950	
Accounts Payable		$15,878
Unearned Revenue		1,730
Common Stock		36,254
	$53,862	$53,862

The July transactions were as follows.

July	8	Received $5,189 in cash on June 30 accounts receivable.
	9	Paid employee salaries $2,100.
	11	Received $4,925 in cash for services provided.
	14	Paid creditors $10,750 of accounts payable.
	17	Purchased supplies on account $618.
	22	Billed customers for services provided $4,700.
	30	Paid employee salaries $3,114, utilities $1,467, and repairs $492.
	31	Paid $700 cash dividend.

Instructions

(a) Prepare a general ledger using T accounts. Enter the opening balances in the ledger accounts as of July 1. Provision should be made for the following additional accounts: Dividends, Dry Cleaning Revenue, Repair Expense, Salaries Expense, and Utilities Expense.

(b) Journalize the transactions.

(c) Post to the ledger accounts.

(d) Prepare a trial balance on July 31, 2005.

(d) Cash $ 4,023
Tot. trial
        balance $53,355

P3-7A This trial balance of Dubuque Company does not balance.

Prepare a correct trial balance.
(SO 8)

DUBUQUE COMPANY
Trial Balance
May 31, 2005

	Debit	Credit
Cash	$ 5,650	
Accounts Receivable		$ 2,750
Prepaid Insurance	700	
Equipment	8,000	
Accounts Payable		4,500
Property Taxes Payable	560	
Common Stock		5,700
Retained Earnings		6,000
Service Revenue	6,690	
Salaries Expense	4,200	
Advertising Expense		1,100
Property Tax Expense	800	
	$26,600	$20,050

Your review of the ledger reveals that each account has a normal balance. You also discover the following errors.

1. The totals of the debit sides of Prepaid Insurance, Accounts Payable, and Property Tax Expense were each understated $100.
2. Transposition errors were made in Accounts Receivable and Service Revenue. Based on postings made, the correct balances were $2,570 and $6,960, respectively.
3. A debit posting to Salaries Expense of $400 was omitted.
4. An $800 cash dividend was debited to Common Stock for $800 and credited to Cash for $800.
5. A $420 purchase of supplies on account was debited to Equipment for $420 and credited to Cash for $420.
6. A cash payment of $250 for advertising was debited to Advertising Expense for $25 and credited to Cash for $25.
7. A collection from a customer for $170 was debited to Cash for $170 and credited to Accounts Payable for $170.

Instructions

Cash $ 5,845
Tot. trial balance $24,670

Prepare the correct trial balance. (*Note:* The chart of accounts also includes the following: Dividends, Supplies, and Supplies Expense.)

Journalize transactions, post, and prepare a trial balance.
(SO 3, 5, 6, 7, 8)

Peachtree

P3-8A Rainbow Theater Inc. was recently formed. All facilities were completed on March 31. On April 1, the ledger showed: Cash $6,000; Land $10,000; Buildings (concession stand, projection room, ticket booth, and screen) $8,000; Equipment $6,000; Accounts Payable $2,000; Mortgage Payable $8,000; and Common Stock $20,000. During April, the following events and transactions occurred.

Apr. 2 Paid film rental fee of $1,100 on first movie.
3 Ordered two additional films at $900 each.
9 Received $3,800 cash from admissions.
10 Paid $2,000 of mortgage payable and $1,000 of accounts payable.
11 Hired R. Thoms to operate concession stand. Thoms agrees to pay Rainbow Theater 17% of gross receipts, payable monthly.
12 Paid advertising expenses $400.
20 Received one of the films ordered on April 3 and was billed $500. The film will be shown in April.
25 Received $3,000 cash from customers for admissions.
29 Paid salaries $1,600.
30 Received statement from R. Thoms showing gross receipts of $1,000 and the balance due to Rainbow Theater of $170 for April. Thoms paid half of the balance due and will remit the remainder on May 5.
30 Prepaid $1,000 rental fee on special film to be run in May.

In addition to the accounts identified above, the chart of accounts shows: Accounts Receivable, Prepaid Rentals, Admission Revenue, Concession Revenue, Advertising Expense, Film Rental Expense, Salaries Expense.

Instructions

(d) Cash $ 5,785
Tot. trial balance $34,470

(a) Enter the beginning balances in the ledger T accounts as of April 1.
(b) Journalize the April transactions, including explanations.
(c) Post the April journal entries to the ledger T accounts.
(d) Prepare a trial balance on April 30, 2005.

Analyze errors and their effects on the trial balance.
(SO 8)

P3-9A A first year co-op student working for Insidz.com recorded the transactions for the month. He wasn't exactly sure how to journalize and post, but he did the best he could. He had a few questions, however, about the following transactions.

1. Cash received from a customer on account was recorded as a debit to Cash of $560 and a credit to Accounts Receivable of $650, instead of $560.
2. A service provided for cash was posted as a debit to Cash of $2,000 and a credit to Service Revenue of $2,000.
3. A debit of $750 for services provided on account was neither recorded nor posted. The credit was recorded correctly.
4. The debit to record $1,000 of cash dividends was posted to the Salary Expense account.

5. The purchase, on account, of a computer that cost $2,500 was recorded as a debit to Supplies and a credit to Accounts Payable.
6. A cash payment of $495 for salaries was recorded as a debit to Salary Expense and a credit to Salaries Payable.
7. Payment of rent for the month was debited to Rent Expense and credited to Cash, $850.
8. Issue of $5,000 of common shares was credited to the Common Stock account, but no debit was recorded.

Instructions
(a) Indicate which of the above transactions are correct, and which are incorrect.
(b) For each error identified in (a), indicate (1) whether the trial balance will balance; (2) the amount of the difference if the trial balance will not balance; and (3) the trial balance column that will have the larger total. Consider each error separately. Use the following form, in which transaction 1 is given as an example.

Error	(1) In Balance	(2) Difference	(3) Larger Column
1.	No	$90	Credit

Problems: Set B

P3-1B   On April 1 Sierra Travel Agency Inc. was established. These transactions were completed during the month.

1. Stockholders invested $20,000 cash in the company in exchange for common stock.
2. Paid $700 cash for April office rent.
3. Purchased office equipment for $2,500 cash.
4. Purchased $300 of advertising in the *Chicago Tribune*, on account.
5. Paid $500 cash for office supplies.
6. Earned $9,000 for services provided: Cash of $1,000 is received from customers, and the balance of $8,000 is billed to customers on account.
7. Paid $400 cash dividends.
8. Paid *Chicago Tribune* amount due in transaction (4).
9. Paid employees' salaries $1,200.
10. Received $8,000 in cash from customers who have previously been billed in transaction (6).

Analyze transactions and compute net income. (SO 1)

Instructions
(a) Prepare a tabular analysis of the transactions using these column headings: Cash, Accounts Receivable, Supplies, Office Equipment, Accounts Payable, Common Stock, and Retained Earnings. Include margin explanations for any changes in Retained Earnings.
(b) From an analysis of the column Retained Earnings, compute the net income or net loss for April.

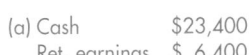
(a) Cash $23,400
    Ret. earnings $ 6,400

P3-2B   Brianna Brunn started her own consulting firm, Brunn Consulting Inc., on May 1, 2005. The following transactions occurred during the month of May.

May	1	Stockholders invested $10,000 cash in the business in exchange for common stock.
	2	Paid $800 for office rent for the month.
	3	Purchased $500 of supplies on account.
	5	Paid $150 to advertise in the *County News*.
	9	Received $1,000 cash for services provided.
	12	Paid $200 cash dividend.
	15	Performed $3,500 of services on account.
	17	Paid $2,500 for employee salaries.

Analyze transactions and prepare financial statements. (SO 1)

20 Paid for the supplies purchased on account on May 3.
23 Received a cash payment of $1,500 for services provided on account on May 15.
26 Borrowed $5,000 from the bank on a note payable.
29 Purchased office equipment for $2,400 on account.
30 Paid $150 for utilities.

Instructions

(a) Cash $13,200
Ret. earnings $ 700

(a) Show the effects of the previous transactions on the accounting equation using the following format. Assume the note payable is to be repaid within the year.

		Assets				Liabilities		Stockholders' Equity	
Date	Cash +	Accounts Receivable	+ Supplies +	Office Equipment	=	Notes Payable +	Accounts Payable +	Common Stock +	Retained Earnings

(b) Net income $900

Include margin explanations for any changes in Retained Earnings.
(b) Prepare an income statement for the month of May.
(c) Prepare a classified balance sheet at May 31, 2005.

Analyze transactions and prepare an income statement, retained earnings statement, and balance sheet.
(SO 1)

P3-3B Shawn Coleman created a corporation providing legal services, Shawn Coleman Inc., on July 1, 2005. On July 31 the balance sheet showed: Cash $4,000; Accounts Receivable $2,500; Supplies $500; Office Equipment $5,000; Accounts Payable $4,200; Common Stock $6,500; and Retained Earnings $1,300. During August the following transactions occurred.

1. Collected $2,000 of accounts receivable due from customers.
2. Paid $2,700 cash for accounts payable due.
3. Earned revenue of $6,400, of which $3,000 is collected in cash and the balance is due in September.
4. Purchased additional office equipment for $2,000, paying $400 in cash and the balance on account.
5. Paid salaries $1,500, rent for August $900, and advertising expenses $350.
6. Declared and paid a cash dividend of $550.
7. Received $2,000 from Standard Federal Bank; the money was borrowed on a 4-month note payable.
8. Incurred utility expenses for month on account $300.

Instructions

(a) Cash $4,600
Ret. earnings $4,100

(a) Prepare a tabular analysis of the August transactions beginning with July 31 balances. The column heading should be: Cash + Accounts Receivable + Supplies + Office Equipment = Notes Payable + Accounts Payable + Common Stock + Retained Earnings. Include margin explanations for any changes in Retained Earnings.

(b) Net income $3,350

(b) Prepare an income statement for August, a retained earnings statement for August, and a classified balance sheet at August 31.

Journalize a series of transactions.
(SO 3, 5)

P3-4B Gager Miniature Golf and Driving Range Inc. was opened on March 1 by Kevin Gager. These selected events and transactions occurred during March.

Mar. 1 Stockholders invested $60,000 cash in the business in exchange for common stock of the corporation.
3 Purchased Lee's Golf Land for $38,000 cash. The price consists of land $23,000, building $9,000, and equipment $6,000. (Record this in a single entry.)
5 Advertised the opening of the driving range and miniature golf course, paying advertising expenses of $1,600 cash.
6 Paid cash $1,800 for a 1-year insurance policy.
10 Purchased golf clubs and other equipment for $1,900 from Tiger Company, payable in 30 days.

18   Received golf fees of $1,200 in cash from customers for golf fees earned.

19   Sold 100 coupon books for $15.00 each in cash. Each book contains ten coupons that enable the holder to play one round of miniature golf or to hit one bucket of golf balls. (*Hint*: The revenue is not earned until the customers use the coupons.)

25   Declared and paid a $500 cash dividend.

30   Paid salaries of $700.

30   Paid Tiger Company in full for equipment purchased on March 10.

31   Received $800 of fees in cash from customers for golf fees earned.

The company uses these accounts: Cash, Prepaid Insurance, Land, Buildings, Equipment, Accounts Payable, Unearned Golf Revenue, Common Stock, Retained Earnings, Dividends, Golf Revenue, Advertising Expense, and Salaries Expense.

Instructions
Journalize the March transactions, including explanations.

P3-5B Kaffen Architects incorporated as licensed architects on April 1, 2005. During the first month of the operation of the business, these events and transactions occurred:

Journalize transactions, post, and prepare a trial balance.
(SO 3, 5, 6, 7, 8)

Apr. 1   Stockholders invested $16,000 cash in exchange for common stock of the corporation.

1   Hired a secretary-receptionist at a salary of $300 per week, payable monthly.

2   Paid office rent for the month $900.

3   Purchased architectural supplies on account from Halo Company $1,500.

10   Completed blueprints on a carport and billed client $1,100 for services.

11   Received $500 cash advance from R. Welk for the design of a new home.

20   Received $1,800 cash for services completed and delivered to P. Donahue.

30   Paid secretary-receptionist for the month $1,200.

30   Paid $600 to Halo Company for accounts payable due.

The company uses these accounts: Cash, Accounts Receivable, Supplies, Accounts Payable, Unearned Revenue, Common Stock, Service Revenue, Salaries Expense, and Rent Expense.

Instructions
(a) Journalize the transactions, including explanations.

(b) Post to the ledger T accounts.

(c) Prepare a trial balance on April 30, 2005.

(c) Cash $15,600
    Tot. trial
        balance $20,300

P3-6B This is the trial balance of Digital Company on September 30.

Journalize transactions, post, and prepare a trial balance.
(SO 3, 5, 6, 7, 8)

DIGITAL COMPANY
Trial Balance
September 30, 2005

	Debit	Credit
Cash	$ 8,500	
Accounts Receivable	2,200	
Supplies	2,100	
Equipment	8,000	
Accounts Payable		$ 5,000
Unearned Revenue		700
Common Stock		15,100
	$20,800	$20,800

The October transactions were as follows.

Oct.   5   Received $1,300 in cash from customers for accounts receivable due.

10   Billed customers for services performed $3,500.

15   Paid employee salaries $1,200.

Oct. 17   Performed $600 of services for customers who paid in advance in August.
    20   Paid $1,100 to creditors for accounts payable due.
    29   Paid a $500 cash dividend.
    31   Paid utilities $700.

Instructions

(a) Prepare a general ledger using T accounts. Enter the opening balances in the ledger accounts as of October 1. Provision should be made for these additional accounts: Dividends, Service Revenue, Salaries Expense, and Utilities Expense.

(d) Cash $ 6,300
    Tot. trial
    balance $23,200

(b) Journalize the transactions, including explanations.
(c) Post to the ledger accounts.
(d) Prepare a trial balance on October 31, 2005.

Prepare a correct trial balance.
(SO 8)

P3-7B   This trial balance of Garstka Co. does not balance.

GARSTKA CO.
Trial Balance
June 30, 2005

	Debit	Credit
Cash		$ 2,440
Accounts Receivable	$ 3,231	
Supplies	800	
Equipment	3,000	
Accounts Payable		2,666
Unearned Revenue	1,200	
Common Stock		9,000
Dividends	800	
Service Revenue		2,380
Salaries Expense	3,600	
Office Expense	910	
	$13,541	$16,486

Each of the listed accounts has a normal balance per the general ledger. An examination of the ledger and journal reveals the following errors:

1. Cash received from a customer on account was debited for $570, and Accounts Receivable was credited for the same amount. The actual collection was for $750.
2. The purchase of a typewriter on account for $340 was recorded as a debit to Supplies for $340 and a credit to Accounts Payable for $340.
3. Services were performed on account for a client for $890. Accounts Receivable was debited for $890 and Service Revenue was credited for $89.
4. A debit posting to Salaries Expense of $800 was omitted.
5. A payment on account for $206 was credited to Cash for $206 and credited to Accounts Payable for $260.
6. Payment of a $600 cash dividend to Garstka's stockholders was debited to Salaries Expense for $600 and credited to Cash for $600.

Instructions

Tot. trial balance $15,581

Prepare the correct trial balance.

Journalize transactions, post, and prepare a trial balance.
(SO 3, 5, 6, 7, 8)

P3-8B   The Good Times Theater Inc. was recently formed. It began operations in March 2005. The Good Times is unique in that it will show only triple features of sequential theme movies. As of February 28, the ledger of The Good Times showed: Cash $16,000; Land $42,000; Buildings (concession stand, projection room, ticket booth, and screen) $18,000; Equipment $16,000; Accounts Payable $12,000; and Common Stock $80,000. During the month of March the following events and transactions occurred.

Mar. 2   Rented the three *Star Wars* movies (*Star Wars®*, *The Empire Strikes Back*, and *The Return of the Jedi*) to be shown for the first three weeks of March. The film rental was $12,000; $4,000 was paid in cash and $8,000 will be paid on March 10.

   3   Ordered the first three *Star Trek* movies to be shown the last 10 days of March. It will cost $400 per night.

   9   Received $8,500 cash from admissions.

   10 Paid balance due on *Star Wars* movies rental and $2,600 on February 28 accounts payable.

   11 Hired M. Brewer to operate concession stand. Brewer agrees to pay The Good Times Theater 15% of gross receipts, payable monthly.

   12 Paid advertising expenses $800.

   20 Received $7,500 cash from customers for admissions.

   20 Received the *Star Trek* movies and paid rental fee of $4,000.

   31 Paid salaries of $3,800.

   31 Received statement from M. Brewer showing gross receipts from concessions of $8,000 and the balance due to The Good Times of $1,200 for March. Brewer paid half the balance due and will remit the remainder on April 5.

   31 Received $20,000 cash from customers for admissions.

In addition to the accounts identified above, the chart of accounts includes: Accounts Receivable, Admission Revenue, Concession Revenue, Advertising Expense, Film Rental Expense, and Salaries Expense.

Instructions
(a) Using T accounts, enter the beginning balances to the ledger.
(b) Journalize the March transactions, including explanations.
(c) Post the March journal entries to the ledger.
(d) Prepare a trial balance on March 31, 2005.

(d) Cash $ 29,400
Tot. trial
  balance $126,600

P3-9B   The bookkeeper for Katie Cater's dance studio made the following errors in journalizing and posting.

Analyze errors and their effects on the trial balance.
(SO 8)

1. A credit to Supplies of $600 was omitted.
2. A debit posting of $300 to Accounts Payable was inadvertently debited to Accounts Receivable.
3. A purchase of supplies on account of $450 was debited to Supplies for $540 and credited to Accounts Payable for $540.
4. A credit posting of $250 to Wages Payable was posted twice.
5. A debit posting to Wages Payable for $250 and a credit posting to Cash for $250 were made twice.
6. A debit posting for $1,000 of Dividends was inadvertently posted to Travel Expense instead.
7. A credit to Service Revenue for $400 was inadvertently posted as a debit to Service Revenue.
8. A credit to Accounts Receivable of $250 was omitted and was credited to Accounts Payable.

Instructions
For each error, indicate (a) whether the trial balance will balance; (b) the amount of the difference if the trial balance will not balance; and (c) the trial balance column that will have the larger total. Consider each error separately. Use the following form, in which error 1 is given as an example.

Error	(a) In Balance	(b) Difference	(c) Larger Column
1.	No	$600	Debit

▶ BROADENING YOUR PERSPECTIVE

Financial Reporting and Analysis

FINANCIAL REPORTING PROBLEM: *Tootsie Roll Industries*

BYP3-1   The financial statements of **Tootsie Roll** in Appendix A at the back of this book contain the following selected accounts, all in thousands of dollars.

Common Stock	$ 23,783
Accounts Payable	12,505
Accounts Receivable	22,686
Selling, Marketing, and Administrative Expense	75,751
Prepaid Expenses	3,819
Property, Plant, and Equipment	248,951
Net Sales	393,185

Instructions
- **(a)** What is the increase and decrease side for each account? What is the normal balance for each account?
- **(b)** Identify the probable other account in the transaction and the effect on that account when:
  - **(1)** Accounts Receivable is decreased.
  - **(2)** Accounts Payable is decreased.
  - **(3)** Prepaid Expenses is increased.
- **(c)** Identify the other account(s) that ordinarily would be involved when:
  - **(1)** Interest Expense is increased.
  - **(2)** Property, Plant, and Equipment is increased.

COMPARATIVE ANALYSIS PROBLEM: *Tootsie Roll vs. Hershey Foods*

BYP3-2   The financial statements of **Hershey Foods** are presented in Appendix B, following the financial statements for **Tootsie Roll** in Appendix A.

Instructions
- **(a)** Based on the information contained in these financial statements, determine the normal balance for:

Tootsie Roll Industries	**Hershey Foods**
(1) Accounts Receivable	(1) Inventories
(2) Property, Plant, and Equipment	(2) Provision for Income Taxes
(3) Accounts Payable	(3) Accrued Liabilities
(4) Retained Earnings	(4) Common Stock
(5) Net Sales	(5) Interest Expense

- **(b)** Identify the other account ordinarily involved when:
  - **(1)** Accounts Receivable is increased.
  - **(2)** Notes Payable is decreased.
  - **(3)** Machinery is increased.
  - **(4)** Interest Income is increased.

RESEARCH CASE

BYP3-3   The North American Industry Classification System (NAICS), a new classification system for organizing economic data, has recently replaced the separate standard classification systems previously used by Canada, the United States, and Mexico. NAICS provides a common standard framework for the collection of economic and financial data for all three nations.

Instructions
At your library, find the *NAICS Manual,* and answer the following.
  (a) The NAICS numbering system uses five levels of detail to identify company activities. What do the first two digits identify? The fourth digit? The sixth digit?
  (b) Identify the sector, subsector, industry group, NAICS industry, and U.S. industry represented by the code 513322.

INTERPRETING FINANCIAL STATEMENTS

BYP3-4   Chieftain International, Inc., is an oil and natural gas exploration and production company. A recent balance sheet reported $208 million in assets with only $4.6 million in liabilities, all of which were short-term accounts payable.

During the year, Chieftain expanded its holdings of oil and gas rights, drilled 37 new wells, and invested in expensive 3-D seismic technology. The company generated $19 million cash from operating activities and paid no dividends. It had a cash balance of $102 million at the end of the year.

Instructions
  (a) Name at least two advantages to Chieftain from having no long-term debt. Can you think of disadvantages?
  (b) What are some of the advantages to Chieftain from having this large a cash balance? What is a disadvantage?
  (c) Why do you suppose Chieftain has the $4.6 million balance in accounts payable, since it appears that it could have made all its purchases for cash?

A GLOBAL FOCUS

BYP3-5   Doman Industries Ltd., whose products are sold in 30 countries worldwide, is an integrated Canadian forest products company.

Doman sells the majority of its lumber products in the United States, and a significant amount of its pulp products in Asia. Doman also has loans from other countries. For example, the Company borrowed US$160 million at an annual interest rate of 12%. Doman must repay this loan, and interest, in U.S. dollars.

One of the challenges global companies face is to make themselves attractive to investors from other countries. This is difficult to do when different accounting rules in different countries blur the real impact of earnings. For example, in a recent year Doman reported a loss of $2.3 million, using Canadian accounting rules. Had it reported under U.S. accounting rules, its loss would have been $12.1 million.

Many companies that want to be more easily compared with U.S. and other global competitors have switched to U.S. accounting principles. **Canadian National Railway, Corel, Cott, Inco,** and **Thomson Corporation** are but a few examples of large Canadian companies whose financial statements are now presented in U.S. dollars, adhere to U.S. GAAP, or are reconciled to U.S. GAAP.

Instructions
  (a) Identify advantages and disadvantages that companies should consider when switching to U.S. reporting standards.
  (b) Suppose you compare Doman Industries to a U.S.-based competitor. Do you believe the use of country-specific accounting policies would hinder your ability to compare the companies? If so, explain how.
  (c) Suppose you compare Doman Industries to a Canadian-based competitor. If the companies apply generally acceptable Canadian accounting policies differently, how could this affect your ability to compare their financial results?
  (d) Do you see any significant distinction between comparing statements prepared using generally accepted accounting principles of different countries and comparing statements prepared using generally accepted accounting principles of the same country (e.g. U.S.) but that apply the principles differently?

FINANCIAL ANALYSIS ON THE WEB

BYP3-6   *Purpose:* This activity provides information about career opportunities for CPAs.

Address: www.futurecpa.org (or go to **www.wiley.com/college/kimmel**)

Careers in Accounting

Steps
1. Go to the address shown above.
2. Click on CPA101.

Instructions
Answer the following questions.
 (a) What does CPA stand for? Where do CPAs work?
 (b) What is meant by "public accounting"?
 (c) What skills does a CPA need?
 (d) What is the salary range for a CPA at a large firm during the first three years? What is the salary range for chief financial officers and treasurers at large corporations?

Critical Thinking

GROUP DECISION CASE

BYP3-7 Lisa Laurel operates Double L Riding Academy, Inc. The academy's primary sources of revenue are riding fees and lesson fees, which are provided on a cash basis. Lisa also boards horses for owners, who are billed monthly for boarding fees. In a few cases, boarders pay in advance of expected use. For its revenue transactions, the academy maintains these accounts: Cash, Accounts Receivable, Unearned Revenue, Riding Revenue, Lesson Revenue, and Boarding Revenue.

The academy owns 10 horses, a stable, a riding corral, riding equipment, and office equipment. These assets are accounted for in accounts Horses, Building, Riding Corral, Riding Equipment, and Office Equipment.

The academy employs stable helpers and an office employee, who receive weekly salaries. At the end of each month, the mail usually brings bills for advertising, utilities, and veterinary service. Other expenses include feed for the horses and insurance. For its expenses, the academy maintains the following accounts: Hay and Feed Supplies, Prepaid Insurance, Accounts Payable, Salaries Expense, Advertising Expense, Utilities Expense, Veterinary Expense, Hay and Feed Expense, and Insurance Expense.

Lisa Laurel's sole source of personal income is dividends from the academy. Thus, the corporation declares and pays periodic dividends. To record stockholders' equity in the business and dividends, two accounts are maintained: Common Stock and Dividends.

During the first month of operations an inexperienced bookkeeper was employed. Lisa Laurel asks you to review the following eight entries of the 50 entries made during the month. In each case, the explanation for the entry is correct.

May	1	Cash	15,000	
		Common Stock		15,000
		(Issued common stock in exchange for $15,000 cash)		
	5	Cash	250	
		Riding Revenue		250
		(Received $250 cash for lesson fees)		
	7	Cash	500	
		Boarding Revenue		500
		(Received $500 for boarding of horses beginning June 1)		
	9	Hay and Feed Expense	1,700	
		Cash		1,700
		(Purchased estimated 5 months' supply of feed and hay for $1,700 on account)		
	14	Riding Equipment	80	
		Cash		800
		(Purchased desk and other office equipment for $800 cash)		

May 15	Salaries Expense	400	
	Cash		400
	(Issued check to Lisa Laurel for personal use)		
20	Cash	145	
	Riding Revenue		154
	(Received $154 cash for riding fees)		
31	Veterinary Expense	75	
	Accounts Payable		75
	(Received bill of $75 from veterinarian for services provided)		

Instructions

With the class divided into groups, answer the following.

(a) For each journal entry that is correct, so state. For each journal entry that is incorrect, prepare the entry that should have been made by the bookkeeper.

(b) Which of the incorrect entries would prevent the trial balance from balancing?

(c) What was the correct net income for May, assuming the bookkeeper originally reported net income of $4,500 after posting all 50 entries?

(d) What was the correct cash balance at May 31, assuming the bookkeeper reported a balance of $12,475 after posting all 50 entries?

COMMUNICATION ACTIVITY

BYP3-8   White Glove Company offers home cleaning service. Two recurring transactions for the company are billing customers for services provided and paying employee salaries. For example, on March 15 bills totaling $6,000 were sent to customers, and $2,000 was paid in salaries to employees.

Instructions

Write a memorandum to your instructor that explains and illustrates the steps in the recording process for each of the March 15 transactions. Use the format illustrated in the text under the heading "The Recording Process Illustrated" (p. 121).

ETHICS CASE

BYP3-9   Sue Bensch is the assistant chief accountant at Digitech Company, a manufacturer of computer chips and cellular phones. The company presently has total sales of $20 million. It is the end of the first quarter and Sue is hurriedly trying to prepare a general ledger trial balance so that quarterly financial statements can be prepared and released to management and the regulatory agencies. The total credits on the trial balance exceed the debits by $1,000.

In order to meet the 4 P.M. deadline, Sue decides to force the debits and credits into balance by adding the amount of the difference to the Equipment account. She chose Equipment because it is one of the larger account balances; percentage-wise it will be the least misstated. Sue plugs the difference! She believes that the difference is quite small and will not affect anyone's decisions. She wishes that she had another few days to find the error but realizes that the financial statements are already late.

Instructions

(a) Who are the stakeholders in this situation?

(b) What ethical issues are involved?

(c) What are Sue's alternatives?

Answers to Self-Study Questions

1. b   2. b   3. b   4. c   5. d   6. d   7. b   8. a   9. c   10. d

11. a   12. c

Answer to Tootsie Roll Review It Question 4, p. 116

Normal balances for accounts in **Tootsie Roll**'s financial statements: Accounts Receivable—debit; Income Taxes Payable —credit; Sales—credit; Selling, Marketing, and Administrative Expense — debit.

Remember to go back to the Navigator box on the chapter-opening page and check off your completed work.

Accrual Accounting Concepts

STUDY OBJECTIVES

After studying this chapter,
you should be able to:

1 Explain the revenue recognition principle and the matching principle.

2 Differentiate between the cash basis and the accrual basis of accounting.

3 Explain why adjusting entries are needed, and identify the major types of adjusting entries.

4 Prepare adjusting entries for prepayments.

5 Prepare adjusting entries for accruals.

6 Describe the nature and purpose of the adjusted trial balance.

7 Explain the purpose of closing entries.

8 Describe the required steps in the accounting cycle.

 THE NAVIGATOR

THE NAVIGATOR ✔

▶ Scan *Study Objectives* ☐

▶ Read *Feature Story* ☐

▶ Read *Preview* ☐

▶ Read text and answer *Before You Go On*
p. 163 ☐   p. 171 ☐   p. 177 ☐
p. 186 ☐

▶ Work Using the *Decision Toolkit* ☐

▶ Review Summary of *Study Objectives* ☐

▶ Work *Demonstration Problem* ☐

▶ Answer *Self-Study Questions* ☐

▶ Complete *Assignments* ☐

FEATURE STORY

Swapping Quarters

The accuracy of the financial reporting system depends on answers to a few fundamental questions. At what point has revenue been earned? At what point is the earnings process complete? When have expenses really been incurred?

To see the significance of these questions consider a simple example. Early one spring morning a brother and sister opened a lemonade stand in front of their house. As their neighbor left for work she bought a glass of lemonade for a quarter. Unfortunately, it was a cool day, and the kids lived on a lightly traveled cul-de-sac. In short, business was slow.

After an hour passed, with no more customers, the brother decided to buy a glass of lemonade. He took the quarter received from the neighbor, passed it to his sister, and then enjoyed a glass of lemonade. A short time later, the sister decided to buy a glass of lemonade. She picked up the quarter, passed it to her brother, and then enjoyed a glass of lemonade.

Within an hour, after passing the quarter back and forth, they had finished off the pitcher of lemonade. They walked in to their house and told their parents how great business had been. They had sold the whole pitcher in less than two hours. The only thing they couldn't figure out was, why, after so many transactions, they had only a quarter to show for their efforts.

Before you're too critical of these siblings consider this: During the 1990s' boom in the stock prices of dot-com companies, many dot-com

companies earned most of their revenue from selling advertising space on their Web sites. To boost reported revenue, some dot-coms began swapping Web-site ad space. Company A would put an ad for its Web site on company B's Web site, and company B would put an ad for its Web site on company A's Web site. No money changed hands, but each company recorded revenue (for the value of the space that it gave up on its site). This practice did little to boost net income and resulted in no additional cash flow—but it did boost *reported revenue*. Regulators eventually put an end to the practice.

Another type of transgression results from companies recording revenue or expenses in the wrong year. In fact, shifting revenues and expenses is one of the most common abuses of financial accounting. **Xerox** recently admitted reporting billions of dollars of lease revenue in periods earlier than it should have been reported. And **WorldCom** stunned the financial markets with its admission that it had boosted 2001 net

income by billions of dollars by delaying the recognition of expenses until later years.

Unfortunately, revelations such as these have become all too common in the corporate world. It is no wonder that in June 2002 the U.S. Trust Survey of affluent Americans reported that 85 percent of its respondents believed that there should be tighter regulation of financial disclosures, and 66 percent said they did not trust the management of publicly traded companies.

Why did so many companies violate basic financial reporting rules and sound ethics? Many speculate that as stock prices climbed, executives were under increasing pressure to meet higher and higher earnings expectations. If actual results weren't as good as hoped for, some gave in to temptation and "adjusted" their numbers to meet market expectations.

☑ THE NAVIGATOR

As indicated in the Feature Story, making adjustments properly is important and necessary. To do otherwise leads to a misstatement of revenues and expenses. In this chapter we introduce you to the accrual accounting concepts that make such adjustments possible.

The organization and content of the chapter are as follows.

ACCRUAL ACCOUNTING CONCEPTS

Timing Issues	The Basics of Adjusting Entries	The Adjusted Trial Balance and Financial Statements	Closing the Books	Summary of the Accounting Cycle
• Revenue recognition principle • Matching principle • Accrual versus cash accounting	• Types of adjusting entries • Adjusting entries for prepayments • Adjusting entries for accruals • Summary of basic relationships	• Preparing the adjusted trial balance • Preparing financial statements	• Preparing closing entries • Preparing a post-closing trial balance	

THE NAVIGATOR

Timing Issues

Consider the following story.

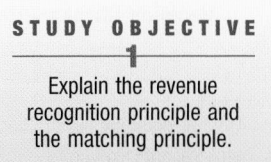

STUDY OBJECTIVE
1
Explain the revenue recognition principle and the matching principle.

> A grocery store owner from the old country kept his accounts payable on a spindle, accounts receivable on a note pad, and cash in a cigar box. His daughter, a certified public accountant, chided her father: "I don't understand how you can run your business this way. How do you know what your profits are?"
>
> "Well," the father replied, "when I got off the boat 40 years ago, I had nothing but the pants I was wearing. Today your brother is a doctor, your sister is a college professor, and you are a CPA. Your mother and I have a nice car, a well-furnished house, and a lake home. We have a good business and everything is paid for. So, you add all that together, subtract the pants, and there's your profit."

Although the old grocer may be correct in his evaluation of how to calculate income over his lifetime, most businesses need more immediate feedback about how well they are doing. For example, management usually wants monthly reports on financial results, most large corporations are required to present quarterly and annual financial statements to stockholders, and the Internal Revenue Service requires all businesses to file annual tax returns. **Accounting divides the economic life of a business into artificial time periods.** As indicated in

Chapter 1, this is the time period assumption. **Accounting time periods are generally a month, a quarter, or a year.**

Many business transactions affect more than one of these arbitrary time periods. For example, a new building purchased by Citigroup or a new airplane purchased by Delta Air Lines will be used for many years. It doesn't make sense to expense the full cost of the building or the airplane at the time of purchase because each will be used for many subsequent periods. Instead, we must determine the impact of each transaction on specific accounting periods.

Determining the amount of revenues and expenses to report in a given accounting period can be difficult. Proper reporting requires an understanding of the nature of the company's business. Two principles are used as guidelines: the revenue recognition principle and the matching principle.

THE REVENUE RECOGNITION PRINCIPLE

Revenue Recognition

Service performed

Customer requests service — At time cash received

Revenue should be recognized in the accounting period in which it is earned (generally when service is performed).

The revenue recognition principle dictates that revenue should be recognized in the accounting period **in which it is earned**. In a service company, revenue is considered to be earned at the time the service is performed. To illustrate, assume a dry cleaning business cleans clothing on June 30, but customers do not claim and pay for their clothes until the first week of July. Under the revenue recognition principle, revenue is earned in June when the service is performed, not in July when the cash is received. At June 30 the dry cleaner would report a receivable on its balance sheet and revenue in its income statement for the service performed.

Improper application of the revenue recognition principle can have devastating consequences for investors. For example, the stock price of outdoor equipment manufacturer The North Face plunged when it announced that $9 million of sales that had been recorded in a previous year were being reversed because North Face had repurchased the goods from the customer. This raised the question of whether a sale should have been recorded in the first place. Recently, investors also lost money because of improper revenue recognition at Xerox, MicroStrategy, and Enron.

DECISION TOOLKIT

Decision Checkpoints	Info Needed for Decision	Tool to Use for Decision	How to Evaluate Results
At what point should the company record revenue?	Need to understand the nature of the company's business	Revenue should be recorded when earned. For a service business, revenue is earned when service is performed.	Recognizing revenue too early overstates current period revenue; recognizing it too late understates current period revenue.

THE MATCHING PRINCIPLE

In recognizing expenses, a simple rule is followed: "Let the expenses follow the revenues." Thus, expense recognition is tied to revenue recognition. Applied to the preceding example, this means that the salary expense incurred in performing the cleaning service on June 30 should be reported in the same period in which the service revenue is recognized. The critical issue in expense recognition is determining when the expense makes its contribution to revenue. This may or may not be the same period in which the expense is paid. If the salary incurred on June 30 is not paid until July, the dry cleaner would report salaries payable on its June 30 balance sheet. The practice of expense recognition is referred to as the **matching principle** because it dictates that efforts (expenses) be matched with accomplishments (revenues). These relationships are shown in Illustration 4-1.

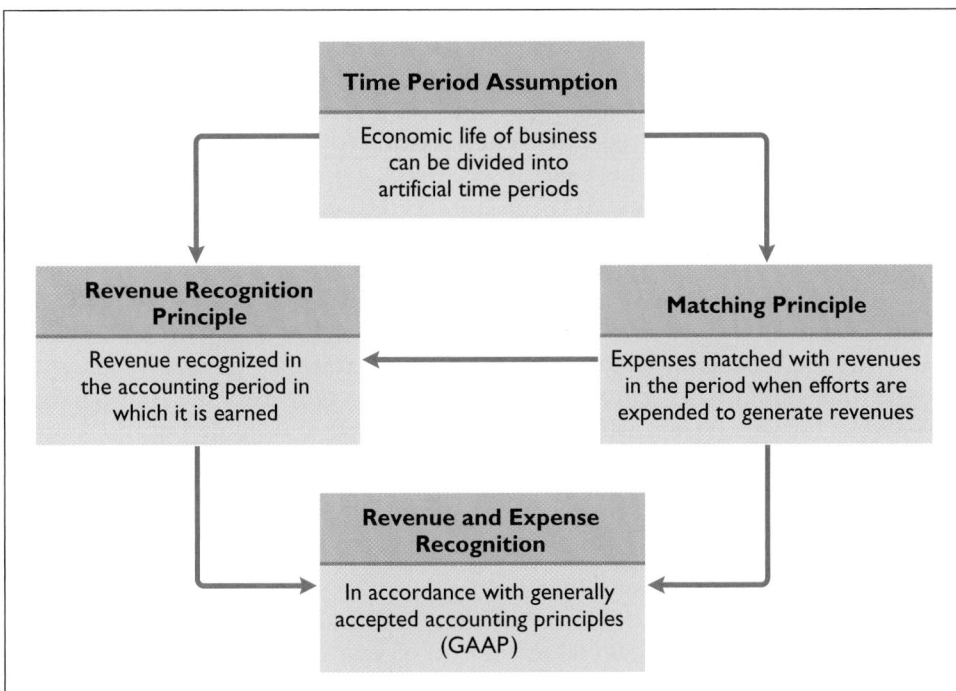

Illustration 4-1 GAAP relationships in revenue and expense recognition

Business Insight
MANAGEMENT PERSPECTIVE

Suppose you are a filmmaker like George Lucas and spend $11 million to produce a film such as *StarWars*. Over what period should the cost be expensed? Of course, it should be expensed over the economic life of the film. But what is its economic life? The filmmaker must estimate how much revenue will be earned from box office sales, video sales, television, and games and toys—a period that could be less than a year or more than 20 years, as is the case for **Twentieth Century Fox**'s *StarWars*. Originally released in 1977, and rereleased in 1997, domestic revenues total nearly $500 million for *StarWars* and continue to grow. This situation demonstrates the difficulty of properly matching expenses to revenues.

SOURCE: StarTrek Newsletter.

DECISION TOOLKIT

Decision Checkpoints	Info Needed for Decision	Tool to Use for Decision	How to Evaluate Results
At what point should the company record expenses?	Need to understand the nature of the company's business	Expenses should "follow" revenues—that is, the effort (expense) should be matched with the result (revenue).	Recognizing expenses too early overstates current period expense; recognizing them too late understates current period expense.

ACCRUAL VERSUS CASH BASIS OF ACCOUNTING

The combined application of the revenue recognition principle and the matching principle results in accrual basis accounting. **Accrual basis accounting** means that transactions that change a company's financial statements are recorded **in the periods in which the events occur**, rather than when the company actually receives or pays cash. For example, using the accrual basis to determine net income means recognizing revenues **when earned** (the revenue recognition principle) **rather than when the cash is received. Likewise, under the accrual basis, expenses are recognized when incurred** (the matching principle) **rather than when paid**.

An alternative to the accrual basis is the cash basis. Under **cash basis accounting**, **revenue is recorded only when the cash is received, and an expense is recorded only when cash is paid. Preparing an income statement under the cash basis of accounting is prohibited under generally accepted accounting principles.** Why? Because it fails to record revenue that has been earned but for which the cash has not been received, thus violating the revenue recognition principle. Nor does a cash-basis income statement match expenses with earned revenues, which violates the matching principle.

Illustration 4-2 compares accrual-based numbers and cash-based numbers, using a simple example. Suppose that you own a painting business and you paint a large building during year 1. In year 1 you incurred and paid total expenses of $50,000, which includes the cost of the paint and your employees' salaries. You billed your customer $80,000 at the end of year 1, but you weren't paid until year 2. On an accrual basis, you would report the revenue during the period earned—year 1—and the expenses would be matched to the period in which the revenues were earned. Thus, your net income for year 1 would be $30,000, and no revenue or expense from this project would be reported in year 2. The $30,000 of income reported for year 1 provides a useful indication of the profitability of your efforts during that period.

If, instead, you were reporting on a cash basis, you would report expenses of $50,000 in year 1 and revenues of $80,000 in year 2. Net income for year 1 would be a loss of $50,000, while net income for year 2 would be $80,000. The

Illustration 4-2 Accrual versus cash basis accounting

	Year 1	Year 2
Activity	Purchased paint, painted building, paid employees	Received payment for work done in year 1
Accrual basis	Revenue $80,000 Expense 50,000 Net income $30,000	Revenue $ 0 Expense 0 Net income $ 0
Cash basis	Revenue $ 0 Expense 50,000 Net loss $(50,000)	Revenue $80,000 Expense 0 Net income $80,000

cash basis measures are not very informative about the results of your efforts during year 1 or year 2.

Although most companies use the accrual basis of accounting, some small companies use the cash basis because they have few receivables and payables. For these companies, the cash basis might approximate the accrual basis.

Business Insight
INTERNATIONAL PERSPECTIVE

The United States government essentially uses a cash-basis accounting system rather than an accrual system. In fact, nearly all governments worldwide use a cash-basis system.

One exception is New Zealand. New Zealand employs accrual accounting to make departmental managers more aware of the costs of various programs (such as the pension plans of government employees) and of the value of government assets, such as buildings and parks. Proponents of governmental accrual-basis accounting suggest that political debates would be less murky if the U.S. government also were to adopt accrual accounting concepts.

BEFORE YOU GO ON . . .

▶ **Review It**

1. What are the revenue recognition and matching principles?
2. What are the differences between the cash and accrual bases of accounting?

☑ THE NAVIGATOR

The Basics of Adjusting Entries

The key idea about accrual accounting is this: Revenues are recognized (recorded) when they are earned; expenses are recognized (recorded) when they are incurred (used up).

In order for revenues to be recorded in the period in which they are earned, and for expenses to be recognized in the period in which they are incurred, adjusting entries are made to revenue and expense accounts at the end of the accounting period. In short, adjusting entries **are needed to ensure that the revenue recognition and matching principles are followed**.

Adjusting entries make it possible to produce accurate financial statements at the end of the accounting period. Thus, the balance sheet reports appropriate assets, liabilities, and stockholders' equity at the statement date, and the income statement shows the proper net income (or loss) for the period. Adjusting entries are necessary because the **trial balance**—the first pulling together of the transaction data—may not contain up-to-date and complete data. This is true for several reasons:

1. Some events are not journalized daily because it would not be useful or efficient to do so. Examples are the use of supplies and the earning of wages by employees.
2. Some costs are not journalized during the accounting period because these costs expire with the passage of time rather than as a result of recurring daily transactions. Examples of such costs are charges to reflect the use of buildings and equipment, rent, and insurance.

STUDY OBJECTIVE
3
Explain why adjusting entries are needed, and identify the major types of adjusting entries.

3. Some items may be unrecorded. An example is a utility service bill that will not be received until the next accounting period.

Adjusting entries are required every time financial statements are prepared. Each account in the trial balance is analyzed to determine whether it is complete and up to date for financial statement purposes.

TYPES OF ADJUSTING ENTRIES

Adjusting entries are classified as either prepayments or accruals. Each of these classes has two subcategories as shown in Illustration 4-3.

Illustration 4-3
Categories of adjusting entries

Prepayments:

1. **Prepaid expenses**: Expenses paid in cash and recorded as assets before they are used or consumed.
2. **Unearned revenues**: Cash received and recorded as liabilities before revenue is earned.

Accruals:

1. **Accrued revenues**: Revenues earned but not yet received in cash or recorded.
2. **Accrued expenses**: Expenses incurred but not yet paid in cash or recorded.

Specific examples and explanations of each type of adjustment are given in subsequent sections. Each example is based on the October 31 trial balance of Sierra Corporation, from Chapter 3, reproduced below in Illustration 4-4. Note that Retained Earnings, with a zero balance, has been added to this trial balance. We will explain its use later.

Illustration 4-4 Trial balance

SIERRA CORPORATION Trial Balance October 31, 2005		
	Debit	**Credit**
Cash	$15,200	
Advertising Supplies	2,500	
Prepaid Insurance	600	
Office Equipment	5,000	
Notes Payable		$ 5,000
Accounts Payable		2,500
Unearned Service Revenue		1,200
Common Stock		10,000
Retained Earnings		0
Dividends	500	
Service Revenue		10,000
Salaries Expense	4,000	
Rent Expense	900	
	$28,700	$28,700

We will assume that Sierra Corporation uses an accounting period of one month. Thus, monthly adjusting entries will be made. The entries will be dated October 31.

ADJUSTING ENTRIES FOR PREPAYMENTS

Prepayments are either prepaid expenses or unearned revenues. Adjusting entries for prepayments are required at the statement date to record the portion of the prepayment that represents the expense incurred or the revenue earned in the current accounting period.

Prepaid Expenses

Payments of expenses that will benefit more than one accounting period are called **prepaid expenses** or **prepayments**. When expenses are prepaid, an asset account is increased (debited) to show the service or benefit that will be received in the future. Examples of common prepayments are insurance, supplies, advertising, and rent. In addition, prepayments are made when buildings and equipment are purchased.

Prepaid expenses are costs that expire either with the passage of time (e.g., rent and insurance) or through use (e.g., supplies). The expiration of these costs does not require daily entries, which would be impractical and unnecessary. Accordingly, we postpone the recognition of such cost expirations until financial statements are prepared. At each statement date, adjusting entries are made to record the expenses applicable to the current accounting period and to show the remaining amounts in the asset accounts.

Prior to adjustment, assets are overstated and expenses are understated. Therefore, as shown in Illustration 4-5, **an adjusting entry for prepaid expenses results in an increase (a debit) to an expense account and a decrease (a credit) to an asset account**.

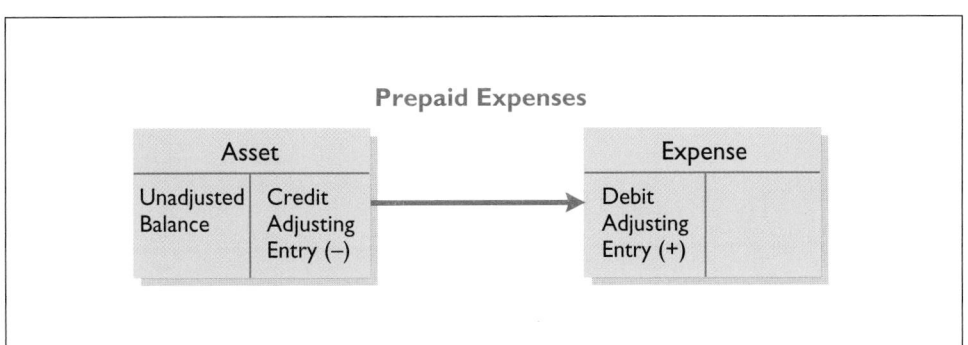

Illustration 4-5 Adjusting entries for prepaid expenses

Let's look in more detail at some specific types of prepaid expenses, beginning with supplies.

SUPPLIES. The purchase of supplies, such as paper and envelopes, results in an increase (a debit) to an asset account. During the accounting period, supplies are used. Rather than record supplies expense as the supplies are used, supplies expense is recognized at the **end** of the accounting period. At the end of the accounting period the company must count the remaining supplies. The difference between the unadjusted balance in the Supplies (asset) account and the actual cost of supplies on hand represents the supplies used (an expense) for that period.

Recall from the facts presented in Chapter 3 that Sierra Corporation purchased advertising supplies costing $2,500 on October 5. The payment was recorded by increasing (debiting) the asset Advertising Supplies. This account shows a balance of $2,500 in the October 31 trial balance. An inventory count at the close of business on October 31 reveals that $1,000 of supplies are still on hand. Thus, the cost of supplies used is $1,500 ($2,500 − $1,000). This use of

Supplies

Oct. 5

Supplies purchased; record asset

Sierra Corporation

Oct. 31
Supplies used; record supplies expense

supplies decreases an asset, Advertising Supplies. It also decreases stockholders' equity by increasing an expense account, Advertising Supplies Expense. The use of supplies affects the accounting equation in the following way.

Assets	=	Liabilities	+	Stockholders' Equity
−$1,500				−$1,500

Thus, the following entry is made:

Oct. 31	Advertising Supplies Expense	1,500	
	Advertising Supplies		1,500
	(To record supplies used)		

After the adjusting entry is posted, the two supplies accounts, in T account form, are as shown in Illustration 4-6.

Illustration 4-6 Supplies accounts after adjustment

Advertising Supplies				Advertising Supplies Expense	
Oct. 5	2,500	Oct. 31 **Adj. 1,500**		Oct. 31 **Adj. 1,500**	
Oct. 31 **Bal. 1,000**				Oct. 31 **Bal. 1,500**	

The asset account Advertising Supplies now shows a balance of $1,000, which is equal to the cost of supplies on hand at the statement date. In addition, Advertising Supplies Expense shows a balance of $1,500, which equals the cost of supplies used in October. **If the adjusting entry is not made, October expenses will be understated and net income overstated by $1,500. Moreover, both assets and stockholders' equity will be overstated by $1,500 on the October 31 balance sheet.**

Business Insight
MANAGEMENT PERSPECTIVE

In the past, the costs of media advertising for burgers, bleaches, athletic shoes, and such products were sometimes recorded as assets and expensed in subsequent periods as sales took place. The reasoning behind this treatment was that long ad campaigns provided benefits over multiple accounting periods. Today this treatment is no longer allowed because it was decided that the benefits were too difficult to measure. Instead, advertising costs must be expensed when the advertising takes place. The issue is important because the outlays for advertising can be substantial. Recent (2001) big spenders: **Coca-Cola** spent $2 billion, **PepsiCo., Inc.** $1.7 billion, **Campbell Soup Company** $1.7 billion, and **JCPenney Company** $947 million.

INSURANCE. Companies purchase insurance to protect themselves from losses due to fire, theft, and unforeseen events. Insurance must be paid in advance, often for more than one year. The cost of insurance (premiums) paid in advance is normally recorded in the asset account Prepaid Insurance. At the financial statement date it is necessary to increase (debit) Insurance Expense and decrease (credit) Prepaid Insurance for the cost of insurance that has expired during the period.

On October 4 Sierra Corporation paid $600 for a one-year fire insurance policy. Coverage began on October 1. The payment was recorded by increasing (debiting) Prepaid Insurance when it was paid. This account shows a balance of $600 in the October 31 trial balance. An analysis of the policy reveals that $50 ($600 ÷ 12) of insurance expires each month. The expiration of Prepaid Insurance would have the following impact on the accounting equation in October (and in each of the next 11 months).

Assets	=	**Liabilities**	+	**Stockholders' Equity**
−$50				−$50

Thus, the following adjusting entry is made.

Oct. 31	Insurance Expense	50	
	Prepaid Insurance		50
	(To record insurance expired)		

After the adjusting entry is posted, the accounts appear as in Illustration 4-7.

Illustration 4-7 Insurance accounts after adjustment

Prepaid Insurance

Oct. 4	600	Oct. 31	**Adj. 50**
Oct. 31	Bal. 550		

Insurance Expense

Oct. 31	**Adj. 50**		
Oct. 31	Bal. 50		

The asset Prepaid Insurance shows a balance of $550, which represents the cost that applies to the remaining 11 months of coverage. At the same time the balance in Insurance Expense is equal to the insurance cost that was used in October. If this adjustment is not made, October expenses would be understated by $50 and net income overstated by $50. Moreover, as the accounting equation shows, both assets and stockholders' equity will be overstated by $50 on the October 31 balance sheet.

DEPRECIATION.   A company typically owns a variety of assets that have long lives, such as buildings, equipment, and motor vehicles. The period of service is referred to as the **useful life** of the asset. Because a building is expected to provide service for many years, it is recorded as an asset, rather than an expense, on the date it is acquired. As explained in Chapter 1, such assets are recorded **at cost**, as required by the cost principle. According to the matching principle, a portion of this cost should then be reported as an expense during each period of the asset's useful life. **Depreciation** is the process of allocating the cost of an asset to expense over its useful life.

Need for Adjustment.   From an accounting standpoint, the acquisition of long-lived assets is essentially a long-term prepayment for services. The need for making periodic adjusting entries for depreciation is therefore the same as described before for other prepaid expenses—that is, to recognize the cost that has been used (an expense) during the period and to report the unused cost (an asset) at the end of the period. One point is very important to understand: **Depreciation is an allocation concept, not a valuation concept.**

Depreciation

Oct. 2

Office equipment purchased; record asset

Office Equipment			
Oct $40	Nov $40	Dec $40	Jan $40
Feb $40	March $40	April $40	May $40
June $40	July $40	Aug $40	Sept $40
Depreciation = $480/year			

Oct. 31
Depreciation recognized; record depreciation expense

That is, we depreciate an asset **to allocate its cost to the periods in which we use it. We are not attempting to reflect the actual change in the value of the asset.**

For Sierra Corporation, assume that depreciation on the office equipment is estimated to be $480 a year, or $40 per month. This would have the following impact on the accounting equation.

Assets	=	Liabilities	+	Stockholders' Equity
−$40				−$40

Accordingly, depreciation for October is recognized by this adjusting entry.

Oct. 31	Depreciation Expense	40	
	Accumulated Depreciation—Office Equipment		40
	(To record monthly depreciation)		

After the adjusting entry is posted, the accounts appear as in Illustration 4-8.

Illustration 4-8 Accounts after adjustment for depreciation

Office Equipment

Oct. 2 5,000	
Oct. 31 Bal. 5,000	

Accumulated Depreciation— Office Equipment

	Oct. 31 **Adj. 40**
	Oct. 31 Bal. 40

Depreciation Expense

Oct. 31 **Adj. 40**	
Oct. 31 Bal. 40	

The balance in the Accumulated Depreciation account will increase $40 each month.

Statement Presentation. Accumulated Depreciation—Office Equipment is a **contra asset account**. That means that it is offset against an asset account (Office Equipment) on the balance sheet, and its normal balance is a credit. This account is used instead of decreasing (crediting) Office Equipment for a simple reason: to disclose *both* the original cost of the equipment and the total cost that has expired to date. In the balance sheet, Accumulated Depreciation—Office Equipment is deducted from the related asset account as shown in Illustration 4-9.

Helpful Hint All contra accounts have increases, decreases, and normal balances **opposite to** the account to which they relate.

Illustration 4-9 Balance sheet presentation of accumulated depreciation

Office equipment	$5,000
Less: Accumulated depreciation—office equipment	40
	$4,960

Alternative Terminology Book value is also referred to as **carrying value**.

The difference between the cost of any depreciable asset and its related accumulated depreciation is referred to as the **book value** of that asset. In Illustration 4-9, the book value of the equipment at the balance sheet date is $4,960. Be sure to understand that the book value and the market value of the asset are generally two different values. As noted earlier, the purpose of depreciation is not valuation, but a means of cost allocation.

Depreciation expense identifies the portion of an asset's cost that expired during the period (in this case, in October). The accounting equation shows that the omission of this adjusting entry would cause total assets, total stockholders' equity, and net income to be overstated and depreciation expense to be understated.

Unearned Revenues

Cash received before revenue is earned is recorded by increasing (crediting) a liability account called **unearned revenues**. Items like rent, magazine subscriptions, and customer deposits for future service may result in unearned revenues. Airlines such as **United**, **American**, and **Delta**, for instance, treat receipts from the sale of tickets as unearned revenue until the flight service is provided. Unearned revenues are the opposite of prepaid expenses. Indeed, unearned revenue on the books of one company is likely to be a prepayment on the books of the company that has made the advance payment. For example, if identical accounting periods are assumed, a landlord will have unearned rent revenue when a tenant has prepaid rent.

When payment is received for services to be provided in a future accounting period, an unearned revenue (a liability) account should be increased (credited) to recognize the obligation that exists. Unearned revenues are subsequently earned by providing service to a customer. During the accounting period it is not practical to make daily entries as the revenue is earned. Instead, we delay recognition of earned revenue until the adjustment process. Then an adjusting entry is made to record the revenue that has been earned during the period and to show the liability that remains at the end of the accounting period. Typically, prior to adjustment, liabilities are overstated and revenues are understated. Therefore, as shown in Illustration 4-10, **the adjusting entry for unearned revenues results in a decrease (a debit) to a liability account and an increase (a credit) to a revenue account**.

Unearned Revenues

Oct.2

Thank you in advance for your work

I will finish by Dec. 31

$1,200

Cash is received in advance; liability is recorded

Oct.31
Some service has been provided; some revenue is recorded

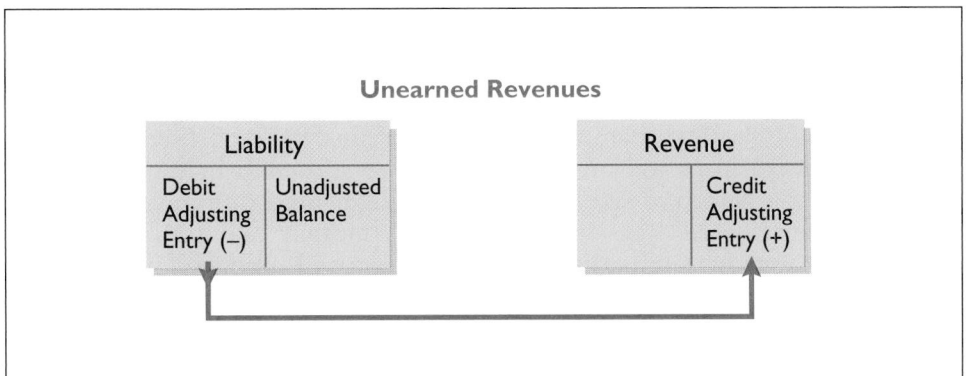

Unearned Revenues

Liability		Revenue	
Debit Adjusting Entry (−)	Unadjusted Balance		Credit Adjusting Entry (+)

Illustration 4-10 Adjusting entries for unearned revenues

Sierra Corporation received $1,200 on October 2 from R. Knox for advertising services expected to be completed by December 31. The payment was credited to Unearned Service Revenue, and this liability account shows a balance of $1,200 in the October 31 trial balance. From an evaluation of the work performed by Sierra for Knox during October, it is determined that $400 has been earned in October. This would affect the accounting equation in the following way.

Assets	=	Liabilities	+	Stockholders' Equity
		−$400		+$400

The following adjusting entry is made.

Oct. 31	Unearned Service Revenue	400	
	Service Revenue		400
	(To record revenue earned)		

After the adjusting entry is posted, the accounts appear as in Illustration 4-11.

Illustration 4-11 Service revenue accounts after adjustment

Unearned Service Revenue				Service Revenue		
Oct. 31 **Adj. 400**	Oct. 2	1,200			Oct. 3	10,000
					31 **Adj.**	**400**
	Oct. 31 Bal. 800				Oct. 31 Bal. 10,400	

The liability Unearned Service Revenue now shows a balance of $800, which represents the remaining advertising services expected to be performed in the future. At the same time, Service Revenue shows total revenue earned in October of $10,400. **If this adjustment is not made, revenues and net income will be understated by $400 in the income statement. Moreover, liabilities will be overstated and stockholders' equity will be understated by $400 on the October 31 balance sheet.**

Business Insight
ETHICS PERSPECTIVE

Companies would rather report steadily increasing profits than fluctuating profits. To "smooth" earnings, companies sometimes shift the reporting of revenues or expenses between periods. A recent *Wall Street Journal* article reported that **Microsoft Corp.** agreed to settle Securities and Exchange Commission charges that it misstated its earnings in some years by illegally maintaining different "reserve" accounts for such expenses as marketing and obsolete inventory. The settlement did not require Microsoft to pay a fine. Microsoft accepted the commission's order without admitting or denying wrongdoing and agreed not to commit accounting violations. "The SEC said Microsoft maintained undisclosed reserve accounts totaling between $200 million and $900 million between 1994 and 1998 and didn't maintain proper internal controls to document them or substantiate their size." The SEC said that the improper use of these reserve accounts resulted in "material inaccuracies" in the financial reports filed with the SEC.

SOURCE: Rebecca Buckman, "Microsoft, SEC Settle Probe Into Earnings Misstatements," *Wall Street Journal Online* (June 4, 2002).

BEFORE YOU GO ON . . .

▶ Review It

1. What are the four types of adjusting entries?
2. What is the effect on assets, stockholders' equity, expenses, and net income if a prepaid expense adjusting entry is not made?
3. What is the effect on liabilities, stockholders' equity, revenues, and net income if an unearned revenue adjusting entry is not made?

▶ Do It

The ledger of Hammond, Inc., on March 31, 2005, includes these selected accounts before adjusting entries are prepared.

	Debit	Credit
Prepaid Insurance	$ 3,600	
Office Supplies	2,800	
Office Equipment	25,000	
Accumulated Depreciation—Office Equipment		$5,000
Unearned Service Revenue		9,200

An analysis of the accounts shows the following.

1. Insurance expires at the rate of $100 per month.
2. Supplies on hand total $800.
3. The office equipment depreciates $200 a month.
4. One-half of the unearned service revenue was earned in March.

Prepare the adjusting entries for the month of March.

Action Plan

• Make adjusting entries at the end of the period for revenues earned and expenses incurred in the period.
• Don't forget to make adjusting entries for prepayments. Failure to adjust for prepayments leads to overstatement of the asset or liability and related understatement of the expense or revenue.

Solution

		Debit	Credit
1. Insurance Expense		100	
Prepaid Insurance			100
(To record insurance expired)			
2. Office Supplies Expense		2,000	
Office Supplies			2,000
(To record supplies used)			
3. Depreciation Expense		200	
Accumulated Depreciation—Office Equipment			200
(To record monthly depreciation)			
4. Unearned Service Revenue		4,600	
Service Revenue			4,600
(To record revenue earned)			

ADJUSTING ENTRIES FOR ACCRUALS

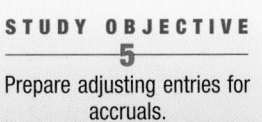

The second category of adjusting entries is **accruals**. Adjusting entries for accruals are required in order to record revenues earned and expenses incurred in the current accounting period that have not been recognized through daily entries and thus are not yet reflected in the accounts. Prior to an accrual

Accrued Revenues

Oct. 31

Revenue and receivable are recorded for unbilled services

Nov.
Cash is received; receivable is reduced

adjustment, the revenue account (and the related asset account) or the expense account (and the related liability account) are understated. Thus, the adjusting entry for accruals will **increase both a balance sheet and an income statement account**.

Accrued Revenues

Revenues earned but not yet recorded at the statement date are **accrued revenues**. Accrued revenues may accumulate (accrue) with the passing of time, as in the case of interest revenue. Or they may result from services that have been performed but neither billed nor collected, as in the case of commissions and fees. The former are unrecorded because the earning of interest does not involve daily transactions. The latter may be unrecorded because only a portion of the total service has been provided and the clients won't be billed until the service has been completed.

An adjusting entry is required to show the receivable that exists at the balance sheet date and to record the revenue that has been earned during the period. Prior to adjustment both assets and revenues are understated. As shown in Illustration 4-12, **an adjusting entry for accrued revenues results in an increase (a debit) to an asset account and an increase (a credit) to a revenue account**.

Illustration 4-12 Adjusting entries for accrued revenues

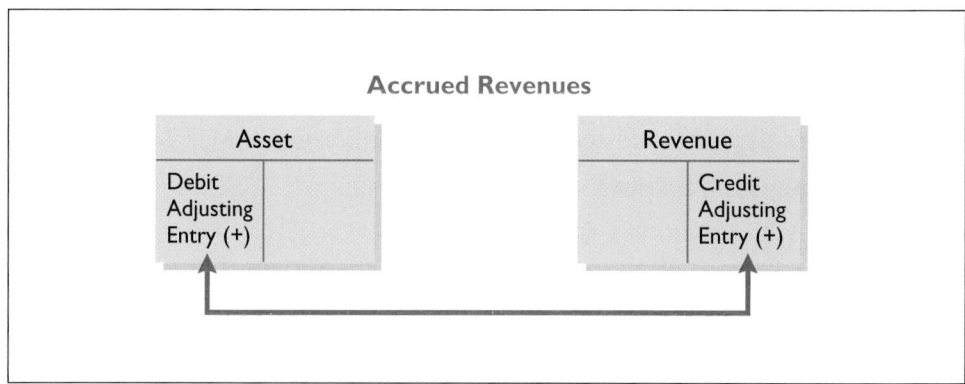

Helpful Hint For accruals, there may have been no prior entry, and the accounts requiring adjustment may both have zero balances prior to adjustment.

In October Sierra Corporation earned $200 for advertising services that were not billed to clients before October 31. Because these services have not been billed, they have not been recorded. Assets and stockholders' equity would be affected as follows.

Assets	=	Liabilities	+	Stockholders' Equity
+$200				+$200

Thus, the following adjusting entry is made.

Oct. 31	Accounts Receivable	200	
	Service Revenue		200
	(To record revenue earned)		

After the adjusting entry is posted, the accounts appear as in Illustration 4-13.

Accounts Receivable		Service Revenue	
Oct. 31 Adj. 200			Oct. 3 10,000
			31 400
			31 Adj. 200
Oct. 31 Bal. 200			Oct. 31 Bal. 10,600

Illustration 4-13
Receivable and revenue
accounts after accrual
adjustments

The asset Accounts Receivable shows that $200 is owed by clients at the balance sheet date. The balance of $10,600 in Service Revenue represents the total revenue earned during the month ($10,000 + $400 + $200). **If the adjusting entry is not made, assets and stockholders' equity on the balance sheet, and revenues and net income on the income statement, will be understated.**

In the next accounting period, the clients will be billed. When this occurs, the entry to record the billing should recognize that $200 of revenue earned in October has already been recorded in the October 31 adjusting entry. To illustrate, assume that bills totaling $3,000 are mailed to clients on November 10. Of this amount, $200 represents revenue earned in October and recorded as Service Revenue in the October 31 adjusting entry. The remaining $2,800 represents revenue earned in November. Assets and stockholders' equity would be affected as follows.

Assets	**=**	**Liabilities**	**+**	**Stockholders' Equity**
+$2,800				+$2,800

Thus, the following entry is made.

Nov. 10	Accounts Receivable	2,800	
	Service Revenue		2,800
	(To record revenue earned)		

This entry records the amount of revenue earned between November 1 and November 10. The subsequent collection of cash from clients (including the $200 earned in October) will be recorded with an increase (a debit) to Cash and a decrease (a credit) to Accounts Receivable.

Accrued Expenses

Expenses incurred but not yet paid or recorded at the statement date are called accrued expenses. Interest, taxes, and salaries are common examples of accrued expenses. Accrued expenses result from the same factors as accrued revenues. In fact, an accrued expense on the books of one company is an accrued revenue to another company. For example, the $200 accrual of service revenue by Sierra Corporation is an accrued expense to the client that received the service.

Adjustments for accrued expenses are necessary to record the obligations that exist at the balance sheet date and to recognize the expenses that apply to the current accounting period. Prior to adjustment, both liabilities and expenses are understated. Therefore, **an adjusting entry for accrued expenses results in an increase (a debit) to an expense account and an increase (a credit) to a liability account**.

Illustration 4-14 Adjusting entries for accrued expenses

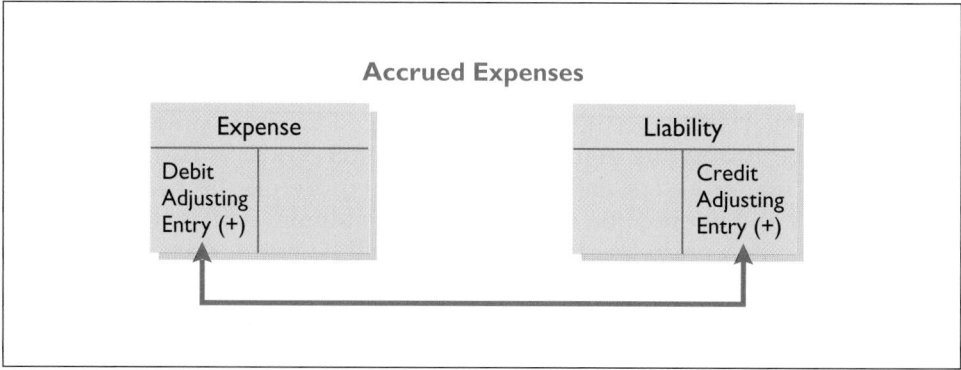

Let's look in more detail at some specific types of accrued expenses, beginning with accrued interest.

ACCRUED INTEREST.   Sierra Corporation signed a three-month note payable in the amount of $5,000 on October 1. The note requires interest at an annual rate of 12%. The amount of the interest accumulation is determined by three factors: (1) the face value of the note, (2) the interest rate, which is always expressed as an annual rate, and (3) the length of time the note is outstanding. In this instance, the total interest due on the $5,000 note at its due date three months in the future is $150 ($5,000 × 12% × $\frac{3}{12}$), or $50 for one month. The formula for computing interest and its application to Sierra Corporation for the month of October are shown in Illustration 4-15.

Illustration 4-15 Formula for computing interest

Face Value of Note	×	Annual Interest Rate	×	Time in Terms of One Year	=	Interest
$5,000	×	12%	×	$\frac{1}{12}$	=	$50

Note that the time period is expressed as a fraction of a year. The accrual of interest at October 31 would have the following effect on the accounting equation.

Assets	=	Liabilities	+	Stockholders' Equity
		+$50		−$50

This would be reflected in an accrued expense adjusting entry at October 31 as follows.

Oct. 31	Interest Expense	50	
	Interest Payable		50
	(To record interest on notes payable)		

After this adjusting entry is posted, the accounts appear as in Illustration 4-16.

Interest Expense				Interest Payable		
Oct. 31	**Adj. 50**				Oct. 31	**Adj. 50**
Oct. 31	Bal. 50				Oct. 31	Bal. 50

Illustration 4-16 Interest accounts after adjustment

Interest Expense shows the interest charges for the month of October. The amount of interest owed at the statement date is shown in Interest Payable. It will not be paid until the note comes due at the end of three months. The Interest Payable account is used, instead of crediting Notes Payable, to disclose the two different types of obligations—interest and principal—in the accounts and statements. **If this adjusting entry is not made, liabilities and interest expense will be understated, and net income and stockholders' equity will be overstated.**

ACCRUED SALARIES.   Some types of expenses, such as employee salaries and commissions, are paid for after the services have been performed. At Sierra Corporation, salaries were last paid on October 26; the next payment of salaries will not occur until November 9. As shown in the calendar in Illustration 4-17, three working days remain in October (October 29–31).

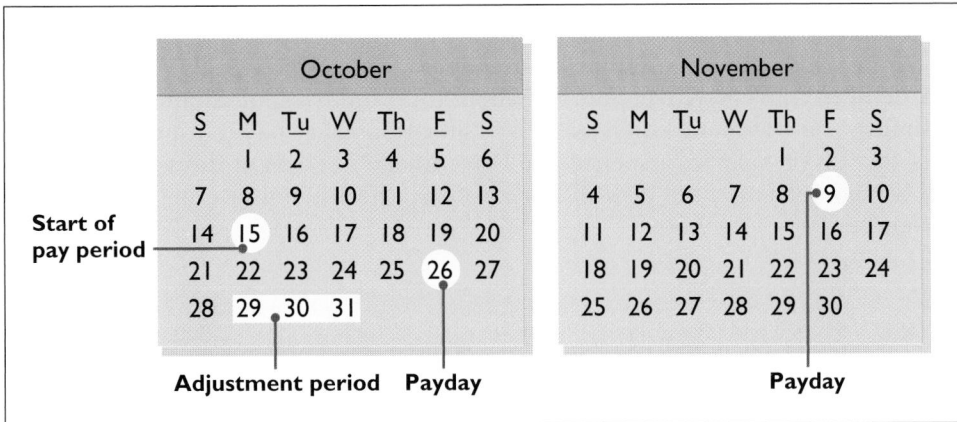

Illustration 4-17
Calendar showing Sierra Corporation's pay periods

At October 31 the salaries for these days represent an accrued expense and a related liability to Sierra. The employees receive total salaries of $2,000 for a five-day work week, or $400 per day. Thus, accrued salaries at October 31 are $1,200 ($400 × 3). This accrual increases a liability, Salaries Payable, and an expense account, Salaries Expense, and has the following effect on the accounting equation.

Assets	=	Liabilities	+	Stockholders' Equity
		+$1,200		−$1,200

The adjusting entry is:

Oct. 31	Salaries Expense		1,200	
	Salaries Payable			1,200
	(To record accrued salaries)			

After this adjusting entry is posted, the accounts are as shown in Illustration 4-18.

Illustration 4-18 Salary accounts after adjustment

Salaries Expense			Salaries Payable	
Oct. 26	4,000			Oct. 31 Adj. 1,200
31 Adj. 1,200				
Oct. 31 Bal. 5,200				Oct. 31 Bal. 1,200

After this adjustment, the balance in Salaries Expense of $5,200 (13 days × $400) is the actual salary expense for October. The balance in Salaries Payable of $1,200 is the amount of the liability for salaries owed as of October 31. **If the $1,200 adjustment for salaries is not recorded, Sierra's expenses will be understated $1,200 and its liabilities will be understated $1,200.**

At Sierra Corporation, salaries are payable every two weeks. Consequently, the next payday is November 9, when total salaries of $4,000 will again be paid. The payment consists of $1,200 of salaries payable at October 31 plus $2,800 of salaries expense for November (7 working days as shown in the November calendar × $400). Therefore, the following entry is made on November 9.

Nov. 9	Salaries Payable		1,200	
	Salaries Expense		2,800	
	Cash			4,000
	(To record November 9 payroll)			

This entry eliminates the liability for Salaries Payable that was recorded in the October 31 adjusting entry and records the proper amount of Salaries Expense for the period between November 1 and November 9.

BEFORE YOU GO ON . . .

▶ **Review It**

1. What is the effect on assets, stockholders' equity, revenues, and net income if an accrued revenue adjusting entry is not made?
2. What is the effect on liabilities, stockholders' equity, expenses, and net income if an accrued expense adjusting entry is not made?
3. What was the amount of **Tootsie Roll**'s 2002 depreciation expense? (*Hint:* The amount is reported in the notes to the financial statements.) The answer to this question is provided on page 216.

▶ **Do It**

Micro Computer Services Inc. began operations on August 1, 2005. At the end of August 2005, management attempted to prepare monthly financial statements. This information relates to August:

1. At August 31 the company owed its employees $800 in salaries that will be paid on September 1.
2. On August 1 the company borrowed $30,000 from a local bank on a 15-year mortgage. The annual interest rate is 10%.
3. Revenue earned but unrecorded for August totaled $1,100.

Prepare the adjusting entries needed at August 31, 2005.

Action Plan

• Make adjusting entries at the end of the period for revenues earned and expenses incurred in the period.
• Don't forget to make adjusting entries for accruals. Adjusting entries for accruals will increase both a balance sheet and an income statement account.

Solution

1. Salaries Expense	800	
Salaries Payable		800
(To record accrued salaries)		
2. Interest Expense	250	
Interest Payable		250
(To record accrued interest: $30,000 \times 10\% \times \frac{1}{12} = \$250$)		
3. Accounts Receivable	1,100	
Service Revenue		1,100
(To record revenue earned)		

☑ THE NAVIGATOR

SUMMARY OF BASIC RELATIONSHIPS

The four basic types of adjusting entries are summarized in Illustration 4-19 (page 178). Take some time to study and analyze the adjusting entries. Be sure to note that **each adjusting entry affects one balance sheet account and one income statement account**.

Illustration 4-19
Summary of adjusting
entries

Type of Adjustment	Accounts Before Adjustment	Adjusting Entry
Prepaid expenses	Assets overstated Expenses understated	Dr. Expenses Cr. Assets
Unearned revenues	Liabilities overstated Revenues understated	Dr. Liabilities Cr. Revenues
Accrued revenues	Assets understated Revenues understated	Dr. Assets Cr. Revenues
Accrued expenses	Expenses understated Liabilities understated	Dr. Expenses Cr. Liabilities

The journalizing and posting of adjusting entries for Sierra Corporation on October 31 are shown in Illustrations 4-20 and 4-21. When reviewing the general ledger in Illustration 4-21, note that the adjustments are highlighted in color.

Illustration 4-20 General journal showing adjusting entries

GENERAL JOURNAL

Date	Account Titles and Explanation	Debit	Credit
2005	Adjusting Entries		

Oct. 31	Advertising Supplies Expense
	  Advertising Supplies
	  (To record supplies used)
		1,500	1,500

31	Insurance Expense
	  Prepaid Insurance
	  (To record insurance expired)
		50	50

31	Depreciation Expense
	  Accumulated Depreciation—Office Equipment
	  (To record monthly depreciation)
		40	40

31	Unearned Service Revenue
	  Service Revenue
	  (To record revenue earned)
		400	400

31	Accounts Receivable
	  Service Revenue
	  (To record revenue earned)
		200	200

31	Interest Expense
	  Interest Payable
	  (To record interest on notes payable)
		50	50

31	Salaries Expense
	  Salaries Payable
	  (To record accrued salaries)
		1,200	1,200

Illustration 4-21 General ledger after adjustments

GENERAL LEDGER

Cash

Oct.	1	10,000	Oct.	2	5,000
	1	5,000		3	900
	2	1,200		4	600
	3	10,000		20	500
				26	4,000

Oct. 31 Bal. 15,200

Accounts Receivable

Oct. 31	200	

Oct. 31 Bal. 200

Advertising Supplies

Oct.	5	2,500	Oct.	31	1,500

Oct. 31 Bal. 1,000

Prepaid Insurance

Oct.	4	600	Oct.	31	50

Oct. 31 Bal. 550

Office Equipment

Oct.	2	5,000

Oct. 31 Bal. 5,000

Accumulated Depreciation—Office Equipment

	Oct. 31	40
	Oct. 31 Bal. 40	

Notes Payable

	Oct. 1	5,000
	Oct. 31 Bal. 5,000	

Accounts Payable

	Oct. 5	2,500
	Oct. 31 Bal. 2,500	

Interest Payable

	Oct. 31	50
	Oct. 31 Bal. 50	

Unearned Service Revenue

Oct. 31	400	Oct.	2	1,200
		Oct.	31 Bal.	800

Salaries Payable

	Oct. 31	1,200
	Oct. 31 Bal. 1,200	

Common Stock

	Oct. 1	10,000
	Oct. 31 Bal.	10,000

Retained Earnings

	Oct. 31	Bal. 0

Dividends

Oct. 20	500	

Oct. 31 Bal. 500

Service Revenue

	Oct. 3	10,000
	31	400
	31	200
	Oct. 31 Bal.	10,600

Salaries Expense

Oct. 26	4,000	
31	1,200	

Oct. 31 Bal. 5,200

Advertising Supplies Expense

Oct. 31	1,500	

Oct. 31 Bal. 1,500

Rent Expense

Oct. 3	900	

Oct. 31 Bal. 900

Insurance Expense

Oct. 31	50	

Oct. 31 Bal. 50

Interest Expense

Oct. 31	50	

Oct. 31 Bal. 50

Depreciation Expense

Oct. 31	40	

Oct. 31 Bal. 40

179

The Adjusted Trial Balance and Financial Statements

STUDY OBJECTIVE
6
Describe the nature and purpose of the adjusted trial balance.

After all adjusting entries have been journalized and posted, another trial balance is prepared from the ledger accounts. This trial balance is called an **adjusted trial balance**. It shows the balances of all accounts, including those that have been adjusted, at the end of the accounting period. The purpose of an adjusted trial balance is to **prove the equality** of the total debit balances and the total credit balances in the ledger after all adjustments have been made. Because the accounts contain all data that are needed for financial statements, the adjusted trial balance is the primary basis for the preparation of financial statements.

PREPARING THE ADJUSTED TRIAL BALANCE

The adjusted trial balance for Sierra Corporation presented in Illustration 4-22 has been prepared from the ledger accounts in Illustration 4-21. The amounts affected by the adjusting entries are highlighted in color.

Illustration 4-22 Adjusted trial balance

SIERRA CORPORATION Adjusted Trial Balance October 31, 2005		
	Dr.	**Cr.**
Cash	$ 15,200	
Accounts Receivable	200	
Advertising Supplies	1,000	
Prepaid Insurance	550	
Office Equipment	5,000	
Accumulated Depreciation—Office Equipment		$ 40
Notes Payable		5,000
Accounts Payable		2,500
Interest Payable		50
Unearned Service Revenue		800
Salaries Payable		1,200
Common Stock		10,000
Retained Earnings		0
Dividends	500	
Service Revenue		10,600
Salaries Expense	5,200	
Advertising Supplies Expense	1,500	
Rent Expense	900	
Insurance Expense	50	
Interest Expense	50	
Depreciation Expense	40	
	$30,190	$30,190

PREPARING FINANCIAL STATEMENTS

Financial statements can be prepared directly from an adjusted trial balance. The interrelationships of data in the adjusted trial balance of Sierra Corporation are presented in Illustrations 4-23 and 4-24. As Illustration 4-23 shows, the income statement is prepared from the revenue and expense accounts. Similarly, the retained earnings statement is derived from the retained earnings account, dividends account, and the net income (or net loss) shown in the income statement. As shown in Illustration 4-24 (on page 182), the balance sheet is then prepared from the asset, liability and equity accounts. The amount reported for retained earnings on the balance sheet is taken from the ending balance in the retained earnings statement.

Illustration 4-23
Preparation of the income statement and retained earnings statement from the adjusted trial balance

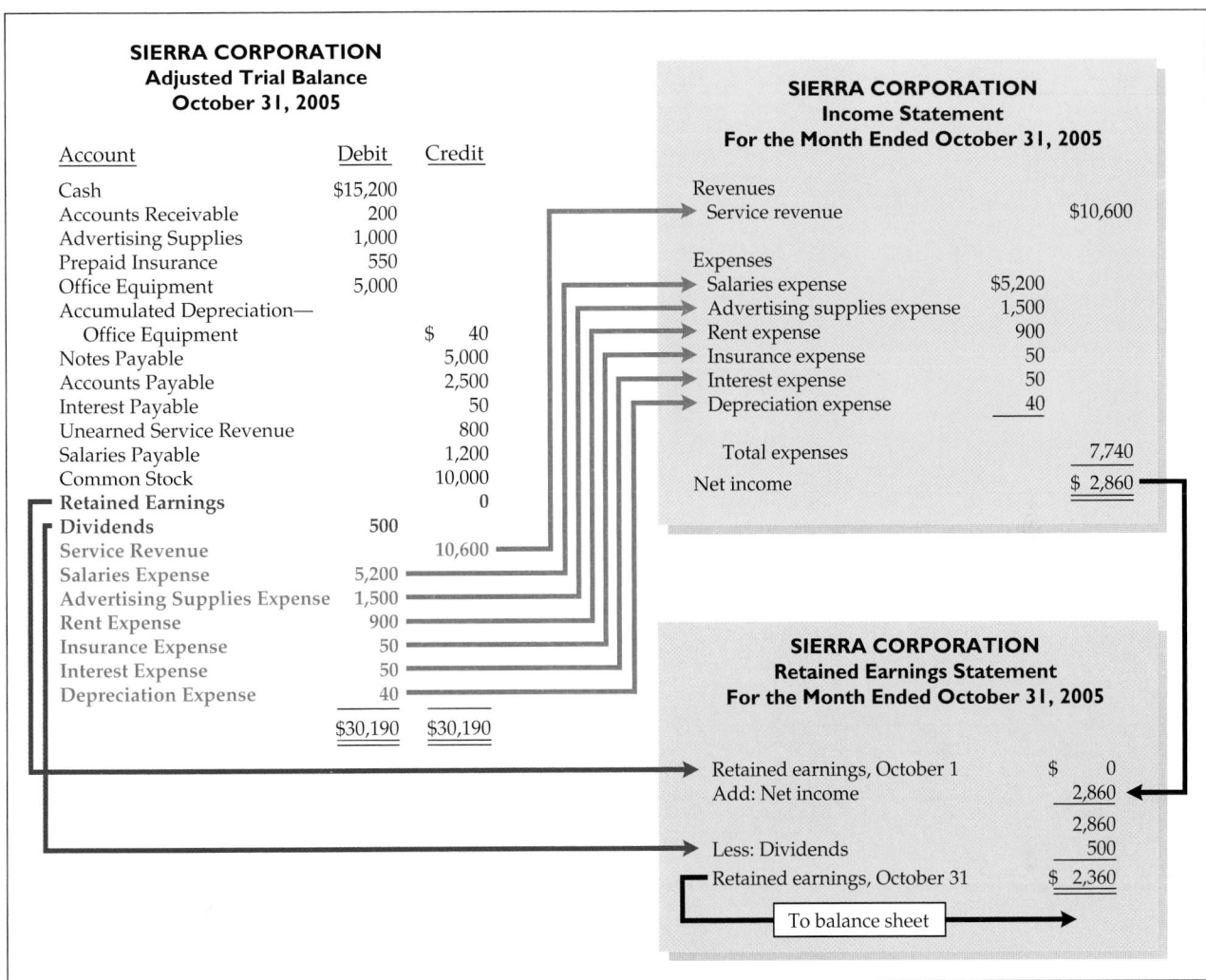

Closing the Books

In previous chapters you learned that revenue and expense accounts and the dividends account are subdivisions of retained earnings, which is reported in the stockholders' equity section of the balance sheet. Because revenues, expenses, and dividends relate to only a given accounting period, they are considered **temporary accounts**. In contrast, all balance sheet accounts are considered **permanent accounts** because their balances are carried forward into future accounting periods. Illustration 4-25 identifies the accounts in each category.

Alternative Terminology
Temporary accounts are sometimes called **nominal accounts**, and permanent accounts are sometimes called **real accounts**.

PREPARING CLOSING ENTRIES

At the end of the accounting period, the temporary account balances are transferred to the permanent stockholders' equity account—Retained Earnings—through the preparation of closing entries. **Closing entries** transfer net income

STUDY OBJECTIVE
7
Explain the purpose of closing entries.

Illustration 4-24 Preparation of the balance sheet from the adjusted trial balance

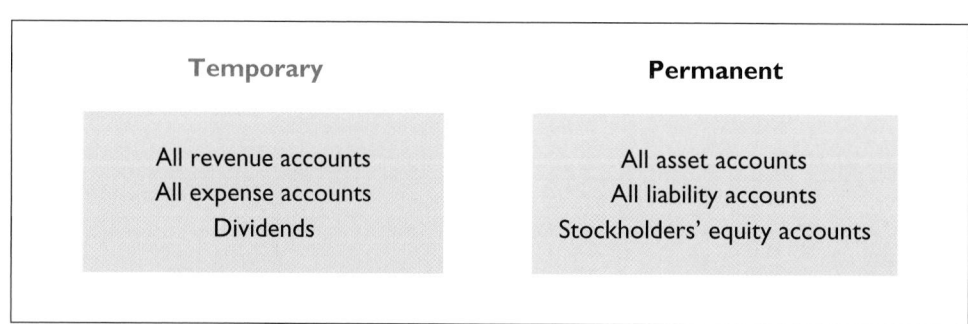

SIERRA CORPORATION
Adjusted Trial Balance
October 31, 2005

Account	Debit	Credit
Cash	$15,200	
Accounts Receivable	200	
Advertising Supplies	1,000	
Prepaid Insurance	550	
Office Equipment	5,000	
Accumulated Depreciation— Office Equipment		$ 40
Notes Payable		5,000
Accounts Payable		2,500
Interest Payable		50
Unearned Service Revenue		800
Salaries Payable		1,200
Common Stock		10,000
Retained Earnings		0
Dividends	500	
Service Revenue		10,600
Salaries Expense	5,200	
Advertising Supplies Expense	1,500	
Rent Expense	900	
Insurance Expense	50	
Interest Expense	50	
Depreciation Expense	40	
	$30,190	$30,190

SIERRA CORPORATION
Balance Sheet
October 31, 2005

Assets

Cash		$15,200
Accounts receivable		200
Advertising supplies		1,000
Prepaid insurance		550
Office equipment	$5,000	
Less: Accumulated depreciation	40	4,960
Total assets		$21,910

Liabilities and Stockholders' Equity

Liabilities		
Notes payable	$ 5,000	
Accounts payable	2,500	
Interest payable	50	
Unearned service revenue	800	
Salaries payable	1,200	
Total liabilities		$ 9,550
Stockholders' equity		
Common stock	10,000	
Retained earnings	2,360	
Total stockholders' equity		12,360
Total liabilities and stockholders' equity		$21,910

Balance at Oct. 31 from Retained Earnings Statement in Illustration 4-23

Illustration 4-25 Temporary versus permanent accounts

Temporary	Permanent
All revenue accounts	All asset accounts
All expense accounts	All liability accounts
Dividends	Stockholders' equity accounts

(or net loss) and dividends to Retained Earnings, so the balance in Retained Earnings agrees with the retained earnings statement. For example, notice that in Illustration 4-24 Retained Earnings has an adjusted balance of zero. Prior to the closing entries, the balance in Retained Earnings will be its beginning-of-the-period balance. For Sierra this is zero because it is Sierra's first year of operations.

In addition to updating Retained Earnings to its correct ending balance, closing entries produce a **zero balance in each temporary account**. As a result, these accounts are ready to accumulate data about revenues, expenses, and dividends in the next accounting period separate from the data in the prior periods. Permanent accounts are not closed.

When closing entries are prepared, each income statement account could be closed directly to Retained Earnings. However, to do so would result in excessive detail in the retained earnings account. Accordingly, the revenue and expense accounts are closed to another temporary account, **Income Summary**, and only the resulting net income or net loss is transferred from this account to Retained Earnings. Illustration 4-26 depicts the closing process. The closing entries for Sierra Corporation are shown in Illustration 4-27.

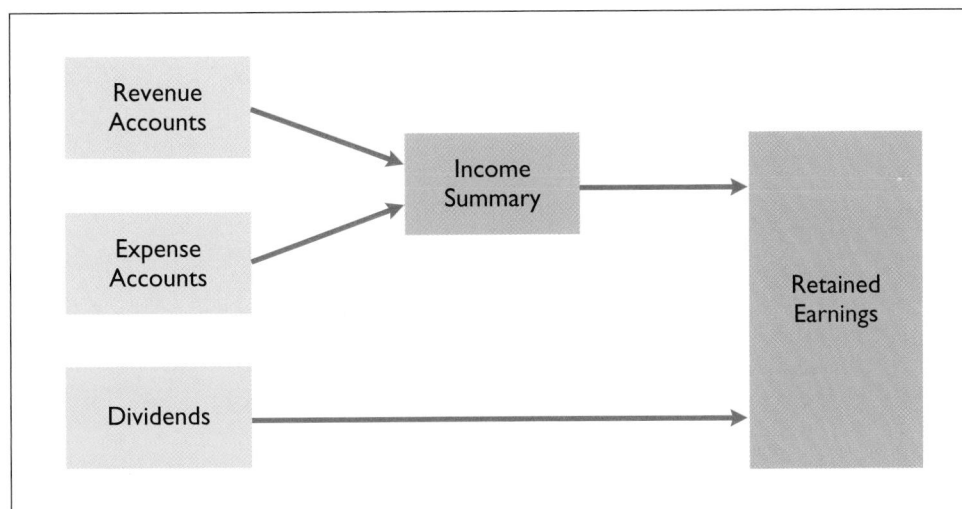

Illustration 4-26 **The closing process**

Illustration 4-27 Closing entries journalized

GENERAL JOURNAL

Date	Account Titles and Explanation	Debit	Credit
	Closing Entries		
2005	(1)		
Oct. 31	Service Revenue	10,600	
	Income Summary		10,600
	(To close revenue account)		
	(2)		
31	Income Summary	7,740	
	Salaries Expense		5,200
	Advertising Supplies Expense		1,500
	Rent Expense		900
	Insurance Expense		50
	Interest Expense		50
	Depreciation Expense		40
	(To close expense accounts)		
	(3)		
31	Income Summary	2,860	
	Retained Earnings		2,860
	(To close net income to retained earnings)		
	(4)		
31	Retained Earnings	500	
	Dividends		500
	(To close dividends to retained earnings)		

Helpful Hint Income Summary is a very descriptive title: Total revenues are closed to Income Summary, total expenses are closed to Income Summary, and the balance in the Income Summary is a net income or net loss.

The posting process for Sierra Corporation's closing entries is diagrammed in Illustration 4-28.

Illustration 4-28 Posting of closing entries

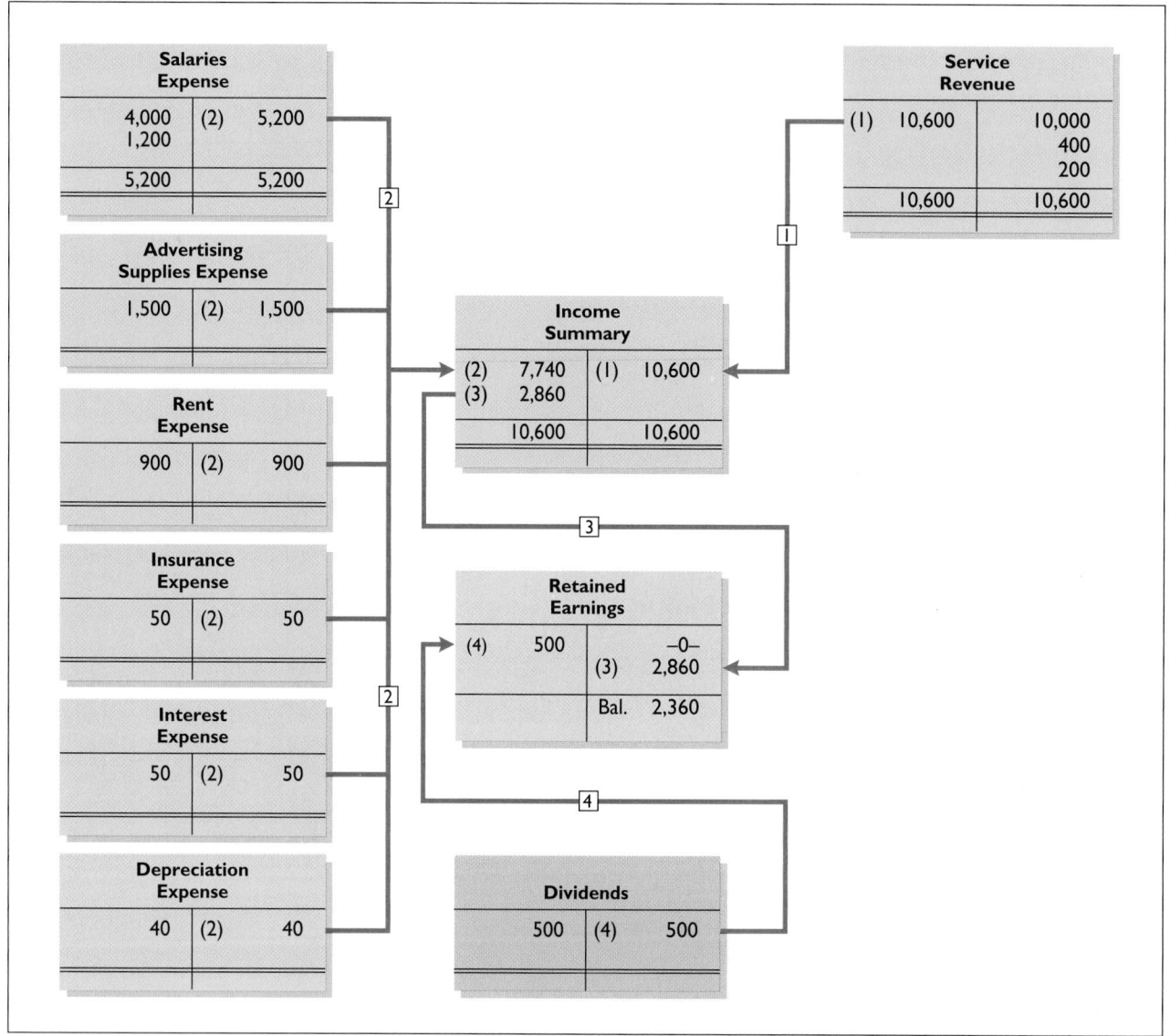

PREPARING A POST-CLOSING TRIAL BALANCE

After all closing entries are journalized and posted, another trial balance, called a **post-closing trial balance**, is prepared from the ledger. A post-closing trial balance is a list of all permanent accounts and their balances after closing entries are journalized and posted. **The purpose of this trial balance is to prove the equality of the permanent account balances that are carried forward into the next accounting period.** Since all temporary accounts will have zero balances, **the post-closing trial balance will contain only permanent—balance sheet—accounts.**

Until Sam Walton had opened 20 **Wal-Mart** stores, he used what he called the "ESP method" of closing the books. ESP was a pretty basic method: If the books didn't balance, Walton calculated the amount by which they were off and entered that amount under the heading ESP—which stood for "Error Some Place." As Walton noted, "It really sped things along when it came time to close those books."

SOURCE: Sam Walton, *Made in America* (New York: Doubleday Publishing Company, 1992), p. 53.

Summary of the Accounting Cycle

STUDY OBJECTIVE
8
Describe the required steps in the accounting cycle.

The required steps in the accounting cycle are shown graphically in Illustration 4-29. You can see that the cycle begins with the analysis of business transactions

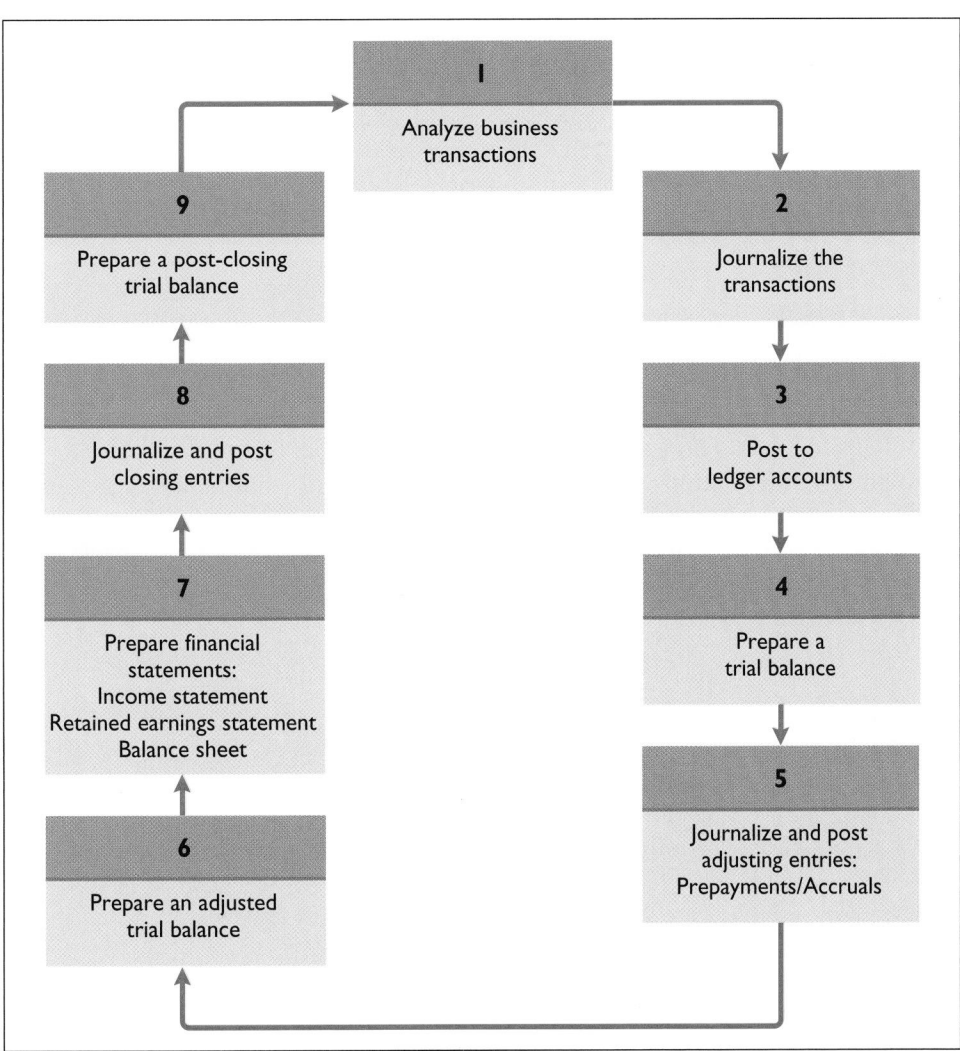

Illustration 4-29 Required steps in the accounting cycle

Helpful Hint Some accountants prefer to reverse certain adjusting entries at the beginning of a new accounting period. A **reversing entry** is made at the beginning of the next accounting period and is the exact opposite of the adjusting entry made in the previous period.

and ends with the preparation of a post-closing trial balance. The steps in the cycle are performed in sequence and are repeated in each accounting period.

Steps 1–3 may occur daily during the accounting period, as explained in Chapter 3. Steps 4–7 are performed on a periodic basis, such as monthly, quarterly, or annually. Steps 8 and 9, closing entries and a post-closing trial balance, are usually prepared only at the end of a company's **annual** accounting period.

Business Insight
MANAGEMENT PERSPECTIVE

Technology has dramatically changed the accounting process. When Larry Carter became chief financial officer of **Cisco Systems**, closing the quarterly accounts would take up to ten days. Within four years he got it down to two days and halved the cost of finance, to 1 percent of sales. Now he is aiming to be able to do a "virtual close"—closing within a day on any day in the quarter. This is not just showing off. Knowing exactly where you are all of the time, says Mr. Carter, allows you to respond faster than your competitors. But it also means that the 600 people who used to spend ten days a quarter tracking transactions can now be more usefully employed on things such as mining data for business intelligence.

SOURCE: Excerpted from "Business and the Internet," *The Economist* (June 26, 1999), p. 12.

BEFORE YOU GO ON . . .

▶ **Review It**

1. How do permanent accounts differ from temporary accounts?
2. What four different types of entries are required in closing the books?
3. What are the content and purpose of a post-closing trial balance?
4. What are the required steps in the accounting cycle?

Using the Decision Toolkit

Humana Corporation provides managed health care services to more than 6.4 million people. Headquartered in Louisville, Kentucky, it has over 14,500 employees in 18 states and Puerto Rico. A simplified version of Humana's December 31, 2001, adjusted trial balance is shown at the top of the next page.

Instructions

From the trial balance, prepare an income statement, retained earnings statement, and classified balance sheet. **Be sure to prepare them in that order, since each statement depends on information determined in the preceding statement.**

HUMANA.

HUMANA CORPORATION
Trial Balance
December 31, 2001
(in millions)

Account	Dr.	Cr.
Cash	$ 651	
Short-Term Investments	1,390	
Receivables	322	
Other Current Assets	260	
Property and Equipment, Net	462	
Long-Term Investments	280	
Other Long-Term Assets	1,039	
Medical Costs Payable		$ 1,086
Accounts Payable		480
Other Current Liabilities		741
Long-Term Debt		589
Common Stock		951
Dividends	0	
Retained Earnings		440
Revenues		10,195
Medical Cost Expense	8,280	
Selling, General, and Administrative Expense	1,545	
Depreciation Expense	162	
Interest Expense	25	
Income Tax Expense	66	
	$14,482	$14,482

Solution

HUMANA.

HUMANA CORPORATION
Income Statement
For the Year Ended December 31, 2001
(in millions)

Revenues		$10,195
Medical cost expense	$8,280	
Selling, general, and administrative expense	1,545	
Depreciation expense	162	
Interest expense	25	
Income tax expense	66	10,078
Net income		$ 117

HUMANA.

HUMANA CORPORATION
Retained Earnings Statement
For the Year Ended December 31, 2001
(in millions)

Beginning retained earnings	$440
Add: Net income	117
Less: Dividends	0
Ending retained earnings	$557

HUMANA CORPORATION
Balance Sheet
December 31, 2001
(in millions)

Assets

Current assets		
Cash	$ 651	
Short-term investments	1,390	
Receivables	322	
Other current assets	260	
Total current assets		$2,623
Long-term investments		280
Property and equipment, net		462
Other long-term assets		1,039
Total assets		$4,404

Liabilities and Stockholders' Equity

Liabilities		
Current liabilities		
Medical costs payable	$1,086	
Accounts payable	480	
Other current liabilities	741	
Total current liabilities		$2,307
Long-term debt		589
Total liabilities		2,896
Stockholders' equity		
Common stock	951	
Retained earnings	557	
Total stockholders' equity		1,508
Total liabilities and stockholders' equity		$4,404

✓ THE
NAVIGATOR

Summary of Study Objectives

1 *Explain the revenue recognition principle and the matching principle.* The revenue recognition principle dictates that revenue be recognized in the accounting period in which it is earned. The matching principle dictates that expenses be recognized when they make their contribution to revenues.

2 *Differentiate between the cash basis and the accrual basis of accounting.* Accrual-based accounting means that events that change a company's financial statements are recorded in the periods in which the events occur. Under the cash basis, events are recorded only in the periods in which the company receives or pays cash.

3 *Explain why adjusting entries are needed, and identify the major types of adjusting entries.* Adjusting entries are made at the end of an accounting period. They ensure that revenues are recorded in the period in which they are earned and that expenses are recognized in the period in which they are incurred. The major types of adjusting entries are prepaid expenses, unearned revenues, accrued revenues, and accrued expenses.

4 *Prepare adjusting entries for prepayments.* Prepayments are either prepaid expenses or unearned revenues. Adjusting entries for prepayments are required at the statement date to record the portion of the prepayment that represents the expense incurred or the revenue earned in the current accounting period.

5 *Prepare adjusting entries for accruals.* Accruals are either accrued revenues or accrued expenses. Adjusting entries for accruals are required to record revenues earned and expenses incurred in the current accounting period that have not been recognized through daily entries.

6 *Describe the nature and purpose of the adjusted trial balance.* An adjusted trial balance is a trial balance that shows the balances of all accounts, including those that have been adjusted, at the end of an accounting period. The purpose of an adjusted trial balance is to show the effects of all financial events that have occurred during the accounting period.

7 *Explain the purpose of closing entries.* One purpose of closing entries is to transfer the results of operations for the period to Retained Earnings. A second purpose is that, to begin a new period, all temporary accounts (revenue accounts, expense accounts, and dividends) must start with a zero balance. To accomplish this, all temporary accounts are "closed" at the end of an accounting period. Separate entries are made to close revenues and expenses to Income Summary, Income Summary to Retained Earnings, and Dividends to Retained Earnings. Only temporary accounts are closed.

8 *Describe the required steps in the accounting cycle.* The required steps in the accounting cycle are: (a) analyze business transactions, (b) journalize the transactions, (c) post to ledger accounts, (d) prepare a trial balance, (e) journalize and post adjusting entries, (f) prepare an adjusted trial balance, (g) prepare financial statements, (h) journalize and post closing entries, and (i) prepare a post-closing trial balance.

DECISION TOOLKIT—A SUMMARY

Decision Checkpoints	Info Needed for Decision	Tool to Use for Decision	How to Evaluate Results
At what point should the company record revenue?	Need to understand the nature of the company's business	Revenue should be recorded when earned. For a service business, revenue is earned when service is performed.	Recognizing revenue too early overstates current period revenue; recognizing it too late understates current period revenue.
At what point should the company record expenses?	Need to understand the nature of the company's business	Expenses should "follow" revenues—that is, the effort (expense) should be matched with the result (revenue).	Recognizing expenses too early overstates current period expense; recognizing expenses too late understates current period expense.

APPENDIX
ADJUSTING ENTRIES IN AN AUTOMATED WORLD—USING A WORK SHEET

STUDY OBJECTIVE
9
Describe the purpose and the basic form of a work sheet.

In the previous discussion we used T accounts and trial balances to arrive at the amounts used to prepare financial statements. Accountants frequently use a device known as a work sheet to determine these amounts. A **work sheet** is a multiple-column form that may be used in the adjustment process and in preparing financial statements. Work sheets can be prepared manually, but today most are prepared on computer spreadsheets. As its name suggests, the work sheet is a working tool for the accountant. **A work sheet is not a permanent accounting record**; it is neither a journal nor a part of the general ledger. The work sheet is merely a supplemental device used to make it easier to prepare adjusting entries and the financial statements. In small companies that have relatively few accounts and adjustments, a work sheet may not be needed. In large companies with numerous accounts and many adjustments, it is almost indispensable.

The basic form of a work sheet is shown in Illustration 4A-1. Note the headings: The work sheet starts with two columns for the Trial Balance. The next two columns record all Adjustments. Next is the Adjusted Trial Balance. The last two sets of columns correspond to the Income Statement and the Balance Sheet. All items listed in the Adjusted Trial Balance columns are recorded in either the Income Statement or the Balance Sheet columns.

Illustration 4A-1 Form and procedure for a work sheet

SIERRA CORPORATION
Work Sheet
For the Month Ended October 31, 2005

Account Titles	Trial Balance Dr.	Trial Balance Cr.	Adjustments Dr.	Adjustments Cr.	Adjusted Trial Balance Dr.	Adjusted Trial Balance Cr.	Income Statement Dr.	Income Statement Cr.	Balance Sheet Dr.	Balance Sheet Cr.
Cash	15,200				15,200				15,200	
Advertising Supplies	2,500			(a) 1,500	1,000				1,000	
Prepaid Insurance	600			(b) 50	550				550	
Office Equipment	5,000				5,000				5,000	
Notes Payable		5,000				5,000				5,000
Accounts Payable		2,500				2,500				2,500
Unearned Service Revenue		1,200	(d) 400			800				800
Common Stock		10,000				10,000				10,000
Retained Earnings		–0–				–0–				–0–
Dividends	500				500				500	
Service Revenue		10,000		(d) 400		10,600		10,600		
				(e) 200						
Salaries Expense	4,000		(g) 1,200		5,200		5,200			
Rent Expense	900				900		900			
Totals	28,700	28,700								
Advertising Supplies Expense			(a) 1,500		1,500		1,500			
Insurance Expense			(b) 50		50		50			
Accum. Depreciation—Office Equipment				(c) 40		40				40
Depreciation Expense			(c) 40		40		40			
Interest Expense			(f) 50		50		50			
Accounts Receivable			(e) 200		200				200	
Interest Payable				(f) 50		50				50
Salaries Payable				(g) 1,200		1,200				1,200
Totals			3,440	3,440	30,190	30,190	7,740	10,600	22,450	19,590
Net Income							2,860			2,860
Totals							10,600	10,600	22,450	22,450

1. Prepare a trial balance on the work sheet

2. Enter adjustment data

3. Enter adjusted balances

4. Extend adjusted balances to appropriate statement columns

5. Total the statement columns, compute net income (or net loss), and complete work sheet

Summary of Study Objective for Appendix

9 *Describe the purpose and the basic form of a work sheet.* The work sheet is a device used to make it easier to prepare adjusting entries and the financial statements. It is often prepared on a computer spreadsheet. The sets of columns of the work sheet are, from left to right, the unadjusted trial balance, adjustments, adjusted trial balance, income statement, and balance sheet.

Glossary

Accrual basis accounting   Accounting basis in which transactions that change a company's financial statements are recorded in the periods in which the events occur, rather than in the periods in which the company receives or pays cash. (p. 162)

Accrued expenses   Expenses incurred but not yet paid in cash or recorded. (p. 173)

Accrued revenues   Revenues earned but not yet received in cash or recorded. (p. 172)

Adjusted trial balance   A list of accounts and their balances after all adjustments have been made. (p. 180)

Adjusting entries   Entries made at the end of an accounting period to ensure that the revenue recognition and matching principles are followed. (p. 163)

Book value   The difference between the cost of a depreciable asset and its related accumulated depreciation. (p. 168)

Cash basis accounting   Accounting basis in which revenue is recorded only when cash is received, and an expense is recorded only when cash is paid. (p. 162)

Closing entries   Entries at the end of an accounting period to transfer the balances of temporary accounts to a permanent stockholders' equity account, Retained Earnings. (p. 181)

Contra asset account   An account that is offset against an asset account on the balance sheet. (p. 168)

Depreciation   The process of allocating the cost of an asset to expense over its useful life. (p. 167)

Fiscal year   An accounting period that is one year long. (p. 160)

Income Summary   A temporary account used in closing revenue and expense accounts. (p. 183)

Matching principle   The principle that dictates that efforts (expenses) be matched with accomplishments (revenues). (p. 161)

Permanent accounts   Balance sheet accounts whose balances are carried forward to the next accounting period. (p. 181)

Post-closing trial balance   A list of permanent accounts and their balances after closing entries have been journalized and posted. (p. 184)

Prepaid expenses (Prepayments)   Expenses paid in cash and recorded as assets before they are used or consumed. (p. 165)

Revenue recognition principle   The principle that revenue be recognized in the accounting period in which it is earned. (p. 160)

Reversing entry   An entry made at the beginning of the next accounting period; the exact opposite of the adjusting entry made in the previous period. (p. 186)

Temporary accounts   Revenue, expense, and dividend accounts whose balances are transferred to Retained Earnings at the end of an accounting period. (p. 181)

Time period assumption   An assumption that the economic life of a business can be divided into artificial time periods. (pp. 159–160)

Unearned revenues   Cash received before revenues were earned and recorded as liabilities until they are earned. (p. 169)

Useful life   The length of service of a productive facility. (p. 167)

Work sheet   A multiple-column form that may be used in the adjustment process and in preparing financial statements. (p. 189)

Demonstration Problem

Terry Thomas and a group of investors incorporate the Green Thumb Lawn Care Corporation on April 1. At April 30 the trial balance shows the following balances for selected accounts.

Prepaid Insurance	$ 3,600
Equipment	28,000
Notes Payable	20,000
Unearned Service Revenue	4,200
Service Revenue	1,800

Analysis reveals the following additional data pertaining to these accounts.

1. Prepaid insurance is the cost of a 2-year insurance policy, effective April 1.
2. Depreciation on the equipment is $500 per month.
3. The note payable is dated April 1. It is a 6-month, 12% note.
4. Seven customers paid for the company's 6 months' lawn service package of $600 beginning in April. These customers were serviced in April

5. Lawn services performed for other customers but not billed at April 30 totaled $1,500.

Instructions

Prepare the adjusting entries for the month of April. Show computations.

Action Plan

- Note that adjustments are being made for 1 month.
- Make computations carefully.
- Select account titles carefully.
- Make sure debits are made first and credits are indented.
- Check that debits equal credits for each entry.

Solution to Demonstration Problem

GENERAL JOURNAL

Date	Account Titles and Explanation	Debit	Credit
	Adjusting Entries		
Apr. 30	Insurance Expense	150	
	Prepaid Insurance		150
	(To record insurance expired:		
	$3,600 ÷ 24 = $150 per month)		
30	Depreciation Expense	500	
	Accumulated Depreciation—Equipment		500
	(To record monthly depreciation)		
30	Interest Expense	200	
	Interest Payable		200
	(To accrue interest on notes payable:		
	$20,000 × 12% × $\frac{1}{12}$ = $200)		
30	Unearned Service Revenue	700	
	Service Revenue		700
	(To record revenue earned: $600 ÷ 6 = $100;		
	$100 per month × 7 = $700)		
30	Accounts Receivable	1,500	
	Service Revenue		1,500
	(To accrue revenue earned but not billed		
	or collected)		

Self-Study Questions

Self-Study/Self-Test

Answers are at the end of this chapter.

(SO 1) **1.** What is the time period assumption?
  (a) Revenue should be recognized in the accounting period in which it is earned.
  (b) Expenses should be matched with revenues.
  (c) The economic life of a business can be divided into artificial time periods.
  (d) The fiscal year should correspond with the calendar year.

(SO 1) **2.** Which principle dictates that efforts (expenses) be recorded with accomplishments (revenues)?
  (a) Matching principle.
  (b) Cost principle.
  (c) Periodicity principle.
  (d) Revenue recognition principle.

(SO 3) **3.** Adjusting entries are made to ensure that:
  (a) expenses are recognized in the period in which they are incurred.
  (b) revenues are recorded in the period in which they are earned.
  (c) balance sheet and income statement accounts have correct balances at the end of an accounting period.
  (d) All of the above.

(SO 4, 5) **4.** Each of the following is a major type (or category) of adjusting entry *except:*
  (a) prepaid expenses.
  (b) accrued revenues.
  (c) accrued expenses.
  (d) earned expenses.

(SO 5) **5.** The trial balance shows Supplies $1,350 and Supplies Expense $0. If $600 of supplies are on hand at the end of the period, the adjusting entry is:

(a)	Supplies	600	
	Supplies Expense		600
(b)	Supplies	750	
	Supplies Expense		750
(c)	Supplies Expense	750	
	Supplies		750
(d)	Supplies Expense	600	
	Supplies		600

(SO 4)   6. Adjustments for unearned revenues:
      (a) decrease liabilities and increase revenues.
      (b) increase liabilities and increase revenues.
      (c) increase assets and increase revenues.
      (d) decrease revenues and decrease assets.

(SO 5)   7. Adjustments for accrued revenues:
      (a) increase assets and increase liabilities.
      (b) increase assets and increase revenues.
      (c) decrease assets and decrease revenues.
      (d) decrease liabilities and increase revenues.

(SO 5)   8. Emily Keshen earned a salary of $400 for the last week of September. She will be paid on October 1. The adjusting entry for Emily's employer at September 30 is:
      (a) No entry is required.
      (b) Salaries Expense   400
           Salaries Payable   400
      (c) Salaries Expense   400
           Cash   400
      (d) Salaries Payable   400
           Cash   400

(SO 6)   9. Which statement is *incorrect* concerning the adjusted trial balance?
      (a) An adjusted trial balance proves the equality of the total debit balances and the total credit balances in the ledger after all adjustments are made.
      (b) The adjusted trial balance provides the primary basis for the preparation of financial statements.
      (c) The adjusted trial balance lists the account balances segregated by assets and liabilities.
      (d) The adjusted trial balance is prepared after the adjusting entries have been journalized and posted.

10. Which one of these statements about the accrual basis of accounting is *false?*   (SO 3)
      (a) Events that change a company's financial statements are recorded in the periods in which the events occur.
      (b) Revenue is recognized in the period in which it is earned.
      (c) This basis is in accord with generally accepted accounting principles.
      (d) Revenue is recorded only when cash is received, and expense is recorded only when cash is paid.

11. Which account will have a zero balance after closing entries have been journalized and posted?   (SO 7)
      (a) Service Revenue.
      (b) Advertising Supplies.
      (c) Prepaid Insurance.
      (d) Accumulated Depreciation.

12. Which types of accounts will appear in the post-closing trial balance?   (SO 7)
      (a) Permanent accounts.
      (b) Temporary accounts.
      (c) Accounts shown in the income statement columns of a work sheet.
      (d) None of the above.

13. All of the following are required steps in the accounting cycle *except:*   (SO 8)
      (a) journalizing and posting closing entries.
      (b) preparing an adjusted trial balance.
      (c) preparing a post-closing trial balance.
      (d) preparing a work sheet.

Note: All asterisked Questions, Exercises, and Problems relate to material in the appendix to the chapter.

Questions

1. (a) How does the time period assumption affect an accountant's analysis of accounting transactions?
   (b) Explain the term *fiscal year.*

2. Identify and state two generally accepted accounting principles that relate to adjusting the accounts.

3. Charles Thon, a lawyer, accepts a legal engagement in March, performs the work in April, and is paid in May. If Thon's law firm prepares monthly financial statements, when should it recognize revenue from this engagement? Why?

4. In completing the engagement in question 3, Thon incurs $2,000 of expenses in March, $2,500 in April, and none in May. How much expense should be deducted from revenues in the month the revenue is recognized? Why?

5. "Adjusting entries are required by the cost principle of accounting." Do you agree? Explain.

6. Why may the financial information in a trial balance not be up-to-date and complete?

7. Distinguish between the two categories of adjusting entries, and identify the types of adjustments applicable to each category.

8. What accounts are debited and credited in a prepaid expense adjusting entry?

9. "Depreciation is a process of valuation that results in the reporting of the fair market value of the asset." Do you agree? Explain.

10. Explain the differences between depreciation expense and accumulated depreciation.

11. Alvarez Company purchased equipment for $12,000. By the current balance sheet date, $7,000 had been depreciated. Indicate the balance sheet presentation of the data.

12. What accounts are debited and credited in an unearned revenue adjusting entry?

13. ⊶——c A company fails to recognize revenue earned but not yet received. Which of the following accounts are involved in the adjusting entry: (a) asset, (b) liability, (c) revenue, or (d) expense? For the accounts selected, indicate whether they would be debited or credited in the entry.

14. ⊶——c A company fails to recognize an expense incurred but not paid. Indicate which of the following accounts is debited and which is credited in the adjusting entry: (a) asset, (b) liability, (c) revenue, or (d) expense.

15. ⊶——c A company makes an accrued revenue adjusting entry for $900 and an accrued expense adjusting entry for $600. How much was net income understated prior to these entries? Explain.

16. On January 9 a company pays $5,000 for salaries, of which $1,700 was reported as Salaries Payable on December 31. Give the entry to record the payment.

17. For each of the following items before adjustment, indicate the type of adjusting entry—prepaid expense, unearned revenue, accrued revenue, and accrued expense—that is needed to correct the misstatement. If an item could result in more than one type of adjusting entry, indicate each of the types.
    (a) Assets are understated.
    (b) Liabilities are overstated.
    (c) Liabilities are understated.
    (d) Expenses are understated.
    (e) Assets are overstated.
    (f) Revenue is understated

18. One-half of the adjusting entry is given below. Indicate the account title for the other half of the entry.
    (a) Salaries Expense is debited.
    (b) Depreciation Expense is debited.
    (c) Interest Payable is credited.
    (d) Supplies is credited.

    (e) Accounts Receivable is debited.
    (f) Unearned Service Revenue is debited.

19. "An adjusting entry may affect more than one balance sheet or income statement account." Do you agree? Why or why not?

20. Why is it possible to prepare financial statements directly from an adjusted trial balance?

21. ⊶——c
    (a) What information do accrual basis financial statements provide that cash basis statements do not?
    (b) What information do cash basis financial statements provide that accrual basis statements do not?

22. What is the relationship, if any, between the amount shown in the adjusted trial balance column for an account and that account's ledger balance?

23. Identify the account(s) debited and credited in each of the four closing entries, assuming the company has net income for the year.

24. Describe the nature of the Income Summary account, and identify the types of summary data that may be posted to this account.

25. What items are disclosed on a post-closing trial balance, and what is its purpose?

26. Which of these accounts would not appear in the post-closing trial balance? Interest Payable, Equipment, Depreciation Expense, Dividends, Unearned Service Revenue, Accumulated Depreciation—Equipment, and Service Revenue.

27. Indicate, in the sequence in which they are made, the three required steps in the accounting cycle that involve journalizing.

28. Identify, in the sequence in which they are prepared, the three trial balances that are required in the accounting cycle.

*29. What is the purpose of a work sheet?

*30. What is the basic form of a work sheet?

Brief Exercises

Identify impact of transactions on cash and retained earnings.
(SO 2)

BE4-1 Transactions that affect earnings do not necessarily affect cash.

Instructions
Identify the effect, if any, that each of the following transactions would have upon cash and retained earnings. The first transaction has been completed as an example.

	Cash	Retained Earnings
(a) Purchased $100 of supplies for cash.	$100	$ 0
(b) Recorded an adjusting entry to record use of $30 of the above supplies.		
(c) Made sales of $1,000, all on account.		
(d) Received $800 from customers in payment of their accounts.		
(e) Purchased capital asset for cash, $2,500.		
(f) Recorded depreciation of building for period used, $800.		

BE4-2 The ledger of H. J. Oslo Company includes the following accounts. Explain why each account may require adjustment.
- **(a)** Prepaid Insurance.
- **(b)** Depreciation Expense.
- **(c)** Unearned Service Revenue.
- **(d)** Interest Payable.

Indicate why adjusting entries are needed.
(SO 3)

BE4-3 J. A. Norris Company accumulates the following adjustment data at December 31. Indicate (1) the type of adjustment (prepaid expense, accrued revenue, and so on) and (2) the status of the accounts before adjustment (overstated or understated).
- **(a)** Supplies of $600 are on hand. Supplies account shows $1,900 balance.
- **(b)** Service Revenue earned but unbilled total $700.
- **(c)** Interest of $200 has accumulated on a note payable.
- **(d)** Rent collected in advance totaling $1,100 has been earned.

Identify the major types of adjusting entries.
(SO 3)

BE4-4 Gonzales Advertising Company's trial balance at December 31 shows Advertising Supplies $8,800 and Advertising Supplies Expense $0. On December 31 there are $1,500 of supplies on hand. Prepare the adjusting entry at December 31 and, using T accounts, enter the balances in the accounts, post the adjusting entry, and indicate the adjusted balance in each account.

Prepare adjusting entry for supplies.
(SO 4)

BE4-5 At the end of its first year, the trial balance of Shumway Company shows Equipment $22,000 and zero balances in Accumulated Depreciation—Equipment and Depreciation Expense. Depreciation for the year is estimated to be $3,000. Prepare the adjusting entry for depreciation at December 31, post the adjustments to T accounts, and indicate the balance sheet presentation of the equipment at December 31.

Prepare adjusting entry for depreciation.
(SO 4)

BE4-6 On July 1, 2005, Gomez Co. pays $16,000 to Richards Insurance Co. for a 2-year insurance contract. Both companies have fiscal years ending December 31. For Gomez Co. journalize and post the entry on July 1 and the adjusting entry on December 31.

Prepare adjusting entry for prepaid expense.
(SO 4)

BE4-7 Using the data in BE4-6, journalize and post the entry on July 1 and the adjusting entry on December 31 for Richards Insurance Co. Richards uses the accounts Unearned Insurance Revenue and Insurance Revenue.

Prepare adjusting entry for unearned revenue.
(SO 4)

BE4-8 The bookkeeper for Sidhu Company asks you to prepare the following accrual adjusting entries at December 31.
- **(a)** Interest on notes payable of $400 is accrued.
- **(b)** Service revenue earned but unbilled totals $1,400.
- **(c)** Salaries of $600 earned by employees have not been recorded.

Use these account titles: Service Revenue, Accounts Receivable, Interest Expense, Interest Payable, Salaries Expense, and Salaries Payable.

Prepare adjusting entries for accruals.
(SO 5)

BE4-9 The trial balance of Downtown Company includes the following balance sheet accounts. Identify the accounts that might require adjustment. For each account that requires adjustment, indicate (1) the type of adjusting entry (prepaid expenses, unearned revenues, accrued revenues, and accrued expenses) and (2) the related account in the adjusting entry.
- **(a)** Accounts Receivable.
- **(b)** Prepaid Insurance.
- **(c)** Equipment.
- **(d)** Accumulated Depreciation—Equipment.
- **(e)** Notes Payable.
- **(f)** Interest Payable.
- **(g)** Unearned Service Revenue.

Analyze accounts in an adjusted trial balance.
(SO 6)

BE4-10 The adjusted trial balance of Verbos Corporation at December 31, 2005, includes the following accounts: Retained Earnings $15,600; Dividends $6,000; Service Revenue $37,000; Salaries Expense $13,000; Insurance Expense $2,000; Rent Expense $3,500; Supplies Expense $1,500; and Depreciation Expense $1,000. Prepare an income statement for the year.

Prepare an income statement from an adjusted trial balance.
(SO 6)

BE4-11 Partial adjusted trial balance data for Verbos Corporation are presented in BE4-10. The balance in Retained Earnings is the balance as of January 1. Prepare a retained earnings statement for the year assuming net income is $14,000.

Prepare a retained earnings statement from an adjusted trial balance.
(SO 6)

BE4-12 The following selected accounts appear in the adjusted trial balance for Matthews Company. Indicate the financial statement on which each account would be reported.

Identify financial statement for selected accounts.
(SO 6)

(a) Accumulated Depreciation.   (e) Service Revenue.
(b) Depreciation Expense.   (f) Supplies.
(c) Retained Earnings.   (g) Accounts Payable.
(d) Dividends.

BE4-13   Using the data in BE4-12, identify the accounts that would be included in a post-closing trial balance.

BE4-14   The required steps in the accounting cycle are listed in random order below. List the steps in proper sequence.
(a) Prepare a post-closing trial balance.
(b) Prepare an adjusted trial balance.
(c) Analyze business transactions.
(d) Prepare a trial balance.
(e) Journalize the transactions.
(f) Journalize and post closing entries.
(g) Prepare financial statements.
(h) Journalize and post adjusting entries.
(i) Post to ledger accounts.

Exercises

E4-1   These are the assumptions, principles, and constraints discussed in this and previous chapters.
1. Economic entity assumption.
2. Matching principle.
3. Monetary unit assumption.
4. Time period assumption.
5. Cost principle.
6. Materiality.
7. Full disclosure principle.
8. Going concern assumption.
9. Revenue recognition principle.
10. Conservatism.

Instructions
Identify by number the accounting assumption, principle, or constraint that describes each situation below. Do not use a number more than once.

_____ (a) Is the rationale for why plant assets are not reported at liquidation value. (Do not use the cost principle.)
_____ (b) Indicates that personal and business record-keeping should be separately maintained.
_____ (c) Ensures that all relevant financial information is reported.
_____ (d) Assumes that the dollar is the "measuring stick" used to report on financial performance.
_____ (e) Requires that accounting standards be followed for all *significant* items.
_____ (f) Separates financial information into time periods for reporting purposes.
_____ (g) Requires recognition of expenses in the same period as related revenues.
_____ (h) Indicates that market value changes subsequent to purchase are not recorded in the accounts.

E4-2   Here are some accounting reporting situations.
(a) Mills Company recognizes revenue at the end of the production cycle but before sale. The price of the product, as well as the amount that can be sold, is not certain.
(b) Healy Company is in its fifth year of operation and has yet to issue financial statements. (Do not use the full disclosure principle.)
(c) Quick, Inc. is carrying inventory at its original cost of $100,000. Inventory has a market value of $110,000.

(d) Fantazzi Hospital Supply Corporation reports only current assets and current liabilities on its balance sheet. Property, plant, and equipment and bonds payable are reported as current assets and current liabilities, respectively. Liquidation of the company is unlikely.

(e) Lee Company has inventory on hand that cost $400,000. Lee reports inventory on its balance sheet at its current market value of $425,000.

(f) Robin Dewitt, president of Classic Music Company, bought a computer for her personal use. She paid for the computer by using company funds and debited the "Computers" account.

Instructions
For each situation, list the assumption, principle, or constraint that has been violated, if any. Some of these assumptions, principles, and constraints were presented in earlier chapters. List only one answer for each situation.

E4-3 Your examination of the records of a company that follows the cash basis of accounting tells you that the company's reported cash basis earnings in 2005 are $35,190. If this firm had followed accrual basis accounting practices, it would have reported the following year-end balances.

Convert earnings from cash to accrual basis.
(SO 2, 4, 5)

	2005	2004
Accounts receivable	$3,400	$2,500
Supplies on hand	1,300	1,160
Unpaid wages owed	1,200	2,400
Other unpaid amounts	1,400	1,600

Instructions
Determine the company's net earnings on an accrual basis for 2005. Show all your calculations in an orderly fashion.

E4-4 In its first year of operations, Patrick Company earned $26,000 in service revenue, $4,000 of which was on account and still outstanding at year-end. The remaining $22,000 was received in cash from customers.

Determine cash basis and accrual basis earnings.
(SO 2)

   The company incurred operating expenses of $14,500. Of these expenses $13,000 were paid in cash; $1,500 was still owed on account at year-end. In addition, Patrick prepaid $2,500 for insurance coverage that would not be used until the second year of operations.

Instructions
(a) Calculate the first year's net earnings under the cash basis of accounting, and calculate the first year's net earnings under the accrual basis of accounting.

(b) Which basis of accounting (cash or accrual) provides more useful information for decision makers?

E4-5 Arseneault Corporation's annual income taxes are estimated to be $12,000 during its first year of operations. It pays its income taxes monthly, a few days after the end of each month. At year-end, selected income tax accounts in the unadjusted trial balance are as follows.

Analyze income tax transactions and prepare adjusting entries.
(SO 2, 5)

Income Tax Expense $11,000   Income Tax Payable $0

Belyea Corporation's annual income taxes are estimated to be $24,000 during its first year of operations. It pays its income taxes quarterly a few days after the end of each quarter (quarters end on the last day of March, June, September, and December). At year-end, selected income tax accounts in the unadjusted trial balance are as follows.

Income Tax Expense $18,000   Income Tax Payable $0

Instructions
(a) How much income tax did Arseneault and Belyea pay during the current year?

(b) How much income tax does each company owe at year-end?

(c) Prepare the adjusting journal entry required to record any accrued income taxes for each company.

E4-6 Coleman Company accumulates the following adjustment data at December 31.

(a) Service Revenue earned but unbilled totals $600.

(b) Store supplies of $300 are on hand. Supplies account shows $2,300 balance.

Identify types of adjustments and accounts before adjustment.
(SO 3, 4, 5)

(c) Utility expenses of $275 are unpaid.

(d) Service revenue of $260 collected in advance has been earned.

(e) Salaries of $800 are unpaid.

(f) Prepaid insurance totaling $400 has expired.

Instructions

For each item indicate (1) the type of adjustment (prepaid expense, unearned revenue, accrued revenue, or accrued expense) and (2) the status of the accounts before adjustment (overstated or understated).

Prepare adjusting entries from selected account data.
(SO 4, 5)

E4-7 The ledger of Easy Rental Agency on March 31 of the current year includes these selected accounts before adjusting entries have been prepared.

	Debits	Credits
Prepaid Insurance	$ 3,600	
Supplies	4,000	
Equipment	25,000	
Accumulated Depreciation—Equipment		$ 8,400
Notes Payable		20,000
Unearned Rent Revenue		10,200
Rent Revenue		60,000
Interest Expense	0	
Wage Expense	14,000	

An analysis of the accounts shows the following.

1. The equipment depreciates $250 per month.

2. One-third of the unearned rent revenue was earned during the quarter.

3. Interest of $500 is accrued on the notes payable.

4. Supplies on hand total $850.

5. Insurance expires at the rate of $300 per month.

Instructions

Prepare the adjusting entries at March 31, assuming that adjusting entries are made quarterly. Additional accounts are: Depreciation Expense, Insurance Expense, Interest Payable, and Supplies Expense.

Prepare adjusting entries.
(SO 4, 5)

E4-8 Donald Patter, D.D.S., opened an incorporated dental practice on January 1, 2005. During the first month of operations the following transactions occurred:

1. Performed services for patients who had dental plan insurance. At January 31, $900 of such services was earned but not yet billed to the insurance companies.

2. Utility expenses incurred but not paid prior to January 31 totaled $520.

3. Purchased dental equipment on January 1 for $80,000, paying $20,000 in cash and signing a $60,000, 3-year note payable (Interest is paid each December 31). The equipment depreciates $400 per month. Interest is $500 per month.

4. Purchased a 1-year malpractice insurance policy on January 1 for $18,000.

5. Purchased $1,600 of dental supplies. On January 31 determined that $500 of supplies were on hand.

Instructions

Prepare the adjusting entries on January 31. Account titles are: Accumulated Depreciation—Dental Equipment, Depreciation Expense, Service Revenue, Accounts Receivable, Insurance Expense, Interest Expense, Interest Payable, Prepaid Insurance, Supplies, Supplies Expense, Utilities Expense, and Utilities Payable.

Prepare adjusting entries.
(SO 4, 5)

E4-9 The unadjusted trial balance for Sierra Corp. is shown in Illustration 4-4, p. 164. In lieu of the adjusting entries shown in the text at October 31, assume the following adjustment data.

1. Advertising supplies on hand at October 31 total $1,100.

2. Expired insurance for the month is $100.

3. Depreciation for the month is $50.

4. As of October 31, $500 of the previously recorded unearned revenue had been earned.

5. Services provided but unbilled (and no receivable has been recorded) at October 31 are $300.

6. Interest expense accrued at October 31 is $70.

7. Accrued salaries at October 31 are $1,400.

Instructions
Prepare the adjusting entries for the items above.

E4-10 The income statement of Rocket Co. for the month of July shows net income of $1,400 based on Service Revenue $5,500; Wages Expense $2,300; Supplies Expense $1,000, and Utilities Expense $800. In reviewing the statement, you discover the following:

Prepare a correct income statement.
(SO 1, 4, 5, 6)

1. Insurance expired during July of $300 was omitted.

2. Supplies expense includes $400 of supplies that are still on hand at July 31.

3. Depreciation on equipment of $150 was omitted.

4. Accrued but unpaid wages at July 31 of $300 were not included.

5. Revenue earned but unrecorded totaled $750.

Instructions
Prepare a correct income statement for July 2005.

E4-11 This is a partial adjusted trial balance of Schweitz Company.

Analyze adjusted data.
(SO 1, 4, 5, 6)

SCHWEITZ COMPANY
Adjusted Trial Balance
January 31, 2005

	Debit	Credit
Supplies	$ 700	
Prepaid Insurance	2,400	
Salaries Payable		$1,200
Unearned Service Revenue		750
Supplies Expense	950	
Insurance Expense	600	
Salaries Expense	1,800	
Service Revenue		2,000

Instructions
Answer these questions, assuming the year begins January 1.

(a) If the amount in Supplies Expense is the January 31 adjusting entry, and $850 of supplies was purchased in January, what was the balance in Supplies on January 1?

(b) If the amount in Insurance Expense is the January 31 adjusting entry, and the original insurance premium was for 1 year, what was the total premium and when was the policy purchased?

(c) If $2,500 of salaries was paid in January, what was the balance in Salaries Payable at December 31, 2004?

(d) If $1,600 was received in January for services performed in January, what was the balance in Unearned Service Revenue at December 31, 2004?

E4-12 Selected accounts of Olympia Company are shown here and on the next page.

Journalize basic transactions and adjusting entries.
(SO 4, 5, 6)

Supplies Expense		Salaries Payable	
July 31	700	July 31	1,200

Salaries Expense				Accounts Receivable		
July 15	1,200			July 31	500	
31	1,200					

Service Revenue				Unearned Service Revenue		
	July 14	3,000	July 31	1,200	July 1	Bal. 1,500
	31	1,200			20	700
	31	500				

Supplies			
July 1	Bal. 1,100	July 31	700
10	200		

Instructions

After analyzing the accounts, journalize (a) the July transactions and (b) the adjusting entries that were made on July 31. [*Hint:* July transactions were for cash.]

Prepare adjusting entries from analysis of trial balances.
(SO 4, 5, 6)

E4-13 The trial balances shown below are before and after adjustment for Rosenberger Company at the end of its fiscal year.

ROSENBERGER COMPANY
Trial Balance
August 31, 2005

	Before Adjustment		After Adjustment	
	Dr.	Cr.	Dr.	Cr.
Cash	$ 9,600		$ 9,600	
Accounts Receivable	8,800		9,400	
Office Supplies	2,300		700	
Prepaid Insurance	4,000		2,500	
Office Equipment	14,000		14,000	
Accumulated Depreciation—Office Equipment		$ 3,600		$ 4,800
Accounts Payable		5,800		5,800
Salaries Payable		0		1,100
Unearned Rent Revenue		1,500		700
Common Stock		10,000		10,000
Retained Earnings		5,600		5,600
Dividends	800		800	
Service Revenue		34,000		34,600
Rent Revenue		11,000		11,800
Salaries Expense	17,000		18,100	
Office Supplies Expense	0		1,600	
Rent Expense	15,000		15,000	
Insurance Expense	0		1,500	
Depreciation Expense	0		1,200	
	$71,500	$71,500	$74,400	$74,400

Instructions

Prepare the adjusting entries that were made.

Prepare financial statements from adjusted trial balance.
(SO 6)

E4-14 The adjusted trial balance for Rosenberger Company is given in E4-13.

Instructions

Prepare the income and retained earnings statements for the year and the classified balance sheet at August 31.

Prepare closing entries.
(SO 7)

E4-15 The adjusted trial balance for Rosenberger Company is given in E4-13.

Instructions

Prepare the closing entries for the temporary accounts at August 31.

Problems: Set A

P4-1A Presented here are the assumptions, principles, and constraints used in this and previous chapters.

Identify accounting assumptions, principles, and constraints.
(SO 1)

1. Economic entity assumption.	**6.** Revenue recognition principle.
2. Materiality.	**7.** Full disclosure principle.
3. Monetary unit assumption.	**8.** Cost principle.
4. Time period assumption.	**9.** Going concern assumption.
5. Matching principle.	**10.** Conservatism.

Instructions
Identify by number the accounting assumption, principle, or constraint that describes each of these situations. Do not use a number more than once.

____ **(a)** Assets are not stated at their liquidation value. (Do not use the cost principle.)
____ **(b)** The death of the president is not recorded in the accounts.
____ **(c)** Pencil sharpeners are expensed when purchased.
____ **(d)** An allowance for doubtful accounts is established. (Do not use conservatism.)
____ **(e)** Each entity is kept as a unit distinct from its owner or owners.
____ **(f)** Reporting must be done at defined intervals.
____ **(g)** Revenue is recorded at the point of sale.
____ **(h)** When in doubt, it is better to understate rather than overstate net income.
____ **(i)** All important information related to inventories is presented in the footnotes or in the financial statements.

P4-2A The following data are taken from the comparative balance sheets of Breakers Billiards Club, which prepares its financial statements using the accrual basis of accounting.

Record transactions on accrual basis; convert revenue to cash receipts.
(SO 2, 4)

December 31	2005	2004
Accounts receivable for member fees	$12,000	$ 9,000
Unearned fees revenue	17,000	22,000

Fees are billed to members based upon their use of the club's facilities. Unearned fees arise from the sale of gift certificates, which members can apply to their future use of club facilities. The 2005 income statement for the club showed that fee revenue of $153,000 was earned during the year.

Instructions
(*Hint:* You will find it helpful to use T accounts to analyze these data.)
(a) Prepare journal entries for each of the following events that took place during 2005.

    1. Fees receivable from 2004 were all collected during 2005.

    2. Gift certificates outstanding at the end of 2004 were all redeemed during 2005.

    3. An additional $30,000 worth of gift certificates were sold during 2005; a portion of these were used by the recipients during the year; the remainder were still outstanding at the end of 2005.

    4. Fees for 2005 were billed to members.

    5. Fees receivable for 2005 (i.e., those billed in item (4) above) were partially collected.

(b) Cash received $145,000

(b) Determine the amount of cash received by the club with respect to fees during 2005.

Prepare adjusting entries, post to ledger accounts, and prepare an adjusted trial balance.
(SO 4, 5, 6)

P4-3A Paula Norby started her own consulting firm, Hometown Consulting, on May 1, 2005. The trial balance at May 31 is as shown on page 202.

Peachtree

HOMETOWN CONSULTING
Trial Balance
May 31, 2005

	Debit	Credit
Cash	$ 6,500	
Accounts Receivable	3,000	
Prepaid Insurance	3,600	
Supplies	1,500	
Office Furniture	12,000	
Accounts Payable		$ 3,500
Unearned Service Revenue		4,000
Common Stock		19,100
Service Revenue		5,000
Salaries Expense	4,000	
Rent Expense	1,000	
	$31,600	$31,600

In addition to those accounts listed on the trial balance, the chart of accounts for Hometown Consulting also contains the following accounts: Accumulated Depreciation—Office Furniture, Travel Payable, Salaries Payable, Depreciation Expense, Insurance Expense, Travel Expense, and Supplies Expense.

Other data:

1. $500 of supplies have been used during the month.

2. Travel costs incurred but not paid are $200.

3. The insurance policy is for 3 years.

4. $1,000 of the balance in the Unearned Service Revenue account remains unearned at the end of the month.

5. May 31 is a Wednesday and employees are paid on Fridays. Hometown Consulting has two employees that are paid $600 each for a 5-day work week.

6. The office furniture has a 5-year life with no salvage value and is being depreciated at $200 per month for 60 months.

7. Invoices representing $2,000 of services performed during the month have not been recorded as of May 31.

Instructions

(a) Prepare the adjusting entries for the month of May.

(b) Post the adjusting entries to the ledger accounts. Enter the totals from the trial balance as beginning account balances. Use T accounts.

(c) Prepare an adjusted trial balance at May 31, 2005.

(c) Tot. trial balance $34,720

Prepare adjusting entries, adjusted trial balance, and financial statements.
(SO 4, 5, 6, 7)

P4-4A Wander In Resort opened for business on June 1 with eight air-conditioned units. Its trial balance before adjustment on August 31 is presented here.

WANDER IN RESORT
Trial Balance
August 31, 2005

	Debit	Credit
Cash	$ 19,600	
Prepaid Insurance	5,400	
Supplies	4,300	
Land	25,000	
Cottages	132,000	
Furniture	26,000	
Accounts Payable		$ 6,500
Unearned Rent Revenue		6,800

	Debit	Credit
Mortgage Payable		90,000
Common Stock		100,000
Dividends	5,000	
Rent Revenue		80,000
Salaries Expense	53,000	
Utilities Expense	9,400	
Repair Expense	3,600	
	$283,300	$283,300

Other data:

1. Insurance expires at the rate of $300 per month.

2. An inventory count on August 31 shows $1,200 of supplies on hand.

3. Annual depreciation is $4,800 on cottages and $2,400 on furniture.

4. Unearned rent of $5,000 was earned prior to August 31.

5. Salaries of $600 were unpaid at August 31.

6. Rentals of $800 were due from tenants at August 31. (Use Accounts Receivable.)

7. The mortgage interest rate is 12% per year. (The mortgage was taken out August 1.)

Instructions

(a) Journalize the adjusting entries on August 31 for the 3-month period June 1–August 31.

(b) Prepare a ledger using T accounts. Enter the trial balance amounts and post the adjusting entries.

(c) Prepare an adjusted trial balance on August 31.

(d) Prepare an income statement and a retained earnings statement for the 3 months ended August 31 and a classified balance sheet as of August 31.

(e) Identify which accounts should be closed on August 31.

(c) Tot. trial
     balance $287,400
(d) Net income $ 12,500

P4-5A E-Z Advertising Agency was founded by Wayne Barlow in January 2000. Presented here are both the adjusted and unadjusted trial balances as of December 31, 2005.

Prepare adjusting entries and financial statements; identify accounts to be closed.
(SO 4, 5, 6, 7)

E-Z ADVERTISING AGENCY
Trial Balance
December 31, 2005

	Unadjusted		Adjusted	
	Dr.	**Cr.**	**Dr.**	**Cr.**
Cash	$ 11,000		$ 11,000	
Accounts Receivable	18,000		21,500	
Art Supplies	8,400		6,000	
Prepaid Insurance	3,350		2,500	
Printing Equipment	60,000		60,000	
Accumulated Depreciation		$ 28,000		$ 35,000
Accounts Payable		5,000		5,000
Interest Payable		0		150
Notes Payable		5,000		5,000
Unearned Advertising Revenue		6,000		5,600
Salaries Payable		0		1,300
Common Stock		20,000		20,000
Retained Earnings		5,500		5,500
Dividends	12,000		12,000	
Advertising Revenue		57,600		61,500
Salaries Expense	10,000		11,300	
Insurance Expense			850	
Interest Expense			150	

	Unadjusted		Adjusted	
	Dr.	**Cr.**	**Dr.**	**Cr.**
Depreciation Expense			7,000	
Art Supplies Expense			2,400	
Rent Expense	4,350		4,350	
	$127,100	$127,100	$139,050	$139,050

Instructions

(a) Journalize the annual adjusting entries that were made.

(b) Prepare an income statement and a retained earnings statement for the year ended December 31, and a classified balance sheet at December 31.

(c) Identify which accounts should be closed on December 31.

(d) If the note has been outstanding 3 months, what is the annual interest rate on that note?

(e) If the company paid $13,500 in salaries in 2005, what was the balance in Salaries Payable on December 31, 2004?

(b) Net income $35,450
Tot. assets $66,000

Prepare adjusting entries.
(SO 4, 5)

P4-6A A review of the ledger of Frazier Company at December 31, 2005, produces the following data pertaining to the preparation of annual adjusting entries.

1. **Salaries Payable $0:** There are eight salaried employees. Salaries are paid every Friday for the current week. Six employees receive a salary of $800 each per week, and two employees earn $500 each per week. December 31 is a Tuesday. Employees do not work weekends. All employees worked the last 2 days of December.

2. **Unearned Rent Revenue $369,000:** The company began subleasing office space in its new building on November 1. Each tenant is required to make a $5,000 security deposit that is not refundable until occupancy is terminated. At December 31 the company had the following rental contracts that are paid in full for the entire term of the lease.

Date	Term (in months)	Monthly Rent	Number of Leases
Nov. 1	6	$4,000	5
Dec. 1	6	8,500	4

3. **Prepaid Advertising $13,200:** This balance consists of payments on two advertising contracts. The contracts provide for monthly advertising in two trade magazines. The terms of the contracts are as follows.

Contract	Date	Amount	Number of Magazine Issues
A650	May 1	$6,000	12
B974	Sept. 1	7,200	24

The first advertisement runs in the month in which the contract is signed.

4. **Notes Payable $80,000:** This balance consists of a note for 1 year at an annual interest rate of 9%, dated June 1, 2005.

Instructions

Prepare the adjusting entries at December 31, 2005. Show all computations.

Prepare adjusting entries and a corrected income statement.
(SO 4, 5)

P4-7A The Try-Us Travel Agency Ltd. was organized on January 1, 2003, by Paul Volpé. Paul is a good manager but a poor accountant. From the trial balance prepared by a part-time bookkeeper, Paul prepared the following income statement for the quarter that ended March 31, 2005.

TRY-US TRAVEL AGENCY LTD.
Income Statement
For the Quarter Ended March 31, 2005

Revenues		
Travel service revenue		$50,000
Operating expenses		
Advertising	$2,600	
Depreciation	400	
Income tax	1,500	
Salaries	6,000	
Utilities	400	10,900
Net income		$39,100

Paul knew that something was wrong with the statement because net income had never exceeded $5,000 in any one quarter. Knowing that you are an experienced accountant, he asks you to review the income statement and other data.

You first look at the trial balance. In addition to the account balances reported above in the income statement, the trial balance contains the following additional selected balances at March 31, 2005.

Supplies	$ 3,200
Prepaid insurance	1,200
Note payable	10,000

You then make inquiries and discover the following:

1. Travel service revenue includes advance payments for cruises, $30,000.

2. There were $800 of supplies on hand at March 31.

3. Prepaid insurance resulted from the payment of a one-year policy on February 1, 2005.

4. The mail on April 1, 2005, brought the utility bill for the month of March's heat, light, and power, $180.

5. There are two employees who receive salaries of $75 each per day. At March 31, three days' salaries have been incurred but not paid.

6. The note payable is a 6-month, 10% note dated January 1, 2005.

Instructions
(a) Prepare any adjusting journal entries required as at March 31, 2005.
(b) Prepare a correct income statement for the quarter ended March 31, 2005.
(c) Explain to Paul the generally accepted accounting principles that he did not recognize in preparing his income statement and their effect on his results.

(b) Net income $5,620

P4-8A   On September 1, 2005, the following were the account balances of Rabbit Ears Equipment Repair.

Journalize transactions and follow through accounting cycle to preparation of financial statements.
(SO 4, 5, 6)

	Debits		**Credits**
Cash	$ 4,880	Accumulated Depreciation	$ 1,500
Accounts Receivable	3,720	Accounts Payable	3,100
Supplies	800	Unearned Service Revenue	400
Store Equipment	15,000	Salaries Payable	700
	$24,400	Common Stock	10,000
		Retained Earnings	8,700
			$24,400

During September the following summary transactions were completed.

Sept. 8 Paid $1,100 for salaries due employees, of which $400 is for September and $700 is for August salaries payable.
10 Received $1,200 cash from customers in payment of account.
12 Received $3,400 cash for services performed in September.
15 Purchased store equipment on account $3,000.

Sept. 17   Purchased supplies on account $1,500.
       20   Paid creditors $4,500 of accounts payable due.
       22   Paid September rent $500.
       25   Paid salaries $1,200.
       27   Performed services on account and billed customers for services provided $700.
       29   Received $650 from customers for services to be provided in the future.

Adjustment data:

1. Supplies on hand $1,800.

2. Accrued salaries payable $400.

3. Depreciation $200 per month.

4. Unearned service revenue of $350 earned.

Instructions

(a) Enter the September 1 balances in the ledger T accounts.
(b) Journalize the September transactions.
(c) Post to the ledger T accounts. Use Service Revenue, Depreciation Expense, Supplies Expense, Salaries Expense, and Rent Expense.
(d) Prepare a trial balance at September 30.
(e) Journalize and post adjusting entries.
(f) Prepare an adjusted trial balance.
(g) Prepare an income statement and a retained earnings statement for September and a classified balance sheet at September 30.

(f) Tot. trial balance $29,050
(g) Tot. assets $24,150

Complete all steps in accounting cycle.
(SO 4, 5, 6, 7, 8)

P4-9A   Jasmine Aladdin opened Flying Carpet Cleaners on March 1, 2005. During March, the following transactions were completed.

Mar. 1   Issued $10,000 of common stock for $10,000 cash.
       1   Purchased used truck for $8,000, paying $5,000 cash and the balance on account.
       3   Purchased cleaning supplies for $1,200 on account.
       5   Paid $1,440 cash on 1-year insurance policy effective March 1.
      14   Billed customers $2,800 for cleaning services.
      18   Paid $1,500 cash on amount owed on truck and $500 on amount owed on cleaning supplies.
      20   Paid $1,500 cash for employee salaries.
      21   Collected $1,600 cash from customers billed on March 14.
      28   Billed customers $4,200 for cleaning services.
      31   Paid $200 for gas and oil used in truck during month.
      31   Declared and paid a $900 cash dividend.

The chart of accounts for Flying Carpet Cleaners contains the following accounts: Cash, Accounts Receivable, Cleaning Supplies, Prepaid Insurance, Equipment, Accumulated Depreciation—Equipment, Accounts Payable, Salaries Payable, Common Stock, Retained Earnings, Dividends, Income Summary, Service Revenue, Gas & Oil Expense, Cleaning Supplies Expense, Depreciation Expense, Insurance Expense, Salaries Expense.

Instructions

(a) Journalize the March transactions.
(b) Post to the ledger accounts. (Use T accounts.)
(c) Prepare a trial balance at March 31.
(d) Journalize the following adjustments.
    1. Earned but unbilled revenue at March 31 was $600.
    2. Depreciation on equipment for the month was $250.
    3. One-twelfth of the insurance expired.
    4. An inventory count shows $400 of cleaning supplies on hand at March 31.
    5. Accrued but unpaid employee salaries were $700.
(e) Post adjusting entries to the T accounts.
(f) Prepare an adjusted trial balance.
(g) Prepare the income statement and a retained earnings statement for March and a classified balance sheet at March 31.
(h) Journalize and post closing entries and complete the closing process.
(i) Prepare a post-closing trial balance at March 31.

(f) Tot. adj. trial
        balance $20,750
(g) Tot. assets $16,030

Problems: Set B

Identify accounting assumptions, principles, and constraints.
(SO 1)

P4-1B Presented below are the assumptions, principles, and constraints used in this and previous chapters.

1. Economic entity assumption.
2. Going concern assumption.
3. Monetary unit assumption.
4. Time period assumption.
5. Full disclosure principle.
6. Revenue recognition principle.
7. Matching principle.
8. Cost principle.
9. Materiality.
10. Conservatism.

Instructions

Identify by number the accounting assumption, principle, or constraint that describes each of these situations. Do not use a number more than once.

_____ **(a)** Repair tools are expensed when purchased. (Do not use conservatism.)
_____ **(b)** Allocates expenses to revenues in proper period.
_____ **(c)** Assumes that the dollar is the measuring stick used to report financial information.
_____ **(d)** Separates financial information into time periods for reporting purposes.
_____ **(e)** Market value changes subsequent to purchase are not recorded in the accounts. (Do not use the revenue recognition principle.)
_____ **(f)** Indicates that personal and business record keeping should be separately maintained.
_____ **(g)** Ensures that all relevant financial information is reported.
_____ **(h)** Lower of cost or market is used to value inventories.

Record transactions on accrual basis; convert revenue to cash receipts.
(SO 2, 4)

P4-2B The following selected data are taken from the comparative financial statements of Hammer Curling Club. The Club prepares its financial statements using the accrual basis of accounting.

September 30	2005	2004
Accounts receivable for member dues	$ 15,000	$ 11,000
Unearned ticket revenue	20,000	25,000
Dues revenue	148,000	132,000

Dues are billed to members based upon their use of the Club's facilities. Unearned ticket revenues arise from the sale of tickets to events such as the Skins Game.

Instructions

(*Hint:* You will find it helpful to use T accounts to analyze the following data. You must analyze these data sequentially, as missing information must first be deduced before moving on. Post your journal entries as you progress, rather than waiting until the end.)

(a) Prepare journal entries for each of the following events that took place during 2005.

1. Dues receivable from members from 2004 were all collected during 2005.
2. Unearned ticket revenue at the end of 2004 was all earned during 2005.
3. Additional tickets were sold for $35,000 cash during 2005; a portion of these were used by the purchasers during the year. The entire balance remaining relates to the upcoming Skins Game in 2005.
4. Dues for the 2004–2005 fiscal year were billed to members.
5. Dues receivable for 2005 (i.e., those billed in item (4) above) were partially collected.

(b) Determine the amount of cash received by the Club from the above transactions during the year ended September 30, 2005.

(b) Cash received $179,000

Prepare adjusting entries, post to ledger accounts, and prepare adjusted trial balance.
(SO 4, 5, 6)

P4-3B Ivan Izo started his own consulting firm, Izo Company, on June 1, 2005. The trial balance at June 30 is as follows.

IZO COMPANY
Trial Balance
June 30, 2005

	Debit	Credit
Cash	$ 6,850	
Accounts Receivable	7,000	
Prepaid Insurance	2,400	
Supplies	2,000	
Office Equipment	15,000	
Accounts Payable		$ 4,500
Unearned Service Revenue		5,000
Common Stock		21,750
Service Revenue		8,000
Salaries Expense	4,000	
Rent Expense	2,000	
	$39,250	$39,250

In addition to those accounts listed on the trial balance, the chart of accounts for Izo Company also contains the following accounts: Accumulated Depreciation—Office Equipment, Utilities Payable, Salaries Payable, Depreciation Expense, Insurance Expense, Utilities Expense, and Supplies Expense.

Other data:

1. Supplies on hand at June 30 total $1,300.
2. A utility bill for $180 has not been recorded and will not be paid until next month.
3. The insurance policy is for a year.
4. $2,500 of unearned service revenue has been earned at the end of the month.
5. Salaries of $1,500 are accrued at June 30.
6. The office equipment has a 5-year life with no salvage value and is being depreciated at $250 per month for 60 months.
7. Invoices representing $3,000 of services performed during the month have not been recorded as of June 30.

Instructions

(a) Prepare the adjusting entries for the month of June.

(b) Service rev. $13,500
(c) Tot. trial balance $44,180

(b) Post the adjusting entries to the ledger accounts. Enter the totals from the trial balance as beginning account balances. Use T accounts.

(c) Prepare an adjusted trial balance at June 30, 2005.

*Prepare adjusting entries,
adjusted trial balance, and
financial statements.*
(SO 4, 5, 6, 7)

P4-4B The Matrix Hotel opened for business on May 1, 2005. Here is its trial balance before adjustment on May 31.

MATRIX HOTEL
Trial Balance
May 31, 2005

	Debit	Credit
Cash	$ 2,500	
Prepaid Insurance	1,800	
Supplies	2,600	
Land	15,000	
Lodge	70,000	
Furniture	16,800	
Accounts Payable		$ 4,700
Unearned Rent Revenue		4,500
Mortgage Payable		35,000
Common Stock		60,000

	Debit	Credit
Rent Revenue		9,000
Salaries Expense	3,000	
Utilities Expense	1,000	
Advertising Expense	500	
	$113,200	$113,200

Other data:

1. Insurance expires at the rate of $300 per month.

2. An inventory of supplies shows $1,200 of unused supplies on May 31.

3. Annual depreciation is $3,600 on the lodge and $3,000 on furniture.

4. The mortgage interest rate is 12%. (The mortgage was taken out on May 1.)

5. Unearned rent of $1,500 has been earned.

6. Salaries of $500 are accrued and unpaid at May 31.

Instructions
(a) Journalize the adjusting entries on May 31.
(b) Prepare a ledger using T accounts. Enter the trial balance amounts and post the adjusting entries.
(c) Prepare an adjusted trial balance on May 31.
(d) Prepare an income statement and a retained earnings statement for the month of May and a classified balance sheet at May 31.
(e) Identify which accounts should be closed on May 31.

(c) Rent revenue $ 10,500
Tot. trial
  balance $114,600
(d) Net income $ 2,900

P4-5B Fantasy Golf Inc. was organized on July 1, 2005. Quarterly financial statements are prepared. The trial balance and adjusted trial balance on September 30 are shown here.

Prepare adjusting entries and financial statements; identify accounts to be closed.
(SO 4, 5, 6, 7)

FANTASY GOLF INC.
Trial Balance
September 30, 2005

	Unadjusted Dr.	Unadjusted Cr.	Adjusted Dr.	Adjusted Cr.
Cash	$ 6,700		$ 6,700	
Accounts Receivable	400		800	
Prepaid Rent	2,000		900	
Supplies	1,200		1,000	
Equipment	15,000		15,000	
Accumulated Depreciation—Equipment				$ 350
Notes Payable		$ 5,000		5,000
Accounts Payable		1,710		1,710
Salaries Payable				600
Interest Payable				50
Unearned Rent Revenue		1,000		600
Common Stock		14,000		14,000
Retained Earnings		0		0
Dividends	600		600	
Commission Revenue		14,000		14,400
Rent Revenue		400		800
Salaries Expense	8,800		9,400	
Rent Expense	900		2,000	
Depreciation Expense			350	
Supplies Expense			200	
Utilities Expense	510		510	
Interest Expense			50	
	$36,110	$36,110	$37,510	$37,510

(b) Net income $ 2,690
Tot. assets $24,050

Instructions
(a) Journalize the adjusting entries that were made.
(b) Prepare an income statement and a retained earnings statement for the 3 months ending September 30 and a classified balance sheet at September 30.
(c) Identify which accounts should be closed on September 30.
(d) If the note bears interest at 12%, how many months has it been outstanding?

Prepare adjusting entries.
(SO 4, 5)

P4-6B   A review of the ledger of Benes Company at December 31, 2005, produces these data pertaining to the preparation of annual adjusting entries.

1. Prepaid Insurance $13,550: The company has separate insurance policies on its buildings and its motor vehicles. Policy B4564 on the building was purchased on July 1, 2004, for $10,500. The policy has a term of 3 years. Policy A2958 on the vehicles was purchased on January 1, 2005, for $4,800. This policy has a term of 2 years.

2. Unearned Subscription Revenue $49,000: The company began selling magazine subscriptions on October 1, 2005 on an annual basis. The selling price of a subscription is $50. A review of subscription contracts reveals the following.

Subscription Start Date	Number of Subscriptions
October 1	200
November 1	300
December 1	480
	980

3. Notes Payable, $40,000: This balance consists of a note for 6 months at an annual interest rate of 9%, dated October 1.

4. Salaries Payable $0: There are eight salaried employees. Salaries are paid every Friday for the current week. Five employees receive a salary of $600 each per week, and three employees earn $700 each per week. December 31 is a Wednesday. Employees do not work weekends. All employees worked the last 3 days of December.

Instructions
Prepare the adjusting entries at December 31, 2005.

Prepare adjusting entries and a corrected income statement.
(SO 4, 5)

P4-7B   The Holiday Travel Court Ltd. was organized on July 1, 2004, by Alice Adare. Alice is a good manager but a poor accountant. From the trial balance prepared by a part-time bookkeeper, Alice prepared the following income statement for her fourth quarter, which ended June 30, 2005.

HOLIDAY TRAVEL COURT LTD.
Income Statement
For the Quarter ended June 30, 2005

Revenues		
Travel court rental revenues		$205,000
Operating expenses		
Advertising	$ 5,200	
Wages	80,500	
Utilities	900	
Depreciation	2,700	
Repairs	4,000	
Total operating expenses		93,300
Net income		$111,700

Alice suspected that something was wrong with the statement because net income had never exceeded $30,000 in any one quarter. Knowing that you are an experienced accountant, she asks you to review the income statement and other data.

You first look at the trial balance. In addition to the account balances reported above in the income statement, the ledger contains the following additional selected balances at June 30, 2005.

Supplies	$ 8,200
Prepaid Insurance	14,400
Note Payable	12,000

You then make inquiries and discover the following.

1. Travel court rental revenues include advanced rental payments received for summer occupancy, in the amount of $47,000.

2. There were $1,300 of supplies on hand at June 30.

3. Prepaid insurance resulted from the payment of a one-year policy on April 1, 2005.

4. The mail in July 2005 brought the following bills: advertising for the week of June 24, $110; repairs made June 18, $4,260; and utilities for the month of June, $215.

5. There are three employees who receive wages that total $250 per day. At June 30, two days' wages have been incurred but not paid.

6. The note payable is a 8% note dated May 1, 2005, and due on July 31, 2005.

7. Income tax of $12,000 for the quarter is due in July but has not yet been recorded.

Instructions
(a) Prepare any adjusting journal entries required as at June 30, 2005.
(b) Prepare a correct income statement for the quarter ended June 30, 2005.
(c) Explain to Alice the generally accepted accounting principles that she did not recognize in preparing her income statement and their effect on her results.

(b) Net income $36,955

P4-8B On November 1, 2005, the following were the account balances of Chambers Equipment Repair.

Journalize transactions and follow through accounting cycle to preparation of financial statements.
(SO 4, 5, 6)

	Debits		**Credits**
Cash	$ 2,790	Accumulated Depreciation	$ 500
Accounts Receivable	2,910	Accounts Payable	2,300
Supplies	1,000	Unearned Service Revenue	400
Store Equipment	10,000	Salaries Payable	500
		Common Stock	10,000
		Retained Earnings	3,000
	$16,700		$16,700

During November the following summary transactions were completed.

Nov.	8	Paid $1,100 for salaries due employees, of which $600 is for November and $500 is for October salaries payable.
	10	Received $1,200 cash from customers in payment of account.
	12	Received $1,700 cash for services performed in November.
	15	Purchased store equipment on account $3,000.
	17	Purchased supplies on account $1,300.
	20	Paid creditors $2,500 of accounts payable due.
	22	Paid November rent $300.
	25	Paid salaries $1,100.
	27	Performed services on account and billed customers for services provided $900.
	29	Received $550 from customers for services to be provided in the future.

Adjustment data:

1. Supplies on hand are valued at $1,600.

2. Accrued salaries payable are $500.

3. Depreciation for the month is $250.

4. Unearned service revenue of $300 is earned.

Instructions

(a) Enter the November 1 balances in the ledger accounts. (Use T accounts.)
(b) Journalize the November transactions.
(c) Post to the ledger accounts. Use Service Revenue, Depreciation Expense, Supplies Expense, Salaries Expense, and Rent Expense.
(d) Prepare a trial balance at November 30.
(e) Journalize and post adjusting entries.
(f) Prepare an adjusted trial balance.
(g) Prepare an income statement and a retained earnings statement for November and a classified balance sheet at November 30.

(f) Cash $ 1,240
   Tot. trial balance $21,900
(g) Net loss $ 550

Complete all steps in accounting cycle.
(SO 4, 5, 6, 7, 8)

P4-9B   Jessica Bell opened Blue Sky Window Washing Inc. on July 1, 2005. During July the following transactions were completed.

July   1   Issued $11,000 of common stock for $11,000 cash.
    1   Purchased used truck for $6,000, paying $3,000 cash and the balance on account.
    3   Purchased cleaning supplies for $800 on account.
    5   Paid $1,200 cash on 1-year insurance policy effective July 1.
   12   Billed customers $2,500 for cleaning services.
   18   Paid $1,000 cash on amount owed on truck and $500 on amount owed on cleaning supplies.
   20   Paid $1,600 cash for employee salaries.
   21   Collected $1,400 cash from customers billed on July 12.
   25   Billed customers $2,000 for cleaning services.
   31   Paid $200 for gas and oil used in the truck during month.
   31   Declared and paid $600 cash dividend.

The chart of accounts for Blue Sky Window Washing contains the following accounts: Cash, Accounts Receivable, Cleaning Supplies, Prepaid Insurance, Equipment, Accumulated Depreciation—Equipment, Accounts Payable, Salaries Payable, Common Stock, Retained Earnings, Dividends, Income Summary, Service Revenue, Gas & Oil Expense, Cleaning Supplies Expense, Depreciation Expense, Insurance Expense, Salaries Expense.

Instructions

(a) Journalize the July transactions.
(b) Post to the ledger accounts. (Use T accounts.)
(c) Prepare a trial balance at July 31.
(d) Journalize the following adjustments.
   (1) Services provided but unbilled and uncollected at July 31 were $1,400.
   (2) Depreciation on equipment for the month was $300.
   (3) One-twelfth of the insurance expired.
   (4) An inventory count shows $600 of cleaning supplies on hand at July 31.
   (5) Accrued but unpaid employee salaries were $400.
(e) Post adjusting entries to the T accounts.
(f) Prepare an adjusted trial balance.

(f) Cash $ 4,300
(g) Tot. assets $16,200

(g) Prepare the income statement and a retained earnings statement for July and a classified balance sheet at July 31.
(h) Journalize and post closing entries and complete the closing process.
(i) Prepare a post-closing trial balance at July 31.

▶ BROADENING YOUR PERSPECTIVE

Financial Reporting and Analysis

FINANCIAL REPORTING PROBLEM: *Tootsie Roll Industries, Inc.*

BYP4-1 The financial statements of **Tootsie Roll** are presented in Appendix A at the end of this book.

Instructions
- **(a)** Using the consolidated income statement and balance sheet, identify items that may result in adjusting entries for prepayments.
- **(b)** Using the consolidated income statement, identify two items that may result in adjusting entries for accruals.
- **(c)** What was the amount of depreciation expense for 2002 and 2001? (You will need to examine the notes to the financial statements.) Where was accumulated depreciation reported?
- **(d)** What was the cash paid for income taxes during 2002, reported at the bottom of the Consolidated Statement of Cash Flows? What was income tax expense (provision for income taxes) for 2002? Where is the remainder presumably reported in the balance sheet?

COMPARATIVE ANALYSIS PROBLEM: *Tootsie Roll vs. Hershey Foods*

BYP4-2 The financial statements of **Hershey Foods** are presented in Appendix B, following the financial statements for **Tootsie Roll** in Appendix A.

Instructions
- **(a)** Identify two accounts on Hershey Foods' balance sheet that provide evidence that Hershey uses accrual accounting. In each case, identify the income statement account that would be affected by the adjustment process.
- **(b)** Identify two accounts on Tootsie Roll's balance sheet that provide evidence that Tootsie Roll uses accrual accounting (different from the two you listed for Hershey). In each case, identify the income statement account that would be affected by the adjustment process.

RESEARCH CASE

BYP4-3 The February 21, 2002, issue of the *Wall Street Journal* includes an article by Ken Brown entitled "Creative Accounting: Four Areas to Buff Up a Company's Picture."

Instructions
Read the article and do the following.
Although the title says "four areas," it actually describes five ways that companies inappropriately manipulate their financial statements. Describe each of these five methods. For each method, give an example of a company that has been accused of using the method, and describe what that specific company was accused of.

INTERPRETING FINANCIAL STATEMENTS

BYP4-4 **Laser Recording Systems**, founded in 1981, produces disks for use in the home market. The following is an excerpt from Laser Recording Systems' financial statements (all dollars in thousands).

> **LASER RECORDING SYSTEMS**
> **Management Discussion**
>
> Accrued liabilities increased to $1,642 at January 31, from $138 at the end of the previous fiscal year. Compensation and related accruals increased $195 due primarily to increases in accruals for severance, vacation, commissions, and relocation expenses. Accrued professional services increased by $137 primarily as a result of legal expenses related to several outstanding contractual disputes. Other expenses increased $35, of which $18 was for interest payable.

Instructions

(a) Can you tell from the discussion whether Laser Recording Systems has prepaid its legal expenses and is now making an adjustment to the asset account Prepaid Legal Expenses, or whether the company is handling the legal expense via an accrued expense adjustment?

(b) Identify each of the adjustments Laser Recording Systems is discussing as one of the four types of possible adjustments discussed in the chapter. How is net income ultimately affected by each of the adjustments?

(c) What journal entry did Laser Recording make to record the accrued interest?

A GLOBAL FOCUS

BYP4-5   IIJ is one of the largest Internet service and network providers in Japan. In its 2001 annual report it reported the following (in million of yen).

	2001	2000
Cash	13,570	16,158
Net income (loss)	(4,700)	(4,784)
Cash provided (used) by operating activities	(270)	1,999

Instructions

(a) Explain how the company could have reported a net loss in 2000, and yet have had positive cash from operations in that year.

(b) Explain how the company's cash from operations could be a negative 270 million yen in 2001, but its cash balance declined by an amount substantially greater than that from 2000 to 2001.

(c) During 2001 the company's revenues were 31,876 million yen. Assume that at the beginning of the year it had no outstanding accounts receivable, but that at the end of the year it had 5,000 yen of accounts receivable outstanding. Based on this data, what was the amount of cash collected from customers during the year?

FINANCIAL ANALYSIS ON THE WEB

BYP4-6   *Purpose:* Using "Edgar Database" to identify and define common corporate filings required by the SEC.

Address: www.sec.gov/index.html (or go to **www.wiley.com/college/kimmel**)

Steps

Under Filings and Forms (EDGAR), choose **Descriptions of SEC Forms**.

Instructions

Describe the following:

(a) Prospectus.   **(d)** Form 10-K.

(b) Schedule 14A.   **(e)** Form 10-Q.

(c) Forms 3, 4, and 5.

Critical Thinking

GROUP DECISION CASE

BYP4-7   Happy Camper Park was organized on April 1, 2004, by Cindy Retzer. Cindy is a good manager but a poor accountant. From the trial balance prepared by a part-time bookkeeper, Cindy prepared the following income statement for the quarter that ended March 31, 2005.

HAPPY CAMPER PARK
Income Statement
For the Quarter Ended March 31, 2005

Revenues		
Rental revenues		$95,000
Operating expenses		
Advertising	$ 5,200	
Wages	29,800	
Utilities	900	
Depreciation	800	
Repairs	4,000	
Total operating expenses		40,700
Net income		$54,300

Cindy knew that something was wrong with the statement because net income had never exceeded $20,000 in any one quarter. Knowing that you are an experienced accountant, she asks you to review the income statement and other data.

You first look at the trial balance. In addition to the account balances reported in the income statement, the ledger contains these selected balances at March 31, 2005.

Supplies	$ 5,200
Prepaid Insurance	7,200
Notes Payable	15,000

You then make inquiries and discover the following.

1. Rental revenues include advanced rentals for summer-month occupancy, $34,000.

2. There were $1,300 of supplies on hand at March 31.

3. Prepaid insurance resulted from the payment of a 1-year policy on January 1, 2005.

4. The mail on April 1, 2005, brought the following bills: advertising for week of March 24, $110; repairs made March 10, $380; and utilities $180.

5. There are four employees who receive wages totaling $350 per day. At March 31, 2 days' wages have been incurred but not paid.

6. The note payable is a 3-month, 10% note dated January 1, 2005.

Instructions
With the class divided into groups, answer the following.
  (a) Prepare a correct income statement for the quarter ended March 31, 2005.
  (b) Explain to Cindy the generally accepted accounting principles that she did not follow in preparing her income statement and their effect on her results.

COMMUNICATION ACTIVITY

BYP4-8   On numerous occasions proposals have surfaced to put the federal government on the accrual basis of accounting. This is no small issue because if this basis were used, it would mean that billions in unrecorded liabilities would have to be booked and the federal deficit would increase substantially.

Instructions

(a) What is the difference between accrual basis accounting and cash basis accounting?

(b) Comment on why politicians prefer a cash basis accounting system over an accrual basis system.

(c) Write a letter to your senators explaining why you think the federal government should adopt the accrual basis of accounting.

ETHICS CASE

BYP4-9 Davito Company is a pesticide manufacturer. Its sales declined greatly this year due to the passage of legislation outlawing the sale of several of Davito's chemical pesticides. During the coming year, Davito will have environmentally safe and competitive replacement chemicals to replace these discontinued products. Sales in the next year are expected to greatly exceed those of any prior year. Therefore, the decline in this year's sales and profits appears to be a one-year aberration.

Even so, the company president believes that a large dip in the current year's profits could cause a significant drop in the market price of Davito's stock and make it a takeover target. To avoid this possibility, he urges Emma Karr, controller, in making this period's year-end adjusting entries to accrue every possible revenue and to defer as many expenses as possible. The president says to Emma, "We need the revenues this year, and next year we can easily absorb expenses deferred from this year. We can't let our stock price be hammered down!" Emma didn't get around to recording the adjusting entries until January 17, but she dated the entries December 31 as if they were recorded then. Emma also made every effort to comply with the president's request.

Instructions

(a) Who are the stakeholders in this situation?

(b) What are the ethical considerations of the president's request and Emma's dating the adjusting entries December 31?

(c) Can Emma accrue revenues and defer expenses and still be ethical?

Answers to Self-Study Questions

1. c   2. a   3. d   4. d   5. c   6. a   7. b   8. b   9. c
10. d   11. a   12. a   13. d

Answer to Tootsie Roll Review It Question 3, p. 177

Under the heading "Property, plant, and equipment" in Note 1, **Tootsie Roll** reports 2002 depreciation expense of $12,354,000.

✔ Remember to go back to the Navigator box on the chapter-opening page and check off your completed work.

Merchandising Operations and the Multiple-Step Income Statement

STUDY OBJECTIVES

After studying this chapter,
you should be able to:

1 Identify the differences between a service enterprise and a merchandising company.

2 Explain the recording of purchases under a perpetual inventory system.

3 Explain the recording of sales revenues under a perpetual inventory system.

4 Distinguish between a single-step and a multiple-step income statement.

5 Determine cost of goods sold under a periodic system.

6 Explain the factors affecting profitability.

THE NAVIGATOR

THE NAVIGATOR ✔

▶ Scan *Study Objectives* ☐

▶ Read *Feature Story* ☐

▶ Read *Preview* ☐

▶ Read text and answer *Before You Go On*
  p. 226 ☐   p. 228 ☐   p. 233 ☐
  p. 234 ☐   p. 238 ☐

▶ Work Using the *Decision Toolkit* ☐

▶ Review Summary of *Study Objectives* ☐

▶ Work *Demonstration Problem* ☐

▶ Answer *Self-Study Questions* ☐

▶ Complete *Assignments* ☐

FEATURE STORY

Who Doesn't Shop at Wal-Mart?

In his book *The End of Work,* Jeremy Rifkin notes that until the 20th century the word *consumption* evoked negative images; to be labeled a "consumer" was an insult. (In fact, one of the deadliest diseases in history, tuberculosis, was often referred to as "consumption.") Twentieth-century merchants realized, however, that in order to prosper, they had to convince people of the need for things not previously needed. For example, **General Motors** made annual changes in its cars so that people would be discontented with the cars they already owned. Thus began consumerism.

Today consumption describes the U.S. lifestyle in a nutshell. We consume twice as much today per person as we did at the end of World War II. The amount of U.S. retail space per person is vastly greater than that of any other country. It appears that we live to shop.

The first great retail giant was **Sears, Roebuck**. It started as a catalog company enabling people in rural areas to buy things by mail. For decades it was the uncontested merchandising leader.

Today **Wal-Mart** is the undisputed champion provider of basic (and perhaps not-so-basic) human needs. Wal-Mart had only 18 stores as recently as 1970. A key cause of its incredible growth is its amazing system of inventory control and distribution. Wal-Mart has a management

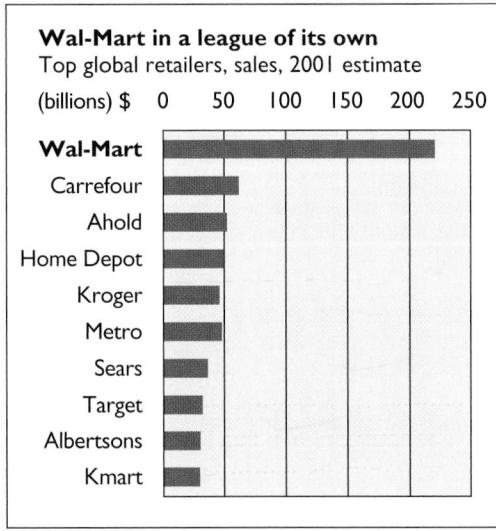

information system that employs six satellite channels. Measured by sales revenues, it is the largest company in the world. In six years it went from selling almost no groceries to being America's largest grocery retailer. Incredibly, Wal-Mart accounts for 60% of U.S. retail sales.

It would appear things have never looked better at Wal-Mart. On the other hand, a *Wall Street Journal* article entitled "How to Sell More to Those Who Think It's Cool to Be Frugal" suggests that consumerism as a way of life might be dying. Don't bet your wide-screen TV on it, though.

THE NAVIGATOR

Wal-Mart in a league of its own
Top global retailers, sales, 2001 estimate

(billions) $	0	50	100	150	200	250
Wal-Mart						
Carrefour						
Ahold						
Home Depot						
Kroger						
Metro						
Sears						
Target						
Albertsons						
Kmart						

On the World Wide Web
Wal-Mart: www.wal-mart.com

Merchandising is one of the largest and most influential industries in the United States. Therefore, understanding the financial statements of merchandising companies is important. In this chapter you will learn the basics about reporting merchandising transactions. In addition, you will learn how to prepare and analyze a commonly used form of the income statement—the multiple-step income statement. The content and organization of the chapter are as follows.

Merchandising Operations

Wal-Mart, **Kmart**, **Sears**, and **Target** are called merchandising companies because they buy and sell merchandise rather than perform services as their primary source of revenue. Merchandising companies that purchase and sell directly to consumers are called **retailers**. Merchandising companies that sell to retailers are known as **wholesalers**. For example, retailer **Walgreens** might buy goods from wholesaler **McKesson**; retailer **Office Depot** might buy office supplies from wholesaler **United Stationers**. The primary source of revenues for merchandising companies is the sale of merchandise, often referred to simply as **sales revenue** or **sales**. Expenses for a merchandising company are divided into two categories: the cost of goods sold and operating expenses.

The **cost of goods sold** is the total cost of merchandise sold during the period. This expense is directly related to the revenue recognized from the sale of goods. The income measurement process for a merchandising company is shown in Illustration 5-1 (page 220). The items in the two blue boxes are unique to a merchandising company; they are not used by a service company.

STUDY OBJECTIVE 1

Identify the differences between a service enterprise and a merchandising company.

Illustration 5-1 Income measurement process for a merchandising company

OPERATING CYCLES

The operating cycle of a merchandising company ordinarily is longer than that of a service company. The purchase of merchandise inventory and its eventual sale lengthen the cycle. The operating cycles of service and merchandising companies are contrasted in Illustration 5-2. Note that the added asset account for a merchandising company is the Merchandise Inventory account.

Illustration 5-2 Operating cycles for a service company and a merchandising company

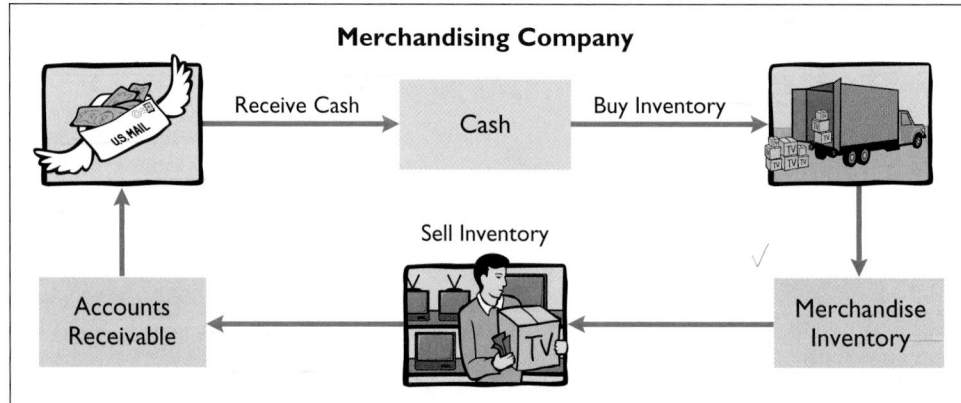

INVENTORY SYSTEMS

A merchandising company keeps track of its inventory to determine what is available for sale and what has been sold. One of two systems is used to account for inventory: a **perpetual inventory system** or a **periodic inventory system**.

Perpetual System

In a **perpetual inventory system**, detailed records of the cost of each inventory purchase and sale are maintained. These records continuously—perpetually—show the inventory that should be on hand for every item. For example, a **Ford** dealership has separate inventory records for each automobile, truck, and van on its lot and showroom floor. Similarly, with the use of bar codes and optical scanners, a grocery store can keep a daily running record of every box of cereal and every jar of jelly that it buys and sells. Under a perpetual inventory system, the cost of goods sold is **determined each time a sale occurs**.

Helpful Hint For control purposes a physical inventory count is taken under the perpetual system, even though it is not needed to determine cost of goods sold.

Periodic System

In a **periodic inventory system**, detailed inventory records of the goods on hand are not kept throughout the period. The cost of goods sold is **determined only at the end of the accounting period**—that is, periodically—when a physical inventory count is taken to determine the cost of goods on hand. To determine the cost of goods sold under a periodic inventory system, the following steps are necessary: (1) Determine the cost of goods on hand at the beginning of the accounting period; (2) add to it the cost of goods purchased; and (3) subtract the cost of goods on hand at the end of the accounting period.

Illustration 5-3 graphically compares the sequence of activities and the timing of the cost of goods sold computation under the two inventory systems.

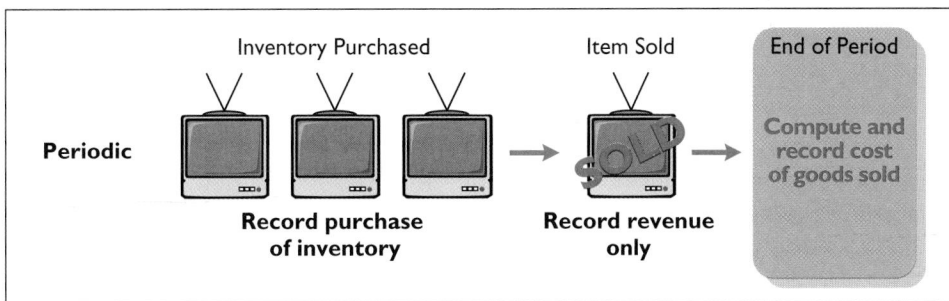

Illustration 5-3
Comparing perpetual and periodic inventory systems

Additional Considerations

Perpetual systems have traditionally been used by companies that sell merchandise with high unit values, such as automobiles, furniture, and major home appliances. The recent widespread use of computers and electronic scanners has enabled many more companies to install perpetual inventory systems. The perpetual inventory system is so named because the accounting records continuously—perpetually—show the quantity and cost of the inventory that should be on hand at any time.

A perpetual inventory system provides better control over inventories than a periodic system. Since the inventory records show the quantities that should be on hand, the goods can be counted at any time to see whether the amount of goods actually on hand agrees with the inventory records. Any shortages uncovered can be investigated immediately. Although a perpetual inventory system requires additional clerical work and additional cost to maintain the subsidiary records, a computerized system can minimize this cost. As noted in the Feature Story, much of Wal-Mart's success is attributed to its sophisticated inventory system.

Some businesses find it either unnecessary or uneconomical to invest in a computerized perpetual inventory system. Many small merchandising businesses, in particular, find that a perpetual inventory system costs more than it is worth. Managers of these businesses can control their merchandise and manage day-to-day operations without detailed inventory records by using a periodic inventory system.

Because the perpetual inventory system is growing in popularity and use, we illustrate it in this chapter. The journal entries for the periodic system are described in an appendix to this chapter.

Business Insight
INVESTOR PERSPECTIVE

Investors are often eager to invest in a company that has a hot new product. However, when snowboard maker **Morrow Snowboards, Inc.,** issued shares of stock to the public for the first time, some investors expressed reluctance to invest in Morrow because of a number of accounting control problems. To reduce investor concerns, Morrow implemented a perpetual inventory system to improve its control over inventory. In addition, it stated that it would perform a physical inventory count every quarter until it felt that the perpetual inventory system was reliable.

Recording Purchases of Merchandise

STUDY OBJECTIVE
2
Explain the recording of purchases under a perpetual inventory system.

Purchases of inventory may be made for cash or on account (credit). Purchases are normally recorded when the goods are received from the seller. Every purchase should be supported by business documents that provide written evidence of the transaction. Each cash purchase should be supported by a canceled check or a cash register receipt indicating the items purchased and amounts paid. Cash purchases are recorded by an increase in Merchandise Inventory and a decrease in Cash.

Each credit purchase should be supported by a **purchase invoice**, which indicates the total purchase price and other relevant information. However, the purchaser does not prepare a separate purchase invoice. Instead, the copy of the sales invoice sent by the seller is used by the buyer as a purchase invoice. In Illustration 5-4 (page 223), for example, the sales invoice prepared by PW Audio Supply, Inc. (the seller) is used as a purchase invoice by Sauk Stereo (the buyer).

The associated entry for Sauk Stereo for the invoice from PW Audio Supply increases Merchandise Inventory and increases Accounts Payable.

Equation analyses summarize the effects of transactions on the three elements of the accounting equation, as well as the effect on cash flows.

A	=	L	+	SE
+3,800		+3,800		

Cash Flows
no effect

May 4	Merchandise Inventory		3,800	
	Accounts Payable			3,800
	(To record goods purchased on account from PW Audio Supply)			

Under the perpetual inventory system, purchases of merchandise for sale are recorded in the Merchandise Inventory account. Thus, **Wal-Mart** would increase (debit) Merchandise Inventory for clothing, sporting goods, and anything else purchased for resale to customers. Not all purchases are debited to Merchandise Inventory, however. Purchases of assets acquired for use and not for resale, such as supplies, equipment, and similar items, are recorded as increases to specific asset accounts rather than to Merchandise Inventory. For example, Wal-Mart would increase Supplies to record the purchase of materials used to make shelf signs or for cash register receipt paper.

PURCHASE RETURNS AND ALLOWANCES

A purchaser may be dissatisfied with the merchandise received because the goods are damaged or defective, of inferior quality, or do not meet the purchaser's specifications. In such cases, the purchaser may return the goods to the seller for credit if the sale was made on credit, or for a cash refund if the purchase was for cash. This transaction is known as a **purchase return**. Alternatively, the purchaser may choose to keep the merchandise if the seller is willing to grant an allowance (deduction) from the purchase price. This transaction is known as a **purchase allowance**.

Assume that Sauk Stereo returned goods costing $300 to PW Audio Supply on May 8. The entry by Sauk Stereo for the returned merchandise decreases Accounts Payable and decreases Merchandise Inventory.

A	=	L	+	SE
−300		−300		

Cash Flows
no effect

May	8	Accounts Payable		300	
		Merchandise Inventory			300
		(To record return of goods received			
		from PW Audio Supply)			

Because Sauk Stereo increased Merchandise Inventory when the goods were received, Merchandise Inventory is decreased when Sauk returns the goods.

FREIGHT COSTS

Freight Costs Incurred by Buyer

The sales invoice indicates whether the seller or the buyer pays the cost of transporting the goods to the buyer's place of business. When the buyer pays the transportation costs, these costs are considered part of the cost of purchasing inventory. As a result, the account **Merchandise Inventory is increased**. For example, if upon delivery of the goods on May 6, Sauk Stereo (the buyer) pays Haul-It Freight Company $150 for freight charges, the entry on Sauk's books is:

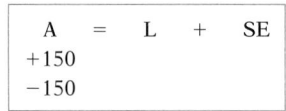

A	=	L	+	SE
+150				
−150				

Cash Flows
−150

May	9	Merchandise Inventory		150	
		Cash			150
		(To record payment of freight on goods			
		purchased)			

Freight Costs Incurred by Seller

In contrast, **freight costs incurred by the seller on outgoing merchandise are an operating expense to the seller**. These costs increase an expense account titled Freight-out or Delivery Expense. For example, if the freight terms on the invoice in Illustration 5-4 had required that PW Audio Supply (the seller) pay the $150 freight charges, the entry by PW Audio would be:

A	=	L	+	SE
−150				−150 Exp

Cash Flows
−150

May	4	Freight-out		150	
		Cash			150
		(To record payment of freight on			
		goods sold)			

When the freight charges are paid by the seller, the seller will usually establish a higher invoice price for the goods, to cover the expense of shipping.

PURCHASE DISCOUNTS

The credit terms of a purchase on account may permit the buyer to claim a cash discount for prompt payment. The buyer calls this cash discount a **purchase discount**. This incentive offers advantages to both parties: The purchaser saves money, and the seller is able to shorten the operating cycle by converting the accounts receivable into cash earlier.

Helpful Hint The term _net_ in "net 30" means the remaining amount due after subtracting any sales returns and allowances and partial payments.

     The **credit terms** specify the amount of the cash discount and time period during which it is offered. They also indicate the length of time in which the purchaser is expected to pay the full invoice price. In the sales invoice in Illustration 5-4, credit terms are 2/10, n/30, which is read "two-ten, net thirty." This means that a 2% cash discount may be taken on the invoice price, less ("net of") any returns or allowances, if payment is made within 10 days of the invoice date (the **discount period**); otherwise, the invoice price, less any returns or allowances, is due 30 days from the invoice date. Alternatively, the discount period may extend to a specified number of days following the month in which the sale occurs. For example, 1/10 EOM (end of month) means that a 1% discount is available if the invoice is paid within the first 10 days of the next month.

When the seller elects not to offer a cash discount for prompt payment, credit terms will specify only the maximum time period for paying the balance due. For example, the time period may be stated as n/30, n/60, or n/10 EOM, meaning, respectively, that the net amount must be paid in 30 days, 60 days, or within the first 10 days of the next month.

When an invoice is paid within the discount period, the amount of the discount decreases Merchandise Inventory because inventory is recorded at its cost and, by paying within the discount period, the merchandiser has reduced its cost. To illustrate, assume Sauk Stereo pays the balance due of $3,500 (gross invoice price of $3,800 less purchase returns and allowances of $300) on May 14, the last day of the discount period. The cash discount is $70 ($3,500 × 2%), and the amount of cash paid by Sauk Stereo is $3,430 ($3,500 − $70). The entry to record the May 14 payment by Sauk Stereo decreases Accounts Payable by the amount of the gross invoice price, reduces Merchandise Inventory by the $70 discount, and reduces Cash by the net amount owed.

May 14	Accounts Payable	3,500	
	Cash		3,430
	Merchandise Inventory		70
	(To record payment within discount period)		

A = L + SE
−3,430 −3,500
−70

Cash Flows
−3,430

If Sauk Stereo failed to take the discount and instead made full payment of $3,500 on June 3, Sauk would debit Accounts Payable and credit Cash for $3,500 each.

June 3	Accounts Payable	3,500	
	Cash		3,500
	(To record payment with no discount taken)		

A = L + SE
−3,500 −3,500

Cash Flows
−3,500

A merchandising company usually should take all available discounts. Passing up the discount may be viewed as **paying interest** for use of the money. For example, if Sauk Stereo passed up the discount, it would be like paying an interest rate of 2% for the use of $3,500 for 20 days. This is the equivalent of an annual interest rate of approximately 36.5% (2% × 365/20). Obviously, it would be better for Sauk Stereo to borrow at prevailing bank interest rates of 8% to 12% than to lose the discount.

Helpful Hint So as not to miss purchase discounts, unpaid invoices should be filed by due dates. This procedure helps the purchaser remember the discount date, prevents early payment of bills, and maximizes the time that cash can be used for other purposes.

SUMMARY OF PURCHASING TRANSACTIONS

A summary of the effect of the previous transactions on Merchandise Inventory is provided in the following T account (with transaction descriptions in parentheses). Sauk originally purchased $3,800 worth of inventory for resale. It then returned $300 of goods. It paid $150 in freight charges, and finally, it received a $70 discount off the balance owed because it paid within the discount period. This results in a balance in Merchandise Inventory of $3,580.

	Merchandise Inventory			
(Purchase)	May 4 3,800	May 8	300	(Purchase return)
(Freight-in)	9 150	May 14	70	(Purchase discount)
(Balance)	3,580			

▶ **Review It**

1. How does the measurement of net income in a merchandising company differ from that in a service enterprise?
2. In what ways is a perpetual inventory system different from a periodic system?
3. Under the perpetual inventory system, what entries are made to record purchases, purchase returns and allowances, purchase discounts, and freight costs?

☑ THE NAVIGATOR

Recording Sales of Merchandise

STUDY OBJECTIVE

3

Explain the recording of sales revenues under a perpetual inventory system.

Sales revenues, like service revenues, are recorded when earned in order to comply with the revenue recognition principle. Typically, sales revenues are earned when the goods are transferred from the seller to the buyer. At this point the sales transaction is completed and the sales price is established.

Sales may be made on credit or for cash. Every sales transaction should be supported by a **business document** that provides written evidence of the sale. **Cash register tapes** provide evidence of cash sales. A **sales invoice**, like the one that was shown in Illustration 5-4 (page 223), provides support for a credit sale. The original copy of the invoice goes to the customer, and a copy is kept by the seller for use in recording the sale. The invoice shows the date of sale, customer name, total sales price, and other relevant information.

Two entries are made for each sale: (1) Accounts Receivable or Cash is increased, and Sales is increased. (2) Cost of Goods Sold is increased, and Merchandise Inventory is decreased. As a result, the Merchandise Inventory account will show at all times the amount of inventory that should be on hand.

To illustrate a credit sales transaction, PW Audio Supply's sale of $3,800 on May 4 to Sauk Stereo (see Illustration 5-4, page 223) is recorded as follows (assume the merchandise cost PW Audio Supply $2,400).

A	=	L	+	SE
+3,800				+3,800 Rev

Cash Flows
no effect

A	=	L	+	SE
−2,400				−2,400 Exp

Cash Flows
no effect

May	4	Accounts Receivable	3,800	
		Sales		3,800
		(To record credit sale to Sauk Stereo per invoice #731)		
	4	Cost of Goods Sold	2,400	
		Merchandise Inventory		2,400
		(To record cost of merchandise sold on invoice #731 to Sauk Stereo)		

Helpful Hint The Sales account is credited only for sales of goods held for resale. Sales of assets not held for resale, such as equipment or land, are credited directly to the asset account.

For internal decision-making purposes, merchandising companies may use more than one sales account. For example, PW Audio Supply may decide to keep separate sales accounts for its sales of TV sets, videocassette recorders, and microwave ovens. **Wal-Mart** might use separate accounts for sporting goods, children's clothing, and hardware—or it might have even more narrowly defined accounts. By using separate sales accounts for major product lines, rather than a single combined sales account, company management can monitor sales trends more closely and respond in a more appropriate strategic fashion to changes in sales patterns. For example, if TV sales are increasing while microwave oven sales are decreasing, the company should reevaluate both its advertising and pricing policies on each of these items to ensure they are optimal.

On its income statement presented to outside investors a merchandising company would normally provide only a single sales figure—the sum of all of its individual sales accounts. This is done for two reasons. First, providing detail on all of its individual sales accounts would add considerable length to its income statement. Second, companies do not want their competitors to know the details of their operating results. However, in 2000 Microsoft decided to expand the number of different types of revenue that it discloses in its annual report from three to five. This disclosure will better enable financial statement users to evaluate the growth of its consumer and Internet businesses.

> **Helpful Hint** How much do you as an investor have a right to know? What is the appropriate level of disclosure?

SALES RETURNS AND ALLOWANCES

We now look at the "flipside" of purchase returns and allowances, which are recorded as **sales returns and allowances** on the books of the seller. PW Audio Supply's entries to record credit for returned goods involve (1) an increase in Sales Returns and Allowances and a decrease in Accounts Receivable at the $300 selling price, and (2) an increase in Merchandise Inventory (assume a $140 cost) and a decrease in Cost of Goods Sold as shown below. (We have assumed that the goods were not defective. If they were defective, an adjustment would be made to the inventory account to reflect their decline in value.)

May	8	Sales Returns and Allowances	300	
		Accounts Receivable		300
		(To record credit granted to Sauk Stereo		
		for returned goods)		
	8	Merchandise Inventory	140	
		Cost of Goods Sold		140
		(To record cost of goods returned)		

$$A = L + SE$$
$$-300 \qquad -300 \text{ Rev}$$
Cash Flows
no effect

$$A = L + SE$$
$$+140 \qquad +140 \text{ Exp}$$
Cash Flows
no effect

Sales Returns and Allowances is a **contra revenue account** to Sales. The normal balance of Sales Returns and Allowances is a debit. A contra account is used, instead of debiting Sales, to disclose in the accounts and in the income statement the amount of sales returns and allowances. Disclosure of this information is important to management. Excessive returns and allowances suggest problems—inferior merchandise, inefficiencies in filling orders, errors in billing customers, or mistakes in delivery or shipment of goods. Moreover, a decrease (debit) recorded directly to Sales would obscure the relative importance of sales returns and allowances as a percentage of sales. It also could distort comparisons between total sales in different accounting periods.

> **Helpful Hint** Remember that the increases, decreases, and normal balances of contra accounts are the opposite of the accounts to which they correspond.

Business Insight
INVESTOR PERSPECTIVE

How high is too high? Returns can become so high that it is questionable whether sales revenue should have been recognized in the first place. An example of high returns is **Florafax International Inc.**, a floral supply company, which was alleged to have shipped its product without customer authorization on ten holiday occasions, including 8,562 shipments of flowers to customers for Mother's Day and 6,575 for Secretary's Day. The return rate on these shipments went as high as 69% of sales. As one employee noted: "Products went out the front door and came in the back door."

SALES DISCOUNTS

As mentioned in our discussion of purchase transactions, the seller may offer the customer a cash discount—called by the seller a **sales discount**—for the prompt payment of the balance due. Like a purchase discount, a sales discount is based on the invoice price less returns and allowances, if any. The Sales Discounts account is increased (debited) for discounts that are taken. The entry by PW Audio Supply to record the cash receipt on May 14 from Sauk Stereo within the discount period is:

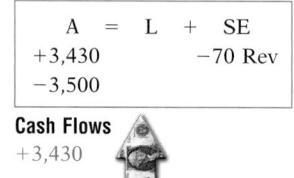

A = L + SE
+3,430   −70 Rev
−3,500

Cash Flows
+3,430

May 14	Cash	3,430	
	Sales Discounts	70	
	Accounts Receivable		3,500
	(To record collection within 2/10, n/30		
	discount period from Sauk Stereo)		

Like Sales Returns and Allowances, Sales Discounts is a **contra revenue account** to Sales. Its normal balance is a debit. This account is used, instead of debiting sales, to disclose the amount of cash discounts taken by customers. If the discount is not taken, PW Audio Supply increases Cash for $3,500 and decreases Accounts Receivable for the same amount at the date of collection.

BEFORE YOU GO ON . . .

▶ Review It

1. Under a perpetual inventory system, what are the two entries that must be recorded at the time of each sale?
2. Why is it important to use the Sales Returns and Allowances account, rather than simply reducing the Sales account, when goods are returned?

▶ Do It

On September 5, De La Hoya Company buys merchandise on account from Junot Diaz Company. The selling price of the goods is $1,500, and the cost to Diaz Company was $800. On September 8, goods with a selling price of $200 and a cost of $105 are returned. Record the transactions on the books of both companies.

Action Plan

• Purchaser records goods at cost.
• Seller records both the sale and the cost of goods sold at the time of the sale.
• When goods are returned, purchaser reduces Merchandise Inventory, but seller records the return in a contra account, Sales Returns and Allowances.

Solution

De La Hoya Company

Sept.	5	Merchandise Inventory	1,500	
		Accounts Payable		1,500
		(To record goods purchased on account)		
Sept.	8	Accounts Payable	200	
		Merchandise Inventory		200
		(To record return of defective goods)		

Junot Diaz Company

Sept.	5	Accounts Receivable	1,500	
		Sales		1,500
		(To record credit sale)		
	5	Cost of Goods Sold	800	
		Merchandise Inventory		800
		(To record cost of goods sold on account)		
Sept.	8	Sales Returns and Allowances	200	
		Accounts Receivable		200
		(To record credit granted for receipt of returned goods)		
	8	Merchandise Inventory	105	
		Cost of Goods Sold		105
		(To record cost of goods returned)		

THE NAVIGATOR

Income Statement Presentation

Two forms of the income statement are widely used by companies. One is the **single-step income statement**. The statement is so named because only one step, subtracting total expenses from total revenues, is required in determining net income (or net loss). In a single-step statement, all data are classified into two categories: (1) **revenues**, which include both operating revenues and nonoperating revenues and gains (for example, interest revenue and gain on sale of equipment); and (2) **expenses**, which include cost of goods sold, operating expenses, and nonoperating expenses and losses (for example, interest expense, loss on sale of equipment, or income tax expense). The single-step income statement is the form we have used thus far in the text. A single-step statement for Wal-Mart is shown in Illustration 5-5.

STUDY OBJECTIVE
4
Distinguish between a single-step and a multiple-step income statement.

Illustration 5-5
Single-step income statements

WAL-MART STORES, INC.
Income Statements
(in millions)

	For the years ended January 31	
	2002	**2001**
Revenues		
Net sales	$217,799	$191,329
Other revenues, net	2,013	1,966
	219,812	193,295
Expenses		
Cost of goods sold	171,562	150,255
Selling, general, and administrative expenses	36,173	31,550
Interest expense	1,326	1,374
Other expense	183	129
Income taxes	3,897	3,692
	213,141	187,000
Net income	$ 6,671	$ 6,295

There are two primary reasons for using the single-step form: (1) A company does not realize any type of profit or income until total revenues exceed total expenses, so it makes sense to divide the statement into these two categories. (2) The form is simple and easy to read.

A second form of the income statement is the **multiple-step income statement**. The multiple-step income statement is often considered more useful because it highlights the components of net income. The Wal-Mart income statement in Illustration 5-6 is an example.

Illustration 5-6
Multiple-step income
statements

WAL★MART
ALWAYS LOW PRICES.
Always

WAL-MART STORES, INC.
Income Statements
(in millions)

	For the years ended January 31	
	2002	**2001**
Net sales	$217,799	$191,329
Cost of goods sold	171,562	150,255
Gross profit	46,237	41,074
Operating expenses		
Selling, general, and administrative expenses	36,173	31,550
Income from operations	10,064	9,524
Other revenues and gains		
Other revenues, net	2,013	1,966
Other expenses and losses		
Interest expense	1,326	1,374
Other expense	183	129
Income before income taxes	10,568	9,987
Income tax expense	3,897	3,692
Net income	$ 6,671	$ 6,295

The multiple-step income statement has three important line items: gross profit, income from operations, and net income. They are determined as follows:

1. Cost of goods sold is subtracted from sales to determine gross profit.
2. Operating expenses are deducted from gross profit to determine income from operations.
3. The results of activities not related to operations are added or subtracted to determine net income.

You should note that income tax expense is reported in a separate section of the income statement before net income. The following discussion provides additional information about the components of a multiple-step income statement.

SALES REVENUES

The income statement for a merchandising company typically presents gross sales revenues for the period and provides details about deductions from that total amount. As contra revenue accounts, sales returns and allowances and sales discounts are deducted from sales in the income statement to arrive at **net sales**. The sales revenues section of the income statement for PW Audio Supply is shown in Illustration 5-7.

Illustration 5-7 Statement
presentation of sales
revenues section

PW AUDIO SUPPLY, INC. Income Statement (partial)		
Sales revenues		
Sales		$480,000
Less: Sales returns and allowances	$12,000	
Sales discounts	8,000	20,000
Net sales		**$460,000**

GROSS PROFIT

Cost of goods sold is deducted from sales revenue to determine **gross profit**. As shown in Illustration 5-6, **Wal-Mart** had a gross profit of $46.2 billion in fiscal year 2002. Sales revenue used for this computation is **net sales**, which takes into account sales returns and allowances and sales discounts. On the basis of the sales data presented in Illustration 5-7 (net sales of $460,000) and the cost of goods sold (assume a balance of $316,000), the gross profit for PW Audio Supply is $144,000, computed as follows.

Alternative Terminology
Gross profit is sometimes
referred to as **gross margin**.

Net sales	$460,000
Cost of goods sold	316,000
Gross profit	**$144,000**

It is important to understand what gross profit is—and what it is not. Gross profit represents the **merchandising profit** of a company. It is *not* a measure of the overall profit of a company because operating expenses have not been deducted. Nevertheless, the amount and trend of gross profit are closely watched by management and other interested parties. Comparisons of current gross profit with past amounts and rates and with those in the industry indicate the effectiveness of a company's purchasing and pricing policies.

OPERATING EXPENSES

Operating expenses are the next component in measuring net income for a merchandising company. At Wal-Mart, operating expenses were $36.2 billion in fiscal year 2002. These expenses are similar in merchandising and service enterprises. At PW Audio Supply, operating expenses were $114,000. The firm's income from operations is determined by subtracting operating expenses from gross profit. Thus, income from operations is $30,000, as shown below.

Gross profit	$144,000
Operating expenses	114,000
Income from operations	$ 30,000

NONOPERATING ACTIVITIES

Nonoperating activities consist of various revenues and expenses and gains and losses that are unrelated to the company's main line of operations. When nonoperating items are included, the label **Income from operations** (or Operating income) precedes them. This label clearly identifies the results of the company's normal operations, an amount determined by subtracting cost of goods sold and operating expenses from net sales. The results of nonoperating activities are shown in the categories **Other revenues and gains** and **Other expenses and losses**. Examples of each are listed in Illustration 5-8.

Illustration 5-8 Other items of nonoperating activities

Other Revenues and Gains	Other Expenses and Losses
Interest revenue from notes receivable and marketable securities	Interest expense on notes and loans payable
Dividend revenue from investments in capital stock	Casualty losses from recurring causes, such as vandalism and accidents
Rent revenue from subleasing a portion of the store	Loss from the sale or abandonment of property, plant, and equipment
Gain from the sale of property, plant, and equipment	Loss from strikes by employees and suppliers

The distinction between operating and nonoperating activities is crucial to many external users of financial data. Operating income is viewed as sustainable, and many nonoperating activities are viewed as nonrecurring. Therefore, when forecasting next year's income, analysts put the most weight on this year's operating income, and less weight on this year's nonoperating activities.

Business Insight
ETHICS PERSPECTIVE

After **Enron**, many companies were forced by increased investor criticism and regulator scrutiny to improve the clarity of their financial disclosures. For example, **IBM** announced that it would begin providing more detail regarding its "Other gains and losses." It had previously included these items in its selling, general, and administrative expenses, with little disclosure.

Disclosing other gains and losses in a separate line item on the income statement won't have any effect on bottom-line income. However, analysts complained that burying these details in the selling, general, and administrative expense line reduced their ability to fully understand how well IBM was performing. For example, previously if IBM sold off one of its buildings at a gain, it would include this gain in the selling, general, and administrative expense line item, thus reducing that expense. This made it appear that the company had done a better job of controlling operating expenses than it actually had. Other companies recently announcing changes to increase the informativeness of their income statements included **PepsiCo**, **Krispy Kreme Doughnuts**, and **General Electric**.

The nonoperating activities are reported in the income statement immediately after the operating activities. Included among these activities in Illustration 5-6 for **Wal-Mart** is net interest expense of $1.3 billion for fiscal year 2002. The amount remaining, after adding the operating and nonoperating sections together, is Wal-Mart's net income of $6.7 billion. Note that the net incomes in Illustrations 5-5 and 5-6 are the same. The difference in the two income statements is the amount of detail displayed and the order presented.

In Illustration 5-9 (on page 233) we have provided the multiple-step income statement of a hypothetical company. This statement provides more detail than that of Wal-Mart.

For homework problems, the multiple-step form of the income statement should be used unless the requirements state otherwise.

Illustration 5-9 Multiple-step income statement

PW AUDIO SUPPLY, INC.
Income Statement
For the Year Ended December 31, 2005

Sales revenues		
Sales		$480,000
Less: Sales returns and allowances	$12,000	
Sales discounts	8,000	20,000
Net sales		460,000
Cost of goods sold		316,000
Gross profit		144,000
Operating expenses		
Store salaries expense	45,000	
Administrative salaries expense	19,000	
Utilities expense	17,000	
Advertising expense	16,000	
Depreciation expense—store equipment	8,000	
Freight-out	7,000	
Insurance expense	2,000	
Total operating expenses		114,000
Income from operations		30,000
Other revenues and gains		
Interest revenue	3,000	
Gain on sale of equipment	600	
	3,600	
Other expenses and losses		
Interest expense	1,800	
Casualty loss from vandalism	200	
	2,000	
		1,600
Income before income taxes		31,600
Income tax expense		10,100
Net income		$ 21,500

Calculation of gross profit

Calculation of income from operations

Results of activities not related to operations

Helpful Hint What is and is not disclosed?
1. Did company sell on credit? Yes, it had sales discounts.
2. Did company take all purchase discounts? Don't know; purchase discounts taken are not reported.

BEFORE YOU GO ON . . .

▶ **Review It**

1. How are sales and contra revenue accounts reported in the income statement?
2. What is the significance of gross profit?
3. What title does **Tootsie Roll** use for gross profit? By what percentage did its gross profit change, and in what direction, in 2002? The answer to this question is provided on p. 264.

✓ THE NAVIGATOR

DETERMINING COST OF GOODS SOLD UNDER A PERIODIC SYSTEM

The determination of cost of goods sold is different under the periodic system than under the perpetual system. When a company uses a perpetual inventory system, all transactions affecting inventory (such as freight costs, returns, and discounts) are recorded directly to the Merchandise Inventory account. In addition, at the time of each sale the perpetual system requires a reduction in

STUDY OBJECTIVE
5
Determine cost of goods sold under a periodic system.

Merchandise Inventory and an increase in Cost of Goods Sold. But under a periodic system separate accounts are used to record freight costs, returns, and discounts. A running account of changes in inventory is not maintained. Instead, the balance in ending inventory, as well as the cost of goods sold for the period, is calculated at the end of the period. The determination of cost of goods sold for PW Audio Supply, using a periodic inventory system, is shown in Illustration 5-10.

Illustration 5-10
Cost of goods sold for a merchandiser using a periodic inventory system

PW AUDIO SUPPLY, INC. Cost of Goods Sold For the Year Ended December 31, 2005			
Cost of goods sold			
Inventory, January 1			$ 36,000
Purchases		$325,000	
Less: Purchases returns and			
allowances	$10,400		
Purchase discounts	6,800	17,200	
Net purchases		307,800	
Add: Freight-in		12,200	
Cost of goods purchased			320,000
Cost of goods available for sale			356,000
Inventory, December 31			40,000
Cost of goods sold			$316,000

Helpful Hint The far right column identifies the primary items that make up cost of goods sold of $316,000. The middle column explains cost of goods purchased of $320,000. The left column reports contra purchase items of $17,200.

The use of the periodic inventory system does not affect the content of the balance sheet. As under the perpetual system, merchandise inventory is reported at the same amount in the current assets section.

Further detail on the use of the periodic system is provided in the appendix to this chapter.

BEFORE YOU GO ON . . .

▶ **Review It**

1. Discuss the three steps in determining cost of goods sold in a periodic inventory system.
2. What accounts are used in determining the cost of goods purchased?
3. In what ways is a perpetual inventory system different from a periodic inventory system?

▶ **Do It**

Aerosmith Company's accounting records show the following at the year-end December 31, 2005: Purchase Discounts $3,400; Freight-in $6,100; Purchases $162,500; Beginning Inventory $18,000; Ending Inventory $20,000; and Purchase Returns $5,200. Compute these amounts for Aerosmith Company using the periodic approach:
(a) Cost of goods purchased.
(b) Cost of goods sold.

Action Plan

• To determine cost of goods purchased, adjust purchases for returns, discounts, and freight-in.

• To determine cost of goods sold, add cost of goods purchased to beginning inventory, and subtract ending inventory.

Solution

(a) Cost of goods purchased:
Purchases − Purchase returns − Purchase discounts + Freight-in
$162,500 − $5,200 − $3,400 + $6,100 = $160,000
(b) Cost of goods sold:
Beginning inventory + Cost of goods purchased −
Ending inventory
$18,000 + $160,000 − $20,000 = $158,000

✓ THE NAVIGATOR

Evaluating Profitability

GROSS PROFIT RATE

A company's gross profit may be expressed as a **percentage** by dividing the amount of gross profit by net sales. This is referred to as the gross profit rate. For PW Audio Supply the gross profit rate is 31.3% ($144,000 ÷ $460,000). The gross profit *rate* is generally considered to be more informative than the gross profit *amount* because it expresses a more meaningful (qualitative) relationship between gross profit and net sales. For example, a gross profit amount of $1,000,000 may sound impressive. But if it was the result of sales of $100,000,000, the company's gross profit rate was only 1%. A 1% gross profit rate is acceptable in only a few industries. Illustration 5-11 presents gross profit rates of a variety of industries.

STUDY OBJECTIVE
6
Explain the factors affecting profitability.

Illustration 5-11 Gross profit rate by industry

A decline in a company's gross profit rate might have several causes. The company may have begun to sell products with a lower "markup"—for example, budget blue jeans versus designer blue jeans. Increased competition may have resulted in a lower selling price. Or, the company may be forced to pay higher prices to its suppliers without being able to pass these costs on to its customers. The gross profit rates for **Wal-Mart** and **Target** are presented in Illustration 5-12 on page 236.

Wal-Mart's gross profit rate declined from 21.5% in 2001 to 21.2% in 2002. In its Management Discussion and Analysis (MD&A), Wal-Mart explained, "This decrease in gross margin occurred primarily due to a shift in customer buying patterns to products that carry lower margins and an increase in food sales as a percent of our total sales." Food products generally carry lower margins than

Illustration 5-12 Gross profit rate

	Gross Profit Rate = $\dfrac{\text{Gross Profit}}{\text{Net Sales}}$	
($ in millions)	**2002**	**2001**
Wal-Mart	$\dfrac{\$46,237}{\$217,799} = 21.2\%$	$\dfrac{\$41,074}{\$191,329} = 21.5\%$
Target	30.5%	30.4%
Industry average	25.0%	

general merchandise. At first glance it might be surprising that Wal-Mart has a lower gross profit rate than Target and the industry average. It is likely, however, that this can be explained by the fact that grocery products are becoming an increasingly large component of Wal-Mart's sales. In fact, in its MD&A, Wal-Mart says, "Management expects our gross margins to continue to decrease as food sales continue to increase as a percentage of total company sales." Also, Wal-Mart has substantial warehouse-style sales in its Sam's Club stores, which are a low-margin, high-volume operation. In later chapters we will provide further discussion of the trade-off between sales volume and gross profit.

Business Insight
INVESTOR PERSPECTIVE

In this section we compared the gross profit rates of **Target** and **Wal-Mart**. Although such comparisons are vital to an analysis of either of these companies, we must now alert you to one problem often encountered in such comparisons: Companies do not always classify expenses in the same way. **Kmart**, another retailing competitor, includes buying and occupancy costs in cost of goods sold, whereas Wal-Mart includes these expenses in the operating expense line item, and Target does not disclose how it treats these costs. Thus, in comparing ratios for these companies, we should recognize that at least some of the difference in the value of the ratios is due simply to this difference in classification. Since these companies do not provide sufficient detail in their notes to enable us to adjust the figures to similar presentation, our ratios may at best be only a rough comparison.

DECISION TOOLKIT

Decision Checkpoints	Info Needed for Decision	Tool to Use for Decision	How to Evaluate Results
Is the price of goods keeping pace with changes in the cost of inventory?	Gross profit and net sales	Gross profit rate $= \dfrac{\text{Gross profit}}{\text{Net sales}}$	Higher ratio suggests the average margin between selling price and inventory cost is increasing. Too high a margin may result in lost sales.

PROFIT MARGIN RATIO

The **profit margin ratio** measures the percentage of each dollar of sales that results in net income. It is computed by dividing net income by net sales (revenue) for the period. How do the gross profit rate and profit margin ratio differ? The gross profit rate measures the margin by which selling price exceeds cost of goods sold. **The profit margin ratio measures the extent by which selling price covers all expenses** (including cost of goods sold). A company can improve its profit margin ratio by either increasing its gross profit rate and/or by controlling its operating expenses and other costs.

Profit margins vary across industries. Businesses with high turnover, such as grocery stores (**Safeway** and **Kroger**) and discount stores (**Target** and **Wal-Mart**), generally experience low profit margins. Low-turnover businesses, such as high-end jewelry stores (**Tiffany and Co.**) or major drug manufacturers (**Merck**), have high profit margins. Profit margin ratios from a variety of industries are provided in Illustration 5-13.

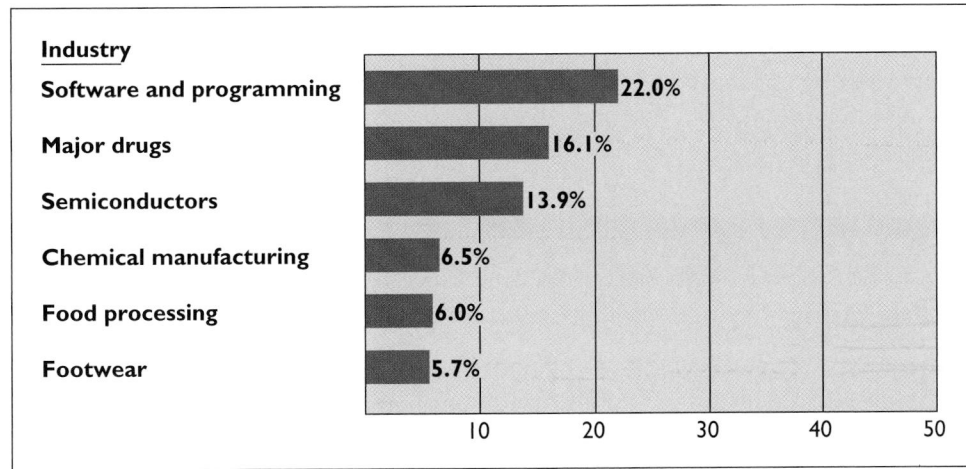

Industry

Software and programming	22.0%
Major drugs	16.1%
Semiconductors	13.9%
Chemical manufacturing	6.5%
Food processing	6.0%
Footwear	5.7%

Illustration 5-13 Profit margin ratio by industry

Profit margins for Wal-Mart and Target and the industry average are presented in Illustration 5-14.

Illustration 5-14 Profit margin ratio

$$\text{Profit Margin Ratio} = \frac{\text{Net Income}}{\text{Net Sales}}$$

	2002	2001
Wal-Mart ($ in millions)	$\frac{\$6,671}{\$217,799} = 3.1\%$	$\frac{\$6,295}{\$191,329} = 3.3\%$
Target	3.5%	3.5%
Industry average	3.47%	

Wal-Mart's profit margin decreased from 3.3% in 2001 to 3.1% in 2002. This means that in 2001 the company generated 3.3 cents on each dollar of sales, and in 2002 it generated 3.1 cents on each dollar of sales. How does Wal-Mart compare to its competitors? Its profit margin ratio was lower than Target's in both 2001 and 2002 and was less than the industry average. Thus, its profit margin ratio does not suggest exceptional profitability. However, we must again keep in mind that an increasing percentage of Wal-Mart's sales is from groceries. The average profit margin ratio for the grocery industry is only 2.0 percent.

Business Insight
MANAGEMENT PERSPECTIVE

In its death spiral toward bankruptcy, **Kmart** appeared to make two very costly strategic errors. First, in an effort to attract customers, it decided to reduce selling prices on over 30,000 items. The problem was that this reduced its gross profit rate—and didn't even have the intended effect of increasing sales because **Wal-Mart** quickly matched these price cuts. Since Wal-Mart operates much more efficiently than Kmart, Wal-Mart could afford to absorb these price cuts and still operate at a profit. Kmart couldn't. Its second error was to try to reduce operating costs by cutting its advertising expenditures. This resulted in a reduction in customers—and sales revenue.

BEFORE YOU GO ON . . .

▶ **Review It**

1. How is the gross profit rate calculated? What might cause it to decline?
2. What effect does improved efficiency of operations have on the profit margin ratio?

☑ THE NAVIGATOR

DECISION TOOLKIT

Decision Checkpoints	Info Needed for Decision	Tool to Use for Decision	How to Evaluate Results
☑	▤▤	⚒	👍👎
Is the company maintaining an adequate margin between sales and expenses?	Net income and net sales	$\text{Profit margin ratio} = \dfrac{\text{Net income}}{\text{Net sales}}$	Higher value suggests favorable return on each dollar of sales.

Using the Decision Toolkit

Sears is currently the number 2 retailer in the United States behind Wal-Mart. Sears has enacted many changes trying to turn itself around. During the 1990s, it shocked and disappointed many loyal customers by closing its catalog business. It also closed 113 stores and eliminated 50,000 jobs. Although Sears wants to surpass Wal-Mart, it is aiming for a different niche. It is directing itself more toward clothing and "hard-line" items rather than toward being a discounter. The following financial data are available for Sears.

($ in millions)	Year ended	
	12/29/01	12/30/00
Net income	$ 735	$ 1,343
Sales	41,078	40,937
Cost of goods sold	26,322	26,721

Instructions

Using the basic facts in the table, evaluate the following components of Sears's profitability for the years ended December 29, 2001 and December 30, 2000.

    Profit margin ratio
    Gross profit rate

How do Sears's profit margin ratio and gross profit rate compare to those of Wal-Mart and Target for 2001? (*Note:* Since the year-end of Sears differs from those of Wal-Mart and Target, compare Sears's 2001 results with the 2002 results of Wal-Mart and Target.)

Solution

($ in millions)	Year ended	
	12/29/01	12/30/00
Profit margin ratio	$\dfrac{\$735}{\$41,078} = 1.8\%$	$\dfrac{\$1,343}{\$40,937} = 3.3\%$
Gross profit rate	$\dfrac{\$41,078 - \$26,322}{\$41,078} = 35.9\%$	$\dfrac{\$40,937 - \$26,721}{\$40,937} = 34.7\%$

Sears's profit margin ratio (income per dollar of sales) declined from 3.3% to 1.8%, while its gross profit rate increased from 34.7% to 35.9%. Comparing Sears's gross profit rate (35.9%) to Wal-Mart's (21.2%) and Target's (30.5%), it appears that Sears has a higher markup on its goods.

    Sears's profit margin ratio of 1.8% compared to Wal-Mart's 3.1% and Target's 3.5% suggests that Sears is not able to control its costs as well as the others.

 THE NAVIGATOR

Summary of Study Objectives

1 ***Identify the differences between a service enterprise and a merchandising company.*** Because of the presence of inventory, a merchandising company has sales revenue, cost of goods sold, and gross profit. To account for inventory, a merchandising company must choose between a perpetual inventory system and a periodic inventory system.

2 ***Explain the recording of purchases under a perpetual inventory system.*** The Merchandise Inventory account is debited for all purchases of merchandise and for freight costs, and it is credited for purchase discounts and purchase returns and allowances.

3 ***Explain the recording of sales revenues under a perpetual inventory system.*** When inventory is sold, Accounts Receivable (or Cash) is debited and Sales is credited for the selling price of the merchandise. At the same time, Cost of Goods Sold is debited and Merchandise Inventory is credited for the cost of inventory items sold. Subsequent entries are required for (a) sales returns and allowances and (b) sales discounts.

4 ***Distinguish between a single-step and a multiple-step income statement.*** In a single-step income statement, all data are classified under two categories, revenues or expenses, and net income is determined in one step. A multiple-step income statement shows numerous steps in determining net income, including results of nonoperating activities.

5 ***Determine cost of goods sold under a periodic system.*** The periodic system uses multiple accounts to keep track of transactions that affect inventory. To determine cost of goods sold, first calculate cost of goods purchased by adjusting purchases for returns, allowances, discounts, and freight-in. Then calculate cost of goods sold by adding cost of goods purchased to beginning inventory and subtracting ending inventory.

6 *Explain the factors affecting profitability.* Profitability is affected by gross profit, as measured by the gross profit rate, and by management's ability to control costs, as measured by the profit margin ratio.

DECISION TOOLKIT—A SUMMARY

Decision Checkpoints	Info Needed for Decision	Tool to Use for Decision	How to Evaluate Results
Is the price of goods keeping pace with changes in the cost of inventory?	Gross profit and net sales	Gross profit rate $= \dfrac{\text{Gross profit}}{\text{Net sales}}$	Higher ratio suggests the average margin between selling price and inventory cost is increasing. Too high a margin may result in lost sales.
Is the company maintaining an adequate margin between sales and expenses?	Net income and net sales	Profit margin ratio $= \dfrac{\text{Net income}}{\text{Net sales}}$	Higher value suggests favorable return on each dollar of sales.

APPENDIX
PERIODIC INVENTORY SYSTEM

As described in this chapter, one of two basic systems of accounting for inventories may be used: (1) the perpetual inventory system or (2) the periodic inventory system. In the chapter we focused on the characteristics of the perpetual inventory system. In this appendix we discuss and illustrate the **periodic inventory system**. One key difference between the two systems is the point at which cost of goods sold is computed. For a visual reminder of this difference, you may want to refer back to Illustration 5-3 on page 221.

Recording Merchandise Transactions

STUDY OBJECTIVE
7
Explain the recording of purchases and sales of inventory under a periodic inventory system.

In a **periodic inventory system**, revenues from the sale of merchandise are recorded when sales are made, just as in a perpetual system. Unlike the perpetual system, however, **no attempt is made on the date of sale to record the cost of the merchandise sold.** Instead, a physical inventory count is taken at the **end of the period** to determine (1) the cost of the merchandise then on hand and (2) the cost of the goods sold during the period. And, **under a periodic system, purchases of merchandise are recorded in the Purchases account rather than the Merchandise Inventory account**. Also, in a periodic system, purchase returns and allowances, purchase discounts, and freight costs on purchases are recorded in separate accounts.

To illustrate the recording of merchandise transactions under a periodic inventory system, we will use purchase/sale transactions between PW Audio Supply, Inc. and Sauk Stereo, as illustrated for the perpetual inventory system in this chapter.

Recording Purchases of Merchandise

On the basis of the sales invoice (Illustration 5-4, shown on page 223) and receipt of the merchandise ordered from PW Audio Supply, Sauk Stereo records the $3,800 purchase as follows.

May	4	Purchases	3,800	
		Accounts Payable		3,800
		(To record goods purchased on account, terms 2/10, n/30)		

Purchases is a temporary account whose normal balance is a debit.

PURCHASE RETURNS AND ALLOWANCES

Because $300 of merchandise received from PW Audio Supply is inoperable, Sauk Stereo returns the goods and prepares the following entry to recognize the return.

May	8	Accounts Payable	300	
		Purchase Returns and Allowances		300
		(To record return of inoperable goods purchased from PW Audio Supply)		

Purchase Returns and Allowances is a temporary account whose normal balance is a credit.

FREIGHT COSTS

When the purchaser directly incurs the freight costs, the account Freight-in (or Transportation-in) is debited. For example, if upon delivery of the goods on May 6, Sauk pays Haul-It Freight Company $150 for freight charges on its purchase from PW Audio Supply, the entry on Sauk's books is:

May	9	Freight-in (Transportation-in)	150	
		Cash		150
		(To record payment of freight on goods purchased)		

Like Purchases, Freight-in is a temporary account whose normal balance is a debit. **Freight-in is part of cost of goods purchased.** The reason is that cost of goods purchased should include any freight charges necessary to bring the goods to the purchaser. Freight costs are not subject to a purchase discount. Purchase discounts apply on the invoice cost of the merchandise.

PURCHASE DISCOUNTS

On May 14 Sauk Stereo pays the balance due on account to PW Audio Supply, taking the 2% cash discount allowed by PW Audio for payment within 10 days. The payment and discount are recorded by Sauk Stereo as follows.

May	14	Accounts Payable ($3,800 − $300)	3,500	
		Purchase Discounts ($3,500 × .02)		70
		Cash		3,430
		(To record payment to PW Audio Supply within the discount period)		

Purchase Discounts is a temporary account whose normal balance is a credit.

Recording Sales of Merchandise

The sale of $3,800 of merchandise to Sauk Stereo on May 4 (sales invoice No. 731, Illustration 5-4) is recorded by the seller, PW Audio Supply, as follows.

May	4	Accounts Receivable	3,800	
		Sales		3,800
		(To record credit sales per invoice #731 to Sauk Stereo)		

SALES RETURNS AND ALLOWANCES

To record the returned goods received from Sauk Stereo on May 8, PW Audio Supply records the $300 sales return as follows.

May	8	Sales Returns and Allowances	300	
		Accounts Receivable		300
		(To record return of goods from Sauk Stereo)		

SALES DISCOUNTS

On May 14, PW Audio Supply receives payment of $3,430 on account from Sauk Stereo. PW Audio honors the 2% cash discount and records the payment of Sauk's account receivable in full as follows.

May	14	Cash	3,430	
		Sales Discounts ($3,500 × .02)	70	
		Accounts Receivable ($3,800 − $300)		3,500
		(To record collection from Sauk Stereo within 2/10, n/30 discount period)		

COMPARISON OF ENTRIES—
PERPETUAL vs. PERIODIC

	ENTRIES ON SAUK STEREO'S BOOKS		
Transaction	**Perpetual Inventory System**	**Periodic Inventory System**	
May 4 Purchase of merchandise on credit.	Merchandise Inventory 3,800 Accounts Payable 3,800	Purchases 3,800 Accounts Payable 3,800	
May 8 Purchase returns and allowances.	Accounts Payable 300 Merchandise Inventory 300	Accounts Payable 300 Purchase Returns and Allowances 300	
May 9 Freight costs on purchases.	Merchandise Inventory 150 Cash 150	Freight-in 150 Cash 150	
May 14 Payment on account with a discount.	Accounts Payable 3,500 Cash 3,430 Merchandise Inventory 70	Accounts Payable 3,500 Cash 3,430 Purchase Discounts 70	

	ENTRIES ON PW AUDIO SUPPLY'S BOOKS		
Transaction	**Perpetual Inventory System**	**Periodic Inventory System**	
May 4 Sale of merchandise on credit.	Accounts Receivable 3,800 Sales Revenue 3,800	Accounts Receivable 3,800 Sales Revenue 3,800	
	Cost of Goods Sold 2,400 Merchandise Inventory 2,400	No entry for cost of goods sold	
May 8 Return of merchandise sold.	Sales Returns and Allowances 300 Accounts Receivable 300	Sales Returns and Allowances 300 Accounts Receivable 300	
	Merchandise Inventory 140 Cost of Goods Sold 140	No entry	
May 14 Cash received on account with a discount.	Cash 3,430 Sales Discounts 70 Accounts Receivable 3,500	Cash 3,430 Sales Discounts 70 Accounts Receivable 3,500	

Summary of Study Objective for Appendix

7 *Explain the recording of purchases and sales of inventory under a periodic inventory system.* To record purchases, entries are required for (a) cash and credit purchases, (b) purchase returns and allowances, (c) purchase discounts, and (d) freight costs. To record sales, entries are required for (a) cash and credit sales, (b) sales returns and allowances, and (c) sales discounts.

Glossary

Contra revenue account An account that is offset against a revenue account on the income statement. (p. 227)

Cost of goods sold The total cost of merchandise sold during the period. (p. 219)

Gross profit The excess of net sales over the cost of goods sold. (p. 231)

Gross profit rate Gross profit expressed as a percentage by dividing the amount of gross profit by net sales. (p. 235)

Net sales Sales less sales returns and allowances and sales discounts. (p. 230)

Periodic inventory system An inventory system in which detailed records of goods on hand are not maintained and the cost of goods sold is determined only at the end of an accounting period. (p. 221)

Perpetual inventory system A detailed inventory system in which the cost of each inventory item is maintained and the records continuously show the inventory that should be on hand. (p. 221)

Profit margin ratio Measures the percentage of each dollar of sales that results in net income, computed by dividing net income by net sales. (p. 237)

Purchase allowance A deduction made to the selling price of merchandise, granted by the seller so that the buyer will keep the merchandise. (p. 223)

Purchase discount A cash discount claimed by a buyer for prompt payment of a balance due. (p. 224)

Purchase invoice A document that supports each credit purchase. (p. 222)

Purchase return A return of goods from the buyer to the seller for cash or credit. (p. 223)

Sales discount A reduction given by a seller for prompt payment of a credit sale. (p. 228)

Sales invoice A document that provides support for credit sales. (p. 226)

Sales returns and allowances Purchase returns and allowances from the seller's perspective. See definitions for purchase returns and purchase allowances. (p. 227)

Sales revenue Primary source of revenue in a merchandising company. (p. 219)

Demonstration Problem

The adjusted trial balance for the year ended December 31, 2005, for Dykstra Company is shown below.

DYKSTRA COMPANY
Adjusted Trial Balance
For the Year Ended December 31, 2005

	Dr.	Cr.
Cash	$ 14,500	
Accounts Receivable	11,100	
Merchandise Inventory	29,000	
Prepaid Insurance	2,500	
Store Equipment	95,000	
Accumulated Depreciation		$ 18,000
Notes Payable		25,000
Accounts Payable		10,600
Common Stock		70,000
Retained Earnings		11,000
Dividends	12,000	

	Dr.	Cr.
Sales		536,800
Sales Returns and Allowances	6,700	
Sales Discounts	5,000	
Cost of Goods Sold	363,400	
Freight-out	7,600	
Advertising Expense	12,000	
Store Salaries Expense	56,000	
Utilities Expense	18,000	
Rent Expense	24,000	
Depreciation Expense	9,000	
Insurance Expense	4,500	
Interest Expense	3,600	
Interest Revenue		2,500
	$673,900	$673,900

Instructions

Prepare a multiple-step income statement for Dykstra Company.

Solution to Demonstration Problem

DYKSTRA COMPANY
Income Statement
For the Year Ended December 31, 2005

Sales revenues		
Sales		$536,800
Less: Sales returns and allowances	$ 6,700	
Sales discounts	5,000	11,700
Net sales		525,100
Cost of goods sold		363,400
Gross profit		161,700
Operating expenses		
Store salaries expense	56,000	
Rent expense	24,000	
Utilities expense	18,000	
Advertising expense	12,000	
Depreciation expense	9,000	
Freight-out	7,600	
Insurance expense	4,500	
Total operating expenses		131,100
Income from operations		30,600
Other revenues and gains		
Interest revenue	2,500	
Other expenses and losses		
Interest expense	3,600	1,100
Net income		$ 29,500

Action Plan

• In preparing the income statement, remember that the key components are net sales, cost of goods sold, gross profit, total operating expenses, and net income (loss). These components are reported in the right-hand column of the income statement.

• Present nonoperating items after income from operations.

☑ THE NAVIGATOR

Note: All Questions, Exercises, and Problems marked with an asterisk relate to material in the appendix to the chapter.

Self-Study Questions

Self-Study/Self-Test

Answers are at the end of the chapter.

(SO 2) **1.** Which of the following statements about a periodic inventory system is true?
(a) Cost of goods sold is determined only at the end of the accounting period.
(b) Detailed records of the cost of each inventory purchase and sale are maintained continuously.
(c) The periodic system provides better control over inventories than a perpetual system.
(d) The increased use of computerized systems has increased the use of the periodic system.

(SO 2) **2.** Which of the following items does *not* result in an adjustment in the merchandise inventory account under a perpetual system?
(a) A purchase of merchandise.
(b) A return of merchandise inventory to the supplier.
(c) Payment of freight costs for goods shipped to a customer.
(d) Payment of freight costs for goods received from a supplier.

(SO 3) **3.** Which sales accounts normally have a debit balance?
(a) Sales discounts.
(b) Sales returns and allowances.
(c) Both (a) and (b).
(d) Neither (a) nor (b).

(SO 3) **4.** A credit sale of $750 is made on June 13, terms 2/10, n/30, on which a return of $50 is granted on June 16. What amount is received as payment in full on June 23?
(a) $700.   (c) $685.
(b) $686.   (d) $650.

(SO 4) **5.** Gross profit will result if:
(a) operating expenses are less than net income.
(b) sales revenues are greater than operating expenses.
(c) sales revenues are greater than cost of goods sold.
(d) operating expenses are greater than cost of goods sold.

(SO 4) **6.** If sales revenues are $400,000, cost of goods sold is $310,000, and operating expenses are $60,000, what is the gross profit?

(a) $30,000.   (c) $340,000.
(b) $90,000.   (d) $400,000.

(SO 4) **7.** The income statement for a merchandising company shows each of these features *except*:
(a) gross profit.
(b) cost of goods sold.
(c) a sales revenue section.
(d) All of these are present.

(SO 5) **8.** If beginning inventory is $60,000, cost of goods purchased is $380,000, and ending inventory is $50,000, what is cost of goods sold under a periodic system?
(a) $390,000.   (c) $330,000.
(b) $370,000.   (d) $420,000.

(SO 6) **9.** Which of the following would affect the gross profit rate? (Assume sales remains constant.)
(a) An increase in advertising expense.
(b) A decrease in depreciation expense.
(c) An increase in cost of goods sold.
(d) A decrease in insurance expense.

(SO 6) **10.** The gross profit *rate* is equal to:
(a) net income divided by sales.
(b) cost of goods sold divided by sales.
(c) net sales minus cost of goods sold, divided by net sales.
(d) sales minus cost of goods sold, divided by cost of goods sold.

(SO 6) **11.** Which factor would *not* affect the gross profit rate?
(a) An increase in the cost of heating the store.
(b) An increase in the sale of luxury items.
(c) An increase in the use of "discount pricing" to sell merchandise.
(d) An increase in the price of inventory items.

(SO 7) *12. When goods are purchased for resale by a company using a periodic inventory system:
(a) purchases on account are debited to Merchandise Inventory.
(b) purchases on account are debited to Purchases.
(c) purchase returns are debited to Purchase Returns and Allowances.
(d) freight costs are debited to Purchases.

☑ THE NAVIGATOR

Questions

1. (a) "The steps in the accounting cycle for a merchandising company are different from the steps in the accounting cycle for a service enterprise." Do you agree or disagree?
(b) Is the measurement of net income in a merchan-

dising company conceptually the same as in a service enterprise? Explain.

2. How do the components of revenues and expenses differ between a merchandising company and a service enterprise?

3. (a) Explain the income measurement process in a merchandising company.
   (b) How does income measurement differ between a merchandising company and a service company?

4. Dan Mozena Co. has sales revenue of $100,000, cost of goods sold of $70,000, and operating expenses of $20,000. What is its gross profit?

5. Carol Brandon believes revenues from credit sales may be earned before they are collected in cash. Do you agree? Explain.

6. (a) What is the primary source document for recording (1) cash sales and (2) credit sales?
   (b) Using XXs for amounts, give the journal entry for each of the transactions in part (a).

7. A credit sale is made on July 10 for $900, terms 2/10, n/30. On July 12, $100 of goods are returned for credit. Give the journal entry on July 19 to record the receipt of the balance due within the discount period.

8. Goods costing $1,600 are purchased on account on July 15 with credit terms of 2/10, n/30. On July 18 a $100 credit memo is received from the supplier for damaged goods. Give the journal entry on July 24 to record payment of the balance due within the discount period.

9. Mark Mader Company reports net sales of $800,000, gross profit of $580,000, and net income of $300,000. What are its operating expenses?

10. Identify the distinguishing features of an income statement for a merchandising company.

11. Why is the normal operating cycle for a merchandising company likely to be longer than for a service company?

12. What merchandising account(s) will appear in the post-closing trial balance?

13. What types of businesses are most likely to use a perpetual inventory system?

14. Identify the accounts that are added to or deducted from purchases to determine the cost of goods purchased under a periodic system. For each account, indicate (a) whether it is added or deducted and (b) its normal balance.

15. In the following cases, use a periodic inventory system to identify the item(s) designated by the letters X and Y.
   (a) Purchases − X − Y = Net purchases.
   (b) Cost of goods purchased − Net purchases = X.
   (c) Beginning inventory + X = Cost of goods available for sale.
   (d) Cost of goods available for sale − Cost of goods sold = X.

16. What two ratios measure factors that affect profitability?

17. What factors affect a company's gross profit rate—that is, what can cause the gross profit rate to increase and what can cause it to decrease?

*18. Goods costing $1,600 are purchased on account on July 15 with credit terms of 2/10, n/30. On July 18 a $100 credit memo is received from the supplier for damaged goods. Give the journal entry on July 24 to record payment of the balance due within the discount period assuming a periodic inventory system.

Brief Exercises

Compute missing amounts in determining net income.
(SO 1, 4)

BE5-1 Presented here are the components in Minh Lo Company's income statement. Determine the missing amounts.

Sales	Cost of Goods Sold	Gross Profit	Operating Expenses	Net Income
$ 75,000	(b)	$ 39,000	(d)	$10,800
$108,000	$65,000	(c)	(e)	$29,500
(a)	$71,900	$109,600	$39,500	(f)

Journalize perpetual inventory entries.
(SO 2, 3)

BE5-2 Janine Company buys merchandise on account from Laura Company. The selling price of the goods is $900 and the cost of goods is $700. Both companies use perpetual inventory systems. Journalize the transactions on the books of both companies.

Journalize sales transactions.
(SO 3)

BE5-3 Prepare the journal entries to record the following transactions on Dave Wier Company's books using a perpetual inventory system.
   (a) On March 2 Dave Wier Company sold $900,000 of merchandise to Lucy Ritter Company, terms 2/10, n/30. The cost of the merchandise sold was $600,000.
   (b) On March 6 Lucy Ritter Company returned $120,000 of the merchandise purchased on March 2. The cost of the merchandise returned was $65,000.
   (c) On March 12 Dave Wier Company received the balance due from Lucy Ritter Company.

Journalize purchase transactions.
(SO 2)

BE5-4 From the information in BE5-3, prepare the journal entries to record these transactions on Lucy Ritter Company's books under a perpetual inventory system.

BE5-5 Mila Company provides this information for the month ended October 31, 2005: sales on credit $300,000; cash sales $100,000; sales discounts $5,000; and sales returns and allowances $18,000. Prepare the sales revenues section of the income statement based on this information.

Prepare sales revenue section of income statement.
(SO 4)

BE5-6 Explain where each of these items would appear on a multiple-step income statement: gain on sale of equipment, cost of goods sold, depreciation expense, and sales returns and allowances.

Identify placement of items on a multiple-step income statement.
(SO 4)

BE5-7 Assume that E. Guard Company uses a periodic inventory system and has these account balances: Purchases $400,000; Purchase Returns and Allowances $11,000; Purchase Discounts $8,000; and Freight-in $16,000. Determine net purchases and cost of goods purchased.

Compute net purchases and cost of goods purchased.
(SO 5)

BE5-8 Assume the same information as in BE5-7 and also that E. Guard Company has beginning inventory of $60,000, ending inventory of $90,000, and net sales of $630,000. Determine the amounts to be reported for cost of goods sold and gross profit.

Compute cost of goods sold and gross profit.
(SO 5)

BE5-9 Bruno Corporation reported net sales of $250,000, cost of goods sold of $100,000, operating expenses of $50,000, net income of $80,000, beginning total assets of $500,000, and ending total assets of $600,000. Calculate each of the following values.
 (a) Profit margin ratio. (b) Gross profit rate.

Calculate profitability ratios.
(SO 6)

BE5-10 Shaunna Corporation reported net sales $550,000; cost of goods sold $300,000; operating expenses $150,000; and net income $70,000. Calculate the following values.
 (a) Profit margin ratio. (b) Gross profit rate.

Calculate profitability ratios.
(SO 6)

*****BE5-11** Prepare the journal entries to record these transactions on H. Hunt Company's books using a periodic inventory system.
 (a) On March 2, H. Hunt Company purchased $900,000 of merchandise from B. Streisand Company, terms 2/10, n/30.
 (b) On March 6 H. Hunt Company returned $130,000 of the merchandise purchased on March 2 because it was defective.
 (c) On March 12 H. Hunt Company paid the balance due to B. Streisand Company.

Journalize purchase transactions.
(SO 7)

Exercises

E5-1 The following transactions are for Anna Company.
 1. On December 3 Anna Company sold $480,000 of merchandise to Nathan Co., terms 2/10, n/30. The cost of the merchandise sold was $320,000.
 2. On December 8 Nathan Co. was granted an allowance of $24,000 for merchandise purchased on December 3.
 3. On December 13 Anna Company received the balance due from Nathan Co.

Journalize sales transactions.
(SO 3)

Instructions
 (a) Prepare the journal entries to record these transactions on the books of Anna Company. Anna uses a perpetual inventory system.
 (b) Assume that Anna Company received the balance due from Nathan Co. on January 2 of the following year instead of December 13. Prepare the journal entry to record the receipt of payment on January 2.

E5-2 Assume that on September 1 **Office Depot** had an inventory that included a variety of calculators. The company uses a perpetual inventory system. During September these transactions occurred.

Journalize perpetual inventory entries.
(SO 2, 3)

Sept. 6 Purchased calculators from Digital Co. at a total cost of $1,440, terms n/30.
  9 Paid freight of $80 on calculators purchased from Digital Co.
  10 Returned calculators to Digital Co. for $38 credit because they did not meet specifications.
  12 Sold calculators costing $520 for $780 to College Book Store, terms n/30.

14 Granted credit of $30 to College Book Store for the return of one calculator that was not ordered. The calculator cost $20.

20 Sold calculators costing $570 for $900 to Student Card Shop, terms n/30.

Instructions

Journalize the September transactions.

Journalize purchase transactions.
(SO 2)

E5-3 This information relates to Plato Co.

1. On April 5 purchased merchandise from Jack Meyer Company for $18,000, terms 2/10, n/30.

2. On April 6 paid freight costs of $900 on merchandise purchased from Jack Meyer.

3. On April 7 purchased equipment on account for $26,000.

4. On April 8 returned some of April 5 merchandise to Jack Meyer Company which cost $2,800.

5. On April 15 paid the amount due to Jack Meyer Company in full.

Instructions

(a) Prepare the journal entries to record the transactions listed above on the books of Plato Co. Plato Co. uses a perpetual inventory system.

(b) Assume that Plato Co. paid the balance due to Jack Meyer Company on May 4 instead of April 15. Prepare the journal entry to record this payment.

Journalize purchase transactions.
(SO 2)

E5-4 On June 10 Disch Company purchased $6,000 of merchandise from Miller Company, terms 2/10, n/30. Disch pays the freight costs of $400 on June 11. Damaged goods totaling $300 are returned to Miller for credit on June 12. On June 19 Disch Company pays Miller Company in full, less the purchase discount. Both companies use a perpetual inventory system.

Instructions

(a) Prepare separate entries for each transaction on the books of Disch Company.

(b) Prepare separate entries for each transaction for Miller Company. The merchandise purchased by Disch on June 10 cost Miller $3,000, and the goods returned cost Miller $180.

Prepare sales revenues section of income statement.
(SO 4)

E5-5 The adjusted trial balance of Lois Company shows these data pertaining to sales at the end of its fiscal year, October 31, 2005: Sales $900,000; Freight-out $12,000; Sales Returns and Allowances $15,000; and Sales Discounts $12,000.

Instructions

Prepare the sales revenues section of the income statement.

E5-6 Presented below is information for Garbo Co. for the month of January 2005.

Prepare an income statement and calculate profitability ratios.
(SO 4, 6)

Cost of goods sold	$208,000	Rent expense	$ 18,000
Freight-out	7,000	Sales discounts	8,000
Insurance expense	12,000	Sales returns and allowances	13,000
Salary expense	61,000	Sales	350,000

Instructions

(a) Prepare an income statement using the format presented on page 233.

(b) Calculate the profit margin ratio and the gross profit rate.

E5-7 Financial information is presented here for two companies.

Compute missing amounts and calculate profitability ratios.
(SO 4, 6)

	Lisa Company	Tamara Company
Sales	$90,000	?
Sales returns	?	$ 5,000
Net sales	81,000	95,000
Cost of goods sold	58,000	?
Gross profit	?	38,000
Operating expenses	15,000	?
Net income	?	18,000

Instructions

(a) Fill in the missing amounts. Show all computations.

(b) Calculate the profit margin ratio and the gross profit rate for each company.

E5-8 In its income statement for the year ended December 31, 2005, Quilt Company reported the following condensed data.

Prepare multiple-step income statement and calculate profitability ratios.
(SO 4, 6)

Administrative expenses	$435,000	Selling expenses	$ 690,000
Cost of goods sold	989,000	Loss on sale of equipment	10,000
Interest expense	75,000	Net sales	2,350,000
Interest revenue	45,000		

Instructions

(a) Prepare a multiple-step income statement.

(b) Calculate the profit margin ratio and gross profit rate.

E5-9 In its income statement for the year ended June 30, 2001, **The Clorox Company** reported the following condensed data (dollars in millions).

Prepare multiple-step income statement and calculate profitability ratios.
(SO 4, 6)

Selling and		Research and	
administrative expenses op	$ 495	development expense	$ 67
Net sales	3,903	Income tax expense 4	162
Interest expense	88	Other losses 3	95
Advertising expense	352	Cost of goods sold l	2,319

Instructions

(a) Prepare a multiple-step income statement.

(b) Calculate the gross profit rate and the profit margin ratio.

E5-10 The trial balance of J. Harlow Company at the end of its fiscal year, August 31, 2005, includes these accounts: Merchandise Inventory $17,200; Purchases $144,000; Sales $190,000; Freight-in $4,000; Sales Returns and Allowances $3,000; Freight-out $1,000; and Purchase Returns and Allowances $2,000. The ending merchandise inventory is $25,000.

Prepare cost of goods sold section.
(SO 5)

Instructions

Prepare a cost of goods sold section for the year ending August 31.

E5-11 Below is a series of cost of goods sold sections for companies X, F, L, and S.

Prepare cost of goods sold section.
(SO 5)

	X	F	L	S
Beginning inventory	$ 250	$ 120	$1,000	$ (j)
Purchases	1,500	1,080	(g)	43,590
Purchase returns and allowances	40	(d)	290	(k)
Net purchases	(a)	1,030	7,210	42,090
Freight-in	110	(e)	(h)	2,240
Cost of goods purchased	(b)	1,230	7,940	(l)
Cost of goods available for sale	1,820	1,350	(i)	49,530
Ending inventory	310	(f)	1,450	6,230
Cost of goods sold	(c)	1,230	7,490	43,300

Instructions

Fill in the lettered blanks to complete the cost of goods sold sections.

*E5-12 This information relates to Hans Olaf Co.

Journalize purchase transactions.
(SO 7)

1. On April 5 purchased merchandise from D. DeVito Company for $18,000, terms 2/10, net/30, FOB shipping point.

2. On April 6 paid freight costs of $900 on merchandise purchased from D. DeVito Company.

3. On April 7 purchased equipment on account for $26,000.

4. On April 8 returned some of April 5 merchandise to D. DeVito Company which cost $2,800.

5. On April 15 paid the amount due to D. DeVito Company in full.

Instructions

(a) Prepare the journal entries to record these transactions on the books of Hans Olaf Co. using a periodic inventory system.

(b) Assume that Hans Olaf Co. paid the balance due to D. DeVito Company on May 4 instead of April 15. Prepare the journal entry to record this payment.

Problems: Set A

Journalize, post, prepare partial income statement, and calculate ratios.
(SO 2, 3, 4, 6)

Peachtree

P5-1A   Paula Norby Distributing Company completed these merchandising transactions in the month of April. At the beginning of April, the ledger of Paula Norby showed Cash of $9,000 and Common Stock of $9,000.

Apr.	2	Purchased merchandise on account from Iowa Supply Co. $6,300, terms 2/10, n/30.
	4	Sold merchandise on account $5,000, terms 2/10, n/30. The cost of the merchandise sold was $4,000.
	5	Paid $200 freight on April 4 sale.
	6	Received credit from Iowa Supply Co. for merchandise returned $300.
	11	Paid Iowa Supply Co. in full, less discount.
	13	Received collections in full, less discounts, from customers billed on April 4.
	14	Purchased merchandise for cash $4,400.
	16	Received refund from supplier for returned merchandise on cash purchase of April 14, $500.
	18	Purchased merchandise from Prairie Distributors $4,200, terms 2/10, n/30.
	20	Paid freight on April 18 purchase $100.
	23	Sold merchandise for cash $8,100. The cost of the merchandise sold was $6,700.
	26	Purchased merchandise for cash $2,300.
	27	Paid Prairie Distributors in full, less discount.
	29	Made refunds to cash customers for returned merchandise $110. The returned merchandise had a cost of $75.
	30	Sold merchandise on account $3,700, terms n/30. The cost of the merchandise sold was $3,000.

Paula Norby Distributing Company's chart of accounts includes Cash, Accounts Receivable, Merchandise Inventory, Accounts Payable, Common Stock, Sales, Sales Returns and Allowances, Sales Discounts, Cost of Goods Sold, and Freight-out.

Instructions

(a) Journalize the transactions.

(b) Post the transactions to T accounts. Be sure to enter the beginning cash and common stock balances.

(c) Gross profit $2,965

(c) Prepare the income statement through gross profit for the month of April 2005.

(d) Calculate the profit margin ratio and the gross profit rate. (Assume operating expenses were $900.)

Journalize purchase and sale transactions under a perpetual inventory system.
(SO 2, 3)

P5-2A   On the Go Warehouse distributes suitcases to retail stores and extends credit terms of 1/10, n/30 to all of its customers. During the month of July the following merchandising transactions occurred.

July	1	Purchased 60 suitcases on account for $30 each from Trunk Manufacturers, terms 1/15, n/30.
	3	Sold 40 suitcases on account to Luggage World for $50 each.
	9	Paid Trunk Manufacturers in full.
	12	Received payment in full from Luggage World.
	17	Sold 30 suitcases on account to The Travel Spot for $50 each.
	18	Purchased 60 suitcases on account for $30 (including freight) each from Vacation Manufacturers, terms 2/10, n/30.

20 Received $300 credit for 10 suitcases returned to Vacation Manufacturers.
21 Received payment in full from The Travel Spot.
22 Sold 40 suitcases on account to Vacations-Are-Us for $52 each.
30 Paid Vacation Manufacturers in full.
31 Granted Vacations-Are-Us $260 credit for 5 suitcases returned costing $150.

Instructions

Journalize the transactions for the month of July for On the Go Warehouse, using a perpetual inventory system. Assume the cost of each suitcase sold was $30.

P5-3A At the beginning of the current season, the ledger of Village Tennis Shop showed Cash $2,500; Merchandise Inventory $1,700; and Common Stock $4,200. The following transactions were completed during April.

Journalize, post, and prepare trial balance and partial income statement.
(SO 2, 3, 4)

Peachtree

Apr. 4 Purchased racquets and balls from Robert Co. $840, terms 3/10, n/30.
6 Paid freight on Robert Co. purchase $60.
8 Sold merchandise to members $900, terms n/30. The merchandise sold cost $600.
10 Received credit of $40 from Robert Co. for a damaged racquet that was returned.
11 Purchased tennis shoes from Newbee Sports for cash $300.
13 Paid Robert Co. in full.
14 Purchased tennis shirts and shorts from Venus Sportswear $500, terms 2/10, n/60.
15 Received cash refund of $50 from Newbee Sports for damaged merchandise that was returned.
17 Paid freight on Venus Sportswear purchase $30.
18 Sold merchandise to members $800, terms n/30. The cost of the merchandise sold was $410.
20 Received $500 in cash from members in settlement of their accounts.
21 Paid Venus Sportswear in full.
27 Granted an allowance of $30 to members for tennis clothing that did not fit properly.
30 Received cash payments on account from members $350.

The chart of accounts for the tennis shop includes Cash, Accounts Receivable, Merchandise Inventory, Accounts Payable, Common Stock, Sales, Sales Returns and Allowances, and Cost of Goods Sold.

Instructions

(a) Journalize the April transactions.
(b) Using T accounts, enter the beginning balances in the ledger accounts and post the April transactions.
(c) Prepare a trial balance on April 30, 2005.
(d) Prepare an income statement through gross profit.

(c) Tot. trial balance $5,900
(d) Gross profit $ 660

P5-4A Skogmo Department Store is located near the Cascade Shopping Mall. At the end of the company's fiscal year on December 31, 2005, the following accounts appeared in its adjusted trial balance.

Prepare financial statements and calculate profitability ratios.
(SO 4, 6)

Accounts Payable	$ 79,300
Accounts Receivable	50,300
Accumulated Depreciation—Building	52,500
Accumulated Depreciation—Equipment	42,600
Building	190,000
Cash	33,000
Common Stock	150,000
Cost of Goods Sold	415,000
Depreciation Expense—Building	10,400
Depreciation Expense—Equipment	13,000
Dividends	28,000
Equipment	100,000

[handwritten: same as net inc]

[handwritten box: is this beg ret]

Account	Amount	[handwritten]
Insurance Expense	7,200	IS
Interest Expense	11,000	IS
Interest Payable	8,000	Liab
Interest Revenue	4,300	IS rev
Merchandise Inventory	75,000	Asset -20,000
Mortgage Payable	80,000	Liabilia Long
Office Salaries Expense	32,000	IS
Prepaid Insurance	2,400	Asset
Property Taxes Payable	4,800	Liability
Property Taxes Expense	4,800	IS
Retained Earnings	26,600	RE, BS
Sales Salaries Expense	76,000	IS
Sales revenue	630,000	IS
Sales Commissions Expense	14,500	IS
Sales Commissions Payable	3,500	Liability
Sales Returns and Allowances	8,000	contra sale IS
Utilities Expense	11,000	IS

[handwritten: contra revenue]

Additional data: $20,000 of the mortgage payable is due for payment next year. *[handwritten: current 20, longterm 60]*

Instructions

(a) Prepare a multiple-step income statement, a retained earnings statement, and a classified balance sheet.

(b) Calculate the profit margin ratio and the gross profit rate.

(a) Net income $ 31,400
Tot. assets $355,600

Prepare a correct multiple-step income statement.
(SO 4)

P5-5A A part-time bookkeeper prepared this income statement for Nashika Company for the year ending December 31, 2005.

NASHIKA COMPANY
Income Statement
December 31, 2005

Revenues		
Sales		$715,000
Less: Freight-out	$10,000	
Sales discounts	11,300	21,300
Net sales		693,700
Other revenues (net)		1,300
Total revenues		695,000
Expenses		
Cost of goods sold		470,000
Selling expenses		100,000
Administrative expenses		50,000
Dividends		12,000
Total expenses		632,000
Net income		$ 63,000

As an experienced, knowledgeable accountant, you review the statement and determine the following facts.

1. Sales include $12,000 of deposits from customers for future sales orders.

2. Other revenues contain two items: interest expense $4,000 and interest revenue $5,300.

3. Selling expenses consist of sales salaries $76,000, advertising $10,000, depreciation on store equipment $7,500, and sales commissions expense $6,500.

4. Administrative expenses consist of office salaries $19,000; utilities expense $8,000; rent expense $16,000; and insurance expense $7,000. Insurance expense includes $1,600 of insurance applicable to 2006.

Operating
expenses $158,400
Net income $ 64,600

Instructions

Prepare a correct detailed multiple-step income statement.

P5-6A The trial balance of Trendy Fashion Center contained the following accounts at November 30, the end of the company's fiscal year.

Journalize, post, and prepare adjusted trial balance and financial statements.
(SO 4)

TRENDY FASHION CENTER
Trial Balance
November 30, 2005

	Debit	Credit
Cash	$ 36,700	
Accounts Receivable	33,700	
Merchandise Inventory	45,000	
Store Supplies	6,800	
Store Equipment	85,000	
Accumulated Depreciation—Store Equipment		$ 38,000
Delivery Equipment	38,000	
Accumulated Depreciation—Delivery Equipment		6,000
Notes Payable		41,000
Accounts Payable		49,800
Common Stock		80,000
Retained Earnings		30,000
Dividends	12,000	
Sales		747,200
Sales Returns and Allowances	4,200	
Cost of Goods Sold	507,400	
Salaries Expense	130,000	
Advertising Expense	26,400	
Utilities Expense	14,000	
Repair Expense	12,100	
Delivery Expense	16,700	
Rent Expense	24,000	
	$992,000	$992,000

Adjustment data:

1. Store supplies on hand total $3,500.
2. Depreciation is $10,000 on the store equipment and $6,000 on the delivery equipment.
3. Interest of $11,000 is accrued on notes payable at November 30.

Other data: $30,000 of notes payable are due for payment next year.

Instructions
(a) Journalize the adjusting entries.
(b) Prepare T accounts for all accounts used in part (a). Enter the trial balance amounts into the T accounts and post the adjusting entries.
(c) Prepare an adjusted trial balance.
(d) Prepare a multiple-step income statement and a retained earnings statement for the year, and a classified balance sheet at November 30, 2005.

(c) Tot. trial
    balance $1,019,000
(d) Net loss $ (17,900)
    Tot. assets $ 181,900

P5-7A At the end of High-Point Department Store's fiscal year on December 31, 2005, these accounts appeared in its adjusted trial balance.

Determine cost of goods sold and gross profit under periodic approach.
(SO 4, 5)

Freight-in	$ 5,600
Merchandise Inventory (beginning)	40,500
Purchases	442,000
Purchase Discounts	12,000
Purchase Returns and Allowances	6,400
Sales	718,000
Sales Returns and Allowances	8,000

Additional facts:

1. Merchandise inventory on December 31, 2005, is $75,000.

2. Note that High-Point Department Store uses a periodic system.

Instructions

Gross profit $315,300

Prepare an income statement through gross profit for the year ended December 31, 2005.

Calculate missing amounts and assess profitability.
(SO 4, 5, 6)

P5-8A   Danielle MacLean operates a clothing retail operation. She purchases all merchandise inventory on credit and uses a perpetual inventory system. The accounts payable account is used for recording inventory purchases only; all other current liabilities are accrued in separate accounts. You are provided with the following selected information for the fiscal years 2003, 2004, 2005, and 2006.

	2003	2004	2005	2006
Inventory (ending)	$13,000	$ 11,300	$ 14,700	$ 12,200
Accounts payable (ending)	20,000			
Sales		225,700	227,600	219,500
Purchases of merchandise inventory on account		141,000	150,000	132,000
Cash payments to suppliers		135,000	161,000	127,000

Instructions

(a) 2005 $146,600
(c) 2005 $15,000

(a) Calculate cost of goods sold for each of the 2004, 2005, and 2006 fiscal years.

(b) Calculate the gross profit for each of the 2004, 2005, and 2006 fiscal years.

(c) Calculate the ending balance of accounts payable for each of the 2004, 2005, and 2006 fiscal years.

(d) Sales declined in fiscal 2006. Does that mean that profitability, as measured by the gross profit rate, necessarily also declined? Explain, calculating the gross profit rate for each fiscal year to help support your answer.

Journalize, post, and prepare trial balance and partial income statement using periodic approach.
(SO 5, 7)

*P5-9A   At the beginning of the current season, the ledger of Village Tennis Shop showed Cash $2,500; Merchandise Inventory $1,700; and Common Stock $4,200. The following transactions were completed during April.

Apr. 4   Purchased racquets and balls from Robert Co. $840, terms 3/10, n/30.
6   Paid freight on Robert Co. purchase $60.
8   Sold merchandise to members $900, terms n/30.
10   Received credit of $40 from Robert Co. for a damaged racquet that was returned.
11   Purchased tennis shoes from Newbee Sports for cash $300.
13   Paid Robert Co. in full.
14   Purchased tennis shirts and shorts from Venus's Sportswear $500, terms 2/10, n/60.
15   Received cash refund of $50 from Newbee Sports for damaged merchandise that was returned.
17   Paid freight on Venus's Sportswear purchase $30.
18   Sold merchandise to members $800, terms n/30.
20   Received $500 in cash from members in settlement of their accounts.
21   Paid Venus's Sportswear in full.
27   Granted an allowance of $30 to members for tennis clothing that did not fit properly.
30   Received cash payments on account from members $500.

The chart of accounts for the tennis shop includes Cash, Accounts Receivable, Merchandise Inventory, Accounts Payable, Common Stock, Sales, Sales Returns and Allowances, Purchases, Purchase Returns and Allowances, Purchase Discounts, and Freight-in.

Instructions

(a) Journalize the April transactions using a periodic inventory system.

(b) Using T accounts, enter the beginning balances in the ledger accounts and post the April transactions.

(c) Tot. trial balance $6,024
(d) Gross profit $ 660

(c) Prepare a trial balance on April 30, 2005.

(d) Prepare an income statement through Gross Profit, assuming merchandise inventory on hand at April 30 is $2,296.

Problems: Set B

P5-1B Schilling Hardware Store completed the following merchandising transactions in the month of May. At the beginning of May, Schilling's ledger showed Cash of $5,000 and Common Stock of $5,000.

Journalize, post, prepare partial income statement, and calculate ratios.
(SO 2, 3, 4, 6)

May	1	Purchased merchandise on account from Midwest Wholesale Supply for $6,000, terms 2/10, n/30.
	2	Sold merchandise on account for $4,500, terms 2/10, n/30. The cost of the merchandise sold was $3,000.
	5	Received credit from Midwest Wholesale Supply for merchandise returned $200.
	9	Received collections in full, less discounts, from customers billed on sales of $4,500 on May 2.
	10	Paid Midwest Wholesale Supply in full, less discount.
	11	Purchased supplies for cash $900.
	12	Purchased merchandise for cash $3,100.
	15	Received $230 refund for return of poor-quality merchandise from supplier on cash purchase.
	17	Purchased merchandise from Cedar Distributors for $1,900, terms 2/10, n/30.
	19	Paid freight on May 17 purchase $250.
	24	Sold merchandise for cash $6,200. The cost of the merchandise sold was $4,340.
	25	Purchased merchandise from Horicon Inc. for $800, terms 2/10, n/30.
	27	Paid Cedar Distributors in full, less discount.
	29	Made refunds to cash customers for returned merchandise $100. The returned merchandise had cost $70.
	31	Sold merchandise on account for $1,600, terms n/30. The cost of the merchandise sold was $1,120.

Schilling Hardware's chart of accounts includes Cash, Accounts Receivable, Merchandise Inventory, Supplies, Accounts Payable, Common Stock, Sales, Sales Returns and Allowances, Sales Discounts, and Cost of Goods Sold.

Instructions
(a) Journalize the transactions using a perpetual inventory system.
(b) Post the transactions to T accounts. Be sure to enter the beginning cash and common stock balances.
(c) Prepare an income statement through gross profit for the month of May 2005.
(d) Calculate the profit margin ratio and the gross profit rate. (Assume operating expenses were $1,500.)

(c) Gross profit $3,720

P5-2B Garden of Reading Warehouse distributes hardback books to retail stores and extends credit terms of 2/10, n/30 to all of its customers. During the month of June the following merchandising transactions occurred.

Journalize purchase and sale transactions under a perpetual inventory system.
(SO 2, 3)

June	1	Purchased 130 books on account for $5 each (including freight) from Book Worm Publishers, terms 1/10, n/30.
	3	Sold 120 books on account to the Book Nook for $10 each.
	6	Received $50 credit for 10 books returned to Book Worm Publishers.
	9	Paid Book Worm Publishers in full.
	15	Received payment in full from the Book Nook.
	17	Sold 110 books on account to Corner Bookstore for $10 each.
	20	Purchased 120 books on account for $5 each from Parrot Publishers, terms 2/15, n/30.
	24	Received payment in full from Corner Bookstore.
	26	Paid Parrot Publishers in full.
	28	Sold 110 books on account to Readers Bookstore for $10 each.
	30	Granted Readers Bookstore $150 credit for 15 books returned costing $75.

Instructions

Journalize the transactions for the month of June for Garden of Reading Warehouse, using a perpetual inventory system. Assume the cost of each book sold was $5.

Journalize, post, and prepare trial balance and partial income statement.
(SO 2, 3, 4)

P5-3B At the beginning of the current season on April 1, the ledger of Tri-State Pro Shop showed Cash $2,500; Merchandise Inventory $3,500; and Common Stock $6,000. The following transactions were completed during April 2005.

Apr. 5 Purchased golf bags, clubs, and balls on account from Gage Co. $1,700, terms 2/10, n/60.
 7 Paid freight on Gage purchase $80.
 9 Received credit from Gage Co. for merchandise returned $200.
 10 Sold merchandise on account to members $950, terms n/30. The merchandise sold had a cost of $630.
 12 Purchased golf shoes, sweaters, and other accessories on account from Brooks Sportswear $660, terms 1/10, n/30.
 14 Paid Gage Co. in full.
 17 Received credit from Brooks Sportswear for merchandise returned $60.
 20 Made sales on account to members $700, terms n/30. The cost of the merchandise sold was $490.
 21 Paid Brooks Sportswear in full.
 27 Granted an allowance to members for clothing that did not fit properly $75.
 30 Received payments on account from members $1,100.

The chart of accounts for the pro shop includes Cash, Accounts Receivable, Merchandise Inventory, Accounts Payable, Common Stock, Sales, Sales Returns and Allowances, and Cost of Goods Sold.

Instructions

(a) Journalize the April transactions using a perpetual inventory system.
(b) Using T accounts, enter the beginning balances in the ledger accounts and post the April transactions.

(c) Tot. trial
balance $7,650
(d) Gross profit $ 455

(c) Prepare a trial balance on April 30, 2005.
(d) Prepare an income statement through gross profit.

Prepare financial statements and calculate profitability ratios.
(SO 4, 6)

P5-4B Stampfer Department Store is located in midtown Metropolis. During the past several years, net income has been declining because suburban shopping centers have been attracting business away from city areas. At the end of the company's fiscal year on November 30, 2005, these accounts appeared in its adjusted trial balance.

Accounts Payable	$ 27,310
Accounts Receivable	11,770
Accumulated Depreciation—Delivery Equipment	19,680
Accumulated Depreciation—Store Equipment	41,800
Cash	8,000
Common Stock	38,000
Cost of Goods Sold	633,220
Delivery Expense	8,200
Delivery Equipment	57,000
Depreciation Expense—Delivery Equipment	4,000
Depreciation Expense—Store Equipment	9,500
Dividends	12,000
Insurance Expense	9,000
Interest Expense	8,000
Interest Revenue	7,000
Merchandise Inventory	36,200
Notes Payable	47,500
Prepaid Insurance	6,000
Property Tax Expense	3,500
Property Taxes Payable	3,500
Rent Expense	29,000
Retained Earnings	14,200

Salaries Expense	110,000
Sales	910,000
Sales Commissions Expense	14,000
Sales Commissions Payable	6,000
Sales Returns and Allowances	20,000
Store Equipment	125,000
Utilities Expense	10,600

Additional data: Notes payable are due in 2009.

Instructions
(a) Prepare a multiple-step income statement, a retained earnings statement, and a classified balance sheet.
(b) Calculate the profit margin ratio and the gross profit rate.

(a) Net income $ 57,980
Tot. assets $182,490

P5-5B An inexperienced accountant prepared this condensed income statement for Sunrise Company, a retail firm that has been in business for a number of years.

Prepare a correct multiple-step income statement.
(SO 4)

SUNRISE COMPANY
Income Statement
For the Year Ended December 31, 2005

Revenues		
Net sales	$840,000	
Other revenues	24,000	
	864,000	
Cost of goods sold	555,000	
Gross profit	309,000	
Operating expenses		
Selling expenses	104,000	
Administrative expenses	89,000	
	193,000	
Net earnings	$116,000	

As an experienced, knowledgeable accountant, you review the statement and determine the following facts.

1. Net sales consist of sales $900,000, less delivery expense on merchandise sold $30,000, and sales returns and allowances $30,000.

2. Other revenues consist of sales discounts $16,000 and rent revenue $8,000.

3. Selling expenses consist of salespersons' salaries $80,000; depreciation on accounting equipment $8,000; advertising $10,000; and sales commissions $6,000. The commissions represent commissions paid. At December 31, $3,000 of commissions have been earned by salespersons but have not been paid.

4. Administrative expenses consist of office salaries $37,000; dividends $14,000; utilities $12,000; interest expense $2,000; and rent expense $24,000, which includes prepayments totaling $4,000 for the first quarter of 2005.

Instructions
Prepare a correct detailed multiple-step income statement.

Net income $99,000

P5-6B The trial balance of Benton Brothers Wholesale Company contained the accounts shown at December 31, the end of the company's fiscal year.

Journalize, post, and prepare adjusted trial balance and financial statements.
(SO 4)

BENTON BROTHERS WHOLESALE COMPANY
Trial Balance
December 31, 2005

	Debit	Credit
Cash	$ 33,400	
Accounts Receivable	37,600	
Merchandise Inventory	110,000	
Land	92,000	

	Debit	**Credit**
Buildings	197,000	
Accumulated Depreciation—Buildings		$ 57,000
Equipment	83,500	
Accumulated Depreciation—Equipment		42,400
Notes Payable		52,000
Accounts Payable		37,500
Common Stock		200,000
Retained Earnings		68,200
Dividends	12,000	
Sales		922,100
Sales Discounts	5,000	
Cost of Goods Sold	709,900	
Salaries Expense	69,800	
Utilities Expense	9,400	
Repair Expense	8,900	
Gas and Oil Expense	7,200	
Insurance Expense	3,500	
	$1,379,200	$1,379,200

Adjustment data:

1. Depreciation is $10,000 on buildings and $9,000 on equipment. (Both are adminis-trative expenses.)

2. Interest of $7,500 is due and unpaid on notes payable at December 31.

Other data: $15,000 of the notes payable are payable next year.

Instructions
(a) Journalize the adjusting entries.
(b) Create T accounts for all accounts used in part (a). Enter the trial balance amounts into the T accounts and post the adjusting entries.

(c) Tot. trial balance
$1,405,700
(d) Net income $ 81,900
Tot. assets $ 435,100

(c) Prepare an adjusted trial balance.
(d) Prepare a multiple-step income statement and a retained earnings statement for the year, and a classified balance sheet at December 31, 2005.

Determine cost of goods sold and gross profit under periodic approach.
(SO 4, 5)

P5-7B At the end of Stampfer Department Store's fiscal year on November 30, 2005, these accounts appeared in its adjusted trial balance.

Freight-in	$ 5,060
Merchandise Inventory (beginning)	44,360
Purchases	630,000
Purchase Discounts	7,000
Purchase Returns and Allowances	3,000
Sales	910,000
Sales Returns and Allowances	20,000

Additional facts:

1. Merchandise inventory on November 30, 2005, is $36,200.

2. Note that Stampfer Department Store uses a periodic system.

Instructions

Gross profit $256,780

Prepare an income statement through gross profit for the year ended November 30, 2005.

Calculate missing amounts and assess profitability.
(SO 4, 5, 6)

P5-8B Psang Inc. operates a retail operation that purchases and sells snowmobiles, amongst other outdoor products. The company purchases all merchandise inventory on credit and uses a perpetual inventory system. The accounts payable account is used for recording inventory purchases only; all other current liabilities are accrued in separate accounts. You are provided with the following selected information for the fiscal years 2003 through 2006, inclusive.

	2003	2004	2005	2006
Income Statement Data				
Sales		$96,850	$ (e)	$82,220
Cost of goods sold		(a)	27,140	26,550
Gross profit		69,260	61,540	(i)
Operating expenses		63,500	(f)	52,060
Net income		$ (b)	$ 4,570	$ (j)
Balance Sheet Data				
Merchandise inventory	$13,000	$ (c)	$14,700	$ (k)
Accounts payable	5,000	6,500	4,600	(l)
Additional Information				
Purchases of merchandise inventory on account		$25,890	$ (g)	$24,050
Cash payments to suppliers		(d)	(h)	24,650

Instructions

(a) Calculate the missing amounts.

(b) Sales declined over the 3-year fiscal period, 2004–2006. Does that mean that profitability necessarily also declined? Explain, computing the gross profit rate and the profit margin ratio for each fiscal year to help support your answer.

*P5-9B   At the beginning of the current season on April 1, the ledger of Tri-State Pro Shop showed Cash $2,500; Merchandise Inventory $3,500; and Common Stock $6,000. These transactions occured during April 2005.

Journalize, post, and prepare trial balance and partial income statement using periodic approach.
(SO 5, 7)

Apr. 5 Purchased golf bags, clubs, and balls on account from Balata Co. $1,700, FOB shipping point, terms 2/10, n/60.

7 Paid freight on Balata Co. purchases $80.

9 Received credit from Balata Co. for merchandise returned $200.

10 Sold merchandise on account to members $950, terms n/30.

12 Purchased golf shoes, sweaters, and other accessories on account from Arrow Sportswear $660, terms 1/10, n/30.

14 Paid Balata Co. in full.

17 Received credit from Arrow Sportswear for merchandise returned $60.

20 Made sales on account to members $700, terms n/30.

21 Paid Arrow Sportswear in full.

27 Granted credit to members for clothing that did not fit $75.

30 Received payments on account from members $1,100.

The chart of accounts for the pro shop includes Cash, Accounts Receivable, Merchandise Inventory, Accounts Payable, Common Stock, Sales, Sales Returns and Allowances, Purchases, Purchase Returns and Allowances, Purchase Discounts, and Freight-in.

Instructions

(a) Journalize the April transactions using a periodic inventory system.

(b) Using T accounts, enter the beginning balances in the ledger accounts and post the April transactions.

(c) Prepare a trial balance on April 30, 2005.

(d) Prepare an income statement through Gross Profit, assuming merchandise inventory on hand at April 30 is $4,524.

(c) Tot. trial
    balance $7,946
    Gross profit $ 455

▶ **BROADENING YOUR PERSPECTIVE**

Financial Reporting and Analysis

FINANCIAL REPORTING PROBLEM: *Tootsie Roll Industries, Inc.*

BYP5-1 The financial statements for **Tootsie Roll Industries** are presented in Appendix A at the end of this book.

Instructions
Answer these questions using the Consolidated Income Statement.
  (a) What was the percentage change in sales and in net income from 2001 to 2002?
  (b) What was the profit margin ratio in each of the 3 years? Comment on the trend.
  (c) What was Tootsie Roll's gross profit rate in each of the 3 years? Comment on the trend.

COMPARATIVE ANALYSIS PROBLEM: *Tootsie Roll vs. Hershey Foods*

BYP5-2 The financial statements of **Hershey Foods** are presented in Appendix B, following the financial statements for **Tootsie Roll** in Appendix A.

Instructions
  (a) Based on the information contained in these financial statements, determine the following values for each company.
    (1) Profit margin ratio for 2002.
    (2) Gross profit for 2002.
    (3) Gross profit rate for 2002.
    (4) Operating income for 2002.
    (5) Percentage change in operating income from 2001 to 2002.
  (b) What conclusions concerning the relative profitability of the two companies can be drawn from these data?

RESEARCH CASE

BYP5-3 The January 25, 2001, issue of the *Wall Street Journal* includes an article by Nick Wingfield entitled "**Webvan** Seeks to Refine Customers in Hopes of Surviving Cash Crunch."

Instructions
Read the article and answer the following questions.
  (a) Describe in a few sentences Webvan's business plan.
  (b) What was the biggest challenge to Webvan's survival?
  (c) What was Webvan's gross profit rate (also called gross margin)? On the average $100 sale of goods, what was its gross profit? How did Webvan's gross profit rate compare to that of a traditional grocer?
  (d) What operating expenses did Webvan have that a traditional grocer wouldn't have?
  (e) According to the article, what were some things that Webvan could try to do to improve its profitability?

INTERPRETING FINANCIAL STATEMENTS

BYP5-4 **Zany Brainy, Inc.** is a specialty retailer of toys, games, books, and multimedia products for kids. As of the end of the fiscal year 2000, the company operated 188 stores in 34 states. On May 15, 2001, the company filed voluntary Chapter 11 bankruptcy. It is in the process of trying to reorganize itself to become more profitable. Provided below is financial information for the 2 years prior to the company's decision to file for bankruptcy, as well as information for a large competitor, **Toys R Us.**

ZANY BRAINY, INC.
(in millions of dollars, except number of shares)

	2/03/2001	1/29/2000
Current assets	$131.5	$142.5
Total assets	199.2	217.6
Current liabilities	117.8	57.3
Total liabilities	129.6	69.2
Average number of shares outstanding	31.3 million	25.2 million
Sales revenue	$400.5	$376.2
Cost of goods sold	312.5	267.8
Net income (loss)	(80.7)	17.1
Preferred stock dividends	0	0
Cash provided (used) by operations	(50.4)	(4.3)

At February 2, 2001, Toys R Us had the following ratio values.

Earnings per share	$ 0.34	Current ratio	1.32:1
Gross profit rate	31.0%	Current cash debt coverage ratio	−6.4%
Profit margin ratio	3.6%	Debt to total assets ratio	58%
Cash debt coverage ratio	11.0%		

Instructions
Use the information above to answer the following questions.

(a) Calculate the company's earnings per share, gross profit rate, and profit margin ratio for both years. Discuss the change in the company's profitability and its profitability relative to Toys R Us.

(b) Calculate the current ratio and current cash debt coverage ratio for both years. Discuss the change in the company's liquidity and its liquidity relative to Toys R Us. The company's current liabilities at January 30, 1999, were $28.0 million.

(c) Calculate the debt to total assets ratio and cash debt coverage ratio for both years. Discuss the change in the company's solvency and its solvency relative to Toys R Us. The company's total liabilities at January 30, 1999, were $33.9 million.

(d) Discuss whether your findings would have been useful in predicting whether the company was going to have to file for bankruptcy. That is, based on this analysis, should investors have been surprised by the company's bankruptcy filing?

A GLOBAL FOCUS

BYP5-5 Recently it was announced that two giant French retailers, **Carrefour SA** and **Promodes SA**, would merge. A headline in the *Wall Street Journal* blared, "French Retailers Create New Wal-Mart Rival." While **Wal-Mart's** total sales would still exceed those of the combined company, Wal-Mart's international sales are far less than those of the combined company. This is a serious concern for Wal-Mart, since its primary opportunity for future growth lies outside of the United States.

Below are basic financial data for the combined corporation (in French francs) and Wal-Mart (in U.S. dollars). Even though their results are presented in different currencies, by employing ratios we can make some basic comparisons.

	Carrefour/ Promodes (in millions)	Wal-Mart (in billions)
Sales	Euros 69,486	$191,329
Cost of goods sold	53,875	150,255
Net income	1,266	6,295
Total assets	43,470	78,130
Current assets	16,910	26,555
Current liabilities	12,997	28,949
Total liabilities	32,773	46,787

Instructions

Compare the two companies by answering the following.

(a) Calculate the gross profit rate for each of the companies, and discuss their relative abilities to control cost of goods sold.

(b) Calculate the profit margin ratio, and discuss the companies' relative profitability.

(c) Calculate the current ratio and debt to total assets ratios for the two companies, and discuss their relative liquidity and solvency.

(d) What concerns might you have in relying on this comparison?

FINANCIAL ANALYSIS ON THE WEB

BYP5-6 *Purpose*: No financial decision maker should ever rely solely on the financial information reported in the annual report to make decisions. It is important to keep abreast of financial news. This activity demonstrates how to search for financial news on the Web.

Address: http://biz.yahoo.com/i (or go to **www.wiley.com/college/kimmel**)

Steps

1. Type in either Wal-Mart, Target Corp., or Kmart.

2. Choose **News**.

3. Select an article that sounds interesting to you and that would be relevant to an investor in these companies.

Instructions

(a) What was the source of the article? (For example, Reuters, Businesswire, Prnewswire.)

(b) Pretend that you are a personal financial planner and that one of your clients owns stock in the company. Write a brief memo to your client summarizing the article and explaining the implications of the article for their investment.

Critical Thinking

GROUP DECISION CASE

BYP5-7 Three years ago Maggie Green and her brother-in-law Joe Longeway opened FedCo Department Store. For the first 2 years, business was good, but the following condensed income results for 2005 were disappointing.

FEDCO DEPARTMENT STORE
Income Statement
For the Year Ended December 31, 2005

Net sales		$700,000
Cost of goods sold		546,000
Gross profit		154,000
Operating expenses		
Selling expenses	$100,000	
Administrative expenses	25,000	
		125,000
Net income		$ 29,000

Maggie believes the problem lies in the relatively low gross profit rate (gross profit divided by net sales) of 22%. Joe believes the problem is that operating expenses are too high. Maggie thinks the gross profit rate can be improved by making two changes: (1) Increase average selling prices by 17%; this increase is expected to lower sales volume so that total sales dollars will increase only 6%. (2) Buy merchandise in larger quantities and take all purchase discounts; these changes are expected to increase the gross profit rate by 3%. Maggie does not anticipate that these changes will have any effect on operating expenses.

Joe thinks expenses can be cut by making these two changes: (1) Cut 2005 sales salaries of $60,000 in half and give sales personnel a commission of 2% of net sales. (2) Reduce store deliveries to one day per week rather than twice a week; this change will reduce 2005 delivery expenses of $30,000 by 40%. Joe feels that these changes will not have any effect on net sales.

Maggie and Joe come to you for help in deciding the best way to improve net income.

Instructions
With the class divided into groups, answer the following.
 (a) Prepare a condensed income statement for 2006 assuming (1) Maggie's changes are implemented and (2) Joe's ideas are adopted.
 (b) What is your recommendation to Maggie and Joe?
 (c) Prepare a condensed income statement for 2006 assuming both sets of proposed changes are made.
 (d) Discuss the impact that other factors might have. For example, would increasing the quantity of inventory increase costs? Would a salary cut affect employee morale? Would decreased morale affect sales? Would decreased store deliveries decrease customer satisfaction? What other suggestions might be considered?

COMMUNICATION ACTIVITY

BYP5-8   The following situation is presented in chronological order.
 1. Dexter decides to buy a surfboard.
 2. He calls Surfing USA Co. to inquire about their surfboards.
 3. Two days later he requests Surfing USA Co. to make him a surfboard.
 4. Three days later Surfing USA Co. sends him a purchase order to fill out.
 5. He sends back the purchase order.
 6. Surfing USA Co. receives the completed purchase order.
 7. Surfing USA Co. completes the surfboard.
 8. Dexter picks up the surfboard.
 9. Surfing USA Co. bills Dexter.
 10. Surfing USA Co. receives payment from Dexter.

Instructions
In a memo to the president of Surfing USA Co., answer the following questions.
 (a) When should Surfing USA Co. record the sale?
 (b) Suppose that with his purchase order, Dexter is required to make a down payment. Would that change your answer to part (a)?

ETHICS CASE

BYP5-9   Melissa Lee was just hired as the assistant treasurer of Yorkshire Stores, a specialty chain store company that has nine retail stores concentrated in one metropolitan area. Among other things, the payment of all invoices is centralized in one of the departments Melissa will manage. Her primary responsibility is to maintain the company's high credit rating by paying all bills when due and to take advantage of all cash discounts.

Travis Brett, the former assistant treasurer, who has been promoted to treasurer, is training Melissa in her new duties. He instructs Melissa that she is to continue the practice of preparing all checks "net of discount" and dating the checks the last day of the discount period. "But," Travis Brett continues, "we always hold the checks at least 4 days beyond the discount period before mailing them. That way we get another 4 days of interest on our money. Most of our creditors need our business and don't complain. And, if they scream about our missing the discount period, we blame it on the mail room or the post office. We've only lost one discount out of every hundred we take that way. I think everybody does it. By the way, welcome to our team!"

Instructions
   (a) What are the ethical considerations in this case?
   (b) What stakeholders are harmed or benefited?
   (c) Should Melissa continue the practice started by Travis? Does she have any choice?

Answers to Self-Study Questions

1. a   2. c   3. c   4. b   5. c   6. b   7. d   8. a   9. c
10. c   11. a   *12. b

Answer to Tootsie Roll Review It Question 3, p. 233

Tootsie Roll's title for gross profit is "gross margin." Its gross profit (gross margin) decreased 1.5% in 2002 ($175,098 − $172,420) ÷ $175,098   .

✔ Remember to go back to the Navigator box on the chapter-opening page and check off your completed work.

Reporting and Analyzing Inventory

STUDY OBJECTIVES

After studying this chapter,
you should be able to:

1 Describe the steps in determining inventory quantities.

2 Explain the basis of accounting for inventories and apply the inventory cost flow methods under a periodic inventory system.

3 Explain the financial statement and tax effects of each of the inventory cost flow assumptions.

4 Explain the lower of cost or market basis of accounting for inventories.

5 Compute and interpret the inventory turnover ratio.

6 Describe the LIFO reserve and explain its importance for comparing results of different companies.

 THE NAVIGATOR

THE NAVIGATOR ✔

▶ Scan *Study Objectives* ☐

▶ Read *Feature Story* ☐

▶ Read *Preview* ☐

▶ Read text and answer *Before You Go On*
   p. 270 ☐   p. 279 ☐   p. 283 ☐

▶ Work Using the *Decision Toolkit* ☐

▶ Review Summary of *Study Objectives* ☐

▶ Work *Demonstration Problem* ☐

▶ Answer *Self-Study Questions* ☐

▶ Complete *Assignments* ☐

FEATURE STORY

Where Is That Spare Bulldozer Blade?

Let's talk inventory—big, bulldozer-size inventory. **Caterpillar Inc.** is the world's largest manufacturer of construction and mining equipment, diesel and natural gas engines, and industrial gas turbines. It sells its products in over 200 countries, making it one of the most successful U.S. exporters. More than 70% of its productive assets are located domestically, while nearly 50% of its sales are foreign.

During the 1980s Caterpillar's profitability suffered, but today it is very successful. A big part of this turnaround can be attributed to effective management of its inventory. Imagine what a bulldozer costs. Now imagine what it costs Caterpillar to have too many bulldozers sitting around in inventory—a situation the company definitely wants to avoid. Conversely, Caterpillar must make sure it has enough inventory to meet demand.

Between 1991 and 1998 Caterpillar's sales increased by 100%, while its inventory increased by only 50%. To achieve this dramatic reduction in the amount of resources tied up in inventory, while continuing to meet customers' needs, Caterpillar used a two-pronged approach. First, it completed a factory modernization program in 1993, which dramatically increased its production efficiency. The program reduced the amount of inventory being processed at any one time by 60%. It also reduced by an incredible 75% the time it takes to manufacture a part.

Second, Caterpillar dramatically improved its parts distribution system. It ships more than 100,000 items daily from its 23 distribution centers strategically located around the world (10 million square feet of warehouse space—remember, we're talking bulldozers). The company can virtually guarantee that it can get any part to anywhere in the world within 24 hours. Although this network services 550,000 part numbers, 99.7% of orders are filled immediately or shipped within hours. In fact, Caterpillar's distribution system is so advanced that it created a subsidiary, **Caterpillar Logistics Services, Inc.**, that warehouses and distributes other companies'

products. This subsidiary distributes products as diverse as running shoes, computer software, and auto parts all around the world. In short, how Caterpillar manages and accounts for its inventory goes a long way in explaining how profitable it is.

On the World Wide Web
Caterpillar Inc.: www.cat.com

In the previous chapter, we discussed the accounting for merchandise inventory using a perpetual inventory system. In this chapter, we explain the methods used to calculate the cost of inventory on hand at the balance sheet date and the cost of goods sold. We conclude by illustrating methods for analyzing inventory.

The content and organization of this chapter are as follows.

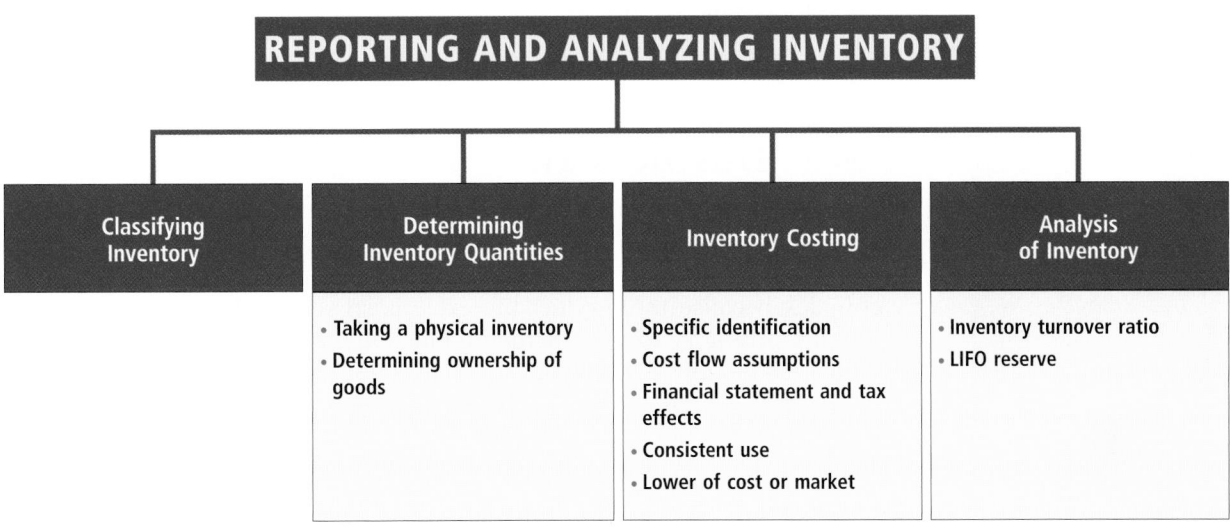

REPORTING AND ANALYZING INVENTORY

Classifying Inventory	Determining Inventory Quantities	Inventory Costing	Analysis of Inventory
	• Taking a physical inventory • Determining ownership of goods	• Specific identification • Cost flow assumptions • Financial statement and tax effects • Consistent use • Lower of cost or market	• Inventory turnover ratio • LIFO reserve

☑ THE NAVIGATOR

Classifying Inventory

How a company classifies its inventory depends on whether the firm is a merchandiser or a manufacturer. In a **merchandising** company, such as those described in Chapter 5, inventory consists of many different items. For example, in a grocery store, canned goods, dairy products, meats, and produce are just a few of the inventory items on hand. These items have two common characteristics: (1) They are owned by the company, and (2) they are in a form ready for sale to customers in the ordinary course of business. Thus, only one inventory classification, **merchandise inventory**, is needed to describe the many different items that make up the total inventory.

In a **manufacturing** company, some inventory may not yet be ready for sale. As a result, inventory is usually classified into three categories: finished goods, work in process, and raw materials. **Finished goods inventory** is manufactured items that are completed and ready for sale. **Work in process** is that portion of manufactured inventory that has been placed into the production process but is not yet complete. **Raw materials** are the basic goods that will be used in production but have not yet been placed into production. For example, **Caterpillar** classifies earth-moving tractors completed and ready for sale as **finished goods**. The tractors on the assembly line in various stages of production are classified as **work in process**. The steel, glass, tires, and other components that are on hand waiting to be used in the production of tractors are identified as **raw materials**.

> **Helpful Hint** Regardless of the classification, all inventories are reported under Current Assets on the balance sheet.

By observing the levels and changes in the levels of these three inventory types, financial statement users can gain insight into management's production plans. For example, low levels of raw materials and high levels of finished goods suggest that management believes it has enough inventory on hand, and production will be slowing down—perhaps in anticipation of a recession. On the other hand, high levels of raw materials and low levels of finished goods probably indicate that management is planning to step up production.

The accounting concepts discussed in this chapter apply to the inventory classifications of both merchandising and manufacturing companies. Our focus here is on merchandise inventory.

Business Insight
MANAGEMENT PERSPECTIVE

Inventory management for companies that make and sell high-tech products is very complex because the product life cycle is so short. The company wants to have enough inventory to meet demand, but doesn't want to have too much, because the introduction of a new product wipes out demand for the "old" product. **Palm**, maker of "personal digital assistants" (PDAs), learned this lesson the hard way in late 2001. Sales of its existing products had been booming, and the company was frequently faced with shortages, so it started increasing its inventories. Then sales started to slow and inventories started to grow faster than wanted. Management panicked and decided to announce that its new product—one that would make its old one obsolete—would be coming out in two weeks. Sales of the old product quickly died—leaving a mountain of inventory. But the new product wasn't actually ready for six weeks, resulting in a loss of sales in the interim.

Determining Inventory Quantities

STUDY OBJECTIVE
1
Describe the steps in determining inventory quantities.

No matter whether they are using a periodic or perpetual inventory system, all companies need to determine inventory quantities at the end of the accounting period. If using a perpetual system, companies take a physical inventory for two purposes: to check the accuracy of their perpetual inventory records, and to determine the amount of inventory lost due to wasted raw materials, shoplifting, or employee theft. Companies using a periodic inventory system must take a physical inventory for two *different* purposes: to determine the inventory on hand at the balance sheet date, and to determine the cost of goods sold for the period.

Determining inventory quantities involves two steps: (1) taking a physical inventory of goods on hand and (2) determining the ownership of goods.

TAKING A PHYSICAL INVENTORY

Taking a physical inventory involves actually counting, weighing, or measuring each kind of inventory on hand. In many companies, taking an inventory is a formidable task. Retailers such as **Target**, **True Value Hardware**, or **Home Depot** have thousands of different inventory items. An inventory count is generally more accurate when goods are not being sold or received during the counting. Consequently, companies often "take inventory" when the business is closed or when business is slow. Many retailers close early on a chosen day in January— after the holiday sales and returns, when inventories are at their lowest level—

to count inventory. Recall from Chapter 5 that **Wal-Mart** had a year-end of January 31. The physical inventory is taken at the end of the accounting period.

Business Insight
ETHICS PERSPECTIVE

Over the years the inventory account has played a role in many fraud cases. A classic involved salad oil. Management filled storage tanks mostly with water. Since oil rises to the top, the auditors thought the tanks were full of oil. In addition, management said they had more tanks than they really did—they repainted numbers on the tanks to confuse auditors. More recently, managers at women's apparel maker **Leslie Fay** were convicted of falsifying inventory records to boost net income—and consequently to boost management bonuses. In another case, executives at **Craig Consumer Electronics** were accused of defrauding lenders by manipulating inventory records. The indictment said the company classified "defective goods as new or refurbished" and claimed that it owned certain shipments "from overseas suppliers when, in fact, Craig either did not own the shipments or the shipments did not exist."

DETERMINING OWNERSHIP OF GOODS

One challenge in determining inventory quantities is making sure a company owns the inventory. To determine ownership of goods, two questions must be answered: Do all of the goods included in the count belong to the company? Does the company own any goods that were not included in the count?

Goods in Transit

A complication in determining ownership is **goods in transit** (on board a truck, train, ship, or plane) at the end of the period. The company may have purchased goods that have not yet been received, or it may have sold goods that have not yet been delivered. To arrive at an accurate count, ownership of these goods must be determined.

Goods in transit should be included in the inventory of the company that has legal title to the goods. Legal title is determined by the terms of the sale, as shown in Illustration 6-1 and described below.

Illustration 6-1
Terms of sale

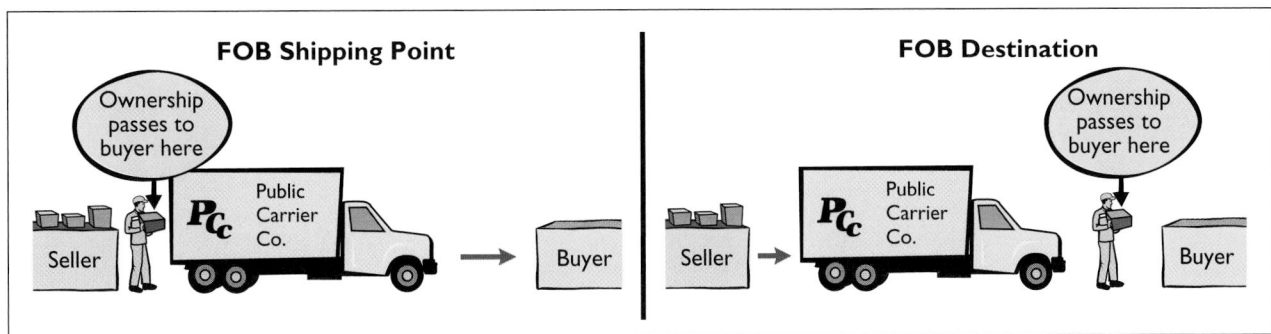

1. When the terms are **FOB (free on board) shipping point**, ownership of the goods passes to the buyer when the public carrier accepts the goods from the seller.

2. When the terms are **FOB destination**, ownership of the goods remains with the seller until the goods reach the buyer.

Consigned Goods

In some lines of business, it is customary to hold the goods of other parties and try to sell the goods for them for a fee, but without taking ownership of the goods. These are called **consigned goods**. For example, you might have a used car that you would like to sell. If you take the item to a dealer, the dealer might be willing to put the car on its lot and charge you a commission if it is sold. Under this agreement the dealer **would not take ownership** of the car, which would still belong to you. Therefore, if an inventory count were taken, the car would not be included in the dealer's inventory. Many car, boat, and antique dealers sell goods on consignment to keep their inventory costs down and to avoid the risk of purchasing an item that they won't be able to sell. Today even some manufacturers are making consignment agreements with their suppliers in order to keep their inventory levels low.

BEFORE YOU GO ON . . .

▶ **Review It**

1. What are the three inventory categories a manufacturing company would be likely to use? Why should financial statement users be aware of these categories?
2. What steps are involved in determining inventory quantities?
3. How is ownership determined for goods in transit?
4. Who has title to consigned goods?

☑ THE NAVIGATOR

Inventory Costing

STUDY OBJECTIVE
2
Explain the basis of accounting for inventories and apply the inventory cost flow methods under a periodic inventory system.

After the quantity of units of inventory has been determined, unit costs are applied to the quantities to determine the total cost of the inventory and the cost of good sold. This process can be complicated if inventory items have been purchased at different times and at different prices. For example, assume that Crivitz TV Company purchases three identical 46-inch TVs at costs of $700, $750, and $800. During the year Crivitz sold two sets at $1,200 each. These facts are summarized in Illustration 6-2.

Illustration 6-2 Data for inventory costing example

Purchases		
February 3	1 set	$ 700
March 5	1 set	$ 750
May 22	1 set	$ 800
Sales		
June 1	2 sets	$2,400 ($1,200 × 2)

Cost of goods sold will differ depending on which of the sets the company sold. For example, it might be $1,450 ($700 + $750), or $1,500 ($700 + $800), or $1,550 ($750 + $800). In this section we discuss alternative costing methods available to Crivitz.

SPECIFIC IDENTIFICATION

If the TVs sold by Crivitz are the ones it purchased on February 3 and May 22, then its cost of goods sold is $1,500 ($700 + $800), and its ending inventory is $750. If Crivitz can positively identify which particular units were sold and which are still in ending inventory, it can use the **specific identification method** of inventory costing (see Illustration 6-3). In this case, ending inventory and cost of goods sold are easily and accurately determined.

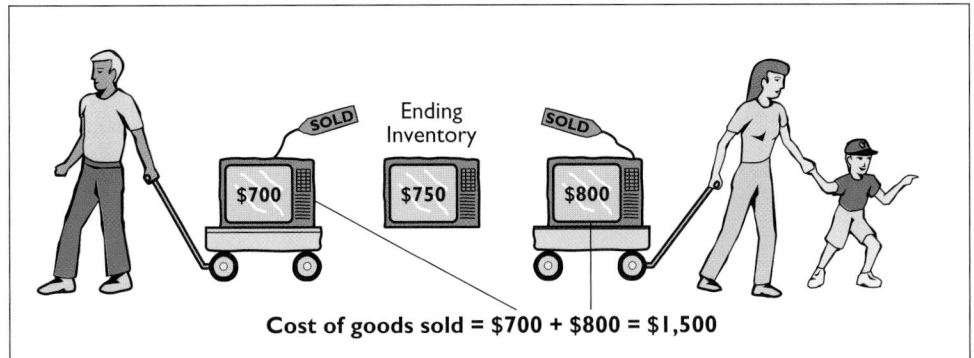

Illustration 6-3 Specific identification method

Specific identification requires that records be kept of the original cost of each individual inventory item. Historically, specific identification was possible only when a company sold a limited variety of high-unit-cost items that could be identified clearly from the time of purchase through the time of sale. Examples of such products are cars, pianos, or expensive antiques. Today, with bar coding it is theoretically possible to do specific identification with nearly any type of product. The reality is, however, that this practice is still relatively rare. Instead, rather than keep track of the cost of each particular item sold, most companies make assumptions, called **cost flow assumptions**, about which units were sold.

Ethics Note A major disadvantage of the specific identification method is that management may be able to manipulate net income. For example, it can boost net income by selling units purchased at a low cost, or reduce net income by selling units purchased at a high cost.

COST FLOW ASSUMPTIONS

Because specific identification is often impractical, other cost flow methods are allowed. These differ from specific identification in that they **assume** flows of costs that may be unrelated to the physical flow of goods. There are three assumed cost flow methods:

1. First-in, first-out (FIFO)

2. Last-in, first-out (LIFO)

3. Average cost

There is no accounting requirement that the cost flow assumption be consistent with the physical movement of the goods. The selection of the appropriate cost flow method is made by management.

The three cost flow assumptions can be illustrated using the data of Crivitz TV Company. Under the FIFO method the first goods purchased are assumed to be the first goods sold. Thus Crivitz's cost of goods sold under FIFO would be $1,450 ($700 + $750). Under the LIFO method the last goods purchased are assumed to be the first goods sold. Thus Crivitz's cost of goods sold under LIFO would be $1,550 ($750 + $800). Finally, under the average cost method, the cost of goods sold is based on the weighted average cost of all units purchased. In this case the average cost would be $750 [($700 + $750 + $800)/3]. The cost of two units sold would be 2 × $750 = $1,500.

To illustrate these three inventory cost flow methods, we will assume that Houston Electronics uses a periodic inventory system and has the information shown in Illustration 6-4 for its Astro condenser.[1] (The use of these methods under a perpetual system is presented in an appendix to this chapter.)

Illustration 6-4 Cost of goods available for sale

HOUSTON ELECTRONICS Astro Condensers				
Date	Explanation	Units	Unit Cost	Total Cost
Jan. 1	Beginning inventory	100	$10	$ 1,000
Apr. 15	Purchase	200	11	2,200
Aug. 24	Purchase	300	12	3,600
Nov. 27	Purchase	400	13	5,200
	Total	1,000		$12,000

The company had a total of 1,000 units available that it could have sold during the period. The total cost of these units was $12,000. A physical inventory at the end of the year determined that during the year 550 units were sold and 450 units were in inventory at December 31. The question then is how to determine what prices to use to value the goods sold and the ending inventory. The sum of the cost allocated to the units sold plus the cost of the units in inventory must add up to $12,000, the total cost of all goods available for sale.

First-In, First-Out (FIFO)

The **FIFO method** assumes that the **earliest goods** purchased are the first to be sold. FIFO often parallels the actual physical flow of merchandise because it generally is good business practice to sell the oldest units first. Under the FIFO method, therefore, the **costs** of the earliest goods purchased are the first to be recognized as cost of goods sold. (Note that this does not necessarily mean that the oldest units *are* sold first, but that the costs of the oldest units are recognized first. In a bin of picture hangers at the hardware store, for example, no one really knows, nor would it matter, which hangers are sold first.) The allocation of the cost of goods available for sale at Houston Electronics under FIFO is shown in Illustration 6-5 (on page 273).

Note that under FIFO, since it is assumed that the first goods purchased were the first goods sold, ending inventory is based on the prices of the most recent units purchased. That is, **under FIFO, the cost of the ending inventory is obtained by taking the unit cost of the most recent purchase and working backward until all units of inventory have been costed**. In this example, the 450 units of ending inventory must be priced using the most recent prices. The last purchase was 400 units at $13 on November 27. The remaining 50 units are priced at the price of the second most recent purchase, $12, on August 24. Next, cost of goods sold is calculated by subtracting the cost of the units **not sold** (ending inventory) from the cost of all goods available for sale.

---

[1]We have chosen to use the periodic approach for a number of reasons. First, many companies that use a perpetual inventory system use it to keep track of units on hand, but then determine cost of goods sold at the end of the period using one of the three cost flow approaches applied under essentially a periodic approach. Second, because of the complexity, few companies use average cost on a perpetual basis. Third, most companies that use perpetual LIFO employ dollar-value LIFO, which is presented in more advanced texts. Fourth, FIFO gives the same results under either perpetual or periodic. And finally, it is easier to demonstrate the cost flow assumptions under the periodic system, which makes it more pedagogically appropriate.

Illustration 6-5 Allocation of costs—FIFO method

COST OF GOODS AVAILABLE FOR SALE

Date	Explanation	Units	Unit Cost	Total Cost
Jan. 1	Beginning inventory	100	$10	$ 1,000
Apr. 15	Purchase	200	11	2,200
Aug. 24	Purchase	300	12	3,600
Nov. 27	Purchase	400	13	5,200
	Total	1,000		$12,000

Helpful Hint Note the sequencing of the allocation: (1) Compute ending inventory and (2) determine cost of goods sold.

STEP 1: ENDING INVENTORY   **STEP 2: COST OF GOODS SOLD**

Date	Units	Unit Cost	Total Cost		
Nov. 27	400	$13	$ 5,200	Cost of goods available for sale	$12,000
Aug. 24	50	12	600	Less: Ending inventory	5,800
Total	450		$5,800	Cost of goods sold	$ 6,200

Helpful Hint Another way of thinking about the calculation of FIFO **ending inventory** is the LISH assumption—last in still here.

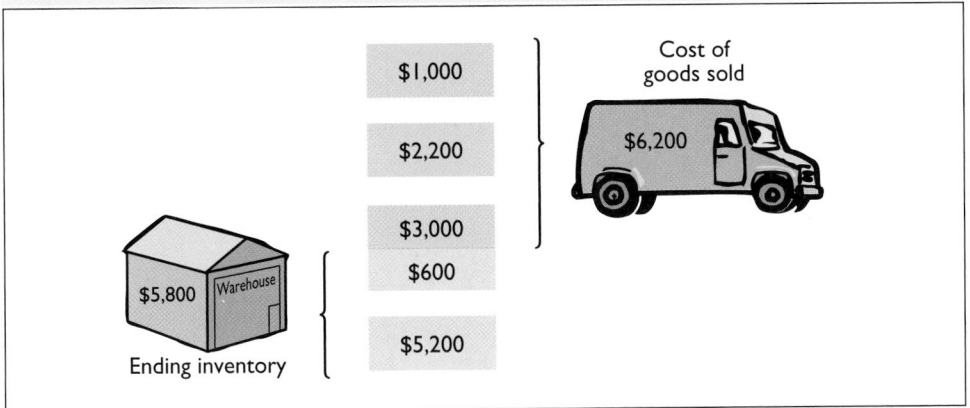

Illustration 6-6 demonstrates that cost of goods sold can also be calculated by pricing the 550 units sold using the prices of the first 550 units acquired. Note that of the 300 units purchased on August 24, only 250 units are assumed sold. This agrees with our calculation of the cost of ending inventory, where 50 of these units were assumed unsold and thus included in ending inventory.

Date	Units	Unit Cost	Total Cost
Jan. 1	100	$10	$ 1,000
Apr. 15	200	11	2,200
Aug. 24	250	12	3,000
Total	550		$6,200

Illustration 6-6 Proof of cost of goods sold

Last-In, First-Out (LIFO)

The **LIFO method** assumes that the **latest goods** purchased are the first to be sold. LIFO seldom coincides with the actual physical flow of inventory. (Exceptions include goods stored in piles, such as coal or hay, where goods are removed from the top of the pile as sold.) Under the LIFO method, the **costs** of the latest goods purchased are the first to be recognized as cost of goods sold. The allocation of the cost of goods available for sale at Houston Electronics under LIFO is shown in Illustration 6-7 (page 274).

Illustration 6-7 Allocation of costs—LIFO method

COST OF GOODS AVAILABLE FOR SALE

Date	Explanation	Units	Unit Cost	Total Cost
Jan. 1	Beginning inventory	100	$10	$ 1,000
Apr. 15	Purchase	200	11	2,200
Aug. 24	Purchase	300	12	3,600
Nov. 27	Purchase	400	13	5,200
	Total	1,000		$12,000

STEP 1: ENDING INVENTORY   **STEP 2: COST OF GOODS SOLD**

Date	Units	Unit Cost	Total Cost		
Jan. 1	100	$10	$ 1,000	Cost of goods available for sale	$12,000
Apr. 15	200	11	2,200	Less: Ending inventory	5,000
Aug. 24	150	12	1,800	Cost of goods sold	$ 7,000
Total	450		$5,000		

Helpful Hint Another way of thinking about the calculation of LIFO **ending inventory** is the FISH assumption—first in still here.

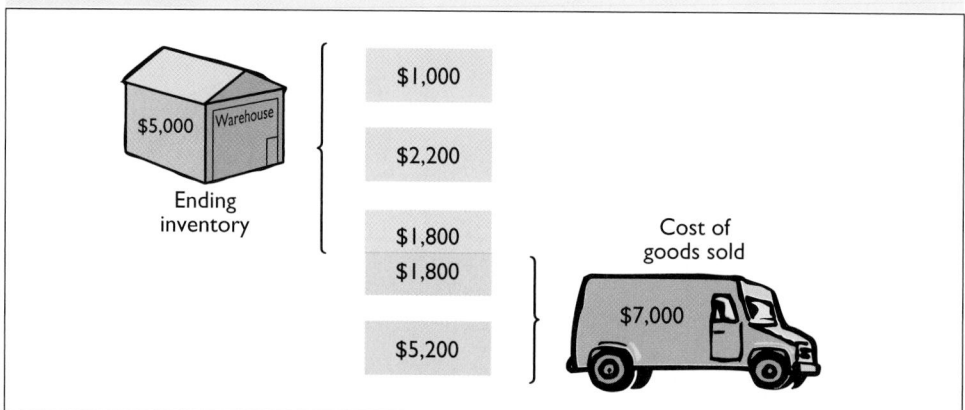

Under LIFO, since it is assumed that the first goods sold were those that were most recently purchased, ending inventory is based on the prices of the oldest units purchased. That is, **under LIFO, the cost of the ending inventory is obtained by taking the unit cost of the earliest goods available for sale and working forward until all units of inventory have been costed**. In this example, the 450 units of ending inventory must be priced using the earliest prices. The first purchase was 100 units at $10 in the January 1 beginning inventory. Then 200 units were purchased at $11. The remaining 150 units needed are priced at $12 per unit (August 24 purchase). Next, cost of goods sold is calculated by subtracting the cost of the units **not sold** (ending inventory) from the cost of all goods available for sale.

Illustration 6-8 demonstrates that cost of goods sold can also be calculated by pricing the 550 units sold using the prices of the last 550 units acquired. Note that of the 300 units purchased on August 24, only 150 units are assumed sold. This agrees with our calculation of the cost of ending inventory, where 150 of these units were assumed unsold and thus included in ending inventory.

Illustration 6-8 Proof of cost of goods sold

Date	Units	Unit Cost	Total Cost
Nov. 27	400	$13	$ 5,200
Aug. 24	150	12	1,800
Total	550		$7,000

Under a periodic inventory system, which we are using here, **all goods purchased during the period are assumed to be available for the first sale, regardless of the date of purchase**.

Average Cost

The **average cost method** allocates the cost of goods available for sale on the basis of the **weighted average unit cost** incurred. The average cost method assumes that goods are similar in nature. The formula and a sample computation of the weighted average unit cost are given in Illustration 6-9.

Cost of Goods Available for Sale	÷	Total Units Available for Sale	=	Weighted Average Unit Cost
$12,000	÷	1,000	=	$12.00

Illustration 6-9 Formula for weighted average unit cost

The weighted average unit cost is then applied to the units on hand to determine the cost of the ending inventory. The allocation of the cost of goods available for sale at Houston Electronics using average cost is shown in Illustration 6-10.

Illustration 6-10 Allocation of costs— average cost method

COST OF GOODS AVAILABLE FOR SALE

Date	Explanation	Units	Unit Cost	Total Cost
Jan. 1	Beginning inventory	100	$10	$ 1,000
Apr. 15	Purchase	200	11	2,200
Aug. 24	Purchase	300	12	3,600
Nov. 27	Purchase	400	13	5,200
	Total	1,000		$12,000

STEP 1: ENDING INVENTORY

$12,000 ÷ 1,000 = $12.00

Units	Unit Cost	Total Cost
450	$12.00	$5,400

STEP 2: COST OF GOODS SOLD

Cost of goods available for sale	$12,000
Less: Ending inventory	5,400
Cost of goods sold	$ 6,600

$$\frac{\$12,000}{1,000 \text{ units}} = \$12 \text{ per unit}$$

Cost per unit

450 units × $12 = $5,400   Warehouse

Ending inventory

$12,000 − $5,400 = $6,600

Cost of goods sold

We can verify the cost of goods sold under this method by multiplying the units sold by the weighted average unit cost (550 × $12 = $6,600). Note that this method does not use the average of the unit costs. That average is $11.50 ($10 + $11 + $12 + $13 = $46; $46 ÷ 4). The average cost method instead uses the average **weighted** by the quantities purchased at each unit cost.

FINANCIAL STATEMENT AND TAX EFFECTS OF COST FLOW METHODS

STUDY OBJECTIVE
3

Explain the financial statement and tax effects of each of the inventory cost flow assumptions.

Each of the three assumed cost flow methods is acceptable for use. For example, **Black & Decker Manufacturing Company** and **Wendy's International** currently use the FIFO method of inventory costing. **Campbell Soup Company**, **Krogers**, and **Walgreen Drugs** use LIFO for part or all of their inventory. **Bristol-Myers Squibb**, **Starbucks**, and **Motorola** use the average cost method. Indeed, a company may also use more than one cost flow method at the same time. **Del Monte Corporation**, for example, uses LIFO for domestic inventories and FIFO for foreign inventories. Illustration 6-11 shows the use of the three cost flow methods in the 600 largest U.S. companies. The reasons companies adopt different inventory cost flow methods are varied, but they usually involve one of three factors:

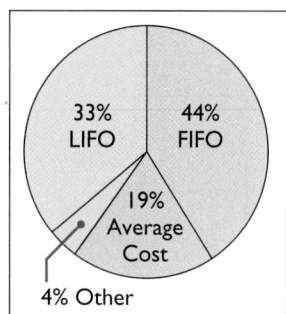

Illustration 6-11 Use of cost flow methods in major U.S. companies

1. Income statement effects
2. Balance sheet effects
3. Tax effects

Income Statement Effects

To understand why companies might choose a particular cost flow method, let's examine the effects of the different cost flow assumptions on the financial statements of Houston Electronics. The condensed income statements in Illustration 6-12 assume that Houston sold its 550 units for $11,500, had operating expenses of $2,000, and is subject to an income tax rate of 30%.

Illustration 6-12
Comparative effects of cost flow methods

HOUSTON ELECTRONICS Condensed Income Statements			
	FIFO	**LIFO**	**Average Cost**
Sales	$11,500	$11,500	$11,500
Beginning inventory	1,000	1,000	1,000
Purchases	11,000	11,000	11,000
Cost of goods available for sale	12,000	12,000	12,000
Ending inventory	5,800	5,000	5,400
Cost of goods sold	6,200	7,000	6,600
Gross profit	5,300	4,500	4,900
Operating expenses	2,000	2,000	2,000
Income before income taxes	3,300	2,500	2,900
Income tax expense (30%)	990	750	870
Net income	$ 2,310	$ 1,750	$ 2,030

Although the cost of goods available for sale ($12,000) is the same under each of the three inventory cost flow methods, the ending inventories and the costs of goods sold are different. This difference is due to the unit costs that are allocated to cost of goods sold and to ending inventory. Each dollar of difference in ending inventory results in a corresponding dollar difference in income before income taxes. For Houston, an $800 difference exists between FIFO and LIFO cost of goods sold.

In periods of changing prices, the cost flow assumption can have a significant impact on income and on evaluations based on income. In most instances, prices are rising (inflation). In a period of inflation, FIFO produces a higher net income because the lower unit costs of the first units purchased are matched against revenues. In a period of rising prices (as is the case here for Houston), FIFO reports the highest net income ($2,310) and LIFO the lowest ($1,750); average cost falls in the middle ($2,030). If prices are falling, the results from the use of FIFO and LIFO are reversed: FIFO will report the lowest net income and LIFO the highest. To management, higher net income is an advantage: It causes external users to view the company more favorably. In addition, if management bonuses are based on net income, FIFO will provide the basis for higher bonuses.

Some argue that the use of LIFO in a period of inflation enables the company to avoid reporting **paper** or **phantom profit** as economic gain. To illustrate, assume that Kralik Company buys 200 units of a product at $20 per unit on January 10 and 200 more on December 31 at $24 each. During the year, 200 units are sold at $30 each. The results under FIFO and LIFO are shown in Illustration 6-13.

	FIFO		**LIFO**	
Sales (200 × $30)	$6,000		$6,000	
Cost of goods sold	4,000	(200 × $20)	4,800	(200 × $24)
Gross profit	$2,000		$1,200	

Under LIFO, Kralik Company has recovered the current replacement cost ($4,800) of the units sold. Thus, the gross profit in economic terms is real. However, under FIFO, the company has recovered only the January 10 cost ($4,000). To replace the units sold, it must reinvest $800 (200 × $4) of the gross profit. Thus, $800 of the gross profit is said to be phantom or illusory. As a result, reported net income is also overstated in real terms.

Balance Sheet Effects

A major advantage of the FIFO method is that in a period of inflation, the costs allocated to ending inventory will approximate their current cost. For example, for Houston, 400 of the 450 units in the ending inventory are costed under FIFO at the higher November 27 unit cost of $13.

Conversely, a major shortcoming of the LIFO method is that in a period of inflation, the costs allocated to ending inventory may be significantly understated in terms of current cost. This is true for Houston, where the cost of the ending inventory includes the $10 unit cost of the beginning inventory. The understatement becomes greater over prolonged periods of inflation if the inventory includes goods purchased in one or more prior accounting periods.

Tax Effects

We have seen that both inventory on the balance sheet and net income on the income statement are higher when FIFO is used in a period of inflation. Yet, many companies have switched to LIFO. The reason is that LIFO results in the lowest income taxes (because of lower net income) during times of rising prices.

DECISION TOOLKIT

Decision Checkpoints	Info Needed for Decision	Tool to Use for Decision	How to Evaluate Results
Which inventory costing method should be used?	Are prices increasing, or are they decreasing?	Income statement, balance sheet, and tax effects	Depends on objective. In a period of rising prices, income and inventory are higher and cash flow is lower under FIFO. LIFO provides opposite results. Average cost can moderate the impact of changing prices.

For example, at Houston Electronics, income taxes are $750 under LIFO, compared to $990 under FIFO. The tax saving of $240 makes more cash available for use in the business.

USING INVENTORY COST FLOW METHODS CONSISTENTLY

Whatever cost flow method a company chooses, it should be used consistently from one accounting period to another. Consistent application enhances the comparability of financial statements over successive time periods. In contrast, using the FIFO method one year and the LIFO method the next year would make it difficult to compare the net incomes of the two years.

Helpful Hint As you learned in Chapter 2, consistency and comparability are important characteristics of accounting information.

Although consistent application is preferred, it does not mean that a company may *never* change its method of inventory costing. When a company adopts a different method, the change and its effects on net income should be disclosed in the financial statements. A typical disclosure is shown in Illustration 6-14 (next page), using information from recent financial statements of the Quaker Oats Company.

 Business Insight
INTERNATIONAL PERSPECTIVE

U.S. companies typically choose between LIFO and FIFO. Many choose LIFO because it reduces inventory profits and taxes. However, in many foreign countries LIFO is not allowed. International regulators recently considered rules that would ban LIFO entirely and force companies to use FIFO. This proposed rule was defeated, but the issue is almost certain to reappear.

The issue is sensitive. As John Wulff, controller for **Union Carbide**, noted, "We were in support of the international effort up until the proposal to eliminate LIFO." Wulff says that if Union Carbide had been suddenly forced to switch from LIFO to FIFO recently, its reported $632 million pretax income would have jumped by $300 million. That would have increased Carbide's income tax bill by as much as $120 million.

Do you believe that accounting principles and rules should be the same around the world?

Illustration 6-14
Disclosure of change in
cost flow method

QUAKER OATS COMPANY
Notes to the Financial statements

Note 1:   Effective July 1, the Company adopted the LIFO cost flow assumption for valuing the majority of U.S. Grocery Products inventories. The Company believes that the use of the LIFO method better matches current costs with current revenues. The effect of this change on the current year was to decrease net income by $16.0 million.

LOWER OF COST OR MARKET

The value of the inventory of companies selling high-technology or fashion goods can drop very quickly due to changes in technology or changes in fashions. These circumstances sometimes call for inventory valuation methods other than those presented so far. For example, suppose you are the owner of a retail store that sells Compaq computers. Imagine that during the recent 12-month period, the cost of the computers dropped $300 per unit. At the end of your fiscal year, you have some of these computers in inventory. Do you think your inventory should be stated at cost, in accordance with the cost principle, or at its lower replacement cost?

As you probably reasoned, this situation requires a departure from the cost basis of accounting. When the value of inventory is lower than its cost, the inventory is written down to its market value. This is done by valuing the inventory at the **lower of cost or market (LCM)** in the period in which the price decline occurs. LCM is an example of the accounting **concept of conservatism**, which means that the best choice among accounting alternatives is the method that is least likely to overstate assets and net income.

LCM is applied to the items in inventory after one of the cost flow methods (specific identification, FIFO, LIFO, or average cost) has been used to determine cost. Under the LCM basis, market is defined as **current replacement cost**, not selling price. For a merchandising company, market is the cost of purchasing the same goods at the present time from the usual suppliers in the usual quantities. Current replacement cost is used because a decline in the replacement cost of an item usually leads to a decline in the selling price of the item.

STUDY OBJECTIVE
4
Explain the lower of cost or market basis of accounting for inventories.

BEFORE YOU GO ON . . .

▶ Review It

1. What factors should be considered by management in selecting an inventory cost flow method?
2. What inventory cost flow method does **Tootsie Roll Industries** use for U.S. inventories? What method does it use for foreign inventories? (*Hint:* You will need to examine the notes for Tootsie Roll's financial statements.) The answer to these questions is provided on page 312.
3. Which inventory cost flow method produces the highest net income in a period of rising prices? The lowest income taxes?
4. When should inventory be reported at a value other than cost?

▶ **Do It**

The accounting records of Shumway Ag Implement show the following data.

Beginning inventory	4,000 units at $ 3
Purchases	6,000 units at $ 4
Sales	5,000 units at $12

Determine the cost of goods sold during the period under a periodic inventory system using (a) the FIFO method, (b) the LIFO method, and (c) the average cost method.

Action Plan

• Understand the periodic inventory system.
• Allocate costs between goods sold and goods on hand (ending inventory) for each cost flow method,
• Compute cost of goods sold for each cost flow method.

Solution

(a) FIFO: (4,000 @ $3) + (1,000 @ $4) = $12,000 + $4,000 = $16,000
(b) LIFO: 5,000 @ $4 = $20,000
(c) Average cost: [(4,000 @ $3) + (6,000 @ $4)] ÷ 10,000
            = ($12,000 + $24,000) ÷ 10,000
            = $3.60 per unit; 5,000 @ $3.60 = $18,000

✓ THE NAVIGATOR

Business Insight
INVESTOR PERSPECTIVE

In January 2002 **Ford Motor Co**. shocked its investors with an announcement that it was going take a $1 billion lower of cost or market charge on the value of its inventory of palladium, a precious metal used in vehicle emission devices. Fearing a shortage of the metal, Ford managers bought a huge amount of it, just before prices plummeted. Investors were angry both because Ford clearly should have taken steps to insulate itself from the effects of such price swings and because they felt the company had not adequately disclosed its risk of losses due to changes in the value of this metal. In fact, one group of investors filed a suit against the company because of the losses they sustained due to the drop in the company's stock price.

Analysis of Inventory

For companies that sell goods, managing inventory levels can be one of the most critical tasks. Having too much inventory on hand costs the company money in storage costs, interest cost (on funds tied up in inventory), and costs associated with the obsolescence of technical goods (e.g., computer chips) or shifts in fashion (e.g., clothes). But having too little inventory on hand results in lost sales. In this section we discuss some issues related to evaluating inventory levels.

INVENTORY TURNOVER RATIO

The **inventory turnover ratio** is calculated as cost of goods sold divided by average inventory. It indicates how quickly a company sells its goods—how many times the inventory "turns over" (is sold) during the year. Inventory turnover can be divided into 365 days to compute **days in inventory**, which indicates the average age of the inventory.

High inventory turnover (low days in inventory) indicates the company is tying up little of its funds in inventory—that it has a minimal amount of inventory on hand at any one time. Although minimizing the funds tied up in inventory is efficient, too high an inventory turnover ratio may indicate that the company is losing sales opportunities because of inventory shortages. For example, investment analysts suggested recently that **Office Depot** had gone too far in reducing its inventory—they said they were seeing too many empty shelves. Thus, management should closely monitor this ratio to achieve the best balance between too much and too little inventory.

In Chapter 5 we discussed the increasingly competitive environment of retailers like **Wal-Mart** and **Target**. We noted that Wal-Mart has implemented many technological innovations to improve the efficiency of its inventory management. The following data are available for Wal-Mart.

(in millions)	2002	2001	2000
Ending inventory	$ 22,614	$ 21,442	$19,793
Cost of goods sold	171,562	150,255	

Illustration 6-15 presents the inventory turnover ratios and days in inventory for Wal-Mart and Target, using data from the financial statements of those corporations for 2002 and 2001.

The calculations in Illustration 6-15 show that Wal-Mart turns its inventory more frequently than Target (7.8 times for Wal-Mart versus 6.3 times for

Illustration 6-15 Inventory turnover ratio and days in inventory

$$\text{Inventory Turnover Ratio} = \frac{\text{Cost of Goods Sold}}{\text{Average Inventory}}$$

$$\text{Days in Inventory} = \frac{365}{\text{Inventory Turnover Ratio}}$$

($ in millions)		2002	2001
Wal-Mart	Inventory turnover ratio	$\dfrac{\$171,562}{(\$22,614 + \$21,442)/2} = 7.8$ times	$\dfrac{\$150,255}{(\$21,442 + \$19,793)/2} = 7.3$ times
	Days in inventory	$\dfrac{365 \text{ days}}{7.8} = 46.8$ days	$\dfrac{365 \text{ days}}{7.3} = 50.0$ days
Target	Inventory turnover ratio	6.3 times	6.3 times
	Days in inventory	57.9 days	57.9 days

Target). Consequently, the average time an item spends on a Wal-Mart shelf is shorter (46.8 days for Wal-Mart versus 57.9 days for Target). This suggests that Wal-Mart is more efficient than Target in its inventory management. Note also that Wal-Mart's inventory turnover, which was already better than Target's in 2001, improved in 2002. Wal-Mart's sophisticated inventory tracking and distribution system allows it to keep minimum amounts of inventory on hand, while still keeping the shelves full of what customers are looking for.

DECISION TOOLKIT

Decision Checkpoints	Info Needed for Decision	Tool to Use for Decision	How to Evaluate Results
How long is an item in inventory?	Cost of goods sold; beginning and ending inventory	$$\text{Inventory turnover ratio} = \frac{\text{Cost of goods sold}}{\text{Average inventory}}$$ $$\text{Days in inventory} = \frac{365 \text{ days}}{\text{Inventory turnover ratio}}$$	A higher inventory turnover ratio or lower average days in inventory suggests that management is reducing the amount of inventory on hand, relative to sales.

STUDY OBJECTIVE
6
Describe the LIFO reserve and explain its importance for comparing results of different companies.

ANALYSTS' ADJUSTMENTS FOR LIFO RESERVE

Earlier we noted that using LIFO rather than FIFO can result in significant differences in the results reported in the balance sheet and the income statement. With increasing prices, FIFO will result in higher income than LIFO. On the balance sheet, FIFO will result in higher reported inventory. The financial statement differences of using LIFO normally increase the longer a company uses LIFO.

Using different inventory cost flow assumptions complicates analysts' attempts to compare the results of companies that use different inventory methods. Fortunately, companies using LIFO are required to report the amount that inventory would increase (or occasionally decrease) if the company had instead been using FIFO. This amount is referred to as the **LIFO reserve**. Reporting the LIFO reserve enables analysts to make adjustments to compare companies that use different cost flow methods.

Illustration 6-16 presents an excerpt from the notes to **Caterpillar**'s 2001 financial statements that discloses and discusses Caterpillar's LIFO reserve.

Illustration 6-16
Caterpillar LIFO reserve

CATERPILLAR®

CATERPILLAR INC.
Notes to the Financial Statements

Inventories: Inventories are stated at the lower of cost or market. Cost is principally determined using the last-in, first-out (LIFO) method. If the FIFO (first-in, first-out) method had been in use, inventories would have been $1,923, $2,065, and $2,000 million higher than reported at December 31, 2001, 2000, and 1999, respectively.

Caterpillar has used LIFO for nearly 50 years. Thus, the cumulative difference between LIFO and FIFO reflected in the inventory account is very large. In fact, the 2001 LIFO reserve of $1,923 million is nearly as large as the 2001 LIFO inventory of $2,925 million. Such a huge difference would clearly distort any comparisons you might try to make with one of Caterpillar's competitors that used FIFO.

To adjust Caterpillar's inventory balance we add the LIFO reserve to reported inventory, as shown in Illustration 6-17. That is, if Caterpillar had used FIFO all along, its inventory would be $4,848 million, rather than $2,925 million.

	(in millions)
2001 inventory using LIFO	$ 2,925
2001 LIFO reserve	1,923
2001 inventory assuming FIFO	**$4,848**

Illustration 6-17
Conversion of inventory
from LIFO to FIFO

The LIFO reserve can have a significant effect on ratios commonly used by analysts. Using the LIFO reserve adjustment, Illustration 6-18 calculates the value of the current ratio (current assets ÷ current liabilities) under both the LIFO and FIFO cost flow assumptions.

Illustration 6-18 Impact of
LIFO reserve on ratios

($ in millions)	LIFO	FIFO
Current ratio	$\dfrac{\$13,400}{\$10,276} = 1.3:1$	$\dfrac{\$13,400 + \$1,923}{\$10,276} = 1.5:1$

As shown in Illustration 6-18, if Caterpillar uses FIFO, its current ratio is 1.5:1 rather than 1.3:1 under LIFO. Thus, Caterpillar's liquidity appears stronger if a FIFO assumption is used in valuing inventories. If a similar adjustment is made for the inventory turnover ratio, Caterpillar's inventory turnover actually looks worse under FIFO than under LIFO, dropping from 5.3 times for LIFO to 3.1 times using the FIFO assumption.[2] The reason: LIFO reports low inventory amounts, which cause inventory turnover to be overstated. **Case Corporation**, a competitor of Caterpillar, uses FIFO to account for its inventory. Comparing Caterpillar to Case Corporation without converting Caterpillar's inventory to FIFO would lead to distortions and potentially erroneous decisions.

BEFORE YOU GO ON . . .

▶ **Review It**

1. What is the purpose of the inventory turnover ratio? What is the relationship between the inventory turnover ratio and average days in inventory?
2. What is the LIFO reserve? What does it tell a financial statement user?

---

[2]The LIFO reserve also affects cost of goods sold, although typically by a much less material amount. The cost of goods sold adjustment is discussed in more advanced financial statement analysis texts.

DECISION TOOLKIT

Decision Checkpoints	Info Needed for Decision	Tool to Use for Decision	How to Evaluate Results
What is the impact of LIFO on the company's reported inventory?	LIFO reserve, cost of goods sold, ending inventory	$\dfrac{\text{LIFO}}{\text{inventory}} + \dfrac{\text{LIFO}}{\text{reserve}} = \dfrac{\text{FIFO}}{\text{inventory}}$	If these adjustments are material, they can significantly affect such measures as the current ratio and the inventory turnover ratio.

Using the Decision Toolkit

The Manitowoc Company is located in Manitowoc, Wisconsin. In recent years it has made a series of strategic acquisitions to grow and enhance its market-leading positions in each of its three business segments. These include: cranes and related products (crawler cranes, tower cranes, and boom trucks); food service equipment (commercial ice-cube machines, ice-beverage dispensers, and commercial refrigeration equipment); and marine operations (shipbuilding and ship-repair services). For 2001 the company reported net income of $45.5 million. Here is the inventory note taken from the 2001 financial statements.

THE MANITOWOC COMPANY
Notes to the Financial Statements

Inventories: The components of inventories are summarized at December 31 as follows (in thousands).

	2001	2000
Components		
Raw materials	$ 44,302	$ 33,935
Work in process	35,517	32,914
Finished goods	62,798	45,880
Total inventories at FIFO cost	142,617	112,729
Excess of FIFO cost over LIFO value	(19,561)	(21,551)
Total inventories at LIFO	$123,056	$ 91,178

Inventory is carried at the lower of cost or market using the first-in, first-out (FIFO) method for 79% and 57% of total inventory for 2001 and 2000, respectively. The remainder of the inventory is costed using the last-in, first-out (LIFO) method.

Additional facts:

2001 Current liabilities	$296,161
2001 Current assets (as reported)	$331,090
2001 Cost of goods sold	$831,768

Instructions

Answer the following questions.

1. Why does the company report its inventory in three components?
2. Why might the company use two methods (LIFO and FIFO) to account for its inventory?
3. Perform each of the following.
   (a) Calculate the inventory turnover ratio and days in inventory using the LIFO inventory.
   (b) Show the conversion of the 2001 and 2000 LIFO inventory values to FIFO values.
   (c) Calculate the 2001 current ratio using LIFO and the current ratio using FIFO. Discuss the difference.

Solution

1. The Manitowoc Company is a manufacturer, so it purchases raw materials and makes them into finished products. At the end of each period, it has some goods that have been started but are not yet complete, referred to as work in process. By reporting all three components of inventory, the company reveals important information about its inventory position. For example, if amounts of raw materials have increased significantly compared to the previous year, we might assume the company is planning to step up production. On the other hand, if levels of finished goods have increased relative to last year and raw materials have declined, we might conclude that sales are slowing down—that the company has too much inventory on hand and is cutting back production.

2. Companies are free to choose different cost flow assumptions for different types of inventory. A company might choose to use FIFO for a product that is expected to decrease in price over time. One common reason for choosing a method other than LIFO is that many foreign countries do not allow LIFO; thus, the company cannot use LIFO for its foreign operations.

3. (a)
$$\frac{\text{Inventory turnover}}{\text{ratio}} = \frac{\text{Cost of goods sold}}{\text{Average inventory}} = \frac{\$831,768}{(\$123,056 + \$91,178)/2} = 7.8$$

$$\frac{\text{Days in}}{\text{inventory}} = \frac{365}{\text{Inventory turnover ratio}} = \frac{365}{7.8} = 46.8 \text{ days}$$

(b) Conversion from LIFO to FIFO values

	2001	**2000**
LIFO inventory	$123,056	$ 91,178
LIFO reserve	19,561	21,551
FIFO inventory	$142,617	$112,729

(c) Current ratio

LIFO	**FIFO**
$\dfrac{\text{Current assets}}{\text{Current liabilities}} = \dfrac{\$331,090}{\$296,161} = 1.12{:}1$	$\dfrac{\$331,090 + \$19,561}{\$296,161} = 1.18{:}1$

This represents a 5% increase in the current ratio $(1.18 - 1.12)/1.12$.

THE NAVIGATOR

Summary of Study Objectives

1 *Describe the steps in determining inventory quantities.* The steps are (1) taking a physical inventory of goods on hand and (2) determining the ownership of goods in transit or on consignment.

2 *Explain the basis of accounting for inventories and apply the inventory cost flow methods under a periodic inventory system.* The primary basis of accounting for inventories is cost. Cost includes all expenditures necessary to acquire goods and place them in condition ready for sale. Cost of goods available for sale includes (a) cost of beginning inventory and (b) cost of goods purchased. The inventory cost flow methods are: specific identification and three assumed cost flow methods—FIFO, LIFO, and average cost.

3 *Explain the financial statement and tax effects of each of the inventory cost flow assumptions.* The cost of goods available for sale may be allocated to cost of goods sold and ending inventory by specific identification or by a method based on an assumed cost flow. When prices are rising, the first-in, first-out (FIFO) method results in lower cost of goods sold and higher net income than the average cost and the last-in, first-out (LIFO) methods. The reverse is true when prices are falling. In the balance sheet, FIFO results in an ending inventory that is closest to current value, whereas the inventory under LIFO is the farthest from current value. LIFO results in the lowest income taxes (because of lower net income).

4 *Explain the lower of cost or market basis of accounting for inventories.* The lower of cost or market (LCM) basis may be used when the current replacement cost (market) is less than cost. Under LCM, the loss is recognized in the period in which the price decline occurs.

5 *Compute and interpret the inventory turnover ratio.* The inventory turnover ratio is calculated as cost of goods sold divided by average inventory. It can be converted to average days in inventory by dividing 365 days by the inventory turnover ratio. A higher turnover ratio or lower average days in inventory suggests that management is trying to keep inventory levels low relative to its sales level.

6 *Describe the LIFO reserve and explain its importance for comparing results of different companies.* The LIFO reserve represents the difference between ending inventory using LIFO and ending inventory if FIFO were employed instead. For some companies this difference can be significant, and ignoring it can lead to inappropriate conclusions when using the current ratio or inventory turnover ratio.

☑ THE NAVIGATOR

DECISION TOOLKIT—A SUMMARY

Decision Checkpoints	Info Needed for Decision	Tool to Use for Decision	How to Evaluate Results
Which inventory costing method should be used?	Are prices increasing, or are they decreasing?	Income statement, balance sheet, and tax effects	Depends on objective. In a period of rising prices, income and inventory are higher and cash flow is lower under FIFO. LIFO provides opposite results. Average cost can moderate the impact of changing prices.
How long is an item in inventory?	Cost of goods sold; beginning and ending inventory	$\text{Inventory turnover ratio} = \dfrac{\text{Cost of goods sold}}{\text{Average inventory}}$ $\text{Days in inventory} = \dfrac{365 \text{ days}}{\text{Inventory turnover ratio}}$	A higher inventory turnover ratio or lower average days in inventory suggests that management is reducing the amount of inventory on hand, relative to sales.
What is the impact of LIFO on the company's reported inventory?	LIFO reserve, cost of goods sold, ending inventory	$\text{LIFO inventory} + \text{LIFO reserve} = \text{FIFO inventory}$	If these adjustments are material, they can significantly affect such measures as the current ratio and the inventory turnover ratio.

APPENDIX 6A
INVENTORY COST FLOW METHODS IN PERPETUAL INVENTORY SYSTEMS

Each of the inventory cost flow methods described in the chapter for a periodic inventory system may be used in a perpetual inventory system. To illustrate the application of the three assumed cost flow methods (FIFO, LIFO, and average cost), we will use the data shown below and in this chapter for Houston Electronic's Astro Condenser.

STUDY OBJECTIVE
7
Apply the inventory cost flow methods to perpetual inventory records.

Illustration 6A-1
Inventoriable units and costs

HOUSTON ELECTRONICS Astro Condensers					
Date	Explanation	Units	Unit Cost	Total Cost	Balance in Units
1/1	Beginning inventory	100	$10	$ 1,000	100
4/15	Purchases	200	11	2,200	300
8/24	Purchases	300	12	3,600	600
9/10	Sale	550			50
11/27	Purchases	400	13	5,200	450
				$12,000	

First-In, First-Out (FIFO)

Under FIFO, the cost of the earliest goods on hand **prior to each sale** is charged to cost of goods sold. Therefore, the cost of goods sold on September 10 consists of the units on hand January 1 and the units purchased April 15 and August 24. The inventory on a FIFO method perpetual system is shown in Illustration 6A-2.

Illustration 6A-2
Perpetual system—FIFO

Date	Purchases	Cost of Goods Sold	Balance
January 1			(100 @ $10) $ 1,000
April 15	(200 @ $11) $2,200		(100 @ $10) (200 @ $11) $ 3,200
August 24	(300 @ $12) $3,600		(100 @ $10) (200 @ $11) $ 6,800 (300 @ $12)
September 10		(100 @ $10) (200 @ $11) (250 @ $12) $6,200	(50 @ $12) $ 600
November 27	(400 @ $13) $5,200		(50 @ $12) (400 @ $13) $5,800

The ending inventory in this situation is $5,800, and the cost of goods sold is $6,200 [(100 @ $10) + (200 @ $11) + (250 @ $12)].

The results under FIFO in a perpetual system are the **same as in a periodic system** (see Illustration 6-5 on page 273 where, similarly, the ending inventory is $5,800 and cost of goods sold is $6,200). Regardless of the system, the first costs in are the costs assigned to cost of goods sold.

Last-In, First-Out (LIFO)

Under the LIFO method using a perpetual system, the cost of the most recent purchase prior to sale is allocated to the units sold. Therefore, the cost of the goods sold on September 10 consists of all the units from the August 24 and April 15 purchases and 50 of the units in beginning inventory. The ending inventory on a LIFO method is computed in Illustration 6A-3.

Illustration 6A-3
Perpetual system—LIFO

Date	Purchases	Cost of Goods Sold	Balance	
January 1			(100 @ $10)	$1,000
April 15	(200 @ $11) $2,200		(100 @ $10) (200 @ $11) }	$3,200
August 24	(300 @ $12) $3,600		(100 @ $10) (200 @ $11) (300 @ $12) }	$6,800
September 10		(300 @ $12) (200 @ $11) (50 @ $10) ────── $6,300	(50 @ $10)	$ 500
November 27	(400 @ $13) $5,200		(50 @ $10) (400 @ $13) }	$5,700

The use of LIFO in a perpetual system will usually produce cost allocations that differ from using LIFO in a periodic system. In a perpetual system, the latest units purchased prior to each sale are allocated to cost of goods sold. In contrast, in a periodic system, the latest units purchased during the period are allocated to cost of goods sold. Thus, when a purchase is made after the last sale, the LIFO periodic system will apply this purchase to the previous sale. See Illustration 6-8 (on page 274) where the proof shows the 400 units at $13 purchased on November 27 applied to the sale of 550 units on September 10.

As shown above, under the LIFO perpetual system the 400 units at $13 purchased on November 27 are all applied to the ending inventory.

The ending inventory in this LIFO perpetual illustration is $5,700 and cost of goods sold is $6,300, as compared to the LIFO periodic illustration (on page 274) where the ending inventory is $5,000 and cost of goods sold is $7,000.

Average Cost

The average cost method in a perpetual inventory system is called the **moving average method**. Under this method a new average is computed **after each purchase**. The average cost is computed by dividing the cost of goods available for sale by the units on hand. The average cost is then applied to: (1) the units sold, to determine the cost of goods sold, and (2) the remaining units on hand, to determine the ending inventory amount. The application of the average cost method by Houston Electronics is shown in Illustration 6A-4.

Illustration 6A-4
Perpetual system—
average cost method

Date	Purchases	Cost of Goods Sold	Balance	
January 1			(100 @ $10)	$1,000
April 15	(200 @ $11) $2,200		(300 @ $10.667)	$3,200
August 24	(300 @ $12) $3,600		(600 @ $11.333)	$6,800
September 10		(550 @ $11.333) ────── $6,233	(50 @ $11.333)	$ 567
November 27	(400 @ $13) $5,200		(450 @ $12.816)	$5,767

As indicated above, **a new average is computed each time a purchase is made**. On April 15, after 200 units are purchased for $2,200, a total of 300 units costing $3,200 ($1,000 + $2,200) are on hand. The average unit cost is $10.667 ($3,200 ÷ 300). On August 24, after 300 units are purchased for $3,600, a total of 600 units costing $6,800 ($1,000 + $2,200 + $3,600) are on hand at an average cost per unit of $11.333 ($6,800 ÷ 600). This unit cost of $11.333 is used in costing sales until another purchase is made, when a new unit cost is computed. Accordingly, the unit cost of the 550 units sold on September 10 is $11.333, and the total cost of goods sold is $6,233. On November 27, following the purchase of 400 units for $5,200, there are 450 units on hand costing $5,767 ($567 + $5,200) with a new average cost of $12.816 ($5,767 ÷ 450).

This moving average cost under the perpetual inventory system should be compared to Illustration 6-10 (on page 275) showing the weighted average method under a periodic inventory system.

Summary of Study Objective for Appendix 6A

7 *Apply the inventory cost flow methods to perpetual inventory records.* Under FIFO, the cost of the earliest goods on hand prior to each sale is charged to cost of goods sold. Under LIFO, the cost of the most recent purchase prior to sale is charged to cost of goods sold. Under the average cost method, a new average cost is computed after each purchase.

APPENDIX 6B
INVENTORY ERRORS

Unfortunately, errors occasionally occur in accounting for inventory. In some cases, errors are caused by failure to count or price the inventory correctly. In other cases, errors occur because proper recognition is not given to the transfer of legal title to goods that are in transit. When errors occur, they affect both the income statement and the balance sheet.

STUDY OBJECTIVE
8
Indicate the effects of inventory errors on the financial statements.

Income Statement Effects

As you know, both the beginning and ending inventories appear in the income statement. The ending inventory of one period automatically becomes the beginning inventory of the next period. Inventory errors affect the computation of cost of goods sold and net income in two periods.

The effects on cost of goods sold can be computed by entering incorrect data in the formula in Illustration 6B-1 and then substituting the correct data.

Illustration 6B-1 Formula for cost of goods sold

| Beginning Inventory | + | Cost of Goods Purchased | − | Ending Inventory | = | Cost of Goods Sold |

If beginning inventory is understated, cost of goods sold will be understated. On the other hand, understating ending inventory will overstate cost of goods sold. The effects of inventory errors on the current year's income statement are shown in Illustration 6B-2.

Illustration 6B-2 Effects of inventory errors on current year's income statement

Inventory Error	Cost of Goods Sold	Net Income
Understate beginning inventory	Understated	Overstated
Overstate beginning inventory	Overstated	Understated
Understate ending inventory	Overstated	Understated
Overstate ending inventory	Understated	Overstated

An error in the ending inventory of the current period will have a **reverse effect on net income of the next accounting period**. This is shown in Illustration 6B-3. Note that the understatement of ending inventory in 2004 results in an understatement of beginning inventory in 2005 and an overstatement of net income in 2005.

Illustration 6B-3 Effects of inventory errors on two years' income statements

SAMPLE COMPANY
Condensed Income Statements

	2004 Incorrect		2004 Correct		2005 Incorrect		2005 Correct	
Sales		$80,000		$80,000		$90,000		$90,000
Beginning inventory	$20,000		$20,000		$12,000		$15,000	
Cost of goods purchased	40,000		40,000		68,000		68,000	
Cost of goods available for sale	60,000		60,000		80,000		83,000	
Ending inventory	12,000		15,000		23,000		23,000	
Cost of goods sold		48,000		45,000		57,000		60,000
Gross profit		32,000		35,000		33,000		30,000
Operating expenses		10,000		10,000		20,000		20,000
Net income		$22,000		$25,000		$13,000		$10,000

$(3,000)
Net income
understated

$3,000
Net income
overstated

The errors cancel. Thus the combined total income for the 2-year period is correct.

Over the two years, total net income is correct because the errors offset each other. Notice that total income using incorrect data is $35,000 ($22,000 + $13,000), which is the same as the total income of $35,000 ($25,000 + $10,000) using correct data. Also note in this example that an error in the beginning inventory does not result in a corresponding error in the ending inventory for that period. The correctness of the ending inventory depends entirely on the accuracy of taking and costing the inventory at the balance sheet date under the periodic inventory system.

Business Insight
INVESTOR PERSPECTIVE

Inventory fraud increases during recessions. Such fraud includes pricing inventory at amounts in excess of its actual value, or claiming to have inventory when no inventory exists. Inventory fraud is usually done to overstate ending inventory, thereby understating cost of goods sold and creating higher income.

Balance Sheet Effects

The effect of ending inventory errors on the balance sheet can be determined by using the basic accounting equation: Assets = Liabilities + Stockholders' equity. Errors in the ending inventory have the effects shown in Illustration 6B-4.

Ending Inventory Error	Assets	Liabilities	Stockholders' Equity
Overstated	Overstated	No effect	Overstated
Understated	Understated	No effect	Understated

Illustration 6B-4 Effects of ending inventory errors on balance sheet

The effect of an error in ending inventory on the subsequent period was shown in Illustration 6B-3. Recall that if the error is not corrected, the combined total net income for the two periods would be correct. Thus, total stockholders' equity reported on the balance sheet at the end of 2005 will also be correct.

Summary of Study Objective for Appendix 6B

8 *Indicate the effects of inventory errors on the financial statements.* In the income statement of the current year: (a) an error in beginning inventory will have a reverse effect on net income (overstatement of inventory results in understatement of net income, and vice versa) and (b) an error in ending inventory will have a similar effect on net income (e.g., overstatement of inventory results in overstatement of net income). If ending inventory errors are not corrected in the following period, their effect on net income for that period is reversed, and total net income for the two years will be correct. In the balance sheet, ending inventory errors will have the same effect on total assets and total stockholders' equity and no effect on liabilities.

Glossary

Average cost method An inventory costing method that uses the weighted average unit cost to allocate the cost of goods available for sale to ending inventory and cost of goods sold. (p. 275)

Consigned goods Goods held for sale by one party (the consignee) although ownership of the goods is retained by another party (the consignor). (p. 270)

Current replacement cost The current cost to replace an inventory item. (p. 279)

Days in inventory Measure of the average number of days inventory is held; calculated as 365 divided by inventory turnover ratio. (p. 281)

Finished goods inventory Manufactured items that are completed and ready for sale. (p. 267)

First-in, first-out (FIFO) method An inventory costing method that assumes that the costs of the earliest goods purchased are the first to be recognized as cost of goods sold. (p. 272)

FOB destination Freight terms indicating that the goods are placed free on board at the buyer's place of business, and the seller pays the freight cost; goods belong to the seller while in transit. (p. 270)

FOB shipping point Freight terms indicating that the goods are placed free on board the carrier by the seller, and the buyer pays the freight cost; goods belong to the buyer while in transit. (p. 269)

Inventory turnover ratio   A ratio that measures the number of times on average the inventory sold during the period; computed by dividing cost of goods sold by the average inventory during the period. (p. 281)

Last-in, first-out (LIFO) method   An inventory costing method that assumes that the costs of the latest units purchased are the first to be allocated to cost of goods sold. (p. 273)

LIFO reserve   For a company using LIFO, the difference between inventory reported using LIFO and inventory using FIFO. (p. 282)

Lower of cost or market (LCM) basis   (inventories) A basis whereby inventory is stated at the lower of cost or market (current replacement cost). (p. 279)

Raw materials   Basic goods that will be used in production but have not yet been placed in production. (p. 267)

Specific identification method   An actual physical flow costing method in which items still in inventory are specifically costed to arrive at the total cost of the ending inventory. (p. 271)

Weighted average unit cost   Average cost that is weighted by the number of units purchased at each unit cost. (p. 275)

Work in process   That portion of manufactured inventory that has begun the production process but is not yet complete. (p. 267)

Demonstration Problem

Englehart Company has the following inventory, purchases, and sales data for the month of March.

Inventory, March 1	200 units @ $4.00	$ 800
Purchases		
March 10	500 units @ $4.50	2,250
March 20	400 units @ $4.75	1,900
March 30	300 units @ $5.00	1,500
Sales		
March 15	500 units	
March 25	400 units	

The physical inventory count on March 31 shows 500 units on hand.

Instructions

Under a **periodic inventory system**, determine the cost of inventory on hand at March 31 and the cost of goods sold for March under (a) the first-in, first-out (FIFO) method; (b) the last-in, first-out (LIFO) method; and (c) the average cost method.

Action Plan

- For FIFO, allocate the latest costs to inventory.
- For LIFO, allocate the earliest costs to inventory.
- For average costs, use a weighted average.
- Remember, the costs allocated to cost of goods sold can be proved.
- Total purchases are the same under all three cost flow assumptions.

Solution to Demonstration Problem

The cost of goods available for sale is $6,450:

Inventory	200 units @ $4.00	$ 800
Purchases		
March 10	500 units @ $4.50	2,250
March 20	400 units @ $4.75	1,900
March 30	300 units @ $5.00	1,500
Total cost of goods available for sale		$6,450

(a)   **FIFO Method**

Ending inventory:

Date	Units	Unit Cost	Total Cost	
Mar. 30	300	$5.00	$1,500	
Mar. 20	200	4.75	950	$2,450

Cost of goods sold: $6,450 − $2,450 = $4,000

(b)   LIFO Method

Ending inventory:

Date	Units	Unit Cost	Total Cost	
Mar. 1	200	$4.00	$ 800	
Mar. 10	300	4.50	1,350	$2,150

Cost of goods sold: $6,450 − $2,150 = $4,300

(c)   **Weighted Average Cost Method**

Weighted average unit cost: $6,450 ÷ 1,400 = $4.607
Ending inventory: 500 × $4.607 = $2,303.50

Cost of goods sold: $6,450 − $2,303.50 = $4,146.50

☑ THE NAVIGATOR

Note: All Questions, Exercises, and Problems marked with an asterisk relate to material in the appendixes to the chapter.

Self-Study Questions

Self-Study/Self-Test

Answers are at the end of the chapter.

(SO 1) **1.** When is a physical inventory usually taken?
   (a) When the company has its greatest amount of inventory.
   (b) When goods are not being sold or received.
   (c) At the end of the company's fiscal year.
   (d) Both (b) and (c).

(SO 1) **2.** Which of the following should *not* be included in the physical inventory of a company?
   (a) Goods held on consignment from another company.
   (b) Goods shipped on consignment to another company.
   (c) Goods in transit from another company shipped FOB shipping point.
   (d) All of the above should be included.

(SO 2) **3.** Kam Company has the following units and costs.

	Units	Unit Cost
Inventory, Jan. 1	8,000	$11
Purchase, June 19	13,000	12
Purchase, Nov. 8	5,000	13

If 9,000 units are on hand at December 31, what is the cost of the ending inventory under FIFO?
   (a) $99,000.   (c) $113,000.
   (b) $108,000.   (d) $117,000.

(SO 2) **4.** From the data in question 3, what is the cost of the ending inventory under LIFO?
   (a) $113,000.   (c) $99,000.
   (b) $108,000.   (d) $100,000.

(SO 3) **5.** ⚙ In periods of rising prices, LIFO will produce:
   (a) higher net income than FIFO.
   (b) the same net income as FIFO.

   (c) lower net income than FIFO.
   (d) higher net income than average costing.

(SO 3) **6.** Considerations that affect the selection of an inventory costing method do *not* include:
   (a) tax effects.
   (b) balance sheet effects.
   (c) income statement effects.
   (d) perpetual versus periodic inventory system.

(SO 4) **7.** The lower of cost or market rule for inventory is an example of the application of:
   (a) the conservatism constraint.
   (b) the historical cost principle.
   (c) the materiality constraint.
   (d) the economic entity assumption.

(SO 5) **8.** ⚙ Which of these would cause the inventory turnover ratio to increase the most?
   (a) Increasing the amount of inventory on hand.
   (b) Keeping the amount of inventory on hand constant but increasing sales.
   (c) Keeping the amount of inventory on hand constant but decreasing sales.
   (d) Decreasing the amount of inventory on hand and increasing sales.

(SO 6) **9.** The LIFO reserve is:
   (a) the difference between the value of the inventory under LIFO and the value under FIFO.
   (b) an amount used to adjust inventory to the lower of cost or market.
   (c) the difference between the value of the inventory under LIFO and the value under average cost.
   (d) an amount used to adjust inventory to historical cost.

(SO 7) *10. In a perpetual inventory system,
   (a) LIFO cost of goods sold will be the same as in a periodic inventory system.
   (b) average costs are based entirely on unit-cost simple averages.
   (c) a new average is computed under the average cost method after each sale.
   (d) FIFO cost of goods sold will be the same as in a periodic inventory system.

*11. Fran Company's ending inventory is understated (SO 8) by $4,000. The effects of this error on the current year's cost of goods sold and net income, respectively, are:
   (a) understated and overstated.
   (b) overstated and understated.
   (c) overstated and overstated.
   (d) understated and understated.

Questions

1. "The key to successful business operations is effective inventory management." Do you agree? Explain.

2. An item must possess two characteristics to be classified as inventory. What are these two characteristics?

3. Your friend Nick Bickler has been hired to help take the physical inventory in Casey's Hardware Store. Explain to Nick Bickler what this job will entail.

4. (a) Lynn Company ships merchandise to Sheri Corporation on December 30. The merchandise reaches the buyer on January 5. Indicate the terms of sale that will result in the goods being included in (1) Lynn's December 31 inventory and (2) Sheri's December 31 inventory.
   (b) Under what circumstances should Lynn Company include consigned goods in its inventory?

5. Rosena's Hat Shop received a shipment of hats for which it paid the wholesaler $2,940. The price of the hats was $3,000, but Rosena's was given a $60 cash discount and required to pay freight charges of $70. In addition, Rosena's paid $100 to cover the travel expenses of an employee who negotiated the purchase of the hats. What amount should Rosena's include in inventory? Why?

6. What is the primary basis of accounting for inventories? What is the major objective in accounting for inventories?

7. Mark Erikson believes that the allocation of cost of goods available for sale should be based on the actual physical flow of the goods. Explain to Mark why this may be both impractical and inappropriate.

8. What are the major advantage and major disadvantage of the specific identification method of inventory costing?

9. "The selection of an inventory cost flow method is a decision made by accountants." Do you agree? Explain. Once a method has been selected, what accounting requirement applies?

10. Which assumed inventory cost flow method:
   (a) usually parallels the actual physical flow of merchandise?
   (b) assumes that goods available for sale during an accounting period are similar in nature?
   (c) assumes that the latest units purchased are the first to be sold?

11. In a period of rising prices, the inventory reported in Plato Company's balance sheet is close to the current cost of the inventory, whereas York Company's inventory is considerably below its current cost. Identify the inventory cost flow method used by each company. Which company probably has been reporting the higher gross profit?

12. Donna Corporation has been using the FIFO cost flow method during a prolonged period of inflation. During the same time period, Donna has been paying out all of its net income as dividends. What adverse effects may result from this policy?

13. Alyssa Jacobsen is studying for the next accounting midterm examination. What should Alyssa know about (a) departing from the cost basis of accounting for inventories and (b) the meaning of "market" in the lower of cost or market method?

14. Today's Music Center has five CD players on hand at the balance sheet date that cost $400 each. The current replacement cost is $320 per unit. Under the lower of cost or market basis of accounting for inventories, what value should be reported for the CD players on the balance sheet? Why?

15. What cost flow assumption may be used under the lower of cost or market basis of accounting for inventories?

16. Why is it inappropriate for a company to include freight-out expense in the Cost of Goods Sold account?

17. Ed & Trish Company's balance sheet shows Inventories $162,800. What additional disclosures should be made?

18. Under what circumstances might the inventory turnover ratio be too high; that is, what possible negative consequences might occur?

19. What is the LIFO reserve? What are the consequences of ignoring a large LIFO reserve when analyzing a company?

*20. "When perpetual inventory records are kept, the results under the FIFO and LIFO methods are the same as they would be in a periodic inventory system." Do you agree? Explain.

*21. How does the average method of inventory costing differ between a perpetual inventory system and a periodic inventory system?

*22. Petra Company discovers in 2005 that its ending inventory at December 31, 2004, was $5,000 understated. What effect will this error have on (a) 2004 net income, (b) 2005 net income, and (c) the combined net income for the 2 years?

Brief Exercises

BE6-1 Michelle Wilson Company identifies the following items for possible inclusion in the physical inventory. Indicate whether each item should be included or excluded from the inventory taking.
(a) Goods shipped on consignment by Wilson to another company.
(b) Goods in transit from a supplier shipped FOB destination.
(c) Goods sold but being held for customer pickup.
(d) Goods held on consignment from another company.

Identify items to be included in taking a physical inventory.
(SO 1)

BE6-2 In its first month of operations, Clare Company made three purchases of merchandise in the following sequence: (1) 300 units at $6, (2) 400 units at $7, and (3) 500 units at $9. Assuming there are 400 units on hand, compute the cost of the ending inventory under (a) the FIFO method and (b) the LIFO method. Clare uses a periodic inventory system.

Compute ending inventory using FIFO and LIFO.
(SO 2)

BE6-3 Data for Clare Company are presented in BE6-2. Compute the cost of the ending inventory under the average cost method, assuming there are 400 units on hand.

Compute the ending inventory using average costs.
(SO 2)

BE6-4 The management of Muni Corp. is considering the effects of various inventory-costing methods on its financial statements and its income tax expense. Assuming that the price the company pays for inventory is increasing, which method will:
(a) provide the highest net income?
(b) provide the highest ending inventory?
(c) result in the lowest income tax expense?
(d) result in the most stable earnings over a number of years?

Explain the financial statement effect of inventory cost flow assumptions.
(SO 3)

BE6-5 In its first month of operation, Marquette Company purchased 100 units of inventory for $6, then 200 units for $7, and finally 150 units for $8. At the end of the month, 200 units remained. Compute the amount of phantom profit that would result if the company used FIFO rather than LIFO. Explain why this amount is referred to as phantom profit. The company uses the periodic method.

Explain the financial statement effect of inventory cost flow assumptions.
(SO 3)

BE6-6 American Video Center accumulates the following cost and market data at December 31.

Determine the LCM valuation.
(SO 4)

Inventory Categories	Cost Data	Market Data
Cameras	$12,000	$10,200
Camcorders	9,000	9,500
VCRs	14,000	12,800

Compute the lower of cost or market valuation for American's total inventory.

BE6-7 At December 31, 2001, the following information (in thousands) was available for sunglasses manufacturer **Oakley, Inc.**: ending inventory $77,270; beginning inventory $61,998; cost of goods sold $174,332; and sales revenue $429,267. Calculate the inventory turnover ratio and days in inventory for Oakley, Inc.

Compute inventory turnover ratio and days in inventory.
(SO 5)

BE6-8 **Winnebago Industries, Inc.** is a leading manufacturer of motor homes. Winnebago reported ending inventory at August 25, 2001, of $79,815,000 under the LIFO inventory method. In the notes to its financial statements, Winnebago reported a LIFO reserve of $23,072,000 at August 25, 2001. What would Winnebago Industries' ending inventory have been if it had used FIFO?

Determine ending inventory and cost of goods sold using LIFO reserve.
(SO 6)

*BE6-9** Roshek's Department Store uses a perpetual inventory system. Data for product E2-D2 include the following purchases.

Apply cost flow methods to records.
(SO 7)

Date	Number of Units	Unit Price
May 7	50	$10
July 28	30	15

On June 1 Roshek sold 30 units, and on August 27, 33 more units. Compute the cost of goods sold using (1) FIFO, (2) LIFO, and (3) average cost.

Determine correct financial statement amount.
(SO 8)

BE6-10   Red Wall Company reports net income of $90,000 in 2005. However, ending inventory was understated by $7,000. What is the correct net income for 2005? What effect, if any, will this error have on total assets as reported in the balance sheet at December 31, 2005?

Exercises

Determine the correct inventory amount.
(SO 1)

E6-1   American Bank and Trust is considering giving Holub Company a loan. Before doing so, they decide that further discussions with Holub's accountant may be desirable. One area of particular concern is the inventory account, which has a year-end balance of $295,000. Discussions with the accountant reveal the following.

1. Holub sold goods costing $55,000 to Burke Company FOB shipping point on December 28. The goods are not expected to reach Burke until January 12. The goods were not included in the physical inventory because they were not in the warehouse.

2. The physical count of the inventory did not include goods costing $95,000 that were shipped to Holub FOB destination on December 27 and were still in transit at year-end.

3. Holub received goods costing $25,000 on January 2. The goods were shipped FOB shipping point on December 26 by Strang Co. The goods were not included in the physical count.

4. Holub sold goods costing $40,000 to Sterling of Canada FOB destination on December 30. The goods were received in Canada on January 8. They were not included in Holub's physical inventory.

5. Holub received goods costing $37,000 on January 2 that were shipped FOB destination on December 29. The shipment was a rush order that was supposed to arrive December 31. This purchase was included in the ending inventory of $295,000.

Instructions
Determine the correct inventory amount on December 31.

Determine the correct inventory amount.
(SO 1)

E6-2   Kale Thompson, an auditor with Sneed CPAs, is performing a review of Platinum Company's inventory account. Platinum did not have a good year, and top management is under pressure to boost reported income. According to its records, the inventory balance at year-end was $740,000. However, the following information was not considered when determining that amount.

1. Included in the company's count were goods with a cost of $250,000 that the company is holding on consignment. The goods belong to Superior Corporation.

2. The physical count did not include goods purchased by Platinum with a cost of $40,000 that were shipped FOB destination on December 28 and did not arrive at Platinum's warehouse until January 3.

3. Included in the inventory account was $17,000 of office supplies that were stored in the warehouse and were to be used by the company's supervisors and managers during the coming year.

4. The company received an order on December 29 that was boxed and was sitting on the loading dock awaiting pick-up on December 31. The shipper picked up the goods on January 1 and delivered them on January 6. The shipping terms were FOB shipping point. The goods had a selling price of $40,000 and a cost of $30,000. The goods were not included in the count because they were sitting on the dock.

5. On December 29 Platinum shipped goods with a selling price of $80,000 and a cost of $60,000 to District Sales Corporation FOB shipping point. The goods arrived on

January 3. District Sales had only ordered goods with a selling price of $10,000 and a cost of $8,000. However, a sales manager at Platinum had authorized the shipment and said that if District wanted to ship the goods back next week, it could.

6. Included in the count was $50,000 of goods that were parts for a machine that the company no longer made. Given the high-tech nature of Platinum's products, it was unlikely that these obsolete parts had any other use. However, management would prefer to keep them on the books at cost, "since that is what we paid for them, after all."

Instructions
Prepare a schedule to determine the correct inventory amount. Provide explanations for each item above, saying why you did or did not make an adjustment for each item.

E6-3   On December 1, Discount Electronics Ltd. has three DVD players left in stock. All are identical, all are priced to sell at $750. One of the three DVD players left in stock, with serial #1012, was purchased on June 1 at a cost of $500. Another, with serial #1045, was purchased on November 1 for $450. The last player, serial #1056, was purchased on November 30 for $400.

Calculate cost of goods sold using specific identification and FIFO periodic.
(SO 2, 3)

Instructions
(a) Calculate the cost of goods sold using the FIFO periodic inventory method assuming that two of the three players were sold by the end of December, Discount Electronic's year-end.
(b) If Discount Electronics used the specific identification method instead of the FIFO method, how might it alter its earnings by "selectively choosing" which particular players to sell to the two customers? What would Discount's cost of goods sold be if the company wished to minimize earnings? Maximize earnings?
(c) Which inventory method, FIFO or specific identification, do you recommend that Discount use? Explain why.

E6-4   Sherpers sells a snowboard, Xpert, that is popular with snowboard enthusiasts. Below is information relating to Sherpers's purchases of Xpert snowboards during September. During the same month, 124 Xpert snowboards were sold. Sherpers uses a periodic inventory system.

Compute inventory and cost of goods sold using periodic FIFO and LIFO.
(SO 2)

Date	Explanation	Units	Unit Cost	Total Cost
Sept. 1	Inventory	26	$ 97	$ 2,522
Sept. 12	Purchases	45	102	4,590
Sept. 19	Purchases	20	104	2,080
Sept. 26	Purchases	50	105	5,250
	Totals	141		$14,442

Instructions
(a) Compute the ending inventory at September 30 using the FIFO and LIFO methods. Prove the amount allocated to cost of goods sold under each method.
(b) For both FIFO and LIFO, calculate the sum of ending inventory and cost of goods sold. What do you notice about the answers you found for each method?

E6-5   In June, Newport Company reports the following for the month of June.

Compute inventory and cost of goods sold using periodic FIFO, LIFO, and average costs.
(SO 2, 3)

Instructions

Date	Explanation	Units	Unit Cost	Total Cost
June 1	Inventory	200	$5	$1,000
12	Purchase	300	6	1,800
23	Purchase	500	7	3,500
30	Inventory	160		

(a) Compute the cost of the ending inventory and the cost of goods sold under (1) FIFO, (2) LIFO, and (3) average cost.
(b) Which costing method gives the highest ending inventory and the highest cost of goods sold? Why?
(c) How do the average cost values for ending inventory and cost of goods sold relate to ending inventory and cost of goods sold for FIFO and LIFO?
(d) Explain why the average cost is not $6.

Calculate inventory and cost of goods sold using FIFO, average, and LIFO in a periodic inventory system.
(SO 2)

E6-6   Mawmey Inc. uses a periodic inventory system. Its records show the following for the month of May, in which 78 units were sold.

Date	Explanation	Units	Unit Cost	Total Cost
May 1	Inventory	30	$ 8	$240
15	Purchase	25	10	250
24	Purchase	35	12	420
	Total	90		$910

Instructions

Calculate the ending inventory at May 31 using the (a) FIFO, (b) average cost, and (c) LIFO methods. Prove the amount allocated to cost of goods sold under each method.

Compute inventory turnover ratio, days in inventory, and gross profit rate.
(SO 5)

E6-7   This information is available for **PepsiCo, Inc.** for 1999, 2000, and 2001.

(in millions)	1999	2000	2001
Beginning inventory	$ 1,016	$ 899	$ 1,192
Ending inventory	899	1,192	1,310
Cost of goods sold	10,326	10,226	10,754
Sales	25,093	25,479	26,935

Instructions

Calculate the inventory turnover ratio, days in inventory, and gross profit rate for PepsiCo., Inc. for 1999, 2000, and 2001. Comment on any trends.

Determine the effect of the LIFO reserve on current ratio.
(SO 5, 6)

E6-8   **Deere & Company** is a global manufacturer and distributor of agricultural, construction, and forestry equipment. It reported the following information in its 2001 annual report.

(in millions)	2001	2000
Inventories (LIFO)	$ 1,506	1,553
Current assets	16,015	
Current liabilities	6,199	
LIFO reserve	1,004	
Cost of goods sold	9,376	

Instructions

(a) Compute Deere's inventory turnover ratio and days in inventory for 2001.
(b) Compute Deere's current ratio using the 2001 data as presented, and then again after adjusting for the LIFO reserve.
(c) Comment on how ignoring the LIFO reserve might affect your evaluation of Deere's liquidity.

Calculate inventory and cost of goods sold using three cost flow methods in a perpetual inventory system.
(SO 7)

*E6-9**   Inventory data for Newport Company are presented in E6-5.

Instructions

(a) Calculate the cost of the ending inventory and the cost of goods sold for each cost flow assumption, using a perpetual inventory system. Assume a sale of 400 units occurred on June 15 for a selling price of $8 and a sale of 440 units on June 27 for $9. (*Note:* For the average cost method, round unit cost to three decimal places.)
(b) How do the results differ from E6-5?
(c) Why is the average unit cost not $6 [($5 + $6 + $7) ÷ 3 = $6]?

Apply cost flow methods to perpetual records.
(SO 7)

*E6-10**   Information about Sherpers is presented in E6-4. Additional data regarding Sherpers' sales of Xpert snowboards are provided below. Assume that Sherpers uses a perpetual inventory system.

Date		Units	Unit Price	Total Cost
Sept. 5	Sale	12	$199	$ 2,388
Sept. 16	Sale	50	199	9,950
Sept. 29	Sale	62	209	12,958
	Totals	124		$25,296

Instructions
(a) Compute ending inventory at September 30 using FIFO, LIFO, and average cost. (*Note:* For average cost, round unit cost to three decimal places.)
(b) Compare ending inventory using a perpetual inventory system to ending inventory using a periodic inventory system (from E6-4).
(c) Which inventory cost flow method (FIFO, LIFO) gives the same ending inventory value under both periodic and perpetual? Which method gives different ending inventory values?

*E6-11   Brighton Hardware reported cost of goods sold as follows.

Determine effects of inventory errors.
(SO 8)

	2006	2005
Beginning inventory	$ 30,000	$ 20,000
Cost of goods purchased	175,000	160,000
Cost of goods available for sale	205,000	180,000
Ending inventory	35,000	30,000
Cost of goods sold	$170,000	$150,000

Brighton made two errors:

1. 2005 ending inventory was overstated by $4,000.

2. 2006 ending inventory was understated by $3,000.

Instructions
Compute the correct cost of goods sold for each year.

*E6-12   Zales Company reported these income statement data for a 2-year period.

Prepare correct income statements.
(SO 8)

	2006	2005
Sales	$250,000	$210,000
Beginning inventory	40,000	32,000
Cost of goods purchased	202,000	173,000
Cost of goods available for sale	242,000	205,000
Ending inventory	52,000	40,000
Cost of goods sold	190,000	165,000
Gross profit	$ 60,000	$ 45,000

Zales Company uses a periodic inventory system. The inventories at January 1, 2005, and December 31, 2006, are correct. However, the ending inventory at December 31, 2005, is overstated by $4,000.

Instructions
(a) Prepare correct income statement data for the 2 years.
(b) What is the cumulative effect of the inventory error on total gross profit for the 2 years?
(c) Explain in a letter to the president of Zales Company what has happened—that is, the nature of the error and its effect on the financial statements.

Problems: Set A

P6-1A   Kananaskis Country Limited is trying to determine the value of its ending inventory as of February 28, 2005, the company's year-end. The following transactions occurred, and the accountant asked your help in determining whether they should be recorded or not.

Determine items and amounts to be recorded in inventory.
(SO 1)

Peachtree

(a) On February 26, Kananaskis shipped goods costing $800 to a customer and charged the customer $1,000. The goods were shipped with terms FOB destination and the receiving report indicates that the customer received the goods on March 2.

(b) On February 26, Seller Inc. shipped goods to Kananaskis under terms FOB shipping point. The invoice price was $350 plus $25 for freight. The receiving report indicates that the goods were received by Kananaskis on March 2.

(c) Kananaskis had $500 of inventory isolated in the warehouse. The inventory is designated for a customer who has requested that the goods be shipped on March 10.

(d) Also included in Kananaskis' warehouse is $400 of inventory that Craft Producers shipped to Kananaskis on consignment.

(e) On February 26, Kananaskis issued a purchase order to acquire goods costing $750. The goods were shipped with terms FOB destination on February 27. Kananaskis received the goods on March 2.

(f) On February 26, Kananaskis shipped goods to a customer under terms FOB shipping point. The invoice price was $350 plus $25 for freight; the cost of the items was $280. The receiving report indicates that the goods were received by the customer on March 2.

Instructions

For each of the above transactions, specify whether the item in question should be included in ending inventory, and if so, at what amount.

Determine cost of goods sold and ending inventory using FIFO, LIFO, and average cost with analysis.
(SO 2, 3)

P6-2A Breathless Distribution markets CDs of the performing artist Christina Spears. At the beginning of October, Breathless had in beginning inventory 1,000 Spears CDs with a unit cost of $5. During October Breathless made the following purchases of Spears CDs.

Oct. 3	3,500 @ $6	Oct. 19	2,000 @ $8
Oct. 9	4,000 @ $7	Oct. 25	2,000 @ $9

During October 10,000 units were sold. Breathless uses a periodic inventory system.

Instructions

(a) Determine the cost of goods available for sale.

(b) Determine (1) the ending inventory and (2) the cost of goods sold under each of the assumed cost flow methods (FIFO, LIFO, and average cost). Prove the accuracy of the cost of goods sold under the FIFO and LIFO methods.

(c) Which cost flow method results in (1) the highest inventory amount for the balance sheet and (2) the highest cost of goods sold for the income statement?

Cost of goods sold:
FIFO $66,000
LIFO $74,000
Average $70,400

Determine cost of goods sold and ending inventory using FIFO, average cost, and LIFO in a periodic inventory system and assess financial statement effects.
(SO 2, 3)

Peachtree

Cost of goods sold:
FIFO $21,200
LIFO $22,400
Average $21,760

P6-3A Kane Company Ltd. had a beginning inventory on January 1 of 100 units of Product SXL at a cost of $20 per unit. During the year, purchases were:

Mar. 15	300 units at $24	Sept. 4	300 units at $28
July 20	200 units at $25	Dec. 2	100 units at $30

Kane Company sold 850 units, and it uses a periodic inventory system.

Instructions

(a) Determine the cost of goods available for sale.

(b) Determine the ending inventory and the cost of goods sold under each of the assumed cost flow methods (FIFO, LIFO, and average cost). Prove the accuracy of the cost of goods sold under each method.

(c) Which cost flow method results in the highest inventory amount for the balance sheet? The highest cost of goods sold for the income statement?

Compute ending inventory, prepare income statements, and answer questions using FIFO and LIFO.
(SO 2, 3)

P6-4A The management of Red Robin Inc. is reevaluating the appropriateness of using its present inventory cost flow method, which is average cost. The company requests your help in determining the results of operations for 2006 if either the FIFO or the LIFO method had been used. For 2005 the accounting records show these data:

Inventories		Purchases and Sales	
Beginning (10,000 units)	$22,800	Total net sales (225,000 units)	$865,000
Ending (15,000 units)		Total cost of goods purchased	
		(230,000 units)	578,500

Purchases were made quarterly as follows.

Quarter	Units	Unit Cost	Total Cost
1	60,000	$2.30	$138,000
2	50,000	2.50	125,000
3	50,000	2.60	130,000
4	70,000	2.65	185,500
	230,000		$578,500

Operating expenses were $147,000, and the company's income tax rate is 32%.

Instructions

(a) Prepare comparative condensed income statements for 2005 under FIFO and LIFO. (Show computations of ending inventory.)

(b) Answer the following questions for management in business-letter form.

Gross profit:
FIFO $303,450
LIFO $298,000

(1) Which cost flow method (FIFO or LIFO) produces the more meaningful inventory amount for the balance sheet? Why?

(2) Which cost flow method (FIFO or LIFO) produces the more meaningful net income? Why?

(3) Which cost flow method (FIFO or LIFO) is more likely to approximate the actual physical flow of goods? Why?

(4) How much more cash will be available for management under LIFO than under FIFO? Why?

(5) Will gross profit under the average cost method be higher or lower than FIFO? Than LIFO? (*Note:* It is not necessary to quantify your answer.)

P6-5A You are provided with the following information for Danielle Inc. for the month ended June 30, 2005. Danielle uses the periodic method for inventory.

Calculate ending inventory, cost of goods sold, gross profit, and gross profit rate under periodic method; compare results.
(SO 2, 3)

Date	Description	Quantity	Unit Cost or Selling Price
June 1	Beginning inventory	25	$60
June 4	Purchase	85	64
June 10	Sale	70	90
June 11	Sale return	10	90
June 18	Purchase	35	68
June 18	Purchase return	5	68
June 25	Sale	50	95
June 28	Purchase	20	72

Instructions

(a) Calculate (i) ending inventory, (ii) cost of goods sold, (iii) gross profit, and (iv) gross profit rate under each of the following methods.

(1) LIFO.

(2) FIFO.

Gross profit:
LIFO $2,830
FIFO $3,210
Average $2,986

(3) Average cost. (Round cost per unit to three decimal places.)

(b) Compare results for the three cost flow assumptions.

P6-6A You are provided with the following information for Gas Guzzlers. Gas Guzzlers uses the periodic method of accounting for its inventory transactions.

Compare specific identification, FIFO, and LIFO under periodic method; use cost flow assumption to justify price increase.
(SO 2, 3)

March 1 Beginning inventory 1,500 litres at a cost of 40¢ per litre.
March 3 Purchased 2,000 litres at a cost of 45¢ per litre.
March 5 Sold 1,800 litres for 60¢ per litre.
March 10 Purchased 3,500 litres at a cost of 49¢ per litre.
March 20 Purchased 2,000 litres at a cost of 55¢ per litre.
March 30 Sold 5,000 litres for 70¢ per litre.

Gross profit:
Specific
identification $1,331
FIFO $1,463
LIFO $1,180

Instructions

(a) Prepare partial income statements through gross profit, and calculate the value of ending inventory that would be reported on the balance sheet, under each of the following cost flow assumptions.

    (1) Specific identification method assuming:

        (i) the March 5 sale consisted of 900 litres from the March 1 beginning inventory and 900 litres from the March 3 purchase; and

        (ii) the March 30 sale consisted of the following number of units sold from each purchase: 400 litres from March 1; 500 litres from March 3; 2,600 litres from March 10; 1,500 litres from March 20.

    (2) FIFO.

    (3) LIFO.

(b) How can companies use a cost flow method to justify price increases? Which cost flow method would best support an argument to increase prices?

Compute inventory turnover ratio, days in inventory, and current ratio based on LIFO and after adjusting for LIFO reserve.
(SO 5, 6)

P6-7A Gehl Company manufactures a full line of construction and agriculture equipment. The following information is available for Gehl for 2001. The company uses the LIFO inventory method.

(in thousands)	**2001**
Beginning inventory	$ 45,598
Ending inventory	52,161
LIFO reserve	20,191
Current assets	163,194
Current liabilities	56,466
Cost of goods sold	187,069
Sales	251,636

Instructions

(a) Calculate the inventory turnover ratio and days in inventory.
(b) Calculate the current ratio based on LIFO inventory.
(c) After adjusting for the LIFO reserve, calculate the current ratio.
(d) Comment on any difference between parts (b) and (c).

Calculate cost of goods sold and ending inventory under LIFO, FIFO, and average under the perpetual system; compare gross profit under each assumption.
(SO 3, 7)

Gross profit:
LIFO $1,730
FIFO $1,820
Average $1,767

***P6-8A** Matthew Inc. is a retailer operating in Dartmouth, Nova Scotia. Matthew uses the perpetual inventory method. All sales returns from customers result in the goods being returned to inventory. (Assume that the inventory is not damaged.) Assume that there are no credit transactions; all amounts are settled in cash. You are provided with the following information for Matthew Inc. for the month of January 2005.

Date	Description	Quantity	Unit Cost or Selling Price
January 1	Beginning inventory	50	$12
January 5	Purchase	100	14
January 8	Sale	80	25
January 10	Sale return	10	25
January 15	Purchase	30	18
January 16	Purchase return	5	18
January 20	Sale	90	25
January 25	Purchase	10	20

Instructions

(a) For each of the following cost flow assumptions, calculate (i) cost of goods sold, (ii) ending inventory, and (iii) gross profit.

    (1) LIFO.

    (2) FIFO.

    (3) Moving average cost. (Round cost per unit to three decimal places.)

(b) Compare results for the three cost flow assumptions.

*P6-9A   Save-Mart Center began operations on July 1. It uses a perpetual inventory system. During July the company had the following purchases and sales.

Determine ending inventory under a perpetual inventory system.
(SO 3, 7)

| | **Purchases** | | |
Date	Units	Unit Cost	Sales Units
July 1	6	$30	
July 6			4
July 11	5	$33	
July 14			3
July 21	3	$36	
July 27			2

Instructions
(a) Determine the ending inventory under a perpetual inventory system using (1) FIFO, (2) average cost, and (3) LIFO. (*Note:* For average cost, round cost per unit to three decimal places.)
(b) Which costing method produces the highest ending inventory valuation?

FIFO $174
Average $169
LIFO $162

Problems: Set B

P6-1B   Banff Limited is trying to determine the value of its ending inventory as of February 28, 2005, the company's year-end. The accountant counted everything that was in the warehouse, as of February 28, which resulted in an ending inventory valuation of $48,000. However, she didn't know how to treat the following transactions so she didn't record them.

Determine items and amounts to be recorded in inventory.
(SO 1)

(a) On February 26, Banff shipped to a customer goods costing $800. The goods were shipped FOB shipping point, and the receiving report indicates that the customer received the goods on March 2.
(b) On February 26, Seller Inc. shipped goods to Banff FOB destination. The invoice price was $350 plus $25 for freight. The receiving report indicates that the goods were received by Banff on March 2.
(c) Banff had $500 of inventory at a customer's warehouse "on approval." The customer was going to let Banff know whether it wanted the merchandise by the end of the week, March 4.
(d) Banff also had $400 of inventory at a Jasper craft shop, on consignment from Banff.
(e) On February 26, Banff ordered goods costing $750. The goods were shipped FOB shipping point on February 27. Banff received the goods on March 1.
(f) On February 28, Banff packaged goods and had them ready for shipping to a customer FOB destination. The invoice price was $350 plus $25 for freight; the cost of the items was $280. The receiving report indicates that the goods were received by the customer on March 2.
(g) Banff had damaged goods set aside in the warehouse because they are no longer saleable. These goods originally cost $400 and, originally, Banff expected to sell these items for $600.

Instructions
For each of the above transactions, specify whether the item in question should be included in ending inventory, and if so, at what amount. For each item that is not included in ending inventory, indicate who owns it and what account, if any, it should have been recorded in.

P6-2B   Doom's Day Distribution markets CDs of the performing artist Harrilyn Hannson. At the beginning of March, Doom's Day had in beginning inventory 1,500 Hannson CDs with a unit cost of $7. During March Doom's Day made the following purchases of Hannson CDs.

Determine cost of goods sold and ending inventory using FIFO, LIFO, and average cost.
(SO 2, 3)

| March 5 | 3,000 @ $8 | March 21 | 4,000 @ $10 |
| March 13 | 5,500 @ $9 | March 26 | 2,000 @ $11 |

During March 13,500 units were sold. Doom's Day uses a periodic inventory system.

Instructions
(a) Determine the cost of goods available for sale.

Cost of goods sold:
FIFO $119,000
LIFO $127,500
Average $123,187

(b) Determine (1) the ending inventory and (2) the cost of goods sold under each of the assumed cost flow methods (FIFO, LIFO, and average cost). Prove the accuracy of the cost of goods sold under the FIFO and LIFO methods. (*Note:* For average cost, round cost per unit to 3 decimal places.)

(c) Which cost flow method results in (1) the highest inventory amount for the balance sheet and (2) the highest cost of goods sold for the income statement?

Determine cost of goods sold and ending inventory using FIFO, average cost, and LIFO in a periodic inventory system, and assess financial statement effect.
(SO 2, 3)

P6-3B Steward Company Inc. had a beginning inventory of 400 units of Product MLN at a cost of $8 per unit. During the year, purchases were:

| Feb. 20 | 700 units at $ 9 | Aug. 12 | 300 units at $11 |
| May 5 | 500 units at $10 | Dec. 8 | 100 units at $12 |

Steward Company uses a periodic inventory system. Sales totalled 1,550 units.

Instructions

(a) Determine the cost of goods available for sale.

Cost of goods sold:
FIFO $14,000
LIFO $15,350
Average $14,725

(b) Determine the ending inventory and the cost of goods sold under each of the assumed cost flow methods (FIFO, LIFO, and average cost). Prove the accuracy of the cost of goods sold under the FIFO and LIFO methods.

(c) Which cost flow method results in the lowest inventory amount for the balance sheet? The lowest cost of goods sold for the income statement?

Compute ending inventory, prepare income statements, and answer questions using FIFO and LIFO.
(SO 2, 3)

P6-4B The management of Zwick Inc. asks your help in determining the comparative effects of the FIFO and LIFO inventory cost flow methods. For 2005 the accounting records show these data.

Inventory, January 1 (10,000 units)	$ 35,000
Cost of 120,000 units purchased	504,500
Selling price of 95,000 units sold	665,000
Operating expenses	120,000

Units purchased consisted of 35,000 units at $4.00 on May 10; 60,000 units at $4.20 on August 15; and 25,000 units at $4.50 on November 20. Income taxes are 28%.

Gross profit:
FIFO $280,000
LIFO $260,500

Instructions

(a) Prepare comparative condensed income statements for 2005 under FIFO and LIFO. (Show computations of ending inventory.)

(b) Answer the following questions for management in the form of a business letter.

(1) Which inventory cost flow method produces the most meaningful inventory amount for the balance sheet? Why?

(2) Which inventory cost flow method produces the most meaningful net income? Why?

(3) Which inventory cost flow method is most likely to approximate the actual physical flow of the goods? Why?

(4) How much more cash will be available for management under LIFO than under FIFO? Why?

(5) How much of the gross profit under FIFO is illusionary in comparison with the gross profit under LIFO?

Calculate ending inventory, cost of goods sold, gross profit, and gross profit rate under periodic method; compare results.
(SO 2, 3)

P6-5B You are provided with the following information for Lahti Inc. for the month ended October 31, 2005. Lahti uses a periodic method for inventory.

Date	Description	Units	Unit Cost or Selling Price
October 1	Beginning inventory	60	$25
October 9	Purchase	120	26
October 11	Sale	100	35
October 17	Purchase	70	27
October 22	Sale	60	40
October 25	Purchase	80	28
October 29	Sale	150	40

Instructions
  (a) Calculate (i) ending inventory, (ii) cost of goods sold, (iii) gross profit, and (iv) gross profit rate under each of the following methods.

  (1) LIFO.

  (2) FIFO.

  (3) Average cost. (Round cost per unit to three decimal places.)

  (b) Compare results for the three cost flow assumptions.

Gross profit:
LIFO $3,650
FIFO $3,710
Average $3,680

P6-6B   You have the following information for Discount Diamonds. Discount Diamonds uses the periodic method of accounting for its inventory transactions. Discount only carries one brand and size of diamonds—all are identical. Each batch of diamonds purchased is carefully coded and marked with its purchase cost.

Compare specific identification and FIFO under periodic method; use cost flow assumption to influence earnings.
(SO 2, 3)

March 1	Beginning inventory 150 diamonds at a cost of $300 per diamond.
March 3	Purchased 200 diamonds at a cost of $350 each.
March 5	Sold 180 diamonds for $600 each.
March 10	Purchased 350 diamonds at a cost of $375 each.
March 25	Sold 500 diamonds for $650 each.

Instructions
  (a) Assume that Discount Diamonds uses the specific identification cost flow method.

  (1) Demonstrate how Discount Diamonds could maximize its gross profit for the month by specifically selecting which diamonds to sell on March 5 and March 25.

  (2) Demonstrate how Discount Diamonds could minimize its gross profit for the month by selecting which diamonds to sell on March 5 and March 25.

  (b) Assume that Discount Diamonds uses the FIFO cost flow assumption. Calculate cost of goods sold. How much gross profit would Discount Diamonds report under this cost flow assumption?

  (c) Assume that Discount Diamonds uses the LIFO cost flow assumption. Calculate cost of goods sold. How much gross profit would the company report under this cost flow assumption?

  (d) Which cost flow method should Discount Diamonds select? Explain.

Gross profit:
Maximum $194,250
Minimum $192,750

P6-7B   This information is available for the Automotive and Electronics Divisions of **General Motors Corporation** for 2001. General Motors uses the LIFO inventory method.

Compute inventory turnover ratio and days in inventory; compute current ratio based on LIFO and after adjusting for LIFO reserve.
(SO 5, 6)

(in millions)	**2001**
Beginning inventory	$ 10,945
Ending inventory	10,034
LIFO reserve	1,814
Current assets	37,063
Current liabilities	56,346
Cost of goods sold	135,620
Sales	151,491

Instructions
  (a) Calculate the inventory turnover ratio and days in inventory.
  (b) Calculate the current ratio based on inventory as reported using LIFO.
  (c) Calculate the current ratio after adjusting for the LIFO reserve.
  (d) Comment on any difference between parts (b) and (c).

*P6-8B Yuan Li Ltd. is a retailer operating in Edmonton, Alberta. Yuan Li uses the perpetual inventory method. All sales returns from customers result in the goods being returned to inventory. (Assume that the inventory is not damaged.) Assume that there are no credit transactions; all amounts are settled in cash. You are provided with the following information for Yuan Li Ltd. for the month of January 2005.

Calculate cost of goods sold and ending inventory for FIFO, average, and LIFO under the perpetual system; compare gross profit under each assumption.
(SO 3, 7)

Date	Description	Quantity	Unit Cost or Selling Price
December 31	Ending inventory	150	$17
January 2	Purchase	100	21
January 6	Sale	150	40
January 9	Sale return	10	40
January 9	Purchase	75	24
January 10	Purchase return	15	24
January 10	Sale	50	45
January 23	Purchase	100	28
January 30	Sale	160	50

Gross profit:
LIFO $7,980
FIFO $8,640
Average $8,395

Instructions

(a) For each of the following cost flow assumptions, calculate (i) cost of goods sold, (ii) ending inventory, and (iii) gross profit.

(1) LIFO. (Assume goods returned on January 9 had $17 cost.)

(2) FIFO. (Assume goods returned on January 9 had $17 cost.)

(3) Moving average cost. (Round cost per unit to three decimal places.)

(b) Compare results for the three cost flow assumptions.

Determine ending inventory under a perpetual inventory system.
(SO 3, 7)

***P6-9B** Save-More Center began operations on July 1. It uses a perpetual inventory system. During July the company had the following purchases and sales.

Date	Purchases Units	Unit Cost	Sales Units
July 1	6	$ 90	
July 6			3
July 11	4	$ 99	
July 14			3
July 21	3	$106	
July 27			5

FIFO $212
Average $200
LIFO $180

Instructions

(a) Determine the ending inventory under a perpetual inventory system using (1) FIFO, (2) average cost (round unit cost to nearest dollar), and (3) LIFO.

(b) Which costing method produces the highest ending inventory valuation?

▶ BROADENING YOUR PERSPECTIVE

Financial Reporting and Analysis

FINANCIAL REPORTING PROBLEM: *Tootsie Roll Industries, Inc.*

BYP6-1 The notes that accompany a company's financial statements provide informative details that would clutter the amounts and descriptions presented in the statements. Refer to the financial statements of **Tootsie Roll** and the accompanying Notes to Consolidated Financial Statements in Appendix A.

Instructions

Answer the following questions. (Give the amounts in thousands of dollars, as shown in Tootsie Roll's annual report.)

(a) What did Tootsie Roll report for the amount of inventories in its Consolidated Balance Sheet at December 31, 2002? At December 31, 2001?

(b) Compute the dollar amount of change and the percentage change in inventories between 2001 and 2002. Compute inventory as a percentage of current assets for 2002.

(c) What are the cost of goods sold reported by Tootsie Roll for 2002, 2001, and 2000? Compute the ratio of cost of goods sold to net sales in 2002.

COMPARATIVE ANALYSIS PROBLEM: *Tootsie Roll vs. Hershey Foods*

BYP6-2   The financial statements of **Hershey Foods** are presented in Appendix B, following the financial statements for **Tootsie Roll** in Appendix A.

Instructions
   (a) Based on the information in the financial statements, compute these 2002 values for each company. (Do not adjust for the LIFO reserve.)

   (1) Inventory turnover ratio.

   (2) Days in inventory.

   (b) What conclusions concerning the management of the inventory can be drawn from these data?

RESEARCH CASE

BYP6-3   The April 27, 2001, issue of the *Wall Street Journal* contains an article by Scott Thurm and Jonathan Weil entitled "Tech Companies Charge Now, May Profit Later."

Instructions
Read the article and answer the following questions.
   (a) What is the amount of the write-off taken by **Cisco**?
   (b) What reason does Cisco give for this write-off? How did Cisco end up with such a large balance of excess inventory?
   (c) Why do some people suggest that Cisco intentionally took a larger than necessary write-off?
   (d) What evidence is there that Cisco may, in fact, sell these parts in the future, even though the company has written them down to a zero value now?
   (e) What are "pro forma" financial results?

INTERPRETING FINANCIAL STATEMENTS

BYP6-4   Snowboarding is a rapidly growing sport in the United States. In 1995 **Morrow Snowboards** announced it would sell shares of stock to the public. In its prospectus (an information-filled document that must be provided by every publicly traded U.S. company the first time it issues shares to the public), Morrow disclosed the following information.

MORROW SNOWBOARDS
Prospectus

Uncertain Ability to Manage Growth: Since inception, the Company has experienced rapid growth in its sales, production, and employee base. These increases have placed significant demands on the Company's management, working capital, and financial and management control systems. The Company's independent auditors used management letters in connection with their audit of the fiscal years ended December 31, 1993 and 1994, and the 9-month period ended September 30, 1995, that identified certain significant deficiencies in the Company's accounting systems, procedures, and controls. To address these growth issues, the Company has, in the past 18 months, relocated its facilities and expanded production capacity, implemented a number of financial accounting control systems, and hired experienced finance, accounting, manufacturing, and marketing personnel. In the accounting area, the Company has begun implementing or improving a perpetual inventory system, a cost accounting system, written accounting policies and procedures, and a comprehensive annual capital expenditure budget. Until the Company develops a reliable perpetual inventory system, it intends to perform physical inventories on a quarterly basis. Although the Company is continuously evaluating and improving its facilities, management, and financial control systems, there can be no assurance that such improvements will meet the demands of future growth. Any inadequacies in these areas could have a material adverse effect on the Company's business, financial condition, and results of operations.

Instructions

(a) What implications does this disclosure have for someone interested in investing in Morrow Snowboards?

(b) Do you think that the price of Morrow's stock will suffer because of these admitted deficiencies in its internal controls, including its controls over inventory?

(c) Why do you think Morrow decided to disclose this negative information?

(d) List the steps that Morrow has taken to improve its control systems.

(e) Do you think that these weaknesses are unusual for a rapidly growing company?

BYP6-5 The following information was taken from the 2001 annual report of **Cooper Tire and Rubber Company** (all dollars in thousands).

	December 31, 2001	2000
Inventories		
Finished goods	$ 207,484	$ 192,357
Work in process	32,838	32,882
Raw materials and supplies	66,156	71,221
	$ 306,478	$ 296,460
Cost of goods sold	$2,724,692	$2,939,815
Current assets	$ 952,100	
Current liabilities	$ 647,900	

From the company's notes: Inventories are valued at cost, which is not in excess of market. Inventory costs have been determined by the last-in, first-out (LIFO) method for substantially all domestic inventories. Costs of other inventories have been determined principally by the first-in, first-out (FIFO) method.

Under the LIFO method, inventories have been reduced by approximately $52,476 and $46,565 at December 31, 2000 and 2001, respectively, from current cost which would be reported under the first-in, first-out method.

Instructions

(a) Define each of the following: finished goods, work-in-process, and raw materials.

(b) The company experienced an increase in finished goods inventory and a decline in raw materials. Discuss the likely cause of this.

(c) What might be a possible explanation for why the company uses FIFO for its non-domestic inventories?

(d) Calculate the company's inventory turnover ratio and days in inventory for 2000 and 2001. (1999 inventory was $274 million.) Discuss the implications of any change in the ratios.

(e) What percentage of total inventory does the 2001 LIFO reserve represent? If the company used FIFO in 2001, what would be the value of its inventory? Do you consider this difference a "material" amount from the perspective of an analyst? Which value accurately represents the value of the company's inventory?

(f) Calculate the company's 2001 current ratio with the numbers as reported, then recalculate after adjusting for the LIFO reserve.

A GLOBAL FOCUS

BYP6-6 **Fuji Photo Film Company** is a Japanese manufacturer of photographic products. Its U.S. counterpart, and arch rival, is **Eastman Kodak**. Together the two dominate the global market for film. The information shown on pages 309 and 310 was extracted from the financial statements of the two companies.

FUJI PHOTO FILM
Notes to the Financial Statements

Summary of significant accounting policies
The Company and its domestic subsidiaries maintain their records and prepare their financial statements in accordance with accounting practices generally accepted in Japan. . . . Certain reclassifications and adjustments, including those relating to tax effects of temporary differences and the accrual of certain expenses, have been incorporated in the accompanying consolidated financial statements to conform with accounting principles generally accepted in the United States.

Inventories
Inventories are valued at the lower of cost or market, cost being determined generally by the moving-average method, except that the cost of the principal raw materials is determined by the last-in, first-out method.

Note 6. Inventories
Inventories at March 31, 2001 and 2000, consisted of the following:

| | (millions of yen) | | (thousands of U.S. dollars) |
	2001	2000	2001
Finished goods	¥218,507	¥125,680	$1,762,153
Work in process	67,399	51,231	543,540
Raw materials and supplies	68,415	54,123	551,734
	¥354,321	¥231,034	$2,857,427

EASTMAN KODAK COMPANY
Notes to the Financial Statements

Inventories
Inventories are valued at cost, which is not in excess of market. The cost of most inventories in the U.S. is determined by the "last-in, first-out" (LIFO) method.

Note 3. Inventories

(in millions)	2001	2000
At FIFO or average cost (approximates current cost)		
Finished goods	$ 851	$1,155
Work in process	318	423
Raw materials and supplies	412	589
	1,581	2,167
LIFO reserve	(444)	(449)
Total	$1,137	$1,718

Inventories valued on the LIFO method are approximately 48% and 47% of total inventories in 2001 and 2000, respectively.

Additional information:

	Fuji Photo Film	Eastman Kodak
2001 Cost of goods sold (millions)	¥803,460	$8,670

Instructions

Answer each of the following questions.

(a) Why do you suppose that Fuji makes adjustments to its accounts so that they conform with U.S. accounting principles when it reports its results?

(b) What are the 2001 inventory turnover ratios and days in inventory of the two companies, using inventory as reported?

(c) Calculate as a percentage of total inventory the portion that each of the components of 2001 inventory (raw materials, work in process, and finished goods) represents. Comment on your findings. (Use FIFO for Kodak.)

FINANCIAL ANALYSIS ON THE WEB

BYP6-7   *Purpose:* Use SEC filings to learn about a company's inventory accounting practices.

Address: http://biz.yahoo.com/p/_capgds-bldmch.html
(or go to **www.wiley.com/college/kimmel**)

Steps

1. Go to this site and click on the name of an equipment manufacturer other than those discussed in the chapter.

2. Click on **SEC filings** from Edgar Online.

3. At the top of the page under "Recent filings" click on Form 10K (annual report).

If the 10K is not listed among the recent filings then click on (**More filings for COMPANY NAME available from EDGAR Online**).

Instructions

Review the 10K to answer the following questions.

(a) What is the name of the company?

(b) How has its inventory changed from the previous year?

(c) What is the amount of raw materials, work-in-process, and finished goods inventory?

(d) What inventory method does the company use?

(e) Calculate the inventory turnover ratio and days in inventory for the current year.

(f) If the company uses LIFO, what was the amount of its LIFO reserve?

Critical Thinking

GROUP DECISION CASE

BYP6-8   Morton International, Inc., headquartered in Chicago, Illinois, manufactures specialty chemicals, automobile airbags, and salt. Recently, its specialty chemicals business was reorganized, and three manufacturing plants were closed. Profits were generally high, however, mostly because of an improved product mix. The automotive airbag business did very well, with sales more than 30% higher than the previous year. However, toward the end of the year, questions were being raised about the safety of airbags, and this put the future of this business in some jeopardy. The salt business had dramatically increased volume because of the demand for ice-control salt due to an unusually severe winter in the northeastern United States. However, ice-control salt has a low profit margin, and so profits were up only modestly.

The current assets portion of Morton International's balance sheet for a recent year is shown on page 311.

MORTON INTERNATIONAL, INC.		
:--	--:	
Balance Sheet (partial)		
(in millions)		
Current assets		
Cash and cash equivalents	$ 138.0	
Receivables, less allowance of $10.8	468.6	
Inventories	381.0	
Other current assets	125.4	
Total current assets	$1,113.0	

Assume that the following transactions occurred during June and July.

1. Office supplies were shipped to Morton by Office Max, FOB destination. The goods were shipped June 29 and received June 30.
2. Morton purchased specialty plastic from Uniroyal Technology for use in airbag manufacture. The goods were shipped FOB shipping point July 1, and were received by Morton July 4.
3. Ford Motor Company purchased 10,000 airbags to be used in the manufacture of new cars. These were shipped FOB shipping point June 30, and were received by Ford July 2.
4. Bassett Furniture shipped office furniture to Morton, FOB destination, June 29. The goods were received July 3.
5. Inland Specialty Chemical shipped Morton chemicals that Morton uses in the manufacture of airbags and other items. The goods were sent FOB shipping point June 29, and were received July 1.
6. Morton purchased new automobiles for its executives from General Motors. The cars were shipped FOB destination June 19, and were received July 2.
7. Morton shipped salt to New York State Public Works, FOB Chicago, June 29. The shipment arrived in Chicago June 30 and in New York July 2.
8. Morton purchased steel, to be used in expanding its manufacturing plant, from Inland Steel, FOB Dallas. The steel was shipped June 30, arrived in Dallas July 2, and at Morton's plant July 6.
9. Morton shipped packaged salt to Associated Wholesale Grocers FOB Kansas City. The salt was shipped June 30, arrived in Kansas City July 1, and at Associated Wholesale Grocers' warehouse July 2.

Instructions
With the class divided into groups, answer the following:
 (a) Which items would be owned by Morton International as of June 30?
 (b) Which transactions involve Morton's inventory account?

COMMUNICATION ACTIVITIES

BYP6-9 In a discussion of dramatic increases in coffee bean prices, a *Wall Street Journal* article noted the following fact about **Starbucks**.

> Before this year's bean-price hike, Starbucks added several defenses that analysts say could help it maintain earnings and revenue. The company last year began accounting for its coffee-bean purchases by taking the average price of all beans in inventory.
>
> *Source:* Aaron Lucchetti, "Crowded Coffee Market May Keep a Lid on Starbucks After Price Rise Hurt Stock," *Wall Street Journal* (June 4, 1997), p. C1.

Prior to this change the company was using FIFO.

Instructions

Your client, the CEO of Hot Cup Coffee, Inc., read this article and sent you an e-mail message requesting that you explain why Starbucks might have taken this action. Your response should explain what impact this change in accounting method has on earnings, why the company might want to do this, and any possible disadvantages of such a change.

BYP6-10   You are the controller of Blue Jays Inc. B. J. Dell, the president, recently mentioned to you that she found an error in the 2004 financial statements which she believes has corrected itself. She determined, in discussions with the purchasing department, that 2004 ending inventory was overstated by $1 million. B. J. says that the 2005 ending inventory is correct, and she assumes that 2005 income is correct. B. J. says to you, "What happened has happened—there's no point in worrying about it anymore."

Instructions

You conclude that B. J. is incorrect. Write a brief, tactful memo to her, clarifying the situation.

ETHICS CASE

BYP6-11   Becker Wholesale Corp. uses the LIFO cost flow method. In the current year, profit at Becker is running unusually high. The corporate tax rate is also high this year, but it is scheduled to decline significantly next year. In an effort to lower the current year's net income and to take advantage of the changing income tax rate, the president of Becker Wholesale instructs the plant accountant to recommend to the purchasing department a large purchase of inventory for delivery 3 days before the end of the year. The price of the inventory to be purchased has doubled during the year, and the purchase will represent a major portion of the ending inventory value.

Instructions

    (a) What is the effect of this transaction on this year's and next year's income statement and income tax expense? Why?

    (b) If Becker Wholesale had been using the FIFO method of inventory costing, would the president give the same directive?

    (c) Should the plant accountant order the inventory purchase to lower income? What are the ethical implications of this order?

Answers to Self-Study Questions

1. d   2. a   3. c   4. d   5. c   6. d   7. a   8. d   9. a
*10. d   *11. b

Answer to Tootsie Roll Review It Question 2, p. 279

Tootsie Roll uses LIFO for U.S. inventories and FIFO for foreign inventories.

Remember to go back to the Navigator box on the chapter-opening page and check off your completed work.

Internal Control and Cash

STUDY OBJECTIVES

After studying this chapter,
you should be able to:

1 Identify the principles of internal control.

2 Explain the applications of internal control to cash receipts.

3 Explain the applications of internal control to cash disbursements.

4 Prepare a bank reconciliation.

5 Explain the reporting of cash.

6 Discuss the basic principles of cash management.

7 Identify the primary elements of a cash budget.

☑ THE NAVIGATOR

THE NAVIGATOR ✔

▶ Scan *Study Objectives*   ❑

▶ Read *Feature Story*   ❑

▶ Read *Preview*   ❑

▶ Read text and answer *Before You Go On*
   p. 321 ❑   p. 324 ❑   p. 331 ❑
   p. 337 ❑

▶ Work Using the *Decision Toolkit*   ❑

▶ Review Summary of *Study Objectives*   ❑

▶ Work *Demonstration Problem*   ❑

▶ Answer *Self-Study Questions*   ❑

▶ Complete *Assignments*   ❑

FEATURE STORY

It Takes a Thief

Have you seen this man? Fifty years old, thinning brown hair, hump on back, bulbous red nose with prominent veins, and wart on upper lip, goes by the name David Shelton—and at least 14 other names. David Shelton is good at what he does. He's a thief who specializes in inside jobs. It's believed that in seven recent years, while working as a bookkeeper for small businesses, he stole at least $600,000.

Ask Celia Imperiale. She hired Mr. Shelton after he responded to an employment ad she placed for a bookkeeper. His resume boasted 20 years of experience with two different employers. He had been with his "current" employer since 1981. When Ms. Imperiale called the number of this "current" employer, she was greeted by a woman who answered with the corporate name and then was transferred to the owner of the company. The owner gave a glowing recommendation. Ms. Imperiale also tried to call the previous employer, but she couldn't find a listing. Since it had been more than 12 years since Mr. Shelton had worked there, she didn't worry about it. But the "current" reference was phony. The phone number that Ms. Imperiale called belonged to a room at a low-rent motel. The glowing reference was given by Mr. Shelton's accomplice.

Mr. Shelton was a reasonably good employee, giving Ms. Imperiale no cause for concern until the day her auditor showed up—which by coincidence was the day after the last time she saw Mr. Shelton. Mr. Shelton had stolen $44,000, mainly by pocketing cash receipts from Ms. Imperiale's three stores. He filled out a proper bank deposit slip, which she always checked. But on his way to the bank he made out a new deposit slip for 10% less than the total; then he deposited 90% and kept 10% for himself. He hid his theft by manipulating the accounting records and by not paying the company's state and federal taxes as they came due. At previous companies Mr. Shelton had pocketed money by creating phony suppliers who billed his employer for work never done. He then made out a check to the phony company and sent it to a bank account that he controlled under another phony name.

Mr. Shelton was careful to leave little evidence. He drove nondescript cars, which he parked far away from where he both worked and lived. He didn't attend corporate social functions and was never in corporate pictures. When he left Ms. Imperiale's company, he stole all of his personnel files. Ms. Imperiale is probably still paying off the loan she had to take out to pay the back taxes that Mr. Shelton didn't pay.

Postscript: David Shelton (whose real name is Donald Peterson) was apprehended when a small business owner recognized him as one of his employees after reading about him in a *Wall Street Journal* article.

Source: Adapted from J. R. Emshwiller, "Looking for a New Bookkeeper? Beware of This One," *Wall Street Journal* (April 19, 1994), p. B1. Copyright 1994 by DOW JONES & CO. INC. Reproduced with permission of DOW JONES & CO. INC. in the format textbook via Copyright Clearance Center.

☑ THE NAVIGATOR

Cash is the lifeblood of any company. Large and small companies alike must guard it carefully. Even companies that are in every other way successful can go bankrupt if they fail to manage cash. Managers must know both how to use cash efficiently and how to protect it. Due to its liquid nature, cash is the easiest asset to steal. As the Feature Story suggests, a particularly difficult problem arises when a company has a dishonest employee.

In this chapter you will learn ways to reduce the risk of theft of cash and other assets, how to report cash in the financial statements, and how to manage cash. The content and organization of the chapter are as follows.

Internal Control

In a 2002 publication sponsored by the Association of Certified Fraud Examiners, it was estimated that fraud costs U.S. organizations more than $600 billion annually. Findings such as these, as well as situations such as the one described in the Feature Story, emphasize the need for a good system of internal control.

Internal control consists of all the related methods and measures adopted within a business to:

1. **Safeguard its assets** from employee theft, robbery, and unauthorized use; and

2. **Enhance the accuracy and reliability of its accounting records** by reducing the risk of errors (unintentional mistakes) and irregularities (intentional mistakes and misrepresentations) in the accounting process.

All major U.S. corporations are required by law to maintain an adequate system of internal control. Companies that fail to comply are subject to fines, and company officers may be imprisoned.

PRINCIPLES OF INTERNAL CONTROL

To safeguard assets and enhance the accuracy and reliability of its accounting records, a company follows internal control principles. The specific control measures used vary with the size and nature of the business and with management's control philosophy. However, the six principles listed in Illustration 7-1 apply to most enterprises. Each principle is explained in the following sections.

315

Illustration 7-1 Principles of internal control

Transfer of cash drawers

Establishment of Responsibility

An essential characteristic of internal control is the assignment of responsibility to specific individuals. **Control is most effective when only one person is responsible for a given task.** To illustrate, assume that the cash on hand at the end of the day in a **Safeway** supermarket is $10 short of the cash rung up on the cash register. If only one person has operated the register, responsibility for the shortage can be assessed quickly. If two or more individuals have worked the register, it may be impossible to determine who is responsible for the error unless each person is assigned a separate cash drawer and register key.

Establishing responsibility includes the authorization and approval of transactions. The vice-president of sales should have the authority to establish policies for making credit sales. These policies ordinarily will require written credit department approval of credit sales.

Segregation of Duties

Segregation of duties is indispensable in a system of internal control. **The rationale for segregation of duties is that the work of one employee should, without a duplication of effort, provide a reliable basis for evaluating the work of another employee.** There are two common applications of this principle:

1. The responsibility for related activities should be assigned to different individuals.

2. The responsibility for record keeping for an asset should be separate from the physical custody of that asset.

RELATED ACTIVITIES. Related activities should be assigned to different individuals in both the purchasing and selling areas. **When one individual is responsible for all of the related activities, the potential for errors and irregularities is increased.**

Related purchasing activities include ordering merchandise, receiving goods, and paying (or authorizing payment) for merchandise. In purchasing, for example, orders could be placed with friends or with suppliers who give kickbacks.

In addition, payment might be authorized without a careful review of the invoice, or, even worse, fictitious invoices might be approved for payment. When the responsibilities for ordering, receiving, and paying are assigned to different individuals, the risk of such abuses is minimized.

Related sales activities also should be assigned to different individuals. Related sales activities include making a sale, shipping (or delivering) the goods to the customer, and billing the customer. When one person is responsible for these related sales transactions, a salesperson could make sales at unauthorized prices to increase sales commissions, a shipping clerk could ship goods to himself, or a billing clerk could understate the amount billed for sales made to friends and relatives. These abuses are less likely to occur when salespersons make the sale, shipping department employees ship the goods on the basis of the sales order, and billing department employees prepare the sales invoice after comparing the sales order with the report of goods shipped.

RECORD KEEPING SEPARATE FROM PHYSICAL CUSTODY. If accounting is to provide a valid basis of accountability for an asset, the accountant (as record keeper) should have neither physical custody of the asset nor access to it. Moreover, the custodian of the asset should not maintain or have access to the accounting records. **The custodian of the asset is not likely to convert the asset to personal use if one employee maintains the record of the asset that should be on hand and a different employee has physical custody of the asset.** The separation of accounting responsibility from the custody of assets is especially important for cash and inventories because these assets are very vulnerable to unauthorized use or misappropriation.

The segregation of duties is shown in Illustration 7-2.

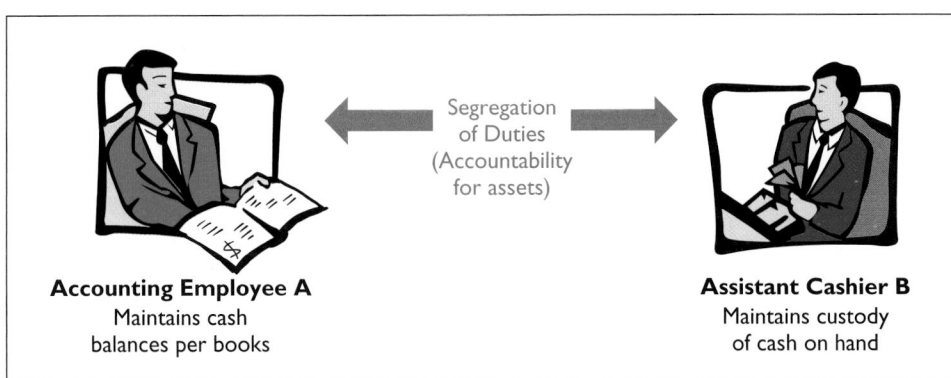

Segregation
of Duties
(Accountability
for assets)

Accounting Employee A
Maintains cash
balances per books

Assistant Cashier B
Maintains custody
of cash on hand

Illustration 7-2 The segregation of duties (accountability for assets) principle

Documentation Procedures

Documents provide evidence that transactions and events have occurred. For example, the shipping document indicates that the goods have been shipped, and the sales invoice indicates that the customer has been billed for the goods. By adding signatures (or initials) to the documents, the individual(s) responsible for the transaction or event can be identified.

Procedures should be established for documents. First, whenever possible, **documents should be prenumbered, and all documents should be accounted for**. Prenumbering helps to prevent a transaction from being recorded more than once or, conversely, to prevent the transactions from not being recorded. Second, documents that are **source documents for accounting entries should be promptly forwarded to the accounting department to help ensure timely recording of the transaction and event**. This control measure contributes directly to the accuracy and reliability of the accounting records.

Helpful Hint An important corollary to prenumbering is that voided documents be kept until all documents are accounted for.

Business Insight
MANAGEMENT PERSPECTIVE

It's said that accountants' predecessors were the scribes of ancient Egypt, who kept the pharaohs' books. They inventoried grain, gold, and other assets. Unfortunately, some fell victim to temptation and stole from their leader, as did other employees of the king. The solution was to have two scribes independently record each transaction (the first internal control). As long as the scribes' totals agreed exactly, there was no problem. But if the totals were materially different, both scribes would be put to death. That proved to be a great incentive for them to carefully check all the numbers and make sure the help wasn't stealing. In fact, fraud prevention and detection became the royal accountants' main duty.

SOURCE: Joseph T. Wells, "So That's Why It's Called a Pyramid Scheme," *Journal of Accountancy* (October 2000), p. 91. Copyright © 2000 from the Journal of Accountancy by the American Institute of Certified Public Accountants, Inc. Opinions of the authors are their own and do not necessarily reflect policies of the AICPA. Reprinted with permission.

Physical, Mechanical, and Electronic Controls

Use of physical, mechanical, and electronic controls is essential. Physical controls relate primarily to the safeguarding of assets. Mechanical and electronic controls safeguard assets and enhance the accuracy and reliability of the accounting records. Examples of these controls are shown in Illustration 7-3.

Illustration 7-3 Physical, mechanical, and electronic controls

Physical Controls

Safes, vaults, and safety deposit boxes for cash and business papers

Locked warehouses and storage cabinets for inventories and records

Computer facilities with pass key access or fingerprint or eyeball scans

Mechanical and Electronic Controls

Alarms to prevent break-ins

Television monitors and garment sensors to deter theft

Time clocks for recording time worked

A crucial consideration in programming computerized systems is building in controls that limit unauthorized or unintentional tampering. Entire books and movies have been produced with computer system tampering as a major theme. Most programmers would agree that tamper-proofing and debugging programs are the most difficult and time-consuming phases of their jobs. Program controls built into the computer prevent intentional or unintentional errors or unauthorized access. To prevent unauthorized access, the computer system may require that passwords be entered and random personal questions be correctly answered, or that biometric controls such as fingerprint or eyeball scans be used, before system access is allowed. Once access has been allowed, other program controls identify data having a value higher or lower than a predetermined amount (limit checks), validate computations (math checks), and detect improper processing order (sequence checks).

Independent Internal Verification

Most systems of internal control provide for independent internal verification. This principle involves the review, comparison, and reconciliation of data prepared by employees. Three measures are recommended to obtain maximum benefit from independent internal verification:

1. The verification should be made periodically or on a surprise basis.
2. The verification should be done by an employee who is independent of the personnel responsible for the information.
3. Discrepancies and exceptions should be reported to a management level that can take appropriate corrective action.

Independent internal verification is especially useful in comparing recorded accountability with existing assets. The reconciliation of the cash register tape with the cash in the register is an example. Another common example is the reconciliation by an independent person of the cash balance per books with the cash balance per bank. The relationship between this principle and the segregation of duties principle is shown graphically in Illustration 7-4.

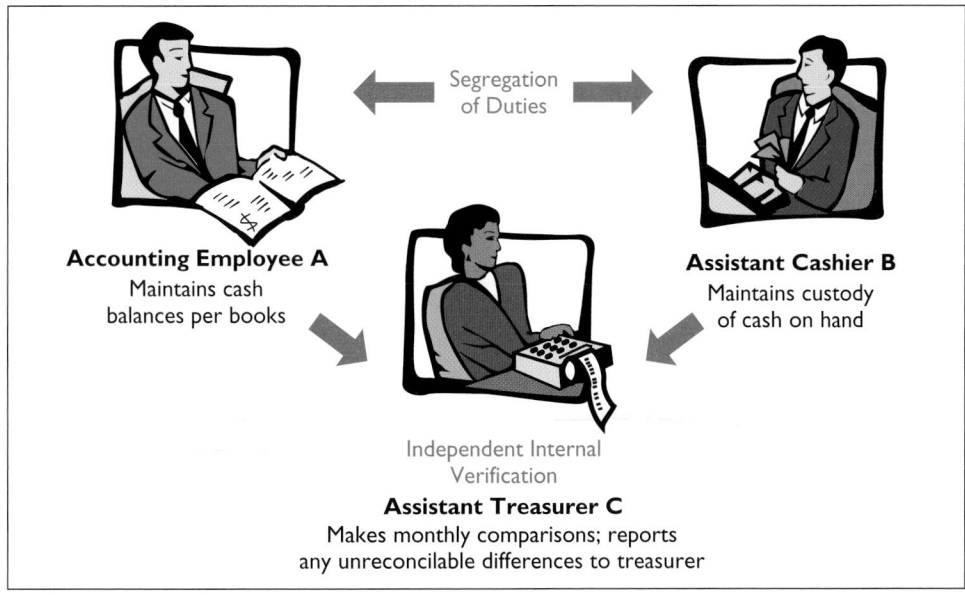

Illustration 7-4
Comparison of segregation of duties principle with independent internal verification principle

Segregation of Duties

Accounting Employee A
Maintains cash balances per books

Assistant Cashier B
Maintains custody of cash on hand

Independent Internal Verification
Assistant Treasurer C
Makes monthly comparisons; reports any unreconcilable differences to treasurer

In large companies, independent internal verification is often assigned to internal auditors. **Internal auditors** are employees of the company who evaluate on a continuous basis the effectiveness of the company's system of internal control. They periodically review the activities of departments and individuals to determine whether prescribed internal controls are being followed. The importance of this function is illustrated by the fact that most fraud is discovered by the company through internal mechanisms, such as existing internal controls and internal audits. The recent alleged fraud at **WorldCom** involving billions of dollars, for example, was uncovered by an internal auditor.

Other Controls

Here are two other control measures:

1. **Bonding of employees who handle cash.** Bonding involves obtaining insurance protection against misappropriation of assets by dishonest employees. This measure contributes to the safeguarding of cash in two ways: First, the insurance company carefully screens all individuals before adding them to the policy and may reject risky applicants. Second, bonded employees know that the insurance company will vigorously prosecute all offenders.

2. **Rotating employees' duties and requiring employees to take vacations.** These measures are designed to deter employees from attempting any thefts, since they will not be able to permanently conceal their improper actions. Many bank embezzlements, for example, have been discovered when the perpetrator has been on vacation or assigned to a new position.

DECISION TOOLKIT

Decision Checkpoints	Info Needed for Decision	Tool to Use for Decision	How to Evaluate Results
Are the company's financial statements supported by adequate internal controls?	Auditor's report, management discussion and analysis, articles in financial press	The required measures of internal control are to (1) establish responsibility, (2) segregate duties, (3) document procedures, (4) employ physical or automated controls, and (5) use independent internal verification.	If any indication is given that these or other controls are lacking, the financial statements should be used with caution.

LIMITATIONS OF INTERNAL CONTROL

A company's system of internal control is generally designed to provide **reasonable assurance** that assets are properly safeguarded and that the accounting records are reliable. **The concept of reasonable assurance rests on the premise that the costs of establishing control procedures should not exceed their expected benefit.**

To illustrate, consider shoplifting losses in retail stores. Such losses could be completely eliminated by having a security guard stop and search customers as they leave the store. Store managers have concluded, however, that the negative effects of this procedure cannot be justified. Instead, stores have attempted to "control" shoplifting losses by less costly procedures such as: (1) posting signs saying, "We reserve the right to inspect all packages" and "All shoplifters will be prosecuted," (2) using hidden TV cameras and store detectives to monitor customer activity, and (3) using sensor equipment at exits.

The **human element** is an important factor in every system of internal control. A good system can become ineffective as a result of employee fatigue, carelessness, or indifference. For example, a receiving clerk may not bother to count goods received or may just "fudge" the counts. Occasionally, two or more individuals may work together to get around prescribed controls. Such **collusion** can significantly impair the effectiveness of a system because it eliminates the protection anticipated from segregation of duties. If a supervisor and a cashier collaborate to understate cash receipts, the system of internal control may be subverted (at least in the short run). No system of internal control is perfect.

The size of the business may impose limitations on internal control. In a small company, for example, it may be difficult to apply the principles of segregation of duties and independent internal verification because of the small number of employees.

It has been suggested that the most important and inexpensive measure any business can take to reduce employee theft and fraud is to conduct thorough background checks. Two tips: (1) Check to see whether job applicants actually graduated from the schools they list. (2) Never use the telephone numbers for previous employers given on the reference sheet; always look them up yourself.

⊕ **International Note**

Other countries also have control problems. For example, a judge in France has issued a 36-page book detailing many of the scams that are widespread, such as kickbacks in public-works contracts, the skimming of development aid money to Africa, and bribes on arms sales.

Business Insight
MANAGEMENT PERSPECTIVE

A study by the Association of Certified Fraud Examiners indicates that businesses with fewer than 100 employees are most at risk for employee theft. Also, the average loss per incident for small companies—$127,500—was actually higher than the average loss for larger companies. The high degree of trust often found in small companies makes them more vulnerable to dishonest employees. For example, in one small company the employee responsible for paying bills would intentionally ask the owner to sign checks only when the owner was extremely busy. The employee would slip in one check that was made out to himself, and the owner didn't notice because he was too busy to carefully review each check.

SOURCE: Joseph T. Wells, "Occupational Fraud: The Audit as Deterrent," *Journal of Accountancy* (April 2002), pp. 24–28.

BEFORE YOU GO ON . . .

▶ Review It

1. What are the two primary objectives of internal control?
2. Identify and describe the principles of internal control.
3. What are the limitations of internal control?

▶ Do It

Li Song owns a small retail store. Li wants to establish good internal control procedures but is confused about the difference between segregation of duties and independent internal verification. Explain the differences to Li.

Action Plan

• Understand and explain the differences between (1) segregation of duties and (2) independent internal verification.

Solution

Segregation of duties relates to the assignment of responsibility so that (1) the work of one employee will check the work of another employee and (2) physical control of assets is separated from the records that keep track of the assets. Segregation of duties occurs daily in using assets and in executing and recording transactions. In contrast, independent internal verification involves reviewing, comparing, and reconciling data prepared by one or several employees. Independent internal verification occurs after the fact, as in reconciling cash register totals at the end of the day with cash on hand.

☑ THE NAVIGATOR

Cash Controls

Just as cash is the beginning of a company's operating cycle, it is usually the starting point for a company's system of internal control. Cash is the one asset that is readily convertible into any other type of asset; it is easily concealed and transported; and it is highly desired. Because of these characteristics, cash is the asset most susceptible to improper diversion and use. Moreover, because of the large volume of cash transactions, numerous errors may occur in executing and recording cash transactions. To safeguard cash and to ensure the accuracy of the accounting records for cash, effective internal control over cash is imperative.

Cash consists of coins, currency (paper money), checks, money orders, and money on hand or on deposit in a bank or similar depository. The general rule is that if the bank will accept it for deposit, it is cash. The application of internal control principles to cash receipts and cash disbursements is explained in the next sections.

STUDY OBJECTIVE
2
Explain the applications of internal control to cash receipts.

Illustration 7-5
Application of internal control principles to cash receipts

INTERNAL CONTROL OVER CASH RECEIPTS

Cash receipts result from a variety of sources: cash sales; collections on account from customers; the receipt of interest, rents, and dividends; investments by owners; bank loans; and proceeds from the sale of noncurrent assets. The internal control principles explained earlier apply to cash receipts transactions as shown in Illustration 7-5. As might be expected, companies vary considerably in how they apply these principles.

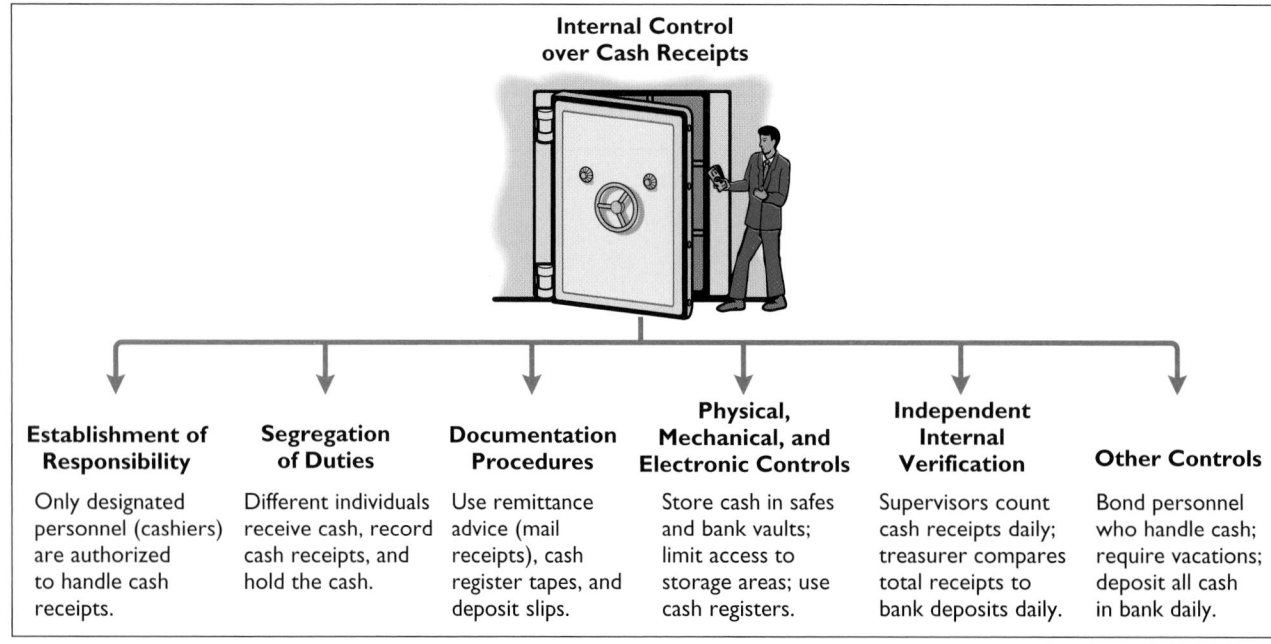

Internal Control over Cash Receipts

Establishment of Responsibility	Segregation of Duties	Documentation Procedures	Physical, Mechanical, and Electronic Controls	Independent Internal Verification	Other Controls
Only designated personnel (cashiers) are authorized to handle cash receipts.	Different individuals receive cash, record cash receipts, and hold the cash.	Use remittance advice (mail receipts), cash register tapes, and deposit slips.	Store cash in safes and bank vaults; limit access to storage areas; use cash registers.	Supervisors count cash receipts daily; treasurer compares total receipts to bank deposits daily.	Bond personnel who handle cash; require vacations; deposit all cash in bank daily.

INTERNAL CONTROL OVER CASH DISBURSEMENTS

STUDY OBJECTIVE
——3——
Explain the applications of internal control to cash disbursements.

Cash is disbursed for a variety of reasons, such as to <u>pay expenses</u> and liabilities or to <u>purchase assets</u>. **Generally, internal control over cash disbursements is more effective when payments are made by check, rather than by cash, except for incidental amounts that are paid out of petty cash.** Payment is made by check generally only after specified control procedures have been followed. In addition, the "paid" check provides proof of payment. The principles of internal control apply to cash disbursements as shown in Illustration 7-6.

Illustration 7-6
Application of internal control principles to cash disbursements

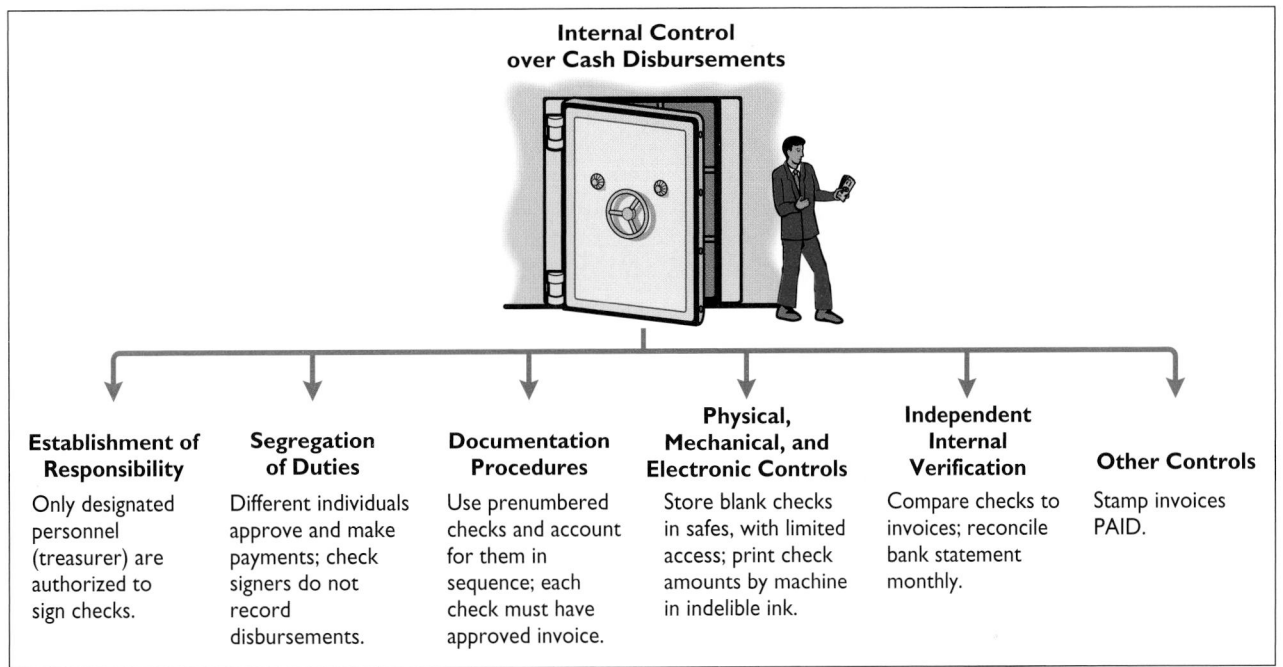

Internal Control over Cash Disbursements

Establishment of Responsibility	Segregation of Duties	Documentation Procedures	Physical, Mechanical, and Electronic Controls	Independent Internal Verification	Other Controls
Only designated personnel (treasurer) are authorized to sign checks.	Different individuals approve and make payments; check signers do not record disbursements.	Use prenumbered checks and account for them in sequence; each check must have approved invoice.	Store blank checks in safes, with limited access; print check amounts by machine in indelible ink.	Compare checks to invoices; reconcile bank statement monthly.	Stamp invoices PAID.

Business Insight
MANAGEMENT PERSPECTIVE

John Patterson suspected pilferage and sloppy bookkeeping by store clerks at his retail business. Frustrated, he placed an order with a Dayton, Ohio, company for two rudimentary cash registers. A year later Patterson's store was in the black.

"What is a good thing for this little store is a good thing for every retail store in the world," he observed. A few months later, in 1884, John Patterson and his brother, Frank, bought the tiny cash register maker for $6,500.

Patterson died in 1922, the year in which his company, **National Cash Register Co.**, sold its two millionth cash register. The Patterson brothers would be surprised to see how technology has changed the cash register. One thing hasn't changed, though: the cash register is still a critical component of internal control.

SOURCE: *Wall Street Journal* (January 28, 1989).

Electronic Funds Transfer (EFT) System

Accounting for and controlling cash is an expensive and time-consuming process. The cost to process a check through a bank system is about $1.00 per check and is increasing. But it costs only 35¢ if the customer uses the telephone and 1¢ if the customer uses the computer. It is not surprising, therefore, that new approaches are being developed to transfer funds among parties without the use of paper (deposit tickets, checks, etc.). Such procedures, called **electronic funds transfers (EFT)**, are disbursement systems that use wire, telephone, telegraph, or computer to transfer cash from one location to another. Use of EFT is quite common. For example, many employees receive no formal payroll checks from their employers, which instead send magnetic tapes to the appropriate banks for deposit. Regular payments such as those for house, car, or utilities are frequently made by EFT.

Petty Cash Fund

As you learned earlier in the chapter, better internal control over cash disbursements is possible when payments are made by check. However, using checks to pay such small amounts as those for postage due, employee working lunches, and taxi fares is both impractical and a nuisance. A common way of handling such payments, while maintaining satisfactory control, is to use a petty cash fund. A **petty cash fund** is a cash fund used to pay relatively small amounts. Information regarding the operation of a petty cash fund is provided in the appendix at the end of this chapter.

BEFORE YOU GO ON . . .

▶ Review It

1. How do the principles of internal control apply to cash receipts?
2. How do the principles of internal control apply to cash disbursements?
3. What is the purpose of a petty cash fund?

▶ Do It

L. R. Cortez is concerned about control over cash receipts in his fast-food restaurant, Big Cheese. The restaurant has two cash registers. At no time do more than two employees take customer orders and ring up sales. Work shifts for employees range from 4 to 8 hours. Cortez asks your help in installing a good system of internal control over cash receipts.

Action Plan
- Differentiate among the internal control principles of (1) establishing responsibility, (2) using electronic controls, and (3) independent internal verification.
- Design an effective system of internal control over cash receipts.

Solution
Cortez should assign a cash register to each employee at the start of each work shift, with register totals set at zero. Each employee should be instructed to use only the assigned register and to ring up all sales. At the end of each work shift, Cortez or a supervisor/manager should total the register and make a cash count to see whether all cash is accounted for.

✔ THE NAVIGATOR

USE OF A BANK

The use of a bank contributes significantly to good internal control over cash. A company can safeguard its cash by using a bank as a depository and clearinghouse for checks received and checks written. The use of a bank minimizes the amount of currency that must be kept on hand. In addition, it facilitates the control of cash because a double record is maintained of all bank transactions—one by the business and the other by the bank. The asset account Cash maintained by the company is the "flip-side" of the bank's liability account for that company. It should be possible to **reconcile these accounts**—make them agree—at any time.

Many companies have more than one bank account. For efficiency of operations and better control, national retailers like **Wal-Mart** and **Target** often have regional bank accounts. Similarly, a company such as **ExxonMobil** with more than 150,000 employees may have a payroll bank account as well as one or more general bank accounts. In addition, a company may maintain several bank accounts in order to have more than one source for obtaining short-term loans when needed.

Bank Statements

Each month, the company receives from the bank a **bank statement** showing its bank transactions and balances.[1] For example, the statement for Laird Company in Illustration 7-7 (on page 326) shows the following: (1) checks paid and other debits that reduce the balance in the depositor's account, (2) deposits and other credits that increase the balance in the depositor's account, and (3) the account balance after each day's transactions. Remember that bank statements are prepared from the *bank's* perspective. For example, every deposit received by the bank is an increase in the bank's liabilities (an account payable to the depositor). Therefore, every deposit received from Laird Company by the National Bank and Trust is *credited* by the bank to Laird Company. The reverse occurs when the bank "pays" a check issued by Laird Company on its checking account balance: Payment reduces the bank's liability and is therefore *debited* to Laird's account with the bank.

All paid checks are listed in numerical sequence on the bank statement along with the date the check was paid and its amount. Upon paying a check, the bank stamps the check "paid"; a paid check is sometimes referred to as a **canceled** check. In addition, the bank includes with the bank statement memoranda explaining other debits and credits made by the bank to the depositor's account.

A debit memorandum is used by the bank when a previously deposited customer's check "bounces" because of insufficient funds. In such a case, the check is marked **NSF** (not sufficient funds) by the customer's bank and is returned to the depositor's bank. The bank then debits (decreases) the depositor's account, as shown by the symbol NSF on the bank statement in Illustration 7-7, and sends the NSF check and debit memorandum to the depositor as notification of the charge. The NSF check creates an account receivable for the depositor and reduces cash in the bank account.

Helpful Hint Essentially, the bank statement is a copy of the bank's records sent to the customer for periodic review.

---

[1] Our presentation assumes that all adjustments are made at the end of the month. In practice, a company may also make journal entries during the month as it receives information from the bank regarding its account.

Illustration 7-7 Bank statement

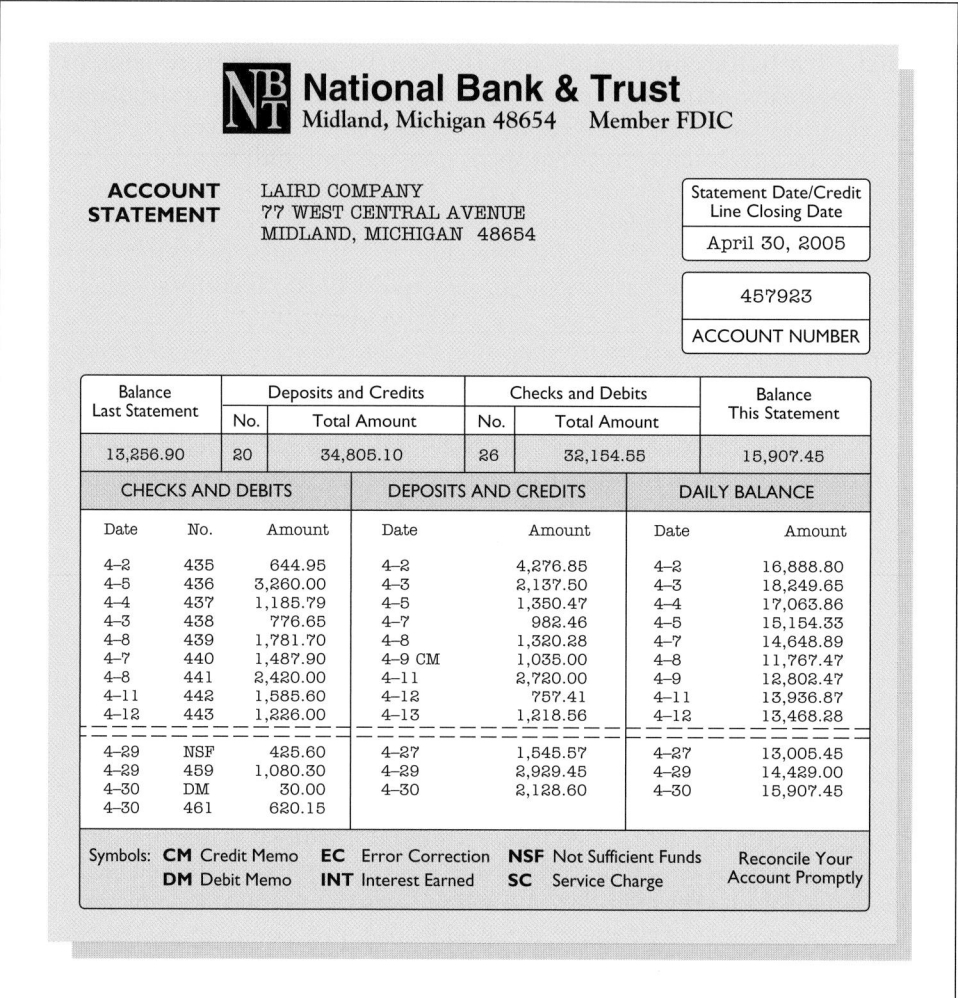

National Bank & Trust
Midland, Michigan 48654   Member FDIC

| ACCOUNT STATEMENT | LAIRD COMPANY 77 WEST CENTRAL AVENUE MIDLAND, MICHIGAN 48654 | Statement Date/Credit Line Closing Date April 30, 2005 |

457923
ACCOUNT NUMBER

Balance Last Statement	Deposits and Credits		Checks and Debits		Balance This Statement
	No.	Total Amount	No.	Total Amount	
13,256.90	20	34,805.10	26	32,154.55	15,907.45

CHECKS AND DEBITS			DEPOSITS AND CREDITS		DAILY BALANCE	
Date	No.	Amount	Date	Amount	Date	Amount
4-2	435	644.95	4-2	4,276.85	4-2	16,888.80
4-5	436	3,260.00	4-3	2,137.50	4-3	18,249.65
4-4	437	1,185.79	4-5	1,350.47	4-4	17,063.86
4-3	438	776.65	4-7	982.46	4-5	15,154.33
4-8	439	1,781.70	4-8	1,320.28	4-7	14,648.89
4-7	440	1,487.90	4-9 CM	1,035.00	4-8	11,767.47
4-8	441	2,420.00	4-11	2,720.00	4-9	12,802.47
4-11	442	1,585.60	4-12	757.41	4-11	13,936.87
4-12	443	1,226.00	4-13	1,218.56	4-12	13,468.28
4-29	NSF	425.60	4-27	1,545.57	4-27	13,005.45
4-29	459	1,080.30	4-29	2,929.45	4-29	14,429.00
4-30	DM	30.00	4-30	2,128.60	4-30	15,907.45
4-30	461	620.15				

Symbols: **CM** Credit Memo   **EC** Error Correction   **NSF** Not Sufficient Funds
          DM Debit Memo   **INT** Interest Earned   **SC** Service Charge

Reconcile Your Account Promptly

Business Insight
MANAGEMENT PERSPECTIVE

Banks charge fees for bounced checks. That is, if you overdraw a business or personal account, you may pay as much as $30 for each bad check. What you might not know is that many banks process checks from largest amount to smallest, in order to maximize the number of bounced checks, and therefore to maximize the revenue they earn from bounced checks. Overdrawing your account could cost you much more than you might think.

STUDY OBJECTIVE
4
Prepare a bank reconciliation.

Reconciling the Bank Account

Because the bank and the company maintain independent records of the company's checking account, you might assume that the respective balances will always agree. In fact, the two balances are seldom the same at any given time. Therefore it is necessary to make the balance per books agree with the balance per bank—a process called **reconciling the bank account**. The lack of agreement between the balances has two causes:

1. **Time lags** that prevent one of the parties from recording the transaction in the same period.
2. **Errors** by either party in recording transactions.

Time lags occur frequently. For example, several days may elapse between the time a company pays by check and the date the check is paid by the bank. Similarly, when a company uses the bank's night depository to make its deposits, there will be a difference of one day between the time the receipts are recorded by the company and the time they are recorded by the bank. A time lag also occurs whenever the bank mails a debit or credit memorandum to the company.

Business Insight
ETHICS PERSPECTIVE

Some companies have used time lags to their advantage. For example, E. F. Hutton managers at one time overdrew their accounts by astronomical amounts—on some days the overdrafts totaled $1 billion—creating interest-free loans they could invest. The loans lasted as long as it took for the covering checks to clear the bank. Although not technically illegal at the time, Hutton's actions were wrong because it did not have bank permission to do so.

The incidence of errors depends on the effectiveness of the internal controls maintained by the company and the bank. Bank errors are infrequent. However, either party could accidentally record a $450 check as $45 or $540. In addition, the bank might mistakenly charge a check drawn by C. D. Berg to the account of C. D. Burg.

RECONCILIATION PROCEDURE.   In reconciling the bank account, it is customary to reconcile the balance per books and balance per bank to their adjusted (correct or true) cash balances. **To obtain maximum benefit from a bank reconciliation, the reconciliation should be prepared by an employee who has no other responsibilities related to cash.** When the internal control principle of independent internal verification is not followed in preparing the reconciliation, cash embezzlements may escape unnoticed. For example, in the Feature Story, a bank reconciliation by someone other than Mr. Shelton might have exposed his embezzlement.

The reconciliation process is shown in Illustration 7-8 (on page 328). The starting point in preparing the reconciliation is to enter the balance per bank statement and balance per books on a schedule. The following steps should reveal all the reconciling items that cause the difference between the two balances.

1. Compare the individual deposits on the bank statement with the deposits in transit from the preceding bank reconciliation and with the deposits per company records or copies of duplicate deposit slips. Deposits recorded by the depositor that have not been recorded by the bank represent **deposits in transit**. These deposits are added to the balance per bank.

Helpful Hint Deposits in transit and outstanding checks are reconciling items because of time lags.

Illustration 7-8 Bank
reconciliation procedures

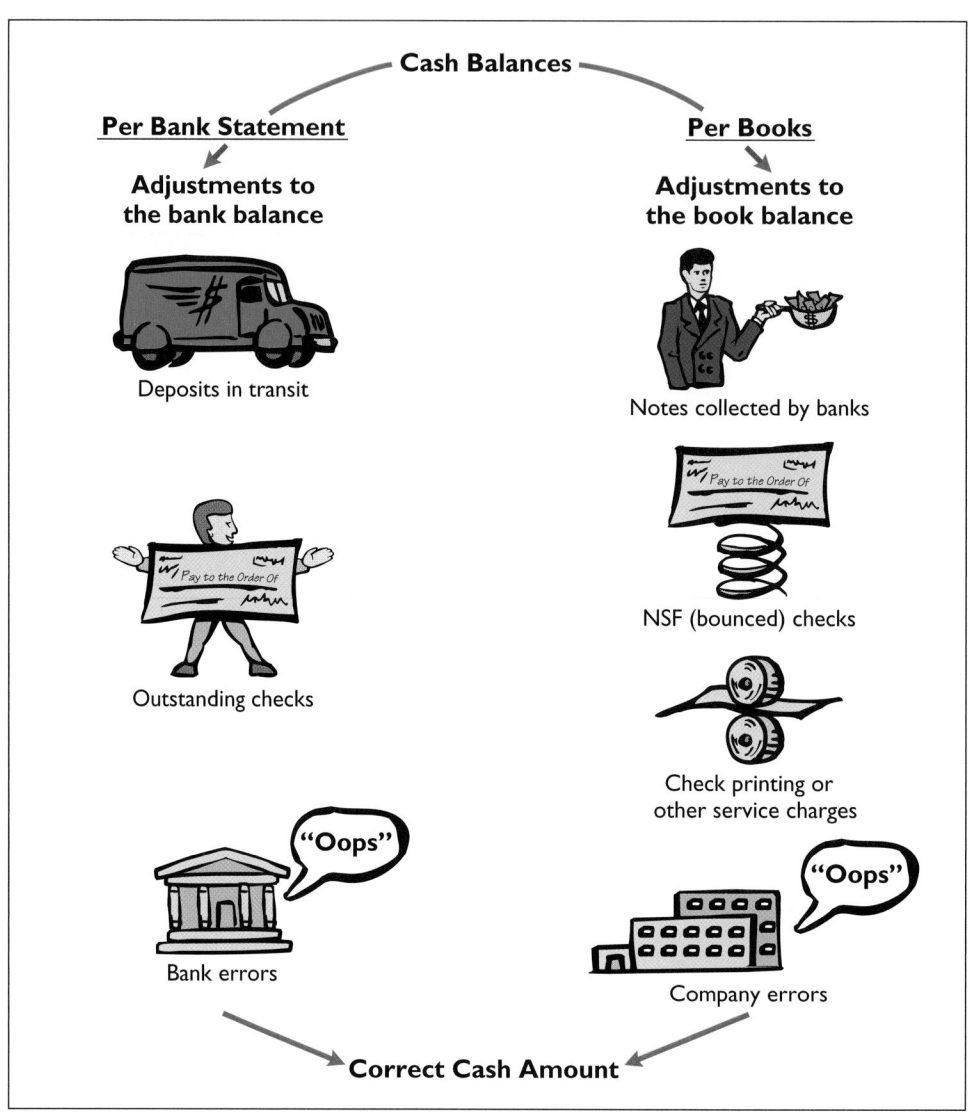

2. Compare the paid checks shown on the bank statement or the paid checks returned with the bank statement with (a) checks outstanding from the preceding bank reconciliation, and (b) checks issued by the company as recorded in the cash payments journal. Issued checks recorded by the company that have not been paid by the bank represent **outstanding checks** that are deducted from the balance per the bank.

3. Note any **errors** discovered in the foregoing steps and list them in the appropriate section of the reconciliation schedule. For example, if a paid check correctly written by the company for $195 was mistakenly recorded by the company for $159, the error of $36 is deducted from the balance per books. All errors made by the depositor are reconciling items in determining the adjusted cash balance per books. In contrast, all errors made by the bank are reconciling items in determining the adjusted cash balance per the bank.

4. Trace **bank memoranda** to the depositor's records. Any unrecorded memoranda should be listed in the appropriate section of the reconciliation schedule. For example, a $5 debit memorandum for bank service charges is

deducted from the balance per books, and a $32 credit memorandum for interest earned is added to the balance per books.

BANK RECONCILIATION ILLUSTRATED.
The bank statement for Laird Company was shown in Illustration 7-7 (page 326). It shows a balance per bank of $15,907.45 on April 30, 2005. On this date the balance of cash per books is $11,589.45. From the foregoing steps, the following reconciling items are determined.

Helpful Hint Note in the bank statement that checks No. 459 and 461 have been paid, but check No. 460 is not listed. Thus, this check is outstanding. If a complete bank statement were provided, checks No. 453 and 457 also would not be listed. The amounts for these three checks are obtained from the company's cash payments records.

1. **Deposits in transit:** April 30 deposit (received by bank on May 1). $2,201.40
2. **Outstanding checks:** No. 453, $3,000.00; No. 457, $1,401.30; No. 460, $1,502.70. 5,904.00
3. **Errors:** Check No. 443 was correctly written by Laird for $1,226.00 and was correctly paid by the bank. However, it was recorded for $1,262.00 by Laird Company. 36.00
4. **Bank memoranda:**
   (a) Debit—NSF check from J. R. Baron for $425.60 425.60
   (b) Debit—Printing company checks charge, $30 30.00
   (c) Credit—Collection of note receivable for $1,000 plus interest earned $50, less bank collection fee $15 1,035.00

The bank reconciliation is shown in Illustration 7-9.

LAIRD COMPANY
Bank Reconciliation
April 30, 2005

Cash balance per bank statement		$ 15,907.45
Add: Deposits in transit		2,201.40
		18,108.85
Less: Outstanding checks		
No. 453	$3,000.00	
No. 457	1,401.30	
No. 460	1,502.70	5,904.00
Adjusted cash balance per bank		**$12,204.85**
Cash balance per books		$ 11,589.45
Add: Collection of note receivable for $1,000 plus interest earned $50, less collection fee $15	$1,035.00	
Error in recording check No. 443	36.00	1,071.00
		12,660.45
Less: NSF check	425.60	
Bank service charge	30.00	455.60
Adjusted cash balance per books		**$12,204.85**

Illustration 7-9 **Bank reconciliation**

Alternative Terminology The terms *adjusted cash balance*, *true cash balance*, and *correct cash balance* may be used interchangeably.

ENTRIES FROM BANK RECONCILIATION.
Each reconciling item used to determine the **adjusted cash balance per books** should be recorded by the depositor. If these items are not journalized and posted, the Cash account will not show the correct balance. The adjusting entries for the Laird Company bank reconciliation on April 30 are as follows.

Helpful Hint These entries are adjusting entries. In prior chapters, Cash was an account that did not require adjustment because a bank reconciliation had not been explained.

Collection of Note Receivable. This entry involves four accounts. Assuming that the interest of $50 has not been recorded and the collection fee is charged to Miscellaneous Expense, the entry is:

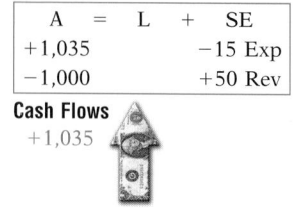

Apr. 30	Cash		1,035	
	Miscellaneous Expense		15	
	Notes Receivable			1,000
	Interest Revenue			50
	(To record collection of note			
	receivable by bank)			

Book Error. An examination of the cash disbursements journal shows that check No. 443 was a payment on account to Andrea Company, a supplier. The correcting entry is:

Apr. 30	Cash		36	
	Accounts Payable—Andrea Company			36
	(To correct error in recording check			
	No. 443)			

NSF Check. As indicated earlier, an NSF check becomes an accounts receivable to the depositor. The entry is:

Apr. 30	Accounts Receivable—J. R. Baron		425.60	
	Cash			425.60
	(To record NSF check)			

Bank Service Charges. Check printing charges (DM) and other bank service charges (SC) are debited to Miscellaneous Expense because they are usually nominal in amount. The entry is:

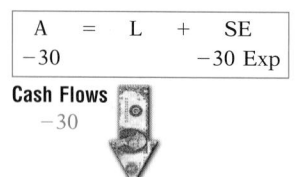

Apr. 30	Miscellaneous Expense		30	
	Cash			30
	(To record charge for printing company			
	checks)			

The foregoing entries could also be combined into one compound entry.

After the entries are posted, the cash account will appear as in Illustration 7-10. The adjusted cash balance in the ledger should agree with the adjusted cash balance per books in the bank reconciliation in Illustration 7-9.

Illustration 7-10 Adjusted balance in cash account

Cash					
Apr. 30	Bal.	11,589.45	Apr. 30		425.60
	30	1,035.00		30	30.00
	30	36.00			
Apr. 30	Bal.	**12,204.85**			

What entries does the bank make? If any bank errors are discovered in preparing the reconciliation, the bank should be notified so it can make the necessary corrections on its records. The bank does not make any entries for deposits in transit or outstanding checks. Only when these items reach the bank will the bank record these items.

BEFORE YOU GO ON . . .

▶ **Review It**

1. Why is it necessary to reconcile a bank account?
2. What steps are involved in the reconciliation procedure?
3. What information is included in a bank reconciliation?

▶ **Do It**

Sally Kist owns Linen Kist Fabrics. Sally asks you to explain how the following reconciling items should be treated in reconciling the bank account at December 31: (1) a debit memorandum for an NSF check, (2) a credit memorandum for a note collected by the bank, (3) outstanding checks, and (4) a deposit in transit.

Action Plan

• Understand the purpose of a bank reconciliation.
• Identify time lags and explain how they cause reconciling items.

Solution

In reconciling the bank account, the reconciling items are treated by Linen Kist Fabrics as follows.

NSF check: Deducted from balance per books.
Collection of note: Added to balance per books.
Outstanding checks: Deducted from balance per bank.
Deposit in transit: Added to balance per bank.

☑ THE NAVIGATOR

Reporting Cash

Cash is reported in two different statements: the balance sheet and the statement of cash flows. The balance sheet reports the amount of cash available at a given point in time. The statement of cash flows shows the sources and uses of cash during a period of time. The cash flow statement was introduced in Chapters 1 and 2 and will be discussed in much detail in Chapter 13. In this section we discuss some important points regarding the presentation of cash in the balance sheet.

When presented in a balance sheet, cash on hand, cash in banks, and petty cash are often combined and reported simply as **Cash**. Because it is the most liquid asset owned by the company, cash is listed first in the current assets section of the balance sheet.

STUDY OBJECTIVE
5
Explain the reporting of cash.

CASH EQUIVALENTS

Many companies use the designation "Cash and cash equivalents" in reporting cash, as shown in Illustration 7-11 for discount car-rental agency **Rent-A-Wreck of America, Inc. Cash equivalents** are short-term, highly liquid investments that are both:

1. Readily convertible to known amounts of cash, and

2. So near their maturity that their market value is relatively insensitive to changes in interest rates.

Examples of cash equivalents are Treasury bills, commercial paper (short-term corporate notes), and money market funds. All typically are purchased with cash that is in excess of immediate needs.

Illustration 7-11
Balance sheet
presentation of cash

RENT‑A‑WRECK

RENT-A-WRECK OF AMERICA, INC.
Balance Sheet (partial)
March 31, 2001
(in thousands)

Assets	
Current assets	
Cash and cash equivalents	$ 554,181
Restricted cash	892,061
Accounts receivable, net	937,377
Prepaid expenses and other	1,031,949
Total current assets	$3,415,568

Occasionally a company will have a net negative balance in its account at a bank. In this case, the negative balance should be reported among current liabilities. For example, farm equipment manufacturer **Ag-Chem** recently reported "Checks outstanding in excess of cash balances" of $2,145,000 among its current liabilities.

RESTRICTED CASH

A company may have cash that is not available for general use but rather is restricted for a special purpose. For example, landfill companies are often required to maintain a fund of restricted cash to ensure they will have adequate resources to cover closing and clean-up costs at the end of a landfill site's useful life. Cash restricted in use should be reported separately on the balance sheet as **restricted cash**. If the restricted cash is expected to be used within the next year, the amount should be reported as a current asset. When this is not the case, the restricted funds should be reported as a noncurrent asset.

Restricted cash is reported in the financial statements of **Rent-A-Wreck** in Illustration 7-11. The company is required to maintain restricted cash as part of

DECISION TOOLKIT

Decision Checkpoints	Info Needed for Decision	Tool to Use for Decision	How to Evaluate Results
Is all of the company's cash available for general use?	Balance sheet and notes to financial statements	Does the company report any cash as being restricted?	A restriction on the use of cash limits management's ability to use those resources for general obligations. This might be considered when assessing liquidity.

a letter of credit agreement with **Bank of America** and as part of a fund held on behalf of its franchisees, to be spent on advertising programs. The company does not have access to these funds for general use, and so they must be reported separately, rather than as part of cash and cash equivalents.

Managing and Monitoring Cash

Many companies struggle, not because they can't generate sales, but because they can't manage their cash. A real-life example of this is a clothing manufacturing company owned by Sharon McCollick. McCollick gave up a stable, high-paying marketing job with **Intel Corporation** to start her own company. Soon she had more orders from stores such as **JCPenney** and **Dayton Hudson** (now **Target**) than she could fill. Yet she found herself on the brink of financial disaster, owing three mortgage payments on her house and $2,000 to the IRS. Her company could generate sales, but it wasn't collecting cash fast enough to support its operations. The bottom line is that a business must have cash.[2]

A merchandising company's operating cycle is generally shorter than a manufacturing company's. The cash to cash operating cycle of a merchandising operation is shown graphically in Illustration 7-12.

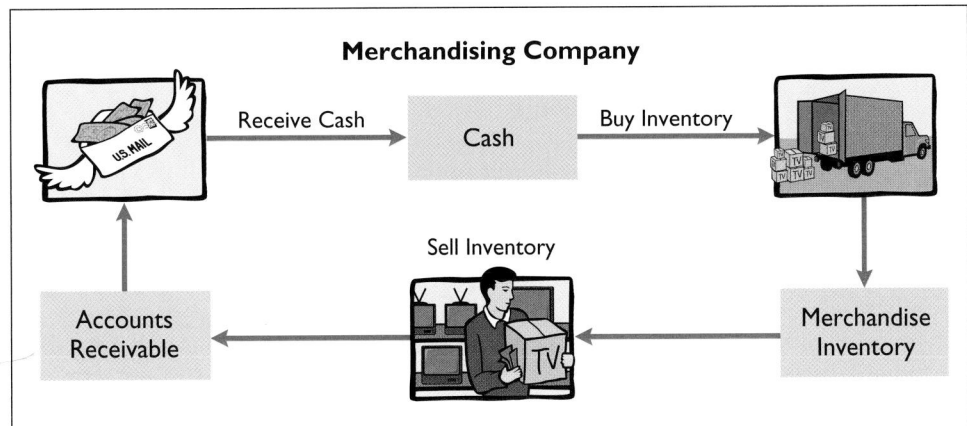

Illustration 7-12
Operating cycle of a merchandising company

To understand cash management, consider the operating cycle of Sharon McCollick's clothing manufacturing company. First, it purchases cloth. Let's assume that it purchases the cloth on credit provided by the supplier, so the company owes its supplier money. Next, employees convert the cloth to clothing. Now the company also owes its employees money. Next, it sells the clothing to retailers, on credit. McCollick's company will have no money to repay suppliers or employees until its customers pay it. In a manufacturing operation there may be a significant lag between the original purchase of raw materials and the ultimate receipt of cash from customers.

Managing the often precarious balance created by the ebb and flow of cash during the operating cycle is one of a company's greatest challenges. The objective is to ensure that a company has sufficient cash to meet payments as they come due, yet minimize the amount of non-revenue-generating cash on hand.

---

[2]Adapted from T. Petzinger, Jr., "The Front Lines—Sharon McCollick Got Mad and Tore Down a Bank's Barriers," *Wall Street Journal* (May 19, 1995), p. B1.

BASIC PRINCIPLES OF CASH MANAGEMENT

STUDY OBJECTIVE
6
Discuss the basic principles
of cash management.

Management of cash is the responsibility of the company **treasurer**. Any company can improve its chances of having adequate cash by following five basic principles of cash management.

1. **Increase the speed of collection of receivables.** Money owed Sharon McCollick by her customers is money that she can't use. The more quickly customers pay her, the more quickly she can use those funds. Thus, rather than have an average collection period of 30 days, she may want an average collection period of 15 days. However, any attempt to force her customers to pay earlier must be carefully weighed against the possibility that she may anger or alienate customers. Perhaps her competitors are willing to provide a 30-day grace period. As noted in Chapter 5, one common way to encourage customers to pay more quickly is to offer cash discounts for early payment under such terms as 2/10, n/30.

2. **Keep inventory levels low.** Maintaining a large inventory of cloth and finished clothing is costly. It ties up large amounts of cash, as well as warehouse space. Increasingly, firms are using techniques to reduce the inventory on hand, thus conserving their cash. Of course, if Sharon McCollick has inadequate inventory, she will lose sales. The proper level of inventory is an important decision.

3. **Delay payment of liabilities.** By keeping track of when her bills are due, Sharon McCollick's company can avoid paying bills too early. Let's say her supplier allows 30 days for payment. If she pays in 10 days, she has lost the use of cash for 20 days. Therefore, she should use the full payment period, but she should not "stretch" payment past the point that could damage her credit rating (and future borrowing ability). Sharon McCollick's company also should conserve cash by taking cash discounts offered by suppliers, when possible.

4. **Plan the timing of major expenditures.** To maintain operations or to grow, all companies must make major expenditures, which normally require some form of outside financing. In order to increase the likelihood of obtaining outside financing, McCollick should carefully consider the timing of major expenditures in light of her company's operating cycle. If at all possible, the expenditure should be made when the company normally has excess cash—usually during the off-season.

5. **Invest idle cash.** Cash on hand earns nothing. An important part of the treasurer's job is to ensure that any excess cash is invested, even if it is only overnight. Many businesses, such as Sharon McCollick's clothing company, are seasonal. During her slow season, when she has excess cash, she should invest it. To avoid a cash crisis, however, it is very important that these investments be highly liquid and risk-free. A *liquid investment* is one with a market in which someone is always willing to buy or sell the investment. A *risk-free investment* means there is no concern that the party will default on its promise to pay its principal and interest. For example, using excess cash to purchase stock in a small company because you heard that it was probably going to increase in value in the near term is totally inappropriate. First, the stock of small companies is often illiquid. Second, if the stock suddenly decreases in value, you might be forced to sell the stock at a loss in order to pay your bills as they come due. The most common form of liquid investments is interest-paying U.S. government securities.

⊕ **International Note**

International sales complicate cash management. For example, if **Nike** must repay a Japanese supplier 30 days from today in Japanese yen, it will be concerned about how the exchange rate of U.S. dollars for yen might change during those 30 days. Often corporate treasurers make investments known as *hedges* to lock in an exchange rate to reduce the company's exposure to exchange rate fluctuation.

These five principles of cash management are summarized in Illustration 7-13 (on the next page).

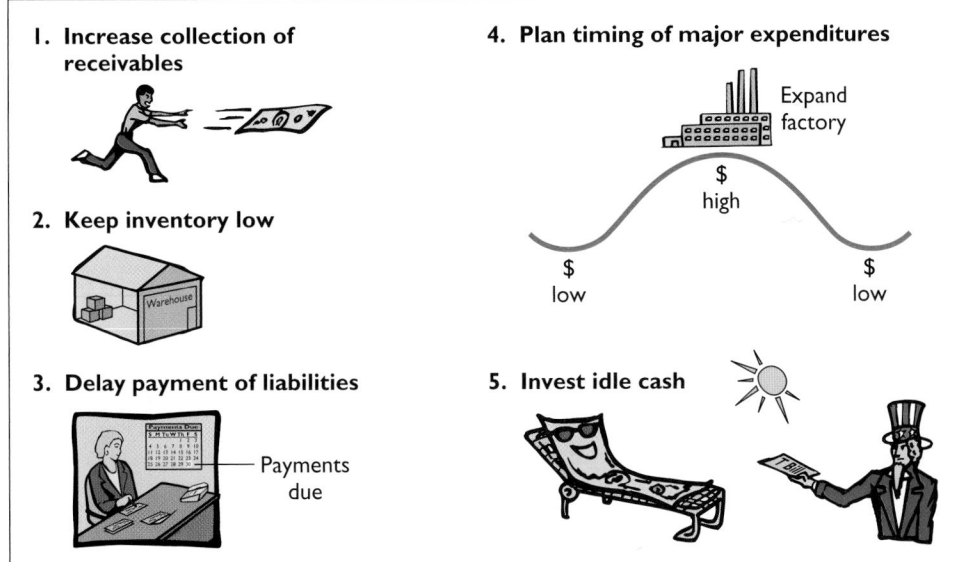

Illustration 7-13 Five principles of sound cash management

1. **Increase collection of receivables**

2. **Keep inventory low**

3. **Delay payment of liabilities** — Payments due

4. **Plan timing of major expenditures** — Expand factory — $ high — $ low — $ low

5. **Invest idle cash**

CASH BUDGETING

Because cash is so vital to a company, **planning the company's cash needs** is a key business activity. It enables the company to plan ahead to cover possible cash shortfalls and to make investments of idle funds. The cash budget shows anticipated cash flows, usually over a one- to two-year period. In this section we introduce the basics of cash budgeting. More advanced discussion of cash budgets and budgets in general is provided in managerial accounting texts.

As shown in Illustration 7-14, the cash budget contains three sections—cash receipts, cash disbursements, and financing—and the beginning and ending cash balances.

STUDY OBJECTIVE
— 7 —
Identify the primary elements of a cash budget.

Illustration 7-14 Basic form of a cash budget

ANY COMPANY Cash Budget	
Beginning cash balance	$X,XXX
Add: **Cash receipts** (itemized)	X,XXX
Total available cash	X,XXX
Less: **Cash disbursements** (itemized)	X,XXX
Excess (deficiency) of available cash over cash disbursements	X,XXX
Financing needed	X,XXX
Ending cash balance	$X,XXX

The **Cash receipts** section includes expected receipts from the company's principal source(s) of cash, such as cash sales and collections from customers on credit sales. This section also shows anticipated receipts of interest and dividends, and proceeds from planned sales of investments, plant assets, and the company's capital stock.

The **Cash disbursements** section shows expected payments for direct materials, direct labor, manufacturing overhead, and selling and administrative expenses. This section also includes projected payments for income taxes, dividends, investments, and plant assets.

The **Financing** section shows expected borrowings and the repayment of the borrowed funds plus interest. This entry is needed when there is a cash deficiency or when the cash balance is less than management's minimum required balance.

Data in the cash budget must be prepared in sequence because the ending cash balance of one period becomes the beginning cash balance for the next period. Data for preparing the cash budget are obtained from other budgets and from information provided by management. In practice, cash budgets are often prepared for the year on a monthly basis.

To minimize detail, we will assume that Hayes Company prepares an annual cash budget by quarters. Preparing a cash budget requires making some assumptions. For example, the cash budget for Hayes Company is based on the company's assumptions regarding collection of accounts receivable, sales of securities, payments for materials and salaries, and purchases of property, plant, and equipment. The accuracy of the cash budget is very dependent on the accuracy of these assumptions.

The cash budget for Hayes Company is shown in Illustration 7-15. The budget indicates that $3,000 of financing will be needed in the second quarter to maintain a minimum cash balance of $15,000. Since there is an excess of available cash over disbursements of $22,500 at the end of the third quarter, the borrowing is repaid in this quarter plus $100 interest.

Illustration 7-15 **Cash budget**

		HAYES COMPANY		
		Cash Budget		
		For the Year Ending December 31, 2005		
			Quarter		
	1	**2**	**3**	**4**
Beginning cash balance	$ 38,000	$ 25,500	$ 15,000	$ 19,400
Add: **Cash receipts**				
Collections from customers	168,000	198,000	228,000	258,000
Sale of securities	2,000	0	0	0
Total receipts	170,000	198,000	228,000	258,000
Total available cash	208,000	223,500	243,000	277,400
Less: **Cash disbursements**				
Materials	23,200	27,200	31,200	35,200
Salaries	62,000	72,000	82,000	92,000
Selling and administrative expenses (excluding depreciation)	94,300	99,300	104,300	109,300
Purchase of truck	0	10,000	0	0
Income tax expense	3,000	3,000	3,000	3,000
Total disbursements	182,500	211,500	220,500	239,500
Excess (deficiency) of available cash over disbursements	25,500	12,000	22,500	37,900
Financing				
Borrowings	0	3,000	0	0
Repayments—plus $100 interest	0	0	3,100	0
Ending cash balance	$ 25,500	$ 15,000	$ 19,400	$ 37,900

A cash budget contributes to more effective cash management. For example, it can show when additional financing will be necessary well before the actual need arises. Conversely, it can indicate when excess cash will be available for investments or other purposes.

DECISION TOOLKIT

Decision Checkpoints	Info Needed for Decision	Tool to Use for Decision	How to Evaluate Results
Will the company be able to meet its projected cash needs?	Cash budget (typically available only to management)	The cash budget shows projected sources and uses of cash. If cash uses exceed internal cash sources, then the company must look for outside sources.	Two issues: (1) Are management's projections reasonable? (2) If outside sources are needed, are they available?

BEFORE YOU GO ON . . .

▶ Review It

1. What are the five principal elements of sound cash management?
2. What are the three sections of the cash budget?
3. What was **Tootsie Roll**'s balance in cash and cash equivalents at December 31, 2002? Did it report any restricted cash? How did Tootsie Roll define cash equivalents? The answer to these questions is provided on p. 364.

▶ Do It

Martian Company's management wants to maintain a minimum monthly cash balance of $15,000. At the beginning of March the cash balance is $16,500; expected cash receipts for March are $210,000; and cash disbursements are expected to be $220,000. How much cash, if any, must be borrowed to maintain the desired minimum monthly balance?

Action Plan
• Insert the dollar data into the basic form of the cash budget.

Solution

Beginning cash balance	$ 16,500
Add: Cash receipts for March	210,000
Total available cash	226,500
Less: Cash disbursements for March	220,000
Excess of available cash over cash disbursements	6,500
Financing	8,500
Ending cash balance	$ 15,000

To maintain the desired minimum cash balance of $15,000, Martian Company must borrow $8,500 of cash.

☑ THE NAVIGATOR

Using the Decision Toolkit

Presented below is hypothetical financial information for **Mattel Corporation**. Included in this information is financial statement data from the year ended December 31, 2004, which should be used to evaluate Mattel's cash position.

Selected Financial Information
Year Ended December 31, 2004
(in millions)

Net cash provided by operations	$325
Capital expenditures	162
Dividends paid	80
Total expenses	680
Depreciation expense	40
Cash balance	206

Also provided are projected data which are management's best estimate of its sources and uses of cash during 2005. This information should be used to prepare a cash budget for 2005.

Projected Sources and Uses of Cash
(in millions)

Beginning cash balance	$206
Cash receipts from sales	355
Cash receipts from sale of short-term investments	20
Cash payments for inventory	357
Cash payments for selling and administrative expense	201
Cash payments for property, plant, and equipment	45
Cash payments for taxes	17

Mattel Corporation's management believes it should maintain a balance of $200 million cash.

Instructions

(a) Using the hypothetical projected sources and uses of cash information presented above, prepare a cash budget for 2005 for Mattel Corporation.
(b) Comment on Mattel's cash adequacy, and discuss steps that might be taken to improve its cash position.

Solution

(a)

MATTEL CORPORATION
Cash Budget
For the Year 2005
(in millions)

Beginning cash balance		$206
Add: Cash receipts		
From sales of product	$355	
From sale of short-term investments	20	375
Total available cash		581
Less: Cash disbursements		
Payments for inventory	357	
Payments for selling and administrative costs	201	

Payments for taxes	17
Payments for property, plant, and equipment	45
Total disbursements	620
Excess (deficiency) of available cash over disbursements	(39)
Financing needed	**239**
Ending cash balance	$200

(b) Mattel's cash position appears adequate. For 2005 Mattel is projecting a cash shortfall. This is not necessarily of concern, but it should be investigated. Given that its primary line of business is toys, and that most toys are sold during December, we would expect Mattel's cash position to vary significantly during the course of the year. After the holiday season it probably has a lot of excess cash. Earlier in the year, when it is making and selling its product but has not yet been paid, it may need to borrow to meet any temporary cash shortfalls.

In the event that Mattel's management is concerned with its cash position, it could take the following steps: (1) Offer its customers cash discounts for early payment, such as 2/10, n/30. (2) Implement inventory management techniques to reduce the need for large inventories of such things as the plastics used to make its toys. (3) Carefully time payments to suppliers by keeping track of when payments are due, so as not to pay too early. (4) If it has plans for major expenditures, time those expenditures to coincide with its seasonal period of excess cash.

Summary of Study Objectives

1 *Identify the principles of internal control.* The principles of internal control are establishment of responsibility; segregation of duties; documentation procedures; physical, mechanical, and electronic controls; independent internal verification; and other controls.

2 *Explain the applications of internal control to cash receipts.* Internal controls over cash receipts include: (a) designating only personnel such as cashiers to handle cash; (b) assigning the duties of receiving cash, recording cash, and having custody of cash to different individuals; (c) obtaining remittance advices for mail receipts, cash register tapes for over-the-counter receipts, and deposit slips for bank deposits; (d) using company safes and bank vaults to store cash with access limited to authorized personnel, and using cash registers in executing over-the-counter receipts; (e) making independent daily counts of register receipts and daily comparisons of total receipts with total deposits; and (f) bonding personnel who handle cash and requiring them to take vacations.

3 *Explain the applications of internal control to cash disbursements.* Internal controls over cash disbursements include: (a) having only specified individuals such as the treasurer authorized to sign checks; (b) assigning the duties of approving items for payment, paying the items, and recording the payment to different individuals; (c) using prenumbered checks and accounting for all checks, with each check supported by an approved invoice; (d) storing blank checks in a safe or vault with access restricted to authorized personnel, and using a machine with indelible ink to imprint amounts on checks; (e) comparing each check with the approved invoice before issuing the check, and making monthly reconciliations of bank and book balances; and (f) after payment, stamping each approved invoice "paid."

4 *Prepare a bank reconciliation.* In reconciling the bank account, it is customary to reconcile the balance per books and the balance per bank to their adjusted balance. The steps in determining the reconciling items are to ascertain deposits in transit, outstanding checks, errors by the depositor or the bank, and unrecorded bank memoranda.

5 *Explain the reporting of cash.* Cash is listed first in the current assets section of the balance sheet. In some cases, cash is reported together with cash equivalents. Cash restricted for a special purpose is reported separately as a current asset or as a noncurrent asset, depending on when the cash is expected to be used.

6 *Discuss the basic principles of cash management.* The basic principles of cash management include: (a) increase collection of receivables, (b) keep inventory levels low, (c) delay payment of liabilities, (d) plan timing of major expenditures, and (e) invest idle cash.

7 *Identify the primary elements of a cash budget.* The three main elements of a cash budget are the cash receipts section, cash disbursements section, and financing section.

DECISION TOOLKIT—A SUMMARY

Decision Checkpoints	Info Needed for Decision	Tool to Use for Decision	How to Evaluate Results
Are the company's financial statements supported by adequate internal controls?	Auditor's report, management discussion and analysis, articles in financial press	The required measures of internal control are to (1) establish responsibility, (2) segregate duties, (3) document procedures, (4) employ physical or automated controls, and (5) use independent internal verification.	If any indication is given that these or other controls are lacking, the financial statements should be used with caution.
Is all of the company's cash available for general use?	Balance sheet and notes to financial statements	Does the company report any cash as being restricted?	A restriction on the use of cash limits management's ability to use those resources for general obligations. This might be considered when assessing liquidity.
Will the company be able to meet its projected cash needs?	Cash budget (typically available only to management)	The cash budget shows projected sources and uses of cash. If cash uses exceed internal cash sources, then the company must look for outside sources.	Two issues: (1) Are management's projections reasonable? (2) If outside sources are needed, are they available?

APPENDIX
OPERATION OF THE PETTY CASH FUND

STUDY OBJECTIVE
8
Explain the operation of a petty cash fund.

The operation of a petty cash fund involves (1) establishing the fund, (2) making payments from the fund, and (3) replenishing the fund.

Establishing the Petty Cash Fund

Two essential steps in establishing a petty cash fund are (1) appointing a petty cash custodian who will be responsible for the fund, and (2) determining the size of the fund. Ordinarily, the amount is expected to cover anticipated disbursements for a three- to four-week period. When the fund is established, a check payable to the petty cash custodian is issued for the stipulated amount. If Laird Company decides to establish a $100 fund on March 1, the entry in general journal form is:

Mar. 1	Petty Cash		100	
	Cash			100
	(To establish a petty cash fund)			

A	=	L	+	SE
+100				
−100				

Cash Flows
no effect

The check is then cashed and the proceeds are placed in a locked petty cash box or drawer. Most petty cash funds are established on a fixed-amount basis. Moreover, no additional entries will be made to the Petty Cash account unless the stipulated amount of the fund is changed. For example, if Laird Company decides on July 1 to increase the size of the fund to $250, it would debit Petty Cash $150 and credit Cash $150.

Helpful Hint Petty cash funds are authorized and legitimate. In contrast, "slush" funds are unauthorized and hidden (under the table).

Making Payments from Petty Cash

The custodian of the petty cash fund has the authority to make payments from the fund that conform to prescribed management policies. Usually management limits the size of expenditures that may be made and does not permit use of the fund for certain types of transactions (such as making short-term loans to employees). Each payment from the fund must be documented on a prenumbered petty cash receipt (or petty cash voucher). The signatures of both the custodian and the individual receiving payment are required on the receipt. If other supporting documents such as a freight bill or invoice are available, they should be attached to the petty cash receipt.

Helpful Hint From the standpoint of internal control, the receipt satisfies two principles: (1) establishing responsibility (signature of custodian), and (2) documentation procedures.

The receipts are kept in the petty cash box until the fund is replenished. As a result, the sum of the petty cash receipts and money in the fund should equal the established total at all times. This means that surprise counts can be made at any time by an independent person, such as an internal auditor, to determine whether the fund is being maintained intact.

No accounting entry is made to record a payment at the time it is taken from petty cash. It is considered both inexpedient and unnecessary to do so. Instead, the accounting effects of each payment are recognized when the fund is replenished.

Replenishing the Petty Cash Fund

When the money in the petty cash fund reaches a minimum level, the fund is replenished. The request for reimbursement is initiated by the petty cash custodian. This individual prepares a schedule (or summary) of the payments that have been made and sends the schedule, supported by petty cash receipts and other documentation, to the treasurer's office. The receipts and supporting documents are examined in the treasurer's office to verify that they were proper payments from the fund. The treasurer then approves the request and a check is prepared to restore the fund to its established amount. At the same time, all supporting documentation is stamped "paid" so that it cannot be submitted again for payment.

Helpful Hint Replenishing involves three internal control procedures: segregation of duties, documentation procedures, and independent internal verification.

To illustrate, assume that on March 15 the petty cash custodian requests a check for $87. The fund contains $13 cash and petty cash receipts for postage

$44, supplies $38, and miscellaneous expenses $5. The entry, in general journal form, to record the check is:

A	=	L	+	SE
+38				−44 Exp
−87				−5 Exp

Cash Flows
−87

Mar.	15	Postage Expense	44	
		Supplies	38	
		Miscellaneous Expense	5	
		Cash		87
		(To replenish petty cash fund)		

Note that the Petty Cash account is not affected by the reimbursement entry. Replenishment changes the composition of the fund by replacing the petty cash receipts with cash, but it does not change the balance in the fund.

Occasionally, in replenishing a petty cash fund it may be necessary to recognize a cash shortage or overage. To illustrate, assume in the preceding example that the custodian had only $12 in cash in the fund plus the receipts as listed. The request for reimbursement would therefore be for $88, and the following entry would be made.

A	=	L	+	SE
+38				−44 Exp
−88				−5 Exp
				−1 Exp

Cash Flows
−88

Mar.	15	Postage Expense	44	
		Supplies	38	
		Miscellaneous Expense	5	
		Cash Over and Short	1	
		Cash		88
		(To replenish petty cash fund)		

Conversely, if the custodian had $14 in cash, the reimbursement request would be for $86, and Cash Over and Short would be credited for $1. A debit balance in Cash Over and Short is reported in the income statement as miscellaneous expense; a credit balance is reported as miscellaneous revenue. Cash Over and Short is closed to Income Summary at the end of the year.

A petty cash fund should be replenished **at the end of the accounting period, regardless of the cash in the fund**. Replenishment at this time is necessary in order to recognize the effects of the petty cash payments on the financial statements.

Internal control over a petty cash fund is strengthened by (1) having a supervisor make surprise counts of the fund to ascertain whether the paid vouchers and fund cash equal the designated amount, and (2) canceling or mutilating the paid vouchers so they cannot be resubmitted for reimbursement.

Summary of Study Objective for Appendix

8 *Explain the operation of a petty cash fund.* In operating a petty cash fund, a company establishes the fund by appointing a custodian and determining the size of the fund. Payments from the fund are made for documented expenditures, and the fund is replenished as needed. The fund is replenished at least at the end of each accounting period, and accounting entries to record payments are made at that time.

Glossary

Bank statement   A statement received monthly from the bank that shows the depositor's bank transactions and balances. (p. 325)

Cash   Resources that consist of coins, currency, checks, money orders, and money on hand or on deposit in a bank or similar depository. (p. 322)

Cash budget A projection of anticipated cash flows, usually over a one- to two-year period. (p. 335)

Cash equivalents Short-term, highly liquid investments that can be converted to a specific amount of cash. (p. 331)

Deposits in transit Deposits recorded by the depositor that have not been recorded by the bank. (p. 327)

Electronic funds transfer (EFT) A disbursement system that uses wire, telephone, telegraph, or computer to transfer cash from one location to another. (p. 324)

Internal auditors Company employees who evaluate on a continuous basis the effectiveness of the company's system of internal control. (p. 319)

Internal control The plan of organization and all the related methods and measures adopted within a business to safeguard its assets and enhance the accuracy and reliability of its accounting records. (p. 315)

NSF check A check that is not paid by a bank because of insufficient funds in a customer's bank account. (p. 325)

Outstanding checks Checks issued and recorded by a company that have not been paid by the bank. (p. 328)

Petty cash fund A cash fund used to pay relatively small amounts. (p. 324)

Restricted cash Cash that is not available for general use, but instead is restricted for a particular purpose. (p. 332)

Treasurer Employee responsible for the management of a company's cash. (p. 334)

Demonstration Problem

Trillo Company's bank statement for May 2005 shows these data.

Balance May 1	$12,650	Balance May 31	$14,280
Debit memorandum:		Credit memorandum:	
NSF check	175	Collection of note receivable	505

The cash balance per books at May 31 is $13,319. Your review of the data reveals the following.

1. The NSF check was from Hup Co., a customer.
2. The note collected by the bank was a $500, 3-month, 12% note. The bank charged a $10 collection fee. No interest has been accrued.
3. Outstanding checks at May 31 total $2,410.
4. Deposits in transit at May 31 total $1,752.
5. A Trillo Company check for $352 dated May 10 cleared the bank on May 25. This check, which was a payment on account, was journalized for $325.

Instructions

(a) Prepare a bank reconciliation at May 31.
(b) Journalize the entries required by the reconciliation.

Solution to Demonstration Problem

(a)

Cash balance per bank statement		$14,280
Add: Deposits in transit		1,752
		16,032
Less: Outstanding checks		2,410
Adjusted cash balance per bank		$13,622
Cash balance per books		$13,319
Add: Collection of note receivable $500,		
plus $15 interest less collection fee $10		505
		13,824
Less: NSF check	$175	
Error in recording check	27	202
Adjusted cash balance per books		$13,622

Action Plan

- Follow the four steps used in reconciling items (pp. 327–329).
- Work carefully to minimize mathematical errors in the reconciliation.
- Prepare entries based on reconciling items per books.
- Make sure the cash ledger balance after posting the reconciling entries agrees with the adjusted cash balance per books.

(b)

May	31	Cash		505	
		Miscellaneous Expense		10	
		Notes Receivable			500
		Interest Revenue			15
		(To record collection of note by bank)			
	31	Accounts Receivable—Hup Co.		175	
		Cash			175
		(To record NSF check from Hup Co.)			
	31	Accounts Payable		27	
		Cash			27
		(To correct error in recording check)			

✓ THE NAVIGATOR

Note: All Questions, Exercises, and Problems marked with an asterisk relate to material in the appendix to the chapter.

Self-Study Questions

Self-Study/Self-Test

Answers are at the end of the chapter.

(SO 1) **1.** Internal control is used in a business to enhance the accuracy and reliability of its accounting records and to:
    (a) safeguard its assets.
    (b) prevent fraud.
    (c) produce correct financial statements.
    (d) deter employee dishonesty.

(SO 1) **2.** The principles of internal control do *not* include:
    (a) establishment of responsibility.
    (b) documentation procedures.
    (c) management responsibility.
    (d) independent internal verification.

(SO 1) **3.** Physical controls do *not* include:
    (a) safes and vaults to store cash.
    (b) independent bank reconciliations.
    (c) locked warehouses for inventories.
    (d) bank safety deposit boxes for important papers.

(SO 2) **4.** Permitting only designated personnel such as cashiers to handle cash receipts is an application of the principle of:
    (a) segregation of duties.
    (b) establishment of responsibility.
    (c) independent internal verification.
    (d) other controls.

(SO 3) **5.** The use of prenumbered checks in disbursing cash is an application of the principle of:
    (a) establishment of responsibility.
    (b) segregation of duties.
    (c) physical, mechanical, and electronic controls.
    (d) documentation procedures.

(SO 3) **6.** The control features of a bank account do *not* include:
    (a) having bank auditors verify the correctness of the bank balance per books.
    (b) minimizing the amount of cash that must be kept on hand.
    (c) providing a double record of all bank transactions.
    (d) safeguarding cash by using a bank as a depository.

(SO 4) **7.** In a bank reconciliation, deposits in transit are:
    (a) deducted from the book balance.
    (b) added to the book balance.
    (c) added to the bank balance.
    (d) deducted from the bank balance.

(SO 5) **8.** Which of the following items in a cash drawer at November 30 is *not* cash?
    (a) Money orders.
    (b) Coins and currency.
    (c) A customer check dated December 1.
    (d) A customer check dated November 28.

(SO 6) **9.** Which of the following is *not* one of the sections of a cash budget?
    (a) Cash receipts section.
    (b) Cash disbursements section.
    (c) Financing section.
    (d) Cash from operations section.

(SO 5) **10.** Which statement correctly describes the reporting of cash?
    (a) Cash cannot be combined with cash equivalents.
    (b) Restricted cash funds may be combined with Cash.

(c) Cash is listed first in the current assets section.

(d) Restricted cash funds cannot be reported as a current asset.

(SO 9) *11. A check is written to replenish a $100 petty cash fund when the fund contains receipts of $94 and $3 in cash. In recording the check:

(a) Cash Over and Short should be debited for $3.

(b) Petty Cash should be debited for $94.

(c) Cash should be credited for $94.

(d) Petty Cash should be credited for $3.

Questions

1. "Internal control is concerned only with enhancing the accuracy of the accounting records." Do you agree? Explain.

2. What principles of internal control apply to most business enterprises?

3. In the corner grocery store, all sales clerks make change out of one cash register drawer. Is this a violation of internal control? Why?

4. Soo Eng is reviewing the principle of segregation of duties. What are the two common applications of this principle?

5. How do documentation procedures contribute to good internal control?

6. What internal control objectives are met by physical, mechanical, and electronic controls?

7. (a) Explain the control principle of independent internal verification.
   (b) What practices are important in applying this principle?

8. As the company accountant, explain the following ideas to the management of Kersee Company.
   (a) The concept of reasonable assurance in internal control.
   (b) The importance of the human factor in internal control.

9. Global Inc. owns the following assets at the balance sheet date.

Cash in bank—savings account	$ 5,000
Cash on hand	1,100
Cash refund due from the IRS	1,000
Checking account balance	12,000
Postdated checks	500

What amount should be reported as Cash in the balance sheet?

10. What principle(s) of internal control is (are) involved in making daily cash counts of over-the-counter receipts?

11. Assume that **May Department Stores** installed new electronic cash registers in its stores. How do cash registers improve internal control over cash receipts?

12. At Patterson Wholesale Company two mail clerks open all mail receipts. How does this strengthen internal control?

13. "To have maximum effective internal control over cash disbursements, all payments should be made by check." Is this true? Explain.

14. Raja Company's internal controls over cash disbursements provide for the treasurer to sign checks imprinted by a checkwriter after comparing the check with the approved invoice. Identify the internal control principles that are present in these controls.

15. How do these principles apply to cash disbursements:
    (a) Physical, mechanical, and electronic controls?
    (b) Other controls?

16. What is the essential feature of an electronic funds transfer (EFT) procedure?

17. "The use of a bank contributes significantly to good internal control over cash." Is this true? Why?

18. Michael Murphy is confused about the lack of agreement between the cash balance per books and the balance per bank. Explain the causes for the lack of agreement to Michael, and give an example of each cause.

19. Describe the basic principles of cash management.

20. Janet Jones asks your help concerning an NSF check. Explain to Janet (a) what an NSF check is, (b) how it is treated in a bank reconciliation, and (c) whether it will require an adjusting entry on the company's books.

21.
    (a) "Cash equivalents are the same as cash." Do you agree? Explain.
    (b) How should restricted cash funds be reported on the balance sheet?

*22. (a) Identify the three activities that pertain to a petty cash fund, and indicate an internal control principle that is applicable to each activity.
    (b) When are journal entries required in the operation of a petty cash fund?

Brief Exercises

Explain the importance of internal control.
(SO 1)

BE7-1 Lauren Andersen is the new owner of Essex Co. She has heard about internal control but is not clear about its importance for her business. Explain to Lauren the two purposes of internal control, and give her one application of each purpose for Essex Co.

Identify internal control principles.
(SO 1)

BE7-2 The internal control procedures in Searcy Company make the following provisions. Identify the principles of internal control that are being followed in each case.
  (a) Employees who have physical custody of assets do not have access to the accounting records.
  (b) Each month the assets on hand are compared to the accounting records by an internal auditor.
  (c) A prenumbered shipping document is prepared for each shipment of goods to customers.

Identify the internal control principles applicable to cash receipts.
(SO 2)

BE7-3 Hutley Company has the following internal control procedures over cash receipts. Identify the internal control principle that is applicable to each procedure.
  (a) All over-the-counter receipts are registered on cash registers.
  (b) All cashiers are bonded.
  (c) Daily cash counts are made by cashier department supervisors.
  (d) The duties of receiving cash, recording cash, and having custody of cash are assigned to different individuals.
  (e) Only cashiers may operate cash registers.

Identify the internal control principles applicable to cash disbursements.
(SO 3)

BE7-4 Massey Company has the following internal control procedures over cash disbursements. Identify the internal control principle that is applicable to each procedure.
  (a) Company checks are prenumbered.
  (b) The bank statement is reconciled monthly by an internal auditor.
  (c) Blank checks are stored in a safe in the treasurer's office.
  (d) Only the treasurer or assistant treasurer may sign checks.
  (e) Check signers are not allowed to record cash disbursement transactions.

Identify the control features of a bank account.
(SO 3)

BE7-5 W. P. Opal is uncertain about the control features of a bank account. Explain the control benefits of (a) a check and (b) a bank statement.

Indicate location of reconciling items in a bank reconciliation.
(SO 4)

BE7-6 The following reconciling items are applicable to the bank reconciliation for Wendy Co. Indicate how each item should be shown on a bank reconciliation.
  (a) Outstanding checks.
  (b) Bank debit memorandum for service charge.
  (c) Bank credit memorandum for collecting a note for the depositor.
  (d) Deposit in transit.

Identify reconciling items that require adjusting entries.
(SO 4)

BE7-7 Using the data in BE7-6, indicate (a) the items that will result in an adjustment to the depositor's records and (b) why the other items do not require adjustment.

Prepare partial bank reconciliation.
(SO 4)

BE7-8 At July 31 Mayfield Company has this bank information: cash balance per bank $7,800; outstanding checks $762; deposits in transit $1,700; and a bank service charge $20. Determine the adjusted cash balance per bank at July 31.

Analyze outstanding checks.
(SO 4)

BE7-9 In the month of November, Jaya Company Inc. wrote checks in the amount of $9,250. In December, checks in the amount of $12,716 were written. In November, $8,578 of these checks were presented to the bank for payment, and $10,889 in December. What is the amount of outstanding checks at the end of November? At the end of December?

Explain the statement presentation of cash balances.
(SO 5)

BE7-10 Santiago Company has these cash balances: cash in bank $12,742; payroll bank account $6,000; and plant expansion fund cash $25,000. Explain how each balance should be reported on the balance sheet.

Prepare a cash budget.
(SO 6)

BE7-11 The following information is available for Croix Company for the month of January: expected cash receipts $60,000; expected cash disbursements $65,000; cash balance on January 1, $12,000. Management wishes to maintain a minimum cash balance of $8,000. Prepare a basic cash budget for the month of January.

Prepare entry to replenish a petty cash fund.
(SO 8)

BE7-12 On March 20 Salizar's petty cash fund of $100 is replenished when the fund contains $24 in cash and receipts for postage $40, supplies $26, and travel expense $10. Prepare the journal entry to record the replenishment of the petty cash fund.

Exercises

Identify the principles of internal control.
(SO 1)

E7-1 Bank employees use a system known as the "maker-checker" system. An employee will record an entry in the appropriate journal, and then a supervisor will verify and approve the entry. These days, as all of a bank's accounts are computerized, the employee first enters a batch of entries into the computer, and then the entries are posted automatically to the general ledger account after the supervisor approves them on the system.

Access to the computer system is password-protected and task-specific, which means that the computer system will not allow the employee to approve a transaction or the supervisor to record a transaction.

Instructions
Identify the principles of internal control inherent in the "maker-checker" procedure used by banks.

Identify the principles of internal control.
(SO 1)

E7-2 Rosati's Pizza operates strictly on a carryout basis. Customers pick up their orders at a counter where a clerk exchanges the pizza for cash. While at the counter, the customer can see other employees making the pizzas and the large ovens in which the pizzas are baked.

Instructions
Identify the six principles of internal control and give an example of each principle that you might observe when picking up your pizza. (*Note:* It may not be possible to observe all the principles.)

List internal control weaknesses over cash receipts and suggest improvements.
(SO 1, 2)

E7-3 The following control procedures are used in Patillo Company for over-the-counter cash receipts.

1. Cashiers are experienced; thus, they are not bonded.

2. All over-the-counter receipts are registered by three clerks who share a cash register with a single cash drawer.

3. To minimize the risk of robbery, cash in excess of $100 is stored in an unlocked attaché case in the stock room until it is deposited in the bank.

4. At the end of each day the total receipts are counted by the cashier on duty and reconciled to the cash register total.

5. The company accountant makes the bank deposit and then records the day's receipts.

Instructions
(a) For each procedure, explain the weakness in internal control and identify the control principle that is violated.
(b) For each weakness, suggest a change in the procedure that will result in good internal control.

List internal control weaknesses for cash disbursements and suggest improvements.
(SO 1, 3)

E7-4 The following control procedures are used in Beverly's Boutique Shoppe for cash disbursements.

1. Each week Beverly leaves 100 company checks in an unmarked envelope on a shelf behind the cash register.

2. The store manager personally approves all payments before signing and issuing checks.

3. The company checks are unnumbered.

4. After payment, bills are "filed" in a paid invoice folder.

5. The company accountant prepares the bank reconciliation and reports any discrepancies to the owner.

Instructions
(a) For each procedure, explain the weakness in internal control and identify the internal control principle that is violated.

(b) For each weakness, suggest a change in the procedure that will result in good internal control.

Identify internal control weaknesses for cash disbursements and suggest improvements.
(SO 3)

E7-5 At Idaho Company checks are not prenumbered because both the purchasing agent and the treasurer are authorized to issue checks. Each signer has access to unissued checks kept in an unlocked file cabinet. The purchasing agent pays all bills pertaining to goods purchased for resale. Prior to payment, the purchasing agent determines that the goods have been received and verifies the mathematical accuracy of the vendor's invoice. After payment, the invoice is filed by vendor and the purchasing agent records the payment in the cash disbursements journal. The treasurer pays all other bills following approval by authorized employees. After payment, the treasurer stamps all bills "paid," files them by payment date, and records the checks in the cash disbursements journal. Idaho Company maintains one checking account that is reconciled by the treasurer.

Instructions
(a) List the weaknesses in internal control over cash disbursements.
(b) ▭▭▭▷ Write a memo indicating your recommendations for improving company procedures.

Prepare bank reconciliation and adjusting entries.
(SO 4)

E7-6 Alana Davis is unable to reconcile the bank balance at January 31. Alana's reconciliation is shown here.

Cash balance per bank	$3,660.20
Add: NSF check	430.00
Less: Bank service charge	25.00
Adjusted balance per bank	$4,065.20
Cash balance per books	$3,975.20
Less: Deposits in transit	590.00
Add: Outstanding checks	730.00
Adjusted balance per books	$4,115.20

Instructions
(a) What is the proper adjusted cash balance per bank?
(b) What is the proper adjusted cash balance per books?
(c) Prepare the adjusting journal entries necessary to determine the adjusted cash balance per books.

Determine outstanding checks.
(SO 4)

E7-7 At April 30 the bank reconciliation of Trisha Company shows three outstanding checks: No. 254 $650, No. 255 $800, and No. 257 $410. The May bank statement and the May cash payments journal are given here.

Bank Statement Checks Paid			Cash Payments Journal Checks Issued		
Date	Check No.	Amount	Date	Check No.	Amount
5-4	254	$650	5-2	258	$159
5-2	257	410	5-5	259	275
5-17	258	159	5-10	260	925
5-12	259	275	5-15	261	500
5-20	261	500	5-22	262	750
5-29	263	480	5-24	263	480
5-30	262	750	5-29	264	360

Prepare bank reconciliation and adjusting entries.
(SO 4)

Instructions
Using step 2 in the reconciliation procedure (see page 328), list the outstanding checks at May 31.

E7-8 The following information pertains to Allied Camera Company.
   1. Cash balance per bank, July 31, $7,238.

2. July bank service charge not recorded by the depositor $40.

3. Cash balance per books, July 31, $7,190.

4. Deposits in transit, July 31, $1,700.

5. Note for $1,000 collected for Allied in July by the bank, plus interest $36 less fee $20. The collection has not been recorded by Allied, and no interest has been accrued.

6. Outstanding checks, July 31, $772.

Instructions

(a) Prepare a bank reconciliation at July 31, 2005.

(b) Journalize the adjusting entries at July 31 on the books of Allied Camera Company.

E7-9 This information relates to the Cash account in the ledger of Garcia Company.

Prepare bank reconciliation and adjusting entries.
(SO 4)

> Balance September 1—$16,400; Cash deposited—$64,000
> Balance September 30—$17,600; Checks written—$62,800

The September bank statement shows a balance of $16,422 at September 30 and the following memoranda.

Credits		Debits	
Collection of $1,800 note plus interest $30	$1,830	NSF check: J. Hower	$410
Interest earned on checking account	45	Safety deposit box rent	30

At September 30 deposits in transit were $4,996 and outstanding checks totaled $2,383.

Instructions

(a) Prepare the bank reconciliation at September 30, 2005.

(b) Prepare the adjusting entries at September 30, assuming (1) the NSF check was from a customer on account, and (2) no interest had been accrued on the note.

E7-10 The cash records of Great Plaines Company show the following.

Compute deposits in transit and outstanding checks for two bank reconciliations.
(SO 4)

1. The June 30 bank reconciliation indicated that deposits in transit total $750. During July the general ledger account Cash shows deposits of $16,200, but the bank statement indicates that only $15,600 in deposits were received during the month.

2. The June 30 bank reconciliation also reported outstanding checks of $920. During the month of July, Great Plaines Company books show that $17,200 of checks were issued, yet the bank statement showed that $16,400 of checks cleared the bank in July.

3. In September deposits per bank statement totaled $25,900, deposits per books were $25,400, and deposits in transit at September 30 were $2,400.

4. In September cash disbursements per books were $23,700, checks clearing the bank were $24,000, and outstanding checks at September 30 were $2,100.

There were no bank debit or credit memoranda, and no errors were made by either the bank or Great Plaines Company.

Instructions

Answer the following questions.

(a) In situation 1, what were the deposits in transit at July 31?

(b) In situation 2, what were the outstanding checks at July 31?

(c) In situation 3, what were the deposits in transit at August 31?

(d) In situation 4, what were the outstanding checks at August 31?

E7-11 Tory, Hachey, and Wedunn, three law students who have joined together to open a law practice, are struggling to manage their cash flow. They haven't yet built up sufficient clientele and revenues to support their legal practice's ongoing costs. Initial costs, such as advertising, renovations to their premises, and the like, all result in outgoing cash flow at a time when little is coming in. Tory, Hachey, and Wedunn haven't had time to establish a billing system since most of their clients' cases haven't yet reached the courts, and the lawyers didn't think it would be right to bill them until "results were achieved."

Unfortunately, Tory, Hachey, and Wedunn's suppliers don't feel the same way. Their suppliers expect them to pay their accounts payable within a few days of receiving their

Review cash management practices.
(SO 6)

bills. So far, there hasn't even been enough money to pay the three lawyers, and they are not sure how long they can keep practicing law without getting some money into their pockets.

Instructions

Can you provide any suggestions for Tory, Hachey, and Wedunn to improve their cash management practices?

Prepare a cash budget for two months.
(SO 7)

E7-12 Hanover Company Limited expects to have a cash balance of $46,000 on January 1, 2005. These are the relevant monthly budget data for the first two months of 2005.

1. Collections from customers: January $70,000, February $150,000
2. Payments to suppliers: January $40,000, February $75,000
3. Wages: January $30,000, February $40,000. Wages are paid in the month they are incurred.
4. Administrative expenses: January $21,000, February $30,000. These costs include depreciation of $1,000 per month. All other costs are paid as incurred.
5. Selling expenses: January $14,000, February $20,000. These costs are exclusive of depreciation. They are paid as incurred.
6. Sales of short-term investments in January are expected to realize $10,000 in cash. Hanover has a line of credit at a local bank that enables it to borrow up to $25,000. The company wants to maintain a minimum monthly cash balance of $20,000.

Instructions

Prepare a cash budget for January and February.

Prepare journal entries for a petty cash fund.
(SO 8)

*E7-13 During October, North Star Company experiences the following transactions in establishing a petty cash fund.

Oct. 1 A petty cash fund is established with a check for $100 issued to the petty cash custodian.

31 A count of the petty cash fund disclosed the following items:

Currency	$4.00
Coins	0.40
Expenditure receipts (vouchers):	
Office supplies	$28.10
Telephone, Internet, and fax	16.40
Postage	44.00
Freight-out	6.80

31 A check was written to reimburse the fund and increase the fund to $200.

Instructions

Journalize the entries in October that pertain to the petty cash fund.

Journalize and post petty cash fund transactions.
(SO 8)

*E7-14 RPM Company maintains a petty cash fund for small expenditures. These transactions occurred during the month of August.

Aug. 1 Established the petty cash fund by writing a check on Metro Bank for $200.

15 Replenished the petty cash fund by writing a check for $170. On this date, the fund consisted of $30 in cash and these petty cash receipts: freight-out $74.40, entertainment expense $36, postage expense $33, and miscellaneous expense $27.50.

16 Increased the amount of the petty cash fund to $400 by writing a check for $200.

31 Replenished the petty cash fund by writing a check for $283. On this date, the fund consisted of $117 in cash and these petty cash receipts: postage expense $145, entertainment expense $90.60, and freight-out $45.40.

Instructions

(a) Journalize the petty cash transactions.
(b) Post to the Petty Cash account.
(c) What internal control features exist in a petty cash fund?

Problems: Set A

P7-1A Guard Dog Company recently changed its system of internal control over cash disbursements. The system includes the following features.

Instead of being unnumbered and manually prepared, all checks must now be prenumbered and written by using the new checkwriter purchased by the company. Before a check can be issued, each invoice must have the approval of Jane Bell, the purchasing agent, and Dennis Kurt, the receiving department supervisor. Checks must be signed by either Tom Kimball, the treasurer, or Karen Thews, the assistant treasurer. Before signing a check, the signer is expected to compare the amounts of the check with the amounts on the invoice.

After signing a check, the signer stamps the invoice "paid" and inserts within the stamp, the date, check number, and amount of the check. The "paid" invoice is then sent to the accounting department for recording.

Blank checks are stored in a safe in the treasurer's office. The combination to the safe is known by only the treasurer and assistant treasurer. Each month the bank statement is reconciled with the bank balance per books by the assistant chief accountant.

Identify internal control principles for cash disbursements.
(SO 1, 3)

accountable

Instructions
Identify the internal control principles and their application to cash disbursements of Guard Dog Company.

P7-2A The board of trustees of a local church is concerned about the internal accounting controls pertaining to the offering collections made at weekly services. They ask you to serve on a three-person audit team with the internal auditor of the university and a CPA who has just joined the church. At a meeting of the audit team and the board of trustees you learn the following.

Identify internal control weaknesses in cash receipts.
(SO 1, 2)

1. The church's board of trustees has delegated responsibility for the financial management and audit of the financial records to the finance committee. This group prepares the annual budget and approves major disbursements but is not involved in collections or recordkeeping. No audit has been made in recent years because the same trusted employee has kept church records and served as financial secretary for 15 years. The church does not carry any fidelity insurance.

2. The collection at the weekly service is taken by a team of ushers who volunteer to serve for 1 month. The ushers take the collection plates to a basement office at the rear of the church. They hand their plates to the head usher and return to the church service. After all plates have been turned in, the head usher counts the cash received. The head usher then places the cash in the church safe along with a notation of the amount counted. The head usher volunteers to serve for 3 months.

3. The next morning the financial secretary opens the safe and recounts the collection. The secretary withholds $150–$200 in cash, depending on the cash expenditures expected for the week, and deposits the remainder of the collections in the bank. To facilitate the deposit, church members who contribute by check are asked to make their checks payable to "Cash."

Petty cash fund

4. Each month the financial secretary reconciles the bank statement and submits a copy of the reconciliation to the board of trustees. The reconciliations have rarely contained any bank errors and have never shown any errors per books.

Instructions
(a) Indicate the weaknesses in internal accounting control in the handling of collections.
(b) List the improvements in internal control procedures that you plan to make at the next meeting of the audit team for (1) the ushers, (2) the head usher, (3) the financial secretary, and (4) the finance committee.
(c) What church policies should be changed to improve internal control?

Prepare bank reconciliation and adjusting entries.
(SO 4)

Peachtree

P7-3A On May 31, 2005, Virtual Company had a cash balance per books of $5,681.50. The bank statement from Community Bank on that date showed a balance of $7,964.60. A comparison of the statement with the cash account revealed the following facts.

1. The statement included a debit memo of $90 for the printing of additional company checks.

2. Cash sales of $836.15 on May 12 were deposited in the bank. The cash receipts journal entry and the deposit slip were incorrectly made for $846.15. The bank credited Virtual Company for the correct amount.

3. Outstanding checks at May 31 totaled $1,276.25, and deposits in transit were $836.15.

4. On May 18 the company issued check No. 1181 for $685 to K. Dorfner, on account. The check, which cleared the bank in May, was incorrectly journalized and posted by Virtual Company for $658.

5. A $3,000 note receivable was collected by the bank for Virtual Company on May 31 plus $80 interest. The bank charged a collection fee of $30. No interest has been accrued on the note.

6. Included with the cancelled checks was a check issued by Brennan Company to C. Young for $600 that was incorrectly charged to Virtual Company by the bank.

7. On May 31 the bank statement showed an NSF charge of $480 for a check issued by R. Cheng, a customer, to Virtual Company on account.

Instructions

(a) Cash bal. $8,124.50

(a) Prepare the bank reconciliation as of May 31, 2005.
(b) Prepare the necessary adjusting entries at May 31, 2005.

Prepare bank reconciliation and adjusting entries from detailed data.
(SO 4)

P7-4A The bank portion of the bank reconciliation for Kenya AA Company at November 30, 2005, is shown here.

KENYA AA COMPANY
Bank Reconciliation
November 30, 2005

Cash balance per bank		$14,367.90
Add: Deposits in transit		2,530.20
		16,898.10
Less: Outstanding checks		

Check Number	Check Amount	
3451	$2,260.40	
3470 NO - outstanding	1,100.10	
3471	844.50	
3472	1,426.80	
3474 NO	1,050.00	6,681.80
Adjusted cash balance per bank		$10,216.30

The adjusted cash balance per bank agreed with the cash balance per books at November 30. The December bank statement showed the following checks and deposits.

Bank Statement				
Checks			**Deposits**	
Date	Number	Amount	Date	Amount
12-1	3451	$ 2,260.40	12-1	$ 2,530.20
12-2	3471	844.50	12-4	1,211.60
12-7	3472	1,426.80	12-8	2,365.10
12-4	3475	1,640.70	12-16	2,672.70
12-8	3476	1,300.00	12-21	2,945.00
12-10	3477	2,130.00	12-26	2,567.30
12-15	3479	3,080.00	12-29	2,836.00
12-27	3480	600.00	12-30	1,025.00
12-30	3482	475.50	Total	$18,152.90
12-29	3483	1,140.00		
12-31	3485	540.80		
	Total	$15,438.70		

The cash records per books for December showed the following.

Cash Payments Journal							Cash Receipts Journal	
Date	**Number**	**Amount**	**Date**	**Number**	**Amount**		**Date**	**Amount**
12-1	3475	$1,640.70	12-20	3482	$ 475.50		12-3	$ 1,211.60
12-2	3476	1,300.00	12-22	3483	1,140.00		12-7	2,365.10
12-2	3477	2,130.00	12-23	3484	832.00		12-15	2,672.70
12-4	3478	538.20	12-24	3485	450.80		12-20	2,954.00
12-8	3479	3,080.00	12-30	3486	1,389.50		12-25	2,567.30
12-10	3480	600.00	Total		$14,384.10		12-28	2,836.00
12-17	3481	807.40					12-30	1,025.00
							12-31	1,190.40
							Total	$16,822.10

The bank statement contained two memoranda.

1. A credit of $3,145 for the collection of a $3,000 note for Kenya AA Company plus interest of $160 and less a collection fee of $15. Kenya AA Company has not accrued any interest on the note.

2. A debit of $1,027.10 for an NSF check written by J. Ardan, a customer. At December 31 the check had not been redeposited in the bank.

At December 31 the cash balance per books was $13,034.30, and the cash balance per bank statement was $19,580.00. The bank did not make any errors, **but two errors were made by Kenya AA Company**.

Instructions
(a) Using the four steps in the reconciliation procedure described on pages 327–329, prepare a bank reconciliation at December 31, 2005.

(b) Prepare the adjusting entries based on the reconciliation. [*Note:* The correction of any errors pertaining to recording checks should be made to Accounts Payable. The correction of any errors relating to recording cash receipts should be made to Accounts Receivable.]

(a) Cash bal. $15,053.20

↳ adjusted cash balance per bank

P7-5A Pro-Ag Company of Omaha, Nebraska, provides liquid fertilizer and herbicides to regional farmers. On July 31, 2005, the company's cash account per its general ledger showed a balance of $6,012.70.

The bank statement from Castle National Bank on that date showed the following balance.

Prepare a bank reconciliation and adjusting entries.
(SO 4)

Peachtree

CASTLE NATIONAL BANK

Checks and Debits	Deposits and Credits	Daily Balance
XXX	XXX	7-31 7,075.80

A comparison of the details on the bank statement with the details in the cash account revealed the following facts.

1. The bank service charge for July was $25.

2. The bank collected a note receivable of $1,200 for Pro-Ag Company on July 15, plus $48 of interest. The bank made a $10 charge for the collection. Pro-Ag has not accrued any interest on the note.

3. The July 31 receipts of $2,115 were not included in the bank deposits for July. These receipts were deposited by the company in a night deposit vault on July 31.

4. Company check No. 2480 issued to K. Charles, a creditor, for $492 that cleared the bank in July was incorrectly entered in the cash payments journal on July 10 for $429.

5. Checks outstanding on July 31 totaled $2,480.10.

6. On July 31, the bank statement showed an NSF charge of $452 for a check received by the company from N. O. Doe, a customer, on account.

Instructions

(a) Cash bal. $6,710.70

(a) Prepare the bank reconciliation as of July 31, 2005.

(b) Prepare the necessary adjusting entries at July 31, 2005.

Prepare a cash budget.
(SO 7)

P7-6A   Haley Co. expects to have a cash balance of $26,000 on January 1, 2005. Relevant monthly budget data for the first two months of 2005 are as follows.

Collections from customers: January $60,000; February $190,000
Payments to suppliers: January $50,000; February $75,000

Salaries: January $30,000; February $50,000. Salaries are paid in the month they are incurred.

Selling and administrative expenses: January $27,000; February $39,000. These costs are exclusive of depreciation and are paid as incurred.

Sales of short-term investments in January are expected to realize $8,000 in cash.

Haley has a line of credit at a local bank that enables it to borrow up to $45,000. The company wants to maintain a minimum monthly cash balance of $25,000. Any excess cash above the $25,000 minimum is used to pay off the line of credit.

Instructions

(a) Jan. cash bal. $25,000

(a) Prepare a cash budget for January and February.

(b) Explain how a cash budget contributes to effective management.

Prepare a cash budget.
(SO 7)

P7-7A   Joplin Inc. prepares monthly cash budgets. Here are relevant data from operating budgets for 2005.

	January	February
Sales	$360,000	$400,000
Purchases	100,000	110,000
Salaries	80,000	95,000
Selling and administrative expenses	135,000	160,000

All sales are on account. Collections are expected to be 50% in the month of sale, 30% in the first month following the sale, and 20% in the second month following the sale. Forty percent (40%) of purchases are paid in cash in the month of purchase, and the balance due is paid in the month following the purchase. All other items above are paid in the month incurred. Depreciation has been excluded from selling and administrative expenses.

Other data.

1. Credit sales—November 2004, $200,000; December 2004, $280,000.

2. Purchases—December 2004, $90,000.

3. Other receipts—January: collection of December 31, 2004, interest receivable $3,000; February: proceeds from sale of short-term investments $5,000.

4. Other disbursements—February: payment of $20,000 for land

The company's cash balance on January 1, 2005, is expected to be $60,000. The company wants to maintain a minimum cash balance of $50,000.

Instructions

(a) Jan. customer
        collections $304,000
(b) Jan. 31 cash bal. $ 58,000

(a) Prepare schedules for (1) expected collections from customers and (2) expected payments for purchases for January and February.

(b) Prepare a cash budget for January and February.

Prepare comprehensive bank reconciliation with theft and internal control deficiencies.
(SO 1, 2, 3, 4)

P7-8A   Mini Company is a very profitable small business. It has not, however, given much consideration to internal control. For example, in an attempt to keep clerical and office expenses to a minimum, the company has combined the jobs of cashier and bookkeeper. As a result, C. Milan handles all cash receipts, keeps the accounting records, and prepares the monthly bank reconciliations.

The balance per the bank statement on October 31, 2005, was $13,155. Outstanding checks were: No. 62 for $126.75, No. 183 for $180, No. 284 for $253.25, No. 862 for $190.71, No. 863 for $226.80, and No. 864 for $165.28. Included with the statement was a credit memorandum of $875 indicating the collection of a note receivable for Mini Company by the bank on October 25. This memorandum has not been recorded by Mini Company.

The company's ledger showed one cash account with a balance of $16,242.72. The balance included undeposited cash on hand. Because of the lack of internal controls, Milan took for personal use all of the undeposited receipts in excess of $2,695.51. He then prepared the following bank reconciliation in an effort to conceal his theft of cash.

Cash balance per books, October 31		$16,242.72
Add: Outstanding checks		
No. 862	$190.71	
No. 863	226.80	
No. 864	165.28	482.79
		16,725.51
Less: Undeposited receipts		2,695.51
Unadjusted balance per bank, October 31		14,030.00
Less: Bank credit memorandum		875.00
Cash balance per bank statement, October 31		$13,155.00

Instructions

(a) Prepare a correct bank reconciliation. (*Hint:* Deduct the amount of the theft from the adjusted balance per books.)

(b) Indicate the three ways that Milan attempted to conceal the theft and the dollar amount pertaining to each method.

(c) What principles of internal control were violated in this case?

(a) Cash bal. $14,707.72

Problems: Set B

P7-1B   Cedar Rapids Theater is in the Cedar Rapids Mall. A cashier's booth is located near the entrance to the theater. Two cashiers are employed. One works from 1:00 to 5:00 P.M., the other from 5:00 to 9:00 P.M. Each cashier is bonded. The cashiers receive cash from customers and operate a machine that ejects serially numbered tickets. The rolls of tickets are inserted and locked into the machine by the theater manager at the beginning of each cashier's shift.

Identify internal control weaknesses for cash receipts.
(SO 1, 2)

After purchasing a ticket, the customer takes the ticket to a doorperson stationed at the entrance of the theater lobby some 60 feet from the cashier's booth. The doorperson tears the ticket in half, admits the customer, and returns the ticket stub to the customer. The other half of the ticket is dropped into a locked box by the doorperson.

At the end of each cashier's shift, the theater manager removes the ticket rolls from the machine and makes a cash count. The cash count sheet is initialed by the cashier. At the end of the day, the manager deposits the receipts in total in a bank night deposit vault located in the mall. In addition, the manager sends copies of the deposit slip and the initialed cash count sheets to the theater company treasurer for verification and to the company's accounting department. Receipts from the first shift are stored in a safe located in the manager's office.

Instructions

(a) Identify the internal control principles and their application to the cash receipts transactions of Cedar Rapids Theater.

(b) If the doorperson and cashier decided to collaborate to misappropriate cash, what actions might they take?

P7-2B   Kettle Moraine Middle School wants to raise money for a new sound system for its auditorium. The primary fund-raising event is a dance at which the famous disc jockey Obnoxious Al will play classic and not-so-classic dance tunes. Rick Gleason, the music

Identify internal control weaknesses in cash receipts and cash disbursements.
(SO 1, 2, 3)

and theater instructor, has been given the responsibility for coordinating the fund-raising efforts. This is Rick's first experience with fund-raising. He decides to put the eighth-grade choir in charge of the event; he will be a relatively passive observer.

Rick had 500 unnumbered tickets printed for the dance. He left the tickets in a box on his desk and told the choir students to take as many tickets as they thought they could sell for $5 each. In order to ensure that no extra tickets would be floating around, he told them to dispose of any unsold tickets. When the students received payment for the tickets, they were to bring the cash back to Rick, and he would put it in a locked box in his desk drawer.

Some of the students were responsible for decorating the gymnasium for the dance. Rick gave each of them a key to the money box and told them that if they took money out to purchase materials, they should put a note in the box saying how much they took and what it was used for. After two weeks the money box appeared to be getting full, so Rick asked Steve Stevens to count the money, prepare a deposit slip, and deposit the money in a bank account Rick had opened.

The day of the dance, Rick wrote a check from the account to pay Obnoxious Al. The DJ said, however, that he accepted only cash and did not give receipts. So Rick took $200 out of the cash box and gave it to Al. At the dance Rick had Sara Billings working at the entrance to the gymnasium, collecting tickets from students and selling tickets to those who had not pre-purchased them. Rick estimated that 400 students attended the dance.

The following day Rick closed out the bank account, which had $250 in it, and gave that amount plus the $180 in the cash box to Principal Skinner. Principal Skinner seemed surprised that, after generating roughly $2,000 in sales, the dance netted only $430 in cash. Rick did not know how to respond.

Instructions
Identify as many internal control weaknesses as you can in this scenario, and suggest how each could be addressed.

Prepare bank reconciliation and adjusting entries.
(SO 4)

P7-3B   On July 31, 2005, Nora Company had a cash balance per books of $6,760. The statement from Tri-County Bank on that date showed a balance of $7,695.80. A comparison of the bank statement with the cash account revealed the following facts.

1. The bank service charge for July was $25.
2. The bank collected a note receivable of $1,800 for Nora Company on July 15, plus $68 of interest. The bank made a $10 charge for the collection. Nora has not accrued any interest on the note.
3. The July 31 receipts of $1,824.30 were not included in the bank deposits for July. These receipts were deposited by the company in a night deposit vault on July 31.
4. Company check No. 2480 issued to J. Pauley, a creditor, for $492 that cleared the bank in July was incorrectly entered in the cash payments journal on July 10 for $429.
5. Checks outstanding on July 31 totaled $1,480.10.
6. On July 31 the bank statement showed an NSF charge of $490 for a check received by the company from C. Rose, a customer, on account.

Instructions
(a) Cash bal. $8,040.00
(a) Prepare the bank reconciliation as of July 31.
(b) Prepare the necessary adjusting entries at July 31.

Prepare bank reconciliation and adjusting entries from detailed data.
(SO 4)

P7-4B   The bank portion of the bank reconciliation for Paris Company at October 31, 2005, is shown here.

PARIS COMPANY
Bank Reconciliation
October 31, 2005

Cash balance per bank	$12,367.90
Add: Deposits in transit	1,530.20
	13,898.10

Less: Outstanding checks

Check Number	Check Amount	
2451	$ 1,260.40	
2470	720.10	
2471	844.50	
2472	426.80	
2474	1,050.00	4,301.80
Adjusted cash balance per bank		$ 9,596.30

The adjusted cash balance per bank agreed with the cash balance per books at October 31. The November bank statement showed the following checks and deposits.

Bank Statement

	Checks			Deposits	
Date	Number	Amount	Date	Amount	
11-1	2470	$ 720.10	11-1	$ 1,530.20	
11-2	2471	844.50	11-4	1,211.60	
11-5	2474	1,050.00	11-8	990.10	
11-4	2475	1,640.70	11-13	2,575.00	
11-8	2476	2,830.00	11-18	1,472.70	
11-10	2477	600.00	11-21	2,945.00	
11-15	2479	1,750.00	11-25	2,567.30	
11-18	2480	1,330.00	11-28	1,650.00	
11-27	2481	695.40	11-30	1,186.00	
11-30	2483	575.50	Total	$16,127.90	
11-29	2486	900.00			
	Total	$12,936.20			

The cash records per books for November showed the following.

Cash Payments Journal

Date	Number	Amount	Date	Number	Amount
11-1	2475	$1,640.70	11-20	2483	$ 575.50
11-2	2476	2,830.00	11-22	2484	829.50
11-2	2477	600.00	11-23	2485	974.80
11-4	2478	538.20	11-24	2486	900.00
11-8	2479	1,570.00	11-29	2487	398.00
11-10	2480	1,330.00	11-30	2488	800.00
11-15	2481	695.40	Total		$14,294.10
11-18	2482	612.00			

Cash Receipts Journal

Date	Amount
11-3	$ 1,211.60
11-7	990.10
11-12	2,575.00
11-17	1,472.70
11-20	2,954.00
11-24	2,567.30
11-27	1,650.00
11-29	1,186.00
11-30	1,155.00
Total	$15,761.70

The bank statement contained two bank memoranda:

1. A credit of $1,875 for the collection of an $1,800 note for Paris Company plus interest of $90 and less a collection fee of $15. Paris Company has not accrued any interest on the note.
2. A debit for the printing of additional company checks $110.

At November 30 the cash balance per books was $11,133.90 and the cash balance per bank statement was $17,394.60. The bank did not make any errors, but **two errors were made by Paris Company**.

(a) Cash bal. $12,709.90

Instructions

(a) Using the four steps in the reconciliation procedure described on pages 327–329, prepare a bank reconciliation at November 30, 2005.
(b) Prepare the adjusting entries based on the reconciliation. (*Note:* The correction of any errors pertaining to recording checks should be made to Accounts Payable. The correction of any errors relating to recording cash receipts should be made to Accounts Receivable.)

Prepare a bank reconciliation and adjusting entries.
(SO 4)

P7-5B   NewAge Genetics Company of Canton, Iowa, spreads herbicides and applies liquid fertilizer for local farmers. On May 31, 2005, the company's cash account per its general ledger showed a balance of $6,738.90.

The bank statement from Canton State Bank on that date showed the following balance.

CANTON STATE BANK

Checks and Debits	Deposits and Credits	Daily Balance
XXX	XXX	5-31 7,112.00

A comparison of the details on the bank statement with the details in the cash account revealed the following facts.

1. The statement included a debit memo of $40 for the printing of additional company checks.
2. Cash sales of $836.15 on May 12 were deposited in the bank. The cash receipts journal entry and the deposit slip were incorrectly made for $846.15. The bank credited NewAge Genetics Company for the correct amount.
3. Outstanding checks at May 31 totaled $276.25, and deposits in transit were $936.15.
4. On May 18, the company issued check No. 1181 for $685 to L. Kingston, on account. The check, which cleared the bank in May, was incorrectly journalized and posted by NewAge Genetics Company for $658.
5. A $2,200 note receivable was collected by the bank for NewAge Genetics Company on May 31 plus $110 interest. The bank charged a collection fee of $20. No interest has been accrued on the note.
6. Included with the cancelled checks was a check issued by Bonner Company to P. Jonet for $480 that was incorrectly charged to NewAge Genetics Company by the bank.
7. On May 31, the bank statement showed an NSF charge of $700 for a check issued by Pete Dell, a customer, to NewAge Genetics Company on account.

Instructions

(a) Cash bal. $8,251.90

(a) Prepare the bank reconciliation at May 31, 2005.
(b) Prepare the necessary adjusting entries for NewAge Genetics Company at May 31, 2005.

Prepare cash budget.
(SO 7)

P7-6B   You are provided with the following information taken from New Bay Inc.'s March 31, 2005, balance sheet.

Cash	$ 8,000
Accounts receivable	20,000
Inventory	36,000
Property, plant, and equipment, net of depreciation	120,000
Accounts payable	21,750
Common stock	150,000
Retained earnings	12,250

Additional information concerning New Bay Inc. is as follows.

1. Gross profit is 25% of sales.

2. Actual and budgeted sales data:

March (actual)	$50,000
April (budgeted)	60,000

3. Sales are 60% for cash and 40% on credit. There are no sales discounts, and credit sales are collected in the month following the sale.

4. Half of a month's purchases are paid for in the month of purchase and half in the following month. Purchases of inventory totalled $43,500 for the month of March and are anticipated to total $52,200 for the month of April. Ending inventory is expected to be $43,200 at the end of April.

5. Cash operating costs are anticipated to be $13,300 for the month of April.

6. Equipment costing $2,500 will be purchased for cash in April.

7. The company wishes to maintain a minimum cash balance of $8,000. An open line of credit is available at the bank. All borrowing is done at the beginning of the month, and all repayments are made at the end of the month. The interest rate is 12% per year, and interest expense is accrued at the end of the month and paid in the following month.

Instructions
(a) Calculate cash collections in April for March and April sales.
(b) Calculate the cash disbursements in April related to March and April purchases.
(c) Prepare a cash budget for the month of April. Determine how much cash New Bay Inc. must borrow, or can repay, in April.

(a) Apr. customer
    collections $56,000
(c) Apr.
    borrowings $ 7,650

P7-7B Badger Corporation prepares monthly cash budgets. Here are relevant data from operating budgets for 2005.

Prepare cash budget.
(SO 7)

	January	**February**
Sales	$350,000	$400,000
Purchases	120,000	130,000
Salaries	80,000	95,000
Administrative expenses	70,000	75,000
Selling expenses	79,000	86,000

All sales are on account. Collections are expected to be 50% in the month of sale, 40% in the first month following the sale, and 10% in the second month following the sale. Fifty percent (50%) of purchases are paid in cash in the month of purchase, and the balance due is paid in the month following the purchase. All other items above are paid in the month incurred except for administrative expenses, which include $1,000 of depreciation per month.

Other data.

1. Credit sales—November 2004, $260,000; December 2004, $300,000

2. Purchases—December 2004, $100,000

3. Other receipts—January: collection of December 31, 2004, notes receivable $15,000; February: proceeds from sale of securities $6,000

4. Other disbursements—February: $5,000 cash dividend

The company's cash balance on January 1, 2005, is expected to be $55,000. The company wants to maintain a minimum cash balance of $50,000.

Instructions
(a) Prepare schedules for (1) expected collections from customers and (2) expected payments for purchases for January and February.
(b) Prepare a cash budget for January and February.

(a) Jan. customer
    collections $321,000
(b) Jan. 31
    cash bal. $ 53,000

Prepare comprehensive bank reconciliation with internal control deficiencies.
(SO 1, 2, 3, 4)

P7-8B Wookies and Ewoks Company is a very profitable small business. It has not, however, given much consideration to internal control. For example, in an attempt to keep clerical and office expenses to a minimum, the company has combined the jobs of cashier and bookkeeper. As a result, Luke Sky handles all cash receipts, keeps the accounting records, and prepares the monthly bank reconciliations.

The balance per the bank statement on October 31, 2005, was $18,430. Outstanding checks were: No. 62 for $126.75, No. 183 for $150, No. 284 for $253.25, No. 862 for $190.71, No. 863 for $226.80, and No. 864 for $165.28. Included with the statement was a credit memorandum of $250 indicating the collection of a note receivable for Wookies and Ewoks Company by the bank on October 25. This memorandum has not been recorded by Wookies and Ewoks.

The company's ledger showed one cash account with a balance of $21,992.72. The balance included undeposited cash on hand. Because of the lack of internal controls, Sky took for personal use all of the undeposited receipts in excess of $3,795.51. He then prepared the following bank reconciliation in an effort to conceal his theft of cash.

Cash balance per books, October 31		$21,992.72
Add: Outstanding checks		
No. 862	$190.71	
No. 863	226.80	
No. 864	165.28	482.79
		22,475.51
Less: Undeposited receipts		3,795.51
Unadjusted balance per bank, October 31		18,680.00
Less: Bank credit memorandum		250.00
Cash balance per bank statement, October 31		$18,430.00

Instructions

(a) Cash bal. $21,112.72

(a) Prepare a correct bank reconciliation. (*Hint:* Deduct the amount of the theft from the adjusted balance per books.)

(b) Indicate the three ways that Sky attempted to conceal the theft and the dollar amount involved in each method.

(c) What principles of internal control were violated in this case?

▶ BROADENING YOUR PERSPECTIVE

Financial Reporting and Analysis

FINANCIAL REPORTING PROBLEM: *Tootsie Roll Industries, Inc.*

BYP7-1 The financial statements of **Tootsie Roll** are presented in Appendix A of this book, together with an auditor's report—Report of Independent Auditors.

Instructions

Using the financial statements and reports, answer these questions about Tootsie Roll's internal controls and cash.

(a) What comments, if any, are made about cash in the report of the independent auditors?

(b) What data about cash and cash equivalents are shown in the consolidated balance sheet (statement of financial condition)?

(c) What activities are identified in the consolidated statement of cash flows as being responsible for the changes in cash during 2002?

(d) How are cash equivalents defined in the Notes to Consolidated Financial Statements?

COMPARATIVE ANALYSIS PROBLEM: *Tootsie Roll vs. Hershey Foods*

BYP7-2   The financial statements of **Hershey Foods** are presented in Appendix B, following the financial statements for **Tootsie Roll** in Appendix A.

Instructions

Answer the following questions for each company.

(a) What is the balance in cash and cash equivalents at December 31, 2002?

(b) How much cash was provided by operating activities during 2002?

RESEARCH CASE

BYP7-3   The September 6, 2001, issue of the *Wall Street Journal* includes an article by Shirley Leung entitled "Checks, Balances Were Needed to Avert Alleged Game Scam by Simon Worldwide."

Instructions

Read the article and answer the following questions.

(a) Describe the nature of the theft that is described in the article.

(b) What were the internal control weaknesses that allowed this theft to occur?

(c) What methods do other companies in this industry use to avoid a similar type of theft?

(d) What was one "clue" that the company managers overlooked that should have alerted them that there was a problem?

INTERPRETING FINANCIAL STATEMENTS

BYP7-4   **Microsoft** is the leading developer of software in the world. To continue to be successful Microsoft must generate new products, and generating new products requires significant amounts of cash. Shown below is the current asset and current liability information from Microsoft's June 30, 2001, balance sheet (in millions). Following the Microsoft data is the current asset and current liability information for **Oracle** (in millions), another major software developer.

MICROSOFT, INC. Balance Sheets (partial) As of June 30 (in millions)		
Current assets	**2001**	**2000**
Cash and equivalents	$ 3,922	$ 4,846
Short-term investments	27,678	18,952
Accounts receivable	3,671	3,250
Other	4,366	3,260
Total current assets	$39,637	$30,308
Total current liabilities	$11,132	$ 9,755

ORACLE®

ORACLE Balance Sheets (partial) As of May 31 (in millions)		
Current assets	**2001**	**2000**
Cash and cash equivalents	$4,449	$ 7,429
Short-term investments	1,438	333
Receivables	2,714	2,790
Other current assets	362	331
Total current assets	$8,963	$10,883
Current liabilities	$3,917	$ 5,862

Instructions

(a) What is the definition of a cash equivalent? Give some examples of cash equivalents. How do cash equivalents differ from other types of short-term investments?

(b) Calculate (1) the current ratio and (2) working capital for each company for 2001 and discuss your results.

(c) Is it possible to have too many liquid assets?

A GLOBAL FOCUS

BYP7-5 The international accounting firm **KPMG** recently performed a global survey on e-fraud. Included in its virtual library, at its Web site, **www.kpmg.com**, is a March 29, 2001, article entitled "E-fraud: Is Technology Running Unchecked?" that summarizes the findings of that global survey.

Address: www.kpmg.com/about/press.asp?cid=469

(or go to **www.wiley.com/college/kimmel**)

Instructions

Read the article at the Web site, and answer the following questions.

(a) What do most senior managers in corporations believe to be the most likely perpetrator of a breach of their network systems, and in fact, what is the actual greatest threat?

(b) What percentage of firms perform security audits of their e-commerce systems?

(c) What is the problem with fixing a security breach immediately upon learning that a breach of the system has occurred?

(d) What percentage of the companies had experienced a security breach in the last year? In these instances, what percentage did not take legal action against the perpetrator of the breach?

(e) How did the findings of the survey vary across countries and across other geographic distinctions?

FINANCIAL ANALYSIS ON THE WEB

BYP7-6 The Financial Accounting Standards Board (FASB) is a private organization established to improve accounting standards and financial reporting. The FASB conducts extensive research before issuing a "Statement of Financial Accounting Standards," which represents an authoritative expression of generally accepted accounting principles.

Address: www.rutgers.edu/accounting/raw

(or go to **www.wiley.com/college/kimmel**)

Steps:

1. Choose FASB.

2. Choose FASB Facts.

Instructions

Answer the following questions.

   (a) What is the mission of the FASB?
   (b) How are topics added to the FASB technical agenda?
   (c) What characteristics make the FASB's procedures an "open" decision-making process?

BYP7-7   All organizations should have systems of internal control. Universities are no exception. This site discusses the basics of internal control in a university setting.

Address: **www.bc.edu/bc_org/fvp/ia/ic/intro.html**
            (or go to **www.wiley.com/college/kimmel**)

Steps: Go to the site shown above.

Instructions

The opening page of this site provides links to pages that answer six critical questions. Use these links to answer the following questions.

   (a) In a university setting, who has responsibility for evaluating the adequacy of the system of internal control?
   (b) What do reconciliations ensure in the university setting? Who should review the reconciliation?
   (c) What are some examples of physical controls?
   (d) What are two ways to accomplish inventory counts?

Critical Thinking

GROUP DECISION CASE

BYP7-8   **Alternative Distributor Corp.**, a distributor of groceries and related products, is headquartered in Medford, Massachusetts.

During a recent audit, Alternative Distributor Corp. was advised that existing internal controls necessary for the company to develop reliable financial statements were inadequate. The audit report stated that the current system of accounting for sales, receivables, and cash receipts constituted a material weakness. Among other items, the report focused on nontimely deposit of cash receipts, exposing Alternative Distributor to potential loss or misappropriation, excessive past due accounts receivable due to lack of collection efforts, disregard of advantages offered by vendors for prompt payment of invoices, absence of appropriate segregation of duties by personnel consistent with appropriate control objectives, inadequate procedures for applying accounting principles, lack of qualified management personnel, lack of supervision by an outside board of directors, and overall poor recordkeeping.

Instructions

With the class divided into groups, identify the principles of internal control violated by Alternative Distributor Corporation.

COMMUNICATION ACTIVITY

BYP7-9   As a new auditor for the CPA firm of Barlow, Meier, and Wacker, you have been assigned to review the internal controls over mail cash receipts of Lazybones Company. Your review reveals that checks are promptly endorsed "For Deposit Only," but no list of the checks is prepared by the person opening the mail. The mail is opened either by the cashier or by the employee who maintains the accounts receivable records. Mail receipts are deposited in the bank weekly by the cashier.

Instructions

Write a letter to P. T. Benes, owner of the Lazybones Company, explaining the weaknesses in internal control and your recommendations for improving the system.

ETHICS CASE

BYP7-10   As noted in the chapter, banks charge fees of up to $30 for "bounced" checks—that is, checks that exceed the balance in the account. It has been estimated that processing bounced checks costs a bank roughly $1.50 per check. Thus, the profit margin on bounced checks is very high. Recognizing this, some banks have started to process checks from largest to smallest. By doing this, they maximize the number of checks that bounce if a customer overdraws an account. For example, **NationsBank** (now **Bank of America**) projected a $14 million increase in fee revenue as a result of processing largest checks first. In response to criticism, banks have responded that their customers prefer to have large checks processed first, because those tend to be the most important. At the other extreme, some banks will cover their customers' bounced checks, effectively extending them an interest-free loan while their account is overdrawn.

Instructions
Answer each of the following questions.
  (a) Antonio Freeman had a balance of $1,500 in his checking account at First National Bank on a day when the bank received the following five checks for processing against his account.

Check Number	Amount	Check Number	Amount
3150	$ 35	3165	$ 550
3162	400	3166	1,510
		3169	180

Assuming a $30 fee assessed by the bank for each bounced check, how much fee revenue would the bank generate if it processed checks (1) from largest to smallest, (2) from smallest to largest, and (3) in order of check number?
  (b) Do you think that processing checks from largest to smallest is an ethical business practice?
  (c) In addition to ethical issues, what other issues must a bank consider in deciding whether to process checks from largest to smallest?
  (d) If you were managing a bank, what policy would you adopt on bounced checks?

BYP7-11 Fraud Bureau is a free service, established to alert consumers and investors about prior complaints relating to online vendors, including sellers at online auctions, and to provide consumers, investors, and users with information and news. One of the services it provides is a collection of online educational articles related to fraud.

Address: www.fraudbureau.com/articles/ (or go to **www.wiley.com/college/kimmel**)

Instructions
Go to this site and choose an article of interest to you. Write a short summary of your findings.

Answers to Self-Study Questions
1. a   2. c   3. b   4. b   5. d   6. a   7. c   8. c   9. d   10. c   *11. a

Answer to Tootsie Roll Review It Question 3, p. 337
At December 31, 2002, **Tootsie Roll** reported cash and cash equivalents of $105,507,000. It reported no restricted cash. In Note 1 to its financial statements it defines cash equivalents as "temporary cash investments with an original maturity of three months or less."

Remember to go back to the Navigator box on the chapter-opening page and check off your completed work.

Reporting and Analyzing Receivables

STUDY OBJECTIVES

After studying this chapter, you should be able to:

1 Identify the different types of receivables.

2 Explain how accounts receivable are recognized in the accounts.

3 Describe the methods used to account for bad debts.

4 Compute the interest on notes receivable.

5 Describe the entries to record the disposition of notes receivable.

6 Explain the statement presentation of receivables.

7 Describe the principles of sound accounts receivable management.

8 Identify ratios to analyze a company's receivables.

9 Describe methods to accelerate the receipt of cash from receivables.

THE NAVIGATOR

THE NAVIGATOR ✔

▶ Scan *Study Objectives* ☐

▶ Read *Feature Story* ☐

▶ Read *Preview* ☐

▶ Read text and answer *Before You Go On*
   p. 374 ☐   p. 379 ☐   p. 380 ☐
   p. 388 ☐

▶ Work Using the *Decision Toolkit* ☐

▶ Review Summary of *Study Objectives* ☐

▶ Work *Demonstration Problem* ☐

▶ Answer *Self-Study Questions* ☐

▶ Complete *Assignments* ☐

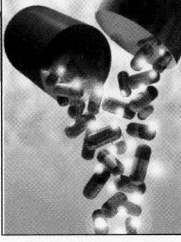

FEATURE STORY

A Dose of Careful Management Keeps Receivables Healthy

"Sometimes you have to know when to be very tough, and sometimes you can give them a bit of a break," says Vivi Su. She's not talking about her children, but about the customers of a subsidiary of pharmaceutical company **Whitehall-Robins**, where she works as supervisor of credit and collections.

For example, while the company's regular terms are 1/15, n/30 (1% discount if paid within 15 days), a customer might ask for and receive a few days of grace and still get the discount. Or a customer might place orders above its credit limit, in which case, depending on their payment history and the circumstances, Ms. Su might authorize the goods to be shipped anyway.

"It's not about drawing a line in the sand, and that's all," she explains. "You want a good relationship with your customers—but you also need to bring in the money."

"The money," in Whitehall-Robins's case amounts to some $170 million in sales a year, nearly all of which comes in through the credit accounts Ms. Su manages. The process starts with the decision to grant a customer an account in the first place, Ms. Su explains. The sales rep gives the customer a credit application. "My department reviews this application very carefully; a customer needs to supply three good references, and we also run a check with a credit firm like **Equifax**. If we accept them, then based on their size and history, we assign a credit limit."

Once accounts are established, they are supervised very carefully. "I get an aging report every single day," says Ms. Su.

"The rule of thumb is that we should always have at least 85% of receivables current—meaning they were billed less than 30 days ago," she continues. "But we try to do even better than that—I like to see 90%." Similarly, her guideline is never to have more than 5% of receivables at over 90 days. But long before that figure is reached, "we jump on it," she says firmly.

At 15 days overdue, the client gets a phone call. Often there's a reasonable explanation for the delay—an invoice may have gone astray, or the payables clerk is away. "But if a customer keeps on delaying, and tells us several times that it'll only be a few more days, we know there's a problem," says Ms. Su. After 45 days, "I send a letter. Then a second notice is sent in writing. After the third and final notice, the client has 10 days to pay, and then I hand it over to a collection agency, and it's out of my hands."

Ms. Su's boss, Terry Norton, records an estimate for bad debts every year, based on a

percentage of receivables. What percentage depends on the current aging history. He also calculates and monitors the company's receivables turnover ratio, which is reported in the financial statements. "I think of it in terms of collection period of DSO—days of sales outstanding," he explains.

Ms. Su knows that she and Mr. Norton are crucial to the profitability of Whitehall-Robins. "Receivables are generally the second-largest asset of any company (after its capital assets)," she points out. "So it's no wonder we keep a very close eye on them."

On the World Wide Web
Whitehall-Robins Healthcare, Inc.
www.whitehall-robins.com

In this chapter we discuss some of the decisions related to reporting and analyzing receivables. As indicated in the Feature Story, receivables are a significant asset on the books of pharmaceutical company **Whitehall-Robins**. Receivables are significant to companies in other industries as well, because a significant portion of sales are done on credit in the United States. As a consequence, companies must pay close attention to their receivables balances and manage them carefully.

The organization and content of the chapter are as follows.

REPORTING AND ANALYZING RECEIVABLES

Types of Receivables	Accounts Receivable	Notes Receivable	Statement Presentation of Receivables	Managing Receivables
	• Recognizing accounts receivable • Valuing accounts receivable	• Computing interest • Recognizing notes receivable • Valuing notes receivable • Disposing of notes receivable		• Extending credit • Establishing a payment period • Monitoring collections • Evaluating liquidity of receivables • Accelerating cash receipts

☑ THE NAVIGATOR

Types of Receivables

The term **receivables** refers to amounts due from individuals and companies. Receivables are claims that are expected to be collected in cash. The management of receivables is a very important activity for any company that sells goods or services on credit. Receivables are important because they represent one of a company's most liquid assets. For many companies, receivables are also one of the largest assets. For example, receivables represented 18% of the current assets of pharmacy giant **Rite Aid** in 2002. Illustration 8-1 lists receivables as a percentage of total assets for five other well-known companies in a recent year.

STUDY OBJECTIVE
1
Identify the different types of receivables.

Illustration 8-1
Receivables as a percentage of assets

Company	Receivables as a Percentage of Total Assets
General Mills	47%
General Electric	45%
Ford Motor Company	41%
Minnesota Mining and Manufacturing Company (3M)	17%
Intel Corporation	6%

The relative significance of a company's receivables as a percentage of its assets differs depending on its industry, the time of year, whether it extends long-term financing, and its credit policies. To reflect important differences among receivables, they are frequently classified as (1) accounts receivable, (2) notes receivable, and (3) other receivables.

Accounts receivable are amounts owed by customers on account. They result from the sale of goods and services. These receivables generally are expected to be collected within 30 to 60 days. They are usually the most significant type of claim held by a company.

Notes receivable represent claims for which formal instruments of credit are issued as evidence of the debt. The credit instrument normally requires the debtor to pay interest and extends for time periods of 60–90 days or longer. Notes and accounts receivable that result from sales transactions are often called **trade receivables**.

Other receivables include non-trade receivables such as interest receivable, loans to company officers, advances to employees, and income taxes refundable. These do not generally result from the operations of the business. Therefore, they are generally classified and reported as separate items in the balance sheet.

Accounts Receivable

Two accounting problems associated with accounts receivable are:

1. Recognizing accounts receivable.
2. Valuing accounts receivable.

A third issue, accelerating cash receipts from receivables, is discussed later in the chapter.

RECOGNIZING ACCOUNTS RECEIVABLE

STUDY OBJECTIVE
2
Explain how accounts receivable are recognized in the accounts.

Initial recognition of accounts receivable is relatively straightforward. For a service organization, a receivable is recorded when service is provided on account. For a merchandiser, accounts receivable are recorded at the point of sale of merchandise on account. When a merchandiser sells goods, both Accounts Receivable and Sales are increased.

Receivables are reduced as a result of sales discounts and sales returns. The seller may offer terms that encourage early payment by providing a discount. For example, terms of 2/10, n/30 provide the buyer with a 2% discount if paid within 10 days. If the buyer chooses to pay within the discount period, the seller's accounts receivable is reduced. Also, the buyer might find some of the goods unacceptable and choose to return the unwanted goods. For example, if merchandise with a selling price of $100 is returned, the seller reduces Accounts Receivable by $100 upon receipt of the returned merchandise.

Business Insight
MANAGEMENT PERSPECTIVE

Sometimes returns can be very significant. Recently pharmacy giant **Rite Aid** sent out return notices to nearly all of its suppliers and reduced the amount it paid each accordingly. In most cases it provided no evidence that the goods were defective—and it did not return the goods, but instead often said that they had been destroyed. In some cases the returns represented 16% of the total goods the supplier had sold to Rite Aid. Analysts suggested that since the move came immediately before the company's accounting year-end, Rite Aid was simply trying to increase its reported net income. Interestingly, in the subsequent year, in the face of lawsuits and threats by suppliers that they would no longer sell to Rite Aid, the company repaid nearly all of the suppliers for the amounts it had deducted.

Illustration 8-2 contains an excerpt from the notes to the financial statements of pharmaceutical manufacturer **Del Laboratories, Inc.** that describes its revenue recognition procedures.

DEL LABORATORIES, INC.
Notes to the Financial Statements

Revenues are recognized and product discounts are recorded when merchandise is shipped. Net sales are comprised of gross revenues less returns, trade discounts, and customer allowances. Merchandise returns are accrued at the earlier of customer deduction or receipt of goods.

Illustration 8-2
Disclosure of revenue
recognition policy

VALUING ACCOUNTS RECEIVABLE

STUDY OBJECTIVE
3
Describe the methods used
to account for bad debts.

Once receivables are recorded in the accounts, the next question is: How should receivables be reported in the financial statements? They are reported on the balance sheet as an asset, but determining the **amount** to report is sometimes difficult because some receivables will become uncollectible.

Although each customer must satisfy the credit requirements of the seller before the credit sale is approved, inevitably some accounts receivable become uncollectible. For example, one of your corporate customers may not be able to pay because it experienced a decline in sales due to a downturn in the economy. Similarly, individuals may be laid off from their jobs or be faced with unexpected hospital bills. Credit losses are debited to **Bad Debts Expense** (or Uncollectible Accounts Expense). Such losses are considered a normal and necessary risk of doing business on a credit basis.

Two methods are used in accounting for uncollectible accounts: (1) the direct write-off method, and (2) the allowance method. Each of these methods is explained in the following sections.

Direct Write-off Method for Uncollectible Accounts

Under the **direct write-off method**, when a particular account is determined to be uncollectible, the loss is charged to Bad Debts Expense. Assume, for example, that Warden Co. writes off M. E. Doran's $200 balance as uncollectible on December 12. The entry is:

Dec. 12	Bad Debts Expense	200	
	Accounts Receivable—M. E. Doran		200
	(To record write-off of M. E. Doran		
	account)		

A	=	L	+	SE
−200				−200 Exp

Cash Flows
no effect

When this method is used, bad debts expense will show only **actual losses** from uncollectibles. Accounts receivable will be reported at its gross amount.

Use of the direct write-off method can reduce the usefulness of both the income statement and balance sheet. Consider the following example. In 2005, Quick Buck Computer Company decided it could increase its revenues by offering computers to college students without requiring any money down, and with no credit-approval process. It went on campuses across the country and distributed one million computers with a selling price of $800 each. This increased Quick Buck's revenues and receivables by $800,000,000. The promotion was a huge success! The 2005 balance sheet and income statement looked wonderful. Unfortunately, during 2006, nearly 40% of the college student customers defaulted on their loans. This made the year 2006 income statement and balance sheet look terrible. Illustration 8-3 shows the effect of these events on the financial statements if the direct write-off method is used.

Illustration 8-3 Effects of direct write-off method

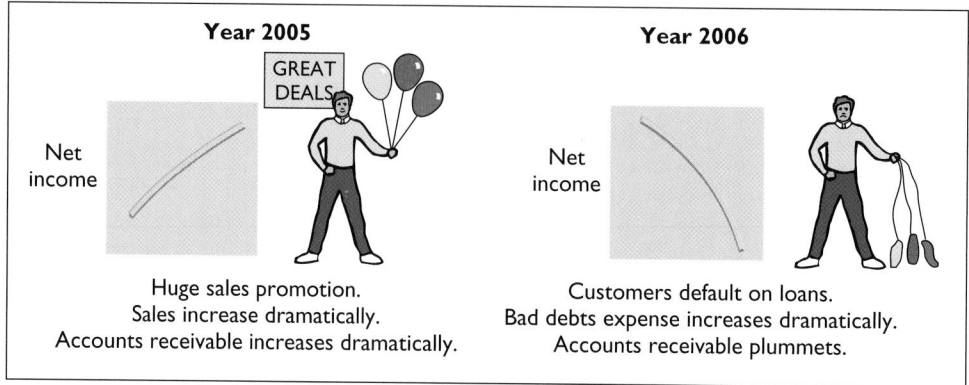

Under the direct write-off method, bad debts expense is often recorded in a period different from the period in which the revenue was recorded. Thus, no attempt is made to match bad debts expense to sales revenues in the income statement or to show accounts receivable in the balance sheet at the amount actually expected to be received. **Consequently, unless bad debts losses are insignificant, the direct write-off method is not acceptable for financial reporting purposes.**

Allowance Method for Uncollectible Accounts

The **allowance method** of accounting for bad debts involves estimating uncollectible accounts at the end of each period. This provides better matching of expenses with revenues on the income statement. It also ensures that receivables are stated at their cash (net) realizable value on the balance sheet. **Cash (net) realizable value** is the net amount expected to be received in cash; it excludes amounts that the company estimates it will not collect. Receivables are therefore reduced by estimated uncollectible receivables on the balance sheet through use of the allowance method.

Helpful Hint In this context, *material* means significant or important to financial statement users.

The allowance method is required for financial reporting purposes when bad debts are material in amount. It has three essential features:

1. Uncollectible accounts receivable are **estimated** and **matched against revenues** in the same accounting period in which the revenues are recorded.

2. Estimated uncollectibles are recorded as an increase (a debit) to Bad Debts Expense and an increase (a credit) to Allowance for Doubtful Accounts (a contra asset account) through an adjusting entry at the end of each period.

3. Actual uncollectibles are debited to Allowance for Doubtful Accounts and credited to Accounts Receivable at the time the specific account is written off as uncollectible.

RECORDING ESTIMATED UNCOLLECTIBLES. To illustrate the allowance method, assume that Hampson Furniture has credit sales of $1,200,000 in 2005, of which $200,000 remains uncollected at December 31. The credit manager estimates that $12,000 of these sales will prove uncollectible. The adjusting entry to record the estimated uncollectibles is:

A	=	L	+	SE
−12,000				−12,000 Exp

Cash Flows
no effect

Dec. 31	Bad Debts Expense		12,000	
	Allowance for Doubtful Accounts			12,000
	(To record estimate of uncollectible accounts)			

<u>Bad Debts Expense</u> is reported in the income statement as an operating expense (usually as a selling expense). Thus, the estimated uncollectibles are matched with sales in 2005 because the expense is recorded in the same year the sales are made.

Allowance for Doubtful Accounts shows the estimated amount of claims on customers that are expected to become uncollectible in the future. A <u>contra account is used instead of a direct credit to Accounts Receivable</u> because we do not know which customers will not pay. The credit balance in the allowance account will absorb the specific write-offs when they occur. It is deducted from Accounts Receivable in the current assets section of the balance sheet as shown in Illustration 8-4.

Illustration 8-4
Presentation of allowance for doubtful accounts

HAMPSON FURNITURE Balance Sheet (partial)		
Current assets		
Cash		$ 14,800
Accounts receivable	$200,000	
Less: Allowance for doubtful accounts	12,000	188,000
Merchandise inventory		310,000
Prepaid expense		25,000
Total current assets		$ 537,800

The amount of $188,000 in Illustration 8-4 represents the expected **cash realizable value** of the accounts receivable at the statement date. **Allowance for Doubtful Accounts is not closed at the end of the fiscal year.**

RECORDING THE WRITE-OFF OF AN UNCOLLECTIBLE ACCOUNT. Companies use various methods of collecting past-due accounts, such as letters, calls, and legal action. When all means of collecting a past-due account have been exhausted and collection appears unlikely, the account should be written off. In the credit card industry it is standard practice to write off accounts that are 210 days past due. To prevent premature or unauthorized write-offs, each write-off should be formally approved in writing by authorized management personnel. To maintain good internal control, authorization to write off accounts should not be given to someone who also has daily responsibilities related to cash or receivables.

To illustrate a receivables write-off, assume that the vice-president of finance of Hampson Furniture on March 1, 2006, authorizes a write-off of the $500 balance owed by R. A. Ware. The entry to record the write-off is:

Mar. 1	Allowance for Doubtful Accounts	500	
	Accounts Receivable—R. A. Ware		500
	(Write-off of R. A. Ware account)		

A	=	L	+	SE
+500				
−500				

Cash Flows
no effect

Bad Debts Expense is not increased when the write-off occurs. **Under the allowance method, every bad debt write-off is debited to the allowance account and not to Bad Debts Expense.** A debit to Bad Debts Expense would be incorrect because the expense has already been recognized, when the adjusting entry was made for estimated bad debts. Instead, the entry to record the write-off of an uncollectible account reduces both Accounts Receivable and the Allowance for Doubtful Accounts. After posting, the general ledger accounts will appear as in Illustration 8-5.

Illustration 8-5 General
ledger balances after
write-off

Accounts Receivable				Allowance for Doubtful Accounts			
Jan. 1 Bal. 200,000		Mar. 1	500	Mar. 1	500	Jan. 1 Bal. 12,000	
Mar. 1 Bal. 199,500						Mar. 1 Bal. 11,500	

A write-off affects only balance sheet accounts. Cash realizable value in the balance sheet, therefore, remains the same, as shown in Illustration 8-6.

Illustration 8-6 Cash
realizable value
comparison

	Before Write-off	After Write-off
Accounts receivable	$ 200,000	$ 199,500
Allowance for doubtful accounts	12,000	11,500
Cash realizable value	**$188,000**	**$188,000**

RECOVERY OF AN UNCOLLECTIBLE ACCOUNT. Occasionally, a company collects from a customer after the account has been written off as uncollectible. Two entries are required to record the recovery of a bad debt: (1) The entry made in writing off the account is reversed to reinstate the customer's account. (2) The collection is journalized in the usual manner. To illustrate, assume that on July 1, R. A. Ware pays the $500 amount that had been written off on March 1. These are the entries:

A	=	L	+	SE
+500				
−500				

Cash Flows
no effect

(1)

July 1	Accounts Receivable—R. A. Ware		500	
	Allowance for Doubtful Accounts			500
	(To reverse write-off of R. A. Ware			
	account)			

A	=	L	+	SE
+500				
−500				

Cash Flows
+500

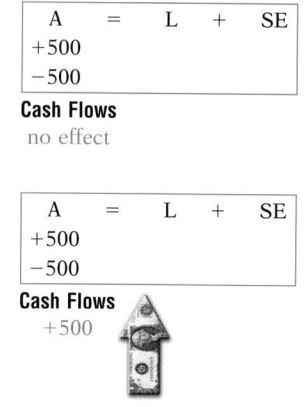

(2)

1	Cash		500	
	Accounts Receivable—R. A. Ware			500
	(To record collection from R. A. Ware)			

Note that the recovery of a bad debt, like the write-off of a bad debt, affects only balance sheet accounts. The net effect of the two entries is an increase in Cash and an increase in Allowance for Doubtful Accounts for $500. Accounts Receivable and the Allowance for Doubtful Accounts both increase in entry (1) for two reasons: First, the company made an error in judgment when it wrote off the account receivable. Second, R. A. Ware did pay, and therefore the Accounts Receivable account should show this collection for possible future credit purposes.

Helpful Hint Like the write-off, a recovery does not involve the income statement.

ESTIMATING THE ALLOWANCE. For Hampson Furniture in Illustration 8-4, the amount of the expected uncollectibles was given. However, in "real life," companies must estimate the amount of expected uncollectible accounts if they use the allowance method. Frequently the allowance is estimated as a percentage of the outstanding receivables.

Under the **percentage of receivables basis**, management establishes a percentage relationship between the amount of receivables and expected losses from uncollectible accounts. A schedule is prepared in which customer balances are classified by the length of time they have been unpaid. Because of its emphasis on time, this schedule is often called an **aging schedule**, and the analysis of it is often called **aging the accounts receivable**.

Business Insight
MANAGEMENT PERSPECTIVE

Companies that provide services and bill on a per hour basis often must spend considerable time preparing detailed bills that specify the billable activities performed. A new company, **TimeBills.com**, has an online product that reduces the amount of time it takes to prepare a bill, while increasing the information provided to the customer. To use the service, you create an electronic record that lists the type of project, customer name, project dates, and billing rate. By clicking on the "timer" function, you can automatically track time spent on a particular project as the work is being performed. TimeBills.com will either mail or e-mail invoices to customers, and keep track of collections, including providing an aging schedule.

After the accounts are arranged by age, the expected bad debt losses are determined by applying percentages, based on past experience, to the totals of each category. The longer a receivable is past due, the less likely it is to be collected. As a result, the estimated percentage of uncollectible debts increases as the number of days past due increases. An aging schedule for Dart Company is shown in Illustration 8-7. Note the increasing uncollectible percentages from 2% to 40%.

Illustration 8-7 Aging schedule

Customer	Total	Not Yet Due	Number of Days Past Due			
			1–30	31–60	61–90	Over 90
T. E. Adert	$ 600		$ 300		$ 200	$ 100
R. C. Bortz	300	$ 300				
B. A. Carl	450		200	$ 250		
O. L. Diker	700	500			200	
T. O. Ebbet	600			300		300
Others	36,950	26,200	5,200	2,450	1,600	1,500
	$39,600	$27,000	$5,700	$3,000	$2,000	$1,900
Estimated percentage uncollectible		2%	4%	10%	20%	40%
Total estimated uncollectible accounts	$ 2,228	$ 540	$ 228	$ 300	$ 400	$ 760

Total estimated uncollectible accounts for Dart Company ($2,228) represent the existing customer claims expected to become uncollectible in the future. Thus, this amount represents the **required balance** in Allowance for Doubtful Accounts at the balance sheet date. Accordingly, **the amount of the bad debts expense adjusting entry is the difference between the required balance and the existing balance in the allowance account**. If the trial balance shows Allowance for Doubtful Accounts with a credit balance of $528, then an adjusting entry for $1,700 ($2,228 − $528) is necessary:

Dec. 31	Bad Debts Expense	1,700	
	Allowance for Doubtful Accounts		1,700
	(To adjust allowance account to total estimated uncollectibles)		

A	=	L	+	SE
−1,700				−1,700 Exp

Cash Flows
no effect

After the adjusting entry is posted, the accounts of Dart Company will appear as in Illustration 8-8.

Illustration 8-8 Bad debts accounts after posting

Bad Debts Expense		Allowance for Doubtful Accounts	
Dec. 31 Adj. **1,700**			Jan. 1 Bal. 528
			Dec. 31 Adj. **1,700**
			Dec. 31 Bal. 2,228

An important aspect of accounts receivable management is simply maintaining a close watch on the accounts. Studies have shown that accounts more than 60 days past due lose approximately 50% of their value if no payment activity occurs within the next 30 days. For each additional 30 days that pass, the collectible value halves once again. As noted in our Feature Story, Vivi Su of **Whitehall-Robins** monitors accounts receivable closely, using an aging schedule to set the percentage of bad debts and computing the company's receivables turnover.

Occasionally the allowance account will have a **debit balance** prior to adjustment because write-offs during the year have **exceeded** previous estimates for bad debts. In such a case, **the debit balance is added to the required balance** when the adjusting entry is made. Thus, if there had been a $500 debit balance in the allowance account before adjustment, the adjusting entry would have been for $2,728 ($2,228 + $500) in order to arrive at a credit balance of $2,228.

The percentage of receivables basis provides an estimate of the cash realizable value of the receivables. It also provides a reasonable matching of expense to revenue.

DECISION TOOLKIT

Decision Checkpoints	Info Needed for Decision	Tool to Use for Decision	How to Evaluate Results
Is the amount of past due accounts increasing? Which accounts require management's attention?	List of outstanding receivables and their due dates	Prepare an aging schedule showing the receivables in various stages: outstanding 0–30 days, 31–60 days, 61–90 days, and over 90 days.	Accounts in the older categories require follow-up: letters, phone calls, and possible renegotiation of terms.

BEFORE YOU GO ON . . .

▶ **Review It**

1. What types of receivables does **Tootsie Roll** report on its balance sheet? Does it use the allowance method or the direct write-off method to account for uncollectibles? The answer to these questions is provided on page 409.
2. To maintain adequate internal controls over receivables, who should authorize receivables write-offs?
3. What are the essential features of the allowance method?
4. What is the primary criticism of the direct write-off method?

▶ Do It

Brule Corporation has been in business for 5 years. The ledger at the end of the current year shows: Accounts Receivable $30,000; Sales $180,000; and Allowance for Doubtful Accounts with a debit balance of $2,000. Bad debts are estimated to be 10% of accounts receivable. Prepare the entry necessary to adjust the Allowance for Doubtful Accounts.

Action Plan

• Report receivables at their cash (net) realizable value—that is, the amount the company expects to collect in cash.
• Estimate the amount the company does not expect to collect.
• Consider the existing balance in the allowance account when using the percentage of receivables basis.

Solution

The following entry should be made, to bring the balance in the Allowance for Doubtful Accounts up to a balance of $3,000 (.1 × $30,000):

Bad Debts Expense	5,000	
Allowance for Doubtful Accounts		5,000
(To record estimate of		
uncollectible accounts)		

Helpful Hint The debit to Bad Debts Expense is calculated as follows:

Allowance for Doubtful Accounts

2,000	5,000
	3,000

Notes Receivable

Credit may also be granted in exchange for a formal credit instrument known as a promissory note. A **promissory note** is a written promise to pay a specified amount of money on demand or at a definite time. Promissory notes may be used (1) when individuals and companies lend or borrow money, (2) when the amount of the transaction and the credit period exceed normal limits, and (3) in settlement of accounts receivable.

In a promissory note, the party making the promise to pay is called the **maker**. The party to whom payment is to be made is called the **payee**. The payee may be specifically identified by name or may be designated simply as the bearer of the note.

In the note shown in Illustration 8-9 (page 376), Brent Company is the maker, and Wilma Company is the payee. To the Wilma Company, the promissory note is a note receivable; to the Brent Company, the note is a note payable.

Notes receivable give the holder a stronger legal claim to assets than accounts receivable. Like accounts receivable, notes receivable can be readily sold to another party. Promissory notes are negotiable instruments (as are checks), which means that, when sold, they can be transferred to another party by endorsement.

Notes receivable are frequently accepted from customers who need to extend the payment of an outstanding account receivable, and they are often required from high-risk customers. In some industries (e.g., the pleasure and sport boat industry) all credit sales are supported by notes. The majority of notes, however, originate from lending transactions. There are three basic issues in accounting for notes receivable:

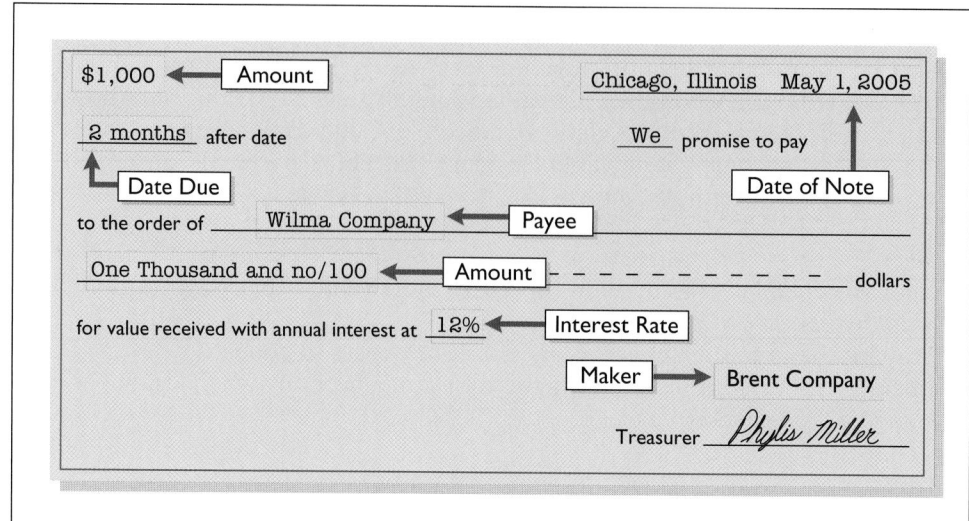

1. **Recognizing** notes receivable.
2. **Valuing** notes receivable.
3. **Disposing** of notes receivable.

We will look at each of these issues, but first we need to consider an issue that did not apply to accounts receivable: computing interest.

COMPUTING INTEREST

The basic formula for computing interest on an interest-bearing note is given in Illustration 8-10.

Illustration 8-10 Formula for computing interest

$$\text{Face Value of Note} \times \text{Annual Interest Rate} \times \text{Time in Terms of One Year} = \text{Interest}$$

The interest rate specified on the note is an **annual** rate of interest. The time factor in the computation expresses the fraction of a year that the note is outstanding. When the maturity date is stated in days, the time factor is frequently the number of days divided by 360. When the due date is stated in months, the time factor is the number of months divided by 12. Computation of interest for various time periods is shown in Illustration 8-11.

Illustration 8-11
Computation of interest

Terms of Note	Interest Computation				
	Face	× Rate ×	Time	= Interest
$ 730, 18%, 120 days	$ 730 ×	18% ×	120/360	=	$ 43.80
$1,000, 15%, 6 months	$1,000 ×	15% ×	6/12	=	$ 75.00
$2,000, 12%, 1 year	$2,000 ×	12% ×	1/1	=	$240.00

There are different ways to calculate interest. For example, the computation in Illustration 8-11 assumed 360 days for the year. Many financial institutions use 365 days to compute interest. (For homework problems, assume 360 days.)

RECOGNIZING NOTES RECEIVABLE

To illustrate the basic entry for notes receivable, we will use Brent Company's $1,000, two-month, 12% promissory note dated May 1. Assuming that the note was written to settle an open account, we record this entry for the receipt of the note by Wilma Company.

May 1	Notes Receivable	1,000	
	Accounts Receivable—Brent Company		1,000
	(To record acceptance of Brent Company note)		

A	=	L	+	SE
+1,000				
−1,000				

Cash Flows
no effect

The note receivable is recorded at its **face value**, the value shown on the face of the note. No interest revenue is reported when the note is accepted because the revenue recognition principle does not recognize revenue until earned. Interest is earned (accrued) as time passes.

If a note is exchanged for cash, the entry is a debit to Notes Receivable and a credit to Cash in the amount of the loan.

VALUING NOTES RECEIVABLE

Like accounts receivable, short-term notes receivable are reported at their **cash (net) realizable value**. The notes receivable allowance account is Allowance for Doubtful Accounts. Valuing short-term notes receivable is the same as valuing accounts receivable. The computations and estimations involved in determining cash realizable value and in recording the proper amount of bad debts expense and related allowance are similar.

Long-term notes receivable, however, pose additional estimation problems. As an example, we need only look at the problems large U.S. banks sometimes have in collecting their receivables. Loans to less-developed countries are particularly worrisome. Developing countries need loans for development but often find repayment difficult. U.S. loans (notes) to less-developed countries at one time totaled approximately $135 billion. In Brazil alone, **Citigroup** at one time had loans equivalent to 80% of its stockholders' equity. In some cases, developed nations have intervened to provide financial assistance to the financially troubled borrowers so as to minimize the political and economic turmoil to the borrower and to ensure the survival of the lender.

DISPOSING OF NOTES RECEIVABLE

Notes may be held to their maturity date, at which time the face value plus accrued interest is due. In some situations, the maker of the note defaults, and appropriate adjustment must be made. In other situations, similar to accounts receivable, the holder of the note speeds up the conversion to cash by selling the receivables. The entries for honoring and dishonoring notes are illustrated next.

STUDY OBJECTIVE
5
Describe the entries to record the disposition of notes receivable.

Honor of Notes Receivable

A note is **honored** when it is paid in full at its maturity date. For each interest-bearing note, the **amount due at maturity** is the face value of the note plus interest for the length of time specified on the note.

To illustrate, assume that Wolder Co. lends Higley Inc. $10,000 on June 1, accepting a four-month, 9% interest note. In this situation, interest is $300 ($10,000 × 9% × $\frac{4}{12}$). The amount due, the maturity value, is $10,300. To obtain payment, Wolder (the payee) must present the note either to Higley Inc. (the maker) or to the maker's agent, such as a bank. If Wolder presents the note to Higley Inc. on October 1, the maturity date, the entry by Wolder to record the collection is:

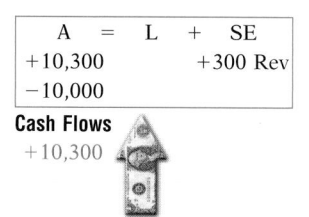

Helpful Hint How many days of interest should be accrued at September 30 for a 90-day note issued on August 16? *Answer:* 45 days (15 days in August plus 30 days in September).

A = L + SE
+10,300   +300 Rev
−10,000
Cash Flows
+10,300

Oct. 1	Cash	10,300	
	Notes Receivable		10,000
	Interest Revenue		300
	(To record collection of Higley Inc. note and interest)		

Accrual of Interest Receivable

If Wolder Co. prepares financial statements as of September 30, it is necessary to accrue interest. In this case, the adjusting entry by Wolder is for four months, or $300, as shown below.

A = L + SE
+300   +300 Rev
Cash Flows
no effect

Sept. 30	Interest Receivable	300	
	Interest Revenue		300
	(To accrue 4 months' interest on Higley note)		

When interest has been accrued, it is necessary to credit Interest Receivable at maturity. The entry by Wolder to record the honoring of the Higley note on October 1 is:

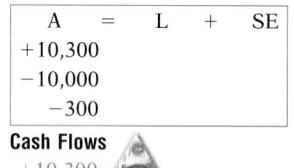

A = L + SE
+10,300
−10,000
−300
Cash Flows
+10,300

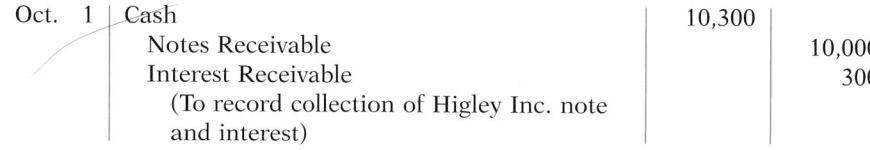

Oct. 1	Cash	10,300	
	Notes Receivable		10,000
	Interest Receivable		300
	(To record collection of Higley Inc. note and interest)		

In this case, Interest Receivable is credited because the receivable was established in the adjusting entry.

Dishonor of Notes Receivable

A **dishonored note** is a note that is not paid in full at maturity. A dishonored note receivable is no longer negotiable; however, the payee still has a claim against the maker of the note for both the note and the interest. If the lender expects that it eventually will be able to collect, the Notes Receivable account is transferred to an Account Receivable for both the face value of the note and the interest due. Sometimes the two parties negotiate new terms to make it easier for the borrower to repay the debt.

If there is no hope of collection, the face value of the note should be written off.

Business Insight
INTERNATIONAL PERSPECTIVE

Nessim Gaon isn't easily intimidated. He says that the Russian government owes him $600 million, and he is determined to get it one way or the other. All the way back in 1991 he provided loans to the Russian Federation, when it was part of the Soviet Union, to buy food, pesticides, medicine, and other items. Russia was to repay the loan with oil. Shortly thereafter the Soviet Union collapsed, and Gaon has been trying to get his money ever since. To get his money he convinced courts to freeze Russian bank accounts in Europe, tried to intercept U.S. payments to Russia for decommissioned nuclear warheads, and even had plans to confiscate Russian President Vladimir Putin's plane as it landed in Paris.

SOURCE: Andrew Higgins, "Bad-Risk Russia Is in Debt to a Guy Who Finds Creative Ways to Collect," *Wall Street Journal Online* (April 24, 2001).

BEFORE YOU GO ON . . .

▶ **Review It**

1. What is the basic formula for computing interest?
2. At what value are notes receivable reported on the balance sheet?
3. Explain the difference between honoring and dishonoring a note receivable.

▶ **Do It**

Gambit Stores accepts from Leonard Co. a $3,400, 90-day, 12% note dated May 10 in settlement of Leonard's overdue open account. The note matures on August 8. What entry is made by Gambit at the maturity date, assuming Leonard pays the note and interest in full at that time?

Action Plan

• Determine whether interest was accrued.
• Compute the accrued interest.
• Prepare the entry for payment of the note and the interest. The entry to record interest at maturity in this solution assumes that no interest has been previously accrued on this note.

Solution

The interest payable at maturity date is $102, computed as follows.

$$\text{Face} \times \text{Rate} \times \text{Time} = \text{Interest}$$

$$\$3,400 \times 12\% \times \frac{90}{360} = \$102$$

This entry is recorded by Gambit Stores at the maturity date.

Cash	3,502	
Notes Receivable		3,400
Interest Revenue		102
(To record collection of Leonard note and interest)		

THE NAVIGATOR

Financial Statement Presentation of Receivables

STUDY OBJECTIVE

6

Explain the statement presentation of receivables.

Each of the major types of receivables should be identified in the balance sheet or in the notes to the financial statements. Short-term receivables are reported in the current assets section of the balance sheet, below short-term investments. Short-term investments appear before short-term receivables because these investments are nearer to cash. Both the gross amount of receivables and the allowance for doubtful accounts should be reported. Illustration 8-12 shows a presentation of receivables for **Deere & Company** from its 2001 balance sheet and notes. Note that notes receivable are listed before accounts receivable because notes are more easily converted to cash.

Illustration 8-12 Balance sheet presentation of receivables

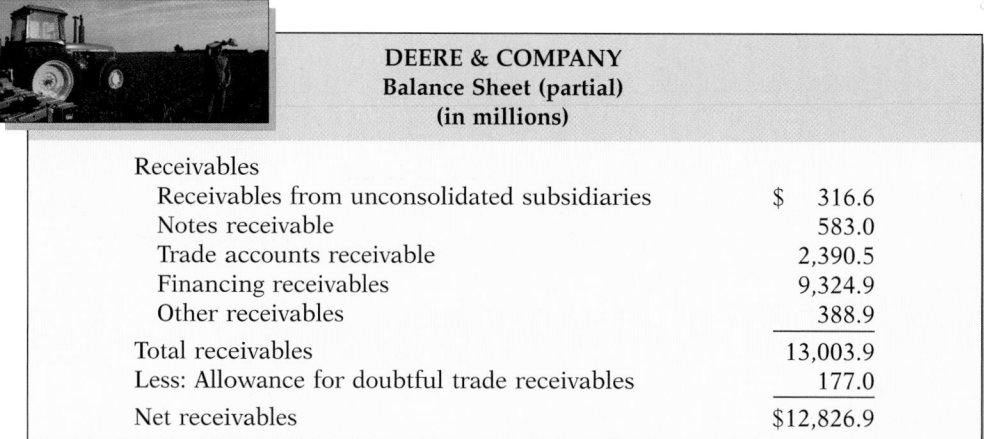

DEERE & COMPANY	
Balance Sheet (partial)	
(in millions)	
Receivables	
Receivables from unconsolidated subsidiaries	$ 316.6
Notes receivable	583.0
Trade accounts receivable	2,390.5
Financing receivables	9,324.9
Other receivables	388.9
Total receivables	13,003.9
Less: Allowance for doubtful trade receivables	177.0
Net receivables	$12,826.9

In the income statement, bad debts expense is reported under "Selling expenses" in the operating expenses section. Interest revenue is shown under "Other revenues and gains" in the nonoperating section of the income statement.

If a company has significant risk of uncollectible accounts or other problems with its receivables, it is required to discuss this possibility in the notes to the financial statements.

BEFORE YOU GO ON . . .

▶ **Review It**

1. Explain where receivables are reported on the balance sheet and in what order.
2. Where are bad debts expense and interest revenue reported on the income statement?

☑ THE NAVIGATOR

Managing Receivables

STUDY OBJECTIVE

7

Describe the principles of sound accounts receivable management.

Managing accounts receivable involves five steps:

1. Determine to whom to extend credit.
2. Establish a payment period.
3. Monitor collections.

4. Evaluate the liquidity of receivables.

5. Accelerate cash receipts from receivables when necessary.

EXTENDING CREDIT

A critical part of managing receivables is determining who should be extended credit and who should not. Many companies increase sales by being generous with their credit policy, but they may end up extending credit to risky customers who do not pay. If the credit policy is too tight, you will lose sales. If it is too loose, you may sell to "deadbeats" who will pay either very late or not at all. One CEO noted that prior to getting his credit and collection department in order, his salespeople had 300 square feet of office space **per person**, while the people in credit and collections had six people crammed into a single 300-square-foot space. Although this arrangement boosted sales, it had very expensive consequences in bad debts expense.

Certain steps can be taken to help minimize losses as credit standards are relaxed. Risky customers might be required to provide letters of credit or bank guarantees. Then if the customer does not pay, the bank that provided the guarantee will do so. Particularly risky customers might be required to pay cash on delivery.

In addition, you should ask potential customers for references from banks and suppliers to determine their payment history. It is important to check these references on potential new customers as well as periodically to check the financial health of continuing customers. Many resources are available for investigating customers. For example, *The Dun & Bradstreet Reference Book of American Business* lists millions of companies and provides credit ratings for many of them.

Business Insight
MANAGEMENT PERSPECTIVE

In the weeks prior to Kmart's decision in early 2002 to file for Chapter 11 bankruptcy protection, many of its suppliers were taking concrete steps to protect themselves. For example, the garden supply company **The Scotts Company**, which in the previous year sold Kmart $175 million in goods, decided to quit shipping to Kmart until its survival plans were more clear. This was a big decision for Scotts, since Kmart represented 10% of its sales in the previous year. One consultant said that in an informal survey of Kmart suppliers, one-third weren't shipping to Kmart, one-third were holding back shipments until they learned more, and one-third were doing business as usual. Many of those that were shipping were demanding cash on delivery (rather than extending credit). All of this meant that Kmart had a lot of empty shelves, at a time when it was hard pressed for cash.

SOURCE: Amy Merrick, "Kmart Suppliers Limit Risk in Case of Chapter 11 Filing," *Wall Street Journal Online* (January 21, 2002).

ESTABLISHING A PAYMENT PERIOD

Companies that extend credit should determine a required payment period and communicate that policy to their customers. It is important to make sure that your company's payment period is consistent with that of your competitors. For example, if you decide to require payment within 15 days, but your competitors require payment within 45 days, you may lose sales to your competitors. However, as noted in Chapter 5, you might allow up to 45 days to pay but offer a sales discount for people paying within 15 days to match competitors' terms yet still encourage prompt payment of accounts.

MONITORING COLLECTIONS

Preparation of the accounts receivable aging schedule was discussed on page 373. An accounts receivable aging schedule should be prepared at least monthly. In addition to estimating the allowance for bad debts, the aging schedule has other uses to management. It aids estimation of the timing of future cash inflows, which is very important to the treasurer's efforts to prepare a cash budget. It provides information about the overall collection experience of the company and identifies problem accounts. For example, management would compute and compare the percentage of receivables that are over 90 days past due.

The aging schedule identifies problem accounts that need to be pursued with phone calls, letters, and occasionally legal action. Sometimes special arrangements must be made with problem accounts. For example, it was reported that **Intel Corporation** (a major manufacturer of computer chips) required that **Packard Bell** (at one time one of the largest U.S. sellers of personal computers) give Intel an interest-bearing note receivable in exchange for its past-due account receivable owed to Intel. This was cause for concern within the investment community, first because it suggested that Packard Bell was in trouble, and second because of the impact on Intel's accounts receivable, since Packard Bell was one of its largest customers.

DECISION TOOLKIT

Decision Checkpoints	Info Needed for Decision	Tool to Use for Decision	How to Evaluate Results
Is the company's credit risk increasing?	Customer account balances and due dates	Accounts receivable aging schedule	Compute and compare the percentage of receivables over 90 days old.

If a company has significant concentrations of credit risk, it is required to discuss this risk in the notes to its financial statements. A **concentration of credit risk** is a threat of nonpayment from a single customer or class of customers that could adversely affect the financial health of the company. An excerpt from the credit risk note from the 2002 annual report of **McKesson Corp.** is shown in Illustration 8-13.

Illustration 8-13
Excerpt from note on concentration of credit risk

McKESSON
Empowering Healthcare

McKESSON CORP.
Notes to the Financial Statements

Concentrations of Credit Risk: A significant proportion of the increase in sales has been to a limited number of large customers and as a result, our credit concentration has increased. Accordingly, any defaults in payment by these large customers could have a significant negative impact on our financial condition, results of operations and liquidity. At March 31, 2002, receivables from our ten largest customers accounted for approximately 41% of total customer accounts receivable. Fiscal 2002 sales to, and March 31, 2002 receivables from, our largest customer, Rite Aid Corporation, represented approximately 14% of consolidated sales and 10% of consolidated customer accounts receivable.

This note to McKesson Corp.'s financial statements indicates it has a high level of credit concentration. A default by any of these large customers could have a significant negative impact on its financial performance.

DECISION TOOLKIT

Decision Checkpoints	Info Needed for Decision	Tool to Use for Decision	How to Evaluate Results
Does the company have significant concentrations of credit risk?	Note to the financial statements on concentrations of credit risk	If risky credit customers are identified, the financial health of those customers should be evaluated to gain an independent assessment of the potential for a material credit loss.	If a material loss appears likely, the potential negative impact of that loss on the company should be carefully evaluated, along with the adequacy of the allowance for doubtful accounts.

EVALUATING LIQUIDITY OF RECEIVABLES

STUDY OBJECTIVE
8
Identify ratios to analyze a company's receivables.

Investors and managers keep a watchful eye on the relationship among sales, accounts receivable, and cash collections. If sales increase, then accounts receivable are also expected to increase. But a disproportionate increase in accounts receivable might signal trouble. Perhaps the company increased its sales by loosening its credit policy, and these receivables may be difficult or impossible to collect. Such receivables are considered less liquid. Recall that liquidity is measured by how quickly certain assets can be converted to cash.

The ratio used to assess the liquidity of the receivables is the **receivables turnover ratio**. This ratio measures the number of times, on average, receivables are collected during the period. The receivables turnover ratio is computed by dividing net credit sales (net sales less cash sales) by the average net accounts receivables during the year. Unless seasonal factors are significant, **average** accounts receivable outstanding can be computed from the beginning and ending balances of the net receivables.[1]

A popular variant of the receivables turnover ratio is to convert it into an **average collection period** in terms of days. This is done by dividing the receivables turnover ratio into 365 days. The average collection period is frequently used to assess the effectiveness of a company's credit and collection policies. The general rule is that the average collection period should not greatly exceed the credit term period (i.e., the time allowed for payment).

The following data (in millions) are available for McKesson Corp.

	For the year ended March 31,	
	2001	**2000**
Sales	$42,010.0	$36,687.0
Accounts receivable (net)	3,439.4	3,034.5

---

[1] If seasonal factors are significant, the average accounts receivable balance might be determined by using monthly amounts.

The receivables turnover ratio and average collection period for McKesson Corp. are shown in Illustration 8-14, along with comparative industry data.

Illustration 8-14
Receivables turnover and
average collection period

$$\text{Receivables Turnover Ratio} = \frac{\text{Net Credit Sales}}{\text{Average Net Receivables}}$$

$$\text{Average Collection Period} = \frac{365}{\text{Receivables Turnover Ratio}}$$

($ in millions)		2001	2000
McKesson	Receivables turnover	$\frac{\$42,010}{(\$3,439.4 + \$3,034.5)/2} = 13.0$ times	$\frac{\$36,687}{(\$3,034.5 + \$2,552.0)/2^*} = 13.1$ times
	Average collection period	$\frac{365}{13.0} = 28.1$ days	$\frac{365}{13.1} = 27.9$ days
Industry average	Receivables turnover	10.4 times	
	Average collection period	35.1 days	

*The receivables balance at March 31, 1999, was $2,552.0 million.

These calculations assume that all sales were credit sales.

McKesson's receivables turnover was 13.0 times in 2001, with a corresponding average collection period of 28.1 days. This was slightly worse than its 2000 collection period of 27.9 days. But it compares favorably with the industry average collection period of 35.1 days. What this means is that McKesson is able to turn its receivables into cash more quickly than most of its competitors. With regard to its receivables, McKesson is more liquid. This means that the company has a better likelihood of paying its current obligations than a company with a slower receivables turnover.

Business Insight
MANAGEMENT PERSPECTIVE

In some cases, receivables turnover may be misleading. Some companies, especially large retail chains, encourage credit and revolving charge sales, and they slow collections in order to earn a healthy return on the outstanding receivables in the form of interest at rates of 18% to 22%. This may explain why **Sears**'s turnover is only 1.63 times (an average collection period of 224 days), for example. In general, however, the faster the turnover, the greater the reliance that can be placed on the current ratio for assessing liquidity.

DECISION TOOLKIT

Decision Checkpoints	Info Needed for Decision	Tool to Use for Decision	How to Evaluate Results
Are collections being made in a timely fashion?	Net credit sales and average receivables balance	$\text{Receivables turnover ratio} = \dfrac{\text{Net credit sales}}{\text{Average net receivables}}$ $\text{Average collection period} = \dfrac{365 \text{ days}}{\text{Receivables turnover ratio}}$	Average collection period should be consistent with corporate credit policy. An increase may suggest a decline in financial health of customers.

ACCELERATING CASH RECEIPTS

In the normal course of events, accounts receivable are collected in cash and removed from the books. However, as credit sales and receivables have grown in size and significance, the "normal course of events" has changed. Two common expressions apply to the collection of receivables: (1) Time is money—that is, waiting for the normal collection process costs money. (2) A bird in the hand is worth two in the bush—that is, getting the cash now is better than getting it later or not at all. Therefore, in order to accelerate the receipt of cash from receivables, companies frequently sell their receivables to another company for cash, thereby shortening the cash-to-cash operating cycle.

There are three reasons for the sale of receivables. The first is their **size**. In recent years, for competitive reasons, sellers (retailers, wholesalers, and manufacturers) often have provided financing to purchasers of their goods. For example, many major companies in the automobile, truck, industrial and farm equipment, computer, and appliance industries have created companies that accept responsibility for accounts receivable financing. **General Motors** has **General Motors Acceptance Corp. (GMAC)**, **Sears** has **Sears Roebuck Acceptance Corp. (SRAC)**, and **Ford** has **Ford Motor Credit Corp. (FMCC)**. These companies are referred to as **captive finance companies** because they are wholly owned by the company selling the product. The purpose of captive finance companies is to encourage the sale of their products by assuring financing to buyers. However, the parent companies involved do not necessarily want to hold large amounts of receivables.

Second, **receivables may be sold because they may be the only reasonable source of cash**. When credit is tight, companies may not be able to borrow money in the usual credit markets. Even if credit is available, the cost of borrowing may be prohibitive.

A final reason for selling receivables is that **billing and collection are often time-consuming and costly**. As a result, it is often easier for a retailer to sell the receivables to another party that has expertise in billing and collection matters. Credit card companies such as **MasterCard**, **Visa**, **American Express**, and **Diners Club** specialize in billing and collecting accounts receivable.

National Credit Card Sales

Approximately one billion credit cards were estimated to be in use recently—more than three credit cards for every man, woman, and child in this country. A common type of credit card is a national credit card such as **Visa** and **Master-**

Card. Three parties are involved when national credit cards are used in making retail sales: (1) the credit card issuer, who is independent of the retailer, (2) the retailer, and (3) the customer. **A retailer's acceptance of a national credit card is another form of selling—factoring—the receivable by the retailer.**

The use of national credit cards translates to more sales and zero bad debts for the retailer. Both are powerful reasons for a retailer to accept such cards. The major advantages of national credit cards to the retailer are shown in Illustration 8-15. In exchange for these advantages, the retailer pays the credit card issuer a fee of 2% to 4% of the invoice price for its services.

Illustration 8-15
Advantages of credit cards to the retailer

Sales resulting from the use of Visa and MasterCard are considered cash sales by the retailer. Upon notification of a credit card charge from a retailer, the bank that issued the card immediately adds the amount to the seller's bank balance. These credit card charges are therefore recorded in the same manner as checks deposited from a cash sale. The banks that issue these cards generally charge retailers a fee of 2% to 4% of the credit card sales slips for this service.

To illustrate, Morgan Marie purchases $1,000 of compact discs for her restaurant from Sondgeroth Music Co., and she charges this amount on her Visa First Bank Card. The service fee that First Bank charges Sondgeroth Music is 3 percent. The entry by Sondgeroth Music to record this transaction is:

A	=	L	+	SE
+970				−30 Exp
				+1,000 Rev

Cash Flows
+970

Cash	970	
Service Charge Expense	30	
Sales		1,000
(To record Visa credit card sales)		

Sale of Receivables to a Factor

A common way to accelerate receivables collection is a sale to a factor. A **factor** is a finance company or bank that buys receivables from businesses for a fee and then collects the payments directly from the customers. Factoring was traditionally associated with the textiles, apparel, footwear, furniture, and home furnishing industries. It has now spread to other types of businesses and is a multi-billion dollar industry. For example, **Sears, Roebuck & Co.** once sold $14.8 billion of customer accounts receivable. **McKesson** has a pre-arranged agreement allowing it to sell up to $850 million of its receivables. McKesson's sale of receivables may explain why its receivables turnover ratio exceeds the industry average.

Factoring arrangements vary widely, but typically the factor charges a commission. It ranges from 1% to 3% of the amount of receivables purchased. To illustrate, assume that Hendredon Furniture factors $600,000 of receivables to Federal Factors, Inc. Federal Factors assesses a service charge of 2% of the amount of receivables sold. The following journal entry records the sale by Hendredon Furniture.

Cash	588,000	
Service Charge Expense (2% × $600,000)	12,000	
Accounts Receivable		600,000
(To record the sale of accounts receivable)		

A = L + SE
+588,000   −12,000 Exp
−600,000

Cash Flows
+588,000

If the company usually sells its receivables, the service charge expense incurred by Hendredon Furniture is recorded as selling expense. If receivables are sold infrequently, this amount may be reported under "Other expenses and losses" in the income statement.

The basic principles of managing accounts receivable are summarized in Illustration 8-16.

Illustration 8-16
Managing receivables

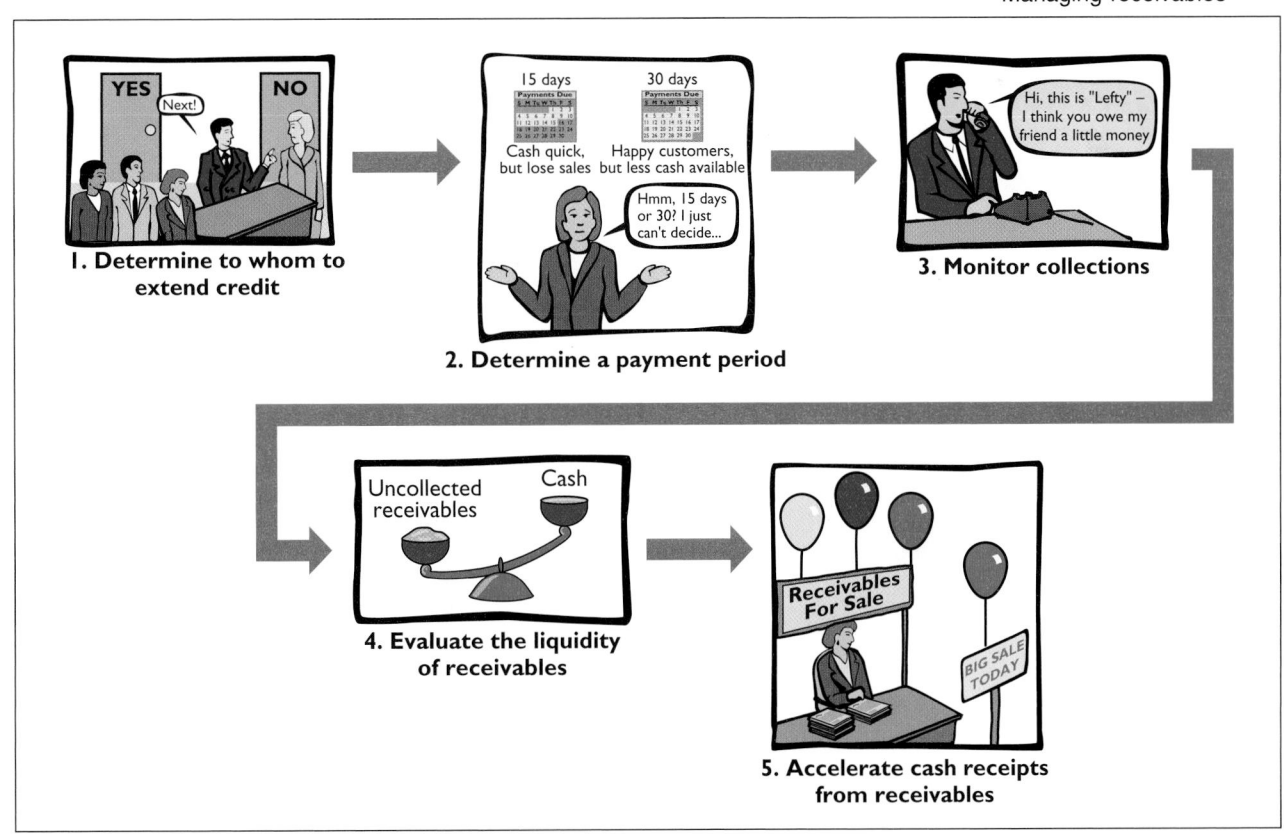

BEFORE YOU GO ON . . .

▶ Review It

1. What is meant by a concentration of credit risk?
2. What is the interpretation of the receivables turnover ratio and the average collection period?
3. For whom is the service charge on a credit card sale an expense?
4. Why do companies sell their receivables?

▶ Do It

Peter M. Dell Wholesalers Co. has been expanding faster than it can raise capital. According to its local banker, the company has reached its debt ceiling. Dell's customers are slow in paying (60–90 days), but its suppliers (creditors) are demanding 30-day payment. Dell has a cash flow problem.

Dell needs to raise $120,000 in cash to safely cover next Friday's employee payroll. Dell's present balance of outstanding receivables totals $750,000. What might Dell do to alleviate this cash crunch? Record the entry that Dell would make when it raises the needed cash. (Assume a 1% service charge.)

Action Plan

• Consider sale of receivables to a factor.
• Weigh cost of factoring against benefit of having cash in hand.

Solution

If Dell Co. factors $125,000 of its accounts receivable at a 1% service charge, this entry would be made.

Cash	123,750	
Service Charge Expense	1,250	
Accounts Receivable		125,000
(To record sale of receivables to factor)		

Using the Decision Toolkit

The information on page 389 was taken from the December 31, 2001, financial statements of **Del Laboratories**, Inc. Similar to **McKesson Corp.**, Del Laboratories manufactures and distributes pharmaceuticals. Del Labs is, however, much smaller than McKesson, and it has not enjoyed the phenomenal growth that McKesson has.

Instructions

Comment on Del Laboratories' accounts receivable management and liquidity relative to that of McKesson, with consideration given to (1) the current ratio and (2) the receivables turnover ratio and average collection period. McKesson's current ratio was 1.40:1. The other ratio values for McKesson were calculated earlier in the chapter.

DEL LABORATORIES, INC.
Selected Financial Information
(in thousands)

	2001		2000	
Sales		$332,679		$294,883
Current assets				
Cash and cash equivalents		$ 2,687		$ 2,910
Accounts receivable	$56,997		$61,196	
Allowance for doubtful accounts	4,200		1,000	
Net accounts receivable		52,797		60,196
Inventories		62,678		58,584
Other current assets		8,602		7,631
Total current assets		$126,764		$129,321
Total current liabilities		$ 51,587		$ 43,656

Solution

(McKesson Corp. figures in millions, Del Labs figures in thousands)

1. Here is the current ratio (Current assets ÷ Current liabilities) for each company.

McKesson	**Del Labs**
$\dfrac{\$9,164,000}{\$6,549,700} = 1.40:1$	$\dfrac{\$126,764}{\$51,587} = 2.46:1$

This suggests that Del Labs is substantially more liquid than McKesson.

2. The receivables turnover ratio and average collection period for each company are:

	McKesson	**Del Labs**
Receivables turnover ratio	13.0 times	$\dfrac{\$332,679}{(\$52,797 + \$60,196)/2} = 5.9$ times
Average collection period	28.1 days	$\dfrac{365}{5.9} = 61.9$ days

McKesson's receivables turnover ratio of 13.0 compared to Del Laboratories' 5.9, and its average collection days of 28.1 days versus Del Labs' 61.9 days, suggest that McKesson is able to collect from its customers much more rapidly. McKesson's more rapid collection of receivables may compensate in part for its lower current ratio. That is, since it can turn its receivables into cash more quickly, its receivables appear to be more liquid than those of Del Labs.

Summary of Study Objectives

1 *Identify the different types of receivables.* Receivables are frequently classified as accounts, notes, and other. Accounts receivable are amounts owed by customers on account. Notes receivable represent claims that are evidenced by formal instruments of credit. Other receivables include nontrade receivables such as interest receivable, loans to company officers, advances to employees, and income taxes refundable.

2 *Explain how accounts receivable are recognized in the accounts.* Accounts receivable are recorded at invoice price. They are reduced by sales returns and allowances. Cash discounts reduce the amount received on accounts receivable.

3 *Describe the methods used to account for bad debts.* The two methods of accounting for uncollectible accounts are the allowance method and the direct write-off method. Under the allowance method, uncollectible accounts are estimated as a percentage of receivables. It emphasizes the cash realizable value of the accounts receivable. An aging schedule is frequently used with this approach.

4 *Compute the interest on notes receivable.* The formula for computing interest is: Face value × Interest rate × Time.

5 *Describe the entries to record the disposition of notes receivable.* Notes can be held to maturity, at which time the face value plus accrued interest is due and the note is removed from the accounts. In many cases, however, similar to accounts receivable, the holder of the note speeds up the conversion by selling the receivable to another party. In some situations, the maker of the note dishonors the note (defaults), and the note is written off.

6 *Explain the statement presentation of receivables.* Each major type of receivable should be identified in the balance sheet or in the notes to the financial statements. Short-term receivables are considered current assets. The gross amount of receivables and allowance

for doubtful accounts should be reported. Bad debts and service charge expenses are reported in the income statement as operating (selling) expenses, and interest revenue is shown as other revenues and gains in the nonoperating section of the statement.

7 *Describe the principles of sound accounts receivable management.* To properly manage receivables, management must (a) determine to whom to extend credit, (b) determine a payment period, (c) monitor collections, (d) evaluate the liquidity of receivables, and (e) accelerate cash receipts from receivables when necessary.

8 *Identify ratios to analyze a company's receivables.* The receivables turnover ratio and the average collection period both are useful in analyzing management's effectiveness in managing receivables. The accounts receivable aging schedule also provides useful information.

9 *Describe methods to accelerate the receipt of cash from receivables.* If the company needs additional cash, management can accelerate the collection of cash from receivables by selling (factoring) its receivables or by allowing customers to pay with bank credit cards.

THE NAVIGATOR

DECISION TOOLKIT—A SUMMARY

Decision Checkpoints	Info Needed for Decision	Tool to Use for Decision	How to Evaluate Results
Is the amount of past due accounts increasing? Which accounts require management's attention?	List of outstanding receivables and their due dates	Prepare an aging schedule showing the receivables in various stages: outstanding 0–30 days, 31–60 days, 61–90 days, and over 90 days.	Accounts in the older categories require follow-up: letters, phone calls, and possible renegotiation of terms.
Is the company's credit risk increasing?	Customer account balances and due dates	Accounts receivable aging schedule	Compute and compare the percentage of receivables over 90 days old.
Does the company have significant concentrations of credit risk?	Note to the financial statements on concentrations of credit risk	If risky credit customers are identified, the financial health of those customers should be evaluated to gain an independent assessment of the potential for a material credit loss.	If a material loss appears likely, the potential negative impact of that loss on the company should be carefully evaluated, along with the adequacy of the allowance for doubtful accounts.
Are collections being made in a timely fashion?	Net credit sales and average receivables balance	$\text{Receivables turnover ratio} = \dfrac{\text{Net credit sales}}{\text{Average net receivables}}$ $\text{Average collection period} = \dfrac{365 \text{ days}}{\text{Receivables turnover ratio}}$	Average collection period should be consistent with corporate credit policy. An increase may suggest a decline in financial health of customers.

Glossary

Accounts receivable Amounts owed by customers on account. (p. 368)

Aging the accounts receivable The analysis of customer balances by the length of time they have been unpaid. (p. 372)

Allowance method A method of accounting for bad debts that involves estimating uncollectible accounts at the end of each period. (p. 370)

Average collection period The average amount of time that a receivable is outstanding, calculated by dividing 365 days by the receivables turnover ratio. (p. 383)

Bad debts expense An expense account to record credit losses. (p. 369)

Cash (net) realizable value The net amount expected to be received in cash. (p. 370)

Concentration of credit risk The threat of nonpayment from a single customer or class of customers that could adversely affect the financial health of the company. (p. 382)

Direct write-off method A method of accounting for bad debts that involves expensing accounts at the time they are determined to be uncollectible. (p. 369)

Dishonored note A note that is not paid in full at maturity. (p. 378)

Factor A finance company or bank that buys receivables from businesses for a fee and then collects the payments directly from the customers. (p. 387)

Maker The party in a promissory note who is making the promise to pay. (p. 375)

Notes receivable Claims for which formal instruments of credit are issued as evidence of the debt. (p. 368)

Payee The party to whom payment of a promissory note is to be made. (p. 375)

Percentage of receivables basis Management establishes a percentage relationship between the amount of receivables and the expected losses from uncollectible accounts. (p. 372)

Promissory note A written promise to pay a specified amount of money on demand or at a definite time. (p. 375)

Receivables Amounts due from individuals and companies that are expected to be collected in cash. (p. 367)

Receivables turnover ratio A measure of the liquidity of receivables, computed by dividing net credit sales by average net receivables. (p. 383)

Trade receivables Notes and accounts receivable that result from sales transactions. (p. 368)

Demonstration Problem

Presented here are selected transactions related to B. Dylan Corp.

Mar.	1	Sold $20,000 of merchandise to Potter Company, terms 2/10, n/30.
	11	Received payment in full from Potter Company for balance due.
	12	Accepted Juno Company's $20,000, 6-month, 12% note for balance due.
	13	Made B. Dylan Corp. credit card sales for $13,200.
	15	Made Visa credit sales totaling $6,700. A 5% service fee is charged by Visa.
Apr.	11	Sold accounts receivable of $8,000 to Harcot Factor. Harcot Factor assesses a service charge of 2% of the amount of receivables sold.
	13	Received collections of $8,200 on B. Dylan Corp. credit card sales.
May	10	Wrote off as uncollectible $16,000 of accounts receivable. (B. Dylan Corp. uses the percentage of receivables basis to estimate bad debts.)
June	30	The balance in accounts receivable at the end of the first 6 months is $200,000 and the bad debt percentage is 10%. At June 30 the credit balance in the allowance account prior to adjustment is $3,500.
July	16	One of the accounts receivable written off in May pays the amount due, $4,000, in full.

Instructions

Prepare the journal entries for the transactions.

Solution to Demonstration Problem

Mar.	1	Accounts Receivable—Potter Company	20,000	
		Sales		20,000
		(To record sales on account)		

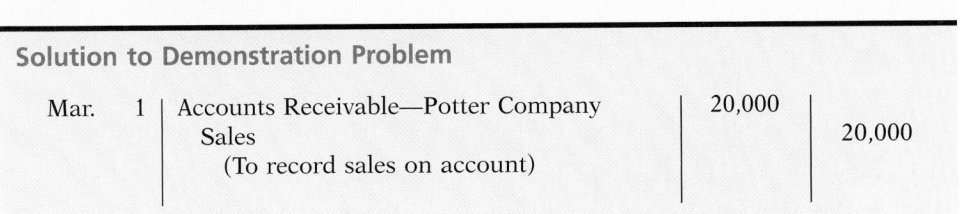

Action Plan

- Generally, record accounts receivable at invoice price.
- Recognize that sales returns and allowances and cash discounts reduce the amount received on accounts receivable.
- Record a service charge expense on the seller's books when accounts receivable are sold.
- Prepare an adjusting entry for bad debts expense.
- Recognize the balance in the allowance account under the percentage of receivables basis.
- Record write-offs of accounts receivable only in balance sheet accounts.

	11	Cash	19,600	
		Sales Discounts (2% × $20,000)	400	
		Accounts Receivable—Potter Company		20,000
		(To record collection of accounts receivable)		
	12	Notes Receivable	20,000	
		Accounts Receivable—Juno Company		20,000
		(To record acceptance of Juno Company note)		
	13	Accounts Receivable	13,200	
		Sales		13,200
		(To record company credit card sales)		
	15	Cash	6,365	
		Service Charge Expense (5% × $6,700)	335	
		Sales		6,700
		(To record credit card sales)		
Apr.	11	Cash	7,840	
		Service Charge Expense (2% × $8,000)	160	
		Accounts Receivable		8,000
		(To record sale of receivables to factor)		
	13	Cash	8,200	
		Accounts Receivable		8,200
		(To record collection of accounts receivable)		
May	10	Allowance for Doubtful Accounts	16,000	
		Accounts Receivable		16,000
		(To record write-off of accounts receivable)		
June	30	Bad Debts Expense	16,500	
		Allowance for Doubtful Accounts		16,500
		[($200,000 × 10%) − $3,500]		
		(To record estimate of uncollectible accounts)		
July	16	Accounts Receivable	4,000	
		Allowance for Doubtful Accounts		4,000
		(To reverse write-off of accounts receivable)		
		Cash	4,000	
		Accounts Receivable		4,000
		(To record collection of accounts receivable)		

Self-Study Questions

Self-Study/Self-Test

Answers are at the end of the chapter.

(SO 2) **1.** Jason Company on June 15 sells merchandise on account to Melody Co. for $1,000, terms 2/10, n/30. On June 20 Melody Co. returns merchandise worth $300 to Jason Company. On June 24 payment is received from Melody Co. for the balance due. What is the amount of cash received?

(a) $700.   (c) $686.
(b) $680.   (d) None of the above.

(SO 3) **2.** Net credit sales for the month are $800,000. The accounts receivable balance is $160,000. The allowance is calculated as 7.5% of the receivables balance using the percentage of receivables basis. If the Allowance for Doubtful Accounts has a credit balance of $5,000 before adjustment, what is the balance after adjustment?
  (a) $12,000.   (c) $17,000.
  (b) $7,000.   (d) $31,000.

(SO 3) **3.** In 2005 F. S. Fitzgerald Company had net credit sales of $750,000. On January 1, 2005, Allowance for Doubtful Accounts had a credit balance of $18,000. During 2005, $30,000 of uncollectible accounts receivable were written off. Past experience indicates that the allowance should be 10% of the balance in receivables (percentage of receivables basis). If the accounts receivable balance at December 31 was $200,000, what is the required adjustment to the Allowance for Doubtful Accounts at December 31, 2005?
  (a) $20,000.   (c) $32,000.
  (b) $75,000.   (d) $30,000.

(SO 3) **4.** An analysis and aging of the accounts receivable of Wells Company at December 31 reveal these data:

Accounts receivable	$800,000
Allowance for doubtful accounts per books before adjustment (credit)	50,000
Amounts expected to become uncollectible	65,000

What is the cash realizable value of the accounts receivable at December 31, after adjustment?
  (a) $685,000.   (c) $800,000.
  (b) $750,000.   (d) $735,000.

(SO 4) **5.** Which of these statements about promissory notes is *incorrect*?
  (a) The party making the promise to pay is called the maker.
  (b) The party to whom payment is to be made is called the payee.
  (c) A promissory note is not a negotiable instrument.
  (d) A promissory note is more liquid than an account receivable.

(SO 4) **6.** Swendson Co. accepts a $1,000, 3-month, 12% promissory note in settlement of an account with Willis Co. The entry to record this transaction is:

(a) Notes Receivable	1,030	
Accounts Receivable		1,030
(b) Notes Receivable	1,000	
Accounts Receivable		1,000
(c) Notes Receivable	1,000	
Sales		1,000

(d) Notes Receivable	1,020	
Accounts Receivable		1,020

(SO 5) **7.** Bright Co. holds Raymond Inc.'s $10,000, 120-day, 9% note. The entry made by Bright Co. when the note is collected, assuming no interest has previously been accrued, is:

(a) Cash	10,300	
Notes Receivable		10,300
(b) Cash	10,000	
Notes Receivable		10,000
(c) Accounts Receivable	10,300	
Notes Receivable		10,000
Interest Revenue		300
(d) Cash	10,300	
Notes Receivable		10,000
Interest Revenue		300

(SO 8) **8.** Jay Corporation had net credit sales during the year of $800,000 and cost of goods sold of $500,000. The balance in receivables at the beginning of the year was $100,000 and at the end of the year was $150,000. What was the receivables turnover ratio?
  (a) 6.4   (b) 8.0   (c) 5.3   (d) 4.0

(SO 8) **9.** Brendal Corporation sells its goods on terms of 2/10, n/30. It has a receivables turnover ratio of 7. What is its average collection period (days)?
  (a) 2,555   (b) 30   (c) 52   (d) 210

(SO 9) **10.** Which of these statements about **Visa** credit card sales is *incorrect*?
  (a) The credit card issuer conducts the credit investigation of the customer.
  (b) The retailer is not involved in the collection process.
  (c) The retailer must wait to receive payment from the issuer.
  (d) The retailer receives cash more quickly than it would from individual customers.

(SO 9) **11.** New Millenium Retailers accepted $50,000 of **Citibank Visa** credit card charges for merchandise sold on July 1. Citibank charges 4% for its credit card use. The entry to record this transaction by New Millenium Retailers will include a credit to Sales of $50,000 and a debit(s) to:
  (a) Cash $48,000 and Service Charge Expense $2,000.
  (b) Accounts Receivable $48,000 and Service Charge Expense $2,000.
  (c) Cash $50,000.
  (d) Accounts Receivable $50,000.

☑ THE NAVIGATOR

Questions

1. What is the difference between an account receivable and a note receivable?

2. What are some common types of receivables other than accounts receivable or notes receivable?

3. What are the essential features of the allowance method of accounting for bad debts?

4. Jo Duma cannot understand why the cash realizable value does not decrease when an uncollectible account is written off under the allowance method. Clarify this point for Jo Duma.

5. Cobo Company has a credit balance of $3,900 in Allowance for Doubtful Accounts before adjustment. The estimated uncollectibles under the percentage of receivables basis is $5,800. Prepare the adjusting entry.

6. How are bad debts accounted for under the direct write-off method? What are the disadvantages of this method?

7. Your roommate is uncertain about the advantages of a promissory note. Compare the advantages of a note receivable with those of an account receivable.

8. How may the maturity date of a promissory note be stated?

9. Compute the missing amounts for each of the following notes.

Principal	Annual Interest Rate	Time	Total Interest
(a)	9%	120 days	$ 360
$30,000	8%	3 years	(d)
$60,000	(b)	5 months	$2,500
$50,000	11%	(c)	$1,375

10. Dent Company dishonors a note at maturity. What are the options available to the lender?

11. **General Motors Company** has accounts receivable and notes receivable. How should the receivables be reported on the balance sheet?

12. What are the steps to good receivables management?

13. How might a company monitor the risk related to its accounts receivable?

14. What is meant by a concentration of credit risk?

15. The President of Ho Inc. proudly announces her company's improved liquidity since its current ratio has increased substantially from one year to the next. Does an increase in the current ratio always indicate improved liquidity? What other ratio or ratios might you review to determine whether or not the increase in the current ratio is an improvement in financial health?

16. The **Coca-Cola Company's** receivables turnover ratio was 10.68 in 2001, and its average amount of net receivables during the period was $1,880 million. What is the amount of its net credit sales for the period? What is the average collection period in days?

17. **JCPenney Company** accepts both its own credit cards and national credit cards. What are the advantages of accepting both types of cards?

18. An article in the *Wall Street Journal* indicated that companies are selling their receivables at a record rate. Why do companies sell their receivables?

19. Midwest Textiles decides to sell $700,000 of its accounts receivable to First Central Factors Inc. First Central Factors assesses a service charge of 3% of the amount of receivables sold. Prepare the journal entry that Midwest Textiles makes to record this sale.

Brief Exercises

Identify different types of receivables.
(SO 1)

BE8-1 Presented below are three receivables transactions. Indicate whether these receivables are reported as accounts receivable, notes receivable, or other receivables on a balance sheet.
  (a) Advanced $10,000 to an employee.
  (b) Received a promissory note of $34,000 for services performed.
  (c) Sold merchandise on account for $60,000 to a customer.

Record basic accounts receivable transactions.
(SO 2)

BE8-2 Record the following transactions on the books of Allen Co.
  (a) On July 1 Allen Co. sold merchandise on account to Manhattan Inc. for $14,000, terms 2/10, n/30.
  (b) On July 8 Manhattan Inc. returned merchandise worth $2,400 to Allen Co.
  (c) On July 11 Manhattan Inc. paid for the merchandise.

Prepare entry for write-off, and determine cash realizable value.
(SO 3)

BE8-3 At the end of 2005, Pascal Co. has accounts receivable of $700,000 and an allowance for doubtful accounts of $54,000. On January 24, 2006, it is learned that the

company's receivable from Mora Inc. is not collectible and therefore management authorizes a write-off of $12,000.
  (a) Prepare the journal entry to record the write-off.
  (b) What is the cash realizable value of the accounts receivable (1) before the write-off and (2) after the write-off?

BE8-4   Assume the same information as BE8-3 and that on March 4, 2006, Pascal Co. receives payment of $12,000 in full from Mora Co. Prepare the journal entries to record this transaction.

Prepare entries for collection of bad debt write-off.
(SO 3)

BE8-5   Marion Co. uses the percentage of receivables basis to record bad debts expense and concludes that 1% of accounts receivable will become uncollectible. Accounts receivable are $500,000 at the end of the year, and the allowance for doubtful accounts has a credit balance of $1,500.
  (a) Prepare the adjusting journal entry to record bad debts expense for the year.
  (b) If the allowance for doubtful accounts had a debit balance of $800 instead of a credit balance of $1,500, prepare the adjusting journal entry for bad debts expense.

Prepare entry using percentage of receivables method.
(SO 3)

BE8-6   Presented below are three promissory notes. Determine the missing amounts.

Compute maturity date and interest on note.
(SO 4)

Date of Note	Terms	Principal	Annual Interest Rate	Total Interest
April 1	60 days	$900,000	10%	(a)
July 2	30 days	79,000	(b)	$592.50
March 7	6 months	56,000	11%	(c)

BE8-7   On January 10, 2005, Tene Co. sold merchandise on account to B. Hills for $12,000, terms n/30. On February 9 B. Hills gave Tene Co. a 9% promissory note in settlement of this account. Prepare the journal entry to record the sale and the settlement of the accounts receivable.

Prepare entry for note receivable exchanged for accounts receivable.
(SO 4)

BE8-8   During its first year of operations, Dana Company had credit sales of $3,000,000, of which $600,000 remained uncollected at year-end. The credit manager estimates that $35,000 of these receivables will become uncollectible.
  (a) Prepare the journal entry to record the estimated uncollectibles. (Assume an unadjusted balance of zero.)
  (b) Prepare the current assets section of the balance sheet for Dana Company, assuming that in addition to the receivables it has cash of $90,000, merchandise inventory of $130,000, and prepaid expenses of $13,000.
  (c) Calculate the receivables turnover ratio and average collection period. Assume that average net receivables were $300,000.

Prepare entry for estimated uncollectibles and classifications, and compute ratios.
(SO 3, 6, 7, 8)

BE8-9   The 2001 financial statements of **3M Company** report net sales of $16.0 billion. Accounts receivable (net) are $3.0 billion at the beginning of the year and $2.6 billion at the end of the year. Compute 3M's receivables turnover ratio. Compute 3M's average collection period for accounts receivable in days.

Analyze accounts receivable.
(SO 8)

BE8-10   Consider these transactions:
  (a) Club Garibaldi Restaurant accepted a Visa card in payment of a $100 lunch bill. The bank charges a 3% fee. What entry should Club Garibaldi make?
  (b) Curtis Company sold its accounts receivable of $80,000. What entry should Curtis make, given a service charge of 3% on the amount of receivables sold?

Prepare entries for credit card sale and sale of accounts receivable.
(SO 9)

Exercises

E8-1   On January 6 Dusk Co. sells merchandise on account to Dawn Inc. for $6,000, terms 2/10, n/30. On January 16 Dawn pays the amount due.

Prepare entries for recognizing accounts receivable.
(SO 2)

Instructions
Prepare the entries on Dusk Co.'s books to record the sale and related collection.

Prepare entries for recognizing accounts receivable.
(SO 2)

E8-2   On January 10 Donna Kozen uses her Marais Co. credit card to purchase merchandise from Marais Co. for $1,300. On February 10 Kozen is billed for the amount due of $1,300. On February 12 Kozen pays $1,000 on the balance due. On March 10 Kozen is billed for the amount due, including interest at 1% per month on the unpaid balance as of February 12.

Instructions

Prepare the entries on Marais Co.'s books related to the transactions that occurred on January 10, February 12, and March 10.

Prepare entries to record allowance for doubtful accounts.
(SO 3)

E8-3   The ledger of Seymor Company at the end of the current year shows Accounts Receivable $90,000; Credit Sales $780,000; and Sales Returns and Allowances $40,000.

Instructions

(a) If Seymor uses the direct write-off method to account for uncollectible accounts, journalize the adjusting entry at December 31, assuming Seymor determines that Copp's $1,400 balance is uncollectible.

(b) If Allowance for Doubtful Accounts has a credit balance of $1,100 in the trial balance, journalize the adjusting entry at December 31, assuming bad debts are expected to be 10% of accounts receivable.

(c) If Allowance for Doubtful Accounts has a debit balance of $500 in the trial balance, journalize the adjusting entry at December 31, assuming bad debts are expected to be 8% of accounts receivable.

Determine bad debt expense, and prepare the adjusting entry.
(SO 3)

E8-4   Galenti Company has accounts receivable of $92,500 at March 31, 2005. An analysis of the accounts shows these amounts.

| | Balance, March 31 | |
Month of Sale	2005	2004
March	$65,000	$75,000
February	12,600	8,000
December and January	8,500	2,400
November and October	6,400	1,100
	$92,500	$86,500

Credit terms are 2/10, n/30. At March 31, 2005, there is a $2,200 credit balance in Allowance for Doubtful Accounts prior to adjustment. The company uses the percentage of receivables basis for estimating uncollectible accounts. The company's estimates of bad debts are as follows.

Age of Accounts	Estimated Percentage Uncollectible
Current	2%
1–30 days past due	7
31–90 days past due	30
Over 90 days	50

Instructions

(a) Determine the total estimated uncollectibles.

(b) Prepare the adjusting entry at March 31, 2005, to record bad debts expense.

(c) Discuss the implications of the changes in the aging schedule from 2004 to 2005.

Prepare entry for estimated uncollectibles, write-off, and recovery.
(SO 3)

E8-5   On December 31, 2005, when its Allowance for Doubtful Accounts had a debit balance of $1,000, Pat Davis Co. estimates that 12% of its accounts receivable balance of $70,000 will become uncollectible and records the necessary adjustment to the Allowance for Doubtful Accounts. On May 11, 2006, Pat Davis Co. determined that Cody Hanover's account was uncollectible and wrote off $900. On June 12, 2006, Hanover paid the amount previously written off.

Instructions
Prepare the journal entries on December 31, 2005, May 11, 2006, and June 12, 2006.

E8-6 Bernard Supply Co. has the following transactions related to notes receivable during the last 2 months of the year.

Prepare entries for notes receivable transactions.
(SO 4, 5)

Nov. 1 Loaned $30,000 cash to T. Crew on a 1-year, 8% note.
Dec. 11 Sold goods to M. F. Hoffman, Inc., receiving a $3,600, 90-day, 12% note.
    16 Received an $8,000, 6-month, 12% note to settle an open account from C. Lampe.
    31 Accrued interest revenue on all notes receivable.

Instructions
Journalize the transactions for Bernard Supply Co.

E8-7 These transactions took place for Blue Diamond Co.

Journalize notes receivable transactions.
(SO 4, 5)

2004

May 1 Received a $6,000, 1-year, 12% note in exchange for an outstanding account receivable from G. Dolphin.
Dec. 31 Accrued interest revenue on the G. Dolphin note.

2005

May 1 Received principal plus interest on the G. Dolphin note. (No interest has been accrued since December 31, 2004.)

Instructions
Record the transactions in the general journal.

E8-8 Winter Corp. had the following balances in receivable accounts at October 31, 2005 (in thousands): Allowance for Doubtful Accounts $51; Accounts Receivable $2,840; Other Receivables $189; Notes Receivable $853.

Prepare a balance sheet presentation of receivables.
(SO 6)

Instructions
Prepare the balance sheet presentation of Winter Corp.'s receivables in good form.

E8-9 The following is a list of activities that companies perform in relation to their receivables.

Identify the principles of receivables management.
(SO 7)

1. Selling receivables to a factor.
2. Reviewing company ratings in *The Dun and Bradstreet Reference Book of American Business.*
3. Collecting information on competitors' payment period policies.
4. Preparing accounts receivable aging schedule and calculating the credit risk ratio.
5. Calculating the receivables turnover ratio and average collection period.

Instructions
Match each of the activities listed above with a purpose of the activity listed below.
(a) Determine to whom to extend credit.
(b) Establish a payment period.
(c) Monitor collections.
(d) Evaluate the receivables balance.
(e) Accelerate cash receipts from receivables when necessary.

E8-10 The following information was taken from the 2001 financial statements of **FedEx Corporation**, a major global transportation/delivery company.

Compute ratios to evaluate a company's receivables balance.
(SO 7, 8)

(in millions)	2001	2000
Accounts receivable (gross)	$ 2,601.8	$ 2,633.0
Accounts receivable (net)	$ 2,506.0	$ 2,547.0
Allowance for uncollectible accounts	95.8	86.0
Sales	19,629.0	18,257.0
Total current assets	3,449.1	3,284.7

Instructions

Answer each of the following questions.

(a) Calculate the receivables turnover ratio and the average collection period for 2001 for FedEx.

(b) Is accounts receivable a material component of the company's total current assets?

(c) Evaluate the balance in FedEx's allowance for uncollectible accounts.

Prepare entry for sale of accounts receivable.
(SO 9)

E8-11   On March 3 Global Appliances sells $700,000 of its receivables to Friendly Factors Inc. Friendly Factors Inc. assesses a finance charge of 4% of the amount of receivables sold.

Instructions

Prepare the entry on Global Appliances' books to record the sale of the receivables.

Identify reason for sale of receivables.
(SO 9)

E8-12   The 2001 annual report of **Office Depot, Inc.** notes that the company entered into an agreement to sell all of its credit card program receivables to financial service companies.

Instructions

Explain why Office Depot, a financially stable company with positive cash flow, would choose to sell its receivables.

Prepare entry for credit card sale.
(SO 9)

E8-13   On May 10 Tran Company sold merchandise for $7,000 and accepted the customer's First Business Bank MasterCard. At the end of the day, the First Business Bank MasterCard receipts were deposited in the company's bank account. First Business Bank charges a 3% service charge for credit card sales.

Instructions

Prepare the entry on Tran Company's books to record the sale of merchandise.

Prepare entry for credit card sale.
(SO 9)

E8-14   On July 4 Blondie's Restaurant accepts a Visa card for a $300 dinner bill. Visa charges a 4% service fee.

Instructions

Prepare the entry on Blondie's books related to the transaction.

Problems: Set A

Journalize transactions related to bad debts.
(SO 2, 3)

P8-1A   The following represents selected information taken from a company's aging schedule to estimate uncollectible accounts receivable at year end.

| | Total | Number of Days Outstanding | | | | |
		0–30	31–60	61–90	91–120	Over 120
Accounts receivable	$260,000	$100,000	$60,000	$50,000	$30,000	$20,000
% uncollectible		1%	5%	7.5%	10%	12%
Estimated bad debts	13,150	1000	3000	3750	3000	2400

Instructions

(a) Calculate the total estimated bad debts based on the above information.

(b) Prepare the year-end adjusting journal entry to record the bad debts using the allowance method and the aged uncollectible accounts receivable determined in (a). Assume the unadjusted balance in the Allowance for Doubtful Accounts account is a $10,000 credit.   *Estimate*

(c) Of the above accounts, $2,000 is determined to be specifically uncollectible. Prepare the journal entry to write off the uncollectible accounts.

(d) The company subsequently collects $1,000 on a specific account that had previously been determined to be uncollectible in (c). Prepare the journal entry(ies) necessary to restore the account and record the cash collection.

(e) Explain how establishing an allowance account satisfies the matching principle.

(a) Tot. est.
    bad debts. $13,150

% uncollectible

P8-2A At December 31, 2005, Zurich Company reported this information on its balance sheet.

Prepare journal entries related to bad debt expense, and compute ratios.
(SO 2, 3, 8)

Accounts receivable	$960,000
Less: Allowance for doubtful accounts	70,000

During 2006 the company had the following transactions related to receivables.

1. Sales on account	$3,800,000
2. Sales returns and allowances	50,000
3. Collections of accounts receivable	3,000,000
4. Write-offs of accounts receivable deemed uncollectible	90,000
5. Recovery of bad debts previously written off as uncollectible	40,000

Instructions
(a) Prepare the journal entries to record each of these five transactions. Assume that no cash discounts were taken on the collections of accounts receivable.
(b) Enter the January 1, 2006, balances in Accounts Receivable and Allowance for Doubtful Accounts, post the entries to the two accounts (use T accounts), and determine the balances.
(c) Prepare the journal entry to record bad debts expense for 2006, assuming that aging the accounts receivable indicates that expected bad debts are $110,000.
(d) Compute the receivables turnover ratio and average collection period.

(b) A/R bal. $1,620,000

P8-3A Presented here is an aging schedule for Northern Iowa Company.

Journalize transactions related to bad debts.
(SO 2, 3)

Customer	Total	Not Yet Due	Number of Days Past Due			
			1–30	**31–60**	**61–90**	**Over 90**
Anita	$ 22,000		$10,000	$12,000		
Barry	40,000	$ 40,000				
Chagnon	57,000	16,000	6,000		$35,000	
David	34,000					$34,000
Others	126,000	96,000	16,000	14,000		
	$279,000	$152,000	$32,000	$26,000	$35,000	$34,000
Estimated percentage uncollectible		4%	9%	15%	25%	50%
Total estimated bad debts	$ 38,610	$ 6,080	$ 2,880	$ 3,900	$ 8,750	$17,000

At December 31, 2005, the unadjusted balance in Allowance for Doubtful Accounts is a credit of $14,000.

Instructions
(a) Journalize and post the adjusting entry for bad debts at December 31, 2005. (Use T accounts.)
(b) Journalize and post to the allowance account these 2006 events and transactions:
1. March 31, a $500 customer balance originating in 2005 is judged uncollectible.
2. May 31, a check for $500 is received from the customer whose account was written off as uncollectible on March 31.
(c) Journalize the adjusting entry for bad debts on December 31, 2006, assuming that the unadjusted balance in Allowance for Doubtful Accounts is a debit of $800 and the aging schedule indicates that total estimated bad debts will be $30,300.

P8-4A Here is information related to Emporia Company for 2005.

Compute bad debt amounts.
(SO 3)

Total credit sales	$2,000,000
Accounts receivable at December 31	800,000
Bad debts written off	36,000

Instructions

(a) What amount of bad debts expense will Emporia Company report if it uses the direct write-off method of accounting for bad debts?

(b) Assume that Emporia Company decides to estimate its bad debts expense based on 4% of accounts receivable. What amount of bad debts expense will the company record if it has an Allowance for Doubtful Accounts credit balance of $4,000?

(c) Assume the same facts as in part (b), except that there is a $2,000 debit balance in Allowance for Doubtful Accounts. What amount of bad debts expense will Emporia record?

(d) What is the weakness of the direct write-off method of reporting bad debts expense?

Journalize entries to record transactions related to bad debts.
(SO 2, 3)

P8-5A   At December 31, 2005, the trial balance of Saratoga Company contained the following amounts before adjustment.

	Debits	Credits
Accounts Receivable	$400,000	
Allowance for Doubtful Accounts		$ 1,800
Sales		950,000

Instructions

(a) Based on the information given, which method of accounting for bad debts is Saratoga Company using—the direct write-off method or the allowance method? How can you tell?

(b) Prepare the adjusting entry at December 31, 2005, for bad debts expense assuming that the aging schedule indicates that $13,200 of accounts receivable will be uncollectible.

(c) Repeat part (b) assuming that instead of a credit balance there is a $1,800 debit balance in the Allowance for Doubtful Accounts.

(d) During the next month, January 2006, a $5,000 account receivable is written off as uncollectible. Prepare the journal entry to record the write-off.

(e) Repeat part (d) assuming that Saratoga uses the direct write-off method instead of the allowance method in accounting for uncollectible accounts receivable.

(f) ▭▭▭➤ What type of account is the allowance for doubtful accounts? How does it affect how accounts receivable is reported on the balance sheet at the end of the accounting period?

Journalize various receivables transactions.
(SO 1, 2, 4, 5)

P8-6A   On January 1, 2005, Della Valle Company had Accounts Receivable $146,000; Notes Receivable $11,000; and Allowance for Doubtful Accounts $13,200. The note receivable is from Lisa Company. It is a 4-month, 12% note dated December 31, 2004. Della Valle Company prepares financial statements annually. During the year the following selected transactions occurred.

Jan.	5	Sold $12,000 of merchandise to Lynn Company, terms n/15.
	20	Accepted Lynn Company's $12,000, 3-month, 9% note for balance due.
Feb.	18	Sold $8,000 of merchandise to Drew Company and accepted Drew's $8,000, 6-month, 10% note for the amount due.
Apr.	20	Collected Lynn Company note in full.
	30	Received payment in full from Lisa Company on the amount due.
May	25	Accepted Shamrock Inc.'s $6,000, 6-month, 8% note in settlement of a past-due balance on account.
Aug.	18	Received payment in full from Drew Company on note due.
Sept.	1	Sold $8,000 of merchandise to Louis Company and accepted an $8,000, 6-month, 10% note for the amount due.

Instructions

Journalize the transactions.

P8-7A   The president of Hanlon Enterprises Ltd., Renée Hanlon, is considering the impact that certain transactions have on its receivables turnover and average collection period ratios. Prior to the following transactions, Hanlon's receivables turnover was 6 times, and its average collection period was 61 days.

Explain the impact of transactions on ratios: discuss acceleration of receipt of cash from receivables.
(SO 8, 9)

Transaction	Receivables Turnover (6×)	Average Collection Period (61 days)
1. Recorded sales on account $100,000.		
2. Collected $25,000 owing from customers.		
3. Recorded bad debt expense for the year $7,500, using the allowance method.		
4. Recorded sales returns of $1,500 and credited the customers' accounts.		
5. Wrote off a $2,500 account from a customer as uncollectible.		

Instructions

(a) Complete the table, indicating whether each transaction will increase (I), decrease (D), or have no effect (NE) on the ratios.

(b) Renée Hanlon was reading through the financial statements for some publicly traded companies and noticed that they had recorded a loss on sale of receivables. She would like you to explain why companies sell their receivables.

P8-8A Kingston Company closes its books on October 31. On September 30 the Notes Receivable account balance is $24,700. Notes Receivable include the following.

Prepare entries for various credit card and notes receivable transactions.
(SO 2, 4, 5, 6, 9)

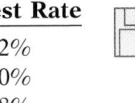

Date	Maker	Face Value	Term	Maturity Date	Interest Rate
Aug. 16	Teller Inc.	$ 8,000	60 days	Oct. 15	12%
Aug. 25	Jonet Co.	6,500	2 months	Oct. 25	10%
Sept. 30	KLH Corp.	10,200	6 months	Mar. 30	8%

Interest is computed using a 360-day year. During October the following transactions were completed.

Oct. 7 Made sales of $6,900 on Kingston credit cards.
   12 Made sales of $750 on Visa credit cards. The credit card service charge is 3%.
   15 Received payment in full from Teller Inc. on the amount due.
   25 Received payment in full from Jonet Co. on amount due.

Instructions

(a) Journalize the October transactions and the October 31 adjusting entry for accrued interest receivable.

(b) Enter the balances at October 1 in the receivable accounts and post the entries to all of the receivable accounts. (Use T accounts.)

(c) Show the balance sheet presentation of the receivable accounts at October 31.

(b) A/R bal. $ 6,900
(c) Tot.
        receivables $17,168

P8-9A Presented here is basic financial information from the 2001 annual reports of **Intel** and **Advanced Micro Devices (AMD)**, the two primary manufacturers of silicon chips for personal computers.

Calculate and interpret various ratios.
(SO 7, 8)

(in millions)	Intel	AMD
Sales	$26,539	$3,891.8
Allowance for doubtful accounts, Jan. 1	84	22.7
Allowance for doubtful accounts, Dec. 31	68	19.3
Accounts receivable balance (gross), Jan. 1	4,213	569.9
Accounts receivable balance (gross), Dec. 31	2,675	679.1

Instructions
Calculate the receivables turnover ratio and average collection period for both companies. Comment on the difference in their collection experiences.

Problems: Set B

*Journalize transactions
related to bad debts.*
(SO 2, 3)

P8-1B Image.com uses the allowance method to estimate uncollectible accounts receivable. The company produced the following aging of the accounts receivable at year end.

| | Total | Number of Days Outstanding | | | | |
		0–30	31–60	61–90	91–120	Over 120
Accounts receivable	$375,000	$220,000	$90,000	$40,000	$10,000	$15,000
% uncollectible		1%	4%	5%	6%	10%
Estimated bad debts						

Instructions

(a) Tot. est. bad debts $9,900

(a) Calculate the total estimated bad debts based on the above information.
(b) Prepare the year-end adjusting journal entry to record the bad debts using the aged uncollectible accounts receivable determined in (a). Assume the unadjusted balance in Allowance for Doubtful Accounts is a $10,000 debit.
(c) Of the above accounts, $5,000 is determined to be specifically uncollectible. Prepare the journal entry to write off the uncollectible account.
(d) The company collects $5,000 subsequently on a specific account that had previously been determined to be uncollectible in (c). Prepare the journal entry(ies) necessary to restore the account and record the cash collection.
(e) Comment on how your answers to (a)–(d) would change if Image.com used 3% of *total* accounts receivable, rather than aging the accounts receivable. What are the advantages to the company of aging the accounts receivable rather than applying a percentage to total accounts receivable?

*Prepare journal entries
related to bad debt expense,
and compute ratios.*
(SO 2, 3, 8)

P8-2B At December 31, 2005, Plaza Imports reported this information on its balance sheet.

Accounts receivable	$1,000,000
Less: Allowance for doubtful accounts	50,000

During 2006 the company had the following transactions related to receivables.

1.	Sales on account	$2,600,000
2.	Sales returns and allowances	40,000
3.	Collections of accounts receivable	2,200,000
4.	Write-offs of accounts receivable deemed uncollectible	65,000
5.	Recovery of bad debts previously written off as uncollectible	25,000

Instructions

(b) A/R bal. $1,295,000

(a) Prepare the journal entries to record each of these five transactions. Assume that no cash discounts were taken on the collections of accounts receivable.
(b) Enter the January 1, 2006, balances in Accounts Receivable and Allowance for Doubtful Accounts, post the entries to the two accounts (use T accounts), and determine the balances.
(c) Prepare the journal entry to record bad debts expense for 2006, assuming that aging the accounts receivable indicates that estimated bad debts are $70,000.
(d) Compute the receivables turnover ratio and average collection period.

P8-3B   Presented below is an aging schedule for Dinah Company.

Journalize transactions related to bad debts.
(SO 2, 3)

Customer	Total	Not Yet Due	Number of Days Past Due			
			1–30	31–60	61–90	Over 90
Aber	$ 20,000		$ 9,000	$11,000		
Bohr	30,000	$30,000				
Case	50,000	15,000	5,000		$30,000	
Datz	38,000					$38,000
Others	120,000	92,000	15,000	13,000		
	$258,000	$137,000	$29,000	$24,000	$30,000	$38,000
Estimated percentage uncollectible		3%	5%	12%	24%	50%
Total estimated bad debts	$ 34,640	$ 4,110	$ 1,450	$ 2,880	$ 7,200	$19,000

At December 31, 2005, the unadjusted balance in Allowance for Doubtful Accounts is a credit of $10,000.

Instructions
(a) Journalize and post the adjusting entry for bad debts at December 31, 2005. (Use T accounts.)
(b) Journalize and post to the allowance account these 2006 events and transactions:
 1. March 1, a $600 customer balance originating in 2005 is judged uncollectible.
 2. May 1, a check for $600 is received from the customer whose account was written off as uncollectible on March 1.
(c) Journalize the adjusting entry for bad debts at December 31, 2006, assuming that the unadjusted balance in Allowance for Doubtful Accounts is a debit of $1,100 and the aging schedule indicates that total estimated bad debts will be $33,200.

P8-4B   Here is information related to Tsunami Company for 2005.

Compute bad debt amounts.
(SO 3)

Total credit sales	$1,500,000
Accounts receivable at December 31	600,000
Bad debts written off	28,000

Instructions
(a) What amount of bad debts expense will Tsunami Company report if it uses the direct write-off method of accounting for bad debts?
(b) Assume that Tsunami Company decides to estimate its bad debts expense based on 3% of accounts receivable. What amount of bad debts expense will the company record if Allowance for Doubtful Accounts has a credit balance of $3,000?
(c) Assume the same facts as in part (b), except that there is a $1,000 debit balance in Allowance for Doubtful Accounts. What amount of bad debts expense will Tsunami record?
(d) What is the weakness of the direct write-off method of reporting bad debts expense?

P8-5B   At December 31, 2005, the trial balance of Bossa Nova Company contained the following amounts before adjustment.

Journalize entries to record transactions related to bad debts.
(SO 2, 3)

	Debits	Credits
Accounts Receivable	$350,000	
Allowance for Doubtful Accounts		$ 1,500
Sales		875,000

Instructions

(a) Prepare the adjusting entry at December 31, 2005, to record bad debt expense assuming that the aging schedule indicates that $17,800 of accounts receivable will be uncollectible.

(b) Repeat part (a) assuming that instead of a credit balance there is a $1,500 debit balance in the Allowance for Doubtful Accounts.

(c) During the next month, January 2006, a $5,200 account receivable is written off as uncollectible. Prepare the journal entry to record the write-off.

(d) Repeat part (c) assuming that Bossa Nova Company uses the direct write-off method instead of the allowance method in accounting for uncollectible accounts receivable.

(e) What are the advantages of using the allowance method in accounting for uncollectible accounts as compared to the direct write-off method?

*Journalize various
receivables transactions.
(SO 1, 2, 4, 5)*

P8-6B On January 1, 2005, Liam Company had Accounts Receivable $54,200 and Allowance for Doubtful Accounts $4,700. Liam Company prepares financial statements annually and uses a perpetual inventory system. During the year the following selected transactions occurred.

Jan. 5 Sold $6,000 of merchandise to Thomas Company, terms n/30. Cost of the merchandise sold was $4,000.

Feb. 2 Accepted a $6,000, 4-month, 12% promissory note from Thomas Company for balance due.

12 Sold $7,800 of merchandise costing $5,000 to Patrick Company and accepted Patrick's $7,800, 2-month, 10% note for the balance due.

26 Sold $5,000 of merchandise costing $3,300 to Jeremiah Co., terms n/10.

Apr. 5 Accepted a $5,000, 3-month, 8% note from Jeremiah Co. for balance due.

12 Collected Patrick Company note in full.

June 2 Collected Thomas Company note in full.

15 Sold $2,000 of merchandise costing $1,500 to Michael Inc. and accepted a $2,000, 6-month, 12% note for the amount due.

Instructions
Journalize the transactions.

*Explain the impact of
transactions on ratios.
(SO 8)*

P8-7B The president of Fort McMurray Enterprises Ltd. asks if you could indicate the impact certain transactions have on the following ratios.

Transaction	Current Ratio (2:1)	Receivables Turnover (10X)	Average Collection Period (36.5 days)
1. Recorded $2,500 sales on account. The cost of the goods sold was $1,500.			
2. Recorded bad debt expense of $500 using allowance method.			
3. Wrote off a $100 account receivable as uncollectible.			
4. Received $3,000 on cash sale. The cost of the goods sold was $1,800.			

Instructions
Complete the table, indicating whether each transaction will increase (I), decrease (D), or have no effect (NE) on the specific ratios provided for Fort McMurray Enterprises.

*Prepare entries for various
credit card and notes
receivable transactions.
(SO 2, 4, 5, 6, 9)*

P8-8B Burlington Company closes its books on July 31. On June 30 the Notes Receivable account balance is $23,800. Notes Receivable include the following.

Date	Maker	Face Value	Term	Maturity Date	Interest Rate
May 21	Alder Inc.	$ 9,000	60 days	July 20	12%
May 25	Dorn Co.	4,800	60 days	July 24	11%
June 30	MJH Corp.	10,000	6 months	December 31	9%

During July the following transactions were completed.

July 5   Made sales of $7,800 on Burlington credit cards.
     14   Made sales of $700 on Visa credit cards. The credit card service charge is 3%.
     20   Received payment in full from Alder Inc. on the amount due.
     25   Received payment in full from Dorn Co. on the amount due.

Instructions
(a) Journalize the July transactions and the July 31 adjusting entry for accrued interest receivable. (Interest is computed using 360 days.)
(b) Enter the balances at July 1 in the receivable accounts and post the entries to all of the receivable accounts. (Use T accounts.)
(c) Show the balance sheet presentation of the receivable accounts at July 31.

(b) A/R bal. $ 7,800
(c) Tot.
   receivables $17,875

P8-9B   Presented here is basic financial information (in millions) from the 2001 annual reports of **Nike** and **Reebok**.

Calculate and interpret various ratios.
(SO 7, 8)

	Nike	Reebok
Sales	$9,488.8	$2,992.9
Allowance for doubtful accounts, Jan. 1	65.4	48.0
Allowance for doubtful accounts, Dec. 31	72.1	55.2
Accounts receivable balance (gross), Jan. 1	1,634.8	471.8
Accounts receivable balance (gross), Dec. 31	1,693.5	438.6

Instructions
Calculate the receivables turnover ratio and average collection period for both companies. Comment on the difference in their collection experiences.

BROADENING YOUR PERSPECTIVE

Financial Reporting and Analysis

FINANCIAL REPORTING PROBLEM: *Tootsie Roll Industries*

BYP8-1   Refer to the financial statements of Tootsie Roll Industries and the accompanying notes to its financial statements in Appendix A.

Instructions
(a) Calculate the receivables turnover ratio and average collection period for 2002.
(b) Did Tootsie Roll have any potentially significant credit risks in 2002? (*Hint:* Review Note 13 to the financial statements.)
(c) What conclusions can you draw from the information in parts (a) and (b)?

COMPARATIVE ANALYSIS PROBLEM: *Tootsie Roll vs. Hershey Foods*

BYP8-2 The financial statements of **Hershey Foods** are presented in Appendix B, following the financial statements for **Tootsie Roll** in Appendix A.

Instructions
(a) Based on the information contained in these financial statements, compute the following 2002 values for each company. Hershey's allowance for uncollectible accounts was $16 million at December 31, 2001, and $16.5 million at December 31, 2002.
  (1) Receivables turnover ratio. (Assume all sales were credit sales.)
  (2) Average collection period for receivables.
(b) What conclusions concerning the management of accounts receivable can be drawn from these data?

RESEARCH CASE

BYP8-3 The May 13, 2002, issue of the *Wall Street Journal* includes an article by Paul Beckett entitled "Is **Citigroup** Set for a Rainy Day? Reserves Make Investors Uneasy."

Instructions
Read the article and answer the following questions.
(a) How do Citigroup's "reserve" accounts (such as allowance for bad debts) compare to those of other large financial institutions?
(b) What reasons are given for expecting that Citigroup should actually have larger reserves than its peer institutions, rather than smaller reserves?
(c) How does the article suggest that a bank's expectations about the future economy affect the amount of reserves that the bank sets up? What does this suggest about Citigroup's expectations about the future economy?
(d) What are some reasons given for not being alarmed about the adequacy of Citigroup's reserves?

INTERPRETING FINANCIAL STATEMENTS

BYP8-4 **Sears** is one of the world's largest retailers. It is also a huge provider of credit through its Sears credit card. Revenue generated from credit operations was $5.2 billion in 2001 from 30 million Sears cardholders. The rate of interest Sears earns on outstanding receivables varies from 10% to 21% in the United States to up to 28% in Canada. In some instances, to acquire cash when needed, the company will sell its receivables. For instance, at December 31, 2000, Sears sold $7.8 billion of its receivables.

The following information (in millions) was available in Sears's 2001 financial statements.

	2001	2000	1999
Accounts receivable (gross)	$29,321	$18,003	$18,793
Accounts receivable (net)	28,155	17,317	18,033
Allowance for doubtful accounts	1,166	686	760
Merchandise sales	35,843	36,366	34,963
Credit revenues	5,235	4,571	4,521
Bad debts expense	1,344	884	871

Instructions
(a) Discuss whether the sale of receivables by Sears in 2000 represented a significant portion of its receivables. Why might Sears have sold these receivables? As an investor, what concerns might you have about these sales?
(b) Calculate and discuss the receivables turnover ratio and average collection period for Sears for 2001 and 2000.
(c) Do you think Sears provides credit cards as a revenue-generating activity or as a convenience for its customers?
(d) Compute the ratio of bad debts expense to merchandise sales for 2001 and 2000. Did this ratio improve or worsen? What considerations should Sears make in deciding whether it wants to have liberal or conservative credit-granting policies?

BYP8-5 The following information was taken from the 2001 financial statements and accompanying notes of **The Scotts Company**, a major manufacturer of lawn-care products.

(in millions)	2001	2000
Accounts receivable	$ 244.7	$ 227.7
Allowance for uncollectible accounts	23.9	11.7
Sales	1,747.7	1,709.0
Total current assets	694.2	643.9

THE SCOTTS COMPANY
Notes to the Financial Statements

Note 16. Concentrations of Credit Risk

Financial instruments which potentially subject the Company to concentration of credit risk consist principally of trade accounts receivable. The Company sells its consumer products to a wide variety of retailers, including mass merchandisers, home centers, independent hardware stores, nurseries, garden outlets, warehouse clubs and local and regional chains. Professional products are sold to commercial nurseries, greenhouses, landscape services, and growers of specialty agriculture crops.

At September 30, 2001, 70% of the Company's accounts receivable was due from customers in North America. Approximately 85% of these receivables were generated from the Company's North American Consumer segment. The most significant concentration of receivables within the segment was from home centers, which accounted for 20%, followed by mass merchandisers at 12% of the Company's receivables balance at September 30, 2001. No other retail concentrations (e.g., independent hardware stores, nurseries, etc. in similar markets) accounted for more than 10% of the Company's accounts receivable balance at September 30, 2001.

The remaining 15% of North American accounts receivable was generated from customers of the Global Professional segment located in North America. As a result of the changes in distribution methods made in fiscal 2000 for the Global Professional segment customers in North America, nearly all products are sold through distributors. Accordingly, nearly all of the Global Professional segment's North American accounts receivable at September 30, 2001 is due from distributors.

The 30% of accounts receivable generated outside of North America is due from retailers, distributors, nurseries and growers. No concentrations of customers or individual customers within this group account for more than 10% of the Company's accounts receivable balance at September 30, 2001.

Instructions

Answer each of the following questions.
  (a) Calculate the receivables turnover ratio and average collection period for 2001 for the company.
  (b) Is accounts receivable a material component of the company's total current assets?
  (c) Scotts sells seasonal products. How might this affect the accuracy of your answer to part (a)?
  (d) Evaluate the credit risk of Scotts' concentrated receivables.
  (e) Comment on the informational value of Scotts' Note 16 on concentrations of credit risk.

A GLOBAL FOCUS

BYP8-6 **Art World Industries, Inc.**, was incorporated in 1986 in Delaware, although it is located in Los Angeles. The company prints, publishes, and sells limited-edition graphics and reproductive prints in the wholesale market.

The company's balance sheet at the end of a recent year showed an allowance for doubtful accounts of $175,477. The allowance was set up against certain Japanese accounts receivable that average more than one year in age. The Japanese acknowledge the amount due, but with the slow economy in Japan, they lack the resources to pay at this time.

Instructions
(a) Which method of accounting for uncollectible accounts does Art World Industries use?
(b) Explain the difference between the direct write-off and percentage of receivables methods. Based on Art World's disclosure above, what important factor would you have to consider in arriving at appropriate percentages to apply for the percentage of receivables method?
(c) What are the implications for a company's receivables management of selling its products internationally?

FINANCIAL ANALYSIS ON THE WEB

BYP8-7 **Purpose:** To learn more about factoring from a Web site that provides factoring services.

Address: www.invoicefinancial.com (or go to **www.wiley.com/college/kimmel**)

Steps: Go to the Web site and answer the following questions.
(a) What are some of the benefits of factoring?
(b) What amount of accounts receivable are factored each year?
(c) What is the range of the percentages of the typical discount rate?
(d) If a company factors its receivables, what percentage of the value of the receivables can it expect to receive from the factor in the form of cash, and how quickly will it receive the cash?

Critical Thinking

GROUP DECISION CASE

BYP8-8 Mary and Michael Wilfer own Campus Fashions. From its inception Campus Fashions has sold merchandise on either a cash or credit basis, but no credit cards have been accepted. During the past several months, the Wilfers have begun to question their credit-sales policies. First, they have lost some sales because of their refusal to accept credit cards. Second, representatives of two metropolitan banks have convinced them to accept their national credit cards. One bank, City National Bank, has stated that (1) its credit card fee is 4% and (2) it pays the retailer 96 cents on each $1 of sales within 3 days of receiving the credit card billings.

The Wilfers decide that they should determine the cost of carrying their own credit sales. From the accounting records of the past 3 years they accumulate these data:

	2005	2004	2003
Net credit sales	$500,000	$600,000	$400,000
Collection agency fees for slow-paying customers	2,600	2,500	1,600
Salary of part-time accounts receivable clerk	3,800	3,800	3,800

Credit and collection expenses as a percentage of net credit sales are as follows: uncollectible accounts 1.6%, billing and mailing costs .5%, and credit investigation fee on new customers .2%.

Mary and Michael also determine that the average accounts receivable balance outstanding during the year is 5% of net credit sales. The Wilfers estimate that they could earn an average of 10% annually on cash invested in other business opportunities.

Instructions
With the class divided into groups, answer the following.
(a) Prepare a tabulation for each year showing total credit and collection expenses in dollars and as a percentage of net credit sales.

   (b) Determine the net credit and collection expenses in dollars and as a percentage of sales after considering the revenue not earned from other investment opportunities. (*Note:* The income lost on the cash held by the bank for 3 days is considered to be immaterial.)

   (c) Discuss both the financial and nonfinancial factors that are relevant to the decision.

COMMUNICATION ACTIVITY

BYP8-9 Home Fibers Corporation is a recently formed business selling the "World's Best Doormat." The corporation is selling doormats faster than Home Fibers can make them. It has been selling the product on a credit basis, telling customers to "pay when they can." Oddly, even though sales are tremendous, the company is having trouble paying its bills.

Instructions

Write a memo to the president of Home Fibers Corporation discussing these questions:

   (a) What steps should be taken to improve the company's ability to pay its bills?

   (b) What accounting steps should be taken to measure its success in improving collections and in recording its collection success?

   (c) If the corporation is still unable to pay its bills, what additional steps can be taken with its receivables to ease its liquidity problems?

ETHICS CASE

BYP8-10 The controller of Zapatos Corporation believes that the company's yearly allowance for doubtful accounts should be 2% of net credit sales. The president of Zapatos Corporation, nervous that the stockholders might expect the company to sustain its 10% growth rate, suggests that the controller increase the allowance for doubtful accounts to 4%. The president thinks that the lower net income, which reflects a 6% growth rate, will be a more sustainable rate for Zapatos Corporation.

Instructions

   (a) Who are the stakeholders in this case?

   (b) Does the president's request pose an ethical dilemma for the controller?

   (c) Should the controller be concerned with Zapatos Corporation's growth rate in estimating the allowance? Explain your answer.

Answers to Self-Study Questions

1. c   2. a   3. c   4. d   5. c   6. b   7. d   8. a   9. c   10. c   11. a

Answer to Tootsie Roll Review It Question 1, p. 374

Tootsie Roll reports two types of receivables on its balance sheet: Accounts receivable trade, and Other receivables. Since Tootsie Roll's balance sheet reports allowance amounts for receivables, we know that Tootsie Roll uses the allowance method rather than the direct write-off method.

Remember to go back to the Navigator box on the chapter-opening page and check off your completed work.

Reporting
and Analyzing
Long-Lived Assets

STUDY OBJECTIVES

After studying this chapter,
you should be able to:

1 Describe how the cost principle applies to plant assets.

2 Explain the concept of depreciation.

3 Compute periodic depreciation using the straight-line method, and contrast its expense pattern with those of other methods.

4 Describe the procedure for revising periodic depreciation.

5 Explain how to account for the disposal of plant assets.

6 Describe methods for evaluating the use of plant assets.

7 Identify the basic issues related to reporting intangible assets.

8 Indicate how long-lived assets are reported on the balance sheet.

☑ THE NAVIGATOR

FEATURE STORY

A Tale of Two Airlines

So, you're interested in starting a new business. Have you given any thought to the airline industry? Your only experience with airlines is as a passenger? Don't let that stop you, advises Ray Novelli. Novelli's airline, **Presidential Air**, was one of 30 new airlines that entered the U.S. market in a recent 30-month period—one per month.

The impetus behind all these upstarts was the tremendous success of two discount, no-frills airlines: **Southwest Airlines** and **Valujet**. What is interesting is the different approach taken by these two airlines to arrive at their success. Southwest Airlines' fleet is composed of primarily sleek, new, highly efficient planes requiring little maintenance. The average age of its planes is 8.3 years, the lowest in the industry. To be able to afford new planes, Southwest had to be very patient in its growth goals. Over a 22-year period, Southwest has risen to the number six spot in size for U.S. airlines—and to even higher rankings in on-time performance, customer service, and baggage handling.

Valujet, on the other hand, opted for old planes, known in the industry as Zombies, which are 25 to 30 years old and cost less than a tenth of the purchase price of a new plane. This practice of buying older planes allowed Valujet to add one or two planes a month to its fleet—an unheard-of expansion. Valujet started with two planes and within a year and a half had 36 planes. Valujet, which was started with a $3.4-million investment, grew to be

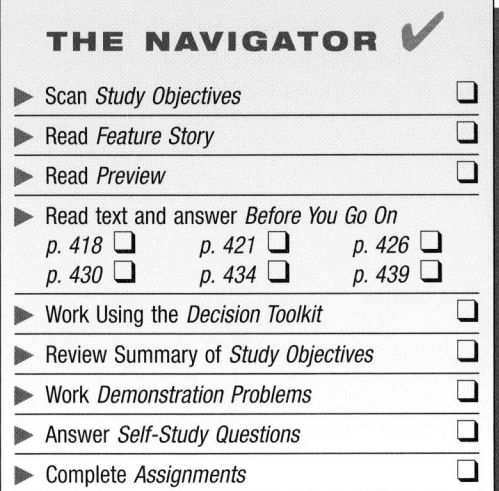

THE NAVIGATOR ✔

▶ Scan *Study Objectives* ☐
▶ Read *Feature Story* ☐
▶ Read *Preview* ☐
▶ Read text and answer *Before You Go On*
   p. 418 ☐   p. 421 ☐   p. 426 ☐
   p. 430 ☐   p. 434 ☐   p. 439 ☐
▶ Work Using the *Decision Toolkit* ☐
▶ Review Summary of *Study Objectives* ☐
▶ Work *Demonstration Problems* ☐
▶ Answer *Self-Study Questions* ☐
▶ Complete *Assignments* ☐

worth $630 million in its first three years. By comparison, it took Southwest Airlines 10 years to acquire that many planes. For a while there was a surplus of these old planes on the market, until Valujet enjoyed such tremendous success that seemingly everyone wanted to buy or lease old planes to start an airline.

However, a terrible crash in May 1996 in Florida focused the spotlight on Valujet and called into question the wisdom of relying on old planes. Although the cause of the crash appears to have been unrelated to the age of its planes, in the aftermath of the crash Valujet struggled to survive under the weight of both government scrutiny and lack of customer confidence. The crash heightened awareness of the age of the U.S. fleet as well as the importance of ongoing maintenance. Whether this spells the end for new discount startups remains to be seen.

In the face of continuing financial problems and customer skepticism, Valujet merged with AirWays Corp. and took the name of its airline, **AirTran Airways**. Perhaps you should proceed with caution in planning the startup of your own airline!

☑ THE NAVIGATOR

On the World Wide Web
Southwest Airlines:
www.southwest.com
Valujet: www.airtran.com

Was **Valujet**'s approach to buying equipment really the "right formula," or was it a recipe for disaster? For airlines and many other companies, making the right decisions regarding long-lived assets is critical because these assets represent huge investments. Management must make many ongoing decisions about long-lived assets—what assets to acquire and when, how to finance them, how to account for them, and when to dispose of them.

In this chapter we address these and other issues surrounding long-lived assets. Our discussion of long-lived assets is presented in two parts: plant assets and intangible assets. *Plant assets* are the property, plant, and equipment (physical assets) that commonly come to mind when we think of a company. Companies also have many important *intangible assets*. These are assets such as copyrights and patents that lack physical substance but can be extremely valuable and vital to a company's success.

The content and organization of this chapter are as follows.

SECTION 1
PLANT ASSETS

Plant assets are resources that have physical substance (a definite size and shape), are used in the operations of a business, and are not intended for sale to customers. They are called various names—property, plant, and equipment; plant and equipment; and fixed assets. By whatever name, these assets are expected to provide services to the company for a number of years. Except for land, plant assets decline in service potential (value) over their useful lives.

Plant assets are critical to a company's success because they determine the company's capacity and therefore its ability to satisfy customers. With too few planes, for example, **AirTran** and **Southwest Airlines** would lose customers to their competitors, but with too many planes, they would be flying with empty seats. Management must constantly monitor its needs and acquire assets accordingly. Failure to do so results in lost business opportunities or inefficient use of existing assets and is likely to show up eventually in poor financial results.

It is important for a company to (1) keep assets in good operating condition, (2) replace worn-out or outdated assets, and (3) expand its productive assets as needed. The decline of rail travel in the United States can be traced in part to the failure of railroad companies to maintain and update their assets. Conversely, the growth of air travel in this country can be attributed in part to the general willingness of airline companies to follow these essential guidelines.

For many companies, investments in plant assets are substantial. Illustration 9-1 shows the percentages of plant assets in relation to total assets in some other companies.

Illustration 9-1
Percentages of plant assets in relation to total assets

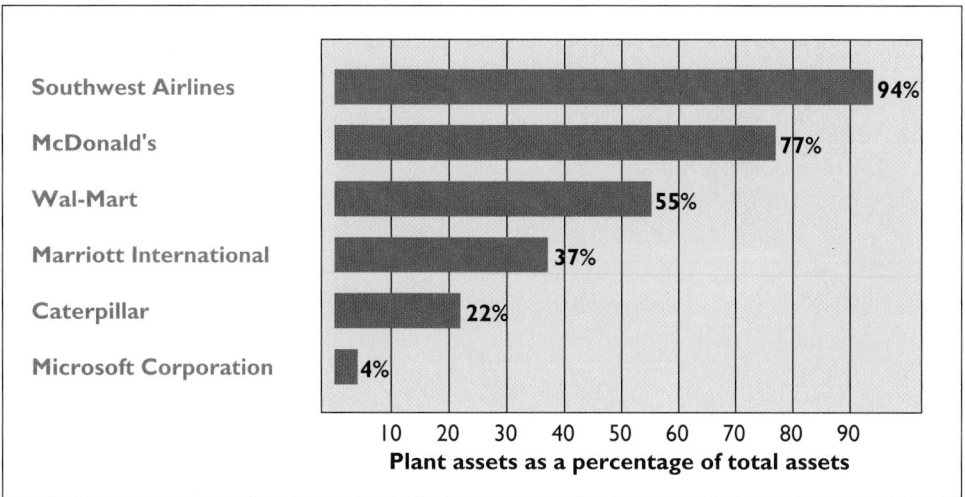

Determining the Cost of Plant Assets

STUDY OBJECTIVE

1

Describe how the cost principle applies to plant assets.

 International Note

The United Kingdom is flexible regarding asset valuation. Companies revalue to fair value when they believe this information is more relevant. Switzerland and the Netherlands also permit revaluations.

The **cost principle** requires that plant assets be recorded at cost. Thus, the planes at AirTran and Southwest Airlines are recorded at cost. **Cost consists of all expenditures necessary to acquire an asset and make it ready for its intended use.** For example, the purchase price, freight costs paid by the purchaser, and installation costs are all considered part of the cost of factory machinery.

Determining which costs to include in a plant asset account and which costs not to include is very important. If a cost is not included in a plant asset account, then it must be expensed immediately. Such costs are referred to as **revenue expenditures**. On the other hand, costs that are not expensed immediately but are instead included in a plant asset account are referred to as **capital expenditures**.

This distinction is important because it has immediate, and often material, implications for the income statement. Some companies, in order to boost current income, have been known to improperly capitalize expenditures that should have been expensed. For example, suppose that $1,000 of maintenance costs incurred at the end of the year are improperly capitalized to a building account. (That is, they are included in the asset account Buildings rather than being expensed immediately.) If the cost of the building is being allocated as an expense (depreciated) over a 40-year life, then the maintenance cost of $1,000 will be incorrectly spread across 40 years instead of being expensed in the current year. Current-year expenses will be understated by $1,000, and current-year income will be overstated by $1,000. Thus, determining which costs to capitalize and which to expense is very important.

Business Insight
ETHICS PERSPECTIVE

In what could become one of the largest accounting frauds in history, **WorldCom** announced the discovery of $7 billion in expenses improperly booked as capital expenditures, a gimmick that boosted profit over a recent five-quarter period. If these expenses had been booked properly, WorldCom, one of the biggest stock market stars of the 1990s, would have reported a net loss for 2001, as well as for the first quarter of 2002. Instead, WorldCom reported a profit of $1.4 billion for 2001 and $130 million for the first quarter of 2002. As a result of these problems, WorldCom declared bankruptcy, to the dismay of its investors and creditors.

Cost is measured by the cash paid in a cash transaction or by the **cash equivalent price** paid when noncash assets are used in payment. **The cash equivalent price is equal to the fair market value of the asset given up or the fair market value of the asset received, whichever is more clearly determinable.** Once cost is established, it becomes the basis of accounting for the plant asset over its useful life. Current market or replacement values are not used to increase the recorded cost after acquisition. The application of the cost principle to each of the major classes of plant assets is explained in the following sections.

LAND

Land is often used as a building site for a manufacturing plant or office site. The cost of land includes (1) the cash purchase price, (2) closing costs such as title and attorney's fees, (3) real estate brokers' commissions, and (4) accrued property taxes and other liens on the land assumed by the purchaser. For example, if the cash price is $50,000 and the purchaser agrees to pay accrued taxes of $5,000, the cost of the land is $55,000.

All necessary costs incurred in making land **ready for its intended use** increase (debit) the Land account. When vacant land is acquired, its cost includes expenditures for clearing, draining, filling, and grading. If the land has a building on it that must be removed to make the site suitable for construction of a new building, all demolition and removal costs, less any proceeds from salvaged materials, are included in the Land account.

To illustrate, assume that Hayes Manufacturing Company acquires real estate at a cash cost of $100,000. The property contains an old warehouse that is razed at a net cost of $6,000 ($7,500 in costs less $1,500 proceeds from salvaged materials). Additional expenditures are for the attorney's fee $1,000 and the real estate broker's commission $8,000. Given these factors, the cost of the land is $115,000, computed as shown in Illustration 9-2.

Land	
Cash price of property	$ 100,000
Net removal cost of warehouse	6,000
Attorney's fee	1,000
Real estate broker's commission	8,000
Cost of land	**$115,000**

Illustration 9-2
Computation of cost of land

When the acquisition is recorded, Land is debited for $115,000 and Cash is credited for $115,000.

LAND IMPROVEMENTS

Land improvements are structural additions made to land, such as driveways, parking lots, fences, landscaping, and underground sprinklers. The cost of land improvements includes all expenditures necessary to make the improvements ready for their intended use. For example, the cost of a new company parking lot includes the amount paid for paving, fencing, and lighting; thus the total of all of these costs would be debited to Land Improvements. Land improvements have limited useful lives, and their maintenance and replacement are the responsibility of the company. Because of their limited useful life, the cost of land improvements are expensed (depreciated) over their useful life.

BUILDINGS

Buildings are facilities used in operations, such as stores, offices, factories, warehouses, and airplane hangers. All necessary expenditures relating to the purchase or construction of a building are charged to the Buildings account. When a building is **purchased**, such costs include the purchase price, closing costs (attorney's fees, title insurance, etc.), and real estate broker's commission. Costs to make the building ready for its intended use consist of expenditures for remodeling rooms and offices and replacing or repairing the roof, floors, electrical wiring, and plumbing. When a new building is **constructed**, its cost consists of the contract price plus payments made by the owner for architects' fees, building permits, and excavation costs.

In addition, interest costs incurred to finance a construction project are included in the cost of the asset when a significant period of time is required to get the asset ready for use. In these circumstances, interest costs are considered as necessary as materials and labor. However, the inclusion of interest costs in the cost of a constructed building is **limited to interest costs incurred during the construction period**. When construction has been completed, subsequent interest payments on funds borrowed to finance the construction are recorded as increases (debits) to Interest Expense.

EQUIPMENT

Equipment includes assets used in operations, such as store check-out counters, office furniture, factory machinery, delivery trucks, and airplanes. The cost of equipment consists of the cash purchase price, sales taxes, freight charges, and insurance during transit paid by the purchaser. It also includes expenditures required in assembling, installing, and testing the unit. However, motor vehicle licenses and accident insurance on company trucks and cars are treated as expenses as they are incurred because they represent annual recurring expenditures and do not benefit future periods. Two criteria apply in determining the cost of equipment: (1) the frequency of the cost—one time or recurring, and (2) the benefit period—the life of the asset or one year.

To illustrate, assume that Lenard Company purchases a delivery truck at a cash price of $22,000. Related expenditures are for sales taxes $1,320, painting and lettering $500, motor vehicle license $80, and a three-year accident insurance policy $1,600. The cost of the delivery truck is $23,820, computed as shown in Illustration 9-3.

Delivery Truck	
Cash price	$ 22,000
Sales taxes	1,320
Painting and lettering	500
Cost of delivery truck	**$23,820**

Illustration 9-3
Computation of cost of
delivery truck

The cost of a motor vehicle license is treated as an expense, and the cost of an insurance policy is considered a prepaid asset. Thus, the entry to record the purchase of the truck and related expenditures is as follows.

Delivery Truck	23,820	
License Expense	80	
Prepaid Insurance	1,600	
Cash		25,500
(To record purchase of delivery truck and related expenditures)		

A	=	L	+	SE
+23,820				−80 Exp
+1,600				
−25,500				

Cash Flows
−25,500

For another example, assume Merten Company purchases factory machinery at a cash price of $50,000. Related expenditures are for sales taxes $3,000, insurance during shipping $500, and installation and testing $1,000. The cost of the factory machinery is $54,500, computed as in Illustration 9-4.

Factory Machinery	
Cash price	$ 50,000
Sales taxes	3,000
Insurance during shipping	500
Installation and testing	1,000
Cost of factory machinery	**$54,500**

Illustration 9-4
Computation of cost of
factory machinery

Thus, the entry to record the purchase and related expenditures is as follows.

Factory Machinery	54,500	
Cash		54,500
(To record purchase of factory machinery and related expenditures)		

A	=	L	+	SE
+54,500				
−54,500				

Cash Flows
−54,500

TO BUY OR LEASE?

In this chapter we focus on assets that are purchased, but we want to expose you briefly to an alternative to purchasing—leasing. In many industries leasing is quite common. For example, one-third of heavy-duty commercial trucks are leased. In a lease, a party that owns an asset (the **lessor**) agrees to allow another party (the **lessee**) to use the asset for an agreed period of time at an agreed price.

Some advantages of leasing an asset versus purchasing it are:

1. **Reduced risk of obsolescence.** Frequently, lease terms allow the party using the asset (the lessee) to exchange the asset for a more modern one if it becomes outdated. This is much easier than trying to sell an obsolete asset.

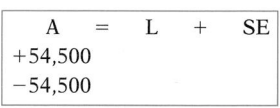

2. **Little or no down payment.** To purchase an asset most companies must borrow money, which usually requires a down payment of at least 20%. Leasing an asset requires little or no down payment.

3. **Shared tax advantages.** Startup companies typically do not make much money in their early years, and so they have little need for the tax deductions available from owning an asset. In a lease, the lessor gets the tax advantage because it owns the asset. It often will pass these tax savings on to the lessee in the form of lower lease payments.

4. **Assets and liabilities not reported.** Many companies prefer to keep assets and especially liabilities off their books. Certain types of leases, called **operating leases**, allow the lessee to account for the transaction as a rental with neither an asset nor a liability recorded.

Airlines often choose to lease many of their airplanes in long-term lease agreements. In its 2001 financial statements, **Southwest Airlines** stated that it leased 92 of its 355 planes under operating leases. Because operating leases are accounted for as a rental, these 92 planes did not show up on its balance sheet.

Under another type of lease, a **capital lease**, both the asset and the liability are shown on the balance sheet. For the lessee under a capital lease, long-term lease agreements are accounted for in a way that is very similar to purchases: On the lessee's balance sheet, the leased item is shown as an asset, and the obligation owed to the lessor is shown as a liability. The leased asset is depreciated by the lessee in a manner similar to purchased assets. About 1% of property, plant, and equipment on Southwest Airlines' balance sheet are accounted for as capital leases. Additional discussion about leasing is presented in Chapter 10 on liabilities.

Business Insight
MANAGEMENT PERSPECTIVE

As an excellent example of the magnitude of leasing, leased planes recently accounted for nearly 40% of the U.S. fleet of commercial airlines. The reasons for leasing include favorable tax treatment, increased flexibility, and low airline income. As passenger volume is expected to significantly increase in the next 20 years, industry analysts expect that many more airplanes will be needed, and it is anticipated that much of the financing will be done through leasing. Leasing is particularly attractive to lessors because airplanes have relatively long lives, a ready secondhand market, and a significant resale value.

BEFORE YOU GO ON . . .

▶ Review It

1. What are plant assets? What are the major classes of plant assets? At what value should plant assets be recorded?
2. What are revenue expenditures? What are capital expenditures?
3. What are the primary advantages of leasing?

▶ Do It

Assume that a delivery truck is purchased for $15,000 cash plus sales taxes of $900 and delivery costs of $500. The buyer also pays $200 for painting and lettering, $600 for an annual insurance policy, and $80 for a motor vehicle license. Explain how each of these costs is accounted for.

Action Plan

- Identify expenditures made in order to get delivery equipment ready for its intended use.
- Expense operating costs incurred during the useful life of the equipment.

Solution

The first four payments ($15,000, $900, $500, and $200) are considered to be expenditures necessary to make the truck ready for its intended use. Thus, the cost of the truck is $16,600. The payments for insurance and the license are considered to be operating expenses incurred during the useful life of the asset.

☑ THE NAVIGATOR

Accounting for Plant Assets

DEPRECIATION

As explained in Chapter 4, **depreciation** **is the process of allocating to expense the cost of a plant asset over its useful (service) life in a rational and systematic manner**. Such cost allocation is designed to properly match expenses with revenues. (See Illustration 9-5.)

STUDY OBJECTIVE
2
Explain the concept of depreciation.

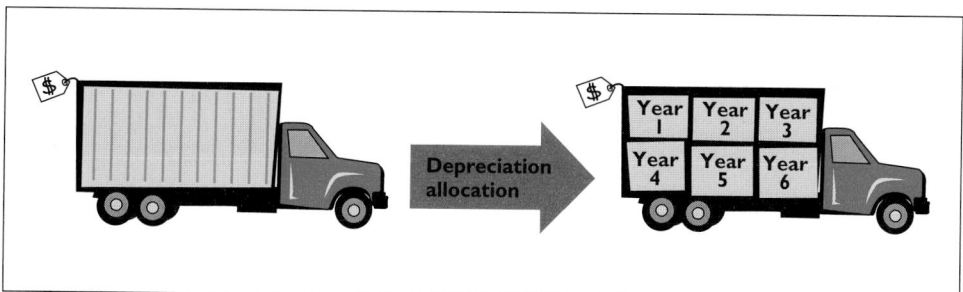

Illustration 9-5
Depreciation as an allocation concept

Depreciation affects the balance sheet through accumulated depreciation, which is reported as a deduction from plant assets. It affects the income statement through depreciation expense.

It is important to understand that **depreciation is a process of cost allocation**, **not a process of asset valuation**. No attempt is made to measure the change in an asset's market value during ownership because plant assets are not held for resale. Thus, the **book value**—cost less accumulated depreciation—of a plant asset may differ significantly from its **market value**. In fact, if an asset is fully depreciated, it can have zero book value but still have a significant market value.

Depreciation applies to three classes of plant assets: land improvements, buildings, and equipment. Each of these classes is considered to be a **depreciable asset** because the usefulness to the company and the revenue-producing ability of each class decline over the asset's useful life. Depreciation **does not apply to land** because its usefulness and revenue-producing ability

Helpful Hint Remember that depreciation is the process of allocating cost over the useful life of an asset. It is not a measure of value.

generally remain intact as long as the land is owned. In fact, in many cases, the usefulness of land increases over time because of the scarcity of good sites. Thus, **land is not a depreciable asset**.

During a depreciable asset's useful life its revenue-producing ability declines because of wear and tear. A delivery truck that has been driven 100,000 miles will be less useful to a company than one driven only 800 miles. Similarly, trucks and cars exposed to snow and salt deteriorate faster than equipment that is not exposed to these elements.

A decline in revenue-producing ability may also occur because of obsolescence. Obsolescence is the process by which an asset becomes out of date before it physically wears out. The rerouting of major airlines from Chicago's Midway Airport to Chicago-O'Hare International Airport because Midway's runways were too short for jumbo jets is an example. Similarly, many companies have replaced their computers long before they had originally planned to do so because improvements in new computers made their old computers obsolete.

Recognizing depreciation for an asset does not result in the accumulation of cash for replacement of the asset. The balance in Accumulated Depreciation represents the total amount of the asset's cost that has been charged to expense to date; **it is not a cash fund**.

Factors in Computing Depreciation

Three factors affect the computation of depreciation, as shown in Illustration 9-6.

Illustration 9-6 Three factors in computing depreciation

Cost: all expenditures necessary to acquire the asset and make it ready for intended use

Useful life: estimate of the expected life based on need for repair, service life, and vulnerability to obsolescence

Salvage value: estimate of the asset's value at the end of its useful life

1. **Cost.**   Considerations that affect the cost of a depreciable asset have been explained earlier in this chapter. Remember that plant assets are recorded at cost, in accordance with the cost principle.

2. **Useful life.**   Useful life is an estimate of the expected productive life, also called service life, of the asset for its owner. Useful life may be expressed in terms of time, units of activity (such as machine hours), or units of output. Useful life is an estimate. In making the estimate, management considers such factors as the intended use of the asset, repair and maintenance policies, and vulnerability of the asset to obsolescence. The company's past experience with similar assets is often helpful in deciding on expected useful life.

3. **Salvage value.**   Salvage value is an estimate of the asset's value at the end of its useful life for its owner. The value may be based on the asset's worth as scrap or on its expected trade-in value. Like useful life, salvage value is an estimate. In making the estimate, management considers how it plans to dispose of the asset and its experience with similar assets.

Business Insight
MANAGEMENT PERSPECTIVE

Willamette Industries, Inc., of Portland, Oregon, said in March 1999 that it would change its accounting estimates relating to depreciation of certain assets, beginning with the first quarter of 1999. The vertically integrated forest products company said the changes were due to advances in technology that have increased the service life on its equipment an extra five years. Willamette expected the accounting changes to increase its 1999 full-year earnings by about $57 million, or $0.52 a share. Its 1998 earnings were $89 million, or $0.80 a share. Imagine a 65% improvement in earnings per share from a mere change in the estimated life of equipment!

BEFORE YOU GO ON . . .

▶ Review It

1. What is the relationship, if any, of depreciation to (a) cost allocation, (b) asset valuation, and (c) cash accumulation?
2. Explain the factors that affect the computation of depreciation.
3. What does **Tootsie Roll** use as the estimated useful life on its buildings? On its machinery and equipment? The answer to this question is provided on page 462.

☑ THE NAVIGATOR

Depreciation Methods

Although a number of methods exist, depreciation is generally computed using one of these three methods:

1. Straight-line
2. Declining-balance
3. Units-of-activity

STUDY OBJECTIVE
3
Compute periodic depreciation using the straight-line method, and contrast its expense pattern with those of other methods.

Like the alternative inventory methods discussed in Chapter 6, each of these depreciation methods is acceptable under generally accepted accounting principles. Management selects the method it believes best measures an asset's contribution to revenue over its useful life. Once a method is chosen, it should be applied consistently over the useful life of the asset. Consistency enhances the comparability of financial statements.

Illustration 9-7 shows the distribution of the *primary* depreciation methods in 600 of the largest U.S. companies. Clearly, straight-line depreciation is the most widely used approach. In fact, because some companies use more than one method, **it can actually be said that straight-line depreciation is used for some or all of the depreciation taken by more than 90% of U.S. companies**. For this reason, we illustrate procedures for straight-line depreciation and discuss the alternative approaches only at a conceptual level. This coverage introduces you to the basic idea of depreciation as an allocation concept without entangling you in too much procedural detail. (Also, note that many hand-held calculators are preprogrammed to perform the basic depreciation methods.) Details on the alternative approaches are presented in the appendix to this chapter (pages 442–445).

Our illustration of depreciation methods, both here and in the appendix, is based on the following data relating to a small delivery truck purchased by Bill's Pizzas on January 1, 2005.

Illustration 9-7 Use of depreciation methods in major U.S. companies

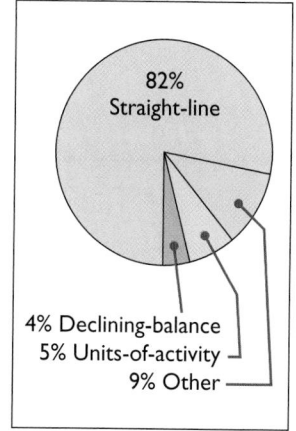

82% Straight-line

4% Declining-balance
5% Units-of-activity
9% Other

Cost	$ 13,000
Expected salvage value	$ 1,000
Estimated useful life (in years)	5
Estimated useful life (in miles)	100,000

STRAIGHT-LINE. Under the **straight-line method**, an equal amount of depreciation is expensed each year of the asset's useful life. Management must choose the useful life of an asset based on its own expectations and experience. To compute the annual depreciation expense, we divide depreciable cost by the estimated useful life. **Depreciable cost** represents the total amount subject to depreciation and is calculated as the cost of the asset less its salvage value. The computation of depreciation expense in the first year for Bill's Pizzas' delivery truck is shown in Illustration 9-8.

Illustration 9-8 Formula for straight-line method

Alternatively, we can compute an annual *rate* at which the delivery truck is being depreciated. In this case, the rate is 20% (100% ÷ 5 years). When an annual rate is used under the straight-line method, the percentage rate is applied to the depreciable cost of the asset, as shown in the **depreciation schedule** in Illustration 9-9.

Illustration 9-9 Straight-line depreciation schedule

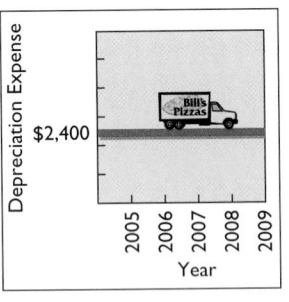

BILL'S PIZZAS

	Computation			Annual	End of Year	
Year	**Depreciable Cost**	×	**Depreciation Rate**	= **Depreciation Expense**	**Accumulated Depreciation**	**Book Value**
2005	$12,000		20%	$ 2,400	$ 2,400	$10,600*
2006	12,000		20	2,400	4,800	8,200
2007	12,000		20	2,400	7,200	5,800
2008	12,000		20	2,400	9,600	3,400
2009	12,000		20	2,400	12,000	1,000
				Total $12,000		

*$13,000 − $2,400

Note that the depreciation expense of $2,400 is the same each year, and that the book value at the end of the useful life is equal to the estimated $1,000 salvage value.

What happens when an asset is purchased **during** the year, rather than on January 1 as in our example? In that case, it is necessary to **prorate the annual depreciation** for the portion of a year used. If Bill's Pizzas had purchased the delivery truck on April 1, 2005, the truck would be used for 9 months in 2005. The depreciation for 2005 would be $1,800 ($12,000 × 20% × $\frac{9}{12}$ of a year).

As indicated earlier, the straight-line method predominates in practice. For example, such large companies as **Campbell Soup**, **Marriott International**, and **General Mills** use the straight-line method. It is simple to apply, and it matches expenses with revenues appropriately when the use of the asset is reasonably uniform throughout the service life. The types of assets that give equal benefits over useful life generally are those for which daily use does not affect productivity. Examples are office furniture and fixtures, buildings, warehouses, and garages for motor vehicles.

DECLINING-BALANCE. The **declining-balance method** computes periodic depreciation using a declining book value. This method is called an **accelerated-depreciation method** because it results in more depreciation in the early years of an asset's life than does the straight-line approach. However, because the total amount of depreciation (the depreciable cost) taken over an asset's life is the same no matter what approach is used, the declining-balance method produces a decreasing annual depreciation expense over the asset's useful life. In early years declining-balance depreciation expense will exceed straight-line, but in later years it will be less than straight-line. Managers might choose an accelerated approach if they think that an asset's utility will decline quickly.

The declining-balance approach can be applied at different rates, which result in varying speeds of depreciation. A common declining-balance rate is double the straight-line rate. As a result, the method is often referred to as the **double-declining-balance method**. If we apply the double-declining-balance method to Bill's Pizzas' delivery truck, assuming a five-year life, we get the pattern of depreciation shown in Illustration 9-10. **The chapter's appendix, page 443, presents the computations behind these numbers.** Again, note that total depreciation over the life of the truck is $12,000, the depreciable cost.

BILL'S PIZZAS			
	Annual Depreciation Expense	**End of Year**	
Year		**Accumulated Depreciation**	**Book Value**
2005	$ 5,200	$ 5,200	$ 7,800
2006	3,120	8,320	4,680
2007	1,872	10,192	2,808
2008	1,123	11,315	1,685
2009	685	12,000	1,000
Total	$12,000		

Illustration 9-10
Declining-balance depreciation schedule

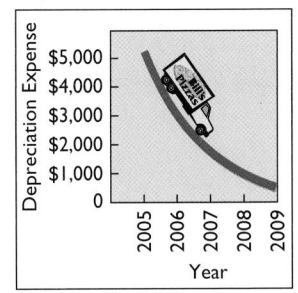

UNITS-OF-ACTIVITY. As indicated earlier, useful life can be expressed in ways other than a time period. Under the **units-of-activity method**, useful life is expressed in terms of the total units of production or the use expected from the asset. The units-of-activity method is ideally suited to factory machinery: Production can be measured in terms of units of output or in terms of machine hours used in operating the machinery. It is also possible to use the method for such items as delivery equipment (miles driven) and airplanes (hours in use). The units-of-activity method is generally not suitable for such assets as buildings or furniture because activity levels are difficult to measure for these assets.

Applying the units-of-activity method to the delivery truck owned by Bill's Pizzas, we first must know some basic information. Bill's expects to be able to drive the truck a total of 100,000 miles. Illustration 9-11 shows depreciation over the five-year life based on an assumed mileage pattern. **The computations used to arrive at these results are presented in the chapter's appendix, pages 444–445.**

Illustration 9-11
Units-of-activity
depreciation schedule

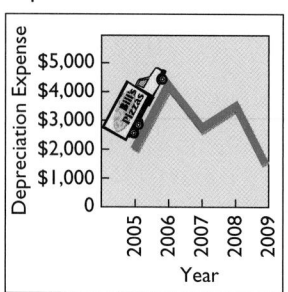

			BILL'S PIZZAS	
	Units of	**Annual**	**End of Year**	
Year	**Activity (miles)**	**Depreciation Expense**	**Accumulated Depreciation**	**Book Value**
2005	15,000	$ 1,800	$ 1,800	$11,200
2006	30,000	3,600	5,400	7,600
2007	20,000	2,400	7,800	5,200
2008	25,000	3,000	10,800	2,200
2009	10,000	1,200	12,000	1,000
Total	100,000	$12,000		

As the name implies, under units-of-activity depreciation, the amount of depreciation is proportional to the activity that took place during that period. For example, the delivery truck was driven twice as many miles in 2006 as in 2005, and depreciation was exactly twice as much in 2006 as it was in 2005.

Management's Choice: Comparison of Methods

Illustration 9-12 presents a comparison of annual and total depreciation expense for Bill's Pizzas under the three methods.

Illustration 9-12
Comparison of
depreciation methods

Year	Straight-Line	Declining-Balance	Units-of-Activity
2005	$ 2,400	$ 5,200	$ 1,800
2006	2,400	3,120	3,600
2007	2,400	1,872	2,400
2008	2,400	1,123	3,000
2009	2,400	685	1,200
	$12,000	$12,000	$12,000

Periodic depreciation varies considerably among the methods, but **total depreciation is the same for the five-year period**. Each method is acceptable in accounting because each recognizes the decline in service potential of the asset in a rational and systematic manner. The depreciation expense pattern under each method is presented graphically in Illustration 9-13.

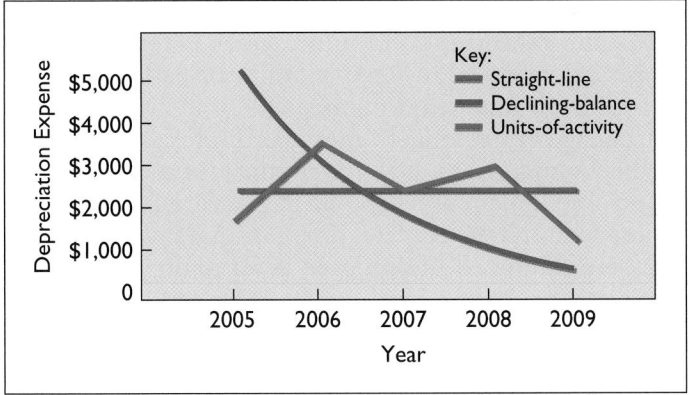

Illustration 9-13 Patterns of depreciation

Depreciation and Income Taxes

The Internal Revenue Service (IRS) allows corporate taxpayers to deduct depreciation expense when computing taxable income. However, the tax regulations of the IRS do not require the taxpayer to use the same depreciation method on the tax return that is used in preparing financial statements. Consequently, many large corporations use straight-line depreciation in their financial statements in order to maximize net income, and at the same time they use a special accelerated-depreciation method on their tax returns in order to minimize their income taxes. For tax purposes, taxpayers must use on their tax returns either the straight-line method or a special accelerated-depreciation method called the **Modified Accelerated Cost Recovery System** (MACRS).

Helpful Hint Depreciation per GAAP is usually different from depreciation per IRS rules.

International Note

In Germany, tax laws have a strong influence on financial accounting. Depreciation expense determined by the tax code must also be used for preparing financial statements.

Depreciation Disclosure in the Notes

The choice of depreciation method must be disclosed in a company's financial statements or in related notes that accompany the statements. Illustration 9-14 shows the "Property and equipment" notes from the financial statements of **Southwest Airlines**.

SOUTHWEST AIRLINES
Notes to the Financial Statements

Property and equipment Depreciation is provided by the straight-line method to estimated residual values over periods ranging from 20 to 25 years for flight equipment and 3 to 30 years for ground property and equipment. Amortization of property under capital leases is on a straight-line basis over the lease term and is included in depreciation expense.

Illustration 9-14
Disclosure of depreciation policies

From this note we learn that Southwest Airlines uses the straight-line method to depreciate its planes. It also uses the straight-line method to depreciate planes that it leases rather than purchases.

Revising Periodic Depreciation

Annual depreciation expense should be reviewed periodically by management. If wear and tear or obsolescence indicates that annual depreciation is either inadequate or excessive, the depreciation expense amount should be changed.

When a change in an estimate is required, the change is made in **current and future years but not to prior periods**. Thus, when a change is made,

STUDY OBJECTIVE
4

Describe the procedure for revising periodic depreciation.

(1) there is no correction of previously recorded depreciation expense, and (2) depreciation expense for current and future years is revised. The rationale for this treatment is that continual restatement of prior periods would adversely affect users' confidence in financial statements.

Significant changes in estimates must be disclosed in the financial statements. Although a company may have a legitimate reason for changing an estimated life, financial statement users should be aware that some companies might change an estimate simply to achieve financial statement goals. For example, extending an asset's estimated life reduces depreciation expense and increases current period income.

Illustration 9-15 shows an example of changes in depreciation estimates for **AirTran Airways** that increased income.

Illustration 9-15
Disclosure of changes in depreciation estimates

AIR TRAN AIRWAYS
Notes to the Financial Statements

Note 1. Property and equipment   Property and equipment is stated on the basis of cost. Flight equipment is depreciated to its salvage values using the straight-line method.

The estimated salvage values and depreciable lives are periodically reviewed for reasonableness, and revised if necessary. The Boeing 717 (B717) fleet has a salvage value of 10 percent. At July 1, 2001, we revised the useful lives on our B717 fleet, as outlined below, in order to more accurately reflect the estimated useful life of the aircraft:

	2001 Useful Life	2000 Useful Life
Airframes	30 years	25 years
Engines	30 years	25 years
Aircraft parts	30 years	5 years

The effect of this change for the year ended December 31, 2001, was to decrease our net loss by approximately $0.6 million, or $0.01 per share.

AirTran was operating at a loss at the time of these changes. Whether these changes are reasonable depends on the accuracy of the assumptions regarding these planes. Our Feature Story suggests that although many planes are lasting a long time, safety concerns might ground many old planes.

BEFORE YOU GO ON . . .

▶ Review It

1. Why is depreciation an allocation concept rather than a valuation concept?
2. What is the formula for computing annual depreciation under the straight-line method?
3. How do the depreciation methods differ in their effects on annual depreciation over the useful life of an asset?
4. Are revisions of periodic depreciation made to prior periods? Explain.

▶ **Do It**

On January 1, 2005, Iron Mountain Ski Corporation purchased a new snow grooming machine for $50,000. The machine is estimated to have a 10-year life with a $2,000 salvage value. What journal entry would Iron Mountain Ski Corporation make at December 31, 2005, if it uses the straight-line method of depreciation?

Action Plan

• Calculate depreciable cost (Cost − Salvage value).
• Divide the depreciable cost by the asset's estimated useful life.

Solution

$$\text{Depreciation expense} = \frac{\text{Cost} - \text{Salvage value}}{\text{Useful life}} = \frac{\$50,000 - \$2,000}{10} = \$4,800$$

The entry to record the first year's depreciation would be:

Dec. 31	Depreciation Expense	4,800	
	Accumulated Depreciation—Machinery		4,800
	(To record annual depreciation on snow grooming machine)		

✓ THE NAVIGATOR

EXPENDITURES DURING USEFUL LIFE

During the useful life of a plant asset, a company may incur costs for ordinary repairs, additions, and improvements. **Ordinary repairs** are expenditures to maintain the operating efficiency and expected productive life of the unit. They usually are fairly small amounts that occur frequently throughout the service life. Motor tune-ups and oil changes, the painting of buildings, and the replacing of worn-out gears on factory machinery are examples. They are debited to Repair (or Maintenance) Expense as incurred. Because they are immediately charged against revenues as an expense, these costs are **revenue expenditures**.

Additions and improvements are costs incurred to increase the operating efficiency, productive capacity, or expected useful life of the plant asset. These expenditures are usually material in amount and occur infrequently during the period of ownership. Expenditures for additions and improvements increase the company's investment in productive facilities and are generally debited to the plant asset affected. Accordingly, they are **capital expenditures**. The accounting for capital expenditures varies depending on the nature of the expenditure.

Northwest Airlines at one time spent $120 million to spruce up 40 DC9-30 jets. The improvements were designed to extend the lives of the planes, meet stricter government noise limits, and save money. The capital expenditure was expected to extend the life of the jets by 10 to 15 years and save about $560 million compared to the cost of buying new planes. The DC9 jets were, on average, 24 years old.

IMPAIRMENTS

As noted earlier, the book value of plant assets is rarely the same as the market value. In instances where the value of a plant asset declines substantially, its market value might fall materially below book value. This may happen because a machine has become obsolete, or the market for the product made by the machine has dried up or has become very competitive. A **permanent decline** in the market value of an asset is referred to as an **impairment**. In order that the asset is not overstated on the books, it is written down to its new market value during the year in which the decline in value occurs. For example, **AirTran** announced a $28 million impairment loss on its DC9s and a $10.8 million impairment loss on its B737s in 2001. AirTran used appraisals and considered recent transactions and market trends involving similar aircraft in determining the fair market values.

In the past, some companies delayed recording losses on impairments until a year when it was "convenient" to do so—when the impact on the company's reported results was minimized. For example, if a company has record profits in one year, it can then afford to write down some of its bad assets without hurting its reported results too much. The practice of timing the recognition of gains and losses to achieve certain income results is known as **earnings management**. A recent FASB standard requires immediate recognition of these write-downs in order to reduce the practice of earnings management.

Write-downs can create problems for users of financial statements. Critics of write-downs note that after a company writes down assets, its depreciation expense will be lower in all subsequent periods. Some companies intentionally write down assets in bad years, when they are going to report poor results anyway. Then in subsequent years, when the company recovers, its results will look even better because of lower depreciation expense.

Business Insight
INVESTOR PERSPECTIVE

In recent years companies such as **IBM**, **3M**, **Westinghouse**, and **Digital Equipment Corporation** have reported huge write-downs. These companies are quick to emphasize that these are "nonrecurring events." That is, they are one-time charges and thus do not represent a recurring drag on future earnings. However, a number of large companies have reported large write-downs in multiple years, which makes analysts suspicious. After one of IBM's recent write-downs, one analyst recommended not buying IBM stock because, with such frequent write-downs, "What confidence do we have the same will not happen again?"

PLANT ASSET DISPOSALS

Companies dispose of plant assets that are no longer useful to them. Illustration 9-16 shows the three ways in which plant asset disposals are made.

Sale	**Retirement**	**Exchange**
Equipment is sold to another party.	Equipment is scrapped or discarded.	Existing equipment is traded for new equipment.

Illustration 9-16 Methods of plant asset disposal

Whatever the disposal method, the company must determine the book value of the plant asset at the time of disposal. Recall that the book value is the difference between the cost of the plant asset and the accumulated depreciation to date. If the disposal occurs at any time during the year, depreciation for the fraction of the year to the date of disposal must be recorded. The book value is then eliminated by reducing (debiting) Accumulated Depreciation for the total depreciation associated with that asset to the date of disposal and reducing (crediting) the asset account for the cost of the asset.

Sale of Plant Assets

In a disposal by sale, the book value of the asset is compared with the proceeds received from the sale. If the proceeds from the sale **exceed** the book value of the plant asset, a **gain on disposal** occurs. If the proceeds from the sale **are less than** the book value of the plant asset sold, a **loss on disposal** occurs.

Only by coincidence will the book value and the fair market value of the asset be the same at the time the asset is sold. Gains and losses on sales of plant assets are therefore quite common. As an example, Delta Air Lines reported a $94,343,000 gain on the sale of five Boeing B-727-200 aircraft and five Lockheed L-1011-1 aircraft.

GAIN ON SALE. To illustrate a gain on sale of plant assets, assume that on July 1, 2005, Wright Company sells office furniture for $16,000 cash. The office furniture originally cost $60,000 and as of January 1, 2005, had accumulated depreciation of $41,000. Depreciation for the first six months of 2005 is $8,000. The entry to record depreciation expense and update accumulated depreciation to July 1 is as follows.

July 1	Depreciation Expense	8,000	
	Accumulated Depreciation—Office Furniture		8,000
	(To record depreciation expense for the		
	first 6 months of 2005)		

A = L + SE
−8,000   −8,000 Exp

Cash Flows
no effect

After the accumulated depreciation balance is updated, a gain on disposal of $5,000 is computed as shown in Illustration 9-17.

Cost of office furniture	$60,000
Less: Accumulated depreciation ($41,000 + $8,000)	49,000
Book value at date of disposal	11,000
Proceeds from sale	16,000
Gain on disposal of plant asset	**$ 5,000**

Illustration 9-17
Computation of gain on disposal

The entry to record the sale and the gain on sale of the plant asset is as follows.

July 1	Cash	16,000	
	Accumulated Depreciation—Office Furniture	49,000	
	Office Furniture		60,000
	Gain on Disposal		5,000
	(To record sale of office furniture at a		
	gain)		

A = L + SE
+16,000   +5,000 Rev
+49,000
−60,000

Cash Flows
+16,000

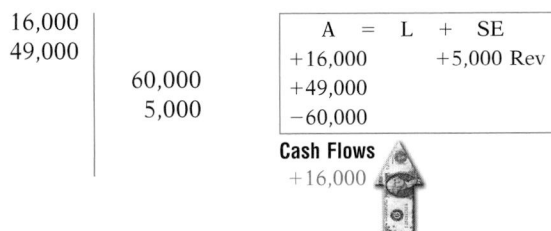

The gain on disposal of the plant asset is reported in the "Other revenues and gains" section of the income statement.

LOSS ON SALE. Assume that instead of selling the office furniture for $16,000, Wright sells it for $9,000. In this case, a loss of $2,000 is computed as in Illustration 9-18.

Illustration 9-18
Computation of loss on disposal

Cost of office furniture	$60,000
Less: Accumulated depreciation	49,000
Book value at date of disposal	11,000
Proceeds from sale	9,000
Loss on disposal of plant asset	**$ 2,000**

The entry to record the sale and the loss on sale of the plant asset is as follows.

A = L + SE
+9,000   −2,000 Exp
+49,000
−60,000

Cash Flows
+9,000

July 1	Cash	9,000	
	Accumulated Depreciation—Office Furniture	49,000	
	Loss on Disposal	2,000	
	Office Furniture		60,000
	(To record sale of office furniture at a loss)		

The loss on disposal of the plant asset is reported in the "Other expenses and losses" section of the income statement.

Retirement of Plant Assets

Some assets are simply retired by the company at the end of their useful life rather than sold. For example, some productive assets used in manufacturing may have very specific uses, and they consequently have no ready market when the company no longer needs them. In such a case the asset is simply retired.

Retirement of an asset is recorded as a special case of a disposal where no cash is received. Accumulated Depreciation is decreased (debited) for the full amount of depreciation taken over the life of the asset. The asset account is reduced (credited) for the original cost of the asset. The loss (a gain is not possible on a retirement) is equal to the asset's book value on the date of retirement.[1]

BEFORE YOU GO ON . . .

▶ **Review It**

1. What is the difference between an ordinary repair and an addition or improvement? Why is this distinction important to financial reporting?
2. What is an impairment? In what way do critics suggest that companies manage their earnings through the write-downs associated with impairments?
3. What is the proper accounting for sales and retirements of plant assets?

---

[1] The accounting for exchanges, the third method of plant asset disposal, is discussed in more advanced courses.

► **Do It**

Overland Trucking has an old truck that cost $30,000 and has accumulated depreciation of $16,000. Assume two different situations: (1) The company sells the old truck for $17,000 cash. (2) The truck is worthless, so the company simply retires it. What entry should Overland use to record each scenario?

Action Plan

• Compare the asset's book value and its fair value to determine whether a gain or loss has occurred.
• Make sure that both the Truck account and Accumulated Depreciation—Truck are reduced upon disposal.

Solution

1. Sale of truck for cash:

Cash	17,000	
Accumulated Depreciation—Truck	16,000	
Truck		30,000
Gain on Disposal [$17,000 − ($30,000 − $16,000)]		3,000
(To record sale of truck at a gain)		

2. Retirement of truck:

Accumulated Depreciation—Truck	16,000	
Loss on Disposal	14,000	
Truck		30,000
(To record retirement of truck at a loss)		

☑ THE NAVIGATOR

Analyzing Plant Assets

The presentation of financial statement information about plant assets enables decision makers to analyze the company's use of its plant assets. We will use two measures to analyze plant assets: return on assets ratio, and asset turnover ratio.

STUDY OBJECTIVE
6
Describe methods for evaluating the use of plant assets.

RETURN ON ASSETS RATIO

An overall measure of profitability is the **return on assets ratio**. This ratio is computed by dividing net income by average assets. (Average assets are commonly calculated by adding the beginning and ending values of assets and dividing by 2.) The return on assets ratio indicates the amount of net income generated by each dollar invested in assets. Thus, the higher the return on assets, the more profitable the company. Information is provided below related to **AirTran** and **Southwest Airlines**.

	AirTran **(in millions)**	**Southwest Airlines** **(in millions)**
Net income, 2001	$ (3)	$ 511
Net income, 2000	47	603
Total assets, 12/31/01	498	8,997
Total assets, 12/31/00	546	6,670
Total assets, 12/31/99	467	5,654
Net sales, 2001	665	5,555
Net sales, 2000	624	5,650

The 2001 and 2000 return on assets of AirTran, Southwest Airlines, and industry averages are presented in Illustration 9-19.

Illustration 9-19 Return on assets ratio

Return on Assets Ratio = $\dfrac{\text{Net Income}}{\text{Average Total Assets}}$		
	2001	**2000**
AirTran **($ in millions)**	$\dfrac{\$(3)}{(\$498 + \$546)/2^*} = -1\%$	$\dfrac{\$47}{(\$546 + \$467)/2} = 9.3\%$
Southwest Airlines **($ in millions)**	$\dfrac{\$511}{(\$8{,}997 + \$6{,}670)/2} = 6.5\%$	$\dfrac{\$603}{(\$6{,}670 + \$5{,}654)/2} = 9.8\%$
Industry average	1.62%	

*Amounts in the ratio calculations have been rounded.

As shown from the information provided, AirTran had a miserable year in 2001 as did the entire airline industry. The events of September 11, 2001, had a devastating impact on the industry. Surprisingly, Southwest Airlines was able to earn a modest rate of return on its assets in contrast to the steep losses of AirTran and other competitors. As shown, the industry average rate of return for 2001 of 1.62% is extremely low. If it continues, many in the industry will be in great financial distress.

DECISION TOOLKIT

Decision Checkpoints	Info Needed for Decision	Tool to Use for Decision	How to Evaluate Results
Is the company using its assets effectively?	Net income and average assets	Return on assets ratio = $\dfrac{\text{Net income}}{\text{Average total assets}}$	Higher value suggests favorable efficiency (use of assets).

ASSET TURNOVER RATIO

The **asset turnover ratio** indicates how efficiently a company uses its assets—that is, how many dollars of sales are generated by each dollar invested in assets. It is calculated by dividing net sales by average total assets. When we compare two companies in the same industry, the one with the higher asset turnover ratio is operating more efficiently; it is generating more sales per dollar invested in assets.

The asset turnover ratios for **AirTran** and **Southwest Airlines** for 2001 are computed in Illustration 9-20 (on page 433).

These asset turnover ratios tell us that for each dollar invested in assets, AirTran generates sales of $1.27 and Southwest $0.71. AirTran is more successful in generating sales per dollar invested in assets, perhaps due in part to

Illustration 9-20 **Asset turnover ratio for 2001**

its decision to purchase older planes. The average asset turnover ratio for the airline industry is .75 times, more in line with Southwest's asset turnover.

Asset turnover ratios vary considerably across industries. The average asset turnover for utility companies is .45, whereas the grocery store industry has an average asset turnover of 3.49. Asset turnover ratios, therefore, are only comparable within—not between—industries.

PROFIT MARGIN RATIO REVISTED

In Chapter 5 you learned about the profit margin ratio. The profit margin ratio is calculated by dividing net income by net sales. It tells how effective a company is in turning its sales into income—that is, how much income is provided by each dollar of sales. Illustration 9-21 shows that the return on assets ratio can be computed from the profit margin ratio and the asset turnover ratio.

Profit Margin	×	Asset Turnover	=	Return on Assets
$\dfrac{\text{Net Income}}{\text{Net Sales}}$	×	$\dfrac{\text{Net Sales}}{\text{Average Total Assets}}$	=	$\dfrac{\text{Net Income}}{\text{Average Total Assets}}$

Illustration 9-21 Composition of return on assets ratio

This relationship has very important strategic implications for management. From Illustration 9-21 we can see that if a company wants to increase its return on assets, it can do so by either increasing the margin it generates from each dollar of goods that it sells (the profit margin ratio), or by trying to increase the volume of goods that it sells (the asset turnover). For example, most grocery stores have very low profit margins, often in the range of 1 or 2 cents for every dollar of goods sold. Grocery stores, therefore, rely on high turnover to increase their return on assets. Alternatively, a store selling luxury goods, such as expensive jewelry, doesn't generally have a high turnover. Consequently, a seller of luxury goods must have a high profit margin.

Let's evaluate the return on assets ratio of Southwest Airlines for 2001 by evaluating its components—the profit margin ratio and the asset turnover ratio. (See Illustration 9-22 on page 434.)

Illustration 9-22
Components of Southwest
Airlines' rate of return

	Profit Margin	×	Asset Turnover	=	Return on Assets
Southwest Airlines	9.2%	×	.71 times	=	6.5%

Southwest Airlines has a profit margin ratio of 9.2% ($511 ÷ $5,555). Compared to the industry average of 1.72%, this suggests that Southwest has better control of its costs than most in the industry. As noted previously, Southwest's asset turnover is about equal to the industry average. Therefore, it would appear that if Southwest can increase its asset turnover by increasing the amount of sales it generates per dollar invested in planes, it will increase its reputation even further as one of the most profitable companies in the industry.

DECISION TOOLKIT

Decision Checkpoints	Info Needed for Decision	Tool to Use for Decision	How to Evaluate Results
How effective is the company at generating sales from its assets?	Net sales and average total assets	$\text{Asset turnover ratio} = \dfrac{\text{Net sales}}{\text{Average total assets}}$	Indicates the sales dollars generated per dollar of assets. A high value suggests the company is effective in using its resources to generate sales.

BEFORE YOU GO ON . . .

▶ **Review It**

1. What is the purpose of the return on assets ratio? How is it calculated?
2. What is the purpose of the asset turnover ratio? How is it computed?
3. What are the two key components that explain the return on assets ratio?

☑ THE NAVIGATOR

SECTION 2
INTANGIBLE ASSETS

Intangible assets are rights, privileges, and competitive advantages that result from ownership of long-lived assets that do not possess physical substance. Many companies' most valuable assets are intangible. Some widely known intangibles are the patents of **Polaroid**, the franchises of **McDonald's**, the trade name **iMac**, and **Nike's** trademark "swoosh."

As you will learn in this section, although financial statements do report numerous intangibles, many other financially significant intangibles are not reported. To give an example, according to its 2002 financial statements, **Microsoft** had a net book value of $52.2 billion. But its *market* value—the total market price of all its shares on that same date—was roughly $260 billion. Thus, its actual market value was about $208 billion greater than what its balance sheet said the company was worth. It is not uncommon for a company's reported book value to differ from its market value, because balance sheets are reported at historical cost. But such an extreme difference seriously diminishes the usefulness of the balance sheet to decision makers. In the case of Microsoft, the difference is due to unrecorded intangibles. For many high-tech or so-called intellectual-property companies, most of their value is from intangibles, many of which are not reported under current accounting rules.

Intangibles may be evidenced by contracts, licenses, and other documents. Intangibles may arise from these sources:

1. Government grants such as patents, copyrights, franchises, trademarks, and trade names.
2. Acquisition of another business in which the purchase price includes a payment for goodwill.
3. Private monopolistic arrangements arising from contractual agreements, such as franchises and leases.

Accounting for Intangible Assets

Intangible assets are recorded at cost. Under a new accounting standard, intangibles are now categorized as having either a limited life or an indefinite life. If an intangible has a **limited life**, its cost should be allocated over its useful life using a process similar to depreciation. The process of allocating the cost of intangibles is referred to as **amortization**. The cost of intangible assets with **indefinite lives should not be amortized**. To record amortization of an intangible asset, Amortization Expense is increased (debited), and the specific intangible asset is decreased (credited). (Unlike depreciation, no contra account, such as Accumulated Amortization, is usually used.)

Intangible assets are typically amortized on a straight-line basis. For example, the legal life of a patent is 20 years. **The cost of a patent should be amortized over its 20-year life or its useful life, whichever is shorter.** To illustrate the computation of patent amortization, assume that National Labs purchases a patent at a cost of $60,000. If the useful life of the patent is estimated to be eight years, the annual amortization expense is $7,500 ($60,000 ÷ 8). The following entry records the annual amortization.

STUDY OBJECTIVE 7
Identify the basic issues related to reporting intangible assets.

Dec. 31	Amortization Expense—Patent	7,500	
	Patent		7,500
	(To record patent amortization)		

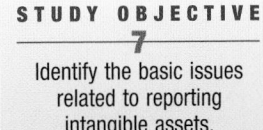

Cash Flows
no effect

When analyzing a company that has significant intangibles, the reasonableness of the estimated useful life should be evaluated. In determining useful life, the company should consider obsolescence, inadequacy, and other factors. These may cause a patent or other intangible to become economically ineffective before the end of its legal life. For example, suppose a computer hardware manufacturer obtained a patent on a new computer chip that it had developed. The legal life of the patent is 20 years. From experience, however, we know that the useful life of a computer chip patent is rarely more than five years. Because new superior chips are developed so rapidly, existing chips become obsolete. Consequently, we would question the amortization expense of a company if it amortized its patent on a computer chip for longer than a five-year period. Amortizing an intangible over a period that is too long will understate amortization expense, overstate the company's net income, and overstate its assets.

DECISION TOOLKIT

Decision Checkpoints	Info Needed for Decision	Tool to Use for Decision	How to Evaluate Results
Is the company's amortization of intangibles reasonable?	Estimated useful life of intangibles from notes to financial statements of this company and its competitors	If the company's estimated useful life significantly exceeds that of competitors or does not seem reasonable in light of the circumstances, the reason for the difference should be investigated.	Too high an estimated useful life will result in understating amortization expense and overstating net income.

Types of Intangible Assets

PATENTS

A **patent** is an exclusive right issued by the United States Patent Office that enables the recipient to manufacture, sell, or otherwise control an invention for a period of 20 years from the date of the grant. **The initial cost of a patent is the cash or cash equivalent price paid to acquire the patent.**

The saying "A patent is only as good as the money you're prepared to spend defending it" is very true. Most patents are subject to some type of litigation by competitors. A well-known example is the patent infringement suit won by **Polaroid** against **Eastman Kodak** in protecting its patent on instant cameras. If the owner incurs legal costs in successfully defending the patent in an infringement suit, such costs are considered necessary to establish the validity of the patent. Thus, **they are added to the Patent account and amortized over the remaining life of the patent**.

Helpful Hint Patent infringement suits are expensive. One estimate of the median cost of a patent case for each side was $280,000 through discovery and $580,000 through trial.

RESEARCH AND DEVELOPMENT COSTS

Research and development costs are expenditures that may lead to patents, copyrights, new processes, and new products. Many companies spend considerable sums of money on research and development in an ongoing effort to develop new products or processes. For example, in a recent year **IBM** spent over $5.2 billion on research and development. There are uncertainties in identifying the extent and timing of the future benefits of these expenditures. As a result, research and development costs are **usually recorded as an expense when incurred**, whether the research and development is successful or not.

Helpful Hint Research and development costs are not intangible costs, but because these expenditures may lead to patents and copyrights, we discuss them in this section.

To illustrate, assume that Laser Scanner Company spent $3 million on research and development that resulted in two highly successful patents. It spent $20,000 on legal fees for the patents. The legal fees are included in the cost of the patents, but the R&D costs cannot be included in the cost of the patents. Rather, they are recorded as an expense when incurred.

Many disagree with this accounting approach. They argue that to expense these costs leads to understated assets and net income. Others, however, argue that capitalizing these costs would lead to highly speculative assets on the balance sheet. Who is right is difficult to determine.

 International Note

Many factors, including differences in accounting treatment of R&D, contribute to differences in R&D expenditures across nations.

COPYRIGHTS

Copyrights are granted by the federal government, giving the owner the exclusive right to reproduce and sell an artistic or published work. Copyrights extend for the life of the creator plus 70 years. The cost of the copyright consists of the **cost of acquiring and defending it**. The cost may be only the $10 fee paid to the U.S. Copyright Office, or it may amount to a great deal more if a copyright infringement suit is involved. The useful life of a copyright generally is significantly shorter than its legal life.

TRADEMARKS AND TRADE NAMES

A **trademark** or **trade name** is a word, phrase, jingle, or symbol that distinguishes or identifies a particular enterprise or product. Trade names like Wheaties, Trivial Pursuit, Sunkist, Kleenex, Coca-Cola, Big Mac, and Jeep create immediate product identification and generally enhance the sale of the product. The creator or original user may obtain the exclusive legal right to the trademark or trade name by registering it with the U.S. Patent Office. Such registration provides 20 years' protection and may be renewed indefinitely as long as the trademark or trade name is in use.

If the trademark or trade name is purchased, the cost is the purchase price. If it is developed by the enterprise itself, the cost includes attorney's fees, registration fees, design costs, successful legal defense costs, and other expenditures directly related to securing it. Because trademarks and trade names have indefinite lives, they are not amortized.

Business Insight
MANAGEMENT PERSPECTIVE

Domain names are a good example of a trade name. Buying domain names is a hot market these days. While the cost of registration is negligible, if a company has to purchase its name from a cybersquatter—people who register names in the hopes of reselling them for a profit—the cost can rise quickly.

When **eBay Inc.**, the world's largest online auction house, recently tried to register www.ebay.ca in Canada, it discovered that the name had been registered previously by an entrepreneur. eBay then had two options to consider. Since eBay is a registered trademark around the world, the company could take legal action, or it could negotiate to buy the name from the current registrant. In the meantime, eBay is using the domain name www.ebaycanada.ca, which had also been registered previously by a self-described " Internet entrepreneur." This entrepreneur said he hoped to make some quick money when he registered www.ebaycanada.ca last year. He eventually gave up the name without a fight rather than go to court and face huge legal bills.

FRANCHISES AND LICENSES

When you drive down the street in your RAV4 purchased from a **Toyota** dealer, fill up your tank at the corner **Shell** station, eat lunch at **Wendy's**, and make plans to vacation at a **Club Med** resort, you are dealing with franchises. A **franchise** is a contractual arrangement under which the franchisor grants the franchisee the right to sell certain products, to render specific services, or to use certain trademarks or trade names, usually within a designated geographic area.

Another type of franchise, granted by a governmental body, permits the enterprise to use public property in performing its services. Examples are the use of city streets for a bus line or taxi service; the use of public land for telephone, electric, and cable television lines; and the use of airwaves for radio or TV broadcasting. Such operating rights are referred to as **licenses**.

Franchises and licenses may be granted for a definite period of time, an indefinite period, or perpetual. **When costs can be identified with the acquisition of the franchise or license, an intangible asset should be recognized.** Annual payments made under a franchise agreement should be recorded as **operating expenses** in the period in which they are incurred. In the case of a limited life, the cost of a franchise (or license) should be amortized as operating expense over the useful life. If the life is indefinite or perpetual, the cost is not amortized.

GOODWILL

Usually the largest intangible asset that appears on a company's balance sheet is goodwill. **Goodwill** represents the value of all favorable attributes that relate to a business enterprise. These include exceptional management, desirable location, good customer relations, skilled employees, high-quality products, fair pricing policies, and harmonious relations with labor unions. Goodwill is therefore unusual: Unlike other assets such as investments, plant assets, and even other intangibles, which can be sold *individually* in the marketplace, goodwill can be identified only with the business *as a whole*.

If goodwill can be identified only with the business as a whole, how can it be determined? Certainly, many business enterprises have many of the factors cited above (exceptional management, desirable location, and so on). However, to determine the amount of goodwill in these situations would be difficult and very subjective. In other words, to recognize goodwill without an exchange transaction that puts a value on the goodwill would lead to subjective valuations that do not contribute to the reliability of financial statements. **Therefore, goodwill is recorded only when there is an exchange transaction that involves the purchase of an entire business. When an entire business is purchased, goodwill is the excess of cost over the fair market value of the net assets (assets less liabilities) acquired.**

In recording the purchase of a business, the net assets are debited at their fair market values, cash is credited for the purchase price, and the difference is recorded as the cost of goodwill. Goodwill is not amortized because it is considered to have an indefinite life. However, it must be written down if its value is determined to have been permanently impaired.

Financial Statement Presentation of Long-Lived Assets

BALANCE SHEET PRESENTATION

STUDY OBJECTIVE
8
Indicate how long-lived assets are reported on the balance sheet.

Usually plant assets are shown in the financial statements under "Property, plant, and equipment," and intangibles are shown separately under "Intangible assets." Illustration 9-23 is adapted from **The Coca-Cola Company**'s 2001 balance sheet.

Intangibles do not usually use a contra asset account like the contra asset account Accumulated Depreciation used for plant assets. Instead, amortization of these accounts is recorded as a direct decrease (credit) to the asset account.

The Coca-Cola Company

THE COCA-COLA COMPANY Balance Sheet (partial) (in millions)	
Property, plant, and equipment	
Land	$ 217
Buildings and improvements	1,812
Machinery and equipment	4,881
Containers	195
	7,105
Less: Accumulated depreciation	2,652
	4,453
Trademarks and other intangible assets	2,579
Total	$7,032

Illustration 9-23
Presentation of property, plant, and equipment and intangible assets

Either within the balance sheet or in the notes, there should be disclosure of the balances of the major classes of assets, such as land, buildings, and equipment, and of accumulated depreciation by major classes or in total. In addition, the depreciation and amortization methods used should be described and the amount of depreciation and amortization expense for the period disclosed.

STATEMENT OF CASH FLOWS PRESENTATION

It is also interesting to examine the statement of cash flows to determine the amount of property, plant, and equipment purchased and the cash received from property, plant, and equipment sold in a given year. For example, the investing activities section of **Coca-Cola** reports the following.

The Coca-Cola Company

THE COCA-COLA COMPANY Statement of Cash Flows (partial) (in millions)	
Cash flow from investing activities	
Purchases of property, plant, and equipment	$(769)
Proceeds from disposals of property, plant, and equipment	91

Illustration 9-24
Purchases and dispositions of property, plant, and equipment

As indicated, Coca-Cola made significant investments in property, plant, and equipment which should be viewed positively given the company's overall profitability. The level of investment suggests that Coca-Cola believes that it can earn a reasonable rate of return on these assets.

BEFORE YOU GO ON . . .

▶ **Review It**

1. Identify the major types of intangible assets and the proper accounting for them.
2. Explain the accounting for research and development costs.
3. How are intangible assets presented on the balance sheet?

 THE NAVIGATOR

Using the Decision Toolkit

Krispy Kreme Doughnuts, Inc. is a specialty retailer of doughnuts. Krispy Kreme's principal business is owning and franchising Krispy Kreme doughnut stores in which it makes and sells over 20 varieties of doughnuts, including its Hot Glazed Original. Each of its stores is a doughnut factory with the capacity to produce from 4,000 dozen doughnuts to over 10,000 dozen doughnuts daily.

Many stock analysts recently have been giving a strong buy recommendation for the stock. A friend of yours, Seth Bloomer, has an interest in investing in Krispy Kreme and has asked you some questions.

Instructions

Review the excerpts below from the company's 2002 annual report and selected financial information and then answer the following questions posed to you by Seth.

1. What method does the company use to depreciate its property and equipment? Over what period are these assets being depreciated?

2. Explain why Krispy Kreme's recently acquired intangible assets are not being amortized.

3. Why is interest capitalized on major capital expenditures during construction, whereas most interest is expensed as incurred?

4. What does the term impairment mean in relation to accounting for intangible assets?

5. Seth was able to get the following information related to Krispy Kreme:

	Krispy Kreme	**Industry average**
Profit margin	7.07%	7.90%
Return on assets	12.23%	10.43%

Seth does not understand how the profit margin can be lower for Krispy Kreme but its return on assets higher. Explain to Seth how this can happen.

KRISPY KREME DOUGHNUTS, INC.
Excerpts from Summary of Significant Accounting Policies

Property and Equipment   Property and equipment are stated at cost less accumulated depreciation. Major renewals and betterments are charged to the property accounts while replacements, maintenance, and repairs which do not improve or extend the lives of the respective assets are expensed currently. Interest is capitalized on major capital expenditures during the period of construction.

Depreciation of property and equipment is provided on the straight-line method over the estimated useful lives: Buildings—15 to 35 years; Machinery and equipment—3 to 15 years; Leasehold improvements—lesser of useful lives of assets or lease term.

Intangible Assets   Intangible assets include goodwill recorded in connection with a business acquisition and the value assigned to reacquired franchise agreements in connection with the acquisition of the rights to certain markets from franchisees. Goodwill and reacquired franchise agreements associated with acquisitions completed on or before June 30, 2001, were amortized on a straight-line basis over an estimated life of 15 years. Reacquired franchise agreements associated with acquisitions completed after June 30 were not amortized. The Company periodically evaluates the recoverability of goodwill and reacquired franchise agreements and will adjust recorded amounts for impairment losses. The Company believes that no impairment of intangible assets existed at February 3, 2002.

Source: Krispy Kreme Doughnut Inc. 2002 annual report.

Solution

1. Depreciation of property and equipment is provided on the straight-line method over the estimated useful lives: Buildings—15 to 35 years; Machinery and equipment—3 to 15 years; Leasehold improvements—lesser of useful lives of assets or lease term.

2. Goodwill and apparently the reacquired franchise agreements are viewed as having an indefinite life. Under a new accounting standard, the cost of intangible assets with indefinite lives should not be amortized.

3. Interest costs incurred to finance construction projects are included in the cost of the asset when a significant period of time is required to get the asset ready for use. In these circumstances, interest costs are considered as necessary as materials and labor. However, the inclusion of interest costs in the cost of a constructed building is limited to the construction period.

4. A permanent decline in the market value of an asset is referred to as impairment. In order that the asset is not overstated on the books, it is written down to its new market value during the year in which the decline in value occurs. Given that the intangible assets for Krispy Kreme have an indefinite life, it is very important that these assets periodically be tested for impairment.

5. The return on assets is a function of two factors: profit margin and asset turnover. The formula to compute rate of return is:

$$\text{Return on assets} = \text{Profit margin} \times \text{Asset turnover}$$

Given that Krispy Kreme has a lower profit margin but a higher rate of return than the industry average, its asset turnover must be higher than the industry average. In this case, Krispy Kreme's asset turnover ratio is 1.73 times (12.23 ÷ 7.07), whereas the industry average is 1.32 (10.43 ÷ 7.90) times. What this analysis indicates is that Krispy Kreme is selling a lot of doughnuts given its asset base.

Summary of Study Objectives

1 *Describe how the cost principle applies to plant assets.* The cost of plant assets includes all expenditures necessary to acquire the asset and make it ready for its intended use. Cost is measured by the cash or cash equivalent price paid.

2 *Explain the concept of depreciation.* Depreciation is the process of allocating to expense the cost of a plant asset over its useful (service) life in a rational and systematic manner. Depreciation is not a process of valuation, and it is not a process that results in an accumulation of cash. Depreciation is caused by wear and tear and by obsolescence.

3 *Compute periodic depreciation using the straight-line method, and contrast its expense pattern with those of other methods.* The formula for straight-line depreciation is:

$$\frac{\text{Cost} - \text{Salvage value}}{\text{Useful life (in years)}}$$

The expense patterns of the three depreciation methods are as follows.

Method	Annual Depreciation Pattern
Straight-line	Constant amount
Declining-balance	Decreasing amount
Units-of-activity	Varying amount

4 *Describe the procedure for revising periodic depreciation.* Revisions of periodic depreciation are made in present and future periods, not retroactively.

5 *Explain how to account for the disposal of plant assets.* The procedure for accounting for the disposal of a plant asset through sale or retirement is: (a) Eliminate the book value of the plant asset at the date of disposal. (b) Record cash proceeds, if any. (c) Account for the difference between the book value and the cash proceeds as a gain or a loss on disposal.

6 *Describe methods for evaluating the use of plant assets.* Plant assets may be analyzed using the return on assets ratio and the asset turnover ratio. The return on assets ratio is comprised of the asset turnover ratio and the profit margin ratio.

7 *Identify the basic issues related to reporting intangible assets.* Intangible assets are reported at their cost less any amounts amortized. If an intangible asset has a limited life, its cost should be allocated over its useful life. Intangible assets with indefinite lives should not be amortized.

8 *Indicate how long-lived assets are reported on the balance sheet.* Plant assets are usually shown under "Property, plant, and equipment"; intangibles are shown separately under "Intangible assets." Either within the balance sheet or in the notes, the balances of the major classes of assets, such as land, buildings, and equipment, and accumulated depreciation by major classes or in total are disclosed. The depreciation and amortization methods used should be described, and the amount of depreciation and amortization expense for the period should be disclosed.

DECISION TOOLKIT—A SUMMARY

Decision Checkpoints	Info Needed for Decision	Tool to Use for Decision	How to Evaluate Results
Is the company using its assets effectively?	Net income and average assets	$\text{Return on assets ratio} = \dfrac{\text{Net income}}{\text{Average total assets}}$	Higher value suggests favorable efficiency (use of assets).
How effective is the company at generating sales from its assets?	Net sales and average total assets	$\text{Asset turnover ratio} = \dfrac{\text{Net sales}}{\text{Average total assets}}$	Indicates the sales dollars generated per dollar of assets. A high value suggests the company is effective in using its resources to generate sales.
Is the company's amortization of intangibles reasonable?	Estimated useful life of intangibles from notes to financial statements of this company and its competitors	If the company's estimated useful life significantly exceeds that of competitors or does not seem reasonable in light of the circumstances, the reason for the difference should be investigated.	Too high an estimated useful life will result in understating amortization expense and overstating net income.

APPENDIX
CALCULATION OF DEPRECIATION USING OTHER METHODS

In this appendix we show the calculations of the depreciation expense amounts used in the chapter for the declining-balance and units-of-activity methods.

Declining-Balance

The **declining-balance method** produces a decreasing annual depreciation expense over the useful life of the asset. The method is so named because the computation of periodic depreciation is based on a **declining book value** (cost less accumulated depreciation) of the asset. Annual depreciation expense is computed by multiplying the book value at the beginning of the year by the declining-balance depreciation rate. **The depreciation rate remains constant from year to year, but the book value to which the rate is applied declines each year.**

Book value for the first year is the cost of the asset because the balance in accumulated depreciation at the beginning of the asset's useful life is zero. In subsequent years, book value is the difference between cost and accumulated depreciation at the beginning of the year. **Unlike other depreciation methods, salvage value is ignored in determining the amount to which the declining-balance rate is applied.** Salvage value, however, does limit the total depreciation that can be taken. Depreciation stops when the asset's book value equals its expected salvage value.

As noted in the chapter, a common declining-balance rate is double the straight-line rate—a method often referred to as the **double-declining-balance method**. If Bill's Pizzas uses the double-declining-balance method, the depreciation rate is 40% (2 × the straight-line rate of 20%). Illustration 9A-1 presents the formula and computation of depreciation for the first year on the delivery truck.

Helpful Hint The straight-line rate is approximated as 1 ÷ Estimated life. In this case it is 1 ÷ 5 = 20%.

Book Value at Beginning of Year	×	Declining-Balance Rate	=	Depreciation Expense
$13,000	×	40%	=	$5,200

Illustration 9A-1 Formula for declining-balance method

The depreciation schedule under this method is given in Illustration 9A-2.

Illustration 9A-2 Double-declining-balance depreciation schedule

BILL'S PIZZAS

| | Computation | | | Annual | End of Year | |
Year	Book Value Beginning of Year	×	Depreciation Rate =	Depreciation Expense	Accumulated Depreciation	Book Value
2005	$13,000		40%	$5,200	$ 5,200	$ 7,800*
2006	7,800		40	3,120	8,320	4,680
2007	4,680		40	1,872	10,192	2,808
2008	2,808		40	1,123	11,315	1,685
2009	1,685		40	685**	12,000	1,000

*$13,000 − $5,200
**Computation of $674 ($1,685 × 40%) is adjusted to $685 in order for book value to equal salvage value.

Helpful Hint Depreciation stops when the asset's book value equals its expected salvage value.

You can see that the delivery equipment is 69% depreciated ($8,320 ÷ $12,000) at the end of the second year. Under the straight-line method it would be depreciated 40% ($4,800 ÷ $12,000) at that time. Because the declining-balance method produces higher depreciation expense in the early years than in the later years, it is considered an **accelerated-depreciation method**.

The declining-balance method is compatible with the matching principle. The higher depreciation expense in early years is matched with the higher benefits received in these years. Conversely, lower depreciation expense is recognized in later years when the asset's contribution to revenue is less. Also, some assets lose their usefulness rapidly because of obsolescence. In these cases, the declining-balance method provides a more appropriate depreciation amount.

When an asset is purchased during the year, it is necessary to prorate the declining-balance depreciation in the first year on a time basis. For example, if Bill's Pizzas had purchased the delivery equipment on April 1, 2005, depreciation for 2005 would be $3,900 ($13,000 × 40% × $\frac{9}{12}$). The book value for computing depreciation in 2006 then becomes $9,100 ($13,000 − $3,900), and the 2006 depreciation is $3,640 ($9,100 × 40%).

Units-of-Activity

Alternative Terminology
Another term often used is the **units-of-production method**.

Under the **units-of-activity method**, useful life is expressed in terms of the total units of production or use expected from the asset. The units-of-activity method is ideally suited to equipment whose activity can be measured in units of output, miles driven, or hours in use. The units-of-activity method is generally not suitable for assets for which depreciation is a function more of time than of use.

To use this method, the total units of activity for the entire useful life are estimated and that amount is divided into the depreciable cost to determine the depreciation cost per unit. The depreciation cost per unit is then multiplied by the units of activity during the year to give the annual depreciation for that year. To illustrate, assume that the delivery truck of Bill's Pizzas is driven 15,000 miles in the first year. Illustration 9A-3 presents the formula and computation of depreciation expense in the first year.

Illustration 9A-3
Formula for units-of-activity method

Depreciable Cost	÷	Total Units of Activity	=	Depreciation Cost per Unit
$12,000	÷	100,000 miles	=	$0.12

Depreciation Cost per Unit	×	Units of Activity during the Year	=	Depreciation Expense
$0.12	×	15,000 miles	=	$1,800

The depreciation schedule, using assumed mileage data, is shown in Illustration 9A-4.

BILL'S PIZZAS					
	Computation		**Annual**	**End of Year**	
Year	**Units of Activity** ×	**Depreciation Cost/Unit** =	**Depreciation Expense**	**Accumulated Depreciation**	**Book Value**
2005	15,000	$0.12	$1,800	$ 1,800	$11,200*
2006	30,000	0.12	3,600	5,400	7,600
2007	20,000	0.12	2,400	7,800	5,200
2008	25,000	0.12	3,000	10,800	2,200
2009	10,000	0.12	1,200	12,000	1,000
*$13,000 − $1,800					

Illustration 9A-4
Units-of-activity depreciation schedule

Helpful Hint Depreciation stops when the asset's book value equals its expected salvage value.

The units-of-activity method is not nearly as popular as the straight-line method, primarily because it is often difficult to make a reasonable estimate of total activity. However, this method is used by some very large companies, such as **Standard Oil Company of California** and **Boise Cascade Corporation**. When the productivity of the asset varies significantly from one period to another, the units-of-activity method results in the best matching of expenses with revenues. This method is easy to apply when assets are purchased during the year. In such a case, the productivity of the asset for the partial year is used in computing the depreciation.

Summary of Study Objective for Appendix

9 *Compute periodic depreciation using the declining-balance method and the units-of-activity method.* The depreciation expense calculation for each of these methods is shown here:

Declining-balance:

$$\text{Book value at beginning of year} \times \text{Declining-balance rate} = \text{Depreciation expense}$$

Units-of-activity:

$$\frac{\text{Depreciable cost}}{} \div \frac{\text{Total units of activity}}{} = \frac{\text{Depreciation cost per unit}}{}$$

$$\text{Depreciation cost per unit} \times \text{Units of activity during year} = \text{Depreciation expense}$$

Glossary

Accelerated-depreciation method A depreciation method that produces higher depreciation expense in the early years than the straight-line approach. (p. 423)

Additions and improvements Costs incurred to increase the operating efficiency, productive capacity, or expected useful life of a plant asset. (p. 427)

Amortization The process of allocating to expense the cost of an intangible asset. (p. 435)

Asset turnover ratio Indicates how efficiently a company uses its assets; calculated as net sales divided by average total assets. (p. 432)

Capital expenditures Expenditures that increase the company's investment in productive facilities. (p. 414)

Capital lease A long-term agreement allowing one party (the lessee) to use another party's asset (the lessor). The arrangement is accounted for like a purchase. (p. 418)

Cash equivalent price An amount equal to the fair market value of the asset given up or the fair market value of the asset received, whichever is more clearly determinable. (p. 415)

Copyright An exclusive right granted by the federal government allowing the owner to reproduce and sell an artistic or published work. (p. 437)

Declining-balance method A depreciation method that applies a constant rate to the declining book value of the asset and produces a decreasing annual depreciation expense over the useful life of the asset. (p. 423)

Depreciable cost The cost of a plant asset less its salvage value. (p. 422)

Depreciation The process of allocating to expense the cost of a plant asset over its useful life in a rational and systematic manner. (p. 419)

Franchise A contractual arrangement under which the franchisor grants the franchisee the right to sell certain products, to render specific services, or to use certain trademarks or trade names, usually within a designated geographic area. (p. 437)

Goodwill The value of all favorable attributes that relate to a business enterprise. (p. 438)

Impairment A permanent decline in the market value of an asset. (p. 427)

Intangible assets Rights, privileges, and competitive advantages that result from the ownership of long-lived assets that do not possess physical substance. (p. 434)

Lessee A party that has made contractual arrangements to use another party's asset without purchasing it. (p. 417)

Lessor A party that has agreed contractually to let another party use its asset. (p. 417)

Licenses Operating rights to use public property, granted by a governmental agency to a business enterprise. (p. 438)

Operating lease An arrangement allowing one party (the lessee) to use the asset of another party (the lessor). The arrangement is accounted for as a rental. (p. 418)

Ordinary repairs Expenditures to maintain the operating efficiency and expected productive life of the asset. (p. 427)

Patent An exclusive right issued by the U.S. Patent Office that enables the recipient to manufacture, sell, or otherwise control an invention for a period of 20 years from the date of the grant. (p. 436)

Plant assets Tangible resources that have physical substance, are used in the operations of the business, and are not intended for sale to customers. (p. 413)

Research and development costs Expenditures that may lead to patents, copyrights, new processes, and new products. (p. 436)

Return on assets ratio A profitability measure that indicates the amount of net income generated by each dollar invested in assets; computed as net income divided by average assets. (p. 431)

Revenue expenditures Expenditures that are immediately charged against revenues as an expense. (p. 414)

Straight-line method A method in which periodic depreciation is the same for each year of the asset's useful life. (p. 422)

Trademark (trade name) A word, phrase, jingle, or symbol that distinguishes or identifies a particular enterprise or product. (p. 437)

Units-of-activity method A depreciation method in which useful life is expressed in terms of the total units of production or use expected from the asset. (p. 423)

Demonstration Problem 1

DuPage Company purchased a factory machine at a cost of $18,000 on January 1, 2005. The machine was expected to have a salvage value of $2,000 at the end of its 4-year useful life.

Instructions

Prepare a depreciation schedule using the straight-line method.

Action Plan
• Under the straight-line method, apply the depreciation rate to depreciable cost.

Solution to Demonstration Problem

DUPAGE COMPANY
Depreciation Schedule—Straight-Line Method

Year	Computation			Annual Depreciation Expense	End of Year	
	Depreciable Cost	×	Depreciation Rate =		Accumulated Depreciation	Book Value
2005	$16,000		25%	$4,000	$ 4,000	$14,000*
2006	16,000		25	4,000	8,000	10,000
2007	16,000		25	4,000	12,000	6,000
2008	16,000		25	4,000	16,000	2,000

*$18,000 − $4,000

Demonstration Problem 2

On January 1, 2002, Skyline Limousine Co. purchased a limousine at an acquisition cost of $28,000. The vehicle has been depreciated by the straight-line method using a 4-year service life and a $4,000 salvage value. The company's fiscal year ends on December 31.

Instructions

Prepare the journal entry or entries to record the disposal of the limousine assuming that it was:
(a) Retired and scrapped with no salvage value on January 1, 2006.
(b) Sold for $5,000 on July 1, 2005.

Solution to Demonstration Problem

(a) Jan. 1, 2006	Accumulated Depreciation—Limousine	24,000	
	Loss on Disposal	4,000	
	Limousine		28,000
	(To record retirement of limousine)		
(b) July 1, 2005	Depreciation Expense	3,000	
	Accumulated Depreciation—Limousine		3,000
	(To record depreciation to date of disposal)		
	Cash	5,000	
	Accumulated Depreciation—Limousine	21,000	
	Loss on Disposal	2,000	
	Limousine		28,000
	(To record sale of limousine)		

Action Plan
- Calculate accumulated depreciation (depreciation expense per year $\times$ years in use).
- At the time of disposal, determine the book value of the asset.
- Recognize any gain or loss from disposal of the asset.

☑ THE NAVIGATOR

Note: All Questions, Exercises, and Problems marked with an asterisk relate to material in the appendix to the chapter.

Self-Study Questions

Self-Study/Self-Test

Answers are at the end of the chapter.

(SO 1) **1.** Corrieten Company purchased equipment and these costs were incurred:

Cash price	$24,000
Sales taxes	1,200
Insurance during transit	200
Installation and testing	400
Total costs	$25,800

What amount should be recorded as the cost of the equipment?
(a) $24,000.   (c) $25,400.
(b) $25,200.   (d) $25,800.

(SO 1) **2.** Harrington Corporation recently leased a number of trucks from Andre Corporation. In inspecting the books of Harrington Corporation, you notice that the trucks have not been recorded as assets on its balance sheet. From this you can conclude that Harrington is accounting for this transaction as a/an:
(a) operating lease.   (c) purchase.
(b) capital lease.   (d) None of the above.

3. Depreciation is a process of: (SO 2)
(a) valuation.   (c) cash accumulation.
(b) cost allocation.   (d) appraisal.

4. Cuso Company purchased equipment on January 1, 2004, at a total invoice cost of $400,000. The equipment has an estimated salvage value of $10,000 and an estimated useful life of 5 years. What is the amount of accumulated depreciation at December 31, 2005, if the straight-line method of depreciation is used? (SO 3)
(a) $80,000.   (c) $78,000.
(b) $160,000.   (d) $156,000.

5. A company would minimize its depreciation expense in the first year of owning an asset if it used: (SO 3)
(a) a high estimated life, a high salvage value, and declining-balance depreciation.
(b) a low estimated life, a high salvage value, and straight-line depreciation.
(c) a high estimated life, a high salvage value, and straight-line depreciation.
(d) a low estimated life, a low salvage value, and declining-balance depreciation.

(SO 4) 6. When there is a change in estimated depreciation:
   (a) previous depreciation should be corrected.
   (b) current and future years' depreciation should be revised.
   (c) only future years' depreciation should be revised.
   (d) None of the above.

(SO 5) 7. Additions to plant assets:
   (a) are revenue expenditures.
   (b) increase a Repair Expense account.
   (c) increase a Purchases account.
   (d) are capital expenditures.

(SO 6) 8. Which of the following measures provides an indication of how efficient a company is in employing its assets?
   (a) Current ratio.
   (b) Profit margin ratio.
   (c) Debt to total assets ratio.
   (d) Asset turnover ratio.

(SO 7) 9. Pierce Company incurred $150,000 of research and development costs in its laboratory to develop a new product. It spent $20,000 in legal fees for a patent granted on January 2, 2005. On July 31, 2005, Pierce paid $15,000 for legal fees in a successful defense of the patent. What is the total amount that should be debited to Patents through July 31, 2005?
   (a) $150,000. (c) $185,000.
   (b) $35,000.   (d) Some other amount.

(SO 7) 10. Indicate which one of these statements is *true*.
   (a) Since intangible assets lack physical substance, they need to be disclosed only in the notes to the financial statements.
   (b) Goodwill should be reported as a contra account in the stockholders' equity section.

   (c) Totals of major classes of assets can be shown in the balance sheet, with asset details disclosed in the notes to the financial statements.
   (d) Intangible assets are typically combined with plant assets and natural resources and then shown in the property, plant, and equipment section.

11. If a company reports goodwill as an intangible asset on its books, what is the one thing you know with certainty? (SO 7)
   (a) The company is a valuable company worth investing in.
   (b) The company has a well-established brand name.
   (c) The company purchased another company.
   (d) The goodwill will generate a lot of positive business for the company for many years to come.

*12. Kant Enterprises purchased a truck for $11,000 on January 1, 2004. The truck will have an estimated salvage value of $1,000 at the end of 5 years. If you use the units-of-activity method, the balance in accumulated depreciation at December 31, 2005, can be computed by the following formula: (SO 9)
   (a) ($11,000 ÷ Total estimated activity) × Units of activity for 2005.
   (b) ($10,000 ÷ Total estimated activity) × Units of activity for 2005.
   (c) ($11,000 ÷ Total estimated activity) × Units of activity for 2004 and 2005.
   (d) ($10,000 ÷ Total estimated activity) × Units of activity for 2004 and 2005.

 ✓ THE NAVIGATOR

Questions

1. Mrs. Whistler is uncertain about how the cost principle applies to plant assets. Explain the principle to Mrs. Whistler.

2. How is the cost for a plant asset measured in a cash transaction? In a noncash transaction?

3. What are the primary advantages of leasing?

4. HaiFat Company acquires the land and building owned by Benz Company. What types of costs may be incurred to make the asset ready for its intended use if HaiFat Company wants to use only the land? If it wants to use both the land and the building?

5. In a recent newspaper release, the president of Heller Company asserted that something has to be done about depreciation. The president said, "Depreciation does not come close to accumulating the cash needed to replace the asset at the end of its useful life." What is your response to the president?

6. Daria is studying for the next accounting examination. She asks your help on two questions: (a) What is salvage value? (b) How is salvage value used in determining depreciable cost under the straight-line method? Answer Daria's questions.

7. Contrast the straight-line method and the units-of-activity method in relation to (a) useful life and (b) the pattern of periodic depreciation over useful life.

8. Contrast the effects of the three depreciation methods on annual depreciation expense.

9. In the fourth year of an asset's 5-year useful life, the company decides that the asset will have a 6-year service life. How should the revision of depreciation be recorded? Why?

10. Distinguish between revenue expenditures and capital expenditures during an asset's useful life.

11. How is a gain or a loss on the sale of a plant asset computed?

12. Ruby Corporation owns a machine that is fully depreciated but is still being used. How should Ruby account for this asset and report it in the financial statements?

13. What are the similarities and differences between depreciation and amortization?

14. Trevelyan Company hires an accounting intern who says that intangible assets should always be amortized over their legal lives. Is the intern correct? Explain.

15. Goodwill has been defined as the value of all favorable attributes that relate to a business enterprise. What types of attributes could result in goodwill?

16. Georgia Lazenby, a business major, is working on a case problem for one of her classes. In this case problem, the company needs to raise cash to market a new product it developed. Timothy Holt, an engineering major, takes one look at the company's balance sheet and says, "This company has an awful lot of goodwill. Why don't you recommend that they sell some of it to raise cash?" How should Georgia respond to Timothy?

17. Under what conditions is goodwill recorded? What is the proper accounting treatment for amortizing goodwill?

18. Often research and development costs provide companies with benefits that last a number of years. (For example, these costs can lead to the development of a patent that will increase the company's income for many years.) However, generally accepted accounting principles require that such costs be recorded as an expense when incurred. Why?

19. In 2001 **Campbell Soup Company** reported average total assets of $5,561 million, net sales of $6,664 million, and net income of $649 million. What was Campbell Soup's return on assets ratio?

20. Give an example of an industry that would be characterized by (a) a high asset turnover ratio and a low profit margin ratio, and (b) a low asset turnover ratio and a high profit margin ratio.

21. Mimi Corporation and Magda Corporation both operate in the same industry. Mimi uses the straight-line method to account for depreciation, whereas Magda uses an accelerated method. Explain what complications might arise in trying to compare the results of these two companies.

22. Helga Corporation uses straight-line depreciation for financial reporting purposes but an accelerated method for tax purposes. Is it acceptable to use different methods for the two purposes? What is Helga Corporation's motivation for doing this?

23. You are comparing two companies in the same industry. You have determined that Tiffany Corp. depreciates its plant assets over a 40-year life, whereas Zales Corp. depreciates its plant assets over a 20-year life. Discuss the implications this has for comparing the results of the two companies.

Brief Exercises

BE9-1 These expenditures were incurred by Velentin Zukovsky Company in purchasing land: cash price $50,000; accrued taxes $7,000; attorney's fees $2,500; real estate broker's commission $2,800; and clearing and grading $3,500. What is the cost of the land?

Determine the cost of land.
(SO 1)

BE9-2 Hector Gonzales Company incurs these expenditures in purchasing a truck: cash price $18,000; accident insurance (during use) $2,000; sales taxes $900; motor vehicle license $300; and painting and lettering $1,200. What is the cost of the truck?

Determine the cost of a truck.
(SO 1)

BE9-3 Empire Chemicals Company acquires a delivery truck at a cost of $22,000 on January 1, 2004. The truck is expected to have a salvage value of $2,000 at the end of its 5-year useful life. Compute annual depreciation for the first and second years using the straight-line method.

Compute straight-line depreciation.
(SO 3)

BE9-4 On January 1, 2005, the Osato Company ledger shows Equipment $32,000 and Accumulated Depreciation $10,000. The depreciation resulted from using the straight-line method with a useful life of 10 years and a salvage value of $2,000. On this date the company concludes that the equipment has a remaining useful life of only 2 years with the same salvage value. Compute the revised annual depreciation.

Compute revised depreciation.
(SO 4)

BE9-5 Prepare journal entries to record these transactions: (a) Lopez Company retires its delivery equipment, which cost $41,000. Accumulated depreciation is also $41,000 on this delivery equipment. No salvage value is received. (b) Assume the same information as in part (a), except that accumulated depreciation for Lopez Company is $38,000 instead of $41,000.

Journalize entries for disposal of plant assets.
(SO 5)

BE9-6 Snooper Company sells office equipment on September 30, 2005, for $18,000 cash. The office equipment originally cost $72,000 and as of January 1, 2005, had accu-

Journalize entries for sale of plant assets.
(SO 5)

mulated depreciation of $42,000. Depreciation for the first 9 months of 2005 is $6,250. Prepare the journal entries to (a) update depreciation to September 30, 2005, and (b) record the sale of the equipment.

Account for intangibles—patents.
(SO 7)

BE9-7 Kananga Company purchases a patent for $180,000 on January 2, 2005. Its estimated useful life is 6 years.
(a) Prepare the journal entry to record amortization expense for the first year.
(b) Show how this patent is reported on the balance sheet at the end of the first year.

Compute return on assets ratio and asset turnover ratio.
(SO 6)

BE9-8 In its 2001 annual report, **McDonald's Corporation** reports beginning total assets of $21.7 billion; ending total assets of $22.5 billion; net sales of $14.9 billion, and net income of $1.6 billion.
(a) Compute McDonald's return on assets ratio.
(b) Compute McDonald's asset turnover ratio.

Classification of long-lived assets on balance sheet.
(SO 8)

BE9-9 **Nike, Inc.** reported the following plant assets and intangible assets for the year ended May 31, 2001 (in millions): other plant assets $562.9; land $177.2; patents and trademarks (at cost) $218.6; machinery and equipment $1,117.3; buildings $695.4; goodwill (at cost) $322.5; accumulated amortization $143.8; accumulated depreciation $934.0. Prepare a partial balance sheet for Nike for these items.

Compute declining-balance depreciation.
(SO 9)

*BE9-10** Depreciation information for Empire Chemicals Company is given in BE9-3. Assuming the declining-balance depreciation rate is double the straight-line rate, compute annual depreciation for the first and second years under the declining-balance method.

Compute depreciation using units-of-activity method.
(SO 9)

*BE9-11** Professor Dent Taxi Service uses the units-of-activity method in computing depreciation on its taxicabs. Each cab is expected to be driven 120,000 miles. Taxi 10 cost $24,500 and is expected to have a salvage value of $500. Taxi 10 was driven 28,000 miles in 2004 and 20,000 miles in 2005. Compute the depreciation for each year.

Exercises

Determine cost of plant acquisitions.
(SO 1)

E9-1 The following expenditures relating to plant assets were made by Gold Company during the first 2 months of 2005.
1. Paid $7,000 of accrued taxes at time plant site was acquired.
2. Paid $200 insurance to cover possible accident loss on new factory machinery while the machinery was in transit.
3. Paid $850 sales taxes on new delivery truck.
4. Paid $21,000 for parking lots and driveways on new plant site.
5. Paid $250 to have company name and advertising slogan painted on new delivery truck.
6. Paid $8,000 for installation of new factory machinery.
7. Paid $900 for a 1-year accident insurance policy on new delivery truck.
8. Paid $75 motor vehicle license fee on new truck.

Instructions
(a) Explain the application of the cost principle in determining the acquisition cost of plant assets.
(b) List the numbers of the transactions, and opposite each indicate the account title to which each expenditure should be debited.

Determine acquisition costs of land.
(SO 1)

E9-2 On March 1, 2005, Domino Company acquired real estate, on which it planned to construct a small office building, by paying $90,000 in cash. An old warehouse on the property was demolished at a cost of $8,200; the salvaged materials were sold for $1,700. Additional expenditures before construction began included $1,100 attorney's fee for work concerning the land purchase, $4,000 real estate broker's fee, $9,100 architect's fee, and $14,000 to put in driveways and a parking lot. *[handwritten: land improvements]* *[handwritten: building]*

Instructions
(a) Determine the amount to be reported as the cost of the land.
(b) For each cost not used in part (a), indicate the account to be debited.

E9-3 Lazar Company purchased a new machine on April 1, 2005, at a cost of $96,000. The company estimated that the machine has a salvage value of $6,000. The machine is expected to be used for 70,000 working hours during its 5-year life.

Determine straight-line depreciation for partial period.
(SO 3)

Instructions
Compute the depreciation expense under the straight-line method for 2005 and 2006, assuming a December 31 year-end.

E9-4 Elliot Carrard, the new controller of Spirit Company, has reviewed the expected useful lives and salvage values of selected depreciable assets at the beginning of 2005. Here are his findings:

Compute revised annual depreciation.
(SO 3,4)

Type of Asset	Date Acquired	Cost	Accumulated Depreciation, Jan. 1, 2005	Useful Life (in years)		Salvage Value	
				Old	Proposed	Old	Proposed
Building	Jan. 1, 1997	$800,000	$152,000	40	50	$40,000	$48,000
Warehouse	Jan. 1, 1999	120,000	27,600	25	20	5,000	3,600

All assets are depreciated by the straight-line method. Spirit Company uses a calendar year in preparing annual financial statements. After discussion, management has agreed to accept Elliot's proposed changes. (The "Proposed" useful life is total life, not remaining life.)

Instructions
(a) Compute the revised annual depreciation on each asset in 2005. (Show computations.)
(b) Prepare the entry (or entries) to record depreciation on the building in 2005.

E9-5 Quarrel Co. has delivery equipment that cost $50,000 and has been depreciated $20,000.

Journalize transactions related to disposals of plant assets.
(SO 5)

Instructions
Record entries for the disposal under the following assumptions.
(a) It was scrapped as having no value.
(b) It was sold for $37,000.
(c) It was sold for $16,000.

E9-6 During 2001 **Federal Express** reported the following information (in millions): net sales of $19,629 and net income of $584. Its balance sheet also showed total assets at the beginning of the year of $11,527 and total assets at the end of the year of $13,340.

Calculate asset turnover ratio and return on assets ratio.
(SO 6)

Instructions
Calculate (a) asset turnover ratio and (b) return on assets ratio.

E9-7 These are selected 2005 transactions for Chang Corporation:

Prepare adjusting entries for amortization.
(SO 7)

Jan. 1   Purchased a copyright from its creator for $140,000. The copyright has a useful life of 10 years and a remaining legal life of 30 years.
May 1   Purchased a patent with an estimated useful life of 4 years and a legal life of 20 years for $30,000.

Instructions
Prepare all adjusting entries at December 31 to record amortization required by the events.

E9-8 Vijay Company, organized in 2005, has these transactions related to intangible assets in that year:

Prepare entries to set up appropriate accounts for different intangibles; calculate amortization.
(SO 7)

Jan. 2   Purchased a patent (5-year life) $450,000.
Apr. 1   Goodwill purchased (indefinite life) $360,000.
July 1   Acquired a 10-year franchise; expiration date July 1, 2015, $450,000.
Sept. 1   Research and development costs $185,000.

Instructions
(a) Prepare the necessary entries to record these intangibles. All costs incurred were for cash.
(b) Make the entries as of December 31, 2005, recording any necessary amortization.
(c) Indicate what the balances should be on December 31, 2005.

Discuss implications of amortization period.
(SO 7)

E9-9   **Alliance Atlantis Communications Inc.** noted in its 1999 annual report that, effective January 1, 1999, the company had changed its accounting policy to amortize broadcast rights over the contracted exhibition period, which is based on the estimated useful life of the program. Previously, the company amortized broadcast rights over the lesser of 2 years or the contracted exhibition period.

Instructions

 Write a short memo to your client explaining the implications this has for the analysis of Alliance Atlantis's results. Also, discuss whether this change in amortization period appears reasonable.

E9-10   The questions listed below are independent of one another.

Answer questions on depreciation and intangibles.
(SO 2, 7)

Instructions

Provide a brief answer to each question.

(a) Why should a company depreciate its buildings?

(b) How can a company have a building that has a zero reported book value but substantial market value?

(c) What are some examples of intangibles that you might find on your college campus?

(d) Give some examples of company or product trademarks or trade names. Are trade names and trademarks reported on a company's balance sheet?

Compute depreciation under units-of-activity method.
(SO 9)

*E9-11   Orient Express Bus Lines uses the units-of-activity method in depreciating its buses. One bus was purchased on January 1, 2005, at a cost of $108,000. Over its 4-year useful life, the bus is expected to be driven 100,000 miles. Salvage value is expected to be $8,000.

Instructions

(a) Compute the depreciation cost per unit.

(b) Prepare a depreciation schedule assuming actual mileage was: 2005, 30,000; 2006, 32,000; 2007, 21,000; and 2008, 17,000.

Compute declining-balance and units-of-activity depreciation.
(SO 9)

*E9-12   Basic information relating to a new machine purchased by Lazar Company is presented in E9-3.

Instructions

Using the facts presented in E9-3, compute depreciation using the following methods in the year indicated.

(a) Declining-balance using double the straight-line rate for 2005 and 2006.

(b) Units-of-activity for 2005, assuming machine usage was 1,900 hours.

Problems: Set A

Determine acquisition costs of land and building.
(SO 1)

P9-1A   Fleming Company was organized on January 1. During the first year of operations, the following plant asset expenditures and receipts were recorded in random order.

Debits

1. Cost of real estate purchased as a plant site (land $180,000 and building $70,000)	$ 250,000
2. Accrued real estate taxes paid at time of purchase of real estate	4,900
3. Cost of demolishing building to make land suitable for construction of new building	27,000
4. Cost of filling and grading the land	7,270
5. Excavation costs for new building	21,900
6. Architect's fees on building plans	51,000
7. Full payment to building contractor	629,500
8. Cost of parking lots and driveways	31,800
9. Real estate taxes paid for the current year on land	5,320
	$1,028,690

Credits

10. Proceeds for salvage of demolished building	$ 12,700

Instructions
Analyze the transactions using the table column headings provided here. Enter the number of each transaction in the Item column, and enter the amounts in the appropriate columns. For amounts in the Other Accounts column, also indicate the account titles.

Item	Land	Building	Other Accounts

Land $276,470

P9-2A   At December 31, 2005, Pouncer Corporation reported these plant assets.

Journalize equipment transactions related to purchase, sale, retirement, and depreciation.
(SO 5, 8)

Land		$ 4,000,000
Buildings	$28,500,000	
Less: Accumulated depreciation—buildings	12,100,000	16,400,000
Equipment	48,000,000	
Less: Accumulated depreciation—equipment	5,000,000	43,000,000
Total plant assets		$63,400,000

During 2006, the following selected cash transactions occurred.

Apr. 1   Purchased land for $2,630,000.
May 1   Sold equipment that cost $675,000 when purchased on January 1, 2001. The equipment was sold for $350,000.
June 1   Sold land purchased on June 1, 1993, for $1,800,000. The land cost $300,000.
July 1   Purchased equipment for $1,000,000.
Dec. 31   Retired equipment that cost $470,000 when purchased on December 31, 1996. No salvage value was received.

Instructions
(a) Journalize the transactions. (*Hint:* You may wish to set up T accounts, post beginning balances, and then post 2006 transactions.) Pouncer uses straight-line depreciation for buildings and equipment. The buildings are estimated to have a 40-year life and no salvage value; the equipment is estimated to have a 10-year useful life and no salvage value. Update depreciation on assets disposed of at the time of sale or retirement.
(b) Record adjusting entries for depreciation for 2006.
(c) Prepare the plant assets section of Pouncer's balance sheet at December 31, 2006.

(c) Tot. plant assets
$60,897,500

P9-3A   Presented here are selected transactions for Harlem Corporation for 2005.

Journalize entries for disposal of plant assets.
(SO 5)

Jan.   1   Retired a piece of machinery that was purchased on January 1, 1995. The machine cost $52,000 and had a useful life of 10 years with no salvage value.
June 30   Sold a computer that was purchased on January 1, 2002. The computer cost $49,000 and had a useful life of 7 years with no salvage value. The computer was sold for $31,000.
Dec. 31   Discarded a delivery truck that was purchased on January 1, 2001. The truck cost $27,000 and was depreciated based on an 8-year useful life with a $3,000 salvage value.

Instructions
Journalize all entries required on the above dates, including entries to update depreciation on assets disposed of, where applicable. Harlem Corporation uses straight-line depreciation.

P9-4A   The intangible assets section of the balance sheet for Chardin Company at December 31, 2005, is presented here.

Prepare entries to record transactions related to acquisition and amortization of intangibles; prepare the intangible assets section and notes.
(SO 7, 8)

Patent ($70,000 cost less $7,000 amortization)	$63,000
Copyright ($48,000 cost less $19,200 amortization)	28,800
Total	$91,800

The patent was acquired in January 2005 and has a useful life of 10 years. The copyright was acquired in January 2002 and also has a useful life of 10 years. The following cash transactions may have affected intangible assets during 2006.

Jan. 2   Paid $22,500 legal costs to successfully defend the patent against infringement by another company.

Jan.–June   Developed a new product, incurring $220,000 in research and development costs. A patent was granted for the product on July 1, and its useful life is equal to its legal life. Legal and other costs for the patent were $10,000.

Sept. 1   Paid $110,000 to an extremely large defensive lineman to appear in commercials advertising the company's products. The commercials will air in September and October.

Oct. 1   Acquired a copyright for $160,000. The copyright has a useful life of 50 years.

Instructions

(a) Prepare journal entries to record the transactions.

(b) Prepare journal entries to record the 2006 amortization expense.

(c) Tot. intangibles $259,200

(c) Prepare the intangible assets section of the balance sheet at December 31, 2006.

(d) Prepare the notes to the financial statements on Chardin Company's intangible assets as of December 31, 2006.

Prepare entries to correct errors in recording and amortizing intangible assets. (SO 7)

P9-5A   Due to rapid employee turnover in the accounting department, the following transactions involving intangible assets were improperly recorded by the Stanhope Company in 2005.

1. Stanhope developed a new manufacturing process, incurring research and development costs of $153,000. The company also purchased a patent for $62,000. In early January Stanhope capitalized $215,000 as the cost of the patents. Patent amortization expense of $10,750 was recorded based on a 20-year useful life.

2. On July 1, 2005, Stanhope purchased a small company and as a result acquired goodwill of $76,000. Stanhope recorded a half-year's amortization in 2005 based on a 50-year life ($760 amortization). The goodwill has an indefinite life.

Instructions

Prepare all journal entries necessary to correct any errors made during 2005. Assume the books have not yet been closed for 2005.

Calculate and comment on return on assets, profit margin, and asset turnover ratio. (SO 6)

P9-6A   Thunder Corporation and Lightning Corporation, two corporations of roughly the same size, are both involved in the manufacture of umbrellas. Each company depreciates its plant assets using the straight-line approach. An investigation of their financial statements reveals the following information.

	Thunder Corp.	Lightning Corp.
Net income	$ 800,000	$1,000,000
Sales	1,600,000	1,300,000
Total assets (average)	2,500,000	1,700,000
Plant assets (average)	1,400,000	1,200,000
Intangible assets (goodwill)	600,000	0

Instructions

(a) For each company, calculate these values:

   (1) Return on assets ratio.

   (2) Profit margin.

   (3) Asset turnover ratio.

(b) ▭▭▭▭▷ Based on your calculations in part (a), comment on the relative effectiveness of the two companies in using their assets to generate sales. What factors complicate your ability to compare the two companies?

*P9-7A   In recent years Columbo Transportation purchased three used buses. Because of frequent employee turnover in the accounting department, a different accountant selected the depreciation method for each bus, and various methods have been used. Information concerning the buses is summarized in the table below.

Compute depreciation under different methods.
(SO 3, 9)

Bus	Acquired	Cost	Salvage Value	Useful Life (in years)	Depreciation Method
1	Jan. 1, 2003	$ 86,000	$ 6,000	5	Straight-line
2	Jan. 1, 2003	150,000	10,000	6	Declining-balance
3	Jan. 1, 2003	100,000	9,000	5	Units-of-activity

For the declining-balance method, Columbo Transportation uses the double-declining rate. For the units-of-activity method, total miles are expected to be 130,000. Actual miles of use in the first 3 years were: 2003, 24,000; 2004, 34,000; and 2005, 30,000.

Instructions
(a) Compute the amount of accumulated depreciation on each bus at December 31, 2005.
(b) If Bus 2 was purchased on May 1 instead of January 1, what would be the depreciation expense for this bus in 2003? In 2004?

(a) Bus 1 $48,000

*P9-8A   Crawford Corporation purchased machinery on January 1, 2005, at a cost of $260,000. The estimated useful life of the machinery is 5 years, with an estimated salvage value at the end of that period of $20,000. The company is considering different depreciation methods that could be used for financial reporting purposes.

Compute depreciation under different methods.
(SO 3, 9)

Instructions
(a) Prepare separate depreciation schedules for the machinery using the straight-line method, and the declining-balance method using double the straight-line rate.
(b) Which method would result in the higher reported 2005 income? In the highest total reported income over the 5-year period?
(c) Which method would result in the lower reported 2005 income? In the lowest total reported income over the 5-year period?

(a) Double-declining-balance exp. 2006 $62,400

Problems: Set B

P9-1B   Pierce Company was organized on January 1. During the first year of operations, the following plant asset expenditures and receipts were recorded in random order.

Determine acquisition costs of land and building.
(SO 1)

Debits

1. Cost of real estate purchased as a plant site (land $235,000 and building $25,000)		$260,000
2. Installation cost of fences around property		7,200
3. Cost of demolishing building to make land suitable for construction of new building		19,000
4. Excavation costs for new building		23,000
5. Accrued real estate taxes paid at time of purchase of real estate		2,179
6. Cost of parking lots and driveways		29,000
7. Architect's fees on building plans		38,000
8. Real estate taxes paid for the current year on land		5,800
9. Full payment to building contractor		600,000
		$984,179

Credits

10. Proceeds from salvage of demolished building		$5,000

Instructions

Analyze the transactions using the following table column headings. Enter the number of each transaction in the Item column, and enter the amounts in the appropriate columns. For amounts in the Other Accounts column, also indicate the account title.

Land $276,179

Item	Land	Building	Other Accounts

Journalize equipment transactions related to purchase, sale, retirement, and depreciation.
(SO 5, 8)

P9-2B   At December 31, 2005, Midas Corporation reported the following plant assets.

Land		$ 3,000,000
Buildings	$26,500,000	
Less: Accumulated depreciation—buildings	12,100,000	14,400,000
Equipment	40,000,000	
Less: Accumulated depreciation—equipment	5,000,000	35,000,000
Total plant assets		$52,400,000

During 2006, the following selected cash transactions occurred.

Apr. 1 Purchased land for $2,200,000.
May 1 Sold equipment that cost $600,000 when purchased on January 1, 1999. The equipment was sold for $200,000.
June 1 Sold land for $1,800,000. The land cost $500,000.
July 1 Purchased equipment for $1,100,000.
Dec. 31 Retired equipment that cost $500,000 when purchased on December 31, 1996. No salvage value was received.

Instructions

(a) Journalize the transactions. (*Hint:* You may wish to set up T accounts, post beginning balances, and then post 2006 transactions.) Midas uses straight-line depreciation for buildings and equipment. The buildings are estimated to have a 40-year useful life and no salvage value; the equipment is estimated to have a 10-year useful life and no salvage value. Update depreciation on assets disposed of at the time of sale or retirement.

(c) Tot. plant assets
            $50,362,500

(b) Record adjusting entries for depreciation for 2006.
(c) Prepare the plant assets section of Midas's balance sheet at December 31, 2006.

Journalize entries for disposal of plant assets.
(SO 5)

P9-3B   Presented here are selected transactions for Melina Company for 2005.

Jan. 1 Retired a piece of machinery that was purchased on January 1, 1995. The machine cost $62,000 on that date and had a useful life of 10 years with no salvage value.
June 30 Sold a computer that was purchased on January 1, 2002. The computer cost $35,000 and had a useful life of 5 years with no salvage value. The computer was sold for $12,000.
Dec. 31 Discarded a delivery truck that was purchased on January 1, 2000. The truck cost $27,000 and was depreciated based on an 8-year useful life with a $3,000 salvage value.

Instructions

Journalize all entries required on the above dates, including entries to update depreciation, where applicable, on assets disposed of. Melina Company uses straight-line depreciation. (Assume depreciation is up to date as of December 31, 2004.)

Prepare entries to record transactions related to acquisition and amortization of intangibles; prepare the intangible assets section and note.
(SO 7, 8)

P9-4B   The intangible assets section of Moore Corporation's balance sheet at December 31, 2005, is presented here.

Patent ($60,000 cost less $6,000 amortization)	$54,000
Copyright ($36,000 cost less $25,200 amortization)	10,800
Total	$64,800

The patent was acquired in January 2005 and has a useful life of 10 years. The copyright was acquired in January 1999 and also has a useful life of 10 years. The following cash transactions may have affected intangible assets during 2006.

Jan. 2   Paid $27,000 legal costs to successfully defend the patent against infringement by another company.

Jan.–June   Developed a new product, incurring $210,000 in research and development costs. A patent was granted for the product on July 1, and its useful life is equal to its legal life. Legal and other costs for the patent were $5,000.

Sept. 1   Paid $60,000 to a quarterback to appear in commercials advertising the company's products. The commercials will air in September and October.

Oct. 1   Acquired a copyright for $180,000. The copyright has a useful life of 50 years.

Instructions
(a) Prepare journal entries to record the transactions.
(b) Prepare journal entries to record the 2006 amortization expense for intangible assets.
(c) Prepare the intangible assets section of the balance sheet at December 31, 2006.   *(c) Tot. intangibles $258,300*
(d) Prepare the note to the financial statements on Moore Corporation's intangible assets as of December 31, 2006.

P9-5B   Due to rapid employee turnover in the accounting department, the following transactions involving intangible assets were improperly recorded by Cramer Corporation in 2005.

Prepare entries to correct errors in recording and amortizing intangible assets. (SO 7)

1. Cramer developed a new manufacturing process, incurring research and development costs of $120,000. The company also purchased a patent for $37,400. In early January Cramer capitalized $157,400 as the cost of the patents. Patent amortization expense of $7,870 was recorded based on a 20-year useful life.
2. On July 1, 2005, Cramer purchased a small company and as a result acquired goodwill of $60,000. Cramer recorded a half-year's amortization in 2005, based on a 50-year life ($600 amortization). The goodwill has an indefinite life.

Instructions
Prepare all journal entries necessary to correct any errors made during 2005. Assume the books have not yet been closed for 2005.

P9-6B   Barnaby Corporation and Smudge Corporation, two companies of roughly the same size, are both involved in the manufacture of shoe-tracing devices. Each company depreciates its plant assets using the straight-line approach. An investigation of their financial statements reveals this information.

Calculate and comment on return on assets, profit margin, and asset turnover ratio. (SO 6)

	Barnaby Corp.	Smudge Corp.
Net income	$ 400,000	$ 600,000
Sales	1,400,000	1,200,000
Total assets (average)	3,200,000	2,500,000
Plant assets (average)	2,400,000	1,800,000
Accumulated depreciation	300,000	625,000
Intangible assets (goodwill)	300,000	0

Instructions
(a) For each company, calculate these values:
   (1) Return on assets ratio.
   (2) Profit margin.
   (3) Asset turnover ratio.

(b) Based on your calculations in part (a), comment on the relative effectiveness of the two companies in using their assets to generate sales. What factors complicate your ability to compare the two companies?

*P9-7B   In recent years Zorin Company has purchased three machines. Because of frequent employee turnover in the accounting department, a different accountant was in

Compute depreciation under different methods. (SO 3, 9)

charge of selecting the depreciation method for each machine, and various methods have been used. Information concerning the machines is summarized in the table.

Machine	Acquired	Cost	Salvage Value	Useful Life (in years)	Depreciation Method
1	Jan. 1, 2002	$96,000	$ 6,000	9	Straight-line
2	July 1, 2003	80,000	10,000	8	Declining-balance
3	Nov. 1, 2003	78,000	6,000	6	Units-of-activity

For the declining-balance method, Zorin Company uses the double-declining rate. For the units-of-activity method, total machine hours are expected to be 24,000. Actual hours of use in the first 3 years were: 2003, 1,500; 2004, 4,500; and 2005, 5,000.

Instructions

(a) Machine 2 $40,625

(a) Compute the amount of accumulated depreciation on each machine at December 31, 2005.

(b) If machine 2 was purchased on October 1 instead of July 1, what would be the depreciation expense for this machine in 2003? In 2004?

Compute depreciation under different methods.
(SO 3, 9)

*P9-8B   Blofeld Corporation purchased machinery on January 1, 2005, at a cost of $170,000. The estimated useful life of the machinery is 4 years, with an estimated residual value at the end of that period of $10,000. The company is considering different depreciation methods that could be used for financial reporting purposes.

Instructions

(a) Double-declining-
balance expense 2007
          $21,250

(a) Prepare separate depreciation schedules for the machinery using the straight-line method, and the declining-balance method using double the straight-line rate. Round to the nearest dollar.

(b) Which method would result in the higher reported 2005 income? In the highest total reported income over the 4-year period?

(c) Which method would result in the lower reported 2005 income? In the lowest total reported income over the 4-year period?

▶ BROADENING YOUR PERSPECTIVE

Financial Reporting and Analysis

FINANCIAL REPORTING PROBLEM: *Tootsie Roll Industries, Inc.*

BYP9-1   Refer to the financial statements and the Notes to Consolidated Financial Statements of **Tootsie Roll Industries** in Appendix A.

Instructions
Answer the following questions.

(a) What were the total cost and book value of property, plant, and equipment at December 31, 2002?

(b) What method or methods of depreciation are used by Tootsie Roll for financial reporting purposes?

(c) What was the amount of depreciation and amortization expense for each of the 3 years 2000–2002? (*Hint:* Use statement of cash flows.)

(d) Using the statement of cash flows, what are the amounts of property, plant, and equipment purchased (capital expenditures) in 2002 and 2001?

(e) Explain how Tootsie Roll accounted for its intangible assets in 2002.

(f) Read Tootsie Roll's note 10 on commitments. Does the company primarily engage in capital leases or operating leases? What are the implications for analysis of its financial statements?

COMPARATIVE ANALYSIS PROBLEM: *Tootsie Roll vs. Hershey Foods*

BYP9-2   The financial statements of **Hershey Foods** are presented in Appendix B, following the financial statements for **Tootsie Roll Industries** in Appendix A.

Instructions
   (a) Based on the information in these financial statements and the accompanying notes and schedules, compute the following values for each company in 2002.
      (1) Return on assets ratio.
      (2) Profit margin.
      (3) Asset turnover ratio.
   (b) What conclusions concerning the management of plant assets can be drawn from these data?

RESEARCH CASE

BYP9-3   The June 26, 2002, issue of the *Wall Street Journal* ran an article by Jared Sandberg, Rebecca Blumenstein, and Shawn Young entitled "**WorldCom** Internal Probe Uncovers Massive Fraud."

Instructions
Read this article and answer the following questions.
   (a) What was the fraud that occurred at WorldCom, and what was its impact on net income in 2001 and 2002?
   (b) How was the massive fraud discovered?
   (c) As a result of this fraud, WorldCom eventually declared bankruptcy. Explain what factors probably led the company to declare bankruptcy.
   (d) The article notes that the fraud helped WorldCom increase its cash flow from operations. Explain how the company's cash flow was increased.
   (e) What happened to WorldCom's stock price as a result of this fraud?

INTERPRETING FINANCIAL STATEMENTS

BYP9-4   **Bob Evans Farms, Inc.** operates 495 restaurants in 22 states and produces fresh and fully cooked sausage products, fresh salads, and related products distributed to grocery stores in the Midwest, Southwest, and Southeast. For a recent 3-year period Bob Evans Farms reported the following selected income statement data (in millions of dollars).

	2002	**2001**	**2000**
Sales	$1,061.8	$1,007.5	$947.9
Cost of goods sold	300.4	292.9	274.4
Net income	67.7	50.8	52.9
Total assets	721.9	678.7	624.4

   In his letters to stockholders, the chief executive officer (CEO) expressed great enthusiasm for the company's future. Here is an excerpt from that letter:

> **BOB EVANS FARMS, INC.**
> **Letter to Stockholders (partial)**
>
> Fiscal 2002 was a record-breaking year for Bob Evans Farms. The company's financial performance on both sides of the business exceeded our expectations. Strategically, the Bob Evans brand is stronger than ever, and we see plenty of opportunities to leverage it and continue building stockholder value in the years ahead.

Instructions
   (a) Compute the percentage change in sales and in net income from 2000 to 2002.
   (b) What contribution, if any, did the company's gross profit rate make to the improved earnings?

(c) What was Bob Evans's profit margin ratio in each of the 3 years? Comment on any trend in this percentage.

(d) The CEO's letter also stated that the company's "same-store sales" have increased by 5% from the previous year. What effect would you expect this change to have on return on assets? Calculate the company's return on assets for 2001 and 2002 to see if it reflects the increase in same-store sales.

(e) Based on the trends in these ratios, does the CEO's optimism seem appropriate?

BYP9-5 **Boeing** and **McDonnell Douglas** were two leaders in the manufacture of aircraft. In 1996 Boeing announced intentions to acquire McDonnell Douglas and create one huge corporation. Competitors, primarily **Airbus of Europe**, were very concerned that they would not be able to compete with such a huge rival. In addition, customers were concerned that this merger would reduce the number of suppliers to a point where Boeing would be able to dictate prices. Provided below are figures taken from the 1995 financial statements of Boeing and McDonnell Douglas, which allow a comparison of the operations of the two corporations prior to their merger.

($ in millions)	Boeing	McDonnell Douglas
Total revenue	$19,515	$14,322
Net income (loss)	393	(416)
Total assets (average)	22,098	10,466
Land (average)	404	91
Buildings and fixtures	5,791	1,647
Machinery and equipment	7,251	2,161
Average property, plant, and equipment (at cost)	13,744	3,899
Accumulated depreciation	7,288	2,541
Depreciation expense	976	196

Instructions

(a) Which company used a longer average estimated useful life for its assets?

(b) Based on the asset turnover ratio, which company used its assets more effectively to generate sales?

(c) Which company generated a better return on assets?

(d) Besides an increase in size, what other factors might have motivated this merger?

A GLOBAL FOCUS

BYP9-6 As noted in the chapter, the accounting for goodwill differs in countries around the world. The discussion of a change in goodwill accounting practices shown at the top of page 461 was taken from the notes to the financial statements of **J Sainsbury Plc**, one of the world's leading retailers. Headquartered in the United Kingdom, it serves 11 million customers a week.

Instructions

Answer the following questions.

(a) How does the initial determination and recording of goodwill compare with that in the United States? That is, is goodwill initially recorded in the same circumstances, and is the calculation of the amount the same in both the United Kingdom and the United States?

(b) Prior to adoption of the new accounting standard (*FRS 10*), how did the company account for goodwill? What were the implications for the income statement?

(c) Under the new accounting standard, how does the company account for its goodwill? Is it possible, under the new standard, for a company to avoid charging goodwill amortization to net income?

(d) In what ways is the new standard similar to U.S. standards, and in what ways is it different?

FINANCIAL ANALYSIS ON THE WEB

BYP9-7 *Purpose:* Use an annual report to identify a company's plant assets and the depreciation method used.

Address: www.reportgallery.com (or go to **www.wiley.com/college/kimmel**)

J SAINSBURY PLC
Notes to the Financial Statements

Accounting Policies Goodwill arising in connection with the acquisition of shares in subsidiaries and associated undertakings is calculated as the excess of the purchase price over the fair value of the net tangible assets acquired. In prior years goodwill has been deducted from reserves in the period of acquisition. FRS 10 is applicable in the current financial year, and in accordance with the standard acquired goodwill is now shown as an asset on the Group's Balance Sheet. As permitted by FRS 10, goodwill written off to reserves in prior periods has not been restated as an asset.

Goodwill is treated as having an indefinite economic life where it is considered that the acquired business has strong customer loyalty built up over a long period of time, based on advantageous store locations and a commitment to maintain the marketing advantage of the retail brand. The carrying value of the goodwill will be reviewed annually for impairment and adjusted to its recoverable amount if required. Where goodwill is considered to have a finite life, amortisation will be applied over that period.

For amounts stated as goodwill which are considered to have indefinite life, no amortisation is charged to the Profit and Loss Account.

Steps
1. From Report Gallery Homepage, choose **View the Library of Annual Reports**.
2. Select a particular company.
3. Choose **Annual Report**.
4. Follow instructions below.

Instructions
Answer the following questions.
   (a) What is the name of the company?
   (b) What is the Internet address of the annual report?
   (c) At fiscal year-end, what is the net amount of its plant assets?
   (d) What is the accumulated depreciation?
   (e) Which method of depreciation does the company use?

Critical Thinking

GROUP DECISION CASE

BYP9-8 Honey Company and Money Company are two companies that are similar in many respects except that Honey Company uses the straight-line method and Money Company uses the declining-balance method at double the straight-line rate. On January 2, 2003, both companies acquired identical depreciable assets listed in the table below.

Asset	Cost	Salvage Value	Useful Life
Building	$320,000	$20,000	40 years
Equipment	110,000	10,000	10 years

Money's depreciation expense was $38,000 in 2003, $32,800 in 2004, and $28,520 in 2005. Including the appropriate depreciation charges, annual net income for the companies in the years 2003, 2004, and 2005 and total income for the 3 years were as follows.

	2003	2004	2005	Total
Honey Company	$82,000	$88,400	$90,000	$260,400
Money Company	68,000	76,000	86,000	230,000

At December 31, 2005, the balance sheets of the two companies are similar except that Money Company has more cash than Honey Company.

Zora is interested in investing in one of the companies, and she comes to you for advice.

Instructions

With the class divided into groups, answer the following.

(a) Determine the annual and total depreciation recorded by Honey Company during the 3 years.

(b) Assuming that Money Company also uses the straight-line method of depreciation instead of the declining-balance method (that is, Money's depreciation expense would equal Honey's), prepare comparative income data for the 3 years.

(c) Which company should Zora invest in? Why?

COMMUNICATION ACTIVITY

BYP9-9 The chapter presented some concerns regarding the current accounting standards for research and development expenditures.

Instructions

Pretend that you are either (a) the president of a company that is very dependent on ongoing research and development, writing a memo to the FASB complaining about the current accounting standards regarding research and development, or (b) the FASB member defending the current standards regarding research and development. Your memo should address the following questions.

1. By requiring expensing of R&D, do you think companies will spend less on R&D? Why or why not? What are the possible implications for the competitiveness of U.S. companies?

2. If a company makes a commitment to spend money for R&D, it must believe it has future benefits. Shouldn't these costs therefore be capitalized just like the purchase of any long-lived asset that you believe will have future benefits?

ETHICS CASE

BYP9-10 Acme Anti-Pollution Company is suffering declining sales of its principal product, nonbiodegradable plastic cartons. The president, Marc Angelo Draco, instructs his controller, Dan Tay, to lengthen asset lives to reduce depreciation expense. A processing line of automated plastic extruding equipment, purchased for $2.7 million in January 2002, was originally estimated to have a useful life of 8 years and a salvage value of $300,000. Depreciation has been recorded for 2 years on that basis. Marc wants the estimated life changed to 12 years total and the straight-line method continued. Dan is hesitant to make the change, believing it is unethical to increase net income in this manner. Marc says, "Hey, the life is only an estimate, and I've heard that our competition uses a 12-year life on their production equipment."

Instructions

(a) Who are the stakeholders in this situation?

(b) Is the proposed change in asset life unethical, or is it simply a good business practice by an astute president?

(c) What is the effect of Marc's proposed change on income before taxes in the year of change?

Answers to Self-Study Questions

1. d   2. a   3. b   4. d   5. c   6. b   7. d   8. d   9. b   10. c   11. c
*12. d

Answer to Tootsie Roll Review It Question 3, p. 421

Tootsie Roll depreciates its buildings over 20 to 35 years and its machinery and equipment over 5 to 20 years.

✔ **Remember to go back to the Navigator box on the chapter-opening page and check off your completed work.**

Reporting and Analyzing Liabilities

STUDY OBJECTIVES

After studying this chapter,
you should be able to:

1 Explain a current liability and identify the major types of current liabilities.

2 Describe the accounting for notes payable.

3 Explain the accounting for other current liabilities.

4 Identify the types of bonds.

5 Prepare the entries for the issuance of bonds and interest expense.

6 Describe the entries when bonds are redeemed.

7 Identify the requirements for the financial statement presentation and analysis of liabilities.

 THE NAVIGATOR

THE NAVIGATOR ✔

▶ Scan *Study Objectives* ☐

▶ Read *Feature Story* ☐

▶ Read *Preview* ☐

▶ Read text and answer *Before You Go On*
  p. 471 ☐   p. 474 ☐   p. 481 ☐
  p. 488 ☐

▶ Work Using the *Decision Toolkit* ☐

▶ Review Summary of *Study Objectives* ☐

▶ Work *Demonstration Problem* ☐

▶ Answer *Self-Study Questions* ☐

▶ Complete *Assignments* ☐

FEATURE STORY

And Then There Were Two

Debt can help a company acquire the things it needs to grow, but it is often the very thing that kills a company. A brief history of **Maxwell Car Company** illustrates the role of debt in the U.S. auto industry. In 1920 Maxwell Car Company was on the brink of financial ruin. Because it was axle-deep in debt and unable to pay its bills, its creditors stepped in and took over. A former **General Motors** executive named Walter Chrysler was hired to reorganize the company. By 1925 he had taken over the company and renamed it **Chrysler**. By 1933 Chrysler was booming, with sales surpassing even those of **Ford**.

But the next few decades saw Chrysler make a series of blunders. During the 1940s, while its competitors were making yearly design changes to boost customer interest, Chrysler made no changes. During the 1960s, when customers wanted large cars, Chrysler produced small cars. During the 1970s, when customers wanted small cars, Chrysler offered big "boats." By 1980, with its creditors pounding at the gates, Chrysler was again on the brink of financial ruin.

At that point Chrysler brought in a former Ford executive named Lee Iacocca to save the company. Iacocca, considered by many as good a politician as a businessman, argued that the United States could not afford to let Chrysler fail because of the loss of jobs. He convinced the federal government to grant loan guarantees—promises that if Chrysler failed to pay its creditors, the government would pay them. Iacocca then streamlined operations and brought out some profitable products. Chrysler repaid all of its government-guaranteed loans by 1983, seven years ahead of the scheduled final payment.

What has happened since? In the 1990s Chrysler knew both feast and famine: In 1991 it operated in the red, with Iacocca leaving the company under pressure in 1992. By 1995 Chrysler was the most profitable U.S.-based car manufacturer and the envy of the entire industry. But to compete in today's global vehicle market, you must be big—really big. So in 1998 Chrysler merged with German automaker **Daimler-Benz**, to form **DaimlerChrysler**. This left just two U.S.-based auto manufacturers—General Motors and Ford.

These companies are giants. In comparison with other U.S. corporations, General Motors and Ford rank, respectively, number three and four in

total assets. But General Motors and Ford have accumulated a truckload of debt on their way to getting this big. Combined, they have *$573 billion* in total outstanding liabilities. Although debt has made it possible to get so big, the Chrysler story makes it clear that debt can also threaten a company's survival.

On the World Wide Web
DaimlerChrysler:
   www.daimlerchrysler.com
Ford: www.ford.com
General Motors: www.gm.com

The Feature Story suggests that **General Motors** and **Ford** have tremendous amounts of debt. It is unlikely that they could have grown so large without this debt, but at times this debt threatens their very existence. Given this risk, why do companies borrow money? Why do they sometimes borrow short-term and other times long-term? Besides bank borrowings, what other kinds of debts does a company incur? In this chapter we address these issues.

The content and organization of the chapter are as follows.

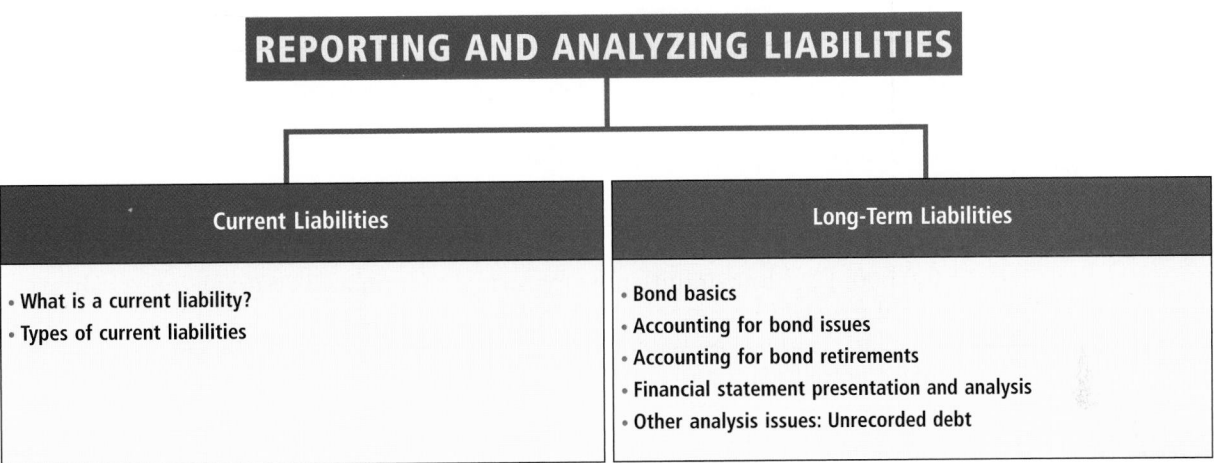

REPORTING AND ANALYZING LIABILITIES

Current Liabilities	Long-Term Liabilities
• What is a current liability? • Types of current liabilities	• Bond basics • Accounting for bond issues • Accounting for bond retirements • Financial statement presentation and analysis • Other analysis issues: Unrecorded debt

☑ THE NAVIGATOR

SECTION 1
CURRENT LIABILITIES

What Is a Current Liability?

You have learned that liabilities are defined as "creditors' claims on total assets" and as "existing debts and obligations." These claims, debts, and obligations must be settled or paid at some time in the future by the transfer of assets or services. The future date on which they are due or payable (the maturity date) is a significant feature of liabilities.

As explained in Chapter 2, a **current liability** is a debt that can reasonably be expected to be paid (1) from existing current assets or through the creation of other current liabilities, and (2) within one year or the operating cycle, whichever is longer. Debts that do not meet both criteria are classified as **long-term liabilities**.

Financial statement users want to know whether a company's obligations are current or long-term. A company, for example, that has more current liabilities than current assets often lacks liquidity, or short-term debt-paying ability. In addition, users want to know the types of liabilities a company has. If a company declares bankruptcy, a specific, predetermined order of payment to creditors exists. Thus, the amount and type of liabilities are of critical importance.

> **STUDY OBJECTIVE**
> **1**
> Explain a current liability and identify the major types of current liabilities.

Types of Current Liabilities

The different types of current liabilities include notes payable, accounts payable, unearned revenues, and accrued liabilities such as taxes, salaries and wages, and interest. In this section we discuss a few of the common and more important types of current liabilities.

NOTES PAYABLE

STUDY OBJECTIVE
2
Describe the accounting for notes payable.

Obligations in the form of written notes are recorded as **notes payable**. Notes payable are often used instead of accounts payable because they give the lender written documentation of the obligation in case legal remedies are needed to collect the debt. Notes payable usually require the borrower to pay interest and frequently are issued to meet short-term financing needs.

Notes are issued for varying periods of time. **Those due for payment within one year of the balance sheet date are usually classified as current liabilities.** Most notes are interest-bearing.

To illustrate the accounting for notes payable, assume that First National Bank agrees to lend $100,000 on September 1, 2005, if Cole Williams Co. signs a $100,000, 12%, four-month note maturing on January 1. With an interest-bearing note, the amount of assets received when the note is issued generally equals the note's face value. Cole Williams Co. therefore will receive $100,000 cash and will make the following journal entry.

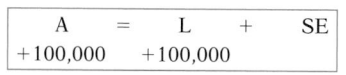

A = L + SE
+100,000   +100,000

Cash Flows
+100,000

Sept. 1	Cash	100,000	
	Notes Payable		100,000
	(To record issuance of 12%, 4-month note to First National Bank)		

Interest accrues over the life of the note and must be recorded periodically. If Cole Williams Co. prepares financial statements annually, an adjusting entry is required to recognize interest expense and interest payable of $4,000 ($100,000 × 12% × $\frac{4}{12}$) at December 31. The adjusting entry is:

A = L + SE
+4,000   −4,000 Exp

Cash Flows
no effect

Dec. 31	Interest Expense	4,000	
	Interest Payable		4,000
	(To accrue interest for 4 months on First National Bank note)		

In the December 31 financial statements, the current liabilities section of the balance sheet will show notes payable $100,000 and interest payable $4,000. In addition, interest expense of $4,000 will be reported under "Other expenses and losses" in the income statement.

At maturity (January 1), Cole Williams Co. must pay the face value of the note ($100,000) plus $4,000 interest ($100,000 × 12% × $\frac{4}{12}$). The entry to record payment of the note and accrued interest is:

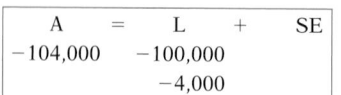

A = L + SE
−104,000   −100,000
           −4,000

Cash Flows
−104,000

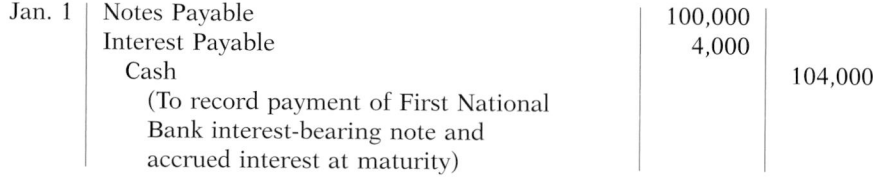

Jan. 1	Notes Payable	100,000	
	Interest Payable	4,000	
	Cash		104,000
	(To record payment of First National Bank interest-bearing note and accrued interest at maturity)		

Appendix 10C at the end of this chapter discusses the accounting for long-term installment notes payable.

SALES TAXES PAYABLE

Many of the products we purchase at retail stores are subject to sales taxes. This tax is expressed as a percentage of the sales price. The retailer (or selling company) collects the tax from the customer when the sale occurs and periodically (usually monthly) remits the collections to the state's department of revenue.

Under most state laws, the amount of the sale and the amount of the sales tax collected must be rung up separately on the cash register. (Gasoline sales are a major exception.) The cash register readings are then used to credit Sales and Sales Taxes Payable. For example, if the March 25 cash register readings for Cooley Grocery show sales of $10,000 and sales taxes of $600 (sales tax rate of 6%), the journal entry is:

Helpful Hint Watch how sales are rung up at local retailers to see whether the sales tax is computed separately.

Mar. 25	Cash	10,600	
	Sales		10,000
	Sales Taxes Payable		600
	(To record daily sales and sales taxes)		

A	=	L	+	SE
+10,600		+600		+10,000 Rev

Cash Flows
+10,600

When the taxes are remitted to the taxing agency, Sales Taxes Payable is decreased (debited) and Cash is decreased (credited). The company does not report sales taxes as an expense; it simply forwards the amount paid by the customer to the government. Thus, Cooley Grocery serves only as a **collection agent** for the taxing authority.

When sales taxes are not rung up separately on the cash register, total receipts are divided by 100% plus the sales tax percentage to determine sales. To illustrate, assume in our example that Cooley Grocery "rings up" total receipts of $10,600. Because the amount received from the sale is equal to the sales price 100% plus 6% of sales, or 1.06 times the sales total, we can compute sales as follows: $10,600 ÷ 1.06 = $10,000. Thus, the sales tax amount of $600 is found by either (1) subtracting sales from total receipts ($10,600 − $10,000) or (2) multiplying sales by the sales tax rate ($10,000 × 6%).

Business Insight
MANAGEMENT PERSPECTIVE

If you buy a book at a bookstore, you pay sales tax. If you buy the same book over the Internet, you don't pay sales tax (in most cases). This is one reason why e-commerce, as it has come to be called, has been growing exponentially and why Web sites like **Amazon.com** have become so popular. A recent study suggested that Internet sales would fall by 30 percent if sales tax were applied. In December 2001 Congress passed and President Bush signed into law a two-year extension to the ban on sales taxes on Internet purchases. While Internet retailers were pleased, the American Booksellers Association protested the ban, saying it gives online booksellers such as Amazon.com an unfair advantage over brick-and-mortar bookstores.

SOURCE: Edward Nawotka, "Bush Extends Internet Tax Ban," *Publishers Weekly* (December 3, 2001), p. 18.

PAYROLL AND PAYROLL TAXES PAYABLE

Assume that Susan Alena works 40 hours this week for Pepitone Inc., earning a wage of $10 per hour. Will Susan receive a $400 check at the end of the week? Not likely. The reason: Pepitone is required to withhold amounts from her wages to pay various governmental authorities. For example, Pepitone will withhold amounts for Social Security taxes and for federal and state income taxes. If these withholdings total $100, Susan will receive a check for only $300. Illustration 10-1 summarizes the types of payroll deductions that normally occur for most companies.

Illustration 10-1
Payroll deductions

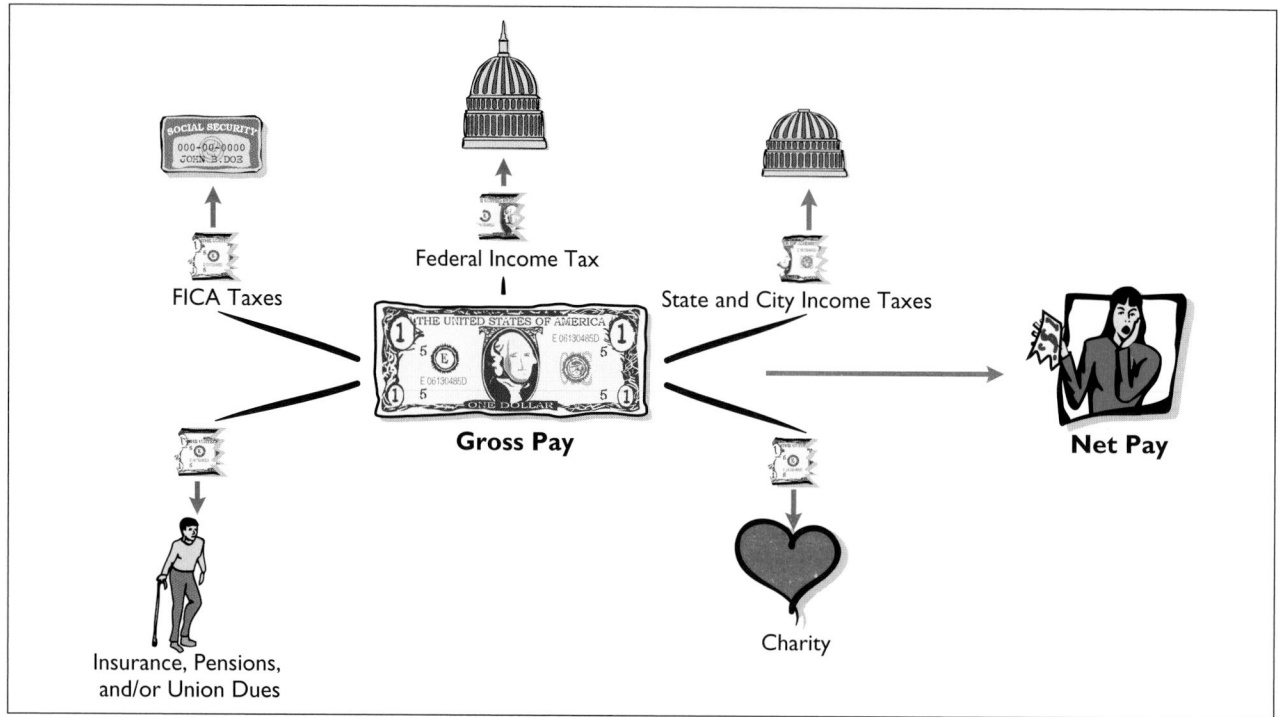

As a result of these deductions, companies withhold from employee paychecks amounts that must be paid to other parties. Pepitone therefore has incurred a liability to pay these third parties, and this liability must be reported in its balance sheet.

To provide a second illustration, assume that Cargo Corporation makes the following journal entry to record its payroll for the week of March 7.

A	=	L	+	SE
		+7,250		−100,000 Exp
		+21,864		
		+2,922		
		+67,964		

Cash Flows
no effect

Mar. 7	Salaries and Wages Expense	100,000	
	FICA Taxes Payable[1]		7,250
	Federal Income Taxes Payable		21,864
	State Income Taxes Payable		2,922
	Salaries and Wages Payable		67,964
	(To record payroll and withholding taxes		
	for the week ending March 7)		

The payment of this payroll on March 7 is then recorded as follows.

A	=	L	+	SE
−67,964		−67,964		

Cash Flows
−67,964

Mar. 7	Salaries and Wages Payable	67,964	
	Cash		67,964
	(To record payment of the March 7		
	payroll)		

---

[1]Social Security taxes are commonly referred to as FICA taxes. In 1937 Congress enacted the Federal Insurance Contribution Act (FICA). As can be seen in this journal entry and the payroll tax journal entry, the employee and employer must make equal contributions to Social Security. The Social Security rate in 2002 was 7.65% for each.

In this case Cargo reports $100,000 in wages and salaries expense. In addition, it reports liabilities for the wages payable as well as liabilities to other governmental agencies. Rather than pay the employees $100,000, Cargo is instead required to withhold the taxes and make the tax payments directly. In summary, Cargo is essentially serving as a tax collector.

In addition to the liabilities incurred as a result of withholdings, employers also incur a second type of payroll-related liability. With every payroll, the employer incurs liabilities to pay various **payroll taxes** levied upon the employer. These payroll taxes include the *employer's share* of Social Security (FICA) taxes and state and federal unemployment taxes. Based on the $100,000 payroll in our Cargo Corp. example, the following entry would be made to record the employer's expense and liability for these payroll taxes.

Mar. 7	Payroll Tax Expense	13,450	
	FICA Taxes Payable		7,250
	Federal Unemployment Taxes Payable		800
	State Unemployment Taxes Payable		5,400
	(To record employer's payroll taxes on March 7 payroll)		

A	=	L	+	SE
		+7,250		−13,450 Exp
		+800		
		+5,400		

Cash Flows
no effect

The payroll and payroll tax liability accounts are classified as current liabilities because they must be paid to employees or remitted to taxing authorities periodically and in the near term. Taxing authorities impose substantial fines and penalties on employers if the withholding and payroll taxes are not computed correctly and paid on time.

UNEARNED REVENUES

A magazine publisher such as **Sports Illustrated** may receive a customer's check when magazines are ordered, and an airline company such as **American Airlines** often receives cash when it sells tickets for future flights. Season tickets for concerts, sporting events, and theatre programs are also paid for in advance. How do companies account for unearned revenues that are received before goods are delivered or services are rendered?

1. When the advance is received, Cash is increased (debited), and a current liability account identifying the source of the unearned revenue is also increased (credited).

2. When the revenue is earned, the unearned revenue account is decreased (debited), and an earned revenue account is increased (credited).

To illustrate, assume that Superior University sells 10,000 season football tickets at $50 each for its five-game home schedule. The entry for the sales of season tickets is:

Aug. 6	Cash	500,000	
	Unearned Football Ticket Revenue		500,000
	(To record sale of 10,000 season tickets)		

A	=	L	+	SE
+500,000		+500,000		

Cash Flows
+500,000

As each game is completed, the following entry is made.

Sept. 7	Unearned Football Ticket Revenue	100,000	
	Football Ticket Revenue		100,000
	(To record football ticket revenues earned)		

A	=	L	+	SE
		−100,000		+100,000 Rev

Cash Flows
no effect

The account Unearned Football Ticket Revenue represents unearned revenue and is reported as a current liability in the balance sheet. As revenue is earned, a reclassification from unearned revenue to earned revenue occurs. Unearned revenue is material for some companies: In the airline industry, tickets sold for future flights represent almost 50% of total current liabilities. At **United Airlines**, unearned ticket revenue is the largest current liability, recently amounting to more than $1 billion.

Illustration 10-2 shows specific unearned and earned revenue accounts used in selected types of businesses.

Illustration 10-2
Unearned and earned
revenue accounts

Type of Business	Account Title	
	Unearned Revenue	**Earned Revenue**
Airline	Unearned Passenger Ticket Revenue	Passenger Ticket Revenue
Magazine publisher	Unearned Subscription Revenue	Subscription Revenue
Hotel	Unearned Rental Revenue	Rental Revenue

CURRENT MATURITIES OF LONG-TERM DEBT

Companies often have a portion of long-term debt that comes due in the current year. As an example, assume that Wendy Construction issues a 5-year, interest-bearing $25,000 note on January 1, 2004. This note specifies that each January 1, starting January 1, 2005, $5,000 of the note should be paid. When financial statements are prepared on December 31, 2004, $5,000 should be reported as a current liability and $20,000 as a long-term liability. Current maturities of long-term debt are often identified on the balance sheet as **long-term debt due within one year**. At December 31, 2001, the Automotive Division of **General Motors** had $64 million of such debt.

It is not necessary to prepare an adjusting entry to recognize the current maturity of long-term debt. At the balance sheet date, all obligations due within one year are classified as current, and all other obligations are classified as long-term.

Business Insight
MANAGEMENT PERSPECTIVE

A decision that all companies must make is to what extent to rely on short-term versus long-term financing. The critical nature of this decision was highlighted in the fall of 2001, after the World Trade Center disaster. Prior to September 11, short-term interest rates had been extremely low relative to long-term rates. In order to minimize interest costs, many companies were relying very heavily on short-term financing to purchase things they normally would have used long-term debt for. The problem with short-term financing is that it requires companies to continually find new financing as each loan comes due. This makes them vulnerable to sudden changes in the economy.

After September 11, lenders and short-term investors became very reluctant to loan money. This put the squeeze on many companies: as short-term loans came due, they were unable to refinance. Some were able to get other financing, but at extremely high rates (for example, 12% as compared to 3%). Others were unable to get loans and instead had to sell assets to generate cash for their immediate needs.

SOURCE: Henny Sender, "Firms Feel Consequences of Short-Term Borrowing," Wall Street Journal Online (October 12, 2001).

BEFORE YOU GO ON . . .

▶ Review It

1. What are the two criteria for classifying a debt as a current liability?
2. What are some examples of current liabilities?
3. What are three items generally withheld from employees' wages or salaries?
4. Identify three examples of unearned revenues.
5. Identify the liabilities classified as current by **Tootsie Roll**. The answer to this question is provided on page 524.

▶ Do It

During the month of September, Lake Corporation's employees earned wages of $60,000. Withholdings related to these wages were $3,500 for Social Security (FICA), $6,500 for federal income tax, and $2,000 for state income tax. Costs incurred for unemployment taxes were $90 for federal and $150 for state.

Prepare the September 30 journal entries for (a) wages expense and wages payable assuming that all September wages will be paid in October and (b) the company's payroll tax expense.

Action Plan

• Remember that wages earned are an expense to the company, but the amount due to be paid to the employee is reduced by withholdings.
• Payroll taxes are taxes the company incurs related to its employees.

Solution

(a) To determine wages payable, reduce wages expense by the withholdings for FICA, federal income tax, and state income tax.

Sept. 30	Wages Expense	60,000	
	FICA Taxes Payable		3,500
	Federal Income Taxes Payable		6,500
	State Income Taxes Payable		2,000
	Wages Payable		48,000

(b) Payroll taxes would be for the company's share of FICA, as well as for federal and state unemployment tax.

Sept. 30	Payroll Tax Expense	3,740	
	FICA Taxes Payable		3,500
	Federal Unemployment Taxes Payable		90
	State Unemployment Taxes Payable		150

SECTION 2
LONG-TERM LIABILITIES

Long-term liabilities are obligations that are expected to be paid after one year. In this section we explain the accounting for the principal types of obligations reported in the long-term liabilities section of the balance sheet. These obligations often are in the form of bonds or long-term notes.

Bond Basics

Bonds are a form of interest-bearing note payable issued by corporations, universities, and governmental agencies. Bonds, like common stock, are sold in small denominations (usually $1,000 or multiples of $1,000). As a result, bonds attract many investors.

TYPES OF BONDS

Bonds may have different features. Some types of bonds commonly issued are described in the following sections.

Secured and Unsecured Bonds

Secured bonds have specific assets of the issuer pledged as collateral for the bonds. **Unsecured bonds** are issued against the general credit of the borrower. These bonds are used extensively by large corporations with good credit ratings. For example, in a recent annual report, **Dupont** reported more than $2 billion of unsecured bonds outstanding.

Convertible and Callable Bonds

Convertible Bonds

Bonds that can be converted into common stock at the bondholder's option are called **convertible bonds**. Bonds subject to retirement at a stated dollar amount prior to maturity at the option of the issuer are known as **callable bonds**. Convertible bonds have features that are attractive both to bondholders and to the issuer. The conversion often gives bondholders an opportunity to benefit if the market price of the common stock increases substantially. Furthermore, until conversion, the bondholder receives interest on the bond. For the issuer, the bonds sell at a higher price and pay a lower rate of interest than comparable debt securities that do not have a conversion option. Many corporations, such as **USAir**, **USX Corp.**, and **General Motors Corporation**, have convertible bonds outstanding.

ISSUING PROCEDURES

A **bond certificate** is issued to the investor to provide evidence of the investor's claim against the company. As shown in Illustration 10-3 (page 473), it provides information such as the name of the company that issued the bonds, the face value of the bonds, the maturity date of the bonds, and the contractual interest rate. The **face value** is the amount due at the maturity date. The **maturity date**

Callable Bonds

Business Insight
INVESTOR PERSPECTIVE

Although bonds are generally secured by solid, substantial assets like land, buildings, and equipment, exceptions occur. For example, **Trans World Airlines Inc. (TWA)**—now part of **American Airlines**—at one time decided to issue $300 million of high-yielding 5-year bonds, secured by a grab-bag of assets—including some durable spare parts but also a lot of disposable items that TWA had in its warehouses, such as light bulbs and gaskets. Some called the planned TWA bonds "light bulb bonds." As one financial expert noted: "You've got to admit that some security is better than none." However, noted another, "They're digging pretty far down the barrel."

SOURCE: Wall Street Journal (June 2, 1989).

Illustration 10-3 Bond certificate

Issuer of bonds

Maturity date

No.

$5000

INTERNATIONAL MINERALS & CHEMICAL CORPORATION

11.875% SINKING FUND DEBENTURE DUE MAY 1, 2008

INTERNATIONAL MINERALS & CHEMICAL CORPORATION, a New York corporation (herein referred to as the "Company"), for value received, hereby promises to pay to

CUSIP 459884 AC 6

SEE REVERSE FOR CERTAIN DEFINITIONS

11.875%
DUE 2008

SPECIMEN

11.875%
DUE 2008

or registered assigns,
the principal sum of

FIVE THOUSAND DOLLARS

on May 1, 2005, in such coin or currency of the United States of America which at the time of payment is legal tender for public and private debts, upon presentation and surrender of this Debenture, at the option of the registered owner, either at the office or agency of the Company in the Borough of Manhattan, City and State of New York, or at the office or agency of the Company in the City of Chicago, Illinois, and to pay interest on such principal sum in like coin or currency, at the rate per annum specified in the title of this Debenture, at either such office or agency, from May 1, 1980, or from the most recent date to which interest has been paid or otherwise provided for, semi-annually on May 1 and November 1 in each year until payment of the principal sum has been made or duly provided for. The interest so payable on any May 1 or November 1 will (subject to certain exceptions provided in the Indenture referred to on the reverse hereof) be paid to the person in whose name this Debenture (or any Debenture evidencing all or a portion of the same debt) was registered at the

close of business on the fifteenth day of the calendar month preceding such May 1 or November 1, or if such day is not a business day, at the close of business on the next preceding business day. Interest on this Debenture may be paid at the option of the Company by check mailed to the registered address of the person entitled to such interest as such address shall appear on the registry books on the record date for such interest payment.

The provisions of this Debenture are continued on the reverse hereof and such continued provisions shall for all purposes have the same effect as though fully set forth at this place.

This Debenture shall not be valid or become obligatory for any purpose until the certificate of authentication hereon shall have been signed by the Trustee or any Authenticating Agent under the Indenture.

IN WITNESS WHEREOF, **INTERNATIONAL MINERALS & CHEMICAL CORPORATION** has caused this Debenture to be signed in its corporate name by its Chairman of the Board, its President, one of its Vice Presidents or its Treasurer by his signature, or a facsimile thereof, and has caused a facsimile of its corporate seal to be affixed hereunto or imprinted hereon and to be attested by its Secretary or an Assistant Secretary by his signature, or a facsimile thereof. Dated:

CERTIFICATE OF AUTHENTICATION
This is one of the Debentures described in the within-mentioned Indenture.

THE FIRST NATIONAL BANK OF CHICAGO, Trustee

By

Authorized Officer

INTERNATIONAL MINERALS & CHEMICAL CORPORATION · NEW YORK · 1909

Attest:

Secretary

INTERNATIONAL MINERALS & CHEMICAL CORPORATION

By

Chairman of the Board

Face or par value

Contractual interest rate

is the date that the final payment is due to the investor from the company. The **contractual interest rate** is the rate used to determine the amount of cash interest the borrower pays and the investor receives. Usually the contractual rate is stated as an annual rate, and interest is generally paid semiannually.

Alternative Terminology
The contractual rate is often referred to as the **stated rate**.

DETERMINING THE MARKET VALUE OF BONDS

If you were an investor interested in purchasing a bond, how would you determine how much to pay? To be more specific, assume that Coronet, Inc. issues a zero-interest (pays no interest) bond with a face value of $1,000,000 due in 20 years. For this bond, the only cash you receive is $1 million at the end of 20 years. Would you pay $1 million for this bond?

We hope not, because $1 million received 20 years from now is not the same as $1 million received today. The reason you should not pay $1 million relates to what is called the **time value of money**. If you had $1 million today, you would invest it and earn interest such that at the end of 20 years, your investment would be worth much more than $1 million. Thus, if someone is going to pay you $1 million 20 years from now, you would want to find its equivalent

Same dollars at different times are not equal.

today, or its **present value**. In other words, you would want to determine how much must be invested today at current interest rates to have $1 million in 20 years.

The current market value (present value) of a bond is therefore a function of three factors: (1) the dollar amounts to be received, (2) the length of time until the amounts are received, and (3) the market rate of interest. The **market interest rate** is the rate investors demand for loaning funds to the corporation. The process of finding the present value is referred to as **discounting** the future amounts.

To illustrate, assume that Acropolis Company on January 1, 2005, issues $100,000 of 9% bonds, due in 5 years, with interest payable annually at year-end. The purchaser of the bonds would receive the following two types of cash payments: (1) **principal** of $100,000 to be paid at maturity, and (2) five $9,000 **interest payments** ($100,000 × 9%) over the term of the bonds. A time diagram depicting both cash flows is shown in Illustration 10-4.

Illustration 10-4 Time diagram depicting cash flows

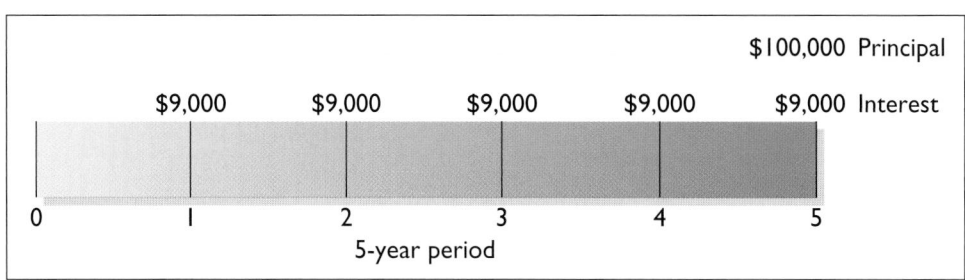

The current market value of a bond is equal to the present value of all the future cash payments promised by the bond. The present values of these amounts are listed in Illustration 10-5.

Illustration 10-5 Computing the market price of bonds

Present value of $100,000 received in 5 years	$ 64,993
Present value of $9,000 received annually for 5 years	35,007
Market price of bonds	**$100,000**

Tables are available to provide the present value numbers to be used, or these values can be determined mathematically.[2] Further discussion of the concepts and the mechanics of the time value of money computations is provided in Appendix C near the end of the book.

BEFORE YOU GO ON . . .

▶ **Review It**

1. What are bonds?
2. What are secured versus unsecured bonds and callable versus convertible bonds?

---

[2]For those knowledgable in the use of present value tables, the computations in this example are: $100,000 × .64993 = $64,993 and $9,000 × 3.88965 = $35,007 (rounded).

3. Explain the terms *face value* and *contractual interest rate*.
4. Explain why you would prefer to receive $1 million today rather than 5 years from now.

☑ THE NAVIGATOR

Accounting for Bond Issues

A corporation records bond transactions when it issues or retires (buys back) bonds and when bondholders convert bonds into common stock. If bondholders sell their bond investment to another investor, the issuing firm receives no further money on the transaction, **nor is the transaction journalized by the issuing corporation** (although it does keep records of the names of bondholders in some cases).

Bonds may be issued at face value, below face value (discount), or above face value (premium). Bond prices for both new issues and existing bonds are quoted as **a percentage of the face value of the bond**, **which is usually $1,000**. Thus, a $1,000 bond with a quoted price of 97 means that the selling price of the bond is 97% of face value, or $970 in this case.

ISSUING BONDS AT FACE VALUE

To illustrate the accounting for its bonds issued at face value, assume that Devor Corporation issues 100, 5-year, 10%, $1,000 bonds dated January 1, 2005, at 100 (100% of face value). The entry to record the sale is:

STUDY OBJECTIVE
5
Prepare the entries for the issuance of bonds and interest expense.

Jan. 1	Cash	100,000	
	Bonds Payable		100,000
	(To record sale of bonds at face value)		

A	=	L	+	SE
+100,000		+100,000		

Cash Flows
+100,000

Bonds payable are reported in the long-term liabilities section of the balance sheet because the maturity date is January 1, 2010 (more than one year away).

Over the term (life) of the bonds, entries are required for bond interest. Interest on bonds payable is computed in the same manner as interest on notes payable, as explained earlier. If it is assumed that interest is payable annually on January 1 on the bonds described above, interest of $10,000 ($100,000 × 10% × $\frac{12}{12}$) must be accrued on December 31.

At December 31 an adjusting entry is required to recognize the $10,000 of interest expense incurred. The entry is:

Helpful Hint Interest Expense = Principal × Rate × Time

Dec. 31	Bond Interest Expense	10,000	
	Bond Interest Payable		10,000
	(To accrue bond interest)		

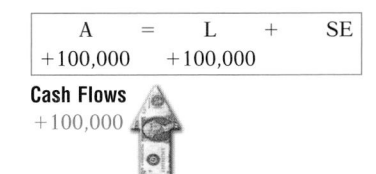

A	=	L	+	SE
		+10,000		−10,000 Exp

Cash Flows
no effect

Bond interest payable is classified as a current liability because it is scheduled for payment within the next year. When the interest is paid on January 1, 2006, Bond Interest Payable is decreased (debited) and Cash is decreased (credited) for $10,000.

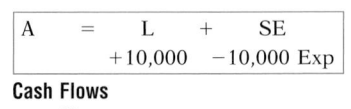

The entry to record the payment on January 1 is:

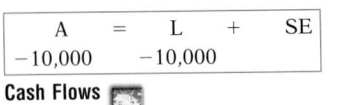

A	=	L	+	SE
−10,000		−10,000		

Cash Flows
−10,000

Jan. 1	Bond Interest Payable	10,000	
	Cash		10,000
	(To record payment of bond interest)		

DISCOUNT OR PREMIUM ON BONDS

The previous illustrations assumed that the interest rates paid on bonds, often referred to as the contractual (stated) interest rate and the market (effective) interest rate, were the same. Recall that the contractual interest rate is the rate applied to the face (par) value to arrive at the interest paid in a year. The market interest rate is the rate investors demand for loaning funds to the corporation. When the contractual interest rate and the market interest rate are the same, bonds sell at face value.

However, market interest rates change daily. They are influenced by the type of bond issued, the state of the economy, current industry conditions, and the company's individual performance. As a result, the contractual and market interest rates often differ, and therefore bonds sell below or above face value.

Helpful Hint Bond prices vary inversely with changes in the market interest rate. As market interest rates decline, bond prices will increase. When a bond is issued, if the market interest rate is below the contractual rate, the price will be higher than the face value.

To illustrate, suppose that a company issues 10% bonds at a time when other bonds of similar risk are paying 12%. Investors will not be interested in buying the 10% bonds, so their value will fall below their face value. In this case, we say the 10% bonds are **selling at a discount**. As a result of the decline in the bonds' selling price, the actual interest rate incurred by the company increases to the level of the current market interest rate.

Conversely, if the market rate of interest is **lower** than the contractual interest rate, investors will have to pay more than face value for the bonds. That is, if the market rate of interest is 8% but the contractual interest rate on the bonds is 10%, the issuer will require more funds from the investor. In these cases, **bonds sell at a premium**. These relationships are shown graphically in Illustration 10-6.

Illustration 10-6 Interest rates and bond prices

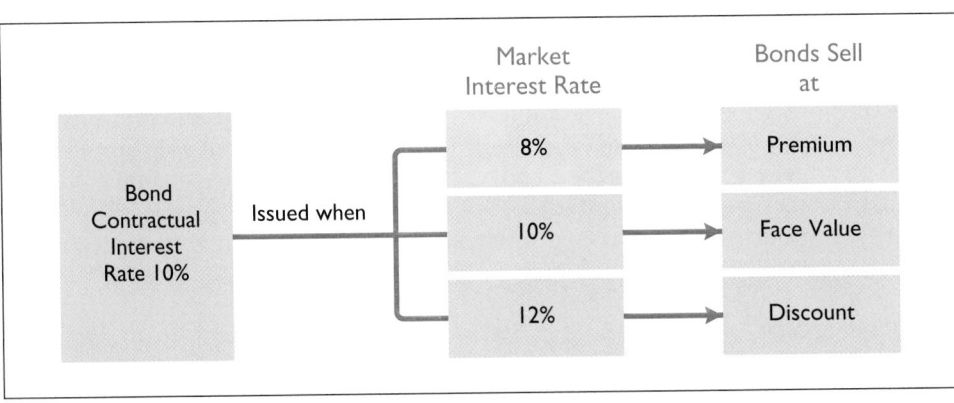

Helpful Hint Some bonds are sold at a discount by design. "Zero-coupon" bonds, which pay no interest, sell at a deep discount to face value.

Issuance of bonds at an amount different from face value is quite common. By the time a company prints the bond certificates and markets the bonds, it will be a coincidence if the market rate and the contractual rate are the same. Thus, the issuance of bonds at a discount does not mean that the financial strength of the issuer is suspect. Conversely, the sale of bonds at a premium does not indicate that the financial strength of the issuer is exceptional.

ISSUING BONDS AT A DISCOUNT

To illustrate the issuance of bonds at a discount, assume that on January 1, 2005, Candlestick Inc. sells $100,000, 5-year, 10% bonds at 98 (98% of face value) with interest payable on January 1. The entry to record the issuance is:

Jan. 1	Cash	98,000	
	Discount on Bonds Payable	2,000	
	Bonds Payable		100,000
	(To record sale of bonds at a discount)		

A	=	L	+	SE
+98,000		−2,000		
		+100,000		

Cash Flows
+98,000

Although Discount on Bonds Payable has a debit balance, **it is not an asset**. Rather it is a **contra account**, which is **deducted from bonds payable** on the balance sheet as in Illustration 10-7.

Illustration 10-7
Statement presentation of discount on bonds payable

CANDLESTICK INC. Balance Sheet (partial)		
Long-term liabilities		
Bonds payable	$100,000	
Less: Discount on bonds payable	**2,000**	$98,000

The $98,000 represents the **carrying (or book) value** of the bonds. On the date of issue this amount equals the market price of the bonds.

The issuance of bonds below face value causes the total cost of borrowing to differ from the bond interest paid. That is, the issuing corporation not only must pay the contractual interest rate over the term of the bonds but also must pay the face value (rather than the issuance price) at maturity. Therefore, the difference between the issuance price and the face value of the bonds—the discount—is an **additional cost of borrowing** that should be recorded as **bond interest expense** over the life of the bonds. The total cost of borrowing $98,000 for Candlestick Inc. is $52,000, computed as shown in Illustration 10-8.

Helpful Hint The carrying value (book value) of bonds issued at a discount is determined by subtracting the balance of the discount account from the balance of the Bonds Payable account.

Illustration 10-8
Computation of total cost of borrowing—bonds issued at discount

Bonds Issued at a Discount	
Annual interest payments	
($100,000 × 10% = $10,000; $10,000 × 5)	$ 50,000
Add: Bond discount ($100,000 − $98,000)	2,000
Total cost of borrowing	$52,000

Alternatively, the total cost of borrowing can be determined as follows (Illustration 10-9).

Illustration 10-9
Alternative computation of total cost of borrowing—bonds issued at discount

Bonds Issued at a Discount	
Principal at maturity	$100,000
Annual interest payments ($10,000 × 5)	50,000
Cash to be paid to bondholders	150,000
Cash received from bondholders	98,000
Total cost of borrowing	$ 52,000

To follow the matching principle, bond discount is allocated to expense in each period in which the bonds are outstanding. This is referred to as **amortizing the discount**. Amortization of the discount **increases** the amount of interest expense reported each period. That is, after amortizing the discount, the amount of interest expense reported in a period will exceed the contractual amount. As shown in Illustration 10-8, for the bonds issued by Candlestick Inc., total interest expense will exceed the contractual interest by $2,000 over the life of the bonds.

As the discount is amortized, its balance declines. As a consequence, the carrying value of the bonds will increase, until at maturity the carrying value of the bonds equals their face amount. This is shown in Illustration 10-10. Procedures for amortizing bond discount are discussed in Appendix 10A and Appendix 10B at the end of this chapter.

Illustration 10-10
Amortization of bond discount

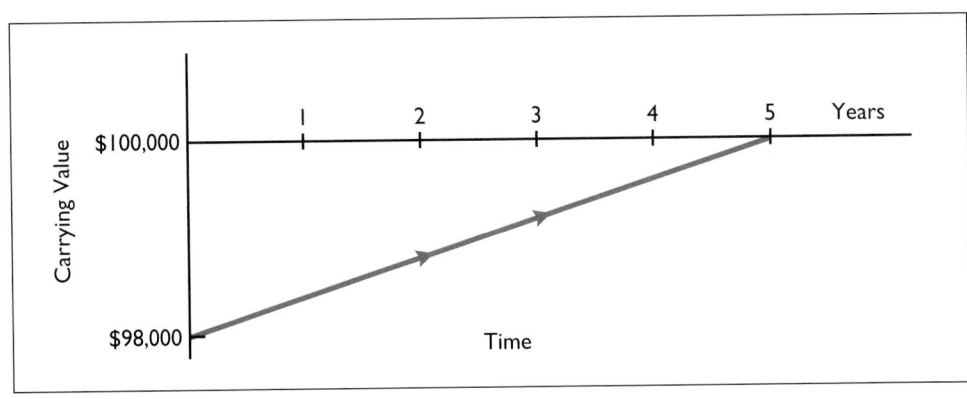

ISSUING BONDS AT A PREMIUM

Helpful Hint Both a discount and a premium account are valuation accounts. A valuation account is one that is needed to value properly the item to which it relates.

A	=	L	+	SE
+102,000		+100,000		
		+2,000		

Cash Flows
+102,000

The issuance of bonds at a premium can be illustrated by assuming the Candlestick Inc. bonds described above are sold at 102 (102% of face value) rather than at 98. The entry to record the sale is:

Jan. 1	Cash	102,000	
	Bonds Payable		100,000
	Premium on Bonds Payable		2,000
	(To record sale of bonds at a premium)		

Premium on bonds payable is **added to bonds payable** on the balance sheet, as shown in Illustration 10-11.

Illustration 10-11
Statement presentation of bond premium

CANDLESTICK INC. Balance Sheet (partial)		
Long-term liabilities		
Bonds payable	$100,000	
Add: Premium on bonds payable	2,000	$102,000

The sale of bonds above face value causes the total cost of borrowing to be **less than the bond interest paid** because the borrower is not required to pay the bond premium at the maturity date of the bonds. Thus, the premium is considered to be **a reduction in the cost of borrowing** that reduces bond interest expense over the life of the bonds. The total cost of borrowing $102,000 for Candlestick Inc. is $48,000, computed as in Illustration 10-12.

Bonds Issued at a Premium	
Annual interest payments	
($100,000 × 10% = $10,000; $10,000 × 5)	$ 50,000
Less: Bond premium ($102,000 − $100,000)	2,000
Total cost of borrowing	**$48,000**

Illustration 10-12
Computation of total cost of borrowing—bonds issued at a premium

Alternatively, the cost of borrowing can be computed as in Illustration 10-13.

Bonds Issued at a Premium	
Principal at maturity	$100,000
Annual interest payments ($10,000 × 5)	50,000
Cash to be paid to bondholders	150,000
Cash received from bondholders	102,000
Total cost of borrowing	**$ 48,000**

Illustration 10-13
Alternative computation of total cost of borrowing—bonds issued at a premium

Similar to bond discount, bond premium is allocated to expense in each period in which the bonds are outstanding. This is referred to as **amortizing the premium**. Amortization of the premium **decreases** the amount of interest expense reported each period. That is, after amortizing the premium, the amount of interest expense reported in a period will be less than the contractual amount. As shown in Illustration 10-12, for the bonds issued by Candlestick Inc., contractual interest will exceed the interest expense by $2,000 over the life of the bonds.

As the premium is amortized its balance will decline. As a consequence, the carrying value of the bonds will decrease, until at maturity the carrying value of the bonds equals their face amount. This is shown in Illustration 10-14.

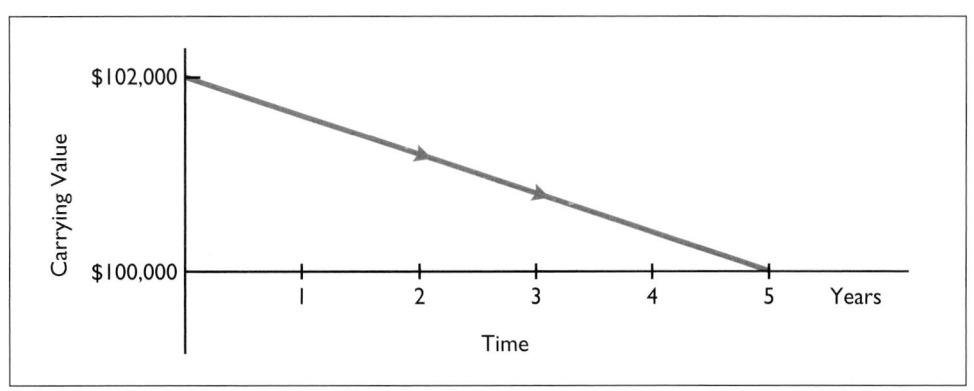

Illustration 10-14
Amortization of bond premium

Procedures for amortizing bond premium are discussed in Appendix 10A and Appendix 10B at the end of this chapter.

Accounting for Bond Retirements

Bonds are retired when they are purchased (redeemed) by the issuing corporation. The appropriate entries for these transactions are explained next.

REDEEMING BONDS AT MATURITY

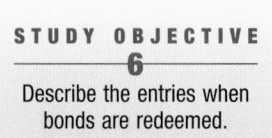

STUDY OBJECTIVE
6
Describe the entries when bonds are redeemed.

Regardless of the issue price of bonds, the book value of the bonds at maturity will equal their face value. Assuming that the interest for the last interest period is paid and recorded separately, the entry to record the redemption of the Candlestick bonds at maturity is:

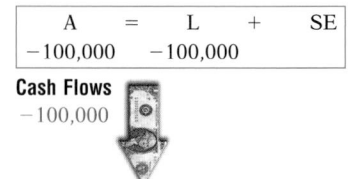

A	=	L	+	SE
−100,000		−100,000		

Cash Flows
−100,000

Bonds Payable	100,000	
Cash		100,000
(To record redemption of bonds at maturity)		

REDEEMING BONDS BEFORE MATURITY

Helpful Hint If a bond is redeemed prior to its maturity date and its carrying value exceeds its redemption price, will the retirement result in a gain or a loss on redemption? Answer: Gain.

Bonds may be redeemed before maturity. A company may decide to retire bonds before maturity in order to reduce interest cost and remove debt from its balance sheet. A company should retire debt early only if it has sufficient cash resources.

When bonds are retired before maturity, it is necessary to: (1) eliminate the carrying value of the bonds at the redemption date, (2) record the cash paid, and (3) recognize the gain or loss on redemption. The carrying value of the bonds is the face value of the bonds less unamortized bond discount or plus unamortized bond premium at the redemption date.

To illustrate, assume at the end of the fourth period Candlestick Inc., having sold its bonds at a premium, retires its bonds at 103 after paying the annual interest. Assume that the carrying value of the bonds at the redemption date is $100,400. The entry to record the redemption at the end of the fourth interest period (January 1, 2009) is:

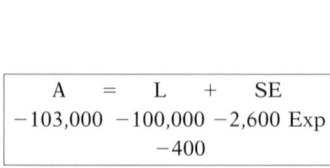

A	=	L	+	SE
−103,000		−100,000		−2,600 Exp
		−400		

Cash Flows
−103,000

Jan. 1	Bonds Payable	100,000	
	Premium on Bonds Payable	400	
	Loss on Bond Redemption	2,600	
	Cash		103,000
	(To record redemption of bonds at 103)		

Note that the loss of $2,600 is the difference between the cash paid of $103,000 and the carrying value of the bonds of $100,400.

Business Insight
INTERNATIONAL PERSPECTIVE

A dramatic example of the importance of bond financing—which literally changed the course of history—is seen in Britain's struggle for supremacy in the 18th and 19th centuries. With only a fraction of the population and wealth of France, Britain ultimately humbled its mightier foe through the use of bonds. Because of its effective central bank and a fair system of collecting taxes, Britain developed the capital markets that enabled its government to issue bonds. Britain was able to borrow money at almost half the cost paid by France and was able to incur more debt as a proportion of the economy than could France. Britain thus could more than match the French navy, raise an army of its own, and lavishly subsidize other armies, eventually destroying Napoleon and his threat to Europe.

SOURCE: "How British Bonds Beat Back Bigger France," *Forbes* (March 13, 1995).

BEFORE YOU GO ON . . .

▶ Review It

1. What entry is made to record the issuance of bonds payable of $1 million at 100? At 96? At 102?
2. Why do bonds sell at a discount? At a premium? At face value?
3. Explain the accounting for redemption of bonds at maturity and before maturity by payment in cash.

▶ Do It

A bond amortization table shows (a) interest to be paid $50,000, (b) interest expense to be recorded $52,000, and (c) amortization $2,000. Answer the following questions: (1) Were the bonds sold at a premium or a discount? (2) After recording the interest expense, will the bond carrying value increase or decrease?

Action Plan

• Know the effects that the amortization of bond discount and bond premium have on bond interest expense and on the carrying value of the bonds.
• Remember bond discount amortization increases both bond interest expense and the carrying value of the bonds. Bond premium amortization has the reverse effect.

Solution

(1) The bond amortization table indicates that interest expense is $2,000 greater than the interest paid. This difference is equal to the amortization amount. Thus, the bonds were sold at a discount. (2) The interest entry will decrease Discount on Bonds Payable and increase the carrying value of the bonds.

☑ THE NAVIGATOR

Financial Statement Presentation and Analysis

BALANCE SHEET PRESENTATION

Current liabilities are the first category under Liabilities on the balance sheet. Each of the principal types of current liabilities is listed separately within the category.

Current liabilities are seldom listed in their order of maturity because of the varying maturity dates that may exist for specific obligations such as notes payable. A more common, and entirely satisfactory, method of presenting current liabilities is to list them by **order of magnitude**, with the largest obligations first. Use this approach for your homework assignments.

Long-term liabilities are reported in a separate section of the balance sheet immediately following "Current liabilities." An example is shown in Illustration 10-15.

Illustration 10-15
Balance sheet
presentation of liabilities

MARAIS COMPANY Balance Sheet (partial)		
Liabilities		
Current liabilities		
Current maturities of long-term debt	$ 300,000	
Notes payable	250,000	
Accounts payable	125,000	
Accrued liabilities	75,000	
Total current liabilities		$ 750,000
Long-term liabilities		
Bonds payable	1,000,000	
Less: Discount on bonds payable	80,000	920,000
Notes payable, secured by plant assets		500,000
Lease liability		540,000
Total long-term liabilities		1,960,000
Total liabilities		$2,710,000

Disclosure of debt is very important. Because of failures at **Enron, WorldCom**, and **Global Crossing**, investors have become very concerned about companies' debt obligations. Summary data regarding debts may be presented in the balance sheet with detailed data (such as interest rates, maturity dates, conversion privileges, and assets pledged as collateral) shown in a supporting schedule in the notes. The current maturities of long-term debt should be reported as current liabilities if they are to be paid from current assets.

STATEMENT OF CASH FLOWS PRESENTATION

The balance sheet presents the balances of a company's debts at a point in time. Information regarding cash inflows and outflows during the year that resulted from the principal portion of debt transactions is provided in the "Financing activities" section of the statement of cash flows. Interest expense is reported in the "Operating activities" section, even though it resulted from debt transactions.

Illustration 10-16 presents the cash flows from financing activities from the statement of cash flows for the Automotive Division of **General Motors**. From this we learn that the division issued new long-term debt of $5.8 billion and repaid long-term debt of $2.6 billion.

GENERAL MOTORS CORPORATION— AUTOMOTIVE DIVISION
Statement of Cash Flows (partial)
2001
(in millions)

Cash flows from financing activities	
Net increase (decrease) in loans payable	$ 194
Long-term debt—borrowings	5,850
Long-term debt—repayments	(2,602)
Repurchases of common and preference stocks	(264)
Proceeds from issuing common and preference stocks	517
Cash dividends paid to stockholders	(1,201)
Net cash (used in) provided by financing activities	$ 2,494

Illustration 10-16
Financing activities section of statement of cash flows

ANALYSIS

Careful examination of debt obligations helps you assess a company's ability to pay its current obligations. It also helps to determine whether a company can obtain long-term financing in order to grow. The following information from the financial statements of **General Motors** will be used to illustrate the analysis of a company's liquidity and solvency.

GENERAL MOTORS CORPORATION— AUTOMOTIVE DIVISION
Balance Sheets
December 31, 2001 and 2000
(in millions)

Assets	2001	2000
Total current assets	$ 37,063	$ 41,147
Noncurrent assets	93,147	92,209
Total assets	$130,210	$133,356
Liabilities and Stockholders' Equity		
Total current liabilities	$ 56,346	$ 55,740
Noncurrent liabilities	69,825	60,964
Total liabilities	126,171	116,704
Total stockholders' equity	4,039	16,652
Total liabilities and stockholders' equity	$130,210	$133,356

Illustration 10-17
Simplified balance sheets for General Motors Corporation

Liquidity

Liquidity ratios measure the short-term ability of a company to pay its maturing obligations and to meet unexpected needs for cash. A commonly used measure of liquidity is the current ratio (presented in Chapter 2). The current ratio is calculated as current assets divided by current liabilities. Illustration 10-18 presents the current ratio for General Motors along with the industry average.

Illustration 10-18
Current ratio

($ in millions)	General Motors		Industry Average
	2001	**2000**	**2001**
Current Ratio	$\frac{\$37,063}{\$56,346} = .66:1$	$\frac{\$41,147}{\$55,740} = .74:1$	1.63:1

General Motors' current assets are less than its current liabilities. Therefore its current ratio is less than 1 in both 2000 and 2001. The industry average current ratio for manufacturers of autos and trucks is 1.63:1.[3] Thus, General Motors appears to lack liquidity.

In recent years many companies have intentionally reduced their liquid assets (such as cash, accounts receivable, and inventory) because they cost too much to hold. This is particularly true of large companies such as GM. Companies that keep fewer liquid assets on hand must rely on other sources of liquidity. One such source is a **bank line of credit**. A line of credit is a prearranged agreement between a company and a lender that permits the company, should it be necessary, to borrow up to an agreed-upon amount. The disclosure regarding debt in General Motors' financial statements states that it has $8.5 billion of unused lines of credit. This represents a substantial amount of available cash. In addition, the Management Discussion and Analysis section of its annual report provides an extensive discussion of the company's liquidity. In it, GM notes that even though its credit rating was downgraded during the year, it "will continue to have excellent access to the capital markets sufficient to meet the Corporation's needs for financial flexibility." Thus, even though General Motors has a low current ratio, its available lines of credit as well as other sources of financing appear adequate to meet any short-term cash deficiency it might experience.

DECISION TOOLKIT

Decision Checkpoints	Info Needed for Decision	Tool to Use for Decision	How to Evaluate Results
Can the company obtain short-term financing when necessary?	Available lines of credit, from notes to the financial statements.	Compare available lines of credit to current liabilities. Also, evaluate liquidity ratios.	If liquidity ratios are low, then lines of credit should be high to compensate.

Solvency

Solvency ratios measure the ability of a company to survive over a long period of time. The Feature Story in this chapter mentioned that although there once were many U.S. automobile manufacturers, only two U.S.-based companies

---

[3]Market Guide based this and subsequent industry ratios used in this chapter on a group of 29 companies that manufacture cars and trucks (see *multex.com*).

Financial Statement Presentation and Analysis

remain today. Many of the others went bankrupt. This highlights the fact that when making a long-term loan or purchasing a company's stock, you must give consideration to a company's solvency.

To reduce the risks associated with having a large amount of debt during an economic downturn, U.S. automobile manufacturers have taken two precautionary steps. First, they have built up large balances of cash and cash equivalents to avoid a cash crisis. Second, recently, they have been reluctant to build new plants or hire new workers to meet their production needs. Instead, they have asked existing workers to put in overtime, or they "outsource" work to other companies. In this way, if an economic downturn occurs, they avoid having to make debt payments on idle production plants, and they minimize layoffs.

In an earlier chapter (Chapter 2) you learned that one measure of a company's solvency is the debt to total assets ratio. This is calculated as total liabilities divided by total assets. This ratio indicates the extent to which a company's debt could be repaid by liquidating its assets. Other measures can also be useful. One such measure is the **times interest earned ratio**, which provides an indication of a company's ability to meet interest payments as they come due. It is computed by dividing income before interest expense and income taxes by interest expense. It uses income before interest expense and taxes because this number best represents the amount available to pay interest.

We can use the balance sheet information presented on page 483 and the additional information below to calculate solvency ratios for the Automotive Division of General Motors.

($ in millions)	2001	2000
Net income (loss)	$(1,167)	$2,839
Interest expense	751	815
Tax expense (refund)	(270)	1,443

The debt to total assets ratios and times interest earned ratios for General Motors and averages for the industry are shown in Illustration 10-19.

Illustration 10-19
Solvency ratios

$$\text{Debt to Total Assets Ratio} = \frac{\text{Total Liabilities}}{\text{Total Assets}}$$

$$\text{Times Interest Earned Ratio} = \frac{\text{Net Income} + \text{Interest Expense} + \text{Tax Expense}}{\text{Interest Expense}}$$

($ in millions)	General Motors 2001	General Motors 2000	Industry Average 2001
Debt to Total Assets Ratio	$\frac{\$126,171}{\$130,210} = 97\%$	$\frac{\$116,704}{\$133,356} = 88\%$	88.9%
Times Interest Earned Ratio	$\frac{\$(1,167) + \$751 - \$270}{\$751}$ = 0 times	$\frac{\$2,839 + \$815 + \$1,443}{\$815}$ = 6.3 times	1.4 times

General Motors' debt to total assets ratio increased substantially from 88% in 2000 to 97% in 2001. The industry average for manufacturers of autos and trucks is 88.9%. Thus, General Motors' ratio is very high, especially considering that we are looking only at the automotive division and have excluded the financing division of the company, which traditionally has a very high debt to assets ratio. This change suggests that the company, which already was very dependent on debt financing, shifted even further in that direction. As a consequence, its solvency declined during this period.

The debt to total assets ratio varies across industries because different capital structures are appropriate for different industries. Illustration 10-20 provides debt to total assets ratios for companies across a variety of industries.

Illustration 10-20 Debt to total assets ratio by industry

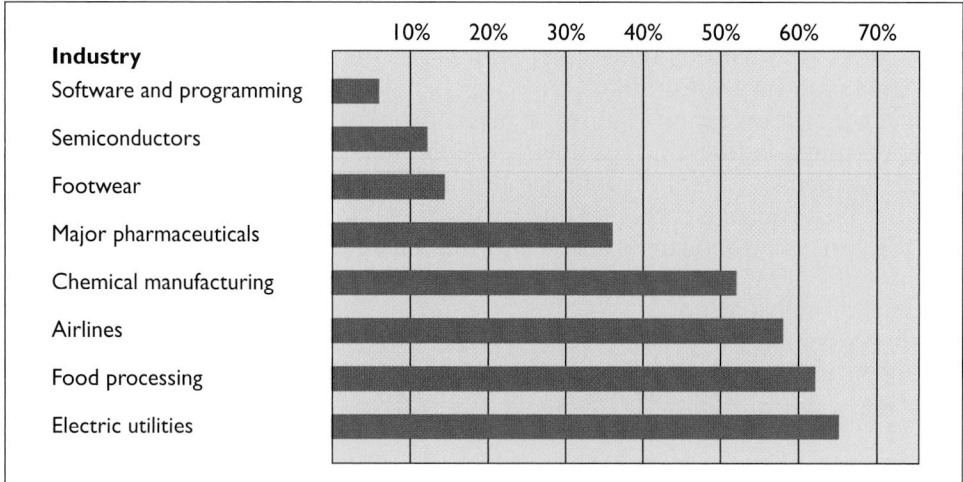

Note that the auto and truck industry's average debt to total assets ratio of 88.9% is extremely high relative to even the highest of these, the electric utility industry, which is typically thought of as being very reliant on debt financing.

General Motors' times interest earned ratio declined from 6.3 times in 2000 to zero in 2001. The industry average for manufacturers of autos and trucks is a low 1.4 times, reflecting the tough times experienced by that sector of the economy during 2001. The reason that General Motors' 2001 measure is zero is that no income was available to cover the company's interest payments. Income before interest expense and taxes—that is, income after adding back interest expense and in this case, deducting a tax refund—was negative. The company's high debt to total assets ratio, combined with its interest coverage ratio of zero, should be of obvious concern to the company's creditors and investors. This concern was reflected in a downgrade to GM's credit rating during 2001.

DECISION TOOLKIT

Decision Checkpoints	Info Needed for Decision	Tool to Use for Decision	How to Evaluate Results
Can the company meet its obligations in the long term?	Interest expense and net income before interest and taxes	Times interest earned ratio $= \dfrac{\text{Net income} + \text{Interest expense} + \text{Tax expense}}{\text{Interest expense}}$	High ratio indicates ability to meet interest payments as scheduled.

Other Analysis Issues: Unrecorded Debt

A concern for analysts when they evaluate a company's liquidity and solvency is whether that company has properly recorded all of its obligations. The bankruptcy of **Enron Corporation**, one of the largest bankruptcies in U.S. history, demonstrated how much damage can result when a company does not properly record or disclose all of its debts.

Sometimes a company's balance sheet does not fully report its actual obligations. One reason a company's balance sheet might not fully reflect its potential obligations is due to contingencies. **Contingencies** are events with uncertain outcomes. A common type of contingency is lawsuits. Suppose, for example, that you were analyzing the financial statements of a cigarette manufacturer and did not consider the possible negative implications of existing unsettled lawsuits. Your analysis of the company's financial position would certainly be misleading. Other common types of contingencies are product warranties and environmental clean-up obligations.

A second reason that a company's balance sheet might understate its actual obligations is that the company might have **"off-balance-sheet financing."** Off-balance-sheet financing is an attempt to borrow funds in such a way that the obligations are not recorded. One very common type of off-balance-sheet financing results from leasing transactions.

Recall from Chapter 9 that many large U.S. airlines lease a substantial portion of their planes without showing the planes or any debt related to them on their balance sheets. For example, the total increase in assets and liabilities that would result if **United Airlines'** off-balance-sheet **"operating" leases** were instead recorded on the balance sheet would be approximately $11.9 billion. Illustration 10-21 presents United Airlines' debt to total assets ratio using the numbers presented in its balance sheet and also shows the ratio after adjusting for the off-balance-sheet debt and assets resulting from its leases. Even without adjusting for leases, United's ratio of .76 is quite high. But after adjusting for the off-balance-sheet leases, United has a ratio of .84. This means that of every dollar of assets, 84 cents was funded by debt. This would be of concern to analysts evaluating the solvency of United Airlines.

	Using numbers as presented on balance sheet	**Adjusted for off-balance-sheet leases**
Debt to total assets ratio	$\frac{\$18.6}{\$24.4} = .76$	$\frac{\$18.6 + \$11.9}{\$24.4 + \$11.9} = .84$

Illustration 10-21 Debt to total assets ratio adjusted for leases

Critics of off-balance-sheet financing contend that many leases represent unavoidable obligations that meet the definition of a liability, and therefore they should be reported as liabilities on the balance sheet. To reduce these concerns, companies are required to report their operating lease obligations for subsequent years in a note. This allows analysts and other financial statement users to adjust a company's financial statements by adding leased assets and lease liabilities if they feel that this treatment is more appropriate.

Appendix 10D at the end of this chapter discusses the criteria used to determine the accounting treatment for contingent liabilities and leases.

DECISION TOOLKIT

Decision Checkpoints	Info Needed for Decision	Tool to Use for Decision	How to Evaluate Results
Does the company have any contingent liabilities?	Knowledge of events with uncertain negative outcomes	Notes to financial statements and financial statements	If negative outcomes are possible, determine the probability, the amount of loss, and the potential impact on financial statements.
Does the company have significant off-balance-sheet financing, such as unrecorded lease obligations?	Information on unrecorded obligations, such as schedule of minimum lease payments from lease note	Compare liquidity and solvency ratios with and without unrecorded obligations included.	If ratios differ significantly after including unrecorded obligations, these obligations should not be ignored in analysis.

BEFORE YOU GO ON . . .

▶ **Review It**

1. What is meant by solvency?
2. What information does the times interest earned ratio provide, and how is the ratio calculated?
3. What is meant by "off-balance-sheet financing"? What is a common example of off-balance-sheet financing?
4. What are contingent liabilities?

THE NAVIGATOR

Using the Decision Toolkit

Ford Motor Company has enjoyed some tremendous successes, including its popular Taurus and Explorer vehicles. Yet observers are looking for the next big hit. Development of a new vehicle costs billions. A flop is financially devastating, and the financial effect is magnified if the company has large amounts of outstanding debt.

The balance sheets on page 489 provide financial information for the Automotive Division of Ford Motor Company as of December 31, 2001 and 2000. We have chosen to analyze only the Automotive Division rather than the total corporation, which includes Ford's giant financing division. In an actual analysis you would want to analyze the major divisions individually as well as the combined corporation as a whole.

Instructions

1. Evaluate Ford's liquidity using appropriate ratios, and compare to those of General Motors and to industry averages.
2. Evaluate Ford's solvency using appropriate ratios, and compare to those of General Motors and to industry averages.
3. Comment on Ford's available lines of credit.

FORD MOTOR COMPANY—
AUTOMOTIVE DIVISION
Balance Sheets
December 31, 2001 and 2000
(in millions)

Assets	2001	2000
Current assets	$33,121	$37,833
Noncurrent assets	55,198	56,479
Total assets	$88,319	$94,312
Liabilities and Shareholders' Equity		
Current liabilities	$44,546	$43,181
Noncurrent liabilities	48,434	44,369
Total liabilities	92,980	87,550
Total shareholders' equity	(4,661)	6,762
Total liabilities and shareholders' equity	$88,319	$94,312
Other Information		
Net income (loss)	$(6,325)	$ 3,529
Tax expense (refund)	(2,711)	1,738
Interest expense	1,378	1,383
Available lines of credit (Automotive Division)	7,516	

Solution

1. Ford's liquidity can be measured using the current ratio:

2001	2000
Current ratio $\dfrac{\$33,121}{\$44,546} = .74:1$	$\dfrac{\$37,833}{\$43,181} = .88:1$

Like that of General Motors, Ford's current ratio is below 1—its current assets are less than its current liabilities. These are increasingly common levels for large companies that have reduced the amount of cash, inventory, and receivables they hold. As noted earlier, these low current ratios are not necessarily cause for concern, but they do require more careful monitoring. Ford must also make sure to have other short-term financing options available, such as lines of credit.

2. Ford's solvency can be measured with the debt to total assets ratio and the times interest earned ratio:

	2001	2000
Debt to total assets ratio	$\dfrac{\$92,980}{\$88,319} = 105\%$	$\dfrac{\$87,550}{\$94,312} = 93\%$
Times interest earned ratio	$\dfrac{\$(6,325) + \$1,378 - \$2,711}{\$1,378}$ $= 0$ times	$\dfrac{\$3,529 + \$1,383 + \$1,738}{\$1,383}$ $= 4.8$ times

The debt to total assets ratio suggests that Ford, like General Motors, relies very heavily on debt financing. The ratio increased from 2000 to 2001, indicating that the company's solvency declined. In fact, in 2001 its ratio exceeds 1. This is possible because we have calculated the ratio for the Automotive Division only, rather than the whole company. The debt to total assets ratio for the entire company is 97%. This is extremely high.

The times interest earned ratio declined from a respectable 4.8 times in 2000 to zero in 2001. The 2001 ratio is zero because, even after adding back interest and taxes, the company's income was negative. It is likely that the decline in the company's solvency was a concern to investors and creditors and would be closely monitored.

3. Ford has available lines of credit of $7.516 billion as well as access to other financing sources. These financing sources significantly improve its liquidity. The company has tremendous resources available to it, should it face a liquidity crunch.

Summary of Study Objectives

1 *Explain a current liability and identify the major types of current liabilities.* A current liability is a debt that can reasonably be expected to be paid (a) from existing current assets or through the creation of other current liabilities, and (b) within one year or the operating cycle, whichever is longer. The major types of current liabilities are notes payable, accounts payable, sales taxes payable, unearned revenues, and accrued liabilities such as taxes, salaries and wages, and interest payable.

2 *Describe the accounting for notes payable.* When a promissory note is interest-bearing, the amount of assets received upon the issuance of the note is generally equal to the face value of the note, and interest expense is accrued over the life of the note. At maturity, the amount paid is equal to the face value of the note plus accrued interest.

3 *Explain the accounting for other current liabilities.* Sales taxes payable are recorded at the time the related sales occur. The company serves as a collection agent for the taxing authority. Sales taxes are not an expense to the company. Until employee withholding taxes are remitted to the governmental taxing authorities, they are credited to appropriate liability accounts. Unearned revenues are initially recorded in an unearned revenue account. As the revenue is earned, a transfer from unearned revenue to earned revenue occurs. The current maturities of long-term debt should be reported as a current liability in the balance sheet.

4 *Identify the types of bonds.* The following different types of bonds may be issued: secured and unsecured bonds, and convertible and callable bonds.

5 *Prepare the entries for the issuance of bonds and interest expense.* When bonds are issued, Cash is debited for the cash proceeds and Bonds Payable is credited for the face value of the bonds. In addition, the accounts Premium on Bonds Payable and Discount on Bonds Payable are used to show the bond premium and bond discount, respectively. Bond discount and bond premium are amortized over the life of the bond.

6 *Describe the entries when bonds are redeemed.* When bonds are redeemed at maturity, Cash is credited and Bonds Payable is debited for the face value of the bonds. When bonds are redeemed before maturity, it is necessary to (a) eliminate the carrying value of the bonds at the redemption date, (b) record the cash paid, and (c) recognize the gain or loss on redemption.

7 *Identify the requirements for the financial statement presentation and analysis of liabilities.* Current liabilities are reported first, followed by long-term liabilities. The nature and amount of each liability should be reported in the balance sheet or in schedules in the notes accompanying the statements. Inflows and outflows of cash related to the principal portion of long-term debts are reported in the financing section of the statement of cash flows. The liquidity of a company may be analyzed by computing the current ratio. The long-run solvency of a company may be analyzed by computing the debt to total assets ratio and the times interest earned ratio. Other factors to consider are contingent liabilities and lease obligations.

DECISION TOOLKIT—A SUMMARY

Decision Checkpoints	Info Needed for Decision	Tool to Use for Decision	How to Evaluate Results
Can the company obtain short-term financing when necessary?	Available lines of credit, from notes to the financial statements	Compare available lines of credit to current liabilities. Also, evaluate liquidity ratios.	If liquidity ratios are low, then lines of credit should be high to compensate.
Can the company meet its obligations in the long term?	Interest expense and net income before interest and taxes	$$\text{Times interest earned ratio} = \frac{\text{Net income} + \text{Interest expense} + \text{Tax expense}}{\text{Interest expense}}$$	High ratio indicates ability to meet interest payments as scheduled.
Does the company have any contingent liabilities?	Knowledge of events with uncertain negative outcomes	Notes to financial statements and financial statements	If negative outcomes are possible, determine the probability, the amount of loss, and the potential impact on financial statements.
Does the company have significant off-balance-sheet financing, such as unrecorded lease obligations?	Information on unrecorded obligations, such as schedule of minimum lease payments from lease note	Compare liquidity and solvency ratios with and without unrecorded obligations included.	If ratios differ significantly after including unrecorded obligations, these obligations should not be ignored in analysis.

APPENDIX 10A
STRAIGHT-LINE AMORTIZATION

Amortizing Bond Discount

STUDY OBJECTIVE
8
Apply the straight-line method of amortizing bond discount and bond premium.

To follow the matching principle, bond discount should be allocated to expense in each period in which the bonds are outstanding. The **straight-line method of amortization** allocates the same amount to interest expense in each interest period. The calculation is presented in Illustration 10A-1.

$$\text{Bond Discount} \div \text{Number of Interest Periods} = \text{Bond Discount Amortization}$$

Illustration 10A-1
Formula for straight-line method of bond discount amortization

In the Candlestick Inc. example (page 477), the company sold $100,000, 5-year, 10% bonds on January 1, 2005, for $98,000. This resulted in a $2,000 bond discount ($100,000 − $98,000). The bond discount amortization is $400

($2,000 ÷ 5) for each of the five amortization periods. The entry to record the first accrual of bond interest and the amortization of bond discount on December 31 is:

A	=	L	+	SE
		+400		−10,400 Exp
		+10,000		

Cash Flows
no effect

Dec. 31	Bond Interest Expense	10,400	
	Discount on Bonds Payable		400
	Bond Interest Payable		10,000
	(To record accrued bond interest and amortization of bond discount)		

Alternative Terminology The amount in the Discount on Bonds Payable account is often referred to as **Unamortized Discount on Bonds Payable**.

Over the term of the bonds, the balance in Discount on Bonds Payable will decrease annually by the same amount until it has a zero balance at the maturity date of the bonds. Thus, the carrying value of the bonds at maturity will be equal to the face value of the bonds.

Preparing a bond discount amortization schedule, as shown in Illustration 10A-2, is useful to determine interest expense, discount amortization, and the carrying value of the bond. As indicated, the interest expense recorded each period is $10,400. Also note that the carrying value of the bond increases $400 each period until it reaches its face value $100,000 at the end of period 5.

Illustration 10A-2 Bond discount amortization schedule

BOND DISCOUNT AMORTIZATION SCHEDULE
Straight-Line Method—Annual Interest Payments
$100,000 of 10%, 5-Year Bonds

Interest Periods	(A) Interest To Be Paid (10% × $100,000)	(B) Interest Expense To Be Recorded (A) + (C)	(C) Discount Amortization ($2,000 ÷ 5)	(D) Unamortized Discount (D) − (C)	(E) Bond Carrying Value ($100,000 − D)
Issue date				$2,000	$ 98,000
1	$10,000	$10,400	$ 400	1,600	98,400
2	10,000	10,400	400	1,200	98,800
3	10,000	10,400	400	800	99,200
4	10,000	10,400	400	400	99,600
5	10,000	10,400	400	0	100,000
	$50,000	$52,000	$2,000		

Column **(A)** remains constant because the face value of the bonds ($100,000) is multiplied by the annual contractual interest rate (10%) each period.
Column **(B)** is computed as the interest paid (Column A) plus the discount amortization (Column C).
Column **(C)** indicates the discount amortization each period.
Column **(D)** decreases each period by the same amount until it reaches zero at maturity.
Column **(E)** increases each period by the amount of discount amortization until it equals the face value at maturity.

Amortizing Bond Premium

The amortization of bond premium parallels that of bond discount. The formula for determining bond premium amortization under the straight-line method is presented in Illustration 10A-3.

Bond Premium	÷	Number of Interest Periods	=	Bond Premium Amortization

Illustration 10A-3
Formula for straight-line method of bond premium amortization

Continuing our example of Candlestick Inc., assume the bonds described above are sold for $102,000, rather than $98,000. This results in a bond premium of $2,000 ($102,000 − $100,000). The premium amortization for each interest period is $400 ($2,000 ÷ 5). The entry to record the first accrual of interest on December 31 is:

Dec. 31	Bond Interest Expense	9,600	
	Premium on Bonds Payable	400	
	Bond Interest Payable		10,000
	(To record accrued bond interest and		
	amortization of bond premium)		

A	=	L	+	SE	
				−400	−9,600 Exp
				+10,000	

Cash Flows
no effect

Over the term of the bonds, the balance in Premium on Bonds Payable will decrease annually by the same amount until it has a zero balance at maturity.

A bond premium amortization schedule, as shown in Illustration 10A-4, is useful to determine interest expense, premium amortization, and the carrying value of the bond. As indicated, the interest expense recorded each period is $9,600. Note that the carrying value of the bond decreases $400 each period until it reaches its face value of $100,000 at the end of period 5.

Illustration 10A-4 Bond premium amortization schedule

BOND PREMIUM AMORTIZATION SCHEDULE
Straight-Line Method—Annual Interest Payments
$100,000 of 10%, 5-Year Bonds

Interest Periods	(A) Interest To Be Paid (10% × $100,000)	(B) Interest Expense To Be Recorded (A) − (C)	(C) Premium Amortization ($2,000 ÷ 5)	(D) Unamortized Premium (D) − (C)	(E) Bond Carrying Value ($100,000 + D)
Issue date				$2,000	$102,000
1	$10,000	$ 9,600	$ 400	1,600	101,600
2	10,000	9,600	400	1,200	101,200
3	10,000	9,600	400	800	100,800
4	10,000	9,600	400	400	100,400
5	10,000	9,600	400	0	100,000
	$50,000	$48,000	$2,000		

Column (A) remains constant because the face value of the bonds ($100,000) is multiplied by the annual contractual interest rate (10%) each period.
Column (B) is computed as the interest paid (Column A) less the premium amortization (Column C).
Column (C) indicates the premium amortization each period.
Column (D) decreases each period by the same amount until it reaches zero at maturity.
Column (E) decreases each period by the amount of premium amortization until it equals the face value at maturity.

Summary of Study Objective for Appendix 10A

8 *Apply the straight-line method of amortizing bond discount and bond premium.* The straight-line method of amortization results in a constant amount of amortization and interest expense per period.

APPENDIX 10B
EFFECTIVE-INTEREST AMORTIZATION

STUDY OBJECTIVE
9
Apply the effective-interest method of amortizing bond discount and bond premium.

To follow the matching principle, bond discount should be allocated to expense in each period in which the bonds are outstanding. However, to completely comply with the matching principle, interest expense as a percentage of carrying value should not change over the life of the bonds. This percentage, referred to as the **effective-interest rate**, is established when the bonds are issued and remains constant in each interest period. Unlike the straight-line method, the effective-interest method of amortization accomplishes this result.

Under the **effective-interest method**, the amortization of bond discount or bond premium results in periodic interest expense equal to a constant percentage of the carrying value of the bonds. The effective-interest method results in varying amounts of amortization and interest expense per period but a constant percentage rate. In contrast, the straight-line method results in constant amounts of amortization and interest expense per period but a varying percentage rate.

The following steps are required under the effective-interest method.

1. Compute the **bond interest expense** by multiplying the carrying value of the bonds at the beginning of the interest period by the effective-interest rate.

2. Compute the **bond interest paid** (or accrued) by multiplying the face value of the bonds by the contractual interest rate.

3. Compute the **amortization amount** by determining the difference between the amounts computed in steps (1) and (2).

These steps are depicted graphically in Illustration 10B-1.

Illustration 10B-1
Computation of amortization using effective-interest method

(1)	(2)	(3)
Bond Interest Expense	**Bond Interest Paid**	
Carrying Value of Bonds at Beginning of Period $\times$ Effective Interest Rate	$-$	Face Amount of Bonds $\times$ Contractual Interest Rate	$=$	Amortization Amount

Both the straight-line and effective-interest methods of amortization result in the same total amount of interest expense over the term of the bonds. Furthermore, interest expense each interest period is generally comparable in amount. However, **when the amounts are materially different, the effective-interest method is required under generally accepted accounting principles (GAAP)**.

Amortizing Bond Discount

To illustrate the effective-interest method of bond discount amortization, assume that Wrightway Corporation issues $100,000 of 10%, 5-year bonds on January 1, 2005, with interest payable each January 1. The bonds sell for $92,790 (92.79% of face value), which results in bond discount of $7,210 ($100,000 − $92,790) and an effective-interest rate of 12%. (Note that the $92,790 can be proven as shown in Appendix C at the end of this book.)

Preparing a bond discount amortization schedule as shown in Illustration 10B-2 facilitates the recording of interest expense and the discount amortization. Note that interest expense as a percentage of carrying value remains constant at 12%.

Illustration 10B-2 Bond discount amortization schedule

		(B) Interest Expense to Be Recorded (12% × Preceding Bond Carrying Value)		(C) Discount Amortization (B) − (A)	(D) Unamortized Discount (D) − (C)	(E) Bond Carrying Value ($100,000 − D)
Interest Periods	(A) Interest to Be Paid (10% × $100,000)					
Issue date					$7,210	$ 92,790
1	$10,000	$11,135	(12% × $92,790)	$1,135	6,075	93,925
2	10,000	11,271	(12% × $ 93,925)	1,271	4,804	95,196
3	10,000	11,424	(12% × $ 95,196)	1,424	3,380	96,620
4	10,000	11,594	(12% × $ 96,620)	1,594	1,786	98,214
5	10,000	11,786	(12% × $ 98,214)	1,786	–0–	100,000
	$ 50,000	$ 57,210		$ 7,210		

WRIGHTWAY CORPORATION
Bond Discount Amortization
Effective-Interest Method—Annual Interest Payments
10% Bonds Issued at 12%

Column (A) remains constant because the face value of the bonds ($100,000) is multiplied by the annual contractual interest rate (10%) each period.
Column (B) is computed as the preceding bond carrying value times the annual effective-interest rate (12%).
Column (C) indicates the discount amortization each period.
Column (D) decreases each period until it reaches zero at maturity.
Column (E) increases each period until it equals face value at maturity.

For the first interest period, the computations of bond interest expense and the bond discount amortization are as follows.

Bond interest expense ($92,790 × 12%)	$11,135
Bond interest paid ($100,000 × 10%)	10,000
Bond discount amortization	**$ 1,135**

Illustration 10B-3 Computation of bond discount amortization

As a result, the entry to record the accrual of interest and amortization of bond discount by Wrightway Corporation on December 31, is:

A = L + SE
+1,135 −11,135 Exp
+10,000

Cash Flows
no effect

Dec. 31	Bond Interest Expense	11,135	
	Discount on Bonds Payable		1,135
	Bond Interest Payable		10,000
	(To record accrued interest and amortization of bond discount)		

For the second interest period, bond interest expense will be $11,271 ($93,925 × 12%), and the discount amortization will be $1,271. At December 31, the following adjusting entry is made.

A = L + SE
+1,271 −11,271 Exp
+10,000

Cash Flows
no effect

Dec. 31	Bond Interest Expense	11,271	
	Discount on Bonds Payable		1,271
	Bond Interest Payable		10,000
	(To record accrued interest and amortization of bond discount)		

Helpful Hint When a bond sells for $107,985 it is quoted at 107.985% of face value. Note that $107,985 can be proven as shown in Appendix C.

Amortizing Bond Premium

The amortization of bond premium by the effective-interest method is similar to the procedures described for bond discount. As an example, assume that Wrightway Corporation issues $100,000, 10%, 5-year bonds on January 1, with interest payable on January 1. In this case, the bonds sell for $107,985, which results in bond premium of $7,985 and an effective-interest rate of 8%. The bond premium amortization schedule is shown in Illustration 10B-4.

Illustration 10B-4 Bond premium amortization schedule

WRIGHTWAY CORPORATION
Bond Premium Amortization
Effective-Interest Method—Annual Interest Payments
10% Bonds Issued at 8%

Interest Periods	(A) Interest to Be Paid (10% × $100,000)	(B) Interest Expense to Be Recorded (8% × Preceding Bond Carrying Value)	(C) Premium Amortization (A) − (B)	(D) Unamortized Premium (D) − (C)	(E) Bond Carrying Value ($100,000 + D)
Issue date				$7,985	$107,985
1	$10,000	$ 8,639 (8% × $107,985)	$1,361	6,624	106,624
2	10,000	8,530 (8% × $ 106,624)	1,470	5,154	105,154
3	10,000	8,412 (8% × $ 105,154)	1,588	3,566	103,566
4	10,000	8,285 (8% × $ 103,566)	1,715	1,851	101,851
5	10,000	8,149* (8% × $ 101,851)	1,851	–0–	100,000
	$50,000	$ 42,015	$7,985		

Column **(A)** remains constant because the face value of the bonds ($100,000) is multiplied by the contractual interest rate (10%) each period.
Column **(B)** is computed as the carrying value of the bonds times the annual effective-interest rate (8%).
Column **(C)** indicates the premium amortization each period.
Column **(D)** decreases each period until it reaches zero at maturity.
Column **(E)** decreases each period until it equals face value at maturity.

*$1 difference due to rounding.

For the first interest period, the computations of bond interest expense and the bond premium amortization are:

Bond interest paid ($100,000 × 10%)	$10,000
Bond interest expense ($107,985 × 8%)	8,639
Bond premium amortization	**$ 1,361**

Illustration 10B-5
Computation of bond premium amortization

The entry on December 31 is:

Dec. 31	Bond Interest Expense	8,639	
	Premium on Bonds Payable	1,361	
	Bond Interest Payable		10,000
	(To record accrued interest and		
	amortization of bond premium)		

A	=	L	+	SE
		+10,000		−8,639 Exp
		−1,361		

Cash Flows
no effect

For the second interest period, interest expense will be $8,530, and the premium amortization will be $1,470. Note that the amount of periodic interest expense decreases over the life of the bond when the effective-interest method is applied to bonds issued at a premium. The reason is that a constant percentage is applied to a decreasing bond carrying value to compute interest expense. The carrying value is decreasing because of the amortization of the premium.

Summary of Study Objective for Appendix 10B

9 *Apply the effective-interest method of amortizing bond discount and bond premium.* The effective-interest method results in varying amounts of amortization and interest expense per period but a constant percentage rate of interest. When the difference between the straight-line and effective-interest method is material, the use of the effective-interest method is required under GAAP.

APPENDIX 10C

ACCOUNTING FOR LONG-TERM NOTES PAYABLE

The use of notes payable in long-term debt financing is quite common. Long-term notes payable are similar to short-term interest-bearing notes payable except that the terms of the notes exceed one year. In periods of unstable interest rates, the interest rate on long-term notes may be tied to changes in the market rate for comparable loans. Examples are the 8.03% adjustable rate notes issued by **General Motors** and the floating-rate notes issued by **American Express Company**.

A long-term note may be secured by a document called a **mortgage** that pledges title to specific assets as security for a loan. **Mortgage notes payable** are widely used in the purchase of homes by individuals and in the acquisition of plant assets by many small and some large companies. For example, approximately 18% of **McDonalds'** long-term debt relates to mortgage notes on land,

STUDY OBJECTIVE
10
Describe the accounting for long-term notes payable.

buildings, and improvements. Like other long-term notes payable, the mortgage loan terms may stipulate either a fixed or an adjustable interest rate. Typically, the terms require the borrower to make installment payments over the term of the loan. Each payment consists of (1) interest on the unpaid balance of the loan and (2) a reduction of loan principal. The interest decreases each period, while the portion applied to the loan principal increases.

Mortgage notes payable are recorded initially at face value, and entries are required subsequently for each installment payment. To illustrate, assume that Porter Technology Inc. issues a $500,000, 12%, 20-year mortgage note on December 31, 2005, to obtain needed financing for the construction of a new research laboratory. The terms provide for semiannual installment payments of $33,231 (not including real estate taxes and insurance). The installment payment schedule for the first two years is as follows.

Helpful Hint Electronic spreadsheet programs can create a schedule of installment loan payments. This allows you to put in the data for your own mortgage loan and get an illustration that really hits home.

Illustration 10C-1
Mortgage installment payment schedule

Semiannual Interest Period	(A) Cash Payment	(B) Interest Expense (D) × 6%	(C) Reduction of Principal (A) − (B)	(D) Principal Balance (D) − (C)
Issue date				$500,000
1	$33,231	$30,000	$3,231	496,769
2	33,231	29,806	3,425	493,344
3	33,231	29,601	3,630	489,714
4	33,231	29,383	3,848	485,866

The entries to record the mortgage loan and first installment payment are as follows.

A = L + SE
+500,000 +500,000

Cash Flows
+500,000

Dec. 31	Cash	500,000	
	Mortgage Notes Payable		500,000
	(To record mortgage loan)		

A = L + SE
−33,231 −3,231 −30,000 Exp

Cash Flows
−33,231

June 30	Interest Expense	30,000	
	Mortgage Notes Payable	3,231	
	Cash		33,231
	(To record semiannual payment on mortgage)		

In the balance sheet, the reduction in principal for the next year is reported as a current liability, and the remaining unpaid principal balance is classified as a long-term liability. At December 31, 2006, the total liability is $493,344, of which $7,478 ($3,630 + $3,848) is current and $485,866 ($493,344 − $7,478) is long-term.

Summary of Study Objective for Appendix 10C

10 *Describe the accounting for long-term notes payable.* Each payment consists of (1) interest on the unpaid balance of the loan, and (2) a reduction of loan principal. The interest decreases each period, while the portion applied to the loan principal increases each period.

APPENDIX 10D
ACCOUNTING FOR CONTINGENCIES AND LEASES

Contingent Liabilities

Contingencies are events with uncertain outcomes. For users of financial statements, contingencies are often very important to understanding a company's financial position. Common types of contingencies are lawsuits, product warranties, and environmental problems.

Accounting rules require that contingencies be disclosed in the notes, and in some cases they must be accrued as liabilities. For example, suppose that Waterbury Inc. is sued by a customer for $1 million due to an injury sustained by a defective product. If at December 31 (the company's year-end) the lawsuit had not yet been resolved, how should the company account for this event? If the company can determine **a reasonable estimate** of the expected loss and if it is **probable** it will lose the suit, then the company should accrue for the loss. The loss is recorded by increasing (debiting) a loss account and increasing (crediting) a liability such as Lawsuit Liability. If *both* of these conditions are not met, then the company discloses the basic facts regarding this suit in the notes to its financial statements.

The liabilities associated with contingencies can be material. For example, **Procter & Gamble** is phasing out its long-time use of promotional coupons, saying that the cost was too high; **ExxonMobil** was ordered to pay billions of dollars as a result of an Alaskan oil spill; cigarette companies have been trying to negotiate a settlement of all their lawsuits with total payments of hundreds of billions of dollars. The notes to recent financial statements of cigarette manufacturer **Philip Morris** contained four and one-half pages of discussion regarding litigation. Illustration 10D-1 is an excerpt from the contingency note from the financial statements of **General Motors**.

GENERAL MOTORS CORPORATION
Notes to the Financial Statements (partial)

GM has established reserves for matters in which losses are probable and can be reasonably estimated. Some of the matters may involve compensatory, punitive, or other treble damage claims, or demands for recall campaigns, environmental remediation programs, or sanctions, that if granted, could require the Corporation to pay damages or make other expenditures in amounts that could not be estimated at December 31, 2001. After discussion with counsel, it is the opinion of management that such liability is not expected to have a material adverse effect on the Corporation's consolidated financial condition or results of operations.

Illustration 10D-1 Excerpt from contingency note disclosure

The note suggests that at this time General Motors does not have any outstanding litigation requiring accrual or disclosure. Sometimes analysts make adjustments to the financial statements for unrecorded contingencies that they feel should have been reported as liabilities on the balance sheet.

DECISION TOOLKIT

Decision Checkpoints	Info Needed for Decision	Tool to Use for Decision	How to Evaluate Results
✔			👍👎
Does the company have any contingent liabilities?	Knowledge of events with uncertain negative outcomes	Notes to financial statements and financial statements	If negative outcomes are possible, determine the probability, the amount of loss, and the potential impact on financial statements.

Lease Liabilities

In most lease contracts, a periodic payment is made by the lessee and is recorded as rent expense in the income statement. The renting of an apartment and the rental of a car at an airport are examples of these types of leases, often referred to as **operating leases**. In an operating lease the intent is **temporary use of the property by the lessee with continued ownership of the property by the lessor**.

In some cases, however, the lease contract transfers substantially **all the benefits and risks of ownership to the lessee**, so that the lease is **in effect, a purchase of the property**. This type of lease is called a **capital lease** because the fair value of the leased asset is *capitalized* by the lessee by recording it on its balance sheet.

Accounting standards have precise criteria that determine whether a lease should be accounted for as a capital lease. The thrust of these criteria is to determine whether the lease transaction more closely resembles a purchase transaction or a rental transaction. This is determined by asking these questions:

- Is it likely that the lessee will end up with the asset at the end of the lease?
- Will the lessee use the asset for most of its useful life?
- Will the payments made by the lessee be approximately the same as the payments it would have made if it had purchased the asset?

If the answer to any of these questions is yes, then the lease should be accounted for as a capital lease. That is, the lessee must record the asset and a related liability for the lease payments. Otherwise, the lessee can account for the transaction as an operating lease, meaning that neither an asset nor liability is shown on its books.

Most lessees do not like to report leases on their balance sheets because the lease liability increases the company's total liabilities. This, in turn, may make it more difficult for the company to obtain needed funds from lenders. **As a result, companies attempt to keep leased assets and lease liabilities off the balance sheet by structuring the lease agreement to avoid meeting the criteria of a capital lease.** Then they account for most of their leases as operating leases. Recall from Chapter 9, for example, that **Southwest Airlines** leased about a third of its planes, and nearly all of these were accounted for as operating leases. Consequently, a third of the planes used by Southwest Airlines do not show up on its balance sheet, nor do the liabilities related to those planes. As noted in this chapter, this procedure of keeping liabilities off the balance sheet is often referred to as **off-balance-sheet financing**.

The financial statement note describing General Motors' obligations under operating leases in 2001 is presented in Illustration 10D-2.

GENERAL MOTORS CORPORATION
Notes to the Financial Statements (partial)

GM had the following minimum commitments under noncancelable operating leases having remaining terms in excess of one year primarily for property: 2002—$630 million; 2003—$666 million; 2004—$464 million; 2005—$411 million; 2006—$468 million; and $2.1 billion in 2007 and thereafter. Certain lease minimum commitments fund the obligations of nonupdated SPEs. Certain of the leases contain escalation clauses of renewal or purchase options. Rental expenses under operating leases were $849 million, $861 million, and $825 million in 2001, 2000, and 1999, respectively.

Summary of Study Objective for Appendix 10D

11 *Describe the accounting for contingencies and leases.* Contingencies are events with uncertain outcomes. If a reasonable estimate of the amount of the outcome can be made, and if the outcome is probable, then it should be recorded in the accounts. If not, the nature of the event should be disclosed. A leased asset should be recorded as a purchase if it meets certain criteria.

Glossary

Bond certificate A legal document that indicates the name of the issuer, the face value of the bonds, and such other data as the contractual interest rate and the maturity date of the bonds. (p. 472)

Bonds A form of interest-bearing notes payable issued by corporations, universities, and governmental entities. (p. 472)

Callable bonds Bonds that are subject to retirement at a stated dollar amount prior to maturity at the option of the issuer. (p. 472)

Capital lease A type of lease whose characteristics make it similar to a debt-financed purchase and that is consequently accounted for in that fashion. (p. 500)

Contingencies Events with uncertain outcomes, such as a potential liability that may become an actual liability sometime in the future. (p. 487)

Contractual (stated) interest rate Rate used to determine the amount of interest the borrower pays and the investor receives. (p. 473)

Convertible bonds Bonds that permit bondholders to convert them into common stock at their option. (p. 472)

Current liability A debt that can reasonably be expected to be paid (1) from existing current assets or through the creation of other current liabilities, and (2) within one year or the operating cycle, whichever is longer. (p. 465)

Discount (on a bond) The difference between the face value of a bond and its selling price, when a bond is sold for less than its face value. (p. 476)

Effective-interest method of amortization A method of amortizing bond discount or bond premium that results in periodic interest expense equal to a constant percentage of the carrying value of the bonds. (p. 494)

Effective-interest rate Rate established when bonds are issued that remains constant in each interest period. (p. 494)

Face value Amount of principal due at the maturity date of the bond. (p. 472)

Long-term liabilities Obligations expected to be paid more than one year in the future. (p. 471)

Market interest rate The rate investors demand for loaning funds to the corporation. (p. 474)

Maturity date The date on which the final payment on a bond is due from the bond issuer to the investor. (p. 472)

Mortgage note payable A long-term note secured by a mortgage that pledges title to specific units of property as security for the loan. (p. 497)

Notes payable An obligation in the form of a written promissory note. (p. 466)

Off-balance-sheet financing The intentional effort by a company to structure its financing arrangements so as to avoid showing liabilities on its books. (p. 487)

Operating lease A contractual arrangement giving the lessee temporary use of the property with continued ownership of the property by the lessor. Accounted for as a rental. (p. 500)

Premium (on a bond) The difference between the selling price and the face value of a bond when a bond is sold for more than its face value. (p. 476)

Present value The value today of an amount to be received at some date in the future after taking into account current interest rates. (p. 474)

Secured bonds Bonds that have specific assets of the issuer pledged as collateral. (p. 472)

Straight-line method of amortization A method of amortizing bond discount or bond premium that allo-

cates the same amount to interest expense in each interest period. (p. 491)

Times interest earned ratio A measure of a company's solvency, calculated by dividing income before interest expense and taxes by interest expense. (p. 485)

Unsecured bonds Bonds issued against the general credit of the borrower. (p. 472)

Demonstration Problem

Snyder Software Inc. successfully developed a new spreadsheet program. However, to produce and market the program, the company needed $2.0 million of additional financing. On January 1, 2005, Snyder borrowed money as follows.

1. Snyder issued $500,000, 11%, 10-year bonds. The bonds sold at face value and pay interest on January 1.
2. Snyder issued $1.0 million, 10%, 10-year bonds for $886,996. Interest is payable on January 1. Snyder uses the straight-line method of amortization.

Instructions

(a) For the 11% bonds, prepare journal entries for the following items.
    (1) The issuance of the bonds on January 1, 2005.
    (2) Accrue interest expense on December 31, 2005.
    (3) The payment of interest on January 1, 2006.
(b) For the 10-year, 10% bonds:
    (1) Journalize the issuance of the bonds on January 1, 2005.
    (2) Prepare the entry for the redemption of the bonds at 101 on January 1, 2008, after paying the interest due on this date. The carrying value of the bonds at the redemption date was $920,897.

Solution to Demonstration Problem

(a) (1) 2005

Jan. 1	Cash	500,000	
	Bonds Payable		500,000
	(To record issue of 11%, 10-year bonds at face value)		

Action Plan
- Record the discount on bonds issued as a contra liability account.
- Compute the loss on bond redemption as the excess of the cash paid over the carrying value of the redeemed bonds.

(2) 2005

Dec. 31	Bond Interest Expense	55,000	
	Bond Interest Payable		55,000
	(To record accrual of bond interest)		

(3) 2006

Jan. 1	Bond Interest Payable	55,000	
	Cash		55,000
	(To record payment of accrued interest)		

(b) (1) 2005

Jan. 1	Cash	886,996	
	Discount on Bonds Payable	113,004	
	Bonds Payable		1,000,000
	(To record issuance of bonds at a discount)		

(2) 2008			
Jan. 1	Bonds Payable	1,000,000	
	Loss on Bond Redemption	89,103*	
	Discount on Bonds Payable		79,103
	Cash		1,010,000
	(To record redemption of bonds at		
	101)		
	*($1,010,000 − $920,897)		

Note: All Questions, Exercises, and Problems marked with an asterisk relate to material in the appendixes to the chapter.

Self-Study Questions

Self-Study/Self-Test

Answers are at the end of the chapter.

(SO 1) **1.** The time period for classifying a liability as current is one year or the operating cycle, whichever is:
  (a) longer.   (c) probable.
  (b) shorter.   (d) possible.

(SO 1) **2.** To be classified as a current liability, a debt must be expected to be paid:
  (a) out of existing current assets.
  (b) by creating other current liabilities.
  (c) within 2 years.
  (d) Either (a) or (b)

(SO 2) **3.** Corricten Company borrows $88,500 on September 1, 2005, from Harrington State Bank by signing an $88,500, 12%, one-year note. What is the accrued interest at December 31, 2005?
  (a) $2,655.   (c) $4,425.
  (b) $3,540.   (d) $10,620.

(SO 3) **4.** Andre Company has total proceeds from sales of $4,515. If the proceeds include sales taxes of 5%, what is the amount to be credited to Sales?
  (a) $4,000.
  (b) $4,300.
  (c) $4,289.25.
  (d) The correct answer is not given.

(SO 4) **5.** ▸——◖ Which of the following is *not* a measure of liquidity?
  (a) Debt to total assets ratio.
  (b) Working capital.
  (c) Current ratio.
  (d) Current cash debt coverage.

(SO 7) **6.** What term is used for bonds that have specific assets pledged as collateral?
  (a) Callable bonds.
  (b) Convertible bonds.
  (c) Secured bonds.
  (d) Discount bonds.

(SO 5) **7.** Cuso Inc. issues 10-year bonds with a maturity value of $200,000. If the bonds are issued at a premium, this indicates that:
  (a) the contractual interest rate exceeds the market interest rate.

  (b) the market interest rate exceeds the contractual interest rate.
  (c) the contractual interest rate and the market interest rate are the same.
  (d) no relationship exists between the two rates.

(SO 5) **8.** On January 1, 2005, Scissors Corp. issues $200,000, 5-year, 7% bonds at face value. The entry to record the issuance of the bonds would include a:
  (a) debit to cash for $14,000.
  (b) debit to bonds payable for $200,000.
  (c) credit to bonds payable for $200,000.
  (d) credit to bond interest expense of $14,000.

(SO 6) **9.** Kant Corporation retires its $100,000 face value bonds at 105 on January 1, following the payment of interest. The carrying value of the bonds at the redemption date is $103,745. The entry to record the redemption will include a:
  (a) credit of $3,745 to Loss on Bond Redemption.
  (b) debit of $3,745 to Premium on Bonds Payable.
  (c) credit of $1,255 to Gain on Bond Redemption.
  (d) debit of $5,000 to Premium on Bonds Payable.

(SO 7) **10.** ▸——◖ In a recent year Day Corporation had net income of $150,000, interest expense of $30,000, and tax expense of $20,000. What was Day Corporation's times interest earned ratio for the year?
  (a) 5.00.   (c) 6.66.
  (b) 4.00.   (d) 7.50.

(SO 8) *__**11.** On January 1 Pierce Corporation issues $500,000, 5-year, 12% bonds at 96 with interest payable on January 1. The entry on December 31 to record accrued bond interest and the amortization of bond discount using the straight-line method will include a:
  (a) debit to Interest Expense, $57,600.

(b) debit to Interest Expense, $60,000.

(c) credit to Discount on Bonds Payable, $4,000.

(d) credit to Discount on Bonds Payable, $2,000.

(SO 8) *12. For the bonds issued in question 11, what is the carrying value of the bonds at the end of the third interest period?
(a) $492,000.   (c) $472,000.
(b) $488,000.   (d) $464,000.

(SO 9) *13. On January 1, Daisey Duke Inc. issued $1,000,000, 9% bonds for $939,000. The market rate of interest for these bonds is 10%. Interest is payable annually on December 31. Daisey Duke uses the effective-interest method of amortizing bond discount. At the end of the first year,

Daisey Duke should report unamortized bond discount of:
(a) $54,900.   (c) $51,610.
(b) $57,100.   (d) $51,000.

*14. On January 1, Anthony Corporation issued (SO 9) $1,000,000, 14%, 5-year bonds with interest payable on December 31. The bonds sold for $1,072,096. The market rate of interest for these bonds was 12%. On the first interest date, using the effective-interest method, the debit entry to Bond Interest Expense is for:
(a) $120,000.
(b) $125,581.
(c) $128,652.
(d) $140,000.

☑ THE NAVIGATOR

Questions

1. Susan Day believes a current liability is a debt that can be expected to be paid in one year. Is Susan correct? Explain.

2. LaBelle Company obtains $25,000 in cash by signing a 9%, 6-month, $25,000 note payable to First Bank on July 1. LaBelle's fiscal year ends on September 30. What information should be reported for the note payable in the annual financial statements?

3. (a) Your roommate says, "Sales taxes are reported as an expense in the income statement." Do you agree? Explain.
(b) Hard Wok Cafe has cash proceeds from sales of $10,400. This amount includes $400 of sales taxes. Give the entry to record the proceeds.

4. Omega University sold 10,000 season football tickets at $90 each for its five-game home schedule. What entries should be made (a) when the tickets are sold and (b) after each game?

5. Identify three taxes commonly withheld by the employer from an employee's gross pay.

6. (a) Identify three taxes commonly paid by employers on employees' salaries and wages.
(b) Where in the financial statements does the employer report taxes withheld from employees' pay?

7. (a) What are long-term liabilities? Give two examples.
(b) What is a bond?

8. Contrast these types of bonds:
(a) Secured and unsecured.
(b) Convertible and callable.

9. Explain each of these important terms in issuing bonds:
(a) Face value.
(b) Contractual interest rate.
(c) Bond certificate.

10. (a) What is a convertible bond?
(b) Discuss the advantages of a convertible bond from the standpoint of the bondholders and of the issuing corporation.

11. Describe the two major obligations incurred by a company when bonds are issued.

12. Assume that Rocky Inc. sold bonds with a face value of $100,000 for $104,000. Was the market interest rate equal to, less than, or greater than the bonds' contractual interest rate? Explain.

13. Caitlin and Samantha are discussing how the market price of a bond is determined. Caitlin believes that the market price of a bond is solely a function of the amount of the principal payment at the end of the term of a bond. Is she right? Discuss.

14. If a 10%, 10-year, $600,000 bond is issued at face and interest is paid annually, what is the amount of the interest payment at the end of the first period?

15. If the Bonds Payable account has a balance of $900,000 and the Discount on Bonds Payable account has a balance of $40,000, what is the carrying value of the bonds?

16. Which accounts are debited and which are credited if a bond issue originally sold at a premium is redeemed before maturity at 97 immediately following the payment of interest?

17. ⌐━━━⌐
(a) In general, what are the requirements for the financial statement presentation of long-term liabilities?
(b) What ratios may be computed to evaluate a company's liquidity and solvency?

18. ⌐━━━⌐ Bob Leno says that liquidity and solvency are the same thing. Is he correct? If not, how do they differ?

19. Gerald Ford needs a few new trucks for his business. He is considering buying the trucks but is concerned that the additional debt he will need to borrow will make his liquidity and solvency ratios look bad. What options does he have other than purchasing the trucks, and how will these options affect his financial statements?

20. Heflin Corporation has a current ratio of 1.1. Tom has always been told that a corporation's current ratio should exceed 2.0. Heflin argues that its ratio is low because it has a minimal amount of inventory on hand so as to reduce operating costs. Heflin also points out that it has significant available lines of credit. Is Tom still correct? What do some companies do to compensate for having fewer liquid assets?

21. What are the implications for analysis if a company has significant operating leases?

*22. Explain the straight-line method of amortizing discount and premium on bonds payable.

*23. Ewing Corporation issues $200,000 of 8%, 5-year bonds on January 1, 2005, at 104. Assuming that the straight-line method is used to amortize the premium, what is the total amount of interest expense for 2005?

*24. Mary Blaska is discussing the advantages of the effective-interest method of bond amortization with her accounting staff. What do you think Mary is saying?

*25. Apex Corporation issues $400,000 of 9%, 5-year bonds on January 1, 2005, at 104. If Apex uses the effective-interest method in amortizing the premium, will the annual interest expense increase or decrease over the life of the bonds? Explain.

*26. What criteria must be met before a contingency must be recorded as a liability? How should the contingency be disclosed if the criteria are not met?

*27. What is the primary difference between the nature of an operating lease and a capital lease? What is the difference in how they are recorded?

Brief Exercises

BE10-1 Carlton Company has these obligations at December 31: (a) a note payable for $100,000 due in 2 years, (b) a 10-year mortgage payable of $200,000 payable in ten $20,000 annual payments, (c) interest payable of $15,000 on the mortgage, and (d) accounts payable of $60,000. For each obligation, indicate whether it should be classified as a current liability.

Identify whether obligations are current liabilities.
(SO 1)

BE10-2 Jazz Company borrows $70,000 on July 1 from the bank by signing a $70,000, 10%, 1-year note payable. Prepare the journal entries to record (a) the proceeds of the note and (b) accrued interest at December 31, assuming adjusting entries are made only at the end of the year.

Prepare entries for an interest-bearing note payable.
(SO 2)

BE10-3 Nicky Supply does not segregate sales and sales taxes at the time of sale. The register total for March 16 is $10,070. All sales are subject to a 6% sales tax. Compute sales taxes payable and make the entry to record sales taxes payable and sales.

Compute and record sales taxes payable.
(SO 3)

BE10-4 Bel Air University sells 3,600 season basketball tickets at $60 each for its 12-game home schedule. Give the entry to record (a) the sale of the season tickets and (b) the revenue earned by playing the first home game.

Prepare entries for unearned revenues.
(SO 3)

BE10-5 Geoffrey Inc. is considering these two alternatives to finance its construction of a new $2 million plant:
  (a) Issuance of 200,000 shares of common stock at the market price of $10 per share.
  (b) Issuance of $2 million, 7% bonds at face value.

Complete the table and indicate which alternative is preferable.

Compare bond financing to stock financing.
(SO 4)

	Issue Stock	Issue Bond
Income before interest and taxes	$1,000,000	$1,000,000
Interest expense from bonds	_____	_____
Income before income taxes		
Income tax expense (30%)	_____	_____
Net income	$_____	$_____
Outstanding shares	_____	700,000
Earnings per share	$_____	$_____

Prepare journal entries for bonds issued at face value.
(SO 5)

BE10-6 Will Smith Corporation issued 1,000 9%, 5-year, $1,000 bonds dated January 1, 2005, at face value. Interest is paid each January 1.
(a) Prepare the journal entry to record the sale of these bonds on January 1, 2005.
(b) Prepare the adjusting journal entry on December 31, 2005, to record interest expense.
(c) Prepare the journal entry on January 1, 2006, to record interest paid.

Prepare journal entry for redemption of bonds.
(SO 6)

BE10-7 The balance sheet for Fresh Prince Company reports the following information on July 1, 2005.

FRESH PRINCE COMPANY
Balance Sheet (partial)

Long-term liabilities		
Bonds payable	$1,000,000	
Less: Discount on bonds payable	60,000	$940,000

Fresh Prince decides to redeem these bonds at 102 after paying annual interest. Prepare the journal entry to record the redemption on July 1, 2005.

Prepare statement presentation of long-term liabilities.
(SO 7)

BE10-8 Presented here are long-term liability items for Pool House Inc. at December 31, 2005. Prepare the long-term liabilities section of the balance sheet for Pool House Inc.

Bonds payable, due 2009	$900,000
Notes payable, due 2007	80,000
Discount on bonds payable	45,000

Analyze liquidity and solvency.
(SO 7)

BE10-9 The 2001 **Reebok** financial statements contain the following selected data (in millions).

Current assets	$1,295	Interest expense	$ 18
Total assets	1,543	Income taxes	48
Current liabilities	449	Net income	103
Total liabilities	823		
Cash	413		
Short-term investments	0		
Accounts receivable	383		

Compute the following values.
(a) Working capital.   **(c)** Debt to total assets ratio.
(b) Current ratio.   **(d)** Times interest earned ratio.

Calculate debt to total assets ratio; discuss effect of operating leases on solvency.
(SO 7)

BE10-10 At December 31, 2000, **Northwest Airlines** reported $765,000,000 in required payments on operating leases. If these assets had been purchased with debt, assets and liabilities would rise by approximately $4,988,000,000. Northwest's total assets in this year were $10,877,000,000, and total liabilities were $9,856,000,000.
(a) Calculate Northwest's debt to total assets ratio, first using the figures as reported, and then after increasing assets and liabilities for the unrecorded operating leases.
(b) Discuss the potential effect of these operating leases on your assessment of Northwest's solvency.

Prepare journal entries for bonds issued at a discount.
(SO 8)

*BE10-11 Hillary Company issues $2 million, 10-year, 9% bonds at 98, with interest payable on December 31. The straight-line method is used to amortize bond discount.
(a) Prepare the journal entry to record the sale of these bonds on January 1, 2005.
(b) Prepare the journal entry to record interest expense and bond discount amortization on December 31, 2005, assuming no previous accrual of interest.

Prepare journal entries for bonds issued at a premium.
(SO 8)

*BE10-12 Banks Inc. issues $5 million, 5-year, 10% bonds at 102, with interest payable on January 1. The straight-line method is used to amortize bond premium.
(a) Prepare the journal entry to record the sale of these bonds on January 1, 2005.
(b) Prepare the journal entry to record interest expense and bond premium amortization on December 31, 2005, assuming no previous accrual of interest.

*BE10-13 Presented below is the partial bond discount amortization schedule for Uncle Phil Corp., which uses the effective-interest method of amortization.

Use effective-interest method of bond amortization.
(SO 9)

Interest Periods	Interest to Be Paid	Interest Expense to Be Recorded	Discount Amortization	Unamortized Discount	Bond Carrying Value
Issue date				$62,311	$937,689
1	$45,000	$46,884	$1,884	60,427	939,573
2	45,000	46,979	1,979	58,448	941,552

Instructions
(a) Prepare the journal entry to record the payment of interest and the discount amortization at the end of period 1.
(b) ▭▬▶ Explain why interest expense is greater than interest paid.
(c) ▭▬▶ Explain why interest expense will increase each period.

Exercises

E10-1 Kassie Neuman and Emily Keshen borrowed $15,000 on an 8-month, 9% note from Garden State Bank to open their business, EZ's Coffee House. The money was borrowed on May 1, 2005, and the note matures January 1, 2006.

Prepare entries for interest-bearing notes.
(SO 2)

Instructions
(a) Prepare the entry to record the receipt of the funds from the loan.
(b) Prepare the entry to accrue the interest on May 31.
(c) Assuming adjusting entries are made at the end of each month, determine the balance in the interest payable account at December 31, 2005.
(d) Prepare the entry required on January 1, 2006, when the loan is paid back.

E10-2 On May 15, Corrietan's Outback Clothiers borrowed some money on a 3-month note to provide cash during the slow season of the year. The interest rate on the note was 8%. At the time the note was due, the amount of interest owed was $260.

Prepare entries for interest-bearing notes.
(SO 2)

Instructions
(a) Determine the amount borrowed by Corrietan's.
(b) Assume the amount borrowed was $18,500. What was the interest rate if the amount of interest owed was $740?
(c) Prepare the entry for the initial borrowing and the repayment for the facts in part (a).

E10-3 On June 1, Cairo Company Ltd. borrows $50,000 from First Bank on a 6-month, $50,000, 12% note. The note matures on December 1.

Prepare entries for interest-bearing notes.
(SO 2)

Instructions
(a) Prepare the entry on June 1.
(b) Prepare the adjusting entry on June 30.
(c) Prepare the entry at maturity (December 1), assuming monthly adjusting entries have been made through November 30.
(d) What was the total financing cost (interest expense)?

E10-4 In providing accounting services to small businesses, you encounter the following situations pertaining to cash sales.
  1. Harrington Company rings up sales and sales taxes separately on its cash register. On April 10 the register totals are sales $25,000 and sales taxes $1,800.
  2. Andre Company does not segregate sales and sales taxes. Its register total for April 15 is $11,660, which includes a 6% sales tax.

Journalize sales and related taxes.
(SO 3)

Instructions
Prepare the entries to record the sales transactions and related taxes for (a) Harrington Company and (b) Andre Company.

E10-5 During the month of March, Cuso Company's employees earned wages of $70,000. Withholdings related to these wages were $4,500 for Social Security (FICA), $7,500 for

Journalize payroll entries.
(SO 3)

federal income tax, $3,100 for state income tax, and $400 for union dues. The company incurred no cost related to these earnings for federal unemployment tax, but incurred $700 for state unemployment tax.

Instructions
(a) Prepare the necessary March 31 journal entry to record wages expense and wages payable. Assume that wages earned during March will be paid during April.
(b) Prepare the entry to record the company's payroll tax expense.

Journalize unearned revenue transactions.
(SO 3)

E10-6 Season tickets for the Chicken Hawks are priced at $230 and include 23 games. Revenue is recognized after each game is played. When the season began, the amount credited to Unearned Season Ticket Revenue was $1,104,000. By the end of October, $768,000 of the Unearned Season Ticket Revenue had been recorded as earned.

Instructions
(a) How many season tickets did the Chicken Hawks sell?
(b) How many home games had the Chicken Hawks played by the end of October?
(c) Prepare the entry for the initial recording of the Unearned Season Ticket Revenue.
(d) Prepare the entry to recognize the revenue after the first home game had been played.

Journalize unearned subscription revenue.
(SO 3)

E10-7 Westwood Company Ltd. publishes a monthly sports magazine, *Fishing Preview*. Subscriptions to the magazine cost $24 per year. During November 2005, Westwood sells 6,000 subscriptions for cash, beginning with the December issue. Westwood prepares financial statements quarterly and recognizes subscription revenue earned at the end of the quarter. The company uses the accounts Unearned Subscription Revenue and Subscription Revenue. The company has a December 31 year-end.

Instructions
(a) Prepare the entry in November for the receipt of the subscriptions.
(b) Prepare the adjusting entry at December 31, 2005, to record subscription revenue earned in December 2005.
(c) Prepare the adjusting entry at March 31, 2006, to record subscription revenue earned in the first quarter of 2006.

Prepare journal entries for issuance of bonds and payment of accrual of interest.
(SO 5)

E10-8 On September 1, 2005, Mooney Corporation issued $400,000, 9%, 10-year bonds at face value. Interest is payable annually on September 1. Mooney's year-end is December 31.

Instructions
Prepare journal entries to record the following events.
(a) The issuance of the bonds.
(b) The accrual of interest on December 31, 2005.
(c) The payment of interest on September 1, 2006.

Prepare journal entries for issuance of bonds and payment and accrual of interest.
(SO 5)

E10-9 On January 1 Pierce Company issued $100,000, 10%, 10-year bonds at face value. Interest is payable annually on January 1.

Instructions
Prepare journal entries to record the following events.
(a) The issuance of the bonds.
(b) The accrual of interest on December 31.
(c) The payment of interest on January 1.

Prepare journal entries to record issuance of bonds, payment of interest, and redemption at maturity.
(SO 5, 6)

E10-10 Pueblo Company Limited issued $240,000 of 9%, 20-year bonds on January 1, 2005, at face value. Interest is payable annually on January 1.

Instructions
Prepare the journal entries to record the following events.
(a) The issuance of the bonds
(b) The accrual of interest on December 31, 2005.
(c) The payment of interest on January 1, 2006.
(d) The redemption of the bonds at maturity, assuming interest for the last interest period has been paid and recorded.

E10-11 The situations presented here are independent of each other.

Prepare journal entries for redemption of bonds. (SO 6)

Instructions

For each situation prepare the appropriate journal entry for the redemption of the bonds.

(a) Joy Corporation retired $130,000 face value, 12% bonds on June 30, 2005, at 101. The carrying value of the bonds at the redemption date was $122,500. The bonds pay annual interest, and the interest payment due on June 30, 2005, has been made and recorded.

(b) Asler, Inc., retired $180,000 face value, 12.5% bonds on June 30, 2005, at 98. The carrying value of the bonds at the redemption date was $183,000. The bonds pay annual interest, and the interest payment due on June 30, 2005, has been made and recorded.

E10-12 The adjusted trial balance for Quebec Corporation at the end of 2005 contained the following accounts.

Prepare statement presentation of long-term liabilities. (SO 7)

Bond Interest Payable	$ 9,000
Note Payable, due 2009	59,500
Bonds Payable, due 2014	160,000
Premium on Bonds Payable	41,000

Instructions

(a) Prepare the long-term liabilities section of the balance sheet.

(b) Indicate the proper balance sheet classification for the account(s) listed above that do not belong in the long-term liabilities section.

E10-13 **McDonald's** 2001 financial statements contain the following selected data (in millions).

Calculate liquidity and solvency ratios; discuss impact of unrecorded obligations on liquidity and solvency. (SO 7)

Current assets	$ 1,819	Interest expense	$ 452
Total assets	22,535	Income taxes	693
Current liabilities	2,248	Net income	1,637
Total liabilities	13,046		
Cash	418		
Accounts receivable	882		

Instructions

(a) Compute the following values.

(1) Working capital. (3) Debt to total assets ratio.

(2) Current ratio. (4) Times interest earned ratio.

(b) The notes to McDonald's financial statements show that subsequent to 2001 the company will have future minimum lease payments under operating leases of $9,915.7 million. If these assets had been purchased with debt, assets and liabilities would rise by approximately $7,600 million. Recompute the debt to total assets ratio after adjusting for this. Discuss your result.

E10-14 The following financial data were reported by **3M Company** for 2001 and 2000 ($ in millions).

Calculate current ratio before and after paying accounts payable. (SO 7)

3M COMPANY
Balance Sheet (partial)

	2001	2000
Current assets		
Cash and cash equivalents	$ 616	$ 302
Accounts receivable, net	2,482	2,891
Inventories	2,091	2,312
Other current assets	1,107	874
Total current assets	$6,296	$6,379
Current liabilities	$4,509	$4,754

Instructions
(a) Calculate the current ratio for 3M for 2001 and 2000.
(b) Suppose that at the end of 2001 3M management used $200 million cash to pay off $200 million of accounts payable. How would its current ratio change?

Calculate current ratio before and after paying accounts payable.
(SO 7)

E10-15 The following financial data were reported by Brian's Re-Gifting Boutique for 2005 and 2004.

BRIAN'S RE-GIFTING BOUTIQUE
Balance Sheet (partial)
September 30 (in thousands)

	2005	2004
Current assets		
Cash and short-term deposits	$2,574	$1,021
Accounts receivable	2,347	1,575
Inventories	1,201	1,010
Other current assets	322	192
Total current assets	$6,444	$3,798
Current liabilities	$5,003	$4,108

Instructions
(a) Calculate the current ratio for Brian's Re-Gifting Boutique for 2005 and 2004.
(b) Suppose that at the end of 2005, the Re-Gifting Boutique used $1.5 million cash to pay off $1.5 million of accounts payable. How would its current ratio change?
(c) At September 30, the Re-Gifting Boutique has an undrawn operating line of credit of $12.5 million. Would this affect any assessment that you might make of the Re-Gifting Boutique's short-term liquidity? Explain.

Prepare journal entries to record issuance of bonds, payment of interest, amortization of premium using straight-line, and redemption at maturity.
(SO 5, 6, 8)

*E10-16 Shumway Company issued $300,000, 9%, 20-year bonds on January 1, 2005, at 104. Interest is payable annually on January 1. Shumway uses straight-line amortization for bond premium or discount.

Instructions
Prepare the journal entries to record the following events.
(a) The issuance of the bonds.
(b) The accrual of interest and the premium amortization on December 31, 2005.
(c) The payment of interest on January 1, 2006.
(d) The redemption of the bonds at maturity, assuming interest for the last interest period has been paid and recorded.

Prepare journal entries to record issuance of bonds, payment of interest, amortization of discount using straight-line, and redemption at maturity.
(SO 5, 6, 8)

*E10-17 Basler Company issued $220,000, 11%, 10-year bonds on December 31, 2004, for $215,000. Interest is payable annually on December 31. Basler uses the straight-line method to amortize bond premium or discount.

Instructions
Prepare the journal entries to record the following events.
(a) The issuance of the bonds.
(b) The payment of interest and the discount amortization on December 31, 2005.
(c) The redemption of the bonds at maturity, assuming interest for the last interest period has been paid and recorded.

Prepare journal entries for issuance of bonds, payment of interest, and amortization of discount using effective-interest method.
(SO 9)

*E10-18 Montreal Corporation issued $260,000, 9%, 10-year bonds on January 1, 2005, for $244,024. This price resulted in an effective interest rate of 10% on the bonds. Interest is payable annually on January 1. Montreal uses the effective-interest method to amortize bond premium or discount.

Instructions
Prepare the journal entries to record (round to the nearest dollar):
(a) The issuance of the bonds.
(b) The accrual of interest and the discount amortization on December 31, 2005.
(c) The payment of interest on January 1, 2006.

*E10-19   Ruiz Company issued $180,000, 11%, 10-year bonds on January 1, 2005, for $191,060. This price resulted in an effective interest rate of 10% on the bonds. Interest is payable annually on January 1. Ruiz uses the effective-interest method to amortize bond premium or discount.

Prepare journal entries for issuance of bonds, payment of interest, and amortization of premium using effective-interest method.
(SO 9)

Instructions
Prepare the journal entries (rounded to the nearest dollar) to record:
  (a) The issuance of the bonds.
  (b) The accrual of interest and the premium amortization on December 31, 2005.
  (c) The payment of interest on January 1, 2006.

*E10-20   Wiley Co. receives $110,000 when it issues a $110,000, 10%, mortgage note payable to finance the construction of a building at December 31, 2005. The terms provide for semiannual installment payments of $7,800 on June 30 and December 31.

Prepare journal entries to record mortgage note and installment payments.
(SO 10)

Instructions
Prepare the journal entries to record the mortgage loan and the first two installment payments.

Problems: Set A

P10-1A   On January 1, 2005, the ledger of El-Gazzar Company contained the following liability accounts.

Prepare current liability entries, adjusting entries, and current liabilities section.
(SO 1, 2, 3, 7)

Peachtree

Accounts Payable	$52,000
Sales Taxes Payable	8,500
Unearned Service Revenue	14,000

During January the following selected transactions occurred.

Jan. 1   Borrowed $18,000 from Midland Bank on a 3-month, 10%, $18,000 note.
      5   Sold merchandise for cash totaling $16,905, which includes 5% sales taxes.
      12   Provided services for customers who had made advance payments of $8,000. (Credit Service Revenue.)
      14   Paid state revenue department for sales taxes collected in December 2004 ($8,500).
      20   Sold 500 units of a new product on credit at $50 per unit, plus 5% sales tax.

During January the company's employees earned wages of $40,000. Withholdings related to these wages were $2,800 for Social Security (FICA), $3,800 for federal income tax, and $1,100 for state income tax. The company owed no money related to these earnings for federal or state unemployment tax. Assume that wages earned during January will be paid during February. No entry had been recorded for wages or payroll tax expense as of January 31.

Instructions
  (a) Journalize the January transactions.
  (b) Journalize the adjusting entries at January 31 for the outstanding notes payable and for wages expense and payroll tax expense.
  (c) Prepare the current liabilities section of the balance sheet at January 31, 2005. Assume no change in accounts payable.

(c) Tot. current liabilities $120,905

P10-2A   Rocky Mountain Bikes markets mountain-bike tours to clients vacationing in various locations in the mountains of Colorado. In preparation for the upcoming summer biking season, Rocky entered into the following transactions related to notes payable.

Journalize and post note transactions; show balance sheet presentation.
(SO 2, 7)

Mar. 1   Purchased Mongoose bikes for use as rentals by issuing an $8,000, 3-month, 9% note payable that is due June 1.
Mar. 31   Recorded accrued interest for the Mongoose note.

Apr. 1   Issued a $21,000 9 month note for the purchase of mountain property on which to build bike trails. The note bears 10% interest and is due January 1.

Apr. 30   Recorded accrued interest for the Mongoose note and the land note.

May 1   Issued a 4-month note to Telluride National Bank for $20,000 at 6%. The funds will be used for working capital for the beginning of the season; the note is due September 1.

May 31   Recorded accrued interest for all three notes.

June 1   Paid principal and interest on the Mongoose note.

June 30   Recorded accrued interest for the land note and the Telluride Bank note.

Instructions

(a) Prepare journal entries for the transactions noted above.

(b) Interest Payable $725   (b) Post the above entries to the Notes Payable, Interest Payable, and Interest Expense accounts. (Use T accounts.)

(c) Assuming that Rocky's year-end is June 30, show the balance sheet presentation of notes payable and interest payable at that date.

(d) How much interest expense relating to notes payable did Rocky incur during the year?

Prepare journal entries to record interest payments and redemption of bonds. (SO 5, 6)

P10-3A The following section is taken from Disch Corp.'s balance sheet at December 31, 2004.

Current liabilities	
Bond interest payable	$ 144,000
Long-term liabilities	
Bonds payable, 9%, due January 1, 2009	1,600,000

Interest is payable annually on January 1. The bonds are callable on any annual interest date.

Instructions

(a) Journalize the payment of the bond interest on January 1, 2005.

(b) Loss $16,000   (b) Assume that on January 1, 2005, after paying interest, Disch Corp. calls bonds having a face value of $400,000. The call price is 104. Record the redemption of the bonds.

(c) Prepare the adjusting entry on December 31, 2005, to accrue the interest on the remaining bonds.

Prepare journal entries to record issuance of bonds, interest, balance sheet presentation, and bond redemption. (SO 5, 6, 7)

P10-4A On May 1, 2004, MEM Corp. issued $800,000, 9%, 5-year bonds at face value. The bonds were dated May 1, 2004, and pay interest annually on May 1. Financial statements are prepared annually on December 31.

Instructions

(a) Prepare the journal entry to record the issuance of the bonds.

(b) Prepare the adjusting entry to record the accrual of interest on December 31, 2004.

(c) Show the balance sheet presentation of bonds payable and bond interest payable on December 31, 2004.

(d) Prepare the journal entry to record the payment of interest on May 1, 2005.

(e) Prepare the adjusting entry to record the accrual of interest on December 31, 2005.

(f) Loss $8,000   (f) Assume that on January 1, 2006, MEM pays the accrued bond interest and calls the bonds. The call price is 101. Record the payment of interest and redemption of the bonds.

Prepare journal entries to record issuance of bonds, show balance sheet presentation, and record bond redemption. (SO 5, 6)

P10-5A Admiral Electric sold $3,000,000, 10%, 20-year bonds on January 1, 2005. The bonds were dated January 1 and pay interest on January 1. The bonds were sold at 104.

Instructions

(a) Prepare the journal entry to record the issuance of the bonds on January 1, 2005.

(b) At December 31, 2005, $6,000 of the bond premium had been amortized. Show the balance sheet presentation of the bond liability at December 31, 2005. (Assume that interest has been paid.)

(c) Loss $42,000   (c) At December 31, 2006, when the carrying value of the bonds was $3,108,000, the company redeemed the bonds at 105. Record the redemption of the bonds assuming that interest for the year had already been paid.

P10-6A The following selected information was taken from the financial statements of Krispy Kreme Doughnuts, Inc.

Calculate and comment on ratios.
(SO 7)

KRISPY KREME DOUGHNUTS, INC.
Balance Sheet (partial)
December 31
(in thousands)

	Jan. 28, 2001	Feb. 3, 2002
Total current assets	$ 67,611	$101,769
Capital assets and other long-term assets	103,882	153,607
	$171,493	$255,376
Current liabilities	$ 38,168	$ 52,533
Long-term liabilities	6,529	12,685
Total liabilities	44,697	65,218
Shareholders' equity	126,796	190,158
Total liabilities and shareholders' equity	$171,493	$255,376

Other information:

	2001	2002
Interest expense	$ 607	$ 337
Tax expense	9,058	16,168
Net income	14,725	26,378
Cash provided by operations	32,112	36,210

Note 8. Lease Commitments

The Company conducts some of its operations from leased facilities and, additionally, leases certain equipment under operating leases. Generally, these have initial lease terms of 5 to 18 years and contain provisions for renewal options of 5 to 10 years.

At February 3, 2002, future minimum annual rental commitments, gross, under non-cancelable operating leases, including lease commitments on consolidated joint ventures, are as follows:

Fiscal Year Ending in	Amount (in thousands)
2003	$ 9,845
2004	7,478
2005	5,640
2006	4,074
2007	3,562
Thereafter	27,402
	$58,001

Rental expense, net of rental income, totaled $6,220,000 in fiscal 2000, $8,540,000 in fiscal 2001 and $10,576,000 in fiscal 2002.

Instructions

(a) Calculate each of the following ratios for 2002 and 2001.
   (1) Current ratio.
   (2) Current cash debt coverage ratio. (Current liabilities as of January 30, 2000, were $29,586.)
   (3) Debt to total assets ratio.
   (4) Times interest earned ratio.
   (5) Cash debt coverage ratio. (Total liabilities as of January 30, 2000, were $57,203.)

(b) Comment on Krispy Kreme's liquidity and solvency.

(c) Read the company's note on leases (Note 8). If the operating leases had instead been accounted for like a purchase, assets and liabilities would have increased by approximately $36,500,000. Recalculate the debt to total assets ratio for 2002 and discuss the implications for analysis.

Prepare journal entries to record interest payments, straight-line premium amortization, and redemption of bonds (SO 5, 6, 8)

*P10-7A The following section is taken from North Slope Oil Company's balance sheet at December 31, 2005.

Current liabilities		
Bond interest payable		$ 432,000
Long-term liabilities		
Bonds payable, 12% due January 1, 2016	$3,600,000	
Add: Premium on bonds payable	400,000	4,000,000

Interest is payable annually on January 1. The bonds are callable on any annual interest date. North Slope uses straight-line amortization for any bond premium or discount. From December 31, 2005, the bonds will be outstanding for an additional 10 years (120 months).

Instructions
(Round all computations to the nearest dollar.)
(a) Journalize the payment of bond interest on January 1, 2006.
(b) Prepare the entry to amortize bond premium and to accrue interest due on December 31, 2006.

(c) Gain $144,000

(c) Assume on January 1, 2007, after paying interest, that North Slope Company calls bonds having a face value of $1,800,000. The call price is 102. Record the redemption of the bonds.
(d) Prepare the adjusting entry at December 31, 2007, to amortize bond premium and to accrue interest on the remaining bonds.

Prepare journal entries to record issuance of bonds, interest, and straight-line amortization of bond premium and discount. (SO 5, 7, 8)

*P10-8A Ghani Company sold $1,500,000, 12%, 10-year bonds on January 1, 2005. The bonds were dated January 1, 2005, and pay interest on January 1. Ghani Company uses the straight-line method to amortize bond premium or discount.

Instructions
(a) Prepare all the necessary journal entries to record the issuance of the bonds and bond interest expense for 2005, assuming that the bonds sold at 101.
(b) Prepare journal entries as in part (a) assuming that the bonds sold at 96.
(c) Show the balance sheet presentation for the bond issue at December 31, 2005, using (1) the 101 selling price, and then (2) the 96 selling price.

Prepare journal entries to record issuance of bonds, interest, and straight-line amortization of bond premium and discount. (SO 5, 7, 8)

*P10-9A La Jolla Corporation sold $3,500,000, 7%, 20-year bonds on December 31, 2004. The bonds were dated December 31, 2004, and pay interest on December 31. The company uses straight-line amortization for premiums and discounts. Financial statements are prepared annually.

Instructions
(a) Prepare the journal entry to record the issuance of the bonds assuming they sold at:
  (1) 98½.
  (2) 103.
(b) Prepare amortization tables for both of the assumed sales for the first three interest payments.

(c) (2) 12/31/05 Interest Expense $239,750

(c) Prepare the journal entries to record interest expense for the first two interest payments under both assumed sales.
(d) Show the balance sheet presentation for both assumed sales at December 31, 2005.

Prepare journal entries to record issuance of bonds, payment of interest, and amortization of bond premium using effective-interest method. (SO 5, 9)

*P10-10A On January 1, 2005, Cordelia Corporation issued $1,500,000 face value, 12%, 10-year bonds at $1,684,337. This price resulted in an effective-interest rate of 10% on the bonds. Cordelia uses the effective-interest method to amortize bond premium or discount. The bonds pay annual interest January 1.

Instructions
(Round all computations to the nearest dollar.)
(a) Prepare the journal entry to record the issuance of the bonds on January 1, 2005.

(b) Prepare an amortization table through December 31, 2007 (three interest periods) for this bond issue.
(c) Prepare the journal entry to record the accrual of interest and the amortization of the premium on December 31, 2005.
(d) Prepare the journal entry to record the payment of interest on January 1, 2006.
(e) Prepare the journal entry to record the accrual of interest and the amortization of the premium on December 31, 2006.

(c) Interest
    Expense $168,434

*P10-11A On January 1, 2005, Lakota Company issued $2,200,000 face value, 10%, 10-year bonds at $1,951,390. This price resulted in an effective interest rate of 12% on the bonds. Lakota uses the effective-interest method to amortize bond premium or discount. The bonds pay annual interest January 1.

Prepare journal entries to record issuance of bonds, payment of interest, and amortization of discount using effective-interest method. In addition, answer questions.
(SO 5, 7, 9)

Instructions
(a) Prepare the journal entries to record the following transactions.

  (1) The issuance of the bonds on January 1, 2005.
  (2) The accrual of interest and the amortization of the discount on December 31, 2005.
  (3) The payment of interest on January 1, 2006.
  (4) The accrual of interest and the amortization of the discount on December 31, 2006.

(b) Show the proper balance sheet presentation for the liability for bonds payable on the December 31, 2006, balance sheet.
(c) ⬛➡ Provide the answers to the following questions in narrative form.

  (1) What amount of interest expense is reported for 2006?
  (2) Would the bond interest expense reported in 2006 be the same as, greater than, or less than the amount that would be reported if the straight-line method of amortization were used?
  (3) Determine the total cost of borrowing over the life of the bond.
  (4) Would the total bond interest expense be greater than, the same as, or less than the total interest expense that would be reported if the straight-line method of amortization were used?

(c) (1) $235,867

*P10-12A Dorothy Corporation purchased a new piece of equipment to be used in its new facility. The $750,000 piece of equipment was purchased with a $50,000 down payment and with cash received through the issuance of a $700,000, 6%, 4-year mortgage note payable issued on October 1, 2005. The terms provide for quarterly installment payments of $49,536 on December 31, March 31, June 30, and September 30.

Prepare installment payments schedule and journal entries for a mortgage note payable.
(SO 7, 10)

Instructions
(Round all computations to the nearest dollar.)
(a) Prepare an installment payments schedule for the first five payments of the notes payable.
(b) Prepare all necessary journal entries related to the notes payable for December 31, 2005.
(c) Show balance sheet presentation for these obligations for December 31, 2005. (*Hint:* Be sure to distinguish between the current and long-term portions of the note.)

*P10-13A Peter Furlong has just approached a venture capitalist for financing for his sailing school. The lenders are willing to loan Peter $50,000 at a high-risk annual interest rate of 24%. The loan is payable over 3 years in monthly installments of $1,962. Each payment includes principal and interest, calculated using the effective-interest method for amortizing debt. Peter receives the loan on May 1, 2005, which is the first day of his fiscal year. Peter makes the first payment on May 31, 2005.

Prepare journal entries to record payments for long-term note payable.
(SO 10)

Instructions
(a) Prepare an amortization schedule for the period from May 1, 2005, to August 31, 2005. Round all calculations to the nearest dollar.
(b) Prepare all journal entries for Peter Furlong for the period beginning May 1, 2005, and ending July 31, 2005. Round all calculations to the nearest dollar.

(b) 6/30 Interest
    Expense $981

Problems: Set B

*Prepare current liability
entries, adjusting entries, and
current liability section.*
(SO 1, 2, 3, 7)

P10-1B On January 1, 2005, the ledger of Popper Company contained these liability accounts.

Accounts Payable	$42,500
Sales Taxes Payable	6,600
Unearned Service Revenue	19,000

During January the following selected transactions occurred.

Jan. 1 Borrowed $15,000 in cash from Midland Bank on a 4-month, 8%, $15,000 note.

   5 Sold merchandise for cash totaling $7,875, which includes 5% sales taxes.

   12 Provided services for customers who had made advance payments of $12,000. (Credit Service Revenue.)

   14 Paid state treasurer's department for sales taxes collected in December 2004, $6,600.

   20 Sold 500 units of a new product on credit at $52 per unit, plus 5% sales tax.

During January the company's employees earned wages of $60,000. Withholdings related to these wages were $4,000 for Social Security (FICA), $5,000 for federal income tax, and $1,500 for state income tax. The company owed no money related to these earnings for federal or state unemployment tax. Assume that wages earned during January will be paid during February. No entry had been recorded for wages or payroll tax expense as of January 31.

Instructions

(a) Journalize the January transactions.

(b) Journalize the adjusting entries at January 31 for the outstanding note payable and for wages expense and payroll tax expense.

(c) Tot. current
    liabilities $130,275

(c) Prepare the current liabilities section of the balance sheet at January 31, 2005. Assume no change in Accounts Payable.

*Journalize and post note
transactions; show balance
sheet presentation.*
(SO 2, 7)

P10-2B Spiderman Company sells rock-climbing products and also operates an indoor climbing facility for climbing enthusiasts. During the last part of 2005, Spiderman had the following transactions related to notes payable.

Sept. 1 Issued a $15,000 note to Black Diamond to purchase inventory. The 3-month note payable bears interest of 8% and is due December 1.

Sept. 30 Recorded accrued interest for the Black Diamond note.

Oct. 1 Issued a $10,000, 9%, 4-month note to Montpelier Bank to finance the building of a new climbing area for advanced climbers. The note is due February 1.

Oct. 31 Recorded accrued interest for the Black Diamond note and the Montpelier Bank note.

Nov. 1 Issued an $18,000 note and paid $8,000 cash to purchase a vehicle to transport clients to nearby climbing sites as part of a new series of climbing classes. This note bears interest of 11% and matures in 12 months.

Nov. 30 Recorded accrued interest for the Black Diamond note, the Montpelier Bank note, and the vehicle note.

Dec. 1 Paid principal and interest on the Black Diamond note.

Dec. 31 Recorded accrued interest for the Montpelier Bank note and the vehicle note.

Instructions

(a) Prepare journal entries for the transactions noted above.

(b) Interest
    Payable $555

(b) Post the above entries to the Notes Payable, Interest Payable, and Interest Expense accounts. (Use T accounts.)

(c) Show the balance sheet presentation of notes payable and interest payable at December 31.

(d) How much interest expense relating to notes payable did Spiderman Company incur during the year?

P10-3B The following section is taken from Peppermint Patty's balance sheet at December 31, 2004.

Prepare journal entries to record interest payments and redemption of bonds. (SO 5, 6)

Current liabilities	
Bond interest payable	$ 16,000
Long-term liabilities	
Bonds payable, 8%, due January 1, 2011	200,000

Interest is payable annually on January 1. The bonds are callable on any annual interest date.

Instructions
(a) Journalize the payment of the bond interest on January 1, 2005.
(b) Assume that on January 1, 2005, after paying interest, Peppermint Patty calls bonds having a face value of $50,000. The call price is 102. Record the redemption of the bonds.
(c) Prepare the adjusting entry on December 31, 2005, to accrue the interest on the remaining bonds.

P10-4B On October 1, 2004, PFQ Corp. issued $600,000, 10%, 10-year bonds at face value. The bonds were dated October 1, 2004, and pay interest annually on October 1. Financial statements are prepared annually on December 31.

Prepare journal entries to record issuance of bonds, interest, balance sheet presentation, and bond redemption. (SO 5, 6, 7)

Instructions
(a) Prepare the journal entry to record the issuance of the bonds.
(b) Prepare the adjusting entry to record the accrual of interest on December 31, 2004.
(c) Show the balance sheet presentation of bonds payable and bond interest payable on December 31, 2004.
(d) Prepare the journal entry to record the payment of interest on October 1, 2005.
(e) Prepare the adjusting entry to record the accrual of interest on December 31, 2005.
(f) Assume that on January 1, 2006, PFQ pays the accrued bond interest and calls the bonds. The call price is 103. Record the payment of interest and redemption of the bonds.

(f) Loss $18,000

P10-5B Bellingham Company sold $4,000,000, 9%, 20-year bonds on January 1, 2005. The bonds were dated January 1, 2005, and pay interest on December 31. The bonds were sold at 97.

Prepare journal entries to record issuance of bonds, show balance sheet presentation, and record bond redemption. (SO 5, 6, 7)

Instructions
(a) Prepare the journal entry to record the issuance of the bonds on January 1, 2005.
(b) At December 31, 2005, $6,000 of the bond discount had been amortized. Show the balance sheet presentation of the bond liability at December 31, 2005. (Assume that interest has been paid.)
(c) At December 31, 2006, when the carrying value of the bonds was $3,892,000, the company redeemed the bonds at 102. Record the redemption of the bonds assuming that interest for the year had already been paid.

(c) Loss $188,000

P10-6B You have been presented with the following selected information taken from the financial statements of **Southwest Airlines Co.**

Calculate and comment on ratios. (SO 7)

SOUTHWEST AIRLINES CO.
Balance Sheet (partial)
December 31
(in millions)

	2001	2000
Total current assets	$2,520	$ 832
Noncurrent assets	6,477	5,838
Total assets	$8,997	$6,670

Current liabilities	$2,239	$1,298
Long-term liabilities	2,744	1,921
Total liabilities	4,983	3,219
Shareholders' equity	4,014	3,451
Total liabilities and shareholders' equity	$8,997	$6,670

Other information:

	2001	2000
Net income (loss)	$ 511	$ 603
Income tax expense	317	392
Interest expense	70	70
Cash provided by operations	1,485	1,298

Note 8. Leases

The majority of the Company's terminal operations space, as well as 92 aircraft, were under operating leases at December 31, 2001. Future minimum lease payments under noncancelable operating leases are as follows: 2002, $290,378; 2003, $275,013; 2004, $242,483; 2005, $217,170; 2006, $185,559; after 2006, $1,589,559.

Instructions

(a) Calculate each of the following ratios for 2001 and 2000.

(1) Current ratio.
(2) Current cash debt coverage. (Current liabilities in 1999 were $962.)
(3) Debt to total assets.
(4) Debt coverage.
(5) Cash debt coverage. (Total liabilities in 1999 were $2,818.)

(b) Comment on the trend in ratios.
(c) Read the company's note on leases. If the operating leases had instead been accounted for like a purchase, assets and liabilities would increase by approximately $1,500 million. Recalculate the debt to total assets ratio for 2001 in light of this information, and discuss the implictions for analysis.

Prepare journal entries to record interest payments, straight-line discount amortization, and redemption of bonds. (SO 5, 6, 8)

*P10-7B The following section is taken from Cunningham Corp.'s balance sheet at December 31, 2005.

Current liabilities		
Bond interest payable		$ 264,000
Long-term liabilities		
Bonds payable, 11%, due January 1, 2016	$2,400,000	
Less: Discount on bonds payable	42,000	2,358,000

Interest is payable annually on January 1. The bonds are callable on any annual interest date. Cunningham uses straight-line amortization for any bond premium or discount. From December 31, 2005, the bonds will be outstanding for an additional 10 years (120 months).

Instructions
(Round all computations to the nearest dollar.)

(a) Journalize the payment of bond interest on January 1, 2006.
(b) Prepare the entry to amortize bond discount and to accrue the interest on December 31, 2006.

(c) Loss $27,450

(c) Assume on January 1, 2007, after paying interest, that Cunningham Corp. calls bonds having a face value of $600,000. The call price is 103. Record the redemption of the bonds.
(d) Prepare the adjusting entry at December 31, 2007, to amortize bond discount and to accrue interest on the remaining bonds.

Prepare journal entries to record issuance of bonds, interest, and straight-line amortization of bond premium and discount. (SO 5, 7, 8)

*P10-8B Salvador Corporation sold $1,500,000, 8%, 10-year bonds on January 1, 2005. The bonds were dated January 1, 2005, and pay interest on January 1. Salvador Corporation uses the straight-line method to amortize bond premium or discount.

Instructions

(a) Prepare all the necessary journal entries to record the issuance of the bonds and bond interest expense for 2005, assuming that the bonds sold at 103.

(b) Prepare journal entries as in part (a) assuming that the bonds sold at 99.

(c) Show the balance sheet presentation for the bond issue at December 31, 2005, using (1) the 103 selling price, and then (2) the 99 selling price.

P10-9B   Tory Amos Co. sold $5,000,000, 9%, 5-year bonds on January 1, 2005. The bonds were dated January 1, 2005, and pay interest on January 1. The company uses straight-line amortization on bond premiums and discounts. Financial statements are prepared annually.

Prepare journal entries to record issuance of bonds, interest, and straight-line amortization of bond premium and discount. (SO 5, 6, 8)

Instructions

(a) Prepare the journal entries to record the issuance of the bonds assuming they sold at:

(1) 102.

(2) 97.

(b) Prepare amortization tables for both assumed sales for the first three interest payments.

(c) Prepare the journal entries to record interest expense for 2005 under both assumed sales.

(d) Show the balance sheet presentation for both assumed sales at December 31, 2005.

P10-10B   On January 1, 2005, Hingis Corporation issued $1,200,000 face value, 9%, 10-year bonds at $1,126,265. This price resulted in an effective-interest rate of 10% on the bonds. Hingis uses the effective-interest method to amortize bond premium or discount. The bonds pay annual interest January 1.

Prepare journal entries to record issuance of bonds, payment of interest, and amortization of bond discount using effective-interest method. (SO 9)

Instructions

(Round all computations to the nearest dollar.)

(a) Prepare the journal entry to record the issuance of the bonds on January 1, 2005.

(b) Prepare an amortization table through December 31, 2007 (three interest periods) for this bond issue.

(c) Prepare the journal entry to record the accrual of interest and the amortization of the discount on December 31, 2005.

(d) Prepare the journal entry to record the payment of interest on January 1, 2006.

(e) Prepare the journal entry to record the accrual of interest and the amortization of the discount on December 31, 2006.

(c) Interest Expense $112,627

P10-11B   On January 1, 2005, IOCO Company issued $2,000,000 face value, 12%, 10-year bonds at $2,245,783. This price resulted in a 10% effective-interest rate on the bonds. IOCO uses the effective-interest method to amortize bond premium or discount. The bonds pay annual interest on each January 1.

Prepare journal entries to record issuance of bonds, payment of interest, and amortization of premium using effective-interest method. In addition, answer questions. (SO 5, 7, 9)

Instructions

(a) Prepare the journal entries to record the following transactions.

(1) The issuance of the bonds on January 1, 2005.

(2) Accrual of interest and amortization of the premium on December 31, 2005.

(3) The payment of interest on January 1, 2006.

(4) Accrual of interest and amortization of the premium on December 31, 2006.

(a) (4) Interest Expense $223,036

(b) Show the proper balance sheet presentation for the liability for bonds payable on the December 31, 2006, balance sheet.

(c) Provide the answers to the following questions in narrative form.

(1) What amount of interest expense is reported for 2006?

(2) Would the bond interest expense reported in 2006 be the same as, greater than, or less than the amount that would be reported if the straight-line method of amortization were used?

P10-12B   Labelle purchased a new piece of equipment to be used in its new facility. The $550,000 piece of equipment was purchased with a $50,000 down payment and with cash received through the issuance of a $500,000, 8%, 3-year mortgage note payable issued on October 1, 2005. The terms provide for quarterly installment payments of $47,280 on December 31, March 31, June 30, and September 30.

Prepare installment payments schedule and journal entries for a mortgage note payable. (SO 7, 10)

Instructions

(Round all computations to the nearest dollar.)

(a) Prepare an installment payments schedule for the first five payments of the notes payable.

(b) Prepare all journal entries related to the notes payable for December 31, 2005.

(c) Show balance sheet presentation for this obligation for December 31, 2005. (*Hint:* Be sure to distinguish between the current and long-term portions of the note.)

Prepare journal entries to record payments for long-term note payable.
(SO 10)

*P10-13B Franca Cudini has just approached a venture capitalist for financing for her new business venture, the development of a local ski hill. On July 1, 2005, the lenders loaned Franca $100,000 at an annual interest rate of 10%. The loan is repayable over 5 years in annual installments of $26,380, principal and interest, due each June 30. The first payment is due June 30, 2006. Franca uses the effective-interest method for amortizing debt. Her ski hill company's year-end will be June 30.

Instructions

(a) Prepare an amortization schedule for the 5 years, 2005–2010. Round all calculations to the nearest dollar.

(b) 6/30/06 Interest
    Expense $10,000

(b) Prepare all journal entries for Franca Cudini for the first 2 fiscal years ended June 30, 2006, and June 30, 2007. Round all calculations to the nearest dollar.

(c) Show the balance sheet presentation of the note payable as of June 30, 2007. (*Hint:* Be sure to distinguish between the current and long-term portions of the note.)

▶ **BROADENING YOUR PERSPECTIVE**

Financial Reporting and Analysis

FINANCIAL REPORTING PROBLEM: *Tootsie Roll Industries*

BYP10-1   Refer to the financial statements of **Tootsie Roll Industries** and the Notes to Consolidated Financial Statements in Appendix A.

Instructions

Answer the following questions.

(a) What were Tootsie Roll's total current liabilities at December 31, 2002? What was the increase/decrease in Tootsie Roll's total current liabilities from the prior year?

(b) How much were the accounts payable at December 31, 2002?

(c) What were the components of total current liabilities on December 31, 2002 (other than accounts payable already discussed above)?

COMPARATIVE ANALYSIS PROBLEM: *Tootsie Roll vs. Hershey Foods*

BYP10-2   The financial statements of **Hershey Foods** are presented in Appendix B, following the financial statements for **Tootsie Roll Industries** in Appendix A.

Instructions

(a) Based on the information contained in these financial statements, compute the following 2002 ratios for each company.

  (1) Current ratio.
  (2) Current cash debt coverage ratio.

What conclusions concerning the companies' liquidity can be drawn from these ratios?

(b) Based on the information contained in these financial statements, compute the following 2002 ratios for each company.

  (1) Debt to total assets.
  (2) Times interest earned. (Hershey's total interest expense for 2002 was $64,393,000.)
  (3) Cash debt coverage ratio.

What conclusions about the companies' long-run solvency can be drawn from the ratios?

RESEARCH CASE

BYP10-3   Rapidly declining stock prices sometimes "trigger" other problems for a company. The May 3, 2002, edition of the *Wall Street Journal* contains an article by John Carreyrou entitled "**Vivendi** Reveals Another Liability from Off-Balance-Sheet Accounting. The July 10, 2002, edition of the *Wall Street Journal* contains an article, also by John Carreyrou, entitled "Vivendi Headquarters Raided in Disclosures-Related Probe," which summarizes the culmination of the liquidity problems brought on by the earlier events.

Instructions

Read the articles and answer the following questions.

(a) What is a put option? What is the total cost that Vivendi incurred in one week due to put options triggered by the drop in its stock price?

(b) In order to pay its obligation related to these options, the company will have to borrow money. What will be the likely outcome of having to borrow more money? What implications does this have for the company's profitability?

(c) Why did French stock market regulators raid Vivendi's headquarters?

(d) Why does the timing of the company's announcement about its liquidity problems matter to investors?

(e) In what significant way does the power of French stock market regulators differ from that of the U.S. Securities and Exchange Commission?

INTERPRETING FINANCIAL STATEMENTS

BYP10-4   Hechinger Co. and **Home Depot** are two home improvement retailers. Compared to Hechinger, founded in the early 1900s, Home Depot is a relative newcomer. But, in recent years, while Home Depot was reporting an average increase in net income of 28% per year between 1995 and 1998, Hechinger was reporting increasingly large net losses. Finally, in 1999, largely due to competition from Home Depot, Hechinger was forced to file for bankruptcy. Here are financial data for both companies (in millions).

	Hechinger 10/3/98	Home Depot 1/31/99
Cash	$ 21	$ 62
Receivables	0	469
Total current assets	1,153	4,933
Beginning total assets	1,668	11,229
Ending total assets	1,577	13,465
Beginning current liabilities	935	2,456
Ending current liabilities	938	2,857
Beginning total liabilities	1,392	4,015
Ending total liabilities	1,339	4,716
Interest expense	67	37
Income tax expense	3	1,040
Cash provided (used) by operations	(257)	1,917
Net income	(93)	1,614
Net sales	3,444	30,219

Instructions

Using the data, perform the following analysis.

(a) Calculate working capital, the current ratio, and the current cash debt coverage ratio for each company. Discuss their relative liquidity.

(b) Calculate the debt to total assets ratio, times interest earned, and cash debt coverage ratio for each company. Discuss their relative solvency.

(c) Calculate the return on assets ratio and profit margin ratio for each company. Comment on their relative profitability.

(d) The notes to Home Depot's financial statements indicate that it leases many of its facilities using operating leases. If these assets had instead been purchased with debt, assets and liabilities would have increased by approximately $2,347 million. Calculate the company's debt to total assets ratio employing this adjustment. Discuss the implications.

BYP10-5 **Lufkin Industries** and **CNH Global N.V.** are two manufacturers of construction and agricultural machinery.

Here are financial data for both companies (in millions).

	Lufkin Industries 12/31/01	CNH Global N.V. 12/31/01
Total current assets	$ 97.6	$ 7,431
Beginning total assets	233.6	17,577
Ending total assets	246.1	17,212
Beginning current liabilities	40.4	9,210
Ending current liabilities	37.0	7,353
Beginning total liabilities	80.9	15,063
Ending total liabilities	75.1	15,303
Interest expense	0.9	726
Income tax expense (refund)	12.7	(105)
Cash provided (used) by operations	34.8	(182)
Net income (loss)	19.5	(332)
Net sales	278.9	9,030

Instructions

Using the data, perform the following analysis.

(a) Calculate working capital, the current ratio, and the current cash debt coverage ratio for each company. Discuss their relative liquidity.

(b) Calculate the debt to total assets ratio, times interest earned, and cash debt coverage ratio for each company. Discuss their relative solvency.

(c) Calculate the return on assets ratio and profit margin ratio for each company. Comment on their relative profitability.

A GLOBAL FOCUS

BYP10-6 Many multinational companies find it beneficial to have their shares listed on stock exchanges in foreign countries. In order to do this, they must comply with the securities laws of those countries. Some of these laws relate to the form of financial disclosure the company must provide, including disclosures related to contingent liabilities. This exercise investigates the **Tokyo Stock Exchange**, the largest stock exchange in Japan.

Address: **www.tse.or.jp/english/index.shtml** (or go to **www.wiley.com/college/kimmel**)

Steps

1. Choose **About TSE**.
2. Choose **History**. Answer questions (a) and (b).
3. Choose **Listed Companies**.
4. Choose **Disclosure**. Answer questions (c) and (d).

Instructions

Answer the following questions.

(a) When was the first stock exchange opened in Japan? How many exchanges does Japan have today?

(b) What event caused trading to stop for a period of time in Japan?

(c) What are four examples of decisions by corporations that must be disclosed at the time of their occurrence?

(d) What are four examples of "occurrence of material fact" that must be disclosed at the time of their occurrence?

FINANCIAL ANALYSIS ON THE WEB

BYP10-7 *Purpose:* Bond or debt securities pay a stated rate of interest. This rate of interest is dependent on the risk associated with the investment. Moody's Investment Service provides ratings for companies that issue debt securities.

Address: **www.moodys.com/** (or go to **www.wiley.com/college/kimmel**)

Steps: From Moody's homepage, choose **About Moody's** and then **Moody's History**.

Instructions

Answer the following questions.

(a) What year did Moody's introduce the first bond rating?

(b) List three basic principles Moody's uses in rating bonds.

(c) What is the definition of Moody's Aaa rating on long-term bonds and preferred stock?

BYP10-8 *Purpose:* To illustrate the usefulness of financial calculators on the Web.

Address: **www.centura.com/tools** (or go to **www.wiley.com/college/kimmel**)

Steps: Go to the site shown above.

Instructions

Choose one of the many financial decisions listed at the site. Fill in inputs based on two different sets of assumptions. Print out your results, and then write up a short description of the decision model for your instructor. Describe the inputs and assumptions the model uses. Also try to identify the strengths and weaknesses of the site.

Critical Thinking

GROUP DECISION CASE

BYP10-9 On January 1, 2003, Helene Corporation issued $1,200,000 of 5-year, 8% bonds at 97. The bonds pay interest annually on January 1. By January 1, 2005, the market rate of interest for bonds of risk similar to those of Helene Corporation had risen. As a result the market value of these bonds was $1,000,000 on January 1, 2005—below their carrying value of $1,178,400.

Helene Riche, president of the company, suggests repurchasing all of these bonds in the open market at the $1,000,000 price. But to do so the company will have to issue $1,000,000 (face value) of new 10-year, 12% bonds at par. The president asks you, as controller, "What is the feasibility of my proposed repurchase plan?"

Instructions

With the class divided into groups, answer the following.

(a) Prepare the journal entry to retire the 5-year bonds on January 1, 2005. Prepare the journal entry to issue the new 10-year bonds.

(b) Prepare a short memo to the president in response to the president's request for advice. List the economic factors that you believe should be considered for her repurchase proposal.

COMMUNICATION ACTIVITY

BYP10-10 Finn Berge, president of the Blue Marlin, is considering the issuance of bonds to finance an expansion of his business. He has asked you to do the following: (1) discuss the advantages of bonds over common stock financing, (2) indicate the type of bonds he might issue, and (3) explain the issuing procedures used in bond transactions.

Instructions

Write a memorandum to the president, answering his request.

ETHICS CASE

BYP10-11 The July 1998 issue of *Inc.* magazine includes an article by Jeffrey L. Seglin entitled "Would You Lie to Save Your Company?" It recounts the following true situation:

"A Chief Executive Officer (CEO) of a $20-million company that repairs aircraft engines received notice from a number of its customers that engines that it had recently repaired had failed, and that the company's parts were to blame. The CEO had not yet determined whether his company's parts were, in fact, the cause of the problem. The Federal Aviation Administration (FAA) had been notified and was investigating the matter.

What complicated the situation was that the company was in the midst of its year-end audit. As part of the audit, the CEO was required to sign a letter saying that he was not aware of any significant outstanding circumstances that could negatively impact the company—in accounting terms, of any contingent liabilities. The auditor was not aware of the customer complaints or the FAA investigation.

The company relied heavily on short-term loans from eight banks. The CEO feared that if these lenders learned of the situation, they would pull their loans. The loss of these loans would force the company into bankruptcy, leaving hundreds of people without jobs. Prior to this problem, the company had a stellar performance record."

Instructions

Answer the following questions.

(a) Who are the stakeholders in this situation?

(b) What are the CEO's possible courses of action? What are the potential results of each course of action? (Take into account the two alternative outcomes: the FAA determines the company (1) was not at fault, and (2) was at fault.)

(c) What would you do, and why?

(d) Suppose the CEO decides to conceal the situation, and that during the next year the company is found to be at fault and is forced into bankruptcy. What losses are incurred by the stakeholders in this situation? Do you think the CEO should suffer legal consequences if he decides to conceal the situation?

BYP10-12   During the summer of 2002 the financial press reported that **Citigroup** was being investigated for allegations that it had arranged transactions for **Enron** so as to intentionally misrepresent the nature of the transactions and consequently achieve favorable balance sheet treatment. Essentially, the deals were structured to make it appear that money was coming into Enron from trading activities, rather than from loans.

A July 23, 2002, *New York Times* article by Richard Oppel and Kurt Eichenwald entitled "Citigroup Said to Mold Deal to Help Enron Skirt Rules" suggested that Citigroup intentionally kept certain parts of a secret oral agreement out of the written record for fear that it would change the accounting treatment. Critics contend that this had the effect of significantly understating Enron's liabilities, thus misleading investors and creditors. Citigroup maintains that, as a lender, it has no obligation to ensure that its clients account for transactions properly. The proper accounting, Citigroup insists, is the responsibility of the client and its auditor.

Instructions

Answer the following questions.

(a) Who are the stakeholders in this situation?

(b) Do you think that a lender, in general, in arranging so called "structured financing" has a responsibility to ensure that its clients account for the financing in an appropriate fashion, or is this the responsibility of the client and its auditor?

(c) What effect did the fact that the written record did not disclose all characteristics of the transaction probably have on the auditor's ability to evaluate the accounting treatment of this transaction?

(d) The *New York Times* article noted that in one presentation made to sell this kind of deal to Enron and other energy companies, Citigroup stated that using such an arrangement "eliminates the need for capital markets disclosure, keeping structure mechanics private." Why might a company wish to conceal the terms of a financing arrangement from the capital markets (investors and creditors)? Is this appropriate? Do you think it is ethical for a lender to market deals in this way?

(e) Why was this deal more potentially harmful to shareholders than other off-balance-sheet transactions (for example, lease financing)?

Answers to Self-Study Questions

1. a   2. d   3. b   4. b   5. a   6. c   7. a   8. c   9. b   10. c   11. c   12. a   13. b   14. c

---

Answer to Tootsie Roll Review It Question 5, p. 471

The liabilities that **Tootsie Roll** has identified as current are: Accounts Payable, Dividends Payable, Accrued Liabilities, and Income Taxes Payable.

Remember to go back to the Navigator box on the chapter-opening page and check off your completed work.

Reporting and Analyzing Stockholders' Equity

STUDY OBJECTIVES

After studying this chapter,
you should be able to:

1 Identify and discuss the major characteristics of a corporation.

2 Record the issuance of common stock.

3 Explain the accounting for the purchase of treasury stock.

4 Differentiate preferred stock from common stock.

5 Prepare the entries for cash dividends and understand the effect of stock dividends and stock splits.

6 Identify the items that affect retained earnings.

7 Prepare a comprehensive stockholders' equity section.

8 Evaluate a corporation's dividend and earnings performance from a stock-holder's perspective.

THE NAVIGATOR

THE NAVIGATOR ✔

▶ Scan *Study Objectives*   ☐

▶ Read *Feature Story*   ☐

▶ Read *Preview*   ☐

▶ Read text and answer *Before You Go On*
　p. 532 ☐   p. 536 ☐   p. 538 ☐
　p. 546 ☐   p. 549 ☐   p. 554 ☐

▶ Work Using the *Decision Toolkit*   ☐

▶ Review Summary of *Study Objectives* ☐

▶ Work *Demonstration Problem*   ☐

▶ Answer *Self-Study Questions*   ☐

▶ Complete *Assignments*   ☐

FEATURE STORY

What's Cooking?

What major U.S. corporation got its start 32 years ago with a waffle iron? Hint: It doesn't sell food. Another hint: Swoosh. Another hint: "Just do it." That's right, **Nike**. In 1971 Nike cofounder Bill Bowerman put a piece of rubber into a kitchen waffle iron, and the trademark waffle sole was born. It seems fair to say that at Nike, "They don't make 'em like they used to."

Nike was co-founded by Bowerman and Phil Knight, a member of Bowerman's University of Oregon track team. Each began in the shoe business independently during the early 1960s. Bowerman got his start by making hand-crafted running shoes for his University of Oregon track team. Knight, after completing graduate school, started a small business importing low-cost, high-quality shoes from Japan. In 1964 the two joined forces, each contributing $500, and formed Blue Ribbon Sports, a partnership, marketing Japanese shoes.

It wasn't until 1971 that the company began manufacturing its own line of shoes. With the new shoes came a new corporate name—Nike—the Greek goddess of victory. It is hard to imagine that the company that now boasts a stable full of world-class athletes as promoters at one time had part-time employees selling shoes out of car trunks at track meets. Nike's success has been achieved through relentless innovation combined with unbridled promotion.

By 1980 Nike was sufficiently established that it was able to issue its first stock to the public. In that same year it also created a stock ownership program for its employees, allowing them to share in the company's success. Since then Nike has enjoyed phenomenal growth, with 2001 sales reaching $9.5 billion. Its dividend per share to stockholders is almost 4 times higher than its level of 11 years ago.

Nike is not alone in its quest for the top of the sport shoe world. Competitor **Reebok** pushes Nike every step of the way. However, Nike's recent success has resulted in sales that are three times those of Reebok.

Is the race over? Probably not. The shoe market is fickle, with new styles becoming popular almost daily and vast international markets still lying untapped. Whether one of these two giants does eventually take control of the planet remains to be seen. Meanwhile the shareholders sit anxiously in the stands as this Olympic-size drama unfolds.

☑ THE NAVIGATOR

On the World Wide Web
Nike: www.nike.com
Reebok: www.reebok.com

Corporations like Nike and Reebok have substantial resources at their disposal. In fact, the corporation is the dominant form of business organization in the United States in terms of sales, earnings, and number of employees. All of the 500 largest U.S. companies are corporations. In this chapter we look at the essential features of a corporation and explain the accounting for a corporation's capital stock transactions.

The content and organization of the chapter are as follows.

REPORTING AND ANALYZING STOCKHOLDERS' EQUITY

The Corporate Form of Organization	Stock Issue Considerations	Accounting for Treasury Stock	Preferred Stock	Dividends	Retained Earnings	Financial Statement Presentation	Measuring Corporate Performance
• Characteristics • Formation • Stockholder rights	• Authorized stock • Issuance • Par and no-par value • Accounting for common stock issues	• Purchase of treasury stock	• Dividend preferences • Liquidation preference	• Cash dividends • Stock dividends • Stock splits	• Retained earnings restrictions	• Balance sheet • Statement of cash flows	• Dividend record • Earnings performance • Debt vs. equity decision

☑ THE NAVIGATOR

The Corporate Form of Organization

A corporation is created by law. As a legal entity, a **corporation** has most of the rights and privileges of a person. The major exceptions relate to privileges that can be exercised only by a living person, such as the right to vote or to hold public office. Similarly, a corporation is subject to the same duties and responsibilities as a person. For example, it must abide by the laws and it must pay taxes.

Corporations may be classified in a variety of ways. Two common classifications are **by purpose** and **by ownership**. A corporation may be organized for the purpose of making a profit (such as **Nike** or **General Motors**), or it may be a nonprofit charitable, medical, or educational corporation (such as the **Salvation Army** or the **American Cancer Society**).

Classification by ownership differentiates publicly held and privately held corporations. A **publicly held corporation** may have thousands of stockholders, and its stock is regularly traded on a national securities market such as the New York Stock Exchange. Examples are **IBM**, **Caterpillar**, and **General Electric**. In contrast, a **privately held corporation**, often referred to as a closely held corporation, usually has only a few stockholders and does not offer its stock for sale to the general public. Privately held companies are generally much smaller than publicly held companies, although some notable exceptions exist. **Cargill Inc.**, a private corporation that trades in grain and other commodities, is one of the largest companies in the United States. This chapter deals primarily with issues related to publicly held companies.

CHARACTERISTICS OF A CORPORATION

In 1964, when Nike's founders, Knight and Bowerman, were just getting started in the running shoe business, they formed their original organization as a partnership. In 1968 they reorganized the company as a corporation. A number of characteristics distinguish a corporation from proprietorships and partnerships. The most important of these characteristics are explained below.

Separate Legal Existence

Stockholders
Legal existence separate from owners

As an entity separate and distinct from its owners, the corporation acts under its own name rather than in the name of its stockholders. **Nike**, for example, may buy, own, and sell property, borrow money, and enter into legally binding contracts in its own name. It may also sue or be sued. It pays taxes as a separate entity.

In contrast to a partnership, in which the acts of the owners (partners) bind the partnership, the acts of the owners (stockholders) do not bind the corporation unless such owners are agents of the corporation. For example, if you owned shares of Nike stock, you would not have the right to purchase inventory for the company unless you were designated as an agent of the corporation.

Limited Liability of Stockholders

Stockholders
Limited liability of stockholders

Since a corporation is a separate legal entity, creditors ordinarily have recourse only to corporate assets to satisfy their claims. The liability of stockholders is normally limited to their investment in the corporation. Creditors have no legal claim on the personal assets of the stockholders unless fraud has occurred. Thus, even in the event of bankruptcy of the corporation, stockholders' losses are generally limited to the amount of capital they have invested in the corporation.

Transferable Ownership Rights

Ownership of a corporation is held in shares of capital stock, which are transferable units. Stockholders may dispose of part or all of their interest in a corporation simply by selling their stock. The transfer of an ownership interest in a partnership requires the consent of each partner. In contrast, the transfer of stock is entirely at the discretion of the stockholder. It does not require the approval of either the corporation or other stockholders.

The transfer of ownership rights among stockholders normally has no effect on the operating activities of the corporation. Nor does it affect the corporation's assets, liabilities, and total stockholders' equity. The transfer of ownership rights is a transaction between individual owners. The company does not participate in the transfer of these ownership rights after the original sale of the capital stock.

Transferable ownership rights

Ability to Acquire Capital

Ability to acquire capital

It is relatively easy for a corporation to obtain capital through the issuance of stock. Buying stock in a corporation is often attractive to an investor because a stockholder has limited liability and shares of stock are readily transferable. Also, numerous individuals can become stockholders by investing small amounts of money. In sum, the ability of a successful corporation to obtain capital is virtually unlimited.

Continuous Life

The life of a corporation is stated in its charter. The life may be perpetual or it may be limited to a specific number of years. If it is limited, the period of existence can be extended through renewal of the charter. Since a corporation is a separate legal entity, its continuance as a going concern is not affected by the withdrawal, death, or incapacity of a stockholder, employee, or officer. As a result, a successful corporation can have a continuous and perpetual life.

Continuous life

Corporation Management

Although stockholders legally own the corporation, they manage it indirectly through a board of directors they elect. Philip Knight is the chairman of **Nike**'s board of directors. The board, in turn, formulates the operating policies for the company. The board also selects officers, such as a president and one or more vice-presidents, to execute policy and to perform daily management functions.

A typical organization chart showing the delegation of responsibility is shown in Illustration 11-1.

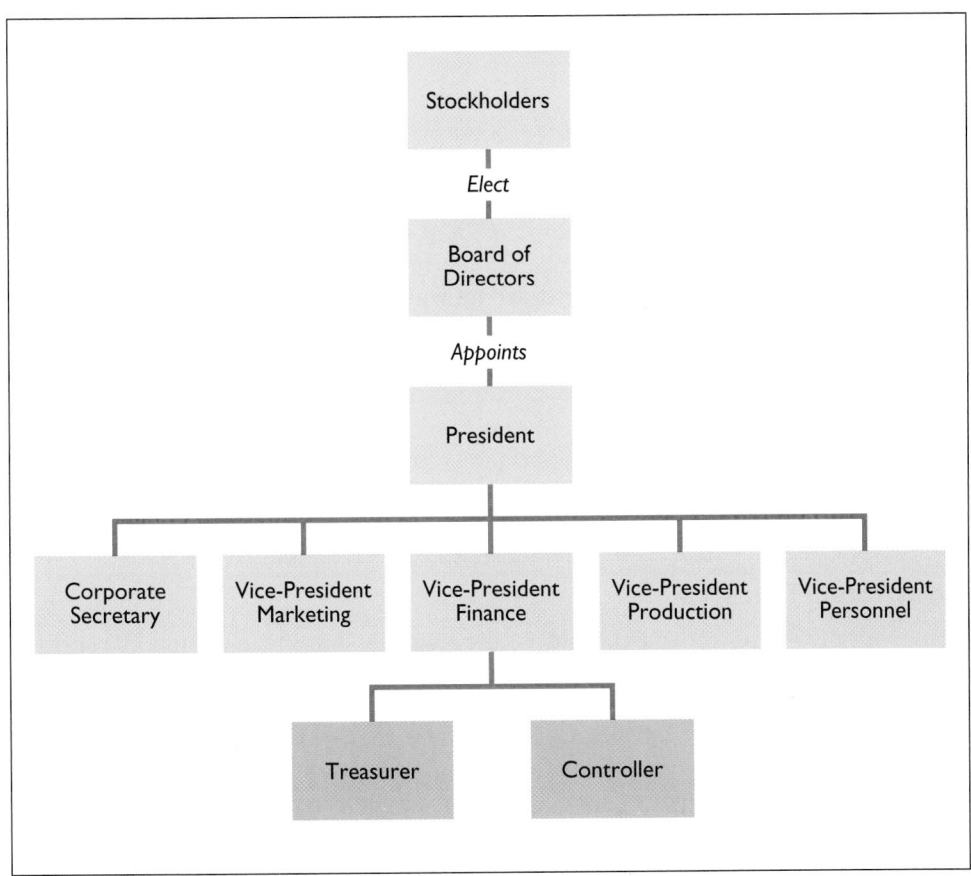

Illustration 11-1
Corporation organization chart

The **president** is the chief executive officer (CEO). He or she has direct responsibility for managing the business. As the organization chart shows, the president delegates responsibility to other officers. The chief accounting officer is the **controller**. The controller's responsibilities include (1) maintaining the accounting records and an adequate system of internal control and (2) preparing financial statements, tax returns, and internal reports. The **treasurer** has custody of the corporation's funds and is responsible for maintaining the company's cash position.

The organizational structure of a corporation enables a company to hire professional managers to run the business. On the other hand, some view this separation as a weakness. The separation of ownership and management prevents owners from playing an active role in managing the company, which some owners prefer.

Business Insight
ETHICS PERSPECTIVE

In the wake of **Enron**'s collapse, the members of Enron's board of directors have been questioned and scrutinized to determine what they knew, and when they knew it. A *Wall Street Journal* story reported that Enron's board contends it was "kept in the dark" by management and by Arthur Andersen—Enron's longtime auditor—and didn't learn about the company's troublesome accounting until October 2001. But, the *Wall Street Journal* reported that according to outside attorneys, "directors on at least two occasions waived Enron's ethical code of conduct to approve partnerships between Enron and its chief financial officer. Those partnerships kept significant debt off of Enron's books and masked actual company finances."

SOURCE: Carol Hymowitz, "Serving on a Board Now Means Less Talk, More Accountability," *Wall Street Journal Online* (January 29, 2002).

Government Regulations

State laws / SEC laws / WKK Corp. / Stock exchange requirements / Federal regulations / **Government regulations**

A corporation is subject to numerous state and federal regulations. For example, state laws usually prescribe the requirements for issuing stock, the distributions of earnings permitted to stockholders, and acceptable methods for retiring stock. Federal securities laws govern the sale of capital stock to the general public. Also, most publicly held corporations are required to make extensive disclosure of their financial affairs to the Securities and Exchange Commission (SEC) through quarterly and annual reports. In addition, when a corporate stock is listed and traded on organized securities markets, the corporation must comply with the reporting requirements of these exchanges.

Additional Taxes

Additional taxes

For proprietorships and partnerships, the owner's share of earnings is reported on his or her personal income tax return. Taxes are then paid on this amount by the individual. Corporations, on the other hand, must pay federal and state income taxes as a separate legal entity. These taxes are substantial: They can amount to as much as 40% of taxable income.

In addition, stockholders are required to pay taxes on cash dividends. Thus, many argue that corporate income is **taxed twice (double taxation)**, once at the corporate level and again at the individual level.

The advantages and disadvantages of a corporation compared to a proprietorship and partnership are shown in Illustration 11-2.

Illustration 11-2
Advantages and disadvantages of a corporation

Advantages	Disadvantages
• Separate legal existence • Limited liability of stockholders • Transferable ownership rights • Ability to acquire capital • Continuous life • Corporation management—professional managers	• Corporation management—separation of ownership and management • Government regulations • Additional taxes

Business Insight
MANAGEMENT PERSPECTIVE

Sometimes you can have your cake, and eat it too. A variety of "hybrid" organizational forms—forms that combine different attributes of partnerships and corporations—now exist. For example, one type of corporate form, called an **S corporation**, allows for legal treatment as a corporation but tax treatment as a partnership—that is, no double taxation. The rules regarding S corporation treatment were recently changed, making it possible for more small- and medium-sized businesses to qualify. One of the primary criteria is that the company cannot have more than 75 shareholders. Other forms include limited partnerships, limited liability partnerships (LLPs), and limited liability corporations (LLCs).

DECISION TOOLKIT

Decision Checkpoints	Info Needed for Decision	Tool to Use for Decision	How to Evaluate Results
Should the company incorporate?	Capital needs, growth expectations, type of business, tax status	Corporations have limited liability, easier capital raising ability, and professional managers; but they suffer from additional taxes, government regulations, and separation of ownership from management.	Must carefully weigh the costs and benefits in light of the particular circumstances.

FORMING A CORPORATION

A corporation is formed by grant of a state **charter**. Regardless of the number of states in which a corporation has operating divisions, it is incorporated in only one state. It is to the company's advantage to incorporate in a state whose laws are favorable to the corporate form of business organization. For example, although **General Motors** has its headquarters in Michigan, it is incorporated in New Jersey. In fact, more and more corporations have been incorporating in states with rules that favor existing management. For example, **Gulf Oil** changed its state of incorporation to Delaware to thwart possible unfriendly takeovers. There, certain defensive tactics against takeovers can be approved by the board of directors alone, without a vote by shareholders.

Upon receipt of its charter from the state of incorporation, the corporation establishes **by-laws**. The by-laws establish the internal rules and procedures for conducting the affairs of the corporation. Corporations engaged in interstate commerce must also obtain a **license** from each state in which they do business. The license subjects the corporation's operating activities to the general corporation laws of the state.

STOCKHOLDER RIGHTS

When chartered, the corporation may begin selling ownership rights in the form of shares of stock. When a corporation has only one class of stock, it is identified as **common stock**. Each share of common stock gives the stockholder the ownership rights pictured in Illustration 11-3 (page 532). The ownership rights of a share of stock are stated in the articles of incorporation or in the by-laws.

Illustration 11-3
Ownership rights of
stockholders

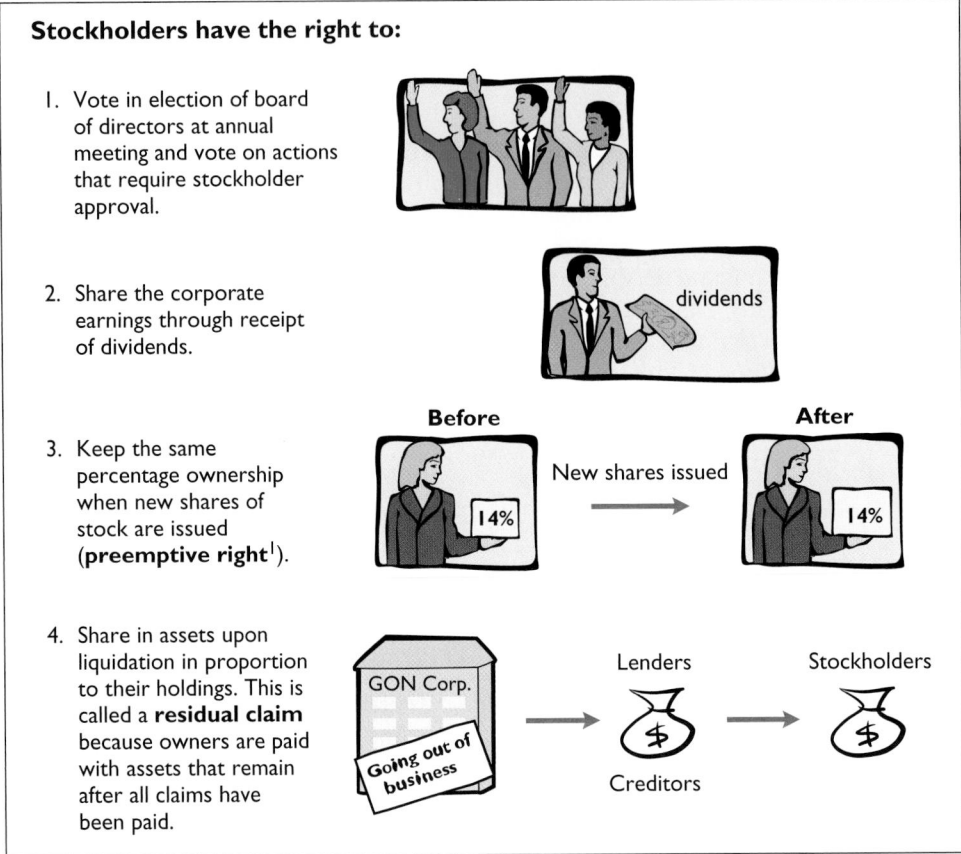

Stockholders have the right to:

1. Vote in election of board of directors at annual meeting and vote on actions that require stockholder approval.

2. Share the corporate earnings through receipt of dividends.

3. Keep the same percentage ownership when new shares of stock are issued (**preemptive right**[1]).

4. Share in assets upon liquidation in proportion to their holdings. This is called a **residual claim** because owners are paid with assets that remain after all claims have been paid.

Proof of stock ownership is evidenced by a printed or engraved form known as a **stock certificate**. As shown in Illustration 11-4, the face of the certificate shows the name of the corporation, the stockholder's name, the class and special features of the stock, the number of shares owned, and the signatures of authorized corporate officials. Certificates are prenumbered to ensure proper control over their use; they may be issued for any quantity of shares.

BEFORE YOU GO ON . . .

▶ Review It

1. What are the advantages and disadvantages of a corporation compared to a proprietorship and a partnership?
2. Identify the principal steps in forming a corporation.
3. What rights are inherent in owning a share of stock in a corporation?

☑ THE NAVIGATOR

---

[1]A number of companies have eliminated the preemptive right because they believe it places an unnecessary and cumbersome demand on management. For example, **IBM**, by stockholder approval, has dropped its preemptive right for stockholders.

Illustration 11-4 A stock certificate

Stock Issue Considerations

Although **Nike** incorporated in 1968, it did not sell stock to the public until
1980. At that time Nike evidently decided it would benefit from the infusion of
cash that a public sale of its shares would bring. When a corporation decides
to issue stock, it must resolve a number of basic questions: How many shares
should be authorized for sale? How should the stock be issued? What value
should be assigned to the stock? These questions are answered in the following sections.

AUTHORIZED STOCK

The amount of stock that a corporation is authorized to sell is indicated in its
charter. If all **authorized stock** is sold, then a corporation must obtain consent
of the state to amend its charter before it can issue additional shares.

**The authorization of common stock does not result in a formal ac-
counting entry** because the event has no immediate effect on either corporate assets or stockholders' equity. However, disclosure of the number of
shares authorized is required in the stockholders' equity section of the balance sheet.

ISSUANCE OF STOCK

A corporation can issue common stock **directly** to investors. Or it can issue common stock **indirectly** through an investment banking firm that specializes in
bringing securities to the attention of prospective investors. Direct issue is typical in closely held companies. Indirect issue is customary for a publicly held
corporation. New issues of stock may be offered for sale to the public through

 International Note

U.S. and U.K. corporations raise
most of their capital through
millions of outside shareholders
and bondholders. In contrast,
companies in Germany, France,
and Japan acquire financing
from large banks or other institutions. Consequently, in the
latter environment, shareholders are less important, and external reporting and auditing
receive less emphasis.

various organized U.S. securities exchanges: the New York Stock Exchange, the American Stock Exchange, and 13 regional exchanges. Stock may also be traded on the NASDAQ national market.

PAR AND NO-PAR VALUE STOCKS

Par value stock is capital stock that has been assigned a value per share in the corporate charter. Years ago, par value was used to determine the **legal capital** per share that must be retained in the business for the protection of corporate creditors. That amount is not available for withdrawal by stockholders. Thus, in the past, most states required the corporation to sell its shares at par or above.

However, the usefulness of par value as a protective device to creditors was questionable because par value was often immaterial relative to the value of the company's stock in the securities markets—even at the time of issue. For example, **Reebok**'s par value is $0.01 per share, yet a new issue in 2002 would have sold at a **market value** in the $22 per share range. Thus, par has no relationship with market value and in the vast majority of cases is an immaterial amount. As a consequence, today many states do not require a par value. Instead, other means are used to determine legal capital to protect creditors.

No-par value stock is capital stock that has not been assigned a value in the corporate charter. No-par value stock is quite common today. For example, **Nike**, **Procter & Gamble**, and **North American Van Lines** all have no-par stock. In many states the board of directors is permitted to assign a **stated value** to the no-par shares.

ACCOUNTING FOR COMMON STOCK ISSUES

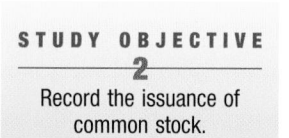

STUDY OBJECTIVE
2
Record the issuance of common stock.

The stockholders' equity section of a corporation's balance sheet includes: (1) **paid-in (contributed) capital** and (2) **retained earnings (earned capital)**. The distinction between paid-in capital and retained earnings is important from both a legal and an economic point of view. **Paid-in capital** is the amount paid to the corporation by stockholders in exchange for shares of ownership. *Retained earnings* is earned capital held for future use in the business. In this section we discuss the accounting for paid-in capital. In a later section we discuss retained earnings.

Let's now look at how to account for new issues of common stock. The primary objectives in accounting for the issuance of common stock are: (1) to identify the specific sources of paid-in capital and (2) to maintain the distinction between paid-in capital and retained earnings. As shown below, **the issuance of common stock affects only paid-in capital accounts**.

Helpful Hint Stock is sometimes issued in exchange for services (payment to attorneys or consultants, for example) or other noncash assets (land or buildings). The accounting for such stock issues is beyond the scope of this book. Here we look at only the issuance of common stock in exchange for cash.

As discussed earlier, par value does not indicate a stock's market value. The cash proceeds from issuing par value stock may be equal to, greater than, or less than par value. When the issuance of common stock for cash is recorded, the par value of the shares is credited to Common Stock, and the portion of the proceeds that is above or below par value is recorded in a separate paid-in capital account.

To illustrate, assume that Hydro-Slide, Inc. issues 1,000 shares of $1 par value common stock at par for cash. The entry to record this transaction is:

A = L + SE
+1,000   +1,000 CS

Cash Flows
+1,000

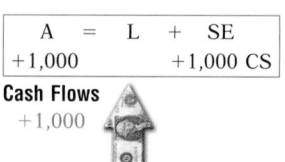

Cash	1,000	
Common Stock		1,000
(To record issuance of 1,000 shares of $1 par common stock at par)		

If Hydro-Slide, Inc. issues an additional 1,000 shares of the $1 par value common stock for cash at $5 per share, the entry is:

Cash	5,000		
Common Stock		1,000	
Paid-in Capital in Excess of Par Value		4,000	
(To record issuance of 1,000 shares of common			
stock in excess of par)			

A	=	L	+	SE
+5,000				+1,000 CS
				+4,000 CS

Cash Flows
+5,000

The total paid-in capital from these two transactions is $6,000. If Hydro-Slide, Inc. has retained earnings of $27,000, the stockholders' equity section of the balance sheet is as shown in Illustration 11-5.

HYDRO-SLIDE, INC.
Balance Sheet (partial)

Stockholders' equity	
Paid-in capital	
Common stock	$ 2,000
Paid-in capital in excess of par value	4,000
Total paid-in capital	6,000
Retained earnings	27,000
Total stockholders' equity	$33,000

Illustration 11-5
Stockholders' equity—
paid-in capital in excess
of par value

Some companies issue no-par stock with a stated value. For accounting purposes, the stated value is treated in the same fashion as the par value. For example, if in our Hydro-Slide example the stock was no-par stock with a stated value of $1, the entries would be the same as those presented for the par stock except the term "Par Value" would be replaced with "Stated Value." If a company issues no-par stock that does not have a stated value, then the full amount received is credited to the Common Stock account. In such a case, there is no need for the Paid-in Capital in Excess of Stated Value account.

Business Insight
INVESTOR PERSPECTIVE

The stock of publicly held companies is traded on organized exchanges at dollar prices per share established by the interaction between buyers and sellers. For each listed security the financial press reports the high and low prices of the stock during the year, the total volume of stock traded on a given day, the high and low prices for the day, and the closing market price, with the net change for the day. **Nike** is listed on the New York Stock Exchange. Here is a recent listing for Nike:

	52 Weeks						
Stock	**High**	**Low**	**Volume**	**High**	**Low**	**Close**	**Net Change**
Nike	64.28	40.75	15309	46.65	44.95	45.48	−1.52

These numbers indicate the following: The high and low market prices for the last 52 weeks have been $64.28 and $40.75. The trading volume for the previous day was 1,530,900 shares. The high, low, and closing prices for that date were $46.65, $44.95, and $45.48, respectively. The net change for the day was a decrease of $1.52 per share.

BEFORE YOU GO ON . . .

▶ **Review It**

1. Of what significance to a corporation is the amount of authorized stock?
2. What alternative approaches may a corporation use to sell new shares to investors?
3. Distinguish between par value and market value.
4. Explain the accounting for par and no-par common stock issued for cash.

▶ **Do It**

Cayman Corporation begins operations on March 1 by issuing 100,000 shares of $10 par value common stock for cash at $12 per share. Journalize the issuance of the shares.

Action Plan

• In issuing shares for cash, credit Common Stock for par value per share.
• Credit any additional proceeds in excess of par value to a separate paid-in capital account.

Solution

Mar. 1	Cash	1,200,000	
	Common Stock		1,000,000
	Paid-in Capital in Excess of Par Value		200,000
	(To record issuance of 100,000 shares at $12 per share)		

☑ THE NAVIGATOR

Accounting for Treasury Stock

STUDY OBJECTIVE
3
Explain the accounting for the purchase of treasury stock.

Treasury stock is a corporation's own stock that has been issued, fully paid for, reacquired by the corporation and held in its treasury for future use. A corporation may acquire treasury stock for various reasons:

1. To reissue the shares to officers and employees under bonus and stock compensation plans.
2. To increase trading of the company's stock in the securities market in the hope of enhancing its market value by signaling that management believes the stock is underpriced.
3. To have additional shares available for use in acquiring other companies.
4. To reduce the number of shares outstanding and thereby increase earnings per share.

Another infrequent reason for purchasing treasury shares is that management may want to eliminate hostile shareholders by buying them out.

Many corporations have treasury stock. For example, in the United States approximately 68% of companies have treasury stock.[2] Specifically, in 2001 **Nike** purchased 4 million treasury shares, **IBM**, 51 million, and **Bristol-Myers Squibb**, 27 million shares. Stock repurchases have been so substantial that a re-

---

[2]*Accounting Trends & Techniques—2001* (New York: American Institute of Certified Public Accountants).

cent study by two Federal Reserve economists suggested that a sharp reduction in corporate purchases of treasury shares might result in as much as a 38% drop in the value of the U.S. stock market.

PURCHASE OF TREASURY STOCK

The purchase of treasury stock is generally accounted for by the **cost method**. This method derives its name from the fact that the Treasury Stock account is maintained at the cost of shares purchased. Under the cost method, **Treasury Stock is increased (debited) by the price paid to reacquire the shares**. **Treasury Stock decreases by the same amount when the shares are later sold**.

To illustrate, assume that on January 1, 2005, the stockholders' equity section for Mead, Inc. has 100,000 shares of $5 par value common stock outstanding (all issued at par value) and Retained Earnings of $200,000. The stockholders' equity section of the balance sheet before purchase of treasury stock is as shown in Illustration 11-6.

Illustration 11-6
Stockholders' equity with no treasury stock

MEAD, INC. Balance Sheet (partial)	
Stockholders' equity	
Paid-in capital	
Common stock, $5 par value, 100,000 shares issued and outstanding	$500,000
Retained earnings	200,000
Total stockholders' equity	$700,000

On February 1, 2005, Mead acquires 4,000 shares of its stock at $8 per share. The entry is:

Feb. 1	Treasury Stock	32,000	
	Cash		32,000
	(To record purchase of 4,000 shares of treasury stock at $8 per share)		

A	=	L	+	SE
−32,000				−32,000 TS

Cash Flows
−32,000

The Treasury Stock account would increase by the cost of the shares purchased ($32,000). The original paid-in capital account, Common Stock, would not be affected because **the number of issued shares does not change**.

Treasury stock is deducted from total paid-in capital and retained earnings in the stockholders' equity section of the balance sheet, as shown in Illustration 11-7 for Mead, Inc. Thus, the acquisition of treasury stock reduces stockholders' equity.

Helpful Hint Treasury Stock is a contra stockholders' equity account.

Illustration 11-7
Stockholders' equity with treasury stock

MEAD, INC. Balance Sheet (partial)	
Stockholders' equity	
Paid-in capital	
Common stock, $5 par value, 100,000 shares issued and 96,000 shares outstanding	$500,000
Retained earnings	200,000
Total paid-in capital and retained earnings	700,000
Less: Treasury stock (4,000 shares)	32,000
Total stockholders' equity	$668,000

Both the number of shares issued (100,000) and the number in the treasury (4,000) are disclosed. The difference is the number of shares of stock outstanding (96,000). The term **outstanding stock** means the number of shares of issued stock that are being held by stockholders.

Business Insight
MANAGEMENT PERSPECTIVE

In a bold (and some would say very risky) move in late 1996, **Reebok** bought back nearly a *third* of its shares. This repurchase of shares dramatically reduced Reebok's available cash. In fact, the company borrowed significant funds to accomplish the repurchase. In a press release, management stated that it was repurchasing the shares because it believed that the stock was severely under-priced. The repurchase of so many shares was meant to signal management's belief in good future earnings.

Skeptics, however, suggested that Reebok's management was repurchasing shares to make it less likely that the company would be acquired by another company (in which case Reebok's top managers would likely lose their jobs). By depleting its cash Reebok became a less likely acquisition target. Acquiring companies like to purchase companies with large cash reserves so they can pay off debt used in the acquisition.

BEFORE YOU GO ON . . .

▶ Review It

1. What is treasury stock, and why do companies acquire it?
2. How is treasury stock recorded?
3. Where is treasury stock reported in the financial statements?

▶ Do It

Santa Anita Inc. purchases 3,000 shares of its $50 par value common stock for $180,000 cash on July 1. The shares are to be held in the treasury until resold. Journalize the treasury stock transaction.

Action Plan

• Record the purchase of treasury stock at cost.
• Report treasury stock as a deduction from stockholders' equity (contra account) at the bottom of the stockholders' equity section.

Solution

July 1	Treasury Stock	180,000	
	Cash		180,000
	(To record the purchase of 3,000 shares		
	at $60 per share)		

☑ THE NAVIGATOR

Preferred Stock

To appeal to a larger segment of potential investors, a corporation may issue an additional class of stock, called preferred stock. **Preferred stock** has contractual provisions that give it preference or priority over common stock in certain areas. Typically, preferred stockholders have a priority in relation to (1) dividends and (2) assets in the event of liquidation. However, they sometimes do not have voting rights. **Reebok** has no outstanding preferred stock, whereas **Nike** has a very minor amount outstanding. Approximately 15% of U.S. companies have one or more classes of preferred stock.[3]

Like common stock, preferred stock may be issued for cash or for noncash consideration. The entries for these transactions are similar to the entries for common stock. When a corporation has more than one class of stock, each paid-in capital account title should identify the stock to which it relates (e.g., Preferred Stock, Common Stock, Paid-in Capital in Excess of Par Value—Preferred Stock, and Paid-in Capital in Excess of Par Value—Common Stock). Assume that Stine Corporation issues 10,000 shares of $10 par value preferred stock for $12 cash per share. The entry to record the issuance is:

STUDY OBJECTIVE
——————4——————
Differentiate preferred stock
from common stock.

Cash	120,000	
Preferred Stock		100,000
Paid-in Capital in Excess of Par Value—Preferred Stock		20,000
(To record the issuance of 10,000 shares of $10 par value preferred stock)		

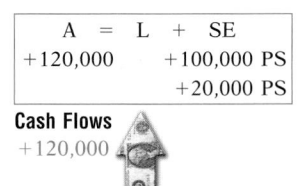

A	=	L	+	SE
+120,000				+100,000 PS
				+20,000 PS

Cash Flows
+120,000

Preferred stock may have either a par value or no-par value. In the stockholders' equity section of the balance sheet, preferred stock is shown first because of its dividend and liquidation preferences over common stock.

DIVIDEND PREFERENCES

As indicated above, **preferred stockholders have the right to share in the distribution of corporate income before common stockholders**. For example, if the dividend rate on preferred stock is $5 per share, common shareholders will not receive any dividends in the current year until preferred stockholders have received $5 per share. The first claim to dividends does not, however, **guarantee** dividends. Dividends depend on many factors, such as adequate retained earnings and availability of cash.

For preferred stock, the per share dividend amount is stated as a percentage of the par value of the stock or as a specified amount. For example, **EarthLink** specifies a 3% dividend, whereas **Nike** pays 10 cents per share on its $1 par preferred stock.

Cumulative Dividend

Preferred stock contracts often contain a **cumulative dividend** feature. This right means that preferred stockholders must be paid both current-year dividends and any unpaid prior-year dividends before common stockholders receive dividends. When preferred stock is cumulative, preferred dividends not declared in a given period are called **dividends in arrears**.

---

[3]*Accounting Trends & Techniques—2001* (New York: American Institute of Certified Public Accountants).

To illustrate, assume that Scientific Leasing has 5,000 shares of 7%, $100 par value cumulative preferred stock outstanding. Each $100 share pays a $7 dividend (.07 × $100). The annual dividend is $35,000 (5,000 × $7 per share). If dividends are two years in arrears, preferred stockholders are entitled to receive the dividends as shown in Illustration 11-8 in the current year.

Illustration 11-8
Computation of total dividends to preferred stock

Dividends in arrears ($35,000 × 2)	$ 70,000
Current-year dividends	35,000
Total preferred dividends	**$105,000**

No distribution can be made to common stockholders until this entire preferred dividend is paid. In other words, dividends cannot be paid to common stockholders while any preferred stock dividend is in arrears.

Dividends in arrears are not considered a liability. No obligation exists until the board of directors formally "declares" that the corporation will pay a dividend. However, the amount of dividends in arrears should be disclosed in the notes to the financial statements. Doing so enables investors to assess the potential impact of this commitment on the corporation's financial position.

Companies that are unable to meet their dividend obligations are not looked upon favorably by the investment community. As a financial officer noted in discussing one company's failure to pay its cumulative preferred dividend for a period of time, "Not meeting your obligations on something like that is a major black mark on your record."

LIQUIDATION PREFERENCE

Most preferred stocks have a preference on corporate assets if the corporation fails. This feature provides security for the preferred stockholder. The preference to assets may be for the par value of the shares or for a specified liquidating value. For example, **Commonwealth Edison** issued preferred stock that entitles the holders to receive $31.80 per share, plus accrued and unpaid dividends, in the event of involuntary liquidation. The liquidation preference is used in litigation pertaining to bankruptcy lawsuits involving the respective claims of creditors and preferred stockholders.

Dividends

STUDY OBJECTIVE
5

Prepare the entries for cash dividends and understand the effect of stock dividends and stock splits.

As noted earlier, a dividend **is a distribution by a corporation to its stockholders on a pro rata basis.** *Pro rata* means that if you own, say, 10% of the common shares, you will receive 10% of the dividend. Dividends can take four forms: cash, property, script (promissory note to pay cash), or stock. Cash dividends, which predominate in practice, and stock dividends, which are declared with some frequency, are the focus of our discussion.

Investors are very interested in a company's dividend practices. In the financial press, **dividends are generally reported quarterly as a dollar amount per share**. (Sometimes they are reported on an annual basis.) For example, **Nike**'s **quarterly** dividend rate in the fourth quarter of 2001 was 12 cents per share, whereas the dividend rate for that quarter for **JCPenney Company** was 12.5 cents, and for **PepsiCo** it was 14.5 cents.

CASH DIVIDENDS

A **cash dividend** is a pro rata distribution of cash to stockholders. For a corporation to pay a cash dividend, it must have the following.

1. **Retained earnings.** In many states, payment of dividends from legal capital is prohibited. However, payment of dividends from paid-in capital in excess of par is legal in some states. **Payment of dividends from retained earnings is legal in all states.** In addition, companies are frequently constrained by agreements with their lenders to pay dividends only from retained earnings.

2. **Adequate cash.** Recently **Nike** had a balance in retained earnings of $3,194 million but a cash balance of only $304 million. If it had wanted pay a dividend equal to its retained earnings, Nike would have had to raise $2,890 million more in cash. It would have been unlikely to do this because a dividend of this size would not be sustainable in the future. (That is, Nike would not be able to pay this much in dividends in future years.) In addition, such a dividend would completely deplete Nike's balance in retained earnings, so it would not be able to pay a dividend in the next year unless it had positive net income.

3. **Declared dividends.** The board of directors has full authority to determine the amount of income to be distributed in the form of dividends and the amount to be retained in the business. Dividends do not accrue like interest on a note payable, and they are not a liability until they are declared.

The amount and timing of a dividend are important issues for management to consider. The payment of a large cash dividend could lead to liquidity problems for the company. Conversely, a small dividend or a missed dividend may cause unhappiness among stockholders who expect to receive a reasonable cash payment from the company on a periodic basis. Many companies declare and pay cash dividends quarterly. On the other hand, a number of high-growth companies pay no dividends, preferring to retain earnings and use them to finance capital expenditures.

In order to remain in business, companies must honor their interest payments to creditors, bankers, and bondholders. But the payment of dividends to stockholders is another matter. Many companies can survive, and even thrive, without such payouts. "Why give money to those strangers?" is the response of one company president. Investors must keep an eye on the company's dividend policy and understand what it may mean. For most companies, for example, regular dividend boosts in the face of irregular earnings can be a warning signal. Companies with high dividends and rising debt may be borrowing money to pay shareholders. On the other hand, low dividends may not be a negative sign because they may mean high returns through increases in the stock price. Presumably, investors for whom regular dividends are important tend to buy stock in companies that pay periodic dividends, and those for whom growth in the stock price (capital gains) is more important tend to buy stock in companies that retain earnings.

Entries for Cash Dividends

Three dates are important in connection with dividends: (1) the declaration date, (2) the record date, and (3) the payment date. Accounting entries are required on the declaration date and the payment date.

On the **declaration date**, the board of directors formally authorizes the cash dividend and announces it to stockholders. The declaration of a cash dividend

commits the corporation to a binding legal obligation. Thus, an entry is required to recognize the decrease in retained earnings and the increase in the liability Dividends Payable.

To illustrate, assume that on December 1, 2005, the directors of Media General declare a $0.50 per share cash dividend on 100,000 shares of $10 par value common stock. The dividend is $50,000 (100,000 × $0.50). The entry to record the declaration is:

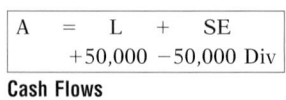

A	=	L	+	SE
		+50,000		−50,000 Div

Cash Flows
no effect

Declaration Date

Dec. 1	Retained Earnings (or Cash Dividends Declared)	50,000	
	Dividends Payable		50,000
	(To record declaration of cash dividend)		

Dividends Payable is a current liability: it will normally be paid within the next several months.

You may recall that in Chapter 3, instead of decreasing Retained Earnings, the account Dividends was used. This account provides additional information in the ledger. For example, a company may have separate dividend accounts for each class of stock or each type of dividend. When a separate dividend account is used, its balance is transferred to Retained Earnings at the end of the year by a closing entry. Whichever account is used for the dividend declaration, the effect is the same: Retained earnings is decreased and a current liability is increased. To avoid additional detail in the textbook, we have chosen to use the Retained Earnings account. For homework problems, you should use the Retained Earnings account for recording dividend declarations.

Helpful Hint The record date is important in determining the dividend to be paid to each stockholder but not the total dividend.

At the **record date**, ownership of the outstanding shares is determined for dividend purposes. The stockholders' records maintained by the corporation supply this information.

For Media General, the record date is December 22. No entry is required on the record date.

Record Date

| Dec. 22 | |
| | No entry necessary |

On the **payment date**, dividend checks are mailed to the stockholders on record as of December 22, and the payment of the dividend is recorded. If January 20 is the payment date for Media General, the entry on that date is:

A	=	L	+	SE
−50,000		−50,000		

Cash Flows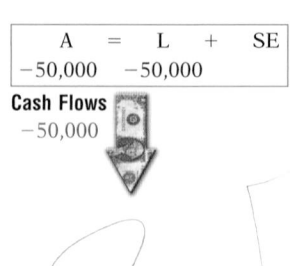
−50,000

Payment Date

Jan. 20	Dividends Payable	50,000	
	Cash		50,000
	(To record payment of cash dividend)		

Note that payment of the dividend reduces both current assets and current liabilities, but it has no effect on stockholders' equity. The cumulative effect of the **declaration and payment** of a cash dividend on a company's financial statements is to **decrease both stockholders' equity and total assets**.

Business Insight
INVESTOR PERSPECTIVE

To pay, or not to pay, that seems to be the question. As stock prices fall and the market becomes more volatile, investors become more interested in dividends. And what they found recently was not too pleasing. One article noted that "According to Standard and Poor's, only 72% of companies in its S&P 500 index paid a dividend last year [2001], down from 94% in 1980. Last year, the average dividend payment shrank by 3.3%, the biggest drop in 50 years. Barely one-fifth of all listed American companies paid a dividend in 1999."

SOURCE: "Dividends' End: Should Technology Companies Pay Dividends?" *The Economist* (January 12, 2002), p. 68.

STOCK DIVIDENDS

A stock dividend is a pro rata distribution of the corporation's own stock to stockholders. Whereas a cash dividend is paid in cash, a stock dividend is paid in stock. **A stock dividend results in a decrease in retained earnings and an increase in paid-in capital.** Unlike a cash dividend, a stock dividend does not decrease total stockholders' equity or total assets.

Because a stock dividend does not result in a distribution of assets, many view it as nothing more than a publicity gesture. Stock dividends are often issued by companies that do not have adequate cash to issue a cash dividend. These companies may not want to announce that they are not going to be issuing a cash dividend at their normal time to do so. By issuing a stock dividend they "save face" by giving the appearance of distributing a dividend. Note that since a stock dividend neither increases nor decreases the assets in the company, investors are not receiving anything they didn't already own. In a sense it is like ordering two pieces of pie and having your host take one piece of pie and cut it into two smaller pieces. You are not better off, but you got your two pieces of pie.

To illustrate a stock dividend, assume that you have a 2% ownership interest in Cetus Inc.; you own 20 of its 1,000 shares of common stock. If Cetus declares a 10% stock dividend, 100 shares (1,000 × 10%) of stock would be issued. You would receive two shares (2% × 100), but your ownership interest would remain at 2% (22 ÷ 1,100). **You now own more shares of stock, but your ownership interest has not changed.** Moreover, no cash is disbursed, and no liabilities have been assumed by the corporation.

What, then, are the purposes and benefits of a stock dividend? Corporations generally issue stock dividends for one of the following reasons.

1. To satisfy stockholders' dividend expectations without spending cash.
2. To increase the marketability of the stock by increasing the number of shares outstanding and thereby decreasing the market price per share. Decreasing the market price of the stock makes it easier for smaller investors to purchase the shares.
3. To emphasize that a portion of stockholders' equity has been permanently reinvested in the business and therefore is unavailable for cash dividends.

Helpful Hint Because of its effects, a stock dividend is also referred to as *capitalizing retained earnings.*

The size of the stock dividend and the value to be assigned to each dividend share are determined by the board of directors when the dividend is declared. In order to meet legal requirements, the per share amount must be at least equal to the par or stated value.

The accounting profession distinguishes between a **small stock dividend** (less than 20%–25% of the corporation's issued stock) and a **large stock dividend** (greater than 20%–25%). It recommends that the directors assign the **fair market value per share** for small stock dividends. The recommendation is based on the assumption that a small stock dividend will have little effect on the market price of the shares previously outstanding. Thus, many stockholders consider small stock dividends to be distributions of earnings equal to the fair market value of the shares distributed. The amount to be assigned for a large stock dividend is not specified by the accounting profession; however, **par or stated value per share** is normally assigned. Small stock dividends predominate in practice. In the appendix at the end of the chapter, we illustrate the journal entries for small stock dividends.

Effects of Stock Dividends

How do stock dividends affect stockholders' equity? They **change the composition of stockholders' equity** because a portion of retained earnings is transferred to paid-in capital. However, **total stockholders' equity remains the same**. Stock dividends also have no effect on the par or stated value per share, but the number of shares outstanding increases. To illustrate, assume that Medland Corp. declares a 10% stock dividend on its $10 par common stock when 50,000 shares were outstanding. The market price was $15 per share.

Illustration 11-9 Stock dividend effects

	Before Dividend	After Dividend
Stockholders' equity		
Paid-in capital		
Common stock, $10 par	$ 500,000	$ 550,000
Paid-in capital in excess of par value	—	25,000
Total paid-in capital	500,000	575,000
Retained earnings	300,000	225,000
Total stockholders' equity	**$800,000**	**$800,000**
Outstanding shares	**50,000**	**55,000**

In this example, total paid-in capital is increased by $75,000 (50,000 shares × 10% × $15), and retained earnings is decreased by the same amount. Note also that total stockholders' equity remains unchanged at $800,000.

STOCK SPLITS

A **stock split**, like a stock dividend, involves the issuance of additional shares of stock to stockholders according to their percentage ownership. However, **a stock split results in a reduction in the par or stated value per share**. The purpose of a stock split is to increase the marketability of the stock by lowering its market value per share. This, in turn, makes it easier for the corporation to issue additional stock.

The effect of a split on market value is generally inversely proportional to the size of the split. For example, after a recent 2-for-1 stock split, the market value of Nike's stock fell from $111 to approximately $55.

Helpful Hint A stock split changes the par value per share but does not affect any balances in stockholders' equity.

In a stock split, the number of shares is increased in the same proportion that the par or stated value per share is decreased. For example, in a 2-for-1 split, one share of $10 par value stock is exchanged for two shares of $5 par value stock. **A stock split does not have any effect on paid-in capital, retained earnings, and total stockholders' equity.** However, the number of shares outstanding increases. These effects are shown in Illustration 11-10, assuming that instead of issuing a 10% stock dividend, Medland splits its 50,000 shares of common stock on a 2-for-1 basis.

	Before Stock Split	After Stock Split
Stockholders' equity		
Paid-in capital		
Common stock (Before: 50,000 $10 par shares; after: 100,000 $5 par shares)	$ 500,000	$ 500,000
Paid-in capital in excess of par value	0	0
Total paid-in capital	500,000	500,000
Retained earnings	300,000	300,000
Total stockholders' equity	$800,000	$800,000
Outstanding shares	50,000	100,000

Illustration 11-10 Stock split effects

Because a stock split does not affect the balances in any stockholders' equity accounts, **it is not necessary to journalize a stock split**. However, a memorandum entry explaining the effect of the split is typically made.

The differences between the effects of stock dividends and stock splits are shown in Illustration 11-11.

Item	Stock Dividend	Stock Split
Total paid-in capital	Increase	No change
Total retained earnings	Decrease	No change
Total par value (common stock)	Increase	No change
Par value per share	No change	Decrease

Illustration 11-11 Effects of stock splits and stock dividends differentiated

Business Insight
MANAGEMENT PERSPECTIVE

Some large institutional investors won't buy stocks that sell for less than $10 per share. In 2002 **AT&T** was concerned that its share price (which had dropped dramatically) would fall into the single digits, so it announced a 1-for-5 reverse stock split. That is, it would reduce the number of outstanding shares to one-fifth of its existing level in an effort to increase the price to five times its existing level. If you owned 100 shares, you would be left with 20, but the total value of your shares would still be the same.

BEFORE YOU GO ON . . .

▶ Review It

1. What factors affect the size of a company's cash dividend?
2. Why do companies issue stock dividends? Why do companies declare stock splits?
3. Distinguish between a small and a large stock dividend and indicate the basis for valuing each kind of dividend.
4. Contrast the effects of a small stock dividend and a 2-for-1 stock split on (a) stockholders' equity and (b) outstanding shares.

▶ Do It

Due to five years of record earnings at Sing CD Corporation, the market price of its 500,000 shares of $2 par value common stock tripled from $15 per share to $45. During this period, paid-in capital remained the same at $2,000,000. Retained earnings increased from $1,500,000 to $10,000,000. President Joan Elbert is considering either a 10% stock dividend or a 2-for-1 stock split. She asks you to show the before and after effects of each option on retained earnings.

Action Plan

• Calculate the stock dividend's effect on retained earnings by multiplying the number of new shares times the market price of the stock (or par value for a large stock dividend).
• Recall that a stock dividend increases the number of shares without affecting total equity.
• Recall that a stock split only increases the number of shares outstanding and decreases the par value per share without affecting total equity.

Solution

The stock dividend amount is $2,250,000 [(500,000 × 10%) × $45]. The new balance in retained earnings is $7,750,000 ($10,000,000 − $2,250,000). The retained earnings balance after the stock split is the same as it was before the split: $10,000,000. The effects on the stockholders' equity accounts are as follows.

	Original Balances	After Dividend	After Split
Paid-in capital	$ 2,000,000	$ 4,250,000	$ 2,000,000
Retained earnings	10,000,000	7,750,000	10,000,000
Total stockholders' equity	$12,000,000	$12,000,000	$12,000,000
Shares outstanding	500,000	550,000	1,000,000

Retained Earnings

STUDY OBJECTIVE
6
Identify the items that affect retained earnings.

Retained earnings is net income that is retained in the business. The balance in retained earnings is part of the stockholders' claim on the total assets of the corporation. It does not, however, represent a claim on any specific asset. Nor can the amount of retained earnings be associated with the balance of any asset account. For example, a $100,000 balance in retained earnings does not mean that there should be $100,000 in cash. The reason is that the cash resulting from the excess of revenues over expenses may have been used to purchase buildings, equipment, and other assets. Illustration 11-12 shows recent amounts of retained earnings and cash in selected companies.

Illustration 11-12
Retained earnings and
cash balances

Company	(in millions) Retained Earnings	Cash
Circuit City Stores, Inc.	$1,597	$446
Nike, Inc.	3,194	304
Starbucks Coffee Company	590	113
Amazon.com	(2,293)	822

When expenses exceed revenues, a **net loss** results. In contrast to net income, a net loss decreases retained earnings. In closing entries a net loss is debited to the Retained Earnings account. **Net losses are not debited to paid-in capital accounts.** To do so would destroy the distinction between paid-in and earned capital. If cumulative losses exceed cumulative income over a company's life, a debit balance in Retained Earnings results. A debit balance in retained earnings, such as that of Amazon.com in 2000, is identified as a deficit. It is reported as a deduction in the stockholders' equity section of the balance sheet, as shown in Illustration 11-13.

Illustration 11-13
Stockholders' equity with
deficit

AMAZON.COM
Balance Sheet (partial)
December 31, 2000
(in thousands)

Stockholders' equity	
Paid-in capital	
Common stock	$ 3,571
Paid-in capital in excess of par value	1,322,479
Total paid-in capital	1,326,050
Accumulated deficit	(2,293,301)
Total stockholders' equity (deficit)	$ (967,251)

RETAINED EARNINGS RESTRICTIONS

The balance in retained earnings is generally available for dividend declarations. Some companies state this fact. In some cases, however, there may be retained earnings restrictions. These make a portion of the balance currently unavailable for dividends. Restrictions result from one or more of these causes: legal, contractual, or voluntary.

Retained earnings restrictions are generally disclosed in the notes to the financial statements. For example, Tektronix Inc., a manufacturer of electronic measurement devices, had total retained earnings of $774 million, but the unrestricted portion was only $223.8 million.

Illustration 11-14
Disclosure of unrestricted
retained earnings

TEKTRONIX INC.
Notes to the Financial Statements

Certain of the Company's debt agreements require compliance with debt covenants. Management believes that the Company is in compliance with such requirements for the fiscal year ended May 26, 2001. The Company had unrestricted retained earnings of $223.8 million after meeting those requirements.

Financial Statement Presentation of Stockholders' Equity

BALANCE SHEET PRESENTATION

In the stockholders' equity section of the balance sheet, paid-in capital and retained earnings are reported, and the specific sources of paid-in capital are identified. Within paid-in capital, two classifications are recognized:

1. **Capital stock**, which consists of preferred and common stock. Preferred stock is shown before common stock because of its preferential rights. Information about the par value, shares authorized, shares issued, and shares outstanding is reported for each class of stock.

2. **Additional paid-in capital**, which includes the excess of amounts paid in over par or stated value and paid-in capital from treasury stock.

The stockholders' equity section of the balance sheet of Graber Inc. is presented in Illustration 11-15. A retained earnings restriction is disclosed in the notes.

Illustration 11-15
Comprehensive stockholders' equity section

🌐 **International Note**

In Switzerland, there are no specific disclosure requirements for shareholders' equity. However, companies typically disclose separate categories of capital on the balance sheet.

GRABER INC.
Balance Sheet (partial)

Stockholders' equity		
Paid-in capital		
Capital stock		
9% preferred stock, $100 par value, cumulative, 10,000 shares authorized, 6,000 shares issued and outstanding		$ 600,000
Common stock, no par, $5 stated value, 500,000 shares authorized, 400,000 shares issued, and 390,000 outstanding		2,000,000
Total capital stock		2,600,000
Additional paid-in capital		
In excess of par value—preferred stock	$ 30,000	
In excess of stated value—common stock	1,050,000	
Total additional paid-in capital		1,080,000
Total paid-in capital		3,680,000
Retained earnings (see Note R)		1,160,000
Total paid-in capital and retained earnings		4,840,000
Less: Treasury stock—common (10,000 shares)		(80,000)
Total stockholders' equity		$4,760,000

Note R: Retained earnings is restricted for the cost of treasury stock, $80,000.

The stockholders' equity section for Graber Inc. includes most of the accounts discussed in this chapter. The disclosures pertaining to Graber's common stock indicate that 400,000 shares are issued; 100,000 shares are unissued (500,000 authorized less 400,000 issued); and 390,000 shares are outstanding (400,000 issued less 10,000 shares in treasury).

In published annual reports, subclassifications within the stockholders' equity section are seldom presented. Moreover, the individual sources of additional paid-in capital are often combined and reported as a single amount, as shown by the excerpts from Kmart's 2001 balance sheet in Illustration 11-16.

KMART CORPORATION
Balance Sheet (partial)
January 30, 2002
(in millions)

Stockholders' equity
  Common stock, $1 par value; 1,500,000,000 shares
    authorized; 503,294,515 shares issued $ 503
  Capital in excess of par value   1,695
  Retained earnings   1,261
Total stockholders' equity $3,459

Illustration 11-16
Stockholders' equity section

STATEMENT OF CASH FLOWS PRESENTATION

The balance sheet presents the balances of a company's stockholders' equity accounts at a point in time. Information regarding cash inflows and outflows during the year that resulted from equity transactions is reported in the "Financing Activities" section of the statement of cash flows. Illustration 11-17 presents the cash flows from financing activities from the statement of cash flows of Sara Lee Corporation. From this information we learn that the company's purchases of treasury stock during the period far exceeded its issuances of new common stock, and its financing activities resulted in a net reduction in its cash balance.

SARA LEE CORPORATION
Statement of Cash Flows (partial)
For the Year Ended June 30, 2001
(in millions)

Cash Flows from Financing Activities
  Issuances of common stock $ 104
  Purchases of common stock   (643)
  Payments of dividends   (486)
  Borrowings of long-term debt   1,023
  Repayments of long-term debt   (390)
  Short-term (repayments) borrowings, net   (1,914)
Net cash used in financing activities $(2,306)

Illustration 11-17
Financing activities of statement of cash flows

BEFORE YOU GO ON . . .

▶ Review It

1. Identify the classifications within the paid-in capital section and the totals that are stated in the stockholders' equity section of a balance sheet.
2. What is a retained earnings restriction?

3. What was the total cost of **Tootsie Roll**'s treasury stock in 2002? What was the total value of the 2002 cash dividend? What was the total charge to retained earnings of the 2002 stock dividend? The answer to these questions is provided on p. 575.

☑ THE NAVIGATOR

Measuring Corporate Performance

Investors are interested in both a company's dividend record and its earnings performance. Although they are often parallel, that is not always the case. Thus, each should be investigated separately.

DIVIDEND RECORD

STUDY OBJECTIVE
8
Evaluate a corporation's dividend and earnings performance from a stockholder's perspective.

One way that companies reward stock investors for their investment is to pay them dividends. The **payout ratio** measures the percentage of earnings distributed in the form of cash dividends to common stockholders. It is computed by **dividing total cash dividends declared to common shareholders by net income**. From the information shown below, the payout ratio for **Nike** in 2001 and 2000 is calculated in Illustration 11-18.

	2001	**2000**
Dividends (in millions)	$129.6	$131.5
Net income (in millions)	589.7	579.1

Illustration 11-18 Nike's payout ratio

$$\text{Payout Ratio} = \frac{\text{Cash Dividends Declared on Common Stock}}{\text{Net Income}}$$

($ in millions)	2001	2000
Payout Ratio	$\dfrac{\$129.6}{\$589.7} = 22\%$	$\dfrac{\$131.5}{\$579.1} = 23\%$

Companies that have high growth rates are characterized by low payout ratios because they reinvest most of their net income in the business. Thus, a low payout ratio is not necessarily bad news. Companies that believe they have many good opportunities for growth, such as **Nike** and **Reebok**, will reinvest those funds in the company rather than pay high dividends. In fact, dividend payout ratios for the 500 largest U.S. companies currently are very low relative to historical rates. However, low dividend payments, or a cut in dividend payments, might signal that a company has liquidity or solvency problems and is trying to free up cash by not paying dividends. Thus, the reason for low dividend payments should be investigated.

Listed in Illustration 11-19 are payout ratios in recent years of four well-known companies.

Company	Payout Ratio
Microsoft	0%
Kellogg	86.6%
Sears	41.0%
Johnson & Johnson	36.1%

Illustration 11-19
Variability of payout ratios among companies

DECISION TOOLKIT

Decision Checkpoints	Info Needed for Decision	Tool to Use for Decision	How to Evaluate Results
What portion of its earnings does the company pay out in dividends?	Net income and total cash dividends paid on common stock	$\text{Payout ratio} = \dfrac{\text{Cash dividends declared on common stock}}{\text{Net income}}$	A low ratio suggests that the company is retaining its earnings for investment in future growth.

EARNINGS PERFORMANCE

Another way to measure corporate performance is through profitability. A widely used ratio that measures profitability from the common stockholders' viewpoint is **return on common stockholders' equity**. This ratio shows how many dollars of net income were earned for each dollar invested by common stockholders. It is computed by dividing net income available to common stockholders (Net income − Preferred stock dividends) by average common stockholders' equity. From the additional information presented below, **Nike's** return on common stockholders' equity ratios are calculated for 2001 and 2000 in Illustration 11-20.

(in thousands)	2001	2000	1999
Net income	$ 589,700	$ 579,100	$ 451,400
Preferred stock dividends	30	30	30
Common stockholders' equity	3,494,500	3,136,000	3,334,600

Illustration 11-20 Nike's return on common stockholders' equity

Return on Common Stockholders' Equity Ratio	$=\dfrac{\text{Net Income − Preferred Stock Dividends}}{\text{Average Common Stockholders' Equity}}$

($ in thousands)	2001	2000
Return on Common Stockholders' Equity Ratio	$\dfrac{\$589,700 - \$30}{(\$3,494,500 + \$3,136,000)/2} = 17.8\%$	$\dfrac{\$579,100 - \$30}{(\$3,136,000 + \$3,334,600)/2} = 17.9\%$

From 2000 to 2001, Nike's return on common shareholders' equity remained steady. As a company grows larger, it becomes increasingly hard to sustain a high return. In Nike's case, since many believe the U.S. market for expensive sports shoes is saturated, it will need to grow either along new product lines, such as hiking shoes and golf equipment, or in new markets, such as Europe and Asia.

DEBT VERSUS EQUITY DECISION

To obtain large amounts of long-term capital, corporate managers must decide whether to issue bonds or to sell common stock. Bonds have three primary advantages relative to common stock, as shown in Illustration 11-21.

Illustration 11-21
Advantages of bond financing over common stock

Bond Financing	Advantages
	1. **Stockholder control is not affected.** Bondholders do not have voting rights, so current owners (stockholders) retain full control of the company.
	2. **Tax savings result.** Bond interest is deductible for tax purposes; dividends on stock are not.
	3. **Return on common stockholders' equity may be higher.** Although bond interest expense reduces net income, return on common stockholders' equity often is higher under bond financing because no additional shares of common stock are issued.

How does the debt versus equity decision affect the return on common stockholders' equity ratio? Illustration 11-22 shows that the return on common stockholders' equity is affected by the return on assets ratio and the amount of leverage a company uses—that is, by the company's reliance on debt (often measured by the debt to total assets ratio). If a company wants to increase its return on common stockholders' equity, it can either increase its return on assets or increase its reliance on debt financing.

Illustration 11-22
Components of the return on common stockholders' equity

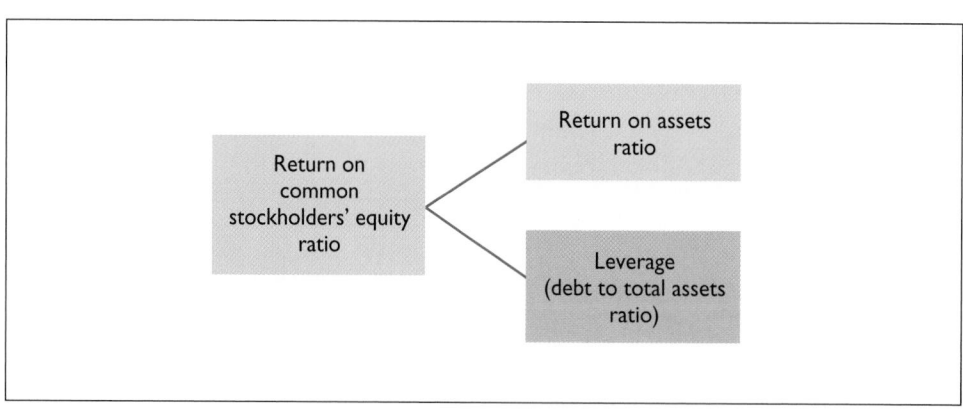

To illustrate the potential effect of debt financing on the return on common stockholders' equity, assume that Microsystems Inc. is considering two plans for financing the construction of a new $5 million plant: Plan A involves issuing

200,000 shares of common stock at the current market price of $25 per share. Plan B involves issuing $5 million of 12% bonds at face value. Income before interest and taxes on the new plant will be $1.5 million; income taxes are expected to be 30%. Microsystems currently has 100,000 shares of common stock outstanding issued at $25 per share. The alternative effects on the return on common stockholders' equity are shown in Illustration 11-23.

	Plan A: Issue stock	Plan B: Issue bonds
Income before interest and taxes	$1,500,000	$1,500,000
Interest (12% × $5,000,000)	—	600,000
Income before income taxes	1,500,000	900,000
Income tax expense (30%)	450,000	270,000
Net income	$1,050,000	$ 630,000
Common stockholders' equity	$7,500,000	$2,500,000
Return on common stockholders' equity	14%	25.2%

Illustration 11-23
Effects on return on common stockholders' equity of issuing debt

Note that with long-term debt financing (bonds), net income is $420,000 ($1,050,000 − $630,000) less. However, the return on common stockholders' equity increases from 14% to 25.2% with the use of debt financing because there is less common stockholders' equity to spread the income across. **In general, as long as the return on assets rate exceeds the rate paid on debt, the return on common stockholders' equity will be increased by the use of debt.**

After seeing this illustration, one might ask, why don't companies rely almost exclusively on debt financing, rather than equity? Debt has one major disadvantage: **The company locks in fixed payments that must be made in good times and bad. Interest must be paid on a periodic basis, and the principal (face value) of the bonds must be paid at maturity.** A company with fluctuating earnings and a relatively weak cash position may experience great difficulty in meeting interest requirements in periods of low earnings. In the extreme, this can result in bankruptcy. With common stock financing, on the other hand, the company can decide to pay low (or no) dividends if earnings are low.

DECISION TOOLKIT

Decision Checkpoints	Info Needed for Decision	Tool to Use for Decision	How to Evaluate Results
What is the company's return on common stockholders' investment?	Earnings available to common stockholders and average common stockholders' equity	Return on common stockholders' equity ratio = $\dfrac{\text{Net income} - \text{Preferred stock dividends}}{\text{Average common stockholders' equity}}$	A high measure suggests strong earnings performance from common stockholders' perspective.

BEFORE YOU GO ON . . .

▶ **Review It**

1. What measure can be used to evaluate a company's dividend record, and how is it calculated?
2. What factors affect the return on common stockholders' equity ratio?
3. What are the advantages and disadvantages of debt and equity financing?

☑ THE NAVIGATOR

Using the Decision Toolkit

Reebok remains one of Nike's fiercest competitors. In such a competitive and rapidly changing environment, one wrong step can spell financial disaster. After bottoming out at the end of 1999, Reebok's stock has rebounded sharply.

Instructions

The following facts are available for **Reebok**. Using this information, evaluate its (1) dividend record and (2) earnings performance, and contrast them with those for **Nike** for 2000 and 2001. Nike's P-E ratio at the end of 2001 was 18.5.

(in thousands except per share data)	2001	2000	1999
Dividends declared	0	0	0
Dividends declared per share	0	0	0
Net income	$102,726	$ 80,878	$ 11,045
Preferred stock dividends	0	0	0
Shares outstanding at end of year	59,039	57,492	55,225
Stock price at end of year	$ 26.50	$ 27.34	$ 8.19
Common stockholders' equity	$719,938	$607,863	$528,816

Solution

1. *Dividend record:* A measure to evaluate dividend record is the payout ratio. For Reebok, this measure in 2001 and 2000 is calculated as shown below.

	2001	**2000**
Payout ratio	$\dfrac{\$0}{\$102,726} = 0\%$	$\dfrac{\$0}{\$80,878} = 0\%$

Nike's payout ratio remained nearly constant at 22%, while Reebok paid no dividends.

2. *Earnings performance:* There are many measures of earnings performance. Some of those presented thus far in the book were earnings per share (page 65), the price-earnings ratio (page 65), and the return on common stockholders' equity ratio (this chapter). These measures for Reebok in 2001 and 2000 are calculated as shown here.

	2001	**2000**
Earnings per share	$\dfrac{\$102,726 - 0}{(59,039 + 57,492)/2} = \$1.76$	$\dfrac{\$80,878 - 0}{(57,492 + 55,225)/2} = \$1.44$
Price-earnings ratio	$\dfrac{\$26.50}{\$1.76} = 15.1$	$\dfrac{\$27.34}{\$1.44} = 19.0$
Return on common stockholders' equity ratio	$\dfrac{\$102,726 - 0}{(\$719,938 + \$607,863)/2} = 15.5\%$	$\dfrac{\$80,878 - 0}{(\$607,863 + \$528,816)/2} = 14.2\%$

From 2000 to 2001 Reebok's earnings increased on both a total and per share basis. Reebok's price-earnings ratio decreased, perhaps hinting that investors believe earnings will decline somewhat in coming years. Compared to Nike's P-E ratio of 18.5, Reebok seems to be slightly lower-priced; that is, Reebok's shareholders are paying less per dollar of earnings than are Nike's. This could be an indication that investors think Nike's future is brighter.

Reebok's return on common stockholders' equity increased from 14.2% to 15.5%. While this represents a healthy increase, it is still less than Nike's 17.8%.

Summary of Study Objectives

1 *Identify and discuss the major characteristics of a corporation.* The major characteristics of a corporation are separate legal existence, limited liability of stockholders, transferable ownership rights, ability to acquire capital, continuous life, corporation management, government regulations, and additional taxes.

2 *Record the issuance of common stock.* When the issuance of common stock for cash is recorded, the par value of the shares is credited to Common Stock; the portion of the proceeds that is above par value is recorded in a separate paid-in capital account. When no-par common stock has a stated value, the entries are similar to those for par value stock. When no-par common stock does not have a stated value, the entire proceeds from the issue become legal capital and are credited to Common Stock.

3 *Explain the accounting for the purchase of treasury stock.* The cost method is generally used in accounting for treasury stock. Under this approach, Treasury Stock is debited at the price paid to reacquire the shares.

4 *Differentiate preferred stock from common stock.* Preferred stock has contractual provisions that give it priority over common stock in certain areas. Typically, preferred stockholders have a preference as to (1) dividends and (2) assets in the event of liquidation. However, they often do not have voting rights.

5 *Prepare the entries for cash dividends and understand the effect of stock dividends and stock splits.* Entries for dividends are required at the declaration date and the payment date. At the declaration date the entries for a cash dividend are: debit Retained Earnings and credit Dividends Payable. The effects

of stock dividends and splits: Small *stock dividends* transfer an amount equal to the fair market value of the shares issued from retained earnings to the paid-in capital accounts. *Stock splits* reduce the par value per share of the common stock while increasing the number of shares so that total par value remains the same.

6 *Identify the items that affect retained earnings.* Additions to retained earnings consist of net income. Deductions consist of net loss and cash and stock dividends. In some instances, portions of retained earnings are restricted, making that portion unavailable for the payment of dividends.

7 *Prepare a comprehensive stockholders' equity section.* In the stockholders' equity section of the balance sheet, paid-in capital and retained earnings are reported, and specific sources of paid-in capital are identified. Within paid-in capital, two classifications are shown: capital stock and additional paid-in capital. If a corporation has treasury stock, the cost of treasury stock is deducted from total paid-in capital and retained earnings to determine total stockholders' equity.

8 *Evaluate a corporation's dividend and earnings performance from a stockholder's perspective.* A company's dividend record can be evaluated by looking at what percentage of net income it chooses to pay out in dividends, as measured by the dividend payout ratio (dividends divided by net income). Earnings performance is measured with the return on common stockholders' equity ratio (income available to common shareholders divided by average common shareholders' equity).

*right of first refusal —
if selling corp can buy
back before you sell to
someone else — usually
smaller, privately owned*

DECISION TOOLKIT—A SUMMARY

Decision Checkpoints	Info Needed for Decision	Tool to Use for Decision	How to Evaluate Results
Should the company incorporate?	Capital needs, growth expectations, type of business, tax status	Corporations have limited liability, easier capital raising ability, and professional managers; but they suffer from additional taxes, government regulations, and separation of ownership from management.	Must carefully weigh the costs and benefits in light of the particular circumstances.
What portion of its earnings does the company pay out in dividends?	Net income and total cash dividends paid on common stock	$\text{Payout ratio} = \dfrac{\text{Cash dividends declared on common stock}}{\text{Net income}}$	A low ratio suggests that the company is retaining its earnings for investment in future growth.
What is the company's return on common stockholders' investment?	Earnings available to common stockholders and average common stockholders' equity	$\text{Return on common stockholders' equity ratio} = \dfrac{\text{Net income} - \text{Preferred stock dividends}}{\text{Average common stockholders' equity}}$	A high measure suggests strong earnings performance from common stockholders' perspective.

APPENDIX
ENTRIES FOR STOCK DIVIDENDS

STUDY OBJECTIVE
9
Prepare entries for stock dividends.

To illustrate the accounting for stock dividends, assume that Medland Corporation has a balance of $300,000 in retained earnings and declares a 10% stock dividend on its 50,000 shares of $10 par value common stock. The current fair market value of its stock is $15 per share. The number of shares to be issued is 5,000 (10% × 50,000), and the total amount to be debited to Retained Earnings is $75,000 (5,000 × $15). The entry to record this transaction at the declaration date is:

A	=	L	+	SE
				−75,000 Div
				+50,000 CS
				+25,000 CS

Cash Flows
no effect

Retained Earnings (or Stock Dividends Declared)	75,000	
Common Stock Dividends Distributable		50,000
Paid-in Capital in Excess of Par Value		25,000
(To record declaration of 10% stock dividend)		

Note that at the declaration date Retained Earnings is decreased (debited) for the fair market value of the stock issued; Common Stock Dividends Distributable is increased (credited) for the par value of the dividend shares (5,000 × $10); and the excess over par (5,000 × $5) is credited to an additional paid-in capital account.

Common Stock Dividends Distributable is a stockholders' equity account; it is not a liability because assets will not be used to pay the dividend. If a balance sheet is prepared before the dividend shares are issued, the distributable account is reported in paid-in capital as an addition to common stock issued, as shown in Illustration 11A-1.

MEDLAND CORPORATION		
Balance Sheet (partial)		
Paid-in capital		
Common stock	$500,000	
Common stock dividends distributable	**50,000**	$550,000

Illustration 11A-1
Statement presentation of common stock dividends distributable

When the dividend shares are issued, Common Stock Dividends Distributable is decreased and Common Stock is increased as follows.

Helpful Hint Note that the dividend account title is *distributable*, not *payable*.

Common Stock Dividends Distributable	50,000	
Common Stock		50,000
(To record issuance of 5,000 shares in a stock dividend)		

A = L + SE
        −50,000 CS
        +50,000 CS

Cash Flows
no effect

Summary of Study Objective for Appendix

9 *Prepare entries for stock dividends.* To record the declaration of a small stock dividend (less than 20%), reduce Retained Earnings for an amount equal to the fair value of the shares issued. Record a credit to a temporary stockholders' equity account—Common Stock Dividends Distributable—for the par value of the shares; the balance is credited to Paid-in Capital in Excess of Par Value. When the shares are issued, debit Common Stock Dividends Distributable and credit Common Stock.

Glossary

Authorized stock The amount of stock that a corporation is authorized to sell as indicated in its charter. (p. 533)

Cash dividend A pro rata distribution of cash to stockholders. (p. 541)

Corporation A company organized as a separate legal entity, with most of the rights and privileges of a person. Evidence of ownership is shares of stock. (p. 527)

Cumulative dividend A feature of preferred stock entitling the stockholder to receive current and unpaid prior-year dividends before common stockholders receive any dividends. (p. 539)

Declaration date The date the board of directors formally declares the dividend and announces it to stockholders. (p. 541)

Deficit A debit balance in retained earnings. (p. 547)

Dividend A distribution by a corporation to its stockholders on a pro rata (equal) basis. (p. 540)

Dividends in arrears Preferred dividends that were supposed to be declared but were not declared during a given period. (p. 539)

Legal capital The amount per share of stock that must be retained in the business for the protection of corporate creditors. (p. 534)

No-par value stock Capital stock that has not been assigned a value in the corporate charter. (p. 534)

Outstanding stock Capital stock that has been issued and is being held by stockholders. (p. 538)

Paid-in capital The amount paid in to the corporation by stockholders in exchange for shares of ownership. (p. 534)

Par value stock Capital stock that has been assigned a value per share in the corporate charter. (p. 534)

Payment date The date dividend checks are mailed to stockholders. (p. 542)

Payout ratio A measure of the percentage of earnings distributed in the form of cash dividends to common stockholders. (p. 550)

Preferred stock Capital stock that has contractual preferences over common stock in certain areas. (p. 539)

Privately held corporation A corporation that has only a few stockholders and whose stock is not available for sale to the general public. (p. 527)

Publicly held corporation A corporation that may have thousands of stockholders and whose stock is regularly traded on a national securities market. (p. 527)

Record date The date when ownership of outstanding shares is determined for dividend purposes. (p. 542)

Retained earnings   Net income that is retained in the business. (p. 546)

Retained earnings restrictions   Circumstances that make a portion of retained earnings currently unavailable for dividends. (p. 547)

Return on common stockholders' equity ratio   A measure of profitability from the stockholders' point of view; computed by dividing net income minus preferred stock dividends by average common stockholders' equity. (p. 551)

Stated value   The amount per share assigned by the board of directors to no-par stock. (p. 534)

Stock dividend   A pro rata distribution of the corporation's own stock to stockholders. (p. 543)

Stock split   The issuance of additional shares of stock to stockholders accompanied by a reduction in the par or stated value per share. (p. 544)

Treasury stock   A corporation's own stock that has been issued, fully paid for, and reacquired by the corporation but not retired. (p. 536)

Demonstration Problem

Peachtree

www.wiley.com/college/kimmel

Rolman Corporation is authorized to issue 1,000,000 shares of $5 par value common stock. In its first year the company has the following stock transactions.

Jan. 10   Issued 400,000 shares of stock at $8 per share.
Sept. 1   Purchased 10,000 shares of common stock for the treasury at $9 per share.
Dec. 24   Declared a cash dividend of 10 cents per share.

Instructions

(a) Journalize the transactions.
(b) Prepare the stockholders' equity section of the balance sheet assuming the company had retained earnings of $150,600 at December 31.

Action Plan

• When common stock has a par value, credit Common Stock for par value and Paid-in Capital in Excess of Par Value for the amount above par value.

• Debit the Treasury Stock account at cost.

Solution to Demonstration Problem

(a)	Jan. 10	Cash	3,200,000	
		Common Stock		2,000,000
		Paid-in Capital in Excess of Par Value		1,200,000
		(To record issuance of 400,000 shares of $5 par value stock)		
	Sept. 1	Treasury Stock	90,000	
		Cash		90,000
		(To record purchase of 10,000 shares of treasury stock at cost)		
	Dec. 24	Retained Earnings	39,000	
		Dividends Payable		39,000
		(To record declaration of 10 cents per share cash dividend)		

(b)

ROLMAN CORPORATION
Balance Sheet (partial)

Stockholders' equity		
Paid-in capital		
Capital stock		
Common stock, $5 par value, 1,000,000 shares authorized, 400,000 shares issued, 390,000 outstanding	$2,000,000	
Additional paid-in capital in excess of par value	1,200,000	
Total paid-in capital		3,200,000
Retained earnings		150,600
Total paid-in capital and retained earnings		3,350,600
Less: Treasury stock (10,000 shares)		90,000
Total stockholders' equity		$3,260,600

THE NAVIGATOR

Note: All Questions, Exercises, and Problems marked with an asterisk relate to material in the appendix to the chapter.

Self-Study Questions

Self-Study/Self-Test

Answers are at the end of the chapter.

(SO 1) **1.** Which of these is *not* a major advantage of a corporation?
(a) Separate legal existence.
(b) Continuous life.
(c) Government regulations.
(d) Transferable ownership rights.

(SO 1) **2.** A major disadvantage of a corporation is:
(a) limited liability of stockholders.
(b) additional taxes.
(c) transferable ownership rights.
(d) None of the above.

(SO 1) **3.** Which of these statements is *false?*
(a) Ownership of common stock gives the owner a voting right.
(b) The stockholders' equity section begins with paid-in capital.
(c) The authorization of capital stock does not result in a formal accounting entry.
(d) Legal capital is intended to protect stockholders.

(SO 2) **4.** ABC Corp. issues 1,000 shares of $10 par value common stock at $12 per share. When the transaction is recorded, credits are made to:
(a) Common Stock $10,000 and Paid-in Capital in Excess of Stated Value $2,000.
(b) Common Stock $12,000.
(c) Common Stock $10,000 and Paid-in Capital in Excess of Par Value $2,000.
(d) Common Stock $10,000 and Retained Earnings $2,000.

(SO 4) **5.** Preferred stock may have which of the following features?
(a) dividend preference.
(b) preference to assets in the event of liquidation.
(c) cumulative dividends.
(d) all of the above.

6. Entries for cash dividends are required on the: (SO 5)
(a) declaration date and the record date.
(b) record date and the payment date.
(c) declaration date, record date, and payment date.
(d) declaration date and the payment date.

7. Which of these statements about stock divi- (SO 5) dends is *true?*
(a) Stock dividends reduce a company's cash balance.
(b) A stock dividend has no effect on total stockholders' equity.
(c) A stock dividend decreases total stockholders' equity.
(d) A stock dividend ordinarily will increase total stockholders' equity.

8. In the stockholders' equity section, the cost of (SO 7) treasury stock is deducted from:
(a) total paid-in capital and retained earnings.
(b) retained earnings.
(c) total stockholders' equity.
(d) common stock in paid-in capital.

9. The return on stockholders' equity is (SO 8) increased by all of the following, except:
(a) an increase in the return on assets ratio.
(b) an increase in the use of debt financing.
(c) an increase in the company's stock price.
(d) an increase in the company's net income.

10. Willie is nearing retirement and (SO 8) would like to invest in a stock that will provide a good steady income supply. Willie should choose a stock with a:
(a) high current ratio.
(b) high dividend payout.
(c) high earnings per share.
(d) high price-earnings ratio.

✓ THE NAVIGATOR

Questions

1. Ralph, a student, asks your help in understanding some characteristics of a corporation. Explain each of these to Ralph.
(a) Separate legal existence.
(b) Limited liability of stockholders.
(c) Transferable ownership rights.

2. (a) Your friend T. R. Cedras cannot understand how the characteristic of corporate management is both an advantage and a disadvantage. Clarify this problem for T. R.
(b) Identify and explain two other disadvantages of a corporation.

3. Maggie Jones believes a corporation must be incorporated in the state in which its headquarters office is located. Is Maggie correct? Explain.

4. What are the basic ownership rights of common stockholders in the absence of restrictive provisions?

5. A corporation has been defined as an entity separate and distinct from its owners. In what ways is a corporation a separate legal entity?

6. What are the two principal components of stockholders' equity?

7. The corporate charter of Shelby Corporation allows the issuance of a maximum of 100,000 shares of common stock. During its first 2 years of operation, Shelby sold 60,000 shares to shareholders and reacquired 7,000 of these shares. After these transactions, how many shares are authorized, issued, and outstanding?

8. Which is the better investment—common stock with a par value of $5 per share or common stock with a par value of $20 per share?

9. For what reasons might a company like **IBM** repurchase some of its stock (treasury stock)?

10. Ogden, Inc. purchases 1,000 shares of its own previously issued $5 par common stock for $11,000. Assuming the shares are held in the treasury, what effect does this transaction have on (a) net income, (b) total assets, (c) total paid-in capital, and (d) total stockholders' equity?

11. (a) What are the principal differences between common stock and preferred stock?
    (b) Preferred stock may be cumulative. Discuss this feature.
    (c) How are dividends in arrears presented in the financial statements?

12. Identify the events that result in credits and debits to retained earnings.

13. Indicate how each of these accounts should be classified in the stockholders' equity section of the balance sheet.
    (a) Common stock.
    (b) Paid-in capital in excess of par value.
    (c) Retained earnings.
    (d) Treasury stock.
    (e) Paid-in capital in excess of stated value.
    (f) Preferred stock.

14. What three conditions must be met before a cash dividend is paid?

15. Three dates associated with Galena Company's cash dividend are May 1, May 15, and May 31. Discuss the significance of each date and give the entry at each date.

16. Contrast the effects of a cash dividend and a stock dividend on a corporation's balance sheet.

17. Jane Apple asks, "Since stock dividends don't change anything, why declare them?" What is your answer to Jane?

18. Marge Corporation has 10,000 shares of $15 par value common stock outstanding when it announces a 2-for-1 split. Before the split, the stock had a market price of $140 per share. After the split, how many shares of stock will be outstanding, and what will be the approximate market price per share?

19. The board of directors is considering a stock split or a stock dividend. They understand that total stockholders' equity will remain the same under either action. However, they are not sure of the different effects of the two actions on other aspects of stockholders' equity. Explain the differences to the directors.

20. (a) What is the purpose of a retained earnings restriction?
    (b) Identify the possible causes of retained earnings restrictions.

21. WAT Inc.'s common stock has a par value of $1 and a current market value of $15. Explain why these amounts are different.

22. ◎━━━◉ What is the formula for the payout ratio? What does it indicate?

23. ◎━━━◉ Explain the circumstances under which debt financing will increase the return on stockholders' equity ratio.

24. Under what circumstances will the return on assets ratio and the return on common stockholders' equity ratio be equal?

25. Sherry Corp has a return on assets ratio of 12%. It plans to issue bonds at 8% and use the cash to retire debt. What effect will this have on its debt to total assets ratio and on its return on common stockholders' equity?

Brief Exercises

Cite advantages and disadvantages of a corporation.
(SO 1)

BE11-1 Patty Reeves is planning to start a business. Identify for Patty the advantages and disadvantages of the corporate form of business organization.

Journalize issuance of par value common stock.
(SO 2)

BE11-2 On May 10 Chalmers Corporation issues 1,000 shares of $10 par value common stock for cash at $13 per share. Journalize the issuance of the stock.

Journalize issuance of no-par common stock.
(SO 2)

BE11-3 On June 1 Mowen Inc. issues 2,000 shares of no-par common stock at a cash price of $9 per share. Journalize the issuance of the shares.

Journalize issuance of preferred stock.
(SO 4)

BE11-4 Smithers Inc. issues 5,000 shares of $100 par value preferred stock for cash at $117 per share. Journalize the issuance of the preferred stock.

Prepare entries for a cash dividend.
(SO 5)

BE11-5 Broden Corporation has 10,000 shares of common stock outstanding. It declares a $1 per share cash dividend on November 1 to stockholders of record on December

1. The dividend is paid on December 31. Prepare the entries on the appropriate dates to record the declaration and payment of the cash dividend.

BE11-6 The stockholders' equity section of Falcon Corporation's balance sheet consists of common stock ($10 par) $1,000,000 and retained earnings $400,000. A 10% stock dividend (10,000 shares) is declared when the market value per share is $15. Show the before and after effects of the dividend on (a) the components of stockholders' equity and (b) the shares outstanding.

Show before and after effects of a stock dividend.
(SO 5)

BE11-7 Burns Corporation has these accounts at December 31: Common Stock, $10 par, 5,000 shares issued, $50,000; Paid-in Capital in Excess of Par Value $10,000; Retained Earnings $32,000; and Treasury Stock—Common, 500 shares, $7,000. Prepare the stockholders' equity section of the balance sheet.

Prepare a stockholders' equity section.
(SO 7)

BE11-8 Paul Dixon, president of Dixon Corporation, believes that it is a good practice for a company to maintain a constant payout of dividends relative to its earnings. Last year net income was $600,000, and the corporation paid $150,000 in dividends. This year, due to some unusual circumstances, the corporation had income of $2,000,000. Paul expects next year's net income to be about $700,000. What was Dixon Corporation's payout ratio last year? If it is to maintain the same payout ratio, what amount of dividends would it pay this year? Is this necessarily a good idea—that is, what are the pros and cons of maintaining a constant payout ratio in this scenario?

Evaluate a company's dividend record.
(SO 8)

BE11-9 SUPERVALU, one of the largest grocery retailers in the United States, is headquartered in Minneapolis. The following financial information (in millions) was taken from the company's 2001 annual report. Net sales $23,194; net income $82; beginning stockholders' equity $1,793; ending stockholders' equity $1,821. Compute the return on stockholders' equity ratio.

Calculate the return on stockholders' equity.
(SO 8)

*****BE11-10** Crawford Corporation has 100,000 shares of $10 par value common stock outstanding. It declares a 10% stock dividend on December 1 when the market value per share is $14. The dividend shares are issued on December 31. Prepare the entries for the declaration and distribution of the stock dividend.

Prepare entries for a stock dividend.
(SO 9)

Exercises

E11-1 During its first year of operations, Dean Corporation had these transactions pertaining to its common stock.

Journalize issuance of common stock.
(SO 2)

> Jan. 10 Issued 90,000 shares for cash at $5 per share.
> July 1 Issued 50,000 shares for cash at $8 per share.

Instructions
(a) Journalize the transactions, assuming that the common stock has a par value of $5 per share.
(b) Journalize the transactions, assuming that the common stock is no-par with a stated value of $1 per share.

E11-2 Deppe Co. had these transactions during the current period.

Journalize issuance of common stock and preferred stock and purchase of treasury stock.
(SO 2, 3, 4)

June 12 Issued 60,000 shares of $1 par value common stock for cash of $300,000.
July 11 Issued 1,000 shares of $100 par value preferred stock for cash at $110 per share.
Nov. 28 Purchased 2,000 shares of treasury stock for $120,000.

Instructions
Prepare the journal entries for the transactions.

E11-3 Homer Corporation is authorized to issue both preferred and common stock. The par value of the preferred is $50. During the first year of operations, the company had the following events and transactions pertaining to its preferred stock.

Journalize preferred stock transactions and indicate statement presentation.
(SO 4, 7)

> Feb. 1 Issued 30,000 shares for cash at $51 per share.
> July 1 Issued 40,000 shares for cash at $56 per share.

Instructions
(a) Journalize the transactions.
(b) Post to the stockholders' equity accounts. (Use T accounts.)
(c) Discuss the statement presentation of the accounts.

Answer questions about stockholders' equity section.
(SO 2, 3, 4, 7)

E11-4 The stockholders' equity section of Camp Corporation's balance sheet at December 31 is presented here.

CAMP CORPORATION
Balance Sheet (partial)

Stockholders' equity	
Paid-in capital	
Preferred stock, cumulative, 10,000 shares authorized,	
6,000 shares issued and outstanding	$ 900,000
Common stock, no par, 750,000 shares authorized,	
600,000 shares issued	1,800,000
Total paid-in capital	2,700,000
Retained earnings	1,158,000
Total paid-in capital and retained earnings	3,858,000
Less: Treasury stock (10,000 common shares)	(52,000)
Total stockholders' equity	$3,806,000

Instructions
From a review of the stockholders' equity section, answer the following questions.
(a) How many shares of common stock are outstanding?
(b) Assuming there is a stated value, what is the stated value of the common stock?
(c) What is the par value of the preferred stock?
(d) If the annual dividend on preferred stock is $45,000, what is the dividend rate on preferred stock?
(e) If dividends of $90,000 were in arrears on preferred stock, what would be the balance reported for retained earnings?

Prepare correct entries for capital stock transactions.
(SO 2, 3, 4)

E11-5 Springfield Corporation recently hired a new accountant with extensive experience in accounting for partnerships. Because of the pressure of the new job, the accountant was unable to review what he had learned earlier about corporation accounting. During the first month, he made the following entries for the corporation's capital stock.

May	2	Cash	120,000	
		Capital Stock		120,000
		(Issued 10,000 shares of $5 par value		
		common stock at $12 per share)		
	10	Cash	550,000	
		Capital Stock		550,000
		(Issued 10,000 shares of $50 par value		
		preferred stock at $55 per share)		
	15	Capital Stock	12,000	
		Cash		12,000
		(Purchased 1,000 shares of common		
		stock for the treasury at $12 per share)		

Instructions
On the basis of the explanation for each entry, prepare the entries that should have been made for the capital stock transactions.

Journalize cash dividends and indicate statement presentation.
(SO 5)

E11-6 On January 1 Dodd Corporation had 75,000 shares of no-par common stock issued and outstanding. The stock has a stated value of $5 per share. During the year, the following transactions occurred.

Apr. 1 Issued 5,000 additional shares of common stock for $11 per share.
June 15 Declared a cash dividend of $1.50 per share to stockholders of record on June 30.
July 10 Paid the $1.50 cash dividend.
Dec. 1 Issued 3,000 additional shares of common stock for $13 per share.
15 Declared a cash dividend on outstanding shares of $1.70 per share to stockholders of record on December 31.

Instructions
(a) Prepare the entries, if any, on each of the three dates that involved dividends.
(b) How are dividends and dividends payable reported in the financial statements prepared at December 31?

E11-7 On October 31 the stockholders' equity section of Capital Company's balance sheet consists of common stock $600,000 and retained earnings $400,000. Capital is considering the following two courses of action: (1) declaring a 5% stock dividend on the 60,000 $10 par value shares outstanding or (2) effecting a 2-for-1 stock split that will reduce par value to $5 per share. The current market price is $15 per share.

Compare effects of a stock dividend and a stock split.
(SO 5)

Instructions
Prepare a tabular summary of the effects of the alternative actions on the company's stockholders' equity, outstanding shares, and book value per share. Use these column headings: **Before Action**, **After Stock Dividend**, and **After Stock Split**.

E11-8 **Wells Fargo & Company**, headquartered in San Francisco, is one of the nation's largest financial institutions. It reported the following selected accounts (in millions) as of December 31, 2001.

Prepare a stockholders' equity section.
(SO 7)

Retained earnings	$16,757
Preferred stock, adjustable-rate, series B	64
Common stock—$1⅔ par value, authorized 6,000,000,000 shares; issued 1,736,381,025 shares	2,894
Treasury stock—40,886,028 shares	(1,937)
Additional paid-in capital—common stock	9,436

Instructions
Prepare the stockholders' equity section of the balance sheet for Wells Fargo as of December 31, 2001.

E11-9 The following stockholders' equity accounts, arranged alphabetically, are in the ledger of Dill Corporation at December 31, 2005.

Prepare a stockholders' equity section.
(SO 7)

Common Stock ($5 stated value)	$1,500,000
Paid-in Capital in Excess of Par Value—Preferred Stock	280,000
Paid-in Capital in Excess of Stated Value—Common Stock	900,000
Preferred Stock (8%, $100 par, noncumulative)	500,000
Retained Earnings	1,134,000
Treasury Stock—Common (6,000 shares)	78,000

Instructions
Prepare the stockholders' equity section of the balance sheet at December 31, 2005.

E11-10 The following accounts appear in the ledger of Clown Inc. after the books are closed at December 31, 2005.

Prepare a stockholders' equity section.
(SO 7)

Common Stock (no-par, $1 stated value, 400,000 shares authorized, 200,000 shares issued)	$ 200,000
Paid-in Capital in Excess of Stated Value—Common Stock	1,200,000
Preferred Stock ($5 par value, 8%, 40,000 shares authorized, 30,000 shares issued)	150,000
Retained Earnings	900,000
Treasury Stock (10,000 common shares)	64,000
Paid-in Capital in Excess of Par Value—Preferred Stock	344,000

Instructions

Prepare the stockholders' equity section at December 31, assuming $100,000 of retained earnings is restricted for plant expansion. (Use Note R.)

Calculate ratios to evaluate dividend and earnings performance.
(SO 8)

E11-11 The following financial information is available for **Sara Lee Corporation**.

(in millions)	2001	2000
Average common stockholders' equity	$1,178	$1,250
Dividends declared for common stockholders	486	485
Dividends declared for preferred stockholders	0	0
Net income	2,266	1,222

Instructions

Calculate the payout ratio and return on common stockholders' equity ratio for 2001 and 2000. Comment on your findings.

Calculate ratios to evaluate dividend and earnings performance.
(SO 8)

E11-12 The following financial information is available for **Walgreen Company**.

(in millions)	2001	2000
Average common stockholders' equity	$4,720.6	$3,859.2
Dividends declared for common stockholders	142.5	136.1
Dividends declared for preferred stockholders	0	0
Net income	885.6	776.9

Instructions

Calculate the payout ratio and return on common stockholders' equity ratio for 2001 and 2000.

Calculate ratios to evaluate profitability and solvency.
(SO 8)

E11-13 Central Corporation decided to issue common stock and used the $400,000 proceeds to retire all of its outstanding bonds on January 1, 2005. The following information is available for the company for 2004 and 2005.

	2005	2004
Net income	$ 200,000	$ 150,000
Average stockholders' equity	1,100,000	700,000
Total assets	1,200,000	1,200,000
Current liabilities	100,000	100,000
Total liabilities	100,000	500,000

Instructions

(a) Compute the return on stockholder's equity ratio for both years.
(b) Explain how it is possible that net income increased, but the return on common stockholders' equity decreased.
(c) Compute the debt to total assets ratio for both years, and comment on the implications of this change in the company's solvency.

Journalize stock dividends.
(SO 5, 9)

*E11-14 On January 1, 2005, Burger Corporation had $1,500,000 of common stock outstanding that was issued at par and retained earnings of $750,000. The company issued 60,000 shares of common stock at par on July 1 and earned net income of $400,000 for the year.

Instructions

Journalize the declaration of a 10% stock dividend on December 10, 2005, for the following two independent assumptions.

(a) Par value is $10 and market value is $12.
(b) Par value is $5 and market value is $18.

Problems: Set A

P11-1A Bart Corporation was organized on January 1, 2005. It is authorized to issue 10,000 shares of 8%, $100 par value preferred stock and 500,000 shares of no-par common stock with a stated value of $2 per share. The following stock transactions were completed during the first year.

Journalize stock transactions, post, and prepare paid-in capital section.
(SO 2, 4, 7)

Jan.	10	Issued 80,000 shares of common stock for cash at $3 per share.
Mar.	1	Issued 5,000 shares of preferred stock for cash at $102 per share.
May	1	Issued 80,000 shares of common stock for cash at $4 per share.
Sept.	1	Issued 10,000 shares of common stock for cash at $5 per share.
Nov.	1	Issued 2,000 shares of preferred stock for cash at $105 per share.

Instructions
(a) Journalize the transactions.
(b) Post to the stockholders' equity accounts. (Use T accounts.)
(c) Prepare the paid-in capital section of stockholders' equity at December 31, 2005.

(c) Tot. paid-in capital
$1,330,000

P11-2A The stockholders' equity accounts of Ewers Corporation on January 1, 2005, were as follows.

Journalize transactions, post, and prepare a stockholders' equity section; calculate ratios.
(SO 2, 3, 5, 7, 8)

Preferred Stock (12%, $50 par cumulative, 10,000 shares authorized)	$ 400,000
Common Stock ($1 stated value, 2,000,000 shares authorized)	1,000,000
Paid-in Capital in Excess of Par Value—Preferred Stock	80,000
Paid-in Capital in Excess of Stated Value—Common Stock	1,400,000
Retained Earnings	1,716,000
Treasury Stock—Common (10,000 shares)	40,000

During 2005 the corporation had these transactions and events pertaining to its stockholders' equity.

Feb.	1	Issued 15,000 shares of common stock for $90,000.
Nov.	10	Purchased 14,000 shares of common stock for the treasury at a cost of $18,000.
Nov.	15	Declared a 12% cash dividend on preferred stock, payable December 15.
Dec.	1	Declared a $0.30 per share cash dividend to stockholders of record on December 15, payable December 31, 2005.
	15	Paid the dividend declared on November 15.
	31	Determined that net income for the year was $408,000. The market price of the common stock on this date was $9 per share. Paid the dividend declared on December 1.

Instructions
(a) Journalize the transactions. (Include entries to close net income to Retained Earnings.)
(b) Enter the beginning balances in the accounts, and post the journal entries to the stockholders' equity accounts. (Use T accounts.)
(c) Prepare the stockholders' equity section of the balance sheet at December 31, 2005.
(d) Calculate the payout ratio, earnings per share, price-earnings ratio, and return on common stockholders' equity ratio. (*Hint:* Use the common shares outstanding on January 1 and December 31 to determine average shares outstanding.)

(c) Tot. paid-in capital
$2,970,000

P11-3A On December 31, 2004, Cow Company had 1,000,000 shares of $1 par common stock issued and outstanding. The stockholders' equity accounts at December 31, 2004, had the balances listed here.

Prepare a stockholders' equity section.
(SO 7)

Common Stock	$1,000,000
Additional Paid-in Capital	500,000
Retained Earnings	900,000

Transactions during 2005 and other information related to stockholders' equity accounts were as follows.

1. On January 9, 2005, issued at $8 per share 100,000 shares of $5 par value, 9% cumulative preferred stock.

2. On February 8, 2005, reacquired 8,000 shares of its common stock for $7 per share.
3. On June 10, 2005, declared a cash dividend of $1 per share on the common stock outstanding, payable on July 10, 2005, to stockholders of record on July 1, 2005.
4. On December 15, 2005, declared the yearly cash dividend on preferred stock, payable December 28, 2005, to stockholders of record on December 15, 2005.
5. Net income for the year is $2,400,000. At December 31, 2005, the market price of the common stock was $15 per share.

Instructions

Tot. stockholders' equity
$4,507,000

Prepare the stockholders' equity section of Cow Company's balance sheet at December 31, 2005.

Reproduce retained earnings account, and prepare a stockholders' equity section.
(SO 5, 6, 7)

P11-4A The post-closing trial balance of Fogarty Corporation at December 31, 2005, contains these stockholders' equity accounts.

Preferred Stock (12,000 shares issued)	$ 600,000
Common Stock (250,000 shares issued)	2,500,000
Paid-in Capital in Excess of Par Value—Preferred Stock	250,000
Paid-in Capital in Excess of Par Value—Common Stock	700,000
Retained Earnings	1,165,000

A review of the accounting records reveals this information:

1. Preferred stock is $50 par, 10%, and cumulative; 12,000 shares have been outstanding since January 1, 2004.
2. Authorized stock is 20,000 shares of preferred and 500,000 shares of common with a $10 par value.
3. The January 1, 2005, balance in Retained Earnings was $980,000.
4. On July 1, 20,000 shares of common stock were sold for cash at $16 per share.
5. A cash dividend of $250,000 was declared and properly allocated to preferred and common stock on October 1. No dividends were paid to preferred stockholders in 2004.
6. Net income for the year was $435,000.
7. On December 31, 2005, the directors authorized disclosure of a $150,000 restriction of retained earnings for plant expansion. (Use Note X.)

Instructions

(b) Tot. paid-in capital
$4,050,000

(a) Reproduce the retained earnings account for the year.
(b) Prepare the stockholders' equity section of the balance sheet at December 31.

Prepare a stockholders' equity section.
(SO 7)

P11-5A The following stockholders' equity accounts, arranged alphabetically, are in the ledger of Repo Corporation at December 31, 2005.

Common Stock ($5 stated value, 800,000 shares authorized)	$2,800,000
Paid-in Capital in Excess of Par Value—Preferred Stock	645,000
Paid-in Capital in Excess of Stated Value—Common Stock	1,500,000
Preferred Stock (8%, $50 par, noncumulative)	750,000
Retained Earnings	1,958,000
Treasury Stock—Common (25,000 shares)	150,000

Instructions

Tot. stockholders' equity
$7,503,000

Prepare the stockholders' equity section of the balance sheet at December 31, 2005.

Prepare a stockholders' equity section.
(SO 7)

P11-6A On January 1, 2005, Anthony Inc. had these stockholder equity balances.

Common Stock, $1 par (1,000,000 shares authorized; 500,000 shares issued and outstanding)	$ 500,000
Paid-in Capital in Excess of Par Value	1,000,000
Retained Earnings	600,000

During 2005, the following transactions and events occurred.

1. Issued 50,000 shares of $1 par common stock for $100,000.
2. Issued 30,000 common shares for cash at $5 per share.
3. Purchased 25,000 shares of common stock for the treasury at $4 per share.
4. Declared and paid a cash dividend of $100,000.
5. Reported net income of $300,000.

Instructions
Prepare the stockholders' equity section of the balance sheet at December 31, 2005.

P11-7A Nancy Company manufactures raingear. During 2005 Nancy Company decided to issue bonds at 14% interest and then used the cash to purchase a significant amount of treasury stock. The following information is available for Nancy Company.

Evaluate a company's profitability and solvency.
(SO 8)

	2005	2004
Sales	$3,000,000	$3,000,000
Net income	850,000	1,000,000
Interest expense	200,000	50,000
Tax expense	100,000	142,000
Total assets	5,000,000	5,625,000
Average total assets	5,312,500	6,250,000
Total liabilities	2,000,000	1,000,000
Average total stockholders' equity	3,312,500	5,250,000
Dividends	340,000	400,000

Instructions
(a) Use the information above to calculate the following ratios for both years: (i) return on assets ratio, (ii) return on common stockholders' equity ratio, (iii) payout ratio, (iv) debt to total assets ratio, (v) times interest earned ratio.
(b) Referring to your findings in part (a), discuss the changes in the company's profitability from 2004 to 2005.
(c) Referring to your findings in part (a), discuss the changes in the company's solvency from 2004 to 2005.
(d) Based on your findings in (b), was the decision to issue debt to purchase common stock a wise one?

P11-8A On January 1, 2005, Frank Corporation had these stockholders' equity accounts.

Prepare dividend entries, prepare a stockholders' equity section, and calculate ratios.
(SO 5, 7, 8, 9)

Common Stock ($20 par value, 60,000 shares issued and outstanding)	$1,200,000
Paid-in Capital in Excess of Par Value	200,000
Retained Earnings	600,000

During the year, the following transactions occurred.

Feb.	1	Declared a $0.50 cash dividend per share to stockholders of record on February 15, payable March 1.
Mar.	1	Paid the dividend declared in February.
July	1	Declared a 5% stock dividend to stockholders of record on July 15, distributable July 31. On July 1 the market price of the stock was $28 per share.
	31	Issued the shares for the stock dividend.
Dec.	1	Declared a $1 per share dividend to stockholders of record on December 15, payable January 5, 2006.
	31	Determined that net income for the year was $410,000. The market price of the common stock on this date was $48.

Instructions
(a) Journalize the transactions. (Include entries to close net income to Retained Earnings.)
(b) Enter the beginning balances and post the entries to the stockholders' equity T accounts. (*Note:* Open additional stockholders' equity accounts as needed.)
(c) Prepare the stockholders' equity section of the balance sheet at December 31.
(d) Calculate the payout ratio, earnings per share, price-earnings ratio, and return on common stockholders' equity ratio. (*Hint:* Use the common shares outstanding on January 1 and December 31 to determine average shares outstanding.)

Problems: Set B

Journalize stock transactions, post, and prepare paid-in capital section.
(SO 2, 4, 7)

P11-1B   Revival Corporation was organized on January 1, 2005. It is authorized to issue 20,000 shares of 6%, $50 par value preferred stock and 500,000 shares of no-par common stock with a stated value of $1 per share. The following stock transactions were completed during the first year.

Jan.	10	Issued 100,000 shares of common stock for cash at $4 per share.
Mar.	1	Issued 12,000 shares of preferred stock for cash at $52 per share.
May	1	Issued 70,000 shares of common stock for cash at $5 per share.
Sept.	1	Issued 5,000 shares of common stock for cash at $6 per share.
Nov.	1	Issued 2,000 shares of preferred stock for cash at $63 per share.

Instructions

(a) Journalize the transactions.

(b) Post to the stockholders' equity accounts. (Use T accounts.)

(c) Prepare the paid-in capital portion of the stockholders' equity section at December 31, 2005.

(c) Tot. paid-in capital
         $1,530,000

Journalize transactions, post, and prepare a stockholders' equity section; calculate ratios.
(SO 2, 3, 5, 7, 8)

P11-2B   The stockholders' equity accounts of Music Corporation on January 1, 2005, were as follows.

Preferred Stock (10%, $100 par noncumulative, 5,000 shares authorized)	$ 400,000
Common Stock ($5 stated value, 300,000 shares authorized)	1,000,000
Paid-in Capital in Excess of Par Value—Preferred Stock	15,000
Paid-in Capital in Excess of Stated Value—Common Stock	380,000
Retained Earnings	488,000
Treasury Stock—Common (5,000 shares)	40,000

During 2005 the corporation had the following transactions and events pertaining to its stockholders' equity.

Feb.	1	Issued 3,000 shares of common stock for $18,000.
Mar.	20	Purchased 1,000 additional shares of common treasury stock at $9 per share.
Oct.	1	Declared a 10% cash dividend on preferred stock, payable November 1.
Nov.	1	Paid the dividend declared on October 1.
Dec.	1	Declared a $0.50 per share cash dividend to common stockholders of record on December 15, payable December 31, 2005.
	31	Determined that net income for the year was $280,000. At December 31 the market price of the common stock was $10 per share. Paid the dividend declared on December 1.

Instructions

(a) Journalize the transactions. (Include entries to close net income to Retained Earnings.)

(b) Enter the beginning balances in the accounts and post the journal entries to the stockholders' equity accounts. (Use T accounts.)

(c) Prepare the stockholders' equity section of the balance sheet at December 31, 2005.

(d) Calculate the payout ratio, earnings per share, price-earnings ratio, and return on common stockholders' equity ratio. (*Note:* Use the common shares outstanding on January 1 and December 31 to determine the average shares outstanding.)

(c) Tot. paid-in capital
         $1,813,000

Prepare a stockholders' equity section.
(SO 7)

P11-3B   On December 31, 2004, Elliott Company had 1,500,000 shares of $5 par common stock issued and outstanding. The stockholders' equity accounts at December 31, 2004, had the balances listed here.

Common Stock	$7,500,000
Additional Paid-in Capital	1,800,000
Retained Earnings	1,200,000

Transactions during 2005 and other information related to stockholders' equity accounts were as follows.

1. On January 10, 2005, issued at $112 per share 100,000 shares of $100 par value, 8% cumulative preferred stock.

2. On February 8, 2005, reacquired 15,000 shares of its common stock for $16 per share.
3. On June 8, 2005, declared a cash dividend of $1.20 per share on the common stock outstanding, payable on July 10, 2005, to stockholders of record on July 1, 2005.
4. On December 9, 2005, declared the yearly cash dividend on preferred stock, payable January 10, 2006, to stockholders of record on December 15, 2005.
5. Net income for the year was $3,600,000. At December 31, 2005, the market price of the common stock was $18 per share.

Instructions

Prepare the stockholders' equity section of Elliott's balance sheet at December 31, 2005.

Tot. stockholders' equity
$22,478,000

P11-4B   The ledger of Java Corporation at December 31, 2005, after the books have been closed, contains the following stockholders' equity accounts.

Reproduce retained earnings account, and prepare a stockholders' equity section.
(SO 5, 6, 7)

Preferred Stock (10,000 shares issued)	$1,000,000
Common Stock (420,000 shares issued)	2,100,000
Paid-in Capital in Excess of Par Value—Preferred Stock	200,000
Paid-in Capital in Excess of Stated Value—Common Stock	1,600,000
Retained Earnings	2,980,000

A review of the accounting records reveals this information:

1. Preferred stock is 10%, $100 par value, noncumulative. Since January 1, 2004, 10,000 shares have been outstanding; 20,000 shares are authorized.
2. Common stock is no-par with a stated value of $5 per share; 600,000 shares are authorized.
3. The January 1, 2005, balance in Retained Earnings was $2,500,000.
4. On October 1, 100,000 shares of common stock were sold for cash at $8 per share.
5. A cash dividend of $400,000 was declared and properly allocated to preferred and common stock on November 1. No dividends were paid to preferred stockholders in 2004.
6. Net income for the year was $880,000.
7. On December 31, 2005, the directors authorized disclosure of a $130,000 restriction of retained earnings for plant expansion. (Use Note A.)

Instructions

(a) Reproduce the retained earnings account (T account) for the year.
(b) Prepare the stockholders' equity section of the balance sheet at December 31.

(b) Tot. paid-in capital
$4,900,000

P11-5B   Planet Corporation has been authorized to issue 20,000 shares of $100 par value, 10%, noncumulative preferred stock and 1,000,000 shares of no-par common stock. The corporation assigned a $5 stated value to the common stock. At December 31, 2005, the ledger contained the following balances pertaining to stockholders' equity.

Prepare entries for stock transactions, and prepare a stockholders' equity section.
(SO 2, 3, 4, 7)

Preferred Stock	$ 120,000
Paid-in Capital in Excess of Par Value—Preferred Stock	30,000
Common Stock	2,000,000
Paid-in Capital in Excess of Stated Value—Common Stock	1,850,000
Treasury Stock—Common (2,000 shares)	66,000
Retained Earnings	82,000

The preferred stock was issued for $150,000 cash. All common stock issued was for cash. In November 2,000 shares of common stock were purchased for the treasury at a per share cost of $33. No dividends were declared in 2005.

Instructions

(a) Prepare the journal entries for the following.

(1) Issuance of preferred stock for cash.
(2) Issuance of common stock for cash.
(3) Purchase of common treasury stock for cash.

(b) Prepare the stockholders' equity section of the balance sheet at December 31, 2005.

(b) Tot. stockholders' equity
$4,016,000

P11-6B   On January 1, 2005, Fair Inc. had these stockholders' equity balances.

Prepare a stockholders' equity section.
(SO 7)

Common Stock, $2 par (2,000,000 shares authorized, 500,000 shares issued and outstanding)	$1,000,000
Paid-in Capital in Excess of Par Value	500,000
Retained Earnings	600,000

During 2005, the following transactions and events occurred.

1. Issued 50,000 shares of $2 par value common stock for $4 per share.
2. Issued 40,000 shares of common stock for cash at $5 per share.
3. Purchased 15,000 shares of common stock for the treasury at $6 per share.
4. Declared and paid a cash dividend of $115,000.
5. Earned net income of $300,000.

Tot. stockholders' equity
$2,595,000

Instructions

Prepare the stockholders' equity section of the balance sheet at December 31, 2005.

Evaluate a company's
profitability and solvency.
(SO 8)

P11-7B Extralite Company manufactures backpacks. During 2005 Extralite issued bonds at 12% interest and used the cash proceeds to purchase treasury stock. The following financial information is available for Extralite Company for the years 2005 and 2004.

	2005	2004
Sales	$ 9,000,000	$ 9,000,000
Net income	2,550,000	3,000,000
Interest expense	600,000	150,000
Tax expense	700,000	826,000
Dividends paid	1,020,000	1,200,000
Total assets (year-end)	14,500,000	16,875,000
Average total assets	14,937,500	17,647,000
Total liabilities (year-end)	6,000,000	3,000,000
Average total stockholders' equity	9,400,000	14,100,000

Instructions

(a) Use the information above to calculate the following ratios for both years: (i) return on assets ratio, (ii) return on common stockholders' equity ratio, (iii) payout ratio, (iv) debt to total assets ratio, (v) times interest earned ratio.
(b) Referring to your findings in part (a), discuss the changes in the company's profitability from 2004 to 2005.
(c) Referring to your findings in part (a), discuss the changes in the company's solvency from 2004 to 2005.
(d) Based on your findings in (b), was the decision to issue debt to purchase common stock a wise one?

Prepare dividend entries,
prepare a stockholders' equity
section, and calculate ratios.
(SO 5, 7, 8, 9)

*P11-8B On January 1, 2005, Nuclear Corporation had these stockholders' equity accounts.

Common Stock ($10 par value, 70,000 shares issued and outstanding)	$700,000
Paid-in Capital in Excess of Par Value	300,000
Retained Earnings	540,000

During the year, the following transactions occurred.

Jan. 15 Declared a $0.60 cash dividend per share to stockholders of record on January 31, payable February 15.
Feb. 15 Paid the dividend declared in January.
Apr. 15 Declared a 10% stock dividend to stockholders of record on April 30, distributable May 15. On April 15 the market price of the stock was $16 per share.
May 15 Issued the shares for the stock dividend.
Dec. 1 Declared a $0.75 per share cash dividend to stockholders of record on December 15, payable January 10, 2006.
31 Determined that net income for the year was $370,000. On December 31 the market price of the stock was $15 per share.

Instructions

(a) Journalize the transactions. (Include entries to close net income to Retained Earnings.)
(b) Enter the beginning balances and post the entries to the stockholders' equity T accounts. (*Note:* Open additional stockholders' equity accounts as needed.)
(c) Prepare the stockholders' equity section of the balance sheet at December 31.
(d) Calculate the payout ratio, earnings per share, price-earnings ratio, and return on common stockholders' equity ratio. (*Hint:* Use the common shares outstanding on January 1 and December 31 to determine average shares outstanding.)

(c) Tot. stockholders' equity
$1,810,250

BROADENING YOUR PERSPECTIVE

Financial Reporting and Analysis

FINANCIAL REPORTING PROBLEM: *Tootsie Roll Industries, Inc.*

BYP11-1 The stockholders' equity section of **Tootsie Roll Industries**' balance sheet is shown in the Consolidated Statement of Financial Position in Appendix A. You will also find data relative to this problem on other pages of Appendix A. (Note that Tootsie Roll has two classes of common stock. To answer the following questions, add the two classes of stock together.)

Instructions
Answer the following questions.
  (a) What is the par or stated value per share of Tootsie Roll's common stock?
  (b) What percentage of Tootsie Roll's authorized common stock was issued at December 31, 2002? (Round to the nearest full percent.)
  (c) How many shares of common stock were outstanding at December 31, 2001, and at December 31, 2002?
  (d) Calculate the payout ratio, earnings per share, price-earnings ratio, and return on common stockholders' equity ratio for 2002. Tootsie Roll's stock price at December 31, 2002, was $30.68. (*Hint:* Use the common shares outstanding on January 1 and December 31 to determine average shares outstanding.)

COMPARATIVE ANALYSIS PROBLEM: *Tootsie Roll vs. Hershey Foods*

BYP11-2 The financial statements of **Hershey Foods** are presented in Appendix B, following the financial statements for **Tootsie Roll** in Appendix A.

Instructions
  (a) Based on the information in these financial statements, compute the 2002 return on common stockholders' equity, debt to total assets ratio, and return on assets ratio for each company.
  (b) What conclusions concerning the companies' profitability can be drawn from these ratios? Which company relies more on debt to boost its return to common shareholders?
  (c) Compute the payout ratio for each company. Which pays out a higher percentage of its earnings?

RESEARCH CASE

BYP11-3 The March 28, 2001, edition of the *Wall Street Journal* contains an article by Cassell Bryan-Low entitled "A Growing Number of Firms Pull Back on Stock Buybacks."

Instructions
Read the article and answer the following questions.
  (a) In what way does the article say that the current trend in treasury stock repurchases is "a reversal of the traditional logic"?
  (b) What are the reasons given in the article for why companies are buying back fewer shares?
  (c) How much did **International Business Machines (IBM)** spend on treasury stock purchases between 1995 and the end of 2000?
  (d) What is given as a possible explanation for the timing of **Yahoo**'s first ever treasury stock repurchase?

INTERPRETING FINANCIAL STATEMENTS

BYP11-4 In recent years the fast-food chain **Wendy's International** has purchased many treasury shares. From January 3, 1999, to December 30, 2001, the number of shares outstanding has fallen from 124 million to 105 million. The following information was drawn from the company's financial statements (in millions).

	Year ended	
	Dec. 30, 2001	**Jan. 3, 1999**
Net income	$ 193.6	$ 123.4
Total assets	2,076.0	1,837.9
Average total assets	2,016.9	1,889.8
Total common stockholders' equity	1,029.8	1,068.1
Average common stockholders' equity	1,078.0	1,126.2
Total liabilities	1,046.3	769.9
Average total liabilities	939.0	763.7
Interest expense	30.2	19.8
Income taxes	113.7	84.3
Cash provided by operations	305.2	233.8
Cash dividends paid on common stock	26.8	31.0
Preferred stock dividends	0	0
Average number of common shares outstanding	109.7	119.9

Instructions
Use the information provided to answer the following questions.
(a) Compute earnings per share, return on common stockholders' equity, and return on assets for both years. Discuss the change in the company's profitability over this period.
(b) Compute the dividend payout ratio. Also compute the average cash dividend paid per share of common stock (dividends paid divided by the average number of common shares outstanding). Discuss any change in these ratios during this period and the implications for the company's dividend policy.
(c) Compute the debt to total assets ratio, interest coverage ratio, and cash debt coverage ratio. Discuss the change in the company's solvency.
(d) Based on your findings in (a) and (c), discuss to what extent any change in the return on common stockholders' equity was the result of increased reliance on debt.
(e) Do the purchase of treasury stock and the shift toward more reliance on debt appear to have been wise strategic moves?

BYP11-5 Marriott Corporation split into two companies: **Host Marriott Corporation** and **Marriott International**. Host Marriott retained ownership of the corporation's vast hotel and other properties, while Marriott International, rather than owning hotels, managed them. The purpose of this split was to free Marriott International from the "baggage" associated with Host Marriott, thus allowing it to be more aggressive in its pursuit of growth. The following information (in millions) is provided for each corporation for their first full year operating as independent companies.

	Host Marriott	**Marriott International**
Sales	$1,501	$8,415
Net income	(25)	200
Total assets	3,822	3,207
Total liabilities	3,112	2,440
Stockholders' equity	710	767

Instructions
(a) The two companies were split by the issuance of shares of Marriott International to all shareholders of the previous combined company. Discuss the nature of this transaction.
(b) Calculate the debt to total assets ratio for each company.
(c) Calculate the return on assets and return on common stockholders' equity ratios for each company.
(d) The company's debtholders were fiercely opposed to the original plan to split the two companies because the original plan had Host Marriott absorbing the majority

of the company's debt. They relented only when Marriott International agreed to absorb a larger share of the debt. Discuss the possible reasons the debtholders were opposed to the plan to split the company.

A GLOBAL FOCUS

BYP11-6 American depositary receipts (ADRs) represent a way for U.S. investors to invest in foreign corporations without directly purchasing actual foreign shares of stock. Instead, a U.S. bank purchases the shares in a foreign company and then issues to investors securities (the ADRs) which pass through the risks and rewards of the underlying stock. For example, when the underlying stock pays a dividend the U.S. bank pays a dividend to the holder of the ADR. The March 1, 2001, issue of the *Wall Street Journal* contains an article by Craig Karmin entitled "ADR Holders Find They Retain Unequal Rights" that discusses one potential drawback of this system.

Instructions
Read the article and answer the following questions.
  (a) What is the nature of the shareholder resolution that the holders of the **BP Amoco** ADRs are trying to pass?
  (b) What do these investors hope to accomplish by getting their resolution on the ballot?
  (c) Are ADRs common?
  (d) What are some of the advantages of ADRs to U.S. investors as compared to owning local shares?

FINANCIAL ANALYSIS ON THE WEB

BYP11-7 *Purpose:* Use the stockholders' equity section of an annual report and identify the major components.

Address: **www.reportgallery.com** (or go to **www.wiley.com/college/kimmel**)

Steps
  1. From Report Gallery Homepage, choose **Viewing Library**.
  2. Select a particular company.
  3. Choose **Annual Report**.
  4. Follow instructions below.

Instructions
Answer the following questions.
  (a) What is the company's name?
  (b) What classes of capital stock has the company issued?
  (c) For each class of stock:
    (1) How many shares are authorized, issued, and/or outstanding?
    (2) What is the par value?
  (d) What are the company's retained earnings?
  (e) Has the company acquired treasury stock? How many shares?

Critical Thinking

GROUP DECISION CASE

BYP11-8 The stockholders' meeting for Simpson Corporation has been in progress for some time. The chief financial officer for Simpson is presently reviewing the company's financial statements and is explaining the items that make up the stockholders' equity section of the balance sheet for the current year. The stockholders' equity section for Simpson Corporation at December 31, 2005, is presented on page 574.

SIMPSON CORPORATION
Balance Sheet (partial)

Stockholders' equity		
Paid-in capital		
Capital stock		
Preferred stock, authorized 1,000,000 shares		
cumulative, $100 par value, $8 per share, 6,000		
shares issued and outstanding		$ 600,000
Common stock, authorized 5,000,000 shares, $1		
par value, 3,000,000 shares issued and 2,700,000		
outstanding		3,000,000
Total capital stock		3,600,000
Additional paid-in capital		
In excess of par value—preferred stock	$ 50,000	
In excess of par value—common stock	$25,000,000	
Total additional paid-in capital		25,050,000
Total paid-in capital		28,650,000
Retained earnings		900,000
Total paid-in capital and retained earnings		29,550,000
Less: Common treasury stock (300,000 shares)		9,300,000
Total stockholders' equity		$20,250,000

A number of questions regarding the stockholders' equity section of Simpson Corporation's balance sheet have been raised at the meeting.

Instructions
With the class divided into groups, answer the following questions as if your group were the chief financial officer for Simpson Corporation.
(a) "What does the cumulative provision related to the preferred stock mean?"
(b) "I thought the common stock was presently selling at $29.75, and yet the company has the stock stated at $1 per share. How can that be?"
(c) "Why is the company buying back its common stock? Furthermore, the treasury stock has a debit balance because it is subtracted from stockholders' equity. Why is treasury stock not reported as an asset if it has a debit balance?"
(d) "Why is it necessary to distinguish between retained earnings and paid-in capital? Why not just show total stockholders' equity?"

COMMUNICATION ACTIVITY

BYP11-9   Phil Nelson, your uncle, is an inventor who has decided to incorporate. Uncle Phil knows that you are an accounting major at U.N.O. In a recent letter to you, he ends with the question, "I'm filling out a state incorporation application. Can you tell me the difference among the following terms: (1) authorized stock, (2) issued stock, (3) outstanding stock, and (4) preferred stock?"

Instructions
In a brief note, differentiate for Uncle Phil the four different stock terms. Write the letter to be friendly, yet professional.

ETHICS CASES

BYP11-10   The R&D division of Water Chemical Corp. has just developed a chemical for sterilizing the vicious Brazilian "killer bees" which are invading Mexico and the southern United States. The president of Water is anxious to get the chemical on the market because Water's profits need a boost—and his job is in jeopardy because of decreasing sales and profits. Water has an opportunity to sell this chemical in Central American countries, where the laws are much more relaxed than in the United States.

The director of Water's R&D division strongly recommends further research in the laboratory to test the side effects of this chemical on other insects, birds, animals, plants, and even humans. He cautions the president, "We could be sued from all sides if the chemical has tragic side effects that we didn't even test for in the lab." The president answers, "We can't wait an additional year for your lab tests. We can avoid losses from such lawsuits by establishing a separate wholly owned corporation to shield Water Chemical Corp. from such lawsuits. We can't lose any more than our investment in the new corporation, and we'll invest just the patent covering this chemical. We'll reap the benefits if the chemical works and is safe, and avoid the losses from lawsuits if it's a disaster." The following week Water creates a new wholly owned corporation called Dock Inc., sells the chemical patent to it for $10, and watches the spraying begin.

Instructions
(a) Who are the stakeholders in this situation?
(b) Are the president's motives and actions ethical?
(c) Can Water shield itself against losses of Dock Inc.?

BYP11-11 Dutchman Corporation has paid 60 consecutive quarterly cash dividends (15 years). The last 6 months have been a real cash drain on the company, however, as profit margins have been greatly narrowed by increasing competition. With a cash balance sufficient to meet only day-to-day operating needs, the president, Herb Barnett, has decided that a stock dividend instead of a cash dividend should be declared. He tells Dutchman's financial vice-president, Betty Fischer, to issue a press release stating that the company is extending its consecutive dividend record with the issuance of a 5% stock dividend. "Write the press release convincing the stockholders that the stock dividend is just as good as a cash dividend," he orders. "Just watch our stock rise when we announce the stock dividend; it must be a good thing if that happens."

Instructions
(a) Who are the stakeholders in this situation?
(b) Is there anything unethical about president Barnett's intentions or actions?
(c) What is the effect of a stock dividend on a corporation's stockholders' equity accounts? Which would you rather receive as a stockholder—a cash dividend or a stock dividend? Why?

Answers to Self-Study Questions
1. c 2. b 3. d 4. c 5. d 6. d 7. b 8. a 9. c 10. b

Answer to Tootsie Roll Review It Question 3, p. 550

The cost of **Tootsie Roll**'s treasury stock in 2002 was $1,992,000. It declared cash dividends of $14,304,000. The stock dividend reduced retained earnings by $64,724,000.

Remember to go back to the Navigator box on the chapter-opening page and check off your completed work.

Reporting and Analyzing Investments

STUDY OBJECTIVES

After studying this chapter,
you should be able to:

1 Identify the reasons corporations invest in stocks and debt securities.

2 Explain the accounting for debt investments.

3 Explain the accounting for stock investments.

4 Describe the purpose and usefulness of consolidated financial statements.

5 Indicate how debt and stock investments are valued and reported in the financial statements.

6 Distinguish between short-term and long-term investments.

THE NAVIGATOR ✔

▶ Scan *Study Objectives* ☐

▶ Read *Feature Story* ☐

▶ Read *Preview* ☐

▶ Read text and answer *Before You Go On*
  p. 583 ☐   p. 588 ☐   p. 592 ☐
  p. 596 ☐

▶ Work Using the *Decision Toolkit* ☐

▶ Review Summary of *Study Objectives* ☐

▶ Work *Demonstration Problem* ☐

▶ Answer *Self-Study Questions* ☐

▶ Complete *Assignments* ☐

FEATURE STORY

"On the Other Hand, It Might Be a Really Bad Idea"

In a rapidly changing world, you must adapt quickly or suffer the consequences. In business, change requires investment. In the entertainment industry, technology is bringing about innovations so quickly that it is nearly impossible to guess which technologies will last and which will soon fade away. For example, will satellite TV and cable TV both survive, or will just one survive? Or will both be replaced by something completely new? Similarly, will CDs be completely replaced by online music? And if so, how will it be sold? Who will win, and who will lose? If you invest in the wrong technology, you lose. But often if you just sit still and fail to invest, you may lose as well.

AOL Time Warner, Inc. exists at the center of this arena. It is not an environment for the timid, and over the years Time Warner's philosophy has been anything but timid. Time Warner lives by the motto, "Eat or be eaten." That is, if we can't beat you, we will buy you. An abbreviated list of the company's holdings (either acquired or developed internally) gives an idea of its reach. Magazines: *People, Time, Life, Sports Illustrated, Fortune.* Book publishers: Time-Life Books, Book-of-the Month Club, Little, Brown and Co., Sunset Books. Music:

Warner Bros. Records, Reprise, Atlantic, Rhino, Electra, Asylum. Television and movies: Warner Bros. ("Friends," "The West Wing," the WB Network), HBO ("The Sopranos"), and movies like *The Lord of the Rings*, the Harry Potter movies, and *The Matrix* and *Matrix Reloaded*. It also owns **Turner Broadcasting**, which includes TNT, CNN, and Turner's incredible collection of thousands of classic movies.

But all of these previous mergers and acquisitions pale next to the granddaddy of them all. In 2000 Time Warner agreed to be acquired by Internet service provider **AOL**. That's right, the company that had swallowed so many others agreed to be swallowed. At the height of the Internet boom, AOL's stock price was astronomical. It used its highly valued shares to buy Time Warner. The brilliance of the idea seemed so obvious: Time Warner had the content, and AOL had tens of millions of customers to sell the content to, as well as a delivery mechanism—the Internet.

At the time of the merger the combined company had a stock market value of $284 billion.

Today it is worth $61 billion—shareholders lost $223 billion. There are no longer any remaining AOL executives in the company's top ranks, and many people think that the company will soon sell off AOL and remove "AOL" from the front of its name, in an effort to "put it all behind them." You can bet the shareholders won't forget that quickly.

☑ THE NAVIGATOR

On the World Wide Web
AOL Time Warner:
www.aoltimewarner.com

The management of **AOL Time Warner** believes in a policy of aggressive growth through investing in the stock of existing companies. In addition to purchasing stock, companies also purchase other securities such as debt securities issued by corporations or by governments. Investments can be purchased for a short or long period of time, as a passive investment, or with the intent to control another company. As you will see later in the chapter, the way in which a company accounts for its investments is determined by a number of factors.

The content and organization of this chapter are as follows.

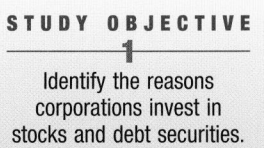

Why Corporations Invest

Corporations purchase investments in debt or equity securities generally for one of three reasons. First, a corporation may **have excess cash** that it does not need for the immediate purchase of operating assets. For example, many companies experience seasonal fluctuations in sales. A Cape Cod marina has more sales in the spring and summer than in the fall and winter, whereas the reverse is true for an Aspen ski shop. Thus, at the end of an operating cycle, many companies may have cash on hand that is temporarily idle pending the start of another operating cycle. Until the cash is needed, these companies may invest the excess funds to earn, through interest and dividends, a greater return than they would get by just holding the funds in the bank. The role played by such temporary investments in the operating cycle is depicted in Illustration 12-1 (page 580).

Excess cash may also result from economic cycles. For example, when the economy is booming, **General Motors** generates considerable excess cash. Although it uses some of this cash to purchase new plant and equipment and

STUDY OBJECTIVE

1

Identify the reasons corporations invest in stocks and debt securities.

Illustration 12-1
Temporary investments
and the operating cycle

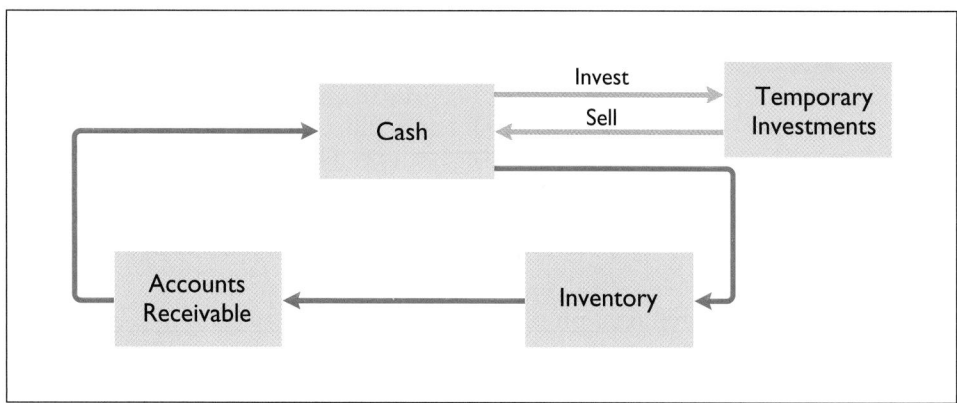

pays out some of the cash in dividends, it may also invest excess cash in liquid assets in anticipation of a future downturn in the economy. It can then liquidate these investments during a recession, when sales slow down and cash is scarce.

When investing excess cash for short periods of time, corporations invest in low-risk, highly liquid securities—most often short-term government securities. It is generally not wise to invest short-term excess cash in shares of common stock because stock investments can experience rapid price changes. If you did invest your short-term excess cash in stock and the price of the stock declined significantly just before you needed cash again, you would be forced to sell your stock investment at a loss.

A second reason some companies such as banks purchase investments is because they generate a **significant portion of their earnings from investment income**. Although banks make most of their earnings by lending money, they also generate earnings by investing in debt and equity securities. Banks purchase investment securities because loan demand varies both seasonally and with changes in the economic climate. Thus, when loan demand is low, a bank must find other uses for its cash. Investing in securities also allows banks to diversify some of their risk. Bank regulators severely limit the ability of banks to invest in common stock; therefore, most investments held by banks are debt securities.

Mutual funds and pension funds are corporations that also regularly invest to generate earnings. However, they do so for *speculative reasons;* that is, they are speculating that the investment will increase in value and thus result in positive returns. Therefore, they invest primarily in the common stock of other corporations. These investments are passive in nature; the pension fund or mutual fund does not usually take an active role in controlling the affairs of the companies in which they invest.

A third reason why companies invest is for **strategic reasons**. A company may purchase a noncontrolling interest in another company in a related industry in which it wishes to establish a presence. For example, as noted in the Feature Story, at one time **Time Warner** (now **AOL Time Warner**) purchased **Turner Broadcasting** to have a stake in Turner's expanding business opportunities. Similarly, AOL acquired Time Warner because it was believed to be a good match of content with distribution capabilities. Thus, not even a huge corporation like Time Warner is at the top of the corporate "food chain." It, too, can be purchased. Alternatively, a company can exercise some influence over one of its customers or suppliers by purchasing a significant, but not controlling, interest in that company.

A corporation may also choose to purchase a controlling interest in another company. This might be done to enter a new industry without incurring the tremendous costs and risks associated with starting from scratch. Or a company might purchase another company in its same industry. The purchase of a company that is in your industry, but involved in a different activity, is called a **vertical acquisition**. For example, Nike might purchase a chain of athletic shoe stores, such as The Athlete's Foot. In a **horizontal acquisition** you purchase a company that does the same activity as your company. For example, Nike might purchase Reebok.

In summary, businesses invest in other companies for the reasons shown in Illustration 12-2.

Illustration 12-2 Why corporations invest

Reason	Typical Investment
To house excess cash until needed	Low-risk, high-liquidity, short-term securities such as government-issued securities
To generate earnings *I need 1,000 Treasury bills by tonight*	Debt securities (banks and other financial institutions); and stock securities (mutual funds and pension funds)
To meet strategic goals	Stocks of companies in a related industry or in an unrelated industry that the company wishes to enter

Accounting for Debt Investments

STUDY OBJECTIVE
2
Explain the accounting for debt investments.

Debt investments are investments in government and corporation bonds. In accounting for debt investments, entries are required to record (1) the acquisition, (2) the interest revenue, and (3) the sale.

RECORDING ACQUISITION OF BONDS

At acquisition, the cost principle applies. Cost includes all expenditures necessary to acquire these investments, such as the price paid plus brokerage fees (commissions), if any. Assume that Kuhl Corporation acquires 50 Doan Inc. 12%, 10-year, $1,000 bonds on January 1, 2005, for $54,000, including brokerage fees of $1,000. The entry to record the investment is:

Jan. 1	Debt Investments	54,000	
	Cash		54,000
	(To record purchase of 50 Doan Inc. bonds)		

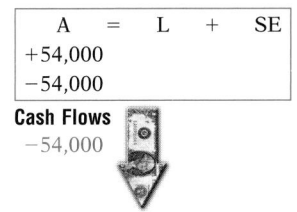

A	=	L	+	SE
+54,000				
−54,000				

Cash Flows
−54,000

Business Insight
INVESTOR PERSPECTIVE

Corporate bonds, like capital stock, are traded on national securities exchanges. They can be bought and sold by investors at any time at the current market price. Bond prices and trading activity are published daily in newspapers and the financial press, in the form shown below.

Bonds	Current Yield	Volume	Close	Net Change
AOL Time Warner $7\frac{3}{4}$ 05	7.1	283	$109\frac{1}{8}$	$+\frac{3}{4}$

This information indicates that **AOL Time Warner** has outstanding $7\frac{3}{4}\%$, $1,000 bonds maturing in 2005 and currently yielding a 7.1% return. In addition, 283 bonds were traded in this week; at the close of trading, the price was $109\frac{1}{8}\%$ of face value, or $1,009.125. The Net Change column indicates the difference between the day's closing price and the previous day's closing price. A slightly different format is used for quotations on government-issued bonds.

RECORDING BOND INTEREST

The Doan Inc. bonds pay interest of $3,000 semiannually on July 1 and January 1 ($50,000 × 12% × $\frac{1}{2}$). The entry for the receipt of interest on July 1 is:

A	=	L	+	SE
+3,000				+3,000 Rev

Cash Flows
+3,000

July 1	Cash	3,000	
	Interest Revenue		3,000
	(To record receipt of interest on Doan Inc. bonds)		

If Kuhl Corporation's fiscal year ends on December 31, it is necessary to accrue the interest of $3,000 earned since July 1. The adjusting entry is:

A	=	L	+	SE
+3,000				+3,000 Rev

Cash Flows
no effect

Dec. 31	Interest Receivable	3,000	
	Interest Revenue		3,000
	(To accrue interest on Doan Inc. bonds)		

Interest Receivable is reported as a current asset in the balance sheet; Interest Revenue is reported under "Other revenues and gains" in the income statement. When the interest is received on January 1, the entry is:

A	=	L	+	SE
+3,000				
−3,000				

Cash Flows
+3,000

Jan. 1	Cash	3,000	
	Interest Receivable		3,000
	(To record receipt of accrued interest)		

A credit to Interest Revenue at this time is incorrect because the interest revenue was earned and accrued in the preceding accounting period.

Helpful Hint The accounting for short-term debt investments and long-term debt investments is similar. Any exceptions are discussed in more advanced courses.

RECORDING SALE OF BONDS

When a bondholder sells bonds, it is necessary to decrease the investment account by the amount of the cost of the bonds. Any difference between the net proceeds from sale (sales price less brokerage fees) and the cost of the bonds is recorded as a gain or loss. Assume, for example, that Kuhl Corporation receives

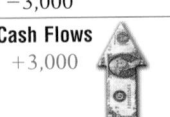

net proceeds of $58,000 on the sale of the Doan Inc. bonds on January 1, 2006, after receiving the interest due. Since the securities cost $54,000, a gain of $4,000 has been realized. The entry to record the sale is:

Jan. 1	Cash	58,000	
	Debt Investments		54,000
	Gain on Sale of Debt Investments		4,000
	(To record sale of Doan Inc. bonds)		

A	=	L	+	SE
+58,000				+4,000 Rev
−54,000				

Cash Flows
+58,000

The gain on the sale of debt investments is reported under "Other revenues and gains" in the income statement.

BEFORE YOU GO ON . . .

▶ Review It

1. What are the reasons corporations invest in securities?
2. What entries are required in accounting for debt investments?

▶ Do It

Waldo Corporation had these transactions pertaining to debt investments:

Jan. 1   Purchased 30 10%, $1,000 Hillary Co. bonds for $30,000 plus brokerage fees of $900. Interest is payable semiannually on July 1 and January 1.
July 1   Received semiannual interest on Hillary Co. bonds.
July 1   Sold 15 Hillary Co. bonds for $15,000 less $400 brokerage fees.

(a) Journalize the transactions.
(b) Prepare the adjusting entry for the accrual of interest on December 31.

Action Plan

• Record bond investments at cost.
• Record interest when received and/or accrued.
• When bonds are sold, credit the investment account for the cost of the bonds.
• Record any difference between the cost and the net proceeds as a gain or loss.

Solution

(a) Jan.	1	Debt Investments	30,900	
		Cash		30,900
		(To record purchase of 30 Hillary Co. bonds)		
	July 1	Cash	1,500	
		Interest Revenue ($30,000 × .10 × $\frac{6}{12}$)		1,500
		(To record receipt of interest on Hillary Co. bonds)		
	July 1	Cash	14,600	
		Loss on Sale of Debt Investments	850	
		Debt Investments ($30,900 × $\frac{15}{30}$)		15,450
		(To record sale of 15 Hillary Co. bonds)		
(b) Dec. 31		Interest Receivable	750	
		Interest Revenue ($15,000 × .10 × $\frac{6}{12}$)		750
		(To accrue interest on Hillary Co. bonds)		

☑ THE NAVIGATOR

Accounting for Stock Investments

STUDY OBJECTIVE
3
Explain the accounting for stock investments.

Stock investments are investments in the capital stock of corporations. When a company holds stock (and/or debt) of several different corporations, the group of securities is identified as an **investment portfolio**.

The accounting for investments in common stock is based on the extent of the investor's influence over the operating and financial affairs of the issuing corporation (the **investee**) as shown in Illustration 12-3. In some cases, depending on the degree of investor influence, net income of the investee is considered to be income to the investor.

Illustration 12-3
Accounting guidelines for stock investments

Investor's Ownership Interest in Investee's Common Stock	Presumed Influence on Investee	Accounting Guidelines
Less than 20%	Insignificant	Cost method
Between 20% and 50%	Significant	Equity method
More than 50%	Controlling	Consolidated financial statements

The presumed influence may be negated by extenuating circumstances. For example, a company that acquires a 25% interest in another company in a "hostile" takeover may not have any significant influence over the investee.[1] In other words, companies are required to use judgment instead of blindly following the guidelines. We explain and illustrate the application of each guideline next.

HOLDINGS OF LESS THAN 20%

In the accounting for stock investments of less than 20%, the cost method is used. Under the cost method, the investment is recorded at cost, and revenue is recognized when cash dividends are received.

Recording Acquisition of Stock

At acquisition, the cost principle applies. Cost includes all expenditures necessary to acquire these investments, such as the price paid plus brokerage fees (commissions), if any. Assume, for example, that on July 1, 2005, Sanchez Corporation acquires 1,000 shares (10% ownership) of Beal Corporation common stock at $40 per share plus brokerage fees of $500. The entry for the purchase is:

---

[1]Among the factors that should be considered in determining an investor's influence are whether (1) the investor has representation on the investee's board of directors, (2) the investor participates in the investee's policy-making process, (3) there are material transactions between the investor and the investee, and (4) the common stock held by other stockholders is concentrated or dispersed.

July 1	Stock Investments	40,500
	Cash	40,500
	(To record purchase of 1,000 shares of	
	Beal common stock)	

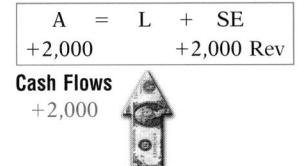

A = L + SE
+40,500
−40,500

Cash Flows
−40,500

Recording Dividends

During the time the stock is held, entries are required for any cash dividends received. Thus, if a $2.00 per share dividend is received by Sanchez Corporation on December 31, the entry is:

Dec. 31	Cash (1,000 × $2)	2,000
	Dividend Revenue	2,000
	(To record receipt of a cash dividend)	

A = L + SE
+2,000   +2,000 Rev

Cash Flows
+2,000

Dividend Revenue is reported under "Other revenues and gains" in the income statement.

Recording Sale of Stock

When stock is sold, the difference between the net proceeds from the sale (sales price less brokerage fees) and the cost of the stock is recognized as a gain or a loss. Assume, for instance, that Sanchez Corporation receives net proceeds of $39,500 on the sale of its Beal Corporation stock on February 10, 2006. Because the stock cost $40,500, a loss of $1,000 has been incurred. The entry to record the sale is:

Feb. 10	Cash	39,500
	Loss on Sale of Stock Investments	1,000
	Stock Investments	40,500
	(To record sale of Beal common stock)	

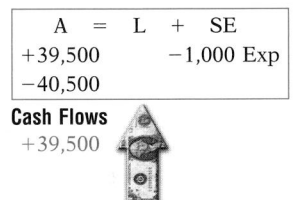

A = L + SE
+39,500   −1,000 Exp
−40,500

Cash Flows
+39,500

The loss account is reported under "Other expenses and losses" in the income statement, whereas a gain on sale is shown under "Other revenues and gains."

HOLDINGS BETWEEN 20% AND 50%

When an investor company owns only a small portion of the shares of stock of another company (the investee), the investor cannot exercise control over the company. When an investor owns between 20% and 50% of the common stock of a corporation, however, it is generally presumed that the investor has significant influence over the financial and operating activities of the investee. The investor probably has a representative on the investee's board of directors. With a representative on the board, the investor begins to exercise some control over the investee—and the investee company in some sense really becomes part of the investor company.

For example, even prior to purchasing all of **Turner Broadcasting, Time Warner** owned 20% of Turner. Because it exercised significant control over major decisions made by Turner, Time Warner used an approach called the equity method. Under the equity method, **the investor records its share of the net income of the investee in the year when it is earned**. To delay recognizing the investor's share of net income until a cash dividend is declared ignores the fact that the investor and investee are, in some sense, one company, so the investor is better off by the investee's earned income.

Under the **equity method**, the investment in common stock is initially recorded at cost, and the investment account is **adjusted annually** to show the investor's equity in the investee. Each year, the investor (1) increases (debits) the investment account and increases (credits) revenue for its share of the investee's net income,[2] and (2) decreases (credits) the investment account for the amount of dividends received. The investment account is reduced for dividends received because the net assets of the investee are decreased when a dividend is paid.

Recording Acquisition of Stock Investments

Assume that Milar Corporation acquires 30% of the common stock of Beck Company for $120,000 on January 1, 2005. The entry to record this transaction is:

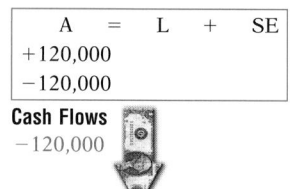

A	=	L	+	SE
+120,000				
−120,000				

Cash Flows
−120,000

Jan. 1	Stock Investments	120,000	
	Cash		120,000
	(To record purchase of Beck common stock)		

Recording Revenue and Dividends

For 2005 Beck reports net income of $100,000 and declares and pays a $40,000 cash dividend. Milar is required to record (1) its share of Beck's income, $30,000 (30% × $100,000), and (2) the reduction in the investment account for the dividends received, $12,000 ($40,000 × 30%). The entries are:

A	=	L	+	SE
+30,000				+30,000 Rev

Cash Flows
no effect

(1)

Dec. 31	Stock Investments	30,000	
	Revenue from Investment in Beck Company		30,000
	(To record 30% equity in Beck's 2005 net income)		

(2)

A	=	L	+	SE
+12,000				
−12,000				

Cash Flows
+12,000

Dec. 31	Cash	12,000	
	Stock Investments		12,000
	(To record dividends received)		

After the transactions for the year are posted, the investment and revenue accounts are as shown in Illustration 12-4.

Illustration 12-4
Investment and revenue accounts after posting

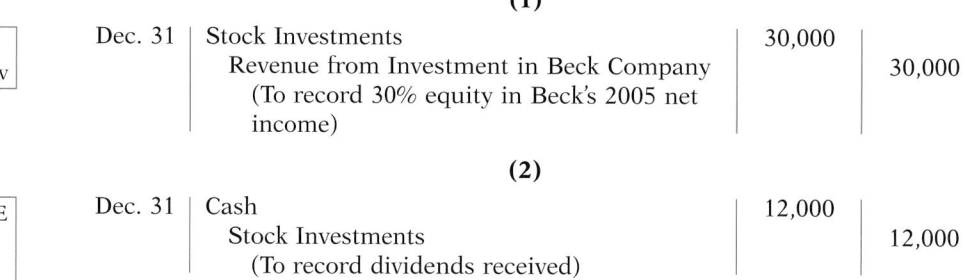

Stock Investments				Revenue from Investment in Beck Company	
Jan. 1	120,000	Dec. 31	12,000		
Dec. 31	30,000			Dec. 31	30,000
Dec. 31 Bal.	138,000				

During the year, the investment account has increased by $18,000. This $18,000 is Milar's 30% equity in the $60,000 increase in Beck's retained earnings ($100,000 − $40,000). In addition, Milar reports $30,000 of revenue from its investment, which is 30% of Beck's net income of $100,000. Note that the difference between reported income under the cost method and reported revenue under the equity method can be significant. For example, Milar would report only $12,000 of dividend revenue (30% × $40,000) if the cost method were used.

---

[2]Conversely, the investor increases (debits) a loss account and decreases (credits) the investment account for its share of the investee's net loss.

HOLDINGS OF MORE THAN 50%

A company that owns more than 50% of the common stock of another entity is known as the **parent company**. The entity whose stock is owned by the parent company is called the **subsidiary (affiliated) company**. Because of its stock ownership, the parent company has a **controlling interest** in the subsidiary company.

When a company owns more than 50% of the common stock of another company, **consolidated financial statements** are usually prepared. Consolidated financial statements present the assets and liabilities controlled by the parent company and the aggregate profitability of the affiliated companies. They are prepared **in addition to** the financial statements for each of the individual parent and subsidiary companies. As noted earlier, prior to acquiring all of Turner Broadcasting, Time Warner accounted for its investment in Turner using the equity method. Time Warner's net investment in Turner was reported in a single line item—Other investments. After the merger, Time Warner instead consolidated Turner's results with its own. Under this approach, the individual assets and liabilities of Turner are included with those of Time Warner; its plant and equipment are added to Time Warner's plant and equipment, its receivables are added to Time Warner's receivables, and so on. A similar sort of consolidation went on when **AOL** merged with **Time Warner** in 2001.

Consolidated statements are especially useful to the stockholders, board of directors, and management of the parent company. Moreover, consolidated statements inform creditors, prospective investors, and regulatory agencies as to the magnitude and scope of operations of the companies under

Helpful Hint If the parent (A) has three wholly owned subsidiaries (B, C, and D), there are four separate legal entities but only one economic entity from the viewpoint of the shareholders of the parent company.

Business Insight
MANAGEMENT PERSPECTIVE

AOL Time Warner, Inc., owns 100% of the common stock of **Home Box Office** (HBO) Corporation. The common stockholders of AOL Time Warner elect the board of directors of the company, who, in turn, select the officers and managers of the company. The board of directors controls the property owned by the corporation, which includes the common stock of HBO. Thus, they are in a position to elect the board of directors of HBO and, in effect, control its operations. These relationships are graphically illustrated here:

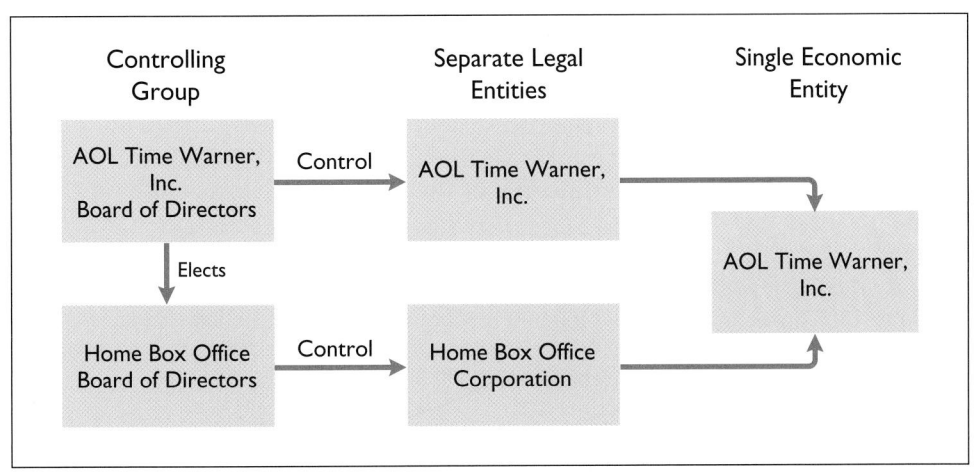

common control. For example, regulators and the courts undoubtedly used the consolidated statements of **AT&T** to determine whether a breakup of AT&T was in the public interest. Listed here are three companies that prepare consolidated statements and some of the companies they have owned. Note that one, **Disney**, is AOL Time Warner's arch rival.

PepsiCo	Cendant	The Walt Disney Company
Frito-Lay	Howard Johnson	Capital Cities/ABC, Inc.
Tropicana	Ramada Inn	Disneyland, Disney World
Quaker Oats	Century 21	Mighty Ducks
Pepsi-Cola	Coldwell Banker	Anaheim Angels
Gatorade	Avis	ESPN

BEFORE YOU GO ON . . .

▶ Review It

1. What are the accounting entries for investments in stock with ownership of less than 20%?
2. What entries are made under the equity method when (a) the investor receives a cash dividend from the investee and (b) the investee reports net income for the year?
3. What is the purpose of consolidated financial statements?

▶ Do It

These are two independent situations:

1. Rho Jean Inc. acquired 5% of the 400,000 shares of common stock of Stillwater Corp. at a total cost of $6 per share on May 18, 2005. On August 30 Stillwater declared and paid a $75,000 dividend. On December 31 Stillwater reported net income of $244,000 for the year.
2. Debbie, Inc., obtained significant influence over North Sails by buying 40% of North Sails' 60,000 outstanding shares of common stock at a cost of $12 per share on January 1, 2005. On April 15 North Sails declared and paid a cash dividend of $45,000. On December 31 North Sails reported net income of $120,000 for the year.

Prepare all necessary journal entries for 2005 for (a) Rho Jean Inc. and (b) Debbie, Inc.

Action Plan

• Presume that the investor has relatively little influence over the investee when an investor owns less than 20% of the common stock of another corporation. In this case, net income earned by the investee is not considered a proper basis for recognizing income from the investment by the investor.

• Presume significant influence for investments of 20%–50%. Therefore, record the investor's share of the net income of the investee.

Solution

(a) May 18	Stock Investments (400,000 × 5% × $6)	120,000	
	Cash		120,000
	(To record purchase of 20,000 shares of Stillwater stock)		
Aug. 30	Cash ~~Interest~~	3,750	
	Dividend Revenue ($75,000 × 5%)		3,750
	(To record receipt of cash dividend)		

(b) Jan. 1	Stock Investments (60,000 × 40% × \$12)	288,000	
	Cash		288,000
	(To record purchase of 24,000 shares of North Sails stock)		
Apr. 15	Cash	18,000	
	Stock Investments (\$45,000 × 40%)		18,000
	(To record receipt of cash dividend)		
Dec. 31	Stock Investments (\$120,000 × 40%)	48,000	
	Revenue from Investment in North Sails		48,000
	(To record 40% equity in North Sails' net income)		

THE NAVIGATOR

Valuation and Reporting of Investments

STUDY OBJECTIVE
5
Indicate how debt and stock investments are valued and reported in the financial statements.

The value of debt and stock investments may fluctuate greatly during the time they are held. For example, in one 12-month period, the stock of Digital Equipment Corporation hit a high of $76\frac{1}{2}$ and a low of $28\frac{3}{8}$. In light of such price fluctuations, how should investments be valued at the balance sheet date? Valuation could be at cost, at fair value (market value), or at the lower of cost or market value. Many people argue that fair value offers the best approach because it represents the expected cash realizable value of securities. **Fair value** is the amount for which a security could be sold in a normal market. Others counter that, unless a security is going to be sold soon, the fair value is not relevant because the price of the security will likely change again.

CATEGORIES OF SECURITIES

For purposes of valuation and reporting at a financial statement date, debt and stock investments are classified into three categories of securities:

1. **Trading securities** are securities bought and held primarily for sale in the near term to generate income on short-term price differences.
2. **Available-for-sale securities** are securities that may be sold in the future.
3. **Held-to-maturity securities** are debt securities that the investor has the intent and ability to hold to maturity.[3]

The valuation guidelines for these securities are presented in Illustration 12-5.

Illustration 12-5 Valuation guidelines

Trading	Available-for-sale	Held-to-maturity
"We'll sell within ten days."	"We'll hold the stock for a while to see how it performs."	"We intend to hold until maturity."
At fair value with changes reported in net income	At fair value with changes reported in the stockholders' equity section	At amortized cost

[3]This category is provided for completeness. The accounting and valuation issues related to held-to-maturity securities are discussed in more advanced accounting courses.

These guidelines apply to all debt securities and all stock investments in which the holdings are less than 20%.

Trading Securities

Trading securities are held with the intention of selling them in a short period of time (generally less than a month). *Trading* means frequent buying and selling. As indicated in Illustration 12-5, trading securities are reported at fair value, referred to as **mark-to-market** accounting, and changes from cost are reported **as part of net income**. The changes are reported as **unrealized gains or losses** because the securities have not been sold. The unrealized gain or loss is the difference between the **total cost** of the securities in the category and their **total fair value**.

As an example, Illustration 12-6 shows the costs and fair values for investments classified as trading securities for Kale Corporation on December 31, 2005.

Illustration 12-6 Valuation of trading securities

Investments	Cost	Fair Value	Unrealized Gain (Loss)
Yorkville Company bonds	$ 50,000	$ 48,000	$(2,000)
Kodak Company stock	90,000	99,000	9,000
Total	$140,000	$147,000	$ 7,000

Helpful Hint An unrealized gain or loss is reported in the income statement because of the likelihood that the securities will be sold at fair value since they are a short-term investment.

Kale Corporation has an unrealized gain of $7,000 because total fair value ($147,000) is $7,000 greater than total cost ($140,000). Fair value and unrealized gain or loss are recorded through an adjusting entry at the time financial statements are prepared. In the entry a valuation allowance account, Market Adjustment—Trading, is used to record the difference between the total cost and the total fair value of the securities. The adjusting entry for Kale Corporation is:

A	=	L	+	SE
+7,000				+7,000 Rev

Cash Flows
no effect

Dec. 31	Market Adjustment—Trading	7,000	
	Unrealized Gain—Income		7,000
	(To record unrealized gain on trading securities)		

The use of the Market Adjustment—Trading account enables the company to maintain a record of the investment cost. Actual cost is needed to determine the gain or loss realized when the securities are sold. The Market Adjustment—Trading balance is added to the cost of the investments to arrive at a fair value for the trading securities.

The fair value of the securities is the amount reported on the balance sheet. The unrealized gain is reported on the income statement under "Other revenues and gains." Why are unrealized gains and losses on trading securities included in income? Trading securities are held for a short period of time; thus, if a company has an unrealized gain or loss on its trading securities portfolio, it is likely that these securities will be sold soon and the gain or loss will be realized.

The term "income" is used in the Unrealized Gain account title to indicate that the gain affects net income. If the total cost of the trading securities is greater than total fair value, an unrealized loss has occurred. In such a case, the adjusting entry is a debit to Unrealized Loss—Income and a credit to Market Adjustment—Trading. The unrealized loss is reported under "Other expenses and losses" in the income statement.

The market adjustment account is carried forward into future accounting periods. No entries are made to this account during the period. At the end of each reporting period, the balance in the account is adjusted to the difference between cost and fair value at that time. The Unrealized Gain or Loss—Income account is closed to Income Summary at the end of the reporting period to bring its balance to zero.

Available-for-Sale Securities

As indicated earlier, available-for-sale securities are held with the intent of selling them sometime in the future. If the intent is to sell the securities within the next year or operating cycle, the securities are classified as current assets in the balance sheet. Otherwise, they are classified as long-term assets in the investments section of the balance sheet.

Available-for-sale securities are also reported at fair value. The procedure for determining fair value and unrealized gain or loss for these securities is the same as that for trading securities. To illustrate, assume that Elbert Corporation has two securities that are classified as available-for-sale. Illustration 12-7 provides information on the cost, fair value, and amount of the unrealized gain or loss on December 31, 2005.

Investments	Cost	Fair Value	Unrealized Gain (Loss)
Campbell Soup Corporation 8% bonds	$ 93,537	$103,600	$10,063
Hershey Foods stock	200,000	180,400	(19,600)
Total	$293,537	$284,000	$(9,537)

Illustration 12-7 Valuation of available-for-sale securities

For Elbert Corporation, there is an unrealized loss of $9,537 because total cost ($293,537) is $9,537 more than total fair value ($284,000). Both the adjusting entry and the reporting of the unrealized gain or loss from available-for-sale securities differ from those illustrated for trading securities. The differences result because these securities are not expected to be sold in the near term. Thus, prior to actual sale there is a much greater likelihood of changes in fair value that may change either unrealized gains or losses. Accordingly, an unrealized gain or loss is not reported in the income statement. Instead, it is reported as **a separate component of stockholders' equity**, referred to as a **contra equity account**. In the adjusting entry, the market adjustment account is identified with available-for-sale securities, and the unrealized gain or loss account is identified with stockholders' equity. The adjusting entry for Elbert Corporation to record the unrealized loss of $9,537 is:

Helpful Hint The entry is the same regardless of whether the securities are considered short-term or long-term.

Dec. 31	Unrealized Gain or Loss—Equity	9,537	
	Market Adjustment—Available-for-Sale		9,537
	(To record unrealized loss on available-for-sale securities)		

A	=	L	+	SE
−9,537				−9,537 Eq

Cash Flows
no effect

If total fair value exceeds total cost, the adjusting entry would be recorded as an increase (debit) to the market adjustment account and an increase (a credit) to an unrealized gain account.

For available-for-sale securities, the unrealized gain or loss account is carried forward to future periods. At each future balance sheet date, it is adjusted with the market adjustment account to show the difference between cost and fair value at that time.

EVALUATING INVESTMENT PORTFOLIO PERFORMANCE

The latest accounting standards for reporting investments in debt securities and equity investments of less than 20% were introduced in 1993. These new rules were intended to improve the information provided about the performance of a company's investment portfolio. Unfortunately, even under these new standards,

Helpful Hint Note that even though gains and losses on held-to-maturity securities also are not reported in income until realized, a company is less likely to window-dress with these securities because penalties are associated with selling these securities prior to maturity.

companies can "window-dress" their reported earnings results—that is, make net income look better than it is in reality.

Companies can choose which of the three categories of securities to use for an investment. Recall that gains and losses on investments classified as available-for-sale are not included in income, but rather are recorded as an adjustment to equity. If a company wanted to manage its reported income, it could simply sell those available-for-sale investments that have unrealized gains, and not sell those available-for-sale investments that have unrealized losses. By doing this, the company is deferring the losses until a later period. For example, refer back to Illustration 12-7. If Elbert Corporation wanted to increase its reported income, it could sell its investment in **Campbell Soup** and realize a gain of $10,063. It would then report an unrealized loss of $19,600 in the equity section of its balance sheet.

Sometimes unrealized losses on available-for-sale securities can be material. For example, in a recent year **KeyCorp**, a bank holding company headquartered in Cleveland, Ohio, reported net income of $853 million. However, the reduction to shareholders' equity for unrealized holding losses on available-for-sale securities was $115 million. That is, if these securities had been sold before year-end, income would have declined by $115 million. This potential loss represented 13% of net income. Similarly, in a recent year **Bank of America** reported a reduction to shareholders' equity of $326 million, when net income for the year was $2,176 million. Clearly, it is important to consider the potential impact of these unrealized losses on current and future income when evaluating the performance of the company's investment portfolio.

DECISION TOOLKIT

Decision Checkpoints	Info Needed for Decision	Tool to Use for Decision	How to Evaluate Results
Is the company window-dressing its results by manipulating its available-for-sale portfolio?	Balance of unrealized gains and unrealized losses	Unrealized gains and losses on available-for-sale securities are not run through net income but are recorded as adjustments to stockholders' equity. A company can window-dress by selling winners and holding losers to increase reported income, or do the opposite to reduce reported income.	Window-dressing is not easy to spot: It is difficult for an outsider to determine why companies chose to either sell or hold a security. A user should evaluate a company's earnings as reported, including any unrealized gains and losses, to see total potential variation.

BEFORE YOU GO ON . . .

▶ **Review It**

1. What are the three categories of investment securities?
2. What are the proper valuation and reporting for each of the three categories of investment securities?
3. Explain why unrealized gains and losses on trading securities are run through the income statement, while unrealized gains and losses on available-for-sale securities are not.
4. How might a company window-dress its reported earnings using its available-for-sale securities portfolio?

THE NAVIGATOR

BALANCE SHEET PRESENTATION OF INVESTMENTS

For balance sheet presentation, investments must be classified as either short-term or long-term.

Short-Term Investments

STUDY OBJECTIVE
6
Distinguish between short-term and long-term investments.

Short-term investments (also called **marketable securities**) are securities held by a company that are (1) **readily marketable** and (2) **intended to be converted into cash** within the next year or operating cycle, whichever is longer. Investments that do not meet **both criteria** are classified as long-term investments. In a recent survey of 600 large U.S. companies, 401 reported short-term investments.

READILY MARKETABLE. **An investment is readily marketable when it can be sold easily whenever the need for cash arises.** Short-term paper[4] meets this criterion because it can be sold readily to other investors. Stocks and bonds traded on organized securities markets, such as the New York Stock Exchange, are readily marketable because they can be bought and sold daily. In contrast, there may be only a limited market for the securities issued by small corporations and no market for the securities of a privately held company.

Helpful Hint Trading securities are always classified as short-term. Available-for-sale securities can be either short-term or long-term.

INTENT TO CONVERT. **Intent to convert means that management intends to sell the investment within the next year or operating cycle, whichever is longer.** Generally, this criterion is satisfied when the investment is considered a resource that will be used whenever the need for cash arises. For example, a ski resort may invest idle cash during the summer months with the intent to sell the securities to buy supplies and equipment shortly before the next winter season. This investment is considered short-term even if lack of snow cancels the next ski season and eliminates the need to convert the securities into cash as intended.

Because of their high liquidity, short-term investments are listed immediately below Cash in the current assets section of the balance sheet. Short-term investments are reported at fair value. For example, Pace Corporation would report its trading securities as shown in Illustration 12-8.

PACE CORPORATION Balance Sheet (partial)	
Current assets	
Cash	$21,000
Short-term investments, at fair value	60,000

Illustration 12-8
Presentation of temporary investments

Long-Term Investments

Long-term investments are generally reported in a separate section of the balance sheet immediately below Current assets, as shown later in Illustration 12-11 (page 595). Long-term investments in available-for-sale securities are reported at fair value, and investments in common stock accounted for under the equity method are reported at their equity value.

---

[4]Short-term paper includes (1) certificates of deposits (CDs) issued by banks, (2) money market certificates issued by banks and savings and loan associations, (3) Treasury bills issued by the U.S. government, and (4) commercial paper (notes) issued by corporations with good credit ratings.

PRESENTATION OF REALIZED AND UNREALIZED GAIN OR LOSS

Gains and losses on investments, whether realized or unrealized, must be presented in the financial statements. In the income statement, gains and losses, as well as interest and dividend revenue, are reported in the nonoperating section under the categories listed in Illustration 12-9.

Illustration 12-9
Nonoperating items related to investments

Other Revenue and Gains	Other Expenses and Losses
Interest Revenue	Loss on Sale of Investments
Dividend Revenue	Unrealized Loss—Income
Gain on Sale of Investments	
Unrealized Gain—Income	

As indicated earlier, an unrealized gain or loss on available-for-sale securities is reported as a separate component of stockholders' equity. To illustrate, assume that Dawson Inc. has common stock of $3,000,000, retained earnings of $1,500,000, and an unrealized loss on available-for-sale securities of $100,000. The financial statement presentation of the unrealized loss is shown in Illustration 12-10.

Illustration 12-10
Unrealized loss in stockholders' equity section

DAWSON INC. Balance Sheet (partial)	
Stockholders' equity	
Common stock	$3,000,000
Retained earnings	1,500,000
Total paid-in capital and retained earnings	4,500,000
Less: **Unrealized loss on available-for-sale securities**	(100,000)
Total stockholders' equity	$4,400,000

Note that the presentation of the loss is similar to the presentation of the cost of treasury stock in the stockholders' equity section. An unrealized gain is added in this section. Reporting the unrealized gain or loss in the stockholders' equity section serves two important purposes: (1) It reduces the volatility of net income due to fluctuations in fair value, and (2) it informs the financial statement user of the gain or loss that would occur if the securities were sold at fair value.

A new accounting standard requires that items such as this, which affect stockholders' equity but are not included in the calculation of net income, must be reported as part of a more inclusive measure called *comprehensive income*. For example, in **Tootsie Roll Industries**' balance sheet, stockholders' equity is reduced by "Accumulated other comprehensive earnings (loss)" of negative $11,052,000. Note 11 to Tootsie Roll's financial statements shows that one component of this amount was unrealized gains and losses on investment securities. Comprehensive income is discussed more fully in Chapter 14.

COMPLETE BALANCE SHEET

Many sections of classified balance sheets have been presented in this and preceding chapters. The balance sheet in Illustration 12-11 (on the next page) includes such topics from previous chapters as the issuance of par value

Illustration 12-11
Complete balance sheet

PACE CORPORATION
Balance Sheet
December 31, 2005

Assets

Current assets			
Cash			$ 21,000
Short-term investments, at fair value			60,000
Accounts receivable		$ 84,000	
Less: Allowance for doubtful accounts		4,000	80,000
Merchandise inventory, at FIFO cost			130,000
Prepaid insurance			23,000
Total current assets			314,000
Investments			
Investments in stock of less than 20% owned companies, at fair value		50,000	
Investment in stock of 20%–50% owned company, at equity		150,000	
Total investments			200,000
Property, plant, and equipment			
Land			300,000
Buildings	$800,000		
Less: Accumulated depreciation	200,000	600,000	
Equipment	180,000		
Less: Accumulated depreciation	54,000	126,000	
Total property, plant, and equipment			1,026,000
Intangible assets			
Goodwill (Note 1)		170,000	
Total intangible assets			170,000
Total assets			$1,710,000

Liabilities and Stockholders' Equity

Current liabilities			
Accounts payable			$ 185,000
Federal income taxes payable			60,000
Bond interest payable			10,000
Total current liabilities			255,000
Long-term liabilities			
Bonds payable, 10%, due 2017		$ 300,000	
Less: Discount on bonds		10,000	
Total long-term liabilities			290,000
Total liabilities			545,000
Stockholders' equity			
Paid-in capital			
Common stock, $10 par value, 200,000 shares authorized, 80,000 shares issued and outstanding		800,000	
Paid-in capital in excess of par value		100,000	
Total paid-in capital		900,000	
Retained earnings (Note 2)		255,000	
Total paid-in capital and retained earnings		1,155,000	
Add: **Unrealized gain on available-for-sale securities**		10,000	
Total stockholders' equity			1,165,000
Total liabilities and stockholders' equity			$1,710,000

Note 1. Goodwill is assumed to have an indefinite life, and therefore is not amortized.
Note 2. Retained earnings of $100,000 is restricted for plant expansion.

common stock, restrictions of retained earnings, and issuance of long-term bonds. From this chapter, the statement includes (highlighted in red) short-term and long-term investments. We have assumed the short-term investments are trading securities; the long-term investments in stock of less than 20% owned companies are assumed to be available-for-sale securities. Illustration 12-11 also includes a long-term investment reported at equity, descriptive notations within the statement such as the basis for valuing merchandise, and two notes to the statement.

BEFORE YOU GO ON . . .

▶ Review It

1. Explain where short-term and long-term investments are reported on a balance sheet.
2. Where are unrealized gains and losses from trading securities reported? Where are unrealized gains and losses from available-for-sale securities reported?

3. What was the amount of Tootsie Roll's investments that were classified as current? What amount was noncurrent? What percentage of total assets was investments? The answer to this question is provided on page 613.

☑ THE NAVIGATOR

Using the Decision Toolkit

KeyCorp is an Ohio bank holding company (a corporation that owns banks). It manages $85 billion in assets, the largest of which is its loan portfolio of $61 billion. In addition to its loan portfolio, however, like other banks it has significant debt and stock investments. The nature of these investments varies from short-term to long-term and as a consequence, consistent with accounting rules, KeyCorp reports its investments in three different categories: trading, available-for-sale, and held-to-maturity. The following facts are from KeyCorp's 2002 annual report.

($ in millions)	Amortized Cost	Gross Unrealized Gains	Gross Unrealized Losses	Fair Value
Trading securities	—	—	—	$1,632
Available-for-sale securities	$8,389	$210	$92	8,507
Held-to-maturity securities	120	9	0	129

Net income: $976 million

Instructions

Answer the following questions.

1. Why do you suppose KeyCorp purchases investments rather than only making loans? Why does it purchase investments that vary in terms of both their maturities and their type (debt versus stock)?

2. How must KeyCorp account for its investments in each of the three categories? In what ways does classifying investments into three different categories assist investors in evaluating the profitability of a company like KeyCorp?

3. Suppose that the management of KeyCorp was not happy with its 2002 net income. What step could it have taken with its investment portfolio that definitely would have increased 2002 reported profit? How much could it have increased reported profit? Why do you suppose it chose not to do this?

vestments in debt and stock securities are classified as trading, available-for-sale, or held-to-maturity securities for valuation and reporting purposes. Trading securities are reported as current assets at fair value, with changes from cost reported in net income. Available-for-sale securities are also reported at fair value, with the changes from cost reported in stockholders' equity. Available-for-sale securities are classified as short-term or long-term depending on their expected realization.

6 *Distinguish between short-term and long-term investments.* Short-term investments are securities held by a company that are readily marketable and intended to be converted to cash within the next year or operating cycle, whichever is longer. Investments that do not meet both criteria are classified as long-term investments.

DECISION TOOLKIT—A SUMMARY

Decision Checkpoints	Info Needed for Decision	Tool to Use for Decision	How to Evaluate Results
Is the company window-dressing its results by manipulating its available-for-sale portfolio?	Balance of unrealized gains and unrealized losses	Unrealized gains and losses on available-for-sale securities are not run through net income but are recorded as adjustments to stockholders' equity. A company can window-dress by selling winners and holding losers to increase reported income, or do the opposite to reduce reported income.	Window-dressing is not easy to spot: It is difficult for an outsider to determine why companies chose to either sell or hold a security. A user should evaluate a company's earnings as reported, including any unrealized gains and losses, to see total potential variation.

Glossary

Available-for-sale securities Securities that may be sold in the future. (p. 589)

Consolidated financial statements Financial statements that present the assets and liabilities controlled by the parent company and the aggregate profitability of the affiliated companies. (p. 587)

Controlling interest Ownership of more than 50% of the common stock of another entity. (p. 587)

Cost method An accounting method in which the investment in common stock is recorded at cost and revenue is recognized only when cash dividends are received. (p. 584)

Debt investments Investments in government and corporation bonds. (p. 581)

Equity method An accounting method in which the investment in common stock is initially recorded at cost, and the investment account is then adjusted annually to show the investor's equity in the investee. (p. 586)

Fair value Amount for which a security could be sold in a normal market. (p. 589)

Held-to-maturity securities Debt securities that the investor has the intent and ability to hold to their maturity date. (p. 589)

Long-term investments Investments that are not readily marketable or that management does not intend to convert into cash within the next year or operating cycle, whichever is longer. (p. 593)

Mark-to-market A method of accounting for certain investments that requires that they be adjusted to their fair value at the end of each period. (p. 590)

Parent company A company that owns more than 50% of the common stock of another entity. (p. 587)

Short-term investments (marketable securities) Investments that are readily marketable and intended to be converted into cash within the next year or operating cycle, whichever is longer. (p. 593)

Stock investments Investments in the capital stock of corporations. (p. 584)

Subsidiary (affiliated) company A company in which more than 50% of its stock is owned by another company. (p. 587)

Trading securities Securities bought and held primarily for sale in the near term to generate income on short-term price differences. (p. 589)

Demonstration Problem

In its first year of operations, DeMarco Company had these selected transactions in stock investments that are considered **trading securities**.

June 1   Purchased for cash 600 shares of Sanburg common stock at $24 per share plus $300 brokerage fees.

July 1   Purchased for cash 800 shares of Cey common stock at $33 per share plus $600 brokerage fees.

Sept. 1   Received a $1 per share cash dividend from Cey Corporation.

Nov. 1   Sold 200 shares of Sanburg common stock for cash at $27 per share less $150 brokerage fees.

Dec. 15   Received a $0.50 per share cash dividend on Sanburg common stock.

Instructions

(a) Journalize the transactions.

(b) Prepare the adjusting entry at December 31 to report the securities at fair value. At December 31 the fair values per share were: Sanburg $25 and Cey $30.

Solution to Demonstration Problem

(a)
Date	Account	Debit	Credit
June 1	Stock Investments	14,700	
	Cash [(600 × $24) + $300]		14,700
	(To record purchase of 600 shares of Sanburg common stock)		
July 1	Stock Investments	27,000	
	Cash [(800 × $33) + $600]		27,000
	(To record purchase of 800 shares of Cey common stock)		
Sept. 1	Cash	800	
	Dividend Revenue		800
	(To record receipt of $1 per share cash dividend from Cey)		
Nov. 1	Cash [(200 × $27) − $150]	5,250	
	Stock Investments (200 × $24.50)		4,900
	Gain on Sale of Stock Investments		350
	(To record sale of 200 shares of Sanburg common stock)		
Dec. 15	Cash [(600 − 200) × $0.50]	200	
	Dividend Revenue		200
	(To record receipt of $0.50 per share dividend from Sanburg)		
(b) Dec. 31	Unrealized Loss—Income	2,800	
	Market Adjustment—Trading		2,800
	(To record unrealized loss on trading securities)		

Investment	Cost	Fair Value	Unrealized Gain (Loss)
Sanburg common stock	$ 9,800	$10,000	$ 200
Cey common stock	27,000	24,000	(3,000)
Total	$36,800	$34,000	$(2,800)

Action Plan

• Include the price paid plus brokerage fees in the cost of the investment.

• Compute the gain or loss on sales as the difference between net selling price and the cost of the securities.

• Base the adjustment to fair value on the total difference between the cost and the fair value of the securities.

Self-Study Questions

Answers are at the end of the chapter.

(SO 2) **1.** Debt investments are initially recorded at:
(a) cost.
(b) cost plus accrued interest.
(c) fair value.
(d) None of the above

(SO 2) **2.** Hanes Company sells debt investments costing $26,000 for $28,000 plus accrued interest that has been recorded. In journalizing the sale, credits are:
(a) Debt Investments and Loss on Sale of Debt Investments.
(b) Debt Investments, Gain on Sale of Debt Investments, and Bond Interest Receivable.
(c) Stock Investments and Bond Interest Receivable.
(d) The correct answer is not given.

(SO 3) **3.** Pryor Company receives net proceeds of $42,000 on the sale of stock investments that cost $39,500. This transaction will result in reporting in the income statement a:
(a) loss of $2,500 under "Other expenses and losses."
(b) loss of $2,500 under "Operating expenses."
(c) gain of $2,500 under "Other revenues and gains."
(d) gain of $2,500 under "Operating revenues."

(SO 3) **4.** The equity method of accounting for long-term investments in stock should be used when the investor has significant influence over an investee and owns:
(a) between 20% and 50% of the investee's common stock.
(b) 20% or more of the investee's common stock.
(c) more than 50% of the investee's common stock.
(d) less than 20% of the investee's common stock.

(SO 4) **5.** Which of these statements is *not* true?

Consolidated financial statements are useful to:
(a) determine the profitability of specific subsidiaries.
(b) determine the aggregate profitability of enterprises under common control.
(c) determine the breadth of a parent company's operations.

(d) determine the full extent of aggregate obligations of enterprises under common control.

(SO 5) **6.** At the end of the first year of operations, the total cost of the trading securities portfolio is $120,000 and the total fair value is $115,000. What should the financial statements show?
(a) A reduction of an asset of $5,000 and a realized loss of $5,000.
(b) A reduction of an asset of $5,000 and an unrealized loss of $5,000 in the stockholders' equity section.
(c) A reduction of an asset of $5,000 in the current assets section and an unrealized loss of $5,000 under "Other expenses and losses."
(d) A reduction of an asset of $5,000 in the current assets section and a realized loss of $5,000 under "Other expenses and losses."

(SO 5) **7.** In the balance sheet, Unrealized Loss—Equity is reported as a:
(a) contra asset account.
(b) contra stockholders' equity account.
(c) loss in the income statement.
(d) loss in the retained earnings statement.

(SO 5) **8.** ⊶⊷ If a company wants to increase its reported income by manipulating its investment accounts, which should it do?
(a) Sell its "winner" trading securities and hold its "loser" trading securities.
(b) Hold its "winner" trading securities and sell its "loser" trading securities.
(c) Sell its "winner" available-for-sale securities and hold its "loser" available-for-sale securities.
(d) Hold its "winner" available-for-sale securities and sell its "loser" available-for-sale securities.

(SO 6) **9.** To be classified as short-term investments, debt investments must be readily marketable and be expected to be sold within:
(a) 3 months from the date of purchase.
(b) the next year or operating cycle, whichever is shorter.
(c) the next year or operating cycle, whichever is longer.
(d) the operating cycle.

☑ THE NAVIGATOR

Questions

1. What are the reasons that corporations invest in securities?

2. (a) What is the cost of an investment in bonds?
(b) When is interest on bonds recorded?

3. Ann Adler is confused about losses and gains on the sale of debt investments. Explain these issues to Ann:
(a) How the gain or loss is computed.
(b) The statement presentation of gains and losses.

4. Clio Company sells Cross's bonds that cost $40,000 for $45,000, including $3,000 of accrued interest. In recording the sale, Clio books a $5,000 gain. Is this correct? Explain.

5. What is the cost of an investment in stock?

6. To acquire Mega Corporation stock, R. L. Duran pays $65,000 in cash plus $1,500 broker's fees. What entry should be made for this investment, assuming the stock is readily marketable?

7. (a) When should a long-term investment in common stock be accounted for by the equity method?
   (b) When is revenue recognized under the equity method?

8. Malon Corporation uses the equity method to account for its ownership of 35% of the common stock of Flynn Packing. During 2005 Flynn reported a net income of $80,000 and declares and pays cash dividends of $10,000. What recognition should Malon Corporation give to these events?

9. What constitutes "significant influence" when an investor's financial interest is less than 50%?

10. Distinguish between the cost and equity methods of accounting for investments in stocks.

11. What are consolidated financial statements?

12. What are the valuation guidelines for investments at a balance sheet date?

13. Wendy Walner is the controller of G-Products, Inc. At December 31 the company's investments in trading securities cost $74,000 and have a fair value of $70,000. Indicate how Wendy would report these data in the financial statements prepared on December 31.

14. Using the data in question 13, how would Wendy report the data if the investment were long-term and the securities were classified as available-for-sale?

15. Reo Company's investments in available-for-sale securities at December 31 show total cost of $192,000 and total fair value of $210,000. Prepare the adjusting entry.

16. Using the data in question 15, prepare the adjusting entry assuming the securities are classified as trading securities.

17. What is the proper statement presentation of the account Unrealized Loss—Equity?

18. What purposes are served by reporting Unrealized Gains (Losses)—Equity in the stockholders' equity section?

19. Kirk Wholesale Supply owns stock in Xerox Corporation, which it intends to hold indefinitely because of some negative tax consequences if sold. Should the investment in Xerox be classified as a short-term investment? Why?

Brief Exercises

BE12-1   Phelps Corporation purchased debt investments for $41,500 on January 1, 2005. On July 1, 2005, Phelps received cash interest of $2,075. Journalize the purchase and the receipt of interest. Assume no interest has been accrued.

Journalize entries for debt investments.
(SO 2)

BE12-2   On August 1 McLain Company buys 1,000 shares of ABC common stock for $35,000 cash plus brokerage fees of $600. On December 1 the stock investments are sold for $38,000 in cash. Journalize the purchase and sale of the common stock.

Journalize entries for stock investments.
(SO 3)

BE12-3   Harmon Company owns 30% of Hook Company. For the current year Hook reports net income of $150,000 and declares and pays a $50,000 cash dividend. Record Harmon's equity in Hook's net income and the receipt of dividends from Hook.

Journalize transactions under the equity method.
(SO 3)

BE12-4   Cost and fair value data for the trading securities of Michele Company at December 31, 2005, are $62,000 and $59,000, respectively. Prepare the adjusting entry to record the securities at fair value.

Prepare adjusting entry using fair value.
(SO 5)

BE12-5   For the data presented in BE12-4, show the financial statement presentation of the trading securities and related accounts.

Indicate statement presentation using fair value.
(SO 6)

BE12-6   In 2005, its first year of operations, Duggen Corporation purchased available-for-sale stock securities costing $72,000 as a long-term investment. At December 31, 2005, the fair value of the securities is $65,000. Prepare the adjusting entry to record the securities at fair value.

Prepare adjusting entry using fair value.
(SO 5)

BE12-7   For the data presented in BE12-6, show the financial statement presentation of the available-for-sale securities and related accounts. Assume the available-for-sale securities are noncurrent.

Indicate statement presentation using fair value.
(SO 6)

BE12-8   Saber Corporation has these long-term investments: common stock of Sword Co. (10% ownership) held as available-for-sale securities, cost $108,000, fair value

Prepare investments section of balance sheet.
(SO 6)

$113,000; common stock of Epee Inc. (30% ownership), cost $210,000, equity $250,000; and a bond sinking fund of $150,000. Prepare the investments section of the balance sheet.

Exercises

Journalize debt investment transactions, and accrue interest.
(SO 2)

E12-1 Greer Corporation had these transactions pertaining to debt investments.

Jan. 1   Purchased 90 10%, $1,000 Ford Co. bonds for $90,000 cash plus brokerage fees of $900. Interest is payable semiannually on July 1 and January 1.
July 1   Received semiannual interest on Ford Co. bonds.
July 1   Sold 40 Ford Co. bonds for $44,000 less $400 brokerage fees.

Instructions
(a) Journalize the transactions.
(b) Prepare the adjusting entry for the accrual of interest at December 31.

Journalize stock investment transactions, and explain income statement presentation.
(SO 3)

E12-2 Puff Daddy Company had these transactions pertaining to stock investments.

Feb. 1   Purchased 800 shares of GET common stock (2%) for $9,000 cash plus brokerage fees of $200.
July 1   Received cash dividends of $1 per share on GET common stock.
Sept. 1   Sold 400 shares of GET common stock for $5,500 less brokerage fees of $100.
Dec. 1   Received cash dividends of $1 per share on GET common stock.

Instructions
(a) Journalize the transactions.
(b) Explain how dividend revenue and the gain (loss) on sale should be reported in the income statement.

Journalize transactions for investments in stock.
(SO 3)

E12-3 Grosby Inc. had these transactions pertaining to investments in common stock.

Jan. 1   Purchased 1,000 shares of Hannah Corporation common stock (5%) for $70,000 cash plus $1,400 broker's commission.
July 1   Received a cash dividend of $7 per share.
Dec. 1   Sold 500 shares of Hannah Corporation common stock for $32,000 cash less $800 broker's commission.
31   Received a cash dividend of $7 per share.

Instructions
Journalize the transactions.

Journalize and post transactions under the equity method.
(SO 3)

E12-4 On January 1 Howell Corporation purchased a 30% equity investment in Bellingham Corporation for $150,000. At December 31 Bellingham declared and paid a $70,000 cash dividend and reported net income of $250,000.

Instructions
(a) Journalize the transactions.
(b) Determine the amount to be reported as an investment in Bellingham stock at December 31.

Journalize entries under cost and equity methods.
(SO 3)

E12-5 Presented below are two independent situations.

1. Ritter Cosmetics acquired 10% of the 200,000 shares of common stock of Mai Fashion at a total cost of $13 per share on March 18, 2005. On June 30 Mai declared and paid a $75,000 dividend. On December 31 Mai reported net income of $122,000 for the year. At December 31 the market price of Mai Fashion was $16 per share. The stock is classified as available-for-sale.

2. Somer Inc. obtained significant influence over Ortiz Corporation by buying 40% of Ortiz's 30,000 outstanding shares of common stock at a total cost of $9 per share on January 1, 2005. On June 15 Ortiz declared and paid a cash dividend of $35,000. On December 31 Ortiz reported a net income of $90,000 for the year.

Instructions
Prepare all the necessary journal entries for 2005 for (a) Ritter Cosmetics and (b) Somer Inc.

E12-6 At December 31, 2005, the trading securities for Yanik, Inc., are as follows.

Security	Cost	Fair Value
A	$17,500	$16,000
B	12,500	14,000
C	23,000	19,000
Total	$53,000	$49,000

Prepare adjusting entry to record fair value, and indicate statement presentation.
(SO 5, 6)

Instructions
(a) Prepare the adjusting entry at December 31, 2005, to report the securities at fair value.
(b) Show the balance sheet and income statement presentation at December 31, 2005, after adjustment to fair value.

E12-7 Data for investments in stock classified as trading securities are presented in E12-6. Assume instead that the investments are classified as available-for-sale securities with the same cost and fair value data. The securities are considered to be a long-term investment.

Prepare adjusting entry to record fair value, and indicate statement presentation.
(SO 5, 6)

Instructions
(a) Prepare the adjusting entry at December 31, 2005, to report the securities at fair value.
(b) Show the statement presentation at December 31, 2005, after adjustment to fair value.
(c) M. Wise, a member of the board of directors, does not understand the reporting of the unrealized gains or losses. Write a letter to Mr. Wise explaining the reporting and the purposes it serves.

E12-8 Bill Bradley Company has these data at December 31, 2005.

Securities	Cost	Fair Value
Trading	$120,000	$128,000
Available-for-sale	100,000	94,000

Prepare adjusting entries for fair value, and indicate statement presentation for two classes of securities.
(SO 5, 6)

The available-for-sale securities are held as a long-term investment.

Instructions
(a) Prepare the adjusting entries to report each class of securities at fair value.
(b) Indicate the statement presentation of each class of securities and the related unrealized gain (loss) accounts.

Problems: Set A

P12-1A Marvel Davis Farms is a grower of hybrid seed corn for **DeKalb Genetics Corporation.** It has had two exceptionally good years and has elected to invest its excess funds in bonds. The following selected transactions relate to bonds acquired as an investment by Marvel Davis Farms, whose fiscal year ends on December 31.

Journalize debt investment transactions and show financial statement presentation.
(SO 2, 5, 6)

2005
Jan. 1 Purchased at par $1,000,000 of Sycamore Corporation 10-year, 9% bonds dated January 1, 2005, directly from the issuing corporation.
July 1 Received the semiannual interest on the Sycamore bonds.
Dec. 31 Accrual of interest at year-end on the Sycamore bonds.

(Assume that all intervening transactions and adjustments have been properly recorded and the number of bonds owned has not changed from December 31, 2005, to December 31, 2007.)

2008
Jan. 1 Received the semiannual interest on the Sycamore bonds.
Jan. 1 Sold $500,000 Sycamore bonds at 114. The broker deducted $7,000 for commissions and fees on the sale.
July 1 Received the semiannual interest on the Sycamore bonds.
Dec. 31 Accrual of interest at year-end on the Sycamore bonds.

Instructions

(a) Gain on sale of debt investment $63,000

(a) Journalize the listed transactions for the years 2005 and 2008.

(b) Assume that the fair value of the bonds at December 31, 2005, was $960,000. These bonds are classified as available-for-sale securities. Prepare the adjusting entry to record these bonds at fair value.

(c) Based on your analysis in part (b), show the balance sheet presentation of the bonds and interest receivable at December 31, 2005. Assume the investments are considered long-term. Indicate where any unrealized gain or loss is reported in the financial statements.

Journalize investment transactions, prepare adjusting entry, and show financial statement presentation.
(SO 2, 3, 6)

Peachtree

P12-2A In January 2005 the management of Mann Company concludes that it has sufficient cash to purchase some short-term investments in debt and stock securities. During the year, these transactions occurred.

Feb. 1 Purchased 800 shares of SRI common stock for $40,000 plus brokerage fees of $800.

Mar. 1 Purchased 500 shares of FGH common stock for $18,000 plus brokerage fees of $500.

Apr. 1 Purchased 70 $1,000, 12% CRT bonds for $70,000 plus $1,200 brokerage fees. Interest is payable semiannually on April 1 and October 1.

July 1 Received a cash dividend of $0.60 per share on the SRI common stock.

Aug. 1 Sold 200 shares of SRI common stock at $42 per share less brokerage fees of $350.

Sept. 1 Received $1 per share cash dividend on the FGH common stock.

Oct. 1 Received the semiannual interest on the CRT bonds.

Oct. 1 Sold the CRT bonds for $68,000 less $1,000 brokerage fees.

At December 31 the fair values of the SRI and FGH common stocks were $39 and $30 per share, respectively.

Instructions

(b) Unrealized loss $10,700

(a) Journalize the transactions and post to the accounts Debt Investments and Stock Investments. (Use the T account form.)

(b) Prepare the adjusting entry at December 31, 2005, to report the investments at fair value. All securities are considered to be trading securities.

(c) Show the balance sheet presentation of investment securities at December 31, 2005.

(d) Identify the income statement accounts and give the statement classification of each account.

Journalize transactions, prepare adjusting entry for stock investments, and show balance sheet presentation.
(SO 3, 5, 6)

P12-3A On December 31, 2004, Kern Associates owned the following securities that are held as long-term investments.

Common Stock	Shares	Cost
A Co.	1,000	$60,000
B Co.	6,000	36,000
C Co.	1,200	24,000

On this date the total fair value of the securities was equal to its cost. The securities are not held for influence or control over the investees. In 2005 these transactions occurred:

July 1 Received $1.50 per share semiannual cash dividend on B Co. common stock.

Aug. 1 Received $0.50 per share cash dividend on A Co. common stock.

Sept. 1 Sold 500 shares of B Co. common stock for cash at $7 per share less brokerage fees of $100.

Oct. 1 Sold 400 shares of A Co. common stock for cash at $56 per share less brokerage fees of $600.

Nov. 1 Received $1 per share cash dividend on C Co. common stock.

Dec. 15 Received $0.50 per share cash dividend on A Co. common stock.

31 Received $1.50 per share semiannual cash dividend on B Co. common stock.

At December 31 the fair values per share of the common stocks were: A Co. $47, B Co. $6, and C Co. $19.

Instructions
(a) Journalize the 2005 transactions and post to the account Stock Investments. (Use the T account form.)
(b) Prepare the adjusting entry at December 31, 2005, to show the securities at fair value. The stock should be classified as available-for-sale securities.
(c) Show the balance sheet presentation of the investments and the unrealized gain (loss) at December 31, 2005. At this date Kern Associates has common stock $2,000,000 and retained earnings $1,200,000.

(b) Unrealized loss $9,000

P12-4A   Wet Concrete acquired 20% of the outstanding common stock of Hawes Inc. on January 1, 2005, by paying $1,200,000 for 50,000 shares. Hawes declared and paid a $0.60 per share cash dividend on June 30 and again on December 31, 2005. Hawes reported net income of $800,000 for the year.

Prepare entries under cost and equity methods, and prepare memorandum.
(SO 3)

Instructions
(a) Prepare the journal entries for Wet Concrete for 2005 assuming Wet cannot exercise significant influence over Hawes. (Use the cost method.)
(b) Prepare the journal entries for Wet Concrete for 2005 assuming Wet can exercise significant influence over Hawes. (Use the equity method.)
(c) The board of directors of Wet Concrete is confused about the differences between the cost and equity methods. Prepare a memorandum for the board that explains each method and shows in tabular form the account balances under each method at December 31, 2005.

(a) Total dividend revenue
$60,000
(b) Revenue from investments
$160,000

P12-5A   Here is Sammy Sosa Company's portfolio of long-term available-for-sale securities at December 31, 2004.

Journalize stock transactions, and show balance sheet presentation.
(SO 3, 5, 6)

	Cost
1,000 shares of McGwire Inc. common stock	$52,000
1,400 shares of B. Ruth Corporation common stock	84,000
800 shares of H. Aaron Corporation preferred stock	33,600

On December 31 the total cost of the portfolio equaled the total fair value. Sosa had these transactions related to the securities during 2005.

Jan. 20   Sold 1,000 shares of McGwire Inc. common stock at $56 per share less brokerage fees of $600.
    28   Purchased 400 shares of $10 par value common stock of M. Mantle Corporation at $78 per share plus brokerage fees of $480.
    30   Received a cash dividend of $1.15 per share on B. Ruth Corporation common stock.
Feb. 8   Received cash dividends of $0.40 per share on H. Aaron Corporation preferred stock.
    18   Sold all 800 shares of H. Aaron preferred stock at $30 per share less brokerage fees of $360.
July 30   Received a cash dividend of $1 per share on B. Ruth Corporation common stock.   .
Sept. 6   Purchased an additional 800 shares of the $10 par value common stock of M. Mantle Corporation at $82 per share plus brokerage fees of $800.
Dec. 1   Received a cash dividend of $1.50 per share on M. Mantle Corporation common stock.

At December 31, 2005, the fair values of the securities were:

B. Ruth Corporation common stock	$64 per share
M. Mantle Corporation common stock	$70 per share

Sosa uses separate account titles for each investment, such as Investment in B. Ruth Corporation Common Stock.

Instructions
(a) Prepare journal entries to record the transactions.
(b) Post to the investment accounts. (Use T accounts.)
(c) Prepare the adjusting entry at December 31, 2005, to report the portfolio at fair value.
(d) Show the balance sheet presentation at December 31, 2005.

(a) Loss on sale $9,960

(c) Unrealized loss $8,480

Prepare a balance sheet.
(SO 6)

P12-6A   The following data, presented in alphabetical order, are taken from the records of Jackson Corporation.

Accounts payable	$ 220,000
Accounts receivable	90,000
Accumulated depreciation—building	180,000
Accumulated depreciation—equipment	52,000
Allowance for doubtful accounts	6,000
Bond investments	400,000
Bonds payable (10%, due 2019)	400,000
Buildings	900,000
Cash	72,000
Common stock ($5 par value; 500,000 shares authorized, 300,000 shares issued)	1,500,000
Discount on bonds payable	20,000
Dividends payable	50,000
Equipment	275,000
Goodwill	220,000
Income taxes payable	70,000
Investment in Houston Inc. stock (30% ownership), at equity	240,000
Land	500,000
Merchandise inventory	170,000
Notes payable (due 2006)	70,000
Paid-in capital in excess of par value	200,000
Prepaid insurance	16,000
Retained earnings	340,000
Short-term stock investment, at fair value	185,000

Total assets $2,830,000

Instructions
Prepare a balance sheet at December 31, 2005.

Problems: Set B

Journalize debt investment transactions and show financial statement presentation.
(SO 2, 5, 6)

P12-1B   Willow Carecenters Inc. provides financing and capital to the health care industry, with a particular focus on nursing homes for the elderly. The following selected transactions relate to bonds acquired as an investment by Willow, whose fiscal year ends on December 31.

2005

Jan. 1   Purchased at par $5,000,000 of Friendship Nursing Centers, Inc., 10-year, 10% bonds dated January 1, 2005, directly from Friendship.

July 1   Received the semiannual interest on the Friendship bonds.

Dec. 31   Accrual of interest at year-end on the Friendship bonds.

(Assume that all intervening transactions and adjustments have been properly recorded and that the number of bonds owned has not changed from December 31, 2005, to December 31, 2007.)

2008

Jan. 1   Received the semiannual interest on the Friendship bonds.

Jan. 1   Sold $2,500,000 Friendship bonds at 106. The broker deducted $10,000 for commissions and fees on the sale.

July 1   Received the semiannual interest on the Friendship bonds.

Dec. 31   Accrual of interest at year-end on the Friendship bonds.

Instructions

(a) Gain on sale of debt investment $140,000

(a) Journalize the listed transactions for the years 2005 and 2008.

(b) Assume that the fair value of the bonds at December 31, 2005, was $5,500,000. These bonds are classified as available-for-sale securities. Prepare the adjusting entry to record these bonds at fair value.

(c) Based on your analysis in part (b), show the balance sheet presentation of the bonds and interest receivable at December 31, 2005. Assume the investments are considered long-term. Indicate where any unrealized gain or loss is reported in the financial statements.

P12-2B In January 2005 the management of Norris Company concludes that it has sufficient cash to permit some short-term investments in debt and stock securities. During the year these transactions occurred.

Journalize investment transactions, prepare adjusting entry, and show financial statement presentation.
(SO 2, 3, 6)

Feb. 1   Purchased 600 shares of Alpha common stock for $28,800 plus brokerage fees of $300.
Mar. 1   Purchased 800 shares of Omega common stock for $20,000 plus brokerage fees of $400.
Apr. 1   Purchased 60 $1,000, 12% Pep bonds for $60,000 plus $1,200 brokerage fees. Interest is payable semiannually on April 1 and October 1.
July 1   Received a cash dividend of $0.60 per share on the Alpha common stock.
Aug. 1   Sold 200 shares of Alpha common stock at $56 per share less brokerage fees of $200.
Sept. 1   Received $1 per share cash dividend on the Omega common stock.
Oct. 1   Received the semiannual interest on the Pep bonds.
Oct. 1   Sold the Pep bonds for $65,000 less $1,000 brokerage fees.

At December 31 the fair values of the Alpha and Omega common stocks were $57 and $24 per share, respectively.

Instructions
(a) Journalize the transactions and post to the accounts Debt Investments and Stock Investments. (Use the T account form.)
(b) Prepare the adjusting entry at December 31, 2005, to report the investment securities at fair value. All securities are considered to be trading securities.
(c) Show the balance sheet presentation of investment securities at December 31, 2005.
(d) Identify the income statement accounts and give the statement classification of each account.

(a) Gain on stock sale $1,300

P12-3B On December 31, 2004, Milner Associates owned the following securities that are held as long-term investments. The securities are not held for influence or control over the investee.

Journalize transactions, prepare adjusting entry for stock investments, and show balance sheet presentation.
(SO 3, 5, 6)

Common Stock	Shares	Cost
D Co.	2,000	$90,000
E Co.	5,000	45,000
F Co.	1,500	30,000

On this date the total fair value of the securities was equal to its cost. In 2005 these transactions occurred.

July 1   Received $0.80 per share semiannual cash dividend on E Co. common stock.
Aug. 1   Received $0.50 per share cash dividend on D Co. common stock.
Sept. 1   Sold 700 shares of E Co. common stock for cash at $7 per share less brokerage fees of $200.
Oct. 1   Sold 500 shares of D Co. common stock for cash at $54 per share less brokerage fees of $500.
Nov. 1   Received $1 per share cash dividend on F Co. common stock.
Dec. 15   Received $0.50 per share cash dividend on D Co. common stock.
    31   Received $0.80 per share semiannual cash dividend on E Co. common stock.

At December 31 the fair values per share of the common stocks were: D Co. $48, E Co. $8, and F Co. $17.

Instructions
(a) Journalize the 2005 transactions and post to the account Stock Investments. (Use the T account form.)
(b) Prepare the adjusting entry at December 31, 2005, to show the securities at fair value. The stock should be classified as available-for-sale securities.

(b) Unrealized loss $4,300

(c) Show the balance sheet presentation of the investments and the unrealized gain (loss) at December 31, 2005. At this date Milner Associates has common stock $1,700,000 and retained earnings $1,000,000.

Prepare entries under cost and equity methods, and tabulate differences.
(SO 3)

P12-4B Nayler Services acquired 30% of the outstanding common stock of Quinn Company on January 1, 2005, by paying $800,000 for the 40,000 shares. Quinn declared and paid $0.40 per share cash dividends on March 15, June 15, September 15, and December 15, 2005. Quinn reported net income of $360,000 for the year.

(a) Total dividend revenue
$64,000

(b) Revenue from investment
$108,000

Instructions

(a) Prepare the journal entries for Nayler Services for 2005 assuming Nayler cannot exercise significant influence over Quinn. (Use the cost method.)

(b) Prepare the journal entries for Nayler Services for 2005 assuming Nayler can exercise significant influence over Quinn. (Use the equity method.)

(c) In tabular form indicate the investment and income statement account balances at December 31, 2005, under each method of accounting.

Journalize stock transactions and show statement presentation.
(SO 3, 5, 6)

P12-5B The following are in Big Head Todd Company's portfolio of long-term available-for-sale securities at December 31, 2004.

	Cost
500 shares of Aglar Corporation common stock	$26,000
700 shares of BAL Corporation common stock	42,000
400 shares of Hicks Corporation preferred stock	16,800

On December 31, the total cost of the portfolio equaled total fair value. Big Head Todd had the following transactions related to the securities during 2005.

Jan. 7 Sold 500 shares of Aglar Corporation common stock at $56 per share less brokerage fees of $700.

10 Purchased 200 shares, $70 par value common stock of Miley Corporation at $78 per share, plus brokerage fees of $240.

26 Received a cash dividend of $1.15 per share on BAL Corporation common stock.

Feb. 2 Received cash dividends of $0.40 per share on Hicks Corporation preferred stock.

10 Sold all 400 shares of Hicks Corporation preferred stock at $30.00 per share less brokerage fees of $180.

July 1 Received a cash dividend of $1.00 per share on BAL Corporation common stock.

Sept. 1 Purchased an additional 400 shares of the $70 par value common stock of Miley Corporation at $82 per share, plus brokerage fees of $400.

Dec. 15 Received a cash dividend of $1.50 per share on Miley Corporation common stock.

At December 31, 2005, the fair values of the securities were:

BAL Corporation common stock	$64 per share
Miley Corporation common stock	$72 per share

Big Head Todd Company uses separate account titles for each investment, such as Investment in BAL Corporation Common Stock.

Instructions

(a) Loss on sale $4,980

(a) Prepare journal entries to record the transactions.

(b) Post to the investment accounts. (Use T accounts.)

(b) Unrealized loss $3,040

(c) Prepare the adjusting entry at December 31, 2005, to report the portfolio at fair value.

(d) Show the balance sheet presentation at December 31, 2005.

Prepare a balance sheet.
(SO 6)

P12-6B The following data, presented in alphabetical order, are taken from the records of Rothchild Corporation.

Accounts payable	$ 220,000
Accounts receivable	90,000
Accumulated depreciation—building	180,000
Accumulated depreciation—equipment	52,000
Allowance for doubtful accounts	6,000

Bond investments	250,000
Bonds payable (10%, due 2014)	500,000
Buildings	950,000
Cash	92,000
Common stock ($10 par value; 500,000 shares authorized, 150,000 shares issued)	1,500,000
Dividends payable	90,000
Equipment	275,000
Goodwill	250,000
Income taxes payable	110,000
Investment in Dodge common stock (10% ownership), at cost	278,000
Investment in Huston common stock (30% ownership), at equity	230,000
Land	400,000
Market adjustment—available-for-sale securities (Dr.)	8,000
Merchandise inventory	170,000
Notes payable (due 2006)	70,000
Paid-in capital in excess of par value	200,000
Premium on bonds payable	40,000
Prepaid insurance	16,000
Retained earnings	213,000
Short-term stock investment, at fair value	180,000
Unrealized gain—available-for-sale securities	8,000

The investment in Dodge common stock is considered to be a long-term available-for-sale security.

Instructions
Prepare a balance sheet at December 31, 2005.

Total assets $2,951,000

BROADENING YOUR PERSPECTIVE

Financial Reporting and Analysis

FINANCIAL REPORTING PROBLEM: *Tootsie Roll Industries, Inc.*

BYP12-1   The financial statements of **Tootsie Roll Industries** are presented in Appendix A.

Instructions
Answer the following questions.
  (a) What information about investments is reported in the consolidated balance sheet?
  (b) Based on the information in Note 12 to Tootsie Roll's financial statements, what is the value of trading securities in 2002?
  (c) What effect did interest income on investments have on Income Before Income Taxes in 2002? (See Note 9.)
  (d) Judging from the statement of cash flows, did purchases of investment securities increase or decrease in 2002, and by how much?

COMPARATIVE ANALYSIS PROBLEM: *Tootsie Roll vs. Hershey Foods*

BYP12-2   The financial statements of **Hershey Foods** are presented in Appendix B, following the financial statements for **Tootsie Roll Industries** in Appendix A.

Instructions
Compare the investing activities sections of the statements of cash flows for the two companies for 2002, 2001, and 2000. What conclusions concerning the nature of investment activity can be drawn from these data?

RESEARCH CASE

BYP12-3   The January 9, 1999, issue of *The Economist* includes an article entitled "How to Make Mergers Work."

Instructions
Read the article and answer the following questions.

 (a) What percentage of mergers actually added value to the combined company? Which investors tend to gain from the merger, and which tend to lose?

 (b) The article suggests that mergers in the past tended to be undertaken to create diversified conglomerates, but that mergers of today tend to be defensive in nature. Give examples of motivations for defensive mergers and industries where they have taken place.

 (c) What are some reasons why mergers often fail?

 (d) What are some methods for increasing the likelihood of success?

INTERPRETING FINANCIAL STATEMENTS

BYP12-4   Delta Air Lines, Inc., is based in Atlanta, Georgia, and is one of the world's largest air carriers. Besides carrying passengers, Delta also provides freight and mail transportation services.

Here is the assets section of a recent Delta balance sheet (excluding dollar amounts):

DELTA AIR LINES
Balance Sheet (partial)

Current assets
  Cash and cash equivalents
  Short-term investments
  Accounts receivable, net of allowance for uncollectible accounts
  Maintenance and operating supplies, at average cost
  Deferred income taxes
  Prepaid expenses and other
Property and equipment
  Flight equipment, less accumulated depreciation
  Flight equipment under capital leases, less accumulated amortization
  Ground property and equipment, less accumulated depreciation
  Advance payments for equipment
Other assets
  Investments in stock of less than 20% owned companies
  Deferred income taxes
  Investments in associated companies
  Cost in excess of net assets acquired, net of accumulated amortization
  Leasehold and operating rights, net of accumulated amortization
  Other

Delta also reported the following information concerning certain of its investments:

1. Investments in **TransQuest Information Solutions** (TransQuest), an information technology joint venture, are accounted for under the equity method.

2. Investments with an original maturity of 3 months or less are stated at cost, which approximates fair value.

3. Cost in excess of net assets acquired (goodwill), which is being amortized over 40 years, is related to the company's acquisition of **Western Air Lines, Inc.,** on December 18, 1986.

4. The company's investments in **Singapore Air Lines Limited** are accounted for under the cost method and are classified as available-for-sale and carried at aggregate market value.

5. Cash in excess of operating requirements is invested in short-term, highly liquid investments. These investments are classified as available-for-sale and are stated at fair value.

Instructions

(a) For each item 1–5 above, determine where it should be shown on Delta's balance sheet, using the account titles listed earlier.

(b) Assume that item 2 includes an investment in **IBM Corporation** bonds consisting of ten bonds of $10,000 each. What accounting treatment is required for the following?

(1) Singapore Air Lines Limited announces net income for the year of $3.15 per share. Assume that Delta holds 3,500 shares.

(2) Western Air Lines announces a net loss of $18,000,000, or $.63 per share for the quarter.

(3) IBM Corporation declares and pays a $.25 dividend per share.

BYP12-5   Firstar Inc. is a large bank holding company. In addition to making loans, it has significant trading activities. During a recent year the company reported net income of $430 million.

The following additional information was available regarding the company's available-for-sale portfolio.

(in millions)	Cost	Gross Unrealized Gains	Gross Unrealized Losses	Fair Value
	$6,064	$159.6	$2.5	$6,221

Instructions

Firstar has a significant available-for-sale portfolio. How much, and by what percentage, could the company have increased its income by selling its "winners" while holding its "losers"? Why do you suppose it chose not to do this?

A GLOBAL FOCUS

BYP12-6   Xerox Corporation has a 50% investment interest in a joint venture with the Japanese corporation Fuji, called **Fuji Xerox**. Xerox accounts for this investment using the equity method. The following additional information regarding this investment was taken from Xerox's 1998 annual report (in millions).

Investment in Fuji Xerox per balance sheet	$ 1,354
Fuji Xerox net income	108
Xerox total assets	30,024
Xerox total liabilities	25,167
Fuji Xerox total assets	6,279
Fuji Xerox total liabilities	3,757

Instructions

(a) What alternative approaches are available for accounting for long-term investments in stock? Discuss whether Xerox is correct in using the equity method to account for this investment.

(b) Under the equity method, how does Xerox report its investment in Fuji Xerox? If Xerox owned a majority of Fuji Xerox, it then would have to consolidate Fuji Xerox instead of using the equity method. Discuss how this would change Xerox's financial statements. That is, in what way and by how much would assets and liabilities change?

(c) The use of 50% joint ventures is becoming a fairly common practice. Why might companies like Xerox and Fuji prefer to participate in a joint venture rather than own a majority share?

FINANCIAL ANALYSIS ON THE WEB

BYP12-7   The Securities and Exchange Commission (SEC) is the primary regulatory agency of U.S. financial markets. Its job is to ensure that the markets remain fair for all investors. The following SEC site provides useful information for investors.

Address: **www.sec.gov/answers.shtml** (or go to **www.wiley.com/college/ kimmel**)

Steps

Go to the site shown above.

Instructions

Find the definition of the following terms:
- **(a)** Ask price.
- **(b)** Margin account.
- **(c)** Prospectus.
- **(d)** Yield.

BYP12-8 Most publicly traded companies are analyzed by numerous analysts. These analysts often don't agree about a company's future prospects. In this exercise you will find analysts' ratings about companies and make comparisons over time and across companies in the same industry. You will also see to what extent the analysts experienced "earnings surprises." Earnings surprises can cause changes in stock prices.

Address: **biz.yahoo.com/i** (or go to **www.wiley.com/college/kimmel**)

Steps

1. Choose a company.
2. Use the index to find the company's name.
3. Choose **Research**.

Instructions

Answer the following questions.
- **(a)** How many brokers rated the company?
- **(b)** What percentage rated it a strong buy?
- **(c)** What was the average rating for the week?
- **(d)** Did the average rating improve or decline relative to the previous week?
- **(e)** How do the brokers rank this company among all the companies in its industry?
- **(f)** What was the amount of the earnings surprise during the last quarter? (That is, to what extent were analysts' expectations of earnings incorrect?)
- **(g)** Are earnings expected to increase or decrease this quarter compared to last?

Critical Thinking

GROUP DECISION CASE

BYP12-9 At the beginning of the question and answer portion of the annual stockholders' meeting of Revell Corporation, stockholder Carol Finstrom asks, "Why did management sell the holdings in AHM Company at a loss when this company has been very profitable during the period its stock was held by Revell?"

Since President Larry Wisdom has just concluded his speech on the recent success and bright future of Revell, he is taken aback by this question and responds, "I remember we paid $1,100,000 for that stock some years ago, and I am sure we sold that stock at a much higher price. You must be mistaken."

Finstrom retorts, "Well, right here in footnote number 7 to the annual report it shows that 240,000 shares, a 30% interest in AHM, was sold on the last day of the year. Also, it states that AHM earned $550,000 this year and paid out $150,000 in cash dividends. Further, a summary statement indicates that in past years, while Revell held AHM stock, AHM earned $1,240,000 and paid out $440,000 in dividends. Finally, the income statement for this year shows a loss on the sale of AHM stock of $180,000. So, I doubt that I am mistaken."

Red-faced, President Wisdom turns to you.

Instructions

With the class divided into groups, answer the following:

Help out President Wisdom: What dollar amount did Revell receive upon the sale of the AHM stock? Explain why both Finstrom and Wisdom are correct.

COMMUNICATION ACTIVITY

BYP12-10 Chapperal Corporation has purchased two securities for its portfolio. The first is a stock investment in Sting Ray Corporation, one of its suppliers. Chapperal purchased 10% of Sting Ray with the intention of holding it for a number of years but has no intention of purchasing more shares. The second investment is a purchase of debt securities. Chapperal purchased the debt securities because its analysts believe that changes in market interest rates will cause these securities to increase in value in a short period of time. Chapperal intends to sell the securities as soon as they have increased in value.

Instructions
Write a memo to Gils Stiles, the chief financial officer, explaining how to account for each of these investments and the implications for reported income from this accounting treatment.

ETHICS CASE

BYP12-11 Scott Kreiter Financial Services Company holds a large portfolio of debt and stock securities as an investment. The total fair value of the portfolio at December 31, 2005, is greater than total cost, with some securities having increased in value and others having decreased. Vicki Lemke, the financial vice-president, and Ula Greenwood, the controller, are in the process of classifying for the first time the securities in the portfolio.

Lemke suggests classifying the securities that have increased in value as trading securities in order to increase net income for the year. She wants to classify the securities that have decreased in value as long-term available-for-sale securities so that the decreases in value will not affect 2005 net income.

Greenwood disagrees. She recommends classifying the securities that have decreased in value as trading securities and those that have increased in value as long-term available-for-sale securities. Greenwood argues that the company is having a good earnings year and that recognizing the losses now will help to smooth income for this year. Moreover, for future years, when the company may not be as profitable, the company will have built-in gains.

Instructions
   (a) Will classifying the securities as Lemke and Greenwood suggest actually affect earnings as each says it will?
   (b) Is there anything unethical in what Lemke and Greenwood propose? Who are the stakeholders affected by their proposals?
   (c) Assume that Lemke and Greenwood properly classify the portfolio. Assume, at year-end, that Lemke proposes to sell the securities that will increase 2005 net income, and that Greenwood proposes to sell the securities that will decrease 2005 net income. Is this unethical?

Answers to Self-Study Questions

1. a   2. b   3. c   4. a   5. a   6. c   7. b   8. c   9. c

Answer to Tootsie Roll Review It Question 3, p. 596

Tootsie Roll had investments of $40,737,000 classified as current, and $116,501,000 classified as noncurrent. Investments represented 24.3% of total assets [($40,737,000 + $116,501,000) ÷ $646,080,000].

Remember to go back to the Navigator box on the chapter-opening page and check off your completed work.

13

Statement of Cash Flows

STUDY OBJECTIVES

After studying this chapter,
you should be able to:

1 Indicate the usefulness of the statement of cash flows.

2 Distinguish among operating, investing, and financing activities.

3 Explain the impact of the product life cycle on a company's cash flows.

4 Prepare a statement of cash flows using one of two approaches: (a) the indirect method or (b) the direct method.

5 Use the statement of cash flows to evaluate a company.

☑ THE NAVIGATOR

THE NAVIGATOR ✔

▶ Scan *Study Objectives* ☐

▶ Read *Feature Story* ☐

▶ Read *Preview* ☐

▶ Read text and answer *Before You Go On*
  p. 621 ☐   p. 625 ☐   p. 633 ☐
  p. 642 ☐   p. 649 ☐

▶ Work Using the *Decision Toolkit* ☐

▶ Review Summary of *Study Objectives* ☐

▶ Work *Demonstration Problem* ☐

▶ Answer *Self-Study Questions* ☐

▶ Complete *Assignments* ☐

FEATURE STORY

I've Got $38 Billion Burning a Hole in My Pocket!

Things move fast in the high technology sector. Very fast. The business story of the turn-of-the-millenium period is surely the explosion of activity in areas such as software, Internet-based services, and high-speed communications.

In today's environment, companies must be ready to respond to changes quickly in order to survive and thrive. They need to produce new products and expand to new markets continually. To do this takes cash—lots and lots of cash. Keeping lots of cash available is a real challenge for a young company. It requires great cash management and careful attention to cash flow.

One technique for cash management that is common in young high-tech companies is paying employees in part through stock options. This frees up cash for business activities, especially in the crucial early phase of the company.

Microsoft, at 27 years of age the great-granddaddy of the software industry, was a pioneer of this and other cash management strategies. By some estimates, more than 1,000 Microsoft employees became millionaires through stock options in the first 20 years of the company's operations.

The story of Microsoft's phenomenal growth—how it was founded in 1975 by Bill Gates and, by 2000, had grown so large and powerful that a U.S.

judge ordered it to be broken up—is well-known. But the numbers are nonetheless startling. Seattle-based Microsoft's 2001 statement of cash flows reported cash provided by operating activities in excess of $13 billion. Its cash flow per share, $2.18, is double the industry average, and more than its earnings per share of $1.38. Its cash and short-term investments amounted to over $31 billion on its balance sheet at its fiscal year-end of June 30, 2001.

That kind of money is astounding, even in this big-money sector. For comparison, consider **Novell, Inc.** Based in Provo, Utah, Novell is an internationally recognized developer of software products, such as NetWare, UnixWare, and Groupware. Founded in 1983, Novell is younger than Microsoft by 8 years—eons in the computing world. Novell may not be the worldwide household name that Microsoft is, but Novell is certainly a major player. It generated cash from operations of $101 million for the year ending October 31, 2001, down from a high of $145 million in 2000. Still, this is only a drop in the bucket compared with Microsoft's billions.

It is impossible to predict what the future will hold for either of these companies. What effect will the *Antitrust Act* decision have on Microsoft, and on the industry as a whole? How will Novell's recent acquisition of **Cambridge Technology Partners** pan out? Will its reorganization into three segments generate greater efficiencies? Will its newly realigned sales force woo new customers? Will Microsoft's video game console, *Xbox*, meet sales expectations?

Cash management is sure to continue to be an important factor for both companies, and for their ever-growing list of upstart competitors. Beyond that, anything is possible in this sector, where change is the only constant. After all, who could have predicted in 1975 that 19-year-old Bill Gates would become the world's best-known billionaire?

☑ THE NAVIGATOR

On the World Wide Web
Microsoft: www.microsoft.com
Novell: www.novell.com

The balance sheet, income statement, and retained earnings statement do not always show the whole picture of the financial condition of a company or institution. In fact, looking at the financial statements of some well-known companies, a thoughtful investor might ask questions like these: How did **Eastman Kodak** finance cash dividends of $649 million in a year in which it earned only $17 million? How could **United Airlines** purchase new planes that cost $1.9 billion in a year in which it reported a net loss of over $2 billion? How did the companies that spent a combined fantastic $3.4 trillion on mergers and acquisitions in a recent year finance those deals? Answers to these and similar questions can be found in this chapter, which presents the statement of cash flows.

The content and organization of this chapter are as follows.

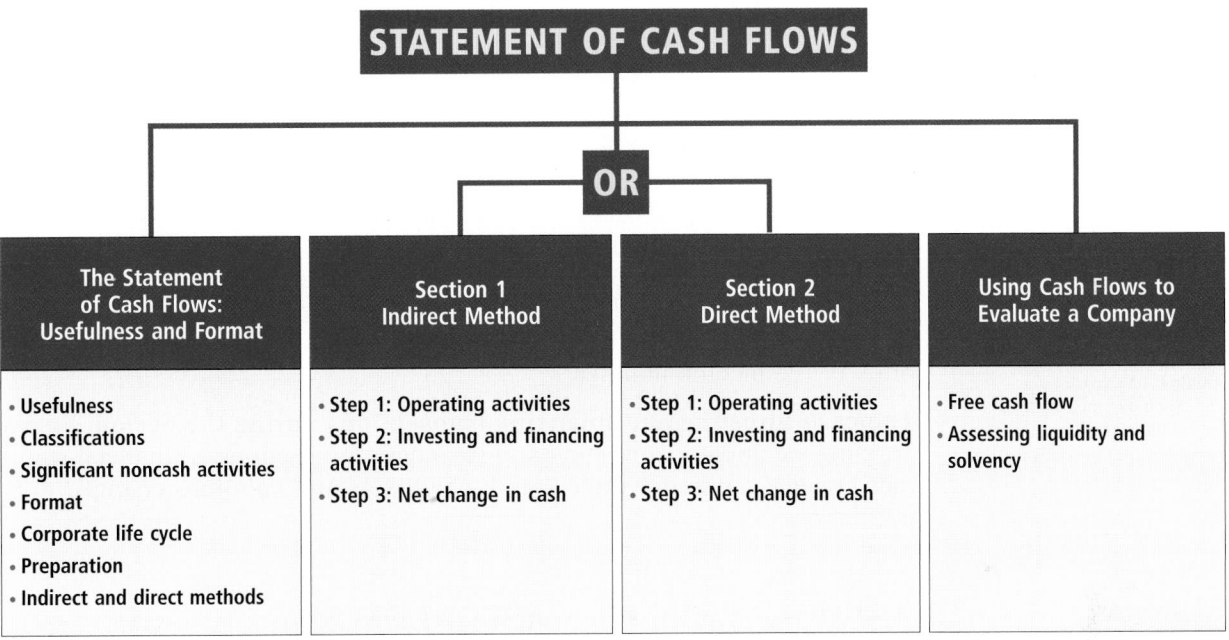

THE NAVIGATOR

The Statement of Cash Flows: Usefulness and Format

The basic financial statements we have presented so far provide only limited information about a company's cash flows (cash receipts and cash payments). For example, comparative balance sheets show the increase in property, plant, and equipment during the year. But they do not show how the additions were financed or paid for. The income statement shows net income. But it does not indicate the amount of cash generated by operating activities. The retained earnings statement shows cash dividends declared but not the cash dividends paid during the year. None of these statements presents a detailed summary of where cash came from and how it was used.

Helpful Hint Recall that the retained earnings statement is often presented in the statement of stockholders' equity.

STUDY OBJECTIVE
1
Indicate the usefulness of the statement of cash flows.

USEFULNESS OF THE STATEMENT OF CASH FLOWS

The **statement of cash flows** reports the cash receipts, cash payments, and net change in cash resulting from operating, investing, and financing activities during a period. The information in a statement of cash flows should help investors, creditors, and others assess:

1. **The entity's ability to generate future cash flows.** By examining relationships between items in the statement of cash flows, investors and others can make predictions of the amounts, timing, and uncertainty of future cash flows better than they can from accrual basis data.

2. **The entity's ability to pay dividends and meet obligations.** If a company does not have adequate cash, it cannot pay employees, settle debts, or pay dividends. Employees, creditors, and stockholders should be particularly interested in this statement, because it alone shows the flows of cash in a business.

3. **The reasons for the difference between net income and net cash provided (used) by operating activities.** Net income provides information on the success or failure of a business enterprise. However, some financial statement users are critical of accrual basis net income because it requires many estimates. As a result, the reliability of the number is often challenged. Such is not the case with cash. Many readers of the statement of cash flows want to know the reasons for the difference between net income and net cash provided by operating activities. Then they can assess for themselves the reliability of the income number.

4. **The cash investing and financing transactions during the period.** By examining a company's investing and financing transactions, a financial statement reader can better understand why assets and liabilities changed during the period.

ETHICS NOTE

Many investors believe that "Cash is cash and everything else is accounting." That is, they feel that cash flow is less susceptible to management manipulation than traditional accounting measures such as net income. Though we would discourage reliance on cash flows to the exclusion of accrual accounting, comparing cash from operations to net income can reveal important information about the "quality" of reported net income. Such a comparison can reveal the extent to which net income provides a good measure of actual performance.

STUDY OBJECTIVE
2
Distinguish among operating, investing, and financing activities.

CLASSIFICATION OF CASH FLOWS

The statement of cash flows classifies cash receipts and cash payments as operating, investing, and financing activities. Transactions and other events characteristic of each kind of activity are described below.

1. **Operating activities** include the cash effects of transactions that create revenues and expenses. They thus enter into the determination of net income.

2. **Investing activities** include (a) acquiring and disposing of investments and property, plant, and equipment, and (b) lending money and collecting the loans.

3. **Financing activities** include (a) obtaining cash from issuing debt and repaying the amounts borrowed, and (b) obtaining cash from stockholders and providing them with a return on their investment.

The category of operating activities is the most important. As noted above, it shows the cash provided by company operations. This source of cash is generally considered to be the best measure of a company's ability to generate sufficient cash to continue as a going concern.

Illustration 13-1 (next page) lists typical cash receipts and cash payments within each of the three classifications. **Study the list carefully.** It will prove very useful in solving homework exercises and problems.

Types of Cash Inflows and Outflows

Operating activities—Income statement items
  Cash inflows:
    From sale of goods or services.
    From returns on loans (interest received) and on equity securities
      (dividends received).
  Cash outflows:
    To suppliers for inventory.
    To employees for services.
    To government for taxes.
    To lenders for interest.
    To others for expenses.

Investing activities—Changes in investments and long-term assets
  Cash inflows:
    From sale of property, plant, and equipment.
    From sale of debt or equity securities of other entities.
    From collection of principal on loans to other entities.
  Cash outflows:
    To purchase property, plant, and equipment.
    To purchase debt or equity securities of other entities.
    To make loans to other entities.

Financing activities—Changes in long-term liabilities and stockholders' equity
  Cash inflows:
    From sale of common stock.
    From issuance of debt (bonds and notes).
  Cash outflows:
    To stockholders as dividends.
    To redeem long-term debt or reacquire capital stock.

**Operating
activities**

Investing activities

**Financing
activities**

Note the following general guidelines: (1) Operating activities involve income statement items. (2) Investing activities involve cash flows resulting from changes in investments and long-term asset items. (3) Financing activities involve cash flows resulting from changes in long-term liability and stockholders' equity items.

Some cash flows related to investing or financing activities are classified as operating activities. For example, receipts of investment revenue (interest and dividends) are classified as operating activities. So are payments of interest to lenders. Why are these considered operating activities? **Because these items are reported in the income statement, where results of operations are shown.**

SIGNIFICANT NONCASH ACTIVITIES

Not all of a company's significant activities involve cash. Examples of significant noncash activities are:

1. Issuance of common stock to purchase assets.

2. Conversion of bonds into common stock.

3. Issuance of debt to purchase assets.

4. Exchanges of plant assets.

Significant financing and investing activities that do not affect cash are not reported in the body of the statement of cash flows. However, these activities are reported in either a **separate schedule** at the bottom of the statement of cash flows or in a **separate note or supplementary schedule** to the financial statements.

The reporting of these noncash activities in a separate schedule satisfies the **full disclosure principle**. In solving homework assignments you should present significant noncash investing and financing activities in a separate schedule at the bottom of the statement of cash flows. (See lower section of Illustration 13-2, at the bottom of this page, for an example.)

Business Insight
INVESTOR PERSPECTIVE

Net income is not the same as net cash provided by operations. The differences are illustrated by the following results from recent annual reports for 2002 ($ in millions).

Company	Net Income	Net Cash Provided by Operations
Kmart Corporation	$(3,219)	$ 252
Wal-Mart Stores, Inc.	6,671	10,260
JCPenney Company, Inc.	378	1,329
Sears, Roebuck & Co.	1,578	2,467
Target Corporation	1,645	2,863

Note the wide disparity among these companies that all engaged in similar types of retail merchandising.

FORMAT OF THE STATEMENT OF CASH FLOWS

The general format of the statement of cash flows presents the results of the three activities discussed previously—operating, investing, and financing—plus the significant noncash investing and financing activities. A widely used form of the statement of cash flows is shown in Illustration 13-2.

Illustration 13-2 Format of statement of cash flows

COMPANY NAME
Statement of Cash Flows
Period Covered

Cash flows from operating activities
  (List of individual items)   XX
    Net cash provided (used) by operating activities   XXX
Cash flows from investing activities
  (List of individual inflows and outflows)   XX
    Net cash provided (used) by investing activities   XXX
Cash flows from financing activities
  (List of individual inflows and outflows)   XX
    Net cash provided (used) by financing activities   XXX
Net increase (decrease) in cash   XXX
Cash at beginning of period   XXX
Cash at end of period   XXX

Noncash investing and financing activities
  (List of individual noncash transactions)   XXX

The cash flows from operating activities section always appears first. It is followed by the investing activities and the financing activities sections.

BEFORE YOU GO ON . . .

▶ Review It

1. Why is the statement of cash flows useful?
2. What are the major classifications of cash flows on the statement of cash flows?
3. What are some examples of significant noncash activities?
4. What is the general format of the statement of cash flows? In what sequence are the three types of business activities presented?

▶ Do It

During its first week, Duffy & Stevenson Company had these transactions.

1. Issued 100,000 shares of $5 par value common stock for $800,000 cash.
2. Borrowed $200,000 from Castle Bank, signing a 5-year note bearing 8% interest.
3. Purchased two semi-trailer trucks for $170,000 cash.
4. Paid employees $12,000 for salaries and wages.
5. Collected $20,000 cash for services rendered.

Classify each of these transactions by type of cash flow activity.

Action Plan

• Identify the three types of activities used to report all cash inflows and outflows.
• Report as operating activities the cash effects of transactions that create revenues and expenses and enter into the determination of net income.
• Report as investing activities transactions that (a) acquire and dispose of investments and productive long-lived assets and (b) lend money and collect loans.
• Report as financing activities transactions that (a) obtain cash from issuing debt and repay the amounts borrowed and (b) obtain cash from stockholders and pay them dividends.

Solution

1. Financing activity   4. Operating activity
2. Financing activity   5. Operating activity
3. Investing activity

☑ THE NAVIGATOR

THE CORPORATE LIFE CYCLE

All products go through a series of phases called the **product life cycle**. The phases (in order of their occurrence) are often referred to as follows: **introductory phase**, **growth phase**, **maturity phase**, and **decline phase**. The introductory phase occurs at the beginning of a company's life, when it is purchasing fixed assets and beginning to produce and sell products. During the growth phase, the company is striving to expand its production and sales. In the maturity phase, sales and production level off. During the decline phase, sales of the product fall due to a weakening in consumer demand.

STUDY OBJECTIVE
3
Explain the impact of the product life cycle on a company's cash flows.

If a company had only one product and that product was nearing the end of its salable life, we could easily say that the company was in the decline phase. Companies generally have more than one product, however, and not all of a company's products are in the same phase of the product life cycle at the same time. Still, we can characterize a company as being in one of the four phases, because the majority of its products are in a particular phase.

Illustration 13-3 shows that the phase a company is in affects its cash flows. In the **introductory phase**, we expect that the company will not be generating positive cash from operations. That is, cash used in operations will exceed cash generated by operations in the introductory phase. Also, the company will be spending considerable amounts to purchase productive assets such as buildings and equipment. To support its asset purchases the company will have to issue stock or debt. Thus, during the introductory phase we expect cash from operations to be negative, cash from investing to be negative, and cash from financing to be positive.

Illustration 13-3
Impact of product life cycle on cash flows

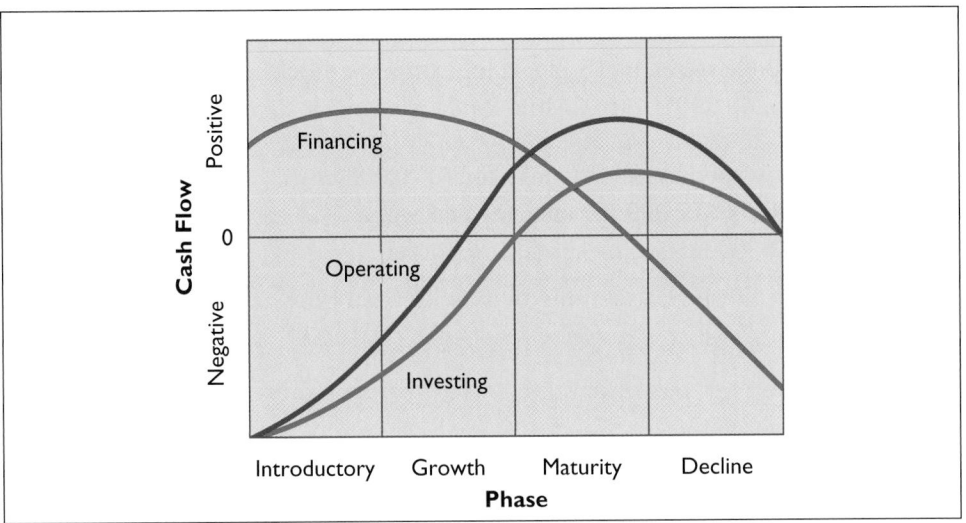

During the **growth phase**, we expect to see the company start to generate small amounts of cash from operations. During this phase, cash from operations on the statement of cash flows will be less than net income on the income statement. One reason income will exceed cash flow from operations during this period is explained by the difference between the cash paid for inventory and the amount expensed as cost of goods sold. Since sales are projected to be increasing, the size of inventory purchases must increase. Thus, less inventory will be expensed on an accrual basis than purchased on a cash basis in the growth phase. Also, collections on accounts receivable will lag behind sales, and accrual sales during a period will exceed cash collections during that period. Cash needed for asset acquisitions will continue to exceed cash provided by operations, requiring that the company make up the deficiency by issuing new stock or debt. Thus, in the growth phase, the company continues to show negative cash from investing and positive cash from financing.

During the **maturity phase**, cash from operations and net income are approximately the same. Cash generated from operations exceeds investing needs. Thus, in the maturity phase the company can actually start to retire debt or buy back stock.

Finally, during the **decline phase**, cash from operations decreases. Cash from investing might actually become positive as the company sells off excess assets. Cash from financing may be negative as the company buys back stock and retires debt.

Business Insight
INVESTOR PERSPECTIVE

Listed here are the amounts of net income and cash from operations, investing, and financing during 2001 for some well-known companies. The final column suggests their likely phase in the life cycle based on these figures.

Company ($ in millions)	Net Income	Cash Provided by Operations	Cash Provided (Used) by Investing	Cash Provided (Used) by Financing	Likely Phase in Life Cycle
Amazon.com	$ (567)	$ (120)	$ (253)	$ 107	Introductory
Iomega	(93)	(12)	(5)	(18)	Introductory
Bethlehem Steel	(1,950)	(208)	(42)	244	Early decline
Kellogg	474	1,132	(4,144)	3,040	Late maturity
Southwest Airlines	511	1,485	(998)	1,270	Early maturity
Starbucks	181	461	(433)	15	Late growth

Consider **Microsoft**: During its early years it had significant product development costs and little revenue. Microsoft was lucky in that its agreement with **IBM** to provide the operating system for IBM PCs gave it an early steady source of cash to support growth. As noted in the Feature Story, one way Microsoft conserved cash was to pay employees with stock options rather than cash. Today Microsoft could best be characterized as being between the growth and maturity phases. It continues to spend considerable amounts on research and development and investment in new assets. For the last three years, however, its cash from operations has exceeded its net income. Also, cash from operations over this period exceeded cash used for investing, and common stock repurchased exceeded common stock issued. For Microsoft, as for any large company, the challenge is to maintain its growth. In the software industry, where products become obsolete very quickly, the challenge is particularly great.

PREPARING THE STATEMENT OF CASH FLOWS

The statement of cash flows is prepared differently from the three other basic financial statements. First, it is not prepared from an adjusted trial balance. The statement requires detailed information concerning the changes in account balances that occurred between two points in time. An adjusted trial balance will not provide the necessary data. Second, the statement of cash flows deals with cash receipts and payments. As a result, the effects of the use of accrual accounting **must be adjusted to determine cash flows**.

The information to prepare this statement usually comes from three sources:

- **Comparative balance sheets.** Information in the comparative balance sheets indicates the amount of the changes in assets, liabilities, and stockholders' equities from the beginning to the end of the period.

- **Current income statement.** Information in this statement helps determine the amount of cash provided or used by operations during the period.

- **Additional information.** Such information includes transaction data that are needed to determine how cash was provided or used during the period.

Preparing the statement of cash flows from these data sources involves three major steps, explained in Illustration 13-4 (page 624).

Illustration 13-4
Three major steps in
preparing the statement of
cash flows

Illustration 13-4
Three major steps in
preparing the statement of
cash flows

Step 1: Determine net cash provided/used by operating activities by converting net income from an accrual basis to a cash basis.

This step involves analyzing not only the current year's income statement but also comparative balance sheets and selected additional data.

Step 2: Analyze changes in noncurrent asset and liability accounts and record as investing and financing activities, or as significant noncash transactions.

This step involves analyzing comparative balance sheet data and selected additional information for their effects on cash.

Step 3: Compare the net change in cash on the statement of cash flows with the change in the cash account reported on the balance sheet to make sure the amounts agree.

The difference between the beginning and ending cash balances can be easily computed from comparative balance sheets.

INDIRECT AND DIRECT METHODS

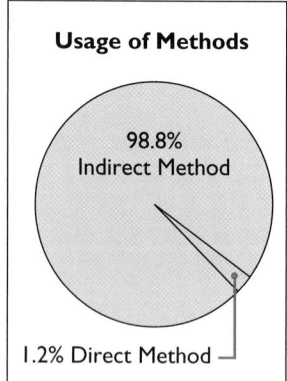

Usage of Methods

98.8% Indirect Method

1.2% Direct Method

In order to perform step 1, **net income must be converted from an accrual basis to a cash basis**. This conversion may be done by either of two methods: (1) the indirect method or (2) the direct method. **Both methods arrive at the same total amount** for "Net cash provided by operating activities." They differ in **how** they arrive at the amount.

The indirect method is used extensively in practice, as shown in the nearby chart.[1] Companies (98.8%) favor the indirect method for two reasons: (1) It is easier and less costly to prepare, and (2) it focuses on the differences between net income and net cash flow from operating activities.

The direct method shows operating cash receipts and payments, making it more consistent with the objective of a statement of cash flows. The FASB has expressed a preference for the direct method, but allows the use of either method.

Beginning at the bottom of page 625, in two separate sections, we describe the use of the two methods. Section 1 illustrates the indirect method. Section 2 illustrates the direct method. These sections are independent of each other. *Only one or the other* need be covered in order to understand and prepare the statement of cash flows. When you have finished the section assigned by your instructor, turn to the next topic—"Using Cash Flows to Evaluate a Company," on page 645.

---

[1] *Accounting Trends and Techniques—2001* (New York: American Institute of Certified Public Accountants, 2001).

Business Insight
INVESTOR PERSPECTIVE

During the 1990s, analysts increasingly used cash-flow-based measures of income, such as cash flow provided by operations, instead of or in addition to net income. The reason for the change was that they were losing faith in accrual-accounting-based net income numbers. Sadly, these days even cash flow from operations isn't always what it seems to be. For example, in 2002 **WorldCom, Inc.** disclosed that it had improperly capitalized expenses: It moved $3.8 billion of cash outflows from the "Cash from operating activities" section of the cash flow statement to the "Investing activities" section, thereby greatly enhancing cash provided by operating activities. Similarly, in 2002 **Dynegy, Inc.** restated its cash flow statement for 2001 so that $300 million tied to its complex natural gas trading operation was removed from cash flow from operations and instead put into the financing section—a drop of 37% in cash flow from operations.

SOURCE: Henny Sender, "Sadly, These Days Even Cash Flow Isn't Always What It Seems To Be," *Wall Street Journal Online* (May 8, 2002).

BEFORE YOU GO ON . . .

▶ **Review It**

1. What are the phases of the product life cycle, and how do they affect the statement of cash flows?

2. Based on its statement of cash flows, in what stage of the product life cycle is **Tootsie Roll Industries**? The answer to this question is provided on page 676.

3. What are the three major steps in the preparation of a statement of cash flows?

4. What is the primary difference between the indirect and direct approaches to the statement of cash flows? Which method is more commonly used in practice?

✓ THE NAVIGATOR

SECTION ONE
STATEMENT OF CASH FLOWS— INDIRECT METHOD

STUDY OBJECTIVE
4a
Prepare a statement of cash flows using the indirect method.

To explain how to prepare a statement of cash flows using the indirect method, we use financial information from Computer Services Company. Illustration 13-5 (page 626) presents Computer Services' current and previous-year balance sheet, its current-year income statement, and related financial information.

Illustration 13-5
Comparative balance
sheets, income statement,
and additional information
for Computer Services
Company

COMPUTER SERVICES COMPANY
Comparative Balance Sheets
December 31

Assets	2005	2004	Change in Account Balance Increase/Decrease
Current assets			
Cash	$ 55,000	$ 33,000	$ 22,000 Increase
Accounts receivable	20,000	30,000	10,000 Decrease
Merchandise inventory	15,000	10,000	5,000 Increase
Prepaid expenses	5,000	1,000	4,000 Increase
Property, plant, and equipment			
Land	130,000	20,000	110,000 Increase
Building	160,000	40,000	120,000 Increase
Accumulated depreciation—building	(11,000)	(5,000)	6,000 Increase
Equipment	27,000	10,000	17,000 Increase
Accumulated depreciation—equipment	(3,000)	(1,000)	2,000 Increase
Total	$398,000	$138,000	
Liabilities and Stockholders' Equity			
Current liabilities			
Accounts payable	$ 28,000	$ 12,000	$ 16,000 Increase
Income tax payable	6,000	8,000	2,000 Decrease
Long-term liabilities			
Bonds payable	130,000	20,000	110,000 Increase
Stockholders' equity			
Common stock	70,000	50,000	20,000 Increase
Retained earnings	164,000	48,000	116,000 Increase
Total liabilities and stockholders' equity	$398,000	$138,000	

COMPUTER SERVICES COMPANY
Income Statement
For the Year Ended December 31, 2005

Revenues		$507,000
Cost of goods sold	$150,000	
Operating expenses (excluding depreciation)	111,000	
Depreciation expense	9,000	
Loss on sale of equipment	3,000	
Interest expense	42,000	$315,000
Income before income tax		192,000
Income tax expense		47,000
Net income		$145,000

Additional information for 2005:
1. The company declared and paid a $29,000 cash dividend.
2. Issued $110,000 of long-term bonds in direct exchange for land.
3. A building costing $120,000 was purchased for cash. Equipment costing $25,000 was also purchased for cash.
4. The company sold equipment with a book value of $7,000 (cost $8,000, less accumulated depreciation $1,000) for $4,000 cash.
5. Issued common stock for $20,000 cash.
6. Depreciation expense was comprised of $6,000 for building and $3,000 for equipment.

We will now apply the three steps to the information provided for Computer Services Company.

Step 1: Operating Activities

DETERMINE NET CASH PROVIDED/USED BY OPERATING ACTIVITIES BY CONVERTING NET INCOME FROM AN ACCRUAL BASIS TO A CASH BASIS

To determine net cash provided by operating activities under the indirect method, **net income is adjusted in numerous ways**. A useful starting point is to understand **why** net income must be converted to net cash provided by operating activities. Under generally accepted accounting principles, most companies use the accrual basis of accounting. As you have learned, this basis requires that revenue be recorded when earned and that expenses be recorded when incurred. Earned revenues may include credit sales that have not yet been collected in cash. Expenses incurred may include some items that have not been paid in cash. Thus, under the accrual basis of accounting, net income is not the same as net cash provided by operating activities. Therefore, under the indirect method, net income must be adjusted to convert certain items to the cash basis. The **indirect method** (or reconciliation method) starts with net income and converts it to net cash provided by operating activities. Illustration 13-6 lists the three types of adjustments.

Net Income	+/−	Adjustments	=	Net Cash Provided/ Used by Operating Activities
		• Add back noncash expenses, such as depreciation expense, amortization, or depletion.		
		• Deduct gains and add losses that resulted from investing and financing activities.		
		• Analyze changes to noncash current asset and current liability accounts.		

Illustration 13-6
Three types of adjustments to convert net income to net cash provided by operating activities

The three types of adjustments are explained in the next three sections.

DEPRECIATION EXPENSE

Computer Services' income statement reports depreciation expense of $9,000. Although depreciation expense reduces net income, it does not reduce cash. In other words, depreciation expense is a noncash charge. It is added back to net income to arrive at net cash provided by operating activities. Depreciation expense is reported as follows in the statement of cash flows.

Helpful Hint Depreciation is similar to any other expense in that it reduces net income. It differs in that it does not involve a current cash outflow; that is why it must be *added back* to net income to arrive at cash provided by operations.

Illustration 13-7
Adjustment for depreciation

Cash flows from operating activities		
Net income		$145,000
Adjustments to reconcile net income to net cash provided by operating activities:		
Depreciation expense		9,000
Net cash provided by operating activities		$154,000

Depreciation and similar noncash charges such as amortization of intangible assets, depletion expense, and bad debt expense are frequently listed in the statement of cash flows as the first adjustment to net income.

LOSS ON SALE OF EQUIPMENT

Computer Services' income statement reports a $3,000 loss on the sale of equipment (book value $7,000, less cash received from sale of equipment $4,000). Illustration 13-1 states that cash received from the sale of plant assets should be reported in the investing activities section. Because of this, **all gains and losses must be eliminated from net income to arrive at cash from operating activities**. In our example, Computer Services Company's loss of $3,000 should not be included in the operating activities section of the statement of cash flows. Illustration 13-8 shows that the $3,000 loss is eliminated by adding $3,000 back to net income to arrive at net cash provided by operating activities.

Illustration 13-8
Adjustment for loss on sale of equipment

Cash flows from operating activities			
Net income			$145,000
Adjustments to reconcile net income to net cash provided by operating activities:			
Depreciation expense		$9,000	
Loss on sale of equipment		3,000	12,000
Net cash provided by operating activities			$157,000

If a gain on sale occurs, the gain is deducted from net income in order to determine net cash provided by operating activities. **In the case of either a gain or a loss, the actual amount of cash received from the sale is reported as a source of cash in the investing activities section of the statement of cash flows.**

CHANGES TO NONCASH CURRENT ASSET AND CURRENT LIABILITY ACCOUNTS

A final adjustment in reconciling net income to net cash provided by operating activities involves examining all changes in current asset and current liability accounts. The accrual accounting process records revenues in the period earned and expenses in the period incurred. For example, Accounts Receivable is used to record amounts owed to the company for sales that have been made but cash collections have not yet been received. The Prepaid Insurance account is used to reflect insurance that has been paid for, but which has not yet expired, and therefore has not been expensed. Similarly, the Salaries Payable account reflects salaries expense that has been incurred by the company but has not been paid. As a result, we need to adjust net income for these accruals and prepayments to determine net cash provided by operating activities. Thus we must analyze the change in each current asset and current liability account to determine its impact on net income and cash.

Changes in Noncash Current Assets

The adjustments required for changes in noncash current asset accounts are as follows: **Increases in current asset accounts are deducted from net income, and decreases in current asset accounts are added to net income, to arrive at net cash provided by operating activities.** We can observe these relationships by analyzing the accounts of Computer Services Company.

DECREASE IN ACCOUNTS RECEIVABLE. Computer Services Company's accounts receivable decreased by $10,000 (from $30,000 to $20,000) during the period. For Computer Services Company this means that cash receipts were $10,000 higher than revenues. Illustration 13-9 shows that Computer Services Company had $507,000 in revenues (as reported on the income statement), but it collected $517,000 in cash. As shown in Illustration 13-10, to adjust net income to net cash provided by operating activities, the decrease of $10,000 in accounts receivable is added to net income.

Accounts Receivable			
1/1/05	Balance	30,000	Receipts from customers 517,000
	Revenues	507,000	
12/31/05	Balance	20,000	

Illustration 13-9 Analysis of accounts receivable

When the Accounts Receivable balance increases, cash receipts are lower than revenue earned under the accrual basis. Therefore, the amount of the increase in accounts receivable is deducted from net income to arrive at net cash provided by operating activities.

INCREASE IN MERCHANDISE INVENTORY. Computer Services Company's Merchandise Inventory balance increased $5,000 (from $10,000 to $15,000) during the period. The Merchandise Inventory account reflects the difference between the amount of inventory that has been purchased and the amount that has been sold. For Computer Services this means that the cost of merchandise purchased exceeded the cost of goods sold by $5,000. As a result, cost of goods sold does not reflect $5,000 of cash payments made for merchandise. This inventory increase of $5,000 during the period is deducted from net income to arrive at net cash provided by operating activities (see Illustration 13-10, below). If inventory decreases, the amount of the change is added to net income to arrive at net cash provided by operating activities.

INCREASE IN PREPAID EXPENSES. Prepaid expenses increased during the period by $4,000. This means that cash paid for expenses is higher than expenses reported on an accrual basis. Cash payments have been made in the current period, but expenses (as charges to the income statement) have been deferred to future periods. To adjust net income to net cash provided by operating activities, the $4,000 increase in prepaid expenses is deducted from net income (see Illustration 13-10).

Cash flows from operating activities		
Net income		$145,000
Adjustments to reconcile net income to net cash provided by operating activities:		
Depreciation expense	$ 9,000	
Loss on sale of equipment	3,000	
Decrease in accounts receivable	10,000	
Increase in merchandise inventory	(5,000)	
Increase in prepaid expenses	(4,000)	13,000
Net cash provided by operating activities		$158,000

Illustration 13-10 Adjustments for changes in current asset accounts

If prepaid expenses decrease, reported expenses are higher than the expenses paid. Therefore, the decrease in prepaid expense is added to net income to arrive at net cash provided by operating activities.

Changes in Current Liabilities

The adjustments required for changes in current liability accounts are as follows: **Increases in current liability accounts are added to net income, and decreases in current liability accounts are deducted from net income, to arrive at net cash provided by operating activities.**

INCREASE IN ACCOUNTS PAYABLE. For Computer Services Company, Accounts Payable increased by $16,000 (from $12,000 to $28,000) during the period. That means the company received $16,000 more in goods than it actually paid for. As shown in Illustration 13-11 (below), to adjust net income to determine net cash provided by operating activities, the $16,000 increase in Accounts Payable is added to net income.

DECREASE IN INCOME TAXES PAYABLE. When a company incurs income tax expense but has not yet paid its taxes, it records income tax payable. A change in the Income Tax Payable account reflects the difference between income tax expense incurred and income tax actually paid. Computer Services' Income Tax Payable account decreased by $2,000. That means the $47,000 of income tax expense reported on the income statement was $2,000 less than the amount of taxes paid during the period of $49,000. As shown in Illustration 13-11, to adjust net income to a cash basis, net income must be reduced by $2,000.

Illustration 13-11
Adjustments for changes in current liability accounts

Cash flows from operating activities		
Net income		$145,000
Adjustments to reconcile net income to net cash provided by operating activities:		
Depreciation expense	$ 9,000	
Loss on sale of equipment	3,000	
Decrease in accounts receivable	10,000	
Increase in merchandise inventory	(5,000)	
Increase in prepaid expenses	(4,000)	
Increase in accounts payable	16,000	
Decrease in income tax payable	(2,000)	27,000
Net cash provided by operating activities		$172,000

Illustration 13-11 shows that, after starting with net income of $145,000, the sum of all of the adjustments to net income was $27,000. This resulted in net cash provided by operating activities of $172,000.

SUMMARY OF CONVERSION TO NET CASH PROVIDED BY OPERATING ACTIVITIES—INDIRECT METHOD

As shown in the previous illustrations, the statement of cash flows prepared by the indirect method starts with net income. It then adds or deducts items to arrive at net cash provided by operating activities. The required adjustments are of three types: (1) noncash charges such as depreciation, amortization, and depletion; (2) gains and losses on the sale of plant assets; and (3) changes in noncash current asset and current liability accounts. A summary of these changes is provided in Illustration 13-12.

		Adjustment Required to Convert Net Income to Net Cash Provided by Operating Activities
Noncash charges	Depreciation expense	Add
	Patent amortization expense	Add
	Depletion expense	Add
Gains and losses	Loss on sale of plant asset	Add
	Gain on sale of plant asset	Deduct
Changes in current assets and current liabilities	Increase in current asset account	Deduct
	Decrease in current asset account	Add
	Increase in current liability account	Add
	Decrease in current liability account	Deduct

Illustration 13-12
Adjustments required to convert net income to net cash provided by operating activities

Step 2: Investing and Financing Activities

ANALYZE CHANGES IN NONCURRENT ASSET AND LIABILITY ACCOUNTS AND RECORD AS INVESTING AND FINANCING ACTIVITIES, OR AS NONCASH INVESTING AND FINANCING ACTIVITIES

INCREASE IN LAND. As indicated from the change in the Land account and the additional information, land of $110,000 was purchased through the issuance of long-term bonds. The issuance of bonds payable for land has no effect on cash. But it is a significant noncash investing and financing activity that merits disclosure in a separate schedule.

Helpful Hint The investing and financing activities are measured and reported the same under both the direct and indirect methods.

INCREASE IN BUILDING. As the additional data indicate, an office building was acquired for $120,000 cash. This is a cash outflow reported in the investing section.

INCREASE IN EQUIPMENT. The Equipment account increased $17,000. The additional information explains that this was a net increase that resulted from two transactions: (1) a purchase of equipment of $25,000 and (2) the sale for $4,000 of equipment costing $8,000. These transactions are classified as investing activities. Each transaction should be reported separately. Thus the purchase of equipment should be reported as an outflow of cash for $25,000. The sale should be reported as an inflow of cash for $4,000. The T account below shows the reasons for the change in this account during the year.

Equipment			
1/1/05 Balance	10,000	Cost of equipment sold	8,000
Purchase of equipment	**25,000**		
12/31/05 Balance	27,000		

Illustration 13-13
Analysis of equipment

The following entry shows the details of the equipment sale transaction.

Cash	4,000	
Accumulated Depreciation	1,000	
Loss on Sale of Equipment	3,000	
Equipment		8,000

A	=	L	+	SE
+4,000				−3,000 Exp
+1,000				
−8,000				

Helpful Hint When stocks or bonds are issued for cash, the actual proceeds will appear in the statement of cash flows as a financing inflow (rather than the par value of the stocks or face value of bonds).

INCREASE IN BONDS PAYABLE. The Bonds Payable account increased $110,000. As indicated in the additional information, land was acquired from the issuance of these bonds. This noncash transaction is reported in a separate schedule at the bottom of the statement.

INCREASE IN COMMON STOCK. The balance sheet reports an increase in Common Stock of $20,000. The additional information section notes that this increase resulted from the issuance of new shares of stock. This is a cash inflow reported in the financing section.

INCREASE IN RETAINED EARNINGS. Retained earnings increased $116,000 during the year. This increase can be explained by two factors: (1) Net income of $145,000 increased retained earnings. (2) Dividends of $29,000 decreased retained earnings. Net income is adjusted to net cash provided by operating activities in the operating activities section. Payment of the dividends is a **cash outflow that is reported as a financing activity**.

Helpful Hint It is the **payment** of dividends, not the declaration, that appears in the cash flow statement.

STATEMENT OF CASH FLOWS—2005

Using the previous information, we can now prepare a statement of cash flows for 2005 for Computer Services Company as shown in Illustration 13-14.

Illustration 13-14
Statement of cash flows, 2005—indirect method

Helpful Hint Note that in the investing and financing activities sections, positive numbers indicate cash inflows (receipts), and negative numbers indicate cash outflows (payments).

COMPUTER SERVICES COMPANY Statement of Cash Flows—Indirect Method For the Year Ended December 31, 2005		
Cash flows from operating activities		
Net income		$ 145,000
Adjustments to reconcile net income to net cash		
provided by operating activities:		
Depreciation expense	$ 9,000	
Loss on sale of equipment	3,000	
Decrease in accounts receivable	10,000	
Increase in merchandise inventory	(5,000)	
Increase in prepaid expenses	(4,000)	
Increase in accounts payable	16,000	
Decrease in income tax payable	(2,000)	27,000
Net cash provided by operating activities		172,000
Cash flows from investing activities		
Purchase of building	(120,000)	
Purchase of equipment	(25,000)	
Sale of equipment	4,000	
Net cash used by investing activities		(141,000)
Cash flows from financing activities		
Issuance of common stock	20,000	
Payment of cash dividends	(29,000)	
Net cash used by financing activities		(9,000)
Net increase in cash		22,000
Cash at beginning of period		33,000
Cash at end of period		$ 55,000
Noncash investing and financing activities		
Issuance of bonds payable to purchase land		$ 110,000

Step 3: Net Change in Cash

COMPARE THE NET CHANGE IN CASH IN THE STATEMENT OF CASH FLOWS WITH THE CHANGE IN THE CASH ACCOUNT REPORTED ON THE BALANCE SHEET TO MAKE SURE THE AMOUNTS AGREE

Illustration 13-14 indicates that the net change in cash during the period was an increase of $22,000. This agrees with the change in Cash account reported on the balance sheet in Illustration 13-5.

BEFORE YOU GO ON . . .

▶ Review It

1. What is the format of the operating activities section of the statement of cash flows using the indirect method?
2. Where is depreciation expense shown on a statement of cash flows using the indirect method?
3. Where are significant noncash investing and financing activities shown in a statement of cash flows? Give some examples.

▶ Do It

Presented below is information related to Reynolds Company. Use it to prepare a statement of cash flows using the indirect method.

REYNOLDS COMPANY Comparative Balance Sheets December 31			
Assets	**2005**	**2004**	**Change Increase/Decrease**
Cash	$ 54,000	$ 37,000	$ 17,000 Increase
Accounts receivable	68,000	26,000	42,000 Increase
Inventories	54,000	–0–	54,000 Increase
Prepaid expenses	4,000	6,000	2,000 Decrease
Land	45,000	70,000	25,000 Decrease
Buildings	200,000	200,000	–0–
Accumulated depreciation—buildings	(21,000)	(11,000)	10,000 Increase
Equipment	193,000	68,000	125,000 Increase
Accumulated depreciation—equipment	(28,000)	(10,000)	18,000 Increase
Totals	$569,000	$386,000	
Liabilities and Stockholders' Equity			
Accounts payable	$ 23,000	$ 40,000	$ 17,000 Decrease
Accrued expenses payable	10,000	–0–	10,000 Increase
Bonds payable	110,000	150,000	40,000 Decrease
Common stock ($1 par)	220,000	60,000	160,000 Increase
Retained earnings	206,000	136,000	70,000 Increase
Totals	$569,000	$386,000	

REYNOLDS COMPANY
Income Statement
For the Year Ended December 31, 2005

Revenues		$890,000
Cost of goods sold	$465,000	
Operating expenses	221,000	
Interest expense	12,000	
Loss on sale of equipment	2,000	700,000
Income before income taxes		190,000
Income tax expense		65,000
Net income		$125,000

Additional information:
1. Operating expenses include depreciation expense of $33,000 and charges from pre-paid expenses of $2,000.
2. Land was sold at its book value for cash.
3. Cash dividends of $55,000 were declared and paid in 2005.
4. Interest expense of $12,000 was paid in cash.
5. Equipment with a cost of $166,000 was purchased for cash. Equipment with a cost of $41,000 and a book value of $36,000 was sold for $34,000 cash.
6. Bonds of $10,000 were redeemed at their book value for cash. Bonds of $30,000 were converted into common stock.
7. Common stock ($1 par) of $130,000 was issued for cash.
8. Accounts payable pertain to merchandise suppliers.

Action Plan

• Determine net cash provided/used by operating activities by adjusting net income for items that did not affect cash.
• Determine net cash provided/used by investing activities and financing activities.
• Determine the net increase/decrease in cash.

Solution

Helpful Hint
1. Determine net cash provided/used by operating activities, recognizing that operating activities generally relate to changes in current assets and current liabilities.
2. Determine net cash provided/used by investing activities, recognizing that investing activities generally relate to changes in noncurrent assets.
3. Determine net cash provided/used by financing activities, recognizing that financing activities generally relate to changes in long-term liabilities and stockholders' equity accounts.

REYNOLDS COMPANY
Statement of Cash Flows—Indirect Method
For the Year Ended December 31, 2005

Cash flows from operating activities		
Net income		$ 125,000
Adjustments to reconcile net income to net cash		
provided by operating activities:		
Depreciation expense	$ 33,000	
Loss on sale of equipment	2,000	
Increase in accounts receivable	(42,000)	
Increase in inventories	(54,000)	
Decrease in prepaid expenses	2,000	
Decrease in accounts payable	(17,000)	
Increase in accrued expenses payable	10,000	(66,000)
Net cash provided by operating activities		59,000
Cash flows from investing activities		
Sale of land	25,000	
Sale of equipment	34,000	
Purchase of equipment	(166,000)	
Net cash used by investing activities		(107,000)

(Continued)		
Cash flows from financing activities		
Redemption of bonds	(10,000)	
Sale of common stock	130,000	
Payment of dividends	(55,000)	
Net cash provided by financing activities		65,000
Net increase in cash		17,000
Cash at beginning of period		37,000
Cash at end of period		$ 54,000
Noncash investing and financing activities		
Conversion of bonds into common stock		$ 30,000

Note: This concludes Section 1 on preparation of the statement of cash flows using the indirect method. Unless your instructor assigns Section 2, you should turn to the concluding section of the chapter, "Using Cash Flows to Evaluate a Company," on page 645.

SECTION 2
STATEMENT OF CASH FLOWS—DIRECT METHOD

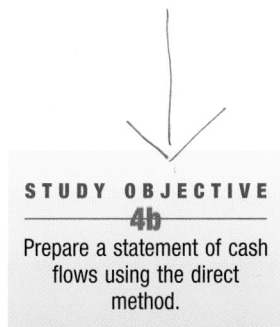

STUDY OBJECTIVE
4b
Prepare a statement of cash flows using the direct method.

To explain and illustrate the direct method, we will use the transactions of Juarez Company for 2005, to prepare a statement of cash flows. Illustration 13-15 presents information related to 2005 for Juarez Company.

Illustration 13-15
Comparative balance sheets, income statement, and additional information for Juarez Company

JUAREZ COMPANY Comparative Balance Sheets December 31			
Assets	**2005**	**2004**	**Change Increase/Decrease**
Cash	$191,000	$159,000	$ 32,000 Increase
Accounts receivable	12,000	15,000	3,000 Decrease
Inventory	170,000	160,000	10,000 Increase
Prepaid expenses	6,000	8,000	2,000 Decrease
Land	140,000	80,000	60,000 Increase
Equipment	160,000	–0–	160,000 Increase
Accumulated depreciation—equipment	(16,000)	–0–	16,000 Increase
Total	$663,000	$422,000	
Liabilities and Stockholders' Equity			
Accounts payable	$ 52,000	$ 60,000	$ 8,000 Decrease
Accrued expenses payable	15,000	20,000	5,000 Decrease
Income taxes payable	12,000	–0–	12,000 Increase
Bonds payable	130,000	–0–	130,000 Increase
Common stock	360,000	300,000	60,000 Increase
Retained earnings	94,000	42,000	52,000 Increase
Total	$663,000	$422,000	

Illustration 13-15 *continued*
Comparative balance sheets, income statement, and additional information for Juarez Company

JUAREZ COMPANY
Income Statement
For the Year Ended December 31, 2005

Revenues		$975,000
Cost of goods sold	$660,000	
Operating expenses (excluding depreciation)	176,000	
Depreciation expense	18,000	
Loss on sale of store equipment	1,000	855,000
Income before income taxes		120,000
Income tax expense		36,000
Net income		$ 84,000

Additional information:
1. In 2005, the company declared and paid a $32,000 cash dividend.
2. Bonds were issued at face value for $130,000 in cash.
3. Equipment costing $180,000 was purchased for cash.
4. Equipment costing $20,000 was sold for $17,000 cash when the book value of the equipment was $18,000.
5. Common stock of $60,000 was issued to acquire land.

To prepare a statement of cash flows under the direct approach, we will apply the three steps outlined in Illustration 13-4 (page 624).

Step 1: Operating Activities

DETERMINE NET CASH PROVIDED/USED BY OPERATING ACTIVITIES BY CONVERTING NET INCOME FROM AN ACCRUAL BASIS TO A CASH BASIS

Under the **direct method**, net cash provided by operating activities is computed by **adjusting each item in the income statement** from the accrual basis to the cash basis. To simplify and condense the operating activities section, **only major classes of operating cash receipts and cash payments are reported**. For these major classes, the difference between cash receipts and cash payments is the net cash provided by operating activities. These relationships are as shown in Illustration 13-16 (next page).

An efficient way to apply the direct method is to analyze the items reported in the income statement in the order in which they are listed. Cash receipts and cash payments related to these revenues and expenses are then determined. The following pages present the adjustments required to prepare a statement of cash flows for Juarez Company using the direct approach.

CASH RECEIPTS FROM CUSTOMERS.
The income statement for Juarez Company reported revenues from customers of $975,000. How much of that was cash receipts? To answer that, it is necessary to consider the change in accounts receivable during the year. When accounts receivable increase during the year, revenues on an accrual basis are higher than cash receipts from customers. Operations led to revenues, but not all of these revenues resulted in cash receipts. To determine the amount of cash receipts, the increase in accounts receivable is deducted from sales revenues. On the other hand, there may be a decrease in accounts receivable. That would occur if cash receipts from customers exceeded sales revenues. In that case, the decrease in accounts receivable is added to sales revenues.

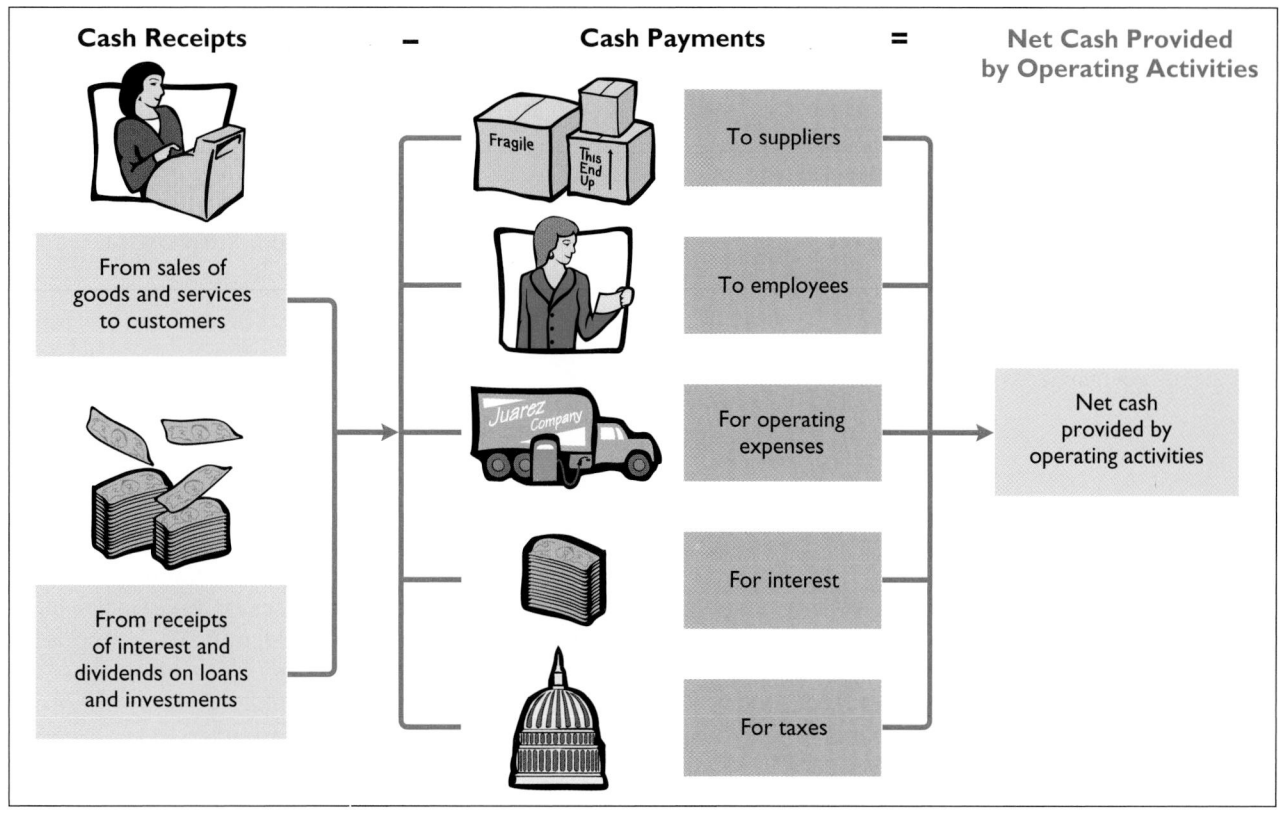

| Cash Receipts | − | Cash Payments | = | Net Cash Provided by Operating Activities |

Illustration 13-16 Major classes of cash receipts and payments

For Juarez Company, accounts receivable decreased $3,000. Thus, cash receipts from customers were $978,000, computed as follows.

Illustration 13-17
Computation of cash receipts from customers

Revenues from sales	$ 975,000
Add: Decrease in accounts receivable	3,000
Cash receipts from customers	**$978,000**

Cash receipts from customers may also be determined from an analysis of the Accounts Receivable account, as shown in Illustration 13-18.

Illustration 13-18 Analysis of accounts receivable

Accounts Receivable

1/1/05	Balance	15,000	**Receipts from customers**	**978,000**
	Revenues from sales	975,000		
12/31/05	Balance	12,000		

Helpful Hint The T account shows that revenue less increase in receivables equals cash receipts.

The relationships among cash receipts from customers, revenues from sales, and changes in accounts receivable are shown in Illustration 13-19.

Illustration 13-19 Formula to compute cash receipts from customers—direct method

| Cash Receipts from Customers | = | Revenues from Sales | { + Decrease in Accounts Receivable
or
− Increase in Accounts Receivable |

CASH PAYMENTS TO SUPPLIERS.   Juarez Company reported cost of goods sold of $660,000 on its income statement. How much of that was cash payments to suppliers? To answer that, it is first necessary to find purchases for the year. To find purchases, cost of goods sold is adjusted for the change in inventory. When inventory increases during the year, purchases for the year have exceeded cost of goods sold. As a result, to determine the amount of purchases, the increase in inventory is added to cost of goods sold.

In 2005, Juarez Company's inventory increased $10,000. Purchases are computed as follows.

Illustration 13-20
Computation of purchases

Cost of goods sold	$ 660,000
Add: Increase in inventory	10,000
Purchases	**$670,000**

After purchases are computed, cash payments to suppliers can be determined. This is done by adjusting purchases for the change in accounts payable. When accounts payable increase during the year, purchases on an accrual basis are higher than they are on a cash basis. As a result, to determine cash payments to suppliers, an increase in accounts payable is deducted from purchases. On the other hand, there may be a decrease in accounts payable. That would occur if cash payments to suppliers exceed purchases. In that case, the decrease in accounts payable is added to purchases.

For Juarez Company, cash payments to suppliers were $678,000, computed as follows.

Illustration 13-21
Computation of cash payments to suppliers

Purchases	$ 670,000
Add: Decrease in accounts payable	8,000
Cash payments to suppliers	**$678,000**

Cash payments to suppliers may also be determined from an analysis of the Accounts Payable account as shown in Illustration 13-22.

Illustration 13-22 Analysis of accounts payable

Accounts Payable				
Payments to suppliers	678,000	1/1/05 Balance		60,000
		Purchases		670,000
		12/31/05 Balance		52,000

Helpful Hint The T account shows that purchases plus decrease in accounts payable equals payments to suppliers.

The relationships among cash payments to suppliers, cost of goods sold, changes in inventory, and changes in accounts payable are shown in the following formula.

Illustration 13-23
Formula to compute cash payments to suppliers—direct method

Cash Payments to Suppliers	=	Cost of Goods Sold	+ Increase in Inventory or − Decrease in Inventory	+ Decrease in Accounts Payable or − Increase in Accounts Payable

CASH PAYMENTS FOR OPERATING EXPENSES. Operating expenses of $176,000 were reported on Juarez's income statement. How much of that amount was cash paid for operating expenses? To answer that, we need to adjust this amount for any changes in prepaid expenses and accrued expenses payable. For example, if prepaid expenses increased during the year, cash paid for operating expenses is higher than operating expenses reported on the income statement. To convert operating expenses to cash payments for operating expenses, the increase must be added to operating expenses. On the other hand, if prepaid expenses decrease during the year, the decrease must be deducted from operating expenses.

Operating expenses must also be adjusted for changes in accrued expenses payable. When accrued expenses payable increase during the year, operating expenses on an accrual basis are higher than they are in a cash basis. As a result, to determine cash payments for operating expenses, an increase in accrued expenses payable is deducted from operating expenses. On the other hand, a decrease in accrued expenses payable is added to operating expenses because cash payments exceed operating expenses.

Juarez Company's cash payments for operating expenses were $179,000, computed as follows.

Operating expenses	$ 176,000	
Deduct: Decrease in prepaid expenses	(2,000)	
Add: Decrease in accrued expenses payable	5,000	
Cash payments for operating expenses	**$179,000**	

Illustration 13-24
Computation of cash payments for operating expenses

The relationships among cash payments for operating expenses, changes in prepaid expenses, and changes in accrued expenses payable are shown in the following formula.

Cash Payments for Operating Expenses	=	Operating Expenses	{ + Increase in Prepaid Expense or − Decrease in Prepaid Expense	{ + Decrease in Accrued Expenses Payable or − Increase in Accrued Expenses Payable

Illustration 13-25 Formula to compute cash payments for operating expenses—direct method

DEPRECIATION EXPENSE AND LOSS ON SALE OF EQUIPMENT. Operating expenses are shown exclusive of depreciation. Depreciation expense in 2005 was $18,000. Depreciation expense is not shown on a statement of cash flows because it is a noncash charge. If the amount for operating expenses includes depreciation expense, operating expenses must be reduced by the amount of depreciation to determine cash payments for operating expenses.

The loss on sale of equipment of $1,000 is also a noncash charge. The loss on sale of equipment reduces net income, but it does not reduce cash. Thus, the loss on sale of equipment is not reported on a statement of cash flows.

Other charges to expense that do not require the use of cash, such as the amortization of intangible assets, depletion expense, and bad debt expense, are treated in the same manner as depreciation.

CASH PAYMENTS FOR INCOME TAXES.   Income tax expense reported on the income statement was $36,000. Income taxes payable, however, increased $12,000. This increase means that $12,000 of the income taxes have not been paid. As a result, income taxes paid were less than income taxes reported in the income statement. Cash payments for income taxes were, therefore, $24,000 as shown below.

Illustration 13-26
Computation of cash payments for income taxes

Income tax expense	$ 36,000
Deduct: Increase in income taxes payable	12,000
Cash payments for income taxes	**$24,000**

The relationships among cash payments for income taxes, income tax expense, and changes in income taxes payable are shown in the following formula.

Illustration 13-27
Formula to compute cash payments for income taxes—direct method

$$\text{Cash Payments for Income Taxes} = \text{Income Tax Expense} \begin{cases} + \textbf{Decrease in Income Taxes Payable} \\ \text{or} \\ - \textbf{Increase in Income Taxes Payable} \end{cases}$$

The results of the previous analysis are presented in the operating activities section of the statement of cash flows of Juarez Company in Illustration 13-28.

Illustration 13-28
Operating activities section of the statement of cash flows

Cash flows from operating activities		
Cash receipts from customers		$978,000
Less: Cash payments:		
To suppliers	$678,000	
For operating expenses	179,000	
For income taxes	24,000	881,000
Net cash provided by operating activities		$ 97,000

When the direct method is used, the net cash flows from operating activities as computed under the indirect method must also be provided in a separate schedule (not shown here).

Step 2: Investing and Financing Activities

ANALYZE CHANGES IN NONCURRENT ASSET AND LIABILITY ACCOUNTS AND RECORD AS INVESTING AND FINANCING ACTIVITIES, OR AS SIGNIFICANT NONCASH TRANSACTIONS

INCREASE IN LAND.   Land increased $60,000. The additional information section indicates that common stock was issued to purchase the land. The issuance of common stock for land has no effect on cash. But it is a **significant noncash investing and financing transaction**. This transaction requires disclosure in a separate schedule at the bottom of the statement of cash flows.

INCREASE IN EQUIPMENT. The comparative balance sheets show that equipment increased $160,000 in 2005. The additional information in Illustration 13-15 indicates that the increase resulted from two investing transactions: (1) Equipment costing $180,000 was purchased for cash. And (2) equipment costing $20,000 was sold for $17,000 cash when its book value was $18,000. The relevant data for the statement of cash flows is the cash paid for the purchase and the cash proceeds from the sale. For Juarez Company, the investing activities section will show the following: The $180,000 purchase of equipment as an outflow of cash, and the $17,000 sale of equipment also as an inflow of cash. The two amounts **should not be netted. Both individual outflows and inflows of cash should be shown.**

The analysis of the changes in equipment should include the related Accumulated Depreciation account. These two accounts for Juarez Company are shown in Illustration 13-29.

Equipment				
1/1/05 Balance	–0–	Cost of equipment sold		20,000
Cash purchase	180,000			
12/31/05 Balance	160,000			

Accumulated Depreciation—Equipment				
Sale of equipment	2,000	1/1/05 Balance		–0–
		Depreciation expense		18,000
		12/31/05 Balance		16,000

Illustration 13-29 Analysis of equipment and related accumulated depreciation

INCREASE IN BONDS PAYABLE. Bonds Payable increased $130,000. The additional information in Illustration 13-15 indicated that bonds with a face value of $130,000 were issued for $130,000 cash. The issuance of bonds is a financing activity. For Juarez Company, there is an inflow of cash of $130,000 from the issuance of bonds.

INCREASE IN COMMON STOCK. The Common Stock account increased $60,000. The additional information indicated that land was acquired from the issuance of common stock. This transaction is a **significant noncash investing and financing transaction** that should be reported separately at the bottom of the statement.

INCREASE IN RETAINED EARNINGS. The $52,000 net increase in Retained Earnings resulted from net income of $84,000 and the declaration and payment of a cash dividend of $32,000. **Net income is not reported in the statement of cash flows under the direct method.** Cash dividends paid of $32,000 are reported in the financing activities section as an outflow of cash.

STATEMENT OF CASH FLOWS—2005

The statement of cash flows for Juarez Company is shown in Illustration 13-30.

JUAREZ COMPANY
Statement of Cash Flows—Direct Method
For the Year Ended December 31, 2005

Cash flows from operating activities		
Cash receipts from customers		$ 978,000
Less: Cash payments:		
To suppliers	$ 678,000	
For operating expenses	179,000	
For income taxes	24,000	881,000
Net cash provided by operating activities		97,000
Cash flows from investing activities		
Purchase of equipment	(180,000)	
Sale of equipment	17,000	
Net cash used by investing activities		(163,000)
Cash flows from financing activities		
Issuance of bonds payable	130,000	
Payment of cash dividends	(32,000)	
Net cash provided by financing activities		98,000
Net increase in cash		32,000
Cash at beginning of period		159,000
Cash at end of period		$ 191,000
Noncash investing and financing activities		
Issuance of common stock to purchase land		$ 60,000

Step 3: Net Change in Cash

COMPARE THE NET CHANGE IN CASH IN THE STATEMENT OF CASH FLOWS WITH THE CHANGE IN THE CASH ACCOUNT REPORTED ON THE BALANCE SHEET TO MAKE SURE THE AMOUNTS AGREE

Illustration 13-30 indicates that the net change in cash during the period was an increase of $32,000. This agrees with the change in balances in the cash account reported on the balance sheets in Illustration 13-15.

BEFORE YOU GO ON . . .

▶ **Review It**

1. What is the format of the operating activities section of the statement of cash flows using the direct method?
2. Where is depreciation expense shown on a statement of cash flows using the direct method?
3. Where are significant noncash investing and financing activities shown on a statement of cash flows? Give some examples.

▶ Do It

Presented below is information related to Reynolds Company. Use it to prepare a statement of cash flows using the direct method.

REYNOLDS COMPANY
Comparative Balance Sheets
December 31

Assets	2005	2004	Change Increase/Decrease
Cash	$ 54,000	$ 37,000	$ 17,000 Increase
Accounts receivable	68,000	26,000	42,000 Increase
Inventories	54,000	–0–	54,000 Increase
Prepaid expenses	4,000	6,000	2,000 Decrease
Land	45,000	70,000	25,000 Decrease
Buildings	200,000	200,000	–0–
Accumulated depreciation—buildings	(21,000)	(11,000)	10,000 Increase
Equipment	193,000	68,000	125,000 Increase
Accumulated depreciation—equipment	(28,000)	(10,000)	18,000 Increase
Totals	$569,000	$386,000	

Liabilities and Stockholders' Equity			
Accounts payable	$ 23,000	$ 40,000	$ 17,000 Decrease
Accrued expenses payable	10,000	–0–	10,000 Increase
Bonds payable	110,000	150,000	40,000 Decrease
Common stock ($1 par)	220,000	60,000	160,000 Increase
Retained earnings	206,000	136,000	70,000 Increase
Totals	$569,000	$386,000	

REYNOLDS COMPANY
Income Statement
For the Year Ended December 31, 2005

Revenues		$890,000
Cost of goods sold	$465,000	
Operating expenses	221,000	
Interest expense	12,000	
Loss on sale of equipment	2,000	700,000
Income before income taxes		190,000
Income tax expense		65,000
Net income		$125,000

Additional information:
1. Operating expenses include depreciation expense of $33,000 and charges from prepaid expenses of $2,000.
2. Land was sold at its book value for cash.
3. Cash dividends of $55,000 were declared and paid in 2005.
4. Interest expense of $12,000 was paid in cash.
5. Equipment with a cost of $166,000 was purchased for cash. Equipment with a cost of $41,000 and a book value of $36,000 was sold for $34,000 cash.
6. Bonds of $10,000 were redeemed at their book value for cash. Bonds of $30,000 were converted into common stock.
7. Common stock ($1 par) of $130,000 was issued for cash.
8. Accounts payable pertain to merchandise suppliers.

Action Plan

- Determine net cash provided/used by operating activities by adjusting each item in the income statement from the accrual basis to the cash basis.
- Determine net cash provided/used by investing activities.
- Determine net cash provided/used by financing activities.
- Determine the net increase/decrease in cash.

Solution

Helpful Hint

1. Determine net cash provided/used by operating activities, recognizing that each item in the income statement must be adjusted to the cash basis.
2. Determine net cash provided/used by investing activities, recognizing that investing activities generally relate to changes in noncurrent assets.
3. Determine net cash provided/used by financing activities, recognizing that financing activities generally relate to changes in long-term liabilities and stockholders' equity accounts.

REYNOLDS COMPANY
Statement of Cash Flows—Direct Method
For the Year Ended December 31, 2005

Cash flows from operating activities		
Cash receipts from customers		$ 848,000[a]
Less: Cash payments:		
To suppliers	$ 536,000[b]	
For operating expenses	176,000[c]	
For interest expense	12,000	
For income taxes	65,000	789,000
Net cash provided by operating activities		59,000
Cash flows from investing activities		
Sale of land	25,000	
Sale of equipment	34,000	
Purchase of equipment	(166,000)	
Net cash used by investing activities		(107,000)
Cash flows from financing activities		
Redemption of bonds	(10,000)	
Sale of common stock	130,000	
Payment of dividends	(55,000)	
Net cash provided by financing activities		65,000
Net increase in cash		17,000
Cash at beginning of period		37,000
Cash at end of period		$ 54,000
Noncash investing and financing activities		
Conversion of bonds into common stock		$ 30,000

Computations:
[a]$848,000 = $890,000 − $42,000
[b]$536,000 = $465,000 + $54,000 + $17,000
[c]$176,000 = $221,000 − $33,000 − $2,000 − $10,000
Technically, an additional schedule reconciling net income to net cash provided by operating activities should be presented as part of the statement of cash flows when using the direct method.

✓ **THE NAVIGATOR**

Note: This concludes Section 2 on preparation of the statement of cash flows using the direct method. You should now proceed to the concluding section of the chapter, "Using Cash Flows to Evaluate a Company."

Using Cash Flows to Evaluate a Company

Traditionally, the ratios most commonly used by investors and creditors have been based on accrual accounting. In previous chapters we introduced cash-based ratios that are gaining increased acceptance among analysts. In this section we review those measures and introduce new ones.

STUDY OBJECTIVE
5
Use the statement of cash flows to evaluate a company.

FREE CASH FLOW

In the statement of cash flows, cash provided by operating activities is intended to indicate the cash-generating capability of the company. Analysts have noted, however, that **cash provided by operating activities fails to take into account that a company must invest in new fixed assets** just to maintain its current level of operations. Companies also must at least **maintain dividends at current levels** to satisfy investors. A measurement to provide additional insight regarding a company's cash generating ability is free cash flow. **Free cash flow** describes the cash remaining from operations after adjustment for capital expenditures and dividends.

Consider the following example: Suppose that MPC produced and sold 10,000 personal computers this year. It reported $100,000 cash provided by operating activities. In order to maintain production at 10,000 computers, MPC invested $15,000 in equipment. It chose to pay $5,000 in dividends. Its free cash flow was $80,000 ($100,000 − $15,000 − $5,000). The company could use this $80,000 either to purchase new assets to expand the business or to pay an $80,000 dividend and continue to produce 10,000 computers. In practice, free cash flow is often calculated with the formula in Illustration 13-31. Alternative definitions also exist.

Illustration 13-31 Free cash flow

Illustration 13-32 provides basic information excerpted from the 2001 statement of cash flows of **Microsoft Corporation**.

Illustration 13-32
Microsoft cash flow information ($ in millions)

MICROSOFT CORPORATION Statement of Cash Flows (partial) 2001		
Cash provided by operations		$13,422
Cash flows from investing activities		
Additions to property, plant, and equipment	$ (1,103)	
Purchases of investments	(66,346)	
Sales of investments	58,715	
Cash used by investing activities		(8,734)
Cash paid for dividends on preferred stock		0

Microsoft's free cash flow is calculated as shown in Illustration 13-33 (page 646).

Illustration 13-33
Calculation of Microsoft's
free cash flow ($ in
millions)

Cash provided by operating activities	$13,422
Less: Expenditures on property, plant, and equipment	1,103
Dividends paid	0
Free cash flow	$12,319

This is a tremendous amount of cash generated in a single year. It is available for the acquisition of new assets, the retirement of stock or debt, or the payment of dividends. It should also be noted that this amount far exceeds Microsoft's 2001 net income of $7,346 million. This lends additional credibility to Microsoft's income number as an indicator of potential future performance. If anything, Microsoft's net income might understate its actual performance.

Oracle Corporation is one of the world's largest sellers of database software and information management services. Like Microsoft, its success depends on continuing to improve its existing products while developing new products to keep pace with rapid changes in technology. Oracle's free cash flow for 2001 was $1,865.8 million. This is impressive, but significantly less than Microsoft's amazing ability to generate cash.

DECISION TOOLKIT

Decision Checkpoints	Info Needed for Decision	Tool to Use for Decision	How to Evaluate Results
How much cash did the company generate to either expand operations or pay dividends?	Cash provided by operating activities, cash spent on fixed assets, and cash dividends	Free cash flow = Cash provided by operations − Capital expenditures − Cash dividends	Significant free cash flow indicates greater potential to finance new investment and pay additional dividends.

Business Insight
INVESTOR PERSPECTIVE

Managers in some industries have long suggested that accrual-based income measures understate the true long-term potential of their companies because of what they suggest are excessive depreciation charges. For example, cable companies frequently suggested that, once they had installed a cable, it would require minimal maintenance and would guarantee the company returns for a long time to come. As a consequence, cable companies, which reported strong operating cash flows but low net income, had high stock prices because investors focused more on their cash flows from operations than on their net income. A *Wall Street Journal* article suggested, however, that investors have grown impatient with the cable companies and have lost faith in cash flow from operations as an indicator of cable company performance. As it turns out, cable companies have had to make many expensive upgrades to previously installed cable systems. Today, after cable stock prices have fallen dramatically, cable industry analysts emphasize that either free cash flows or net income is a better indicator of a cable TV company's long-term potential than cash provided by operating activities.

SOURCE: Susan Pulliam and Mark Robichaux, "Heard on the Street: Cash Flow Stops Propping Cable Stock," *Wall Street Journal* (January 9, 1997), p. C1.

ASSESSING LIQUIDITY AND SOLVENCY USING CASH FLOWS

Previous chapters have presented ratios used to analyze a company's liquidity and solvency. Many of those ratios used accrual-based numbers from the income statement and balance sheet. In this section we focus on ratios that are *cash-based* rather than accrual-based. That is, instead of using numbers from the income statement, these ratios use numbers from the statement of cash flows.

As discussed earlier, many analysts are critical of accrual-based numbers because they feel that the adjustment process allows too much management discretion. These analysts like to supplement accrual-based analysis with measures that use the cash flow statement. One disadvantage of these cash-based measures is that, unlike the more commonly employed accrual-based measures, there are no readily available industry averages for comparison. In the following discussion we use cash flow-based ratios to analyze Microsoft. In addition to the cash flow information provided in Illustration 13-32, we need the following information related to **Microsoft**.

($ in millions)	2001	2000
Current liabilities	$11,132	$ 9,755
Total liabilities	11,968	10,782

Liquidity

Liquidity is the ability of a business to meet its immediate obligations. You learned (in Chapter 2) that one measure of liquidity is the *current ratio*: current assets divided by current liabilities. A disadvantage of the current ratio is that it uses year-end balances of current asset and current liability accounts. These year-end balances may not be representative of the company's position during most of the year.

A ratio that partially corrects this problem is the **current cash debt coverage ratio**. It is computed as cash provided by operating activities divided by average current liabilities. Because cash provided by operating activities involves the entire year rather than a balance at one point in time, it is often considered a better representation of liquidity on the average day. The ratio for **Microsoft Corporation** is calculated as shown in Illustration 13-34, with comparative numbers given for **Oracle**. For comparative purposes, we have also provided each company's current ratio.

Illustration 13-34 Current cash debt coverage ratio

Current Cash Debt Coverage Ratio	=	Cash Provided by Operations / Average Current Liabilities

($ in millions)	Current cash debt coverage ratio	Current ratio
Microsoft	$\dfrac{\$13,422}{(\$11,132 + \$9,755)/2} = 1.29$ times	3.56:1
Oracle	.45 times	2.29:1

Microsoft's net cash provided by operating activities is approximately one-third greater than its average current liabilities. Oracle's ratio of .45 times, though not a cause for concern, is substantially lower than that of Microsoft. Keep in mind that Microsoft's cash position is extraordinary. For example, many large companies now have current ratios in the range of 1.0. By this standard, Oracle's current ratio of 2.29:1 is respectable. Microsoft's current ratio of 3.56:1 is very strong.

DECISION TOOLKIT

Decision Checkpoints	Info Needed for Decision	Tool to Use for Decision	How to Evaluate Results
Is the company generating sufficient cash provided by operating activities to meet its current obligations?	Cash provided by operating activities and average current liabilities	Current cash debt coverage ratio $= \dfrac{\text{Cash provided by operations}}{\text{Average current liabilities}}$	A high value suggests good liquidity. Since the numerator contains a "flow" measure, it provides a good supplement to the current ratio.

Solvency

Solvency is the ability of a company to survive over the long term. A measure of solvency that uses cash figures is the **cash debt coverage ratio**. It is computed as the ratio of cash provided by operating activities to total debt as represented by average total liabilities. This ratio indicates a company's ability to repay its liabilities from cash generated from operations—that is, without having to liquidate productive assets such as property, plant, and equipment. The cash debt coverage ratios for **Microsoft** and **Oracle** for 2001 are given in Illustration 13-35. For comparative purposes, the debt to total assets ratios for each company are also provided.

Illustration 13-35 Cash debt coverage ratio

$$\text{Cash Debt Coverage Ratio} = \frac{\text{Cash Provided by Operations}}{\text{Average Total Liabilities}}$$

($ in millions)	Cash debt coverage ratio	Debt to total assets ratio
Microsoft	$\dfrac{\$13,422}{(\$11,968 + \$10,782)/2} = 1.18$ times	20%
Oracle	.38 times	43%

Microsoft has few long-term obligations. Thus, its cash debt coverage ratio is similar to its current cash debt coverage ratio. Obviously, Microsoft is very solvent. Oracle has some long-term debt with a debt to total assets ratio of 43%. Its cash debt coverage ratio of .38 times is one-third as strong as Microsoft's. Neither the cash nor accrual measures suggest any cause for concern for either company.

DECISION TOOLKIT

Decision Checkpoints	Info Needed for Decision	Tool to Use for Decision	How to Evaluate Results
Is the company generating sufficient cash provided by operating activities to meet its long-term obligations?	Cash provided by operating activities and average total liabilities	Cash debt coverage ratio $=\dfrac{\text{Cash provided by operations}}{\text{Average total liabilities}}$	A high value suggests the company is solvent; that is, it will meet its obligations in the long term.

Business Insight
MANAGEMENT PERSPECTIVE

While **Microsoft**'s cash position is enviable, it does present some challenges. Foremost among these is that management can't find enough ways to spend the cash. For example, unlike computer chip manufacturer **Intel Corporation** (another huge generator of cash), Microsoft has few manufacturing costs, so it cannot spend huge sums on new plant and equipment. Microsoft's management would like to purchase other major software companies, but the federal government won't let it, for fear that it will reduce competition. (For example, the Justice Department blocked Microsoft's proposed purchase of software maker **Intuit**.) Instead, Microsoft is constrained to purchasing small software makers with promising new products. Ironically, even this does not use much of its cash because, first of all, the companies are small, and second, the owners of these small companies prefer to be paid with Microsoft stock rather than cash.

Microsoft's huge holdings of liquid assets could eventually hurt its stock performance. Liquid assets typically provide about a 5% return, whereas Microsoft investors are accustomed to 30% returns. If Microsoft's performance starts to decline because it can't find enough good investment projects, it should distribute cash to its common stockholders in the form of dividends. There's a problem with this plan, though: Bill Gates owns roughly 20% of Microsoft, and the last thing he wants to do is pay personal income tax on billions of dollars of dividend income. In 2003, under severe pressure from stockholders, Microsoft paid its first cash dividend.

SOURCE: David Bank, "Microsoft's Problem Is What Many Firms Just Wish They Had," *Wall Street Journal* (January 17, 1997), p. A9.

BEFORE YOU GO ON . . .

▶ Review It

1. What is the difference between cash from operations and free cash flow?
2. What does it mean if a company has negative free cash flow?
3. Why might an analyst want to supplement accrual-based ratios with cash-based ratios? What are some cash-based ratios?

THE NAVIGATOR

Using the Decision Toolkit

Intel Corporation is the leading producer of computer chips for personal computers. It makes the hugely successful Pentium chip. Its primary competitor is **AMD** (formerly Advanced Micro Devices). The two are vicious competitors, with frequent lawsuits filed between them. Financial statement data for Intel are provided below.

Instructions

Calculate the following cash-based measures for Intel, and compare them with those for AMD provided on page 651.

1. Free cash flow.
2. Current cash debt coverage ratio.
3. Cash debt coverage ratio.

INTEL CORPORATION
Balance Sheets
December 31, 2001 and 2000
(in millions)

Assets	2001	2000
Current assets	$17,633	$21,150
Noncurrent assets	26,762	26,795
Total assets	$44,395	$47,945
Liabilities and Stockholders' Equity		
Current liabilities	$ 6,570	$ 8,650
Long-term liabilities	1,995	1,973
Total liabilities	8,565	10,623
Stockholders' equity	35,830	37,322
Total liabilities and stockholders' equity	$44,395	$47,945

INTEL CORPORATION
Income Statements
For the Years Ended December 31, 2001 and 2000
(in millions)

	2001	2000
Net revenues	$26,539	$33,726
Expenses	25,248	23,191
Net income	$ 1,291	$10,535

INTEL CORPORATION
Statements of Cash Flows
For the Years Ended December 31, 2001 and 2000
(in millions)

	2001	2000
Net cash provided by operating activities	$ 8,654	$ 12,827
Net cash used for investing activities	(195)	(10,035)
Net cash used for financing activities	(3,465)	(3,511)
Net increase (decrease) in cash and cash equivalents	$ 4,994	$ (719)

Note. Cash spent on property, plant, and equipment in 2001 was $7,309. Cash paid for dividends was $538.

Here are the comparative data for **AMD**:

1. Free cash flow — −$511 million
2. Current cash debt coverage ratio — .13 times
3. Cash debt coverage ratio — .07 times

Solution

1. Intel's free cash flow is $807 million ($8,654 − $7,309 − $538). AMD's is actually a negative $511 million. This gives Intel a huge advantage in the ability to move quickly to invest in new projects.

2. The current cash debt coverage ratio for Intel is calculated as follows.

$$\frac{\$8,654}{(\$6,570 + \$8,650)/2} = 1.14 \text{ times}$$

Compared to AMD's value of .13 times, Intel appears to be significantly more liquid.

3. The cash debt coverage ratio for Intel is calculated as follows.

$$\frac{\$8,654}{(\$8,565 + \$10,623)/2} = .90 \text{ times}$$

Compared to AMD's value of .07 times, Intel appears to be significantly more solvent.

Summary of Study Objectives

1 *Indicate the usefulness of the statement of cash flows.* The statement of cash flows provides information about the cash receipts, cash payments, and net change in cash resulting from the operating, investing, and financing activities of a company during the period.

2 *Distinguish among operating, investing, and financing activities.* Operating activities include the cash effects of transactions that enter into the determination of net income. Investing activities involve cash flows resulting from changes in investments and long-term asset items. Financing activities involve cash flows resulting from changes in long-term liability and stockholders' equity items.

3 *Explain the impact of the product life cycle on a company's cash flows.* During the introductory stage, cash provided by operating activities and cash from investing are negative, and cash from financing is positive. During the growth stage, cash provided by operating activities becomes positive. During the maturity stage, cash provided by operating activities exceeds investing needs, so the company begins to retire debt.

During the decline stage, cash provided by operating activities is reduced, cash from investing becomes positive, and cash from financing becomes more negative.

4a *Prepare a statement of cash flows using the indirect method.* The preparation of a statement of cash flows involves three major steps: (1) Determine net cash provided (used) by operating activities. (2) Determine net cash provided (used) by investing and financing activities.(3) Determine the net increase or decrease in cash. Under the indirect method, accrual-basis net income is adjusted to net cash provided by operating activities.

4b *Prepare a statement of cash flows using the direct method.* The preparation of the statement of cash flows involves three major steps: (1) Determine net cash provided (used) by operating activities. (2) Determine net cash provided (used) by investing and financing activities. (3) Determine the net increase or decrease in cash. The direct method reports cash receipts less cash payments to arrive at net cash provided by operating activities.

5 *Use the statement of cash flows to evaluate a company.* A number of measures can be derived by using information from the statement of cash flows as well as the other required financial statements. Free cash flow indicates the amount of cash a company generated during the current year that is available for the payment of dividends or for expansion. Liquidity can be mea- sured with the current cash debt coverage ratio (cash provided by operating activities divided by average current liabilities). Solvency can be measured by the cash debt coverage ratio (cash provided by operating activities divided by average total liabilities).

DECISION TOOLKIT—A SUMMARY

Decision Checkpoints	Info Needed for Decision	Tool to Use for Decision	How to Evaluate Results
How much cash did the company generate to either expand operations or pay dividends?	Cash provided by operating activities, cash spent on fixed assets, and cash dividends	$$\text{Free cash flow} = \text{Cash provided by operations} - \text{Capital expenditures} - \text{Cash dividends}$$	Significant free cash flow indicates greater potential to finance new investment and pay additional dividends.
Is the company generating sufficient cash provided by operating activities to meet its current obligations?	Cash provided by operating activities and average current liabilities	$$\text{Current cash debt coverage ratio} = \frac{\text{Cash provided by operations}}{\text{Average current liabilities}}$$	A high value suggests good liquidity. Since the numerator contains a "flow" measure, it provides a good supplement to the current ratio.
Is the company generating sufficient cash provided by operating activities to meet its long-term obligations?	Cash provided by operating activities and average total liabilities	$$\text{Cash debt coverage ratio} = \frac{\text{Cash provided by operations}}{\text{Average total liabilities}}$$	A high value suggests the company is solvent; that is, it will meet its obligations in the long term.

Glossary

Cash debt coverage ratio A cash-basis ratio used to evaluate solvency, calculated as cash provided by operating activities divided by average total liabilities. (p. 648)

Current cash debt coverage ratio A cash-basis ratio used to evaluate liquidity, calculated as cash provided by operations divided by average current liabilities. (p. 647)

Direct method A method of determining net cash provided by operating activities by adjusting each item in the income statement from the accrual basis to the cash basis. (p. 636)

Financing activities Cash flow activities that include (a) obtaining cash from issuing debt and repaying the amounts borrowed and (b) obtaining cash from stockholders and providing them with a return on their investment. (p. 618)

Free cash flow Cash provided by operating activities adjusted for capital expenditures and dividends paid. (p. 645)

Indirect method A method of preparing a statement of cash flows in which net income is adjusted for items that do not affect cash, to determine net cash provided by operating activities. (p. 627)

Investing activities Cash flow activities that include (a) purchasing and disposing of investments and productive long-lived assets using cash and (b) lending money and collecting the loans. (p. 618)

Operating activities Cash flow activities that include the cash effects of transactions that create revenues and expenses and thus enter into the determination of net income. (p. 618)

Product life cycle   A series of phases in a product's sales and cash flows over time; these phases, in order of occurrence, are introductory, growth, maturity, and decline. (p. 621)

Statement of cash flows   A basic financial statement that provides information about the cash receipts and

cash payments of an entity during a period, classified as operating, investing, and financing activities, in a format that reconciles the beginning and ending cash balances. (p. 618)

Demonstration Problem

The income statement for Kosinski Manufacturing Company contains the following condensed information.

Peachtree

KOSINSKI MANUFACTURING COMPANY
Income Statement
For the Year Ended December 31, 2005

Revenues		$6,583,000
Operating expenses, excluding depreciation	$4,920,000	
Depreciation expense	880,000	5,800,000
Income before income taxes		783,000
Income tax expense		353,000
Net income		$ 430,000

Included in operating expenses is a $24,000 loss resulting from the sale of machinery for $270,000 cash. Machinery was purchased at a cost of $750,000. The following balances are reported on Kosinski's comparative balance sheet at December 31.

	2005	**2004**
Cash	$672,000	$130,000
Accounts receivable	775,000	610,000
Inventories	834,000	867,000
Accounts payable	521,000	501,000

Income tax expense of $353,000 represents the amount paid in 2005. Dividends declared and paid in 2005 totaled $200,000.

Instructions

(a) Prepare the statement of cash flows using the indirect method.
(b) Prepare the statement of cash flows using the direct method.

Solution to Demonstration Problem

(a)   **KOSINSKI MANUFACTURING COMPANY**
Statement of Cash Flows—Indirect Method
For the Year Ended December 31, 2005

Cash flows from operating activities		
Net income		$ 430,000
Adjustments to reconcile net income to net cash provided by operating activities:		
Depreciation expense	$ 880,000	
Loss on sale of machinery	24,000	
Increase in accounts receivable	(165,000)	
Decrease in inventories	33,000	
Increase in accounts payable	20,000	792,000
Net cash provided by operating activities		1,222,000

Action Plan

• Apply the same data to the preparation of a statement of cash flows under both the indirect and direct methods.

• Note the similarities of the two methods: Both methods report the same information in the investing and financing sections.

• Note the differences between the two methods: The cash flows from operating activities sections report different information (but the amount of net cash provided by operating activities is the same for both methods).

Cash flows from investing activities		
Sale of machinery	270,000	
Purchase of machinery	(750,000)	
Net cash used by investing activities		(480,000)
Cash flows from financing activities		
Payment of cash dividends	(200,000)	
Net cash used by financing activities		(200,000)
Net increase in cash		542,000
Cash at beginning of period		130,000
Cash at end of period		$ 672,000

(b) **KOSINSKI MANUFACTURING COMPANY**
Statement of Cash Flows—Direct Method
For the Year Ended December 31, 2005

Cash flows from operating activities		
Cash collections from customers		$6,418,000*
Cash payments:		
For operating expenses	$4,843,000**	
For income taxes	353,000	5,196,000
Net cash provided by operating activities		1,222,000
Cash flows from investing activities		
Sale of machinery	270,000	
Purchase of machinery	(750,000)	
Net cash used by investing activities		(480,000)
Cash flows from financing activities		
Payment of cash dividends	(200,000)	
Net cash used by financing activities		(200,000)
Net increase in cash		542,000
Cash at beginning of period		130,000
Cash at end of period		$ 672,000

Direct Method Computations:

*Computation of cash collections from customers:	
Revenues per the income statement	$6,583,000
Deduct: Increase in accounts receivable	(165,000)
Cash collections from customers	$6,418,000
**Computation of cash payments for operating expenses:	
Operating expenses per the income statement	$4,920,000
Deduct: Loss from sale of machinery	(24,000)
Deduct: Decrease in inventories	(33,000)
Deduct: Increase in accounts payable	(20,000)
Cash payments for operating expenses	$4,843,000

Self-Study Questions

Self-Study/Self-Test

(SO 1) **1.** Which of the following is *incorrect* about the statement of cash flows?
 (a) It is a fourth basic financial statement.
 (b) It provides information about cash receipts and cash payments of an entity during a period.
 (c) It reconciles the ending cash account balance to the balance per the bank statement.

(d) It provides information about the operating, investing, and financing activities of the business.

(SO 2) **2.** The statement of cash flows classifies cash receipts and cash payments by these activities:
(a) operating and nonoperating.
(b) investing, financing, and operating.
(c) financing, operating, and nonoperating.
(d) investing, financing, and nonoperating.

(SO 2) **3.** Which is an example of a cash flow from an operating activity?
(a) Payment of cash to lenders for interest.
(b) Receipt of cash from the sale of capital stock.
(c) Payment of cash dividends to the company's stockholders.
(d) None of the above.

(SO 2) **4.** Which is an example of a cash flow from an investing activity?
(a) Receipt of cash from the issuance of bonds payable.
(b) Payment of cash to repurchase outstanding capital stock.
(c) Receipt of cash from the sale of equipment.
(d) Payment of cash to suppliers for inventory.

(SO 2) **5.** Cash dividends paid to stockholders are classified on the statement of cash flows as:
(a) operating activities.
(b) investing activities.
(c) a combination of (a) and (b).
(d) financing activities.

(SO 2) **6.** Which is an example of a cash flow from a financing activity?
(a) Receipt of cash from sale of land.
(b) Issuance of debt for cash.
(c) Purchase of equipment for cash.
(d) None of the above

(SO 2) **7.** Which of the following is *incorrect* about the statement of cash flows?
(a) The direct method may be used to report cash provided by operations.
(b) The statement shows the cash provided (used) for three categories of activity.
(c) The operating section is the last section of the statement.
(d) The indirect method may be used to report cash provided by operations.

(SO 3) **8.** During the introductory phase of a company's life cycle, one would normally expect to see:
(a) negative cash from operations, negative cash from investing, and positive cash from financing.
(b) negative cash from operations, positive cash from investing, and positive cash from financing.

(c) positive cash from operations, negative cash from investing, and negative cash from financing.
(d) positive cash from operations, negative cash from investing, and positive cash from financing.

Questions 9 and 10 apply only to the indirect method.

9. Net income is $132,000, accounts payable increased $10,000 during the year, inventory decreased $6,000 during the year, and accounts receivable increased $12,000 during the year. Under the indirect method, what is net cash provided by operations? (SO 4a)
(a) $102,000.   (c) $124,000.
(b) $112,000.   (d) $136,000.

10. Items that are added back to net income in determining cash provided by operations under the indirect method do *not* include: (SO 4a)
(a) depreciation expense.
(b) an increase in inventory.
(c) amortization expense.
(d) loss on sale of equipment.

Questions 11 and 12 apply only to the direct method.

11. The beginning balance in accounts receivable is $44,000, the ending balance is $42,000, and sales during the period are $129,000. What are cash receipts from customers? (SO 4b)
(a) $127,000.   (c) $131,000.
(b) $129,000.   (d) $141,000.

12. Which of the following items is reported on a cash flow statement prepared by the direct method? (SO 4b)
(a) Loss on sale of building.
(b) Increase in accounts receivable.
(c) Depreciation expense.
(d) Cash payments to suppliers.

13. The statement of cash flows should *not* be used to evaluate an entity's ability to: (SO 5)
(a) earn net income.
(b) generate future cash flows.
(c) pay dividends.
(d) meet obligations.

14. Free cash flow provides an indication of a company's ability to: (SO 5)
(a) generate net income.
(b) generate cash to pay dividends.
(c) generate cash to invest in new capital expenditures.
(d) both (b) and (c).

Questions

1. (a) What is a statement of cash flows?
   (b) John Stiller maintains that the statement of cash flows is an optional financial statement. Do you agree? Explain.

2. What questions about cash are answered by the statement of cash flows?

3. Distinguish among the three activities reported in the statement of cash flows.

4. (a) What are the major sources (inflows) of cash in a statement of cash flows?
   (b) What are the major uses (outflows) of cash?

5. Why is it important to disclose certain noncash transactions? How should they be disclosed?

6. Wilma Flintstone and Barny Rublestone were discussing the format of the statement of cash flows of Rock Candy Co. At the bottom of Rock Candy's statement of cash flows was a separate section entitled "Noncash investing and financing activities." Give three examples of significant noncash transactions that would be reported in this section.

7. Why is it necessary to use comparative balance sheets, a current income statement, and certain transaction data in preparing a statement of cash flows?

8. (a) What are the phases of the corporate life cycle?
   (b) What effect does each phase have on the numbers reported in a statement of cash flows?

9. Contrast the advantages and disadvantages of the direct and indirect methods of preparing the statement of cash flows. Are both methods acceptable? Which method is preferred by the FASB? Which method is more popular?

10. When the total cash inflows exceed the total cash outflows in the statement of cash flows, how and where is this excess identified?

11. Describe the indirect method for determining net cash provided (used) by operating activities.

12. Why is it necessary to convert accrual-based net income to cash-basis income when preparing a statement of cash flows?

13. The president of Frogger Company is puzzled. During the last year, the company experienced a net loss of $800,000, yet its cash increased $300,000 during the same period of time. Explain to the president how this could occur.

14. Identify five items that are adjustments to convert net income to net cash provided by operating activities under the indirect method.

15. Why and how is depreciation expense reported in a statement prepared using the indirect method?

16. Why is the statement of cash flows useful?

17. During 2005 Steinbrenner Company converted $1,700,000 of its total $2,000,000 of bonds payable into common stock. Indicate how the transaction would be reported on a statement of cash flows, if at all.

18. Describe the direct method for determining net cash provided by operating activities.

19. Give the formulas under the direct method for computing (a) cash receipts from customers and (b) cash payments to suppliers.

20. Armani Inc. reported sales of $2 million for 2005. Accounts receivable decreased $100,000 and accounts payable increased $300,000. Compute cash receipts from customers, assuming that the receivable and payable transactions related to operations.

21. In the direct method, why is depreciation expense not reported in the cash flows from operating activities section?

22. Give examples of accrual-based and cash-based ratios to measure each of these characteristics of a company:
   (a) Liquidity.
   (b) Solvency.

Brief Exercises

Indicate statement presentation of selected transactions.
(SO 2)

BE13-1 Each of these items must be considered in preparing a statement of cash flows for Jerry Co. for the year ended December 31, 2005. For each item, state how it should be shown in the statement of cash flows for 2005.
   (a) Issued bonds for $200,000 cash.
   (b) Purchased equipment for $150,000 cash.
   (c) Sold land costing $20,000 for $20,000 cash.
   (d) Declared and paid a $50,000 cash dividend.

Classify items by activities.
(SO 2)

BE13-2 Classify each item as an operating, investing, or financing activity. Assume all items involve cash unless there is information to the contrary.
   (a) Purchase of equipment.   (d) Depreciation.
   (b) Sale of building.   (e) Payment of dividends.
   (c) Redemption of bonds.   (f) Issuance of capital stock.

BE13-3 The following T account is a summary of the cash account of Elkhart Company.

Identify financing activity transactions.
(SO 2)

T ACCt

Cash (Summary Form)

Balance, Jan. 1	8,000		
Receipts from customers	364,000	Payments for goods	200,000
Dividends on stock investments	6,000	Payments for operating expenses	140,000
Proceeds from sale of equipment	36,000	Interest paid	10,000
Proceeds from issuance of		Taxes paid	8,000
bonds payable	200,000	Dividends paid	50,000
Balance, Dec. 31	206,000		

Which side is Dvd on

What amount of net cash provided (used) by financing activities should be reported in the statement of cash flows?

BE13-4

(a) Why is cash from operations likely to be lower than reported net income during the growth phase?

(b) Why is cash from investing often positive during the late maturity phase and during the decline phase?

Answer questions related to the phases of product life cycle.
(SO 3)

BE13-5 Salvador, Inc. reported net income of $2.5 million in 2005. Depreciation for the year was $260,000, accounts receivable decreased $350,000, and accounts payable decreased $280,000. Compute net cash provided by operating activities using the indirect approach.

Compute cash provided by operating activities—indirect method.
(SO 4a)

BE13-6 The net income for Castle Co. for 2005 was $280,000. For 2005 depreciation on plant assets was $60,000, and the company incurred a loss on sale of plant assets of $12,000. Compute net cash provided by operating activities under the indirect method.

Compute cash provided by operating activities—indirect method.
(SO 4a)

BE13-7 The comparative balance sheets for Holders Company show these changes in noncash current asset accounts: accounts receivable decrease $80,000, prepaid expenses increase $18,000, and inventories increase $30,000. Compute net cash provided by operating activities using the indirect method assuming that net income is $200,000.

Compute net cash provided by operating activities—indirect method.
(SO 4a)

BE13-8 The T accounts for Equipment and the related Accumulated Depreciation for Triangle Art Company at the end of 2005 are shown here.

Determine cash received from sale of equipment.
(SO 4a, 4b)

Equipment				**Accumulated Depreciation**			
Beg. bal.	80,000	Disposals	22,000	Disposals	5,500	Beg. bal.	44,500
Acquisitions	41,600					Depr. exp.	12,000
End. bal.	99,600					End. bal.	51,000

In addition, Triangle Art Company's income statement reported a loss on the sale of equipment of $7,500. What amount was reported on the statement of cash flows as "cash flow from sale of equipment"?

BE13-9 **Columbia Sportswear Company** had accounts receivable of $129,500,000 at January 1, 2001, and $155,300,000 at December 31, 2001. Sales revenues were $779,600,000 for the year 2001. What is the amount of cash receipts from customers in 2001?

Compute receipts from customers—direct method.
(SO 4b)

BE13-10 **Boeing Corporation** reported income taxes of $738,000,000 on its 2001 income statement and income taxes payable of $1,866,000,000 at December 31, 2000, and $909,000,000 at December 31, 2001. What amount of cash payments were made for income taxes during 2001? (Ignore deferred taxes.)

Compute cash payments for income taxes—direct method.
(SO 4b)

BE13-11 Drake Corporation reports operating expenses of $75,000 excluding depreciation expense of $15,000 for 2005. During the year prepaid expenses decreased $6,600 and accrued expenses payable increased $4,400. Compute the cash payments for operating expenses in 2005.

Compute cash payments for operating expenses—direct method.
(SO 4b)

BE13-12 During 2001 **Cypress Semiconductor Corporation** reported cash provided by operations of $95,100,000, cash used in investing of $322,500,000, and cash used in financing of $213,700,000. In addition, cash spent for fixed assets during the period was

Calculate cash-based ratios.
(SO 5)

$176,800,000. Average current liabilities were $276,950,000, and average total liabilities were $1,026,050,000. No dividends were paid. Calculate these values:

(a) Free cash flow.

(b) Current cash debt coverage ratio.

Calculate cash-based ratios.
(SO 5)

BE13-13 Jain Corporation reported cash provided by operating activities of $300,000, cash used by investing activities of $250,000, and cash provided by financing activities of $70,000. In addition, cash spent for capital assets during the period was $200,000. Average current liabilities were $150,000, and average total liabilities were $225,000. No dividends were paid. Calculate these values:

(a) Free cash flow.

(b) Current cash debt coverage ratio.

Calculate cash-based ratios.
(SO 5)

BE13-14 **Alliance Atlantis Communications Inc.** reported a 30% increase in cash flow for its first quarter of 1999-2000. It attributes this increase in cash flow to the overwhelming success of its movie *Austin Powers: The Spy Who Shagged Me*. To date, the film has earned more than $20 million in box office sales. Alliance reported cash provided by operating activities of $234,983,000 and revenues of $163,309,000. An amount of $258,000 was paid for preferred dividends. Cash spent on plant asset additions during the quarter was $4,318,000. Calculate free cash flow.

Exercises

Classify transactions by
type of activity.
(SO 2)

E13-1 Big Salad Corporation had these transactions during 2005.

(a) Issued $50,000 par value common stock for cash.

(b) Purchased a machine for $30,000, giving a long-term note in exchange.

(c) Issued $200,000 par value common stock upon conversion of bonds having a face value of $200,000.

(d) Declared and paid a cash dividend of $18,000.

(e) Sold a long-term investment with a cost of $15,000 for $15,000 cash.

(f) Collected $16,000 of accounts receivable.

(g) Paid $18,000 on accounts payable.

Instructions

Analyze the transactions and indicate whether each transaction resulted in a cash flow from operating activities, investing activities, financing activities, or noncash investing and financing activities.

Classify transactions by
type of activity.
(SO 2)

E13-2 An analysis of comparative balance sheets, the current year's income statement, and the general ledger accounts of Coffee Table Corp. uncovered the following items. Assume all items involve cash unless there is information to the contrary.

(a) Payment of interest on notes payable.

(b) Exchange of land for patent.

(c) Sale of building at book value.

(d) Payment of dividends.

(e) Depreciation.

(f) Receipt of dividends on investment in stock.

(g) Receipt of interest on notes receivable.

(h) Issuance of capital stock.

(i) Amortization of patent.

(j) Issuance of bonds for land.

(k) Purchase of land.

(l) Conversion of bonds into common stock.

(m) Loss on sale of land.

(n) Retirement of bonds.

Instructions

Indicate how each item should be classified in the statement of cash flows using these four major classifications: operating activity (indirect method), investing activity, financing activity, and significant noncash investing and financing activity.

Identify phases of product
life cycle.
(SO 3)

E13-3 The information in the table is from the statement of cash flows for a company at four different points in time (A, B, C, and D). Negative values are presented in parentheses.

	A	B	C	D
	Point in Time			
Cash provided by operations	$ (60,000)	$ 30,000	$120,000	$(10,000)
Cash provided by investing	(100,000)	25,000	30,000	(40,000)
Cash provided by financing	70,000	(110,000)	(50,000)	120,000
Net income	(40,000)	10,000	100,000	(5,000)

Instructions
For each point in time, state whether the company is most likely characterized as being in the introductory phase, growth phase, maturity phase, or decline phase. In each case explain your choice.

E13-4 Poppy Company reported net income of $195,000 for 2005. Poppy also reported depreciation expense of $45,000 and a loss of $5,000 on the sale of equipment. The comparative balance sheet shows a decrease in accounts receivable of $15,000 for the year, a $12,000 increase in accounts payable, and a $4,000 decrease in prepaid expenses.

Prepare the operating activities section—indirect method.
(SO 4a)

Instructions
Prepare the operating activities section of the statement of cash flows for 2005. Use the indirect method.

E13-5 The current sections of DoubleDip Inc.'s balance sheets at December 31, 2004 and 2005, are presented here.

Prepare the operating activities section—indirect method.
(SO 4a)

	2005	2004
Current assets		
Cash	$105,000	$ 99,000
Accounts receivable	120,000	89,000
Inventory	148,000	172,000
Prepaid expenses	27,000	22,000
Total current assets	$400,000	$382,000
Current liabilities		
Accrued expenses payable	$ 15,000	$ 5,000
Accounts payable	85,000	92,000
Total current liabilities	$100,000	$ 97,000

DoubleDip's net income for 2005 was $153,000. Depreciation expense was $19,000.

Instructions
Prepare the net cash provided by operating activities section of the company's statement of cash flows for the year ended December 31, 2005, using the indirect method.

E13-6 These three accounts appear in the general ledger of Bosco Corp. during 2005:

Prepare partial statement of cash flows—indirect method.
(SO 4a)

Equipment

Date		Debit	Credit	Balance
Jan. 1	Balance			160,000
July 31	Purchase of equipment	70,000		230,000
Sept. 2	Cost of equipment constructed	53,000		283,000
Nov. 10	Cost of equipment sold		39,000	244,000

Accumulated Depreciation—Equipment

Date		Debit	Credit	Balance
Jan. 1	Balance			71,000
Nov. 10	Accumulated depreciation on equipment sold	30,000		41,000
Dec. 31	Depreciation for year		28,000	69,000

Retained Earnings

Date		Debit	Credit	Balance
Jan. 1	Balance			105,000
Aug. 23	Dividends (cash)	14,000		91,000
Dec. 31	Net income		67,000	158,000

Instructions

From the postings in the accounts, indicate how the information is reported on a statement of cash flows using the indirect method. The loss on sale of equipment was $3,000. (*Hint:* Purchase of equipment is reported in the investing activities section as a decrease in cash of $70,000.)

Prepare a statement of cash flows—indirect method, and compute cash-based ratios.
(SO 4a, 5)

E13-7 Here are comparative balance sheets for Puffed Up Company:

PUFFED UP COMPANY
Comparative Balance Sheets
December 31

Assets	2005	2004
Cash	$ 63,000	$ 22,000
Accounts receivable	85,000	76,000
Inventories	170,000	189,000
Land	75,000	100,000
Equipment	270,000	200,000
Accumulated depreciation	(66,000)	(32,000)
Total	$597,000	$555,000

Liabilities and Stockholders' Equity	2005	2004
Accounts payable	$ 39,000	$ 47,000
Bonds payable	150,000	200,000
Common stock ($1 par)	216,000	174,000
Retained earnings	192,000	134,000
Total	$597,000	$555,000

Additional information:
1. Net income for 2005 was $98,000.
2. Cash dividends of $40,000 were declared and paid.
3. Bonds payable amounting to $50,000 were redeemed for cash $50,000.
4. Common stock was issued for $42,000 cash.
5. Sales for 2005 were $978,000.

Instructions

(a) Prepare a statement of cash flows for 2005 using the indirect method.
(b) Compute these cash-basis ratios:

   (1) Current cash debt coverage.
   (2) Cash debt coverage.

Compute cash provided by operating activities—direct method.
(SO 4b)

E13-8 Beltless Company completed its first year of operations on December 31, 2005. Its initial income statement showed that Beltless had revenues of $182,000 and operating expenses of $78,000. Accounts receivable and accounts payable at year-end were $60,000 and $18,000, respectively. Assume that accounts payable related to operating expenses. Ignore income taxes.

Instructions

Compute net cash provided by operating activities using the direct method.

Compute cash payments—direct method.
(SO 4b)

E13-9 The 2001 income statement for **McDonald's Corporation** shows cost of goods sold $3,802.1 million and operating expenses (including depreciation expense of $1,086.3 million) $8,370.9 million. The comparative balance sheet for the year shows that inventory increased $6.2 million, prepaid expenses increased $68.9 million, accounts payable (merchandise suppliers) increased $4.6 million, and accrued expenses payable increased $150.3 million.

Instructions

Using the direct method, compute (a) cash payments to suppliers and (b) cash payments for operating expenses.

Compute cash flow from operating activities—direct method.
(SO 4b)

E13-10 The 2005 accounting records of Running on Vapors Transport reveal these transactions and events.

Payment of interest	$ 10,000	Collection of accounts receivable	$192,000
Cash sales	48,000	Payment of salaries and wages	53,000
Receipt of dividend revenue	18,000	Depreciation expense	16,000
Payment of income taxes	12,000	Proceeds from sale of vehicles	812,000
Net income	38,000	Purchase of equipment for cash	22,000
Payment of accounts payable		Loss on sale of vehicles	3,000
for merchandise	110,000	Payment of dividends	14,000
Payment for land	74,000	Payment of operating expenses	28,000

Instructions
Prepare the cash flows from operating activities section using the direct method. (Not all of the items will be used.)

E13-11 The following information is taken from the 2005 general ledger of Lone Ranger Company.

Calculate cash flows—direct method.
(SO 4b)

Rent	Rent expense	$ 35,000
	Prepaid rent, January 1	5,900
	Prepaid rent, December 31	9,000
Salaries	Salaries expense	$ 54,000
	Salaries payable, January 1	10,000
	Salaries payable, December 31	8,000
Sales	Revenue from sales	$180,000
	Accounts receivable, January 1	16,000
	Accounts receivable, December 31	7,000

Instructions
In each case, compute the amount that should be reported in the operating activities section of the statement of cash flows under the direct method.

E13-12 Presented here is 2001 information for **PepsiCo, Inc.** and **The Coca-Cola Company**.

Compare two companies by using cash-based ratios.
(SO 5)

($ in millions)	PepsiCo	Coca-Cola
Cash provided by operations	$ 4,201	$ 4,110
Average current liabilities	4,897	8,875
Average total liabilities	13,100	11,285
Net income	2,662	3,969
Sales	26,935	20,092

Instructions
Using the cash-based ratios presented in this chapter, compare the (a) liquidity and (b) solvency of the two companies.

E13-13 Information for two companies in the same industry, Rita Corporation and Les Corporation, is presented here.

Compare two companies by using cash-based ratios.
(SO 5)

	Rita Corporation	Les Corporation
Cash provided by operating activities	$200,000	$200,000
Average current liabilities	50,000	100,000
Average total liabilities	200,000	250,000
Net earnings	200,000	200,000
Sales	400,000	800,000

Instructions
Using the cash-based ratios presented in this chapter, compare the (a) liquidity and (b) solvency of the two companies.

Problems: Set A

Distinguish among operating, investing, and financing activities.
(SO 2)

P13-1A You are provided with the following transactions that took place during a recent fiscal year.

Transaction	Where Reported on Statement	Cash Inflow, Outflow, or No Effect?
(a) Recorded depreciation expense on the plant assets.		
(b) Incurred a loss on disposal of plant assets.		
(c) Acquired a building by paying cash.		
(d) Made principal repayments on a mortgage.		
(e) Issued common stock.		
(f) Purchased shares of another company to be held as a long-term equity investment.		
(g) Paid dividends to common stockholders.		
(h) Sold inventory on credit. The company uses a perpetual inventory system.		
(i) Purchased inventory on credit.		
(j) Paid wages to employees.		

Instructions
Complete the table indicating whether each item (1) should be reported as an operating (O) activity, investing (I) activity, financing (F) activity, or as a noncash (NC) transaction reported in a separate schedule, and (2) represents a cash inflow or cash outflow or has no cash flow effect. Assume use of the indirect approach.

Determine cash flow effects of changes in plant asset accounts.
(SO 4)

P13-2A The following selected account balances relate to the plant asset accounts of Trudeau Inc. at year-end.

	2005	2004
Accumulated depreciation—buildings	$337,500	$300,000
Accumulated depreciation—equipment	144,000	96,000
Buildings	750,000	750,000
Depreciation expense	101,500	85,500
Equipment	300,000	240,000
Land	100,000	70,000
Loss on sale of equipment	1,000	0

Additional information:

1. Trudeau purchased $80,000 of equipment and $30,000 of land for cash in 2005.
2. Trudeau also sold equipment in 2005.
3. Depreciation expense in 2005 was $37,500 on building and $64,000 on equipment.

Instructions

(a) Cash proceeds $3,000

(a) Determine the amounts of any cash inflows or outflows related to the plant asset accounts in 2005.
(b) Indicate where each of the cash inflows or outflows identified in (a) would be classified on the statement of cash flows.

Prepare the operating activities section—indirect method.
(SO 4a)

P13-3A The income statement of Kroncke Company is presented on page 663.
Additional information:

1. Accounts receivable decreased $510,000 during the year.
2. Prepaid expenses increased $170,000 during the year.
3. Accounts payable to merchandise suppliers increased $50,000 during the year.
4. Accrued expenses payable increased $165,000 during the year.

KRONCKE COMPANY
Income Statement
For the Year Ended December 31, 2005

Sales		$5,400,000
Cost of goods sold		
Beginning inventory	$1,780,000	
Purchases	3,430,000	
Goods available for sale	5,210,000	
Ending inventory	1,920,000	
Total cost of goods sold		3,290,000
Gross profit		2,110,000
Operating expenses		
Selling expenses	400,000	
Administrative expense	525,000	
Depreciation expense	125,000	
Amortization expense	20,000	1,070,000
Net income		$1,040,000

Instructions
Prepare the operating activities section of the statement of cash flows for the year ended December 31, 2005, for Kroncke Company, using the indirect method.

P13-4A   Data for Kroncke Company are presented in P13-3A.

Instructions
Prepare the operating activities section of the statement of cash flows using the direct method.

P13-5A   The income statement of Kraemer Inc. reported the following condensed information.

KRAEMER INC.
Income Statement
For the Year Ended December 31, 2005

Revenues	$545,000
Operating expenses	400,000
Income from operations	145,000
Income tax expense	47,000
Net income	$ 98,000

Kraemer's balance sheet contained these comparative data at December 31.

	2005	2004
Accounts receivable	$50,000	$70,000
Accounts payable	30,000	41,000
Income taxes payable	10,000	4,000

Kraemer has no depreciable assets. Accounts payable pertain to operating expenses.

Instructions
Prepare the operating activities section of the statement of cash flows using the direct method.

P13-6A   Data for Kraemer are presented in P13-5A.

Instructions
Prepare the operating activities section of the statement of cash flows using the indirect method.

Cash from operations
$1,600,000

Prepare the operating activities section—direct method.
(SO 4b)
Cash from operations
$1,600,000

Prepare the operating activities section—direct method.
(SO 4b)

Cash from operations
$113,000

Prepare the operating activities section—indirect method.
(SO 4a)   Cash from operations
$113,000

Prepare a statement of cash flows—indirect method, and compute cash-based ratios.
(SO 4a, 5)

P13-7A Here are the financial statements of YoYo Company.

YOYO COMPANY
Comparative Balance Sheets
December 31

Assets		2005		2004
Cash		$ 26,000		$ 33,000
Accounts receivable		28,000		14,000
Merchandise inventory		38,000		25,000
Property, plant, and equipment	$ 70,000		$ 78,000	
Less: Accumulated depreciation	(27,000)	43,000	(24,000)	54,000
Total		$135,000		$126,000

Liabilities and Stockholders' Equity		2005		2004
Accounts payable		$ 31,000		$ 43,000
Income taxes payable		26,000		20,000
Bonds payable		20,000		10,000
Common stock		25,000		25,000
Retained earnings		33,000		28,000
Total		$135,000		$126,000

YOYO COMPANY
Income Statement
For the Year Ended December 31, 2005

Sales		$286,000
Cost of goods sold		194,000
Gross profit		92,000
Selling expenses	$28,000	
Administrative expenses	9,000	37,000
Income from operations		55,000
Interest expense		7,000
Income before income taxes		48,000
Income tax expense		7,000
Net income		$ 41,000

Additional data:

1. Dividends of $36,000 were declared and paid.
2. During the year equipment was sold for $10,000 cash. This equipment cost $15,000 originally and had a book value of $10,000 at the time of sale.
3. All depreciation expense, $8,000, is in the selling expense category.
4. All sales and purchases are on account.
5. Additional equipment was purchased for $7,000 cash.

Instructions

(a) Cash from operations $16,000

(a) Prepare a statement of cash flows using the indirect method.
(b) Compute these cash-basis measures:
   (1) Current cash debt coverage ratio.
   (2) Cash debt coverage ratio.
   (3) Free cash flow.

P13-8A Data for YoYo Company are presented in P13-7A. Further analysis reveals the following.

Prepare a statement of cash flows—direct method, and compute cash-based ratios.
(SO 4b, 5) (a) Cash from operations $16,000

1. Accounts payable pertains to merchandise creditors.
2. All operating expenses except for depreciation are paid in cash.

Instructions
(a) Prepare a statement of cash flows using the direct method.

(b) Compute these cash-basis measures:
   (1) Current cash debt coverage ratio.
   (2) Cash debt coverage ratio.
   (3) Free cash flow.

P13-9A Condensed financial data of George Company follow.

Prepare a statement of cash flows—indirect method.
(SO 4a)

GEORGE COMPANY
Comparative Balance Sheets
December 31

Assets	2005	2004
Cash	$ 92,700	$ 33,400
Accounts receivable	80,800	37,000
Inventories	121,900	102,650
Investments	84,500	107,000
Plant assets	310,000	205,000
Accumulated depreciation	(49,500)	(40,000)
Total	$640,400	$445,050

Liabilities and Stockholders' Equity		
Accounts payable	$ 62,700	$ 48,280
Accrued expenses payable	12,100	18,830
Bonds payable	140,000	70,000
Common stock	250,000	200,000
Retained earnings	175,600	107,940
Total	$640,400	$445,050

GEORGE COMPANY
Income Statement Data
For the Year Ended December 31, 2005

Sales		$297,500
Gain on sale of plant assets		5,000
		302,500
Less:		
Cost of goods sold	$99,460	
Operating expenses, excluding depreciation expense	14,670	
Depreciation expense	35,500	
Income taxes	7,270	
Interest expense	2,940	159,840
Net income		$142,660

Additional information:

1. New plant assets costing $141,000 were purchased for cash during the year.
2. Investments were sold at cost.
3. Plant assets costing $36,000 were sold for $15,000, resulting in a gain of $5,000.
4. A cash dividend of $75,000 was declared and paid during the year.

Instructions
Prepare a statement of cash flows using the indirect method.

Cash from operations
$117,800

P13-10A Data for George Company are presented in P13-9A. Further analysis reveals that accounts payable pertain to merchandise creditors.

Prepare a statement of cash flows—direct method.
(SO 4b)

Instructions
Prepare a statement of cash flows for George Company using the direct method.

Cash from operations
$117,800

P13-11A Presented on the next page are the comparative balance sheets for Perry Company at December 31.

Prepare a statement of cash flows—indirect method.
(SO 4a)

PERRY COMPANY
Comparative Balance Sheets
December 31

Assets	2005	2004
Cash	$ 26,000	$ 57,000
Accounts receivable	77,000	64,000
Inventory	192,000	140,000
Prepaid expenses	12,140	16,540
Land	105,000	150,000
Equipment	215,000	175,000
Accumulated depreciation—equipment	(70,000)	(42,000)
Building	250,000	250,000
Accumulated depreciation—building	(70,000)	(50,000)
Total	$737,140	$760,540

Liabilities and Stockholders' Equity		
Accounts payable	$ 63,000	$ 45,000
Bonds payable	235,000	265,000
Common stock, $1 par	280,000	250,000
Retained earnings	159,140	200,540
Total	$737,140	$760,540

Additional information:
1. Operating expenses include depreciation expense $65,000 and charges from prepaid expenses of $4,400.
2. Land was sold for cash at cost.
3. Cash dividends of $74,290 were paid.
4. Net income for 2005 was $32,890.
5. Equipment was purchased for $80,000 cash. In addition, equipment costing $40,000 with a book value of $23,000 was sold for $25,000 cash.
6. Bonds were converted at face value by issuing 30,000 shares of $1 par value common stock.

Cash from operations
$53,290

Instructions
Prepare a statement of cash flows for 2005 using the indirect method.

Identify the impact of transactions on ratios.
(SO 5)

P13-12A You are provided with the following transactions that took place during the year.

Transactions	Free Cash Flow ($125,000)	Current Cash Debt Coverage Ratio (0.5 times)	Cash Debt Coverage Ratio (0.3 times)
(a) Recorded cash sales $8,000.			
(b) Purchased inventory for $1,500 cash.			
(c) Purchased new equipment $10,000; signed a short-term note payable for the cost of the equipment.			
(d) Paid a $20,000 cash dividend to common stockholders.			
(e) Acquired a building for $750,000, by signing a mortgage payable for $450,000 and issuing common stock for the balance.			
(f) Made a principal payment on the mortgage currently due, $45,000.			

Instructions

For each transaction listed above, indicate whether it will increase (I), decrease (D), or have no effect (NE) on the ratios.

Problems: Set B

P13-1B You are provided with the following transactions that took place during a recent fiscal year.

Distinguish among operating, investing, and financing activities.
(SO 2)

Transaction	Where Reported on Statement	Cash Inflow, Outflow, or No Effect?
(a) Recorded depreciation expense on the plant assets.		
(b) Recorded and paid interest expense.		
(c) Recorded cash proceeds from a sale of plant assets.		
(d) Acquired land by issuing common stock.		
(e) Paid a cash dividend to preferred stockholders.		
(f) Distributed a stock dividend to common stockholders.		
(g) Recorded cash sales.		
(h) Recorded sales on account.		
(i) Purchased inventory for cash.		
(j) Purchased inventory on account.		

Instructions

Complete the table indicating whether each item (1) should be reported as an operating (O) activity, investing (I) activity, financing (F) activity, or as a noncash (NC) transaction reported in a separate schedule, and (2) represents a cash inflow or cash outflow or has no cash flow effect. Assume use of the indirect approach.

P13-2B The following account balances relate to the stockholders' equity accounts of Wood Corp. at year-end.

Determine cash flow effects of changes in equity accounts.
(SO 4)

	2005	2004
Common stock, 10,500 and 10,000 shares, respectively, for 2005 and 2004	$160,000	$140,000
Preferred stock, 5,000 shares	125,000	125,000
Retained earnings	300,000	240,000

A small stock dividend was declared and issued in 2005. The market value of the shares was $10,500. Cash dividends were $10,000 in both 2005 and 2004. The common stock has no par or stated value.

Instructions

(a) What was the amount of net income reported by Wood Corp. in 2005?

(b) Determine the amounts of any cash inflows or outflows related to the common stock and dividend accounts in 2005.

(c) Indicate where each of the cash inflows or outflows identified in (b) would be classified on the statement of cash flows.

(a) Net income $80,500

P13-3B The income statement of Talker Company is presented here.

TALKER COMPANY
Income Statement
For the Year Ended November 30, 2005

Sales		$7,700,000
Cost of goods sold		
Beginning inventory	$1,900,000	
Purchases	4,400,000	
Goods available for sale	6,300,000	
Ending inventory	1,400,000	
Total cost of goods sold		4,900,000
Gross profit		2,800,000
Operating expenses		
Selling expenses	450,000	
Administrative expenses	700,000	1,150,000
Net income		$1,650,000

Additional information:
1. Accounts receivable increased $200,000 during the year.
2. Prepaid expenses increased $150,000 during the year.
3. Accounts payable to suppliers of merchandise decreased $340,000 during the year.
4. Accrued expenses payable decreased $100,000 during the year.
5. Administrative expenses include depreciation expense of $110,000.

Instructions
Prepare the operating activities section of the statement of cash flows for the year ended November 30, 2005, for Talker Company, using the indirect method.

P13-4B Data for Talker Company are presented in P13-3B.

Instructions
Prepare the operating activities section of the statement of cash flows using the direct method.

P13-5B No Soup Company's income statement contained the condensed information below.

NO SOUP COMPANY
Income Statement
For the Year Ended December 31, 2005

Revenues		$970,000
Operating expenses, excluding depreciation	$624,000	
Depreciation expense	60,000	
Loss on sale of equipment	16,000	700,000
Income before income taxes		270,000
Income tax expense		40,000
Net income		$230,000

No Soup's balance sheet contained these comparative data at December 31.

	2005	2004
Accounts receivable	$65,000	$60,000
Accounts payable	41,000	33,000
Income taxes payable	11,000	7,000

Accounts payable pertain to operating expenses.

Instructions
Prepare the operating activities section of the statement of cash flows using the direct method.

P13-6B   Data for No Soup Company are presented in P13-5B.

Prepare the operating activities section—indirect method.
(SO 4a)

Instructions
Prepare the operating activities section of the statement of cash flows using the indirect method.

Cash from operations
$313,000

P13-7B   Presented below are the financial statements of Newman Company.

Prepare a statement of cash flows—indirect method, and compute cash-based ratios.
(SO 4a, 5)

NEWMAN COMPANY
Comparative Balance Sheets
December 31

Assets	2005	2004
Cash	$ 31,000	$ 20,000
Accounts receivable	38,000	14,000
Merchandise inventory	27,000	20,000
Property, plant, and equipment	60,000	78,000
Accumulated depreciation	(30,000)	(24,000)
Total	$126,000	$108,000

Liabilities and Stockholders' Equity	2005	2004
Accounts payable	$ 29,000	$ 15,000
Income taxes payable	7,000	8,000
Bonds payable	27,000	33,000
Common stock	18,000	14,000
Retained earnings	45,000	38,000
Total	$126,000	$108,000

NEWMAN COMPANY
Income Statement
For the Year Ended December 31, 2005

Sales		$242,000
Cost of goods sold		175,000
Gross profit		67,000
Selling expenses	$18,000	
Administrative expenses	6,000	24,000
Income from operations		43,000
Interest expense		3,000
Income before income taxes		40,000
Income tax expense		6,000
Net income		$ 34,000

Additional data:
1. Dividends declared and paid were $27,000.
2. During the year equipment was sold for $8,500 cash. This equipment cost $18,000 originally and had a book value of $8,500 at the time of sale.
3. All depreciation expense is in the selling expense category.
4. All sales and purchases are on account.

(a) Cash from operations
$31,500

Instructions
(a) Prepare a statement of cash flows using the indirect method.
(b) Compute these cash-basis measures:
   (1) Current cash debt coverage ratio.
   (2) Cash debt coverage ratio.
   (3) Free cash flow.

Prepare a statement of cash flows—direct method, and compute cash-based ratios.
(SO 4b, 5)

P13-8B   Data for Newman Company are presented in P13-7B. Further analysis reveals the following.

1. Accounts payable pertain to merchandise suppliers.
2. All operating expenses except for depreciation were paid in cash.

Instructions

(a) Cash from operations
$31,500

(a) Prepare a statement of cash flows for Newman Company using the direct method.

(b) Compute these cash-basis measures:
 (1) Current cash debt coverage ratio.
 (2) Cash debt coverage ratio.
 (3) Free cash flow.

Prepare a statement of cash flows—indirect method. (SO 4a)

P13-9B Condensed financial data of Elly Inc. follow.

ELLY INC.
Comparative Balance Sheets
December 31

Assets	2005	2004
Cash	$ 97,800	$ 48,400
Accounts receivable	95,800	33,000
Inventories	112,500	102,850
Prepaid expenses	28,400	26,000
Investments	128,000	114,000
Plant assets	270,000	242,500
Accumulated depreciation	(50,000)	(52,000)
Total	$682,500	$514,750

Liabilities and Stockholders' Equity		
Accounts payable	$102,000	$ 67,300
Accrued expenses payable	16,500	17,000
Bonds payable	110,000	150,000
Common stock	220,000	175,000
Retained earnings	234,000	105,450
Total	$682,500	$514,750

ELLY INC.
Income Statement Data
For the Year Ended December 31, 2005

Sales		$392,780
Less:		
Cost of goods sold	$135,460	
Operating expenses, excluding depreciation	12,410	
Depreciation expense	46,500	
Income taxes	7,280	
Interest expense	4,730	
Loss on sale of plant assets	7,500	213,880
Net income		$178,900

Additional information:
1. New plant assets costing $85,000 were purchased for cash during the year.
2. Old plant assets having an original cost of $57,500 were sold for $1,500 cash.
3. Bonds matured and were paid off at face value for cash.
4. A cash dividend of $50,350 was declared and paid during the year.

Cash from operations
$192,250

Instructions

Prepare a statement of cash flows using the indirect method.

Prepare a statement of cash flows—direct method. (SO 4b)

P13-10B Data for Elly Inc. are presented in P13-9B. Further analysis reveals that accounts payable pertain to merchandise creditors.

Cash from operations
$192,250

Instructions

Prepare a statement of cash flows for Elly Inc. using the direct method.

P13-11B   The comparative balance sheets for Festivals Company as of December 31 are presented on the next page.

Prepare a statement of cash flows—indirect method.
(SO 4a)

FESTIVALS COMPANY
Comparative Balance Sheets
December 31

Assets	2005	2004
Cash	$ 81,000	$ 45,000
Accounts receivable	49,000	62,000
Inventory	151,450	142,000
Prepaid expenses	15,280	21,000
Land	90,000	130,000
Equipment	228,000	155,000
Accumulated depreciation—equipment	(45,000)	(35,000)
Building	200,000	200,000
Accumulated depreciation—building	(60,000)	(40,000)
Total	$709,730	$680,000

Liabilities and Stockholders' Equity		
Accounts payable	$ 57,730	$ 40,000
Bonds payable	260,000	300,000
Common stock, $1 par	200,000	160,000
Retained earnings	192,000	180,000
Total	$709,730	$680,000

Additional information:
1. Operating expenses include depreciation expense of $42,000 and charges from prepaid expenses of $5,720.
2. Land was sold for cash at book value.
3. Cash dividends of $25,000 were paid.
4. Net income for 2005 was $37,000.
5. Equipment was purchased for $95,000 cash. In addition, equipment costing $22,000 with a book value of $10,000 was sold for $6,000 cash.
6. Bonds were converted at face value by issuing 40,000 shares of $1 par value common stock.

Instructions
Prepare a statement of cash flows for the year ended December 31, 2005, using the indirect method.

Cash from operations
$110,000

P13-12B   You are provided with the following transactions that took place during the year.

Identify the impact of transactions on ratios.
(SO 5)

Transactions	Free Cash Flow ($125,000)	Current Cash Debt Coverage Ratio (0.5 times)	Cash Debt Coverage Ratio (0.3 times)
(a) Recorded credit sales $2,500.			
(b) Collected $1,500 owing from customers.			
(c) Paid amount owing to suppliers $2,750.			
(d) Recorded sales returns of $500 and credited the customer's account.			
(e) Purchased new equipment $5,000; signed a long-term note payable for the cost of the equipment.			
(f) Purchased a patent and paid $15,000 cash for the asset.			

Instructions

For each transaction listed above, indicate whether it will increase (I), decrease (D), or have no effect (NE) on the ratios.

▶ BROADENING YOUR PERSPECTIVE

Financial Reporting and Analysis

FINANCIAL REPORTING PROBLEM: *Tootsie Roll Industries, Inc.*

BYP13-1 The financial statements of **Tootsie Roll Industries** are presented in Appendix A.

Instructions

Answer the following questions.

(a) What was the amount of net cash provided by operating activities for 2002? For 2001? What were some causes of any significant changes in cash from operations between 2001 and 2002?

(b) What was the amount of increase or decrease in cash and cash equivalents for the year ended December 31, 2002?

(c) Which method of computing net cash provided by operating activities does Tootsie Roll use?

(d) From your analysis of the 2002 statement of cash flows, was the change in accounts receivable a decrease or an increase? Was the change in inventories a decrease or an increase? Was the change in accounts payable a decrease or an increase?

(e) What was the net cash used by investing activities for 2002?

(f) What was the amount of interest paid in 2002? What was the amount of income taxes paid in 2002?

COMPARATIVE ANALYSIS PROBLEM: *Tootsie Roll vs. Hershey Foods*

BYP13-2 The financial statements of **Hershey Foods** are presented in Appendix B, following the financial statements for **Tootsie Roll Industries** in Appendix A.

Instructions

(a) Based on the information in these financial statements, compute these 2002 ratios for each company:
  (1) Current cash debt coverage.
  (2) Cash debt coverage.

(b) What conclusions concerning the management of cash can be drawn from these data?

RESEARCH CASE

BYP13-3 The March 5, 2002, issue of the *Wall Street Journal* contains an article by Mark Maremont entitled "'Cash Flow,' a Highly Touted Measure of Strength, Is Open to Interpretation."

Instructions

Read the article and answer the following questions.

(a) What does the article say is the "conventional wisdom" regarding the measurement of cash flow versus that of net income?

(b) Describe the two methods by which **Tyco** acquires customer contracts.

(c) Explain briefly how it is that the method by which Tyco acquires customer contracts can have a dramatic effect on its reported cash flow.

(d) What measure does Tyco's chief financial officer want investors to focus on, rather than reported earnings?

INTERPRETING FINANCIAL STATEMENTS

BYP13-4   The incredible growth of Amazon.com has put fear into the hearts of traditional retailers. Amazon.com's stock price has soared to amazing levels. However, it is often pointed out in the financial press that the company has never reported a profit for the year. The following financial information is taken from the 2001 financial statements of Amazon.com.

($ in millions)	2001	2000
Current assets	$1,207.9	$ 1,361.1
Total assets	1,637.5	2,135.2
Current liabilities	921.4	975.0
Total liabilities	3,077.5	3,102.4
Cash provided by operations	(119.8)	(130.4)
Capital expenditures	50.3	134.8
Dividends paid	0	0
Net loss	(567.3)	(1,411.3)
Sales	3,122.4	2,762.0

Instructions
(a) Calculate the current ratio and current cash debt coverage ratio for Amazon.com for 2001 and discuss its liquidity.
(b) Calculate the cash debt coverage ratio and the debt to total assets ratio for Amazon.com for 2001 and discuss its solvency.
(c) Calculate free cash flow for Amazon.com for 2001 and discuss its ability to finance expansion from internally generated cash. Thus far Amazon.com has avoided purchasing large warehouses. Instead, it has used those of others. It is possible, however, that in order to increase customer satisfaction the company may have to build its own warehouses. If this happens, how might your impression of its ability to finance expansion change?
(d) Discuss any potential implications of the change in Amazon.com's cash provided by operations and its net loss from 2000 to 2001.
(e) Based on your findings in parts (a) through (d), can you conclude whether or not Amazon.com's amazing stock price is justified?

A GLOBAL FOCUS

BYP13-5   The statement of cash flows has become a commonly provided financial statement by companies throughout the world. It is interesting to note, however, that its format does vary across countries. The statement of cash flows on page 674 is from the 2001 financial statements of Irish pharmaceutical company Elan Corporation.

Instructions
(a) What similarities to U.S. cash flow statements do you notice in terms of general format, as well as terminology?
(b) What differences do you notice in terms of general format, as well as terminology?

ELAN CORPORATION
Consolidated Statement of Cash Flows

	Notes	Year Ended 31 December	
		2001 $m	2000 $m
Cash Flow from Operating Activities	28(a)	524.6	272.2
Returns on Investments and Servicing of Finance			
Interest received		80.3	111.8
Interest paid		(124.1)	(76.4)
Cash (outflow)/inflow from returns on investments and servicing of finance		(43.8)	35.4
Taxation		(6.5)	(3.6)
Capital Expenditure and Financial Investment			
Additions to property, plant and equipment		(120.8)	(64.4)
Receipts from disposal of property, plant and equipment		2.0	9.8
Payments to acquire intangible assets		(286.7)	(79.5)
Receipts from disposal of intangible assets		11.2	—
Payments to acquire financial current assets		(148.2)	(54.6)
Sale and maturity of financial current assets		143.3	100.1
Payments to acquire financial fixed assets		(624.3)	(411.9)
Receipts from disposal of financial fixed assets		76.2	6.7
Cash outflow from capital expenditure and financial investment		(947.3)	(493.8)
Acquisitions and Disposals			
Cash paid on acquisitions	28(d)	(9.5)	(8.0)
Receipts from part disposal of subsidiary		41.9	—
Cash inflow/(outflow) from acquisitions and disposals		32.4	(8.0)
Cash outflow before use of liquid resources and financing		(440.6)	(197.8)
Management of Liquid Resources	28(b)	106.8	399.1
Financing			
Proceeds from issue of share capital		304.8	76.9
Purchase of treasury shares		—	—
Issue of loan notes		1,185.7	444.1
Repayment of loans		(555.7)	(496.0)
Bank borrowing		342.8	200.0
Cash inflow from financing		1,277.6	225.0
Net increase in cash		943.8	426.3
Reconciliation of Net Cash Flow to Movement in Net Debt			
Increase in cash for the period		943.8	426.3
Cash inflow from movement in liquid resources		(106.8)	(399.1)
		837.0	27.2
Other borrowing		(347.4)	(200.0)
Repayment of loans		557.6	512.4
Issue of loan notes		(1,185.7)	(444.1)
Change in net debt resulting from cash flows		(138.5)	(104.5)
Liquid resources acquired with subsidiary undertaking		—	214.2
Loans acquired with subsidiary undertaking		(0.3)	(363.7)
Non-cash movement — translation differences		(1.4)	(1.1)
Non-cash movement — notes		255.3	(54.4)
Non-cash movement — other		1.1	(1.3)
Decrease/(increase) in net debt	28(c)	116.2	(310.8)

FINANCIAL ANALYSIS ON THE WEB

BYP13-6 *Purpose:* Use the Internet to view SEC filings.

Address: biz.yahoo.com/i (or go to **www.wiley.com/college/kimmel**)

Steps
1. Enter a company's name.
2. Choose **Quote**. Answer questions (a) and (b).
3. Choose **Profile**.
4. Choose **SEC**. Answer questions (c) and (d).

Instructions
Answer the following questions.
 (a) What company did you select?
 (b) What is its stock symbol? What is its selling price?
 (c) What recent SEC filings are available for your viewing?
 (d) Which filing is the most recent? What is the date?

Critical Thinking

GROUP DECISION CASE

BYP13-7 Rex Nord and Sara Smith are examining the following statement of cash flows for Collector Company for the year ended January 31, 2005.

COLLECTOR COMPANY
Statement of Cash Flows
For the Year Ended January 31, 2005

Sources of cash	
From sales of merchandise	$370,000
From sale of capital stock	420,000
From sale of investment (purchased below)	80,000
From depreciation	55,000
From issuance of note for truck	20,000
From interest on investments	6,000
Total sources of cash	951,000
Uses of cash	
For purchase of fixtures and equipment	340,000
For merchandise purchased for resale	258,000
For operating expenses (including depreciation)	160,000
For purchase of investment	75,000
For purchase of truck by issuance of note	20,000
For purchase of treasury stock	10,000
For interest on note payable	3,000
Total uses of cash	866,000
Net increase in cash	$ 85,000

Rex claims that Collector's statement of cash flows is an excellent portrayal of a superb first year with cash increasing $85,000. Sara replies that it was not a superb first year. Rather, she says, the year was an operating failure, that the statement is presented incorrectly, and that $85,000 is not the actual increase in cash. The cash balance at the beginning of the year was $140,000.

Instructions
With the class divided into groups, answer the following.
 (a) With whom do you agree, Rex or Sara? Explain your position.
 (b) Using the data provided, prepare a statement of cash flows in proper form using the indirect method. The only noncash items in the income statement are depreciation and the gain from the sale of the investment.

COMMUNICATION ACTIVITY

BYP13-8   Kyle Benson, the owner-president of Iris Co., is unfamiliar with the statement of cash flows that you, as his accountant, prepared. He asks for further explanation.

Instructions
Write him a brief memo explaining the form and content of the statement of cash flows as shown in Illustration 13-14 (page 632).

ETHICS CASE

BYP13-9   On The Road Again Corp. is a medium-sized wholesaler of automotive parts. It has 10 stockholders who have been paid a total of $1 million in cash dividends for 8 consecutive years. The board's policy requires that, for this dividend to be declared, net cash provided by operating activities as reported in On The Road Again's current year's statement of cash flows must exceed $1 million. President and CEO Willie Nelson's job is secure so long as he produces annual operating cash flows to support the usual dividend.

At the end of the current year, controller Waylon Jennings presents president Willie Nelson with some disappointing news: The net cash provided by operating activities is calculated by the indirect method to be only $970,000. The president says to Waylon, "We must get that amount above $1 million. Isn't there some way to increase operating cash flow by another $30,000?" Waylon answers, "These figures were prepared by my assistant. I'll go back to my office and see what I can do." The president replies, "I know you won't let me down, Waylon."

Upon close scrutiny of the statement of cash flows, Waylon concludes that he can get the operating cash flows above $1 million by reclassifying a $60,000, 2-year note payable listed in the financing activities section as "Proceeds from bank loan—$60,000." He will report the note instead as "Increase in payables—$60,000" and treat it as an adjustment of net income in the operating activities section. He returns to the president, saying, "You can tell the board to declare their usual dividend. Our net cash flow provided by operating activities is $1,030,000." "Good man, Waylon! I knew I could count on you," exults the president.

Instructions
  (a) Who are the stakeholders in this situation?
  (b) Was there anything unethical about the president's actions? Was there anything unethical about the controller's actions?
  (c) Are the board members or anyone else likely to discover the misclassification?

Answers to Self-Study Questions
1. c   2. b   3. a   4. c   5. d   6. b   7. c   8. a   9. d   10. b
11. c   12. d   13. a   14. d

Answer to Tootsie Roll Review It Question 2, p. 625

Tootsie Roll has positive cash from operations that exceeds its net income. Its cash from operations exceeded its dividends paid and its capital expenditures. It had negative cash from financing because of significant repurchases of common stock. Tootsie Roll appears to be in the middle to late maturity phase.

✓ Remember to go back to the Navigator box on the chapter-opening page and check off your completed work.

Financial Statement Analysis

After studying this chapter,
you should be able to:

1 Understand the concept of sustainable income.

2 Indicate how irregular items are presented.

3 Explain the concept of comprehensive income.

4 Describe and apply horizontal analysis.

5 Describe and apply vertical analysis.

6 Identify and compute ratios used in analyzing a company's liquidity, solvency, and profitability.

7 Understand the concept of quality of earnings.

☑ THE
NAVIGATOR

THE NAVIGATOR ✔

▶ Scan *Study Objectives*   ❑
▶ Read *Feature Story*   ❑
▶ Read *Preview*   ❑
▶ Read text and answer *Before You Go On*
    p. 686 ❑   p. 694 ❑   p. 695 ❑
▶ Work Using the *Decision Toolkit*   ❑
▶ Review Summary of *Study Objectives*   ❑
▶ Work *Demonstration Problem*   ❑
▶ Answer *Self-Study Questions*   ❑
▶ Complete *Assignments*   ❑

Making the Numbers

There it is again, perched atop *Fortune*'s "Most Admired Companies" list for the fifth year in a row. But when the guys who run **General Electric** go out in public these days, they don't exactly get to bask in adulation. Instead, they have to explain how their company is *not* like **Enron**, or **Global Crossing**, or **Tyco**.

At one level, that's a pretty easy argument to make. GE is not about to collapse or to break up. It has tons of cash, and its businesses generate upwards of a billion dollars every month. It is one of only a handful of companies with a triple-A credit rating. It makes real things like turbines and refrigerators that people spend real money to buy.

GE also has an enviable record of pleasing Wall Street. Quarter after quarter, year after year, GE's earnings come gushing in, usually at least 10% higher than the year before, and almost invariably in line with analysts' estimates.

This used to be seen as a good thing. "Making the numbers" became the most watched measure of corporate performance. By missing only once in the past ten years (by a penny, in the fourth quarter of 1997), GE ensured itself a hallowed place in the corporate hall of fame.

But as one analyst noted, "Smoking used to be chic and fashionable and cool; now it's not. The companies that reliably deliver 15% earnings growth year after year are the new smokers." All of which means that GE's chief executive, Jeffrey Immelt, now finds himself having to tell interviewer after interviewer that no, he's not an earnings cheat.

"Would a miss be more honest?" Immelt asks, with exasperation in his voice. "I think that's terrible. That's where the world has gotten totally turned on its head, where somewhere I'd walk up to a podium and get a Nobel Peace Prize for saying 'I missed my numbers—aren't you proud of me?' "

Source: Adapted from Justin Fox, "What's So Great About GE?" *Fortune* (March 4, 2002), pp. 65–66.

On the World Wide Web
General Electric: www.ge.com

As indicated in our Feature Story, even the most admired companies in the United States are under attack regarding their earnings and disclosure practices. A climate of skepticism has caused many companies to lose billions of dollars in market value if there is even the slightest hint that the company is involved in some form of creative accounting. The purpose of this chapter is to explain the importance of **performance measurement** and to highlight the difficulties of developing **high-quality earnings numbers**, given the complexities of modern business transactions.

The content and organization of this chapter are as follows.

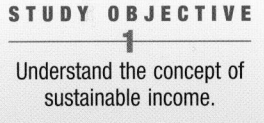

Sustainable Income

Ultimately, the value of a company is a function of its future cash flows. When analysts use this year's net income to estimate future cash flows, they must make sure that this year's net income does not include irregular (i.e., out of the ordinary) revenues, expenses, gains, or losses. Net income adjusted for irregular items is referred to as **sustainable income**. **Sustainable income is the most likely level of income to be obtained in the future.** Sustainable income differs from actual net income by the amount of irregular revenues, expenses, gains, and losses included in this year's net income.

STUDY OBJECTIVE
1
Understand the concept of sustainable income.

Users are interested in sustainable income because it helps them derive an estimate of future earnings without the "noise" of irregular items. For example, suppose Rye Corporation reports that this year's net income is $500,000 but included in that amount is a once-in-a-lifetime gain of $400,000. In estimating next year's net income for Rye Corporation, we would likely ignore this $400,000 gain and estimate that next year's net income will be in the neighborhood of $100,000. That is, based on this year's results, the company's sustainable income is roughly $100,000. Therefore, identifying irregular items is important if you are going to use reported earnings to estimate a company's value.

In earlier chapters you learned how to prepare and use a basic multiple-step income statement. In this chapter we will explain additional components of the income statement as well as a broader measure of performance called comprehensive income. Illustration 14-1 (page 680) presents the components of the income statement and comprehensive income; new items are presented in red. When estimating future cash flows, analysts must consider the implications that each of these components has for future cash flows.

Illustration 14-1
Components of the
income statement

Income Statement

Sales	$XX
Cost of goods sold	XX
Gross profit	XX
Operating expenses	XX
Income from operations	XX
Other revenues (expenses) and gains (losses)	XX
Income before income taxes	XX
Income tax expense	XX
Income before irregular items	XX
Irregular items	XX
Net income	XX
Other comprehensive income items	XX
Comprehensive income	$XX

IRREGULAR ITEMS

As an aid in determining sustainable income, irregular items are identified by type on the income statement. Three types of irregular items are reported:

1. Discontinued operations
2. Extraordinary items
3. Changes in accounting principle

All these irregular items are reported net of income taxes. That is, first income tax expense is calculated for the income before irregular items. Then it is calculated for each individual irregular item. The general concept is, "Let the tax follow the income or loss."

Discontinued Operations

To downsize its operations, **General Dynamics Corp.** sold its missile business to **Hughes Aircraft Co.** for $450 million. In its income statement, General Dynamics was required to report the sale in a separate section entitled "Discontinued operations." **Discontinued operations** refers to the disposal of a significant component of a business, such as the elimination of a major class of customers or an entire activity. When the disposal of a significant component occurs, the income statement should report the gain (or loss) from discontinued operations, net of tax.

To illustrate, assume that Rozek Inc. has revenues of $2.5 million and expenses of $1.7 million from continuing operations in 2005. The company therefore has income before income taxes of $800,000. During 2005 the company discontinued and sold its unprofitable chemical division. The loss on disposal of the chemical division (net of $90,000 taxes) was $210,000. Assuming a 30% tax rate on income before income taxes, we show the income statement presentation in Illustration 14-2.

Illustration 14-2
Statement presentation of
discontinued operations

ROZEK INC.
Income Statement (partial)
For the Year Ended December 31, 2005

Income before income taxes	$ 800,000
Income tax expense	240,000
Income before irregular items	560,000
Discontinued operations	
Loss from disposal of chemical division, net of	
$90,000 income tax savings	(210,000)
Net income	$ 350,000

This presentation clearly indicates the separate effects of continuing operations and discontinued operations on net income.

DECISION TOOLKIT

Decision Checkpoints	Info Needed for Decision	Tool to Use for Decision	How to Evaluate Results
Has the company sold any major components of its business?	Discontinued operations section of income statement	Anything reported in this section indicates that the company has discontinued a major component of its business.	If a major component has been discontinued, its results during the current period should not be included in estimates of future net income.

Extraordinary Items

Extraordinary items are events and transactions that meet two conditions: They are **unusual in nature** and **infrequent in occurrence**. To be considered *unusual*, the item should be abnormal and only incidentally related to the customary activities of the entity. To be regarded as *infrequent*, the event or transaction should not be reasonably expected to recur in the foreseeable future. Both criteria must be evaluated in terms of the environment in which the entity operates. Thus, **Weyerhaeuser Co.** reported the $36 million in damages to its timberland caused by the eruption of Mount St. Helens as an extraordinary item because the event was both unusual and infrequent. In contrast, **Florida Citrus Company** does not report frost damage to its citrus crop as an extraordinary item because frost damage is not viewed as infrequent.

Extraordinary items are reported net of taxes in a separate section of the income statement immediately below discontinued operations. To illustrate, assume that in 2005 a revolutionary foreign government expropriated property held as an investment by Rozek Inc. If the loss is $70,000 before applicable income taxes of $21,000, the income statement presentation will show a deduction of $49,000, as in Illustration 14-3.

Helpful Hint Ordinary gains and losses are reported at pretax amounts in arriving at income before income taxes.

Illustration 14-3
Statement presentation of extraordinary items

ROZEK INC. Income Statement (partial) For the Year Ended December 31, 2005	
Income before income taxes	$ 800,000
Income tax expense	240,000
Income before irregular items	560,000
Discontinued operations: Loss from disposal of chemical division, net of $90,000 income tax savings	(210,000)
Extraordinary item: Expropriation of investment, net of $21,000 income tax savings	(49,000)
Net income	$ 301,000

If a transaction or event meets one but not both of the criteria for an extraordinary item, it should be reported in a separate line item in the upper half of the income statement, rather than being reported in the bottom half as an extraordinary item. Usually these items are reported under either "Other revenues and gains" or "Other expenses and losses" at their gross amount (not net of tax). This is true, for example, of gains (losses) resulting from the sale of property, plant, and equipment, as explained in Chapter 9. Illustration 14-4 (page 682) shows the appropriate classification of extraordinary and ordinary items.

Illustration 14-4
Classification of extraordinary and ordinary items

Extraordinary items

1. Effects of major casualties (acts of God), if rare in the area.

2. Expropriation (takeover) of property by a foreign government.

3. Effects of a newly enacted law or regulation, such as a condemnation action.

Ordinary items

1. Effects of major casualties (acts of God), not uncommon in the area.

2. Write-down of inventories or write-off of receivables.

3. Losses attributable to labor strikes.

4. Gains or losses from sales of property, plant, or equipment.

Business Insight
INVESTOR PERSPECTIVE

Many companies these days are incurring restructuring charges as a result of attempting to reduce costs. Are these costs ordinary or extraordinary? Some companies report "one-time" restructuring charges over and over. Case in point: Toothpaste and diapers giant **Procter & Gamble Co.** reported a restructuring charge in 12 consecutive quarters. On the other hand, some companies take a restructuring charge only once in five years. The one-size-fits-all classification therefore will not work. There appears to be no substitute for a careful analysis of the numbers that comprise net income.

DECISION TOOLKIT

Decision Checkpoints	Info Needed for Decision	Tool to Use for Decision	How to Evaluate Results
Has the company experienced any extraordinary events or transactions?	Extraordinary item section of income statement	Anything reported in this section indicates that the company experienced an event that was both unusual and infrequent.	These items should usually be ignored in estimating future net income.

Changes in Accounting Principle

For ease of comparison, financial statements are expected to be prepared on a basis **consistent** with that used for the preceding period. That is, where a choice of accounting principles is available, the principle initially chosen should be applied consistently from period to period. A change in accounting principle occurs when the principle used in the current year is different from the one used in the preceding year. A change is permitted when (1) management can show that the new principle is preferable to the old principle and (2) the effects of the change are clearly disclosed in the income statement. Two examples are a change in depreciation methods (such as declining-balance to straight-line) and a change in inventory costing methods (such as FIFO to average cost). The effect of a change in an accounting principle on net income can be significant. When **U.S. West**, one of the six regional Bell telephone companies, changed the depreciation method for its telecommunications equipment, it posted a $3.2 billion loss (net of tax).

Sometimes a change in accounting principle is mandated by the Financial Accounting Standards Board (FASB). An example is the change in accounting for start-up costs and customer-acquisition costs. In its income statement in the change period, **Tenneco Automotive** reported a charge of $134 million, net of income taxes of $72 million, under "Cumulative effect of accounting change." An accompanying note explained that the charge resulted from adopting the new standard for these costs.

A change in an accounting principle affects reporting in two ways:

1. The new principle should be used in reporting the results of operations of the current year.
2. The cumulative effect of the change on all prior-year income statements should be disclosed net of applicable taxes in a special section immediately preceding "Net income."

To illustrate, we will assume that at the beginning of 2005, Rozek Inc. changes from the straight-line method to the declining-balance method for equipment that was purchased on January 1, 2002. The cumulative effect on prior-year income statements (statements for 2002–2004) is to increase depreciation expense and decrease income before income taxes by $24,000. If there is a 30% tax rate, the net-of-tax effect of the change is $16,800 ($24,000 × 70%). The income statement presentation is shown in Illustration 14-5.

ROZEK INC. Income Statement (partial) For the Year Ended December 31, 2005	
Income before income taxes	$ 800,000
Income tax expense	240,000
Income before irregular items	560,000
Discontinued operations: Loss from disposal of chemical division, net of $90,000 income tax savings	(210,000)
Extraordinary item: Expropriation of investment, net of $21,000 income tax savings	(49,000)

**Change in accounting principle: Effect on prior
    years of change in depreciation method, net of
    $7,200 income tax savings**
	(16,800)

Net income	$ 284,200

Illustration 14-5
Statement presentation of a change in accounting principle

The income statement for Rozek will also show depreciation expense for the current year. The amount is based on the new depreciation method.

In summary, in evaluating a company, it generally makes sense to eliminate all irregular items in estimating future sustainable income.

DECISION TOOLKIT

Decision Checkpoints	Info Needed for Decision	Tool to Use for Decision	How to Evaluate Results
Has the company changed any of its accounting policies?	Cumulative effect of change in accounting principle section of income statement	Anything reported in this section indicates that the company has changed an accounting policy during the current year.	The cumulative effect should be ignored in estimating the future net income.

COMPREHENSIVE INCOME

Most revenues, expenses, gains, and losses are included in net income. However, certain gains and losses now bypass net income. Instead, these items are recorded as direct adjustments to stockholders' equity. Many analysts have expressed concern about this practice because they believe it reduces the usefulness of the income statement. To address this concern, the FASB now requires companies to report not only net income, but also comprehensive income. **Comprehensive income** includes all changes in stockholders' equity during a period except those changes resulting from investments by stockholders and distributions (dividends) to stockholders.

Illustration of Comprehensive Income

Accounting standards require that most investments in stocks and bonds be adjusted up or down to their market value at the end of each accounting period. For example, assume that during 2005 Stassi Company purchased **IBM** stock for $10,000 as an investment. At the end of 2005 Stassi was still holding the investment, but its market value was now $8,000. In this case, Stassi is required to reduce the recorded value of its IBM investment by $2,000. The $2,000 difference is an unrealized loss.

Should Stassi include this $2,000 unrealized loss in net income? It depends on whether the IBM stock is classified as a trading security or an available-for-sale security. A **trading security** is bought and held primarily for sale in the near term to generate income on short-term price differences. Unrealized losses on trading securities are reported in the "Other expenses and losses" section of the income statement. The rationale: It is likely that the unrealized loss (or an unrealized gain) will be realized, so the loss (gain) should be reported as part of net income.

If Stassi did not purchase the investment for trading purposes, it is classified as available for sale. **Available-for-sale securities** are held with the intent of selling them sometime in the future. Unrealized gains or losses on available-for-sale securities are not included in the determination of net income. Instead, they are reported as part of "Other comprehensive income." For example, if Stassi does not intend to sell its IBM stock in the near term, it may not ever have to realize the loss. By the time Stassi sells the IBM stock, its value may have recovered, and Stassi may actually end up with a gain.

Format

One format for reporting comprehensive income is to report a combined statement of income and comprehensive income.[1] For example, assuming that Stassi

---

[1]Computation of comprehensive income is often shown in a separate statement of comprehensive income or as a section in the stockholders' equity statement. Discussion of these alternatives is left for more advanced courses.

Company has a net income of $300,000, the unrealized loss would adjust net income as follows.

STASSI CORPORATION Combined Statement of Income and Comprehensive Income (partial)	
Net income	$300,000
Unrealized loss on available-for-sale securities	2,000
Comprehensive income	$298,000

Illustration 14-6 Lower portion of combined statement of income and comprehensive income

The unrealized loss on available-for-sale securities is also reported as a separate component of stockholders' equity. To illustrate, assume Stassi Corporation has common stock of $3,000,000, retained earnings of $1,500,000, and an unrealized loss on available-for-sale securities of $2,000. The balance sheet presentation of the unrealized loss is shown in Illustration 14-7.

STASSI CORPORATION Balance Sheet (partial)	
Stockholders' equity	
Common stock	$3,000,000
Retained earnings	1,500,000
Total paid-in capital and retained earnings	4,500,000
Less: **Unrealized loss on available-for-sale securities**	(2,000)
Total stockholders' equity	$4,498,000

Illustration 14-7 Unrealized loss in stockholders' equity section

Note that the presentation of the loss is similar to the presentation of the cost of treasury stock in the stockholders' equity section. An unrealized gain is added in this section. Reporting the unrealized gain or loss in the stockholders' equity section serves two important purposes: (1) It reduces the volatility of net income due to fluctuations in fair value, and (2) it informs the financial statement user of the gain or loss that would occur if the securities were sold at fair value.

Complete Income Statement

The income statement for Pace Corporation in Illustration 14-8 (page 686) presents the types of items found on this statement, such as net sales, cost of goods sold, operating expenses, and income taxes. In addition, it shows how the irregular items (highlighted in red) are reported.

CONCLUDING REMARKS

We have shown that the computation of the correct net income number can be elusive. In assessing the future prospects of a company, some investors focus on income from operations and therefore ignore all irregular and other items. Others use measures such as net income, comprehensive income, or some modified version of one of these amounts.

Illustration 14-8
Complete income
statement

PACE CORPORATION
Income Statement and
Statement of Comprehensive Income
For the Year Ended December 31, 2005

Net sales		$440,000
Cost of goods sold		260,000
Gross profit		180,000
Operating expenses		110,000
Income from operations		70,000
Other revenues and gains	$ 5,600	
Other expenses and losses	(9,600)	(4,000)
Income before income taxes		66,000
Income tax expense ($66,000 × 30%)		19,800
Income before irregular items		46,200
Discontinued operations: Gain on disposal of		
Plastics Division, net of $15,000 income taxes		
($50,000 × 30%)		35,000
Extraordinary item: Tornado loss, net of income		
tax savings $18,000 ($60,000 × 30%)		(42,000)
Change in accounting principle: Effect on prior		
years of change in depreciation method, net of		
$9,000 income tax savings ($30,000 × 30%)		(21,000)
Net income		18,200
Add: Unrealized gain on available-for-sale securities		10,000
Comprehensive income		$ 28,200

BEFORE YOU GO ON . . .

▶ **Review It**

1. What is sustainable income?
2. What are irregular items, and what effect might they have on the estimation of future earnings and future cash flows?
3. What amount did **Tootsie Roll Industries** report as "Other comprehensive earnings (loss)" in 2002? What was the percentage decrease of Tootsie Roll's "Comprehensive earnings (loss)" over its "Net earnings"? The answer to this question is provided on page 735.

☑ THE
NAVIGATOR

Comparative Analysis

As indicated, in assessing the financial performance of a company, investors are interested in the core or sustainable earnings of a company. In addition, investors are interested in making comparisons from period to period. Throughout this book, we have relied on three types of comparisons to improve the decision usefulness of financial information.

1. **Intracompany basis.** Comparisons within a company are often useful to detect changes in financial relationships and significant trends. For example, a comparison of **Kellogg**'s current year's cash amount with the prior year's cash amount shows either an increase or a decrease. Likewise, a comparison of Kellogg's year-end cash amount with the amount of its total assets at year-end shows the proportion of total assets in the form of cash.

2. **Intercompany basis.** Comparisons with other companies provide insight into a company's competitive position. For example, Kellogg's total sales for the year can be compared with the total sales of its competitors in the breakfast cereal area, such as **Quaker Oats** and **General Mills**.

3. **Industry averages.** Comparisons with industry averages provide information about a company's relative position within the industry. For example, Kellogg's financial data can be compared with the averages for its industry compiled by financial ratings organizations such as **Dun & Bradstreet**, **Moody's**, and **Standard & Poor's**, or with information provided on the Internet by organizations such as **Yahoo!** on its financial site.

Three basic tools are used in financial statement analysis to highlight the significance of financial statement data:

1. Horizontal analysis
2. Vertical analysis
3. Ratio analysis

In previous chapters we relied primarily on ratio analysis, supplemented with some basic horizontal and vertical analysis. In the remainder of this section, we introduce more formal forms of horizontal and vertical analysis. In the next section we review ratio analysis in some detail.

HORIZONTAL ANALYSIS

Horizontal analysis, also known as trend analysis, is a technique for evaluating a series of financial statement data over a period of time. Its purpose is to determine the increase or decrease that has taken place, expressed as either an amount or a percentage. For example, here are recent net sales figures (in millions) of **Kellogg Company**:

2001	2000	1999	1998	1997
$8,853.3	$6,954.7	$6,984.2	$6,762.1	$6,830.1

> **STUDY OBJECTIVE 4**
> Describe and apply horizontal analysis.

If we assume that 1997 is the base year, we can measure all percentage increases or decreases relative to this base-period amount with the formula shown in Illustration 14-9.

> **Alternative Terminology**
> Horizontal analysis is also often referred to as **trend analysis**.

$$\text{Change Since Base Period} = \frac{\text{Current-Year Amount} - \text{Base-Year Amount}}{\text{Base-Year Amount}}$$

> **Illustration 14-9**
> Horizontal analysis—computation of changes since base period

dollar

For example, we can determine that net sales for Kellogg Company decreased approximately 1.0% [($6,762.1 − $6,830.1) ÷ $6,830.1] from 1997 to 1998. Similarly, we can also determine that net sales increased by 29.6% [($8,853.3 − $6,830.1) ÷ $6,830.1] from 1997 to 2001.

Alternatively, we can express current-year sales as a percentage of the base period. To do so, we would divide the current-year amount by the base-year amount, as shown in Illustration 14-10.

$$\text{Current Results in Relation to Base Period} = \frac{\text{Current-Year Amount}}{\text{Base-Year Amount}}$$

> **Illustration 14-10**
> Horizontal analysis—computation of current year in relation to base year

%

Current-period sales expressed as a percentage of the base period for each of the five years, using 1997 as the base period, are shown in Illustration 14-11.

Illustration 14-11
Horizontal analysis of net sales

KELLOGG COMPANY				
Net Sales (in millions)				
Base Period 1997				
2001	**2000**	**1999**	**1998**	**1997**
$8,853.3	$6,954.7	$6,984.2	$6,762.1	$6,830.1
129.62%	101.82%	102.26%	99%	100%

The large increase in net sales during 2001 would raise questions regarding possible reasons for such a significant change. Kellogg's 2001 notes to the financial statements explain that "the Company completed its acquisition of Keebler Foods Company" during 2001. This major acquisition would help explain the increase in sales highlighted by horizontal analysis.

To further illustrate horizontal analysis, we use the financial statements of **Kellogg Company**. Its two-year condensed balance sheets for 2001 and 2000, showing dollar and percentage changes, are presented in Illustration 14-12.

Illustration 14-12
Horizontal analysis of a balance sheet

KELLOGG COMPANY, INC.
Condensed Balance Sheets
December 31
(in millions)

	2001	2000	Increase (Decrease) during 2001 Amount	Percent
Assets				
Current assets	$ 1,902.0	$1,617.1	$ 284.9	17.6
Property assets (net)	2,952.8	2,526.9	425.9	16.9
Other assets	5,513.8	742.0	4,771.8	643.1
Total assets	$10,368.6	$4,886.0	$5,482.6	112.2
Liabilities and Stockholders' Equity				
Current liabilities	$ 2,207.6	$2,482.3	$ (274.7)	(11.1)
Long-term liabilities	7,289.5	1,506.2	5,783.3	384.0
Total liabilities	9,497.1	3,988.5	5,508.6	138.1
Stockholders' equity				
Common stock	195.3	205.8	(10.5)	(5.1)
Retained earnings	1,013.3	1,065.7	(52.4)	(4.9)
Treasury stock (cost)	(337.1)	(374.0)	36.9	9.9
Total stockholders' equity	871.5	897.5	(26.0)	(2.9)
Total liabilities and stockholders' equity	$10,368.6	$4,886.0	$5,482.6	112.2

Helpful Hint It is difficult to comprehend the significance of a change when only the dollar amount of change is examined. When the change is expressed in percentage form, it is easier to grasp the true magnitude of the change.

Helpful Hint When using horizontal analysis, both dollar amount changes and percentage changes need to be examined. It is not necessarily bad if a company's earnings are growing at a declining rate. The **amount** of increase may be the same as or more than the base year, but the **percentage** change may be less because the base is greater each year.

The comparative balance sheet shows that a number of changes occurred in Kellogg's financial position from 2000 to 2001. In the assets section, current assets increased $284.9 million, or 17.6% ($284.9 ÷ $1,617.1), and property assets (net) increased $425.9 million, or 16.9%. Other assets increased $4,771.8, or 643.1%. In the liabilities section, current liabilities decreased $274.7 million, or 11.1%, while long-term liabilities increased $5,783.3 million, or 384.0%. In the stockholders' equity section, we find that retained earnings decreased $52.4 million, or 4.9%. The company expanded its asset base, by purchasing Keebler Foods during 2001 and financed this expansion primarily by assuming additional long-term debt. Presented in Illustration 14-13 is a two-year comparative income statement of Kellogg Company for 2001 and 2000 in a condensed format.

Illustration 14-13
Horizontal analysis of
an income statement

Kellogg's

KELLOGG COMPANY, INC.
Condensed Income Statements
For the Years Ended December 31
(in millions)

	2001	2000	Increase (Decrease) during 2001 Amount	Percent
Net sales	$8,853.3	$6,954.7	$1,898.6	27.3
Cost of goods sold	4,128.5	3,327.0	801.5	24.1
Gross profit	4,724.8	3,627.7	1,097.1	30.2
Selling and administrative expenses	3,523.6	2,551.4	972.2	38.1
Nonrecurring charges	33.3	86.5	(53.2)	(61.5)
Income from operations	1,167.9	989.8	178.1	18.0
Interest expense	351.5	137.5	214.0	155.6
Other income (expense), net	(12.3)	15.4	(27.7)	(179.9)
Income before income taxes	804.1	867.7	(63.6)	(7.3)
Income tax expense	322.1	280.0	42.1	15.0
Net income*	$ 482.0	$ 587.7	$ (105.7)	(18.0)

*During 2001, Kellogg Company reported an extraordinary loss and a loss due to the cumulative effect of an accounting change. These items were excluded from Illustration 14-13 to allow for a more meaningful comparison with 2000.

Helpful Hint Note that, in a horizontal analysis, while the amount column is additive (the total is negative $105.7 million), the percentage column is not additive (18.0% is **not** a total).

Horizontal analysis of the income statements shows the following changes: Net sales increased $1,898.6 million, or 27.3% ($1,898.6 ÷ $6,954.7). Cost of goods sold increased $801.5 million, or 24.1% ($801.5 ÷ $3,327.0). Selling and administrative expenses increased $972.2 million, or 38.1% ($972.2 ÷ $2,551.4). Overall, gross profit increased 30.2% and net income decreased 18.0%. The decrease in net income can be attributed to the increase in interest expense.

The measurement of changes from period to period in percentages is relatively straightforward and quite useful. However, complications can result in making the computations. If an item has no value in a base year or preceding year and a value in the next year, no percentage change can be computed. And if a negative amount appears in the base or preceding period and a positive amount exists the following year, no percentage change can be computed.

DECISION TOOLKIT

Decision Checkpoints	Info Needed for Decision	Tool to Use for Decision	How to Evaluate Results
How do the company's financial position and operating results compare with those of the previous period?	Income statement and balance sheet	Comparative financial statements should be prepared over at least two years, with the first year reported being the base year. Changes in each line item relative to the base year should be presented both by amount and by percentage. This is called horizontal analysis.	Significant changes should be investigated to determine the reason for the change.

VERTICAL ANALYSIS

STUDY OBJECTIVE
5
Describe and apply vertical
analysis.

Alternative Terminology
Vertical analysis is sometimes
referred to as **common-size
analysis**.

Vertical analysis, also called common-size analysis, is a technique for evaluating financial statement data that expresses each item in a financial statement as a percent of a base amount. For example, on a balance sheet we might say that current assets are 22% of total assets (total assets being the base amount). Or on an income statement we might say that selling expenses are 16% of net sales (net sales being the base amount).

Presented in Illustration 14-14 is the comparative balance sheet of **Kellogg** for 2001 and 2000, analyzed vertically. The base for the asset items is **total assets**, and the base for the liability and stockholders' equity items is **total liabilities and stockholders' equity**.

Illustration 14-14
Vertical analysis of a
balance sheet

KELLOGG COMPANY, INC.
Condensed Balance Sheets
December 31
(in millions)

	2001		2000	
Assets	**Amount**	**Percent***	**Amount**	**Percent***
Current assets	$ 1,902.0	18.3	$1,617.1	33.1
Property assets (net)	2,952.8	28.5	2,526.9	51.7
Other assets	5,513.8	53.2	742.0	15.2
Total assets	$10,368.6	100.0	$4,886.0	100.0
Liabilities and Stockholders' Equity				
Current liabilities	$ 2,207.6	21.3	$2,482.3	50.8
Long-term liabilities	7,289.5	70.3	1,506.2	30.8
Total liabilities	9,497.1	91.6	3,988.5	81.6
Stockholders' equity				
Common stock	195.3	1.9	205.8	4.2
Retained earnings	1,013.3	9.8	1,065.7	21.8
Treasury stock (cost)	(337.1)	(3.3)	(374.0)	(7.6)
Total stockholders' equity	871.5	8.4	897.5	18.4
Total liabilities and stockholders' equity	$10,368.6	100.0	$4,886.0	100.0

*Numbers have been rounded to total 100%.

In addition to showing the relative size of each category on the balance sheet, vertical analysis may show the percentage change in the individual asset, liability, and stockholders' equity items. In this case, even though current assets increased $284.9 million from 2000 to 2001, they decreased from 33.1% to 18.3% of total assets. Property assets (net) decreased from 51.7% to 28.5% of total assets. Other assets increased from 15.2% to 53.2% of total assets. The other assets in 2001 include $4,818 million of trademarks, trade names, and goodwill that resulted from the acquisition of Keebler Foods. Also, retained earnings decreased by $52.4 million from 2000 to 2001, and total stockholders' equity decreased from 18.4% to 8.4% of total liabilities and stockholders' equity. This switch to a higher percentage of debt financing has two causes: First, total liabilities increased by $5,508.6 million, going from 81.6% to 91.6% of total liabilities and stockholders' equity. Second, common stock decreased by $10.5 million, going from 4.2% to 1.9% of total liabilities and stockholders' equity.

Thus, the company shifted toward a heavier reliance on debt financing both by using more long-term debt and by reducing the amount of outstanding equity.

Vertical analysis of the comparative income statements of Kellogg, shown in Illustration 14-15, reveals that cost of goods sold **as a percentage of net sales** decreased from 47.8% to 46.6%, and selling and administrative expenses increased from 36.7% to 39.8%. Net income as a percent of net sales decreased from 8.4% to 5.5%. Kellogg's decline in net income as a percentage of sales is due primarily to the increase in both selling and administrative expenses and interest expense as a percent of sales. The drop in cost of goods sold and nonrecurring charges was not sufficient to offset the increase in these costs.

KELLOGG COMPANY, INC. Condensed Income Statements For the Years Ended December 31 (in millions)	2001		2000	
	Amount	Percent*	Amount	Percent*
Net sales	$8,853.3	100.0	$6,954.7	100.0
Cost of goods sold	4,128.5	46.6	3,327.0	47.8
Gross profit	4,724.8	53.4	3,627.7	52.2
Selling and administrative expenses	3,523.6	39.8	2,551.4	36.7
Nonrecurring charges	33.3	.4	86.5	1.3
Income from operations	1,167.9	13.2	989.8	14.2
Interest expense	351.5	4.0	137.5	2.0
Other income (expense), net	(12.3)	(.1)	15.4	.2
Income before income taxes	804.1	9.1	867.7	12.4
Income tax expense	322.1	3.6	280.0	4.0
Net income	$ 482.0	5.5	$ 587.7	8.4

*Numbers have been rounded to total 100%.

Illustration 14-15
Vertical analysis of an income statement

Vertical analysis also enables you to compare companies of different sizes. For example, one of Kellogg's main competitors is **General Mills**. Using vertical analysis, we can more meaningfully compare the condensed income statements of Kellogg and General Mills, as shown in Illustration 14-16.

CONDENSED INCOME STATEMENTS For the Year Ended December 31, 2001 (in millions)	Kellogg Company, Inc.		General Mills, Inc.	
	Amount	Percent*	Amount	Percent*
Net sales	$8,853.3	100.0	$7,949.0	100.0
Cost of goods sold	4,128.5	46.6	4,767.0	60.0
Gross profit	4,724.8	53.4	3,182.0	40.0
Selling and administrative expenses	3,523.6	39.8	1,909.0	24.0
Nonrecurring charges	33.3	.4	190.0	2.4
Income from operations	1,167.9	13.2	1,083.0	13.6
Other expenses and revenues (including income taxes)	685.9	7.7	622.0	7.8
Net income	$ 482.0	5.5	$ 461.0	5.8

*Numbers have been rounded to total 100%.

Illustration 14-16
Intercompany comparison by vertical analysis

Although Kellogg's net sales are 11% greater than those of General Mills, vertical analysis eliminates the impact of this size difference for our analysis. Kellogg has a higher gross profit, 53.4%, compared to 40% for General Mills, but Kellogg's selling and administrative expenses are 39.8% of net sales, while those of General Mills are 24% of net sales. Looking at income from operations, we see that the companies report similar percentages: Kellogg's income from operations as a percentage of net sales is 13.2%, compared to 13.6% for General Mills.

DECISION TOOLKIT

Decision Checkpoints	Info Needed for Decision	Tool to Use for Decision	How to Evaluate Results
How do the relationships between items in this year's financial statements compare with those of last year or those of competitors?	Income statement and balance sheet	Each line item on the income statement should be presented as a percentage of net sales, and each line item on the balance sheet should be presented as a percentage of total assets or total liabilities and stockholders' equity. These percentages should be investigated for differences either across years in the same company or in the same year across different companies. This is called vertical analysis.	Any differences either across years or between companies should be investigated to determine the cause.

Ratio Analysis

STUDY OBJECTIVE
6
Identify and compute ratios used in analyzing a company's liquidity, solvency, and profitability.

In previous chapters we presented many ratios used for evaluating the financial health and performance of a company. Here we provide a summary listing of those ratios. Page references to prior discussions are provided if you feel you need to review any individual ratios. An example of a comprehensive financial analysis employing these ratios is provided in the appendix to this chapter.

LIQUIDITY RATIOS

Liquidity ratios (Illustration 14-17) measure the short-term ability of the enterprise to pay its maturing obligations and to meet unexpected needs for cash. Short-term creditors such as bankers and suppliers are particularly interested in assessing liquidity.

SOLVENCY RATIOS

Solvency ratios (Illustration 14-18) measure the ability of the enterprise to survive over a long period of time. Long-term creditors and stockholders are interested in a company's long-run solvency, particularly its ability to pay interest as it comes due and to repay the face value of debt at maturity.

PROFITABILITY RATIOS

Profitability ratios (Illustration 14-19) measure the income or operating success of an enterprise for a given period of time. A company's income, or lack of it, affects its ability to obtain debt and equity financing, its liquidity position, and its ability to grow.

Liquidity Ratios

Illustration 14-17
Summary of liquidity ratios

Working capital	Current assets − Current liabilities	p. 69
Current ratio	$\dfrac{\text{Current assets}}{\text{Current liabilities}}$	p. 69
Current cash debt coverage ratio	$\dfrac{\text{Cash provided by operations}}{\text{Average current liabilities}}$	p. 73
Inventory turnover ratio	$\dfrac{\text{Cost of goods sold}}{\text{Average inventory}}$	p. 281
Days in inventory	$\dfrac{\text{365 days}}{\text{Inventory turnover ratio}}$	p. 281
Receivables turnover ratio	$\dfrac{\text{Net credit sales}}{\text{Average net receivables}}$	p. 384
Average collection period	$\dfrac{\text{365 days}}{\text{Receivables turnover ratio}}$	p. 384

Solvency Ratios

Illustration 14-18
Summary of solvency ratios

Debt to total assets ratio	$\dfrac{\text{Total liabilities}}{\text{Total assets}}$	p. 70
Cash debt coverage ratio	$\dfrac{\text{Cash provided by operations}}{\text{Average total liabilities}}$	p. 73
Times interest earned ratio	$\dfrac{\text{Net income + Interest expense + Tax expense}}{\text{Interest expense}}$	p. 485
Free cash flow	$\dfrac{\text{Cash provided by}}{\text{operations}} - \dfrac{\text{Capital}}{\text{expenditures}} - \dfrac{\text{Cash}}{\text{dividends}}$	p. 645

Profitability Ratios

Illustration 14-19
Summary of profitability ratios

Earnings per share	$\dfrac{\text{Net income − Preferred stock dividends}}{\text{Average common shares outstanding}}$	p. 65
Price-earnings ratio	$\dfrac{\text{Stock price per share}}{\text{Earnings per share}}$	p. 65
Gross profit rate	$\dfrac{\text{Gross profit}}{\text{Net sales}}$	p. 236
Profit margin ratio	$\dfrac{\text{Net income}}{\text{Net sales}}$	p. 237
Return on assets ratio	$\dfrac{\text{Net income}}{\text{Average total assets}}$	p. 432
Asset turnover ratio	$\dfrac{\text{Net sales}}{\text{Average total assets}}$	p. 433
Payout ratio	$\dfrac{\text{Cash dividends declared on common stock}}{\text{Net income}}$	p. 550
Return on common stockholders' equity ratio	$\dfrac{\text{Net income − Preferred stock dividends}}{\text{Average common stockholders' equity}}$	p. 551

As a consequence, creditors and investors alike are interested in evaluating profitability. Profitability is frequently used as the ultimate test of management's operating effectiveness.

BEFORE YOU GO ON . . .

▶ **Review It**

1. What different bases can be used to compare financial information?
2. What is horizontal analysis?
3. What is vertical analysis?
4. Describe ratios that measure liquidity, solvency, and profitability.

☑ THE
NAVIGATOR

Quality of Earnings

STUDY OBJECTIVE
7
Understand the concept of quality of earnings.

In evaluating the financial performance of a company, the quality of a company's earnings is of extreme importance to analysts. A company that has a high **quality of earnings** provides full and transparent information that will not confuse or mislead users of the financial statements. The issue of quality of earnings has taken on increasing importance because recent accounting scandals suggest that some companies are spending too much time managing their income and not enough time managing their business. Here are some of the factors affecting quality of earnings.

ALTERNATIVE ACCOUNTING METHODS

Variations among companies in the application of generally accepted accounting principles may hamper comparability and reduce quality of earnings. For example, one company may use the FIFO method of inventory costing, while another company in the same industry may use LIFO. If inventory is a significant asset to both companies, it is unlikely that their current ratios are comparable. For example, if **General Motors Corporation** had used FIFO instead of LIFO in valuing its inventories, its inventories in a recent year would have been 26% higher, which significantly affects the current ratio (and other ratios as well).

In addition to differences in inventory costing methods, differences also exist in reporting such items as depreciation, depletion, and amortization. Although these differences in accounting methods might be detectable from reading the notes to the financial statements, adjusting the financial data to compensate for the different methods is difficult, if not impossible, in some cases.

PRO FORMA INCOME

Companies whose stock is publicly traded are required to present their income statement following generally accepted accounting principles (GAAP). In recent years, many companies have been also reporting a second measure of income, in addition to their GAAP measure, called pro forma income. **Pro forma income** is a measure that usually excludes items that the company thinks are unusual or nonrecurring. For example, in a recent year, **Cisco Systems** (a high-tech company) reported quarterly net income under GAAP as a quarterly loss of $2.7 billion. However, Cisco also reported pro forma income for the same quarter as a profit of $230 million. This large difference in profits between GAAP income numbers and pro forma income is not unusual these days. For example, during one recent 9-month period the 100 largest firms on the Nasdaq stock exchange reported a total pro forma income of $19.1 billion, but a total loss as measured by GAAP of $82.3 billion—a difference of about $100 billion!

There are no rules as to how to prepare pro forma earnings. Companies have a free rein to exclude any items they deem inappropriate for measuring their performance. Many analysts and investors are critical of the practice of using pro forma income because these numbers often make companies look better than they really are. As noted in the financial press, pro forma numbers might be called EBS, which stands for "earnings before bad stuff." Companies, on the other hand, argue that pro forma numbers more clearly indicate sustainable income because unusual and nonrecurring expenses are excluded. "Cisco's technique gives readers of financial statements a clear picture of Cisco's normal business activities," the company said in a statement issued in response to questions about its accounting.

Recently, regulators stated that they will crack down on companies that use creative accounting to artificially inflate poor earnings results. Stay tuned: Everyone seems to agree that pro forma numbers can be useful if they provide insights into determining a company's sustainable income. However, many companies have abused the flexibility that pro forma numbers allow and have used the measure as a way to put their companies in a good light.

IMPROPER RECOGNITION

Because some managers have felt pressure to continually increase earnings to meet Wall Street's expectations, they have manipulated the earnings numbers to meet these expectations. The most common abuse is the improper recognition of revenue. One practice that companies are using is called channel stuffing. Offering deep discounts on their products to customers, companies encourage their customers to buy early (stuff the channel) rather than later. This lets the company report good earnings in the current period, but it often leads to a disaster in subsequent periods because customers have no need for additional goods. To illustrate, **Bristol-Myers Squibb** recently indicated that it used sales incentives to encourage wholesalers to buy more drugs than needed to meet patients' demands. As a result, the company had to issue revised financial statements showing corrected revenues and income.

Another practice is the improper capitalization of operating expenses. The classic case is **WorldCom**, which capitalized over $7 billion dollars of operating expenses to ensure that it would report positive net income. In other situations, companies fail to report all their liabilities. For example, **Enron** had promised to make payments on certain contracts if financial difficulty developed, but these guarantees were not reported as liabilities. In addition, disclosure was so lacking in transparency that it was impossible to understand what was happening at the company.

BEFORE YOU GO ON . . .

▶ **Review It**

1. Explain what is meant by pro forma income.
2. Describe factors that reduce the quality of earnings.
3. Give an example of improper recognition.

 THE NAVIGATOR

Using the Decision Toolkit

In analyzing a company, you should always investigate an extended period of time in order to determine whether the condition and performance of the company are changing. The condensed financial statements of **Kellogg Company** for 1999 and 1998 are presented here.

KELLOGG COMPANY, INC.
Balance Sheets
December 31
(in millions)

Assets	1999	1998
Current assets		
Cash and short-term investments	$ 150.6	$ 136.4
Accounts receivable (net)	678.5	693.0
Inventories	503.8	451.4
Prepaid expenses and other current assets	236.3	215.7
Total current assets	1,569.2	1,496.5
Property assets (net)	2,640.9	2,888.8
Intangibles and other assets	598.6	666.2
Total assets	$4,808.7	$5,051.5
Liabilities and Stockholders' Equity		
Current liabilities	$1,587.8	$1,718.5
Long-term liabilities	2,407.7	2,443.2
Stockholders' equity—common	813.2	889.8
Total liabilities and stockholders' equity	$4,808.7	$5,051.5

KELLOGG COMPANY, INC.
Condensed Income Statements
For the Years Ended December 31
(in millions)

	1999	1998
Net sales	$6,984.2	$6,762.1
Cost of goods sold	3,325.1	3,282.6
Gross profit	3,659.1	3,479.5
Selling and administrative expenses	2,585.7	2,513.9
Nonrecurring charges	244.6	70.5
Income from operations	828.8	895.1
Interest expense	118.8	119.5
Other income (expense), net	(173.3)	6.9
Income before income taxes	536.7	782.5
Income tax expense	198.4	279.9
Net income	$ 338.3	$ 502.6

Instructions

Compute the following ratios for Kellogg for 1999 and 1998 and discuss your findings.

1. Liquidity:
   (a) Current ratio.
   (b) Inventory turnover ratio. (Inventory on December 31, 1997, was $434.3 million.)

2. Solvency:
   (a) Debt to total assets ratio.
   (b) Times interest earned ratio.

3. Profitability:
   (a) Return on common stockholders' equity ratio. (Equity on December 31, 1997, was $997.5 million.)
   (b) Return on assets ratio. (Assets on December 31, 1997, were $4,877.6 million.)
   (c) Profit margin ratio.

Solution

1. Liquidity
   (a) Current ratio:

   1999: $\dfrac{\$1,569.2}{\$1,587.8} = .99:1$

   1998: $\dfrac{\$1,496.5}{\$1,718.5} = .87:1$

   (b) Inventory turnover ratio:

   1999: $\dfrac{\$3,325.1}{(\$503.8 + \$451.4)/2} = 7.0 \text{ times}$

   1998: $\dfrac{\$3,282.6}{(\$451.4 + \$434.3)/2} = 7.4 \text{ times}$

   We see that between 1998 and 1999 the current ratio increased. The inventory turnover ratio decreased slightly. The faster the inventory turns over (is sold), the more liquid it is. That is, the company can accept a lower current ratio if it can turn over its inventory and receivables more quickly.

2. Solvency
   (a) Debt to total assets ratio:

   1999: $\dfrac{\$3,995.5}{\$4,808.7} = 83\%$

   1998: $\dfrac{\$4,161.7}{\$5,051.5} = 82\%$

   (b) Times interest earned ratio:

   1999: $\dfrac{\$338.3 + \$198.4 + \$118.8}{\$118.8} = 5.5 \text{ times}$

   1998: $\dfrac{\$502.6 + \$279.9 + \$119.5}{\$119.5} = 7.5 \text{ times}$

   Kellogg's solvency as measured by the debt to total assets ratio declined slightly in 1999. We also can see that the times interest earned ratio declined.

3. Profitability
   (a) Return on common stockholders' equity ratio:

   1999: $\dfrac{\$338.3}{(\$813.2 + \$889.8)/2} = 40\%$

   1998: $\dfrac{\$502.6}{(\$889.8 + \$997.5)/2} = 53\%$

   (b) Return on assets ratio:

   1999: $\dfrac{\$338.3}{(\$4,808.7 + \$5,051.5)/2} = 7\%$

   1998: $\dfrac{\$502.6}{(\$5,051.5 + \$4,877.6)/2} = 10\%$

(c) Profit margin ratio:

1999: $\dfrac{\$338.3}{\$6,984.2} = 5\%$

1998: $\dfrac{\$502.6}{\$6,762.1} = 7\%$

Kellogg's return on common stockholders' equity ratio declined sharply. This decline was the result of declines in both its return on assets and its profit margin ratios.

Summary of Study Objectives

1 *Understand the concept of sustainable income.* Sustainable income refers to a company's ability to sustain its profits from operations.

2 *Indicate how irregular items are presented.* Irregular items—discontinued operations, extraordinary items, and changes in accounting principles—are presented on the income statement net of tax below "Income before irregular items" to highlight their unusual nature.

3 *Explain the concept of comprehensive income.* Comprehensive income includes all changes in stockholders' equity during a period except those resulting from investments by stockholders and distributions to stockholders. "Other comprehensive income" is added to net income to arrive at comprehensive income.

4 *Describe and apply horizontal analysis.* Horizontal analysis is a technique for evaluating a series of data over a period of time to determine the increase or decrease that has taken place, expressed as either an amount or a percentage.

5 *Describe and apply vertical analysis.* Vertical analysis is a technique that expresses each item in a financial statement as a percentage of a relevant total or a base amount.

6 *Identify and compute ratios used in analyzing a company's liquidity, solvency, and profitability.* Financial ratios are provided in Illustration 14-17 (liquidity), Illustration 14-18 (solvency), and Illustration 14-19 (profitability).

7 *Understand the concept of quality of earnings.* A high quality of earnings provides full and transparent information that will not confuse or mislead users of the financial statements. Issues related to quality of earnings are (1) alternative accounting methods, (2) pro forma income, and (3) improper recognition.

DECISION TOOLKIT—A SUMMARY

Decision Checkpoints	Info Needed for Decision	Tool to Use for Decision	How to Evaluate Results
Has the company sold any major components of its business?	Discontinued operations section of income statement	Anything reported in this section indicates that the company has discontinued a major component of its business.	If a major component has been discontinued, its results during the current period should not be included in estimates of future net income.
Has the company experienced any extraordinary events or transactions?	Extraordinary item section of income statement	Anything reported in this section indicates that the company experienced an event that was both unusual and infrequent.	These items should usually be ignored in estimating future net income.
Has the company changed any of its accounting policies?	Cumulative effect of change in accounting principle section of income statement	Anything reported in this section indicates that the company has changed an accounting policy during the current year.	The cumulative effect should be ignored in estimating the future net income.
How do the company's financial position and operating results compare with those of the previous period?	Income statement and balance sheet	Comparative financial statements should be prepared over at least two years, with the first year reported being the base year. Changes in each line item relative to the base year should be presented both by amount and by percentage. This is called horizontal analysis.	Significant changes should be investigated to determine the reason for the change.
How do the relationships between items in this year's financial statements compare with those of last year or those of competitors?	Income statement and balance sheet	Each line item on the income statement should be presented as a percentage of net sales, and each line item on the balance sheet should be presented as a percentage of total assets or total liabilities and stockholders' equity. These percentages should be investigated for differences either across years in the same company or in the same year across different companies. This is called vertical analysis.	Any differences either across years or between companies should be investigated to determine the cause.

APPENDIX
COMPREHENSIVE ILLUSTRATION OF RATIO ANALYSIS

In previous chapters we presented many ratios used for evaluating the financial health and performance of a company. In this appendix we provide a comprehensive review of those ratios and discuss some important relationships among them. Since earlier chapters demonstrated the calculation of each of these ratios, in this chapter we instead focus on their interpretation. Page references to prior discussions are provided if you feel you need to review any individual ratios.

The financial information in Illustrations 14A-1 through 14A-4 (pages 700 and 701) was used to calculate **Kellogg**'s 2001 ratios. You can use these data to review the computations.

Illustration 14A-1
Kellogg Company's balance sheet

KELLOGG COMPANY, INC.
Balance Sheets
December 31
(in millions)

Assets	2001	2000
Current assets		
Cash and short-term investments	$ 231.8	$ 204.4
Accounts receivable (net allowance of $15.5 in 2001 and $8.6 in 2000)	762.3	685.3
Inventories	574.5	443.8
Prepaid expenses and other current assets	333.4	283.6
Total current assets	1,902.0	1,617.1
Property assets (net)	2,952.8	2,526.9
Intangibles and other assets	5,513.8	742.0
Total assets	$10,368.6	$4,886.0
Liabilities and Stockholders' Equity		
Current liabilities	$ 2,207.6	$2,482.3
Long-term liabilities	7,289.5	1,506.2
Stockholders' equity—common	871.5	897.5
Total liabilities and stockholders' equity	$10,368.6	$4,886.0

As indicated in the chapter, for analysis of the primary financial statements, ratios can be classified into three types:

1. **Liquidity ratios:** Measures of the short-term ability of the enterprise to pay its maturing obligations and to meet unexpected needs for cash.
2. **Solvency ratios:** Measures of the ability of the enterprise to survive over a long period of time.
3. **Profitability ratios:** Measures of the income or operating success of an enterprise for a given period of time.

As a tool of analysis, ratios can provide clues to underlying conditions that may not be apparent from an inspection of the individual components of a particular ratio. But a single ratio by itself is not very meaningful. Accordingly, in this discussion we use the three comparisons listed on the top of page 702.

KELLOGG COMPANY, INC.
Condensed Income Statements
For the Years Ended December 31
(in millions)

	2001	2000
Net sales	$8,853.3	$6,954.7
Cost of goods sold	4,128.5	3,327.0
Gross profit	4,724.8	3,627.7
Selling and administrative expenses	3,523.6	2,551.4
Nonrecurring charges	33.3	86.5
Income from operations	1,167.9	989.8
Interest expense	351.5	137.5
Other income (expense), net	(12.3)	15.4
Income before income taxes	804.1	867.7
Income tax expense	322.1	280.0
Net income	$ 482.0	$ 587.7

Illustration 14A-2 Kellogg Company's income statement

KELLOGG COMPANY, INC.
Condensed Statements of Cash Flows
For the Years Ended December 31
(in millions)

	2001	2000
Cash flows from operating activities		
Cash receipts from operating activities	$ 8,776.3	$6,951.3
Cash payments for operating activities	7,644.3	6,070.4
Net cash provided by operating activities	1,132.0	880.9
Cash flows from investing activities		
Purchases of property, plant, and equipment	(4,124.4)	(363.3)
Other investing activities	(19.4)	(16.0)
Net cash used in investing activities	(4,143.8)	(379.3)
Cash flows from financing activities		
Issuance of common stock	27.0	4.5
Issuance of debt	5,551.0	294.0
Reductions of debt	(2,128.0)	(336.4)
Payment of dividends	(409.8)	(403.9)
Net cash provided by (used in) financing activities	3,040.2	(441.8)
Other	(1.0)	(6.0)
Increase (decrease) in cash and cash equivalents	27.4	53.8
Cash and cash equivalents at beginning of year	204.4	150.6
Cash and cash equivalents at end of year	$ 231.8	$ 204.4

Illustration 14A-3 Kellogg Company's statement of cash flows

Additional information	2001	2000
Average number of shares (millions)	406.1	405.6
Stock price at year-end	$ 30.1	$ 26.3

Illustration 14A-4 Additional information for Kellogg Company

1. **Intracompany comparisons** covering two years for Kellogg Company (using comparative financial information from Illustrations 14A-1, 14A-2, and 14A-3).

2. **Intercompany comparisons** using **General Mills** as one of Kellogg's principal competitors.

3. **Industry average comparisons** based on Robert Morris Associates' median ratios for manufacturers of flour and other grain mill products and comparisons with other sources. For some of the ratios that we use, industry comparisons are not available. (These are denoted "na.")

Liquidity Ratios

Liquidity ratios measure the short-term ability of the enterprise to pay its maturing obligations and to meet unexpected needs for cash. Short-term creditors such as bankers and suppliers are particularly interested in assessing liquidity. The measures that can be used to determine the enterprise's short-term debt-paying ability are the current ratio, the current cash debt coverage ratio, the receivables turnover ratio, the average collection period, the inventory turnover ratio, and average days in inventory.

1. **Current ratio.** The **current ratio** expresses the relationship of current assets to current liabilities, computed by dividing current assets by current liabilities. It is widely used for evaluating a company's liquidity and short-term debt-paying ability. The 2001 and 2000 current ratios for **Kellogg** and comparative data are shown in Illustration 14A-5.

Illustration 14A-5
Current ratio

Ratio	Formula	Indicates:	Kellogg 2001	Kellogg 2000	General Mills 2001	Industry 2001	Page in book
Current ratio	Current assets / Current liabilities	Short-term debt-paying ability	.86	.65	.60	1.36	69

What do the measures tell us? Kellogg's 2001 current ratio of .86 means that for every dollar of current liabilities, Kellogg has $0.86 of current assets. We sometimes state such ratios as .86 : 1 to reinforce this interpretation. Kellogg's current ratio—and therefore its liquidity—increased significantly in 2001. It is well below the industry average but higher than that of **General Mills**.

Business Insight
INVESTOR PERSPECTIVE

The apparent simplicity of the current ratio can have real-world limitations because adding equal amounts to both the numerator and the denominator causes the ratio to decrease.

Assume, for example, that a company has $2,000,000 of current assets and $1,000,000 of current liabilities; its current ratio is 2 : 1. If it purchases $1,000,000 of inventory on account, it will have $3,000,000 of current assets and $2,000,000 of current liabilities; its current ratio decreases to 1.5 : 1. If, instead, the company pays off $500,000 of its current liabilities, it will have $1,500,000 of current assets and $500,000 of current liabilities; its current ratio increases to 3 : 1. Thus, any trend analysis should be done with care because the ratio is susceptible to quick changes and is easily influenced by management.

2. Current cash debt coverage ratio. A disadvantage of the current ratio is that it uses year-end balances of current asset and current liability accounts. These year-end balances may not be representative of the company's current position during most of the year. A ratio that partially corrects for this problem is the ratio of cash provided by operating activities to average current liabilities, called the **current cash debt coverage ratio**. Because it uses cash provided by operating activities rather than a balance at one point in time, it may provide a better representation of liquidity. Kellogg's current cash debt coverage ratio is shown in Illustration 14A-6.

Illustration 14A-6 Current cash debt coverage ratio

Ratio	Formula	Indicates:	Kellogg 2001	Kellogg 2000	General Mills 2001	Industry 2001	Page in book
Current cash debt coverage ratio	Cash provided by operations / Average current liabilities	Short-term debt-paying ability (cash basis)	.48	.43	.23	na	73

Like the current ratio, this ratio increased in 2001 for Kellogg. Is the coverage adequate? Probably so. Kellogg's operating cash flow coverage of average current liabilities is twice that of General Mills, and it exceeds a commonly accepted threshold of .40. No industry comparison is available.

3. Receivables turnover ratio. Liquidity may be measured by how quickly certain assets can be converted to cash. Low values of the previous ratios can sometimes be compensated for if some of the company's current assets are highly liquid. How liquid, for example, are the receivables? The ratio used to assess the liquidity of the receivables is the **receivables turnover ratio**, which measures the number of times, on average, receivables are collected during the period. The receivables turnover ratio is computed by dividing net credit sales (net sales less cash sales) by average net receivables during the year. The receivables turnover ratio for Kellogg is shown in Illustration 14A-7.

Illustration 14A-7 Receivables turnover ratio

Ratio	Formula	Indicates:	Kellogg 2001	Kellogg 2000	General Mills 2001	Industry 2001	Page in book
Receivables turnover ratio	Net credit sales / Average net receivables	Liquidity of receivables	12.2	10.2	8.6	11.6	384

We have assumed that all Kellogg's sales are credit sales. The receivables turnover ratio for Kellogg rose in 2001. The turnover of 12.2 times compares favorably with the industry median of 11.6, and is much higher than General Mills' turnover of 8.6.

Business Insight
INVESTOR PERSPECTIVE

In some cases, the receivables turnover ratio may be misleading. Some companies, especially large retail chains, issue their own credit cards. They encourage customers to use these cards, and they slow their collections in order to earn a healthy return on the outstanding receivables in the form of interest at rates of 18% to 22%. In general, however, the faster the turnover, the greater the reliance that can be placed on the current ratio for assessing liquidity.

4. **Average collection period.** A popular variant of the receivables turnover ratio converts it into an **average collection period** in days. This is done by dividing the receivables turnover ratio into 365 days. The average collection period for Kellogg is shown in Illustration 14A-8.

Illustration 14A-8
Average collection period

Ratio	Formula	Indicates:	Kellogg 2001	Kellogg 2000	General Mills 2001	Industry 2001	Page in book
Average collection period	$\dfrac{\text{365 days}}{\text{Receivables turnover ratio}}$	Liquidity of receivables and collection success	29.9	35.8	42.5	31.5	384

Kellogg's 2001 receivables turnover of 12.2 times is divided into 365 days to obtain approximately 29.9 days. This means that the average collection period for receivables is about 30 days. Analysts frequently use the average collection period to assess the effectiveness of a company's credit and collection policies. The general rule is that the collection period should not greatly exceed the credit term period (i.e., the time allowed for payment). General Mills' average collection period is significantly longer than those of Kellogg and the industry. This difference may be due to less aggressive collection practices, but it is more likely due to a difference in credit terms granted.

5. **Inventory turnover ratio.** The **inventory turnover ratio** measures the number of times on average the inventory is sold during the period. Its purpose is to measure the liquidity of the inventory. The inventory turnover ratio is computed by dividing the cost of goods sold by the average inventory during the period. Unless seasonal factors are significant, average inventory can be computed from the beginning and ending inventory balances. Kellogg's inventory turnover ratio is shown in Illustration 14A-9.

Illustration 14A-9
Inventory turnover ratio

Ratio	Formula	Indicates:	Kellogg 2001	Kellogg 2000	General Mills 2001	Industry 2001	Page in book
Inventory turnover ratio	$\dfrac{\text{Cost of goods sold}}{\text{Average inventory}}$	Liquidity of inventory	8.1	7.0	5.6	6.9	281

Kellogg's inventory turnover ratio increased in 2001. The turnover ratio of 8.1 times is higher than the industry average of 6.9 and significantly better than General Mills' 5.6. Generally, the faster the inventory turnover, the less cash is tied up in inventory and the less the chance of inventory becoming obsolete. Of course, a downside of high inventory turnover is that the company can run out of inventory when it is needed.

6. **Days in inventory.** A variant of the inventory turnover ratio is the **days in inventory**, which measures the average number of days it takes to sell the inventory. The days in inventory for Kellogg is shown in Illustration 14A-10.

Illustration 14A-10 Days in inventory

Ratio	Formula	Indicates:	Kellogg 2001	Kellogg 2000	General Mills 2001	Industry 2001	Page in book
Days in inventory	$\dfrac{\text{365 days}}{\text{Inventory turnover ratio}}$	Liquidity of inventory and inventory management	45.1	52.1	65.2	52.9	281

Kellogg's 2001 inventory turnover ratio of 8.1 divided into 365 is approximately 45.1 days. An average selling time of 45 days is faster than the industry average and significantly faster than that of General Mills. Some of this difference might be explained by differences in product lines across the two companies, although in many ways the types of products of these two companies are quite similar.

Inventory turnover ratios vary considerably among industries. For example, grocery store chains have a turnover of 10 times and an average selling period of 37 days. In contrast, jewelry stores have an average turnover of 1.3 times and an average selling period of 281 days. Within a company there may even be significant differences in inventory turnover among different types of products. Thus, in a grocery store the turnover of perishable items such as produce, meats, and dairy products is faster than the turnover of soaps and detergents.

To conclude, nearly all of these liquidity measures suggest that Kellogg's liquidity increased during 2001. Its liquidity appears acceptable when compared to the industry as a whole and much better than that of General Mills.

Solvency Ratios

Solvency ratios measure the ability of the enterprise to survive over a long period of time. Long-term creditors and stockholders are interested in a company's long-run solvency, particularly its ability to pay interest as it comes due and to repay the face value of debt at maturity. The debt to total assets ratio, the times interest earned ratio, and the cash debt coverage ratio provide information about debt-paying ability. In addition, free cash flow provides information about the company's solvency and its ability to pay additional dividends or invest in new projects.

7. **Debt to total assets ratio.** The debt to total assets ratio measures the percentage of the total assets provided by creditors. It is computed by dividing total liabilities (both current and long-term) by total assets. This ratio indicates the degree of financial leveraging. It also provides some indication of the company's ability to withstand losses without impairing the interests of its creditors. The higher the percentage of debt to total assets, the greater the risk that the company may be unable to meet its maturing obligations. The lower the ratio, the more equity "buffer" is available to creditors if the company becomes insolvent. Thus, from the creditors' point of view, a low ratio of debt to total assets is desirable. **Kellogg**'s debt to total assets ratio is shown in Illustration 14A-11.

Illustration 14A-11 Debt to total assets ratio

Ratio	Formula	Indicates:	Kellogg 2001	Kellogg 2000	General Mills 2001	Industry 2001	Page in book
Debt to total assets ratio	Total liabilities / Total assets	Percentage of total assets provided by creditors	.92	.82	.78	.59	70

Kellogg's 2001 ratio of .92 means that creditors have provided financing sufficient to cover 92% of the company's total assets. Alternatively, it says that Kellogg would have to liquidate 92% of its assets at their book value in order to pay off all of its debts. Kellogg's 92% is above the industry average of 59% as well as the 78% ratio of **General Mills**. Kellogg's solvency declined during the year. In that time, Kellogg's use of debt financing changed in two ways: First, Kellogg increased its use of long-term debt by 384%, and second, its equity decreased slightly. Both these factors reduced its solvency.

The adequacy of this ratio is often judged in light of the company's earnings. Generally, companies with relatively stable earnings, such as public utilities, have higher debt to total assets ratios than cyclical companies with widely fluctuating earnings, such as many high-tech companies.

Another ratio with a similar meaning is the **debt to equity ratio**. It shows the relative use of borrowed funds (total liabilities) compared with resources invested by the owners. Because this ratio can be computed in several ways, care should be taken when making comparisons. Debt may be defined to include only the noncurrent portion of liabilities, and intangible assets may be excluded from stockholders' equity (which would equal tangible net worth). If debt and assets are defined as above (all liabilities and all assets), then when the debt to total assets ratio equals 50%, the debt to equity ratio is 1 : 1.

8. **Times interest earned ratio.** The **times interest earned ratio** (also called interest coverage) indicates the company's ability to meet interest payments as they come due. It is computed by dividing income before interest expense and income taxes by interest expense. Note that this ratio uses income before interest expense and income taxes because this amount represents what is available to cover interest. Kellogg's times interest earned ratio is shown in Illustration 14A-12.

Illustration 14A-12 Times interest earned ratio

Ratio	Formula	Indicates:	Kellogg 2001	Kellogg 2000	General Mills 2001	Industry 2001	Page in book
Times interest earned ratio	$\dfrac{\text{Net Income} + \text{Interest expense} + \text{Tax expense}}{\text{Interest expense}}$	Ability to meet interest payments as they come due	3.3	7.3	2.6	6.8	485

For Kellogg the 2001 interest coverage was 3.3, which indicates that income before interest and taxes was 3.3 times the amount needed for interest expense. This exceeds the rate for General Mills, but it is less than half the average rate for the industry. The debt to total assets ratio increased for Kellogg during 2001, and its times interest earned ratio declined dramatically. These ratios indicate that Kellogg is less able to service its debt.

9. **Cash debt coverage ratio.** The ratio of cash provided by operating activities to average total liabilities, called the **cash debt coverage ratio**, is a cash-basis measure of solvency. This ratio indicates a company's ability to repay its liabilities from cash generated from operating activities without having to liquidate the assets used in its operations. Illustration 14A-13 shows Kellogg's cash debt coverage ratio.

Illustration 14A-13 Cash debt coverage ratio

Ratio	Formula	Indicates:	Kellogg 2001	Kellogg 2000	General Mills 2001	Industry 2001	Page in book
Cash debt coverage ratio	$\dfrac{\text{Cash provided by operations}}{\text{Average total liabilities}}$	Long-term debt-paying ability (cash basis)	.17	.22	.10	na	73

An industry average for this measure is not available. Kellogg's .17 is higher than General Mills' .10, but it did decline from .22 in 2000. One way of interpreting this ratio is to say that net cash generated from one year of operations would be sufficient to pay off 17% of Kellogg's total liabilities. If 17% of this year's liabilities were retired each year, it would take approximately six years to retire all of its debt. It would take General Mills approximately ten years to do so. A general rule of thumb is that a measure above .20 is acceptable.

10. **Free cash flow.** One indication of a company's solvency, as well as of its ability to pay dividends or expand operations, is the amount of excess cash it generated after investing to maintain its current productive capacity and paying dividends. This amount is referred to as **free cash flow**. For example, if you generate $100,000 of cash from operations but you spend $30,000 to maintain and replace your productive facilities at their current levels and pay $10,000 in dividends, you have $60,000 to use either to expand operations or to pay additional dividends. Kellogg's free cash flow is shown in Illustration 14A-14.

Illustration 14A-14
Free cash flow

Ratio	Formula			Indicates:	Kellogg 2001	Kellogg 2000	General Mills 2001	Industry 2001	Page in book
Free cash flow	Cash provided by operations	− Capital expenditures	− Cash dividends	Cash available for paying dividends or expanding operations	−$3,402.2 (in millions)	$113.7	$49.0 (in millions)	na	645

Kellogg's free cash flow declined considerably from 2000 to 2001. In fact, it was negative in 2001. During 2001, Kellogg used a large portion of free cash flow to acquire Keebler Foods. It is unlikely that Kellogg will have a similar large purchase in the near future.

Profitability Ratios

Profitability ratios measure the income or operating success of an enterprise for a given period of time. A company's income, or the lack of it, affects its ability to obtain debt and equity financing, its liquidity position, and its ability to grow. As a consequence, creditors and investors alike are interested in evaluating profitability. Profitability is frequently used as the ultimate test of management's operating effectiveness.

Throughout this book we have introduced numerous measures of profitability. The relationships among measures of profitability are very important. Understanding them can help management determine where to focus its efforts to improve profitability. Illustration 14A-15 diagrams these relationships. Our discussion of **Kellogg**'s profitability is structured around this diagram.

Illustration 14A-15
Relationships among profitability measures

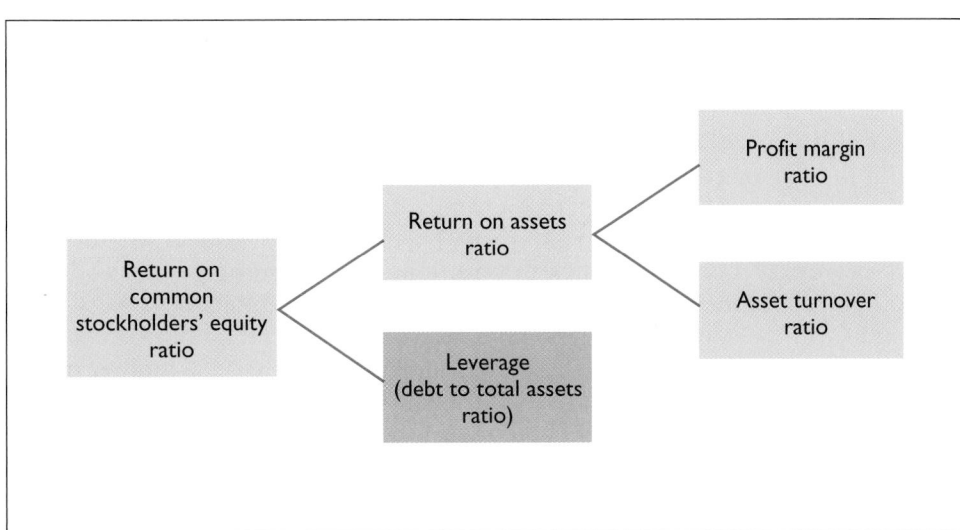

11. Return on common stockholders' equity ratio. A widely used measure of profitability from the common stockholder's viewpoint is the **return on common stockholders' equity ratio**. This ratio shows how many dollars of net income were earned for each dollar invested by the owners. It is computed by dividing net income minus any preferred stock dividends—that is, income available to common stockholders—by average common stockholders' equity. The return on common stockholders' equity for Kellogg is shown in Illustration 14A-16.

Illustration 14A-16
Return on common stockholders' equity ratio

Ratio	Formula	Indicates:	Kellogg 2001	Kellogg 2000	General Mills 2001	Industry 2001	Page in book
Return on common stockholders' equity ratio	Net income − Preferred stock dividends / Average common stockholders' equity	Profitability of common stockholders' investment	.54	.69	.22	.26	551

Kellogg's 2001 rate of return on common stockholders' equity is unusually high at 54%, considering an industry average of 26% and **General Mills'** return of 22%. In the subsequent sections we investigate the causes of this high return.

12. Return on assets ratio. The return on common stockholders' equity ratio is affected by two factors: the **return on assets ratio** and the degree of leverage. The return on assets ratio measures the overall profitability of assets in terms of the income earned on each dollar invested in assets. It is computed by dividing net income by average total assets. Kellogg's return on assets ratio is shown in Illustration 14A-17.

Illustration 14A-17
Return on assets ratio

Ratio	Formula	Indicates:	Kellogg 2001	Kellogg 2000	General Mills 2001	Industry 2001	Page in book
Return on assets ratio	Net income / Average total assets	Overall profitability of assets	.06	.12	.04	.07	432

Kellogg had a 6% return on assets in 2001. This rate is higher than that of General Mills but close to the industry average.

Note that Kellogg's rate of return on stockholders' equity (54%) is substantially higher than its rate of return on assets (6%). The reason is that Kellogg has made effective use of **leverage**. **Leveraging** or **trading on the equity** at a gain means that the company has borrowed money at a lower rate of interest than the rate of return it earns on the assets it purchased with the borrowed funds. Leverage enables management to use money supplied by nonowners to increase the return to owners.

A comparison of the rate of return on assets with the rate of interest paid for borrowed money indicates the profitability of trading on the equity. If you borrow money at 8% and your rate of return on assets is 11%, you are trading on the equity at a gain. Note, however, that trading on the equity is a two-way street: For example, if you borrow money at 11% and earn only 8% on it, you are trading on the equity at a loss.

Kellogg earns more on its borrowed funds than it has to pay in interest. Thus, the return to stockholders exceeds the return on the assets because of the positive benefit of leverage. Recall from our earlier discussion that Kellogg's percentage of debt financing as measured by the ratio of debt to total assets (or debt to equity) increased in 2001. It appears that Kellogg's high return on stockholders' equity is largely a function of its significant use of leverage.

13. **Profit margin ratio.** The return on assets ratio is affected by two factors, the first of which is the profit margin ratio. The **profit margin ratio**, or rate of return on sales, is a measure of the percentage of each dollar of sales that results in net income. It is computed by dividing net income by net sales for the period. Kellogg's profit margin ratio is shown in Illustration 14A-18.

Illustration 14A-18
Profit margin ratio

Ratio	Formula	Indicates:	Kellogg 2001	Kellogg 2000	General Mills 2001	Industry 2001	Page in book
Profit margin ratio	Net income / Net sales	Net income generated by each dollar of sales	.05	.085	.05	.06	237

Kellogg experienced a decline in its profit margin ratio from 2000 to 2001 of 8.5% to 5%. Its profit margin ratio was less than the industry average of 6% but equal to General Mills' 5%.

High-volume (high inventory turnover) enterprises such as grocery stores and pharmacy chains generally have low profit margins, whereas low-volume enterprises such as jewelry stores and airplane manufacturers have high profit margins.

14. **Asset turnover ratio.** The other factor that affects the return on assets ratio is the asset turnover ratio. The **asset turnover ratio** measures how efficiently a company uses its assets to generate sales. It is determined by dividing net sales by average total assets for the period. The resulting number shows the dollars of sales produced by each dollar invested in assets. Illustration 14A-19 shows the asset turnover ratio for Kellogg.

Illustration 14A-19
Asset turnover ratio

Ratio	Formula	Indicates:	Kellogg 2001	Kellogg 2000	General Mills 2001	Industry 2001	Page in book
Asset turnover ratio	Net sales / Average total assets	How efficiently assets are used to generate sales	1.16	1.43	.65	1.37	433

The asset turnover ratio shows that in 2001 Kellogg generated sales of $1.16 for each dollar it had invested in assets. The ratio declined significantly from 2000 to 2001. Kellogg's asset turnover ratio is below the industry average of 1.37 times but well above General Mills' ratio of .65.

Asset turnover ratios vary considerably among industries. The average asset turnover for utility companies is .45, for example, while the grocery store industry has an average asset turnover of 3.49.

In summary, Kellogg's return on assets ratio declined from 12% in 2000 to 6% in 2001. Underlying this decline was a decreased profitability on each dollar of sales (as measured by the profit margin ratio) and a decline in the sales-generating efficiency of its assets (as measured by the asset turnover ratio). The combined effects of profit margin and asset turnover on return on assets for Kellogg can be analyzed as shown in Illustration 14A-20 (page 710).

Ratios:	Profit Margin	×	Asset Turnover	=	Return on Assets
	$\dfrac{\text{Net Income}}{\text{Net Sales}}$	×	$\dfrac{\text{Net Sales}}{\text{Average Total Assets}}$	=	$\dfrac{\text{Net Income}}{\text{Average Total Assets}}$
Kellogg					
2001	5%	×	1.16 times	=	6%
2000	8.5%	×	1.43 times	=	12%

Illustration 14A-20
Composition of return on assets ratio

15. Gross profit rate. Two factors strongly influence the profit margin ratio. One is the gross profit rate. The **gross profit rate** is determined by dividing gross profit (net sales less cost of goods sold) by net sales. This rate indicates a company's ability to maintain an adequate selling price above its cost of goods sold. As an industry becomes more competitive, this ratio declines. For example, in the early years of the personal computer industry, gross profit rates were quite high. Today, because of increased competition and a belief that most brands of personal computers are similar in quality, gross profit rates have become thin. Gross profit rates should be closely monitored over time. Illustration 14A-21 shows Kellogg's gross profit rate.

Illustration 14A-21
Gross profit rate

Ratio	Formula	Indicates:	Kellogg 2001	Kellogg 2000	General Mills 2001	Industry 2001	Page in book
Gross profit rate	$\dfrac{\text{Gross profit}}{\text{Net sales}}$	Margin between selling price and cost of goods sold	.53	.52	.40	.38	236

Kellogg's gross profit rate increased slightly from 2000 to 2001.

16. Earnings per share (EPS). Stockholders usually think in terms of the number of shares they own or plan to buy or sell. Expressing net income earned on a per share basis provides a useful perspective for determining profitability. **Earnings per share** is a measure of the net income earned on each share of common stock. It is computed by dividing net income by the average number of common shares outstanding during the year. The terms "net income per share" or "earnings per share" refer to the amount of net income applicable to each share of *common stock*. Therefore, when we compute earnings per share, if there are preferred dividends declared for the period, they must be deducted from net income to arrive at income available to the common stockholders. Kellogg's earnings per share is shown in Illustration 14A-22.

Illustration 14A-22
Earnings per share

Ratio	Formula	Indicates:	Kellogg 2001	Kellogg 2000	General Mills 2001	Industry 2001	Page in book
Earnings per share (EPS)	$\dfrac{\text{Net income} - \text{Preferred stock dividends}}{\text{Average common shares outstanding}}$	Net income earned on each share of common stock	$1.19	$1.45	$1.39	na	65

Note that no industry average is presented in Illustration 14A-22. Industry data for earnings per share are not reported, and in fact the Kellogg and General Mills ratios should not be compared. Such comparisons are not meaningful because of the wide variations in the number of shares of outstanding stock among companies. Kellogg's earnings per share decreased 26 cents per share in 2001. This represents a 17.9% decrease from the 2000 EPS of $1.45.

17. Price-earnings ratio. The price-earnings ratio is an oft-quoted statistic that measures the ratio of the market price of each share of common stock to the earnings per share. The price-earnings (P-E) ratio is a reflection of investors' assessments of a company's future earnings. It is computed by dividing the market price per share of the stock by earnings per share. Kellogg's price-earnings ratio is shown in Illustration 14A-23.

Illustration 14A-23
Price-earnings ratio

Ratio	Formula	Indicates:	Kellogg 2001	Kellogg 2000	General Mills 2001	Industry 2001	Page in book
Price-earnings ratio	Stock price per share / Earnings per share	Relationship between market price per share and earnings per share	25.3	18.1	29.6	23.8	65

At the end of 2001 and 2000 the market price of Kellogg's stock was $30.1 and $26.3, respectively. General Mills stock was selling for $41.1 at the end of 2001.

In 2001 each share of Kellogg's stock sold for 25.3 times the amount that was earned on each share. Kellogg's price-earnings ratio is higher than the industry average of 23.8 times and significantly higher than its previous year's ratio of 18.1 but lower than General Mills' ratio of 29.6. These higher P-E ratios suggest that the market is more optimistic about Kellogg and General Mills than about the other companies in the industry. However, it might also signal that their stock is overpriced.

18. Payout ratio. The payout ratio measures the percentage of earnings distributed in the form of cash dividends. It is computed by dividing cash dividends declared on common stock by net income. Companies that have high growth rates are characterized by low payout ratios because they reinvest most of their net income in the business. The payout ratio for Kellogg is shown in Illustration 14A-24.

Illustration 14A-24
Payout ratio

Ratio	Formula	Indicates:	Kellogg 2001	Kellogg 2000	General Mills 2001	Industry 2001	Page in book
Payout ratio	Cash dividends declared on common stock / Net income	Percentage of earnings distributed in the form of cash dividends	.85	.69	.74	.43	550

The 2001 and 2000 payout ratios for Kellogg and General Mills are comparatively high in relation to the industry average of .43.

Management has some control over the amount of dividends paid each year, and companies are generally reluctant to reduce a dividend below the amount paid in a previous year. Therefore, the payout ratio will actually increase if a company's net income declines but the company keeps its total dividend payment the same. Of course, unless the company returns to its previous level of profitability, maintaining this higher dividend payout ratio is probably not possible over the long run. Before drawing any conclusions regarding Kellogg's dividend payout ratio, we should calculate this ratio over a longer period of time to evaluate any trends, and also try to find out whether management's philosophy regarding dividends has changed recently. The "Selected financial data" section of Kellogg's Management Discussion and Analysis shows that over a 5-year period earnings per share have declined 12.5%, while dividends per share have grown 16%. Unless earnings growth improves, this rapid dividend growth is not sustainable over the long term.

Business Insight
MANAGEMENT PERSPECTIVE

Generally, companies with stable earnings have high payout ratios. For example, a utility such as **Potomac Electric Company** had an 86% payout ratio over a recent five-year period, and **Amoco Corporation** had a 63% payout ratio over the same period. Conversely, companies that are expanding rapidly, such as **Toys 'R' Us** and **Microsoft**, have never paid a cash dividend.

In terms of the types of financial information available and the ratios used by various industries, what can be practically covered in this textbook gives you only the "Titanic approach": That is, you are seeing only the tip of the iceberg compared to the vast databases and types of ratio analysis that are available on computers. The availability of information is not a problem. The real trick is to be discriminating enough to perform relevant analysis and select pertinent comparative data.

Glossary

Asset turnover ratio A measure of how efficiently a company uses its assets to generate sales, computed as net sales divided by average total assets. (p. 709)

Available-for-sale securities Securities that are held with the intent of selling them sometime in the future. (p. 684)

Average collection period The average number of days that receivables are outstanding, calculated as receivables turnover divided into 365 days. (p. 704)

Cash debt coverage ratio A cash-basis measure used to evaluate solvency, computed as cash from operations divided by average total liabilities. (p. 706)

Change in accounting principle Use of an accounting principle in the current year different from the one used in the preceding year. (p. 683)

Comprehensive income Includes all changes in stockholders' equity during a period except those resulting from investments by stockholders and distributions to stockholders. (p. 684)

Current cash debt coverage ratio A cash-basis measure of short-term debt-paying ability, computed as cash provided by operations divided by average current liabilities. (p. 703)

Current ratio A measure that expresses the relationship of current assets to current liabilities, calculated as current assets divided by current liabilities. (p. 702)

Days in inventory A measure of the average number of days it takes to sell the inventory, computed as inventory turnover divided into 365 days. (p. 704)

Debt to total assets ratio A measure of the percentage of total assets provided by creditors, computed as total debt divided by total assets. (p. 705)

Discontinued operations The disposal of a significant component of a business. (p. 680)

Earnings per share The net income earned by each share of common stock, computed as net income divided by the average common shares outstanding. (p. 710)

Extraordinary items Events and transactions that meet two conditions: (1) unusual in nature and (2) infrequent in occurrence. (p. 681)

Free cash flow The amount of cash from operations after adjusting for capital expenditures and cash dividends paid. (p. 707)

Gross profit rate An indicator of a company's ability to maintain an adequate selling price of goods above their cost, computed as gross profit divided by net sales. (p. 710)

Horizontal analysis A technique for evaluating a series of financial statement data over a period of time to determine the increase (decrease) that has taken place, expressed as either an amount or a percentage. (p. 687)

Inventory turnover ratio A measure of the liquidity of inventory, computed as cost of goods sold divided by average inventory. (p. 704)

Leveraging Borrowing money at a lower rate of interest than can be earned by using the borrowed money; also referred to as trading on the equity. (p. 708)

Liquidity ratios Measures of the short-term ability of the enterprise to pay its maturing obligations and to meet unexpected needs for cash. (p. 692)

Payout ratio A measure of the percentage of earnings distributed in the form of cash dividends, calculated as cash dividends divided by net income. (p. 711)

Price-earnings ratio A comparison of the market price of each share of common stock to the earnings per share, computed as the market price of the stock divided by earnings per share. (p. 711)

Pro forma income A measure of income that usually excludes items that a company thinks are unusual or nonrecurring. (p. 694)

Profit margin ratio A measure of the net income generated by each dollar of sales, computed as net income divided by net sales. (p. 709)

Profitability ratios Measures of the income or operating success of an enterprise for a given period of time. (p. 692)

Quality of earnings Indicates the level of full and transparent information that is provided to users of the financial statements. (p. 694)

Receivables turnover ratio A measure of the liquidity of receivables, computed as net credit sales divided by average net receivables. (p. 703)

Return on assets ratio An overall measure of profitability, calculated as net income divided by average total assets. (p. 708)

Return on common stockholders' equity ratio A measure of the dollars of net income earned for each dollar invested by the owners, computed as income available to common stockholders divided by average common stockholders' equity. (p. 708)

Solvency ratios Measures of the ability of the enterprise to survive over a long period of time. (p. 692)

Times interest earned ratio A measure of a company's ability to meet interest payments as they come due, calculated as income before interest expense and income taxes divided by interest expense. (p. 706)

Trading on the equity Same as leveraging. (p. 708)

Trading securities Securities bought and held primarily for sale in the near term to generate income on short-term price differences. (p. 684)

Vertical analysis A technique for evaluating financial statement data that expresses each item in a financial statement as a percent of a base amount. (p. 690)

Demonstration Problem

The events and transactions of Dever Corporation for the year ending December 31, 2005, resulted in these data.

Cost of goods sold	$2,600,000
Net sales	4,400,000
Other expenses and losses	9,600
Other revenues and gains	5,600
Selling and administrative expenses	1,100,000
Gain from discontinued division	570,000
Loss from tornado disaster (extraordinary loss)	600,000
Cumulative effect of changing from straight-line depreciation to double-declining-balance (increase in depreciation expense)	300,000

Analysis reveals the following.

1. All items are before the applicable income tax rate of 30%.
2. The plastics division was sold on July 1.
3. All operating data for the plastics division have been segregated.

Instructions

Prepare an income statement for the year, excluding the presentation of earnings per share.

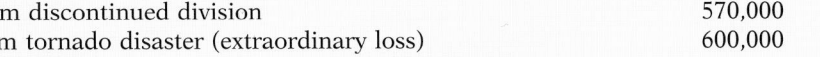

Solution to Demonstration Problem

DEVER CORPORATION
Income Statement
For the Year Ended December 31, 2005

Net sales		$4,400,000
Cost of goods sold		2,600,000
Gross profit		1,800,000
Selling and administrative expenses		1,100,000
Income from operations		700,000
Other revenues and gains	$ 5,600	
Other expenses and losses	(9,600)	(4,000)
Income before income taxes		696,000
Income tax expense ($696,000 × 30%)		208,800
Income before irregular items		487,200
Discontinued operations: Gain from discontinued division, net of taxes of $171,000 ($570,000 × 30%)		399,000
Extraordinary item: Tornado loss, net of income tax savings $180,000 ($600,000 × 30%)		(420,000)
Change in accounting principle: Effect on prior years of change in depreciation method, net of $90,000 income tax savings ($300,000 × 30%)		(210,000)
Net income		$ 256,200

THE NAVIGATOR

Self-Study Questions

Self-Study/Self-Test

Answers are at the end of the chapter.

All of the Self-Study Questions in this chapter employ decision tools.

(SO 2) **1.** In reporting discontinued operations, the income statement should show in a special section:
(a) gains on the disposal of the discontinued component.
(b) losses on the disposal of the discontinued component.
(c) Neither (a) nor (b).
(d) Both (a) and (b).

(SO 2) **2.** Cool Stools Corporation has income before taxes of $400,000 and an extraordinary loss of $100,000. If the income tax rate is 25% on all items, the income statement should show income before irregular items and extraordinary items, respectively, of
(a) $325,000 and $100,000.
(b) $325,000 and $75,000.
(c) $300,000 and $100,000.
(d) $300,000 and $75,000.

(SO 3) **3.** Which of the following would be considered an "Other comprehensive income" item?
(a) gain on disposal of discontinued operations.
(b) unrealized loss on available-for-sale securities.

(c) extraordinary loss related to flood.
(d) net income.

(SO 4) **4.** In horizontal analysis, each item is expressed as a percentage of the:
(a) net income amount.
(b) stockholders' equity amount.
(c) total assets amount.
(d) base-year amount.

(SO 4) **5.** Adams Corporation reported net sales of $300,000, $330,000, and $360,000 in the years 2003, 2004, and 2005, respectively. If 2003 is the base year, what percentage do 2005 sales represent of the base?
(a) 77%.   (c) 120%.
(b) 108%.   (d) 130%.

(SO 5) **6.** The following schedule is a display of what type of analysis?

	Amount	Percent
Current assets	$200,000	25%
Property, plant, and equipment	600,000	75%
Total assets	$800,000	

(a) Horizontal analysis.
(b) Differential analysis.
(c) Vertical analysis.
(d) Ratio analysis.

(SO 5)   **7.** In vertical analysis, the base amount for depreciation expense is generally:
(a) net sales.
(b) depreciation expense in a previous year.
(c) gross profit.
(d) fixed assets.

(SO 6)   **8.** Which measure is an evaluation of a company's ability to pay current liabilities?
(a) Current cash debt coverage ratio.
(b) Current ratio.
(c) Both (a) and (b).
(d) None of the above.

(SO 6)   **9.** Which measure is useful in evaluating the efficiency in managing inventories?
(a) Inventory turnover ratio.
(b) Days in inventory.
(c) Both (a) and (b).
(d) None of the above.

(SO 6)   **10.** Which of these is *not* a liquidity ratio?
(a) Current ratio.
(b) Asset turnover ratio.

(c) Inventory turnover ratio.
(d) Receivables turnover ratio.

(SO 6)   **11.** Plano Corporation reported net income $24,000; net sales $400,000; and average assets $600,000 for 2005. What is the 2005 profit margin?
(a) 6%.
(b) 12%.
(c) 40%.
(d) 200%.

(SO 7)   **12.** Which situation below might indicate a company has a low quality of earnings?
(a) The same accounting principles are used each year.
(b) Revenue is recognized when earned.
(c) Maintenance costs are capitalized and then depreciated.
(d) The financial statements are prepared in accordance with generally accepted accounting principles.

Questions

🔧 All of the Questions in this chapter employ decision tools.

1. Explain sustainable income. What relationship does this concept have to the treatment of irregular items on the income statement?

2. Indicate which of the following items would be reported as an extraordinary item on Thought for Food Corporation's income statement.
(a) Loss from damages caused by a volcano eruption.
(b) Loss from the sale of short-term investments.
(c) Loss attributable to a labor strike.
(d) Loss caused when the Food and Drug Administration prohibited the manufacture and sale of a product line.
(e) Loss of inventory from flood damage because a warehouse is located on a flood plain that floods every 5 to 10 years.
(f) Loss on the write-down of outdated inventory.
(g) Loss from a foreign government's expropriation of a production facility.
(h) Loss from damage to a warehouse in southern California from a minor earthquake.

3. Blue Print Inc. reported 2004 earnings per share of $3.26 and had no extraordinary items. In 2005 earnings per share on income before extraordinary items was $2.99, and earnings per share on net income was $3.49. Do you consider this trend to be favorable? Why or why not?

4. Grand Gourmet Inc. has been in operation for 3 years. All of its manufacturing equipment, which has a useful life of 10 to 12 years, has been depreciated on a straight-line basis. During the fourth year, Grand

Gourmet changes to an accelerated depreciation method for all of its equipment.
(a) Will Grand Gourmet post a gain or a loss on this change?
(b) How will this change be reported?

5. (a) Ilana Hadar believes that the analysis of financial statements is directed at two characteristics of a company: liquidity and profitability. Is Ilana correct? Explain. *3 ratios*
(b) Are short-term creditors, long-term creditors, and stockholders interested in primarily the same characteristics of a company? Explain.

6. (a) Distinguish among the following bases of comparison: intracompany, industry averages, and intercompany.
(b) Give the principal value of using each of the three bases of comparison.

7. Two popular methods of financial statement analysis are horizontal analysis and vertical analysis. Explain the difference between these two methods.

8. (a) If Belman Company had net income of $380,000 in 2004 and it experienced a 24.5% increase in net income for 2005, what is its net income for 2005?
(b) If 6 cents of every dollar of Belman's revenue is net income in 2004, what is the dollar amount of 2004 revenue?

9. Name the major ratios useful in assessing (a) liquidity and (b) solvency.

10. Daniel Shapson is puzzled. His company had a profit margin of 10% in 2005. He feels that this is an indication that the company is doing well. Suzie Franklin, his accountant, says that more information is needed to determine the company's financial well-being. Who is correct? Why?

11. What does each type of ratio measure?
    (a) Liquidity ratios.
    (b) Solvency ratios.
    (c) Profitability ratios.

12. What is the difference between the current ratio and working capital?

13. Quick Buys, a retail store, has a receivables turnover ratio of 4.5 times. The industry average is 12.5 times. Does Quick Buys have a collection problem with its receivables?

14. Which ratios should be used to help answer each of these questions?
    (a) How efficient is a company in using its assets to produce sales?
    (b) How near to sale is the inventory on hand?
    (c) How many dollars of net income were earned for each dollar invested by the owners?
    (d) How able is a company to meet interest charges as they fall due?

15. In September 2002 the price-earnings ratio of **General Motors** was 14, and the price-earnings ratio of **Microsoft** was 33. Which company did the stock market favor? Explain.

16. What is the formula for computing the payout ratio? Do you expect this ratio to be high or low for a growth company?

17. Holding all other factors constant, indicate whether each of the following changes generally signals good or bad news about a company.
    (a) Increase in profit margin ratio.
    (b) Decrease in inventory turnover ratio.
    (c) Increase in current ratio.

(d) Decrease in earnings per share.
(e) Increase in price-earnings ratio.
(f) Increase in debt to total assets ratio.
(g) Decrease in times interest earned ratio.

18. The return on assets for Syed Corporation is 7.6%. During the same year Syed's return on common stockholders' equity is 12.8%. What is the explanation for the difference in the two rates?

19. Which two ratios do you think should be of greatest interest in each of the following cases?
    (a) A pension fund considering the purchase of 20-year bonds.
    (b) A bank contemplating a short-term loan.
    (c) A common stockholder.

20. Merit Grafixx Inc. has net income of $300,000, average shares of common stock outstanding of 50,000, and preferred dividends for the period of $40,000. What is Merit's earnings per share of common stock? Eric Roskopf, the president of Merit Grafixx, believes that the computed EPS of the company is high. Comment.

21. Identify and explain factors that affect quality of earnings.

22. Explain how the choice of one of the following accounting methods over the other raises or lowers a company's net income during a period of continuing inflation.
    (a) Use of FIFO instead of LIFO for inventory costing.
    (b) Use of a 6-year life for machinery instead of a 9-year life.
    (c) Use of straight-line depreciation instead of accelerated declining-balance depreciation.

Brief Exercises

◎━━━━━C   All of the Brief Exercises in this chapter employ decision tools.

Prepare a discontinued operations section of an income statement.
(SO 2)

BE14-1   On June 30 Spinnaker Corporation discontinued its operations in Mexico. On September 1 Spinnaker disposed of the Mexico facility at a pretax loss of $550,000. The applicable tax rate is 25%. Show the discontinued operations section of Spinnaker's income statement.

Prepare a corrected income statement with an extraordinary item.
(SO 2)

BE14-2   An inexperienced accountant for Murf Corporation showed the following in Murf's 2005 income statement: Income before income taxes $300,000; Income tax expense $72,000; Extraordinary loss from flood (before taxes) $60,000; and Net income $168,000. The extraordinary loss and taxable income are both subject to a 25% tax rate. Prepare a corrected income statement beginning with "Income before income taxes."

Prepare a change in accounting principles section of an income statement.
(SO 2)

BE14-3   On January 1, 2005, Porter-Haus Inc. changed from the straight-line method of depreciation to the declining-balance method. The cumulative effect of the change was to increase the prior years' depreciation by $40,000 and 2005 depreciation by $8,000. Show the change in accounting principle section of the 2005 income statement, assuming the tax rate is 25%.

Prepare horizontal analysis.
(SO 4)

BE14-4   Using these data from the comparative balance sheet of Unisource Company, perform horizontal analysis.

	December 31, 2005	December 31, 2004
Accounts receivable	$ 600,000	$ 400,000
Inventory	780,000	600,000
Total assets	3,136,000	2,800,000

BE14-5 Using the data presented in BE14-4 for Unisource Company, perform vertical analysis.

Prepare vertical analysis. (SO 5)

BE14-6 Net income was $500,000 in 2003, $460,000 in 2004, and $519,800 in 2005. What is the percentage of change from (a) 2003 to 2004, and (b) from 2004 to 2005? Is the change an increase or a decrease?

Calculate percentage of change. (SO 4)

BE14-7 If Pyramid Company had net income of $672,300 in 2005 and it experienced a 21% increase in net income over 2004, what was its 2004 net income?

Calculate net income. (SO 4)

BE14-8 Vertical analysis (common-size) percentages for Thombet Company's sales, cost of goods sold, and expenses are listed here.

Calculate change in net income. (SO 5)

Vertical Analysis	2005	2004	2003
Sales	100.0%	100.0%	100.0%
Cost of goods sold	59.2	62.4	64.5
Expenses	25.0	26.6	27.5

Did Thombet's net income as a percent of sales increase, decrease, or remain unchanged over the 3-year period? Provide numerical support for your answer.

BE14-9 Horizontal analysis (trend analysis) percentages for Dunvegan Company's sales, cost of goods sold, and expenses are listed here.

Calculate change in net income. (SO 4)

Horizontal Analysis	2005	2004	2003
Sales	96.2%	106.8%	100.0%
Cost of goods sold	102.0	97.0	100.0
Expenses	110.6	95.4	100.0

Explain whether Dunvegan's net income increased, decreased, or remained unchanged over the 3-year period.

BE14-10 These selected condensed data are taken from a recent balance sheet of Bob Evans Farms (in thousands).

Calculate current ratio. (SO 6)

Cash	$ 7,900
Accounts receivable	11,600
Inventories	15,300
Other current assets	9,900
Total current assets	$ 44,700
Total current liabilities	$130,500

What is the current ratio?

BE14-11 The following data are taken from the financial statements of Lite Wait Company.

Evaluate collection of accounts receivable. (SO 6)

	2005	2004
Accounts receivable (net), end of year	$ 560,000	$ 540,000
Net sales on account	4,800,000	4,100,000
Terms for all sales are 1/10, n/45.		

Compute for each year (a) the receivables turnover ratio and (b) the average collection period. What conclusions about the management of accounts receivable can be drawn from these data? At the end of 2003, accounts receivable was $490,000.

Evaluate management of inventory.
(SO 6)

BE14-12   The following data were taken from the income statements of Menu Masters Company.

	2005	2004
Sales revenue	$6,420,000	$6,240,000
Beginning inventory	960,000	837,000
Purchases	4,640,000	4,661,000
Ending inventory	1,020,000	960,000

 Compute for each year (a) the inventory turnover ratio and (b) days in inventory. What conclusions concerning the management of the inventory can be drawn from these data?

Calculate profitability ratios.
(SO 6)

BE14-13   **Staples, Inc.** is one of the largest suppliers of office products in the United States. It had net income of $265.0 million and net revenue of $10,744.4 million in 2001. Its total assets were $3,983.9 million at the beginning of the year and $4,093.0 million at the end of the year. What is Staples, Inc.'s (a) asset turnover ratio and (b) profit margin ratio? (Round to two decimals.)

Calculate profitability ratios.
(SO 6)

BE14-14   Gem Products Company has stockholders' equity of $400,000 and net income of $56,000. It has a payout ratio of 20% and a return on assets ratio of 16%. How much did Gem Products pay in cash dividends, and what were its average total assets?

Calculate cash-basis liquidity and solvency ratios.
(SO 6)

BE14-15   Selected data taken from the 2002 financial statements of trading card company **Topps Company, Inc.** are as follows (in millions).

Net sales for 2002	$302.9
Current liabilities, March 4, 2001	70.3
Current liabilities, March 2, 2002	47.2
Net cash provided by operating activities	1.6
Total liabilities, March 4, 2001	83.7
Total liabilities, March 2, 2002	63.9

Compute these ratios at March 2, 2002: (a) current cash debt coverage ratio and (b) cash debt coverage ratio.

Exercises

All of the Exercises in this chapter employ decision tools.

Prepare irregular items portion of an income statement.
(SO 2)

E14-1   Chatfield Company has income before irregular items of $270,000 for the year ended December 31, 2005. It also has the following items (before considering income taxes): (1) an extraordinary fire loss of $50,000, (2) a gain of $40,000 from the disposal of a division, and (3) a cumulative change in accounting principle that resulted in an increase in the prior year's depreciation of $30,000. Assume all items are subject to income taxes at a 30% tax rate.

Instructions
Prepare Chatfield Company's income statement for 2005, beginning with "Income before irregular items."

Evaluate the effects of unusual or irregular items.
(SO 1, 2, 6)

E14-2   The *Wall Street Journal* routinely publishes summaries of corporate quarterly and annual earnings reports in a feature called the "Earnings Digest." A typical "digest" report takes the following form.

ENERGY ENTERPRISES (A)
Quarter ending July 31

	2005	2004
Revenues	$2,049,000,000	$1,754,000,000
Net income	97,000,000	(a) 68,750,000
EPS: Net income	1.31	0.93

9 months ending July 31

	2005	2004
Revenues	$5,578,500,000	$5,065,300,000
Extraordinary item	(b) 1,900,000	
Net income	102,700,000	(a) 33,250,000
EPS: Net income	1.36	0.53

(a) Includes a net charge of $26,000,000 from loss on the sale of electrical equipment
(b) Extraordinary gain on Middle East property expropriation

The letter in parentheses following the company name indicates the exchange on which Energy Enterprises' stock is traded—in this case, the American Stock Exchange.

Instructions
Answer the following questions.
(a) How was the loss on the electrical equipment reported on the income statement? Was it reported in the third quarter of 2004? How can you tell?
(b) Why did the *Wall Street Journal* list the extraordinary item separately?
(c) What is the extraordinary item? Was it included in income for the third quarter? How can you tell?
(d) Did Energy Enterprises have an operating loss in any quarter of 2004? Of 2005? How do you know?
(e) Approximately how many shares of stock were outstanding in 2005? Did the number of outstanding shares change from July 31, 2004 to July 31, 2005?
(f) As an investor, what numbers should you use to determine Energy Enterprises' profit margin ratio? Calculate the 9-month profit margin ratio for 2004 and 2005 that you consider most useful. Explain your decision.

E14-3 Here is financial information for Canvas Mark Inc.

Prepare horizontal analysis.
(SO 4)

	December 31, 2005	December 31, 2004
Current assets	$128,000	$100,000
Plant assets (net)	400,000	350,000
Current liabilities	91,000	70,000
Long-term liabilities	144,000	95,000
Common stock, $1 par	150,000	115,000
Retained earnings	143,000	170,000

Instructions
Prepare a schedule showing a horizontal analysis for 2005 using 2004 as the base year.

E14-4 Operating data for Nautilus Corporation are presented here.

Prepare vertical analysis.
(SO 5)

	2005	2004
Sales	$800,000	$600,000
Cost of goods sold	500,000	390,000
Selling expenses	120,000	72,000
Administrative expenses	80,000	54,000
Income tax expense	38,400	25,200
Net income	61,600	58,800

Instructions
Prepare a schedule showing a vertical analysis for 2005 and 2004.

Prepare horizontal and vertical analyses.
(SO 4, 5)

E14-5 The comparative balance sheets of **Philip Morris Companies, Inc.** are presented here.

PHILIP MORRIS COMPANIES, INC.
Comparative Balance Sheets
December 31
($ in millions)

Assets	2001	2000
Current assets	$17,275	$17,238
Property, plant, and equipment (net)	15,137	15,303
Other assets	52,556	46,526
Total assets	$84,968	$79,067

Liabilities and Stockholders' Equity		
Current liabilities	$20,653	$26,976
Long-term liabilities	44,695	37,086
Stockholders' equity	19,620	15,005
Total liabilities and stockholders' equity	$84,968	$79,067

Instructions
(a) Prepare a horizontal analysis of the balance sheet data for Philip Morris using 2000 as a base. (Show the amount of increase or decrease as well.)
(b) Prepare a vertical analysis of the balance sheet data for Philip Morris for 2001.

Prepare horizontal and vertical analyses.
(SO 4, 5)

E14-6 Here are the comparative income statements of Viking Corporation.

VIKING CORPORATION
Comparative Income Statements
For the Years Ended December 31

	2005	2004
Net sales	$550,000	$550,000
Cost of goods sold	440,000	450,000
Gross profit	$110,000	$100,000
Operating expenses	58,000	55,000
Net income	$ 52,000	$ 45,000

100%

Instructions
(a) Prepare a horizontal analysis of the income statement data for Viking Corporation using 2004 as a base. (Show the amounts of increase or decrease.)
(b) Prepare a vertical analysis of the income statement data for Viking Corporation for both years.

Compute liquidity ratios and compare results.
(SO 6)

E14-7 **Nordstrom, Inc.** operates department stores in numerous states. Selected financial statement data (in millions) for 2002 are presented here.

	End of Year	Beginning of Year
Cash and cash equivalents	$ 331.3	$ 25.3
Receivables (net)	698.5	722.0
Merchandise inventory	888.2	945.7
Other current assets	136.6	120.0
Total current assets	$2,054.6	$1,813.0
Total current liabilities	$ 947.7	$ 950.6

For the year, net credit sales were $5,634.1 million, cost of goods sold was $3,765.9 million, and cash from operations was $413.7 million. The allowance for doubtful accounts was $24.3 at the end of the year and $16.5 at the beginning.

Instructions
Compute the current ratio, current cash debt coverage ratio, receivables turnover ratio, average collection period, inventory turnover ratio, and days in inventory at the end of the current year.

E14-8 Gnomes Incorporated had the following transactions involving current assets and current liabilities during February 2005.

Perform current ratio analysis.
(SO 6)

Feb. 3 Collected accounts receivable of $15,000. 3.25
       7 Purchased equipment for $25,000 cash. 2.63
      11 Paid $3,000 for a 3-year insurance policy. 3.5
      14 Paid accounts payable of $14,000. 2.84
      18 Declared cash dividends, $6,000.

Additional information:
As of February 1, 2005, current assets were $130,000 and current liabilities were $40,000.

Instructions
Compute the current ratio as of the beginning of the month and after each transaction.

E14-9 Tedd Company has these comparative balance sheet data:

Compute selected ratios.
(SO 6)

TEDD COMPANY
Balance Sheets
December 31

	2005	2004
Cash	$ 20,000	$ 30,000
Receivables (net)	65,000	60,000
Inventories	60,000	50,000
Plant assets (net)	200,000	180,000
	$345,000	$320,000
Accounts payable	$ 50,000	$ 60,000
Mortgage payable (15%)	100,000	100,000
Common stock, $10 par	140,000	120,000
Retained earnings	55,000	40,000
	$345,000	$320,000

Additional information for 2005:
1. Net income was $25,000.
2. Sales on account were $420,000. Sales returns and allowances amounted to $20,000.
3. Cost of goods sold was $198,000.
4. The allowance for doubtful accounts was $10,000 on December 31, 2005, and $8,000 on December 31, 2004.
5. Net cash provided by operating activities was $41,000.

Instructions
Compute the following ratios at December 31, 2005.
(a) Current. (e) Days in inventory.
(b) Receivables turnover. (f) Cash debt coverage.
(c) Average collection period. (g) Current cash debt coverage.
(d) Inventory turnover.

E14-10 Selected comparative statement data for the giant bookseller **Barnes & Noble** are presented here. All balance sheet data are as of December 31 (in millions).

Compute selected ratios.
(SO 6)

	2001	2000
Net sales	$4,870.4	$4,375.8
Cost of goods sold	3,560.0	3,169.7
Net income	64.0	(52.0)
Accounts receivable	98.6	84.5
Inventory	1,285.0	1,238.6
Total assets	2,623.2	2,557.5
Total common stockholders' equity	888.1	777.7

Instructions

Compute the following ratios for 2001:

(a) Profit margin.

(b) Asset turnover.

(c) Return on assets.

(d) Return on common stockholders' equity.

(e) Gross profit rate.

Compute selected ratios.
(SO 6)

E14-11 Here is the income statement for Life Style, Inc.

LIFE STYLE, INC.
Income Statement
For the Year Ended December 31, 2005

Sales	$400,000
Cost of goods sold	230,000
Gross profit	170,000
Expenses (including $15,000 interest and $24,000 income taxes)	90,000
Net income	$ 80,000

Additional information:

1. Common stock outstanding January 1, 2005, was 30,000 shares, and 40,000 shares were outstanding at December 31, 2005.
2. The market price of Life Style, Inc., stock was $15 in 2005.
3. Cash dividends of $21,000 were paid, $5,000 of which were to preferred stockholders.
4. Cash provided by operating activities was $98,000.

Instructions

Compute the following measures for 2005.

(a) Earnings per share.

(b) Price-earnings ratio.

(c) Payout ratio.

(d) Times interest earned ratio.

Compute amounts from
ratios.
(SO 6)

E14-12 Saylor Corporation experienced a fire on December 31, 2005, in which its financial records were partially destroyed. It has been able to salvage some of the records and has ascertained the following balances.

	December 31, 2005	December 31, 2004
Cash	$ 30,000	$ 10,000
Receivables (net)	72,500	126,000
Inventory	200,000	180,000
Accounts payable	50,000	10,000
Notes payable	30,000	20,000
Common stock, $100 par	400,000	400,000
Retained earnings	113,500	101,000

Additional information:

1. The inventory turnover is 3.6 times.
2. The return on common stockholders' equity is 19%. The company had no additional paid-in capital.
3. The receivables turnover is 9.4 times.
4. The return on assets is 14%.
5. Total assets at December 31, 2004, were $605,000.

Instructions

Compute the following for Saylor Corporation.

(a) Cost of goods sold for 2005.

(b) Net credit sales for 2005.

(c) Net income for 2005.

(d) Total assets at December 31, 2005.

Problems: Set A

    All of the Problems in this chapter employ decision tools.

P14-1A Here are comparative statement data for Here Today Company and Gone Tomorrow Company, two competitors. All balance sheet data are as of December 31, 2005, and December 31, 2004.

Prepare vertical analysis and comment on profitability.
(SO 5, 6)

	Here Today Company		Gone Tomorrow Company	
	2005	**2004**	**2005**	**2004**
Net sales	$350,000		$1,400,000	
Cost of goods sold	180,000		720,000	
Operating expenses	51,000		278,000	
Interest expense	3,000		10,000	
Income tax expense	11,000		68,000	
Current assets	130,000	$100,000	700,000	$650,000
Plant assets (net)	405,000	270,000	1,000,000	750,000
Current liabilities	60,000	52,000	250,000	275,000
Long-term liabilities	50,000	68,000	200,000	150,000
Common stock	360,000	210,000	950,000	700,000
Retained earnings	65,000	40,000	300,000	275,000

Instructions
(a) Prepare a vertical analysis of the 2005 income statement data for Today Company and Tomorrow Company.
(b) Comment on the relative profitability of the companies by computing the return on assets and the return on common stockholders' equity ratios for both companies.

P14-2A The comparative statements of Classic Rock Company are presented here.

Compute ratios from balance sheet and income statement.
(SO 6)

CLASSIC ROCK COMPANY
Income Statements
For the Years Ended December 31

	2005	**2004**
Net sales	$780,000	$624,000
Cost of goods sold	440,000	405,600
Gross profit	340,000	218,400
Selling and administrative expense	143,880	149,760
Income from operations	196,120	68,640
Other expenses and losses		
Interest expense	9,920	7,200
Income before income taxes	186,200	61,440
Income tax expense	29,000	24,000
Net income	$157,200	$ 37,440

CLASSIC ROCK COMPANY
Balance Sheets
December 31

Assets	**2005**	**2004**
Current assets		
Cash	$ 23,100	$ 21,600
Short-term investments	34,800	33,000
Accounts receivable (net allowance for doubtful accounts of $4,800 for 2005 and $4,200 for 2004)	106,200	93,800
Inventory	116,400	64,000
Total current assets	280,500	212,400
Plant assets (net)	455,300	459,600
Total assets	$735,800	$672,000

Liabilities and Stockholders' Equity

Current liabilities		
Accounts payable	$168,200	$132,000
Income taxes payable	25,300	24,000
Total current liabilities	193,500	156,000
Bonds payable	132,000	120,000
Total liabilities	325,500	276,000
Stockholders' equity		
Common stock ($10 par)	140,000	150,000
Retained earnings	270,300	246,000
Total stockholders' equity	410,300	396,000
Total liabilities and stockholders' equity	$735,800	$672,000

All sales were on account. Net cash provided by operating activities was $41,000.

Instructions

Compute the following ratios for 2005.

(a) Earnings per share.
(b) Return on common stockholders' equity.
(c) Return on assets.
(d) Current.
(e) Receivables turnover.
(f) Average collection period.
(g) Inventory turnover.

(h) Days in inventory.
(i) Times interest earned.
(j) Asset turnover.
(k) Debt to total assets.
(l) Current cash debt coverage.
(m) Cash debt coverage.

Perform ratio analysis, and discuss change in financial position and operating results.
(SO 6)

P14-3A The following are condensed balance sheet and income statement data for Juan Valdez Corporation.

JUAN VALDEZ CORPORATION
Balance Sheets
December 31

	2005	2004	2003
Cash	$ 40,000	$ 24,000	$ 20,000
Receivables (net)	120,000	45,000	48,000
Other current assets	80,000	75,000	62,000
Investments	90,000	70,000	50,000
Plant and equipment (net)	603,000	400,000	360,000
	$933,000	$614,000	$540,000
Current liabilities	$ 98,000	$ 75,000	$ 70,000
Long-term debt	250,000	75,000	65,000
Common stock, $10 par	400,000	340,000	300,000
Retained earnings	185,000	124,000	105,000
	$933,000	$614,000	$540,000

JUAN VALDEZ CORPORATION
Income Statements
For the Years Ended December 31

	2005	2004
Sales	$800,000	$750,000
Less: Sales returns and allowances	40,000	50,000
Net sales	760,000	700,000
Cost of goods sold	420,000	400,000
Gross profit	340,000	300,000
Operating expenses (including income taxes)	194,000	225,000
Net income	$146,000	$ 75,000

Additional information:
  1. The market price of Juan Valdez's common stock was $5.00, $3.50, and $2.30 for 2003, 2004, and 2005, respectively.
  2. You must compute dividends paid. All dividends were paid in cash.

Instructions
  (a) Compute the following ratios for 2004 and 2005.
      (1) Profit margin.   **(5)** Price-earnings.
      (2) Gross profit rate.   **(6)** Payout.
      (3) Asset turnover.   **(7)** Debt to total assets.
      (4) Earnings per share.

  (b) Based on the ratios calculated, discuss briefly the improvement or lack thereof in the financial position and operating results from 2004 to 2005 of Juan Valdez Corporation.

P14-4A Financial information for M. L. Kurt Company is presented here.

Compute ratios; comment on overall liquidity and profitability.
(SO 6)

M. L. KURT COMPANY
Balance Sheets
December 31

Assets	2005	2004
Cash	$ 50,000	$ 42,000
Short-term investments	80,000	50,000
Receivables (net allowance for doubtful accounts of $4,000 for 2005 and $3,000 for 2004)	100,000	87,000
Inventories	440,000	300,000
Prepaid expenses	25,000	31,000
Land	75,000	75,000
Building and equipment (net)	570,000	400,000
Total assets	$1,340,000	$985,000
Liabilities and Stockholders' Equity		
Notes payable	$ 125,000	$ 25,000
Accounts payable	160,000	90,000
Accrued liabilities	50,000	50,000
Bonds payable, due 2007	200,000	100,000
Common stock, $5 par	500,000	500,000
Retained earnings	305,000	220,000
Total liabilities and stockholders' equity	$1,340,000	$985,000

M. L. KURT COMPANY
Income Statements
For the Years Ended December 31

	2005	2004
Sales	$1,000,000	$940,000
Cost of goods sold	650,000	635,000
Gross profit	350,000	305,000
Operating expenses	235,000	225,000
Net income	$ 115,000	$ 80,000

Additional information:
  1. Inventory at the beginning of 2004 was $350,000.
  2. Receivables at the beginning of 2004 were $80,000, net an allowance for doubtful accounts of $3,000.
  3. Total assets at the beginning of 2004 were $1,175,000.
  4. No common stock transactions occurred during 2004 or 2005.
  5. All sales were on account.

Instructions

(a) Indicate, by using ratios, the change in liquidity and profitability of the company from 2004 to 2005. (*Note:* Not all profitability ratios can be computed nor can cash-basis ratios be computed.)

(b) Given below are three independent situations and a ratio that may be affected. For each situation, compute the affected ratio (1) as of December 31, 2005, and (2) as of December 31, 2006, after giving effect to the situation. Net income for 2006 was $125,000. Total assets on December 31, 2006, were $1,450,000.

Situation	Ratio
1. 65,000 shares of common stock were sold at par on July 1, 2006.	Return on common stockholders' equity
2. All of the notes payable were paid in 2006.	Debt to total assets
3. The market price of common stock on December 31, 2006, was $6.25. The market price on December 31, 2005, was $5.	Price-earnings

Compute selected ratios, and compare liquidity, profitability, and solvency for two companies.
(SO 6)

P14-5A Selected financial data for **Black & Decker** and **Snap-On Tools** for 2001 are presented here (in millions).

	Black & Decker	Snap-On Tools
	Income Statement Data for Year	
Net sales	$4,333.1	$2,095.7
Cost of goods sold	2,846.6	1,146.7
Selling and administrative expenses	1,138.9	848.7
Interest expense	84.3	35.5
Other income (expense)	(108.0)	(17.2)
Income tax expense	47.3	26.1
Net income (before irregular items)	$ 108.0	$ 21.5
	Balance Sheet Data (End of Year)	
Current assets	$1,892.3	$1,139.4
Property, plant, and equipment (net)	687.5	327.7
Other assets	1,434.4	507.2
Total assets	$4,014.2	$1,974.3
Current liabilities	$1,070.6	$ 549.4
Long-term debt	2,192.6	649.1
Total stockholders' equity	751.0	775.8
Total liabilities and stockholders' equity	$4,014.2	$1,974.3
	Beginning-of-Year Balances	
Total assets	$4,089.7	$2,069.1
Total stockholders' equity	692.4	844.0
Current liabilities	1,632.3	538.0
Total liabilities	3,397.3	1,225.1
	Other Data	
Average receivables (net)	$ 797.7	$ 670.1
Average inventory	778.1	397.1
Net cash provided by operating activities	379.1	163.7

Instructions

(a) For each company, compute the following ratios.
  (1) Current ratio.
  (2) Receivables turnover.
  (3) Average collection period.
  (4) Inventory turnover.
  (5) Days in inventory.

(6) Profit margin.
(7) Asset turnover.
(8) Return on assets.
(9) Return on common stockholders' equity.
(10) Debt to total assets.
(11) Times interest earned.
(12) Current cash debt coverage.
(13) Cash debt coverage.

(b) Compare the liquidity, solvency, and profitability of the two companies.

Problems: Set B

P14-1B Here are comparative statement data for North Company and South Company, two competitors. All balance sheet data are as of December 31, 2005, and December 31, 2004.

Prepare vertical analysis and comment on profitability.
(SO 5, 6)

	North Company		South Company	
	2005	**2004**	**2005**	**2004**
Net sales	$1,849,035		$539,038	
Cost of goods sold	1,080,490		238,006	
Operating expenses	300,000		82,000	
Interest expense	6,800		1,252	
Income tax expense	52,030		6,650	
Current assets	325,975	$312,410	83,336	$ 79,467
Plant assets (net)	526,800	500,000	139,728	125,812
Current liabilities	66,325	75,815	35,348	30,281
Long-term liabilities	113,990	90,000	29,620	25,000
Common stock, $10 par	500,000	500,000	120,000	120,000
Retained earnings	172,460	146,595	38,096	29,998

Instructions
(a) Prepare a vertical analysis of the 2005 income statement data for North Company and South Company.
(b) Comment on the relative profitability of the companies by computing the 2005 return on assets and the return on common stockholders' equity ratios for both companies.

P14-2B The comparative statements of Nathan Hale Company are presented here.

Compute ratios from balance sheet and income statement.
(SO 6)

NATHAN HALE COMPANY
Income Statements
For the Years Ended December 31

	2005	**2004**
Net sales	$1,918,500	$1,750,500
Cost of goods sold	1,005,500	996,000
Gross profit	913,000	754,500
Selling and administrative expenses	506,000	479,000
Income from operations	407,000	275,500
Other expenses and losses		
Interest expense	25,000	19,000
Income before income taxes	382,000	256,500
Income tax expense	87,400	77,000
Net income	$ 294,600	$ 179,500

NATHAN HALE COMPANY
Balance Sheets
December 31

Assets	2005	2004
Current assets		
Cash	$ 60,100	$ 64,200
Short-term investments	54,000	50,000
Accounts receivable (less allowance for doubtful accounts of $4,200 in 2005 and $3,600 in 2004)	107,800	102,800
Inventory	143,000	115,500
Total current assets	364,900	332,500
Plant assets (net)	625,300	520,300
Total assets	$990,200	$852,800
Liabilities and Stockholders' Equity		
Current liabilities		
Accounts payable	$170,000	$145,400
Income taxes payable	43,500	42,000
Total current liabilities	213,500	187,400
Bonds payable	210,000	200,000
Total liabilities	423,500	387,400
Stockholders' equity		
Common stock ($5 par)	280,000	300,000
Retained earnings	286,700	165,400
Total stockholders' equity	566,700	465,400
Total liabilities and stockholders' equity	$990,200	$852,800

All sales were on account. Net cash provided by operating activities for 2005 was $302,000.

Instructions
Compute the following ratios for 2005.

(a) Earnings per share.
(b) Return on common stockholders' equity.
(c) Return on assets.
(d) Current ratio.
(e) Receivables turnover.
(f) Average collection period.
(g) Inventory turnover.

(h) Days in inventory.
(i) Times interest earned.
(j) Asset turnover.
(k) Debt to total assets.
(l) Current cash debt coverage.
(m) Cash debt coverage.

Perform ratio analysis, and discuss change in financial position and operating results.
(SO 6)

P14-3B Condensed balance sheet and income statement data for Click and Clack Corporation are presented here.

CLICK AND CLACK CORPORATION
Balance Sheets
December 31

	2005	2004	2003
Cash	$ 40,000	$ 20,000	$ 18,000
Receivables (net)	50,000	45,000	48,000
Other current assets	90,000	85,000	64,000
Investments	55,000	70,000	45,000
Plant and equipment (net)	500,000	370,000	258,000
	$735,000	$590,000	$433,000
Current liabilities	$ 85,000	$ 80,000	$ 30,000
Long-term debt	165,000	85,000	20,000
Common stock, $10 par	340,000	300,000	300,000
Retained earnings	145,000	125,000	83,000
	$735,000	$590,000	$433,000

CLICK AND CLACK CORPORATION
Income Statements
For the Years Ended December 31

	2005	2004
Sales	$640,000	$500,000
Less: Sales returns and allowances	40,000	50,000
Net sales	600,000	450,000
Cost of goods sold	425,000	300,000
Gross profit	175,000	150,000
Operating expenses (including income taxes)	121,000	88,000
Net income	$ 54,000	$ 62,000

Additional information:

1. The market price of Click and Clack's common stock was $4.00, $6.00, and $7.95 for 2003, 2004, and 2005, respectively.
2. You must compute dividends paid. All dividends were paid in cash.

Instructions

(a) Compute the following ratios for 2004 and 2005.
   (1) Profit margin.
   (2) Gross profit.
   (3) Asset turnover.
   (4) Earnings per share.
   (5) Price-earnings.
   (6) Payout.
   (7) Debt to total assets.

(b) Based on the ratios calculated, discuss briefly the improvement or lack thereof in the financial position and operating results from 2004 to 2005 of Click and Clack Corporation.

P14-4B The following financial information is for Azteca Company.

Compute ratios; comment on overall liquidity and profitability.
(SO 6)

AZTECA COMPANY
Balance Sheets
December 31

Assets	2005	2004
Cash	$ 70,000	$ 65,000
Short-term investments	45,000	40,000
Receivables (net allowance for doubtful accounts of $6,000 for 2005 and $5,000 for 2004)	94,000	90,000
Inventories	230,000	125,000
Prepaid expenses	25,000	23,000
Land	130,000	130,000
Building and equipment (net)	260,000	175,000
Total assets	$854,000	$648,000

Liabilities and Stockholders' Equity	2005	2004
Notes payable	$170,000	$100,000
Accounts payable	45,000	42,000
Accrued liabilities	40,000	40,000
Bonds payable, due 2007	250,000	150,000
Common stock, $10 par	200,000	200,000
Retained earnings	149,000	116,000
Total liabilities and stockholders' equity	$854,000	$648,000

AZTECA COMPANY
Income Statements
For the Years Ended December 31

	2005	2004
Sales	$850,000	$790,000
Cost of goods sold	620,000	575,000
Gross profit	230,000	215,000
Operating expenses	194,000	180,000
Net income	$ 36,000	$ 35,000

Additional information:

1. Inventory at the beginning of 2004 was $115,000.
2. Receivables (net) at the beginning of 2004 were $88,000, with a $5,000 allowance for doubtful accounts.
3. Total assets at the beginning of 2004 were $630,000.
4. No common stock transactions occurred during 2004 or 2005.
5. All sales were on account.

Instructions
(a) Indicate, by using ratios, the change in liquidity and profitability of Azteca Company from 2004 to 2005. (*Note:* Not all profitability ratios can be computed nor can cash-basis ratios be computed.)
(b) Given below are three independent situations and a ratio that may be affected. For each situation, compute the affected ratio (1) as of December 31, 2005, and (2) as of December 31, 2006, after giving effect to the situation. Net income for 2006 was $40,000. Total assets on December 31, 2006, were $900,000.

Situation	Ratio
1. 18,000 shares of common stock were sold at par on July 1, 2006.	Return on common stockholders' equity
2. All of the notes payable were paid in 2006.	Debt to total assets
3. The market price of common stock was $9 and $12.80 on December 31, 2005 and 2006, respectively.	Price-earnings

Compute selected ratios, and compare liquidity, profitability, and solvency for two companies.
(SO 6)

P14-5B Selected financial data of **Target** and **Wal-Mart** for 2001 are presented here (in millions).

	Target Corporation	Wal-Mart Stores, Inc.
	Income Statement Data for Year	
Net sales	$39,176	$217,799
Cost of goods sold	27,246	171,562
Selling and administrative expenses	9,962	36,173
Interest expense	464	1,326
Other income (expense)	712	2,013
Income tax expense	842	3,897
Net income	$ 1,374	$ 6,854
	Balance Sheet Data (End of Year)	
Current assets	$ 9,648	$ 28,246
Noncurrent assets	14,506	55,205
Total assets	$24,154	$ 83,451
Current liabilities	$ 7,054	$ 27,282
Long-term debt	9,240	21,067
Total stockholders' equity	7,860	35,102
Total liabilities and stockholders' equity	$24,154	$ 83,451

	Beginning-of-Year Balances	
Total assets	$19,490	$ 78,130
Total stockholders' equity	6,519	31,343
Current liabilities	6,301	28,949
Total liabilities	12,971	46,787

	Other Data	
Average net receivables	$ 1,916	$ 1,884
Average inventory	4,349	22,028
Net cash provided by operating activities	1,992	10,260

Instructions

(a) For each company, compute the following ratios.

(1) Current.	(8) Return on assets.
(2) Receivables turnover.	(9) Return on common stockholders' equity.
(3) Average collection period.	(10) Debt to total assets.
(4) Inventory turnover.	(11) Times interest earned.
(5) Days in inventory.	(12) Current cash debt coverage.
(6) Profit margin.	(13) Cash debt coverage.
(7) Asset turnover.	

(b) Compare the liquidity, solvency, and profitability of the two companies.

▶ BROADENING YOUR PERSPECTIVE

Financial Reporting and Analysis

FINANCIAL REPORTING PROBLEM: *Tootsie Roll Industries, Inc.*

BYP14-1   Your parents are considering investing in Tootsie Roll Industries common stock. They ask you, as an accounting expert, to make an analysis of the company for them. Fortunately, excerpts from a recent annual report of Tootsie Roll are presented in Appendix A of this textbook.

Instructions

(a) Make a 5-year trend analysis, using 1998 as the base year, of (1) net revenues and (2) net earnings. Comment on the significance of the trend results.

(b) Compute for 2002 and 2001 the (1) debt to total assets ratio and (2) times interest earned ratio. How would you evaluate Tootsie Roll's long-term solvency?

(c) Compute for 2002 and 2001 the (1) profit margin ratio, (2) asset turnover ratio, (3) return on assets ratio, and (4) return on common stockholders' equity ratio. How would you evaluate Tootsie Roll's profitability? Total assets at December 31, 2000, were $562,442,000, and total stockholders' equity at December 31, 2000, was $458,696,000.

(d) What information outside the annual report may also be useful to your parents in making a decision about Tootsie Roll?

COMPARATIVE ANALYSIS PROBLEM: *Tootsie Roll vs. Hershey Foods*

BYP14-2   The financial statements of Hershey Foods are presented in Appendix B, following the financial statements for Tootsie Roll Industries in Appendix A.

Instructions

(a) Based on the information in the financial statements, determine each of the following for each company:

(1) The percentage increase (i) in net sales and (ii) in net income from 2001 to 2002.

(2) The percentage increase (i) in total assets and (ii) in total stockholders' equity from 2001 to 2002.

(3) The earnings per share for 2002.

(b) What conclusions concerning the two companies can be drawn from these data?

RESEARCH CASE

BYP14-3 The August 21, 2001, issue of the *Wall Street Journal* included an article by Jonathan Weil entitled "Companies Pollute Earnings Reports, Leaving P/E Ratios Hard to Calculate."

Instructions

Read the article and answer the following questions.

(a) At the time of the article, what was the overall P-E ratio of the Standard & Poor's 500-stock index of large companies as reported by Thomson Financial/First Call? How did that compare with the long-term historical average?

(b) What earnings measure does Thomson Financial/First Call use to calculate P-E? If, instead, the P-E was measured using earnings as reported under GAAP, what was the P-E for this index? What would this measure suggest about stock prices at the time?

(c) What are "pro forma" earnings? What other names are used for pro forma earnings? Are there any standards or guidelines for determining pro forma income? What justification do companies give for reporting pro forma income?

(d) According to the article, at what point did the use of pro forma earnings "get out of hand"?

(e) What did the article cite as an example of a "start of a backlash" against pro forma earnings measures?

BYP14-4 The October 15, 2002, issue of the *Wall Street Journal* included an article by Jesse Drucker entitled "Motorola's Profit: 'Special' Again?"

Instructions

Read the article and answer the following questions.

(a) For how many consecutive quarters, including the quarter anticipated in the article, has Motorola reported a "special" item on its income statement? What is the total amount of these special charges over this period?

(b) What justification does Motorola give for reporting these charges as special items on its income statement, rather than reporting them as ordinary expenses?

(c) In the second quarter of 2002, what was Motorola's pro forma income, and what was its net income according to generally accepted accounting principles (GAAP)?

(d) According to the article, do Wall Street analysts give more attention to GAAP income or pro forma income? Do analysts agree on how to treat special charges, such as those of Motorola?

INTERPRETING FINANCIAL STATEMENTS

BYP14-5 The Coca-Cola Company and PepsiCo, Inc. provide refreshments to every corner of the world. Selected data from the 2001 consolidated financial statements for The Coca-Cola Company and for PepsiCo, Inc., are presented here (in millions).

	Coca-Cola	PepsiCo
Total current assets	$ 7,171	$ 5,853
Total current liabilities	8,429	4,998
Net sales	20,092	26,935
Cost of goods sold	6,044	10,754
Net income	3,979	2,662
Average (net) receivables for the year	1,880	2,259
Average inventories for the year	1,061	1,251
Average total assets	21,626	21,226
Average common stockholders' equity	10,341	8,126
Average current liabilities	8,870	4,897
Average total liabilities	11,285	13,100
Total assets	22,417	21,695
Total liabilities	11,051	13,047
Income taxes	1,691	1,367
Interest expense	289	219
Cash provided by operating activities	4,110	4,201

Instructions

(a) Compute the following liquidity ratios for 2001 for Coca-Cola and for PepsiCo and comment on the relative liquidity of the two competitors.
  (1) Current ratio.
  (2) Receivables turnover.
  (3) Average collection period.
  (4) Inventory turnover.
  (5) Days in inventory.
  (6) Current cash debt coverage.

(b) Compute the following solvency ratios for the two companies and comment on the relative solvency of the two competitors.
  (1) Debt to total assets ratio.
  (2) Times interest earned.
  (3) Cash debt coverage ratio.

(c) Compute the following profitability ratios for the two companies and comment on the relative profitability of the two competitors.
  (1) Profit margin.
  (2) Asset turnover.
  (3) Return on assets.
  (4) Return on common stockholders' equity.

A GLOBAL FOCUS

BYP14-6 The use of railroad transportation has changed dramatically around the world. Attitudes about railroads and railroad usage differ across countries. In England, the railroads were run by the government until recently. Five years ago, **Railtrack Group PLC** became a publicly traded company. The largest railroad company in the United States is **Burlington Northern Railroad Company**. The following data were taken from the 2001 financial statements of each company.

Financial Highlights	Railtrack Group (pounds in millions)		Burlington Northern (dollars in millions)	
	2001	2000	2001	2000
Total current assets	£ 602	£ 1,177	$ 723	$ 976
Total assets	9,443	11,484	24,721	24,375
Current liabilities	2,517	1,314	2,161	2,186
Total liabilities	6,795	8,411	16,872	16,895
Total stockholders' equity	2,648	3,073	7,849	7,480
Sales	2,476		9,208	
Operating costs and other	2,188		7,563	
Interest expense	89		463	
Income tax expense (credit)	(53)		445	
Net income	252		737	
Cash provided by operations	718		2,197	

Instructions

(a) Calculate the following 2001 liquidity ratios and discuss the relative liquidity of the two companies.
  (1) Current ratio.
  (2) Current cash debt coverage.

(b) Calculate the following 2001 solvency ratios and discuss the relative solvency of the two companies.
  (1) Debt to total assets.
  (2) Times interest earned.
  (3) Cash debt coverage.

(c) Calculate the following 2001 profitability ratios and discuss the relative profitability of the two companies.
  (1) Asset turnover.
  (2) Profit margin.
  (3) Return on assets.
  (4) Return on common stockholders' equity.

(d) What other issues must you consider when comparing these two companies?

FINANCIAL ANALYSIS ON THE WEB

BYP14-7 *Purpose:* To use the Management Discussion and Analysis (MD&A) section of an annual report to evaluate corporate performance for the year.

Addresses: www.ge.com/investor/ (or go to **www.wiley.com/college/kimmel**)

Steps
1. From General Electric's Web site, choose the most recent annual report.
2. Choose financial section.
3. Download annual report.

Instructions
(a) Compare current-year earnings with the previous year's earnings.
(b) What were some of management's explanations for the change in net earnings?

BYP14-8 *Purpose:* To employ comparative data and industry data to evaluate a company's performance and financial position.

Address: http://biz.yahoo.com/i (or go to **www.wiley.com/college/kimmel**)

Steps
(1) Identify two competing companies.
(2) Go to the above address.
(3) Type in the first company's name and choose **Search**.
(4) Choose **Profile**.
(5) Choose **Ratio Comparisons**.
(6) Print out the results.
(7) Repeat steps 3–6 for the competitor.

Instructions
(a) Evaluate the company's liquidity relative to the industry averages and to the competitor that you chose.
(b) Evaluate the company's solvency relative to the industry averages and to the competitor that you chose.
(c) Evaluate the company's profitability relative to the industry averages and to the competitor that you chose.

Critical Thinking

GROUP DECISION CASE

BYP14-9 You are a loan officer for Premier Bank of Port Washington. Rick Gleason, president of R. Gleason Corporation, has just left your office. He is interested in an 8-year loan to expand the company's operations. The borrowed funds would be used to purchase new equipment. As evidence of the company's debt-worthiness, Gleason provided you with the following facts.

	2005	**2004**
Current ratio	3.1	2.1
Asset turnover ratio	2.8	2.2
Cash debt coverage ratio	.1	.2
Net income	Up 32%	Down 8%
Earnings per share	$3.30	$2.50

Rick Gleason is a very insistent (some would say pushy) man. When you told him that you would need additional information before making your decision, he acted offended, and said, "What more could you possibly want to know?" You responded that, at a minimum, you would need complete, audited financial statements.

Instructions
With the class divided into groups, answer the following.
(a) Explain why you would want the financial statements to be audited.

(b) Discuss the implications of the ratios provided for the lending decision you are to make. That is, does the information paint a favorable picture? Are these ratios relevant to the decision?

(c) List three other ratios that you would want to calculate for this company, and explain why you would use each.

COMMUNICATION ACTIVITY

BYP14-10 M. F. Hoffman is the chief executive officer of Hi-Tech Electronics. Hoffman is an expert engineer but a novice in accounting. Hoffman asks you, as an accounting major, to explain (a) the bases for comparison in analyzing Hi-Tech's financial statements and (b) the limitations, if any, in financial statement analysis.

Instructions
Write a memo to M. F. Hoffman that explains the basis for comparison and the factors affecting quality of earnings.

ETHICS CASE

BYP14-11 Grace McQuillan, president of McQ Industries, wishes to issue a press release to bolster her company's image and maybe even its stock price, which has been gradually falling. As controller, you have been asked to provide a list of 20 financial ratios along with some other operating statistics relative to McQ Industries' first-quarter financials and operations.

Two days after you provide the ratios and data requested, you are asked by Minh Ly, the public relations director of McQ, to prove the accuracy of the financial and operating data contained in the press release written by the president and edited by Minh. In the news release, the president highlights the sales increase of 25% over last year's first quarter and the positive change in the current ratio from 1.5:1 last year to 3:1 this year. She also emphasizes that production was up 50% over the prior year's first quarter.

You note that the release contains only positive or improved ratios and none of the negative or deteriorated ratios. For instance, no mention is made that the debt to total assets ratio has increased from 35% to 55%, that inventories are up 89%, and that although the current ratio improved, the current cash debt coverage ratio fell from .15 to .05. Nor is there any mention that the reported profit for the quarter would have been a loss had not the estimated lives of McQ's plant and machinery been increased by 30%. Minh emphasized, "The Pres wants this release by early this afternoon."

Instructions
(a) Who are the stakeholders in this situation?
(b) Is there anything unethical in president McQ's actions?
(c) Should you as controller remain silent? Does Minh have any responsibility?

Answers to Self-Study Questions
1. d   2. d   3. b   4. d   5. c   6. c   7. a   8. c   9. c   10. b
11. a   12. c

Answer to Tootsie Roll Review It Question 3, p. 686

Tootsie Roll reported "Other comprehensive earnings (loss)" of ($1,139,000) in 2002. "Comprehensive earnings (loss)" reduced "Net earnings" by 1.7% [($66,388 − $65,249) ÷ $66,388].

 Remember to go back to the Navigator box on the chapter-opening page and check off your completed work.

Managerial Accounting

STUDY OBJECTIVES

After studying this chapter,
you should be able to:

1 Explain the distinguishing features of managerial accounting.

2 Identify the three broad functions of management.

3 Define the three classes of manufacturing costs.

4 Distinguish between product and period costs.

5 Explain the difference between a merchandising and a manufacturing income statement.

6 Indicate how cost of goods manufactured is determined.

7 Explain the difference between a merchandising and a manufacturing balance sheet.

 ☑ THE NAVIGATOR

THE NAVIGATOR ✔

▶ Scan *Study Objectives* ☐

▶ Read *Feature Story* ☐

▶ Read *Preview* ☐

▶ Read text and answer *Before You Go On*
   p. 741 ☐   p. 744 ☐   p. 754 ☐

▶ Work Using the *Decision Toolkit* ☐

▶ Review Summary of *Study Objectives* ☐

▶ Work *Demonstration Problem* ☐

▶ Answer *Self-Study Questions* ☐

▶ Complete *Assignments* ☐

FEATURE STORY

What a Difference a Day Makes

In January 1998 **Compaq Computer** had just become the largest seller of personal computers, and it was *Forbes* magazine's "company of the year." Its chief executive, Eckhard Pfeiffer, was riding high. But during the next two years Compaq lost $2 billion. The company was in chaos, and Mr. Pfeiffer was out of a job. What happened?

First, Dell happened. **Dell Computer** pioneered a new way of making and selling personal computers. Its customers "custom design" their computer over the Internet or phone. Dell reengineered its "supply chain": It coordinated its efforts with its suppliers and streamlined its order-taking and production process, and it can ship a computer within two days of taking an order. Personal computers lose 1 percent of their value every week they sit on a shelf. Thus, having virtually no inventory is a great advantage to Dell. Compaq tried to adopt Dell's approach, but with limited success.

The second shock to Compaq came when it acquired a company even larger than itself—**Digital Equipment**. Digital was famous as much for its technical service as it was for its products. Mr. Pfeiffer believed that the purchase of Digital, with its huge and respected technical sales force, opened new opportunities for Compaq as a global service company. Now it could sell to and service high-end

737

corporate customers. But combining the two companies proved to be hugely expensive and extremely complicated.

In the end, in order to survive, Compaq was forced to merge with **Hewlett-Packard**. Even this decision caused heated debate between H-P's largest shareholders and its managers. Managers in today's rapidly changing global environment often must make decisions that determine their company's fate, and their own. The chapters from this point on discuss techniques used to assist managers in making these decisions.

On the World Wide Web
Dell: www.dell.com
Hewlett-Packard: www.hp.com

This part of the book focuses on issues illustrated in the Feature Story about **Compaq Computer**. These include determining and controlling the costs of material, labor, and overhead and the relationship between costs and profits. In earlier chapters, which focused on financial accounting, you learned about the form and content of **financial statements for external users** of financial information, such as stockholders and creditors. These financial statements represent the principal product of financial accounting. Managerial accounting focuses primarily on the preparation of **reports for internal users** of financial information, such as the managers and officers of a company. Managerial accounting provides tools for assisting management in making decisions and for evaluating the effectiveness of those decisions.

The content and organization of this chapter are as follows.

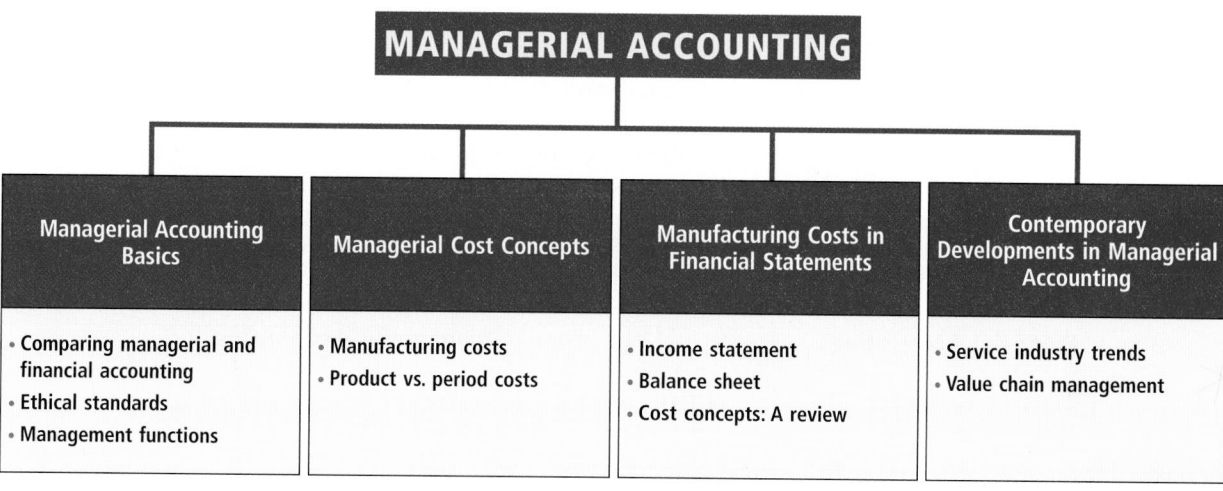

THE NAVIGATOR

Managerial Accounting Basics

Managerial accounting, also called management accounting, is a field of accounting that provides economic and financial information for managers and other internal users. The activities that are part of managerial accounting (and the chapters in which they are discussed) are as follows.

NO 17 or 21

1. Explaining manufacturing and nonmanufacturing costs and how they are reported in the financial statements (Chapter 15).
2. Computing the cost of providing a service or manufacturing a product (Chapters 16 and 17).
3. Determining the behavior of costs and expenses as activity levels change and analyzing cost–volume–profit relationships within a company (Chapter 18). test
4. Assisting management in profit planning and formalizing these plans in the form of budgets (Chapter 19).
5. Providing a basis for controlling costs and expenses by comparing actual results with planned objectives and standard costs (Chapters 20 and 21). 19+20
6. Accumulating and presenting relevant data for management decision making (Chapter 22).

Managerial accounting applies to all types of businesses—service, merchandising, and manufacturing. It also applies to all forms of business organizations—proprietorships, partnerships, and corporations. Managerial accounting is needed in not-for-profit entities as well as in profit-oriented enterprises.

Not long ago, the managerial accountant was primarily engaged in cost accounting—collecting and reporting manufacturing costs to management. Today, the managerial accountant's responsibilities extend to **strategic cost management**—providing managers with data on the efficient use of company resources in both manufacturing and service industries.

STUDY OBJECTIVE

1

Explain the distinguishing features of managerial accounting.

COMPARING MANAGERIAL AND FINANCIAL ACCOUNTING

There are both similarities and differences between managerial and financial accounting. First, each field of accounting deals with the economic events of a business. Thus, their interests overlap. For example, determining the unit cost of manufacturing a product is part of managerial accounting. Reporting the total cost of goods manufactured and sold is part of financial accounting. In addition, both managerial and financial accounting require that a company's economic events be quantified and communicated to interested parties.

The principal differences between financial accounting and managerial accounting are summarized in Illustration 15-1. The diverse needs for economic data among interested parties are responsible for many of the differences.

Illustration 15-1
Differences between financial and managerial accounting

	Financial Accounting		Managerial Accounting
	• External users: stockholders, creditors, and regulators.	**Primary Users of Reports**	• Internal users: officers and managers.
	• Financial statements. • Quarterly and annually.	**Types and Frequency of Reports**	• Internal reports. • As frequently as needed.
	• General-purpose.	**Purpose of Reports**	• Special-purpose for specific decisions.
	• Pertains to business as a whole. • Highly aggregated (condensed). • Limited to double-entry accounting and cost data. • Generally accepted accounting principles.	**Content of Reports**	• Pertains to subunits of the business. • Very detailed. • Extends beyond double-entry accounting to any relevant data. • Standard is relevance to decisions.
	• Audit by CPA.	**Verification Process**	• No independent audits.

publicly held firms   *internal auditors*

ETHICAL STANDARDS FOR MANAGERIAL ACCOUNTANTS

Managerial accountants have an ethical obligation to their companies and the public. To provide guidance for managerial accountants, the Institute of Management Accountants (IMA) has developed a code of ethical standards, entitled *Standards of Ethical Conduct for Practitioners of Management Accounting and Financial Management*. This code divides the managerial accountants' responsibilities into four areas: (1) competence, (2) confidentiality, (3) integrity, and (4) objectivity. The code states that management accountants should not commit acts in violation of these standards. Nor should they condone such acts by others within their organizations.

MANAGEMENT FUNCTIONS

Management's activities and responsibilities can be classified into three broad functions. They are:

1. Planning.
2. Directing and motivating.
3. Controlling.

In performing these functions, managers make decisions that have a significant impact on the organization.

Planning requires management to look ahead and to establish objectives. These objectives are often diverse: maximizing short-term profits and market share, maintaining a commitment to environmental protection, and contributing to social programs. A key objective of management is to add **value** to the business under its control. Value is usually measured by the trading price of the company's stock and by the potential selling price of the company.

Directing and **motivating** involves coordinating a company's diverse activities and human resources to produce a smooth-running operation. This function relates to implementing planned objectives and providing necessary incentives. For example, manufacturers such as **Campbell Soup Company**, **General Motors**, and **Hewlett-Packard** must coordinate purchasing, manufacturing, warehousing, and selling. Service corporations such as **American Airlines**, **Federal Express**, and **AT&T** must coordinate scheduling, sales, and acquisitions of equipment and supplies. Directing also involves selecting executives, appointing managers and supervisors, and hiring and training employees. Most companies prepare **organization charts** to show the interrelationship of activities and the delegation of authority and responsibility within the company.

The third management function, **controlling**, is the process of keeping the company's activities on track. In controlling operations, managers determine whether planned goals are being met. When there are deviations from targeted objectives, they must decide what changes are needed to get back on track.

How do managers achieve control? A smart manager in a small operation should make personal observations, ask good questions, and know how to evaluate the answers. But such a system in a large organization would be chaotic. Imagine the president of Hewlett-Packard attempting to determine whether planned objectives are being met without some record of what has happened and what is expected to occur. Thus, a formal system of evaluation is typically used in large businesses. It would include such items as budgets, responsibility centers, and performance evaluation reports.

Decision making is not a separate management function. Rather, it is the outcome of the exercise of good judgment in planning, directing, motivating, and controlling.

You are now ready to study specific applications of managerial accounting. As you study the managerial chapters, you will encounter many new terms, concepts, and reports. At the same time, you will find some new uses and interpretations of a number of familiar financial accounting terms.

BEFORE YOU GO ON . . .

▶ **Review It**

1. Compare financial accounting and managerial accounting, identifying the principal differences.
2. Identify and discuss the three broad functions of management.

Business Insight
MANAGEMENT PERSPECTIVE

The trend toward more automated and computerized factories has changed the way managers and employees interact. For one thing, managers have fewer direct labor employees to supervise because fewer are needed on the line. Instead of standing in one spot all day, employees and managers have become more mobile, monitoring the computers that control production, and involving themselves in a variety of jobs.

Recently, two technology giants, **General Electric** and **Cisco Systems**, joined forces to build computerized infrastructures for manufacturers. Their goal is to improve productivity by making better use of data generated by factory-automation equipment. Ultimately their systems should provide a closer link between the factory and corporate offices.

Managerial Cost Concepts

To perform the three management functions effectively, management needs information. One very important type of information is related to costs. For example, questions such as the following should be asked.

1. What costs are involved in making a product or providing a service?

2. If production volume is decreased, will costs decrease?

3. What impact will automation have on total costs?

4. How can costs best be controlled?

To answer these questions, management needs reliable and relevant cost information. We now explain and illustrate the costs that management uses.

MANUFACTURING COSTS

STUDY OBJECTIVE
3
Define the three classes of manufacturing costs.

Manufacturing consists of activities and processes that convert raw materials into finished goods. Contrast this type of operation with merchandising, which sells merchandise in the form in which it is purchased. Manufacturing costs are typically classified as shown in Illustration 15-2.

Illustration 15-2
Classifications of manufacturing costs

Direct Materials

To obtain the materials that will be converted into the finished product, the manufacturer purchases raw materials. **Raw materials** are the basic materials and parts used in the manufacturing process. For example, auto manufacturers such as **General Motors**, **Ford**, and **DaimlerChrysler** use steel, plastics, and tires as raw materials in making cars.

Raw materials that can be physically and directly associated with the finished product during the manufacturing process are called direct materials. Examples include flour in the baking of bread, syrup in the bottling of soft drinks, and steel in the making of automobiles. In the Feature Story, direct materials for **Hewlett-Packard** and **Dell Computer** include plastic, glass, hard drives, and processing chips.

But some raw materials cannot be easily associated with the finished product. These are considered indirect materials. Indirect materials (1) do not physically become part of the finished product, such as lubricants and polishing compounds, or (2) cannot be traced because their physical association with the finished product is too small in terms of cost, such as cotter pins and lock washers. Indirect materials are accounted for as part of **manufacturing overhead**.

Helpful Hint A manufacturer uses masking tape to protect certain sections of its product while other sections are painted. The tape is removed and thrown away when the paint is dry. Is the tape a direct or an indirect material? Answer: Indirect.

Direct Labor

The work of factory employees that can be physically and directly associated with converting raw materials into finished goods is considered direct labor. Bottlers at **Coca-Cola**, bakers at **Sara Lee**, and typesetters at **TechBooks** are employees whose activities are usually classified as direct labor. In contrast, the wages of maintenance people, time-keepers, and supervisors are usually identified as indirect labor. Their efforts have no physical association with the finished product, or it is impractical to trace the costs to the goods produced. Like indirect materials, indirect labor is classified as **manufacturing overhead**.

Business Insight
MANAGEMENT PERSPECTIVE

Recently a closely watched study of productivity reported that a U.S. manufacturer, **Ford**, outperformed the North American plants of many of its Japanese rivals. It also reported that productivity at **General Motors** had improved the most of all auto makers. On a per car basis, GM spends $1,979 on labor and benefits. Ford spends $1,667, and **Nissan**, the most efficient of all North American operators, spends just $1,055. If GM were as efficient as Nissan it would reduce labor spending by $5.3 billion.

SOURCE: Karen Lundegaard, "Ford Plant, GM Receive High Marks in Study of Auto Makers' Productivity." *Wall Street Journal* (June 16, 2000).   lowest cost = best

Manufacturing Overhead

Manufacturing overhead consists of costs that are indirectly associated with the manufacture of the finished product. These costs may also be manufacturing costs that cannot be classified as direct materials or direct labor. Manufacturing overhead includes indirect materials, indirect labor, depreciation on factory buildings and machines, and insurance, taxes, and maintenance on factory facilities.

One study found the following magnitudes of the three different product costs as a percentage of the total product cost: direct materials 54.4 percent, direct labor 12.9 percent, and manufacturing overhead 32.6 percent. Note that the direct labor component is the smallest. This component of product cost is dropping substantially because of automation. In some companies, direct labor has become as little as 5 percent of the total cost.

Allocating materials and labor costs to specific products is fairly straightforward. But dealing with overhead presents problems. How much of the purchasing agent's salary is attributable to the hundreds of products made in the same plant? What about the grease that keeps the machines humming, or the computers that make sure paychecks come out on time? Boiled down to its simplest form, the question becomes: Which products cause which costs? In subsequent chapters we show various methods of allocating overhead to products.

PRODUCT VERSUS PERIOD COSTS

Each of the manufacturing cost components (direct materials, direct labor, and manufacturing overhead) are product costs. As the term suggests, **product costs** are costs that are a necessary and integral part of producing the finished product. Product costs are recorded as inventory when incurred. Under the matching principle, these costs do not become expenses until the finished goods inventory is sold. The expense is cost of goods sold.

Period costs are costs that are matched with the revenue of a specific time period rather than included as part of the cost of a salable product. These are nonmanufacturing costs. Period costs include selling and administrative expenses. They are deducted from revenues in the period in which they are incurred.

The foregoing relationships and cost terms are summarized in Illustration 15-3. Our main concern in this chapter is with product costs.

Alternative Terminology
Terms such as *factory overhead*, *indirect manufacturing costs*, and *burden* are sometimes used instead of manufacturing overhead.

STUDY OBJECTIVE
4
Distinguish between product and period costs.

Alternative Terminology
Product costs are also called *inventoriable costs*.

Helpful Hint An unethical manager may choose to inflate the company's earnings by assigning period costs (such as selling and administrative expenses not pertaining to production) to the ending inventory balances.

Illustration 15-3 Product versus period costs

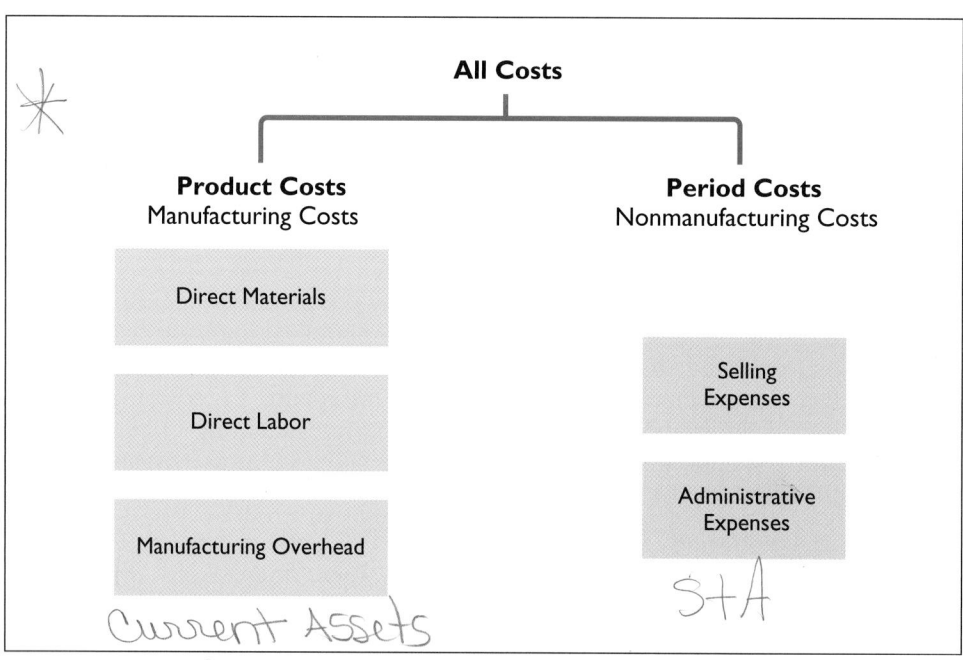

BEFORE YOU GO ON . . .

▶ Review It

1. What are the major cost classifications involved in manufacturing a product?
2. What are product and period costs, and what is their relationship to the manufacturing process?

▶ Do It

A bicycle company has these costs: tires, salaries of employees who put tires on the wheels, factory building depreciation, wheel nuts, spokes, salary of factory manager, handle bars, and salaries of factory maintenance employees. Classify each cost as direct materials, direct labor, or overhead.

Action Plan

- Classify as direct materials any raw materials that can be physically and directly associated with the finished product.
- Classify as direct labor the work of factory employees that can be physically and directly associated with the finished product.
- Classify as manufacturing overhead any costs that are indirectly associated with the finished product.

Solution

Tires, spokes, and handle bars are direct materials. Salaries of employees who put tires on the wheels are direct labor. All of the other costs are manufacturing overhead.

Related exercise material: BE15-4, BE15-5, BE15-7, E15-1, and E15-2.

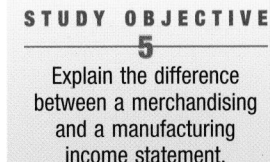

Manufacturing Costs in Financial Statements

The financial statements of a manufacturer are very similar to those of a merchandiser. The principal differences pertain to the cost of goods sold section in the income statement and the current assets section in the balance sheet.

INCOME STATEMENT

Under a periodic inventory system, the income statements of a merchandiser and a manufacturer differ in the cost of goods sold section. For a merchandiser, cost of goods sold is computed by adding the beginning merchandise inventory and the **cost of goods purchased** and subtracting the ending merchandise inventory. For a manufacturer, cost of goods sold is computed by adding the beginning finished goods inventory and **cost of goods manufactured** and subtracting the ending finished goods inventory. (See Illustration 15-4.)

STUDY OBJECTIVE 5
Explain the difference between a merchandising and a manufacturing income statement.

Illustration 15-4 Cost of goods sold components

Helpful Hint A periodic inventory system is assumed here.

Illustration 15-5 Cost of goods sold sections of merchandising and manufacturing income statements

The cost of goods sold sections for merchandising and manufacturing companies in Illustration 15-5 show the different presentations. The other sections of an income statement are similar for merchandisers and manufacturers.

MERCHANDISING COMPANY Income Statement (partial) For the Year Ended December 31, 2005			MANUFACTURING COMPANY Income Statement (partial) For the Year Ended December 31, 2005		
Cost of goods sold			Cost of goods sold		
Merchandise inventory, January 1	$ 70,000		Finished goods inventory, January 1	$ 90,000	
Cost of goods purchased	650,000		Cost of goods manufactured		
			(see Illustration 15-7)	370,000	
Cost of goods available for sale	720,000		Cost of goods available for sale	460,000	
Merchandise inventory, December 31	400,000		Finished goods inventory, December 31	80,000	
Cost of goods sold		$ 320,000	Cost of goods sold		$ 380,000

A number of accounts are involved in determining the cost of goods manufactured. To eliminate excessive detail, it is customary to show in the income statement only the total cost of goods manufactured. The details are presented in a Cost of Goods Manufactured Schedule. The form and content of this schedule are shown in Illustration 15-7 (page 747).

Determining the Cost of Goods Manufactured

STUDY OBJECTIVE
6
Indicate how cost of goods manufactured is determined.

An example may help show how the cost of goods manufactured is determined. Assume that **Hewlett-Packard** has a number of computers in various stages of production on January 1. In total, these partially completed units are called **beginning work in process inventory**. The costs assigned to beginning work in process inventory are based on the **manufacturing costs incurred in the prior period**.

The manufacturing costs incurred in the current year are used first to complete the work in process on January 1. They then are used to start the production of other computers. The sum of the direct materials costs, direct labor costs, and manufacturing overhead incurred in the current year is the total manufacturing costs for the current period.

Helpful Hint Does the amount of "total manufacturing costs for the current year" include the amount of "beginning work in process inventory?" Answer: No.

We now have two cost amounts: (1) the cost of the beginning work in process and (2) the total manufacturing costs for the current period. The sum of these costs is the total cost of work in process for the year.

At the end of the year, some computers may be only partially completed. The costs of these units become the cost of the **ending work in process inventory**. To find the cost of goods manufactured, we subtract this cost from the total cost of work in process. The determination of the cost of goods manufactured is shown graphically in Illustration 15-6 below.

Illustration 15-6 Cost of goods manufactured formula

Cost of Goods Manufactured Schedule

An internal report shows each of the cost elements shown in Illustration 15-6. This report is called the **cost of goods manufactured schedule**. The schedule for Olsen Manufacturing Company (using assumed data) is shown in Illustration 15-7. Note that the schedule presents detailed data for direct materials and for manufacturing overhead.

Review Illustration 15-6 and then examine the cost of goods manufactured schedule in Illustration 15-7. You should be able to distinguish between "total manufacturing costs" and "cost of goods manufactured." The difference is the effect of the change in work in process during the period.

OLSEN MANUFACTURING COMPANY
Cost of Goods Manufactured Schedule
For the Year Ended December 31, 2005

Work in process, January 1			$ 18,400
Direct materials			
Raw materials inventory, January 1	$ 16,700		
Raw materials purchases	152,500		
Total raw materials available for use	169,200		
Less: Raw materials inventory, December 31	22,800		
Direct materials used		$146,400	
Direct labor		175,600	
Manufacturing overhead			
Indirect labor	14,300		
Factory repairs	12,600		
Factory utilities	10,100		
Factory depreciation	9,440		
Factory insurance	8,360		
Total manufacturing overhead		54,800	
Total manufacturing costs			376,800
Total cost of work in process			395,200
Less: Work in process, December 31			25,200
Cost of goods manufactured			$370,000

Illustration 15-7 Cost of goods manufactured schedule

DECISION TOOLKIT

Decision Checkpoints	Info Needed for Decision	Tool to Use for Decision	How to Evaluate Results
Is the company maintaining control over the costs of production?	Cost of material, labor, and overhead	Cost of goods manufactured schedule	Compare the cost of goods manufactured to revenue expected from product sales.

BALANCE SHEET

The balance sheet for a merchandising company shows just one category of inventory. In contrast, the balance sheet for a manufacturer may have three inventory accounts as shown in Illustration 15-8.

STUDY OBJECTIVE 7

Explain the difference between a merchandising and a manufacturing balance sheet.

Illustration 15-8
Inventory accounts for a manufacturer

Raw Materials Inventory	Work in Process Inventory	Finished Goods Inventory
Shows the cost of raw materials on hand.	Shows the cost applicable to units that have been started into production but are only partially completed.	Shows the cost of completed goods on hand.

Finished Goods Inventory is to a manufacturer what Merchandise Inventory is to a merchandiser. It represents the goods that are available for sale.

The current assets sections presented in Illustration 15-9 contrast the presentations of inventories for merchandising and manufacturing companies. Manufacturing inventories are generally listed in the order of their liquidity—the order in which they are expected to be realized in cash. Thus, finished goods inventory is listed first. The remainder of the balance sheet is similar for the two types of companies.

Illustration 15-9
Current assets sections of merchandising and manufacturing balance sheets

MERCHANDISING COMPANY Balance Sheet December 31, 2005			MANUFACTURING COMPANY Balance Sheet December 31, 2005		
Current assets			Current assets		
Cash		$ 100,000	Cash		$180,000
Receivables (net)		210,000	Receivables (net)		210,000
Merchandise inventory		400,000	**Inventories**		
Prepaid expenses		22,000	**Finished goods**	$80,000	
			Work in process	25,200	
Total current assets		$ 732,000	**Raw materials**	22,800	128,000
			Prepaid expenses		18,000
			Total current assets		$536,000

(handwritten: (Can't invent labor) work in process (3) – mat – lab)

Each step in the accounting cycle for a merchandiser applies to a manufacturer. For example, prior to preparing financial statements, adjusting entries are required. The adjusting entries are essentially the same as those of a merchandiser. The closing entries are also similar for manufacturers and merchandisers. (For more detail, see the appendix at the end of the chapter.)

DECISION TOOLKIT

Decision Checkpoints	Info Needed for Decision	Tool to Use for Decision	How to Evaluate Results
What is the composition of a manufacturing company's inventory?	Amount of raw materials, work in process, and finished goods inventory	Balance sheet	Determine whether there is sufficient finished goods inventory, raw materials, and work in process to meet forecasted demand.

COST CONCEPTS—A REVIEW

You have learned a number of cost concepts in this chapter. Because many of these concepts are new, we believe an extended example will help illustrate how they are used.

Assume that Northridge Company manufactures and sells pre-hung metal doors. Recently, it also has decided to start selling pre-hung wood doors. An old warehouse that the company owns will be used to manufacture the new product. Northridge identifies the following costs associated with manufacturing and selling the pre-hung wood doors.

1. The material cost (wood) for each door is $10.
2. Labor costs required to construct a wood door are $8 per door.
3. Depreciation on the new equipment used to make the wood doors using the straight-line method is $25,000 per year.
4. Property taxes on the warehouse used to make the wood doors are $6,000 per year.
5. Advertising costs for the pre-hung wood doors total $2,500 per month or $30,000 per year.
6. Sales commissions related to pre-hung wood doors sold are $4 per door.
7. Salaries for employees who maintain the warehouse are $28,000.
8. The salary of the plant manager in charge of pre-hung wood doors is $70,000.
9. The cost of shipping pre-hung wood doors is $12 per door sold.

These manufacturing and selling costs can be assigned to the various categories shown in Illustration 15-10.

Cost Item	Direct Materials	Direct Labor	Manufacturing Overhead	Period Costs
1. Material cost ($10) per door	X			
2. Labor costs ($8) per door		X		
3. Depreciation on new equipment ($25,000 per year)			X	
4. Property taxes ($6,000 per year)			X	
5. Advertising costs ($30,000 per year)				X
6. Sales commissions ($4 per door)				X
7. Maintenance salaries ($28,000 per year)			X	
8. Salary of plant manager ($70,000)			X	
9. Cost of shipping pre-hung doors ($12 per door)				X

Heading: Product Costs (spanning Direct Materials, Direct Labor, Manufacturing Overhead)

Illustration 15-10
Assignment of costs to cost categories

Remember that total manufacturing costs are the sum of the **product costs**—direct materials, direct labor, and manufacturing overhead. If Northridge

Company produces 10,000 pre-hung wood doors the first year, the total manufacturing costs would be $309,000 as shown in Illustration 15-11.

Illustration 15-11
Computation of total
manufacturing costs

Cost Number and Item	Manufacturing Cost
1. Material cost ($10 × 10,000)	$ 100,000
2. Labor cost ($8 × 10,000)	80,000
3. Depreciation on new equipment	25,000
4. Property taxes	6,000
7. Maintenance salaries	28,000
8. Salary of plant manager	70,000
Total manufacturing costs	**$309,000**

Knowing the total manufacturing costs, Northridge can compute the manufacturing cost per unit, assuming 10,000 units: The cost to produce one pre-hung wood door is $30.90 ($309,000 ÷ 10,000 units).

The cost concepts discussed in this chapter will be used extensively in subsequent chapters. Study Illustration 15-10 carefully. If you do not understand any of these classifications, go back and reread the appropriate section.

Contemporary Developments in Managerial Accounting

Since the 1970s, the competitive environment for U.S. businesses has changed significantly. For example, the airline, financial services, and telecommunications industries have been deregulated. Global competition has intensified, particularly in the automotive and electronics industries. Today, business managers demand different and better information from managerial accountants than they needed just a few years ago. Factors such as those discussed below will contribute to the expanding role of managerial accounting in the twenty-first century.

SERVICE INDUSTRY TRENDS

The Feature Story notes that at the peak of its success as a personal computer manufacturer, **Compaq** purchased **Digital Equipment**. Its management believed that the future of computing lies in providing computer services, rather than in manufacturing hardware. In fact, during the most recent decade, the U.S. economy in general shifted toward an emphasis on providing services, rather than goods. Today over 50 percent of U.S. workers are employed by service compa-

Business Insight
MANAGEMENT PERSPECTIVE

At **South Central Bell (Telephone)**, management accountants have shed their scorekeeping image. A corporate reorganization plan challenged the accountants to "show their stuff." They took on the roles of interpreter, advisor, and partner. To do so, they had to understand what the accounting numbers mean, relate the numbers to business activity, and recommend alternative courses of action. In addition, they must evaluate these alternatives and make decisions to maximize business efficiency.

nies, and that percentage is projected to increase in coming years. Much of this chapter focused on manufacturers. But most of the techniques that you will learn in this course are equally applicable to service entities.

In some respects, the challenges for managerial accounting are greater in service companies than in manufacturing companies. Further complicating matters in recent years, many service industries have been deregulated (for example: trucking, airlines, telecommunications, and banking). In a deregulated environment the information provided by managerial accounting is even more important. Illustration 15-12 presents examples of questions faced by service-company managers.

Managers of service companies look to managerial accounting to answer these questions. In some instances the managerial accountant may need to develop new systems for measuring the cost of serving individual customers. In

Illustration 15-12 Service industries and companies and the managerial accounting questions they face

	Industry/Company	Questions Faced by Service-Company Managers
	Transportation (**American Airlines, Amtrak**)	Whether to buy new or used planes? Whether to service a new route?
	Package delivery services (**FedEx, UPS**)	What fee structure to use? What mode of transportation to use?
	Telecommunications (**AT&T, AOL Time Warner**)	What fee structure to use? Whether to service a new community? How many households will it take to break even? Whether to invest in a new satellite or lay new cable?
	Professional services (attorneys, accountants, physicians)	How much to charge for particular services? How much office overhead to allocate to particular jobs? How efficient and productive are individual staff members?
	Financial institutions (**Wells Fargo, Merrill Lynch**)	Which services to charge for, and which to provide for free? Whether to build a new branch office or to install a new ATM? Should fees vary depending on the size of the customers' accounts?
	Health care (**Blue Cross-Blue Shield**, HMOs)	Whether to invest in new equipment? How much to charge for various services? How to measure the quality of services provided?

others, he or she may need new operating controls to improve the quality and efficiency of specific services. Many of the examples we present in subsequent chapters will be based on service companies.

VALUE CHAIN MANAGEMENT

The **value chain** is the term that describes all activities associated with providing a product or service. The value chain includes activities such as research and development, ordering raw materials, manufacturing, marketing, delivery, and customer relations. Each of these activities should be designed and operated so that they add value to the product or service. A critical component of the value chain is the supply chain. The **supply chain** is all of the activities from receipt of an order to delivery of a product or service. A number of factors affect efforts to manage the value chain and supply chain.

Technological Change

Many companies now employ **enterprise resource planning (ERP)** software systems to manage their value chain. ERP systems provide a comprehensive, centralized, integrated source of information used to manage all major business processes, from purchasing to manufacturing to recording human resources. In large companies, an ERP system might replace as many as 200 individual software packages. For example, an ERP system can eliminate the need for individual software packages for personnel, inventory management, receivables, and payroll. Because the value chain extends beyond the walls of the company, ERP systems both collect and provide information from and to the company's major suppliers, customers, and business partners.

Business Insight
MANAGEMENT PERSPECTIVE

Through **computer-integrated manufacturing (CIM)**, many companies can now manufacture products that are untouched by human hands. An example is the use of robotic equipment in the steel and automobile industries. Automation significantly reduces direct labor costs in many cases. The worker simply monitors the manufacturing process by watching instrument panels.

Also, the widespread use of computers has greatly reduced the cost of accumulating, storing, and reporting managerial accounting information. Computers now make it possible to do more detailed costing of products, processes, and services than was possible under manual processing.

Technology is also affecting the value chain through business-to-business e-commerce on the Internet. The Internet has dramatically changed the way corporations do business with one another. It enables customers and suppliers to share information nearly instantaneously. In addition, it has changed the marketplace, often having the effect of cutting out the "middle man." Industries such as the automobile, airline, hotel, and electronics have made commitments to purchase some or all of their supplies and raw materials in the huge business-to-business electronic marketplaces. For example, **Hilton Hotels** recently committed to purchase as much as $1.5 billion of bed sheets, pest control services, and other items from an Internet supplier, **PurchasePro.com**.

Just-in-Time Inventory Methods

Many companies have significantly lowered inventory levels and costs using just-in-time (JIT) inventory methods. Under a just-in-time method, goods are manufactured or purchased just in time for use. As noted in the Feature Story, Dell Computer is famous for having developed a system for making computers in response to individual customer requests. Even though each computer is custom-made to meet each customer's particular specifications, it takes Dell less than 48 hours to assemble the computer and put it on a truck. By integrating its information systems with those of its suppliers, Dell reduced its inventories to nearly zero. This is a huge advantage in an industry where products become obsolete nearly overnight.

Quality

JIT inventory systems require an increased emphasis on product quality. If products are produced only as they are needed, it is very costly for the company to have to stop production because of defects or machine breakdowns. Many companies have installed total quality management (TQM) systems to reduce defects in finished products. The goal is to achieve zero defects. These systems require timely data on defective products, rework costs, and the cost of honoring warranty contracts. Often this information is used to help redesign the product in a way that makes it less prone to defect. Or it may be used to reengineer the production process to reduce setup time and decrease the potential for error. TQM systems also provide information on nonfinancial measures such as customer satisfaction, number of service calls, and time to generate reports. Attention to these measures, which employees can control, leads to increased profitability.

Business Insight
MANAGEMENT PERSPECTIVE

When it comes to total quality management, few companies can compare with Chiquita Brands International. Grocery store customers are very picky about bananas—bad bananas are consistently the number one grocery store complaint. Because bananas often account for up to 3 percent of a grocery store's sales, Chiquita goes to great lengths to protect the popular fruit. While bananas are in transit from Central America, "black box" recording devices attached to shipping crates ensure that they are kept in an environment of 90 percent humidity and an unvarying 55-degree temperature. Upon arrival in the U.S., bananas are ripened in airtight warehouses that use carefully monitored levels of ethylene gas. Regular checks are made of each warehouse using ultrasonic detectors that can detect leaks the size of a pinhole. Says one grocery store executive, "No other item in the store has this type of attention and resources devoted to it."

SOURCE: Devon Spurgeon, "When Grocers in U.S. Go Bananas Over Bad Fruit, They Call Laubenthal," *Wall Street Journal* (August 14, 2000), p. A1.

Focus on Activities

As discussed earlier, overhead costs have become an increasingly large component of product and service costs. By definition, overhead costs cannot be directly traced to individual products. But to determine each product's cost, overhead must be **allocated** to the various products. In order to obtain more accurate product costs, many companies now allocate overhead using activity-based costing (ABC). Under ABC, overhead is allocated based on each product's use of activities in making the product. For example, the company can keep track of the cost of setting up machines for each batch of a production process. Then a particular product can be allocated part of the total set-up cost based on the number of set-ups that product required. Activity-based costing is beneficial because it results in more accurate product costing and in more careful scrutiny of all activities in the supply chain. For example, if a product's cost is high because it requires a high number of set-ups, management will be motivated to determine how to produce the product using the optimal number of machine set-ups.

BEFORE YOU GO ON . . .

▶ Review It

1. How does the content of an income statement for a merchandiser differ from that for a manufacturer?
2. How are the work in process inventories reported in the cost of goods manufactured schedule?
3. How does the content of the balance sheet for a merchandiser differ from that for a manufacturer?
4. Identify a number of factors that affect the management of a company's value chain.

✓ THE NAVIGATOR

Using the Decision Toolkit

Giant Manufacturing Co. Ltd. specializes in manufacturing many different models of bicycles. Assume that a new model, the Jaguar, has been well accepted. As a result, the company has established a separate manufacturing facility to produce these bicycles. The company produces 1,000 bicycles per month. Giant's monthly manufacturing cost and other expenses data related to these bicycles are as follows.

1. Rent on manufacturing equipment (lease cost) $2,000/month
2. Insurance on manufacturing building $750/month
3. Raw materials (frames, tires, etc.) $80/bicycle
4. Utility costs for manufacturing facility $1,000/month
5. Supplies for general office $800/month
6. Wages for assembly line workers in manufacturing facility $30/bicycle
7. Depreciation on office equipment $650/month

8. Miscellaneous materials (lubricants, solders, etc.) $1.20/bicycle
9. Property taxes on manufacturing building $2,400/year
10. Manufacturing supervisor's salary $3,000/month
11. Advertising for bicycles $30,000/year
12. Sales commissions $10/bicycle
13. Depreciation on manufacturing building $1,500/month

Instructions

(a) Prepare an answer sheet with the following column headings.

| | Product Costs | | | |
Cost Item	Direct Materials	Direct Labor	Manufacturing Overhead	Period Costs

Enter each cost item on your answer sheet, placing an "X" mark under the appropriate headings.

(b) Compute total manufacturing costs for the month.

Solution

(a)

Cost Item	Product Costs			Period Costs
	Direct Materials	**Direct Labor**	**Manufacturing Overhead**	
1. Rent on equipment ($2,000/month)			X	
2. Insurance on manufacturing building ($750/month)			X	
3. Raw materials ($80/bicycle)	X			
4. Manufacturing utilities ($1,000/month)			X	
5. Office supplies ($800/month)				X
6. Wages for workers ($30/bicycle)		X		
7. Depreciation on office equipment ($650/month)				X
8. Miscellaneous materials ($1.20/bicycle)			X	
9. Property taxes on building ($2,400/year)			X	
10. Manufacturing supervisor's salary ($3,000/month)			X	
11. Advertising cost ($30,000/year)				X
12. Sales commissions ($10/bicycle)				X
13. Depreciation on manufacturing building ($1,500/month)			X	

(b)

Cost Item	Manufacturing Cost
Rent on equipment	$ 2,000
Insurance	750
Raw materials ($80 × 1,000)	80,000
Manufacturing utilities	1,000
Labor ($30 × 1,000)	30,000
Miscellaneous materials ($1.20 × 1,000)	1,200
Property taxes ($2,400 ÷ 12)	200
Manufacturing supervisor's salary	3,000
Depreciation on building	1,500
Total manufacturing costs	$119,650

☑ THE NAVIGATOR

Summary of Study Objectives

1 *Explain the distinguishing features of managerial accounting.* The distinguishing features of managerial accounting are:

Primary users of reports—internal users, who are officers, department heads, managers, and supervisors in the company.

Type and frequency of reports—internal reports that are issued as frequently as the need arises.

Purpose of reports—to provide special-purpose information for a particular user for a specific decision.

Content of reports—pertains to subunits of the business and may be very detailed; may extend beyond double-entry accounting system; the reporting standard is relevance to the decision being made.

Verification of reports—no independent audits.

2 *Identify the three broad functions of management.* The three functions are planning, directing and motivating, and controlling. Planning requires management to look ahead and to establish objectives. Directing and motivating involves coordinating the diverse activities and human resources of a company to produce a smooth-running operation. Controlling is the process of keeping the activities on track.

3 *Define the three classes of manufacturing costs.* Manufacturing costs are typically classified as either (1) direct materials, (2) direct labor, or (3) manufacturing overhead. Raw materials that can be physically and directly associated with the finished product during the manufacturing process are called direct materials. The work of factory employees that can be physically and directly associated with converting raw materials into finished goods is considered direct labor. Manufacturing overhead consists

of costs that are indirectly associated with the manufacture of the finished product.

4 *Distinguish between product and period costs.* Product costs are costs that are a necessary and integral part of producing the finished product. Product costs are also called inventoriable costs. Under the matching principle, these costs do not become expenses until the inventory to which they attach is sold. Period costs are costs that are identified with a specific time period rather than with a salable product. These costs relate to nonmanufacturing costs and therefore are not inventoriable costs.

5 *Explain the difference between a merchandising and a manufacturing income statement.* The difference between a merchandising and a manufacturing income statement is in the cost of goods sold section. A manufacturing cost of goods sold section shows beginning and ending finished goods inventories and the cost of goods manufactured.

6 *Indicate how cost of goods manufactured is determined.* The cost of the beginning work in process is added to the total manufacturing costs for the current year to arrive at the total cost of work in process for the year. The ending work in process is then subtracted from the total cost of work in process to arrive at the cost of goods manufactured.

7 *Explain the difference between a merchandising and a manufacturing balance sheet.* The difference between a merchandising and a manufacturing balance sheet is in the current assets section. In the current assets section of a manufacturing company's balance sheet, three inventory accounts are presented: finished goods inventory, work in process inventory, and raw materials inventory.

☑ THE NAVIGATOR

DECISION TOOLKIT—A SUMMARY

Decision Checkpoints	Info Needed for Decision	Tool to Use for Decision	How to Evaluate Results
Is the company maintaining control over the costs of production?	Cost of material, labor, and overhead	Cost of goods manufactured schedule	Compare the cost of goods manufactured to revenue expected from product sales.
What is the composition of a manufacturing company's inventory?	Amount of raw materials, work in process, and finished goods inventory	Balance sheet	Determine whether there is sufficient finished goods inventory, raw materials, and work in process to meet forecasted demand.

APPENDIX
ACCOUNTING CYCLE FOR A
MANUFACTURING COMPANY

The accounting cycle for a manufacturing company is the same as for a merchandising company when a periodic inventory system is used. The journalizing and posting of transactions is the same, except for the additional manufacturing inventories and manufacturing cost accounts. Similarly, the preparation of a trial balance and the journalizing and posting of adjusting entries are the same. Some changes, however, occur in the use of a work sheet and in preparing closing entries.

To illustrate the changes in the work sheet, we will use the cost of goods manufactured schedule for Olsen Manufacturing presented in Illustration 15-7 (page 747), along with other assumed data. For convenience, the cost of goods manufactured schedule is reproduced in Illustration 15A-1.

STUDY OBJECTIVE
8
Prepare a work sheet and closing entries for a manufacturing company.

Illustration 15A-1 Cost of goods manufactured schedule

OLSEN MANUFACTURING COMPANY Cost of Goods Manufactured Schedule For the Year Ended December 31, 2005			
Work in process, January 1			$ 18,400
Direct materials			
Raw materials inventory, January 1	$ 16,700		
Raw materials purchases	152,500		
Total raw materials available for use	169,200		
Less: Raw materials inventory, December 31	22,800		
Direct materials used		$146,400	
Direct labor		175,600	
Manufacturing overhead			
Indirect labor	14,300		
Factory repairs	12,600		
Factory utilities	10,100		
Factory depreciation	9,440		
Factory insurance	8,360		
Total manufacturing overhead		54,800	
Total manufacturing costs			376,800
Total cost of work in process			395,200
Less: Work in process, December 31			25,200
Cost of goods manufactured			$370,000

Work Sheet

When a work sheet is used in preparing financial statements, two additional columns are needed for the cost of goods manufactured schedule. As shown in the work sheet in Illustration 15A-2 (page 758), debit and credit columns for this schedule are inserted before the income statement columns.

In the cost of goods manufactured columns, the beginning inventories of raw materials and work in process are entered as debits. In addition, all the manufacturing costs are entered as debits. The reason is that each of these amounts increases cost of goods manufactured. Ending inventories for raw materials and work in process are entered as credits in the cost of goods manufactured columns because they have the opposite effect—they decrease cost of goods manufactured. The balancing amount for these columns is the cost of goods manufactured. Note that the amount ($370,000) agrees with the amount reported

OLSEN MANUFACTURING COMPANY
Work Sheet (partial)
For the Year Ended December 31, 2005

	Adjusted Trial Balance		Cost of Goods Manufactured		Income Statement		Balance Sheet	
	Dr.	Cr.	Dr.	Cr.	Dr.	Cr.	Dr.	Cr.
Cash	42,500						42,500	
Accounts Receivable (Net)	71,900						71,900	
Finished Goods Inv.	24,600				24,600	19,500	19,500	
Work in Process Inv.	18,400		18,400	25,200			25,200	
Raw Materials Inv.	16,700		16,700	22,800			22,800	
Plant Assets	724,000						724,000	
Accumulated Depr.		278,400						278,400
Notes Payable		100,000						100,000
Accounts Payable		40,000						40,000
Income Taxes Payable		5,000						5,000
Common Stock		200,000						200,000
Retained Earnings		205,100						205,100
Sales		680,000				680,000		
Raw Materials Purchases	152,500		152,500					
Direct Labor	175,600		175,600					
Indirect Labor	14,300		14,300					
Factory Repairs	12,600		12,600					
Factory Utilities	10,100		10,100					
Factory Depreciation	9,440		9,440					
Factory Insurance	8,360		8,360					
Selling Expenses	114,900				114,900			
Administrative Exp.	92,600				92,600			
Income Tax Exp.	20,000				20,000			
Totals	1,508,500	1,508,500	418,000	48,000				
Cost of Goods Manufactured				370,000	370,000			
Totals			418,000	418,000	622,100	699,500	905,900	828,500
Net Income					77,400			77,400
Totals					699,500	699,500	905,900	905,900

Illustration 15A-2 Partial work sheet

for cost of goods manufactured in Illustration 15A-1. This amount is also entered in the income statement debit column.

The income statement and balance sheet columns for a manufacturing company are basically the same as for a merchandising company. For example, the treatment of the finished goods inventories is identical with the treatment of merchandise inventory. That is, the beginning inventory is entered in the debit column, and the ending finished goods inventory is entered in the income statement credit column and in the balance sheet debit column.

As in the case of a merchandising company, financial statements can be prepared from the statement columns of the work sheet. In addition, the cost of goods manufactured schedule can also be prepared directly from the work sheet.

Closing Entries

The closing entries for a manufacturing company are different than for a merchandising company. **A Manufacturing Summary account is used to close all accounts that appear in the cost of goods manufactured schedule.** The balance of the Manufacturing Summary account is the Cost of Goods Manufactured for the period. Manufacturing Summary is then closed to Income Summary. The closing entries can be prepared from the work sheet. As illustrated below, the closing entries for the manufacturing accounts are prepared first. The closing entries for Olsen Manufacturing are as follows.

Dec. 31	Work in Process Inventory (Dec. 31)		25,200	
	Raw Materials Inventory (Dec. 31)		22,800	
	Manufacturing Summary			48,000
	(To record ending raw materials and work in process inventories)			
31	**Manufacturing Summary**		418,000	
	Work in Process Inventory (Jan. 1)			18,400
	Raw Materials Inventory (Jan. 1)			16,700
	Raw Materials Purchases			152,500
	Direct Labor			175,600
	Indirect Labor			14,300
	Factory Repairs			12,600
	Factory Utilities			10,100
	Factory Depreciation			9,440
	Factory Insurance			8,360
	(To close beginning raw materials and work in process inventories and manufacturing cost accounts)			
31	Finished Goods Inventory (Dec. 31)		19,500	
	Sales		680,000	
	Income Summary			699,500
	(To record ending finished goods inventory and close sales account)			
31	Income Summary		622,100	
	Finished Goods Inventory (Jan. 1)			24,600
	Manufacturing Summary			**370,000**
	Selling Expenses			114,900
	Administrative Expenses			92,600
	Income Tax Expense			20,000
	(To close beginning finished goods inventory, manufacturing summary, and expense accounts)			
31	Income Summary		77,400	
	Retained Earnings			77,400
	(To close net income to retained earnings)			

After posting, the summary accounts will show the following.

Manufacturing Summary

Dec. 31	Close	418,000	Dec. 31	Close	48,000
			31	Close	370,000

Income Summary

Dec. 31	Close	622,100	Dec. 31	Close	699,500
31	Close	77,400			

Illustration 15A-3
Summary accounts for a manufacturing company, after posting

These data precisely track the closing entries. It also would be possible to post each account balance to the Manufacturing Summary account.

Summary of Study Objective for Appendix

8 *Prepare a work sheet and closing entries for a manufacturing company.* Two additional columns are needed in the work sheet for the cost of goods manufactured. In these columns, the beginning inventories of raw materials and work in process are entered as debits, and the ending inventories are entered as credits. All manufacturing costs are entered as debits. To close all of the accounts that appear in the cost of goods manufactured schedule, a Manufacturing Summary account is used.

Glossary

Activity-based costing (ABC) A method of allocating overhead based on each product's use of activities in making the product. (p. 753)

Cost of goods manufactured Total cost of work in process less the cost of the ending work in process inventory. (p. 746)

Direct labor The work of factory employees that can be physically and directly associated with converting raw materials into finished goods. (p. 743)

Direct materials Raw materials that can be physically and directly associated with manufacturing the finished product. (p. 743)

Enterprise resource planning (ERP) system Software that provides a comprehensive, centralized, integrated source of information used to manage all major business processes. (p. 752)

Indirect labor Work of factory employees that has no physical association with the finished product, or for which it is impractical to trace the costs to the goods produced. (p. 743)

Indirect materials Raw materials that do not physically become part of the finished product or cannot be traced because their physical association with the finished product is too small. (p. 743)

Just-in-time (JIT) inventory Inventory system in which goods are manufactured or purchased just in time for use. (p. 753)

Managerial accounting A field of accounting that provides economic and financial information for managers and other internal users. (p. 739)

Manufacturing overhead Manufacturing costs that are indirectly associated with the manufacture of the finished product. (p. 743)

Period costs Costs that are matched with the revenue of a specific time period and charged to expense as incurred. (p. 744)

Product costs Costs that are a necessary and integral part of producing the finished product. (p. 744)

Supply chain All activities from receipt of an order to delivery of a product or service. (p. 752)

Total cost of work in process Cost of the beginning work in process plus total manufacturing costs for the current period. (p. 746)

Total manufacturing costs The sum of direct materials, direct labor, and manufacturing overhead incurred in the current period. (p. 746)

Total quality management (TQM) Systems implemented to reduce defects in finished products with the goal of achieving zero defects. (p. 753)

Value chain All activities associated with providing a product or service. (p. 752)

Demonstration Problem

Superior Manufacturing Company has the following cost and expense data for the year ending December 31, 2005.

Raw materials, 1/1/05	$ 30,000	Insurance, factory	$ 14,000
Raw materials, 12/31/05	20,000	Property taxes, factory building	6,000
Raw materials purchased	205,000	Sales (net)	1,500,000
Indirect materials	15,000	Delivery expenses	100,000
Work in process, 1/1/05	80,000	Sales commissions	150,000
Work in process, 12/31/05	50,000	Indirect labor	90,000
Finished goods, 1/1/05	110,000	Factory machinery rent	40,000
Finished goods, 12/31/05	120,000	Factory utilities	65,000
Direct labor	350,000	Depreciation, factory building	24,000
Factory manager's salary	35,000	Administrative expenses	300,000

Instructions

(a) Prepare a cost of goods manufactured schedule for Superior Company for 2005.

(b) Prepare an income statement for Superior Company for 2005.

(c) Assume that Superior Company's ledgers show the balances of the following current asset accounts: Cash $17,000, Accounts Receivable (net) $120,000, Prepaid Expenses $13,000, and Short-term Investments $26,000. Prepare the current assets section of the balance sheet for Superior Company as of December 31, 2005.

Solution to Demonstration Problem

(a)

SUPERIOR MANUFACTURING COMPANY
Cost of Goods Manufactured Schedule
For the Year Ended December 31, 2005

Work in process, 1/1			$ 80,000
Direct materials			
Raw materials inventory, 1/1	$ 30,000		
Raw materials purchased	205,000		
Total raw materials available for use	235,000		
Less: Raw materials inventory, 12/31	20,000		
Direct materials used		$215,000	
Direct labor		350,000	
Manufacturing overhead			
Indirect labor	90,000		
Factory utilities	65,000		
Factory machinery rent	40,000		
Factory manager's salary	35,000		
Depreciation on factory building	24,000		
Indirect materials	15,000		
Insurance on factory building	14,000		
Property taxes—factory building	6,000		
Total manufacturing overhead		289,000	
Total manufacturing costs			854,000
Total cost of work in process			934,000
Less: Work in process, 12/31			50,000
Cost of goods manufactured			$884,000

Action Plan

- Start with beginning work in process as the first item in the cost of goods manufactured schedule.

- Sum direct materials used, direct labor, and total manufacturing overhead to determine total current manufacturing costs.

- Sum beginning work in process and total current manufacturing costs to determine total cost of work in process.

- Cost of goods manufactured is the total cost of work in process less ending work in process.

- In the cost of goods sold section of the income statement, show beginning and ending finished goods inventory and cost of goods manufactured.

- In the balance sheet, list manufacturing inventories in the order of their expected realization in cash, with finished goods first.

(b)

SUPERIOR MANUFACTURING COMPANY
Income Statement
For the Year Ended December 31, 2005

Sales (net)		$1,500,000
Cost of goods sold		
Finished goods inventory, January 1	$110,000	
Cost of goods manufactured	884,000	
Cost of goods available for sale	994,000	
Less: Finished goods inventory, December 31	120,000	
Cost of goods sold		874,000
Gross profit		626,000
Operating expenses		
Administrative expenses	300,000	
Sales commissions	150,000	
Delivery expenses	100,000	
Total operating expenses		550,000
Net income		$ 76,000

(c)

SUPERIOR MANUFACTURING COMPANY
Balance Sheet (partial)
December 31, 2005

Current assets		
Cash		$ 17,000
Short-term investments		26,000
Accounts receivable (net)		120,000
Inventories		
Finished goods	$120,000	
Work in process	50,000	
Raw materials	20,000	190,000
Prepaid expenses		13,000
Total current assets		$366,000

☑ THE NAVIGATOR

Note: All Questions, Exercises, and Problems marked with an asterisk relate to material in the appendix to the chapter.

Self-Study Questions

Self-Study/Self-Test

Answers are at the end of the chapter.

(SO 1) **1.** Managerial accounting:
   (a) is governed by generally accepted accounting principles.
   (b) places emphasis on special-purpose information.
   (c) pertains to the entity as a whole and is highly aggregated.
   (d) is limited to cost data.

(SO 1) **2.** Which of the following is *not* one of the categories in *Standards of Ethical Conduct for Management Accountants?*
   (a) Confidentiality.
   (b) Competence.
   (c) Integrity.
   (d) Independence.

(SO 2) **3.** The management of an organization performs several broad functions. They are:
   (a) planning, directing and motivating, and selling.
   (b) planning, directing and motivating, and controlling.
   (c) planning, manufacturing, and controlling.
   (d) directing and motivating, manufacturing, and controlling.

(SO 3) **4.** Direct materials are a:

	Product Cost	Manufacturing Overhead	Period Cost
(a)	Yes	Yes	No
(b)	Yes	No	No
(c)	Yes	Yes	Yes
(d)	No	No	No

(SO 4) **5.** Indirect labor is a:
   (a) nonmanufacturing cost.
   (b) raw material cost.
   (c) product cost.
   (d) period cost.

(SO 3) **6.** Which of the following costs would be included in manufacturing overhead of a computer manufacturer?
   (a) The cost of the $3\frac{1}{2}$-inch disk drives.
   (b) The wages earned by computer assemblers.
   (c) The cost of the memory chips.
   (d) Depreciation on testing equipment.

(SO 3) **7.** Which of the following is *not* an element of manufacturing overhead?
   (a) Sales manager's salary.
   (b) Plant manager's salary.
   (c) Factory repairman's wages.
   (d) Product inspector's salary.

(SO 5) **8.** For the year, Redder Company has cost of goods manufactured of $600,000, beginning finished goods inventory of $200,000, and ending finished goods inventory of $250,000. The cost of goods sold is:
   (a) $450,000.   (c) $550,000.
   (b) $500,000.   (d) $600,000.

(SO 6) **9.** A cost of goods manufactured schedule shows beginning and ending inventories for:
   (a) raw materials and work in process only.
   (b) work in process only.
   (c) raw materials only.
   (d) raw materials, work in process, and finished goods.

(SO 7) **10.** In a manufacturer's balance sheet, three inventories may be reported: (1) raw materials, (2) work in process, and (3) finished goods. Indicate in what sequence these inventories generally appear on a balance sheet.
   (a) (1), (2), (3)
   (b) (2), (3), (1)
   (c) (3), (1), (2)
   (d) (3), (2), (1)

☑ THE NAVIGATOR

Questions

1. (a) "Managerial accounting is a field of accounting that provides economic information for all interested parties." Do you agree? Explain.
   (b) Pat Gonzalez believes that managerial accounting serves only manufacturing firms. Is Pat correct? Explain.

2. Distinguish between managerial and financial accounting as to (a) primary users of reports, (b) types and frequency of reports, and (c) purpose of reports.

3. How does the content of reports and the verification of reports differ between managerial and financial accounting?

4. (a) Identify the four categories of ethical standards for management accountants.
   (b) Is the responsibility of the management accountant limited to only his or her own acts? Explain.

5. Karen Gish is studying for the next accounting midterm examination. Summarize for Karen what she should know about management functions.

6. "Decision making is management's most important function." Do you agree? Why or why not?

7. Sue Sablow is studying for her next accounting examination. Explain to Sue what she should know about the differences between the income statements for a manufacturing and for a merchandising company.

8. Bob Jackson is unclear as to the difference between the balance sheets of a merchandising company and a manufacturing company. Explain the difference to Bob.

9. How are manufacturing costs classified?

10. Gene Toni claims that the distinction between direct and indirect materials is based entirely on physical association with the product. Is Gene correct? Why?

11. Jane Diaz is confused about the differences between a product cost and a period cost. Explain the differences to Jane.

12. Identify the differences in the cost of goods sold section of an income statement between a merchandising company and a manufacturing company.

13. The determination of the cost of goods manufactured involves the following factors: (A) beginning work in process inventory, (B) total manufacturing costs, and (C) ending work in process inventory. Identify the meaning of x in the following formulas:
    (a) $A + B = x$
    (b) $A + B - C = x$

14. Sajjad Manufacturing has beginning raw materials inventory $12,000, ending raw materials inventory $18,000, and raw materials purchases $180,000. What is the cost of direct materials used?

15. Jam Manufacturing Inc. has beginning work in process $27,200, direct materials used $240,000, direct labor $200,000, total manufacturing overhead $150,000, and ending work in process $32,000. What are total manufacturing costs?

16. Using the data in Q15, what are (a) the total cost of work in process and (b) the cost of goods manufactured?

17. In what order should manufacturing inventories be listed in a balance sheet?

*18. How, if at all, does the accounting cycle differ between a manufacturing company and a merchandising company?

*19. What typical account balances are carried into the cost of goods manufactured columns of the manufacturing work sheet?

*20. Prepare the closing entries for (a) ending work in process and raw materials inventories and (b) manufacturing summary. Use XXXs for amounts.

Brief Exercises

BE15-1 Complete the following comparison table between managerial and financial accounting.

Distinguish between managerial and financial accounting.
(SO 1)

	Financial Accounting	**Managerial Accounting**
Primary users		
Type of reports		
Frequency of reports		
Purpose of reports		
Content of reports		
Verification		

BE15-2 The Institute of Management Accountants has promulgated ethical standards for managerial accountants. Identify the four specific standards.

Identify ethical standards.
(SO 1)

BE15-3 Listed below are the three functions of the management of an organization.
   1. Planning   2. Directing and motivating   3. Controlling

Identify the three management functions.
(SO 2)

Identify which of the following statements best describes each of the above functions.

(a) _____ require(s) management to look ahead and to establish objectives. A key objective of management is to add value to the business.

(b) _____ involve(s) coordinating the diverse activities and human resources of a company to produce a smooth-running operation. This function relates to the implementation of planned objectives.

(c) _____ is the process of keeping the activities on track. Management must determine whether goals are being met and what changes are necessary when there are deviations.

Classify manufacturing costs.
(SO 3)

BE15-4 Determine whether each of the following costs should be classified as direct materials (DM), direct labor (DL), or manufacturing overhead (MO).

(a) _____ Frames and tires used in manufacturing bicycles.
(b) _____ Wages paid to production workers.
(c) _____ Insurance on factory equipment and machinery.
(d) _____ Depreciation on factory equipment.

Classify manufacturing costs.
(SO 3)

BE15-5 Indicate whether each of the following costs of an automobile manufacturer would be classified as direct materials, direct labor, or manufacturing overhead.

(a) _____ Windshield.   **(e)** _____ Factory machinery lubricants.
(b) _____ Engine.   **(f)** _____ Tires.
(c) _____ Wages of assembly line worker.   **(g)** _____ Steering wheel.
(d) _____ Depreciation of factory machinery. **(h)** _____ Salary of painting supervisor.

Identify product and period costs.
(SO 4)

BE15-6 Identify whether each of the following costs should be classified as product costs or period costs.

(a) _____ Manufacturing overhead.   **(d)** _____ Advertising expenses.
(b) _____ Selling expenses.   **(e)** _____ Direct labor.
(c) _____ Administrative expenses. **(f)** _____ Direct material.

Classify manufacturing costs.
(SO 3, 4)

BE15-7 Presented below are Hyde Company's monthly manufacturing cost data related to its personal computer products.

(a) Utilities for manufacturing equipment $116,000
(b) Raw materials (CPU, chips, etc.) $ 85,000
(c) Depreciation on manufacturing building $880,000
(d) Wages for production workers $191,000

Enter each cost item in the following table, placing an "X" under the appropriate headings.

| | Product Costs | | |
	Direct Materials	Direct Labor	Factory Overhead
(a)			
(b)			
(c)			
(d)			

Compute total manufacturing costs and total cost of work in process.
(SO 6)

BE15-8 Buslik Manufacturing Company has the following data: direct labor $242,000, direct materials used $180,000, total manufacturing overhead $208,000, and beginning work in process $25,000. Compute (a) total manufacturing costs and (b) total cost of work in process.

Prepare current assets section.
(SO 7)

BE15-9 In alphabetical order below are current asset items for Ivy Company's balance sheet at December 31, 2005. Prepare the current assets section (including a complete heading).

Accounts receivable	$200,000
Cash	62,000
Finished goods	75,000
Prepaid expenses	38,000
Raw materials	68,000
Work in process	87,000

BE15-10 Presented below are incomplete 2005 manufacturing cost data for Hyun Corporation. Determine the missing amounts.

Determine missing amounts in computing total manufacturing costs.
(SO 6)

	Direct Materials Used	Direct Labor Used	Factory Overhead	Total Manufacturing Costs
(a)	$35,000	$61,000	$ 50,000	?
(b)	?	$75,000	$120,000	$296,000
(c)	$55,000	?	$111,000	$300,000

BE15-11 Use the same data from BE15-10 above and the data below. Determine the missing amounts.

Determine missing amounts in computing cost of goods manufactured.
(SO 6)

	Total Manufacturing Costs	Work in Process (1/1)	Work in Process (12/31)	Cost of Goods Manufactured
(a)	?	$120,000	$86,000	?
(b)	$296,000	?	$98,000	$321,000
(c)	$300,000	$463,000	?	$715,000

***BE15-12** A work sheet is used in preparing financial statements for Lawney Manufacturing Company. The following accounts are included in the adjusted trial balance: Finished Goods Inventory $28,000, Work in Process Inventory $21,600, Raw Materials Purchases $175,000, and Direct Labor $140,000. Indicate the work sheet column(s) to which each account should be extended.

Identify work sheet columns for selected accounts.
(SO 8)

Exercises

E15-1 Presented below is a list of costs and expenses usually incurred by Iguana Corporation, a manufacturer of furniture, in its factory.

1. Salaries for assembly line inspectors.
2. Insurance on factory machines.
3. Property taxes on the factory building.
4. Factory repairs.
5. Upholstery used in manufacturing furniture.
6. Wages paid to assembly line workers.
7. Factory machinery depreciation.
8. Glue, nails, paint, and other small parts used in production.
9. Factory supervisors' salaries.
10. Wood used in manufacturing furniture.

Classify costs into three classes of manufacturing costs.
(SO 3)

Instructions
Classify the above items into the following categories: (a) direct materials, (b) direct labor, and (c) manufacturing overhead.

E15-2 Honmura Company reports the following costs and expenses in May.

Determine the total amount of various types of costs.
(SO 3, 4)

Factory utilities	$ 8,500	Direct labor	$69,100
Depreciation on factory equipment	12,650	Sales salaries	49,400
Depreciation on delivery trucks	3,500	Property taxes on factory building	2,500
Indirect factory labor	48,900	Repairs to office equipment	1,300
Indirect materials	89,800	Factory repairs	2,000
Direct materials used	137,600	Advertising	18,000
Factory manager's salary	8,000	Office supplies used	2,640

Instructions
From the information, determine the total amount of:
(a) Manufacturing overhead.
(b) Product costs.
(c) Period costs.

E15-3 Karpman Company is a manufacturer of personal computers. Various costs and expenses associated with its operations are as follows.

1. Property taxes on the factory building.
2. Production superintendents' salaries.
3. Memory boards and chips used in assembling computers.
4. Depreciation on the factory equipment.
5. Salaries for assembly line quality control inspectors.
6. Sales commissions paid to sell personal computers.
7. Electrical wiring in assembling computers.
8. Wages of workers assembling personal computers.
9. Soldering materials used on factory assembly lines.
10. Salaries for the night security guards for the factory building.

The company intends to classify these costs and expenses into the following categories: (a) direct materials, (b) direct labor, (c) manufacturing overhead, and (d) period costs.

Instructions
List the items (1)–(10). For each item, indicate the cost category to which the item belongs.

E15-4 The cost of goods manufactured schedule shows each of the cost elements. Complete the following schedule for Salazar Manufacturing Company.

SALAZAR MANUFACTURING COMPANY
Cost of Goods Manufactured Schedule
For the Year Ended December 31, 2005

Work in process (1/1)		$200,000
Direct materials		
Raw materials inventory (1/1)	$?	
Add: Raw materials purchases	158,000	
Less: Raw materials inventory (12/31)	7,500	
Direct materials used		$190,000
Direct labor		?
Manufacturing overhead		
Indirect labor	$ 18,000	
Factory depreciation	36,000	
Factory utilities	68,000	
Total overhead		122,000
Total manufacturing costs		?
Total cost of work in process		?
Less: Work in process (12/31)		81,000
Cost of goods manufactured		$560,000

E15-5 Manufacturing cost data for Hermes Company are presented below.

	Case A	Case B	Case C
Direct materials used	(a)	$68,400	$130,000
Direct labor	$ 57,000	86,000	(g)
Manufacturing overhead	42,500	81,600	102,000
Total manufacturing costs	180,650	(d)	253,700
Work in process 1/1/05	(b)	16,500	(h)
Total cost of work in process	221,500	(e)	327,000
Work in process 12/31/05	(c)	9,000	70,000
Cost of goods manufactured	185,275	(f)	(i)

Instructions
Indicate the missing amount for each letter (a) through (i).

E15-6 Incomplete manufacturing cost data for Hollis Company for 2005 are presented in the table below.

Determine the missing amount of different cost items, and prepare a condensed cost of goods manufactured schedule.
(SO 5, 6)

Instructions
(a) Indicate the missing amount for each letter in the table below.
(b) Prepare a condensed cost of goods manufactured schedule for situation (1) for the year ended December 31, 2005.

	Direct Materials Used	Direct Labor Used	Manufacturing Overhead	Total Manufacturing Costs	Work in Process 1/1	Work in Process 12/31	Cost of Goods Manufactured
(1)	$117,000	$140,000	$ 77,000	(a)	$30,000	(b)	$360,000
(2)	(c)	200,000	132,000	$440,000	(d)	$40,000	470,000
(3)	80,000	100,000	(e)	255,000	60,000	80,000	(f)
(4)	70,000	(g)	75,000	294,000	45,000	(h)	270,000

E15-7 Issey Corporation has the following cost records for June 2005.

Prepare a cost of goods manufactured schedule and a partial income statement.
(SO 5, 6)

Indirect factory labor	$ 4,500	Factory utilities	$ 400
Direct materials used	20,000	Depreciation, factory equipment	1,400
Work in process, 6/1/05	3,000	Direct labor	25,000
Work in process, 6/30/05	3,500	Maintenance, factory equipment	1,300
Finished goods, 6/1/05	5,000	Indirect materials	2,200
Finished goods, 6/30/05	7,500	Factory manager's salary	3,000

Instructions
(a) Prepare a cost of goods manufactured schedule for June 2005.
(b) Prepare an income statement through gross profit for June 2005 assuming net sales are $97,100.

E15-8 Hippo Manufacturing Company produces blankets. From its accounting records it prepares the following schedule and financial statements on a yearly basis.
(a) Cost of goods manufactured schedule.
(b) Income statement.
(c) Balance sheet.

Indicate in which schedule or financial statement(s) different cost items will appear.
(SO 5, 6, 7)

The following items are found in its ledger and accompanying data.

1. Direct labor
2. Raw materials inventory, 1/1
3. Work in process inventory, 12/31
4. Finished goods inventory, 1/1
5. Indirect labor
6. Depreciation on factory machinery
7. Work in process, 1/1
8. Finished goods inventory, 12/31
9. Factory maintenance salaries
10. Cost of goods manufactured
11. Depreciation on delivery equipment
12. Cost of goods available for sale
13. Direct materials used
14. Heat and electricity for factory
15. Repairs to roof of factory building
16. Cost of raw materials purchases

Instructions
List the items (1)–(16). For each item, indicate by using the appropriate letter or letters, the schedule and/or financial statement(s) in which the item will appear.

E15-9 An analysis of the accounts of Lanier Manufacturing reveals the following manufacturing cost data for the month ended June 30, 2005.

Prepare a cost of goods manufactured schedule, and present the ending inventories of the balance sheet.
(SO 5, 6, 7)

Inventories	Beginning	Ending
Raw materials	$9,000	$11,100
Work in process	5,000	8,000
Finished goods	8,000	6,000

Costs incurred:

Raw materials purchases $64,000, direct labor $50,000, manufacturing overhead $19,900. The specific overhead costs were: indirect labor $5,500, factory insurance $4,000, machinery depreciation $4,000, machinery repairs $1,800, factory utilities $3,100, miscellaneous factory costs $1,500.

Instructions

(a) Prepare the cost of goods manufactured schedule for the month ended June 30, 2005.

(b) Show the presentation of the ending inventories on the June 30, 2005, balance sheet.

Determine the amount of cost to appear in various accounts, and indicate in which financial statements these accounts would appear.
(SO 5, 6, 7)

E15-10 Jazz Motor Company manufactures automobiles. During September 2005 the company purchased 5,000 head lamps at a cost of $9 per lamp. Jazz withdrew 4,650 lamps from the warehouse during the month. Fifty of these lamps were used to replace the head lamps in autos used by traveling sales staff. The remaining 4,600 lamps were put in autos manufactured during the month.

Of the autos put into production during September 2005, 90% were completed and transferred to the company's storage lot. Of the cars completed during the month, 70% were sold by September 30.

Instructions

(a) Determine the cost of head lamps that would appear in each of the following accounts at September 30, 2005: Raw Materials, Work in Process, Finished Goods, Cost of Goods Sold, and Selling Expenses.

(b) ▭▤▤▷ Write a short memo to the chief accountant, indicating whether and where each of the accounts in (a) would appear on the income statement or on the balance sheet at September 30, 2005.

Prepare a partial work sheet for a manufacturing firm.
(SO 8)

***E15-11** Data for Lanier Manufacturing are presented in Exercise 15-9.

Instructions

Prepare a partial work sheet for Lanier Manufacturing.

Problems: Set A

Classify manufacturing costs into different categories and compute the unit cost.
(SO 3, 4)

P15-1A Snapper Company specializes in manufacturing a unique model of bicycle helmet. The model is well accepted by consumers, and the company has enough orders to keep the factory production at 10,000 helmets per month (80% of its full capacity). Snapper's monthly manufacturing cost and other expense data are as follows.

Rent on factory equipment	$ 6,000
Insurance on factory building	1,500
Raw materials (plastics, polystyrene, etc.)	70,000
Utility costs for factory	900
Supplies for general office	300
Wages for assembly line workers	46,000
Depreciation on office equipment	800
Miscellaneous materials (lubricants, solders, etc.)	1,100
Factory manager's salary	5,700
Property taxes on factory building	400
Advertising for helmets	11,000
Sales commissions	7,000
Depreciation on factory building	1,500

Instructions

(a) Prepare an answer sheet with the following column headings.

(a) Manufacturing
overhead $17,000

	Product Costs			
Cost Item	**Direct Materials**	**Direct Labor**	**Manufacturing Overhead**	**Period Costs**

Enter each cost item on your answer sheet, placing the dollar amount under the appropriate headings. Total the dollar amounts in each of the columns.

(b) Compute the cost to produce one helmet

P15-2A Galex Company, a manufacturer of stereo systems, started its production in October 2005. For the preceding 3 years Galex had been a retailer of stereo systems. After a thorough survey of stereo system markets, Galex decided to turn its retail store into a stereo equipment factory.

Raw materials cost for a stereo system will total $70 per unit. Workers on the production lines are on average paid $10 per hour. A stereo system usually takes 5 hours to complete. In addition, the rent on the equipment used to assemble stereo systems amounts to $4,500 per month. Indirect materials cost $5 per system. A supervisor was hired to oversee production; her monthly salary is $2,700.

Janitorial costs for the factory were $1,300 monthly. Advertising costs for the stereo system will be $8,500 per month. The factory building depreciation expense is $7,200 per year. Property taxes on the factory building will be $6,000 per year.

Classify manufacturing costs into different categories and compute the unit cost.
(SO 3, 4)

Instructions
(a) Prepare an answer sheet with the following column headings.

(a) Manufacturing
overhead $16,100

		Product Costs		
Cost Item	Direct Materials	Direct Labor	Manufacturing Overhead	Period Costs

Assuming that Galex manufactures, on average, 1,300 stereo systems per month, enter each cost item on your answer sheet, placing the dollar amount per month under the appropriate headings. Total the dollar amounts in each of the columns.

(b) Compute the cost to produce one stereo system.

P15-3A Incomplete manufacturing costs, expenses, and selling data for two different cases are as follows.

Indicate the missing amount of different cost items, and prepare a condensed cost of goods manufactured schedule, an income statement, and a partial balance sheet.
(SO 5, 6, 7)

	Case	
	1	2
Direct Materials Used	$ 7,600	$ (g)
Direct Labor	6,000	8,000
Manufacturing Overhead	5,000	4,000
Total Manufacturing Costs	(a)	19,000
Beginning Work in Process Inventory	1,000	(h)
Ending Work in Process Inventory	(b)	3,000
Sales	24,500	(i)
Sales Discounts	2,500	1,400
Cost of Goods Manufactured	16,000	22,000
Beginning Finished Goods Inventory	(c)	3,300
Goods Available for Sale	18,000	(j)
Cost of Goods Sold	(d)	(k)
Ending Finished Goods Inventory	3,400	2,500
Gross Profit	(e)	7,000
Operating Expenses	2,500	(l)
Net Income	(f)	3,000

Instructions
(a) Indicate the missing amount for each letter.
(b) Prepare a condensed cost of goods manufactured schedule for Case 1.
(c) Prepare an income statement and the current assets section of the balance sheet for Case 1. Assume that in Case 1 the other items in the current assets section are as follows: Cash $4,000, Receivables (net) $15,000, Raw Materials $600, and Prepaid Expenses $400.

(b) CGM $16,000
(c) Net income $ 4,900

Prepare a cost of goods manufactured schedule, a partial income statement, and a partial balance sheet.
(SO 5, 6, 7)

P15-4A The data shown on page 770 were taken from the records of Gamma Manufacturing Company for the fiscal year ended June 30, 2005.

Raw Materials			Factory Insurance	$ 4,600
Inventory 7/1/04	$ 48,000		Factory Machinery	
Raw Materials			Depreciation	15,000
Inventory 6/30/05	39,600		Freight-in on Raw Materials	
Finished Goods			Purchased	8,600
Inventory 7/1/04	96,000		Factory Utilities	24,600
Finished Goods			Office Utilities Expense	8,650
Inventory 6/30/05	95,900		Sales	547,000
Work in Process			Sales Discounts	4,200
Inventory 7/1/04	19,800		Plant Manager's Salary	29,000
Work in Process			Factory Property Taxes	9,600
Inventory 6/30/05	17,600		Factory Repairs	1,400
Direct Labor	147,250		Raw Materials Purchases	89,800
Indirect Labor	24,460		Cash	32,000
Accounts Receivable	27,000			

Instructions

(a) CGM $364,910
(b) Gross profit $177,790
(c) Current assets $212,100

(a) Prepare a cost of goods manufactured schedule.
(b) Prepare an income statement through gross profit.
(c) Prepare the current assets section of the balance sheet at June 30, 2005.

Prepare a cost of goods manufactured schedule and a correct income statement. (SO 5, 6)

P15-5A Istanbul Company is a manufacturer of computers. Its controller resigned in October 2005. An inexperienced assistant accountant has prepared the following income statement for the month of October 2005.

ISTANBUL COMPANY
Income Statement
For the Month Ended October 31, 2005

Sales (net)		$780,000
Less: Operating expenses		
Raw materials purchased	$260,000	
Direct labor cost	190,000	
prd Advertising expense	92,000	
Selling and administrative salaries	75,000	
product Rent on factory facilities	60,000	
Depreciation on sales equipment	45,000	
Depreciation on factory equipment	35,000	
Indirect labor cost	25,000	
Utilities expense	12,000	
Insurance expense	8,000	802,000
Net loss		$ (22,000)

Prior to October 2005 the company had been profitable every month. The company's president is concerned about the accuracy of the income statement. As his friend, you have been asked to review the income statement and make necessary corrections. After examining other manufacturing cost data, you have acquired additional information as follows.

1. Inventory balances at the beginning and end of October were:

	October 1	October 31
Raw materials	$18,000	$31,000
Work in process	16,000	14,000
Finished goods	30,000	48,000

2. Only 70% of the utilities expense and 60% of the insurance expense apply to factory operations. The remaining amounts should be charged to selling and administrative activities.

Instructions
(a) Prepare a schedule of cost of goods manufactured for October 2005.
(b) Prepare a correct income statement for October 2005.

(a) CGM $572,200
(b) Net income $ 7,000

*P15-6A Everheart Manufacturing Company uses a simple manufacturing accounting system. At the end of its fiscal year on August 31, 2005, the adjusted trial balance contains the following accounts.

Complete a work sheet; prepare a cost of goods manufactured schedule, an income statement, and a balance sheet; journalize and post the closing entries.
(SO 8)

Debits		Credits	
Cash	$ 16,700	Accumulated Depreciation	$ 353,000
Accounts Receivable (net)	62,900	Notes Payable	45,000
Finished Goods Inventory	56,000	Accounts Payable	38,200
Work in Process Inventory	27,800	Income Taxes Payable	9,000
Raw Materials Inventory	37,200	Common Stock	352,000
Plant Assets	890,000	Retained Earnings	205,300
Raw Materials Purchases	236,500	Sales	996,000
Direct Labor	280,900		$1,998,500
Indirect Labor	27,400		
Factory Repairs	17,200		
Factory Depreciation	19,000		
Factory Manager's Salary	40,000		
Factory Insurance	11,000		
Factory Property Taxes	12,900		
Factory Utilities	13,300		
Selling Expenses	98,500		
Administrative Expenses	115,200		
Income Tax Expense	36,000		
	$1,998,500		

Physical inventory accounts on August 31, 2005, show the following inventory amounts: Finished Goods $54,600, Work in Process $23,400, and Raw Materials $46,500.

Instructions
(a) Enter the adjusted trial balance data on a work sheet in financial statement order and complete the work sheet.
(b) Prepare a cost of goods manufactured schedule for the year.
(c) Prepare an income statement for the year and a balance sheet at August 31, 2005.
(d) Journalize the closing entries.
(e) Post the closing entries to Manufacturing Summary and to Income Summary.

(a) CGM $653,300
(b) Net income $ 91,600

Problems: Set B

P15-1B Kanjo Company specializes in manufacturing motorcycles. The company has enough orders to keep the factory production at 1,000 motorcycles per month. Kanjo's monthly manufacturing cost and other expense data are as follows.

Classify manufacturing costs into different categories and compute the unit cost.
(SO 3, 4)

Maintenance costs on factory building	$ 300
Factory manager's salary	5,000
Advertising for motorcycles	10,000
Sales commissions	5,000
Depreciation on factory building	700
Rent on factory equipment	5,000
Insurance on factory building	3,000
Raw materials (frames, tires, etc.)	20,000
Utility costs for factory	800
Supplies for general office	200
Wages for assembly line workers	40,000
Depreciation on office equipment	500
Miscellaneous materials (lubricants, solders, etc.)	1,000

(a) Manufacturing
 overhead $15,800

Instructions

(a) Prepare an answer sheet with the following column headings.

| | Product Costs | | | |
Cost Item	Direct Materials	Direct Labor	Manufacturing Overhead	Period Costs

Enter each cost item on your answer sheet, placing the dollar amount under the appropriate headings. Total the dollar amounts in each of the columns.

(b) Compute the cost to produce one motorcycle.

Classify manufacturing costs into different categories and compute the unit cost.
(SO 3, 4)

P15-2B Match Company, a manufacturer of tennis rackets, started production in November 2002. For the preceding 5 years Match had been a retailer of sports equipment. After a thorough survey of tennis racket markets, Match decided to turn its retail store into a tennis racket factory.

Raw materials cost for a tennis racket will total $20 per racket. Workers on the production lines are paid on average $13 per hour. A racket usually takes 2 hours to complete. In addition, the rent on the equipment used to produce rackets amounts to $1,000 per month. Indirect materials cost $3 per racket. A supervisor was hired to oversee production; her monthly salary is $3,500.

Janitorial costs for the factory are $1,200 monthly. Advertising costs for the rackets will be $6,000 per month. The factory building depreciation expense is $8,400 per year. Property taxes on the factory building will be $4,320 per year.

Instructions

(a) Manufacturing
 overhead $12,760

(a) Prepare an answer sheet with the following column headings.

| | Product Costs | | | |
Cost Item	Direct Materials	Direct Labor	Manufacturing Overhead	Period Costs

Assuming that Match manufactures, on average, 2,000 tennis rackets per month, enter each cost item on your answer sheet, placing the dollar amount per month under the appropriate headings. Total the dollar amounts in each of the columns.

(b) Compute the cost to produce one racket.

Indicate the missing amount of different cost items, and prepare a condensed cost of goods manufactured schedule, an income statement, and a partial balance sheet.
(SO 5, 6, 7)

P15-3B Incomplete manufacturing costs, expenses, and selling data for two different cases are as follows.

| | Case | |
	1	2
Direct Materials Used	$ 8,300	$ (g)
Direct Labor	3,000	4,000
Manufacturing Overhead	4,000	5,000
Total Manufacturing Costs	(a)	22,000
Beginning Work in Process Inventory	1,000	(h)
Ending Work in Process Inventory	(b)	2,000
Sales	21,500	(i)
Sales Discounts	1,500	1,200
Cost of Goods Manufactured	12,800	21,000
Beginning Finished Goods Inventory	(c)	4,000
Goods Available for Sale	17,300	(j)
Cost of Goods Sold	(d)	(k)
Ending Finished Goods Inventory	1,200	2,500
Gross Profit	(e)	6,000
Operating Expenses	2,700	(l)
Net Income	(f)	2,800

Instructions

(a) Indicate the missing amount for each letter.

(b) CGM $12,800

(b) Prepare a condensed cost of goods manufactured schedule for Case 1.

(c) Prepare an income statement and the current assets section of the balance sheet for Case 1. Assume that in Case 1 the other items in the current assets section are as follows: Cash $3,000, Receivables (net) $10,000, Raw Materials $700, and Prepaid Expenses $200.

(c) Net income $1,200

P15-4B The following data were taken from the records of Mauro Manufacturing Company for the year ended December 31, 2005.

Prepare a cost of goods manufactured schedule, a partial income statement, and a partial balance sheet.
(SO 5, 6, 7)

Raw Materials		Factory Insurance	$ 5,400
Inventory 1/1/05	$ 45,000	Factory Machinery	
Raw Materials		Depreciation	7,700
Inventory 12/31/05	44,200	Freight-in on Raw Materials	
Finished Goods		Purchased	3,900
Inventory 1/1/05	85,000	Factory Utilities	15,900
Finished Goods		Office Utilities Expense	8,600
Inventory 12/31/05	77,800	Sales	475,000
Work in Process		Sales Discounts	3,500
Inventory 1/1/05	9,500	Plant Manager's Salary	30,000
Work in Process		Factory Property Taxes	6,100
Inventory 12/31/05	8,000	Factory Repairs	800
Direct Labor	145,100	Raw Materials Purchases	64,600
Indirect Labor	19,100	Cash	28,000
Accounts Receivable	27,000		

Instructions
(a) Prepare a cost of goods manufactured schedule.
(b) Prepare an income statement through gross profit.
(c) Prepare the current assets section of the balance sheet at December 31.

(a) CGM $300,900
(b) Gross profit $163,400
(c) Current assets $185,000

P15-5B Chelsea Company is a manufacturer of toys. Its controller, Marie Klinger, resigned in August 2005. An inexperienced assistant accountant has prepared the following income statement for the month of August 2005.

Prepare a cost of goods manufactured schedule and a correct income statement.
(SO 5, 6)

CHELSEA COMPANY
Income Statement
For the Month Ended August 31, 2005

Sales (net)		$670,000
Less: Operating expenses		
Raw materials purchased	$200,000	
Direct labor cost	150,000	
Advertising expense	75,000	
Selling and administrative salaries	70,000	
Rent on factory facilities	60,000	
Depreciation on sales equipment	55,000	
Depreciation on factory equipment	35,000	
Indirect labor cost	20,000	
Utilities expense	10,000	
Insurance expense	5,000	680,000
Net loss		$(10,000)

Prior to August 2005 the company had been profitable every month. The company's president is concerned about the accuracy of the income statement. As her friend, you have been asked to review the income statement and make necessary corrections. After examining other manufacturing cost data, you have acquired additional information as follows.

1. Inventory balances at the beginning and end of August were:

	August 1	August 31
Raw materials	$19,500	$33,000
Work in process	25,000	21,000
Finished goods	40,000	62,000

2. Only 60% of the utilities expense and 70% of the insurance expense apply to factory operations; the remaining amounts should be charged to selling and administrative activities.

Instructions

(a) CGM $465,000
(b) Net income $ 21,500

(a) Prepare a cost of goods manufactured schedule for August 2005.
(b) Prepare a correct income statement for August 2005.

▶ BROADENING YOUR PERSPECTIVE

Group Decision Case

BYP15-1 Intermix Manufacturing Company specializes in producing fashion outfits. On July 31, 2005, a tornado touched down at its factory and general office. The inventories in the warehouse and the factory were completely destroyed as was the general office nearby. Next morning, through a careful search of the disaster site, however, Ed Loder, the company's controller, and Susan Manning, the cost accountant, were able to recover a small part of manufacturing cost data for the current month.

"What a horrible experience," sighed Ed. "And the worst part is that we may not have enough records to use in filing an insurance claim."

"It was terrible," replied Susan. "However, I managed to recover some of the manufacturing cost data that I was working on yesterday afternoon. The data indicate that our direct labor cost in July totaled $250,000 and that we had purchased $345,000 of raw materials. Also, I recall that the amount of raw materials used for July was $350,000. But I'm not sure this information will help. The rest of our records are blown away."

"Well, not exactly," said Ed. "I was working on the year-to-date income statement when the tornado warning was announced. My recollection is that our sales in July were $1,250,000 and our gross profit ratio has been 40% of sales. Also, I can remember that our cost of goods available for sale was $790,000 for July."

"Maybe we can work something out from this information!" exclaimed Susan. "My experience tells me that our manufacturing overhead is usually 60% of direct labor."

"Hey, look what I just found," cried Susan. "It's a copy of this June's balance sheet, and it shows that our inventories as of June 30 are Finished goods $36,000, Work in process $22,000, and Raw materials $19,000."

"Super," yelled Ed. "Let's go work something out."

In order to file an insurance claim Intermix Company must determine the amount of its inventories as of July 31, 2005, the date of the tornado touchdown.

Instructions

With the class divided into groups, determine the amount of cost in the Raw Materials, Work in Process, and Finished Goods inventory accounts as of the date of the tornado touchdown.

Managerial Analysis

BYP15-2 Tennis, Anyone? is a fairly large manufacturing company located in the southern United States. The company manufactures tennis rackets, tennis balls, tennis clothing, and tennis shoes, all bearing the company's distinctive logo, a large green question mark on a white flocked tennis ball. The company's sales have been increasing over the past 10 years.

The tennis racket division has recently implemented several advanced manufacturing techniques. Robot arms hold the tennis rackets in place while glue dries, and machine vision systems check for defects. The engineering and design team uses computerized drafting and testing of new products. The following managers work in the tennis racket division.

Wayne Gryer, Sales Manager (supervises all sales representatives)
Tommye Stevens, technical specialist (supervises computer programmers)
Martie Lefever, cost accounting manager (supervises cost accountants)

Jack Marler, production supervisor (supervises all manufacturing employees)
Tina Roy, engineer (supervises all new-product design teams)

Instructions
  (a) What are the primary information needs of each manager?
  (b) Which, if any, financial accounting report(s) is each likely to use?
  (c) Name one special-purpose management accounting report that could be designed
      for each manager. Include the name of the report, the information it would contain,
      and how frequently it should be issued.

Real-World Focus

BYP15-3 **Anchor Glass Container Corporation**, the third largest manufacturer of glass
containers in the U.S., supplies beverage and food producers and consumer products
manufacturers nationwide. Parent company **Consumers Packaging Inc.** *(Toronto Stock
Exchange:* CGC) is a leading international designer and manufacturer of glass containers.
    The following management discussion appeared in a recent annual report of Anchor
Glass.

ANCHOR GLASS CONTAINER CORPORATION
Management Discussion

Cost of Products Sold Cost of products sold as a percentage of net sales was 89.3%
in the current year compared to 87.6% in the prior year. The increase in cost of
products sold as a percentage of net sales principally reflected the impact of operational problems during the second quarter of the current year at a major furnace at
one of the Company's plants, higher downtime, and costs and expenses associated
with an increased number of scheduled capital improvement projects, increases in
labor, and certain other manufacturing costs (with no corresponding selling price
increases in the current year). Reduced fixed costs from the closing of the Streator,
Illinois, plant in June of the current year and productivity and efficiency gains partially offset these cost increases.

Instructions
What factors affect the costs of products sold at Anchor Glass Container Corporation?

Exploring the Web

BYP15-4 **The Institute of Management Accountants (IMA)** is the largest organization
of its kind in the world, dedicated to excellence in the practice of management accounting
and financial management.

Address: **www.imanet.org** (or go to **www.wiley.com/college/kimmel**)

Instructions
At the IMA's home page, locate the answers to the following questions.
  (a) How many members does the IMA have, and what are their job titles?
  (b) What are some of the benefits of joining the IMA as a student?
  (c) Use the chapter locator function to locate the IMA chapter nearest you, and find
      the name of the chapter president.

Communication Activity

BYP15-5 Refer to Problem 15-5B and add the following requirement.
    Prepare a letter to the president of the company, Ruth Chelsea, describing the changes
you made. Explain clearly why net income is different after the changes. Keep the following points in mind as you compose your letter.

1. This is a letter to the president of a company, who is your friend. The style should be generally formal, but you may relax some requirements. For example, you may call the president by her first name.
2. Executives are very busy. Your letter should tell the president your main results first (for example, the amount of net income).
3. You should include brief explanations so that the president can understand the changes you made in the calculations.

Research Assignment

BYP15-6   The December 1995 issue of *Management Accounting* includes an article by William L. Ferrara entitled "Cost/Management Accounting: The 21st Century Paradigm." The article contains a historical perspective on management accounting as well as a prediction of the future.

Instructions
Read the article and answer the following questions.
   (a) What are the four eras into which management accounting is divided? (Identify the dates of each era. These are labeled paradigm A, B, C, and D in the article.)
   (b) What is the costing/pricing formula shown in Table 1 for paradigm (model) D, the fourth era?
   (c) What are the three "provocative new issues" created by the future model of management accounting (paradigm D)?

Ethics Case

BYP15-7   Carlos Morales, controller for Tredway Industries, was reviewing production cost reports for the year. One amount in these reports continued to bother him—advertising. During the year, the company had instituted an expensive advertising campaign to sell some of its slower-moving products. It was still too early to tell whether the advertising campaign was successful.

There had been much internal debate as how to report advertising cost. The vice president of finance argued that advertising costs should be reported as a cost of production, just like direct materials and direct labor. He therefore recommended that this cost be identified as manufacturing overhead and reported as part of inventory costs until sold. Others disagreed. Morales believed that this cost should be reported as an expense of the current period, based on the conservatism principle. Others argued that it should be reported as Prepaid Advertising and reported as a current asset.

The president finally had to decide the issue. He argued that these costs should be reported as inventory. His arguments were practical ones. He noted that the company was experiencing financial difficulty and expensing this amount in the current period might jeopardize a planned bond offering. Also, by reporting the advertising costs as inventory rather than as prepaid advertising, less attention would be directed to it by the financial community.

Instructions
   (a) Who are the stakeholders in this situation?
   (b) What are the ethical issues involved in this situation?
   (c) What would you do if you were Carlos Morales?

Answers to Self-Study Questions
   1. b   2. d   3. b   4. b   5. c   6. d   7. a   8. c   9. a   10. d

 Remember to go back to the Navigator box on the chapter-opening page and check off your completed work.

Job Order Cost Accounting

STUDY OBJECTIVES

After studying this chapter,
you should be able to:

1 Explain the characteristics and purposes of cost accounting.

2 Describe the flow of costs in a job order cost accounting system.

3 Explain the nature and importance of a job cost sheet.

4 Indicate how the predetermined overhead rate is determined and used.

5 Prepare entries for jobs completed and sold.

6 Distinguish between under- and over-applied manufacturing overhead.

 THE NAVIGATOR

THE NAVIGATOR ✔

▶ Scan *Study Objectives* ☐

▶ Read *Feature Story* ☐

▶ Read *Preview* ☐

▶ Read text and answer *Before You Go On*
  p. 781 ☐   p. 792 ☐   p. 798 ☐

▶ Work Using the *Decision Toolkit* ☐

▶ Review Summary of *Study Objectives* ☐

▶ Work *Demonstration Problem* ☐

▶ Answer *Self-Study Questions* ☐

▶ Complete *Assignments* ☐

FEATURE STORY

"… And We'd Like It in Red"

Western States Fire Apparatus, Inc., of Cornelius, Oregon, is one of the few U.S. companies that makes fire trucks. The company builds about 25 trucks per year. Founded in 1941, the company is run by the children and grandchildren of the original founder.

"We buy the chassis, which is the cab and the frame," says Susan Scott, the company's bookkeeper. "In our computer, we set up an account into which all of the direct material that is purchased for that particular job is charged." Other direct materials include the water pump—which can cost $10,000—the lights, the siren, ladders, and hoses.

As for direct labor, the production workers fill out time tickets that tell what jobs they worked on. Usually, the company is building four trucks at any one time. On payday, the controller allocates the payroll to the appropriate job record.

Indirect materials, such as nuts and bolts, wiring, lubricants, and abrasives, are allocated to each job in proportion to direct material dollars. Other costs, such as insurance and supervisors' salaries, are allocated based on direct labor hours. "We need to allocate overhead in order to know what kind of price we have to charge when we submit our bids," she says.

Western gets orders through a "blind-bidding" process. That is, Western submits its bid without knowing the bid prices made by its competitors. "If we bid too low, we won't make a profit. If we bid too high, we don't get the job."

Regardless of the final price for the truck, the quality had better be first-rate. "The fire departments let you know if they don't like what you did, and you usually end up fixing it."

THE NAVIGATOR

The Feature Story about **Western States Fire Apparatus** described the manufacturing costs used in making a fire truck. It demonstrated that accurate costing is critical to the company's success. For example, in order to submit accurate bids on new jobs and to know whether it profited from past jobs, the company needs a good costing system. This chapter illustrates how these manufacturing costs would be assigned to specific jobs, such as the manufacture of individual fire trucks. We begin the discussion in this chapter with an overview of the flow of costs in a job order cost accounting system. We then use a case study to explain and illustrate the documents, entries, and accounts in this type of cost accounting system.

The content and organization of Chapter 16 are as follows.

JOB ORDER COST ACCOUNTING

Cost Accounting Systems	Job Order Cost Flow	Reporting Job Cost Data	Under- or Overapplied Manufacturing Overhead
• Job order cost system • Process cost system	• Accumulating manufacturing costs • Assigning manufacturing costs to work in process • Assigning costs to finished goods • Assigning costs to cost of goods sold • Summary		• Interim balances • Year-end balance

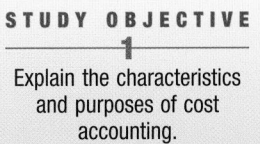
☑ THE NAVIGATOR

Cost Accounting Systems

Cost accounting involves the measuring, recording, and reporting of product costs. From the data accumulated, both the total cost and the unit cost of each product is determined. The accuracy of the product cost information produced by the cost accounting system is critical to the success of the company. As you will see in later chapters, this information is used to determine which products to produce, what price to charge, and the amounts to produce. Accurate product cost information is also vital for effective evaluation of employee performance.

A **cost accounting system** consists of accounts for the various manufacturing costs. These accounts are fully integrated into the general ledger of a company. **An important feature of a cost accounting system is the use of a perpetual inventory system.** Such a system **provides immediate, up-to-date information on the cost of a product**. There are two basic types of cost accounting systems: (1) a job order cost system and (2) a process cost system. Although cost accounting systems differ widely from company to company, most are based on one of these two traditional product costing systems.

STUDY OBJECTIVE
1
Explain the characteristics and purposes of cost accounting.

JOB ORDER COST SYSTEM

Under a **job order cost system**, costs are assigned to each **job** or to each **batch** of goods. An example of a job would be the manufacture of a mainframe computer by **IBM**, the production of a movie by **Disney**, or the making of a fire truck by **Western States**. An example of a batch would be the printing of 225 wedding invitations by a local print shop, or the printing of a weekly issue of *Fortune* magazine by a hi-tech printer such as **Quad Graphics**. Jobs or batches may be completed to fill a specific customer order or to replenish inventory.

An important feature of job order costing is that each job (or batch) has its own distinguishing characteristics. For example, each house is custom built, each consulting engagement by a CPA firm is unique, and each printing job is different. **The objective is to compute the cost per job.** At each point in the manufacturing of a product or the providing of a service, the job and its associated costs can be identified. A job order cost system measures costs for each completed job, rather than for set time periods. The recording of costs in a job order cost system is shown in Illustration 16-1.

Illustration 16-1 Job order cost system

Job Order Cost System
Two jobs: Wedding Invitations and Menus

Black ink $
Typesetting $
225 Invitations $
225 Envelopes $
Vellum stock, pure white $
Job # 9501

Typesetting $
Lamination $
Yellow stock $
50 Copies $
Job # 9502

Each job has distinguishing characteristics and related costs.

PROCESS COST SYSTEM

A **process cost system** is used when a series of connected manufacturing processes or departments produce a large volume of similar products. Production is continuous to ensure that adequate inventories of the finished product(s) are on hand. A process cost system is used in the manufacture of cereal by **Kellogg**, the refining of petroleum by **ExxonMobil**, and the production of automobiles by **General Motors**. Process costing accumulates product-related costs **for a period of time** (such as a week or a month) instead of assigning costs to specific products or job orders. In process costing, the costs are assigned to departments or processes for a set period of time. The recording of costs in a process cost system is shown in Illustration 16-2. The process cost system will be discussed further in Chapter 17.

Illustration 16-2 Process cost system

Process Cost System
Compact Disc Production

1. Oil is pumped.
2. Benzene is removed.
3. The benzene is made into pellets...
4. ...from which compact discs are produced.

Similar products are produced over a specified time period.

A company may use both types of cost systems. For example, **General Motors** uses process cost accounting for its standard model cars, such as Saturns and Corvettes, and job order cost accounting for a custom-made limousine for the President of the United States. The objective of both systems is to provide unit cost information for product pricing, cost control, inventory valuation, and financial statement presentation. End-of-period inventory values are computed by using unit cost data.

Business Insight
MANAGEMENT PERSPECTIVE

Many companies suffer from poor cost accounting. As a result, they sometimes make products they ought not to be selling at all and buy others that they could more profitably make themselves. Also, inaccurate cost data lead companies to misallocate capital and frustrate efforts by plant managers to improve efficiency.

For example, consider the case of a diversified company in the business of rebuilding diesel locomotives. The managers thought they were making money, but a consulting firm found that costs had been seriously underestimated. The company bailed out of the business, and not a moment too soon. Says the consultant who advised the company: "The more contracts it won, the more money it lost."

BEFORE YOU GO ON . . .

▶ Review It

1. What is cost accounting?
2. What does a cost accounting system consist of?
3. How does a job order cost system differ from a process cost system?

✓ THE NAVIGATOR

Job Order Cost Flow

The flow of costs (direct materials, direct labor, and manufacturing overhead) in job order cost accounting parallels the physical flow of the materials as they are converted into finished goods. As shown in Illustration 16-3 (page 782), manufacturing costs are assigned to the Work in Process Inventory account. When a job is completed, the cost of the job is transferred to Finished Goods Inventory. Later when the goods are sold, their cost is transferred to Cost of Goods Sold.

Illustration 16-3 provides a basic overview of the flow of costs in a manufacturing setting. A more detailed presentation of the flow of costs is shown in Illustration 16-4 (page 782). It indicates that there are two major steps in the flow of costs: (1) *accumulating* the manufacturing costs incurred and (2) *assigning* the accumulated costs to the work done. As shown, manufacturing costs incurred are accumulated in entries 1–3 by debits to Raw Materials Inventory, Factory Labor, and Manufacturing Overhead. When these costs are incurred no attempt is made to associate the costs with specific jobs. The remaining entries (entries 4–8) assign manufacturing costs incurred. In the remainder of this chapter (pages 783–797), we will use a case study to explain how a job order system operates.

> STUDY OBJECTIVE
> **2**
> Describe the flow of costs in a job order cost accounting system.

Illustration 16-3 Flow of costs in job order cost accounting

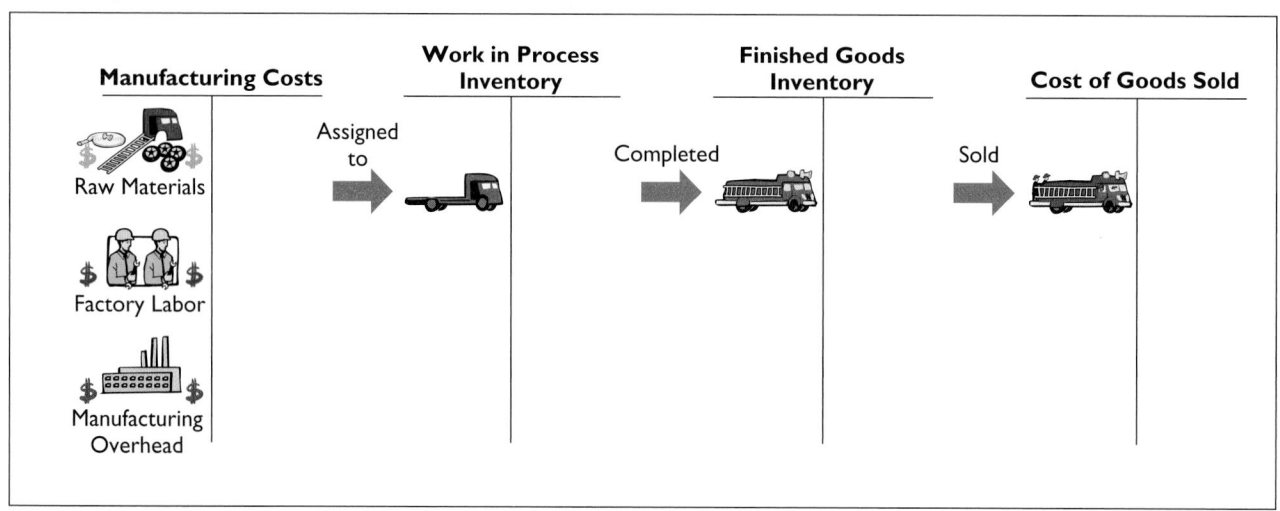

Manufacturing Costs — Raw Materials, Factory Labor, Manufacturing Overhead → Assigned to → **Work in Process Inventory** → Completed → **Finished Goods Inventory** → Sold → **Cost of Goods Sold**

Illustration 16-4 Job order cost accounting system

Job Order Cost Accounting

Raw Materials Inventory

(1) Purchases	(4) Materials used

→ [4] →

Work in Process Inventory

(4) Direct materials used	(7) Cost of completed jobs
(5) Direct labor used	
(6) Overhead applied	

→ [7] →

Finished Goods Inventory

(7) Cost of completed jobs	(8) Cost of goods sold

→ [8] →

Factory Labor

(2) Factory labor incurred	(5) Factory labor used

→ [5]

Cost of Goods Sold

(8) Cost of goods sold	

Manufacturing Overhead

Actual overhead incurred:	(6) Overhead applied
(3) Depreciation Insurance Repairs	
(4) Indirect materials used	
(5) Indirect labor used	

→ [6]

Key to Entries:

Accumulation	Assignment
1. Purchase raw materials	4. Raw materials are used
2. Incur factory labor	5. Factory labor is used
3. Incur manufacturing overhead	6. Overhead is applied
	7. Completed goods are recognized
	8. Cost of goods sold is recognized

ACCUMULATING MANUFACTURING COSTS

In a job order cost system, manufacturing costs are recorded in the period in which they are incurred. To illustrate, we will use the January transactions of Wallace Manufacturing Company, which makes machine tools and dies. (Dies are devices used for cutting out, stamping, or forming metals and plastics.)

Raw Materials Costs

The costs of raw materials purchased are debited to Raw Materials Inventory when the materials are received. This account is debited for the invoice cost and freight costs chargeable to the purchaser. It is credited for purchase discounts taken and purchase returns and allowances. **No effort is made at this point to associate the cost of materials with specific jobs or orders.** The procedures for ordering, receiving, recording, and paying for raw materials are similar to the purchasing procedures of a merchandising company.

To illustrate, assume that Wallace Manufacturing purchases 2,000 handles (Stock No. AA2746) at $5 per unit ($10,000) and 800 modules (Stock No. AA2850) at $40 per unit ($32,000) for a total cost of $42,000 ($10,000 + $32,000). The entry to record this purchase on January 4 is:

	(1)		
Jan. 4	Raw Materials Inventory	42,000	
	Accounts Payable		42,000
	(Purchase of raw materials on account)		

Raw Materials Inventory is a control account. That is, it is a general ledger account that summarizes the detailed data on specific inventory items contained in the subsidiary ledger. The subsidiary ledger consists of individual records for each item of raw materials. The records may take the form of accounts (or cards) that are manually or mechanically prepared. Or the records may be kept as data files maintained electronically on disks or magnetic tape. The records are referred to as **materials inventory records** (or **stores ledger cards**). The card for Stock No. AA2746 following the purchase is shown in Illustration 16-5.

Item: Handles							Part No: AA2746			
	Receipts			Issues			Balance			
Date	Units	Cost	Total	Units	Cost	Total	Units	Cost	Total	
1/4	2,000	$5	$10,000				2,000	$5	$10,000	

Illustration 16-5
Materials inventory card

Helpful Hint

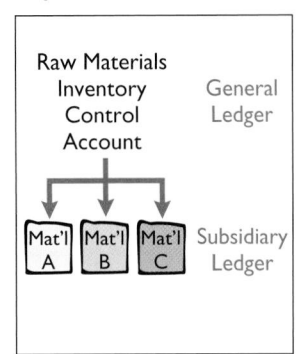

Postings are made daily to the subsidiary ledger. After all postings have been completed, the sum of the balances in the raw materials subsidiary ledger should equal the balance in the Raw Materials Inventory control account.

Factory Labor Costs

The procedures for accumulating factory labor costs are similar to those for computing the payroll for a merchandising company. Time clocks and time cards are used to determine total hours worked; gross and net earnings for each employee are listed in a payroll register; and individual employee earnings records are maintained. To help ensure the accuracy of data, a company should follow the principles of internal control.

In a manufacturing company, the cost of factory labor consists of (1) gross earnings of factory workers, (2) employer payroll taxes on such earnings, and (3) fringe benefits (such as sick pay, pensions, and vacation pay) incurred by the employer. **Labor costs are debited to Factory Labor when they are incurred.**

To illustrate, assume that Wallace Manufacturing incurs $32,000 of factory labor costs. Of that amount, $27,000 relates to wages payable and $5,000 relates to payroll taxes payable in January. The entry is:

	(2)		
Jan. 31	Factory Labor	32,000	
	Factory Wages Payable		27,000
	Employer Payroll Taxes Payable		5,000
	(To record factory labor costs)		

Factory labor is subsequently assigned to work in process or manufacturing overhead, as explained later in the chapter.

Manufacturing Overhead Costs

A company may have many types of overhead costs. These costs may be recognized **daily**, as in the case of machinery repairs and the use of indirect materials and indirect labor. Or overhead costs may be recorded **periodically** through adjusting entries. Property taxes, depreciation, and insurance are recorded periodically, for example. Using assumed data, a **summary entry** for manufacturing overhead in Wallace Manufacturing Company is:

Helpful Hint This is referred to as a summary entry because it summarizes the totals from multiple transactions.

	(3)		
Jan. 31	Manufacturing Overhead	13,800	
	Utilities Payable		4,800
	Prepaid Insurance		2,000
	Accounts Payable (for repairs)		2,600
	Accumulated Depreciation		3,000
	Property Taxes Payable		1,400
	(To record overhead costs)		

Manufacturing Overhead is a control account. Its subsidiary ledger consists of individual accounts for each type of cost, such as Factory Utilities, Factory Insurance, and Factory Repairs.

ASSIGNING MANUFACTURING COSTS TO WORK IN PROCESS

STUDY OBJECTIVE
3
Explain the nature and importance of a job cost sheet.

As shown in Illustration 16-4, assigning manufacturing costs to work in process results in the following entries: (1) **Debits** are made to Work in Process Inventory. (2) **Credits** are made to Raw Materials Inventory, Factory Labor, and Manufacturing Overhead. Journal entries to assign costs to work in process are usually made and posted **monthly**.

An essential accounting record in assigning costs to jobs is a **job cost sheet** shown in Illustration 16-6. A job cost sheet is a form used to record the costs chargeable to a specific job and to determine the total and unit costs of the completed job.

Illustration 16-6
Job cost sheet

Job Cost Sheet

Job No. _____   Quantity _____
Item _____   Date Requested _____
For _____   Date Completed _____

Date	Direct Materials	Direct Labor	Manufacturing Overhead

Cost of completed job
   Direct materials $ _____
   Direct labor   _____
   Manufacturing overhead   _____
Total cost $ _____
Unit cost (total dollars ÷ quantity) $ _____

Helpful Hint In today's electronic environment, job cost sheets are maintained as computer files.

Postings to job cost sheets are made daily, directly from supporting documents.

    A separate job cost sheet is kept for each job. The job cost sheets constitute the subsidiary ledger for the Work in Process Inventory account. **Each entry to Work in Process Inventory must be accompanied by a corresponding posting to one or more job cost sheets.**

Business Insight
MANAGEMENT PERSPECTIVE

General Motors recently launched a new Internet-based ordering system intended to deliver custom vehicles in 15 to 20 days instead of the 55 to 60 days it previously took. Customers interested in a GM car can search online to see if any dealers have a car with the options they want. If not, the customer uses an online program to configure a car with the desired options and then places the order. While this online approach could potentially provide savings for automakers by reducing inventory costs, some people are skeptical. One auto analyst stated, "I don't think it's going to lead to a massive change in the way vehicles are built and sold in the next 10 years."

SOURCE: Karen Lundegaard, "GM Tests Web-Based Ordering System, Seeking to Slash Custom-Delivery Time," *Wall Street Journal* (November 17, 2000).

Raw Materials Costs

Raw materials costs are assigned when the materials are issued by the storeroom. To achieve effective internal control over the issuance of materials, the storeroom worker should receive a written authorization before materials are released to production. Such authorization for issuing raw materials is made on a prenumbered materials requisition slip. This form is signed by an au-

Helpful Hint Approvals are an important part of a materials requisition slip because they help to establish individual accountability over inventory.

thorized employee such as a department supervisor. The materials issued may be used directly on a job, or they may be considered indirect materials. As shown in Illustration 16-7, the requisition should indicate the quantity and type of materials withdrawn and the account to be charged. Direct materials will be charged to Work in Process Inventory, and indirect materials to Manufacturing Overhead.

Illustration 16-7 Materials requisition slip

Helpful Hint The internal control principle of documentation includes prenumbering to enhance accountability.

Wallace Manufacturing Company				
Materials Requisition Slip				

Deliver to: Assembly Department   Req. No. R247
Charge to: Work in Process–Job No. 101   Date: 1/6/05

Quantity	Description	Stock No.	Cost per Unit	Total
200	Handles	AA2746	$5.00	$1,000

Requested by *Bruce Howart*   Received by *Herb Crowley*
Approved by *Kap Shin*   Costed by *Heather Remmers*

The requisition is prepared in duplicate. A copy is retained in the storeroom as evidence of the materials released. The original is sent to accounting, where the cost per unit and total cost of the materials used are determined. Any of the inventory costing methods (FIFO, LIFO, or average cost) may be used in costing the requisitions. After the requisition slips have been costed, they are posted daily to the materials inventory records. Also, **requisitions for direct materials are posted daily to the individual job cost sheets**.

Periodically, the requisitions are sorted, totaled, and journalized. For example, if $24,000 of direct materials and $6,000 of indirect materials are used by Wallace Manufacturing in January, the entry is:

	(4)		
Jan. 31	Work in Process Inventory	24,000	
	Manufacturing Overhead	6,000	
	Raw Materials Inventory		30,000
	(To assign materials to jobs and overhead)		

The requisition slips show total direct materials costs of $12,000 for Job No. 101, $7,000 for Job No. 102, and $5,000 for Job No. 103. The posting of requisition slip R247 and other assumed postings to the job cost sheets for materials are shown in Illustration 16-8. After all postings have been completed, the sum of the direct materials columns of the job cost sheets should equal the direct materials debited to Work in Process Inventory.

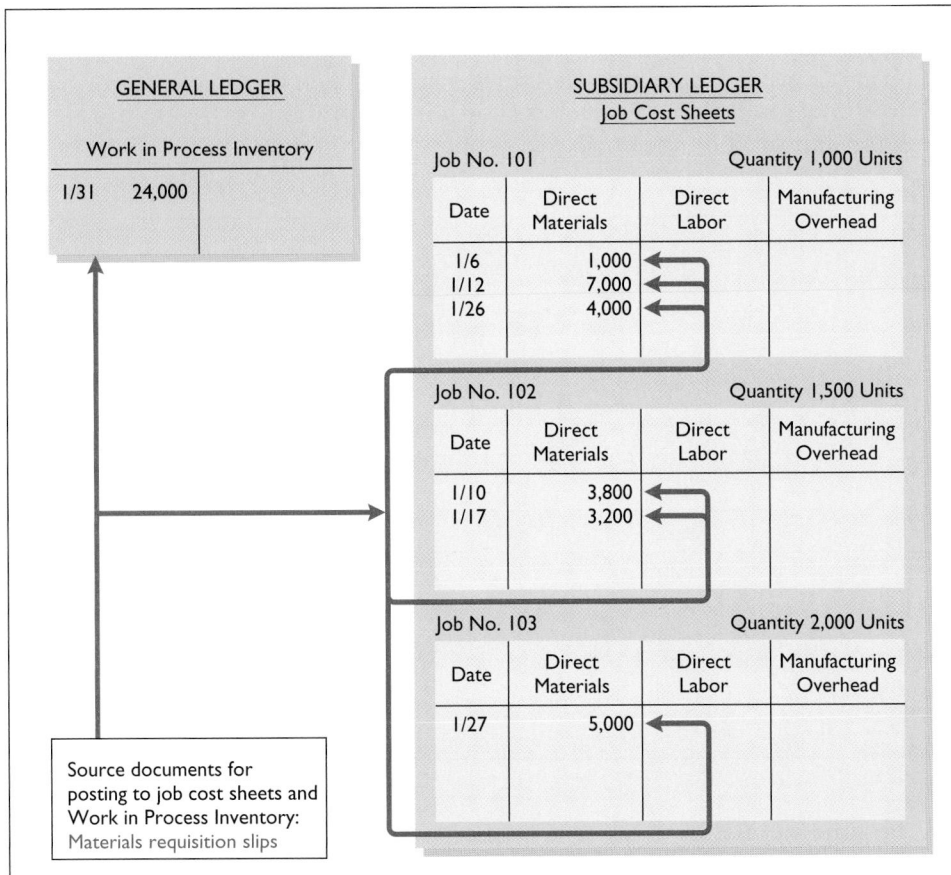

Illustration 16-8 Job cost sheets—direct materials

Helpful Hint Postings to control accounts are made monthly, and postings to job cost sheets are made daily.

The materials inventory record for Part No. AA2746 is shown in Illustration 16-9. It shows the posting of requisition slip R247 for 200 handles and an assumed requisition slip for 760 handles costing $3,800 on January 10 for Job 102.

Illustration 16-9 Materials inventory card following issuances

Item: Handles										Part No: AA2746
	Receipts			Issues			Balance			
Date	Units	Cost	Total	Units	Cost	Total	Units	Cost	Total	
1/4	2,000	$5	$10,000				2,000	$5	$10,000	
1/6				200	$5	$1,000	1,800	$5	9,000	
1/10				760	$5	3,800	1,040	$5	5,200	

Factory Labor Costs

Factory labor costs are assigned to jobs on the basis of time tickets prepared when the work is performed. The time ticket should indicate the employee, the hours worked, the account and job to be charged, and the total labor cost. In many companies these data are accumulated through the use of bar coding and scanning devices. When they start and end work, employees scan bar codes on their identification badges and bar codes associated with each job they work on. The account Work in Process Inventory is debited for direct labor, and Manufacturing Overhead is debited for indirect labor. When direct labor is involved, the job number must be indicated, as shown in Illustration 16-10. All time tickets should be approved by the employee's supervisor.

Illustration 16-10
Time ticket

Helpful Hint In some companies, different colored time tickets are used for direct and indirect labor.

Wallace Manufacturing Company
Time Ticket

Date: 1/6/05

Employee ___John Nash___   Employee No. ___124___
Charge to: ___Work in Process___   Job No. ___101___

Time			Hourly Rate	Total Cost
Start	Stop	Total Hours		
0800	1200	4	10.00	40.00

Approved by _Bob Kadler_   Costed by _M Cher_

The time tickets are later sent to the payroll department. There, the total time reported for an employee for a pay period is reconciled with total hours worked, as shown on the employee's time card. Then the employee's hourly wage rate is applied, and the total labor cost is computed. Finally, the time tickets are sorted, totaled, and journalized. For example, if the $32,000 total factory labor cost consists of $28,000 of direct labor and $4,000 of indirect labor, the entry is:

(5)

Jan. 31	Work in Process Inventory	28,000	
	Manufacturing Overhead	4,000	
	Factory Labor		32,000
	(To assign labor to jobs and overhead)		

As a result of this entry, Factory Labor is left with a zero balance, and employees' gross wages are assigned to the appropriate manufacturing accounts.

Let's assume that the labor costs chargeable to Wallace's three jobs are $15,000, $9,000, and $4,000. The Work in Process Inventory and job cost sheets after posting are shown in Illustration 16-11 (next page). As in the case of direct materials, the postings to the direct labor columns of the job cost sheets should equal the posting of direct labor to Work in Process Inventory.

Manufacturing Overhead Costs

We've seen that direct materials and direct labor can be applied to specific jobs. In contrast, manufacturing overhead relates to production operations **as a whole**. As a result, overhead costs cannot be assigned to specific jobs on the basis of actual costs incurred. Instead, manufacturing overhead is assigned to work in process and to specific jobs **on an estimated basis through the use of a predetermined overhead rate**.

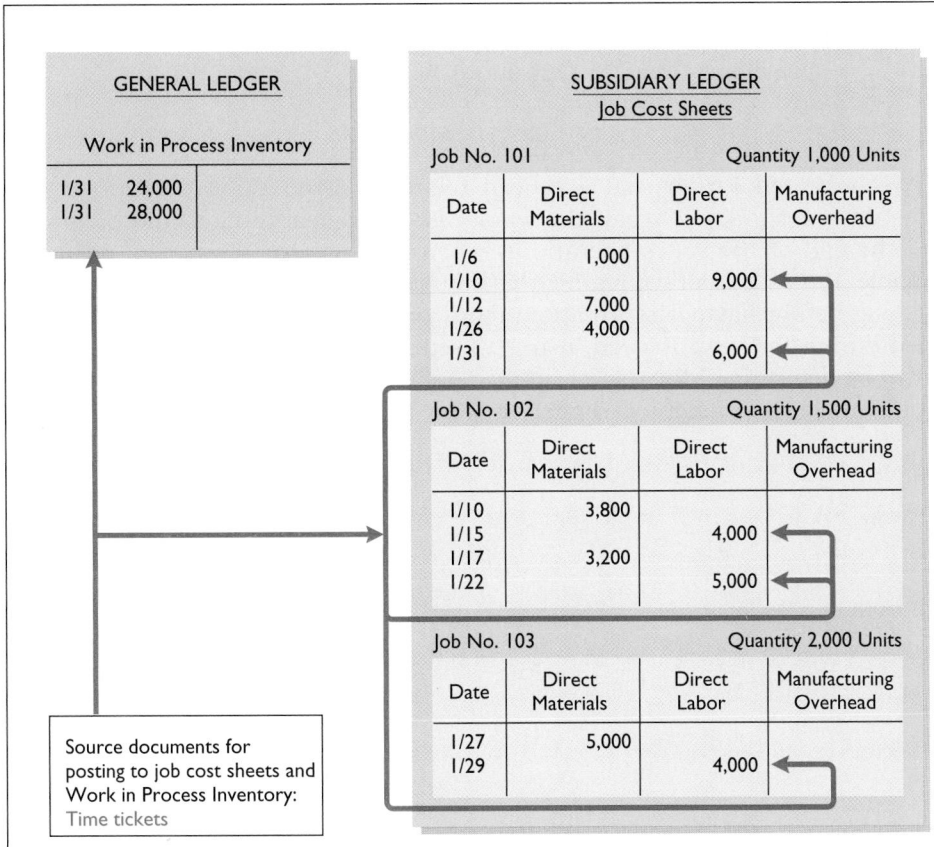

Illustration 16-11 Job cost sheets—direct labor

Helpful Hint Prove the $28,000 by totaling the charges by jobs:

101	$15,000
102	9,000
103	4,000
	$28,000

Business Insight
MANAGEMENT PERSPECTIVE

A job cost computer program provides summaries of material and labor costs by job. The program accumulates costs by jobs, provides data to accounts receivable for billings, assigns overhead costs, and provides up-to-date management reports. The reports generated by such systems are basically the same as those shown for Wallace Manufacturing. The major difference between manual and computerized systems is the time involved in converting data into information and in getting feedback (reports) to management.

The **predetermined overhead rate** is based on the relationship between estimated annual overhead costs and expected annual operating activity. This relationship is expressed in terms of a common **activity base**. The activity may be stated in terms of direct labor costs, direct labor hours, machine hours, or any other measure that will provide an equitable basis for applying overhead costs to jobs. The predetermined overhead rate is established at the beginning of the year. Small companies often will have a single, company-wide predetermined overhead rate. Large companies, however, often have rates that vary from department to department. The formula for a predetermined overhead rate is:

Illustration 16-12
Formula for predetermined
overhead rate

$$\text{Estimated Annual Overhead Costs} \div \text{Expected Annual Operating Activity} = \text{Predetermined Overhead Rate}$$

Helpful Hint In contrast to overhead, actual costs for direct materials and direct labor are used to assign costs to Work in Process.

We indicated earlier that overhead relates to production operations as a whole. In order to know what "the whole" is, the logical thing would be to wait until the end of the year's operations, when all costs for the period would be available. But as a practical matter, that wouldn't work: managers could not wait that long before having information about product costs of specific jobs completed during the year. Instead, using a predetermined overhead rate enables a cost to be determined for the job immediately. Illustration 16-13 indicates how manufacturing overhead is assigned to work in process.

Illustration 16-13 Using predetermined overhead rates

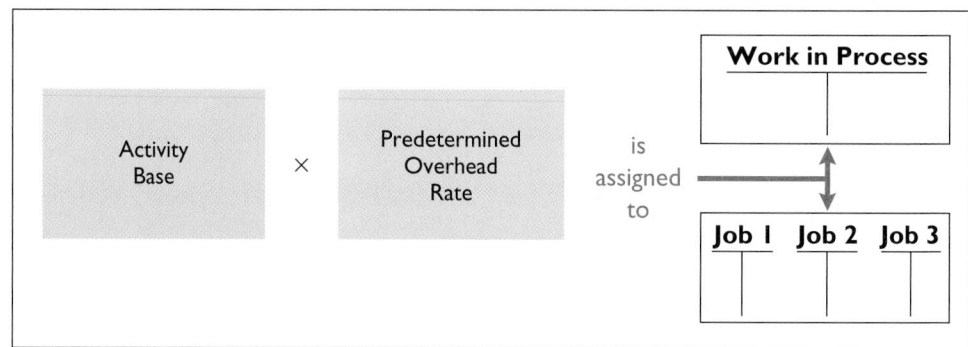

Wallace Manufacturing uses direct labor cost as the activity base. Assuming that annual overhead costs are expected to be $280,000 and that $350,000 of direct labor costs are anticipated for the year, the overhead rate is 80 percent, computed as follows:

$$\$280,000 \div \$350,000 = 80\%$$

This means that for every dollar of direct labor, 80 cents of manufacturing overhead will be assigned to a job. The use of a predetermined overhead rate enables the company to determine the approximate total cost of each job **when the job is completed**.

Historically, direct labor costs or direct labor hours have often been used as the activity base. The reason was the relatively high correlation between direct labor and manufacturing overhead. In recent years, **there has been a trend toward use of machine hours as the activity base**, **due to increased reliance on automation in manufacturing operations**. Or, as mentioned in Chapter 15, activity-based costing has resulted in more accurate allocation of overhead costs based on the activities that give rise to the costs.

A company may use more than one activity base. For example, if a job order is manufactured in more than one factory department, each department may have its own overhead rate. In the Feature Story about fire trucks, two bases were used in assigning overhead to jobs: direct materials dollars for indirect materials, and direct labor hours for such costs as insurance and supervisors' salaries.

For Wallace Manufacturing, the total amount of manufacturing overhead is assigned to work in process. It then is **charged to jobs when direct labor costs are assigned**. Overhead applied for January is $22,400 ($28,000 × 80%). This application is recorded through the following entry.

	(6)		
Jan. 31	Work in Process Inventory	22,400	
	Manufacturing Overhead		22,400
	(To assign overhead to jobs)		

The overhead assigned to each job will be 80 percent of the direct labor cost of the job for the month. After posting, the Work in Process Inventory account and the job cost sheets will appear as shown in Illustration 16-14. Note that the debit of $22,400 to Work in Process Inventory equals the sum of the overhead assigned to jobs: Job 101 $12,000 + Job 102 $7,200 + Job 103 $3,200.

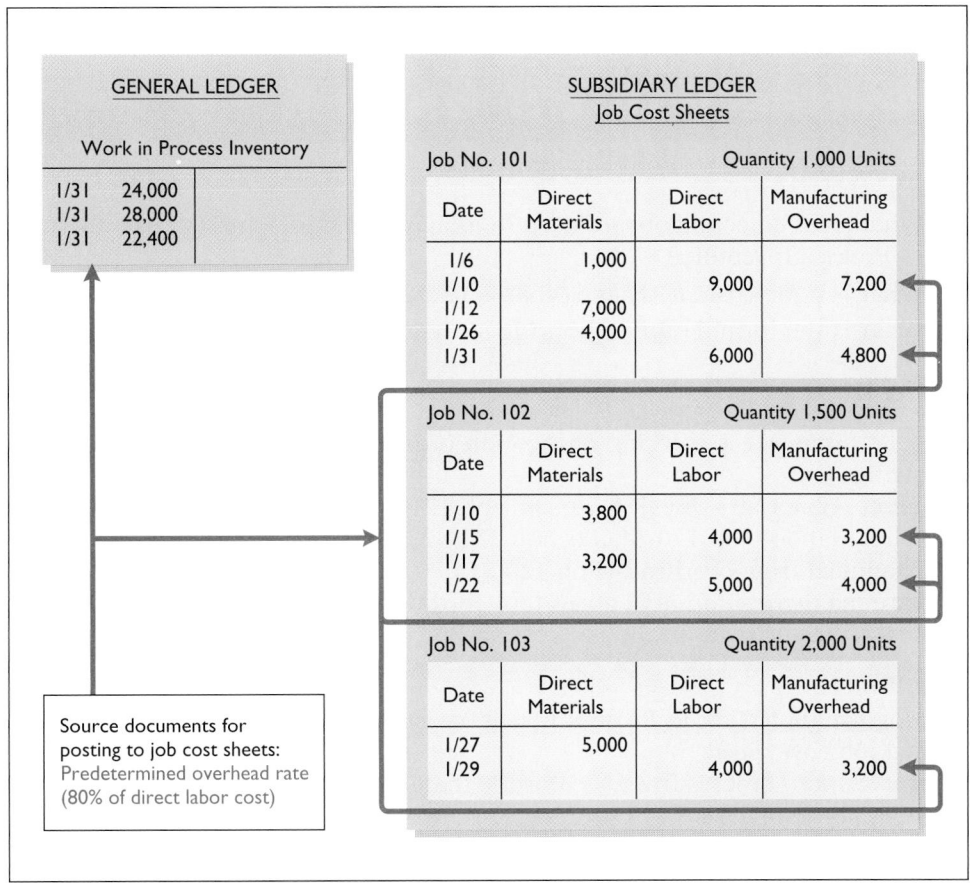

Illustration 16-14
Job cost sheets—
manufacturing overhead
applied

At the end of each month, **the balance in Work in Process Inventory should equal the sum of the costs shown on the job cost sheets of unfinished jobs**. Assuming that all jobs are unfinished, proof of the agreement of the control and subsidiary accounts in Wallace Manufacturing is shown below.

Work in Process Inventory		**Job Cost Sheets**	
Jan. 31	24,000	No. 101	$ 39,000
31	28,000	102	23,200
31	22,400	103	12,200
	74,400 ⟵		**$74,400**

Illustration 16-15 Proof of job cost sheets to work in process inventory

DECISION TOOLKIT

Decision Checkpoints	Info Needed for Decision	Tool to Use for Decision	How to Evaluate Results
What is the cost of a job?	Cost of material, labor, and overhead assigned to a specific job	Job cost sheet	Compare costs to those of previous periods and to those of competitors to ensure that costs are in line. Compare costs to expected selling price or service fees charged to determine overall profitability.

BEFORE YOU GO ON . . .

▶ Review It

1. What source documents are used in assigning manufacturing costs to Work in Process Inventory?
2. What is a job cost sheet, and what is its primary purpose?
3. What is the formula for computing a predetermined overhead rate?

▶ Do It

Danielle Company is working on two job orders. The job cost sheets show the following:

    Direct materials—Job 120 $6,000, Job 121 $3,600
    Direct labor—Job 120 $4,000, Job 121 $2,000
    Manufacturing overhead—Job 120 $5,000, Job 121 $2,500

Prepare the three summary entries to record the assignment of costs to Work in Process from the data on the job cost sheets.

Action Plan

• Recognize that Work in Process Inventory is the control account for all unfinished job cost sheets.
• Debit Work in Process Inventory for the materials, labor, and overhead charged to the job cost sheets.
• Credit the accounts that were debited when the manufacturing costs were accumulated.

Solution

The three summary entries are:

Work in Process Inventory ($6,000 + $3,600)	9,600	
Raw Materials Inventory		9,600
(To assign materials to jobs)		
Work in Process Inventory ($4,000 + $2,000)	6,000	
Factory Labor		6,000
(To assign labor to jobs)		
Work in Process Inventory ($5,000 + $2,500)	7,500	
Manufacturing Overhead		7,500
(To assign overhead to jobs)		

Related exercise material: BE16-3, BE16-4, BE16-7, E16-2, E16-3, E16-7, and E16-8.

☑ THE NAVIGATOR

ASSIGNING COSTS TO FINISHED GOODS

When a job is completed, the costs are summarized and the lower portion of the applicable job cost sheet is completed. For example, if we assume that Job No. 101 is completed on January 31, the job cost sheet will show the following.

Illustration 16-16
Completed job cost sheet

Wallace Manufacturing Company
Job Cost Sheet

Job No. 101 Quantity 1,000
Item Magnetic Sensors Date Requested February 5
For Tanner Company Date Completed January 31

Date	Direct Materials	Direct Labor	Manufacturing Overhead
1/6	$ 1,000		
1/10		$ 9,000	$ 7,200
1/12	7,000		
1/26	4,000		
1/31		6,000	4,800
	$12,000	$15,000	$12,000

Cost of completed job
Direct materials $ 12,000
Direct labor 15,000
Manufacturing overhead 12,000
Total cost $ 39,000
Unit cost ($39,000 ÷ 1,000) $ 39.00

When a job is finished, an entry is made to transfer its total cost to finished goods inventory. The entry for Wallace Manufacturing is:

(7)
Jan. 31 | Finished Goods Inventory | 39,000 |
| Work in Process Inventory | | 39,000 |
| (To record completion of Job No. 101) | |

Finished Goods Inventory is a control account. It controls individual finished goods records in a finished goods subsidiary ledger. Postings to the receipts columns are made directly from completed job cost sheets. The finished goods inventory record for Job No. 101 is shown in Illustration 16-17.

Illustration 16-17
Finished goods record

Item: Magnetic Sensors Job No: 101

	Receipts			Issues			Balance		
Date	Units	Cost	Total	Units	Cost	Total	Units	Cost	Total
1/31	1,000	$39	$39,000				1,000	$39	$39,000
1/31				1,000	$39	$39,000			–0–

ASSIGNING COSTS TO COST OF GOODS SOLD

Cost of goods sold is recognized when each sale occurs. To illustrate the entries when a completed job is sold, assume that on January 31 Wallace Manufacturing sells on account Job 101, costing $39,000, for $50,000. The entries to record the sale and recognize cost of goods sold are:

		(8)		
Jan. 31	Accounts Receivable		50,000	
	Sales			50,000
	(To record sale of Job No. 101)			
31	Cost of Goods Sold		39,000	
	Finished Goods Inventory			39,000
	(To record cost of Job No. 101)			

The units sold, the cost per unit, and the total cost of goods sold for each job sold are recorded in the issues section of the finished goods record, as shown in Illustration 16-17 (on page 793).

SUMMARY OF JOB ORDER COST FLOWS

A completed flow chart for a job order cost accounting system is shown in Illustration 16-18. All postings are keyed to entries 1–8 in Wallace Manufacturing's accounts presented in the cost flow graphic in Illustration 16-4. Illustration 16-19 provides a summary of the flow of documents in a job order cost system.

Illustration 16-18 Flow of costs in a job order cost system

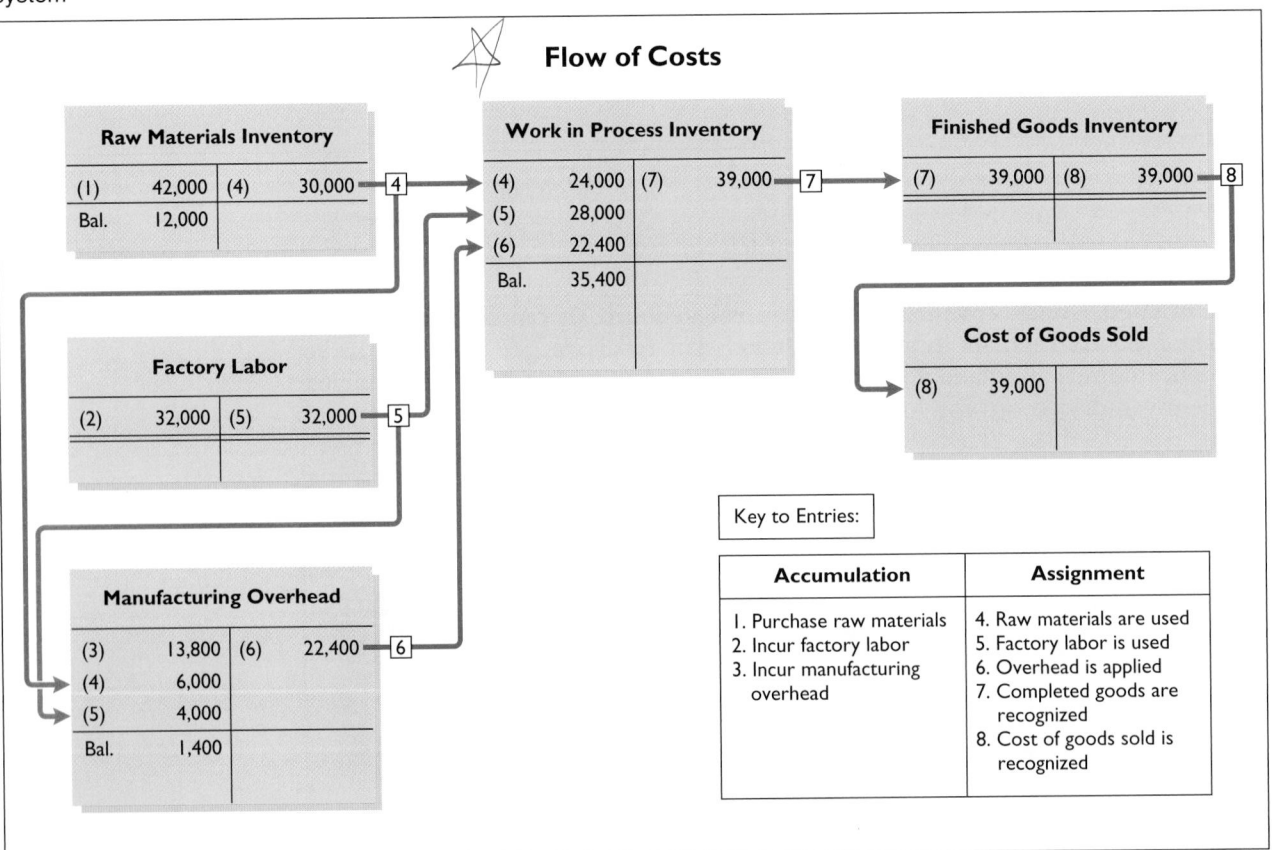

Flow of Costs

Key to Entries:

Accumulation	Assignment
1. Purchase raw materials	4. Raw materials are used
2. Incur factory labor	5. Factory labor is used
3. Incur manufacturing overhead	6. Overhead is applied
	7. Completed goods are recognized
	8. Cost of goods sold is recognized

Illustration 16-19 Flow of documents in a job order cost system

Flow of Documents

Source Documents

Materials Requisition Slips

Labor Time Tickets

Predetermined Overhead Rate

Job Cost Sheet

The job cost sheet summarizes the cost of jobs completed and not completed at the end of the accounting period. Jobs completed are transferred to finished goods to await sale.

Business Insight
MANAGEMENT PERSPECTIVE

With the increased sophistication of microcomputers, small manufacturers can now use micros to perform (1) computer-aided manufacturing (CAM), (2) computer-aided testing (CAT), (3) computer-aided design (CAD), (4) electronic data interchange (EDI), and (5) materials requirement planning (MRP). For a small investment, manufacturers can now use software with capabilities only dreamed about a few years ago.

Reporting Job Cost Data

At the end of a period, financial statements are prepared that present aggregate data on all jobs manufactured and sold. The cost of goods manufactured schedule in job order costing is the same as in Chapter 15 with one exception: **Manufacturing overhead applied is shown, rather than actual overhead costs. This amount is added to direct materials and direct labor to determine total manufacturing costs.** The schedule is prepared directly from the Work in Process Inventory account. A condensed schedule for Wallace Manufacturing Company for January is as follows.

Helpful Hint Monthly financial statements are usually prepared for management use only.

Illustration 16-20 Cost of goods manufactured schedule

WALLACE MANUFACTURING COMPANY
Cost of Goods Manufactured Schedule
For the Month Ended January 31, 2005

Work in process, January 1		$ –0–
Direct materials used	$ 24,000	
Direct labor	28,000	
Manufacturing overhead applied	22,400	
Total manufacturing costs		74,400
Total cost of work in process		74,400
Less: Work in process, January 31		35,400
Cost of goods manufactured		$39,000

Note that the cost of goods manufactured ($39,000) agrees with the amount transferred from Work in Process Inventory to Finished Goods Inventory in journal entry no. 7 in Illustration 16-18.

The income statement and balance sheet are the same as those illustrated in Chapter 15. For example, the partial income statement for Wallace Manufacturing for the month of January is shown in Illustration 16-21.

Illustration 16-21 Partial income statement

WALLACE MANUFACTURING COMPANY		
Income Statement (partial)		
For the Month Ending January 31, 2005		
Sales		$50,000
Cost of goods sold		
Finished goods inventory, January 1	$ –0–	
Cost of goods manufactured (See Illustration 16-20)	39,000	
Cost of goods available for sale	39,000	
Less: Finished goods inventory, January 31	–0–	
Cost of goods sold		39,000
Gross profit		$11,000

Under- or Overapplied Manufacturing Overhead

STUDY OBJECTIVE
6
Distinguish between under- and overapplied manufacturing overhead.

When Manufacturing Overhead has a **debit balance**, overhead is said to be underapplied. **Underapplied overhead** means that the overhead assigned to work in process is less than the overhead incurred. Conversely, when manufacturing overhead has a **credit balance**, overhead is overapplied. **Overapplied overhead** means that the overhead assigned to work in process is greater than the overhead incurred. These concepts are shown in Illustration 16-22.

Manufacturing Overhead	
Actual (Costs incurred)	Applied (Costs assigned)

If actual is *greater* than applied, manufacturing overhead is underapplied.

If actual is *less* than applied, manufacturing overhead is overapplied.

Illustration 16-22 Under- and overapplied overhead

INTERIM BALANCES

The existence of under- or overapplied overhead at the end of a month is expected. It usually does not require corrective action by management. Monthly differences between actual and applied overhead will usually be offsetting over the course of the year.

When monthly financial statements are prepared, under- or overapplied overhead is reported on the balance sheet. **Underapplied overhead is shown as a prepaid expense in the current assets section. Overapplied overhead is reported as unearned revenue in the current liabilities section.**

YEAR-END BALANCE

At the end of the year, all manufacturing overhead transactions are complete. There is no further opportunity for offsetting events to occur. Accordingly, any balance in Manufacturing Overhead is eliminated by an adjusting entry. Usually, under- or overapplied overhead is considered to be an **adjustment to cost of goods sold**. Thus, **underapplied overhead is debited to Cost of Goods Sold. Overapplied overhead is credited to Cost of Goods Sold.** To illustrate, assume that Wallace Manufacturing has a $2,500 credit balance in Manufacturing Overhead at December 31. The adjusting entry for the overapplied overhead is:

Dec. 31	Manufacturing Overhead	2,500	
	Cost of Goods Sold		2,500
	(To transfer overapplied overhead to		
	cost of goods sold)		

After this entry is posted, Manufacturing Overhead will have a zero balance. In preparing an income statement for the year, the amount reported for cost of goods sold will be the account balance **after the adjustment** for either under- or overapplied overhead.

Business Insight
MANAGEMENT PERSPECTIVE

Overhead also applies in nonmanufacturing companies. The State of Michigan found that auto dealers were charging documentary and service fees ranging from $18 to $445 per automobile and inspection fees from $88 to $360. These fees often were charged auto buyers after a base sales price for the car had been negotiated. The Attorney General of the State of Michigan ruled that auto dealers cannot charge customers additional fees for routine overhead costs. The attorney general said: "Overhead is part of the sales price of a motor vehicle. Processing paper work, dealer incurred costs, and inspection fees to qualify cars for extended warranty plans are ordinary overhead expenses."

Conceptually, it can be argued that under- or overapplied overhead at the end of the year should be allocated among ending work in process, finished goods, and cost of goods sold. However, most management accountants do not believe allocation is worth the cost and effort. The bulk of the under- or overapplied amount will be allocated to cost of goods sold anyway, because most of the jobs will be sold during the year.

DECISION TOOLKIT

Decision Checkpoints	Info Needed for Decision	Tool to Use for Decision	How to Evaluate Results
Has the company over- or underapplied overhead for the period?	Actual overhead costs and overhead applied	Manufacturing overhead account	If the account balance is a credit, overhead applied exceeded actual overhead costs. If the account balance is a debit, overhead applied was less than actual overhead costs.

BEFORE YOU GO ON . . .

▶ **Review It**

1. When are entries made to record the completion and sale of a job?
2. What costs are included in total manufacturing costs in the cost of goods manufactured schedule?
3. How is under- or overapplied manufacturing overhead reported in monthly financial statements?

Using the Decision Toolkit

Martinez Building Products Company is one of the largest manufacturers and marketers of unique, custom-made residential garage doors in the U.S. as well as a major supplier of industrial and commercial doors, grills, and counter shutters for the new construction, repair, and remodel markets. Martinez has developed plans for continued expansion of a network of service operations that sell, install, and service manufactured fireplaces, garage doors, and related products.

Martinez uses a job cost system and applies overhead to production on the basis of direct labor cost. In computing a predetermined overhead rate for the year 2005, the company estimated manufacturing overhead to be $24 million and direct labor costs to be $20 million. In addition the following information is provided.

Actual costs incurred during 2005

Direct materials used	$30,000,000
Direct labor cost incurred	21,000,000

Manufacturing costs incurred during 2005

Insurance, factory	$ 500,000
Indirect labor	7,500,000
Maintenance	1,000,000
Rent on building	11,000,000
Depreciation on equipment	2,000,000

Instructions

Answer each of the following.

(a) Why is Martinez Building Products Company using a job order costing system?

(b) On what basis does Martinez allocate its manufacturing overhead? Compute the predetermined overhead rate for the current year.

(c) Compute the amount of the under- or overapplied overhead for 2005.

(d) Martinez had balances in the beginning and ending work in process and finished goods accounts as follows.

	1/1/05	12/31/05
Work in process	$ 5,000,000	$ 4,000,000
Finished goods	13,000,000	11,000,000

Determine the (1) cost of goods manufactured and (2) cost of goods sold for Martinez during 2005. Assume that any under- or overapplied overhead should be included in the cost of goods sold.

(e) During 2005, Job G408 was started and completed. Its cost sheet showed a total cost of $100,000, and the company prices its product at 50% above its cost. What is the price to the customer if the company follows this pricing strategy?

Solution

(a) The company is using a job order system because each job (or batch) must have its own distinguishing characteristics. For example, each type of garage door would be different, and therefore a different cost per garage door should be assigned.

(b) The company allocates its overhead on the basis of direct labor cost. The predetermined overhead rate is 120%, computed as follows.

$$\$24,000,000 \div \$20,000,000 = 120\%$$

(c)		
Actual manufacturing overhead	$22,000,000	
Applied overhead cost ($21,000,000 × 120%)	25,200,000	
Overapplied overhead	$ 3,200,000	

(d) (1)		
Work in process, 1/1/05		$ 5,000,000
Direct materials used	$30,000,000	
Direct labor	21,000,000	
Manufacturing overhead applied	25,200,000	
Total manufacturing costs		76,200,000
Total cost of work in process		81,200,000
Less: Work in process, 12/31/05		4,000,000
Cost of goods manufactured		$77,200,000

(2)		
Finished goods inventory, 1/1/05	$13,000,000	
Cost of goods manufactured (see above)	77,200,000	
Cost of goods available for sale	90,200,000	
Finished goods inventory, 12/31/05	11,000,000	
Cost of goods sold (unadjusted)	79,200,000	
Less: Overapplied overhead	3,200,000	
Cost of goods sold	$76,000,000	

(e)		
G408 cost	$ 100,000	
Markup percentage	× 50%	
Profit	$ 50,000	

Price to customer: $150,000 ($100,000 + $50,000)

Summary of Study Objectives

1 *Explain the characteristics and purposes of cost accounting.* Cost accounting involves the procedures for measuring, recording, and reporting product costs. From the data accumulated, the total cost and the unit cost of each product is determined. The two basic types of cost accounting systems are job order cost and process cost.

2 *Describe the flow of costs in a job order cost accounting system.* In job order cost accounting, manufacturing costs are first accumulated in three accounts: Raw Materials Inventory, Factory Labor, and Manufacturing Overhead. The accumulated costs are then assigned to Work in Process Inventory and eventually to Finished Goods Inventory and Cost of Goods Sold.

3 *Explain the nature and importance of a job cost sheet.* A job cost sheet is a form used to record the costs chargeable to a specific job and to determine the total and unit costs of the completed job. Job cost sheets constitute the subsidiary ledger for the Work in Process Inventory control account.

4 *Indicate how the predetermined overhead rate is determined and used.* The predetermined overhead rate is based on the relationship between estimated annual overhead costs and expected annual operating activity. This is expressed in terms of a common activity base, such as direct labor cost. The rate is used in assigning overhead costs to work in process and to specific jobs.

5 *Prepare entries for jobs completed and sold.* When jobs are completed, the cost is debited to Finished Goods Inventory and credited to Work in Process Inventory. When a job is sold the entries are: (a) Debit Cash or Accounts Receivable and credit Sales for the selling price. And (b) debit Cost of Goods Sold and credit Finished Goods Inventory for the cost of the goods.

6 *Distinguish between under- and overapplied manufacturing overhead.* Underapplied manufacturing overhead means that the overhead assigned to work in process is less than the overhead incurred. Overapplied overhead means that the overhead assigned to work in process is greater than the overhead incurred.

DECISION TOOLKIT—A SUMMARY

Decision Checkpoints	Info Needed for Decision	Tool to Use for Decision	How to Evaluate Results
What is the cost of a job?	Cost of material, labor, and overhead assigned to a specific job	Job cost sheet	Compare costs to those of previous periods and to those of competitors to ensure that costs are in line. Compare costs to expected selling price or service fees charged to determine overall profitability.
Has the company over- or underapplied overhead for the period?	Actual overhead costs and overhead applied	Manufacturing overhead account	If the account balance is a credit, overhead applied exceeded actual overhead costs. If the account balance is a debit, overhead applied was less than actual overhead costs.

Glossary

Cost accounting An area of accounting that involves measuring, recording, and reporting product costs. (p. 779)

Cost accounting system Manufacturing cost accounts that are fully integrated into the general ledger of a company. (p. 779)

Job cost sheet A form used to record the costs chargeable to a job and to determine the total and unit costs of the completed job. (p. 784)

Job order cost system A cost accounting system in which costs are assigned to each job or batch. (p. 780)

Materials requisition slip A document authorizing the issuance of raw materials from the storeroom to production. (p. 785)

Overapplied overhead A situation in which overhead assigned to work in process is greater than the overhead incurred. (p. 796)

Predetermined overhead rate A rate based on the relationship between estimated annual overhead costs and expected annual operating activity, expressed in terms of a common activity base. (p. 789)

Process cost system A system of accounting used by companies that manufacture relatively similar products through a series of continuous processes or operations. (p. 780)

Summary entry A journal entry that summarizes the totals from multiple transactions. (p. 784)

Time ticket A document that indicates the employee, the hours worked, the account and job to be charged, and the total labor cost. (p. 787)

Underapplied overhead A situation in which overhead assigned to work in process is less than the overhead incurred. (p. 796)

Demonstration Problem

During February, Cardella Manufacturing works on two jobs: A16 and B17. Summary data concerning these jobs are as follows.

Manufacturing Costs Incurred

Purchased $54,000 of raw materials on account.
Factory labor $76,000, plus $4,000 employer payroll taxes.
Manufacturing overhead $59,800, not including indirect materials and indirect labor.

Assignment of Costs

Direct materials:	Job A16 $27,000, Job B17 $21,000
Indirect materials:	$3,000
Direct labor:	Job A16 $52,000, Job B17 $26,000
Indirect labor:	$2,000
Manufacturing overhead rate:	80% of direct labor costs.

Job A16 was completed and sold on account for $150,000. Job B17 was only partially completed.

Instructions

(a) Journalize the February transactions in the sequence followed in the chapter (page 794).
(b) What was the amount of under- or overapplied manufacturing overhead?

Solution to Demonstration Problem

(a)

1.

Feb. 28	Raw Materials Inventory	54,000	
	Accounts Payable		54,000
	(Purchase of raw materials on account)		

2.

28	Factory Labor	80,000	
	Factory Wages Payable		76,000
	Employer Payroll Taxes Payable		4,000
	(To record factory labor costs)		

3.

28	Manufacturing Overhead	59,800	
	Accounts Payable, Accumulated		
	Depreciation, and Prepaid Insurance		59,800
	(To record overhead costs)		

4.

28	Work in Process Inventory	48,000	
	Manufacturing Overhead	3,000	
	Raw Materials Inventory		51,000
	(To assign raw materials to production)		

5.

28	Work in Process Inventory	78,000	
	Manufacturing Overhead	2,000	
	Factory Labor		80,000
	(To assign factory labor to production)		

6.

28	Work in Process Inventory	62,400	
	Manufacturing Overhead		62,400
	(To assign overhead to jobs—		
	80% × $78,000)		

Action Plan

- In accumulating costs, debit three accounts: Raw Materials Inventory, Factory Labor, and Manufacturing Overhead.
- When Work in Process Inventory is debited, credit one of the three accounts listed above.
- Debit Finished Goods Inventory for the cost of completed jobs. Debit Cost of Goods Sold for the cost of jobs sold.
- Overhead is underapplied when Manufacturing Overhead has a debit balance.

7.

Feb. 28	Finished Goods Inventory	120,600	
	Work in Process Inventory		120,600
	(To record completion of Job A16: direct materials $27,000, direct labor $52,000, and manufacturing overhead $41,600)		

8.

28	Accounts Receivable	150,000	
	Sales		150,000
	(To record sale of Job A16)		
28	Cost of Goods Sold	120,600	
	Finished Goods Inventory		120,600
	(To record cost of Job A16)		

(b) Manufacturing Overhead has a debit balance of $2,400 as shown below.

Manufacturing Overhead

(3)	59,800	(6)	62,400
(4)	3,000		
(5)	2,000		
Bal.	2,400		

Thus, manufacturing overhead is underapplied for the month.

✓ THE NAVIGATOR

Self-Study Questions

Answers are at the end of the chapter.

(SO 1) **1.** Cost accounting involves the measuring, recording, and reporting of:
(a) product costs.
(b) future costs.
(c) manufacturing processes.
(d) managerial accounting decisions.

(SO 2) **2.** In accumulating raw materials costs, the cost of raw materials purchased in a perpetual system is debited to:
(a) Raw Materials Purchases.
(b) Raw Materials Inventory.
(c) Purchases.
(d) Work in Process.

(SO 2) **3.** When incurred, factory labor costs are debited to:
(a) Work in Process.
(b) Factory Wages Expense.
(c) Factory Labor.
(d) Factory Wages Payable.

(SO 3) **4.** The source documents for assigning costs to job cost sheets are:
(a) invoices, time tickets, and the predetermined overhead rate.
(b) materials requisition slips, time tickets, and the actual overhead costs.
(c) materials requisition slips, payroll register, and the predetermined overhead rate.
(d) materials requisition slips, time tickets, and the predetermined overhead rate.

(SO 3) **5.** In recording the issuance of raw materials in a job order cost system, it would be *incorrect* to:
(a) debit Work in Process Inventory.
(b) debit Finished Goods Inventory.
(c) debit Manufacturing Overhead.
(d) credit Raw Materials Inventory.

(SO 3) **6.** The entry when direct factory labor is assigned to jobs is a debit to:
(a) Work in Process Inventory and a credit to Factory Labor.
(b) Manufacturing Overhead and a credit to Factory Labor.
(c) Factory Labor and a credit to Manufacturing Overhead.
(d) Factory Labor and a credit to Work in Process Inventory.

(SO 4) **7.** The formula for computing the predetermined manufacturing overhead rate is estimated annual overhead costs divided by an expected annual operating activity, expressed as:
(a) direct labor cost.
(b) direct labor hours.
(c) machine hours.
(d) any of the above.

(SO 4)   8. In Cleo Company, the predetermined overhead rate is 80% of direct labor cost. During the month, $210,000 of factory labor costs are incurred, of which $180,000 is direct labor and $30,000 is indirect labor. Actual overhead incurred was $200,000. The amount of overhead debited to Work in Process Inventory should be:

    (a) $120,000.
    (b) $144,000.
    (c) $168,000.
    (d) $160,000.

(SO 5)   9. In BAC Company, Job No. 26 is completed at a cost of $4,500 and later sold for $7,000 cash. A correct entry is:

(a) Debit Finished Goods Inventory $7,000 and credit Work in Process Inventory $7,000.
(b) Debit Cost of Goods Sold $7,000 and credit Finished Goods Inventory $7,000.
(c) Debit Finished Goods Inventory $4,500 and credit Work in Process Inventory $4,500.
(d) Debit Accounts Receivable $7,000 and credit Sales $7,000.

10. In preparing monthly financial statements, over- (SO 6) applied overhead is reported in the balance sheet as a(an):
    (a) prepaid expense.
    (b) unearned revenue.
    (c) noncurrent asset.
    (d) noncurrent liability.

Questions

1. Hal Adelman is studying for an accounting midterm examination. What should Hal know about how management may use job cost data?

2. (a) Marc Tucci is not sure about the differences between cost accounting and a cost accounting system. Explain the difference to Marc. (b) What is an important feature of a cost accounting system?

3. (a) Distinguish between the two types of cost accounting systems. (b) May a company use both types of cost accounting systems?

4. What type of industry is likely to use a job order cost system? Give some examples.

5. What type of industry is likely to use a process cost system? Give some examples.

6. Your roommate asks your help in understanding the major steps in the flow of costs in a job order cost system. Identify the steps for your roommate.

7. There are three inventory control accounts in a job order system. Identify the control accounts and their subsidiary ledgers.

8. What source documents are used in accumulating direct labor costs?

9. "Only normal daily entries are made to manufacturing overhead." Do you agree? Explain.

10. Phil Remmers is confused about the source documents used in assigning materials and labor costs. Identify the documents and give the entry for each document.

11. What is the purpose of a job cost sheet?

12. Indicate the source documents that are used in charging costs to specific jobs.

13. Differentiate between a "materials inventory record" and a "materials requisition slip" as used in a job order cost system.

14. John Simon believes actual manufacturing overhead should be charged to jobs. Do you agree? Why or why not?

15. What relationships are involved in computing a predetermined overhead rate?

16. How can the agreement of Work in Process Inventory and job cost sheets be verified?

17. Pam Smith believes that the cost of goods manufactured schedule in job order cost accounting (Illustration 16-20) is the same as the cost of goods manufactured schedule in general manufacturing accounting (see Illustration 15-7 in Chapter 15). Is Pam correct? Explain.

18. Greg Carnes is confused about under- and overapplied manufacturing overhead. Define the terms for Greg, and indicate the balance in the manufacturing overhead account applicable to each term.

19. "Under- or overapplied overhead is reported in the income statement when monthly financial statements are prepared." Do you agree? If not, indicate the proper presentation.

20. "At the end of the year, under- or overapplied overhead is closed to Income Summary." Is this correct? If not, indicate the customary treatment of this account.

Brief Exercises

BE16-1   Sinason Tool & Die begins operations on January 1. Because all work is done to customer specifications, the company decides to use a job cost accounting system. Prepare a flow chart of a typical job order system with arrows showing the flow of costs. Identify the eight transactions.

Prepare a flowchart of a job order cost accounting system, and identify transactions.
(SO 2)

Prepare entries in accumulating manufacturing costs.
(SO 2)

BE16-2 During January, its first month of operations, Sinason Tool & Die accumulated the following manufacturing costs: raw materials $3,000 on account, factory labor $4,000 of which $3,600 relates to factory wages payable and $400 relates to payroll taxes payable, and utilities payable $2,000. Prepare separate journal entries for each type of manufacturing cost.

Prepare entry for the assignment of raw materials costs.
(SO 2)

BE16-3 In January, Sinason Tool & Die requisitions raw materials for production as follows: Job 1 $900, Job 2 $1,200, Job 3 $200, and general factory use $600. Prepare a summary journal entry to record raw materials used.

Prepare entry for the assignment of factory labor costs.
(SO 2)

BE16-4 Factory labor data for Sinason Tool & Die is given in BE16-2. During January, time tickets show that the factory labor of $4,000 was used as follows: Job 1 $1,200, Job 2 $1,600, Job 3 $700, and general factory use $500. Prepare a summary journal entry to record factory labor used.

Prepare job cost sheets.
(SO 3)

BE16-5 Data pertaining to job cost sheets for Sinason Tool & Die are given in BE16-3 and BE16-4. Prepare the job cost sheets for each of the three jobs. (*Note:* You may omit the column for Manufacturing Overhead.)

Compute predetermined overhead rates.
(SO 4)

BE16-6 Carlos Company estimates that annual manufacturing overhead costs will be $400,000. Estimated annual operating activity bases are: direct labor cost $500,000, direct labor hours 50,000, and machine hours 100,000. Compute the predetermined overhead rate for each activity base.

Assign manufacturing overhead to production.
(SO 4)

BE16-7 During the first quarter, Carlos Company incurs the following direct labor costs: January $40,000, February $30,000, and March $50,000. For each month, prepare the entry to assign overhead to production using a predetermined rate of 80% of direct labor cost.

Prepare entries for completion and sale of completed jobs.
(SO 5)

BE16-8 In March, Santana Company completes Jobs 10 and 11. Job 10 cost $20,000 and Job 11 $32,000. On March 31, Job 10 is sold to the customer for $35,000 in cash. Journalize the entries for the completion of the two jobs and the sale of Job 10.

Indicate statement classification of under- or overapplied overhead.
(SO 6)

BE16-9 On September 30, balances in Manufacturing Overhead are: Wendy Company—debit $1,800, Mahmoud Company—credit $3,000. Indicate how each company should report its balance at September 30, assuming each company prepares annual financial statements on December 31.

Prepare adjusting entries for under- and overapplied overhead.
(SO 6)

BE16-10 At December 31, balances in Manufacturing Overhead are: Sanchez Company—debit $1,000, Gomez Company—credit $900. Prepare the adjusting entry for each company at December 31, assuming the adjustment is made to cost of goods sold.

Exercises

Prepare entries for factory labor.
(SO 2)

E16-1 The gross earnings of the factory workers for Cerrato Company during the month of January are $90,000. The employer's payroll taxes for the factory payroll are $9,000. The fringe benefits to be paid by the employer on this payroll are $4,000. Of the total accumulated cost of factory labor, 85% is related to direct labor and 15% is attributable to indirect labor.

Instructions
(a) Prepare the entry to record the factory labor costs for the month of January.
(b) Prepare the entry to assign factory labor to production.

Prepare journal entries for manufacturing costs.
(SO 2, 3, 4, 5)

E16-2 Alvarez Manufacturing uses a job order cost accounting system. On May 1, the company has a balance in Work in Process Inventory of $3,200 and two jobs in process: Job No. 429 $2,000, and Job No. 430 $1,200. During May, a summary of source documents reveals the following.

Job Number	Materials Requisition Slips	Labor Time Tickets
429	$2,500	$ 2,400
430	2,000	3,000
431	4,400	7,600
General use	800	1,200
	$9,700	$14,200

Alvarez Manufacturing applies manufacturing overhead to jobs at an overhead rate of 80% of direct labor cost. Job No. 429 is completed during the month.

Instructions

(a) Prepare summary journal entries to record the requisition slips, time tickets, the assignment of manufacturing overhead to jobs, and the completion of Job No. 429.

(b) Post the entries to Work in Process Inventory, and prove the agreement of the control account with the job cost sheets.

E16-3   A job order cost sheet for Stan Free Company is shown below.

Analyze a job cost sheet and prepare entries for manufacturing costs.
(SO 2, 3, 4, 5)

Job No. 92			For 2,000 Units
Date	Direct Materials	Direct Labor	Manufacturing Overhead
Beg. bal. Jan. 1	5,000	6,000	3,900
8	6,000		
12		8,000	6,000
25	2,000		
27		4,000	3,000
	13,000	18,000	12,900

Cost of completed job:	
Direct materials	$13,000
Direct labor	18,000
Manufacturing overhead	12,900
Total cost	$43,900
Unit cost ($43,900 ÷ 2,000)	$ 21.95

Instructions

(a) ▭▭▭▷ On the basis of the foregoing data answer the following questions.

(1) What was the balance in Work in Process Inventory on January 1 if this was the only unfinished job?

(2) If manufacturing overhead is applied on the basis of direct labor cost, what overhead rate was used in each year?

(b) Prepare summary entries at January 31 to record the current year's transactions pertaining to Job No. 92.

E16-4   Manufacturing cost data for Lopez Company, which uses a job order cost system, are presented below.

Analyze costs of manufacturing and determine missing amounts.
(SO 2, 5)

	Case A	Case B	Case C
Direct materials used	$ (a)	$83,000	$ 63,150
Direct labor used	50,000	90,000	(h)
Manufacturing overhead applied	42,500	(d)	(i)
Total manufacturing costs	185,650	(e)	287,000
Work in process 1/1/05	(b)	15,500	18,000
Total cost of work in process	201,500	(f)	(j)
Work in process 12/31/05	(c)	11,800	(k)
Cost of goods manufactured	192,300	(g)	262,000

Compute the manufacturing overhead rate and under- or overapplied overhead.
(SO 4, 6)

Instructions

Indicate the missing amount for each letter. Assume that in all cases manufacturing overhead is applied on the basis of direct labor cost and the rate is the same.

E16-5 Ramirez Company applies manufacturing overhead to jobs on the basis of machine hours used. Overhead costs are expected to total $275,000 for the year, and machine usage is estimated at 125,000 hours.

In January, $26,000 of overhead costs are incurred and 12,000 machine hours are used. For the remainder of the year, $274,000 of overhead costs are incurred and 118,000 machine hours are worked.

Instructions

(a) Compute the manufacturing overhead rate for the year.

(b) What is the amount of under- or overapplied overhead at January 31? How should this amount be reported in the financial statements prepared on January 31?

(c) What is the amount of under- or overapplied overhead at December 31?

(d) Assuming the under- or overapplied overhead for the year is not allocated to inventory accounts, prepare the adjusting entry to assign the amount to cost of goods sold.

Analyze job cost sheet and prepare entry for completed job.
(SO 2, 3, 4, 5)

E16-6 A job cost sheet of Serrano Company is given below.

Job Cost Sheet

JOB NO.   469   Quantity   2,000
ITEM   White Lion Cages   Date Requested   7/2
FOR   Tesla Company   Date Completed   7/31

Date	Direct Materials	Direct Labor	Manufacturing Overhead
7/10	825		
12	900		
15		440	572
22		380	494
24	1,600		
27	1,500		
31		540	702

Cost of completed job:
   Direct materials   _____
   Direct labor   _____
   Manufacturing overhead   _____
Total cost   ======
Unit cost   ======

Instructions

(a)   Answer the following questions.

  (1) What are the source documents for direct materials, direct labor, and manufacturing overhead costs assigned to this job?

  (2) What is the predetermined manufacturing overhead rate?

  (3) What are the total cost and the unit cost of the completed job?

(b) Prepare the entry to record the completion of the job.

Prepare entries for manufacturing costs.
(SO 2, 4, 5)

E16-7 Tejada Corporation incurred the following transactions.

1. Purchased raw materials on account $46,300.

2. Raw materials of $36,000 were requisitioned to the factory. An analysis of the materials requisition slips indicated that $8,800 was classified as indirect materials.

3. Factory labor costs incurred were $64,900, of which $59,000 pertained to factory wages payable and $5,900 pertained to employer payroll taxes payable.

4. Time tickets indicated that $60,000 was direct labor and $4,900 was indirect labor.
5. Overhead costs incurred on account were $80,500.
6. Manufacturing overhead was applied at the rate of 150% of direct labor cost.
7. Goods costing $88,000 were completed and transferred to finished goods.
8. Finished goods costing $68,000 to manufacture were sold on account for $103,000.

Instructions
Journalize the transactions. (Omit explanations.)

E16-8 Barajas Printing Corp. uses a job order cost system. The following data summarize the operations related to the first quarter's production.
1. Materials purchased on account $172,000, and factory wages incurred $87,300.
2. Materials requisitioned and factory labor used by job:

Prepare entries for manufacturing costs.
(SO 2, 3, 4, 5)

Job Number	Materials	Factory Labor
A20	$ 32,240	$18,000
A21	42,920	26,000
A22	36,100	15,000
A23	39,270	25,000
General factory use	4,470	3,300
	$155,000	$87,300

3. Manufacturing overhead costs incurred on account $39,500.
4. Depreciation on machinery and equipment $14,550.
5. Manufacturing overhead rate is 75% of direct labor cost.
6. Jobs completed during the quarter: A20, A21, and A23.

Instructions
Prepare entries to record the operations summarized above. (Prepare a schedule showing the individual cost elements and total cost for each job in item 6.)

E16-9 At May 31, 2005, the accounts of Corrales Manufacturing Company show the following.
1. May 1 inventories—finished goods $12,600, work in process $14,700, and raw materials $8,200.
2. May 31 inventories—finished goods $10,500, work in process $17,900, and raw materials $7,100.
3. Debit postings to work in process were: direct materials $62,400, direct labor $32,000, and manufacturing overhead applied $64,000.
4. Sales totaled $200,000.

Prepare a cost of goods manufactured schedule and partial financial statements.
(SO 2, 5)

Instructions
(a) Prepare a condensed cost of goods manufactured schedule.
(b) Prepare an income statement for May through gross profit.
(c) Indicate the balance sheet presentation of the manufacturing inventories at May 31, 2005.

E16-10 Mendoza Company begins operations on April 1. Information from job cost sheets shows the following.

Compute work in process and finished goods from job cost sheets.
(SO 3, 5)

Job Number	Manufacturing Costs Assigned		
	April	May	June
10	$5,200	$4,400	
11	4,100	3,900	$3,000
12	1,200		
13		4,700	4,500
14		3,900	3,600

Job 12 was completed in April. Job 10 was completed in May. Jobs 11 and 13 were completed in June. Each job was sold for 60% above its cost in the month following completion.

Instructions
(a) What is the balance in Work in Process Inventory at the end of each month?
(b) What is the balance in Finished Goods Inventory at the end of each month?
(c) What is the gross profit for May, June, and July?

Problems: Set A

Prepare entries in a job cost system and job cost sheets.
(SO 2, 3, 4, 5, 6)

P16-1A Don Tidrick Manufacturing uses a job order cost system and applies overhead to production on the basis of direct labor costs. On January 1, 2005, Job No. 50 was the only job in process. The costs incurred prior to January 1 on this job were as follows: direct materials $20,000, direct labor $12,000, and manufacturing overhead $21,000. As of January 1, Job No. 49 had been completed at a cost of $90,000 and was part of finished goods inventory. There was a $15,000 balance in the Raw Materials inventory account.

During the month of January, Don Tidrick Manufacturing began production on Jobs 51 and 52, and completed Jobs 50 and 51. Jobs 49 and 50 were sold on account during the month for $122,000 and $158,000, respectively. The following additional events occurred during the month.

1. Purchased additional raw materials of $90,000 on account.
2. Incurred factory labor costs of $63,000. Of this amount $13,000 related to employer payroll taxes.
3. Incurred manufacturing overhead costs as follows: indirect materials $14,000; indirect labor $15,000; depreciation expense $19,000, and various other manufacturing overhead costs on account $23,000.
4. Assigned direct materials and direct labor to jobs as follows.

Job No.	Direct Materials	Direct Labor
50	$10,000	$ 6,000
51	39,000	24,000
52	30,000	18,000

Instructions
(a) Calculate the predetermined overhead rate for 2005, assuming Don Tidrick Manufacturing estimates total manufacturing overhead costs of $1,050,000, direct labor costs of $700,000, and direct labor hours of 20,000 for the year.
(b) Open job cost sheets for Jobs 50, 51, and 52. Enter the January 1 balances on the job cost sheet for Job No. 50.
(c) Prepare the journal entries to record the purchase of raw materials, the factory labor costs incurred, and the manufacturing overhead costs incurred during the month of January.
(d) Prepare the journal entries to record the assignment of direct materials, direct labor, and manufacturing overhead costs to production. In assigning manufacturing overhead costs, use the overhead rate calculated in (a). Post all costs to the job cost sheets as necessary.

(e) Job 50 $78,000
Job 51 $99,000

(e) Total the job cost sheets for any job(s) completed during the month. Prepare the journal entry (or entries) to record the completion of any job(s) during the month.
(f) Prepare the journal entry (or entries) to record the sale of any job(s) during the month.
(g) What is the balance in the Finished Goods Inventory account at the end of the month? What does this balance consist of?
(h) What is the amount of over- or underapplied overhead for the month? How would this be reported on the financial statements for the month of January?

Prepare entries in a job cost system and partial income statement.
(SO 2, 3, 4, 5, 6)

P16-2A For the year ended December 31, 2005, the job cost sheets of Chicago Company contained the following data.

Job Number	Explanation	Direct Materials	Direct Labor	Manufacturing Overhead	Total Costs
7640	Balance 1/1	$25,000	$24,000	$28,800	$ 77,800
	Current year's costs	34,000	36,000	43,200	113,200
7641	Balance 1/1	11,000	18,000	21,600	50,600
	Current year's costs	40,000	48,000	57,600	145,600
7642	Current year's costs	48,000	55,000	66,000	169,000

Other data:

1. Raw materials inventory totaled $15,000 on January 1. During the year, $140,000 of raw materials were purchased on account.
2. Finished goods on January 1 consisted of Job No. 7638 for $87,000 and Job No. 7639 for $92,000.
3. Job No. 7640 and Job No. 7641 were completed during the year.
4. Jobs No. 7638, 7639, and 7641 were sold on account for $530,000.
5. Manufacturing overhead incurred on account totaled $115,000.
6. Other manufacturing overhead consisted of indirect materials $14,000, indirect labor $20,000, and depreciation on factory machinery $8,000.

Instructions

(a) Prove the agreement of Work in Process Inventory with job cost sheets pertaining to unfinished work. *Hint:* Use a single T account for Work in Process Inventory. Calculate each of the following, then post each to the T account: (1) beginning balance, (2) direct materials, (3) direct labor, (4) manufacturing overhead, and (5) completed jobs.

(b) Prepare the adjusting entry for manufacturing overhead, assuming the balance is allocated entirely to Cost of Goods Sold.

(c) Determine the gross profit to be reported for 2005.

(a) Job 7642 $169,000

P16-3A Peoria Inc. is a construction company specializing in custom patios. The patios are constructed of concrete, brick, fiberglass, and lumber, depending upon customer preference. On June 1, 2005, the general ledger for Peoria Inc. contains the following data.

Prepare entries in a job cost system and cost of goods manufactured schedule.
(SO 2, 3, 4, 5)

Raw Materials Inventory	$4,200	Manufacturing Overhead Applied	$32,640
Work in Process Inventory	$5,900	Manufacturing Overhead Incurred	$31,650

Subsidiary data for Work in Process Inventory on June 1 are as follows.

Job Cost Sheets

Customer Job

Cost Element	Rockford	Aurora	Moline
Direct materials	$ 600	$ 800	$ 900
Direct labor	320	540	580
Manufacturing overhead	480	810	870
	$1,400	$2,150	$2,350

A summary of materials requisition slips and time tickets for June shows the following.

Customer Job	Materials Requisition Slips	Time Tickets
Rockford	$ 800	$ 450
Elgin	2,000	800
Aurora	500	360
Moline	1,300	800
Rockford	300	250
	4,900	2,660
General use	1,500	1,200
	$6,400	$3,860

During June, raw materials purchased on account were $3,900, and all wages were paid. Additional overhead costs consisted of depreciation on equipment $700 and miscellaneous costs of $400 incurred on account. Overhead was charged to jobs at the same rate that was used in May. The patios for customers Rockford, Aurora, and Moline were completed during June and sold for a total of $18,900. Each customer paid in full.

Instructions
(a) Journalize the June transactions.
(b) Post the entries to Work in Process Inventory.
(c) Reconcile the balance in Work in Process Inventory with the costs of unfinished jobs.
(d) Prepare a cost of goods manufactured schedule for June.

(d) Cost of goods manufactured $13,450

Compute predetermined overhead rate, apply overhead, and indicate statement presentation of under- or overapplied overhead.
(SO 4, 6)

P16-4A Urbana Manufacturing Company uses a job order cost system in each of its three manufacturing departments. Manufacturing overhead is applied to jobs on the basis of direct labor cost in Department D, direct labor hours in Department E, and machine hours in Department K.

In establishing the predetermined overhead rates for 2006 the following estimates were made for the year.

	Department		
	D	**E**	**K**
Manufacturing overhead	$1,170,000	$1,500,000	$960,000
Direct labor costs	$1,500,000	$1,250,000	$450,000
Direct labor hours	100,000	120,000	40,000
Machine hours	400,000	500,000	120,000

During January, the job cost sheets showed the following costs and production data.

	Department		
	D	**E**	**K**
Direct materials used	$140,000	$126,000	$78,000
Direct labor costs	$120,000	$110,000	$37,500
Manufacturing overhead incurred	$ 98,000	$129,000	$80,000
Direct labor hours	8,000	11,000	3,500
Machine hours	34,000	45,000	10,400

Instructions
(a) Compute the predetermined overhead rate for each department.
(b) Compute the total manufacturing costs assigned to jobs in January in each department.
(c) Compute the under- or overapplied overhead for each department at January 31.
(d) Indicate the statement presentation of the under- or overapplied overhead at January 31.
(e) If the amount in (d) was the same at December 31, how would it be reported in the year-end financial statements?

(b) Dept. E $373,000

(c) Dept. K $ (3,200)

Analyze manufacturing accounts and determine missing amounts.
(SO 2, 3, 4, 5, 6)

P16-5A Florida Boot Corporation's fiscal year ends on November 30. The following accounts are found in its job order cost accounting system for the first month of the new fiscal year.

Raw Materials Inventory

Dec. 1	Beginning balance	(a)	Dec. 31	Requisitions	14,850
31	Purchases	19,225			
Dec. 31	Ending balance	7,975			

Work in Process Inventory

Dec. 1	Beginning balance	(b)	Dec. 31	Jobs completed	(f)
31	Direct materials	(c)			
31	Direct labor	8,100			
31	Overhead	(d)			
Dec. 31	Ending balance	(e)			

Finished Goods Inventory

Dec. 1	Beginning balance	(g)	Dec. 31	Cost of goods sold	(i)
31	Completed jobs	(h)			
Dec. 31	Ending balance	(j)			

Factory Labor

Dec. 31	Factory wages	10,800	Dec. 31	Wages assigned	(k)

Manufacturing Overhead

Dec. 31	Indirect materials	1,900	Dec. 31	Overhead applied	(m)
31	Indirect labor	(l)			
31	Other overhead	1,245			

Other data:

1. On December 1, two jobs were in process: Job No. 154 and Job No. 155. These jobs had combined direct materials costs of $9,750 and direct labor costs of $12,000. Overhead was applied at a rate that was 75% of direct labor cost. $= 9\,000$

2. During December, Job Nos. 156, 157, and 158 were started. On December 31, Job No. 158 was unfinished. This job had charges for direct materials $3,800 and direct labor $4,400, plus manufacturing overhead. All jobs, except for Job No. 158, were completed in December. $3\,800 + 4\,400 + 3\,300 = 11\,500$

3. On December 1, Job No. 153 was in the finished goods warehouse. It had a total cost of $5,000. On December 31, Job No. 157 was the only job finished that was not sold. It had a cost of $4,000.

4. Manufacturing overhead was $230 overapplied in December.

Instructions

List the letters (a) through (m) and indicate the amount pertaining to each letter.

16-5A
egrade

Problems: Set B

P16-1B Han Wu Manufacturing uses a job order cost system and applies overhead to production on the basis of direct labor hours. On January 1, 2005, Job No. 25 was the only job in process. The costs incurred prior to January 1 on this job were as follows: direct materials $10,000; direct labor $6,000; and manufacturing overhead $10,500. Job No. 23 had been completed at a cost of $45,000 and was part of finished goods inventory. There was a $5,000 balance in the Raw Materials inventory account.

During the month of January, the company began production on Jobs 26 and 27, and completed Jobs 25 and 26. Jobs 23 and 25 were sold on account during the month for $67,000 and $74,000, respectively. The following additional events occurred during the month.

1. Purchased additional raw materials of $45,000 on account.
2. Incurred factory labor costs of $31,500. Of this amount $6,500 related to employer payroll taxes.
3. Incurred manufacturing overhead costs as follows: indirect materials $10,000; indirect labor $7,500; depreciation expense $12,000; and various other manufacturing overhead costs on account $15,000.
4. Assigned direct materials and direct labor to jobs as follows.

Prepare entries in a job cost system and job cost sheets.
(SO 2, 3, 4, 5, 6)

Job No.	Direct Materials	Direct Labor
25	$ 5,000	$ 3,000
26	20,000	12,000
27	15,000	9,000

5. The company uses direct labor hours as the activity base to assign overhead. Direct labor hours incurred on each job were as follows: Job No. 25, 200; Job No. 26, 800; and Job No. 27, 600.

Instructions

(a) Calculate the predetermined overhead rate for the year 2005, assuming Han Wu Manufacturing estimates total manufacturing overhead costs of $500,000, direct labor costs of $300,000, and direct labor hours of 20,000 for the year.

(b) Open job cost sheets for Jobs 25, 26, and 27. Enter the January 1 balances on the job cost sheet for Job No. 25.

(c) Prepare the journal entries to record the purchase of raw materials, the factory labor costs incurred, and the manufacturing overhead costs incurred during the month of January.

(d) Prepare the journal entries to record the assignment of direct materials, direct labor, and manufacturing overhead costs to production. In assigning manufacturing overhead costs, use the overhead rate calculated in (a). Post all costs to the job cost sheets as necessary.

(e) Job 26 $52,000

(e) Total the job cost sheets for any job(s) completed during the month. Prepare the journal entry (or entries) to record the completion of any job(s) during the month.

(f) Prepare the journal entry (or entries) to record the sale of any job(s) during the month.

(g) What is the balance in the Work in Process Inventory account at the end of the month? What does this balance consist of?

(h) What is the amount of over- or underapplied overhead for the month? How would this be reported on the financial statements for the month of January?

Prepare entries in a job cost system and partial income statement.
(SO 2, 3, 4, 5, 6)

P16-2B For the year ended December 31, 2005, the job cost sheets of Ying Chen Company contained the following data.

Job Number	Explanation	Direct Materials	Direct Labor	Manufacturing Overhead	Total Costs
7650	Balance 1/1	$18,000	$20,000	$25,000	$ 63,000
	Current year's costs	22,000	30,000	37,500	89,500
7651	Balance 1/1	12,000	18,000	22,500	52,500
	Current year's costs	28,000	40,000	50,000	118,000
7652	Current year's costs	40,000	60,000	75,000	175,000

Other data:

1. Raw materials inventory totaled $20,000 on January 1. During the year, $100,000 of raw materials were purchased on account.

2. Finished goods on January 1 consisted of Job No. 7648 for $98,000 and Job No. 7649 for $62,000.

3. Job No. 7650 and Job No. 7651 were completed during the year.

4. Jobs No. 7648, 7649, and 7650 were sold on account for $390,000.

5. Manufacturing overhead incurred on account totaled $120,000.

6. Other manufacturing overhead consisted of indirect materials $12,000, indirect labor $18,000, and depreciation on factory machinery $19,500.

Instructions

(a) Job 7652 $175,000

(a) Prove the agreement of Work in Process Inventory with job cost sheets pertaining to unfinished work. *Hint:* Use a single T account for Work in Process Inventory. Calculate each of the following, then post each to the T account: (1) beginning balance, (2) direct materials, (3) direct labor, (4) manufacturing overhead, and (5) completed jobs.

(b) Prepare the adjusting entry for manufacturing overhead, assuming the balance is allocated entirely to cost of goods sold.

(c) Determine the gross profit to be reported for 2005.

P16-3B   Richard E. Baker is a contractor specializing in custom-built jacuzzis. On May 1, 2005, his ledger contains the following data.

Prepare entries in a job cost system and cost of goods manufactured schedule.
(SO 2, 3, 4, 5)

Raw Materials Inventory	$30,000
Work in Process Inventory	12,400
Manufacturing Overhead	2,500 (dr.)

The Manufacturing Overhead account has debit totals of $12,500 and credit totals of $10,000. Subsidiary data for Work in Process Inventory on May 1 include:

Job Cost Sheets

Job by Customer	Direct Materials	Direct Labor	Manufacturing Overhead
Engstrom	$2,500	$2,000	$1,500
Hendricks	2,000	1,200	900
Keys	900	800	600
	$5,400	$4,000	$3,000

A summary of materials requisition slips and time tickets for the month of May reveals the following.

Job by Customer	Materials Requisition Slips	Time Tickets
Engstrom	$ 500	$ 400
Hendricks	600	1,000
Keys	2,300	1,300
Bennett	2,400	3,300
	5,800	6,000
General use	1,500	2,600
	$7,300	$8,600

During May, the following costs were incurred: (a) raw materials purchased on account $5,000, (b) labor paid $8,600, (c) manufacturing overhead paid $1,400. Overhead was charged to jobs on the basis of direct labor cost at the same rate as in the previous month.

The jacuzzis for customers Engstrom, Hendricks, and Keys were completed during May. Each jacuzzi was sold for $12,500 cash.

Instructions
  (a) Prepare journal entries for the May transactions.
  (b) Post the entries to Work in Process Inventory.
  (c) Reconcile the balance in Work in Process Inventory with the costs of unfinished jobs.
  (d) Prepare a cost of goods manufactured schedule for May.

(d) Cost of goods manufactured
$20,525

P16-4B   Hopkins Manufacturing uses a job order cost system in each of its three manufacturing departments. Manufacturing overhead is applied to jobs on the basis of direct labor cost in Department A, direct labor hours in Department B, and machine hours in Department C.

In establishing the predetermined overhead rates for 2005 the following estimates were made for the year.

Compute predetermined overhead rates, apply overhead, and indicate statement presentation of under- or overapplied overhead.
(SO 4, 6)

	Department		
	A	**B**	**C**
Manufacturing overhead	$900,000	$760,000	$780,000
Direct labor cost	$600,000	$400,000	$600,000
Direct labor hours	50,000	50,000	40,000
Machine hours	100,000	120,000	150,000

During January, the job cost sheets showed the following costs and production data.

	Department		
	A	**B**	**C**
Direct materials used	$92,000	$86,000	$64,000
Direct labor cost	$48,000	$35,000	$50,400
Manufacturing overhead incurred	$76,000	$54,000	$64,500
Direct labor hours	4,000	3,500	4,200
Machine hours	8,000	10,500	12,600

(a) Dept. B $15.20

(c) Dept. C $1,020 overapplied

Analyze manufacturing cost accounts and determine missing amounts.
(SO 2, 3, 4, 5, 6)

Instructions

(a) Compute the predetermined overhead rate for each department.

(b) Compute the total manufacturing costs assigned to jobs in January in each department.

(c) Compute the under- or overapplied overhead for each department at January 31.

(d) Indicate the statement presentation of the under- or overapplied overhead at January 31.

(e) If the amount in (d) was the same at December 31, how would it be reported in the year-end financial statements?

P16-5B Devona Company's fiscal year ends on June 30. The following accounts are found in its job order cost accounting system for the first month of the new fiscal year.

Raw Materials Inventory

July	1	Beginning balance	19,000	July 31	Requisitions	(a)
	31	Purchases	90,400			
July	31	Ending balance	(b)			

Work in Process Inventory

July	1	Beginning balance	(c)	July 31	Jobs completed	(f)
	31	Direct materials	75,000			
	31	Direct labor	(d)			
	31	Overhead	(e)			
July	31	Ending balance	(g)			

Finished Goods Inventory

July	1	Beginning balance	(h)	July 31	Cost of goods sold	(j)
	31	Completed jobs	(i)			
July	31	Ending balance	(k)			

Factory Labor

July	31	Factory wages	(l)	July 31	Wages assigned	(m)

Manufacturing Overhead

July	31	Indirect materials	8,900	July 31	Overhead applied	91,000
	31	Indirect labor	16,000			
	31	Other overhead	(n)			

Other data:

1. On July 1, two jobs were in process: Job No. 4085 and Job No. 4086, with costs of $17,000 and $8,200, respectively.

2. During July, Job Nos. 4087, 4088, and 4089 were started. On July 31, only Job No. 4089 was unfinished. This job had charges for direct materials $2,000 and direct labor $1,500, plus manufacturing overhead.

3. On July 1, Job No. 4084, costing $135,000, was in the finished goods warehouse. On July 31, Job No. 4088, costing $143,000, was in finished goods.
4. Manufacturing overhead was applied at the rate of 130% of direct labor cost. Overhead was $3,000 underapplied in July.

Instructions
List the letters (a) through (n) and indicate the amount pertaining to each letter. Show computations.

▶ BROADENING YOUR PERSPECTIVE

Group Decision Case

BYP16-1 Du Page Products Company uses a job order cost system. For a number of months there has been an ongoing rift between the sales department and the production department concerning a special-order product, TC-1. TC-1 is a seasonal product that is manufactured in batches of 1,000 units. TC-1 is sold at cost plus a markup of 40% of cost.

The sales department is unhappy because fluctuating unit production costs significantly affect selling prices. Sales personnel complain that this has caused excessive customer complaints and the loss of considerable orders for TC-1.

The production department maintains that each job order must be fully costed on the basis of the costs incurred during the period in which the goods are produced. Production personnel maintain that the only real solution to the problem is for the sales department to increase sales in the slack periods.

Sandra Devona, president of the company, asks you as the company accountant to collect quarterly data for the past year on TC-1. From the cost accounting system, you accumulate the following production quantity and cost data.

Costs	Quarter 1	2	3	4
Direct materials	$100,000	$220,000	$ 80,000	$200,000
Direct labor	60,000	132,000	48,000	120,000
Manufacturing overhead	105,000	123,000	97,000	125,000
Total	$265,000	$475,000	$225,000	$445,000
Production in batches	5	11	4	10
Unit cost (per batch)	$ 53,000	$ 43,182	$ 56,250	$ 44,500

Instructions
With the class divided into groups, answer the following questions.
(a) What manufacturing cost element is responsible for the fluctuating unit costs? Why?
(b) What is your recommended solution to the problem of fluctuating unit costs?
(c) Restate the quarterly data on the basis of your recommended solution.

Managerial Analysis

BYP16-2 In the course of routine checking of all journal entries prior to preparing month-end reports, Sally Weber discovered several strange entries. She recalled that the president's son Jeff had come in to help out during an especially busy time and that he had recorded some journal entries. She was relieved that there were only a few of his entries, and even more relieved that he had included rather lengthy explanations. The entries Jeff made were:

1.

Work in Process Inventory	20,000	
Cash		20,000

(This is for materials put into process. I don't find the record that we paid for these, so I'm crediting Cash, because I know we'll have to pay for them sooner or later.)

2.

Manufacturing Overhead	12,000	
Cash		12,000

(This is for bonuses paid to salespeople. I know they're part of overhead, and I can't find an account called "Non-factory Overhead" or "Other Overhead" so I'm putting it in Manufacturing Overhead. I have the check stubs, so I know we paid these.)

3.

Wages Expense	120,000	
Cash		120,000

(This is for the factory workers' wages. I have a note that payroll taxes are $8,000. I still think that's part of wages expense, and that we'll have to pay it all in cash sooner or later, so I credited Cash for the wages and the taxes.)

4.

Work in Process Inventory	3,000	
Raw Materials Inventory		3,000

(This is for the glue used in the factory. I know we used this to make the products, even though we didn't use very much on any one of the products. I got it out of inventory, so I credited an inventory account.)

Instructions
  (a) How should Jeff have recorded each of the four events?
  (b) If the entry was not corrected, which financial statements (income statement or balance sheet) would be affected? What balances would be overstated or understated?

Real-World Focus

BYP16-3 Founded in 1970, **Parlex Corporation** is a world leader in the design and manufacture of flexible interconnect products. Utilizing proprietary and patented technologies, Parlex produces custom flexible interconnects including flexible circuits, polymer thick film, laminated cables, and value-added assemblies for sophisticated electronics used in automotive, telecommunications, computer, diversified electronics, and aerospace applications. In addition to manufacturing sites in Methuen, Massachusetts; Salem, New Hampshire; Cranston, Rhode Island; San Jose, California; Shanghai, China; Isle of Wight, UK; and Empalme, Mexico, Parlex has logistic support centers and strategic alliances throughout North America, Asia, and Europe.

    The following information was provided in the company's annual report.

PARLEX COMPANY
Notes to the Financial Statements

The Company's products are manufactured on a job order basis to customers' specifications. Customers submit requests for quotations on each job, and the Company prepares bids based on its own cost estimates. The Company attempts to reflect the impact of changing costs when establishing prices. However, during the past several years, the market conditions for flexible circuits and the resulting price sensitivity haven't always allowed this to transpire. Although still not satisfactory, the Company was able to reduce the cost of products sold as a percentage of sales to 85% this year versus 87% that was experienced in the two immediately preceding years. Management continues to focus on improving operational efficiency and further reducing costs.

Instructions
  (a) Parlex management discusses the job order cost system employed by their company. What are several advantages of using the job order approach to costing?
  (b) Contrast the products produced in a job order environment, like Parlex, to those produced when process cost systems are used.

Exploring the Web

BYP16-4 The Institute of Management Accountants sponsors a certification for management accountants, allowing them to obtain the title of Certified Management Accountant.

Address: www.imanet.org (or go to **www.wiley.com/college/kimmel**)

Steps
  1. Go to the site shown above.
  2. Choose **Certification**.

Instructions
  (a) What are the objectives of the certification program?
  (b) What is the "experience requirement"?
  (c) How many hours of continuing education are required, and what types of courses qualify?

Communication Activity

BYP16-5 You are the management accountant for Modine Manufacturing. Your company does custom carpentry work and uses a job order cost accounting system. Modine sends detailed job cost sheets to its customers, along with an invoice. The job cost sheets show the date materials were used, the dollar cost of materials, and the hours and cost of labor. A predetermined overhead application rate is used, and the total overhead applied is also listed.

Cindy Ross is a customer who recently had custom cabinets installed. Along with her check in payment for the work done, she included a letter. She thanked the company for including the detailed cost information but questioned why overhead was estimated. She stated that she would be interested in knowing exactly what costs were included in overhead, and she thought that other customers would, too.

Instructions
Prepare a letter to Ms. Ross (address: 123 Cedar Lane, Altoona, Kansas 66651) and tell her why you did not send her information on exact costs of overhead included in her job. Respond to her suggestion that you provide this information.

Research Case

BYP16-6 The February 1994 issue of *Ohio CPA Journal* includes an article by Eun-Sup Shim and Joseph M. Larkin entitled "A Survey of Current Managerial Accounting Practices: Where Do We Stand?"

Instructions
Read the article and answer the following questions.
  (a) What percent of manufacturers surveyed used job order costing?
  (b) What was the smallest cost component of the three factors of production? What portion of total manufacturing costs does it represent?
  (c) What percent of manufacturers surveyed operate in a single product environment—that is, what percent produce only one product?
  (d) What two managerial decisions were considered most affected by overhead allocation?

Ethics Case

BYP16-7 NIU Printing provides printing services to many different corporate clients. Although NIU bids most jobs, some jobs, particularly new ones, are often negotiated on a "cost-plus" basis. Cost-plus means that the buyer is willing to pay the actual cost plus a return (profit) on these costs to NIU.

Cathrine Traynor, controller for NIU, has recently returned from a meeting where NIU's president stated that he wanted her to find a way to charge most costs to any project that was on a cost-plus basis. The president noted that the company needed more profits to meet its stated goals this period. By charging more costs to the cost-plus projects and therefore less cost to the jobs that were bid, the company should be able to increase its profits for the current year.

Cathrine knew why the president wanted to take this action. Rumors were that he was looking for a new position and if the company reported strong profits, the president's opportunities would be enhanced. Cathrine also recognized that she could probably increase the cost of certain jobs by changing the basis used to allocate manufacturing overhead.

Instructions

(a) Who are the stakeholders in this situation?

(b) What are the ethical issues in this situation?

(c) What would you do if you were Cathrine Traynor?

Answers to Self-Study Questions

1. a   2. b   3. c   4. d   5. b   6. a   7. d   8. b   9. c   10. b

✔ Remember to go back to the Navigator box on the chapter-opening page and check off your completed work.

Process Cost Accounting

STUDY OBJECTIVES

After studying this chapter,
you should be able to:

1 Understand who uses process cost systems.

2 Explain the similarities and differences between job order cost and process cost systems.

3 Explain the flow of costs in a process cost system.

4 Make the journal entries to assign manufacturing costs in a process cost system.

5 Compute equivalent units.

6 Explain the four steps necessary to prepare a production cost report.

7 Prepare a production cost report.

8 Explain just-in-time (JIT) processing.

9 Explain activity-based costing (ABC).

FEATURE STORY

Ben & Jerry's Tracks Its Mix-Ups

At one time, one of the fastest growing companies in the nation was **Ben & Jerry's Homemade, Inc.**, based in Waterbury, Vermont. The ice cream company that started out of a garage in 1978 is now a public company.

Making ice cream is a process—a movement of product from a mixing department to a prepping department to a pint department. The mixing department is where the ice cream is created. The prep area is where extras such as cherries and walnuts are added to make plain ice cream into "Cherry Garcia." And the pint department is where the ice cream is actually put into containers. As the product is processed from one department to the next, the appropriate materials, labor, and overhead are added to it.

"The incoming ingredients from the shipping and receiving departments are stored in certain locations, either in a freezer or dry warehouse," says Beecher Eurich, staff accountant. "As ingredients get added, so do the costs associated with them." How much ice cream is actually produced? Running the plant around the clock, 24,000 pints are produced per 8-hour shift, or 72,000 pints per day.

Using a process costing system, Eurich can tell you how much a certain batch of ice cream costs to make—its materials, labor, and overhead in each of the production departments. She generates reports for the production department heads, but makes sure not to overdo it. "You can get bogged down in

THE NAVIGATOR ✔

▶ Scan *Study Objectives* ☐
▶ Read *Feature Story* ☐
▶ Read *Preview* ☐
▶ Read text and answer *Before You Go On*
   p. 826 ☐   p. 836 ☐   p. 841 ☐
▶ Work Using the *Decision Toolkit* ☐
▶ Review Summary of *Study Objectives* ☐
▶ Work *Demonstration Problem* ☐
▶ Answer *Self-Study Questions* ☐
▶ Complete *Assignments* ☐

numbers," says Eurich. "If you're generating a report that no one can use, then that's a waste of time." More likely, though, Ben & Jerry's production people want to know how efficient they are. Why? Many own stock in the company.

☑ THE NAVIGATOR

www.benjerry.com

The cost accounting system used by companies such as **Ben & Jerry's** is called a **process cost accounting** system. In contrast to job order cost accounting, which focuses on the individual job, process cost accounting focuses on the processes involved in mass-producing products that are identical or very similar in nature. The primary objective of the chapter is to explain and illustrate process cost accounting.

The content and organization of Chapter 17 are as follows.

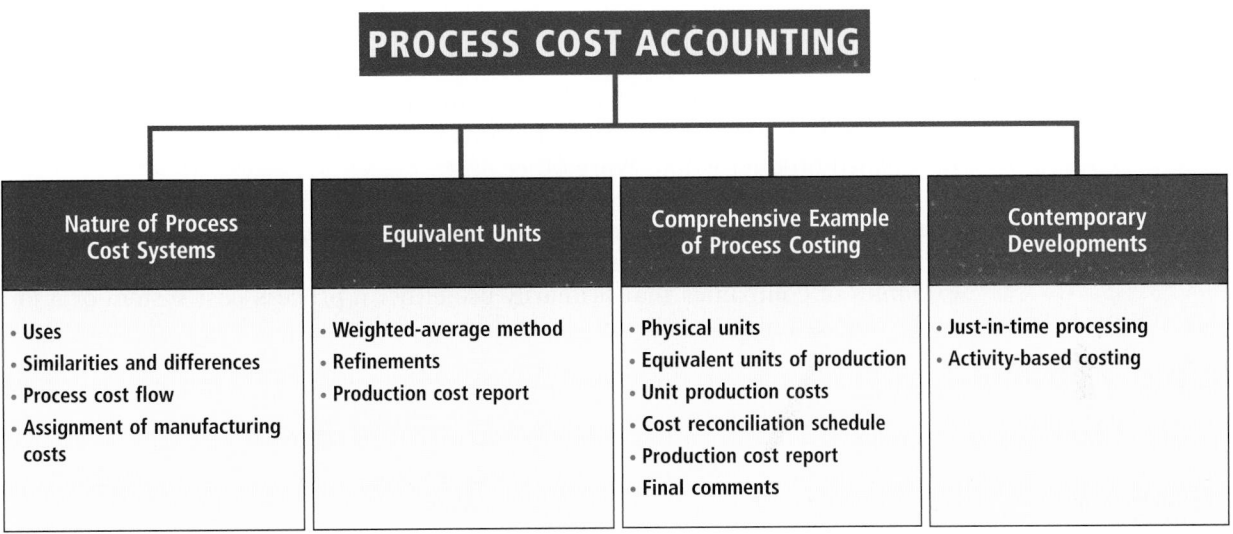

PROCESS COST ACCOUNTING

Nature of Process Cost Systems	Equivalent Units	Comprehensive Example of Process Costing	Contemporary Developments
• Uses • Similarities and differences • Process cost flow • Assignment of manufacturing costs	• Weighted-average method • Refinements • Production cost report	• Physical units • Equivalent units of production • Unit production costs • Cost reconciliation schedule • Production cost report • Final comments	• Just-in-time processing • Activity-based costing

☑ THE NAVIGATOR

The Nature of Process Cost Systems

USES OF PROCESS COST SYSTEMS

Process cost systems are used to apply costs to similar products that are mass-produced in a continuous fashion. Ben & Jerry's uses a process cost system: Production of the ice cream, once it begins, continues until the ice cream emerges, and the processing is the same for the entire run—with precisely the same amount of materials, labor, and overhead. Each finished pint of ice cream is indistinguishable from another.

A company such as **USX** uses process costing in the manufacturing of steel. **Kellogg** and **General Mills** use process costing for cereal production. **Exxon-Mobil** uses process costing for its oil refining. And **Sherwin Williams** uses process costing for its paint products. At a bottling company like **Coca-Cola**, the manufacturing process begins with the blending of the beverages. Next the beverage is dispensed into bottles that are moved into position by automated machinery. The bottles are then capped, packaged, and forwarded to the finished goods warehouse. This process is shown in Illustration 17-1 (page 822).

STUDY OBJECTIVE

1

Understand who uses process cost systems.

Illustration 17-1
Manufacturing processes

Illustration 17-1
Manufacturing processes

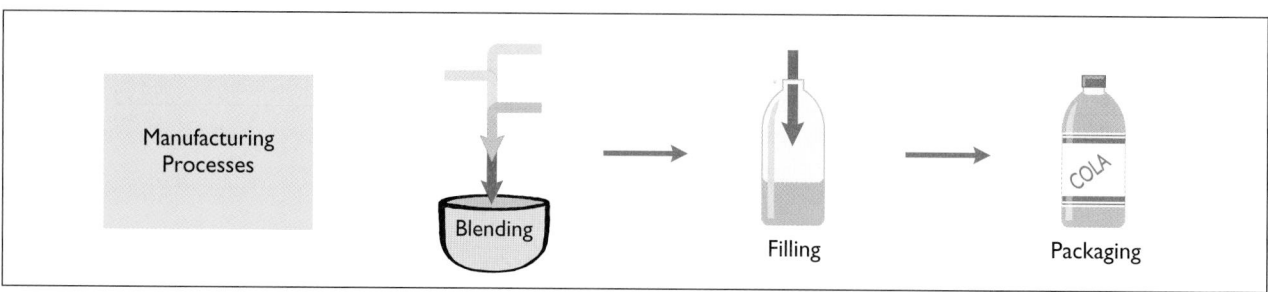

For Coca-Cola, as well as the other companies just mentioned, once the production begins, it continues until the finished product emerges, and each unit of finished product is like every other unit.

In comparison, costs in a job order cost system are assigned to a specific job. Examples are the construction of a customized home, the making of a motion picture, or the manufacturing of a specialized machine. Illustration 17-2 provides examples of companies that primarily use either a process cost system or a job order cost system.

Illustration 17-2 Process cost and job order cost companies and products

Process Cost System Company	Product	Job Order Cost System Company	Product
Coca-Cola, PepsiCo	Soft drinks	Young & Rubicam, J. Walter Thompson	Advertising
ExxonMobil, Shell Oil	Oil	Walt Disney, Warner Brothers	Motion pictures
Intel, Advanced Micro Devices	Computer chips	Center Ice Consultants, Ice Pro	Ice rinks
Dow Chemical, DuPont	Chemicals	Kaiser, Mayo Clinic	Patient health care

SIMILARITIES AND DIFFERENCES BETWEEN JOB ORDER COST AND PROCESS COST SYSTEMS

STUDY OBJECTIVE 2

Explain the similarities and differences between job order cost and process cost systems.

In a job order cost system, costs are assigned to each job. In a process cost system, costs are tracked through a series of connected manufacturing processes or departments, rather than by individual jobs. Thus, process cost systems are used when a large volume of uniform or relatively homogeneous products are produced. The basic flow of costs in these two systems is shown in Illustration 17-3.

The basic similarities and differences between job order cost and process cost systems are highlighted in the two lists on the next page.

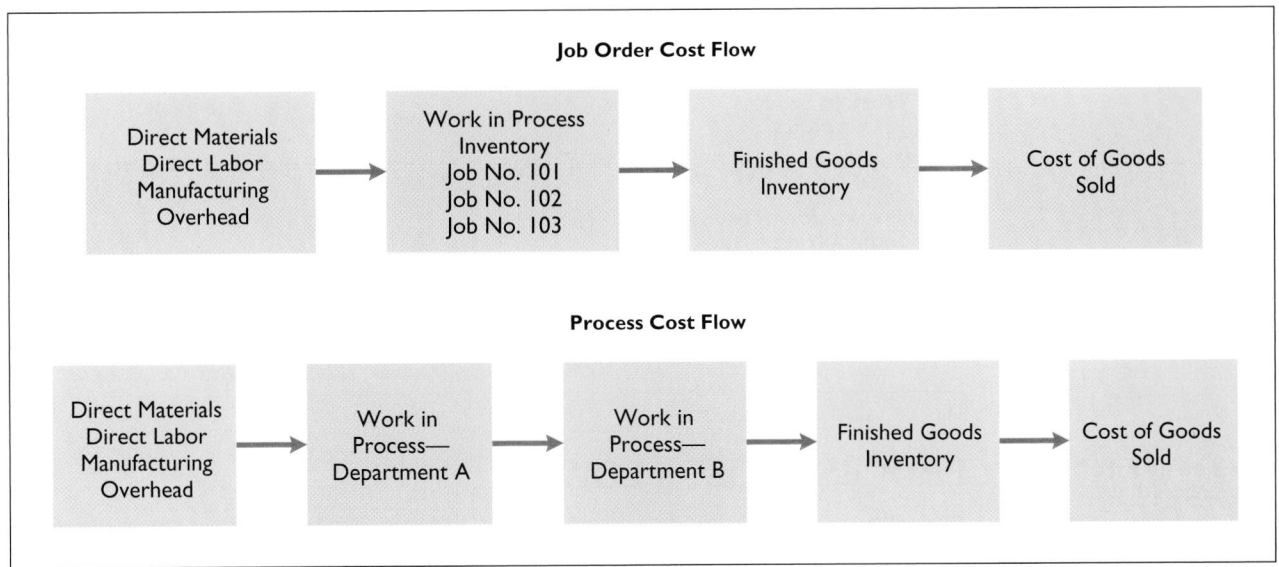

Illustration 17-3 Job order cost and process cost flow

Similarities Between Systems

1. **The manufacturing cost elements.** Both a job order cost and a process cost system track the same three manufacturing cost elements—direct materials, direct labor, and manufacturing overhead.

2. **The accumulation of the costs of materials, labor, and overhead.** In both costing systems, all raw materials are debited to Raw Materials Inventory; all factory labor is debited to Factory Labor; and all manufacturing overhead costs are debited to Manufacturing Overhead.

3. **The flow of costs.** As noted above, all manufacturing costs are accumulated by debits to Raw Materials Inventory, Factory Labor, and Manufacturing Overhead. These costs are then assigned to the same accounts in both costing systems—Work in Process, Finished Goods Inventory, and Cost of Goods Sold. **The methods of assigning costs, however, differ significantly.** These differences are explained and illustrated later in the chapter.

Differences Between Systems

1. **The number of work in process accounts used.** In a job order cost system, only one work in process account is used. In a process cost system, multiple work in process accounts are used; separate accounts are maintained for each production department or manufacturing process.

2. **Documents used to track costs.** In a job order cost system, costs are charged to individual jobs and summarized in a job cost sheet. In a process cost system, costs are summarized in a production cost report for each department.

3. **The point at which costs are totaled.** In a job order cost system, total costs are determined when the job is completed. In a process cost system, total costs are determined at the end of a period of time, such as a month or year.

4. **Unit cost computations.** In a job order cost system, the unit cost is the total cost per job divided by the units produced. In a process cost system, the unit cost is total manufacturing costs for the period divided by the units produced during the period.

The major differences between a job order cost and a process cost system are summarized in Illustration 17-4 (page 824).

Illustration 17-4 Job order versus process cost systems

Features	Job Order Cost System	Process Cost System
Work in process accounts	• One for each job	• One for each process
Documents used	• Job cost sheets	• Production cost reports
Determination of total manufacturing costs	• Each job	• Each period
Unit-cost computations	• Cost of each job ÷ Units produced for the job	• Total manufacturing costs ÷ Units produced during the period

STUDY OBJECTIVE
3
Explain the flow of costs in a process cost system.

Illustration 17-5 Flow of costs in process cost system

PROCESS COST FLOW

Illustration 17-5 shows the flow of costs in the process cost system for Tyler Company. Tyler Company manufactures automatic can openers that are sold to retail outlets. Manufacturing consists of two processes: machining and assembly. In the Machining Department, the raw materials are shaped, honed, and drilled. In the Assembly Department, the parts are assembled and packaged.

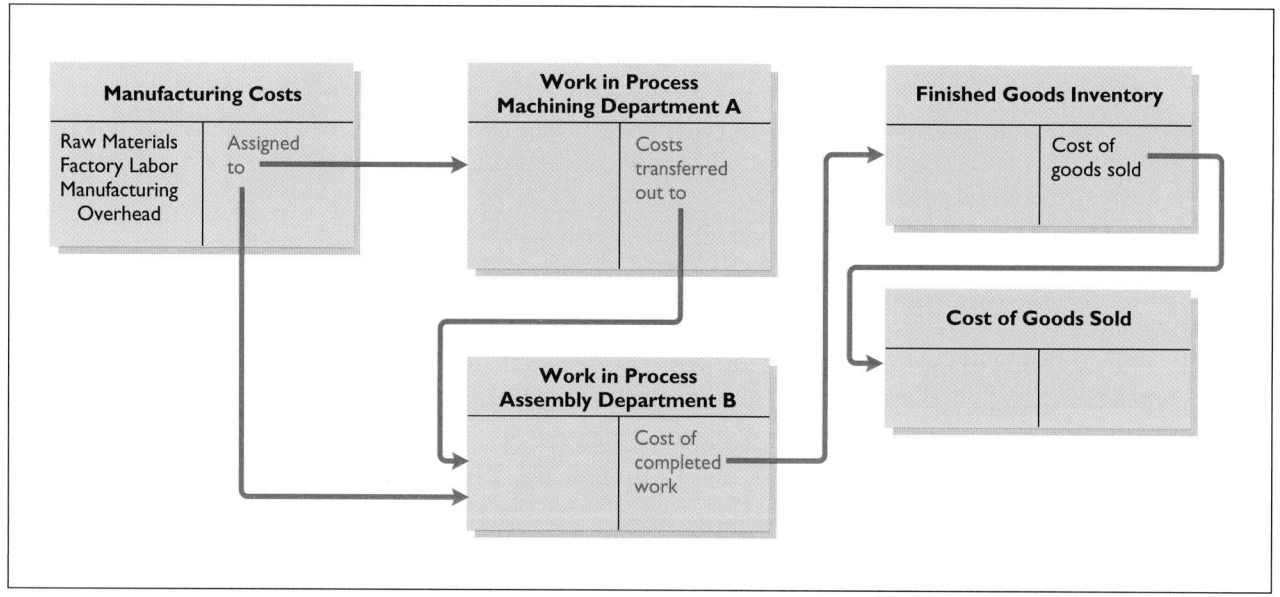

As the flow of costs indicates, materials, labor, and manufacturing overhead can be added in both the Machining and Assembly Departments. When the Machining Department finishes its work, the partially completed units are transferred to the Assembly Department. In the Assembly Department, the goods are finished and are then transferred to the finished goods inventory. Upon sale, the goods are removed from the finished goods inventory. Within each department, a similar set of activities is performed on each unit processed.

STUDY OBJECTIVE
4
Make the journal entries to assign manufacturing costs in a process cost system.

ASSIGNMENT OF MANUFACTURING COSTS—JOURNAL ENTRIES

As indicated earlier, the accumulation of the costs of materials, labor, and manufacturing overhead is the same in a process cost system as in a job order cost system. All raw materials are debited to Raw Materials Inventory when the materials are purchased. All factory labor is debited to Factory Labor when the labor costs are incurred. And overhead costs are debited to Manufacturing Overhead as they are incurred. However, the assignment of the three manufacturing cost elements to Work in Process in a process cost system is different from a job order cost system. Here we'll look at how these manufacturing cost elements are assigned in a process cost system.

Materials Costs

All raw materials issued for production are a materials cost to the producing department. Materials requisition slips may be used in a process cost system, but **fewer requisitions are generally required than in a job order cost system, because the materials are used for processes rather than for specific jobs**. Requisitions are issued less frequently in a process cost system because the requisitions are for larger quantities.

Materials are usually added to production at the beginning of the first process. However, in subsequent processes, other materials may be added at various points. For example, in the manufacture of **Hershey** candy bars, the chocolate and other ingredients are added at the beginning of the first process, and the wrappers and cartons are added at the end of the packaging process. At Tyler Company, materials are entered at the beginning of each process. The entry to record the materials used is:

Work in Process—Machining	XXXX	
Work in Process—Assembly	XXXX	
Raw Materials Inventory		XXXX
(To record materials used)		

In the Feature Story at the beginning of the chapter, materials are added to the ice cream in three departments: milk and flavoring in the mixing department; extras such as cherries and walnuts in the prepping department; and cardboard containers in the pinting (packaging) department.

Factory Labor Costs

In a process cost system, as in a job order cost system, time tickets may be used to determine the cost of labor assignable to production departments. Since labor costs are assigned to a process rather than a job, the labor cost chargeable to a process can be obtained from the payroll register or departmental payroll summaries.

All labor costs incurred within a producing department are a cost of processing the raw materials. Thus, labor costs for the Machining Department will include the wages of employees who shape, hone, and drill the raw materials. The entry to assign these costs for Tyler Company is:

Work in Process—Machining	XXXX	
Work in Process—Assembly	XXXX	
Factory Labor		XXXX
(To assign factory labor to production)		

Manufacturing Overhead Costs

The objective in assigning overhead in a process cost system is to allocate the overhead costs to the production departments on an objective and equitable basis. That basis is the activity that "drives" or causes the costs. A primary driver of overhead costs in continuous manufacturing operations is **machine time used**, not direct labor. Thus, **machine hours are widely used** in allocating manufacturing overhead costs. The entry to allocate overhead to the two processes is:

Work in Process—Machining	XXXX	
Work in Process—Assembly	XXXX	
Manufacturing Overhead		XXXX
(To assign overhead to production)		

Business Insight
MANAGEMENT PERSPECTIVE

In one of **Caterpillar**'s automated cost centers, work is fed into the cost center, processed by robotic machines, and transferred to the next cost center without human intervention. One person tends all of the machines and spends more time maintaining machines than operating them. In such cases, overhead rates based on direct labor hours may be misleading. Surprisingly, some companies continue to assign manufacturing overhead on the basis of direct labor despite the fact that there is no cause-and-effect relationship between labor and overhead.

Transfer to Next Department

At the end of the month, an entry is needed to record the cost of the goods transferred out of the department. In this case, the transfer is to the Assembly Department, and the following entry is made:

Work in Process—Assembly	XXXXX	
Work in Process—Machining		XXXXX
(To record transfer of units to the Assembly		
Department)		

Transfer to Finished Goods

The units completed in the Assembly Department are transferred to the finished goods warehouse. The entry for this transfer is as follows.

Finished Goods Inventory	XXXXX	
Work in Process—Assembly		XXXXX
(To record transfer of units to finished goods)		

Transfer to Cost of Goods Sold

When finished goods are sold, the entry to record the cost of goods sold is as follows.

Cost of Goods Sold	XXXXX	
Finished Goods Inventory		XXXXX
(To record cost of units sold)		

BEFORE YOU GO ON . . .

▶ Review It

1. What type of manufacturing companies might use a process cost accounting system?
2. What are the principal similarities and differences between a job order cost system and a process cost system?

▶ Do It

Ruth Company manufactures ZEBO through two processes: Blending and Bottling. In June, raw materials used were Blending $18,000 and Bottling $4,000. Factory labor costs were Blending $12,000 and Bottling $5,000. Manufacturing overhead costs were Blending $6,000 and Bottling $2,500. Units completed at a cost of $19,000 in the Blending Department are transferred to the Bottling Department. Units completed at a cost of $11,000 in the Bottling Department are transferred to Finished Goods. Journalize the assignment of these costs to the two processes and the transfer of units as appropriate.

Action Plan

- In process cost accounting, keep separate work in process accounts for each process.
- When the costs are assigned to production, debit the separate work in process accounts.
- Transfer cost of completed units to the next process or to Finished Goods.

Solution

The entries are:

Work in Process—Blending	18,000	
Work in Process—Bottling	4,000	
Raw Materials Inventory		22,000
(To record materials used)		
Work in Process—Blending	12,000	
Work in Process—Bottling	5,000	
Factory Labor		17,000
(To assign factory labor to production)		
Work in Process—Blending	6,000	
Work in Process—Bottling	2,500	
Manufacturing Overhead		8,500
(To assign overhead to production)		
Work in Process—Bottling	19,000	
Work in Process—Blending		19,000
(To record transfer of units to the Bottling Department)		
Finished Goods Inventory	11,000	
Work in Process—Bottling		11,000
(To record transfer of units to finished goods)		

Related exercise material: BE17-1, BE17-2, BE17-3, E17-7, and E17-10.

Equivalent Units

STUDY OBJECTIVE
5
Compute equivalent units.

Suppose you were asked to compute the cost of instruction at your college per full-time equivalent student. You are provided the following information.

Illustration 17-6
Information for full-time
student example

Costs:	
Total cost of instruction	$900,000
Student population:	
Full-time students	900
Part-time students	1,000

Part-time students take 60 percent of the classes of a full-time student during the year. To compute the number of full-time equivalent students per year, you would make the following computation.

Illustration 17-7
Full-time equivalent unit
computation

Full-time Students	+	Equivalent Units of Part-time Students	=	Full-time Equivalent Students
900	+	(60% × 1,000)	=	1,500

Helpful Hint Equivalent units is
an expression of the number of
units that would have been
started and finished if all of the
effort were directed at that
purpose.

The cost of instruction per full-time equivalent student is therefore the total cost of instruction ($900,000) divided by the number of full-time equivalent students (1,500), which is $600 ($900,000 ÷ 1,500).

In a process cost system, the same idea, called equivalent units of production, is used. **Equivalent units of production** measure the work done during the period, expressed in fully completed units. This concept is used to determine the cost per unit of completed product.

WEIGHTED-AVERAGE METHOD

The formula to compute equivalent units of production is as follows.

Illustration 17-8
Equivalent units of
production formula

Units Completed and Transferred Out	+	Equivalent Units of Ending Work in Process	=	Equivalent Units of Production

To better understand this concept of equivalent units, consider the following two examples.

Example 1: The Blending Department's entire output during the period consists of ending work in process of 4,000 units which are 60 percent complete as to materials, labor, and overhead. The equivalent units of production for the Blending Department are therefore 2,400 units (4,000 × 60%).

Example 2: The Packaging Department's output during the period consists of 10,000 units completed and transferred out, and 5,000 units in ending work in process which are 70 percent completed. The equivalent units of production are therefore 13,500 [10,000 + (5,000 × 70%)].

This method of computing equivalent units is referred to as the **weighted-average method**. It considers the degree of completion (weighting) of the units completed and transferred out and the ending work in process. It is the method most widely used in practice. A lesser used method, called the FIFO method, is discussed in advanced cost accounting courses.

REFINEMENTS ON THE WEIGHTED-AVERAGE METHOD

Kellogg Company has produced Eggo® Waffles since 1970. Three departments are used to produce these waffles: Mixing, Baking, and Freezing and Packaging. In the Mixing Department dry ingredients, including flour, salt, and baking powder, are mixed with liquid ingredients, including eggs and vegetable oil, to make waffle batter. Information related to the Mixing Department at the end of June is provided in Illustration 17-9.

Illustration 17-9
Information for Mixing
Department

Mixing Department

	Physical Units	Percentage Complete	
		Materials	Conversion Costs
Work in process, June 1	100,000	100%	70%
Started into production	800,000		
Total units	900,000		
Units transferred out	700,000		
Work in process, June 30	200,000	100%	60%
Total units	900,000		

Illustration 17-9 indicates that the beginning work in process is 100 percent complete as to materials cost and 70 percent complete as to conversion costs. In other words, both the dry and liquid ingredients (materials) are added at the beginning of the process to make Eggo® Waffles. The conversion costs (labor and overhead) related to the mixing of these ingredients were incurred uniformly and are 70 percent complete. The ending work in process is 100 percent complete as to materials cost and 60 percent complete as to conversion costs.

Helpful Hint Question: When are separate unit cost computations needed for materials and conversion costs? Answer: Whenever the two types of costs do not occur in the process at the same time.

We then use the Mixing Department information to determine equivalent units. **In computing equivalent units, the beginning work in process is not part of the equivalent units of production formula.** The units transferred out to the Baking Department are fully complete as to both materials and conversion costs. The ending work in process is fully complete as to materials, but only 60 percent complete as to conversion cost. **Two equivalent unit computations are therefore necessary**: one for materials and the other for conversion costs. Illustration 17-10 shows these computations.

Illustration 17-10
Computation of equivalent
units—Mixing Department

	Equivalent Units	
	Materials	Conversion Costs
Units transferred out	700,000	700,000
Work in process, June 30		
200,000 × 100%	200,000	
200,000 × 60%		120,000
Total equivalent units	900,000	820,000

The earlier formula used to compute equivalent units of production can be refined to show the computations for materials and for conversion costs, as follows.

Illustration 17-11
Refined equivalent unit of
production formula

Units Completed and Transferred Out— Materials	+	Equivalent Units of Ending Work in Process—Materials	=	Equivalent Units of Production— Materials
Units Completed and Transferred Out— Conversion Costs	+	Equivalent Units of Ending Work in Process—Conversion Costs	=	Equivalent Units of Production— Conversion Costs

PRODUCTION COST REPORT

As mentioned earlier, a production cost report is prepared for each department in a process cost system. A **production cost report** is the key document used by management to understand the activities in a department. It shows the production quantity and cost data related to that department. For example, in producing Eggo® Waffles, **Kellogg Company** would have three production cost reports: Mixing, Baking, and Freezing and Packaging. Illustration 17-12 shows the flow of costs to make an Eggo® Waffle and the related production cost reports for each department.

Illustration 17-12 Flow of costs in making Eggo® Waffles

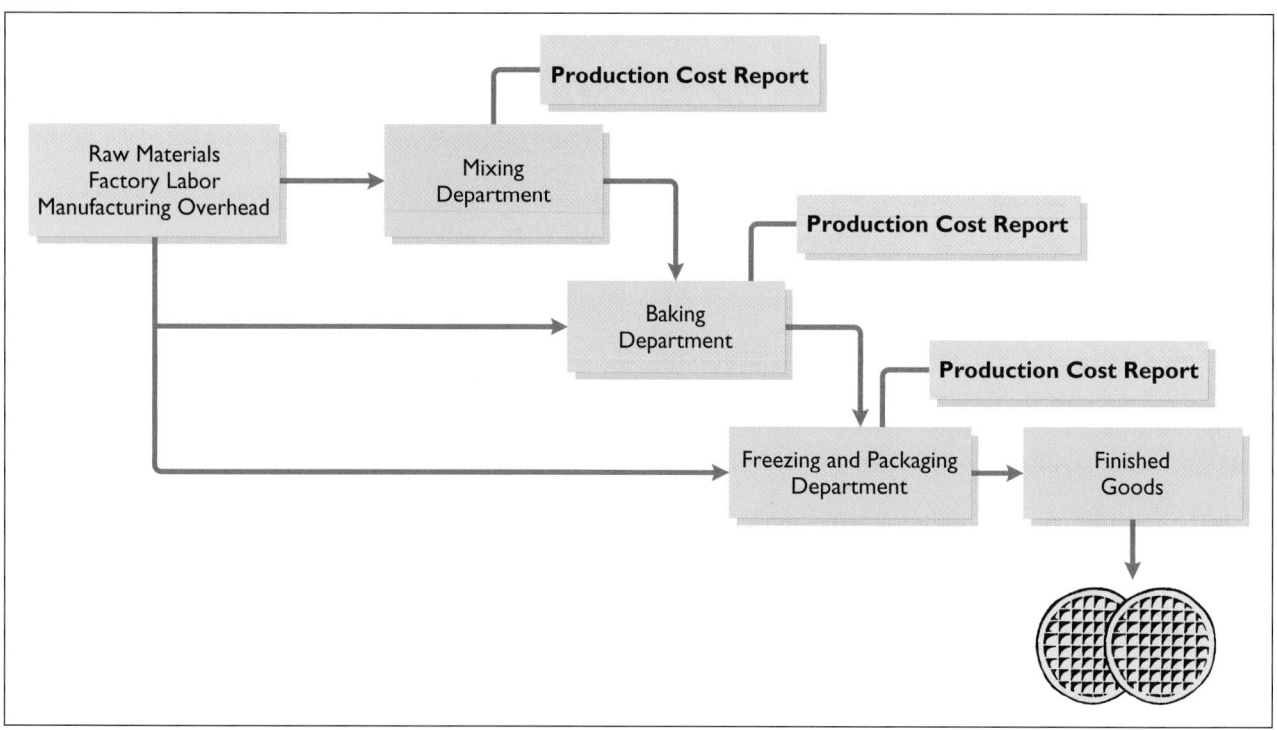

In order to be ready to complete a production cost report, the company must perform four steps:

1. Compute the physical unit flow.
2. Compute the equivalent units of production.
3. Compute unit production costs.
4. Prepare a cost reconciliation schedule.

As a whole, these four steps make up the process costing system. The next section explores these steps in an extended example.

Comprehensive Example of Process Costing

Assumed data for the Mixing Department at **Kellogg Company** for the month of June are shown in Illustration 17-13. We will use this information to complete a production cost report for the Mixing Department.

MIXING DEPARTMENT	
Units:	
Work in process, June 1	100,000
Direct materials: 100% complete	
Conversion costs: 70% complete	
Units started into production during June	800,000
Units completed and transferred out to Baking Department	700,000
Work in process, June 30	200,000
Direct materials: 100% complete	
Conversion costs: 60% complete	
Costs:	
Work in process, June 1	
Direct materials: 100% complete	$ 50,000
Conversion costs: 70% complete	35,000
Cost of work in process, June 1	$ 85,000
Costs incurred during production in June	
Direct materials	$400,000
Conversion costs	170,000
Costs incurred in June	$570,000

Illustration 17-13 Unit and cost data—Mixing Department

COMPUTE THE PHYSICAL UNIT FLOW (STEP 1)

Physical units are the actual units to be accounted for during a period, irrespective of any work performed. To keep track of these units, it is necessary to add the units started (or transferred) into production during the period to the units in process at the begining of the period. This amount is referred to as the **total units to be accounted for**.

The total units then are accounted for by the output of the period. The output consists of units transferred out during the period and any units in process at the end of the period. This amount is referred to as the **total units accounted for**. Illustration 17-14 shows the flow of physical units for Kellogg Company for the month of June for the Mixing Department.

MIXING DEPARTMENT	Physical Units
Units to be accounted for	
Work in process, June 1	100,000
Started (transferred) into production	800,000
Total units	900,000
Units accounted for	
Completed and transferred out	700,000
Work in process, June 30	200,000
Total units	900,000

Illustration 17-14 Physical unit flow—Mixing Department

The records indicate that 900,000 units must be accounted for in the Mixing Department. Of this sum, 700,000 units were transferred to the Baking Department and 200,000 units were still in process.

COMPUTE EQUIVALENT UNITS OF PRODUCTION (STEP 2)

Once the physical flow of the units is established, it is necessary to measure the Mixing Department's productivity in terms of equivalent units of production. In the Mixing Department, materials are added at the beginning of the process, and conversion costs are incurred uniformly during the process. Thus, two computations of equivalent units are required: one for materials and one for conversion costs. The equivalent unit computation is as follows.

Illustration 17-15
Computation of equivalent units—Mixing Department

	Equivalent Units	
	Materials	**Conversion Costs**
Units transferred out	700,000	700,000
Work in process, June 30		
200,000 × 100%	200,000	
200,000 × 60%		120,000
Total equivalent units	**900,000**	**820,000**

Remember that the beginning work in process is ignored in this computation.

COMPUTE UNIT PRODUCTION COSTS (STEP 3)

Armed with the knowledge of the equivalent units of production, we can now compute the unit production costs. **Unit production costs** are costs expressed in terms of equivalent units of production. When equivalent units of production are different for materials and conversion costs, three unit costs are computed: (1) materials, (2) conversion, and (3) total manufacturing.

The computation of total materials cost related to Eggo® Waffles is as follows.

Illustration 17-16
Materials cost computation

Work in process, June 1	
Direct materials cost	$ 50,000
Costs added to production during June	
Direct materials cost	400,000
Total materials cost	**$450,000**

The computation of unit materials cost is as follows.

Illustration 17-17
Unit materials cost computation

Total Materials Cost	÷	Equivalent Units of Materials	=	Unit Materials Cost
$450,000	÷	900,000	=	**$0.50**

The computation of total conversion costs is as follows.

Illustration 17-18
Conversion costs computation

Work in process, June 1	
Conversion costs	$ 35,000
Costs added to production during June	
Conversion costs	170,000
Total conversion costs	**$205,000**

The computation of unit conversion cost is as follows.

Illustration 17-19
Unit conversion cost
computation

Total Conversion Costs	÷	Equivalent Units of Conversion Costs	=	Unit Conversion Cost
$205,000	÷	820,000	=	$0.25

Total manufacturing cost per unit is therefore computed as follows.

Illustration 17-20 Total
manufacturing cost per
unit

Unit Materials Cost	+	Unit Conversion Cost	=	Total Manufacturing Cost per Unit
$0.50	+	$0.25	=	$0.75

PREPARE A COST RECONCILIATION SCHEDULE (STEP 4)

We are now ready to determine the cost of goods transferred out of the Mixing Department to the Baking Department and the costs in ending work in process. The total costs that were charged to the Mixing Department in June are as follows.

Illustration 17-21 Costs
charged to Mixing
Department (total costs to
be accounted for)

Costs to be accounted for	
Work in process, June 1	$ 85,000
Started into production	570,000
Total costs	$655,000

The total costs charged to the Mixing Department in June are therefore $655,000. A cost reconciliation schedule is then prepared to assign these costs to (1) units transferred out to the Baking Department and (2) ending work in process.

Illustration 17-22 Cost
reconciliation schedule—
Mixing Department (total
costs accounted for)

MIXING DEPARTMENT Cost Reconciliation Schedule		
Costs accounted for		
Transferred out (700,000 × $0.75)		$525,000
Work in process, June 30		
Materials (200,000 × $0.50)	$100,000	
Conversion costs (120,000 × $0.25)	30,000	130,000
Total costs		$655,000

The total manufacturing cost per unit, $0.75, is used in costing the units completed and transferred to the Baking Department. In contrast, the unit cost of materials and the unit cost of conversion are needed in costing units in process. The **cost reconciliation schedule** shows that the **total costs accounted for** (Illustration 17-22) equal the **total costs to be accounted for** (see Illustration 17-21).

PREPARING THE PRODUCTION COST REPORT

At this point, we are ready to prepare the production cost report for the Mixing Department. As indicated earlier, this report is an internal document for management that shows production quantity and cost data for a production department.

As noted earlier, there are four steps in preparing a production cost report. They are: (1) Prepare a physical unit schedule. (2) Compute equivalent units. (3) Compute unit costs. (4) Prepare a cost reconciliation schedule. The production cost report for the Mixing Department is shown in Illustration 17-23. The four steps are identified in the report.

Illustration 17-23
Production cost report

Helpful Hint What are the two self-checks in the report? Answer: (1) Total physical units accounted for must equal the total units to be accounted for. (2) Total costs accounted for must equal the total costs to be accounted for.

		Equivalent Units	
QUANTITIES	Physical Units	Materials	Conversion Costs
Units to be accounted for	Step 1		Step 2
Work in process, June 1	100,000		
Started into production	800,000		
Total units	900,000		
Units accounted for			
Transferred out	700,000	700,000	700,000
Work in process, June 30	200,000	200,000	120,000 (200,000 × 60%)
Total units	900,000	900,000	820,000

COSTS		Materials	Conversion Costs	Total
Unit costs Step 3				
Costs in June	(a)	$450,000	$205,000	$655,000
Equivalent units	(b)	900,000	820,000	
Unit costs [(a) ÷ (b)]		$0.50	$0.25	$0.75
Costs to be accounted for				
Work in process, June 1				$ 85,000
Started into production				570,000
Total costs				$655,000

Cost Reconciliation Schedule Step 4

Costs accounted for			
Transferred out (700,000 × $0.75)			$525,000
Work in process, June 30			
Materials (200,000 × $0.50)		$100,000	
Conversion costs (120,000 × $0.25)		30,000	130,000
Total costs			$655,000

MIXING DEPARTMENT
Production Cost Report
for the Month Ended June 30, 2005

Production cost reports provide a basis for evaluating the productivity of a department. In addition, the cost data can be used to assess whether unit costs and total costs are reasonable. By comparing the quantity and cost data with predetermined goals, top management can also judge whether current performance is meeting planned objectives.

Helpful Hint Because production cost reports are used as the basis for evaluation, the data reported therein should be independently accumulated and analyzed to prevent misstatements by department managers.

DECISION TOOLKIT

Decision Checkpoints	Info Needed for Decision	Tool to Use for Decision	How to Evaluate Results
What is the cost of a product?	Costs of materials, labor, and overhead assigned to processes used to make the product	Production cost report	Compare costs to previous periods and to competitors to ensure that costs are in line. Compare to expected selling price to determine overall profitability.

FINAL COMMENTS

Companies often use a combination of a process cost and a job order cost system, called **operations costing**. Operations costing is similar to process costing in that standardized methods are used to manufacture the product. At the same time, the product may have some customized, individual features that require the use of a job order cost system. Consider, for example, the automobile manufacturer **Ford Motor Company**. Each automobile at a given plant goes through the same assembly line, but different materials (such as seat coverings, paint, and tinted glass) may be used for different automobiles. Similarly, **Kellogg's** Pop-Tarts Toaster Pastries® go through numerous processes—mixing, filling, baking, frosting, and packaging. The pastry dough, however, comes in three flavors and there is a variety of fillings.

A cost–benefit tradeoff occurs as a company decides which costing system to use. A job order system, for example, provides detailed information related to the cost of the product. Because each job has its own distinguishing charac-

Business Insight
MANAGEMENT PERSPECTIVE

Frequently when we think of service companies we think of specific, nonroutine tasks, such as rebuilding an automobile engine, providing consulting services on a business acquisition, or working on a major lawsuit. Clearly, such nonroutine situations would call for job order costing. However, many service companies specialize in performing repetitive, routine aspects of a particular business. For example, auto-care vendors such as **Jiffy Lube** focus on the routine aspects of car care; **H&R Block** focuses on the routine aspects of basic tax practice; and many large law firms focus on routine legal services, such as uncomplicated divorces. For service companies that perform routine, repetitive services, process costing provides a simple solution to their accounting needs. In fact, since in many instances there is little or no work in process at the end of the period, applying process costing in this setting can be even easier than for a manufacturer.

teristics, an accurate cost per job can be provided. This information is useful in controlling costs and pricing products. However, the cost of implementing a job order cost system is often expensive because of the accounting costs involved.

On the other hand, for a company like **Intel**, which makes computer chips, is there a benefit in knowing whether the cost of the one hundredth chip produced is different from the one thousandth chip produced? Probably not. An average cost of the product will suffice for control and pricing purposes. In summary, when deciding to use one of these systems, or a combination system, a company must weigh the cost of implementing the system against the benefits from the additional information provided.

BEFORE YOU GO ON . . .

▶ Review It

1. How do physical units differ from equivalent units of production?
2. What are the formulas for computing unit costs of production?
3. How are costs assigned to units transferred out and in process?
4. What are the four sections of a production cost report?
5. What is operations costing, and in what circumstances would a manufacturer use operations costing instead of process costing?
6. Describe the cost–benefit tradeoff involved in deciding what costing system to use.

▶ Do It

In March, Rodayo Manufacturing had the following unit production costs: materials $6 and conversion costs $9. On March 1, it had zero work in process. During March, 12,000 units were transferred out, and 800 units that were 25 percent complete as to conversion costs and 100 percent complete as to materials were in ending work in process at March 31. Assign the costs to the units transferred out and in process.

Action Plan

• Assign the total manufacturing cost of $15 per unit to the 12,000 units transferred.
• Assign the materials cost and conversion cost based on equivalent units of production to units in process.

Solution

The assignment of costs is as follows:

Costs accounted for		
Transferred out (12,000 × $15)		$180,000
Work in process, March 31		
Materials (800 × $6)	$4,800	
Conversion costs (200[a] × $9)	1,800	6,600
Total costs		$186,600

[a]800 × 25%

Related exercise material: BE17-4, BE17-5, BE17-6, BE17-7, BE17-8, E17-1, E17-2, E17-4, E17-6, E17-8, E17-9, and E17-10.

✓ THE NAVIGATOR

DECISION TOOLKIT

Decision Checkpoints	Info Needed for Decision	Tool to Use for Decision	How to Evaluate Results
What costing method should be used?	Type of product produced	Cost of accounting system; benefits of additional information	The benefits of providing the additional information should exceed the costs of the accounting system needed to develop the information.

Contemporary Developments

As indicated in Chapter 15, two contemporary developments in managerial accounting are just-in-time processing and activity-based costing. We explain these innovations in the following sections.

JUST-IN-TIME PROCESSING

Traditionally, continuous process manufacturing has been based on a **just-in-case** philosophy: Inventories of raw materials are maintained *just in case* some items are of poor quality or a key supplier is shut down by a strike. Subassembly parts are manufactured and stored *just in case* they are needed later in the manufacturing process. Finished goods are completed and stored *just in case* unexpected and rush customer orders are received. This philosophy often results in a **"push approach"**: Raw materials and subassembly parts are pushed through each process. Traditional processing often results in the buildup of extensive manufacturing inventories.

Primarily in response to foreign competition, many U.S. firms have switched to **just-in-time (JIT) processing**. JIT manufacturing is dedicated to producing the right products (or parts) at the right time as they are needed. Under JIT processing, raw materials are received **just in time** for use in production, subassembly parts are completed **just in time** for use in finished goods, and finished goods are completed **just in time** to be sold. Illustration 17-24 (on page 838) shows the sequence of activities in just-in-time processing.

STUDY OBJECTIVE

8

Explain just-in-time (JIT) processing.

Objective of JIT Processing

A primary objective of JIT is to eliminate all manufacturing inventories. Inventories are considered to have an adverse effect on net income because they tie up funds and storage space that could be made available for more productive purposes. JIT strives to eliminate inventories by using a **"pull approach"** in manufacturing: At the final process (work station) a signal is sent via a computer to the preceding work station. This signal indicates the exact materials (parts and subassemblies) needed to complete the production of a specified product for a specified time period (such as an eight-hour shift). The preceding process, in turn, sends its signal to other processes back up the line. The goal is a smooth continuous flow in the manufacturing process and no buildup of inventories at any point.

Illustration 17-24
Just-in-time processing

Elements of JIT Processing

There are three important elements in JIT processing:

1. A company must have **dependable suppliers**. Suppliers must be willing to deliver on short notice exact quantities of raw materials according to precise quality specifications (even including multiple deliveries within the same day). Suppliers must also be willing to deliver the raw materials at specified work stations rather than at a central receiving department. This type of purchasing requires constant and direct communication. Such communication is facilitated by an online computer linkage between the company and its suppliers.

2. A **multiskilled workforce** must be developed. Under JIT, machines are often strategically grouped around work cells or work stations. Much of the work is automated. As a result, one worker may have the responsibility to operate and maintain several different types of machines.

3. A **total quality control system** must be established throughout the manufacturing operations. Total quality control means **no defects**. Since only required quantities are signaled by the **pull approach**, any defects at any work station will shut down operations at subsequent work stations. Total quality control requires continuous monitoring by both employees and supervisors at each work station.

Benefits of JIT Processing

The major benefits of JIT processing are:

1. Manufacturing inventories are significantly reduced or eliminated.
2. Product quality is enhanced.

Business Insight
MANAGEMENT PERSPECTIVE

JIT first hit the United States in the early 1980s when it was adopted by auto-mobile companies to meet foreign competition. It is now being successfully used in many companies, including **General Electric**, **Caterpillar**, and **Harley-Davidson**. The effects in most cases have been dramatic. For example, after us-ing JIT for two years, a major division of **Hewlett-Packard** found that work-in-process inventories (in dollars) were down 82 percent, scrap/rework costs were down 30 percent, space utilization improved 40 percent, and labor efficiency im-proved 50 percent. As indicated, JIT not only reduces inventory but also enables a manufacturer to produce a better product faster and with less waste.

3. Rework costs and inventory storage costs are reduced or eliminated.
4. Production cost savings are realized from the improved flow of goods through the processes.

One of the major accounting benefits of JIT is the elimination of raw mate-rials and work in process inventory accounts. In place of these accounts is **one account**, Raw and In-Process Inventory. All materials and conversion costs are charged to this account. Because of the reduction (or elimination) of in-process inventories, the computation of equivalent units of production is simplified.

DECISION TOOLKIT

Decision Checkpoints	Info Needed for Decision	Tool to Use for Decision	How to Evaluate Results
Can we benefit from installation and implementation of JIT processing?	Amounts of raw materials, work-in-process, and finished goods inventory; days that inventory is in storage or waiting to be processed or sold	Establish that we have dependable suppliers, a multiskilled work force, and a total quality control system.	JIT should reduce or nearly eliminate inventories, storage, and waiting time, and should minimize waste and defects. Inventory should be pulled rather than pushed through each production process.

ACTIVITY-BASED COSTING

Activity-based costing (ABC) is a development in product costing that has re-ceived much attention in recent years. **Activity-based costing** focuses on the activities performed in producing a product. An ABC system is similar to con-ventional costing systems in accounting for direct materials and direct labor, but it differs in regard to manufacturing overhead.

In a conventional cost system, a **single unit-level** basis is used to allocate overhead costs to products. The basis may be direct labor or machine hours used to manufacture the product. The assumption in this approach is that as volume of units produced increases, so does the cost of overhead. However, in recent years, the amount of direct labor used in many industries has greatly decreased, and total overhead costs resulting from depreciation on expensive equipment and machinery, utilities, repairs, and maintenance have significantly increased.

STUDY OBJECTIVE
9
Explain activity-based costing (ABC).

In ABC, the cost of a product is equal to the sum of the costs of all activities performed to manufacture it. ABC recognizes that to have accurate and meaningful cost data, **more than one basis** of allocating activity costs to products is needed.

In selecting the allocation basis, ABC seeks to identify the **cost drivers** that measure the activities performed on the product. A cost driver may be any factor or activity that has a direct cause–effect relationship with the resources consumed. Examples of activities and possible cost drivers are as follows.

Illustration 17-25
Activities and cost drivers in ABC

Activity	Cost Driver
Ordering raw materials	Ordering hours; number of orders
Receiving raw materials	Receiving hours; number of shipments
Materials handling	Number of requisitions; weight of materials; handling hours
Production scheduling	Number of orders
Machine setups	Setup hours; number of setups
Machining (fabricating, assembling, etc.)	Machine hours
Quality control inspections	Number of inspections
Factory supervision	Number of employees

Two important assumptions must be met in order to obtain accurate product costs under ABC:

1. All overhead costs related to the activity must be driven by the cost driver used to assign costs to products.

2. All overhead costs related to the activity should respond proportionally to changes in the activity level of the cost driver.

For example, if there is little or no correlation between changes in the cost driver and consumption of the overhead cost, inaccurate product costs are inevitable. A case example in the use of ABC is explained and illustrated in the appendix at the end of this chapter.

Activity-based costing may be used with either a job order or a process cost accounting system. The primary benefit of ABC is more accurate and meaningful product costing. Also, improved cost data about an activity can lead to reduced costs for the activity. In sum, ABC makes managers realize that it is activities and not products that determine the profitability of a company—a realization that should lead to better management decisions.

Business Insight
INTERNATIONAL PERSPECTIVE

Contrary to popular opinion, ABC was not a Japanese invention. ABC was developed in France in the 1950s, but most Japanese corporations have used a form of ABC since that time. In Japan, ABC is called "target costing." Exhaustive market research is done on a new product to determine a price the market will accept. This becomes the target cost that designers, engineers, and production managers must meet. The use of target costing has resulted in products that are priced properly and profitably and that promptly win market share.

BEFORE YOU GO ON . . .

▶ **Review It**

1. What are the principal accounting effects of just-in-time (JIT) processing?
2. What are the primary differences between activity-based costing (ABC) and traditional costing?

☑ THE NAVIGATOR

Using the Decision Toolkit

Essence Company manufactures a high-end after-shave lotion, called Eternity, packaged in 10-ounce plastic bottles. Because the market for after-shave lotion is highly competitive, the company is very concerned about keeping its costs under control.

Eternity is manufactured through three processes: mixing, filling, and corking. Materials are added at the beginning of the process, and labor and overhead are incurred uniformly throughout each process. The company uses a weighted-average method to cost its product. A partially completed production cost report for the month of May for the Mixing Department is shown below.

ESSENCE COMPANY
Mixing Department
Production Cost Report
For the Month Ended May 31, 2005

		Equivalent Units	
QUANTITIES	Physical Units	Materials	Conversion Costs
Units to be accounted for	Step 1		Step 2
Work in process, May 1	1,000		
Started into production	2,000		
Total units	3,000		
Units accounted for			
Transferred out	2,200	?	?
Work in process, May 31	800	?	?
Total units	3,000	?	?

COSTS		Materials	Conversion Costs	Total
Unit costs Step 3				
Costs in May	(a)	?	?	?
Equivalent units	(b)	?	?	
Unit costs [(a) ÷ (b)]		?	?	?
Costs to be accounted for				
Work in process, May 1				$ 56,300
Started into production				119,320
Total costs				$175,620

Cost Reconciliation Schedule Step 4			
Costs accounted for			
Transferred out			?
Work in process, May 31			
Materials		?	
Conversion costs		?	?
Total costs			?

Additional information:
Work in process, May 1, 1000 units

Materials cost, 1,000 units (100% complete)	$49,100	
Conversion costs, 1,000 units (70% complete)	7,200	$ 56,300

Materials cost for 2,000 units started during May. $100,000
Work in process, May 31, 800 units, 100% complete as to materials and
50% complete as to conversion costs.

Instructions

(a) Prepare a production cost report for the Mixing Department for the month of
May.

(b) Prepare the journal entry to record the transfer of goods from the Mixing Department to the Filling Department.

(c) Explain why Essence Company is using a process cost system to account for its
costs.

Solution

(a) A completed production cost report for the Mixing Department is shown below.
Computations to support the amounts reported follow the report.

ESSENCE COMPANY
Mixing Department
Production Cost Report
For the Month Ended May 31, 2005

		Equivalent Units	
QUANTITIES	Physical Units	Materials	Conversion Costs
Units to be accounted for	Step 1		Step 2
Work in process, May 1	1,000		
Started into production	2,000		
Total units	3,000		
Units accounted for			
Transferred out	2,200	2,200	2,200
Work in process, May 31	800	800	400 (800 × 50%)
Total units	3,000	3,000	2,600

COSTS		Materials	Conversion Costs	Total
Unit costs Step 3				
Costs in May	(a)	$149,100	$26,520	$175,620
Equivalent units	(b)	3,000	2,600	
Unit costs [(a) ÷ (b)]		$ 49.70	$ 10.20	$ 59.90

Costs to be accounted for		
Work in process, May 1		$ 56,300
Started into production		119,320
Total costs		$175,620

Cost Reconciliation Schedule Step 4

Costs accounted for		
Transferred out (2,200 × $59.90)		$131,780
Work in process, May 31		
Materials (800 × $49.70)	$39,760	
Conversion costs (400 × $10.20)	4,080	43,840
Total costs		$175,620

Additional computations to support production cost report data:
  Materials cost—$49,100 + $100,000
  Conversion costs—$7,200 + $19,320 ($119,320 − $100,000)

(b) Work in Process—Filling		131,780	
Work in Process—Mixing			131,780

(c) Process cost systems are used to apply costs to similar products that are mass-produced in a continuous fashion. Essence Company uses a process cost system: production of the after-shave lotion, once it begins, continues until the after-shave lotion emerges. The processing is the same for the entire run—with precisely the same amount of materials, labor, and overhead. Each bottle of Eternity after-shave lotion is indistinguishable from another.

☑ THE NAVIGATOR

Summary of Study Objectives

1 *Understand who uses process cost systems.* Process cost systems are used by companies that mass-produce similar products in a continuous fashion. Once production begins, it continues until the finished product emerges. Each unit of finished product is indistinguishable from every other unit.

2 *Explain the similarities and differences between job order cost and process cost systems.* Job order cost systems are similar to process cost systems in three ways: (1) Both systems track the same cost elements—direct materials, direct labor, and manufacturing overhead. (2) Costs are accumulated in the same accounts—Raw Materials Inventory, Factory Labor, and Manufacturing Overhead. (3) Accumulated costs are assigned to the same accounts—Work in Process, Finished Goods Inventory, and Cost of Goods Sold. However, the method of assigning costs differs significantly.

There are four main differences between the two cost systems: (1) A process cost system uses separate accounts for each production department or manufacturing process, rather than only one work in process account used in a job order cost system. (2) In a process cost system, costs are summarized in a production cost report for each department. In a job cost system, costs are charged to individual jobs and summarized in a job cost sheet. (3) Costs are totaled at the end of a time period in a process cost system and at the completion of a job in a job cost system. (4) In a process cost system, unit cost is calculated as: Total manufacturing costs for the period ÷ Units produced during the period. Unit cost in a job cost system is: Total cost per job ÷ Units produced.

3 *Explain the flow of costs in a process cost system.* Manufacturing costs for raw materials, labor, and overhead are assigned to work in process accounts for various departments or manufacturing processes. The costs of units completed in a department are transferred from one department to another as those units move through the manufacturing process. The costs of completed work are transferred to Finished Goods Inventory. When inventory is sold, costs are transferred to Cost of Goods Sold.

4 *Make the journal entries to assign manufacturing costs in a process cost system.* Entries to assign the costs of raw materials, labor, and overhead consist of a credit to Raw Materials Inventory, Factory Labor, and Manufacturing Overhead, and a debit to Work in Process for each of the departments doing the processing. Entries to record the cost of goods transferred to another department are a credit to Work in Process for the department whose work is finished and a debit to the department to which the goods are transferred. The entry to record units completed and transferred to the warehouse is a credit for the department whose work is finished and a debit to Finished Goods Inventory. Finally, the entry to record the sale of goods is a credit to Finished Goods Inventory and a debit to Cost of Goods Sold.

5 *Compute equivalent units.* Equivalent units of production measure work done during a period, expressed in fully completed units. This concept is used to determine the cost per unit of completed product. Equivalent units are the sum of units completed and transferred out plus equivalent units of ending work in process.

6 *Explain the four steps necessary to prepare a production cost report.* The four steps to complete a production cost report are: (1) Compute the physical unit flow—that is, the total units to be accounted for. (2) Compute the equivalent units of production. (3) Compute the unit production costs, expressed in terms of equivalent units of production. (4) Prepare a cost reconciliation schedule, which shows that the total costs accounted for equal the total costs to be accounted for.

7 *Prepare a production cost report.* The production cost report contains both quantity and cost data for a production department. There are four sections in the report: (1) number of physical units, (2) equivalent units determination, (3) unit costs, and (4) cost reconciliation schedule.

8 *Explain just-in-time (JIT) processing.* JIT is a manufacturing technique dedicated to producing the right products at the right time as needed. One of the principal accounting effects is that a Raw and In-Process Inventory account replaces both the raw materials and work in process inventory accounts.

9 *Explain activity-based costing (ABC).* ABC is a method of product costing that focuses on the activities performed to produce products. It assigns the cost of the activities to products by using cost drivers that measure the activities performed. The primary objective of ABC is accurate and meaningful product costs.

THE NAVIGATOR

DECISION TOOLKIT—A SUMMARY

Decision Checkpoints	Info Needed for Decision	Tool to Use for Decision	How to Evaluate Results
What is the cost of a product?	Costs of materials, labor, and overhead assigned to processes used to make the product	Production cost report	Compare costs to previous periods and to competitors to ensure that costs are in line. Compare to expected selling price to determine overall profitability.
Which costing method should be used?	Type of product produced	Cost of accounting system; benefits of additional information	The benefits of providing the additional information should exceed the costs of the accounting system needed to develop the information.
Can we benefit from installation and implementation of JIT processing?	Amounts of raw materials, work-in-process, and finished goods inventory; days that inventory is in storage or waiting to be processed or sold	Establish that we have dependable suppliers, a multiskilled work force, and a total quality control system.	JIT should reduce or nearly eliminate inventories, storage, and waiting time, and should minimize waste and defects. Inventory should be pulled rather than pushed through each production process.

APPENDIX
CASE EXAMPLE OF TRADITIONAL COSTING VERSUS ACTIVITY-BASED COSTING

Production and Cost Data

STUDY OBJECTIVE
10
Apply activity-based costing to specific company data.

In this appendix we present a case example that compares activity-based costing to traditional costing. Assume that Atlas Company produces two products, The Boot and The Club. The Boot is a high-volume item totaling 25,000 units annually. The Club is a low-volume item totaling only 5,000 units per year. Each product requires one hour of direct labor for completion. Therefore, total annual direct labor hours are 30,000 (25,000 + 5,000). Expected annual manufacturing overhead costs are $900,000. The predetermined overhead rate is $30 ($900,000 ÷ 30,000) per direct labor hour.

The direct materials cost per unit is $40 for The Boot and $30 for The Club. The direct labor cost is $12 per unit for each product.

UNIT COSTS UNDER TRADITIONAL COSTING

The unit cost for each product under traditional costing is shown below.

Illustration 17A-1 Unit costs—traditional costing

	Products	
Manufacturing Costs	**The Boot**	**The Club**
Direct materials	$40	$30
Direct labor	12	12
Overhead	30*	30*
Total unit cost	$82	$72

*Predetermined overhead rate × direct labor hours ($30 × 1 hr. = $30).

DETERMINING OVERHEAD RATES UNDER ABC

Analysis reveals that Atlas Company's expected annual overhead costs of $900,000 relate to three activities—machine setups, machining, and inspections. The cost driver and overhead rate for each activity are shown in Illustration 17A-2.

Illustration 17A-2 Computing overhead rates—ABC

Activity	Cost Driver	Total Expected Overhead Cost	Total Expected Use of Cost Driver	Activity-Based Overhead Rate
Machine setups	Number of setups	$300,000	1,500	$200 per setup
Machining	Machine hours	500,000	50,000	$ 10 per machine hour
Inspections	Number of inspections	100,000	2,000	$ 50 per inspection
		$900,000		

ASSIGNING OVERHEAD COSTS TO PRODUCTS UNDER ABC

In assigning costs, it is necessary to know the expected number of cost drivers for each product. Because of its low volume, The Club requires more setups and inspections than The Boot. The expected number of cost drivers for each product is as follows.

Illustration 17A-3 Expected number of cost drivers

	Products		Total
Cost Driver	**The Boot**	**The Club**	**Usage**
Number of machine setups	500	1,000	1,500
Machine hours	30,000	20,000	50,000
Number of inspections	500	1,500	2,000

Using these data, Atlas can assign the expected annual overhead cost to each product as shown in Illustration 17A-4 (page 846).

Illustration 17A-4
Assignment of overhead
costs to products

| Activity | The Boot | | The Club | | Total |
	Number	Cost	Number	Cost	Cost
Machine setups ($200)	500	$100,000	1,000	$200,000	$300,000
Machining ($10)	30,000	300,000	20,000	200,000	500,000
Inspections ($50)	500	25,000	1,500	75,000	100,000
Total assigned costs (a)		$425,000		$475,000	$900,000
Units produced (b)		25,000		5,000	
Overhead cost per unit [(a) ÷ (b)]		$17		$95	

These data show that under ABC, overhead costs are shifted from the high-volume product (The Boot) to the low-volume product (The Club). This shift results in more accurate costing for two reasons:

1. Low-volume products often require more special handling, such as more machine setups and inspections, than high-volume products. This is true for Atlas Company. Thus, the low-volume product frequently is responsible for more overhead costs per unit than a high-volume product.

2. The overhead costs incurred by the low-volume product often are disproportionate to a traditional allocation base. For example, direct labor hours is usually a poor cost driver for assigning overhead costs to low-volume products. When overhead is properly assigned in ABC, it will usually increase the unit cost of low-volume products.

Comparing Unit Costs

A comparison of unit manufacturing costs under traditional costing and ABC shows the following significant differences.

| Manufacturing Costs | The Boot | | The Club | |
	Traditional Costing	ABC	Traditional Costing	ABC
Direct materials	$40	$40	$30	$ 30
Direct labor	12	12	12	12
Overhead	30	17	30	95
Total cost per unit	$82	$69	$72	$137
	Overstated $13		Understated $65	

The comparison shows that unit costs under traditional costing have been significantly distorted. The cost of The Boot has been overstated $13 per unit ($82 − $69). The cost of The Club has been understated $65 per unit ($137 − $72). The differences are attributable to how manufacturing overhead is assigned. A likely consequence of the differences is that Atlas Company has been overpricing The Boot and possibly losing market share to competitors. It also has been sacrificing profitability by underpricing The Club.

As illustrated in the above case, ABC involves the following steps.

1. Identify the major activities that pertain to the manufacture of specific products.

2. Accumulate manufacturing overhead costs by activities.

3. Identify the cost driver(s) that accurately measure(s) each activity's contribution to the finished product.

4. Assign manufacturing overhead costs for each activity to products, using the cost driver(s).

Benefits and Limitations of Activity-Based Costing

We have already seen that a primary benefit of ABC is more accurate product costing. In addition, ABC offers the following other benefits:

1. **Control over overhead costs** is enhanced. Many overhead costs are incurred directly by activities. Thus, managers become more aware of their responsibility to control the activities that generate the costs.

2. **Better management decisions** can be made. More accurate product costing should contribute to setting selling prices that will achieve desired profitability levels. The cost data also should be helpful in deciding whether to discontinue or expand a product line or whether to make or buy a component.

The principal disadvantages of ABC generally focus on two factors. First, **the expense of obtaining the cost data** required by the system is relatively high. ABC requires data that are not normally generated within a company. Examples of such data are the number of setups, inspections, orders placed, and orders received. In addition, many computations are involved in assigning overhead costs to individual products.

Second, **ABC does not eliminate arbitrary assignments** of overhead. For example, plant-wide overhead costs such as depreciation, insurance, and property taxes on the factory building should be allocated to the activity centers in determining the cost of a product. With ABC, these allocations may be more difficult to do accurately because of the increased number of activity centers. As a result, accuracy of product costs could be adversely affected.

Summary of Study Objective for Appendix

10 *Apply activity-based costing to specific company data.* In applying ABC, it is necessary to compute the overhead rate for each activity by dividing total expected overhead by the total expected usage of the cost driver. The overhead cost for each activity is then assigned to products on the basis of each product's use of the cost driver.

Glossary

Activity-based costing A cost accounting system that focuses on the activities performed in manufacturing a specific product. (p. 839).

Cost reconciliation schedule A schedule that shows that the total costs accounted for equal the total costs to be accounted for. (p. 834).

Equivalent units of production A measure of the work done during the period, expressed in fully completed units. (p. 828).

Just-in-time processing A processing system dedicated to producing the right products (or parts) as they are needed. (p. 837).

Operations costing A combination of a process cost and a job order cost system, in which products are manufactured primarily by standardized methods, with some customization. (p. 835).

Physical units Actual units to be accounted for during a period, irrespective of any work performed. (p. 831).

Process cost systems An accounting system used to apply costs to similar products that are mass-produced in a continuous fashion. (p. 821).

Production cost report An internal report for management that shows both production quantity and cost data for a production department. (p. 830).

Total units (costs) accounted for The sum of the units (costs) transferred out during the period plus the units (costs) in process at the end of the period. (p. 831).

Total units (costs) to be accounted for The sum of the units (costs) started (or transferred) into production during the period plus the units (costs) in process at the beginning of the period. (p. 831).

Unit production costs Costs expressed in terms of equivalent units of production. (p. 832).

Weighted-average method Method used to compute equivalent units of production which considers the degree of completion (weighting) of the units completed and transferred out and the ending work in process. (p. 828).

Demonstration Problem

Karlene Industries produces plastic ice cube trays in two processes: heating and stamping. All materials are added at the beginning of the Heating Department. Karlene uses the weighted-average method to compute equivalent units.

On November 1, 1,000 trays that were 70% complete were in process in the Heating Department. During November 12,000 trays were started into production. On November 30, 2,000 trays that were 60% complete were in process.

The following cost information for the Heating Department was also available.

Work in process, November 1		Costs incurred in November	
Materials	$ 640	Material	$3,000
Conversion costs	360	Labor	2,300
Cost of work in process, Nov. 1	$1,000	Overhead	4,050

Instructions

(a) Prepare a production cost report for the Heating Department for the month of November 2005, using the weighted-average method.

(b) Journalize the transfer of costs to the Stamping Department.

Solution to Demonstration Problem

(a)

KARLENE INDUSTRIES
Heating Department
Production Cost Report
For the Month Ended November 30, 2005

		Equivalent Units	
QUANTITIES	Physical Units	Materials	Conversion Costs
Units to be accounted for	Step 1	Step 2	
Work in process, November 1	1,000		
Started into production	12,000		
Total units	13,000		
Units accounted for			
Transferred out	11,000	11,000	11,000
Work in process, November 30	2,000	2,000	1,200
Total units	13,000	13,000	12,200

COSTS		Materials	Conversion Costs	Total
Unit costs Step 3				
Costs in November	(a)	$ 3,640	$ 6,710	$10,350
Equivalent units	(b)	13,000	12,200	
Unit costs [(a) ÷ (b)]		$0.28	$0.55	$0.83

Costs to be accounted for
Work in process, November 1 .... $ 1,000
Started into production 9,350
Total costs $10,350

Cost Reconciliation Schedule Step 4

Costs accounted for
Transferred out (11,000 × $0.83) .... $ 9,130
Work in process, November 30

	Conversion Costs	
Materials (2,000 × $0.28)	$ 560	
Conversion costs (1,200 × $0.55)	660	1,220

Total costs $10,350

(b) Work in Process—Stamping   9,130
    Work in Process—Heating   9,130
       (To record transfer of units to the Stamping
       Department)

Note: All **asterisked** Questions, Exercises, and Problems relate to material in the appendix to the chapter.

Self-Study Questions

Self-Study/Self-Test

Answers are at the end of the chapter.

(SO 1) **1.** Which of the following items is *not* a characteristic of a process cost system?
  (a) Once production begins, it continues until the finished product emerges.
  (b) The products produced are heterogeneous in nature.
  (c) The focus is on continually producing homogeneous products.
  (d) When the finished product emerges, all units have precisely the same amount of materials, labor, and overhead.

(SO 2) **2.** Indicate which of the following statements is *not* correct.
  (a) Both a job order and a process cost system track the same three manufacturing cost elements—direct materials, direct labor, and manufacturing overhead.
  (b) In a job order cost system, only one work in process account is used, whereas in a process cost system, multiple work in process accounts are used.
  (c) Manufacturing costs are accumulated the same way in a job order and in a process cost system.
  (d) Manufacturing costs are assigned the same way in a job order and in a process cost system.

3. In a process cost system, costs are assigned only: (SO 3)
  (a) to one work in process account.
  (b) to work in process and finished goods inventory.
  (c) to work in process, finished goods, and cost of goods sold.
  (d) to work in process accounts.

4. In making the journal entry to assign raw materials costs: (SO 4)
  (a) the debit is to Finished Goods Inventory.
  (b) the debit is often to two or more work in process accounts.
  (c) the credit is generally to two or more work in process accounts.
  (d) the credit is to Finished Goods Inventory.

5. The Mixing Department's output during the period consists of 20,000 units completed and transferred out, and 5,000 units in ending work in process 60% complete as to materials and conversion costs. Beginning inventory is 1,000 units, 40% complete as to materials and conversion costs. The equivalent units of production are: (SO 5)
  (a) 22,600.
  (b) 23,000.
  (c) 24,000.
  (d) 25,000.

(SO 6)   **6.** In RYZ Company, there are zero units in beginning work in process, 7,000 units started into
production, and 500 units in ending work in
process 20% completed. The physical units to be
accounted for are:
   (a) 7,000.   (c) 7,600.
   (b) 7,360.   (d) 7,340.

(SO 5)   **7.** Stock Company has 2,000 units in beginning
work in process, 20% complete as to conversion
costs, 23,000 units transferred out to finished
goods, and 3,000 units in ending work in process
33$\frac{1}{3}$% complete as to conversion costs. The beginning and ending inventory is fully complete
as to materials costs. Equivalent units for materials and conversion costs are, respectively:
   (a) 22,000, 24,000.   (c) 26,000, 24,000.
   (b) 24,000, 26,000.   (d) 26,000, 26,000.

(SO 6)   **8.** Fortner Company has no beginning work in
process; 9,000 units are transferred out and
3,000 units in ending work in process are one-
third finished as to conversion costs and fully
complete as to materials cost. If total materials
cost is $60,000, the unit materials cost is:
   (a) $5.00.
   (b) $5.45 rounded.
   (c) $6.00.
   (d) No correct answer is given.

(SO 6)   **9.** Largo Company has unit costs of $10 for mate-
rials and $30 for conversion costs. If there are
2,500 units in ending work in process, 40% complete as to conversion costs, and fully complete

as to materials cost, the total cost assignable to
the ending work in process inventory is:
   (a) $45,000.   (c) $75,000.
   (b) $55,000.   (d) $100,000.

10. A production cost report   (SO 7)
   (a) is an external report.
   (b) shows costs charged to department and
       costs accounted for.
   (c) shows equivalent units of production but
       not physical units.
   (d) contains six sections.

11. Just-in-time processing (JIT):   (SO 8)
   (a) strives to eliminate inventories.
   (b) uses a pull approach in manufacturing.
   (c) Neither of the above.
   (d) Both (a) and (b).

12. Activity-based costing (ABC):   (SO 9)
   (a) can be used only in a process cost system.
   (b) focuses on units of production.
   (c) focuses on activities performed to produce
       a product.
   (d) uses only a single basis of allocation.

****13.** The overhead rate for Machine Setups is $100   (SO 10)
per setup. Products A and B have 80 and 60
setups, respectively. The overhead assigned to
each product is:
   (a) Product A $8,000, Product B $8,000.
   (b) Product A $8,000, Product B $6,000.
   (c) Product A $6,000, Product B $6,000.
   (d) Product A $6,000, Product B $8,000.

Questions

1. Identify which costing system—job order or process
cost—the following companies would use: (a) **Quaker
Oats**, (b) **Ford Motor Company**, (c) **Kinko's Print
Shop**, and (d) **Warner Bros. Motion Pictures**.

2. Contrast the primary focus of job order cost accounting and of process cost accounting.

3. What are the similarities between a job order and a
process cost system?

4. Your roommate is confused about the features of
process cost accounting. Identify and explain the distinctive features for your roommate.

5. Tina Turner believes there are no significant differences in the flow of costs between job order cost
accounting and process cost accounting. Is Turner
correct? Explain.

6. (a) What source documents are used in assigning
       (1) materials and (2) labor to production?
   (b) What criterion and basis are commonly used in
       allocating overhead to processes?

7. At Kun Company, overhead is assigned to production
departments at the rate of $15 per machining hour.
In July, machine hours were 3,000 in the Machining

Department and 2,400 in the Assembly Department.
Prepare the entry to assign overhead to production.

8. Kent Krause is uncertain about the steps used to prepare a production cost report. State the procedures
that are required in the sequence in which they are
performed.

9. Alan Bruski is confused about computing physical
units. Explain to Alan how physical units to be accounted for and physical units accounted for are
determined.

10. What is meant by the term "equivalent units of production"?

11. How are equivalent units of production computed?

12. Sandy Company had zero units of beginning work in
process. During the period, 9,000 units were completed, and there were 600 units of ending work in
process. What were the units started into production?

13. Cesska Co. has zero units of beginning work in
process. During the period 12,000 units were completed, and there were 600 units of ending work in
process one-fifth complete as to conversion cost and
100% complete as to materials cost. What were the

equivalent units of production for (a) materials and (b) conversion costs?

14. Hipp Co. started 3,000 units for the period. Its beginning inventory is 800 units one-fourth complete as to conversion costs and 100% complete as to materials cost. Its ending inventory is 400 units one-fifth complete as to conversion cost and 100% complete as to materials costs. How many units were transferred out this period?

15. Gruber Company transfers out 14,000 units and has 2,000 units of ending work in process that are 25% complete. Materials are entered at the beginning of the process and there is no beginning work in process. Assuming unit materials costs of $3 and unit conversion costs of $9, what are the costs to be assigned to units (a) transferred out and (b) in ending work in process?

16. (a) Jane Jelk believes the production cost report is an external report for stockholders. Is Jane correct? Explain.
(b) Identify the sections in a production cost report.

17. What purposes are served by a production cost report?

18. At Apex Company, there are 800 units of ending work in process that are 100% complete as to materials and

40% complete as to conversion costs. If the unit cost of materials is $4 and the costs assigned to the 800 units is $6,600, what is the per-unit conversion cost?

19. What is the difference between operations costing and a process costing system?

20. How does a company decide whether to use a job order or a process cost system?

21. (a) Describe the philosophy and approach of just-in-time processing.
(b) Identify the major elements of JIT processing.

22. (a) What are the principal differences between activity-based costing (ABC) and traditional product costing?
(b) What assumptions must be met for ABC costing to be useful?

23. Hoy Co. identifies the following activities that pertain to manufacturing overhead: Materials Handling, Machine Setups, Factory Machine Maintenance, Factory Supervision, and Quality Control. For each activity identify an appropriate cost driver.

*24. (a) Identify the steps that pertain to activity-based costing.
(b) What are the advantages of ABC costing?

Brief Exercises

BE17-1 Table Manufacturing purchases $50,000 of raw materials on account, and it incurs $40,000 of factory labor costs. Journalize the two transactions on March 31 assuming the labor costs are not paid until April.

Journalize entries for accumulating costs. (SO 4)

BE17-2 Data for Table Manufacturing are given in BE17-1. Supporting records show that (a) the Assembly Department used $24,000 of raw materials and $28,000 of the factory labor, and (b) the Finishing Department used the remainder. Journalize the assignment of the costs to the processing departments on March 31.

Journalize the assignment of materials and labor costs. (SO 4)

BE17-3 Factory labor data for Table Manufacturing are given in BE17-2. Manufacturing overhead is assigned to departments on the basis of 200% of labor costs. Journalize the assignment of overhead to the Assembly and Finishing Departments.

Journalize the assignment of overhead costs. (SO 4)

BE17-4 Burrand Manufacturing Company has the following production data for selected months.

Compute physical units of production. (SO 6)

Month	Beginning Work in Process	Units Transferred Out	Ending Work in Process Units	Ending Work in Process % Complete as to Conversion Cost
January	–0–	30,000	5,000	40%
March	–0–	40,000	4,000	75
July	–0–	40,000	10,000	25

Compute the physical units for each month.

BE17-5 Using the data in BE17-4, compute equivalent units of production for materials and conversion costs, assuming materials are entered at the beginning of the process.

Compute equivalent units of production. (SO 5)

BE17-6 In Caroline Company, total material costs are $48,000, and total conversion costs are $60,000. Equivalent units of production are materials 10,000 and conversion 12,000. Compute the unit costs for materials, conversion costs, and total manufacturing costs.

Compute unit costs of production. (SO 6)

Assign costs to units transferred out and in process.
(SO 6)

BE17-7   Sota Company has the following production data for April: units transferred out 40,000, and ending work in process 5,000 units that are 100% complete for materials and 40% complete for conversion costs. If unit materials cost is $8 and unit conversion cost is $12, determine the costs to be assigned to the units transferred out and the units in ending work in process.

Compute unit costs.
(SO 6)

BE17-8   Production costs chargeable to the Finishing Department in June in Madlock Company are materials $9,000, labor $20,000, overhead $18,000. Equivalent units of production are materials 20,000 and conversion costs 19,000. Compute the unit costs for materials and conversion costs.

Prepare cost reconciliation schedule.
(SO 6)

BE17-9   Data for Madlock Company are given in BE17-8. Production records indicate that 18,000 units were transferred out, and 2,000 units in ending work in process were 50% complete as to conversion cost and 100% complete as to materials. Prepare a cost reconciliation schedule.

Compute equivalent units of production.
(SO 5)

BE17-10   The Smelting Department of Darlinda Manufacturing Company has the following production and cost data for November.

> Production: Beginning work in process 2,000 units that are 100% complete as to materials and 20% complete as to conversion costs; units transferred out 8,000 units; and ending work in process 2,000 units that are 100% complete as to materials and 40% complete as to conversion costs.

Compute the equivalent units of production for (a) materials and (b) conversion costs for the month of November.

Compute overhead rates for activities.
(SO 10)

*BE17-11   Dooley Company identifies three activities in its manufacturing process: machine setups, machining, and inspections. Estimated annual overhead cost for each activity is $180,000, $300,000, and $70,000, respectively. The cost driver for each activity and the expected annual usage are: number of setups 1,000, machine hours 25,000, and number of inspections 1,400. Compute the overhead rate for each activity.

Exercises

Compute physical units and equivalent units of production.
(SO 5, 6)

E17-1   In Kam Company, materials are entered at the beginning of each process. Work in process inventories, with the percentage of work done on conversion costs, and production data for its Sterilizing Department in selected months during 2005 are as follows.

	Beginning Work in Process		Units Transferred Out	Ending Work in Process	
Month	**Units**	**Conversion Cost %**		**Units**	**Conversion Cost %**
January	–0–	—	7,000	2,000	60
March	–0–	—	12,000	3,000	30
May	–0–	—	16,000	4,000	80
July	–0–	—	10,000	1,500	40

Instructions
(a) Compute the physical units for January and May.
(b) Compute the equivalent units of production for (1) materials and (2) conversion costs for each month.

Determine equivalent units, unit costs, and assignment of costs.
(SO 5, 6)

E17-2   The Cutting Department of Bjerg Manufacturing has the following production and cost data for July.

Production	Costs	
1. Transferred out 8,000 units.	Beginning work in process	$ –0–
2. Started 1,000 units that are 40% complete as to conversion costs and 100% complete as to materials at July 31.	Materials	45,000
	Labor	14,700
	Manufacturing overhead	18,900

Materials are entered at the beginning of the process. Conversion costs are incurred uniformly during the process.

Instructions
  (a) Determine the equivalent units of production for (1) materials and (2) conversion costs.
  (b) Compute unit costs and prepare a cost reconciliation schedule.

E17-3 The Sanding Department of Copa Furniture Company has the following production and manufacturing cost data for March 2005.

Prepare a production cost report.
(SO 5, 6, 7)

    Production: 12,000 units finished and transferred out; 3,000 units started that are 100% complete as to materials and 30% complete as to conversion costs.

    Manufacturing costs: Materials $33,000; labor $30,000; overhead $35,790.

Instructions
Prepare a production cost report.

E17-4 The Blending Department of Battle Company has the following cost and production data for the month of April.

Determine equivalent units, unit costs, and assignment of costs.
(SO 5, 6)

Costs:	
Work in process, April 1	
Direct materials: 100% complete	$ 100,000
Conversion costs: 20% complete	70,000
Cost of work in process, April 1	$ 170,000
Costs incurred during production in April	
Direct materials	$ 800,000
Conversion costs	350,000
Costs incurred in April	$1,150,000

    Units transferred out totaled 8,000. Ending work in process was 1,000 units that are 100% complete as to materials and 40% complete as to conversion costs.

Instructions
  (a) Compute the equivalent units of production for (1) materials and (2) conversion costs for the month of April.
  (b) Compute the unit costs for the month.
  (c) Determine the costs to be assigned to the units transferred out and in ending work in process.

E17-5 Larry Lair has recently been promoted to production manager, and so he has just started to receive various managerial reports. One of the reports he has received is the production cost report that you prepared. It showed that his department had 1,000 equivalent units in ending inventory. His department has had a history of not keeping enough inventory on hand to meet demand. He has come to you, very angry, and wants to know why you credited him with only 1,000 units when he knows he had at least twice that many on hand.

Explain the production cost report.
(SO 7)

Instructions
  ▱▱▱➡ Explain to him why his production cost report showed only 1,000 equivalent units in ending inventory. Write an informal memo. Be kind and explain very clearly why he is mistaken.

E17-6 The ledger of Tombert Company has the following work in process account.

Answer questions on costs and production.
(SO 3, 5, 6)

Work in Process—Painting

5/1	Balance	3,590	5/31	Transferred out	?
5/31	Materials	6,060			
5/31	Labor	2,500			
5/31	Overhead	1,650			
5/31	Balance	?			

    Production records show that there were 700 units in the beginning inventory, 30% complete, 1,100 units started, and 1,300 units transferred out. The beginning work in process had materials cost of $2,040 and conversion costs of $1,550. The units in ending inventory were 40% complete. Materials are entered at the beginning of the painting process.

Instructions
(a) How many units are in process at May 31?
(b) What is the unit materials cost for May?
(c) What is the unit conversion cost for May?
(d) What is the total cost of units transferred out in May?
(e) What is the cost of the May 31 inventory?

Journalize transactions for two processes.
(SO 4)

E17-7 Yellowknife Manufacturing Company has two production departments: Cutting and Assembly. July 1 inventories are Raw Materials $4,200, Work in Process—Cutting $2,900, Work in Process—Assembly $10,600, and Finished Goods $31,000. During July, the following transactions occurred.

1. Purchased $56,300 of raw materials on account.
2. Incurred $56,000 of factory labor. (Credit Wages Payable.)
3. Incurred $70,000 of manufacturing overhead; $36,000 was paid and the remainder is unpaid.
4. Requisitioned materials for Cutting $15,700 and Assembly $8,900.
5. Used factory labor for Cutting $29,000 and Assembly $27,000.
6. Applied overhead at the rate of $20 per machine hour. Machine hours were Cutting 1,640 and Assembly 1,720.
7. Transferred goods costing $77,600 from the Cutting Department to the Assembly Department.
8. Transferred goods costing $134,900 from Assembly to Finished Goods.
9. Sold goods costing $130,000 for $200,000 on account.

Instructions
Journalize the transactions. (Omit explanations.)

Compute equivalent units, unit costs, and costs assigned.
(SO 5, 6)

E17-8 The Polishing Department of Medina Manufacturing Company has the following production and manufacturing cost data for September. Materials are entered at the beginning of the process.

Production: Beginning inventory 1,600 units that are 100% complete as to materials and 30% complete as to conversion costs; units started during the period are 12,000; ending inventory of 3,000 units 10% complete as to conversion costs.

Manufacturing costs: Beginning inventory costs, comprised of $20,000 of materials and $43,180 of conversion costs; materials costs added in Polishing during the month, $177,200; labor and overhead applied in Polishing during the month, $100,080 and $257,860, respectively.

Instructions
(a) Compute the equivalent units of production for materials and conversion costs for the month of September.
(b) Compute the unit costs for materials and conversion costs for the month.
(c) Determine the costs to be assigned to the units transferred out and in process.

Prepare a production cost report.
(SO 5, 6, 7)

E17-9 The Welding Department of Tomlin Manufacturing Company has the following production and manufacturing cost data for February 2005. All materials are added at the beginning of the process.

Manufacturing Costs			Production Data	
Beginning work in			Beginning work in	
process			process	15,000 units
Materials	$18,000			1/10 complete
Conversion costs	14,175	$ 32,175	Units transferred out	49,000
Materials		180,000	Units started	60,000
Labor		35,100	Ending work in process	26,000
Overhead		64,545		1/5 complete

Instructions
Prepare a production cost report for the Welding Department for the month of February.

Journalize transactions.
(SO 3, 4)

E17-10 Mary Lou Company manufactures pizza sauce through two production departments: Cooking and Canning. In each process, materials and conversion costs are incurred evenly throughout the process. For the month of April, the work in process accounts show the following debits.

	Cooking	Canning
Beginning work in process	$ –0–	$ 4,000
Materials	15,000	6,000
Labor	8,500	7,000
Overhead	29,500	21,800
Costs transferred in		45,000

Instructions

Journalize the April transactions.

*E17-11   Amend Instrument Inc. manufactures two products: missile range instruments and space pressure gauges. During January, 50 range instruments and 300 pressure gauges were produced, and overhead costs of $81,000 were incurred. An analysis of overhead costs reveals the following activities.

Compute overhead rates and assign overhead using ABC.
(SO 10)

Activity	Cost Driver	Total Cost
1. Materials handling	Number of requisitions	$30,000
2. Machine setups	Number of setups	27,000
3. Quality inspections	Number of inspections	24,000

The cost driver volume for each product was as follows.

Cost Driver	Instruments	Gauges	Total
Number of requisitions	400	600	1,000
Number of setups	150	300	450
Number of inspections	200	400	600

Instructions

(a) Determine the overhead rate for each activity.

(b) Assign the manufacturing overhead costs for January to the two products using activity-based costing.

(c) ▭▭▭▷ Write a memo to the president of Amend Instrument, explaining the benefits of activity-based costing.

Problems: Set A

P17-1A   Zion Company manufactures bowling balls through two processes: Molding and Packaging. In the Molding Department, the urethane, rubber, plastics, and other materials are molded into bowling balls. In the Packaging Department, the balls are placed in cartons and sent to the finished goods warehouse. All materials are entered at the beginning of each process. Labor and manufacturing overhead are incurred uniformly throughout each process. Production and cost data for the Molding Department during June 2005 are presented below.

Complete four steps necessary to prepare a production cost report.
(SO 5, 6, 7)

Production Data	June
Beginning work in process units	–0–
Units started into production	22,000
Ending work in process units	2,000
Percent complete—ending inventory	45%

Cost Data	
Materials	$286,000
Labor	114,000
Overhead	136,800
Total	$536,800

Instructions

(a) Prepare a schedule showing physical units of production.

(b) Determine the equivalent units of production for materials and conversion costs.

(c) Compute the unit costs of production.

(d) Determine the costs to be assigned to the units transferred and in process for June.

(e) Prepare a production cost report for the Molding Department for the month of June only.

(c) Materials $13
Conversion costs $12

*Complete four steps
necessary to prepare a
production cost report.*
(SO 5, 6, 7)

P17-2A Stein Industries Inc. manufactures in separate processes furniture for homes. In each process, materials are entered at the beginning, and conversion costs are incurred uniformly. Production and cost data for the first process in making two products in two different manufacturing plants are as follows.

	Cutting Department	
Production Data—July	**Plant 1** **T12-Tables**	**Plant 2** **C10-Chairs**
Work in process units, July 1	–0–	–0–
Units started into production	20,000	18,000
Work in process units, July 31	1,000	500
Work in process percent complete	60	80
Cost Data—July		
Work in process, July 1	$ –0–	$ –0–
Materials	380,000	288,000
Labor	190,000	118,100
Overhead	104,000	96,700
Total	$674,000	$502,800

Instructions

(a) (3) T12:
Materials $19
Conversion costs $15

(a) For each plant:

   (1) Compute the physical units of production.
   (2) Compute equivalent units of production for materials and for conversion costs.
   (3) Determine the unit costs of production.
   (4) Show the assignment of costs of units transferred out and in process.

(b) Prepare the production cost report for Plant 1 for July 2005.

Journalize transactions.
(SO 3, 4)

P17-3A Vargas Company manufactures its product, Vitadrink, through two manufacturing processes: Mixing and Packaging. All materials are entered at the beginning of each process. On October 1, 2005, inventories consisted of Raw Materials $26,000, Work in Process—Mixing $0, Work in Process—Packaging $250,000, and Finished Goods $89,000. The beginning inventory for Packaging consisted of 10,000 units that were 50% complete as to conversion costs and fully complete as to materials. During October, 50,000 units were started into production in the Mixing Department and the following transactions were completed.

1. Purchased $400,000 of raw materials on account.
2. Issued raw materials for production: Mixing $210,000 and Packaging $45,000.
3. Incurred labor costs of $238,900.
4. Used factory labor: Mixing $182,500 and Packaging $56,400.
5. Incurred $790,000 of manufacturing overhead on account.
6. Applied indirect manufacturing overhead on the basis of $25 per machine hour. Machine hours were 28,000 in Mixing and 7,000 in Packaging.
7. Transferred 45,000 units from Mixing to Packaging at a cost of $999,000.
8. Transferred 53,000 units from Packaging to Finished Goods at a cost of $1,455,000.
9. Sold goods costing $1,640,000 for $2,500,000 on account.

Instructions
Journalize the October transactions.

*Assign costs and prepare
production cost report.*
(SO 5, 6, 7)

P17-4A Elite Company has several processing departments. Costs charged to the Assembly Department for November 2005 totaled $2,129,000 as follows.

Work in process, November 1		
Materials	$69,000	
Conversion costs	48,150	$ 117,150
Materials added		1,405,000
Labor		225,920
Overhead		380,930

Production records show that 30,000 units were in beginning work in process 30% complete as to conversion costs, 640,000 units were started into production, and 25,000 units were in ending work in process 40% complete as to conversion costs. Materials are entered at the beginning of each process.

Instructions

(a) Determine the equivalent units of production and the unit costs for the Assembly Department.

(b) Determine the assignment of costs to goods transferred out and in process.

(c) Prepare a production cost report for the Assembly Department.

(b) Transf'd out $2,064,000
      WIP $ 65,000

P17-5A   Sprague Company manufactures basketballs. Materials are added at the beginning of the production process and conversion costs are incurred uniformly. Production and cost data for the month of July 2005 are as follows.

Determine equivalent units and unit costs and assign costs.
(SO 5, 6, 7)

Production Data—Basketballs	Units	Percent Complete
Work in process units, July 1	500	60%
Units started into production	1,600	
Work in process units, July 31	600	40%

Cost Data—Basketballs		
Work in process, July 1		
Materials	$750	
Conversion costs	600	$1,350
Direct materials		2,400
Direct labor		1,580
Manufacturing overhead		1,300

Instructions

(a) Calculate the following.

(1) The equivalent units of production for materials and conversion.

(2) The unit costs of production for materials and conversion costs.

(3) The assignment of costs to units transferred out and in process at the end of the accounting period.

(b) Prepare a production cost report for the month of July for the basketballs.

(a) Materials:
   (1) 2,100
   (2) $1.50
   (3) Transferred out $5,250
        WIP $1,380

P17-6A   Taylor Processing Company uses a weighted-average process costing system and manufactures a single product—a premium rug shampoo and cleaner. The manufacturing activity for the month of October has just been completed. A partially completed production cost report for the month of October for the mixing department is shown below.

Compute equivalent units and complete production cost report.
(SO 5, 7)

TAYLOR PROCESSING COMPANY
Mixing Department
Production Cost Report
For the Month Ended October 31

		Equivalent Units	
QUANTITIES	Physical Units	Materials	Conversion Costs
Units to be accounted for			
Work in process, October 1 (all materials, 70% conversion costs)	20,000		
Started into production	160,000		
Total units	180,000		
Units accounted for			
Transferred out	140,000	?	?
Work in process, October 31 (50% materials, 25% conversion costs)	40,000	?	?
Total units accounted for	180,000	?	?

	Equivalent Units		
		Conversion	
COSTS	**Materials**	**Costs**	**Total**
Unit costs			
Costs in October	$240,000	$90,000	$330,000
Equivalent units	?	?	
Unit costs	$?	+ $?	= $?
Costs to be accounted for			
Work in process, October 1			$ 30,000
Started into production			300,000
Total costs			$330,000
Cost Reconciliation Schedule			
Costs accounted for			
Transferred out			$?
Work in process, October 31			
Materials		?	
Conversion costs		?	?
Total costs			?

Instructions

(a) Prepare a schedule that shows how the equivalent units were computed so that you can complete the "Quantities: Units accounted for" equivalent units section shown in the production cost report above, and compute October unit costs.

(b) Transferred out $294,000
    WIP $ 36,000

(b) Complete the "Cost Reconciliation Schedule" part of the production cost report above.

Assign overhead to products using ABC.
(SO 10)

*P17-7A   Becky Electronics manufactures two large-screen television models: the Royale which sells for $1,500, and a new model, the Majestic, which sells for $1,200. The production cost per unit for each model in 2005 was as follows.

	Royale	**Majestic**
Direct materials	$ 700	$420
Direct labor ($20 per hour)	100	80
Manufacturing overhead ($40 per DLH)	200	160
Total per unit cost	$1,000	$660

In 2005, Becky manufactured 30,000 units of the Royale and 10,000 units of the Majestic. The overhead rate of $40 per direct labor hour was determined by dividing total expected manufacturing overhead of $7,600,000 by the total direct labor hours (190,000) for the two models.

The gross profit on the model was: Royale $500 ($1,500 − $1,000) and Majestic $540 ($1,200 − $660). Because of this difference, management is considering phasing out the Royale model and increasing the production of the Majestic model.

Before finalizing its decision, management asks the controller, Rebecca Sherrick, to prepare an analysis using activity-based costing. Rebecca accumulates the following information about overhead for the year ended December 31, 2005.

Activity	**Cost Driver**	**Total Cost**	**Cost Driver Volume**	**Overhead Rate**
Purchase orders	Number of orders	$1,200,000	30,000	$40
Machine setups	Number of setups	900,000	15,000	60
Machining	Machine hours	4,800,000	160,000	30
Quality control	Number of inspections	700,000	35,000	20

The cost driver volume for each product was:

Cost Driver	Royale	Majestic	Total
Purchase orders	10,000	20,000	30,000
Machine setups	5,000	10,000	15,000
Machine hours	100,000	60,000	160,000
Inspections	10,000	25,000	35,000

Instructions

(a) Assign the total 2005 manufacturing overhead costs to the two products using activity-based costing (ABC).

(b) What was the cost per unit and gross profit of each model using ABC costing?

(c) Are management's future plans for the two models sound?

(a) Majestic $3,700,000

Problems: Set B

P17-1B Acquatic Corporation manufactures water skis through two processes: Molding and Packaging. In the Molding Department fiberglass is heated and shaped into the form of a ski. In the Packaging Department, the skis are placed in cartons and sent to the finished goods warehouse. Materials are entered at the beginning of both processes. Labor and manufacturing overhead are incurred uniformly throughout each process. Production and cost data for the Molding Department for January 2005 are presented below.

Complete four steps necessary to prepare a production cost report. (SO 5, 6, 7)

Production Data	January
Beginning work in process units	–0–
Units started into production	42,500
Ending work in process units	2,500
Percent complete—ending inventory	40%

Cost Data	
Materials	$552,500
Labor	117,000
Overhead	170,000
Total	$839,500

Instructions

(a) Compute the physical units of production.

(b) Determine the equivalent units of production for materials and conversion costs.

(c) Compute the unit costs of production.

(d) Determine the costs to be assigned to the units transferred out and in process.

(e) Prepare a production cost report for the Molding Department for the month of January.

(c) Materials $13
Conversion costs $ 7

P17-2B Freedo Corporation manufactures in separate processes refrigerators and freezers for homes. In each process, materials are entered at the beginning and conversion costs are incurred uniformly. Production and cost data for the first process in making two products in two different manufacturing plants are as follows.

Complete four steps necessary to prepare a production cost report. (SO 5, 6, 7)

	Stamping Department	
	Plant A	**Plant B**
Production Data—June	**R12 Refrigerators**	**F24 Freezers**
Work in process units, June 1	–0–	–0–
Units started into production	20,000	20,000
Work in process units, June 30	2,000	2,500
Work in process percent complete	75	60

Cost Data—June		
Work in process, June 1	$ –0–	$ –0–
Materials	840,000	700,000
Labor	223,500	251,000
Overhead	420,000	319,000
Total	$1,483,500	$1,270,000

(a) (3) R12:
Materials $42
Conversion costs $33

Instructions
(a) For each plant:

(1) Compute the physical units of production.
(2) Compute equivalent units of production for materials and for conversion costs.
(3) Determine the units costs of production.
(4) Show the assignment of costs to units transferred out and in process.

(b) Prepare the production cost report for Plant A for June 2005.

Journalize transactions.
(SO 3, 4)

P17-3B Pepi Company manufactures a nutrient, Everlife, through two manufacturing processes: Blending and Packaging. All materials are entered at the beginning of each process. On August 1, 2005, inventories consisted of Raw Materials $5,000, Work in Process—Blending $0, Work in Process—Packaging $3,945, and Finished Goods $7,500. The beginning inventory for Packaging consisted of 500 units, two-fifths complete as to conversion costs and fully complete as to materials. During August, 9,000 units were started into production in Blending, and the following transactions were completed.

1. Purchased $25,000 of raw materials on account.
2. Issued raw materials for production: Blending $16,930 and Packaging $7,140.
3. Incurred labor costs of $18,770.
4. Used factory labor: Blending $13,320 and Packaging $5,450.
5. Incurred $41,500 of manufacturing overhead on account.
6. Applied manufacturing overhead at the rate of $35 per machine hour. Machine hours were Blending 900 and Packaging 300.
7. Transferred 8,200 units from Blending to Packaging at a cost of $54,940.
8. Transferred 8,600 units from Packaging to Finished Goods at a cost of $74,490.
9. Sold goods costing $62,000 for $90,000 on account.

Instructions
Journalize the August transactions.

Assign costs and prepare
production cost report.
(SO 5, 6, 7)

P17-4B Wang Company has several processing departments. Costs charged to the Assembly Department for October 2005 totaled $1,347,200 as follows.

Work in process, October 1		
Materials	$29,000	
Conversion costs	26,200	$ 55,200
Materials added		1,071,000
Labor		90,000
Overhead		131,000

Production records show that 25,000 units were in beginning work in process 40% complete as to conversion cost, 415,000 units were started into production, and 35,000 units were in ending work in process 20% complete as to conversion costs. Materials are entered at the beginning of each process.

Instructions
(a) Determine the equivalent units of production and the unit costs for the Assembly Department.

(b) Transferred out $1,255,500
WIP $ 91,700

(b) Determine the assignment of costs to goods transferred out and in process.
(c) Prepare a production cost report for the Assembly Department.

Determine equivalent units
and unit costs and assign
costs.
(SO 5, 6, 7)

P17-5B Clemente Company manufactures bicycles and tricycles. For both products, materials are added at the beginning of the production process, and conversion costs are incurred uniformly. Production and cost data for the month of May are as follows.

Production Data—Bicycles	Units	Percent Complete
Work in process units, May 1	500	80%
Units started in production	1,000	
Work in process units, May 31	600	9.5%

Cost Data—Bicycles		
Work in process, May 1		
Materials	$10,000	
Conversion costs	9,280	$19,280
Direct materials		50,000
Direct labor		18,140
Manufacturing overhead		30,000

Instructions

(a) Calculate the following.

    (1) The equivalent units of production for materials and conversion.

    (2) The unit costs of production for materials and conversion costs.

    (3) The assignment of costs to units transferred out and in process at the end of the accounting period.

(b) Prepare a production cost report for the month of May for the bicycles.

(a) Materials:
(1) 1,500
(2) $40
(3) Transf'd out $90,000
WIP $27,420

P17-6B Magic Cleaner Company uses a weighted-average process costing system and manufactures a single product—an all-purpose liquid cleaner. The manufacturing activity for the month of March has just been completed. A partially completed production cost report for the month of March for the mixing and blending department is shown below.

Compute equivalent units and complete production cost report.
(SO 5, 7)

MAGIC CLEANER COMPANY
Mixing and Blending Department
Production Cost Report
For the Month Ended March 31

QUANTITIES	Physical Units	Equivalent Units Materials	Equivalent Units Conversion Costs
Units to be accounted for			
Work in process, March 1 (40% materials, 20% conversion costs)	10,000		
Started into production	100,000		
Total units	110,000		
Units accounted for			
Transferred out	95,000	?	?
Work in process, March 31 (2/3 materials, 1/3 conversion costs)	15,000	?	?
Total units accounted for	110,000	?	?

COSTS	Materials	Conversion Costs	Total
Unit costs			
Costs in March	$170,100	$98,000	$268,100
Equivalent units	?	?	
Unit costs	$? +	$? =	$?
Costs to be accounted for			
Work in process, March 1			$ 15,700
Started into production			252,400
Total costs			$268,100

Cost Reconciliation Schedule

Costs accounted for			
Transferred out			$?
Work in process, March 31			
Materials		?	
Conversion costs		?	?
Total costs			?

Instructions

(a) Prepare a schedule that shows how the equivalent units were computed so that you can complete the "Quantities: Units accounted for" equivalent units section shown in the production cost report above, and compute March unit costs.

(b) Complete the "Cost Reconciliation Schedule" part of the production cost report above.

(b) Transferred out $247,000
WIP $ 21,100

Group Decision Case

BYP17-1   English Bay Beach Company manufactures suntan lotion, called Surtan, in 11-ounce plastic bottles. Surtan is sold in a competitive market. As a result, management is very cost-conscious. Surtan is manufactured through two processes: mixing and filling. Materials are entered at the beginning of each process and labor and manufacturing overhead occur uniformly throughout each process. Unit costs are based on the cost per gallon of Surtan using the weighted-average costing approach.

On June 30, 2005, Sara Simmons, the chief accountant for the past 20 years, opted to take early retirement. Her replacement, Joe Jacobs, had extensive accounting experience with motels in the area but only limited contact with manufacturing accounting.

During July, Joe correctly accumulated the following production quantity and cost data for the Mixing Department.

Production quantities: Work in process, July 1, 8,000 gallons 75% complete; started into production 100,000 gallons; work in process, July 31, 5,000 gallons 20% complete. Materials are added at the beginning of the process.

Production costs: Beginning work in process $88,000, comprised of $21,000 of materials costs and $67,000 of conversion costs; incurred in July: materials $600,000, conversion costs $785,800.

Joe then prepared a production cost report on the basis of physical units started into production. His report showed a production cost of $14.738 per gallon of Surtan. The management of English Bay Beach was surprised at the high unit cost. The president comes to you, as Sara's top assistant, to review Joe's report and prepare a correct report if necessary.

Instructions
With the class divided into groups, answer the following questions.
(a) Show how Joe arrived at the unit cost of $14.738 per gallon of Surtan.
(b) What error(s) did Joe make in preparing his production cost report?
(c) Prepare a correct production cost report for July.

Managerial Analysis

BYP17-2   Logan Furniture Company manufactures living room furniture through two departments: Framing and Upholstering. Materials are entered at the beginning of each process. For May, the following cost data are obtained from the two work in process accounts.

	Framing	**Upholstering**
Work in process, May 1	$ –0–	$?
Materials	420,000	?
Conversion costs	210,000	330,000
Costs transferred in	–0–	550,000
Costs transferred out	550,000	?
Work in process, May 31	80,000	?

Instructions
Answer the following questions.
(a) If 3,000 sofas were started into production on May 1 and 2,500 sofas were transferred to Upholstering, what was the unit cost of materials for May in the Framing Department?
(b) Using the data in (a) above, what was the per unit conversion cost of the sofas transferred to Upholstering?
(c) Continuing the assumptions in (a) above, what is the percentage of completion of the units in process at May 31 in the Framing Department?

Real-World Focus

BYP17-3 General Microwave Corp. is engaged primarily in the design, development, manufacture, and marketing of microwave, electronic, and fiber optic test equipment, components, and subsystems. A substantial portion of the company's microwave product is sold to manufacturers and users of microwave systems and equipment for applications in the defense electronics industry.

General Microwave Corp. reports the following information in one of the notes to its financial statements.

 GENERAL MICROWAVE CORPORATION
5500 New Horizons Boulevard • Amityville, New York 11701

GENERAL MICROWAVE CORPORATION
Notes to the Financial Statement

Work in process inventory reflects all accumulated production costs, which are comprised of direct production costs and overhead, reduced by amounts attributable to units delivered. Work in process inventory is reduced to its estimated net realizable value by a charge to cost of sales in the period [in which] excess costs are identified. Raw materials and finished goods inventories are reflected at the lower of cost or market.

Instructions

(a) What types of manufacturing costs are accumulated in the work in process inventory account?
(b) What types of information must General Microwave have to be able to compute equivalent units of production?
(c) How does General Microwave assign costs to the units transferred out of work in process that are completed?

Exploring the Web

BYP17-4 Search the Internet and find the Web sites of two manufacturers that you think are likely to use process costing. Are there any specifics included in their Web sites that confirm the use of process costing for each of these companies?

Communication Activity

BYP17-5 Catherine Harper was a good friend of yours in high school and is from your home town. While you chose to major in accounting when you both went away to college, she majored in marketing and management. You have recently been promoted to accounting manager for the Snack Foods Division of Clark Enterprises, and your friend was promoted to regional sales manager for the same division of Clark. Catherine recently telephoned you. She explained that she was familiar with job cost sheets, which had been used by the Special Projects division where she had formerly worked. She was, however, very uncomfortable with the production cost reports prepared by your division. She faxed you a list of her particular questions. These included the following.

1. Since Clark occasionally prepares snack foods for special orders in the Snack Foods Division, why don't we track costs of the orders separately?
2. What is an equivalent unit?
3. Why am I getting four production cost reports? Isn't there only one Work in Process account?

Instructions

Prepare a memo to Catherine. Answer her questions, and include any additional information you think would be helpful. You may write informally, but be careful to use proper grammar and punctuation.

Research Case

BYP17-6 The April 1998 issue of *Management Accounting* includes an article by Kip R. Krumwiede entitled "ABC: Why It's Tried and How It Succeeds."

Instructions

Read the article and answer the following questions.

(a) What is the adoption and implementation status of ABC according to the survey conducted in 1996 by the Institute of Management Accountants?

(b) What did Krumwiede's survey attempt to determine?

(c) In Krumwiede's survey, what factors appeared to separate those companies that adopted ABC from those that did not adopt ABC?

(d) Identify at least five "Basic ABC Implementation Tips" recommended in the article.

Ethics Case

BYP17-7 R. B. Robin Company manufactures a high-tech component that passes through two production processing departments, Molding and Assembly. Department managers are partially compensated on the basis of units of products completed and transferred out relative to units of product put into production. This was intended as encouragement to be efficient and to minimize waste.

Barb Crusmer is the department head in the Molding Department, and Wayne Terrago is her quality control inspector. During the month of June, Barb had three new employees who were not yet technically skilled. As a result, many of the units produced in June had minor molding defects. In order to maintain the department's normal high rate of completion, Barb told Wayne to pass through inspection and on to the Assembly Department all units that had defects nondetectable to the human eye. "Company and industry tolerances on this product are too high anyway," says Barb. "Less than 2% of the units we produce are subjected in the market to the stress tolerance we've designed into them. The odds of those 2% being any of this month's units are even less. Anyway, we're saving the company money."

Instructions

(a) Who are the potential stakeholders involved in this situation?

(b) What alternatives does Wayne have in this situation? What might the company do to prevent this situation from occurring?

Answers to Self-Study Questions

1. b   2. d   3. c   4. b   5. b   6. a   7. c   8. a   9. b   10. b   11. d
12. c   13. b

Remember to go back to the Navigator box on the chapter-opening page and check off your completed work.

CHAPTER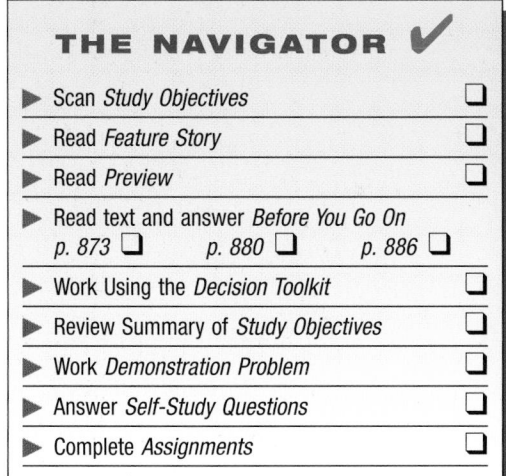

Cost-Volume-Profit Relationships

STUDY OBJECTIVES

After studying this chapter,
you should be able to:

1 Distinguish between variable and fixed costs.

2 Explain the significance of the relevant range.

3 Explain the concept of mixed costs.

4 List the five components of cost-volume-profit analysis.

5 Indicate what contribution margin is and how it can be expressed.

6 Identify the three ways to determine the break-even point.

7 Define margin of safety, and give the formulas for computing it.

8 Give the formulas for determining sales required to earn target net income.

9 Describe the essential features of a cost-volume-profit income statement.

☑ THE NAVIGATOR

THE NAVIGATOR ✔

▶ Scan *Study Objectives* ☐

▶ Read *Feature Story* ☐

▶ Read *Preview* ☐

▶ Read text and answer *Before You Go On*
   p. 873 ☐   p. 880 ☐   p. 886 ☐

▶ Work Using the *Decision Toolkit* ☐

▶ Review Summary of *Study Objectives* ☐

▶ Work *Demonstration Problem* ☐

▶ Answer *Self-Study Questions* ☐

▶ Complete *Assignments* ☐

FEATURE STORY

Growing by Leaps and Leotards

When the last of her three children went off to school, Amy began looking for a job. At this same time, her daughter asked to take dance classes. The nearest dance studio was over 20 miles away, and Amy didn't know how she would balance a new job and drive her daughter to dance class. Suddenly it hit her—why not start her own dance studio?

Amy sketched out a business plan: A local church would rent its basement for $6 per hour. The size of the basement limited the number of students she could teach, but the rent was low. Insurance for a small studio was $50 per month. Initially she would teach classes only for young kids since that was all she felt qualified to do. She thought she could charge $2.50 for a one-hour class. There was room for 8 students per class. She wouldn't get rich—but at least it would be fun, and she didn't have much at risk.

Amy soon realized that the demand for dance classes far exceeded her capacity. She considered renting a bigger space that could serve 15 students per class. But her rent would also increase significantly. Also, rather than paying rent by the hour, she would have to pay $600 per month, even during the summer months when demand for dance classes was low. She also would have to pay utilities—roughly $70 per month.

However, with a bigger space Amy could offer classes for teens and adults. Teens and adults would pay a higher fee—$5 per hour—though the number of students per class would have to be smaller, probably only 8 per class. She could hire a part-time

865

instructor at about $18 per hour to teach advanced classes. Insurance costs could increase to $100 per month. In addition, she would need a part-time administrator at $100 per month to keep records. Amy also realized she could increase her income by selling dance supplies such as shoes, towels, and leotards.

Amy laid out a new business plan based on these estimates. If she failed, she stood to lose real money. Convinced she could make a go of it, she made the big plunge.

Her planning paid off: Within 10 years of starting her business in a church basement Amy had over 800 students, seven instructors, two administrators, and a facility with three separate studios.

☑ THE NAVIGATOR

As the Feature Story indicates, to manage any size business you must understand how costs respond to changes in sales volume and the effect of costs and revenues on profits. A prerequisite to understanding cost-volume-profit (CVP) relationships is knowledge of how costs behave. In this chapter, we first explain the considerations involved in cost behavior analysis. Then we discuss and illustrate CVP analysis and variable costing.

The content and organization of Chapter 18 are as follows.

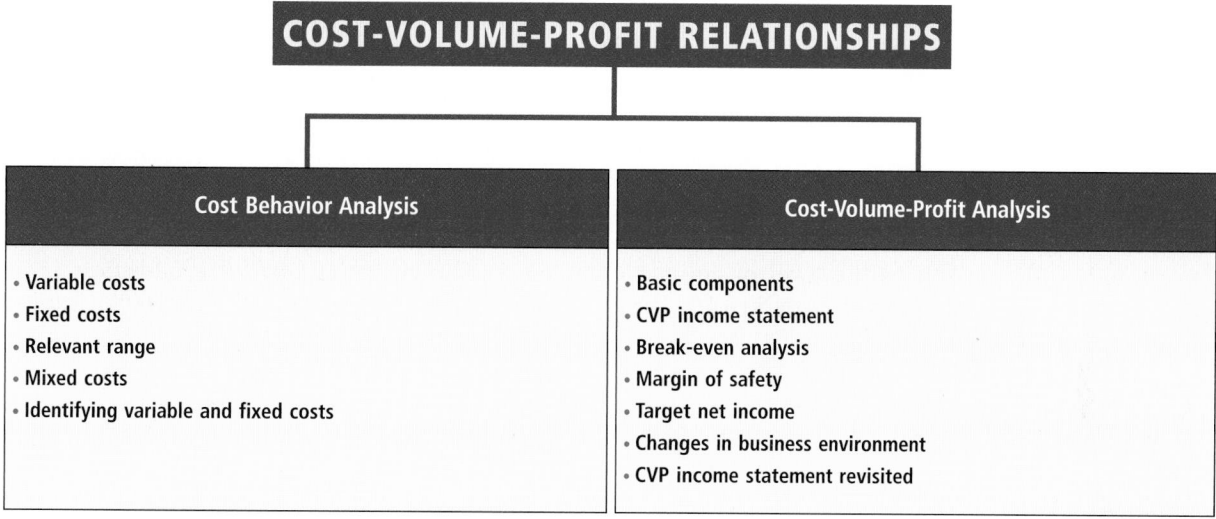

COST-VOLUME-PROFIT RELATIONSHIPS

Cost Behavior Analysis

- Variable costs
- Fixed costs
- Relevant range
- Mixed costs
- Identifying variable and fixed costs

Cost-Volume-Profit Analysis

- Basic components
- CVP income statement
- Break-even analysis
- Margin of safety
- Target net income
- Changes in business environment
- CVP income statement revisited

☑ THE NAVIGATOR

Cost Behavior Analysis

Cost behavior analysis is the study of how specific costs respond to changes in the level of business activity. As you might expect, some costs change, and others remain the same. For example, for an airline company such as **Southwest** or **United**, the longer the flight the higher the fuel costs. On the other hand, **Massachusetts General Hospital**'s employee costs to run the emergency room on any given night are relatively constant regardless of the number of patients serviced. A knowledge of cost behavior helps management plan operations and decide between alternative courses of action. Cost behavior analysis applies to all types of entities, as the Feature Story about Amy's dance studio indicates.

The starting point in cost behavior analysis is measuring the key business activities. Activity levels may be expressed in terms of sales dollars (in a retail company), miles driven (in a trucking company), room occupancy (in a hotel), or dance classes taught (by a dance studio). Many companies use more than one measurement base. A manufacturer, for example, may use direct labor hours or units of output for manufacturing costs and sales revenue or units sold for selling expenses.

For an activity level to be useful in cost behavior analysis, changes in the level or volume of activity should be correlated with changes in costs. The activity level selected is referred to as the activity (or volume) index. The **activity index** identifies the activity that causes changes in the behavior of costs. With an appropriate activity index, it is possible to classify the behavior of costs in response to changes in activity levels into three categories: variable, fixed, or mixed.

VARIABLE COSTS

STUDY OBJECTIVE

1

Distinguish between variable and fixed costs.

Variable costs are costs that vary **in total** directly and proportionately with changes in the activity level. If the level increases 10 percent, total variable costs will increase 10 percent. If the level of activity decreases by 25 percent, variable costs will decrease 25 percent. Examples of variable costs include direct materials and direct labor for a manufacturer; cost of goods sold, sales commissions, and freight-out for a merchandiser; and gasoline in airline and trucking companies. A variable cost may also be defined as a cost that **remains the same *per unit* at every level of activity**.

To illustrate the behavior of a variable cost, assume that Damon Company manufactures radios that contain a $10 digital clock. The activity index is the number of radios produced. As each radio is manufactured, the total cost of the clocks increases by $10. As shown in part (a) of Illustration 18-1, total cost of the clocks will be $20,000 if 2,000 radios are produced, and $100,000 when 10,000 radios are produced. We also can see that a variable cost remains the same per unit as the level of activity changes. As shown in part (b) of Illustration 18-1, the unit cost of $10 for the clocks is the same whether 2,000 or 10,000 radios are produced.

Illustration 18-1 Behavior of total and unit variable costs

Helpful Hint True or false: Variable cost per unit changes directly and proportionately with changes in activity. Answer: False. Per unit cost remains constant at all levels of activity.

Companies that rely heavily on labor to manufacture a product, such as **Nike** or **Reebok**, or to provide a service, such as **Hilton** or **Marriott**, are likely to have many variable costs. In contrast, companies that use a high proportion of machinery and equipment in producing revenue, such as **AT&T** or **Duke Energy Co.**, may have few variable costs.

FIXED COSTS

Fixed costs are costs that **remain the same in total** regardless of changes in the activity level. Examples include property taxes, insurance, rent, supervisory salaries, and depreciation on buildings and equipment. Because total fixed costs remain constant as activity changes, it follows that **fixed costs *per unit* vary inversely with activity: As volume increases, unit cost declines, and vice versa**.

To illustrate the behavior of fixed costs, assume that Damon Company leases its productive facilities at a cost of $10,000 per month. Total fixed costs of the facilities will remain constant at every level of activity, as shown in part (a) of Illustration 18-2. But, on a per unit basis, the cost of rent will decline as activity increases, as shown in part (b) of Illustration 18-2. At 2,000 units, the unit cost is $5 ($10,000 ÷ 2,000). When 10,000 radios are produced, the unit cost is only $1 ($10,000 ÷ 10,000).

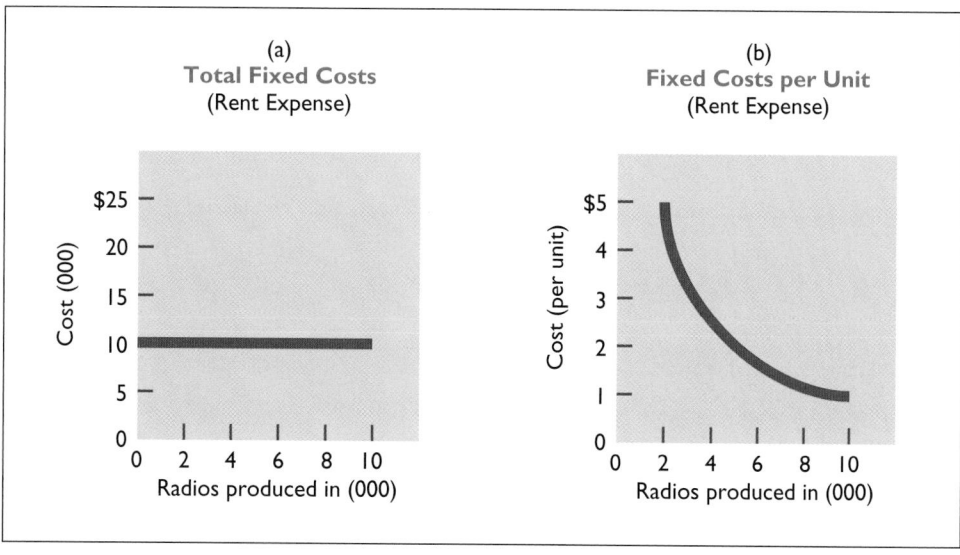

Illustration 18-2 Behavior of total and unit fixed costs

The trend for many manufacturers is to have more fixed costs and fewer variable costs. This trend is the result of increased use of automation and less use of employee labor. As a result, depreciation and lease charges (fixed costs) increase, whereas direct labor costs (variable costs) decrease.

Business Insight
MANAGEMENT PERSPECTIVE

When Thomas Moser quit teaching communications at Bates College 25 years ago, he turned to what he loved doing—furniture woodworking. Today he has over 120 employees. In a business where profit margins are seldom thicker than wood shavings, cost control is everything. Moser keeps no inventory; a 50 percent deposit buys the wood. Because computer-driven machines cut most of the standardized parts and joints, "we're free to be inefficient in assembly and finishing work, where the craft is most obviously expressed," says Moser. Direct labor costs are a manageable 30 percent of revenues. By keeping a tight lid on costs and running an efficient operation, Moser is free to spend most of his time doing what he enjoys most—designing furniture.

SOURCE: Excerpts from "Out of the Woods," *Forbes* (April 5, 1999), p. 74.

RELEVANT RANGE

In Illustrations 18-1 and 18-2, straight lines were drawn throughout the entire activity index for total variable costs and total fixed costs. In essence, the assumption was made that the costs were **linear**. It is now necessary to ask: Is the straight-line relationship realistic? Does the linear assumption produce useful data for CVP analysis?

STUDY OBJECTIVE
2
Explain the significance of the relevant range.

In most business situations, a straight-line relationship **does not exist** for variable costs throughout the entire range of possible activity. At abnormally low levels of activity, it may be impossible to be cost efficient. Small-scale operations may not allow the company to obtain quantity discounts for raw materials or to use specialized labor. In contrast, at abnormally high levels of activity, labor costs may increase sharply because of overtime pay. Also at high activity levels, materials costs may jump significantly because of excess spoilage caused by worker fatigue. As a result, in the real world, the relationship between the behavior of a variable cost and changes in the activity level is often **curvilinear**, as shown in part (a) of Illustration 18-3.

Illustration 18-3
Nonlinear behavior of variable and fixed costs

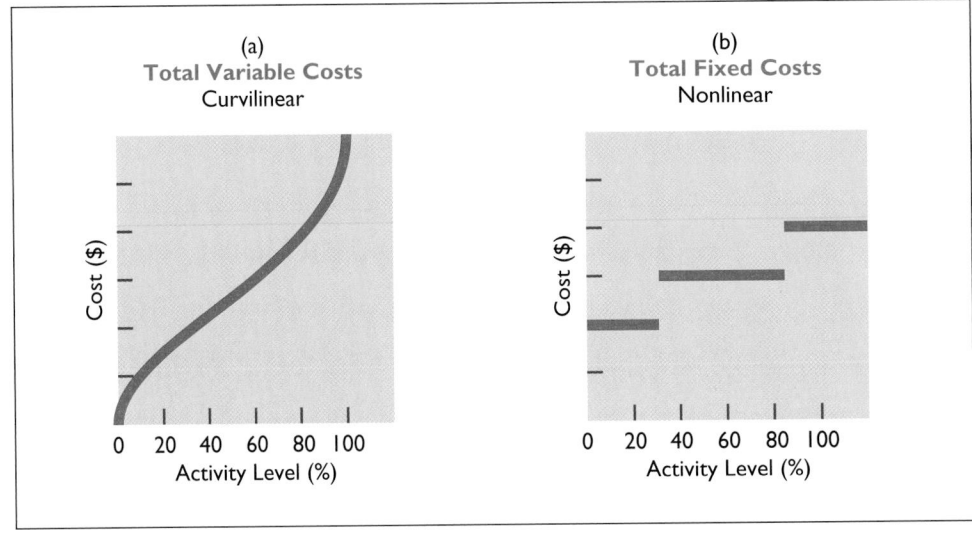

Total fixed costs also do not have a straight-line relationship over the entire range of activity. Some fixed costs will not change. But it is possible for management to change other fixed costs. For example, in the Feature Story the dance studio's rent was originally variable and then became fixed at a certain amount. It then increased to a new fixed amount when the size of the studio increased beyond a certain point. An example of the behavior of total fixed costs through all potential levels of activity is shown in part (b) of Illustration 18-3.

Helpful Hint Fixed costs that may be changeable include research, such as new product development, and management training programs.

For most companies, operating at almost zero or at 100 percent capacity is the exception rather than the rule. Instead, companies often operate over a somewhat narrower range, such as 40–80 percent of capacity. The range over which a company expects to operate during a year is called the **relevant range** of the activity index. Within the relevant range, as shown in both diagrams in Illustration 18-4 (next page), a straight-line relationship generally exists for both variable and fixed costs.

Alternative Terminology The relevant range is also called the *normal* or *practical range*.

As you can see, although the straight-line relationship may not be completely realistic, **the linear assumption produces useful data for CVP analysis as long as the level of activity remains within the relevant range.**

MIXED COSTS

STUDY OBJECTIVE
3
Explain the concept of mixed costs.

Mixed costs are costs that contain both a variable element and a fixed element. Sometimes called **semivariable costs**, **mixed costs change in total but not proportionately with changes in the activity level**. The rental of a **U-Haul** truck is a good example of a mixed cost. Assume that local rental terms for a 17-foot truck, including insurance, are $50 per day plus 50 cents per mile. The per diem charge is a fixed cost with respect to miles driven, whereas the mileage charge is a variable cost. The graphic presentation of the rental cost for a one-day rental is shown in Illustration 18-5.

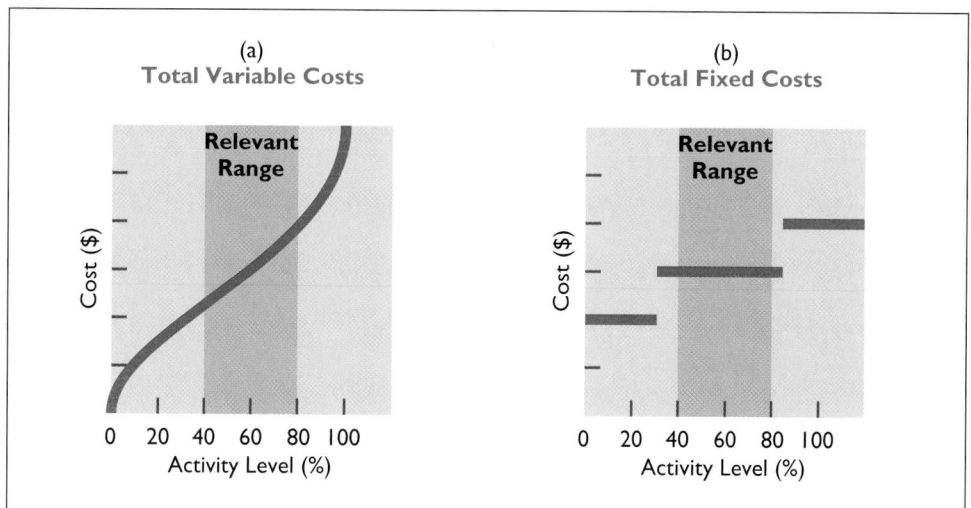

Illustration 18-4 Linear behavior within relevant range

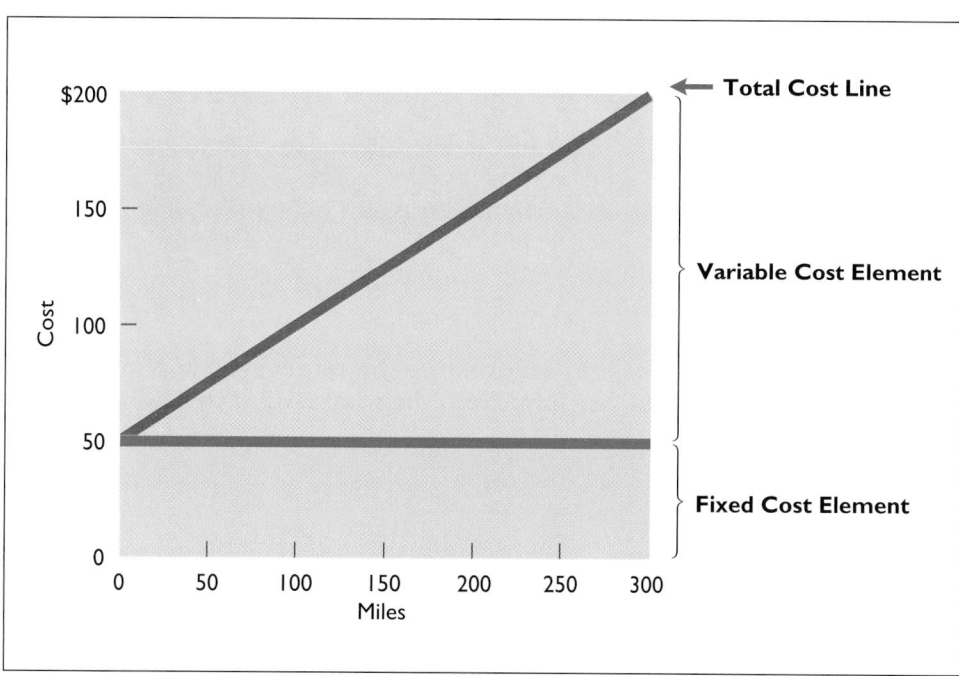

Illustration 18-5 Behavior of a mixed cost

In this case, the fixed cost element is the cost of having the service available. The variable cost element is the cost of actually using the service. Another example of a mixed cost is utility costs (electric, telephone, and so on), where there is a flat service fee plus a usage charge.

For purposes of CVP analysis, **mixed costs must be classified into their fixed and variable elements**. How does management make the classification? One possibility is to determine the variable and fixed components each time a mixed cost is incurred. But because of time and cost constraints, this approach is rarely followed. Instead, the customary approach is to determine variable and fixed costs on an **aggregate basis at the end of a period of time**. The company does this by using its past experience with the behavior of the mixed cost at various levels of activity. Management may use any of several methods in making the determination. We will explain the **high-low method** here. Other methods are more appropriately explained in cost accounting courses.[1]

---

[1]Other methods include the scatter diagram method and least squares regression analysis.

High-Low Method

The high-low method uses the total costs incurred at the high and low levels of activity. The difference in costs between the high and low levels represents variable costs, since only the variable cost element can change as activity levels change. The steps in computing fixed and variable costs under this method are as follows.

1. Determine variable cost per unit from the following formula.

Illustration 18-6 Formula for variable cost per unit using high-low method

Change in Total Costs	÷	High minus Low Activity Level	=	Variable Cost per Unit

To illustrate, assume that Metro Transit Company has the following maintenance costs and mileage data for its fleet of buses over a 4-month period.

Illustration 18-7 Assumed maintenance costs and mileage data

Month	Miles Driven	Total Cost	Month	Miles Driven	Total Cost
January	20,000	$30,000	March	35,000	$49,000
February	40,000	48,000	April	50,000	63,000

The high and low levels of activity are 50,000 miles in April and 20,000 miles in January. The maintenance costs at these two levels are $63,000 and $30,000, respectively. The difference in maintenance costs is $33,000 ($63,000 − $30,000) and the difference in miles is 30,000 (50,000 − 20,000). Therefore, for Metro Transit, variable cost per unit is $1.10, computed as follows.

$$\$33,000 \div 30,000 = \$1.10$$

2. Determine the fixed cost by subtracting the total variable cost at either the high or the low activity level from the total cost at that activity level.

For Metro Transit, the computations are shown in Illustration 18-8.

Illustration 18-8 High-low method computation of fixed costs

	Activity Level	
	High	**Low**
Total cost	$63,000	$30,000
Less: Variable costs		
50,000 × $1.10	55,000	
20,000 × $1.10		22,000
Total fixed costs	**$ 8,000**	**$ 8,000**

Maintenance costs are therefore $8,000 per month plus $1.10 per mile. For example, at 45,000 miles, estimated maintenance costs would be $8,000 fixed and $49,500 variable (45,000 × $1.10).

The high-low method generally produces a reasonable estimate for analysis. However, it does not produce a precise measurement of the fixed and variable elements in a mixed cost because other activity levels are ignored in the computation.

IMPORTANCE OF IDENTIFYING VARIABLE AND FIXED COSTS

Why is it important to segregate costs into variable and fixed elements? The answer may become apparent if we look at the following four business decisions.

1. If **American Airlines** is to make a profit when it reduces all domestic fares by 30 percent, what reduction in costs or increase in passengers will be required? **Answer:** To make a profit when it cuts domestic fares by 30 percent, American Airlines will have to increase the number of passengers or cut its variable costs for those flights. Its fixed costs will not change.

2. If **Ford Motor Company** meets the United Auto Workers' demands for higher wages, what increase in sales revenue will be needed to maintain current profit levels? **Answer:** Higher wages to UAW members at Ford Motor Company will increase the variable costs of manufacturing automobiles. To maintain present profit levels, Ford will have to cut other variable costs or increase the price of its automobiles.

3. If **USX Corp.**'s program to modernize plant facilities reduces the work force by 50 percent, what will be the effect on the cost of producing one ton of steel? **Answer:** The modernizing of plant facilities at USX Corp. changes the proportion of fixed and variable costs of producing one ton of steel. Fixed costs increase because of higher depreciation charges, whereas variable costs decrease due to the reduction in the number of steelworkers.

4. What happens if **Kellogg Company** increases its advertising expenses but cannot increase prices because of competitive pressure? **Answer:** Sales volume must be increased to cover three items: (1) the increase in advertising, (2) the variable cost of the increased sales volume, and (3) the desired additional net income.

BEFORE YOU GO ON . . .

▶ Review It

1. What are the effects on (a) a variable cost and (b) a fixed cost due to a change in activity?
2. What is the relevant range, and how do costs behave within this range?
3. What are the steps in applying the high-low method to mixed costs?

▶ Do It

Helena Company reports the following total costs at two levels of production.

	10,000 units	20,000 units
Direct materials	$20,000	$40,000
Maintenance	8,000	10,000
Depreciation	4,000	4,000

Classify each cost as either variable, fixed, or mixed.

Action Plan

• Recall that a variable cost varies in total directly and proportionately with each change.
• Recall that a fixed cost remains the same in total with each change.
• Recall that a mixed cost changes in total but not proportionately with each change.

Solution

Direct materials is a variable cost. Maintenance is a mixed cost. Depreciation is a fixed cost.

Related exercise material: BE18-1, E18-1, and E18-2.

Cost-Volume-Profit Analysis

Cost-volume-profit (CVP) analysis is the study of the effects of changes in costs and volume on a company's profits. CVP analysis is important in profit planning. It also is a critical factor in such management decisions as setting selling prices, determining product mix, and maximizing use of production facilities.

BASIC COMPONENTS

Illustration 18-9
Components of CVP analysis

CVP analysis considers the interrelationships among the components shown in Illustration 18-9.

The following assumptions underlie each CVP analysis.

1. The behavior of both costs and revenues is linear throughout the relevant range of the activity index.
2. All costs can be classified with reasonable accuracy as either variable or fixed.
3. Changes in activity are the only factors that affect costs.
4. All units produced are sold.
5. When more than one type of product is sold, the sales mix will remain constant. That is, the percentage that each product represents of total sales will stay the same. Sales mix complicates CVP analysis because different products will have different cost relationships. In this chapter we assume a single product. Sales mix issues are addressed in Chapter 22.

When these five assumptions are not valid, the results of CVP analysis may be inaccurate.

CVP INCOME STATEMENT

STUDY OBJECTIVE

5

Indicate what contribution margin is and how it can be expressed.

Because CVP is so important for decision making, management often wants this information reported in a **CVP income statement** format for internal use. The CVP income statement classifies costs as variable and fixed and computes a contribution margin. **Contribution margin** is the amount of revenue remaining after deducting variable costs. It is often stated both as a total amount and on a per unit basis. We will use Vargo Video Company to illustrate a CVP income statement. Relevant data for the CD/DVD players made by this company are as follows.

Illustration 18-10
Assumed selling and cost data for Vargo Video

Unit selling price of CD/DVD	$500
Unit variable costs	$300
Total monthly fixed costs	$200,000
Units sold	1,600

The CVP income statement for Vargo Video therefore would be reported as follows.

VARGO VIDEO COMPANY CVP Income Statement For the Month Ended June 30, 2005		
	Total	**Per Unit**
Sales (1,600 CD/DVDs)	$ 800,000	$ 500
Variable costs	480,000	300
Contribution margin	320,000	$200
Fixed costs	200,000	
Net income	$120,000	

Illustration 18-11 CVP income statement, with net income

A traditional income statement and a CVP income statement both report the same bottom-line net income of $120,000. However a traditional income statement does not classify costs as variable and fixed, and therefore a contribution margin would not be reported. In addition, both a total and a per unit amount are often shown on a CVP income statement to facilitate CVP analysis. In the applications of CVP analysis that follow, we will assume that the term "cost" includes all costs and expenses pertaining to production and sale of the product. That is, cost includes manufacturing costs plus selling and administrative expenses.

Contribution Margin Per Unit

From Vargo Video's CVP income statement, we can see that the contribution margin is $320,000, and the contribution margin per unit is $200 ($500 − $300). The formula for **contribution margin per unit** and the computation for Vargo Video are:

Unit Selling Price	−	Unit Variable Costs	=	Contribution Margin per Unit
$500	−	$300	=	$200

Illustration 18-12 Formula for contribution margin per unit

Contribution margin per unit indicates that for every CD/DVD sold, Vargo will have $200 to cover fixed costs and contribute to net income. Because Vargo Video has fixed costs of $200,000, it must sell 1,000 CD/DVDs ($200,000 ÷ $200) before it earns any net income. Vargo's CVP income statement, assuming a zero net income, would report the following.

VARGO VIDEO COMPANY CVP Income Statement For the Month Ended June 30, 2005		
	Total	**Per Unit**
Sales (1,000 CD/DVDs)	$500,000	$ 500
Variable costs	300,000	300
Contribution margin	200,000	$200
Fixed costs	200,000	
Net income	$ –0–	

Illustration 18-13 CVP income statement, with zero net income

It follows that for every CD/DVD sold above 1,000 units, net income is increased $200. For example, assume that Vargo sold one more CD/DVD, for a total of 1,001 CD/DVDs sold. In this case it would report net income of $200 as shown in Illustration 18-14.

Illustration 18-14 CVP income statement, with net income

VARGO VIDEO COMPANY CVP Income Statement For the Month Ended June 30, 2005		
	Total	**Per Unit**
Sales (1,001 CD/DVDs)	$ 500,500	$ 500
Variable costs	300,300	300
Contribution margin	200,200	$200
Fixed costs	200,000	
Net income	$ 200	

Contribution Margin Ratio

Some managers prefer to use a contribution margin ratio in CVP analysis. The **contribution margin ratio** is the contribution margin per unit divided by the unit selling price. For Vargo Video, the ratio is as follows.

Illustration 18-15 Formula for contribution margin ratio

Contribution Margin per Unit	÷	**Unit Selling Price**	=	**Contribution Margin Ratio**
$200	÷	$500	=	40%

The contribution margin ratio of 40 percent means that $0.40 of each sales dollar ($1 × 40%) is available to apply to fixed costs and to contribute to net income.

This expression of contribution margin is very helpful in determining the effect of changes in sales on net income. For example, net income will increase $40,000 (40% × $100,000) if sales increase $100,000. Thus, by using the contribution margin ratio, managers can quickly determine increases in net income from any change in sales. We can also see this effect through a CVP income statement. Assume that Vargo Video's current sales are $500,000 and it wants to know the effect of a $100,000 increase in sales. It could prepare a comparative CVP income statement analysis as follows.

Illustration 18-16 Comparative CVP income statements

VARGO VIDEO COMPANY CVP Income Statements For the Month Ended June 30, 2005				
	No Change		**With Change**	
	Total	**Per Unit**	**Total**	**Per Unit**
Sales	$500,000	$ 500	$600,000	$ 500
Variable costs	300,000	300	360,000	300
Contribution margin	200,000	$200	240,000	$200
Fixed costs	200,000		200,000	
Net income	$ –0–		$ 40,000	

Study these CVP income statements carefully. The concepts used in these statements will be used extensively in this and later chapters.

DECISION TOOLKIT

Decision Checkpoints	Info Needed for Decision	Tool to Use for Decision	How to Evaluate Results
What was the contribution toward fixed costs and income from each unit sold?	Selling price per unit and variable cost per unit	Contribution margin per unit = Unit selling price − Unit variable cost	Every unit sold will increase income by the contribution margin.
What was the percentage increase in income as a result of an increase in sales?	Contribution margin per unit and unit selling price	Contribution margin ratio = Contribution margin per unit ÷ Unit selling price	Every dollar of sales will increase income by the contribution margin ratio.

BREAK-EVEN ANALYSIS

A key relationship in CVP analysis is the level of activity at which total revenues equal total costs (both fixed and variable). This level of activity is called the **break-even point**. At this volume of sales, the company will realize no income and will suffer no loss. The process of finding the break-even point is called **break-even analysis**. Knowledge of the break-even point is useful to management when it decides whether to introduce new product lines, change sales prices on established products, or enter new markets. The break-even point can be:

> **STUDY OBJECTIVE**
> **6**
> Identify the three ways to determine the break-even point.

1. Computed from a mathematical equation.
2. Computed by using contribution margin.
3. Derived from a cost-volume-profit (CVP) graph.

The break-even point can be expressed **either in sales units or sales dollars**.

Mathematical Equation

A common equation used for CVP analysis is shown in Illustration 18-17.

$$\text{Sales} = \text{Variable Costs} + \text{Fixed Costs} + \text{Net Income}$$

Illustration 18-17
Basic CVP equation

The break-even point **in units** can be computed directly from the equation by **using unit selling prices** and **unit variable costs**. The computation for Vargo Video is:

$$\$500Q = \$300Q + \$200,000 + \$0$$
$$\$200Q = \$200,000$$
$$Q = \textbf{1,000 units}$$

where

$$Q = \text{sales volume}$$
$$\$500 = \text{selling price}$$
$$\$300 = \text{variable cost per unit}$$
$$\$200,000 = \text{total fixed costs}$$

Illustration 18-18
Computation of break-even point in units

Thus, Vargo Video must sell 1,000 units to break even.

To find **sales dollars** required to break even, we multiply the units sold at the break-even point times the selling price per unit, as shown below.

$$1,000 \times \$500 = \$500,000 \text{ (break-even sales dollars)}$$

Identifying the break-even point using the mathematical equation is a special case of CVP analysis. Because at the break-even point net income is zero, **break-even** (whether expressed in sales units or in sales dollars) **occurs where total sales equal variable costs plus fixed costs**.

Business Insight
MANAGEMENT PERSPECTIVE

The Internet is wringing inefficiencies out of nearly every industry. While commercial aircraft spend roughly 4,000 hours a year in the air, chartered aircraft spend only 500 hours flying. That means that they are sitting on the ground—not making any money—nearly 90 percent of the time. Enter flightserve.com. For about the same cost as a first-class ticket, flightserve.com matches up executives with charter flights in small "private jets." The executive gets a more comfortable ride and can avoid the hassle of big airports. Flightserve.com says that the average charter jet has eight seats. When all eight seats are full, the company has an 80 percent profit margin. It breaks even at an average of 3.3 full seats per flight.

SOURCE: "Jet Set Go," *The Economist* (March 18, 2000), p. 68.

Contribution Margin Technique

We know that contribution margin equals total revenues less variable costs. It follows that at the break-even point, **contribution margin must equal total fixed costs**. On the basis of this relationship, we can compute the break-even point using either the contribution margin per unit or the contribution margin ratio.

When the contribution margin per unit is used, the formula to compute break-even point in units is as follows.

Illustration 18-19 Formula for break-even point in units using contribution margin

Fixed Costs	÷	Contribution Margin per Unit	=	Break-even Point in Units

For Vargo Video, the contribution margin per unit is $200, as explained earlier. Thus, the break-even point in units is:

$$\$200,000 \div \$200 = 1,000 \text{ units}$$

When the contribution margin ratio is used, the formula to compute break-even point in dollars is:

Illustration 18-20 Formula for break-even point in dollars using contribution margin ratio

Fixed Costs	÷	Contribution Margin Ratio	=	Break-even Point in Dollars

We know that the contribution margin ratio for Vargo Video is 40 percent. Thus, the break-even point in dollars is:

$$\$200,000 \div 40\% = \$500,000$$

Graphic Presentation

An effective way to find the break-even point is to prepare a break-even graph. Because this graph also shows costs, volume, and profits, it is referred to as a **cost-volume-profit (CVP) graph**.

As shown in the CVP graph in Illustration 18-21, sales volume is recorded along the horizontal axis. This axis should extend to the maximum level of expected sales. Both total revenues (sales) and total costs (fixed plus variable) are recorded on the vertical axis.

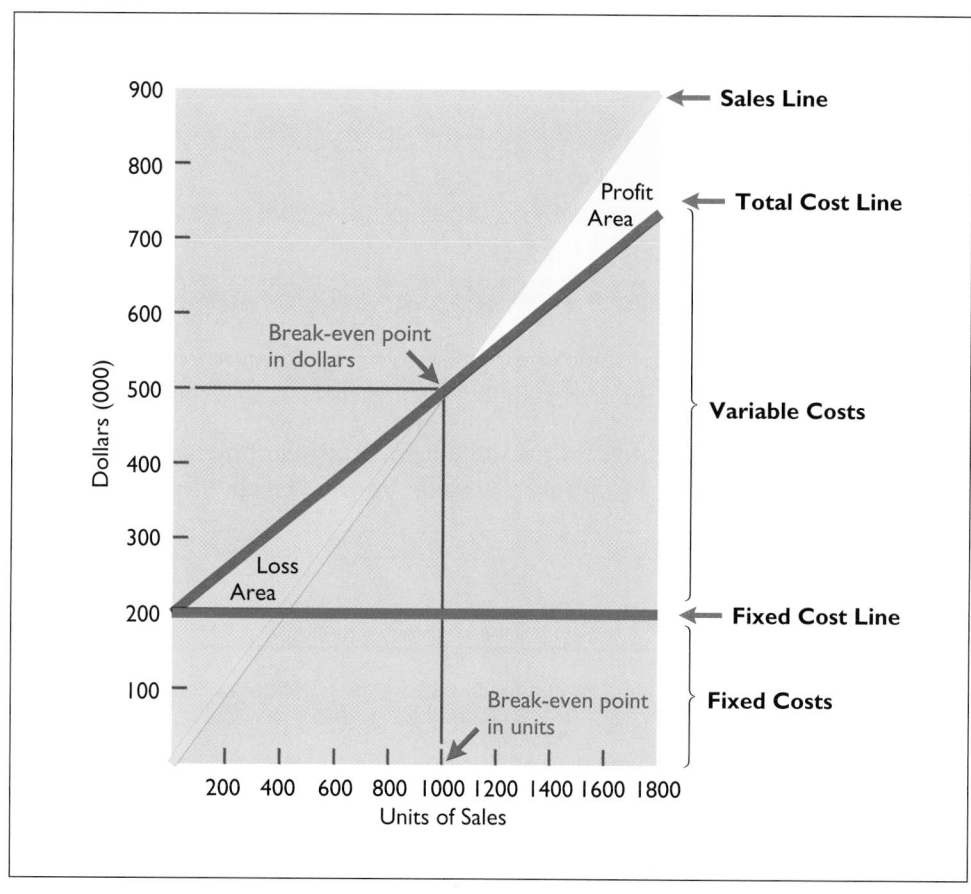

Illustration 18-21
CVP graph

The construction of the graph, using the data for Vargo Video, is as follows.

1. Plot the total-revenue line, starting at the zero activity level. For every CD/DVD sold, total revenue increases by $500. For example, at 200 units, sales are $100,000. At the upper level of activity (1,800 units), sales are $900,000. Note that the revenue line is assumed to be linear throughout the full range of activity.

2. Plot the total fixed cost using a horizontal line. For the CD/DVDs, this line is plotted at $200,000. The fixed cost is the same at every level of activity.

3. Plot the total cost line. This starts at the fixed-cost line at zero activity. It increases by the variable cost at each level of activity. For each CD/DVD, variable costs are $300. Thus, at 200 units, total variable cost is $60,000, and

the total cost is $260,000. At 1,800 units total variable cost is $540,000, and total cost is $740,000. On the graph, the amount of the variable cost can be derived from the difference between the total cost and fixed cost lines at each level of activity.

4. Determine the break-even point from the intersection of the total cost line and the total revenue line. The break-even point in dollars is found by drawing a horizontal line from the break-even point to the vertical axis. The break-even point in units is found by drawing a vertical line from the break-even point to the horizontal axis. For the CD/DVDs, the break-even point is $500,000 of sales, or 1,000 units. At this sales level, Vargo Video will cover costs but make no profit.

The CVP graph also shows both the net income and net loss areas. Thus, the amount of income or loss at each level of sales can be derived from the total sales and total cost lines.

A CVP graph is useful because the effects of a change in any element in the CVP analysis can be quickly seen. For example, a 10 percent increase in selling price will change the location of the total revenue line. Likewise, the effects on total costs of wage increases can be quickly observed.

Business Insight
MANAGEMENT PERSPECTIVE

Computer graphics are a valuable companion to many computer software packages. Color graphs can be instantly changed to provide visual "what if" analysis.

Current technology allows for stunning graphs in a variety of different formats (pie charts, bar, stacked bar, two-dimensional, three-dimensional, etc.). In the appropriate situation, a graph can literally be worth a thousand words.

DECISION TOOLKIT

Decision Checkpoints	Info Needed for Decision	Tool to Use for Decision	How to Evaluate Results
At what amount of sales does a company cover its costs?	Unit selling price, unit variable cost, and total fixed costs	Break-even point analysis *In units:* $$\text{Break-even point} = \frac{\text{Fixed costs}}{\text{Unit contribution margin}}$$ *In dollars:* $$\text{Break-even point} = \frac{\text{Fixed costs}}{\text{Contribution margin ratio}}$$	Below the break-even point—the point at which total sales equal total costs—the company is unprofitable.

BEFORE YOU GO ON . . .

▶ **Review It**

1. What are the assumptions that underlie each CVP application?
2. What is contribution margin, and how can it be expressed?
3. How can the break-even point be determined?

▶ Do It

Lombardi Company has a unit selling price of $400, variable costs per unit of $240, and fixed costs of $160,000. Compute the break-even point in units using (a) a mathematical equation and (b) contribution margin per unit.

Action Plan

- Apply the formula: Sales = Variable costs + Fixed costs + Net income.
- Apply the formula: Fixed costs ÷ Contribution margin per unit = Break-even point in units.

Solution

(a) The formula is $400Q = $240Q + $160,000. The break-even point in units is 1,000 ($160,000 ÷ $160Q). (b) Contribution margin per unit is $160 ($400 − $240). The formula is $160,000 ÷ $160, and the break-even point in units is 1,000.

Related exercise material: BE18-5, BE18-6, E18-3, E18-4, E18-5, E18-6, and E18-7.

MARGIN OF SAFETY

The margin of safety is another relationship that may be calculated in CVP analysis. **Margin of safety** is the difference between actual or expected sales and sales at the break-even point. This relationship measures the "cushion" that management has, allowing it to still break even if expected sales fail to materialize. The margin of safety may be expressed in dollars or as a ratio.

The formula for stating the **margin of safety in dollars** is as follows.

STUDY OBJECTIVE
7
Define margin of safety, and give the formulas for computing it.

Actual (Expected) Sales	−	Break-even Sales	=	Margin of Safety in Dollars

Illustration 18-22 Formula for margin of safety in dollars

Assuming that actual (expected) sales for Vargo Video are $750,000, the computation is:

$$\$750,000 - \$500,000 = \$250,000$$

The formula and computation for determining the **margin of safety ratio** are:

Margin of Safety in Dollars	÷	Actual (Expected) Sales	=	Margin of Safety Ratio
$250,000	÷	$750,000	=	33%

Illustration 18-23 Formula for margin of safety ratio

The higher the dollars or the percentage, the greater the margin of safety. The adequacy of the margin of safety should be evaluated by management in terms of such factors as the vulnerability of the product to competitive pressures and to downturns in the economy.

Business Insight
MANAGEMENT PERSPECTIVE

Computation of break-even and margin of safety is important for service companies as well. Consider how the promoter for the Rolling Stones' tour used the break-even point and margin of safety. For example, one outdoor show should bring 70,000 individuals for a gross of $2.45 million. The promoter guarantees $1.2 million to the Rolling Stones. In addition, 20 percent of gross, or approximately $500,000, goes to the stadium in which the performance is staged. Add another $400,000 for other expenses such as ticket takers, parking attendants, advertising, and so on. This leaves $350,000 to the promoter per show, if it sells out. At 75 percent, the promoter breaks about even. At 50 percent, the promoter loses hundreds of thousands of dollars. However, the promoter also shares in sales of T-shirts and memorabilia for which the promoter will net over $7 million during the tour. From a successful Rolling Stones' tour, the promoter could make $35 million!

TARGET NET INCOME

STUDY OBJECTIVE
8
Give the formulas for determining sales required to earn target net income.

Management usually sets an income objective for individual product lines. This objective is called **target net income**. It indicates the sales necessary to achieve a specified level of income. The sales necessary to achieve target net income can be determined from each of the approaches used to determine break-even sales.

Mathematical Equation

We know that at the break-even point no profit or loss results for the company. By instead adding an amount for target net income to the same basic equation, we obtain the following formula for determining required sales.

Illustration 18-24 Formula for required sales to meet target net income

$$\begin{array}{c}\text{Required} \\ \text{Sales}\end{array} = \begin{array}{c}\text{Variable} \\ \text{Costs}\end{array} + \begin{array}{c}\text{Fixed} \\ \text{Costs}\end{array} + \begin{array}{c}\text{Target Net} \\ \text{Income}\end{array}$$

Required sales may be expressed in **either sales units or sales dollars**. Assuming that target net income is $120,000 for Vargo Video, the computation of required sales in units is as follows.

Illustration 18-25
Computation of required sales

$$\$500Q = 300Q + \$200,000 + \$120,000$$
$$\$200Q = \$320,000$$
$$Q = \mathbf{1{,}600}$$

where:
$$Q = \text{sales volume}$$
$$\$500 = \text{selling price}$$
$$\$300 = \text{variable costs per unit}$$
$$\$200,000 = \text{total fixed costs}$$
$$\$120,000 = \text{target net income}$$

The sales dollars required to achieve the target net income is found by multiplying the units sold by the unit selling price [(1,600 × $500) = $800,000].

Contribution Margin Technique

As in the case of break-even sales, the sales required to meet a target net income can be computed in either units or dollars. The formula using the contribution margin per unit is as follows.

Fixed Costs + Target Net Income	÷	Contribution Margin Per Unit	=	Required Sales in Units

Illustration 18-26 Formula for required sales in units using contribution margin per unit

The computation for Vargo Video is as follows.

$$(\$200,000 + \$120,000) \div \$200 = 1,600 \text{ units}$$

The formula using the contribution margin ratio is as follows.

Fixed Costs + Target Net Income	÷	Contribution Margin Ratio	=	Required Sales in Dollars

Illustration 18-27 Formula for required sales in dollars using contribution margin ratio

The computation for Vargo Video is as follows.

$$\$320,000 \div 40\% = \$800,000$$

Graphic Presentation

The CVP graph in Illustration 18-21 (on page 879) can also be used to find the sales required to meet target net income. In the profit area of the graph, the distance between the sales line and the total cost line at any point equals net income. Required sales are found by analyzing the differences between the two lines until the desired net income is found.

CVP AND CHANGES IN THE BUSINESS ENVIRONMENT

When the **IBM** personal computer (PC) was introduced, it sold for $2,500. Today the same type of computer sells for much less. Recently, when oil prices rose, the break-even point for airline companies such as **American**, **Southwest**, and **United** rose dramatically. Because of lower prices for imported steel, the demand for domestic steel dropped significantly. The point should be clear: Business conditions change rapidly, and management must respond intelligently to these changes. CVP analysis can help.

To illustrate how CVP analysis can be used in responding to change, we will look at three independent situations that might occur at Vargo Video. Each case is based on the original CD/DVD sales and cost data, which were:

Unit selling price	$500
Unit variable cost	$300
Total fixed costs	$200,000
Break-even sales	$500,000 or 1,000 units

Illustration 18-28 Original CD/DVD sales and cost data

CASE 1. A competitor is offering a 10% discount on the selling price of its CD/DVDs. Management must decide whether to offer a similar discount. **Question**: What effect will a 10 percent discount on selling price have on the break-even point for CD/DVDs? **Answer**: A 10 percent discount on selling price reduces the selling price per unit to $450 [$500 − ($500 × 10%)]. Variable costs per unit remain unchanged at $300. Thus, the contribution margin per unit is $150. Assuming no change in fixed costs, break-even sales are 1,333 units, computed as follows.

Illustration 18-29
Computation of break-even sales in units

Fixed Costs	÷	Contribution Margin per Unit	=	Break-even Sales
$200,000	÷	$150	=	1,333 units (rounded)

For Vargo Video, this change would require monthly sales to increase by 333 units, or $33\frac{1}{3}$ percent, in order to break even. In reaching a conclusion about offering a 10 percent discount to customers, management must determine how likely it is to achieve the increased sales. Also, management should estimate the possible loss of sales if the competitor's discount price is not matched.

CASE II. To meet the threat of foreign competition, management invests in new robotic equipment that will lower the amount of direct labor required to make CD/DVDs. It is estimated that total fixed costs will increase 30 percent and that variable cost per unit will decrease 30 percent. **Question**: What effect will the new equipment have on the sales volume required to break even? **Answer**: Total fixed costs become $260,000 [$200,000 + (30% × $200,000)]. The variable cost per unit becomes $210 [$300 − (30% × $300)]. The new break-even point is approximately 900 units, computed as follows.

Illustration 18-30
Computation of break-even sales in units

Fixed Costs	÷	Contribution Margin per Unit	=	Break-even Sales
$260,000	÷	($500 − $210)	=	900 units (rounded)

These changes appear to be advantageous for Vargo Video. The break-even point is reduced by 10 percent, or 100 units.

CASE III. Vargo's principal supplier of raw materials has just announced a price increase. The higher cost is expected to increase the variable cost of CD/DVDs by $25 per unit. Management would like to hold the line on the selling price of CD/DVDs. It plans a cost-cutting program that will save $17,500 in fixed costs per month. Vargo is currently realizing monthly net income of $80,000 on sales of 1,400 CD/DVDs. **Question**: What increase in units sold will be needed to maintain the same level of net income? **Answer**: The variable cost per unit increases to $325 ($300 + $25). Fixed costs are reduced to $182,500 ($200,000 − $17,500). Because of the change in variable cost, the contribution margin per unit becomes $175 ($500 − $325). The required number of units sold to achieve the target net income is computed as follows.

Illustration 18-31
Computation of required sales

Fixed Costs + Target Net Income	÷	Contribution Margin per Unit	=	Required Sales in Units
($182,500 + $80,000)	÷	$175	=	1,500

To achieve the required sales, 1,500 CD/DVDs will have to be sold, an increase of 100 units. If this does not seem to be a reasonable expectation, management will either have to make further cost reductions or accept less net income if the selling price remains unchanged.

Business Insight
MANAGEMENT PERSPECTIVE

When analyzing an Internet business, the so-called "conversion rate" is closely watched. It is calculated by dividing the number of people who actually take action at an Internet site (e.g., buy something) by the total number of people who visit the site. Average conversion rates are from 3 to 5 percent. A rate below 2 percent is poor, while a rate above 10 percent is great.

Conversion rates have an obvious effect on break-even point. Suppose you spend $10,000 on your site, and you attract 5,000 visitors. If you get a 2 percent conversion rate (100 purchases), your site costs $100 per purchase ($10,000 ÷ 100). A 4 percent conversion rate gets you down to a cost of $50 per transaction, and an 8 percent conversion rate gets you down to $25. Studies have shown that conversion rates increase if the site has an easy-to-use interface, fast-performing screens, a convenient ordering process, and advertising that is both clever and clear.

SOURCE: J. William Gurley, "The One Internet Metric That Really Counts," *Fortune* (March 6, 2000), p. 392.

DECISION TOOLKIT

Decision Checkpoints	Info Needed for Decision	Tool to Use for Decision	How to Evaluate Results
How can a company use CVP analysis to improve profitability?	Data on what effect a price change, a fixed-cost change, or a trade-off between fixed and variable costs would have on volume and costs	Measurement of income at new volume levels	If profitability increases under proposed change, adopt change.

CVP INCOME STATEMENT REVISITED

At the beginning of the chapter we presented a simple CVP income statement. When companies prepare a CVP income statement, they provide more detail about specific variable and fixed-cost items.

To illustrate a more detailed CVP income statement, we will assume that Vargo Video reaches its target net income of $120,000 (see Illustration 18-25 on page 882). The following information is obtained on the $680,000 of costs that were incurred in June.

STUDY OBJECTIVE
9
Describe the essential features of a cost-volume-profit income statement.

	Variable	Fixed	Total
Cost of goods sold	$400,000	$120,000	$520,000
Selling expenses	60,000	40,000	100,000
Administrative expenses	20,000	40,000	60,000
	$480,000	$200,000	$680,000

Illustration 18-32
Assumed cost and expense data

The detailed CVP income statement for Vargo is shown below.

Illustration 18-33 Detailed
CVP income statement

VARGO VIDEO COMPANY
CVP Income Statement
For the Month Ended June 30, 2005

		Total	Per Unit
Sales		$ 800,000	$ 500
Variable expenses			
Cost of goods sold	$400,000		
Selling expenses	60,000		
Administrative expenses	20,000		
Total variable expenses		480,000	300
Contribution margin		320,000	$200
Fixed expenses			
Cost of goods sold	120,000		
Selling expenses	40,000		
Administrative expenses	40,000		
Total fixed expenses		200,000	
Net income		$120,000	

BEFORE YOU GO ON . . .

▶ **Review It**

1. What is the formula for computing the margin of safety (a) in dollars and (b) as a ratio?
2. What is the equation to compute target net income?

☑ THE NAVIGATOR

Using the Decision Toolkit

B.T. Hernandez Company, maker of high-quality flashlights, has experienced steady growth over the last 6 years. However, increased competition has led Mr. Hernandez, the president, to believe that an aggressive campaign is needed next year to maintain the company's present growth. The company's accountant has presented Mr. Hernandez with the following data for the current year, 2005, for use in preparing next year's advertising campaign.

Cost Schedules

Variable costs	
Direct labor per flashlight	$ 8.00
Direct materials	4.00
Variable overhead	3.00
Variable cost per flashlight	$ 15.00
Fixed costs	
Manufacturing	$ 25,000
Selling	40,000
Administrative	70,000
Total fixed costs	$135,000
Selling price per flashlight	$25.00
Expected sales, 2005 (20,000 flashlights)	$500,000

Mr. Hernandez has set the sales target for the year 2006 at a level of $550,000 (22,000 flashlights).

Instructions

(Ignore any income tax considerations.)

(a) What is the projected operating income for 2005?

(b) What is the contribution margin per unit for 2005?

(c) What is the break-even point in units for 2005?

(d) Mr. Hernandez believes that to attain the sales target in the year 2006, the company must incur an additional selling expense of $10,000 for advertising in 2006, with all other costs remaining constant. What will be the break-even point in dollar sales for 2006 if the company spends the additional $10,000?

(e) If the company spends the additional $10,000 for advertising in 2006, what is the sales level in dollars required to equal 2005 operating income?

Solution

(a)

Expected sales	$500,000
Less:	
Variable cost (20,000 flashlights × $15)	300,000
Fixed costs	135,000
Projected operating income	$ 65,000

(b) $500,000 ÷ 20,000 = $25 selling price per flashlight

Selling price per flashlight	$25
Variable cost per flashlight	15
Contribution margin per unit	$10

(c) Fixed costs ÷ Contribution margin per unit = Break-even point in units
$135,000 ÷ $10 = 13,500 units

(d) Fixed costs ÷ Contribution margin ratio = Break-even point in dollars
$145,000 ÷ 40% = $362,500

Fixed costs (from 2005)	$135,000
Additional advertising expense	10,000
Fixed costs (2006)	$145,000

Contribution margin = Sales − Variable costs

Expected sales	$550,000
Variable costs (22,000 × $15)	330,000
Contribution margin	$220,000

Contribution margin ratio = Contribution margin ÷ Sales
40% = $220,000 ÷ $550,000

(e) Required sales = (Fixed costs + Target net income) ÷ Contribution margin ratio
$525,000 = ($145,000 + $65,000) ÷ 40%

THE NAVIGATOR

Summary of Study Objectives

1 *Distinguish between variable and fixed costs.* Variable costs are costs that vary in total directly and proportionately with changes in the activity index. Fixed costs are costs that remain the same in total regardless of changes in the activity index.

2 *Explain the significance of the relevant range.* The relevant range is the range of activity in which a company expects to operate during a year. It is important in CVP analysis because the behavior of costs is linear throughout the relevant range.

3 *Explain the concept of mixed costs.* Mixed costs increase in total but not proportionately with changes in the activity level. For purposes of CVP analysis, mixed costs must be classified into their fixed and variable elements. One method that management may use is the high-low method.

4 *List the five components of cost-volume-profit analysis.* The five components of CVP analysis are (a) volume or level of activity, (b) unit selling prices, (c) variable cost per unit, (d) total fixed costs, and (e) sales mix.

5 *Indicate what contribution margin is and how it can be expressed.* Contribution margin is the amount of revenue remaining after deducting variable costs. It can be expressed as a per unit amount or as a ratio.

6 *Identify the three ways to determine the break-even point.* The break-even point can be (a) computed from a mathematical equation, (b) computed by using a contribution margin technique, and (c) derived from a CVP graph.

7 *Define margin of safety, and give the formulas for computing it.* Margin of safety is the difference between actual or expected sales and sales at the break-even point. The formulas for margin of safety are: Actual (expected) sales − Break-even sales = Margin of safety in dollars; Margin of safety in dollars ÷ Actual (expected) sales = Margin of safety ratio.

8 *Give the formulas for determining sales required to earn target net income.* One formula is: Required sales = Variable costs + Fixed costs + Target net income. Another formula is: Fixed costs + Target net income ÷ Contribution margin ratio = Required sales.

9 *Describe the essential features of a cost-volume-profit income statement.* The CVP income statement classifies costs and expenses as variable or fixed and reports contribution margin in the body of the statement.

☑ THE NAVIGATOR

DECISION TOOLKIT—A SUMMARY

Decision Checkpoints ☑	Info Needed for Decision	Tool to Use for Decision	How to Evaluate Results
What was the contribution toward fixed costs and income from each unit sold?	Selling price per unit and variable cost per unit	Contribution margin per unit = Unit selling price − Unit variable cost	Every unit sold will increase income by the contribution margin.
What was the percentage increase in income as a result of an increase in sales?	Contribution margin per unit and unit selling price	Contribution margin ratio = Contribution margin per unit ÷ Unit selling price	Every dollar of sales will increase income by the contribution margin ratio.
At what amount of sales does a company cover its costs?	Unit selling price, unit variable cost, and total fixed costs	Break-even point analysis *In units:* $$\text{Break-even point} = \frac{\text{Fixed costs}}{\text{Unit contribution margin}}$$ *In dollars:* $$\text{Break-even point} = \frac{\text{Fixed costs}}{\text{Contribution margin ratio}}$$	Below the break-even point—the point at which total sales equal total costs—the company is unprofitable.
How can a company use CVP analysis to improve profitability?	Data on what effect a price change, a fixed-cost change, or a trade-off between fixed and variable costs would have on volume and costs	Measurement of income at new volume levels	If profitability increases under proposed change, adopt change.

APPENDIX
VARIABLE COSTING

In the earlier chapters, both variable and fixed manufacturing costs have been classified as product costs. In job order costing, for example, a job is assigned the costs of direct materials, direct labor, and both variable and fixed manufacturing overhead. This costing approach is referred to as **full** or absorption costing. It is so named because all manufacturing costs are charged to, or absorbed by, the product.

An alternative approach is to use variable costing. Under variable costing only direct materials, direct labor, and variable manufacturing overhead costs are considered product costs. Fixed manufacturing overhead costs are recognized as period costs (expenses) when incurred. The difference between absorption costing and variable costing is graphically shown as follows.

Illustration 18A-1
Difference between absorption costing and variable costing

Selling and administrative expenses are period costs under both absorption and variable costing.

To illustrate the computation of unit production cost under absorption and variable costing, assume that Premium Products Corporation manufactures a polyurethane sealant called Fix-it for car windshields. Relevant data for Fix-it in January 2005, the first month of production, are as follows.

Selling price	$20 per unit.
Units	Produced 30,000; sold 20,000; beginning inventory zero.
Variable unit costs	Manufacturing $9 (direct materials $5, direct labor $3, and variable overhead $1). Selling and administrative expenses $2.
Fixed costs	Manufacturing overhead $120,000. Selling and administrative expenses $15,000.

Illustration 18A-2 Sealant sales and cost data for Premium Products Corporation

The per unit production cost under each costing approach is:

Type of Cost	Absorption Costing	Variable Costing
Direct materials	$ 5	$5
Direct labor	3	3
Variable manufacturing overhead	1	1
Fixed manufacturing overhead ($120,000 ÷ 30,000 units produced)	4	0
Total unit cost	**$13**	**$9**

Illustration 18A-3
Computation of per unit production cost

The total unit cost is $4 ($13 − $9) higher for absorption costing. This occurs because fixed manufacturing costs are a product cost under absorption costing. They are a period cost under variable costing and so are expensed, instead. Based on these data, each unit sold and each unit remaining in inventory are costed at $13 under absorption costing and at $9 under variable costing.

Effects of Variable Costing on Income

The income statements under the two costing approaches are shown in Illustrations 18A-4 and 18A-5. The traditional income statement format is used with absorption costing. The cost-volume-profit format is used with variable costing. Computations are inserted parenthetically in the statements to facilitate your understanding of the amounts.

Illustration 18A-4
Absorption costing income statement

Helpful Hint This is the traditional statement that would result from job order and processing costing explained in Chapters 16 and 17.

PREMIUM PRODUCTS CORPORATION		
Income Statement		
For the Month Ended January 31, 2005		
(Absorption Costing)		
Sales (20,000 units × $20)		$400,000
Cost of goods sold		
Inventory, January 1	$ –0–	
Cost of goods manufactured (30,000 units × $13)	390,000	
Cost of goods available for sale	390,000	
Inventory, January 31 (10,000 units × $13)	**130,000**	
Cost of goods sold (20,000 units × $13)		260,000
Gross profit		140,000
Selling and administrative expenses		
(Variable 20,000 units × $2 + fixed $15,000)		55,000
Income from operations		**$ 85,000**

Illustration 18A-5
Variable costing income statement

Helpful Hint Note the difference in the computation of the ending inventory: $9 per unit here, $13 per unit above.

PREMIUM PRODUCTS CORPORATION		
Income Statement		
For the Month Ended January 31, 2005		
(Variable Costing)		
Sales (20,000 units × $20)		$400,000
Variable expenses		
Variable cost of goods sold		
Inventory, January 1	$ –0–	
Variable manufacturing costs (30,000 units × $9)	270,000	
Cost of goods available for sale	270,000	
Inventory, January 31 (10,000 units × $9)	**90,000**	
Variable cost of goods sold	180,000	
Variable selling and administrative expenses		
(20,000 units × $2)	40,000	
Total variable expenses		220,000
Contribution margin		180,000
Fixed expenses		
Manufacturing overhead	120,000	
Selling and administrative expenses	15,000	
Total fixed expenses		135,000
Income from operations		**$ 45,000**

Income from operations under absorption costing shown in Illustration 18A-4 is $40,000 higher than under variable costing ($85,000 − $45,000) shown in Illustration 18A-5.

As highlighted in the two income statements, there is a $40,000 difference in the ending inventories ($130,000 under absorption costing versus $90,000 under variable costing). Under absorption costing, $40,000 of the fixed overhead costs (10,000 units × $4) has been deferred to a future period as a product cost. In contrast, under variable costing the entire fixed manufacturing costs are expensed when incurred.

As shown, when units produced exceed units sold, income under absorption costing is higher. When units produced are less than units sold, income under absorption costing is lower.

When units produced and sold are the same, income from operations will be equal under the two costing approaches. In this case, there is no increase in ending inventory. So fixed overhead costs of the current period are not deferred to future periods through the ending inventory.

The foregoing effects of the two costing approaches on income from operations may be summarized as follows.

Illustration 18A-6
Summary of income effects

Rationale for Variable Costing

The rationale for variable costing centers on the purpose of fixed manufacturing costs. That purpose is **to have productive facilities available for use**. These costs are incurred whether a company operates at zero or at 100 percent of capacity. Thus, proponents of variable costing argue that these costs should be expensed in the period in which they are incurred.

Supporters of absorption costing defend the assignment of fixed manufacturing overhead costs to inventory. They say that these costs are as much a cost of getting a product ready for sale as direct materials or direct labor. Accordingly, these costs should not be matched with revenues until the product is sold.

The use of variable costing is acceptable **only for internal use by management**. It cannot be used in determining product costs in financial statements prepared in accordance with generally accepted accounting principles because it understates inventory costs. To comply with the matching principle, a company must use absorption costing for its work in process and finished goods inventories. Similarly, absorption costing must be used for income tax purposes.

Summary of Study Objective for Appendix

10 *Explain the difference between absorption costing and variable costing.* Under absorption costing, fixed manufacturing costs are product costs. Under variable costing, fixed manufacturing costs are period costs.

Glossary

Absorption costing A costing approach in which all manufacturing costs are charged to the product. (p. 889)

Activity index The activity that causes changes in the behavior of costs. (p. 867)

Break-even point The level of activity at which total revenues equal total costs. (p. 877)

Contribution margin (CM) The amount of revenue remaining after deducting variable costs. (p. 874)

Contribution margin per unit The amount of revenue remaining per unit after deducting variable costs; calculated as unit selling price minus unit variable cost. (p. 875)

Contribution margin ratio The percentage of each dollar of sales that is available to contribute to net income; calculated as contribution margin per unit divided by unit selling price. (p. 876)

Cost behavior analysis The study of how specific costs respond to changes in the level of business activity. (p. 867)

Cost-volume-profit (CVP) analysis The study of the effects of changes in costs and volume on a company's profits. (p. 874)

Cost-volume-profit (CVP) graph A graph showing the relationship between costs, volume, and profits. (p. 879)

Cost-volume-profit (CVP) income statement A statement for internal use that classifies costs and expenses as fixed or variable and reports contribution margin in the body of the statement. (p. 874)

Fixed costs Costs that remain the same in total regardless of changes in the activity level. (p. 868)

High-low method A mathematical method that uses the total costs incurred at the high and low levels of activity to determine the fixed and variable elements of a mixed cost. (p. 872)

Margin of safety The difference between actual or expected sales and sales at the break-even point. (p. 881)

Mixed costs Costs that contain both a variable and a fixed cost element and change in total but not proportionately with changes in the activity level. (p. 870)

Relevant range The range of the activity index over which the company expects to operate during the year. (p. 870)

Target net income The income objective for individual product lines. (p. 882)

Variable costing A costing approach in which only variable manufacturing costs are product costs, and fixed manufacturing costs are period costs (expenses). (p. 889)

Variable costs Costs that vary in total directly and proportionately with changes in the activity level. (p. 868)

Demonstration Problem

Mabo Company makes calculators that sell for $20 each. For the coming year, management expects fixed costs to total $220,000 and variable costs to be $9 per unit.

Instructions

(a) Compute break-even point in units using the mathematical equation.
(b) Compute break-even point in dollars using the contribution margin (CM) ratio.
(c) Compute the margin of safety percentage assuming actual sales are $500,000.
(d) Compute the sales required in dollars to earn net income of $165,000.

Solution to Demonstration Problem

(a) Sales = Variable costs + Fixed costs + Net income
$$\$20Q = \$9Q + \$220,000 + \$0$$
$$\$11Q = \$220,000$$
$$Q = 20,000 \text{ units}$$

(b) Contribution margin per unit = Unit selling price − Unit variable costs
$$\$11 = \$20 - \$9$$
Contribution margin ratio = Contribution margin per unit ÷ Unit selling price
$$55\% = \$11 \div \$20$$
Break-even point in dollars = Fixed cost ÷ Contribution margin ratio
$$= \$220,000 \div 55\%$$
$$= \$400,000$$

(c) Margin of safety $= \dfrac{\text{Actual sales} - \text{Break-even sales}}{\text{Actual sales}}$

$$= \dfrac{\$500,000 - \$400,000}{\$500,000}$$
$$= 20\%$$

(d) Required sales = Variable costs + Fixed costs + Net income
$$\$20Q = \$9Q + \$220,000 + \$165,000$$
$$\$11Q = \$385,000$$
$$Q = 35,000 \text{ units}$$
$$35,000 \text{ units} \times \$20 = \$700,000 \text{ required sales}$$

Action Plan
- Know the formulas.
- Recognize that variable costs change with sales volume; fixed costs do not.
- Avoid computational errors.

Note: All asterisked Questions, Exercises, and Problems relate to material contained in the appendix to the chapter.

Self-Study Questions

Self-Study/Self-Test

Answers are at the end of the chapter.

(SO 1)   **1.** Variable costs are costs that:
    (a) vary in total directly and proportionately with changes in the activity level.
    (b) remain the same per unit at every activity level.
    (c) Neither of the above.
    (d) Both (a) and (b) above.

(SO 2)   **2.** The relevant range is:
    (a) the range of activity in which variable costs will be curvilinear.
    (b) the range of activity in which fixed costs will be curvilinear.
    (c) the range over which the company expects to operate during a year.
    (d) usually from zero to 100% of operating capacity.

(SO 3)   **3.** Mixed costs consist of a:
    (a) variable cost element and a fixed cost element.
    (b) fixed cost element and a controllable cost element.
    (c) relevant cost element and a controllable cost element.
    (d) variable cost element and a relevant cost element.

4. One of the following is *not* involved in CVP   (SO 4)
analysis. That factor is:
    (a) sales mix.
    (b) unit selling prices.
    (c) fixed costs per unit.
    (d) volume or level of activity.

5. Contribution margin: (SO 5)
    (a) is revenue remaining after deducting variable costs.
    (b) may be expressed as contribution margin per unit.
    (c) is selling price less cost of goods sold.
    (d) Both (a) and (b) above.

6. Gossen Company is planning to sell 200,000   (SO 6)
pliers for $4 per unit. The contribution margin ratio is 25%. If Gossen will break even at this level of sales, what are the fixed costs?
    (a) $100,000.   (c) $200,000.
    (b) $160,000.   (d) $300,000.

7. Marshall Company had actual sales of $600,000   (SO 7)
when break-even sales were $420,000. What is the margin of safety ratio?
    (a) 25%.   (c) 33⅓%.
    (b) 30%.   (d) 45%.

(SO 8) 8. The mathematical equation for computing required sales to obtain target net income is: Required sales =
   (a) Variable costs + Target net income.
   (b) Variable costs + Fixed costs + Target net income.
   (c) Fixed costs + Target net income.
   (d) No correct answer is given.

(SO 9) 9. Cournot Company sells 100,000 wrenches for $12 a unit. Fixed costs are $300,000, and net in-

come is $200,000. What should be reported as variable expenses in the CVP income statement?
   (a) $700,000.   (c) $500,000.
   (b) $900,000.   (d) $1,000,000.

*10. Under variable costing, fixed manufacturing   (SO 10) costs are classified as:
   (a) period costs.
   (b) product costs.
   (c) both (a) and (b).
   (d) neither (a) nor (b).

Questions

1. (a) What is cost behavior analysis?
   (b) Why is cost behavior analysis important to management?

2. (a) Jenny Beason asks your help in understanding the term "activity index." Explain the meaning and importance of this term for Jenny.
   (b) State the two ways that variable costs may be defined.

3. Contrast the effects of changes in the activity level on total fixed costs and on unit fixed costs.

4. R.E. Leon claims that the relevant range concept is important only for variable costs.
   (a) Explain the relevant range concept.
   (b) Do you agree with R.E.'s claim? Explain.

5. "The relevant range is indispensable in cost behavior analysis." Is this true? Why or why not?

6. Bart Gomez is confused. He does not understand why rent on his apartment is a fixed cost and rent on a Hertz rental truck is a mixed cost. Explain the difference to Bart.

7. How should mixed costs be classified in CVP analysis? What approach is used to effect the appropriate classification?

8. At the high and low levels of activity during the month, direct labor hours are 90,000 and 40,000, respectively. The related costs are $175,000 and $100,000. What are the fixed and variable costs at any level of activity within the relevant range?

9. "Cost-volume-profit (CVP) analysis is based entirely on unit costs." Do you agree? Explain.

10. Patty Dye defines contribution margin as the amount of profit available to cover operating expenses. Discuss.

11. Doolin Company's Speedo pocket calculator sells for $40. Variable costs per unit are estimated to be $24. What are the contribution margin per unit and the contribution margin ratio?

12. "Break-even analysis is of limited use to management because a company cannot survive by just breaking even." Do you agree? Explain.

13. Total fixed costs are $22,000 for Froelich Inc. It has a contribution margin per unit of $15, and a contribution margin ratio of 20%. Compute the break-even sales in dollars.

14. Linda Fearn asks your help in constructing a CVP graph. Explain to Linda (a) how the break-even point is plotted, and (b) how the level of activity and dollar sales at the break-even point are determined.

15. Define the term "margin of safety." If Hancock Company expects to sell 1,500 units of its product at $12 per unit, and break-even sales for the product are $12,000, what is the margin of safety ratio?

16. Jung Company's break-even sales are $600,000. Assuming fixed costs are $240,000, what sales volume is needed to achieve a target net income of $56,000?

17. The traditional income statement for Reeves Company shows sales $900,000, cost of goods sold $600,000, and operating expenses $200,000. Assuming all costs and expenses are 70% variable and 30% fixed, prepare a CVP income statement through contribution margin.

*18. Distinguish between absorption costing and variable costing.

*19. (a) What is the major rationale for the use of variable costing? (b) Discuss why variable costing may not be used for financial reporting purposes.

Brief Exercises

Classify costs as variable, fixed, or mixed.
(SO 1, 3)

BE18-1 Monthly production costs in Obianwu Company for two levels of production are as follows.

Cost	2,000 units	4,000 units
Indirect labor	$10,000	$20,000
Supervisory salaries	5,000	5,000
Maintenance	3,000	4,000 *1000*

Indicate which costs are variable, fixed, and mixed, and give the reason for each answer.

BE18-2   For Lundy Company, the relevant range of production is 40–80% of capacity. At 40% of capacity, a variable cost is $2,000 and a fixed cost is $4,000. Diagram the behavior of each cost within the relevant range assuming the behavior is linear.

Diagram the behavior of costs within the relevant range.
(SO 2)

BE18-3   For Skole Company, a mixed cost is $40,000 plus $8 per direct labor hour. Diagram the behavior of the cost using increments of 1,000 hours up to 5,000 hours on the horizontal axis and increments of $20,000 up to $80,000 on the vertical axis.

Diagram the behavior of a mixed cost.
(SO 3)

BE18-4   Sass Company accumulates the following data concerning a mixed cost, using miles as the activity level.

Determine variable and fixed cost elements using the high-low method.
(SO 3)

	Miles Driven	Total Cost		Miles Driven	Total Cost
January	8,000	$14,100	March	8,500	$15,000
February	7,500	13,400	April	8,200	14,400

Compute the variable and fixed cost elements using the high-low method.

BE18-5   Determine the missing amounts.

Determine missing amounts for contribution margin.
(SO 5)

	Unit Selling Price	Unit Variable Costs	Contribution Margin per Unit	Contribution Margin Ratio
1.	$250	$160	(a) *90*	(b) *36%*
2.	$500	(c) *350*	$150	(d) *30%*
3.	(e)	(f)	$360	30%

BE18-6   Low Company has a unit selling price of $400, variable costs per unit of $280, and fixed costs of $150,000. Compute the break-even point in units using (a) the mathematical equation and (b) contribution margin per unit.

Compute the break-even point.
(SO 6)

BE18-7   For Koren Company actual sales are $1,200,000 and break-even sales are $900,000. Compute (a) the margin of safety in dollars and (b) the margin of safety ratio.

Compute the margin of safety and the margin of safety ratio.
(SO 7)

BE18-8   For Bianco Company, variable costs are 75% of sales, and fixed costs are $180,000. Management's net income goal is $60,000. Compute the required sales in dollars needed to achieve management's target net income of $60,000. (Use the contribution margin approach.)

Compute sales for target net income.
(SO 8)

BE18-9   Friedman Manufacturing Inc. has sales of $1,800,000 for the first quarter of 2005. In making the sales, the company incurred the following costs and expenses.

Prepare CVP income statement.
(SO 9)

	Variable	Fixed
Cost of goods sold	$760,000	$540,000
Selling expenses	95,000	60,000
Administrative expenses	79,000	66,000

Prepare a CVP income statement for the quarter ended March 31, 2005.

*BE18-10 Gigliuto Company's fixed overhead costs are $4 per unit, and its variable overhead costs are $8 per unit. In the first month of operations, 50,000 units are produced, and 45,000 units are sold. Write a short memo to the chief financial officer explaining which costing approach will produce the higher income and what the difference will be.

Compute net income under absorption and variable costing.
(SO 10)

Exercises

Define and classify variable, fixed, and mixed costs.
(SO 1, 3)

E18-1 Fox Company manufactures a single product. Annual production costs incurred in the manufacturing process are shown below for two levels of production.

	Costs Incurred			
Production in Units	**5,000**		**10,000**	
Production Costs	**Total Cost**	**Cost/ Unit**	**Total Cost**	**Cost/ Unit**
Direct materials	$8,250	$1.65	$16,500	$1.65
Direct labor	9,500	1.90	19,000	1.90
Utilities	1,400	0.28	2,300	0.23
Rent	4,000	0.80	4,000	0.40
Maintenance	800	0.16	1,100	0.11
Supervisory salaries	1,000	0.20	1,000	0.10

Instructions
(a) Define the terms variable costs, fixed costs, and mixed costs.
(b) Classify each cost above as either variable, fixed, or mixed.

Determine fixed and variable costs using the high-low method and prepare graph.
(SO 1, 3)

E18-2 The controller of Getty Industries has collected the following monthly expense data for use in analyzing the cost behavior of maintenance costs.

Month	Total Maintenance Costs	Total Machine Hours
January	$2,900	3,000
February	3,000	4,000
March	3,600	6,000
April	4,500	7,900
May	3,200	5,000
June	4,900	8,000

Instructions
(a) Determine the fixed and variable cost components using the high-low method.
(b) Prepare a graph showing the behavior of maintenance costs, and identify the fixed and variable cost elements. Use 2,000 unit increments and $1,000 cost increments.

Compute contribution margin, break-even point, and margin of safety.
(SO 5, 6, 7)

E18-3 In the month of June, Andrea's Beauty Salon gave 2,500 haircuts, shampoos, and permanents at an average price of $30. During the month, fixed costs were $18,000 and variable costs were 70% of sales.

Instructions
(a) Determine the contribution margin in dollars, per unit, and as a ratio.
(b) Using the contribution margin technique, compute the break-even point in dollars and in units.
(c) Compute the margin of safety in dollars and as a ratio.

Prepare a CVP graph and compute break-even point and margin of safety.
(SO 6, 7)

E18-4 Ewing Company estimates that variable costs will be 50% of sales, and fixed costs will total $800,000. The selling price of the product is $4.

Instructions
(a) Prepare a CVP graph, assuming maximum sales of $3,200,000. (*Note:* Use $400,000 increments for sales and costs and 100,000 increments for units.)
(b) Compute the break-even point in (1) units and (2) dollars.
(c) Compute the margin of safety in (1) dollars and (2) as a ratio, assuming actual sales are $2 million.

Compute variable cost per unit, contribution margin ratio, and increase in fixed costs.
(SO 5)

E18-5 In 2005, Donnin Company had a break-even point of $350,000 based on a selling price of $7 per unit and fixed costs of $140,000. In 2006, the selling price and the variable cost per unit did not change, but the break-even point increased to $455,000.

Instructions
(a) Compute the variable cost per unit and the contribution margin ratio for 2005.
(b) Compute the increase in fixed costs for 2006.

E18-6 Jain Company had $150,000 of net income in 2005 when the selling price per unit was $150, the variable costs per unit were $90, and the fixed costs were $750,000. Management expects per unit data and total fixed costs to remain the same in 2006. The president of Jain Company is under pressure from stockholders to increase net income by $60,000 in 2006.

Compute various components to derive target net income under different assumptions.
(SO 6, 8)

Instructions
(a) Compute the number of units sold in 2005.
(b) Compute the number of units that would have to be sold in 2006 to reach the stockholders' desired profit level.
(c) Assume that Jain Company sells the same number of units in 2006 as it did in 2005. What would the selling price have to be in order to reach the stockholders' desired profit level?

E18-7 Gomez Company reports the following operating results for the month of August: Sales $300,000 (units 5,000); variable costs $210,000; and fixed costs $80,000. Management is considering the following independent courses of action to increase net income.

Compute net income under different alternatives.
(SO 8)

1. Increase selling price by 10% with no change in total variable costs.

2. Reduce variable costs to 65% of sales.

3. Reduce fixed costs by $10,000.

Instructions
Compute the net income to be earned under each alternative. Which course of action will produce the highest net income?

E18-8 Halko Company had sales in 2005 of $1,500,000 on 60,000 units. Variable costs totaled $720,000, and fixed costs totaled $500,000.

A new raw material is available that will decrease the variable costs per unit by 20% (or $2.40). However, to process the new raw material, fixed operating costs will increase by $50,000. Management feels that one-half of the decline in the variable costs per unit should be passed on to customers in the form of a sales price reduction. The marketing department expects that this sales price reduction will result in a 5% increase in the number of units sold.

Prepare a CVP income statement before and after changes in business environment.
(SO 9)

Instructions
Prepare a CVP income statement for 2005, assuming the changes are made as described.

E18-9 Wu Equipment Company manufactures and distributes industrial air compressors. The following costs are available for the year ended December 31, 2005. The company has no beginning inventory. In 2005, 1,500 units were produced, but only 1,200 units were sold. The unit selling price was $4,500. Costs and expenses were:

Compute total product cost and prepare an income statement using variable costing.
(SO 10)

Variable costs per unit	
Direct materials	$ 800
Direct labor	1,500
Variable manufacturing overhead	300
Variable selling and administrative expenses	70
Annual fixed costs and expenses	
Manufacturing overhead	$1,200,000
Selling and administrative expenses	100,000

Instructions
(a) Compute the manufacturing cost of one unit of product using variable costing.
(b) Prepare a 2005 income statement for Wu Company using variable costing.

Problems: Set A

P18-1A Joe Vida owns the Peace Barber Shop. He employs five barbers and pays each a base rate of $1,200 per month. One of the barbers serves as the manager and receives an extra $600 per month. In addition to the base rate, each barber also receives a commission of $3.50 per haircut.

Determine variable and fixed costs, compute break-even point, prepare a CVP graph, and determine net income.
(SO 1, 3, 5, 6)

Other costs are as follows.

Advertising	$200 per month
Rent	$800 per month
Barber supplies	$0.30 per haircut
Utilities	$175 per month plus $0.20 per haircut
Magazines	$25 per month

Joe currently charges $10 per haircut.

Instructions

(a) Determine the variable cost per haircut and the total monthly fixed costs.

(b) 1,300 units

(b) Compute the break-even point in units and dollars.

(c) Prepare a CVP graph, assuming a maximum of 1,800 haircuts in a month. Use increments of 300 haircuts on the horizontal axis and $3,000 on the vertical axis.

(d) Determine net income, assuming 1,500 haircuts are given in a month.

Prepare a CVP income statement, compute break-even point, contribution margin ratio, margin of safety ratio, and sales for target net income.
(SO 5, 6, 7, 8, 9)

P18-2A Tyson Company bottles and distributes NO-KAL, a diet soft drink. The beverage is sold for 40 cents per 16-ounce bottle to retailers, who charge customers 60 cents per bottle. At full (100%) plant capacity, management estimates the following revenues and costs.

Net sales	$1,800,000	Selling expenses—variable	$80,000
Direct materials	400,000	Selling expenses—fixed	65,000
Direct labor	280,000	Administrative expenses—	
Manufacturing overhead—		variable	20,000
variable	300,000	Administrative expenses—	
Manufacturing overhead—		fixed	52,000
fixed	283,000		

Instructions

(a) Prepare a CVP income statement for 2005 based on management's estimates.

(b) (2) $1,000,000

(b) Compute the break-even point in (1) units and (2) dollars.

(c) Compute the contribution margin ratio and the margin of safety ratio. (Round to full percents.)

(d) Determine the sales required to earn net income of $150,000.

Compute break-even point under alternative courses of action.
(SO 5, 6)

P18-3A Cruz Manufacturing's sales slumped badly in 2005. For the first time in its history, it operated at a loss. The company's income statement showed the following results from selling 600,000 units of product: Net sales $2,400,000; total costs and expenses $2,600,000; and net loss $200,000. Costs and expenses consisted of the following.

	Total	Variable	Fixed
Cost of goods sold	$2,100,000	$1,440,000	$ 660,000
Selling expenses	300,000	72,000	228,000
Administrative expenses	200,000	48,000	152,000
	$2,600,000	$1,560,000	$1,040,000

Management is considering the following independent alternatives for 2006.

1. Increase unit selling price 25% with no change in costs, expenses, and sales volume.

2. Change the compensation of salespersons from fixed annual salaries totaling $210,000 to total salaries of $70,000 plus a 4% commission on net sales.

3. Purchase new automated equipment that will change the proportion between variable and fixed cost of goods sold to 60% variable and 40% fixed.

(b) (2) $2,903,226

Instructions

(a) Compute the break-even point in dollars for 2005.

Compute break-even point and margin of safety ratio, and prepare a CVP income statement before and after changes in business environment.
(SO 6, 7, 9)

(b) Compute the break-even point in dollars under each of the alternative courses of action. (Round to nearest dollar.) Which course of action do you recommend?

P18-4A Lois Baiser is the advertising manager for Value Shoe Store. She is currently working on a major promotional campaign. Her ideas include the installation of a new lighting system and increased display space that will add $44,000 in fixed costs to the $280,000 currently spent. In addition, Lois is proposing that a 5% price decrease ($40 to

$38) will produce a 20% increase in sales volume (20,000 to 24,000). Variable costs will remain at $20 per pair of shoes. Management is impressed with Lois's ideas but concerned about the effects that these changes will have on the break-even point and the margin of safety.

Instructions
(a) Compute the current break-even point in units, and compare it to the break-even point in units if Lois's ideas are used.
(b) Compute the margin of safety ratio for current operations and after Lois's changes are introduced. (Round to nearest full percent.)
(c) Prepare a CVP income statement for current operations and after Lois's changes are introduced. Would you make the changes suggested?

P18-5A AFN produces plastic that is used for injection molding applications such as gears for small motors. In 2005, the first year of operations, AFN produced 4,000 tons of plastic and sold 3,000 tons. In 2006, the production and sales results were exactly reversed. In each year, selling price per ton was $2,000, variable manufacturing costs were 15% of the sales price of units produced, variable selling expenses were 10% of the selling price of units sold, fixed manufacturing costs were $2,400,000, and fixed administrative expenses were $600,000.

(b) New approach 25%

*Prepare income statements under absorption and variable costing.
(SO 10)*

Instructions
(a) Prepare comparative income statements for each year using variable costing.
(b) Prepare comparative income statements for each year using absorption costing.
(c) Reconcile the differences each year in income from operations under the two costing approaches.
(d) Comment on the effects of production and sales on net income under the two costing approaches.

*(b) 2005 net income
$2,100,000*

Problems: Set B

P18-1B The College Barber Shop employs four barbers. One barber, who also serves as the manager, is paid a salary of $2,000 per month. The other barbers are paid $1,400 per month. In addition, each barber is paid a commission of $4 per haircut. Other monthly costs are: store rent $800 plus 60 cents per haircut, depreciation on equipment $500, barber supplies 40 cents per haircut, utilities $300, and advertising $200. The price of a haircut is $10.

*Determine variable and fixed costs, compute break-even point, prepare a CVP graph, and determine net income.
(SO 1, 3, 5, 6)*

Instructions
(a) Determine the variable cost per haircut and the total monthly fixed costs.
(b) Compute the break-even point in units and dollars.
(c) Prepare a CVP graph, assuming a maximum of 1,800 haircuts in a month. Use increments of 300 haircuts on the horizontal axis and $3,000 increments on the vertical axis.
(d) Determine the net income, assuming 1,800 haircuts are given in a month.

(b) 1,600 units

P18-2B Corbin Company bottles and distributes LO-KAL, a fruit drink. The beverage is sold for 50 cents per 16-ounce bottle to retailers, who charge customers 70 cents per bottle. At full (100%) plant capacity, management estimates the following revenues and costs.

*Prepare a CVP income statement, compute break-even point, contribution margin ratio, margin of safety ratio, and sales for target net income.
(SO 5, 6, 7, 8, 9)*

Net sales	$2,000,000	Selling expenses—variable	$ 90,000
Direct materials	360,000	Selling expenses—fixed	150,000
Direct labor	650,000	Administrative expenses—	
Manufacturing overhead—		variable	30,000
variable	270,000	Administrative expenses—	
Manufacturing overhead—		fixed	70,000
fixed	260,000		

Instructions
(a) Prepare a CVP income statement for 2005 based on management's estimates.
(b) Compute the break-even point in (1) units and (2) dollars.
(c) Compute the contribution margin ratio and the margin of safety ratio.
(d) Determine the sales required to earn net income of $240,000.

(b) (2) $1,600,000

Compute break-even point under alternative courses of action.
(SO 5, 6)

P18-3B   Griffey Manufacturing had a bad year in 2005. For the first time in its history it operated at a loss. The company's income statement showed the following results from selling 60,000 units of product: Net sales $1,500,000; total costs and expenses $1,740,000; and net loss $240,000. Costs and expenses consisted of the following.

	Total	Variable	Fixed
Cost of goods sold	$1,200,000	$780,000	$420,000
Selling expenses	420,000	75,000	345,000
Administrative expenses	120,000	45,000	75,000
	$1,740,000	$900,000	$840,000

Management is considering the following independent alternatives for 2006.

1. Increase unit selling price 20% with no change in costs, expenses, and sales volume.

2. Change the compensation of salespersons from fixed annual salaries totaling $200,000 to total salaries of $40,000 plus a 5% commission on net sales.

3. Purchase new high-tech factory machinery that will change the proportion between variable and fixed cost of goods sold to 50:50.

Instructions

(a) Compute the break-even point in dollars for 2005.

(b) (3) $1,961,538

(b) Compute the break-even point in dollars under each of the alternative courses of action. Which course of action do you recommend?

Compute break-even point and margin of safety ratio, and prepare a CVP income statement before and after changes in business environment.
(SO 6, 7, 9)

P18-4B   Barb Tsai is the advertising manager for Thrifty Shoe Store. She is currently working on a major promotional campaign. Her ideas include the installation of a new lighting system and increased display space that will add $35,000 in fixed costs to the $225,000 currently spent. In addition, Barb is proposing that a $6\frac{2}{3}\%$ price decrease (from $30 to $28) will produce an increase in sales volume from 17,000 to 22,000 units. Variable costs will remain at $15 per pair of shoes. Management is impressed with Barb's ideas but concerned about the effects that these changes will have on the break-even point and the margin of safety.

Instructions

(a) Compute the current break-even point in units, and compare it to the break-even point in units if Barb's ideas are used.

(b) New approach 9%

(b) Compute the margin of safety ratio for current operations and after Barb's changes are introduced. (Round to nearest full percent.)

(c) Prepare a CVP income statement for current operations and after Barb's changes are introduced. Would you make the changes suggested?

Prepare income statements under absorption and variable costing.
(SO 10)

P18-5B   Zaki Metal Company produces the steel wire that goes into the production of paper clips. In 2005, the first year of operations, Zaki produced 40,000 miles of wire and sold 30,000 miles. In 2006, the production and sales results were exactly reversed. In each year, selling price per mile was $80, variable manufacturing costs were 25% of the sales price, variable selling expenses were $6.00 per mile sold, fixed manufacturing costs were $1,200,000, and fixed administrative expenses were $200,000.

Instructions

(a) Prepare comparative income statements for each year using variable costing.

(b) 2006 net income
$760,000

(b) Prepare comparative income statements for each year using absorption costing.

(c) Reconcile the differences each year in income from operations under the two costing approaches.

(d) Comment on the effects of production and sales on net income under the two costing approaches.

Group Decision Case

BYP18-1 Cedeno Company has decided to introduce a new product. The new product can be manufactured by either a capital-intensive method or a labor-intensive method. The manufacturing method will not affect the quality of the product. The estimated manufacturing costs by the two methods are as follows.

	Capital- Intensive	Labor- Intensive
Direct materials	$5 per unit	$5.50 per unit
Direct labor	$6 per unit	$7.20 per unit
Variable overhead	$3 per unit	$4.80 per unit
Fixed manufacturing costs	$2,440,000	$1,390,000

Cedeno's market research department has recommended an introductory unit sales price of $30. The incremental selling expenses are estimated to be $500,000 annually plus $2 for each unit sold, regardless of manufacturing method.

Instructions

With the class divided into groups, answer the following.
  (a) Calculate the estimated break-even point in annual unit sales of the new product if Cedeno Company uses the:

   (1) capital-intensive manufacturing method.

   (2) labor-intensive manufacturing method.

  (b) Determine the annual unit sales volume at which Cedeno Company would be indifferent between the two manufacturing methods.
  (c) Explain the circumstance under which Cedeno should employ each of the two manufacturing methods.

(CMA adapted)

Managerial Analysis

BYP18-2 The condensed income statement for the Rivera and Santos partnership for 2005 is as follows.

RIVERA AND SANTOS COMPANY
Income Statement
For the Year Ended December 31, 2005

Sales (200,000 units)		$1,200,000
Cost of goods sold		800,000
Gross profit		400,000
Operating expenses		
Selling	$320,000	
Administrative	160,000	480,000
Net loss		($80,000)

A cost behavior analysis indicates that 75% of the cost of goods sold are variable, 50% of the selling expenses are variable, and 25% of the administrative expenses are variable.

Instructions

(Round to nearest unit, dollar, and percentage, where necessary. Use the CVP income statement format in computing profits.)
  (a) Compute the break-even point in total sales dollars and in units for 2005.
  (b) Rivera has proposed a plan to get the partnership "out of the red" and improve its profitability. She feels that the quality of the product could be substantially improved

by spending $0.55 more per unit on better raw materials. The selling price per unit could be increased to only $6.50 because of competitive pressures. Rivera estimates that sales volume will increase by 30%. What effect would Rivera's plan have on the profits and the break-even point in dollars of the partnership?

(c) Santos was a marketing major in college. He believes that sales volume can be increased only by intensive advertising and promotional campaigns. He therefore proposed the following plan as an alternative to Rivera's. (1) Increase variable selling expenses to $0.85 per unit, (2) lower the selling price per unit by $0.20, and (3) increase fixed selling expenses by $20,000. Santos quoted an old marketing research report that said that sales volume would increase by 50% if these changes were made. What effect would Santos's plan have on the profits and the break-even point in dollars of the partnership?

(d) Which plan should be accepted? Explain your answer.

Real-World Focus

BYP18-3   The **Coca-Cola Company** hardly needs an introduction. A line taken from the cover of a recent annual report says it all: If you measured time in servings of Coca-Cola, "a billion Coca-Cola's ago was yesterday morning." On average, every U.S. citizen drinks 363 8-ounce servings of Coca-Cola products each year. Coca-Cola's primary line of business is the making and selling of syrup to bottlers. These bottlers then sell the finished bottles and cans of Coca-Cola to the consumer.

In the annual report of Coca-Cola, the following information was provided.

THE COCA-COLA COMPANY
Management Discussion

Our gross margin declined to 61 percent in 1995 from 62 percent in 1994, primarily due to costs for materials such as sweeteners and packaging.

The increases [in selling expenses] in 1996 and 1995 were primarily due to higher marketing expenditures in support of our Company's volume growth.

We measure our sales volume in two ways: (1) gallon shipments of concentrates and syrups and (2) unit cases of finished product (bottles and cans of Coke sold by bottlers).

Instructions
Answer the following questions.

(a) Are sweeteners and packaging a variable cost or a fixed cost? What is the impact on the contribution margin of an increase in the per unit cost of sweeteners or packaging? What are the implications for profitability?

(b) In your opinion, are marketing expenditures a fixed cost, variable cost, or mixed cost to The Coca-Cola Company? Give justification for your answer.

(c) Which of the two measures cited for measuring volume represents the activity index as defined in this chapter? Why might Coca-Cola use two different measures?

Exploring the Web

BYP18-4   Ganong Bros. Ltd., located in St. Stephen, New Brunswick, is Canada's oldest independent candy company. Its products are distributed worldwide. In 1885, Ganong invented the popular "chicken bone," a cinnamon flavored, pink, hard candy jacket over a chocolate center. The home page of Ganong, listed below, includes information about the company and its products.

Address: **www.pcsolutions.nb.ca/ganong/times.htm**
          (or go to **www.wiley.com/college/kimmel**)

Instructions
Read the description of "chicken bones," and answer the following.
  (a) Describe the steps in making "chicken bones."
  (b) Identify at least two variable and two fixed costs that are likely to affect the production of "chicken bones."

Communication Activity

BYP18-5   Your roommate asks your help on the following questions about CVP analysis formulas.
  (a) How can the mathematical equation for break-even sales show both sales units and sales dollars?
  (b) How do the formulas differ for contribution margin per unit and contribution margin ratio?
  (c) How can contribution margin be used to determine break-even sales in units and in dollars?

Instructions
Write a memo to your roommate stating the relevant formulas and answering each question.

Research Case

BYP18-6   The February 1998 issue of *Management Accounting* includes an article by Bonnie Stivers, Teresa Covin, Nancy Green Hall, and Steven Smalt entitled "How Nonfinancial Performance Measures Are Used."

Instructions
Read the article and answer the following questions.
  (a) The article is based on a study and survey. What is the objective of this study? Describe the specific nature of the survey that was conducted.
  (b) What were the five categories of nonfinancial performance measures identified and surveyed in this study?
  (c) What factors were identified, as a result of the survey, to be the most important nonfinancial measures?
  (d) What are the "three red flags" (conclusions) that the study results highlight?

Ethics Case

BYP18-7   Donny Blake is an accountant for Swenson Company. Early this year Donny made a highly favorable projection of sales and profits over the next 3 years for Swenson's hot-selling computer PLEX. As a result of the projections Donny presented to senior management, they decided to expand production in this area. This decision led to dislocations of some plant personnel who were reassigned to one of the company's newer plants in another state. However, no one was fired, and in fact the company expanded its work force slightly.

Unfortunately Donny rechecked his computations on the projections a few months later and found that he had made an error that would have reduced his projections substantially. Luckily, sales of PLEX have exceeded projections so far, and management is satisfied with its decision. Donny, however, is not sure what to do. Should he confess his honest mistake and jeopardize his possible promotion? He suspects that no one will catch the error because sales of PLEX have exceeded his projections, and it appears that profits will materialize close to his projections.

Instructions

(a) Who are the stakeholders in this situation?

(b) Identify the ethical issues involved in this situation.

(c) What are the possible alternative actions for Donny? What would you do in Donny's position?

Answers to Self-Study Questions

1. d   2. c   3. a   4. c   5. d   6. c   7. b   8. b   9. a   10. a

 ✓ Remember to go back to the Navigator box on the chapter-opening page and check off your completed work.

Budgetary Planning

STUDY OBJECTIVES

After studying this chapter, you should be able to:

1 Indicate the benefits of budgeting.

2 State the essentials of effective budgeting.

3 Identify the budgets that comprise the master budget.

4 Describe the sources for preparing the budgeted income statement.

5 Explain the principal sections of a cash budget.

6 Indicate the applicability of budgeting in nonmanufacturing companies.

THE NAVIGATOR

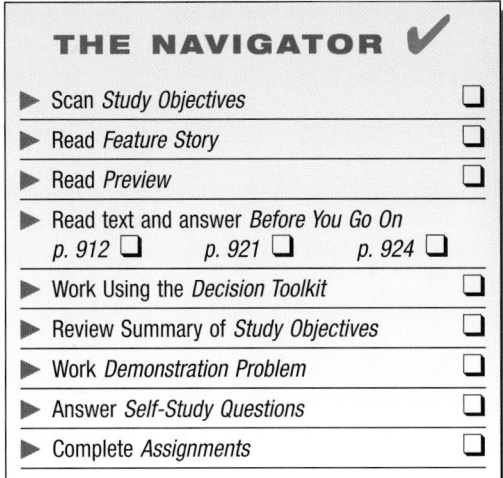

THE NAVIGATOR ✔

▶ Scan *Study Objectives*   ☐

▶ Read *Feature Story*   ☐

▶ Read *Preview*   ☐

▶ Read text and answer *Before You Go On*
   p. 912 ☐   p. 921 ☐   p. 924 ☐

▶ Work Using the *Decision Toolkit*   ☐

▶ Review Summary of *Study Objectives*   ☐

▶ Work *Demonstration Problem*   ☐

▶ Answer *Self-Study Questions*   ☐

▶ Complete *Assignments*   ☐

FEATURE STORY

The Next Amazon. com? Not Quite

The bursting of the dot-com bubble resulted in countless stories of dot-com failures. Many of these ventures were half-baked, get-rich-quick schemes, rarely based on sound business practices. Initially they saw money flowing in faster than they knew what to do with—which was precisely the problem. Without proper planning and budgeting, much of the money went to waste. In some cases, failure was actually brought on by rapid, uncontrolled growth.

One such example was the online discount bookseller PositivelyYou.com. One of the co-founders, Lyle Bowline, had never run a business. However, his experience as an assistant director of an entrepreneurial center had provided him with knowledge about the do's and don'ts of small business. To minimize costs, he started the company off small and simple. He invested $5,000 in computer equipment and ran the business out of his basement. In the early months, even though sales were only about $2,000 a month, the company actually made a profit because it kept its costs low (a feat few other dot-coms could boast of).

Things changed dramatically when the company received national publicity in the financial press. Suddenly the company's sales increased to $50,000 a month—fully 25 times the previous level. The "simple" little business suddenly needed a business plan, a strategic plan, and a budget. It needed to rent office space and hire employees. Initially, members of a local book club donated time to help meet the sudden demand. But quickly the number of paid employees ballooned. The sudden growth necessitated detailed planning and budgeting. The need for a proper budget was accentuated by the fact that the company's gross profit was only 16 cents on each dollar of goods sold. This meant that after paying for its inventory, the company had only 16 cents of every dollar to cover its remaining operating costs.

Unfortunately, the company never got things under control. Within a few months, sales had plummeted to $12,000 per month. At this level of sales the company could not meet the mountain of monthly expenses that it had accumulated in

trying to grow. Ironically, the company's sudden success, and the turmoil it created, appears to have been what eventually caused the company to fail.

THE NAVIGATOR

As the Feature Story about **Positively-You.com** indicates, budgeting is critical to financial well-being. As a student, you budget your study time and your money. Families budget income and expenses. Governmental agencies budget revenues and expenditures. Business enterprises use budgets in planning and controlling their operations.

Our primary focus in this chapter is budgeting—specifically, how budgeting is used as a **planning tool** by management. Through budgeting, it should be possible for management to maintain enough cash to pay creditors, have sufficient raw materials to meet production requirements, and have adequate finished goods to meet expected sales.

The content and organization of Chapter 19 are as follows.

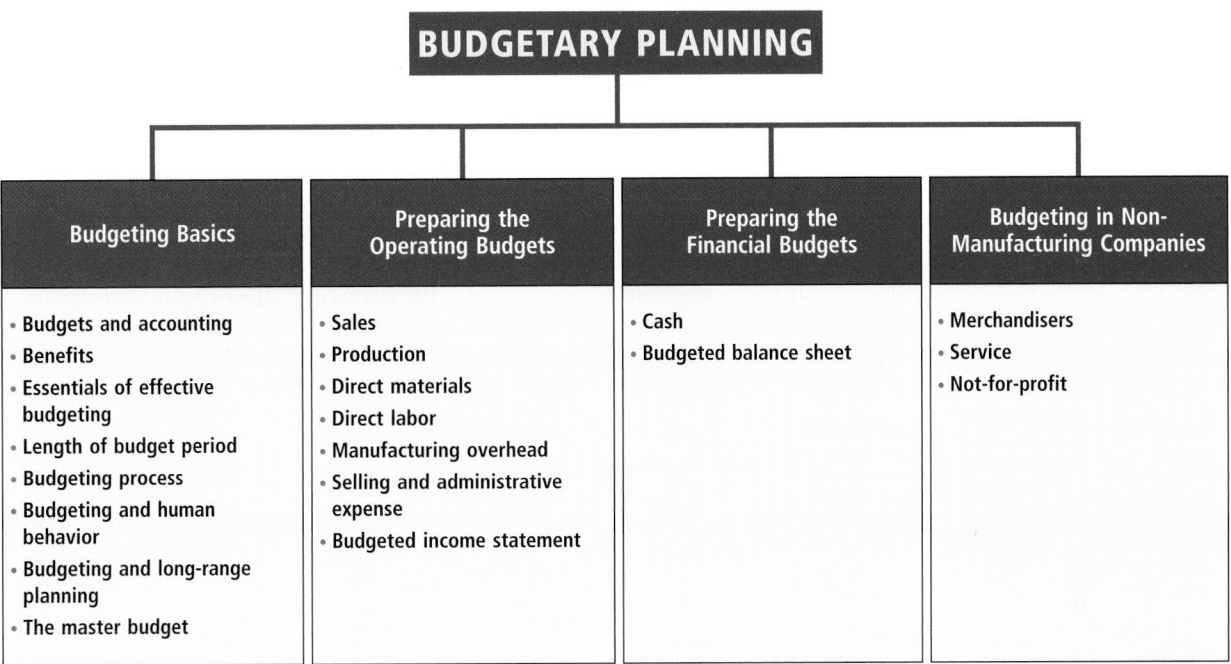

BUDGETARY PLANNING

Budgeting Basics	Preparing the Operating Budgets	Preparing the Financial Budgets	Budgeting in Non-Manufacturing Companies
• Budgets and accounting • Benefits • Essentials of effective budgeting • Length of budget period • Budgeting process • Budgeting and human behavior • Budgeting and long-range planning • The master budget	• Sales • Production • Direct materials • Direct labor • Manufacturing overhead • Selling and administrative expense • Budgeted income statement	• Cash • Budgeted balance sheet	• Merchandisers • Service • Not-for-profit

☑ THE NAVIGATOR

Budgeting Basics

One of management's major responsibilities is planning. As explained in Chapter 15, **planning** is the process of establishing enterprise-wide objectives. A successful organization makes both long-term and short-term plans. These plans set forth the objectives of the company and the proposed way of accomplishing them.

A **budget** is a formal written statement of management's plans for a specified future time period, expressed in financial terms. It normally represents the primary method of communicating agreed-upon objectives throughout the organization. Once adopted, a budget becomes an important basis for evaluating performance. It promotes efficiency and serves as a deterrent to waste and inefficiency. We consider the role of budgeting as a **control device** in Chapter 20.

BUDGETING AND ACCOUNTING

Accounting information makes major contributions to the budgeting process. From the accounting records, historical data on revenues, costs, and expenses can be obtained. These data are helpful in formulating future budget goals.

Normally, accountants have the responsibility for expressing management's budgeting goals in financial terms. In this role, they translate management's plans and communicate the budget to all areas of responsibility. Accountants also prepare periodic budget reports that provide the basis for measuring performance and comparing actual results with planned objectives. The budget itself, and the administration of the budget, however, are entirely management responsibilities.

THE BENEFITS OF BUDGETING

The primary benefits of budgeting are:

STUDY OBJECTIVE
1
Indicate the benefits of budgeting.

1. It requires all levels of management to **plan ahead** and to formalize their goals on a recurring basis.
2. It provides **definite objectives** for evaluating performance at each level of responsibility.
3. It creates an **early warning system** for potential problems. With early warning, management has time to make changes before things get out of hand.
4. It facilitates the **coordination of activities** within the business. It does this by correlating the goals of each segment with overall company objectives. Thus, production and sales promotion can be integrated with expected sales.
5. It results in greater **management awareness** of the entity's overall operations and the impact on operations of external factors, such as economic trends.
6. It **motivates personnel** throughout the organization to meet planned objectives.

A budget is an aid to management; it is not a substitute for management. A budget cannot operate or enforce itself. The benefits of budgeting will be realized only when budgets are carefully prepared and properly administered by management.

ESSENTIALS OF EFFECTIVE BUDGETING

STUDY OBJECTIVE
2
State the essentials of effective budgeting.

Effective budgeting depends on a **sound organizational structure**. In such a structure, authority and responsibility for all phases of operations are clearly defined. Budgets based on **research and analysis** should result in realistic goals that will contribute to the growth and profitability of a company. And, the effectiveness of a budget program is directly related to its **acceptance by all levels of management**.

Once the budget has been adopted, it should be an important tool for evaluating performance. Variations between actual and expected results should be systematically and periodically reviewed to determine their cause(s). However, individuals should not be held responsible for variations that are beyond their control.

LENGTH OF THE BUDGET PERIOD

The budget period is not necessarily one year in length. **A budget may be prepared for any period of time.** Various factors influence the length of the budget period. These factors include the type of budget, the nature of the organization, the need for periodic appraisal, and prevailing business conditions. For example, cash may be budgeted monthly, whereas a plant expansion budget may cover a ten-year period.

The budget period should be long enough to provide an attainable goal under normal business conditions. Ideally, the time period should minimize the impact of seasonal or cyclical fluctuations. On the other hand, the budget period should not be so long that reliable estimates are impossible.

The **most common budget period is one year**. The annual budget, in turn, is often supplemented by monthly and quarterly budgets. Many companies use **continuous twelve-month budgets**. These budgets drop the month just ended and add a future month. One advantage of continuous budgeting is that it keeps management planning a full year ahead.

THE BUDGETING PROCESS

The development of the budget for the coming year generally starts several months before the end of the current year. The budgeting process usually begins with the collection of data from each organizational unit of the company. Past performance is often the starting point from which future budget goals are formulated.

The budget is developed within the framework of a **sales forecast**. This forecast shows potential sales for the industry and the company's expected share of such sales. Sales forecasting involves a consideration of various factors: (1) general economic conditions, (2) industry trends, (3) market research studies, (4) anticipated advertising and promotion, (5) previous market share, (6) changes in prices, and (7) technological developments. The input of sales personnel and top management are essential to the sales forecast.

In small companies like **PositivelyYou.com**, the budgeting process is often informal. In larger companies, responsibility for coordinating the preparation of the budget is assigned to a **budget committee**. The committee ordinarily includes the president, treasurer, chief accountant (controller), and management personnel from each of the major areas of the company, such as sales, production, and research. The budget committee serves as a review board where managers can defend their budget goals and requests. Differences are reviewed, modified if necessary, and reconciled. The budget is then put in its final form by the budget committee, approved, and distributed.

Business Insight
MANAGEMENT PERSPECTIVE

A recent study by Willard & Shullman Group Ltd. found that fewer than 14 percent of businesses with fewer than 500 employees do an annual budget or have a written business plan. In all, nearly 60 percent of these businesses have no plans on paper at all. A few small business owners even say that they see no need for budgeting and planning. Most small business owners, though, say that they understand that budgeting and planning are critical for survival and growth. But given the long hours that they already work addressing day-to-day challenges, they also say that they are "just too busy to plan for the future." Unfortunately, however, by not setting aside time for budgeting and planning, these small businesses are reducing the likelihood that they will grow to be big businesses.

BUDGETING AND HUMAN BEHAVIOR

A budget can have a significant impact on human behavior. It may inspire a manager to higher levels of performance. Or, it may discourage additional effort and pull down the morale of a manager. Why do these diverse effects occur? The answer is found in how the budget is developed and administered.

In **developing the budget**, each level of management should be invited to participate. The overall goal is to reach agreement on a budget that the manager considers fair and achievable. When this objective is met, the budget will have a positive effect on the manager. In contrast, if the manager views the budget as being unfair and unrealistic, he or she may feel discouraged and uncommitted to the budget goals. The risk of having unrealistic budgets is generally greater when the budget is developed from top management down to lower management than vice versa. Illustration 19-1 graphically displays the appropriate flow of budget data from bottom to top in an organization.

Illustration 19-1 Flow of budget data from lower levels of management to top levels

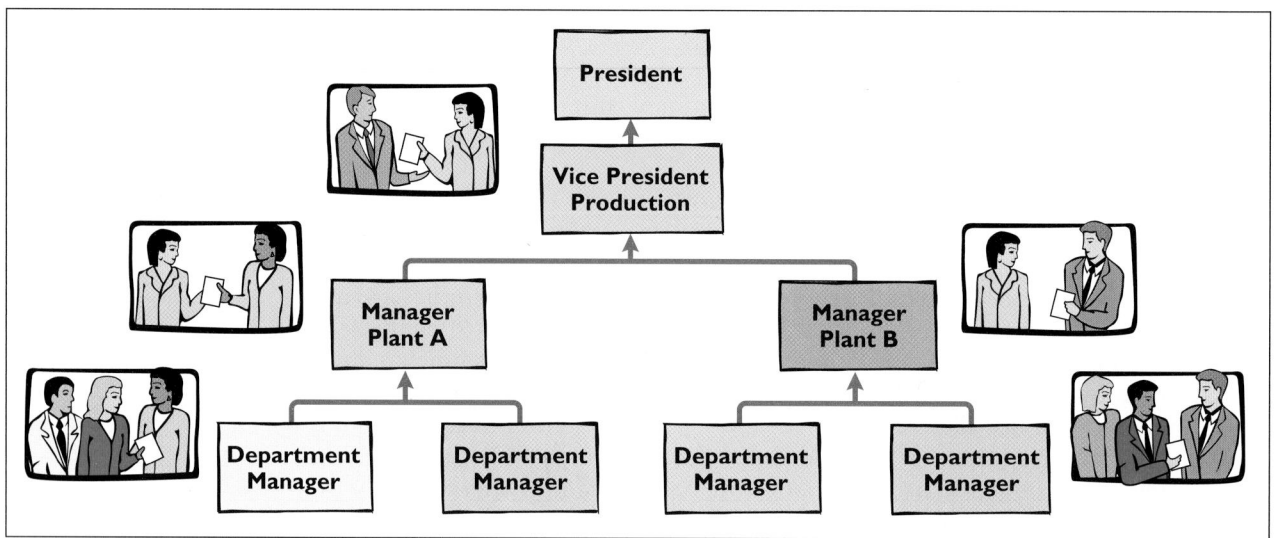

Helpful Hint Unrealistic budgets can lead to unethical employee behavior such as cutting corners on the job or distorting internal financial reports.

Administering the budget relates to how the budget is used by top management. As explained earlier, the budget should have the complete support of top management. The budget also should be an important basis for evaluating performance. The effect of an evaluation will be positive when top management tempers criticism with advice and assistance. In contrast, a manager is likely to respond negatively if the budget is used exclusively to assess blame.

A budget may be used improperly as a pressure device to force improved performance. Or, it can be used as a positive aid in achieving projected goals. In sum, a budget can become a manager's friend or a foe.

BUDGETING AND LONG-RANGE PLANNING

In business, you may hear talk about the need for long-range planning. Budgeting and long-range planning are not the same. One important difference is the **time period involved**. The maximum length of a budget is usually one year, and budgets are often prepared for shorter periods of time, such as a month or a quarter. In contrast, long-range planning usually encompasses a period of at least five years.

A second significant difference is in **emphasis**. Budgeting focuses on achieving specific short-term goals, such as meeting annual profit objectives. **Long-range planning**, on the other hand, identifies long-term goals, selects strategies

Budgeting Basics **911**

to achieve those goals, and develops policies and plans to implement the strategies. In long-range planning, management also considers anticipated trends in the economic and political environment and how the company should cope with them.

The final difference between budgeting and long-range planning pertains to the **amount of detail presented**. Budgets, as you will see in this chapter, can be very detailed. Long-range plans contain considerably less detail. The data in long-range plans are intended more for a review of progress toward long-term goals than as a basis of control for achieving specific results. The primary objective of long-range planning is to develop the best strategy to maximize the company's performance over an extended future period.

THE MASTER BUDGET

The term "budget" is actually a shorthand term to describe a variety of budget documents. All of these documents are combined into a master budget. The **master budget** is a set of interrelated budgets that constitutes a plan of action for a specified time period. The individual budgets included in a master budget are pictured in Illustration 19-2.

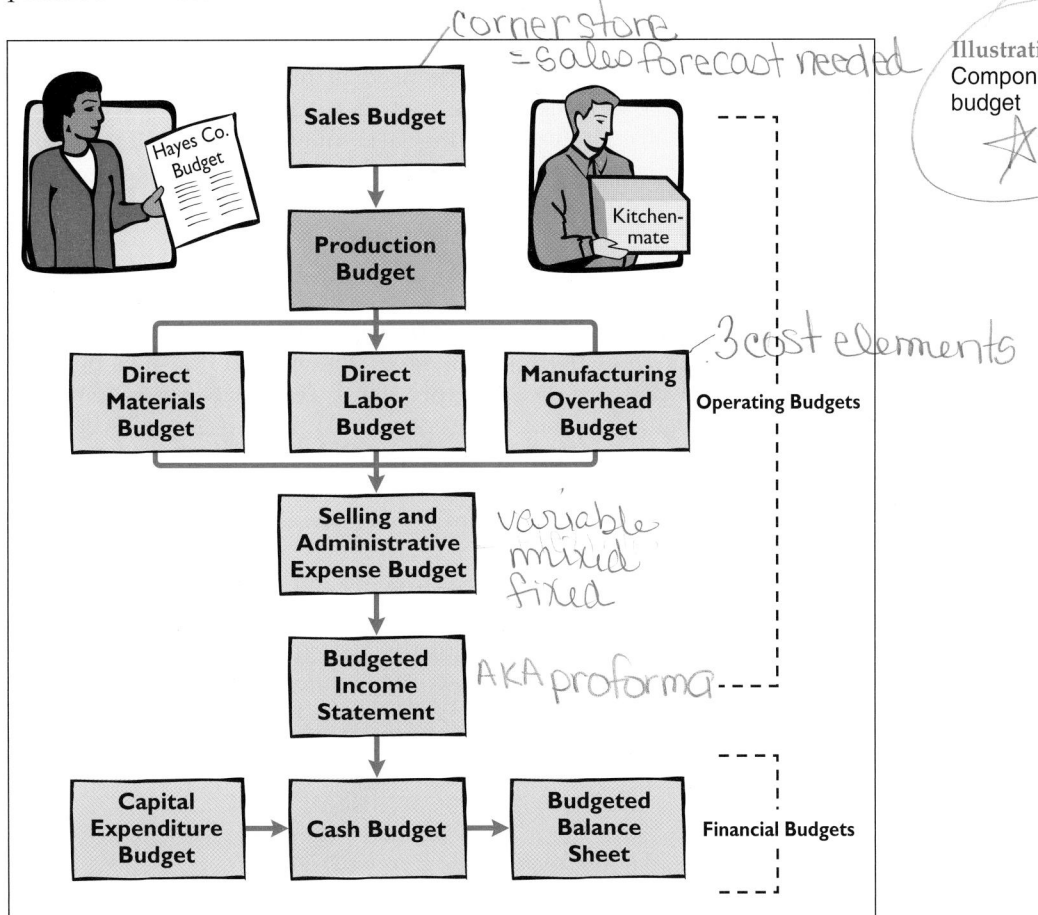

Illustration 19-2
Components of the master budget

As the illustration shows, the master budget contains two classes of budgets. **Operating budgets** are the individual budgets that result in the preparation of the budgeted income statement. These budgets establish goals for the company's sales and production personnel. In contrast, **financial budgets** are the capital expenditure budget, the cash budget, and the budgeted balance sheet. These budgets focus primarily on the cash resources needed to fund expected operations and planned capital expenditures.

The master budget is prepared in the sequence shown in Illustration 19-2. The operating budgets are developed first, beginning with the sales budget. Then the financial budgets are prepared. We will explain and illustrate each budget shown in Illustration 19-2 except the capital expenditure budget. This budget is discussed under the topic Capital Budgeting in Chapter 22.

BEFORE YOU GO ON . . .

▶ **Review It**

1. What are the benefits of budgeting?
2. What are the factors essential to effective budgeting?
3. How does the budget process work?
4. How does budgeting differ from long-range planning?
5. What is a master budget?

☑ THE NAVIGATOR

Preparing the Operating Budgets

A case study of Hayes Company will be used in preparing the operating budgets. Hayes manufactures and sells a single product, Kitchen-mate. The budgets will be prepared by quarters for the year ending December 31, 2005. Hayes Company begins its annual budgeting process on September 1, 2004, and it completes the budget for 2005 by December 1, 2004.

SALES BUDGET

Helpful Hint For a retail or manufacturing company, what is the starting point in preparing the master budget, and why? Answer: Preparation of the sales budget is the starting point for the master budget. It sets the level of activity for other functions such as production and purchasing.

As shown in the master budget in Illustration 19-2, **the sales budget is the first budget prepared**. Each of the other budgets depends on the sales budget. The sales budget is derived from the sales forecast. It represents management's best estimate of sales revenue for the budget period. An inaccurate sales budget may adversely affect net income. For example, an overly optimistic sales budget may result in excessive inventories that may have to be sold at reduced prices. In contrast, an unduly conservative budget may result in loss of sales revenue due to inventory shortages.

The sales budget is prepared by multiplying the expected unit sales volume for each product by its anticipated unit selling price. For Hayes Company, sales volume is expected to be 3,000 units in the first quarter, with 500-unit increments in each succeeding quarter. Based on a sales price of $60 per unit, the sales budget for the year, by quarters, is shown in Illustration 19-3.

Illustration 19-3 Sales budget

HAYES COMPANY					
Sales Budget					
For the Year Ending December 31, 2005					
	Quarter				
	1	**2**	**3**	**4**	**Year**
Expected unit sales	3,000	3,500	4,000	4,500	15,000
Unit selling price	× $60	× $60	× $60	× $60	× $60
Total sales	$180,000	$210,000	$240,000	$270,000	$900,000

Some companies classify the anticipated sales revenue as cash or credit sales and by geographical regions, territories, or salespersons.

PRODUCTION BUDGET

The **production budget** shows the units that must be produced to meet anticipated sales. Production requirements are determined from the following formula.[1]

Budgeted Sales Units	+	Desired Ending Finished Goods Units	−	Beginning Finished Goods Units	=	Required Production Units

Illustration 19-4
Production requirements formula

A realistic estimate of ending inventory is essential in scheduling production requirements. Excessive inventories in one quarter may lead to cutbacks in production and employee layoffs in a subsequent quarter. On the other hand, inadequate inventories may result either in added costs for overtime work or in lost sales. Hayes Company believes it can meet future sales requirements by maintaining an ending inventory equal to 20 percent of the next quarter's budgeted sales volume. For example, the ending finished goods inventory for the first quarter is 700 units (20% × anticipated second-quarter sales of 3,500 units). The production budget is shown in Illustration 19-5.

Illustration 19-5
Production budget

HAYES COMPANY
Production Budget
For the Year Ending December 31, 2005

	Quarter				
	1	**2**	**3**	**4**	**Year**
Expected unit sales (Illustration 19-3)	3,000	3,500	4,000	4,500	
Add: Desired ending finished goods units[a]	700	800	900	1,000[b]	
Total required units	3,700	4,300	4,900	5,500	
Less: Beginning finished goods units	600[c]	700	800	900	
Required production units	**3,100**	**3,600**	**4,100**	**4,600**	**15,400**

[a]20% of next quarter's sales
[b]Expected 2006 first-quarter sales, 5,000 units × 20%
[c]20% of estimated first-quarter 2005 sales units

The production budget, in turn, provides the basis for determining the budgeted costs for each manufacturing cost element, as explained in the following pages.

Business Insight
MANAGEMENT PERSPECTIVE

Wrong move, wrong time, poor planning. When **Fruit of the Loom Inc.** saw underwear and apparel sales slowing, it cut back production sharply. Too sharply, in fact: almost overnight, demand soared. Caught with its shorts down, the company hired back thousands of workers and frantically increased production. The mistimed production cuts contributed to a 43 percent fall in first-quarter profits. For the year, Fruit stood to lose $200 million in sales, and analysts expected an 11 percent drop in profits for the year.

---

[1]This formula ignores any work in process inventories, which are assumed to be nonexistent in Hayes Company.

DIRECT MATERIALS BUDGET

The **direct materials budget** shows both the quantity and cost of direct materials to be purchased. The quantities of direct materials are derived from the following formula.

Illustration 19-6 Formula for direct materials quantities

$$\text{Direct Materials Units Required for Production} + \text{Desired Ending Direct Materials Units} - \text{Beginning Direct Materials Units} = \text{Required Direct Materials Purchases Units}$$

The budgeted cost of direct materials to be purchased is then computed by multiplying the required units of direct materials by the anticipated cost per unit.

The desired ending inventory is again a key component in the budgeting process. For example, inadequate inventories could result in temporary shutdowns of production. Because of its close proximity to suppliers, Hayes Company has found that an ending inventory of raw materials equal to 10 percent of the next quarter's production requirements is sufficient. The manufacture of each Kitchen-mate requires 2 pounds of raw materials, and the expected cost per pound is $4. The direct materials budget is shown in Illustration 19-7.

Illustration 19-7 Direct materials budget

HAYES COMPANY Direct Materials Budget For the Year Ending December 31, 2005					
	Quarter				
	1	**2**	**3**	**4**	**Year**
Units to be produced (Illustration 19-5)	3,100	3,600	4,100	4,600	
Direct materials per unit	× 2	× 2	× 2	× 2	
Total pounds needed for production	6,200	7,200	8,200	9,200	
Add: Desired ending direct materials (pounds)[a]	720	820	920	1,020[b]	
Total materials required	6,920	8,020	9,120	10,220	
Less: Beginning direct materials (pounds)	620[c]	720	820	920	
Direct materials purchases	6,300	7,300	8,300	9,300	
Cost per pound	× $4	× $4	× $4	× $4	
Total cost of direct materials purchases	$25,200	$29,200	$33,200	$37,200	$124,800

[a]10% of next quarter's production requirements
[b]Estimated 2006 first-quarter pounds needed for production, 10,200 × 10%
[c]10% of estimated first-quarter pounds needed for production

DIRECT LABOR BUDGET

Like the direct materials budget, the **direct labor budget** contains the quantity (hours) and cost of direct labor necessary to meet production requirements. Direct labor hours are determined from the production budget. At Hayes Company, two hours of direct labor are required to produce each unit of finished goods. The anticipated hourly wage rate is $10. These data are shown in Illustration 19-8. The direct labor budget is critical in maintaining a labor force that can meet the expected levels of production.

HAYES COMPANY
Direct Labor Budget
For the Year Ending December 31, 2005

	Quarter				
	1	2	3	4	Year
Units to be produced (Illustration 19-5)	3,100	3,600	4,100	4,600	
Direct labor time (hours) per unit	× 2	× 2	× 2	× 2	
Total required direct labor hours	6,200	7,200	8,200	9,200	
Direct labor cost per hour	× $10	× $10	× $10	× $10	
Total direct labor cost	$62,000	$72,000	$82,000	$92,000	$308,000

Illustration 19-8 Direct labor budget

Helpful Hint An important assumption here is that the company can add to and subtract from its work force as needed so that the $10 per hour labor cost applies to a wide range of possible production activity.

MANUFACTURING OVERHEAD BUDGET

The **manufacturing overhead budget** shows the expected manufacturing overhead costs for the budget period. As shown in Illustration 19-9, **this budget distinguishes between variable and fixed overhead costs**. Hayes Company expects variable costs to fluctuate with production volume on the basis of the following rates per direct labor hour: indirect materials $1.00, indirect labor $1.40, utilities $0.40, and maintenance $0.20. Thus, for 6,200 direct labor hours, budgeted indirect materials are $6,200 (6,200 × $1), and budgeted indirect labor is $8,680 (6,200 × $1.40). Hayes also recognizes that some maintenance is fixed. The amounts reported for fixed costs are assumed.

At Hayes Company, overhead is applied to production on the basis of direct labor hours. Thus, as shown in Illustration 19-9, the annual rate is $8 per hour ($246,400 ÷ 30,800).

HAYES COMPANY
Manufacturing Overhead Budget
For the Year Ending December 31, 2005

	Quarter				
	1	2	3	4	Year
Variable costs					
Indirect materials	$ 6,200	$ 7,200	$ 8,200	$ 9,200	$ 30,800
Indirect labor	8,680	10,080	11,480	12,880	43,120
Utilities	2,480	2,880	3,280	3,680	12,320
Maintenance	1,240	1,440	1,640	1,840	6,160
Total variable	18,600	21,600	24,600	27,600	92,400
Fixed costs					
Supervisory salaries	20,000	20,000	20,000	20,000	80,000
Depreciation	3,800	3,800	3,800	3,800	15,200
Property taxes and insurance	9,000	9,000	9,000	9,000	36,000
Maintenance	5,700	5,700	5,700	5,700	22,800
Total fixed	38,500	38,500	38,500	38,500	154,000
Total manufacturing overhead	$57,100	$60,100	$63,100	$66,100	$246,400
Direct labor hours	6,200	7,200	8,200	9,200	30,800
Manufacturing overhead rate per direct labor hour ($246,400 ÷ 30,800)					$8.00

Illustration 19-9 Manufacturing overhead budget

SELLING AND ADMINISTRATIVE EXPENSE BUDGET

Hayes Company combines its operating expenses into one budget, the **selling and administrative expense budget**. This budget projects anticipated selling and administrative expenses for the budget period. In this budget, as in the preceding one, expenses are classified as either variable or fixed. In this case, the variable expense rates per unit of sales are sales commissions $3.00 and freight-out $1.00. Variable expenses per quarter are based on the unit sales from the sales budget (Illustration 19-3). For example, sales in the first quarter are expected to be 3,000 units. Thus, Sales Commissions Expense is $9,000 (3,000 × $3), and Freight-out is $3,000 (3,000 × $1). Fixed expenses are based on assumed data. The selling and administrative expense budget is shown in Illustration 19-10.

Illustration 19-10 Selling and administrative expense budget

HAYES COMPANY Selling and Administrative Expense Budget For the Year Ending December 31, 2005					
	Quarter				
	1	**2**	**3**	**4**	**Year**
Variable expenses					
Sales commissions	$ 9,000	$10,500	$12,000	$13,500	$ 45,000
Freight-out	3,000	3,500	4,000	4,500	15,000
Total variable	12,000	14,000	16,000	18,000	60,000
Fixed expenses					
Advertising	5,000	5,000	5,000	5,000	20,000
Sales salaries	15,000	15,000	15,000	15,000	60,000
Office salaries	7,500	7,500	7,500	7,500	30,000
Depreciation	1,000	1,000	1,000	1,000	4,000
Property taxes and insurance	1,500	1,500	1,500	1,500	6,000
Total fixed	30,000	30,000	30,000	30,000	120,000
Total selling and administrative expenses	$42,000	$44,000	$46,000	$48,000	$180,000

Business Insight
MANAGEMENT PERSPECTIVE

Good budgeting depends on good information, and good information is what e-business is all about. As manufacturers, suppliers, and customers become electronically linked, each benefits by being better informed. **Dell Computer** not only is directly linked to **Solectron**, one of its main suppliers, but also to **Texas Instruments**, one of the main suppliers of parts to Solectron. This linking takes a lot of guesswork out of planning and budgeting for all three companies.

To further improve planning and budgeting, Dell hopes that some day everyone in its industry will anonymously provide their up-to-the-minute production and sales information at a central, electronic exchange. A centralized database such as this would provide valuable information about the supply and demand of computer goods in the marketplace. This information might dramatically improve sales projections, leading to significant improvements in the budgeting process.

SOURCE: "E-Management," *The Economist* (November 11, 2000).

BUDGETED INCOME STATEMENT

The **budgeted income statement** is the important end-product of the operating budgets. This budget indicates the expected profitability of operations for the budget period. The budgeted income statement provides the basis for evaluating company performance.

STUDY OBJECTIVE

4

Describe the sources for preparing the budgeted income statement.

As you would expect, this budget is prepared from the various operating budgets. For example, to find the cost of goods sold, it is first necessary to determine the total unit cost of producing one Kitchen-mate, as follows.

Cost of One Kitchen-mate

Cost Element	Illustration	Quantity	Unit Cost	Total
Direct materials	6-7	2 pounds	$ 4.00	$ 8.00
Direct labor	6-8	2 hours	$10.00	20.00
Manufacturing overhead	6-9	2 hours	$ 8.00	16.00
Total unit cost				$44.00

Illustration 19-11
Computation of total unit cost

Cost of goods sold can then be determined by multiplying the units sold by the unit cost. For Hayes Company, budgeted cost of goods sold is $660,000 (15,000 × $44). All data for the statement are obtained from the individual operating budgets except the following: (1) interest expense is expected to be $100, and (2) income taxes are estimated to be $12,000. The budgeted income statement is shown in Illustration 19-12.

Illustration 19-12
Budgeted income statement

HAYES COMPANY	
Budgeted Income Statement	
For the Year Ending December 31, 2005	
Sales (Illustration 19-3)	$900,000
Cost of goods sold (15,000 × $44)	660,000
Gross profit	240,000
Selling and administrative expenses (Illustration 19-10)	180,000
Income from operations	60,000
Interest expense	100
Income before income taxes	59,900
Income tax expense	12,000
Net income	$ 47,900

DECISION TOOLKIT

Decision Checkpoints	Info Needed for Decision	Tool to Use for Decision	How to Evaluate Results
Has the company met its targets for sales, production expenses, selling and administrative expenses, and net income?	Sales forecasts, inventory levels, projected materials, labor, overhead, and selling and administrative requirements	Master budget—a set of interrelated budgets including sales, production, materials, labor, overhead, and selling and administrative budgets	Results are favorable if revenues exceed budgeted amounts, or if expenses are less than budgeted amounts.

Preparing the Financial Budgets

As shown in Illustration 19-2, the financial budgets consist of the capital expenditure budget, the cash budget, and the budgeted balance sheet. The capital expenditure budget is discussed in Chapter 22; the other budgets are explained in the following sections.

CASH BUDGET

STUDY OBJECTIVE

5

Explain the principal sections of a cash budget.

The **cash budget** shows anticipated cash flows. Because cash is so vital, this budget is considered to be the most important output in preparing financial budgets. The cash budget contains three sections (cash receipts, cash disbursements, and financing) and the beginning and ending cash balances, as shown in Illustration 19-13.

Illustration 19-13 Basic form of a cash budget

ANY COMPANY Cash Budget	
Beginning cash balance	$X,XXX
Add: Cash receipts (Itemized)	X,XXX
Total available cash	X,XXX
Less: Cash disbursements (Itemized)	X,XXX
Excess (deficiency) of available cash over cash disbursements	X,XXX
Financing	X,XXX
Ending cash balance	$X,XXX

Helpful Hint Why is the cash budget prepared after the other budgets are prepared? Answer: Because the information generated by the other budgets dictates the need for inflows and outflows of cash.

The **cash receipts section** includes expected receipts from the company's principal source(s) of revenue. These are usually cash sales and collections from customers on credit sales. This section also shows anticipated receipts of interest and dividends, and proceeds from planned sales of investments, plant assets, and the company's capital stock.

The **cash disbursements section** shows expected cash payments. Such payments include direct materials, direct labor, manufacturing overhead, and selling and administrative expenses. This section also includes projected payments for income taxes, dividends, investments, and plant assets.

The **financing section** shows expected borrowings and the repayment of the borrowed funds plus interest. This section is needed when there is a cash deficiency or when the cash balance is below management's minimum required balance.

Data in the cash budget must be prepared in sequence. The ending cash balance of one period becomes the beginning cash balance for the next period. Data for preparing the cash budget are obtained from other budgets and from information provided by management. In practice, cash budgets are often prepared for the year on a monthly basis.

To minimize detail, we will assume that Hayes Company prepares an annual cash budget by quarters. The cash budget for Hayes Company is based on the following assumptions.

1. The January 1, 2005, cash balance is expected to be $38,000.
2. Sales (Illustration 19-3): 60 percent are collected in the quarter sold and 40 percent are collected in the following quarter. Accounts receivable of $60,000 at December 31, 2004, are expected to be collected in full in the first quarter of 2005.

3. Short-term investments are expected to be sold for $2,000 cash in the first quarter.

4. Direct materials (Illustration 19-7): 50 percent are paid in the quarter purchased and 50 percent are paid in the following quarter. Accounts payable of $10,600 at December 31, 2004, are expected to be paid in full in the first quarter of 2005.

5. Direct labor (Illustration 19-8): 100 percent is paid in the quarter incurred.

6. Manufacturing overhead (Illustration 19-9) and selling and administrative expenses (Illustration 19-10): All items except depreciation are paid in the quarter incurred.

7. Management plans to purchase a truck in the second quarter for $10,000 cash.

8. Hayes makes equal quarterly payments of its estimated annual income taxes.

9. Loans are repaid in the earliest quarter in which there is sufficient cash (i.e., when the cash on hand exceeds the $15,000 minimum required balance).

In preparing the cash budget, it is useful to prepare schedules for collections from customers (assumption No. 2, above) and cash payments for direct materials (assumption No. 4, above). The schedules are shown in Illustrations 19-14 and 19-15.

Illustration 19-14
Collections from customers

SCHEDULE OF EXPECTED COLLECTIONS FROM CUSTOMERS				
	Quarter			
	1	**2**	**3**	**4**
Accounts receivable, 12/31/04	$ 60,000			
First quarter ($180,000)	108,000	$ 72,000		
Second quarter ($210,000)		126,000	$ 84,000	
Third quarter ($240,000)			144,000	$ 96,000
Fourth quarter ($270,000)				162,000
Total collections	$168,000	$198,000	$228,000	$258,000

Illustration 19-15
Payments for direct materials

SCHEDULE OF EXPECTED PAYMENTS FOR DIRECT MATERIALS				
	Quarter			
	1	**2**	**3**	**4**
Accounts payable, 12/31/04	$10,600			
First quarter ($25,200)	12,600	$12,600		
Second quarter ($29,200)		14,600	$14,600	
Third quarter ($33,200)			16,600	$16,600
Fourth quarter ($37,200)				18,600
Total payments	$23,200	$27,200	$31,200	$35,200

The cash budget for Hayes Company is shown in Illustration 19-16 (page 920). The budget indicates that $3,000 of financing will be needed in the second quarter to maintain a minimum cash balance of $15,000. Since there is an excess of available cash over disbursements of $22,500 at the end of the third quarter, the borrowing, plus $100 interest, is repaid in this quarter.

		Quarter			
	Assumption	**1**	**2**	**3**	**4**
Beginning cash balance	1	$ 38,000	$ 25,500	$ 15,000	$ 19,400
Add: Receipts					
Collections from customers	2	168,000	198,000	228,000	258,000
Sale of securities	3	2,000	0	0	0
Total receipts		170,000	198,000	228,000	258,000
Total available cash		208,000	223,500	243,000	277,400
Less: Disbursements					
Direct materials	4	23,200	27,200	31,200	35,200
Direct labor	5	62,000	72,000	82,000	92,000
Manufacturing overhead	6	53,300[1]	56,300	59,300	62,300
Selling and administrative expenses	6	41,000[2]	43,000	45,000	47,000
Purchase of truck	7	0	10,000	0	0
Income tax expense	8	3,000	3,000	3,000	3,000
Total disbursements		182,500	211,500	220,500	239,500
Excess (deficiency) of available cash over disbursements		25,500	12,000	22,500	37,900
Financing					
Borrowings		0	**3,000**	0	0
Repayments—plus $100 interest	9	0	0	3,100	0
Ending cash balance		$ 25,500	$ 15,000	$ 19,400	$ 37,900

HAYES COMPANY
Cash Budget
For the Year Ending December 31, 2005

[1]$57,100 − $3,800 depreciation
[2]$42,000 − $1,000 depreciation

Illustration 19-16
Cash budget

A cash budget contributes to more effective cash management. It can show managers when additional financing will be necessary well before the actual need arises. And, it can indicate when excess cash will be available for investments or other purposes.

DECISION TOOLKIT

Decision Checkpoints	Info Needed for Decision	Tool to Use for Decision	How to Evaluate Results
Is the company going to need to borrow funds in the coming quarter?	Beginning cash balance, cash receipts, cash disbursements, and desired cash balance	Cash budget	The company will need to borrow money if the cash budget indicates a projected cash deficiency of available cash over cash disbursements for the quarter.

BUDGETED BALANCE SHEET

The **budgeted balance sheet** is a projection of financial position at the end of the budget period. This budget is developed from the budgeted balance sheet for the preceding year and the budgets for the current year. Pertinent data from the budgeted balance sheet at December 31, 2004, are as follows.

| Buildings and equipment | $182,000 | Common stock | $225,000 |
| Accumulated depreciation | $ 28,800 | Retained earnings | $ 46,480 |

The budgeted balance sheet at December 31, 2005, is shown below.

Illustration 19-17
Budgeted balance sheet

HAYES COMPANY
Budgeted Balance Sheet
December 31, 2005

Assets

Cash		$ 37,900
Accounts receivable		108,000
Finished goods inventory		44,000
Raw materials inventory		4,080
Buildings and equipment	$192,000	
Less: Accumulated depreciation	48,000	144,000
Total assets		$337,980

Liabilities and Stockholders' Equity

Accounts payable	$ 18,600
Common stock	225,000
Retained earnings	94,380
Total liabilities and stockholders' equity	$337,980

The computations and sources of the amounts are explained below.

Cash: Ending cash balance $37,900, shown in the cash budget (Illustration 19-16).

Accounts receivable: 40 percent of fourth-quarter sales $270,000, shown in the schedule of expected collections from customers (Illustration 19-14).

Finished goods inventory: Desired ending inventory 1,000 units, shown in the production budget (Illustration 19-5) times the total unit cost $44 (shown in Illustration 19-11).

Raw materials inventory: Desired ending inventory 1,020 pounds, times the cost per pound $4, shown in the direct materials budget (Illustration 19-7).

Buildings and equipment: December 31, 2004, balance $182,000, plus purchase of truck for $10,000.

Accumulated depreciation: December 31, 2004, balance $28,800, plus $15,200 depreciation shown in manufacturing overhead budget (Illustration 19-9) and $4,000 depreciation shown in selling and administrative expense budget (Illustration 19-10).

Accounts payable: 50 percent of fourth-quarter purchases $37,200, shown in schedule of expected payments for direct materials (Illustration 19-15).

Common stock: Unchanged from the beginning of the year.

Retained earnings: December 31, 2004, balance $46,480, plus net income $47,900, shown in budgeted income statement (Illustration 19-12).

BEFORE YOU GO ON . . .

▶ **Review It**

1. What are the two classifications of the individual budgets in the master budget?

2. What is the sequence for preparing the budgets that comprise the operating budgets?

3. Identify some of the source documents that would be used in preparing each of the operating budgets.

4. What are the three principal sections of the cash budget?

▶ Do It

In Martian Company, management wants to maintain a minimum monthly cash balance of $15,000. At the beginning of March 2005, the cash balance is $16,500, expected cash receipts for March are $210,000, and cash disbursements are expected to be $220,000. How much cash, if any, must be borrowed to maintain the desired minimum monthly balance?

Action Plan

• Write down the basic form of the cash budget, starting with the beginning cash balance, adding cash receipts for the period, deducting cash disbursements, and identifying the needed financing to achieve the desired minimum ending cash balance.

• Insert the data given into the outlined form of the cash budget.

Solution

MARTIAN COMPANY
Cash Budget
For the Month Ending March 31, 2005

Beginning cash balance	$ 16,500
Add: Cash receipts for March	210,000
Total available cash	226,500
Less: Cash disbursements for March	220,000
Excess of available cash over cash disbursements	6,500
Financing	8,500
Ending cash balance	$ 15,000

To maintain the desired minimum cash balance of $15,000, Martian Company must borrow $8,500 of cash.

Related exercise material: BE19-9 and E19-9.

THE NAVIGATOR

Budgeting in Nonmanufacturing Companies

STUDY OBJECTIVE
6
Indicate the applicability of budgeting in nonmanufacturing companies.

Budgeting is not limited to manufacturers. Budgets may also be used by merchandisers, service enterprises, and not-for-profit organizations.

MERCHANDISERS

As in manufacturing operations, the sales budget for a merchandiser is both the starting point and the key factor in the development of the master budget. The major differences between the master budgets of a merchandiser and a manufacturer are these: (1) A merchandiser **uses a merchandise purchases budget instead of a production budget.** (2) A merchandiser **does not use the manufacturing budgets (direct materials, direct labor, and manufacturing over-**

head). The **merchandise purchases budget** shows the estimated cost of goods to be purchased to meet expected sales. The formula for determining budgeted merchandise purchases is:

Budgeted Cost of Goods Sold	+	Desired Ending Merchandise Inventory	−	Beginning Merchandise Inventory	=	Required Merchandise Purchases

Illustration 19-18
Merchandise purchases formula

To illustrate, assume that the budget committee of Lima Company is preparing the merchandise purchases budget for July. It estimates that budgeted sales will be $300,000 in July and $320,000 in August. Cost of goods sold is expected to be 70 percent of sales. The company's desired ending inventory is 30 percent of the following month's cost of goods sold. Required merchandise purchases for July are $214,200, computed as follows.

Budgeted cost of goods sold (budgeted sales for July of $300,000 × 70%)	$210,000
Desired ending merchandise inventory (budgeted sales for August of $320,000 × 70% × 30%)	67,200
Total	277,200
Less: Beginning merchandise inventory (budgeted sales for July of $300,000 × 70% × 30%)	63,000
Required merchandise purchases for July	**$214,200**

Illustration 19-19
Computation of required merchandise purchases

When a merchandiser is departmentalized, separate budgets are prepared for each department. For example, a grocery store may start by preparing sales budgets and purchases budgets for each of its major departments, such as meats, dairy, and produce. These budgets are then combined into a master budget for the store. When a retailer has branch stores, separate master budgets are prepared for each store. Then these budgets are incorporated into master budgets for the company as a whole.

SERVICE ENTERPRISES

In a service enterprise, such as a public accounting firm, a law office, or a medical practice, the critical factor in budgeting is **coordinating professional staff needs with anticipated services**. If a firm is overstaffed, several problems may result: (1) Labor costs will be disproportionately high. (2) Profits will be lower because of the additional salaries. (3) Staff turnover may increase because of lack of challenging work. In contrast, if an enterprise is understaffed, revenue may be lost because existing and prospective client needs for service cannot be met. Also, professional staff may seek other jobs because of excessive work loads.

Budget data for service revenue may be obtained from **expected output** or **expected input**. When output is used, it is necessary to determine the expected billings of clients for services rendered. In a public accounting firm, for example, output would be the sum of its billings in auditing, tax, and consulting services. When input data are used, each professional staff member is required to project his or her billable time. Billing rates are then applied to billable time to produce expected service revenue.

Dairy Dept.   Meat Dept.   Produce Dept.

Master Budget for Grocery Store

Departmentalized budgets

Gross Profit

Business Insight
MANAGEMENT PERSPECTIVE

Lucy Carter, managing partner of a small CPA firm in Nashville, uses formal budgets as the principal tool for keeping cash flow on an even keel throughout the year. The firm budgets annually for both revenues and expenses on a month-by-month basis. For example, the revenue budget is derived from chargeable-hour goals set by the staff. The firm sets a threshold of 1,800 hours for each staff member and 1,700 hours for each manager. Each month the budget is compared with the financial statements, and adjustments are made if necessary.

NOT-FOR-PROFIT ORGANIZATIONS

Budgeting is just as important for not-for-profit organizations as for profit-oriented enterprises. The budget process, however, is significantly different. In most cases not-for-profit entities budget **on the basis of cash flows (expenditures and receipts)**, **rather than on a revenue and expense basis**. Further, the starting point in the process is usually expenditures, not receipts. For the not-for-profit entity, management's task generally is to find the receipts needed to support the planned expenditures. The activity index is also likely to be significantly different. For example, in a not-for-profit entity, such as a university, budgeted faculty positions may be based on full-time equivalent students or credit hours expected to be taught in a department.

For some governmental units, the budget must be approved by voters. In other cases, such as state governments and the federal government, legislative approval is required. After the budget is adopted, it must be strictly followed. Overspending is often illegal. In governmental budgets, authorizations tend to be on a line-by-line basis. That is, the budget for a municipality may have a specified authorization for police and fire protection, garbage collection, street paving, and so on. The line-item authorization of governmental budgets significantly limits the amount of discretion management can exercise. The city manager often cannot use savings from one line item, such as street paving, to cover increased spending in another line item, such as snow removal.

BEFORE YOU GO ON . . .

▶ **Review It**

1. What is the formula for computing required merchandise purchases?
2. How does budgeting in service and not-for-profit organizations differ from budgeting for manufacturers and merchandisers?

✔ THE NAVIGATOR

Using the Decision Toolkit

The **University of Wisconsin** and its subunits must prepare budgets. One unique subunit of the University of Wisconsin is **Babcock Ice Cream**, a functioning producer of dairy products (and famous, at least on campus, for its delicious ice cream).

Assume that Babcock Ice Cream prepares monthly cash budgets. Relevant data from assumed operating budgets for 2005 are:

	January	February
Sales	$460,000	$412,000
Direct materials purchases	185,000	210,000
Direct labor	70,000	85,000
Manufacturing overhead	50,000	65,000
Selling and administrative expenses	85,000	95,000

Babcock sells 50% of its ice cream in its shops on campus, as well as selling to local stores. Collections from local stores are expected to be 50% in the month of sale, and 50% in the month following sale. Sixty percent (60%) of direct materials purchases are paid in cash in the month of purchase, and the balance due is paid in the month following the purchase. All other items above are paid in the month incurred. (Depreciation has been excluded from manufacturing overhead and selling and administrative expenses.)

Other data:

(1) Sales: November 2004, $370,000; December 2004, $320,000

(2) Purchases of direct materials: December 2004, $175,000

(3) Other receipts: January—Donation received, $2,000
                              February—Sale of used equipment, $4,000

(4) Other disbursements: February—Purchased equipment, $10,000

(5) Repaid debt: January, $30,000

The company's cash balance on January 1, 2005, is expected to be $50,000. The company wants to maintain a minimum cash balance of $45,000.

Instructions

(a) Prepare schedules for (1) expected collections from customers and (2) expected payments for direct materials purchases.
(b) Prepare a cash budget for January and February in columnar form.

Solution

(a) (1)

Expected Collections from Customers

	January	February
December ($320,000)	$ 80,000	$ 0
January ($460,000)	345,000	115,000
February ($412,000)	0	309,000
Totals	$425,000	$424,000

(2)

Expected Payments for Direct Materials

	January	February
December ($175,000)	$ 70,000	$ 0
January ($185,000)	111,000	74,000
February ($210,000)	0	126,000
Totals	$181,000	$200,000

(b)

BABCOCK ICE CREAM
Cash Budget
For the Two Months Ending February 28, 2005

	January	February
Beginning cash balance	$ 50,000	$ 61,000
Add: Receipts		
Collections from customers	425,000	424,000
Donations received	2,000	0
Sale of used equipment	0	4,000
Total receipts	427,000	428,000
Total available cash	477,000	489,000
Less: Disbursements		
Direct materials	181,000	200,000
Direct labor	70,000	85,000
Manufacturing overhead	50,000	65,000
Selling and administrative expenses	85,000	95,000
Purchase of equipment	0	10,000
Total disbursements	386,000	455,000
Excess (deficiency) of available cash over disbursements	91,000	34,000
Financing		
Borrowings	0	11,000
Repayments	30,000	0
Ending cash balance	$ 61,000	$ 45,000

☑ THE NAVIGATOR

Summary of Study Objectives

1 *Indicate the benefits of budgeting.* The primary advantages of budgeting are that it (a) requires management to plan ahead, (b) provides definite objectives for evaluating performance, (c) creates an early warning system for potential problems, (d) facilitates coordination of activities, (e) results in greater management awareness, and (f) motivates personnel to meet planned objectives.

2 *State the essentials of effective budgeting.* The essentials of effective budgeting are (a) sound organizational structure, (b) research and analysis, and (c) acceptance by all levels of management.

3 *Identify the budgets that comprise the master budget.* The master budget consists of the following budgets: (a) sales, (b) production, (c) direct materials, (d) direct labor, (e) manufacturing overhead, (f) selling and administrative expense, (g) budgeted income statement, (h) capital expenditure budget, (i) cash budget, and (j) budgeted balance sheet.

4 *Describe the sources for preparing the budgeted income statement.* The budgeted income statement is prepared from (a) the sales budget, (b) the budgets for direct materials, direct labor, and manufacturing overhead, and (c) the selling and administrative expense budget.

5 *Explain the principal sections of a cash budget.* The cash budget has three sections (receipts, disbursements, and financing) and the beginning and ending cash balances.

6 *Indicate the applicability of budgeting in nonmanufacturing companies.* Budgeting may be used by merchandisers for development of a master budget. In service enterprises budgeting is a critical factor in coordinating staff needs with anticipated services. In not-for-profit organizations, the starting point in budgeting is usually expenditures, not receipts.

☑ THE NAVIGATOR

DECISION TOOLKIT—A SUMMARY

Decision Checkpoints	Info Needed for Decision	Tool to Use for Decision	How to Evaluate Results
Has the company met its targets for sales, production expenses, selling and administrative expenses, and net income?	Sales forecasts, inventory levels, projected materials, labor, overhead, and selling and administrative requirements	Master budget—a set of interrelated budgets including sales, production, materials, labor, overhead, and selling and administrative budgets	Results are favorable if revenues exceed budgeted amounts, or if expenses are less than budgeted amounts.
Is the company going to need to borrow funds in the coming quarter?	Beginning cash balance, cash receipts, cash disbursements, and desired cash balance	Cash budget	The company will need to borrow money if the cash budget indicates a projected cash deficiency of available cash over cash disbursements for the quarter.

Glossary

Budget A formal written statement of management's plans for a specified future time period, expressed in financial terms. (p. 907)

Budget committee A group responsible for coordinating the preparation of the budget. (p. 909)

Budgeted balance sheet A projection of financial position at the end of the budget period. (p. 920)

Budgeted income statement An estimate of the expected profitability of operations for the budget period. (p. 917)

Cash budget A projection of anticipated cash flows. (p. 918)

Direct labor budget A projection of the quantity and cost of direct labor to be incurred to meet production requirements. (p. 914)

Direct materials budget An estimate of the quantity and cost of direct materials to be purchased. (p. 914)

Financial budgets Individual budgets that indicate the cash resources needed for expected operations and planned capital expenditures. (p. 911)

Long-range planning A formalized process of selecting strategies to achieve long-term goals and developing policies and plans to implement the strategies. (p. 910)

Manufacturing overhead budget An estimate of expected manufacturing overhead costs for the budget period. (p. 915)

Master budget A set of interrelated budgets that constitutes a plan of action for a specific time period. (p. 911)

Merchandise purchases budget The estimated cost of goods to be purchased by a merchandiser to meet expected sales. (p. 923)

Operating budgets Individual budgets that result in a budgeted income statement. (p. 911)

Production budget A projection of the units that must be produced to meet anticipated sales. (p. 913)

Sales budget An estimate of expected sales for the budget period. (p. 912)

Sales forecast The projection of potential sales for the industry and the company's expected share of such sales. (p. 909)

Selling and administrative expense budget A projection of anticipated selling and administrative expenses for the budget period. (p. 916)

Demonstration Problem

Soroco Company is preparing its master budget for 2005. Relevant data pertaining to its sales and production budgets are as follows:

Sales: Sales for the year are expected to total 1,200,000 units. Quarterly sales are 20%, 25%, 30%, and 25% respectively. The sales price is expected to be $50 per unit for the first three quarters and $55 per unit beginning in the fourth quarter. Sales in the first quarter of 2006 are expected to be 10% higher than the budgeted sales volume for the first quarter of 2005.

Production: Management desires to maintain ending finished goods inventories at 25% of the next quarter's budgeted sales volume.

Instructions

Prepare the sales budget and production budget by quarters for 2005.

Action Plan

- Know the form and content of the sales budget.
- Prepare the sales budget first as the basis for the other budgets.
- Determine the units that must be produced to meet anticipated sales.
- Know how to compute the beginning and ending finished goods units.

Solution to Demonstration Problem

SOROCO COMPANY
Sales Budget
For the Year Ending December 31, 2005

	Quarter				
	1	**2**	**3**	**4**	**Year**
Expected unit sales	240,000	300,000	360,000	300,000	1,200,000
Unit selling price	× $50	× $50	× $50	× $55	—
	$12,000,000	$15,000,000	$18,000,000	$16,500,000	$61,500,000

SOROCO COMPANY
Production Budget
For the Year Ending December 31, 2005

	Quarter				
	1	**2**	**3**	**4**	**Year**
Expected unit sales	240,000	300,000	360,000	300,000	
Add: Desired ending finished goods units	75,000	90,000	75,000	66,000[1]	
Total required units	315,000	390,000	435,000	366,000	
Less: Beginning finished goods units	60,000[2]	75,000	90,000	75,000	
Units to be produced	255,000	315,000	345,000	291,000	1,206,000

[1]Estimated first-quarter 2006 sales volume 240,000 + (240,000 × 10%) = 264,000; 264,000 × 25%.
[2]25% of estimated first-quarter 2005 sales units.

Self-Study Questions

Self-Study/Self-Test

Answers are at the end of the chapter.

(SO 1) **1.** The benefits of budgeting include *all but one* of the following:
 (a) Management can plan ahead.
 (b) An early warning system is provided for potential problems.
 (c) It enables disciplinary action to be taken at every level of responsibility.
 (d) The coordination of activities is facilitated.

(SO 2) **2.** The essentials of effective budgeting do *not* include:
 (a) top-down budgeting.
 (b) management acceptance.
 (c) research and analysis.
 (d) sound organizational structure.

3. Compared to budgeting, long-range planning (SO 2) generally has the:
 (a) same amount of detail.
 (b) longer time period.
 (c) same emphasis.
 (d) same time period.

4. A sales budget is: (SO 3)
 (a) derived from the production budget.
 (b) management's best estimate of sales revenue for the year.
 (c) not the starting point for the master budget.
 (d) prepared only for credit sales.

5. The formula for the production budget is bud- (SO 3) geted sales in units plus:

(a) desired ending merchandise inventory less beginning merchandise inventory.
(b) beginning finished goods units less desired ending finished goods units.
(c) desired ending direct materials units less beginning direct materials units.
(d) desired ending finished goods units less beginning finished goods units.

(SO 3)   6. Direct materials inventories are kept in pounds in Byrd Company, and the total pounds of direct materials needed for production is 9,500. If the beginning inventory is 1,000 pounds and the desired ending inventory is 2,200 pounds, the total pounds to be purchased is:
(a) 9,400.
(b) 9,500.
(c) 9,700.
(d) 10,700.

(SO 3)   7. The formula for computing the direct labor cost budget is to multiply the direct labor cost per hour by the:
(a) total required direct labor hours.
(b) physical units to be produced.
(c) equivalent units to be produced.
(d) No correct answer is given.

8. Each of the following budgets is used in preparing the budgeted income statement *except* the: (SO 4)
(a) sales budget.
(b) selling and administrative budget.
(c) capital expenditure budget.
(d) direct labor budget.

9. Expected direct materials purchases in Read Company are $70,000 in the first quarter and $90,000 in the second quarter. Forty percent of the purchases are paid in cash as incurred, and the balance is paid in the following quarter. The budgeted cash payments for purchases in the second quarter are: (SO 5)
(a) $96,000.
(b) $90,000.
(c) $78,000.
(d) $72,000.

10. The budget for a merchandiser differs from a budget for a manufacturer because: (SO 6)
(a) a merchandise purchases budget replaces the production budget.
(b) the manufacturing budgets are not applicable.
(c) None of the above.
(d) Both (a) and (b) above.

Questions

1. (a) What is a budget?
   (b) How does a budget contribute to good management?

2. Valerie Flynn and Ken Leask are discussing the benefits of budgeting. They ask you to identify the primary advantages of budgeting. Comply with their request.

3. Lorraine Scott asks your help in understanding the essentials of effective budgeting. Identify the essentials for Lorraine.

4. (a) "Accounting plays a relatively unimportant role in budgeting." Do you agree? Explain.
   (b) What responsibilities does management have in budgeting?

5. What criteria are helpful in determining the length of the budget period? What is the most common budget period?

6. Mary Miller maintains that the only difference between budgeting and long-range planning is time. Do you agree? Why or why not?

7. Distinguish between a master budget and a sales budget.

8. What budget is the starting point in preparing the master budget? What may result if this budget is inaccurate?

9. "The production budget shows both unit production data and unit cost data." Is this true? Explain.

10. Wheaton Company has 8,000 beginning finished goods units. Budgeted sales units are 160,000. If management desires 20,000 ending finished goods units, what are the required units of production?

11. In preparing the direct materials budget for Dukane Company, management concludes that required purchases are 54,000 units. If 50,000 direct materials units are required in production and there are 7,000 units of beginning direct materials, what is the desired units of ending direct materials?

12. The production budget of Hinsdale Company calls for 90,000 units to be produced. If it takes 30 minutes to make one unit and the direct labor rate is $14 per hour, what is the total budgeted direct labor cost?

13. Villanova Company's manufacturing overhead budget shows total variable costs of $168,000 and total fixed costs of $147,000. Total production in units is expected to be 160,000. It takes 15 minutes to make one unit, and the direct labor rate is $15 per hour. Express the manufacturing overhead rate as (a) a percentage of direct labor cost, and (b) an amount per direct labor hour.

14. Westphal Company's variable selling and administrative expenses are 15% of net sales. Fixed expenses are $60,000 per quarter. The sales budget shows expected sales of $200,000 and $250,000 in the first and second quarters, respectively. What are the total budgeted selling and administrative expenses for each quarter?

15. For Advent Company, the budgeted cost for one unit of product is direct materials $10, direct labor $20, and manufacturing overhead 80% of direct labor cost. If 25,000 units are expected to be sold at $77 each, what is the budgeted gross profit?

16. Indicate the supporting schedules used in preparing a budgeted income statement through gross profit for a manufacturer.

17. Identify the three sections of a cash budget. What balances are also shown in this budget?

18. Andrew Manion Company has credit sales of $500,000 in January. Past experience suggests that 45% is collected in the month of sale, 50% in the month following the sale, and 4% in the second month following the sale. Compute the cash collections from January sales in January, February, and March.

19. What is the formula for determining required merchandise purchases for a merchandiser?

20. How may expected revenues in a service enterprise be computed?

Brief Exercises

Prepare a diagram of a master budget.
(SO 3)

BE19-1   Sharon Livingston Manufacturing Company uses the following budgets: Balance Sheet, Capital Expenditure, Cash, Direct Labor, Direct Materials, Income Statement, Manufacturing Overhead, Production, Sales, and Selling and Administrative. Prepare a diagram of the interrelationships of the budgets in the master budget. Indicate whether each budget is an operating or a financial budget.

Prepare a sales budget.
(SO 3)

BE19-2   Emil Company estimates that unit sales will be 10,000 in quarter 1; 12,000 in quarter 2; 14,000 in quarter 3; and 15,000 in quarter 4. Using a sales price of $70 per unit, prepare the sales budget by quarters and for the year ending December 31, 2005.

Prepare a production budget for 2 quarters.
(SO 3)

BE19-3   Sales budget data for Emil Company are given in BE19-2. Management desires to have an ending finished goods inventory equal to 30% of the next quarter's expected unit sales. Prepare a production budget by quarters for the first 6 months of 2005.

Prepare a direct materials budget for 1 month.
(SO 3)

BE19-4   Korenewych Company has 1,200 pounds of raw materials in its December 31, 2005, ending inventory. Required production for January and February are 4,000 and 5,000 units, respectively. Two pounds of raw materials are needed for each unit, and the estimated cost per pound is $6. Management desires an ending inventory equal to 15% of next month's materials requirements. Prepare the direct materials budget for January.

Prepare a direct labor budget for 2 quarters.
(SO 3)

BE19-5   For Shawn Green Company, units to be produced are 5,000 in quarter 1 and 6,000 in quarter 2. It takes 1.8 hours to make a finished unit, and the expected hourly wage rate is $12 per hour. Prepare a direct labor budget by quarters and for the 6 months ending June 30, 2005.

Prepare a manufacturing overhead budget.
(SO 3)

BE19-6   For John Dunham Inc. variable manufacturing overhead costs are expected to be $20,000 in the first quarter of 2005, with $3,000 increments in each of the remaining three quarters. Fixed overhead costs are estimated to be $35,000 in each quarter. Prepare the manufacturing overhead budget by quarters and for the year.

Prepare a selling and administrative expense budget.
(SO 3)

BE19-7   Chudzick Company classifies its selling and administrative expense budget into variable and fixed components. Variable expenses are expected to be $25,000 in the first quarter, and $5,000 increments are expected in the remaining quarters of 2005. Fixed expenses are expected to be $40,000 in each quarter. Prepare the selling and administrative expense budget by quarters and for 2005.

Prepare a budgeted income statement for the year.
(SO 4)

BE19-8   Bitterman Company has completed all of its operating budgets. The sales budget for the year shows 50,000 units and total sales of $2,000,000. The total unit cost of making one unit of sales is $28. Selling and administrative expenses are expected to be $300,000. Income taxes are estimated to be $50,000. Prepare a budgeted income statement for the year ending December 31, 2005.

Prepare data for a cash budget.
(SO 5)

BE19-9   Jorie Aloisio Industries expects credit sales for January, February, and March to be $200,000, $275,000, and $310,000, respectively. It is expected that 70% of the sales will be collected in the month of sale, and 30% will be collected in the following month. Compute cash collections from customers for each month.

Determine required merchandise purchases for 1 month.
(SO 6)

BE19-10   Maggie Sharrer Wholesalers is preparing its merchandise purchases budget. Budgeted sales are $400,000 for April and $450,000 for May. Cost of goods sold is expected to be 75% of sales. The company's desired ending inventory is 20% of the following month's cost of goods sold. Compute the required purchases for April.

Exercises

E19-1 L. Quick Electronics Inc. produces and sells two models of pocket calculators, XQ-103 and XQ-104. The calculators sell for $12 and $20, respectively. Because of the intense competition Quick faces, management budgets sales semiannually. Its projections for the first 2 quarters of 2005 are as follows.

Prepare a sales budget for 2 quarters.
(SO 3)

	Unit Sales	
Product	**Quarter 1**	**Quarter 2**
XQ-103	30,000	27,000
XQ-104	12,000	13,000

No changes in selling prices are anticipated.

Instructions

Prepare a sales budget for the 2 quarters ending June 30, 2005. List the products and show for each quarter and for the 6 months, units, selling price, and total sales by product and in total.

E19-2 S. Stahl Company produces and sells two types of automobile batteries, the heavy-duty HD-240 and the long-life LL-250. The 2005 sales budget for the two products is as follows.

Prepare quarterly production budgets.
(SO 3)

Quarter	HD-240	LL-250
1	5,000	10,000
2	7,000	18,000
3	8,000	20,000
4	10,000	35,000

The January 1, 2005, inventory of HD-240 and LL-250 units is 3,000 and 6,000, respectively. Management desires an ending inventory each quarter equal to 60% of the next quarter's sales. Sales in the first quarter of 2006 are expected to be 30% higher than sales in the same quarter in 2005.

Instructions

Prepare separate quarterly production budgets for each product by quarters for 2005.

E19-3 Gosh-by-Golly Industries has adopted the following production budget for the first 4 months of 2006.

Prepare a direct materials budget.
(SO 3)

Month	**Units**	**Month**	**Units**
January	10,000	March	6,000
February	8,000	April	4,000

Each unit requires 5 pounds of raw materials costing $1.50 per pound. On December 31, 2005, the ending raw materials inventory was 25,000 pounds. Management wants to have a raw materials inventory at the end of each month equal to 50% of next month's production requirements.

Instructions

Prepare a direct materials budget by months for the first quarter.

E19-4 The W. Sublette Company budget committee has reached agreement on the following data for the 6 months ending June 30, 2006.

Prepare production and direct materials budgets by quarters for 6 months.
(SO 3)

Sales units: First quarter 5,000; second quarter 8,000
Ending raw materials inventory: 40% of the next quarter's production requirements
Ending finished goods inventory: 20% of the next quarter's expected sales units

The ending raw materials and finished goods inventories at December 31, 2005, follow the same percentage relationships to production and sales that occur in 2006. Three pounds of raw materials are required to make each unit of finished goods. Raw materials purchased are expected to cost $4 per pound. Sales of 7,000 units and required production of 7,250 units are expected in the third quarter of 2006.

Instructions
(a) Prepare a production budget by quarters for the 6 months.
(b) Prepare a direct materials budget by quarters for the 6 months.

Prepare a direct labor budget.
(SO 3)

E19-5   Twyla, Inc., is preparing its direct labor budget for 2005 from the following production budget based on a calendar year.

Quarter	Units	Quarter	Units
1	20,000	3	35,000
2	25,000	4	30,000

Each unit requires 1.5 hours of direct labor.

Instructions
Prepare a direct labor budget by quarter and for 2005. Wage rates are expected to be $14 for the first 2 quarters and $16 for quarters 3 and 4.

Prepare a manufacturing
overhead budget for the year.
(SO 3)

E19-6   Vincent Nathan Company is preparing its manufacturing overhead budget for 2005. Relevant data consist of the following.

Units to be produced (by quarters):   10,000, 12,000, 14,000, 16,000.

Direct labor: Time is 1.5 hours per unit.

Variable overhead costs per direct labor hour: Indirect materials $0.70; indirect labor $1.20; and maintenance $0.30.

Fixed overhead costs per quarter: Supervisory salaries $35,000; depreciation $12,000; and maintenance $9,000.

Instructions
Prepare the manufacturing overhead budget by quarter and for the year in total.

Prepare a selling and
administrative expense
budget for 2 quarters.
(SO 3)

E19-7   Marcum Company combines its operating expenses for budget purposes in a selling and administrative expense budget. For the first 6 months of 2005, the following data are available.
1. Sales: 15,000 units quarter 1; 18,000 units quarter 2.
2. Variable costs per dollar of sales: Sales commissions 5%, delivery expense 2%, and advertising 3%.
3. Fixed costs per quarter: Sales salaries $10,000, office salaries $6,000, depreciation $4,200, insurance $1,500, utilities $800, and repairs expense $600.
4. Unit selling price: $20.

Instructions
Prepare a selling and administrative expense budget by quarters and for the first 6 months of 2005.

Prepare a budgeted income
statement for the year.
(SO 3, 4)

E19-8   Longhead Company has accumulated the following budget data for the year 2005.
1. Sales: 30,000 units, unit selling price $80.
2. Cost of one unit of finished goods: Direct materials 3 pounds at $5 per pound, direct labor 3 hours at $12 per hour, and manufacturing overhead $6 per direct labor hour.
3. Inventories (raw materials only): Beginning, 10,000 pounds; ending, 15,000 pounds.
4. Raw materials cost: $5 per pound.
5. Selling and administrative expenses: $150,000.
6. Income taxes: 30% of income before income taxes.

Instructions
Prepare a budgeted income statement for 2005. Show the computation of cost of goods sold.

Prepare a cash budget for
2 months.
(SO 5)

E19-9   Campagna Company expects to have a cash balance of $46,000 on January 1, 2005. Relevant monthly budget data for the first 2 months of 2005 are as follows.

Collections from customers: January $80,000, February $150,000.

Payments to suppliers: January $40,000, February $75,000.

Direct labor: January $30,000, February $45,000. Wages are paid in the month they are incurred.

Manufacturing overhead: January $21,000, February $30,000. These costs include depreciation of $1,000 per month. All other overhead costs are paid as incurred.

Selling and administrative expenses: January $15,000, February $20,000. These costs are exclusive of depreciation. They are paid as incurred.

Sales of marketable securities in January are expected to realize $10,000 in cash. Campagna Company has a line of credit at a local bank that enables it to borrow up to $25,000. The company wants to maintain a minimum monthly cash balance of $20,000.

Instructions
Prepare a cash budget for January and February.

E19-10   In May 2005, the budget committee of Sherrick Stores assembles the following data in preparation of budgeted merchandise purchases for the month of June.
1. Expected sales: June $500,000, July $600,000.
2. Cost of goods sold is expected to be 65% of sales.
3. Desired ending merchandise inventory is 40% of the following (next) month's cost of goods sold.
4. The beginning inventory at June 1 will be the desired amount.

Prepare a purchases budget and budgeted income statement for a merchandiser.
(SO 6)

Instructions
(a) Compute the budgeted merchandise purchases for June.
(b) Prepare the budgeted income statement for June through gross profit on sales.

Problems: Set A

P19-1A   Oakbrook Farm Supply Company manufactures and sells a pesticide called Snare. The following data are available for preparing budgets for Snare for the first 2 quarters of 2006.
1. Sales: Quarter 1, 35,000 bags; quarter 2, 50,000 bags. Selling price is $60 per bag.
2. Direct materials: Each bag of Snare requires 5 pounds of Gumm at a cost of $3 per pound and 8 pounds of Tarr at $1.50 per pound.
3. Desired inventory levels:

Prepare budgeted income statement and supporting budgets.
(SO 3, 4)

Type of Inventory	January 1	April 1	July 1
Snare (bags)	8,000	12,000	18,000
Gumm (pounds)	9,000	10,000	13,000
Tarr (pounds)	14,000	20,000	25,000

4. Direct labor: Direct labor time is 15 minutes per bag at an hourly rate of $12 per hour.
5. Selling and administrative expenses are expected to be 8% of sales plus $175,000 per quarter.
6. Income taxes are expected to be 30% of income from operations.

Your assistant has prepared two budgets: (1) The manufacturing overhead budget shows expected costs to be 150% of direct labor cost. (2) The direct materials budget for Tarr shows the cost of Tarr to be $477,000 in quarter 1 and $679,500 in quarter 2.

Instructions
Prepare the budgeted income statement for the first 6 months and all required supporting budgets by quarters and in total. (*Note:* Use variable and fixed in the selling and administrative expense budget.)

Net income $986,650
Standard cost
  per bag $ 34.50

Prepare sales, production, direct materials, direct labor, and income statement budgets.
(SO 3, 4)

P19-2A   Joe Dunham Inc. is preparing its annual budgets for the year ending December 31, 2006. Accounting assistants furnish the following data.

	Product JB 50	Product JB 60
Sales budget:		
Anticipated volume in units	480,000	180,000
Unit selling price	$20.00	$25.00
Production budget:		
Desired ending finished goods units	25,000	15,000
Beginning finished goods units	30,000	10,000
Direct materials budget:		
Direct materials per unit (pounds)	2	3
Desired ending direct materials pounds	30,000	15,000
Beginning direct materials pounds	40,000	10,000
Cost per pound	$3.00	$4.00
Direct labor budget:		
Direct labor hours per unit	0.4	0.6
Direct labor rate per hour	$11.00	$11.00
Budgeted income statement:		
Total unit cost	$12.00	$20.00

An accounting assistant has prepared the detailed manufacturing overhead budget and the selling and administrative expense budget. The latter shows selling expenses of $660,000 for product JB 50 and $360,000 for product JB 60, and administrative expenses of $420,000 for product JB 50 and $340,000 for product JB 60. Income taxes are expected to be 30%.

Instructions

(a) Total sales $14,100,000

(b) Total cost of
   direct materials
   purchases,
   JB50 $ 2,820,000

(c) Net income $ 2,072,000

Prepare the following budgets for the year. Show data for each product. Quarterly budgets should not be prepared.

(a) Sales
(b) Production
(c) Direct materials
(d) Direct labor
(e) Income statement (*Note:* Income taxes are not allocated to the products.)

Prepare sales and production budgets and compute cost per unit under two plans.
(SO 3, 4)

P19-3A   Hindu Industries had sales in 2005 of $6,300,000 and gross profit of $1,500,000. Management is considering two alternative budget plans to increase its gross profit in 2006.

Plan A would increase the selling price per unit from $9.00 to $9.40. Sales volume would decrease by 5% from its 2005 level. Plan B would decrease the selling price per unit by $0.50. The marketing department expects that the sales volume would increase by 150,000 units.

At the end of 2005, Hindu has 30,000 units of inventory on hand. If Plan A is accepted, the 2006 ending inventory should be equal to 4% of the 2006 sales. If Plan B is accepted, the ending inventory should be equal to 40,000 units. Each unit produced will cost $1.60 in direct labor, $2.00 in direct materials, and $0.90 in variable overhead. The fixed overhead for 2006 should be $1,800,000.

Instructions

(c) Unit cost, Plan A $7.22

(a) Prepare a sales budget for 2006 under each plan.
(b) Prepare a production budget for 2006 under each plan.
(c) Compute the production cost per unit under each plan. Why is the cost per unit different for each of the two plans? (Round to two decimals.)
(d) Which plan should be accepted? (*Hint:* Compute the gross profit under each plan.)

Prepare cash budget for 2 months.
(SO 5)

P19-4A   Yaeger Company prepares monthly cash budgets. Relevant data from operating budgets for 2006 are:

	January	February
Sales	$360,000	$400,000
Direct materials purchases	125,000	130,000
Direct labor	90,000	100,000
Manufacturing overhead	70,000	75,000
Selling and administrative expenses	79,000	86,000

All sales are on account. Collections are expected to be 50% in the month of sale, 30% in the first month following the sale, and 20% in the second month following the sale. Sixty percent (60%) of direct materials purchases are paid in cash in the month of purchase, and the balance due is paid in the month following the purchase. All other items above are paid in the month incurred except for selling and administrative expenses that include $1,000 of depreciation per month.

Other data:

1. Credit sales: November 2005, $260,000; December 2005, $300,000.
2. Purchases of direct materials: December 2005, $100,000.
3. Other receipts: January—Collection of December 31, 2005, notes receivable $15,000;
   February—Proceeds from sale of securities $6,000.
4. Other disbursements: February—Dividend payment $5,000.

The company's cash balance on January 1, 2006, is expected to be $70,000. The company wants to maintain a minimum cash balance of $50,000.

Instructions

(a) Prepare schedules for (1) expected collections from customers and (2) expected payments for direct materials purchases.

(b) Prepare a cash budget for January and February in columnar form.

(a) January:
  Collections $322,000
  Payments $115,000
(b) Ending cash balance,
  February $ 50,000

P19-5A   The budget committee of Henning Company collects the following data for its San Miguel Store in preparing budgeted income statements for May and June 2006.

1. Sales for May are expected to be $600,000. Sales in June and July are expected to be 10% higher than the preceding month.
2. Cost of goods sold is expected to be 70% of sales.
3. Company policy is to maintain ending merchandise inventory at 25% of the following month's cost of goods sold.
4. Operating expenses are estimated to be:

Prepare purchases and income statement budgets for a merchandiser.
(SO 6)

Sales salaries	$25,000 per month
Advertising	5% of monthly sales
Delivery expense	3% of monthly sales
Sales commissions	4% of monthly sales
Rent expense	$5,000 per month
Depreciation	$800 per month
Utilities	$600 per month
Insurance	$500 per month

5. Income taxes are estimated to be 30% of income from operations.

Instructions

(a) Prepare the merchandise purchases budget for each month in columnar form.

(b) Prepare budgeted income statements for each month in columnar form. Show in the statements the details of cost of goods sold.

(a) May purchases $430,500
(b) June net income $ 60,830

P19-6A   East Asian Industries' balance sheet at December 31, 2005, is presented below.

Prepare budgeted income statement and balance sheet.
(SO 3, 4)

EAST ASIAN INDUSTRIES
Balance Sheet
December 31, 2005

Assets

Current assets		
Cash		$ 7,500
Accounts receivable		82,500
Finished goods inventory (2,000 units)		30,000
Total current assets		120,000
Property, plant, and equipment		
Equipment	$40,000	
Less: Accumulated depreciation	10,000	30,000
Total assets		$150,000

Liabilities and Stockholders' Equity

Liabilities		
Notes payable		$ 25,000
Accounts payable		45,000
Total liabilities		70,000
Stockholders' equity		
Common stock	$50,000	
Retained earnings	30,000	
Total stockholders' equity		80,000
Total liabilities and stockholders' equity		$150,000

Additional information accumulated for the budgeting process is as follows. Budgeted data for the year 2006 include the following.

	4th Quarter of 2006	Year 2006 Total
Sales budget (8,000 units at $35)	$80,000	$280,000
Direct materials used	17,000	72,400
Direct labor	8,500	38,600
Manufacturing overhead applied	10,000	42,000
Selling and administrative expenses	18,000	76,000

To meet sales requirements and to have 2,500 units of finished goods on hand at December 31, 2006, the production budget shows 8,500 required units of output. The total unit cost of production is expected to be $18. East Asian Industries uses the first-in, first-out (FIFO) inventory costing method. Total depreciation for the year is $4,000. Interest expense is expected to be $3,500 for the year. Income taxes are expected to be 30% of income before income taxes.

All sales and purchases are on account. It is expected that 60% of quarterly sales are collected in cash within the quarter and the remainder is collected in the following quarter. Direct materials purchased from suppliers are paid 50% in the quarter incurred and the remainder in the following quarter. Purchases in the fourth quarter were the same as the materials used. In 2006, the company expects to purchase additional equipment costing $24,000. It expects to pay $8,000 on notes payable plus all interest due and payable to December 31 (included in interest expense $3,500, above). Accounts payable at December 31, 2006, includes amounts due suppliers (see above) plus other accounts payable of $7,500. In 2006, the company expects to declare and pay a $5,000 cash dividend. Unpaid income taxes at December 31 will be $5,000. The company's cash budget shows an expected cash balance of $29,750 at December 31, 2006.

Instructions

Net income $ 43,750
Total assets $156,750

Prepare a budgeted income statement for 2006 and a budgeted balance sheet at December 31, 2006. In preparing the income statement, you will need to compute cost of goods manufactured and finished goods inventory (December 31, 2006).

Problems: Set B

Prepare a budgeted income statement and supporting budgets.
(SO 3, 4)

P19-1B Alcorn Farm Supply Company manufactures and sells a fertilizer called Basic II. The following data are available for preparing budgets for Basic II for the first 2 quarters of 2005.

1. Sales: Quarter 1, 50,000 bags; quarter 2, 70,000 bags. Selling price is $60 per bag.
2. Direct materials: Each bag of Basic II requires 5 pounds of Crup at a cost of $3 per pound and 10 pounds of Dert at $1.50 per pound.
3. Desired inventory levels:

Type of Inventory	January 1	April 1	July 1
Basic II (bags)	10,000	15,000	20,000
Crup (pounds)	9,000	12,000	15,000
Dert (pounds)	15,000	20,000	25,000

4. Direct labor: Direct labor time is 15 minutes per bag at an hourly rate of $10 per hour.
5. Selling and administrative expenses are expected to be 10% of sales plus $150,000 per quarter.
6. Income taxes are expected to be 30% of income from operations.

Your assistant has prepared two budgets: (1) The manufacturing overhead budget shows expected costs to be 100% of direct labor cost. (2) The direct materials budget for Dert which shows the cost of Dert to be $832,500 in quarter 1 and $132,500 in quarter 2.

Instructions
Prepare the budgeted income statement for the first 6 months of 2005 and all required supporting budgets by quarters and in total. (*Note:* Use variable and fixed in the selling and administrative expense budget.)

Net income $1,386,000
Standard cost
per bag $ 35

P19-2B   Borealis Inc. is preparing its annual budgets for the year ending December 31, 2005. Accounting assistants furnish the following data.

Prepare sales, production, direct materials, direct labor, and income statement budgets.
(SO 3, 4)

	Product LN 35	Product LN 40
Sales budget:		
Anticipated volume in units	300,000	150,000
Unit selling price	$20.00	$30.00
Production budget:		
Desired ending finished goods units	30,000	25,000
Beginning finished goods units	20,000	15,000
Direct materials budget:		
Direct materials per unit (pounds)	2	3
Desired ending direct materials pounds	50,000	20,000
Beginning direct materials pounds	40,000	10,000
Cost per pound	$2.00	$3.00
Direct labor budget:		
Direct labor hours per unit	0.5	0.75
Direct labor rate per hour	$9.00	$9.00
Budgeted income statement:		
Total unit cost	$10.00	$20.00

An accounting assistant has prepared the detailed manufacturing overhead budget and the selling and administrative expense budget. The latter shows selling expenses of $460,000 for product LN 35 and $440,000 for product LN 40, and administrative expenses of $420,000 for product LN 35 and $380,000 for product LN 40. Income taxes are expected to be 30%.

Instructions
Prepare the following budgets for the year. Show data for each product. Quarterly budgets should not be prepared.
  (a) Sales
  (b) Production
  (c) Direct materials
  (d) Direct labor
  (e) Income statement (*Note:* Income taxes are not allocated to the products.)

(a) Total sales $10,500,000
(c) Total cost of
*   direct materials*
*   purchases,*
*   LN 40 $ 1,470,000*
(e) Net income $ 1,960,000

P19-3B   David Chambers Industries has sales in 2005 of $5,250,000 (656,250 units) and gross profit of $1,587,500. Management is considering two alternative budget plans to increase its gross profit in 2006.

Plan A would increase the selling price per unit from $8.00 to $8.60. Sales volume would decrease by 10% from its 2005 level. Plan B would decrease the selling price per

Prepare sales and production budgets and compute cost per unit under two plans.
(SO 3, 4)

unit by 5%. The marketing department expects that the sales volume would increase by 100,000 units.

At the end of 2005, Chambers has 75,000 units on hand. If Plan A is accepted, the 2006 ending inventory should be equal to 87,500 units. If Plan B is accepted, the ending inventory should be equal to 100,000 units. Each unit produced will cost $2.00 in direct materials, $1.50 in direct labor, and $0.50 in variable overhead. The fixed overhead for 2006 should be $965,000.

Instructions
(a) Prepare a sales budget for 2006 under (1) Plan A and (2) Plan B.
(b) Prepare a production budget for 2006 under (1) Plan A and (2) Plan B.

(c) Unit cost,
  Plan A $5.60

(c) Compute the cost per unit under (1) Plan A and (2) Plan B. Explain why the cost per unit is different for each of the two plans. (Round to two decimals.)
(d) Which plan should be accepted? (*Hint:* Compute the gross profit under each plan.)

Prepare cash budget for 2 months.
(SO 5)

P19-4B Flypaper Company prepares monthly cash budgets. Relevant data from operating budgets for 2006 are:

	January	February
Sales	$350,000	$400,000
Direct materials purchases	95,000	110,000
Direct labor	100,000	115,000
Manufacturing overhead	60,000	75,000
Selling and administrative expenses	75,000	85,000

All sales are on account. Collections are expected to be 60% in the month of sale, 30% in the first month following the sale, and 10% in the second month following the sale. Thirty percent (30%) of direct materials purchases are paid in cash in the month of purchase, and the balance due is paid in the month following the purchase. All other items above are paid in the month incurred. Depreciation has been excluded from manufacturing overhead and selling and administrative expenses.

Other data:
1. Credit sales: November 2005, $200,000; December 2005, $280,000.
2. Purchases of direct materials: December 2005, $90,000.
3. Other receipts: January—Collection of December 31, 2005, interest receivable $3,000;
  February—Proceeds from sale of securities $5,000.
4. Other disbursements: February—payment of $20,000 for land.

The company's cash balance on January 1, 2006, is expected to be $60,000. The company wants to maintain a minimum cash balance of $50,000.

(a) February:
  Collections $373,000
  Payments $ 99,500
(b) Ending cash
  balance, Jan. $ 50,500

Instructions
(a) Prepare schedules for (1) expected collections from customers and (2) expected payments for direct materials purchases.
(b) Prepare a cash budget for January and February in columnar form.

Prepare purchases and income statement budgets for a merchandiser.
(SO 6)

P19-5B The budget committee of Oriental Company collects the following data for its Westwood Store in preparing budgeted income statements for July and August 2005.
1. Expected sales: July $400,000, August $450,000, September $500,000.
2. Cost of goods sold is expected to be 75% of sales.
3. Company policy is to maintain ending merchandise inventory at 30% of the following month's cost of goods sold.
4. Operating expenses are estimated to be:

Sales salaries	$20,000 per month
Advertising	4% of monthly sales
Delivery expense	2% of monthly sales
Sales commissions	3% of monthly sales
Rent expense	$3,000 per month
Depreciation	$700 per month
Utilities	$500 per month
Insurance	$300 per month

5. Income taxes are estimated to be 30% of income from operations.

Instructions

(a) Prepare the merchandise purchases budget for each month in columnar form.

(b) Prepare budgeted income statements for each month in columnar form. Show the details of cost of goods sold in the statements.

(a) August
  purchases $348,750
(b) August net
  income $ 33,250

▶ **BROADENING YOUR PERSPECTIVE**

Group Decision Case

BYP19-1 Castle Corporation operates on a calendar-year basis. It begins the annual budgeting process in late August when the president establishes targets for the total dollar sales and net income before taxes for the next year.

The sales target is given first to the marketing department. The marketing manager formulates a sales budget by product line in both units and dollars. From this budget, sales quotas by product line in units and dollars are established for each of the corporation's sales districts. The marketing manager also estimates the cost of the marketing activities required to support the target sales volume and prepares a tentative marketing expense budget.

The executive vice president uses the sales and profit targets, the sales budget by product line, and the tentative marketing expense budget to determine the dollar amounts that can be devoted to manufacturing and corporate office expense. The executive vice president prepares the budget for corporate expenses. She then forwards to the production department the product-line sales budget in units and the total dollar amount that can be devoted to manufacturing.

The production manager meets with the factory managers to develop a manufacturing plan that will produce the required units when needed within the cost constraints set by the executive vice president. The budgeting process usually comes to a halt at this point because the production department does not consider the financial resources allocated to be adequate.

When this standstill occurs, the vice president of finance, the executive vice president, the marketing manager, and the production manager meet together to determine the final budgets for each of the areas. This normally results in a modest increase in the total amount available for manufacturing costs and cuts in the marketing expense and corporate office expense budgets. The total sales and net income figures proposed by the president are seldom changed. Although the participants are seldom pleased with the compromise, these budgets are final. Each executive then develops a new detailed budget for the operations in his or her area.

None of the areas has achieved its budget in recent years. Sales often run below the target. When budgeted sales are not achieved, each area is expected to cut costs so that the president's profit target can be met. However, the profit target is seldom met because costs are not cut enough. In fact, costs often run above the original budget in all functional areas (marketing, production, and corporate office).

The president is disturbed that Castle has not been able to meet the sales and profit targets. He hired a consultant with considerable experience with companies in Castle's industry. The consultant reviewed the budgets for the past 4 years. He concluded that the product-line sales budgets were reasonable and that the cost and expense budgets were adequate for the budgeted sales and production levels.

Instructions

With the class divided into groups, answer the following.

(a) Discuss how the budgeting process employed by Castle Corporation contributes to the failure to achieve the president's sales and profit targets.

(b) Suggest how Castle Corporation's budgeting process could be revised to correct the problems.

(c) Should the functional areas be expected to cut their costs when sales volume falls below budget? Explain your answer.   (CMA adapted.)

Managerial Analysis

BYP19-2   Thebeau & Lewis Inc. manufactures ergonomic devices for computer users. Some of their more popular products include glare screens (for computer monitors), keyboard stands with wrist rests, and carousels that allow easy access to floppy disks. Over the past 5 years, they experienced rapid growth, with sales of all products increasing 20% to 50% each year.

Last year, some of the primary manufacturers of computers began introducing new products with some of the ergonomic designs, such as glare screens and wrist rests, already built in. As a result, sales of Thebeau & Lewis's accessory devices have declined somewhat. The company believes that the disk carousels will probably continue to show growth, but that the other products will probably continue to decline. When the next year's budget was prepared, increases were built in to research and development so that replacement products could be developed or the company could expand into some other product line. Some product lines being considered are general-purpose ergonomic devices including back supports, foot rests, and sloped writing pads.

The most recent results have shown that sales decreased more than was expected for the glare screens. As a result, the company may have a shortage of funds. Top management has therefore asked that all expenses be reduced 10% to compensate for these reduced sales. Summary budget information is as follows.

Raw materials	$240,000
Direct labor	110,000
Insurance	50,000
Depreciation	90,000
Machine repairs	30,000
Sales salaries	50,000
Office salaries	80,000
Factory salaries (indirect labor)	50,000
Total	$700,000

Instructions
Using the information above, answer the following questions.
- (a) What are the implications of reducing each of the costs? For example, if the company reduces raw materials costs, it may have to do so by purchasing lower-quality materials. This may affect sales in the long run.
- (b) Based on your analysis in (a), what do you think is the best way to obtain the $70,000 in cost savings requested? Be specific. Are there any costs that cannot or should not be reduced? Why?

Real-World Focus

BYP19-3   Network Computing Devices Inc. was founded in 1988 in Mountain View, Calif. The company develops hardware and software thin-client computing products. (Thin clients are computers that do not have a hard drive but, rather, are served from a central computer through a network.) Presented at the top of page 941 is a discussion by management in an annual report.

Instructions
- (a) Identify the factors that affect the budgeting process at Network Computing Devices Inc.
- (b) Explain the additional budgeting concerns created by the international operations of the company.

Communication Activity   **941**

NETWORK COMPUTING DEVICES, INC.
Management Discussion

The Company's operating results have varied significantly, particularly on a quarterly basis, as a result of a number of factors, including general economic conditions affecting industry demand for computer products, the timing and market acceptance of new product introductions by the Company and its competitors, the timing of significant orders from large customers, periodic changes in product pricing and discounting due to competitive factors, and the availability of key components, such as video monitors and electronic subassemblies, some of which require substantial order lead times. The Company's operating results may fluctuate in the future as a result of these and other factors, including the Company's success in developing and introducing new products, its product and customer mix, and the level of competition which it experiences. The Company operates with a small backlog. Sales and operating results, therefore, generally depend on the volume and timing of orders received, which are difficult to forecast. The Company has experienced slowness in orders from some customers during the first quarter of each calendar year due to budgeting cycles common in the computer industry. In addition, sales in Europe typically are adversely affected in the third calendar quarter as many European customers reduce their business activities during the month of August.

Due to the Company's rapid growth rate and the effect of new product introductions on quarterly revenues, these seasonal trends have not materially impacted the Company's results of operations to date. However, as the Company's product lines mature and its rate of revenue growth declines, these seasonal factors may become more evident. Additionally, the Company's international sales are denominated in U.S. dollars, and an increase or decrease in the value of the U.S. dollar relative to foreign currencies could make the Company's products less or more competitive in those markets.

Exploring the Web

BYP19-4 The opportunities for business consulting in the areas of corporate planning, budgeting, and strategy are almost limitless as new, more powerful software continues to be developed. This exercise takes you to the Web site of **CP Corporate Planning**, a European consulting firm.

Address: **www.corporate-planning.com/us/index.html**
        (or go to **www.wiley.com/college/kimmel**)

Steps:
1. Go to the site above.
2. Choose **Sitemap**.
3. Choose **Case Studies**.

Instructions
Choose three case studies, and in each case identify the problem the company faced and how the situation was resolved.

Communication Activity

BYP19-5 In order to better serve their rural patients, Drs. Jim and Jeff Howell (brothers) began giving safety seminars. Especially popular were their "emergency-preparedness" talks given to farmers. Many people asked whether the "kit" of materials the doctors recommended for common farm emergencies was commercially available.

After checking with several suppliers, the doctors realized that no other company offered the supplies they recommended in their seminars, packaged in the way they described. Their wives, Marie and Pam, agreed to make a test package by ordering supplies from various medical supply companies and assembling them into a "kit" that could be sold at the seminars. When these kits proved a runaway success, the sisters-in-law decided to market them. At the advice of their accountant, they organized this venture as a separate company, called Life Protection Products (LPP), with Marie Howell as CEO and Pam Howell as Secretary-Treasurer.

LPP soon started receiving requests for the kits from all over the country, as word spread about their availability. Even without advertising, LPP was able to sell its full inventory every month. However, the company was becoming financially strained. Marie and Pam had about $100,000 in savings, and they invested about half that amount initially. They believed that this venture would allow them to make money. However, at the present time, only about $30,000 of the cash remains, and the company is constantly short of cash.

Marie Howell has come to you for advice. She does not understand why the company is having cash flow problems. She and Pam have not even been withdrawing salaries. However, they have rented a local building and have hired two more full-time workers to help them cope with the increasing demand. They do not think they could handle the demand without this additional help.

Marie is also worried that the cash problems mean that the company may not be able to support itself. She has prepared the cash budget shown on the next page. All seminar customers pay for their products in full at the time of purchase. In addition, several large companies have ordered the kits for use by employees who work in remote sites. They have requested credit terms and have been allowed to pay in the month following the sale. These large purchasers amount to about 25% of the sales at the present time. LPP purchases the materials for the kits about 2 months ahead of time. Marie and Pam are considering slowing the growth of the company by simply purchasing less materials, which will mean selling fewer kits.

The workers are paid in cash weekly. Marie and Pam need about $15,000 cash on hand at the beginning of the month to pay for purchases of raw materials. Right now they have been using cash from their savings, but as noted, only $30,000 is left.

The cash budget that Marie Howell has given you is shown below.

LIFE PROTECTION PRODUCTS
Cash Budget
For the Quarter Ending June 30, 2006

	April	**May**	**June**
Cash balance, beginning	$15,000	$15,000	$15,000
Cash received			
From prior month sales	5,000	7,500	12,500
From current sales	15,000	22,500	37,500
Total cash on hand	35,000	45,000	65,000
Cash payments			
To employees	3,000	3,000	3,000
For products	25,000	35,000	45,000
Miscellaneous expenses	5,000	6,000	7,000
Postage	1,000	1,000	1,000
Total cash payments	34,000	45,000	56,000
Cash balance	$ 1,000	$ 0	$ 9,000
Borrow from savings	$14,000	$15,000	$ 1,000
Borrow from bank?	$ 0	$ 0	$ 7,000

Instructions

Write a response to Marie Howell. Explain why LPP is short of cash. Will this company be able to support itself? Explain your answer. Make any recommendations you deem appropriate.

Research Case

BYP19-6 The April 2000 issue of the *Journal of Accountancy* contains an article by Lawrence B. Macgregor Serven entitled "The Planning Peril."

Instructions
Read the article and answer the following questions.
- **(a)** Describe the three reasons why revamping the planning process can be perilous.
- **(b)** What four recommendations does the author provide to improve the chances of success of efforts to revamp the planning and budgeting process?
- **(c)** Review the sample survey. Identify what you believe are the three most important questions in this survey, and explain why you think they are important.

Ethics Case

BYP19-7 You are an accountant in the budgetary, projections, and special projects department of American Bare Conductor, Inc., a large manufacturing company. The president, Robert Boey, asks you on very short notice to prepare some sales and income projections covering the next 2 years of the company's much heralded new product lines. He wants these projections for a series of speeches he is making while on a 2-week trip to eight East Coast brokerage firms. The president hopes to bolster American Bare's stock sales and price.

You work 23 hours in 2 days to compile the projections, hand deliver them to the president, and are swiftly but graciously thanked as he departs. A week later you find time to go over some of your computations and discover a miscalculation that makes the projections grossly overstated. You quickly inquire about the president's itinerary and learn that he has made half of his speeches and has half yet to make. You are in a quandary as to what to do.

Instructions
- **(a)** What are the consequences of telling the president of your gross miscalculations?
- **(b)** What are the consequences of *not* telling the president of your gross miscalculations?
- **(c)** What are the ethical considerations to you and the president in this situation?

Answers to Self-Study Questions

1. c   2. a   3. b   4. b   5. d   6. d   7. a   8. c   9. c   10. d

Remember to go back to the Navigator box on the chapter-opening page and check off your completed work.

Budgetary Control and Responsibility Accounting

STUDY OBJECTIVES

After studying this chapter,
you should be able to:

1 Describe the concept of budgetary control.

2 Evaluate the usefulness of static budget reports.

3 Explain the development of flexible budgets and the usefulness of flexible budget reports.

4 Describe the concept of responsibility accounting.

5 Indicate the features of responsibility reports for cost centers.

6 Identify the content of responsibility reports for profit centers.

7 Explain the basis and formula used in evaluating performance in investment centers.

 THE NAVIGATOR

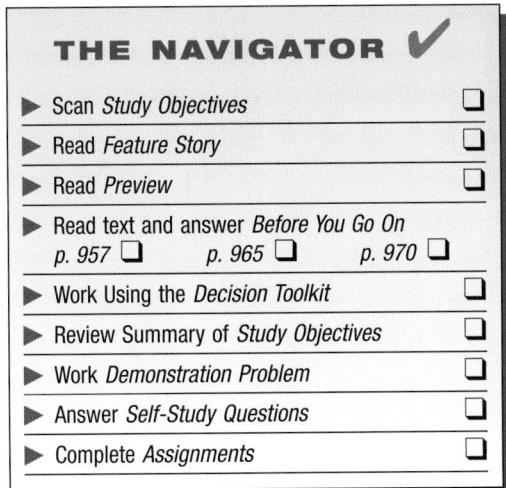

THE NAVIGATOR ✔

▶ Scan *Study Objectives* ☐

▶ Read *Feature Story* ☐

▶ Read *Preview* ☐

▶ Read text and answer *Before You Go On*
   p. 957 ☐   p. 965 ☐   p. 970 ☐

▶ Work Using the *Decision Toolkit* ☐

▶ Review Summary of *Study Objectives* ☐

▶ Work *Demonstration Problem* ☐

▶ Answer *Self-Study Questions* ☐

▶ Complete *Assignments* ☐

FEATURE STORY

Trying to Avoid an Electric Shock

Budgets are critical to evaluating an organization's success. They are based on management's expectations of what is most likely to happen in the future. In order to be useful, they must be accurate. But what if management's expectations are wrong? Estimates are never exactly correct, and sometimes, especially in volatile industries, estimates can be "off by a mile."

In recent years the electric utility industry has become very volatile. Deregulation, volatile prices for natural gas, coal, and oil, changes in environmental regulations, and economic swings have all contributed to large changes in the profitability of electric utility companies. This means that for planning and budgeting purposes, utilities must plan and budget based on multiple "what if" scenarios that take into account factors beyond management's control. For example, in recent years, **Duke Energy Corporation**, headquartered in Charlotte, North Carolina, built budgeting and planning models based on three different scenarios of what the future might hold. One scenario assumes that the U.S. economy will slow considerably. A second scenario assumes that the company will experience "pricing pressure" as the market for energy becomes more efficient as a result of more energy being traded in Internet auctions. A third scenario assumes a continuation of the current environment of rapid growth, changing regulation, and large swings in the prices for the fuels the company uses to create energy.

Compounding this budgeting challenge is the fact that changes in many indirect costs can also significantly affect the company. For example, even a tiny change in market interest rates has a huge effect on the company because it has massive amounts of outstanding debt. And finally, as a result of the California energy crisis, there is mounting pressure for government intervention and regulation. This pressure has resulted in setting "rate caps" that limit the amount that

utilities and energy companies can charge, thus lowering profits. The bottom line is that for budgeting and planning purposes, utility companies must remain alert and flexible.

☑ THE NAVIGATOR

In contrast to Chapter 19, we now consider how budgets are used by management to control operations. In the Feature Story on **Duke Energy**, we saw that budgeting must take into account factors beyond management's control. This chapter focuses on two aspects of management control: (1) budgetary control and (2) responsibility accounting.

The content and organization of Chapter 20 are as follows.

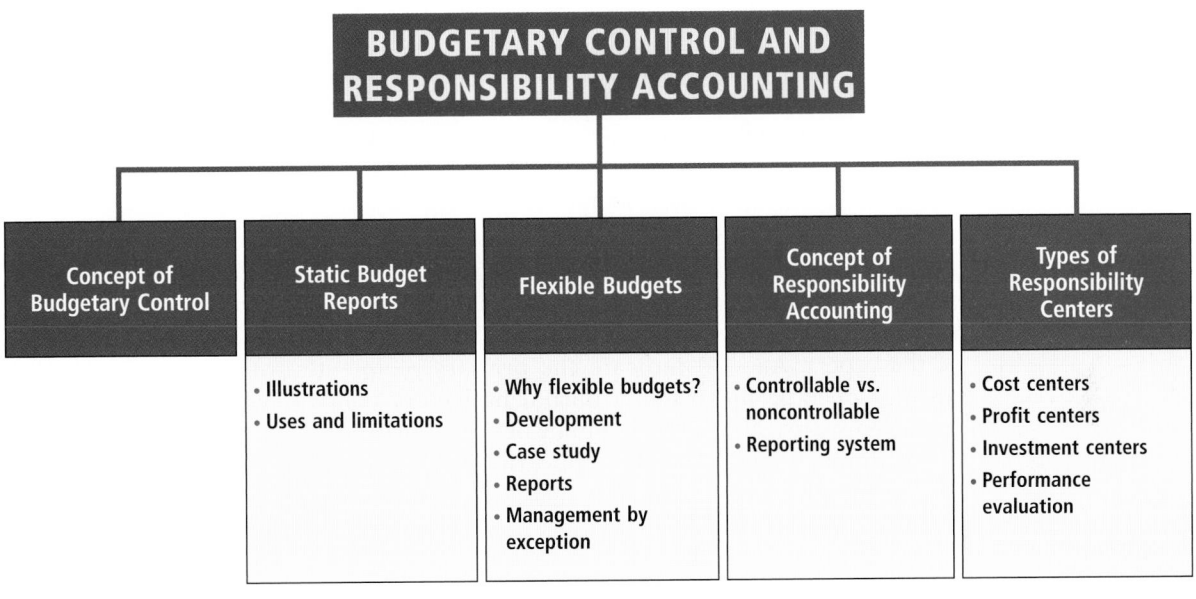

BUDGETARY CONTROL AND RESPONSIBILITY ACCOUNTING

Concept of Budgetary Control	Static Budget Reports	Flexible Budgets	Concept of Responsibility Accounting	Types of Responsibility Centers
	• Illustrations • Uses and limitations	• Why flexible budgets? • Development • Case study • Reports • Management by exception	• Controllable vs. noncontrollable • Reporting system	• Cost centers • Profit centers • Investment centers • Performance evaluation

☑ THE NAVIGATOR

Concept of Budgetary Control

One of management's major functions is to control company operations. Control consists of the steps taken by management to see that planned objectives are met. We now ask: How do budgets contribute to control of operations?

The use of budgets in controlling operations is known as **budgetary control**. Such control takes place by means of **budget reports** that compare actual results with planned objectives. The use of budget reports is based on the belief that planned objectives lose much of their potential value without some monitoring of progress along the way. Just as your professors give midterm exams to evaluate your progress, so top management requires periodic reports on the progress of department managers toward their planned objectives.

Budget reports provide management with feedback on operations. The feedback for a crucial objective, such as having enough cash on hand to pay bills, may be made daily. For other objectives, such as meeting budgeted annual sales and operating expenses, monthly budget reports may suffice. Budget reports can be prepared as frequently as needed. From these reports, management analyzes any differences between actual and planned results and determines their causes. Management then may take corrective action, or it may decide to modify future plans.

STUDY OBJECTIVE
1
Describe the concept of budgetary control.

Budgetary control involves the following activities.

Illustration 20-1
Budgetary control

Budgetary control works best when a company has a formalized reporting system. The system should do the following: (1) Identify the name of the budget report, such as the sales budget or the manufacturing overhead budget. (2) State the frequency of the report, such as weekly or monthly. (3) Specify the purpose of the report. And (4) indicate the primary recipient(s) of the report. The following schedule illustrates a partial budgetary control system for a manufacturing company. Note the frequency of the reports and their emphasis on control. For example, there is a daily report on scrap and a weekly report on labor.

Illustration 20-2
Budgetary control
reporting system

Name of Report	Frequency	Purpose	Primary Recipient(s)
Sales	Weekly	Determine whether sales goals are being met	Top management and sales manager
Labor	Weekly	Control direct and indirect labor costs	Vice president of production and production department managers
Scrap	Daily	Determine efficient use of materials	Production manager
Departmental overhead costs	Monthly	Control overhead costs	Department manager
Selling expenses	Monthly	Control selling expenses	Sales manager
Income statement	Monthly and quarterly	Determine whether income objectives are being met	Top management

Static Budget Reports

STUDY OBJECTIVE
2
Evaluate the usefulness of
static budget reports.

You learned in Chapter 19 that the master budget formalizes management's planned objectives for the coming year. When used in budgetary control, each budget included in the master budget is considered to be static. A **static budget** is a projection of budget data **at one level of activity**. Data for different levels of activity are not considered. As a result, actual results are always compared with budget data at the activity level that was used in developing the master budget.

ILLUSTRATIONS

To illustrate the role of a static budget in budgetary control, we will use selected data prepared for Hayes Company in Chapter 19. Budget and actual sales data for the Kitchen-mate product in the first and second quarters of 2005 are as follows.

Sales	First Quarter	Second Quarter	Total
Budgeted	$180,000	$210,000	$390,000
Actual	179,000	199,500	378,500
Difference	$ 1,000	$ 10,500	$ 11,500

Illustration 20-3 Budget and actual sales data

The sales budget report for Hayes Company's first quarter is shown below. The right-most column reports the difference between the budgeted and actual amounts.

Illustration 20-4 Sales budget report—first quarter

HAYES COMPANY
Sales Budget Report
For the Quarter Ended March 31, 2005

Product Line	Budget	Actual	Difference Favorable F Unfavorable U
Kitchen-mate[a]	$180,000	$179,000	$1,000 U

[a]In practice, each product line would be included in the report.

Alternative Terminology
The difference between budget and actual is sometimes called a *budget variance*.

The report shows that sales are $1,000 under budget—an unfavorable result. This difference is less than 1 percent of budgeted sales ($1,000 ÷ $180,000 = .0056). Top management's reaction to unfavorable differences is often influenced by the materiality (significance) of the difference. Since the difference of $1,000 is immaterial in this case, we will assume that Hayes Company management takes no specific corrective action.

The budget report for the second quarter is presented in Illustration 20-5. It contains one new feature: cumulative year-to-date information. This report indicates that sales for the second quarter were $10,500 below budget. This is 5 percent of budgeted sales ($10,500 ÷ $210,000). Top management may now conclude that the difference between budgeted and actual sales requires investigation.

Illustration 20-5 Sales budget report—second quarter

HAYES COMPANY
Sales Budget Report
For the Quarter Ended June 30, 2005

Product Line	Second Quarter			Year-to-Date		
	Budget	Actual	Difference Favorable F Unfavorable U	Budget	Actual	Difference Favorable F Unfavorable U
Kitchen-mate	$210,000	$199,500	$10,500 U	$390,000	$378,500	$11,500 U

Management's analysis should start by asking the sales manager the cause(s) of the shortfall. The need for corrective action should be considered. For example, management may decide to spur sales by offering sales incentives to customers or by increasing the advertising of Kitchen-mates. Or, if management concludes that a downturn in the economy is responsible for the lower sales, it may modify planned sales and profit goals for the remainder of the year.

Static budgets are best for fixed costs and expenses

USES AND LIMITATIONS

From these examples, you can see that a master sales budget is useful in evaluating the performance of a sales manager. It is now necessary to ask: Is the master budget appropriate for evaluating a manager's performance in controlling costs? Recall that in a static budget, data are not modified or adjusted, regardless of changes in activity. It follows, then, that a static budget is appropriate in evaluating a manager's effectiveness in controlling costs when:

1. The actual level of activity closely approximates the master budget activity level, and/or

2. The behavior of the costs in response to changes in activity is fixed.

A static budget report is, therefore, appropriate for **fixed manufacturing costs** and for **fixed selling and administrative expenses**. But, as you will see shortly, static budget reports may not be a proper basis for evaluating a manager's performance in controlling variable costs.

STUDY OBJECTIVE
3

Explain the development of flexible budgets and the usefulness of flexible budget reports.

Flexible budgets are static budgets at different activity levels

Flexible Budgets

In contrast to a static budget, which is based on one level of activity, a flexible budget projects budget data for various levels of activity. In essence, **the flexible budget is a series of static budgets at different levels of activity**. The flexible budget recognizes that the budgetary process is more useful if it is adaptable to changed operating conditions.

Flexible budgets can be prepared for each of the types of budgets included in the master budget. For example, **Marriott Hotels** can budget revenues and net income on the basis of 60 percent, 80 percent, and 100 percent of room occupancy. Similarly, **American Van Lines** can budget its operating expenses on the basis of various levels of truck miles driven. Likewise, in the Feature Story, **Duke Energy** can budget revenue and net income on the basis of estimated billions of kwh (kilowatt hours) of residential, commercial, and industrial electricity generated. In the following pages, we will illustrate a flexible budget for manufacturing overhead.

WHY FLEXIBLE BUDGETS?

Assume that you are the manager in charge of manufacturing overhead in the Forging Department of Barton Steel. In preparing the manufacturing overhead budget for 2005, you prepare the following static budget based on a production volume of 10,000 units of steel ingots.

Illustration 20-6 Static overhead budget

Helpful Hint The static budget is the master budget of Chapter 19.

BARTON STEEL Manufacturing Overhead Budget (Static) Forging Department For the Year Ended December 31, 2005	
Budgeted production in units (steel ingots)	10,000
Budgeted costs	
Indirect materials	$ 250,000
Indirect labor	260,000
Utilities	190,000
Depreciation	280,000
Property taxes	70,000
Supervision	50,000
	$1,100,000

Fortunately for the company, the demand for steel ingots has increased, and 12,000 units are produced and sold during the year, rather than 10,000. You are elated: Increased sales means increased profitability, which should mean a bonus or a raise for you and the employees in your department. Unfortunately, a comparison of Forging Department actual and budgeted costs has put you on the spot. The budget report is shown below.

Helpful Hint Which of the following is likely to be of little use when costs are variable—the static budget or the flexible budget? Answer: The static budget.

BARTON STEEL
Manufacturing Overhead Budget Report (Static)
Forging Department
For the Year Ended December 31, 2005

	Budget	Actual	Difference Favorable F Unfavorable U
Production in units	10,000	12,000	
Costs			
Indirect materials	$ 250,000	$ 295,000	$ 45,000 U
Indirect labor	260,000	312,000	52,000 U
Utilities	190,000	225,000	35,000 U
Depreciation	280,000	280,000	–0–
Property taxes	70,000	70,000	–0–
Supervision	50,000	50,000	–0–
	$1,100,000	$1,232,000	$132,000 U

Illustration 20-7 Static overhead budget report

This comparison uses budget data based on the original activity level (10,000 steel ingots). It indicates that the Forging Department is significantly **over budget** for three of the six overhead costs. And, there is a total unfavorable difference of $132,000, which is 12 percent over budget ($132,000 ÷ $1,100,000). Your supervisor is very unhappy! Instead of sharing in the company's success, you may find yourself looking for another job. What went wrong?

When you calm down and carefully examine the manufacturing overhead budget, you identify the problem: The budget data are not relevant! At the time the budget was developed, the company anticipated that only 10,000 units of steel ingots would be produced, **not** 12,000 ingots. Comparing actual with budgeted variable costs is meaningless. As production increases, the budget allowances for variable costs should increase both directly and proportionately. The variable costs in this example are indirect materials, indirect labor, and utilities.

Analyzing the budget data for these costs at 10,000 units, you arrive at the following per unit results.

Helpful Hint A static budget will not work if a company has substantial variable costs.

Item	Total Cost	Per Unit
Indirect materials	$250,000	$25
Indirect labor	260,000	26
Utilities	190,000	19
	$700,000	$70

Illustration 20-8 Variable costs per unit

You then can calculate the budgeted variable costs at 12,000 units as follows.

Illustration 20-9
Budgeted variable costs,
12,000 units

Item	Computation	Total
Indirect materials	$25 × 12,000	$300,000
Indirect labor	26 × 12,000	312,000
Utilities	19 × 12,000	228,000
		$840,000

Because fixed costs do not change in total as activity changes, the budgeted amounts for these costs remain the same. The budget report based on the flexible budget for **12,000 units** of production is shown in Illustration 20-10. (Compare this with Illustration 20-7.)

Illustration 20-10 Flexible overhead budget report

BARTON STEEL
Manufacturing Overhead Budget Report (Flexible)
Forging Department
For the Year Ended December 31, 2005

	Budget	Actual	Difference Favorable F Unfavorable U
Production in units	12,000	12,000	
Variable costs			
Indirect materials	$ 300,000	$ 295,000	$5,000 F
Indirect labor	312,000	312,000	–0–
Utilities	228,000	225,000	3,000 F
Total variable	840,000	832,000	8,000 F
Fixed costs			
Depreciation	280,000	280,000	–0–
Property taxes	70,000	70,000	–0–
Supervision	50,000	50,000	–0–
Total fixed	400,000	400,000	–0–
Total costs	$1,240,000	$1,232,000	$8,000 F

This report indicates that the Forging Department is below budget—a favorable difference. Instead of worrying about being fired, you may be in line for a bonus or a raise after all! As this analysis shows, the only appropriate comparison is between actual costs at 12,000 units of production and budgeted costs at 12,000 units. Flexible budget reports provide this comparison.

DEVELOPING THE FLEXIBLE BUDGET

The flexible budget uses the master budget as its basis. To develop the flexible budget, management should take the following steps.

1. Identify the activity index and the relevant range of activity.
2. Identify the variable costs, and determine the budgeted variable cost per unit of activity for each cost.

3. Identify the fixed costs, and determine the budgeted amount for each cost.
4. Prepare the budget for selected increments of activity within the relevant range.

The activity index chosen should be one that significantly influences the costs that are being budgeted. For manufacturing overhead costs, for example, the activity index is usually the same as the index used in developing the predetermined overhead rate—that is, direct labor hours or machine hours. For selling and administrative expenses, the activity index usually is sales or net sales.

The choice of the increment of activity is largely a matter of judgment. For example, if the relevant range is 8,000 to 12,000 direct labor hours, increments of 1,000 hours may be selected. The flexible budget is then prepared for each increment within the relevant range.

DECISION TOOLKIT

Decision Checkpoints	Info Needed for Decision	Tool to Use for Decision	How to Evaluate Results
Are the increased costs resulting from increased production reasonable?	Variable costs projected at different levels of production	Flexible budget	After taking into account different production levels, results are favorable if expenses are less than budgeted amounts.

FLEXIBLE BUDGET—A CASE STUDY

To illustrate the flexible budget, we will use Fox Manufacturing Company. Fox's management wants to use a **flexible budget for monthly comparisons** of actual and budgeted manufacturing overhead costs of the Finishing Department. The master budget for the year ending December 31, 2005, shows expected annual operating capacity of 120,000 direct labor hours and the following overhead costs.

Illustration 20-11 Master budget data

Variable Costs		**Fixed Costs**	
Indirect materials	$180,000	Depreciation	$180,000
Indirect labor	240,000	Supervision	120,000
Utilities	60,000	Property taxes	60,000
Total	$480,000	Total	$360,000

The four steps for developing the flexible budget are applied as follows.

STEP 1. **Identify the activity index and the relevant range of activity.** The activity index is direct labor hours. Management concludes that the relevant range is 8,000–12,000 direct labor hours per month.

STEP 2. **Identify the variable costs, and determine the budgeted variable cost per unit of activity for each cost.** There are three variable costs. The variable cost per unit is found by dividing each total budgeted cost by the direct labor hours used in preparing the master budget (120,000 hours). For Fox Manufacturing, the computations are:

Illustration 20-12
Computation of variable
costs per direct labor hour

Variable Cost	Computation	Variable Cost per Direct Labor Hour
Indirect materials	$180,000 ÷ 120,000	$1.50
Indirect labor	$240,000 ÷ 120,000	2.00
Utilities	$ 60,000 ÷ 120,000	0.50
Total		$4.00

STEP 3. **Identify the fixed costs, and determine the budgeted amount for each cost.** There are three fixed costs. Since Fox desires **monthly budget data**, the budgeted amount is found by dividing each annual budgeted cost by 12. For Fox Manufacturing, the monthly budgeted fixed costs are: depreciation $15,000, supervision $10,000, and property taxes $5,000.

STEP 4. **Prepare the budget for selected increments of activity within the relevant range.** Management decides to prepare the budget in increments of 1,000 direct labor hours.

The flexible budget is shown in Illustration 20-13.

Illustration 20-13 **Flexible monthly overhead budget**

FOX MANUFACTURING COMPANY
Flexible Monthly Manufacturing Overhead Budget
Finishing Department
For the Year 2005

Activity level					
Direct labor hours	8,000	9,000	10,000	11,000	12,000
Variable costs					
Indirect materials	$12,000	$13,500	$15,000	$16,500	$18,000
Indirect labor	16,000	18,000	20,000	22,000	24,000
Utilities	4,000	4,500	5,000	5,500	6,000
Total variable	32,000	36,000	40,000	44,000	48,000
Fixed costs					
Depreciation	15,000	15,000	15,000	15,000	15,000
Supervision	10,000	10,000	10,000	10,000	10,000
Property taxes	5,000	5,000	5,000	5,000	5,000
Total fixed	30,000	30,000	30,000	30,000	30,000
Total costs	$62,000	$66,000	$70,000	$74,000	$78,000

From the budget, the following formula may be used to determine total budgeted costs at any level of activity.

Illustration 20-14 **Formula for total budgeted costs**

$$\text{Fixed Costs} + \frac{\text{Variable Cost Per Unit}}{\times} \text{Activity Level} = \text{Total Budgeted Costs}$$

For Fox Manufacturing, fixed costs are $30,000, and total variable cost per unit is $4.00. Thus, at 9,000 direct labor hours, total budgeted costs are $66,000 [$30,000 + ($4.00 × 9,000)]. Similarly, at 8,622 direct labor hours, total budgeted costs are $64,488 [$30,000 + ($4.00 × 8,622)].

Total budgeted costs can also be shown graphically, as in Illustration 20-15. In the graph, the activity index is shown on the horizontal axis, and costs are indicated on the vertical axis. The graph highlights two activity levels (10,000 and 12,000). As shown, total budgeted costs at these activity levels are $70,000 [$30,000 + ($4.00 × 10,000)] and $78,000 [$30,000 + ($4.00 × 12,000)], respectively.

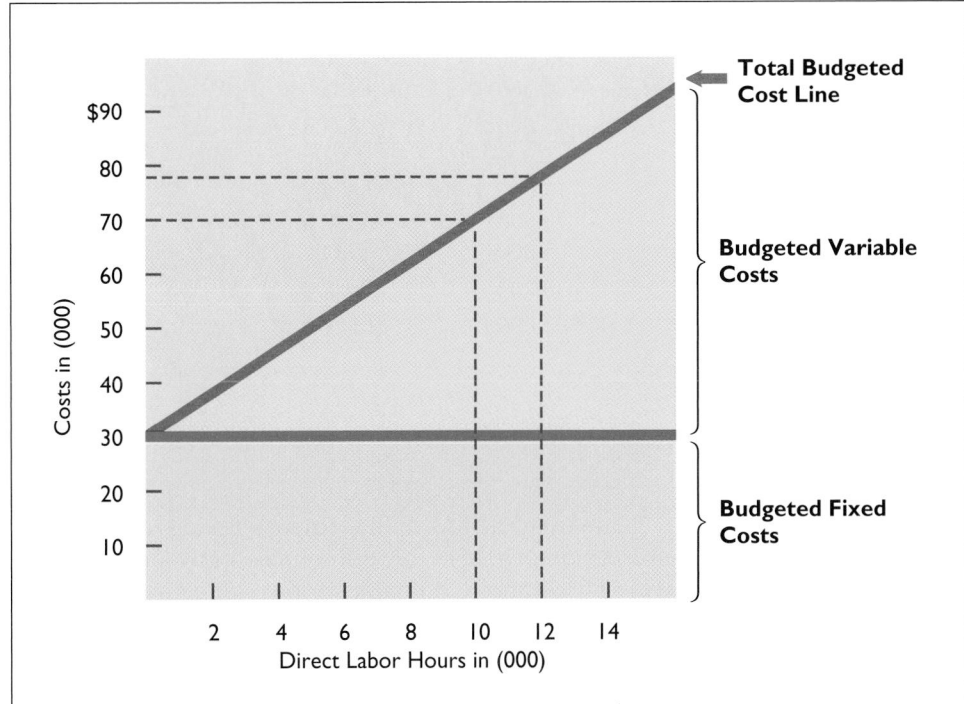

Costs in (000)

Direct Labor Hours in (000)

Illustration 20-15
Graphic flexible budget data highlighting 10,000 and 12,000 activity levels

Helpful Hint Using the data given for the Fox Manufacturing Company, what amount of total costs would be budgeted for 10,600 direct labor hours?
Answer:

Fixed	$30,000
Variable (10,600 × $4)	42,400
Total	$72,400

FLEXIBLE BUDGET REPORTS

Flexible budget reports are another type of internal report. The flexible budget report consists of two sections: (1) production data for a selected activity index, such as direct labor hours, and (2) cost data for variable and fixed costs. The report provides a basis for evaluating a manager's performance in two areas: production control and cost control. Flexible budget reports are widely used in production and service departments.

A budget report for the Finishing Department of Fox Company for the month of January is shown in Illustration 20-16 (page 956). In this month, 9,000 hours were worked. The budget data are therefore based on the flexible budget for 9,000 hours in Illustration 20-13. The actual cost data are assumed.

How appropriate is this report in evaluating the Finishing Department manager's performance in controlling overhead costs? The report clearly provides a reliable basis. Both actual and budget costs are based on the activity level worked during January. Since variable costs generally are incurred directly by the department, the difference between the budget allowance for those hours and the actual costs are the responsibility of the department manager.

In subsequent months, other flexible budget reports will be prepared. For each month, the budget data are based on the actual activity level attained. In February that level may be 11,000 direct labor hours, in July 10,000, and so on.

Helpful Hint An assembly department is a production department, and a maintenance department is a service department, as explained on page 962.

Illustration 20-16 **Flexible overhead budget report**

FOX MANUFACTURING COMPANY Flexible Manufacturing Overhead Budget Report Finishing Department For the Month Ended January 31, 2005			
			Difference
Direct labor hours (DLH)	**Budget at 9,000 DLH**	**Actual Costs 9,000 DLH**	**Favorable F Unfavorable U**
Variable costs			
Indirect materials	$13,500	$14,000	$ 500 U
Indirect labor	18,000	17,000	1,000 F
Utilities	4,500	4,600	100 U
Total variable	36,000	35,600	400 F
Fixed costs			
Depreciation	15,000	15,000	–0–
Supervision	10,000	10,000	–0–
Property taxes	5,000	5,000	–0–
Total fixed	30,000	30,000	–0–
Total costs	$66,000	$65,600	$ 400 F

Helpful Hint Note that this flexible budget is based on a single cost driver. A more accurate budget often can be developed using the activity-based costing concepts explained in Chapter 17.

MANAGEMENT BY EXCEPTION

Management by exception means that top management's review of a budget report is focused either entirely or primarily on differences between actual results and planned objectives. This approach enables top management to focus on problem areas. Management by exception does not mean that top management will investigate every difference. For this approach to be effective, there must be guidelines for identifying an exception. The usual criteria are materiality and controllability.

Materiality

Without quantitative guidelines, management would have to investigate every budget difference regardless of the amount. Materiality is usually expressed as a percentage difference from budget. For example, management may set the percentage difference at 5 percent for important items and 10 percent for other items. All differences either over or under budget by the specified percentage will be investigated. Costs over budget warrant investigation to determine why they were not controlled. Likewise, costs under budget merit investigation to determine whether costs critical to profitability are being curtailed. For example, if maintenance costs are budgeted at $80,000 but only $40,000 is spent, major unexpected breakdowns in productive facilities may occur in the future.

Alternatively, a company may specify a single percentage difference from budget for all items and supplement this guideline with a minimum dollar limit. For example, the exception criteria may be stated at 5 percent of budget or more than $10,000.

Controllability of the Item

Exception guidelines are more restrictive for controllable items than for items that are not controllable by the manager. In fact, there may be no guidelines for noncontrollable items. For example, a large unfavorable difference between actual and budgeted property tax expense may not be flagged for investigation because the only possible causes are an unexpected increase in the tax rate or in the assessed value of the property. An investigation into the difference will be useless: the manager cannot control either cause.

BEFORE YOU GO ON . . .

▶ Review It

1. What is the meaning of budgetary control?
2. When is a static budget appropriate for evaluating a manager's effectiveness in controlling costs?
3. What is a flexible budget?
4. How is a flexible budget developed?
5. What are the criteria used in management by exception?

▶ Do It

Your roommate asks your help in understanding how total budgeted costs are computed at any level of activity. Compute total budgeted costs at 30,000 direct labor hours, assuming that in the flexible budget graph, the fixed cost line and the total budgeted cost line intersect the vertical axis at $36,000 and that the total budget cost line is $186,000 at an activity level of 50,000 direct labor hours.

Action Plan

• Apply the formula: Fixed costs + Variable costs (Total variable costs per unit × Activity level) = Total budgeted costs.

Solution

Using the graph, fixed costs are $36,000, and variable costs are $3 per direct labor hour [($186,000 − $36,000) ÷ 50,000]. Thus, at 30,000 direct labor hours, total budgeted costs are $126,000 [$36,000 + ($3 × 30,000)].

Related exercise material: BE20-3, BE20-4, BE20-5, E20-1, E20-2, E20-3, E20-4, E20-5, E20-6, and E20-7.

☑ THE NAVIGATOR

The Concept of Responsibility Accounting

Like budgeting, responsibility accounting is an important part of management accounting. **Responsibility accounting** involves accumulating and reporting costs (and revenues, where relevant) on the basis of the manager who has the authority to make the day-to-day decisions about the items. Under responsibility accounting, a manager's performance is evaluated on matters directly under that manager's control. Responsibility accounting can be used at every level of management in which the following conditions exist.

STUDY OBJECTIVE
4
Describe the concept of responsibility accounting.

1. Costs and revenues can be directly associated with the specific level of management responsibility.

2. The costs and revenues are controllable at the level of responsibility with which they are associated.

3. Budget data can be developed for evaluating the manager's effectiveness in controlling the costs and revenues.

Levels of responsibility for controlling costs are depicted in Illustration 20-17.

Under responsibility accounting, any individual who has control and is accountable for a specified set of activities can be recognized as a responsibility center. Thus, responsibility accounting may extend from the lowest level of control to the top strata of management. Once responsibility has been established, the effectiveness of the individual's performance is first measured and reported for the specified activity. It is then reported upward throughout the organization.

Responsibility accounting is especially valuable in a decentralized company. **Decentralization** means that the control of operations is delegated to many managers throughout the organization. The term **segment** is sometimes used to identify an area of responsibility in decentralized operations. Under responsibility accounting, segment reports are prepared periodically such as monthly, quarterly, and annually, to evaluate managers' performance.

Responsibility accounting is an essential part of any effective system of budgetary control. The reporting of costs and revenues under responsibility accounting differs from budgeting in two respects.

1. A distinction is made between controllable and noncontrollable items.
2. Performance reports either emphasize or include only items controllable by the individual manager.

Responsibility accounting applies to both profit and not-for-profit entities. The former seek to maximize net income. The latter wish to minimize the cost of providing services.

CONTROLLABLE VERSUS NONCONTROLLABLE REVENUES AND COSTS

All costs and revenues are controllable at some level of responsibility within a company. This truth underscores the adage by the CEO of any organization that "the buck stops here." Under responsibility accounting, the critical issue is

Business Insight
MANAGEMENT PERSPECTIVE

Since devising its budgeting and control system, JKL, Inc., a large New York advertising agency, has become aware of which specific customer accounts are unprofitable and the reasons why. As a result, the agency has dropped several unprofitable accounts that otherwise would have gone unnoticed. Account managers now feel responsible for the profitability of their accounts. They carefully monitor actual hours spent on each account to make sure the account is being managed and run as efficiently as possible. For example, an account manager noticed a large amount of supervisory creative time was being spent on one account. Further investigation showed that the supervisors, rather than the creative department, were doing the actual creative work. The account manager pointed this out, and a junior creative team was appointed to the account, saving JKL a great deal of money.

whether the cost or revenue is controllable at the level of responsibility with which it is associated.

A cost is considered to be controllable at a given level of managerial responsibility if the manager has the power to incur it within a given period of time. From this criterion, it follows that:

> **Helpful Hint** Are there more or fewer controllable costs as you move to higher levels of management? Answer: More.

1. All costs are controllable by top management because of the broad range of its authority.
2. Fewer costs are controllable as one moves down to each lower level of managerial responsibility because of the manager's decreasing authority.

In general, **costs incurred directly by a level of responsibility are controllable at that level**. In contrast, costs incurred indirectly and allocated to a responsibility level are considered to be noncontrollable at that level.

> **Helpful Hint** The longer the time span, the more likely that the cost becomes controllable.

RESPONSIBILITY REPORTING SYSTEM

A responsibility reporting system involves the preparation of a report for each level of responsibility in the company's organization chart. To illustrate such a system, we will use the partial organization chart and production departments of Francis Chair Company in Illustration 20-18 (page 960).

The responsibility reporting system begins with the lowest level of responsibility for controlling costs and moves upward to each higher level. The connections between levels are detailed in Illustration 20-19 (page 961). A brief description of the four reports for Francis Chair Company is as follows.

1. **Report D** is typical of reports that go to managers at the lowest level of responsibility shown in the organization chart—department managers. Similar reports are prepared for the managers of the Fabricating, Assembling, and Enameling Departments.
2. **Report C** is an example of reports that are sent to plant managers. It shows the costs of the Chicago plant that are controllable at the second level of responsibility. In addition, Report C shows summary data for each department

Illustration 20-18 Partial
organization chart

Report A
President sees summary
data of vice presidents.

Report B
Vice president sees
summary of controllable
costs in his/her functional
area.

Report C
Plant manager sees
summary of controllable
costs for each
department in the plant.

Report D
Department manager sees
controllable costs of
his/her department.

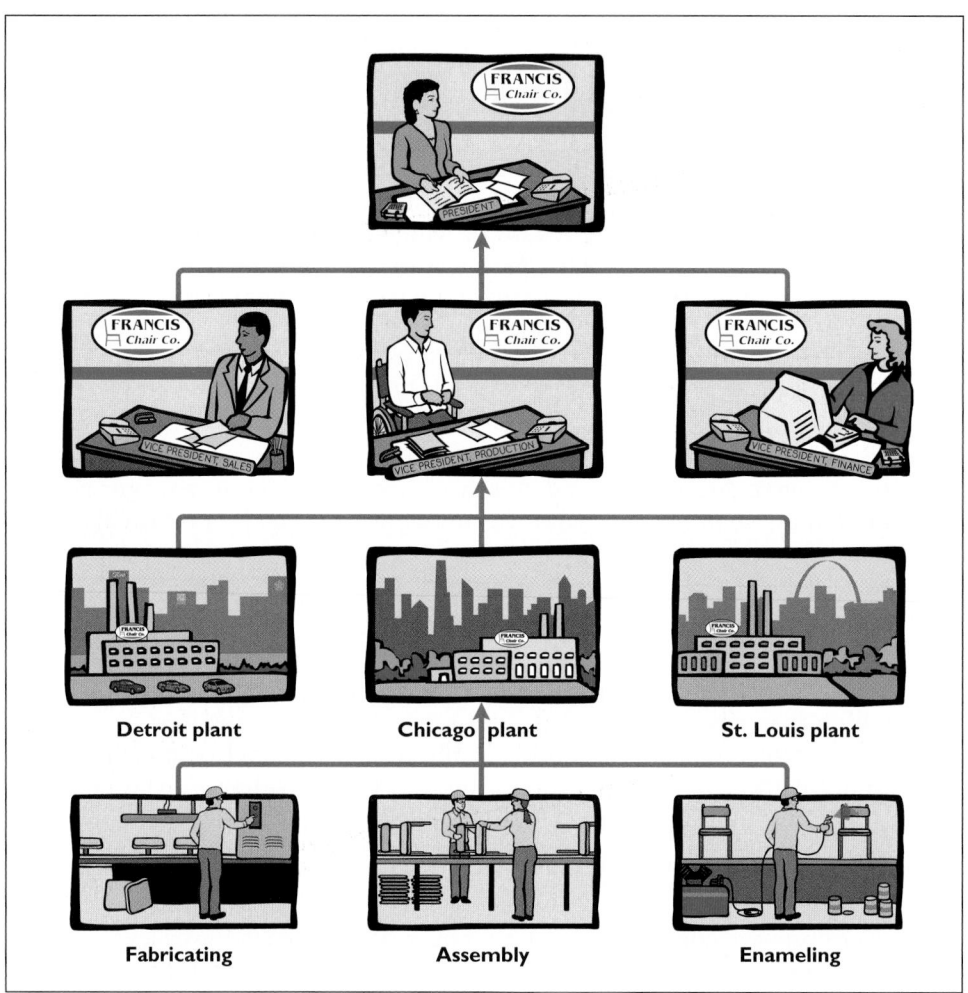

that is controlled by the plant manager. Similar reports are prepared for the Detroit and St. Louis plant managers.

3. **Report B** illustrates the reports at the third level of responsibility. It shows the controllable costs of the vice president of production and summary data on the three assembly plants for which this officer is responsible.

4. **Report A** is typical of the reports that go to the top level of responsibility—the president. This report shows the controllable costs and expenses of this office and summary data on the vice presidents that are accountable to the president.

A responsibility reporting system permits management by exception at each level of responsibility. And, each higher level of responsibility can obtain the detailed report for each lower level of responsibility. For example, the vice president of production in the Francis Chair Company may request the Chicago plant manager's report because this plant is $5,300 over budget.

This type of reporting system also permits comparative evaluations. In Illustration 20-19, the Chicago plant manager can easily rank the department managers' effectiveness in controlling manufacturing costs. Comparative rankings provide further incentive for a manager to control costs. For example, the Detroit plant manager will want to continue to be No. 1 in the report to the vice president of production. The Chicago plant manager will not want to remain No. 3 in future reporting periods.

Illustration 20-19
Responsibility reporting
system

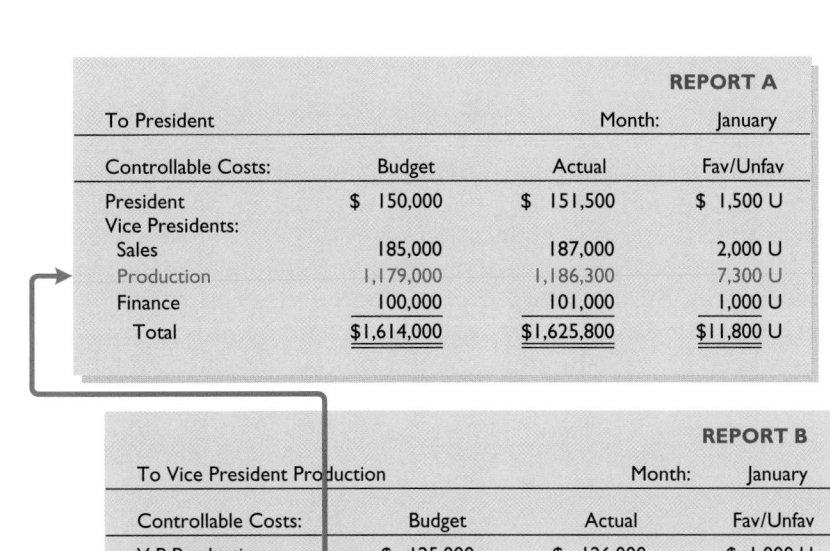

Report A
President sees summary
data of vice presidents.

Report B
Vice president sees
summary of controllable
costs in his/her functional
area.

Report C
Plant manager sees
summary of controllable
costs for each
department in the plant.

Report D
Department manager sees
controllable costs of
his/her department.

REPORT A

To President   Month: January

Controllable Costs:	Budget	Actual	Fav/Unfav
President	$ 150,000	$ 151,500	$ 1,500 U
Vice Presidents:			
Sales	185,000	187,000	2,000 U
Production	1,179,000	1,186,300	7,300 U
Finance	100,000	101,000	1,000 U
Total	$1,614,000	$1,625,800	$11,800 U

REPORT B

To Vice President Production   Month: January

Controllable Costs:	Budget	Actual	Fav/Unfav
V P Production	$ 125,000	$ 126,000	$ 1,000 U
Assembly Plants:			
Detroit	420,000	418,000	2,000 F
Chicago	304,000	309,300	5,300 U
St. Louis	330,000	333,000	3,000 U
Total	$1,179,000	$1,186,300	$ 7,300 U

REPORT C

To Plant Manager-Chicago   Month: January

Controllable Costs:	Budget	Actual	Fav/Unfav
Chicago Plant	$110,000	$113,000	$ 3,000 U
Departments:			
Fabricating	84,000	85,300	1,300 U
Enameling	62,000	64,000	2,000 U
Assembly	48,000	47,000	1,000 F
Total	$304,000	$309,300	$ 5,300 U

REPORT D

To Fabricating Department Manager   Month: January

Controllable Costs:	Budget	Actual	Fav/Unfav
Direct Materials	$ 20,000	$ 20,500	$ 500 U
Direct Labor	40,000	41,000	1,000 U
Overhead	24,000	23,800	200 F
Total	$ 84,000	$ 85,300	$ 1,300 U

Business Insight
MANAGEMENT PERSPECTIVE

In Chapter 15 we discussed enterprise resource planning (ERP) software packages that collect all information regarding the results of the supply chain. A recent innovation is to attach enterprise application systems (EAS) to ERP systems. EAS systems are budgeting and planning tools. By attaching an EAS system called Hyperion Pillar to its ERP system, **Fujitsu Computer Products of America** found that it could more easily compare its budgeted amounts to its actual results. It also reduced its typical time spent on planning and budgeting from 6 to 8 weeks down to 10 to 15 days. Finally, the new system has enabled the company to respond quickly to new developments. For example, in 1999, the software forewarned the company of a potential oversupply problem, and provided recommendations for changes in staffing and capital needs.

SOURCE: Russ Banham, "Better Budgets," *Journal of Accountancy* (February 2000), p. 37.

Types of Responsibility Centers

There are three basic types of responsibility centers: cost centers, profit centers, and investment centers. The type of center indicates the degree of responsibility the manager has for the performance of the center.

A **cost center** incurs costs (and expenses) but does not directly generate revenues. Managers of cost centers have the authority to incur costs. They are evaluated on their ability to control costs. **Cost centers are usually either production departments or service departments.** The former participate directly in making the product. The latter provide only support services. In a **Ford Motor Company** automobile plant, the welding, painting, and assembling departments are production departments; the maintenance, cafeteria, and human resources departments are service departments. All of them are cost centers.

A **profit center** incurs costs (and expenses) and also generates revenues. Managers of profit centers are judged on the profitability of their centers. Examples of profit centers include the individual departments of a retail store, such as clothing, furniture, and automotive products, and branch offices of banks.

Like a profit center, an **investment center** incurs costs (and expenses) and generates revenues. In addition, an investment center has control over the investment funds available for use. Managers of investment centers are evaluated on both the profitability of the center and the rate of return earned on the funds invested. Investment centers are often associated with subsidiary companies. For example, **General Mills's** product lines include cereals, helper dinner mixes, fruit snacks, popcorn, and yogurt. And, our Feature Story utility, **Duke Energy**, has operating divisions such as electric utility, energy, trading, and natural gas. The manager of the investment center (product line) is able to control or significantly influence investment decisions pertaining to such matters as plant expansion and entry into new market areas. These three types of responsibility centers are depicted in Illustration 20-20.

The evaluation of a manager's performance in each type of responsibility center is explained in the remainder of this chapter.

> **Helpful Hint** (1) Is the jewelry department of **Marshall Field's** department store a profit center or a cost center? (2) Is the props department of a movie studio a profit center or a cost center? Answers: (1) Profit center. (2) Cost center.

Illustration 20-20 Types
of responsibility centers

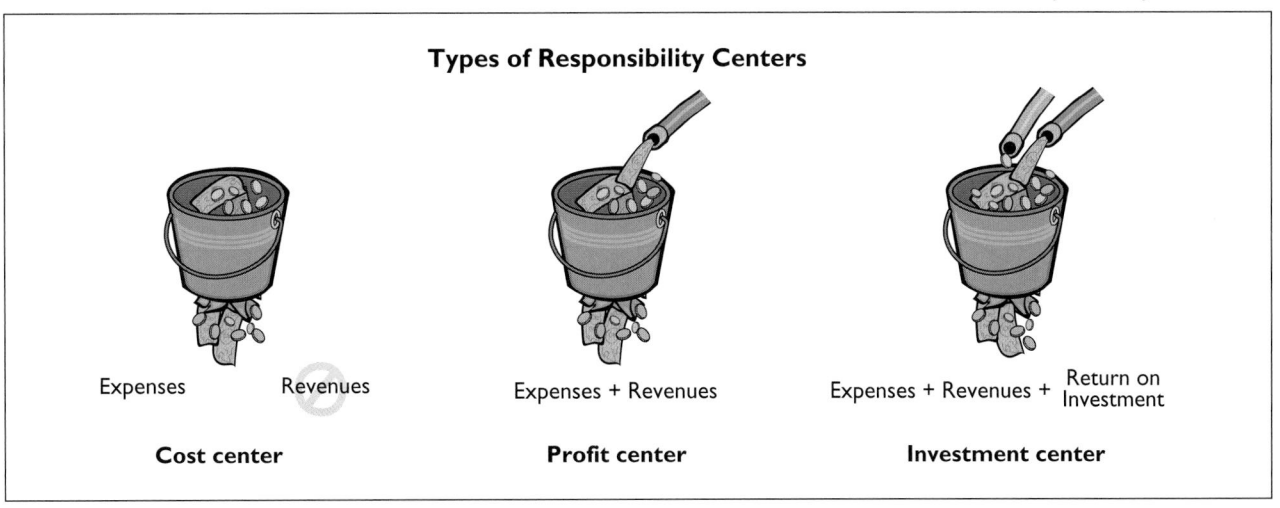

RESPONSIBILITY ACCOUNTING FOR COST CENTERS

The evaluation of a manager's performance for cost centers is based on his or her ability to meet budgeted goals for controllable costs. **Responsibility reports for cost centers compare actual controllable costs with flexible budget data.**

A responsibility report is illustrated in Illustration 20-21. The report is adapted from the budget report for Fox Manufacturing Company in Illustration 20-16 (on page 956). It assumes that the Finishing Department manager is able to control all manufacturing overhead costs except depreciation, property taxes, and his own monthly salary of $6,000. The remaining $4,000 of supervision costs are assumed to apply to other supervisory personnel within the Finishing Department, whose salaries are controllable by the manager.

STUDY OBJECTIVE
5
Indicate the features of responsibility reports for cost centers.

Illustration 20-21
Responsibility report for a cost center

			Difference
			Favorable F
Controllable Cost	**Budget**	**Actual**	**Unfavorable U**
Indirect materials	$13,500	$14,000	$ 500 U
Indirect labor	18,000	17,000	1,000 F
Utilities	4,500	4,600	100 U
Supervision	4,000	4,000	–0–
	$40,000	$39,600	$ 400 F

FOX MANUFACTURING COMPANY
Finishing Department
Responsibility Report
For the Month Ended January 31, 2005

Only controllable costs are included in the report, and no distinction is made between variable and fixed costs. The responsibility report continues the concept of management by exception. In this case, top management may request an explanation of the $1,000 favorable difference in indirect labor and/or the $500 unfavorable difference in indirect materials.

RESPONSIBILITY ACCOUNTING FOR PROFIT CENTERS

STUDY OBJECTIVE
6
Identify the content of responsibility reports for profit centers.

To evaluate the performance of a manager of a profit center, detailed information is needed about both controllable revenues and controllable costs. The operating revenues earned by a profit center, such as sales, are controllable by the manager. All variable costs (and expenses) incurred by the center are also controllable by the manager because they vary with sales. However, to determine the controllability of fixed costs, it is necessary to distinguish between direct and indirect fixed costs.

Direct and Indirect Fixed Costs

A profit center may have both direct and indirect fixed costs. **Direct fixed costs** are costs that relate specifically to one center and are incurred for the sole benefit of that center. Examples of such costs include the salaries established by the profit center manager for supervisory personnel and the cost of a timekeeping department for the center's employees. Since these fixed costs can be traced directly to a center, they are also called **traceable costs**. **Most direct fixed costs are controllable by the profit center manager.**

In contrast, **indirect fixed costs** pertain to a company's overall operating activities and are incurred for the benefit of more than one profit center. Indirect fixed costs are allocated to profit centers on some type of equitable basis. For example, property taxes on a building occupied by more than one center may be allocated on the basis of square feet of floor space used by each center. Or, the costs of a company's human resources department may be allocated to profit centers on the basis of the number of employees in each center. Because these fixed costs apply to more than one center, they are also called **common costs**. **Most indirect fixed costs are not controllable by the profit center manager.**

Responsibility Report

The responsibility report for a profit center shows budgeted and actual **controllable revenues and costs**. The report is prepared using the cost-volume-profit income statement explained in Chapter 18. In the report:

1. Controllable fixed costs are deducted from contribution margin.
2. The excess of contribution margin over controllable fixed costs is identified as **controllable margin**.
3. Noncontrollable fixed costs are not reported.

The responsibility report for the manager of the Marine Division, a profit center of Mantle Manufacturing Company, is shown in Illustration 20-22 (next page). For the year, the Marine Division also had $60,000 of indirect fixed costs that were not controllable by the profit center manager.

Controllable margin is considered to be the best measure of the manager's performance **in controlling revenues and costs**. This report shows that the manager's performance was below budgeted expectations by approximately 10 percent ($36,000 ÷ $360,000). Top management would likely investigate the causes of this unfavorable result. Note that the report does not show the Marine Division's noncontrollable fixed costs of $60,000. These costs would be included in a report on the profitability of the profit center.

Responsibility reports for profit centers may also be prepared monthly. In addition, they may include cumulative year-to-date results.

Helpful Hint Responsibility reports are helpful tools for evaluating managerial performance. Too much emphasis on profits or investments, however, can be harmful because it ignores other important performance issues such as quality and social responsibility.

MANTLE MANUFACTURING COMPANY
Marine Division
Responsibility Report
For the Year Ended January 31, 2005

	Budget	Actual	Difference Favorable F Unfavorable U
Sales	$1,200,000	$1,150,000	$ 50,000 U
Variable costs			
Cost of goods sold	500,000	490,000	10,000 F
Selling and administrative	160,000	156,000	4,000 F
Total	660,000	646,000	14,000 F
Contribution margin	540,000	504,000	36,000 U
Controllable fixed costs			
Cost of goods sold	100,000	100,000	–0–
Selling and administrative	80,000	80,000	–0–
Total	180,000	180,000	–0–
Controllable margin	$ 360,000	$ 324,000	$36,000 U

Illustration 20-22
Responsibility report for profit center

Helpful Hint Recognize that we are emphasizing financial measures of performance. These days companies are also making an effort to stress nonfinancial performance measures such as product quality, labor productivity, market growth, materials' yield, manufacturing flexibility, and technological capability.

DECISION TOOLKIT

Decision Checkpoints	Info Needed for Decision	Tool to Use for Decision	How to Evaluate Results
Have the individual managers been held accountable for the costs and revenues under their control?	Relevant costs and revenues, where the individual manager has authority to make day-to-day decisions about the items	Responsibility reports focused on cost centers, profit centers, and investment centers as appropriate	Compare budget to actual costs and revenues for controllable items.

BEFORE YOU GO ON . . .

▶ Review It

1. What conditions are essential for responsibility accounting?
2. What is involved in a responsibility reporting system?
3. What is the primary objective of a responsibility report for a cost center?
4. How does contribution margin differ from controllable margin in a responsibility report for a profit center?

▶ Do It

Midwest Division operates as a profit center. It reports the following actual results for the year: Sales $1,700,000, variable costs $800,000, controllable fixed costs $400,000, noncontrollable fixed costs $200,000. Annual budgeted amounts were $1,500,000, $700,000, $400,000, and $200,000, respectively. Prepare a responsibility report for the Midwest Division for December 31, 2005.

Action Plan

- Deduct variable costs from sales to show contribution margin.
- Deduct controllable fixed costs from the contribution margin to show controllable margin.
- Do not report noncontrollable fixed costs.

Solution

MIDWEST DIVISION
Responsibility Report
For the Year Ended December 31, 2005

	Budget	**Actual**	**Difference** **Favorable F** **Unfavorable U**
Sales	$1,500,000	$1,700,000	$200,000 F
Variable costs	700,000	800,000	100,000 U
Contribution margin	800,000	900,000	100,000 F
Controllable fixed costs	400,000	400,000	–0–
Controllable margin	$ 400,000	$ 500,000	$100,000 F

Related exercise material: BE20-7 and E20-9.

 THE NAVIGATOR

RESPONSIBILITY ACCOUNTING FOR INVESTMENT CENTERS

As explained earlier, an investment center manager can control or significantly influence the investment funds available for use. Thus, the primary basis for evaluating the performance of a manager of an investment center is **return on investment (ROI)**. The return on investment is considered to be superior to any other performance measurement because it shows the **effectiveness of the manager in utilizing the assets at his or her disposal**.

Return on Investment (ROI)

The formula for computing ROI for an investment center, together with assumed illustrative data, is shown in Illustration 20-23. Both factors in the formula are controllable by the investment center manager. Operating assets consist of current assets and plant assets used in operations by the center and controlled by the manager. Nonoperating assets such as idle plant assets and land held for future use are excluded. Average operating assets are usually based on the cost or book value of the assets at the beginning and end of the year.

Illustration 20-23
ROI formula

Controllable Margin	÷	**Average** **Operating** **Assets**	=	**Return on** **Investment** **(ROI)**
$1,000,000	÷	$5,000,000	=	20%

Responsibility Report

The scope of the investment center manager's responsibility significantly affects the content of the performance report. Since an investment center is an independent entity for operating purposes, **all fixed costs are controllable by its manager**. For example, the manager is responsible for depreciation on investment center assets. Therefore, more fixed costs are identified as controllable in the performance report for an investment center manager than in a performance report for a profit center manager. The report also shows budgeted and actual ROI below controllable margin.

To illustrate this responsibility report, we will now assume that the Marine Division of Mantle Manufacturing Company is an investment center. It has budgeted and actual average operating assets of $2,000,000. We now will assume that the manager can control the $60,000 of fixed costs that were not controllable when the division was a profit center. The responsibility report is shown in Illustration 20-24.

Illustration 20-24
Responsibility report for investment center

MANTLE MANUFACTURING COMPANY
Marine Division
Responsibility Report
For the Year Ended December 31, 2005

	Budget	Actual	Difference Favorable F Unfavorable U
Sales	$1,200,000	$1,150,000	$50,000 U
Variable costs			
Cost of goods sold	500,000	490,000	10,000 F
Selling and administrative	160,000	156,000	4,000 F
Total	660,000	646,000	14,000 F
Contribution margin	540,000	504,000	36,000 U
Controllable fixed costs			
Cost of goods sold	100,000	100,000	–0–
Selling and administrative	80,000	80,000	–0–
Other fixed costs	60,000	60,000	–0–
Total	240,000	240,000	–0–
Controllable margin	$ 300,000	$ 264,000	$36,000 U
Return on investment	15% (a)	13.2% (b)	1.8% U (c)

$$(a)\ \frac{\$300,000}{\$2,000,000} \qquad (b)\ \frac{\$264,000}{\$2,000,000} \qquad (c)\ \frac{\$36,000}{\$2,000,000}$$

The report shows that the manager's performance based on ROI was 12 percent (1.8% ÷ 15%) below budget expectations. Top management would likely want an explanation of the reasons for this unfavorable result.

Judgmental Factors in ROI

The return on investment approach includes two judgmental factors:

1. **Valuation of operating assets.** Operating assets may be valued at acquisition cost, book value, appraised value, or market value. The first two bases are readily available from the accounting records.
2. **Margin (income) measure.** This measure may be controllable margin, income from operations, or net income.

Each of the alternative values for operating assets can provide a reliable basis for evaluating a manager's performance as long as it is consistently applied between reporting periods. However, the use of income measures other than controllable margin will not result in a valid basis for evaluating the performance of an investment center manager.[1]

Improving ROI

The manager of an investment center can improve ROI in two ways: (1) increase controllable margin, and/or (2) reduce average operating assets. To illustrate, we will use the following assumed data for the Marine Division of Mantle Manufacturing.

Illustration 20-25
Assumed data for Marine
Division

Sales	$2,000,000
Variable cost	1,100,000
Contribution margin (45%)	900,000
Controllable fixed costs	300,000
Controllable margin (a)	$ 600,000
Average operating assets (b)	$5,000,000
Return on investment (a) ÷ (b)	12%

INCREASING CONTROLLABLE MARGIN. Controllable margin can be increased by increasing sales or by reducing variable and controllable fixed costs as follows.

1. **Increase sales 10 percent.** Sales will increase $200,000 ($2,000,000 × .10). Assuming no change in the contribution margin percentage of 45 percent, contribution margin will increase $90,000 ($200,000 × .45). Controllable margin will increase by the same amount because controllable fixed costs will not change. Thus, controllable margin becomes $690,000 ($600,000 + $90,000). The new ROI is 13.8 percent, computed as follows.

Illustration 20-26 ROI
computation—increase in
sales

$$ROI = \frac{\text{Controllable margin}}{\text{Average operating assets}} = \frac{\$690,000}{\$5,000,000} = 13.8\%$$

An increase in sales benefits both the investment center and the company if it results in new business. It would not benefit the company if the increase was achieved at the expense of other investment centers.

2. **Decrease variable and fixed costs 10 percent.** Total costs will decrease $140,000 [($1,100,000 + $300,000) × .10]. This reduction will result in a corresponding increase in controllable margin. Thus, controllable margin becomes $740,000 ($600,000 + $140,000). The new ROI is 14.8 percent, computed as follows.

Illustration 20-27 ROI
computation—decrease in
costs

$$ROI = \frac{\text{Controllable margin}}{\text{Average operating assets}} = \frac{\$740,000}{\$5,000,000} = 14.8\%$$

This course of action is clearly beneficial when waste and inefficiencies are eliminated. But, a reduction in vital costs such as required maintenance and inspections is not likely to be acceptable to top management.

---

[1]Although the ROI approach is often used in evaluating investment performance, it has some disadvantages. The appendix to this chapter illustrates a second method for evaluation referred to as the residual income approach.

REDUCING AVERAGE OPERATING ASSETS. Assume that average operating assets are reduced 10 percent or $500,000 ($5,000,000 × .10). Average operating assets become $4,500,000 ($5,000,000 − $500,000). Since controllable margin remains unchanged at $600,000, the new ROI is 13.3 percent, computed as follows.

$$ROI = \frac{\text{Controllable margin}}{\text{Average operating assets}} = \frac{\$600,000}{\$4,500,000} = 13.3\%$$

Illustration 20-28 ROI computation—decrease in operating assets

Reductions in operating assets may or may not be prudent. It is beneficial to eliminate overinvestment in inventories and to dispose of excessive plant assets. However, it is unwise to reduce inventories below expected needs or to dispose of essential plant assets.

DECISION TOOLKIT

Decision Checkpoints	Info Needed for Decision	Tool to Use for Decision	How to Evaluate Results
Has the investment center performed up to expectations?	Controllable margin (contribution margin minus controllable fixed costs), and average investment center operating assets	Return on investment	Compare actual ROI to expected ROI.

PRINCIPLES OF PERFORMANCE EVALUATION

Performance evaluation is at the center of responsibility accounting. **Performance evaluation** is a management function that compares actual results with budget goals. Performance evaluation involves both behavioral and reporting principles.

Behavioral Principles

The human factor is critical in evaluating performance. Behavioral principles include the following.

1. **Managers of responsibility centers should have direct input into the process of establishing budget goals of their area of responsibility.** Without such input, managers may view the goals as unrealistic or arbitrarily set by top management. Such views adversely affect the managers' motivation to meet the targeted objectives.

2. **The evaluation of performance should be based entirely on matters that are controllable by the manager being evaluated.** Criticism of a manager on matters outside his or her control reduces the effectiveness of the evaluation process. It leads to negative reactions by a manager and to doubts about the fairness of the company's evaluation policies.

3. **Top management should support the evaluation process.** As explained earlier, the evaluation process begins at the lowest level of responsibility and extends upward to the highest level of management. Managers quickly lose

faith in the process when top management ignores, overrules, or bypasses established procedures for evaluating a manager's performance.

4. **The evaluation process must allow managers to respond to their evaluations.** Evaluation is not a one-way street. Managers should have the opportunity to defend their performance. Evaluation without feedback is both impersonal and ineffective.

5. **The evaluation should identify both good and poor performance.** Praise for good performance is a powerful motivating factor for a manager. This is especially true when a manager's compensation includes rewards for meeting budget goals.

Reporting Principles of Performance Evaluation

Performance evaluation under responsibility accounting should be based on certain reporting principles. These principles pertain primarily to the internal reports that provide the basis for evaluating performance. Performance reports should:

1. Contain only data that are controllable by the manager of the responsibility center.
2. Provide accurate and reliable budget data to measure performance.
3. Highlight significant differences between actual results and budget goals.
4. Be tailor-made for the intended evaluation.
5. Be prepared at reasonable intervals.

BEFORE YOU GO ON . . .

▶ **Review It**

1. What is the formula for computing return on investment (ROI)?
2. Identify three actions a manager may take to improve ROI.

☑ THE NAVIGATOR

Using the Decision Toolkit

The manufacturing overhead budget for Reebles Company contains the following items.

Variable expenses	
Indirect materials	$25,000
Indirect labor	12,000
Maintenance expenses	10,000
Manufacturing supplies	6,000
Total variable	$53,000
Fixed expenses	
Supervision	$17,000
Inspection costs	1,000
Insurance expenses	2,000
Depreciation	15,000
Total fixed	$35,000

The budget was based on an estimated 2,000 units being produced. During November, 1,500 units were produced, and the following costs incurred.

Variable expenses	
Indirect materials	$25,200
Indirect labor	13,500
Maintenance expenses	8,200
Manufacturing supplies	5,100
Total variable	$52,000
Fixed expenses	
Supervision	$19,300
Inspection costs	1,200
Insurance expenses	2,200
Depreciation	14,700
Total fixed	$37,400

Instructions

(a) Determine which items would be controllable by Ed Lopat, the production manager. (Assume "supervision" excludes Lopat's own salary.)

(b) How much should have been spent during the month for the manufacture of the 1,500 units?

(c) Prepare a flexible manufacturing overhead budget report for Mr. Lopat.

(d) Prepare a responsibility report. Include only the costs that would have been controllable by Mr. Lopat. In an attached memo, describe clearly for Mr. Lopat the areas in which his performance needs to be improved.

Solution

(a) Ed Lopat should be able to control all the variable expenses and the fixed expenses of supervision and inspection. Insurance and depreciation ordinarily are not the responsibility of the department manager.

(b) The total variable cost per unit is $26.50 ($53,000 ÷ 2,000). The total budgeted cost during the month to manufacture 1,500 units is variable costs $39,750 (1,500 × $26.50) plus fixed costs ($35,000), for a total of $74,750 ($39,750 + $35,000).

(c)

REEBLES COMPANY
Production Department
Manufacturing Overhead Budget Report (Flexible)
For the Month Ended November 30, 2005

	Budget at 1,500 units	Actual at 1,500 units	Difference Favorable F Unfavorable U
Variable costs			
Indirect materials	$18,750	$25,200	$ 6,450 U
Indirect labor	9,000	13,500	4,500 U
Maintenance	7,500	8,200	700 U
Manufacturing supplies	4,500	5,100	600 U
Total variable	39,750	52,000	12,250 U
Fixed costs			
Supervision	17,000	19,300	2,300 U
Inspection	1,000	1,200	200 U
Insurance	2,000	2,200	200 U
Depreciation	15,000	14,700	300 F
Total fixed	35,000	37,400	2,400 U
Total costs	$74,750	$89,400	$14,650 U

(d) Because a production department is a cost center, the responsibility report should include only the costs that are controllable by the production manager. In this type of report, no distinction is made between variable and fixed costs. Budget data in the report should be based on the units actually produced.

REEBLES COMPANY
Production Department
Manufacturing Overhead Responsibility Report
For the Month Ended November 30, 2005

Controllable Cost	Budget	Actual	Difference Favorable F Unfavorable U
Indirect materials	$18,750	$25,200	$ 6,450 U
Indirect labor	9,000	13,500	4,500 U
Maintenance	7,500	8,200	700 U
Manufacturing supplies	4,500	5,100	600 U
Supervision	17,000	19,300	2,300 U
Inspection	1,000	1,200	200 U
Total	$57,750	$72,500	$14,750 U

To: Mr. Ed Lopat, Production Manager

From: _____, Vice-President of Production

Subject: Performance Evaluation for the Month of November

Your performance in controlling costs that are your responsibility was very disappointing in the month of November. As indicated in the accompanying responsibility report, total costs were $14,750 over budget. On a percentage basis, costs were 26% over budget. As you can see, actual costs were over budget for every cost item. In three instances, costs were significantly over budget (indirect materials 34%, indirect labor 50%, and supervision 14%).

Ed, it is imperative that you get costs under control in your department as soon as possible.

I think we need to talk about ways to implement more effective cost control measures. I would like to meet with you in my office at 9 a.m. on Wednesday to discuss possible alternatives.

THE NAVIGATOR

Summary of Study Objectives

1 *Describe the concept of budgetary control.* Budgetary control consists of (a) preparing periodic budget reports that compare actual results with planned objectives, (b) analyzing the differences to determine their causes, (c) taking appropriate corrective action, and (d) modifying future plans, if necessary.

2 *Evaluate the usefulness of static budget reports.* Static budget reports are useful in evaluating the progress toward planned sales and profit goals. They are also appropriate in assessing a manager's effectiveness in controlling fixed costs and expenses when (a) actual activity closely approximates the master budget activity level, and/or (b) the behavior of the costs in response to changes in activity is fixed.

3 *Explain the development of flexible budgets and the usefulness of flexible budget reports.* To develop the flexible budget it is necessary to:
(a) Identify the activity index and the relevant range of activity.
(b) Identify the variable costs, and determine the budgeted variable cost per unit of activity for each cost.
(c) Identify the fixed costs, and determine the budgeted amount for each cost.
(d) Prepare the budget for selected increments of activity within the relevant range.

Flexible budget reports permit an evaluation of a manager's performance in controlling production and costs.

4 *Describe the concept of responsibility accounting.* Responsibility accounting involves accumulating and reporting revenues and costs on the basis of the individual manager who has the authority to make the day-to-day decisions about the items. The evaluation of a manager's performance is based on the matters directly under the manager's control. In responsibility accounting, it is necessary to distinguish between controllable and noncontrollable fixed costs and to identify three types of responsibility centers: cost, profit, and investment.

5 *Indicate the features of responsibility reports for cost centers.* Responsibility reports for cost centers compare actual costs with flexible budget data. The reports show only controllable costs, and no distinction is made between variable and fixed costs.

6 *Identify the content of responsibility reports for profit centers.* Responsibility reports show contribution margin, controllable fixed costs, and controllable margin for each profit center.

7 *Explain the basis and formula used in evaluating performance in investment centers.* The primary basis for evaluating performance in investment centers is return on investment (ROI). The formula for computing ROI for investment centers is: Controllable margin ÷ Average operating assets.

☑ THE NAVIGATOR

DECISION TOOLKIT——A SUMMARY

Decision Checkpoints	Info Needed for Decision	Tool to Use for Decision	How to Evaluate Results
Are the increased costs resulting from increased production reasonable?	Variable costs projected at different levels of production	Flexible budget	After taking into account different production levels, results are favorable if expenses are less than budgeted amounts.
Have the individual managers been held accountable for the costs and revenues under their control?	Relevant costs and revenues, where the individual manager has authority to make day-to-day decisions about the items	Responsibility reports focused on cost centers, profit centers, and investment centers as appropriate	Compare budget to actual costs and revenues for controllable items.
Has the investment center performed up to expectations?	Controllable margin (contribution margin minus controllable fixed costs), and average investment center operating assets	Return on investment	Compare actual ROI to expected ROI.

APPENDIX
RESIDUAL INCOME—ANOTHER PERFORMANCE MEASUREMENT

Although most companies use ROI in evaluating their investment performance, ROI has a significant disadvantage. To illustrate, let's look at the Marine Division of Mantle Manufacturing Company. It has an ROI of 20 percent computed as follows.

STUDY OBJECTIVE 8
Explain the difference between ROI and residual income.

Controllable Margin	÷	Average Operating Assets	=	Return on Investment (ROI)
$1,000,000	÷	$5,000,000	=	20%

Illustration 20A-1 ROI formula

The Marine Division is considering producing a new product, a GPS satellite tracker (hereafter referred to as Tracker), for its boats. To produce Tracker, operating assets will have to increase $2,000,000. Tracker is expected to generate an additional $260,000 of controllable margin. A comparison of how Tracker will affect ROI is shown in Illustration 20A-2.

Illustration 20A-2
ROI comparison

	Without Tracker	Tracker	With Tracker
Controllable margin (a)	$1,000,000	$ 260,000	$1,260,000
Average operating assets (b)	$5,000,000	$2,000,000	$7,000,000
Return on investment [(a) ÷ (b)]	20%	13%	18%

The investment in Tracker reduces ROI from 20 percent to 18 percent.

Let's suppose that you are the manager of the Marine Division and must make the decision to produce or not produce Tracker. If you were evaluated using ROI, you probably would not produce Tracker because your ROI would drop from 20 percent to 18 percent. The problem with this ROI analysis is that it ignores an important variable, the minimum rate of return on a company's operating assets. The **minimum rate of return** is the rate at which the Marine Division can cover its costs and earn a profit. Assuming that the Marine Division has a minimum rate of return of 10 percent, it should invest in Tracker because its ROI of 13 percent is greater than 10 percent.

Residual Income Compared to ROI

To evaluate performance using the minimum rate of return, companies use the residual income approach. **Residual income** is the income that remains after subtracting from the controllable margin the minimum rate of return on a company's average operating assets. The residual income for Tracker would be computed as follows.

Illustration 20A-3
Residual income formula

Controllable Margin	−	(Minimum Rate of Return × Average Operating Assets)	=	Residual Income
$260,000	−	(10% × $2,000,000)	=	$60,000

As shown, the residual income related to the Tracker investment is $60,000. Illustration 20A-4 indicates how residual income changes as the additional investment is made.

Illustration 20A-4
Residual income comparison

	Without Tracker	Tracker	With Tracker
Controllable margin (a)	$1,000,000	$260,000	$1,260,000
Average operating assets × 10% (b)	500,000	200,000	700,000
Residual income [(a) − (b)]	$ 500,000	$ 60,000	$ 560,000

This example illustrates how performance evaluation based on ROI can be misleading and can even cause managers to reject projects that would actually increase income for the company. As a result, many companies such as **Coca-Cola**, **Briggs and Stratton**, **Eli Lilly**, and **Siemens AG** use residual income (or a variant often referred to as economic value added) to evaluate investment alternatives and measure company performance.

Residual Income Weakness

The goal of residual income is to maximize the total amount of residual income. This goal, however, ignores the fact that one division might use substantially fewer assets to attain the same level of residual income as another division. For example, we know that to produce Tracker, the Marine Division of Mantle Manufacturing used $2,000,000 of average operating assets to generate $260,000 of controllable margin. Now let's say a different division produced a product called SeaDog, which used $4,000,000 to generate $460,000 of controllable margin, as shown in Illustration 20A-5.

	Tracker	SeaDog
Controllable margin (a)	$260,000	$460,000
Average operating assets × 10% (b)	200,000	400,000
Residual income [(a) − (b)]	$ 60,000	$ 60,000

Illustration 20A-5
Comparison of two products

If the performance of these two investments were evaluated using residual income, they would be considered equal: Both products have the same total residual income. This ignores, however, the fact that SeaDog required **twice** as many operating assets to achieve the same level of residual income.

Summary of Study Objective for Appendix

8 *Explain the difference between ROI and residual income.* ROI is controllable margin divided by average operating assets. Residual income is the income that remains after subtracting the minimum rate of return on a company's average operating assets. ROI sometimes provides misleading results because profitable investments are often rejected when the investment reduces ROI but increases overall profitability.

Glossary

Budgetary control The use of budgets to control operations. (p. 947)

Controllable costs Costs that a manager has the authority to incur within a given period of time. (p. 959)

Controllable margin Contribution margin less controllable fixed costs. (p. 964)

Cost center A responsibility center that incurs costs but does not directly generate revenues. (p. 962)

Decentralization Control of operations is delegated to many managers throughout the organization. (p. 958)

Direct fixed costs Costs that relate specifically to a responsibility center and are incurred for the sole benefit of the center. (p. 964)

Flexible budget A projection of budget data for various levels of activity. (p. 950)

Indirect fixed costs Costs that are incurred for the benefit of more than one profit center. (p. 964)

Investment center A responsibility center that incurs costs, generates revenues, and has control over the investment funds available for use. (p. 962)

Management by exception The review of budget reports by top management focused entirely or primarily on differences between actual results and planned objectives. (p. 956)

Noncontrollable costs Costs incurred indirectly and allocated to a responsibility center that are not controllable at that level. (p. 959)

Profit center A responsibility center that incurs costs and also generates revenues. (p. 962)

Residual income The income that remains after subtracting from the controllable margin the minimum rate of return on a company's operating assets. (p. 974)

Responsibility accounting A part of management accounting that involves accumulating and reporting revenues and costs on the basis of the manager who has the authority to make the day-to-day decisions about the items. (p. 957)

Responsibility reporting system The preparation of reports for each level of responsibility in the company's organization chart. (p. 959)

Return on investment (ROI) A measure of management's effectiveness in utilizing assets at its disposal in an investment center. (p. 966)

Segment An area of responsibility in decentralized operations. (p. 958)

Static budget A projection of budget data at one level of activity. (p. 948)

Demonstration Problem

Glenda Company uses a flexible budget for manufacturing overhead based on direct labor hours. For 2005 the master overhead budget for the Packaging Department at normal capacity of 300,000 direct labor hours was as follows.

Variable Costs		Fixed Costs	
Indirect labor	$360,000	Supervision	$ 60,000
Supplies and lubricants	150,000	Depreciation	24,000
Maintenance	210,000	Property taxes	18,000
Utilities	120,000	Insurance	12,000
	$840,000		$114,000

During July, 24,000 direct labor hours were worked. The company incurred the following variable costs in July: indirect labor $30,200, supplies and lubricants $11,600, maintenance $17,500, and utilities $9,200. Actual fixed overhead costs were the same as monthly budgeted fixed costs.

Instructions

Prepare a flexible budget report for the Packaging Department for July.

Action Plan

- Use budget data for actual direct labor hours worked.

- Classify each cost as variable or fixed.

- Determine the difference between budgeted and actual costs.

- Identify the difference as favorable or unfavorable.

- Determine the difference in total variable costs, total fixed costs, and total costs.

Solution to Demonstration Problem

GLENDA COMPANY
Manufacturing Overhead Budget Report (Flexible)
Packaging Department
For the Month Ended July 31, 2005

	Budget 24,000 DLH	Actual Costs 24,000 DLH	Difference Favorable F Unfavorable U
Direct labor hours (DLH)	**24,000 DLH**	**24,000 DLH**	
Variable costs			
Indirect labor	$28,800	$30,200	$1,400 U
Supplies and lubricants	12,000	11,600	400 F
Maintenance	16,800	17,500	700 U
Utilities	9,600	9,200	400 F
Total variable	67,200	68,500	1,300 U

	Budget	Actual Costs	Difference Favorable F Unfavorable U
Direct labor hours (DLH)	**24,000 DLH**	**24,000 DLH**	
Fixed costs			
Supervision	$ 5,000	$ 5,000	–0–
Depreciation	2,000	2,000	–0–
Property taxes	1,500	1,500	–0–
Insurance	1,000	1,000	–0–
Total fixed	9,500	9,500	–0–
Total costs	$76,700	$78,000	$1,300 U

Note: All asterisked Questions, Exercises, and Problems relate to the material contained in the appendix to the chapter.

Self-Study Questions

Self-Study/Self-Test

Answers are at the end of the chapter.

(SO 1) **1.** Budgetary control involves *all but one* of the following:
(a) modifying future plans.
(b) analyzing differences.
(c) using static budgets.
(d) determining differences between actual and planned results.

(SO 2) **2.** A static budget is useful in controlling costs when cost behavior is:
(a) mixed.   (c) variable.
(b) fixed.   (d) linear.

(SO 3) **3.** At zero direct labor hours in a flexible budget graph, the total budgeted cost line intersects the vertical axis at $30,000. At 10,000 direct labor hours, a horizontal line drawn from the total budgeted cost line intersects the vertical axis at $90,000. Fixed and variable costs may be expressed as:
(a) $30,000 fixed plus $6 per direct labor hour variable.
(b) $30,000 fixed plus $9 per direct labor hour variable.
(c) $60,000 fixed plus $3 per direct labor hour variable.
(d) $60,000 fixed plus $6 per direct labor hour variable.

(SO 3) **4.** At 9,000 direct labor hours, the flexible budget for indirect materials is $27,000. If $28,000 of indirect materials costs are incurred at 9,200 direct labor hours, the flexible budget report should show the following difference for indirect materials:
(a) $1,000 unfavorable.
(b) $1,000 favorable.
(c) $400 favorable.
(d) $400 unfavorable.

(SO 4) **5.** Under responsibility accounting, the evaluation of a manager's performance is based on matters that the manager:
(a) directly controls.
(b) directly and indirectly controls.
(c) indirectly controls.
(d) has shared responsibility for with another manager.

(SO 4) **6.** Responsibility centers include:
(a) cost centers.
(b) profit centers.
(c) investment centers.
(d) all of the above.

(SO 5) **7.** Responsibility reports for cost centers:
(a) distinguish between fixed and variable costs.
(b) use static budget data.
(c) include both controllable and noncontrollable costs.
(d) include only controllable costs.

(SO 6) **8.** In a responsibility report for a profit center, controllable fixed costs are deducted from contribution margin to show:
(a) profit center margin.
(b) controllable margin.
(c) net income.
(d) income from operations.

(SO 7) **9.** In the formula for return on investment (ROI), the factors for controllable margin and operating assets are, respectively:
(a) controllable margin percentage and total operating assets.
(b) controllable margin dollars and average operating assets.
(c) controllable margin dollars and total assets.
(d) controllable margin percentage and average operating assets.

(SO 7) **10.** A manager of an investment center can improve ROI by:
  (a) increasing average operating assets.
  (b) reducing sales.
  (c) increasing variable costs.
  (d) reducing variable and/or controllable fixed costs.

(SO 8) *11. In the formula for residual income, the factors for computing residual income are:

  (a) contribution margin, controllable margin, and average total assets.
  (b) controllable margin, average total assets, and ROI.
  (c) controllable margin, average total assets, and minimum rate of return.
  (d) controllable margin, ROI, and minimum rate of return.

Questions

1. (a) What is budgetary control?
   (b) Tony Crespino is describing budgetary control. What steps should be included in Tony's description?

2. The following purposes are part of a budgetary reporting system: (a) Determine efficient use of materials. (b) Control overhead costs. (c) Determine whether income objectives are being met. For each purpose, indicate the name of the report, the frequency of the report, and the primary recipient(s) of the report.

3. How may a budget report for the second quarter differ from a budget report for the first quarter?

4. Don Cox questions the usefulness of a master sales budget in evaluating sales performance. Is there justification for Don's concern? Explain.

5. Under what circumstances may a static budget be an appropriate basis for evaluating a manager's effectiveness in controlling costs?

6. "A flexible budget is really a series of static budgets." Is this true? Why?

7. The static manufacturing overhead budget based on 40,000 direct labor hours shows budgeted indirect labor costs of $56,000. During March, the department incurs $66,000 of indirect labor while working 45,000 direct labor hours. Is this a favorable or unfavorable performance? Why?

8. A static overhead budget based on 40,000 direct labor hours shows Factory Insurance $6,500 as a fixed cost. At the 50,000 direct labor hours worked in March, factory insurance costs were $6,200. Is this a favorable or unfavorable performance? Why?

9. Kate Coulter is confused about how a flexible budget is prepared. Identify the steps for Kate.

10. Alou Company has prepared a graph of flexible budget data. At zero direct labor hours, the total budgeted cost line intersects the vertical axis at $25,000. At 10,000 direct labor hours, the line drawn from the total budgeted cost line intersects the vertical axis at $85,000. How may the fixed and variable costs be expressed?

11. The flexible budget formula is fixed costs $40,000 plus variable costs of $2 per direct labor hour. What is the total budgeted cost at (a) 9,000 hours and (b) 12,345 hours?

12. What is management by exception? What criteria may be used in identifying exceptions?

13. What is responsibility accounting? Explain the purpose of responsibility accounting.

14. Ann Wilkins is studying for an accounting examination. Describe for Ann what conditions are necessary for responsibility accounting to be used effectively.

15. Distinguish between controllable and noncontrollable costs.

16. How do responsibility reports differ from budget reports?

17. What is the relationship, if any, between a responsibility reporting system and a company's organization chart?

18. Distinguish among the three types of responsibility centers.

19. (a) What costs are included in a performance report for a cost center? (b) In the report, are variable and fixed costs identified?

20. How do direct fixed costs differ from indirect fixed costs? Are both types of fixed costs controllable?

21. Lori Quan is confused about controllable margin reported in an income statement for a profit center. How is this margin computed, and what is its primary purpose?

22. What is the primary basis for evaluating the performance of the manager of an investment center? Indicate the formula for this basis.

23. Explain the ways that ROI can be improved.

24. Indicate two behavioral principles that pertain to (a) the manager being evaluated and (b) top management.

*25. What is a major disadvantage of using ROI to evaluate investment and company performance?

*26. What is residual income, and what is one of its major weaknesses?

Brief Exercises

BE20-1 For the quarter ended March 31, 2005, Russo Company accumulates the following sales data for its product, Garden-Tools: $315,000 budget; $302,000 actual. Prepare a static budget report for the quarter.

Prepare static budget report. (SO 2)

BE20-2 Data for Russo Company are given in BE20-1. In the second quarter, budgeted sales were $380,000, and actual sales were $389,000. Prepare a static budget report for the second quarter and for the year to date.

Prepare static budget report for 2 quarters. (SO 2)

BE20-3 In Maltz Company, direct labor is $20 per hour. The company expects to operate at 10,000 direct labor hours each month. In January 2005, direct labor totaling $207,000 is incurred in working 10,400 hours. Prepare (a) a static budget report and (b) a flexible budget report. Evaluate the usefulness of each report.

Show usefulness of flexible budgets in evaluating performance. (SO 3)

BE20-4 Gomez Company expects to produce 1,200,000 units of Product XX in 2005. Monthly production is expected to range from 80,000 to 120,000 units. Budgeted variable manufacturing costs per unit are: direct materials $5, direct labor $6, and overhead $9. Prepare a flexible manufacturing budget for the relevant range value using 20,000 unit increments.

Prepare a flexible budget for variable costs. (SO 3)

BE20-5 Data for Gomez Company are given in BE20-4. In March 2005, the company incurs the following costs in producing 100,000 units: direct materials $520,000, direct labor $590,000, and variable overhead $915,000. Prepare a flexible budget report for March. Were costs controlled?

Prepare flexible budget report. (SO 3)

BE20-6 In the Assembly Department of Rado Company, budgeted and actual manufacturing overhead costs for the month of April 2005 were as follows.

Prepare a responsibility report for a cost center. (SO 5)

	Budget	**Actual**
Indirect materials	$15,000	$14,500
Indirect labor	20,000	20,800
Utilities	10,000	10,750
Supervision	5,000	5,000

All costs are controllable by the department manager. Prepare a responsibility report for April for the cost center.

BE20-7 Savage Manufacturing Company accumulates the following summary data for the year ending December 31, 2005, for its Water Division which it operates as a profit center: sales—$2,000,000 budget, $2,080,000 actual; variable costs—$1,000,000 budget, $1,050,000 actual; and controllable fixed costs—$300,000 budget, $307,000 actual. Prepare a responsibility report for the Water Division.

Prepare a responsibility report for a profit center. (SO 6)

BE20-8 For the year ending December 31, 2005, Stoker Company accumulates the following data for the Plastics Division which it operates as an investment center: contribution margin—$700,000 budget, $715,000 actual; controllable fixed costs—$300,000 budget, $295,000 actual. Average operating assets for the year were $1,600,000. Prepare a responsibility report for the Plastics Division beginning with contribution margin.

Prepare a responsibility report for an investment center. (SO 7)

BE20-9 For its three investment centers, Chow Company accumulates the following data.

Compute return on investment using the ROI formula. (SO 7)

	I	**II**	**III**
Sales	$2,000,000	$3,000,000	$ 4,000,000
Controllable margin	1,200,000	2,400,000	3,200,000
Average operating assets	6,000,000	8,000,000	10,000,000

Compute the return on investment (ROI) for each center.

BE20-10 Data for the investment centers for Chow Company are given in BE20-9. The centers expect the following changes in the next year: (I) increase sales 10%; (II) decrease costs $200,000; (III) decrease average operating assets $400,000. Compute the expected return on investment (ROI) for each center. Assume center I has a contribution margin percentage of 80%.

Compute return on investment under changed conditions. (SO 7)

Compute ROI and residual income.
(SO 8)

*BE20-11 Napstem, Inc. reports the following financial information.

Average operating assets	$2,400,000
Controllable margin	$ 600,000
Minimum rate of return	9%

Compute the return on investment and the residual income.

Compute ROI and residual income.
(SO 8)

*BE20-12 Presented below is information related to the Pulp Division of Wood Products, Inc.

Contribution margin	$1,000,000
Controllable margin	$ 800,000
Average operating assets	$4,000,000
Minimum rate of return	15%

Compute the Pulp Division's return on investment and residual income.

Exercises

Prepare flexible manufacturing overhead budget.
(SO 3)

E20-1 Voss Company uses a flexible budget for manufacturing overhead based on direct labor hours. Variable manufacturing overhead costs per direct labor hour are as follows.

Indirect labor	$1.00
Indirect materials	0.50
Utilities	0.30

Fixed overhead costs per month are: Supervision $4,000, Depreciation $1,500, and Property Taxes $800. The company believes it will normally operate in a range of 7,000–10,000 direct labor hours per month.

Instructions
Prepare a monthly flexible manufacturing overhead budget for 2005 for the expected range of activity, using increments of 1,000 direct labor hours.

Prepare flexible budget reports for manufacturing overhead costs, and comment on findings.
(SO 3)

E20-2 Using the information in E20-1, assume that in July 2005, Voss Company incurs the following manufacturing overhead costs.

Variable Costs		**Fixed Costs**	
Indirect labor	$8,700	Supervision	$4,000
Indirect materials	4,300	Depreciation	1,500
Utilities	2,500	Property taxes	800

Instructions
(a) Prepare a flexible budget performance report, assuming that the company worked 9,000 direct labor hours during the month. The company expected to work 9,000 direct labor hours.
(b) Prepare a flexible budget performance report, assuming that the company worked 8,500 direct labor hours during the month. The company expected to work 8,500 direct labor hours.
(c) ▭▭▭▭▷ Comment on your findings.

Prepare flexible selling expense budget.
(SO 3)

E20-3 Samano Company uses flexible budgets to control its selling expenses. Monthly sales are expected to range from $170,000 to $200,000. Variable costs and their percentage relationship to sales are: Sales Commissions 5%, Advertising 4%, Traveling 3%, and Delivery 2%. Fixed selling expenses will consist of Sales Salaries $30,000, Depreciation on Delivery Equipment $7,000, and Insurance on Delivery Equipment $1,000.

Instructions
Prepare a monthly flexible budget for each $10,000 increment of sales within the relevant range for the year ending December 31, 2005.

Prepare flexible budget reports for selling expenses.
(SO 3)

E20-4 The actual selling expenses incurred in March 2005 by Samano Company are as follows.

Variable Expenses		Fixed Expenses	
Sales commissions	$9,200	Sales salaries	$30,000
Advertising	7,000	Depreciation	7,000
Travel	5,100	Insurance	1,000
Delivery	3,500		

Instructions

(a) Prepare a flexible budget performance report for March using the budget data in E20-3, assuming that March sales were $170,000. Expected and actual sales are the same.

(b) Prepare a flexible budget performance report, assuming that March sales were $180,000. Expected sales and actual sales are the same.

(c) ▭▭▭▷ Comment on the importance of using flexible budgets in evaluating the performance of the sales manager.

E20-5 Sanchez Company's manufacturing overhead budget for the first quarter of 2005 contained the following data.

Prepare flexible budget and responsibility report for manufacturing overhead. (SO 3, 5)

Variable Costs		Fixed Costs	
Indirect materials	$12,000	Supervisory salaries	$30,000
Indirect labor	10,000	Depreciation	7,000
Utilities	8,000	Property taxes and insurance	8,000
Maintenance	5,000	Maintenance	5,000

Actual variable costs were: indirect materials $14,200, indirect labor $9,600, utilities $8,700, and maintenance $4,200. Actual fixed costs equaled budgeted costs except for property taxes and insurance, which were $8,300.

All costs are considered controllable by the production department manager except for depreciation, and property taxes and insurance.

Instructions

(a) Prepare a flexible overhead budget report for the first quarter.

(b) Prepare a responsibility report for the first quarter.

E20-6 As sales manager, Todd Keyser was given the following static budget report for selling expenses in the Clothing Department of Pace Company for the month of October.

Prepare flexible budget report, and answer question. (SO 2, 3)

PACE COMPANY
Clothing Department
Budget Report
For the Month Ended October 31, 2005

	Budget	Actual	Difference Favorable F Unfavorable U
Sales in units	8,000	10,000	2,000 F
Variable costs			
Sales commissions	$ 2,000	$ 2,500	$ 500 U
Advertising expense	800	850	50 U
Travel expense	4,400	4,900	500 U
Free samples given out	1,000	1,300	300 U
Total variable	8,200	9,550	1,350 U
Fixed costs			
Rent	1,500	1,500	–0–
Sales salaries	1,200	1,200	–0–
Office salaries	800	800	–0–
Depreciation—autos (sales staff)	500	500	–0–
Total fixed	4,000	4,000	–0–
Total costs	$12,200	$13,550	$1,350 U

As a result of this budget report, Todd was called into the president's office and congratulated on his fine sales performance. He was reprimanded, however, for allowing his costs to get out of control. Todd knew something was wrong with the performance report that he had been given. However, he was not sure what to do, and comes to you for advice.

Instructions
(a) Prepare a budget report based on flexible budget data to help Todd.
(b) Should Todd have been reprimanded? Explain.

State total budgeted cost formulas, and prepare flexible budget graph.
(SO 3)

E20-7 Lockwood Company has two production departments, Fabricating and Assembling. At a department managers' meeting, the controller uses flexible budget graphs to explain total budgeted costs. Separate graphs based on direct labor hours are used for each department. The graphs show the following.
1. At zero direct labor hours, the total budgeted cost line and the fixed cost line intersect the vertical axis at $50,000 in the Fabricating Department and $45,000 in the Assembling Department.
2. At normal capacity of 50,000 direct labor hours, the line drawn from the total budgeted cost line intersects the vertical axis at $160,000 in the Fabricating Department, and $110,000 in the Assembling Department.

Instructions
(a) State the total budgeted cost formula for each department.
(b) Compute the total budgeted cost for each department, assuming actual direct labor hours worked were 53,000 and 47,000, in the Fabricating and Assembling Departments, respectively.
(c) Prepare the flexible budget graph for the Fabricating Department, assuming the maximum direct labor hours in the relevant range is 100,000. Use increments of 10,000 direct labor hours on the horizontal axis and increments of $50,000 on the vertical axis.

Prepare reports in a responsibility reporting system.
(SO 4)

E20-8 Loebs Company's organization chart includes the president; the vice president of production; three assembly plants—Dallas, Atlanta, and Tucson; and two departments within each plant—Machining and Finishing. Budget and actual manufacturing cost data for July 2005 are as follows.

Finishing Department—Dallas: Direct materials $41,000 actual, $46,000 budget; direct labor $83,000 actual, $82,000 budget; manufacturing overhead $51,000 actual, $49,200 budget.

Machining Department—Dallas: Total manufacturing costs $218,000 actual, $214,000 budget.

Atlanta Plant: Total manufacturing costs $426,000 actual, $421,000 budget.

Tucson Plant: Total manufacturing costs $494,000 actual, $499,000 budget.

The Dallas plant manager's office costs were $95,000 actual and $92,000 budget. The vice president of production's office costs were $132,000 actual and $130,000 budget. Office costs are not allocated to departments and plants.

Instructions
Using the format on page 961, prepare the reports in a responsibility system for:
(a) The Finishing Department—Dallas.
(b) The plant manager—Dallas.
(c) The vice president of production.

Compute missing amounts in responsibility reports for three profit centers, and prepare a report.
(SO 6)

E20-9 Haven Manufacturing Inc. has three divisions which are operated as profit centers. Operating data for the divisions listed alphabetically are as follows.

Operating Data	Women's Shoes	Men's Shoes	Children's Shoes
Contribution margin	$270,000	(3)	$160,000
Controllable fixed costs	100,000	(4)	(5)
Controllable margin	(1)	$ 90,000	96,000
Sales	600,000	450,000	(6)
Variable costs	(2)	310,000	250,000

Instructions

(a) Compute the missing amounts. Show computations.

(b) Prepare a responsibility report for the Women's Shoe Division assuming (1) the data are for the month ended June 30, 2005, and (2) all data equal budget except variable costs which are $10,000 over budget.

E20-10 The Hackcraft Division of Nunez Company reported the following data for the current year.

Compute ROI for current year and for possible future changes.
(SO 7)

Sales	$3,000,000
Variable costs	1,800,000
Controllable fixed costs	600,000
Average operating assets	6,000,000

Top management is unhappy with the investment center's return on investment (ROI). It asks the manager of the Hackcraft Division to submit plans to improve ROI in the next year. The manager believes it is feasible to consider the following independent courses of action.

1. Increase sales by $320,000 with no change in the contribution margin percentage.
2. Reduce variable costs by $100,000.
3. Reduce average operating assets by 5%.

Instructions

(a) Compute the return on investment (ROI) for the current year.

(b) Using the ROI formula, compute the ROI under each of the proposed courses of action. (Round to one decimal.)

*E20-11 Presented below is selected information for three regional divisions of Sako Company.

Compare ROI and residual income.
(SO 8)

	Divisions		
	West	**East**	**South**
Contribution margin	$ 200,000	$ 600,000	$ 300,000
Controllable margin	$ 140,000	$ 400,000	$ 225,000
Average operating assets	$1,000,000	$2,000,000	$1,500,000
Minimum rate of return	13%	18%	10%

Instructions

(a) Compute the return on investment for each division.

(b) Compute the residual income for each division.

(c) Assume that each division has an investment opportunity that would provide a rate of return of 19%.
   (1) If ROI is used to measure performance, which division or divisions will probably make the additional investment?
   (2) If residual income is used to measure performance, which division or divisions will probably make the additional investment?

*E20-12 Presented below is selected financial information for two divisions of Ashahi Brewery. You are to supply the missing information.

Fill in information related to ROI and residual income.
(SO 8)

	Lager	Lite Lager
Contribution margin	$600,000	$ 500,000
Controllable margin	200,000	(c) 330,000
Average operating assets	(a) 1,000,000	$1,000,000
Minimum rate of return	(b) 11%	13%
Return on investment	20%	(d)
Residual income	$ 90,000	$ 200,000

[handwritten: Use formulas, All info here]

Problems: Set A

Prepare flexible budget and budget report for manufacturing overhead.
(SO 3)

P20-1A Tick Company estimates that 360,000 direct labor hours will be worked during the coming year, 2005, in the Packaging Department. On this basis, the following budgeted manufacturing overhead cost data are computed for the year.

Fixed Overhead Costs		Variable Overhead Costs	
Supervision	$ 90,000	Indirect labor	$144,000
Depreciation	60,000	Indirect materials	90,000
Insurance	27,000	Repairs	54,000
Rent	36,000	Utilities	108,000
Property taxes	18,000	Lubricants	18,000
	$231,000		$414,000

It is estimated that direct labor hours worked each month will range from 27,000 to 36,000 hours.

During October, 27,000 direct labor hours were worked and the following overhead costs were incurred.

Fixed overhead costs: Supervision $7,500, Depreciation $5,000, Insurance $2,225, Rent $3,000, and Property taxes $1,500.

Variable overhead costs: Indirect labor $11,760, Indirect materials, $6,400, Repairs $4,000, Utilities $8,550, and Lubricants $1,640.

Instructions

(a) Total costs:
27,000, DLH $50,300

(a) Prepare a monthly flexible manufacturing overhead budget for each increment of 3,000 direct labor hours over the relevant range for the year ending December 31, 2005.

(b) Total $ 1,275 U

(b) Prepare a flexible budget report for October, when 27,500 direct labor hours were expected.

(c) Comment on management's efficiency in controlling manufacturing overhead costs in October.

Prepare flexible budget, budget report, and graph for manufacturing overhead.
(SO 3)

P20-2A Wahlen Company manufactures tablecloths. Sales have grown rapidly over the past 2 years. As a result, the president has installed a budgetary control system for 2005. The following data were used in developing the master manufacturing overhead budget for the Ironing Department, which is based on an activity index of direct labor hours.

Variable Costs	Rate per Direct Labor Hour	Annual Fixed Costs	
Indirect labor	$0.40	Supervision	$30,000
Indirect materials	0.50	Depreciation	18,000
Factory utilities	0.30	Insurance	12,000
Factory repairs	0.20	Rent	24,000

The master overhead budget was prepared on the expectation that 480,000 direct labor hours will be worked during the year. In June, 42,000 direct labor hours were worked and 42,000 were expected. At that level of activity, actual costs were as follows.

Variable—per direct labor hour: Indirect labor $0.43, Indirect materials $0.50, Factory utilities $0.32, and Factory repairs $0.24.

Fixed: same as budgeted.

Instructions

(a) Total costs:
35,000, DLH $56,000

(a) Prepare a monthly flexible manufacturing overhead budget for the year ending December 31, 2005, assuming production levels range from 35,000 to 50,000 direct labor hours. Use increments of 5,000 direct labor hours.

(b) Budget $65,800
Actual $69,580

(b) Prepare a budget performance report for June comparing actual results with budget data based on the flexible budget.

(c) Were costs effectively controlled? Explain.

(d) State the formula for computing the total budgeted costs for Wahlen Company.
(e) Prepare the flexible budget graph, showing total budgeted costs at 35,000 and 45,000 direct labor hours. Use increments of 5,000 direct labor hours on the horizontal axis and increments of $10,000 on the vertical axis.

P20-3A Nigh Company uses budgets in controlling costs. The August 2005 budget report for the company's Assembling Department is as follows.

State total budgeted cost formula, and prepare flexible budget reports for 2 time periods.
(SO 2, 3)

NIGH COMPANY
Budget Report
Assembling Department
For the Month Ended August 31, 2005

Manufacturing Costs	Budget	Actual	Difference Favorable F Unfavorable U
Variable costs			
Direct materials	$ 48,000	$ 47,000	$1,000 F
Direct labor	78,000	74,100	3,900 F
Indirect materials	24,000	24,200	200 U
Indirect labor	18,000	17,500	500 F
Utilities	15,000	14,900	100 F
Maintenance	9,000	9,200	200 U
Total variable	192,000	186,900	5,100 F
Fixed costs			
Rent	10,000	10,000	–0–
Supervision	17,000	17,000	–0–
Depreciation	7,000	7,000	–0–
Total fixed	34,000	34,000	–0–
Total costs	$226,000	$220,900	$5,100 F

The budget data in the report are based on the master budget for the year, which assumed that 720,000 units would be produced. The Assembling Department manager is pleased with the report and expects a raise, or at least praise for a job well done. The company president, however, is unhappy with the results for August, because only 58,000 units were produced. (*Hint:* The budget amounts above are one-twelfth of the master budget.)

Instructions
(a) State the total monthly budgeted cost formula.
(b) Prepare a budget report for August using flexible budget data. Why does this report provide a better basis for evaluating performance than the report based on static budget data? Assume 62,000 units were expected to be produced.
(c) In September, 64,000 units were produced when 65,000 were expected. Prepare the budget report using flexible budget data, assuming (1) each variable cost was 10% higher than its actual cost in August, and (2) fixed costs were the same in September as in August.

(b) Budget $219,600
(c) Budget $238,800
     Actual $239,590

P20-4A Lococo Manufacturing Inc. operates the Patio Furniture Division as a profit center. Operating data for this division for the year ended December 31, 2005, are as follows.

Prepare responsibility report for a profit center.
(SO 6)

	Budget	Difference from Budget
Sales	$2,500,000	$50,000 F
Cost of goods sold		
Variable	1,300,000	43,000 F
Controllable fixed	200,000	5,000 U
Selling and administrative		
Variable	220,000	7,000 U
Controllable fixed	50,000	2,000 U
Noncontrollable fixed costs	70,000	4,000 U

In addition, Lococo Manufacturing incurs $180,000 of indirect fixed costs that were budgeted at $175,000. Twenty percent (20%) of these costs are allocated to the Patio Furniture Division.

(a) Contribution
   margin $86,000 F
Controllable
   margin $79,000 F

Instructions

(a) Prepare a responsibility report for the Patio Furniture Division for the year.
(b) ▭▭▭▭▶ Comment on the manager's performance in controlling revenues and costs.
(c) Identify any costs excluded from the responsibility report and explain why they were excluded.

Prepare responsibility report for an investment center, and compute ROI.
(SO 7)

P20-5A   Kurian Manufacturing Company manufactures a variety of tools and industrial equipment. The company operates through three divisions. Each division is an investment center. Operating data for the Home Division for the year ended December 31, 2005, and relevant budget data are as follows.

	Actual	Comparison with Budget
Sales	$1,500,000	$100,000 favorable
Variable cost of goods sold	700,000	$100,000 unfavorable
Variable selling and administrative expenses	125,000	$ 25,000 unfavorable
Controllable fixed cost of goods sold	170,000	On target
Controllable fixed selling and administrative expenses	100,000	On target

Average operating assets for the year for the Home Division were $2,000,000 which was also the budgeted amount.

Instructions

(a) Contribution margin
   Budget $430
   Actual $405

(c) (2) 22.5%

(a) Prepare a responsibility report (in thousands of dollars) for the Home Division.
(b) Evaluate the manager's performance. Which items will likely be investigated by top management?
(c) Compute the expected ROI in 2006 for the Home Division, assuming the following changes.
  (1) Variable cost of goods sold is decreased by 6%.
  (2) Average operating assets are decreased by 10%.
  (3) Sales are increased by $200,000, and this increase is expected to increase contribution margin by $90,000.

Prepare reports for cost centers under responsibility accounting, and comment on performance of managers.
(SO 4, 5)

P20-6A   Tilg Company uses a responsibility reporting system. It has divisions in Denver, Seattle, and San Diego. Each division has three production departments: Cutting, Shaping, and Finishing. The responsibility for each department rests with a manager who reports to the division production manager. Each division manager reports to the vice president of production. There are also vice presidents for marketing and finance. All vice presidents report to the president.

In January 2005, controllable actual and budget manufacturing overhead cost data for the departments and divisions were as follows.

Manufacturing Overhead	Actual	Budget
Individual costs—Cutting Department—Seattle		
Indirect labor	$ 73,000	$ 70,000
Indirect materials	46,700	46,000
Maintenance	20,500	18,000
Utilities	20,100	17,000
Supervision	31,000	30,000
	$ 191,300	$ 181,000
Total costs		
Shaping Department—Seattle	$ 158,000	$ 148,000
Finishing Department—Seattle	210,000	208,000
Denver division	676,000	673,000
San Diego division	722,000	715,000
	$1,766,000	$1,744,000

Additional overhead costs were incurred as follows: Seattle division production manager—actual costs $52,500, budget $51,000; vice president of production—actual costs $65,000, budget $64,000; president—actual costs $76,400, budget $74,200. These expenses are not allocated.

The vice presidents who report to the president, other than the vice president of production, had the following expenses.

Vice president	Actual	Budget
Marketing	$133,600	$130,000
Finance	$107,000	$105,000

Instructions
(a) Using the format on page 961, prepare the following responsibility reports.
  (1) Manufacturing overhead—Cutting Department manager—Seattle division.
  (2) Manufacturing overhead—Seattle division manager.
  (3) Manufacturing overhead—vice president of production.
  (4) Manufacturing overhead and expenses—president.

(b) Comment on the comparative performances of:
  (1) Department managers in the Seattle division.
  (2) Division managers.
  (3) Vice presidents.

P20-7A Sawtell Industries has manufactured prefabricated houses for over 20 years. The houses are constructed in sections to be assembled on customers' lots. Sawtell expanded into the precut housing market when it acquired Baron Company, one of its suppliers. In this market, various types of lumber are precut into the appropriate lengths, banded into packages, and shipped to customers' lots for assembly. Sawtell designated the Baron Division as an investment center.

Sawtell uses return on investment (ROI) as a performance measure with investment defined as average operating assets. Management bonuses are based in part on ROI. All investments are expected to earn a minimum rate of return of 15%. Baron's ROI has ranged from 19.3% to 22.1% since it was acquired. Baron had an investment opportunity in 2005 that had an estimated ROI of 18%. Baron's management decided against the investment because it believed the investment would decrease the division's overall ROI.

Selected financial information for Baron are presented below. The division's average operating assets were $12,300,000 for the year 2005.

BARON DIVISION
Selected Financial Information
For the Year Ended December 31, 2005

Sales	$24,000,000
Contribution margin	8,200,000
Controllable margin	2,460,000

Instructions
(a) Calculate the following performance measures for 2005 for the Baron Division.
  (1) Return on investment (ROI).
  (2) Residual income.

(b) Would the management of Baron Division have been more likely to accept the investment opportunity it had in 2005 if residual income were used as a performance measure instead of ROI? Explain your answer.

(CMA, adapted)

(a) (3) $34,800 U

Compare ROI and residual income.
(SO 8)

Problems: Set B

P20-1B Greish Company estimates that 240,000 direct labor hours will be worked during 2005 in the Assembly Department. On this basis, the following budgeted manufacturing overhead data are computed.

Prepare flexible budget and budget report for manufacturing overhead.
(SO 3)

Variable Overhead Costs		Fixed Overhead Costs	
Indirect labor	$ 72,000	Supervision	$ 72,000
Indirect materials	48,000	Depreciation	36,000
Repairs	24,000	Insurance	9,600
Utilities	19,200	Rent	7,200
Lubricants	9,600	Property taxes	6,000
	$172,800		$130,800

It is estimated that direct labor hours worked each month will range from 18,000 to 24,000 hours.

During January, 20,000 direct labor hours were worked and the following overhead costs were incurred.

Variable Overhead Costs		Fixed Overhead Costs	
Indirect labor	$ 6,200	Supervision	$ 6,000
Indirect materials	3,600	Depreciation	3,000
Repairs	1,600	Insurance	800
Utilities	1,250	Rent	700
Lubricants	830	Property taxes	500
	$13,480		$11,000

Instructions

(a) Total costs:
*   18,000 DLH $23,860*

(b) Budget $25,300
*   Actual $24,480*

(a) Prepare a monthly flexible manufacturing overhead budget for each increment of 2,000 direct labor hours over the relevant range for the year ending December 31, 2005.

(b) Prepare a manufacturing overhead budget report for January, assuming 20,500 direct labor hours were expected.

(c) ▭▭▭▭▷ Comment on management's efficiency in controlling manufacturing overhead costs in January.

Prepare flexible budget, budget report, and graph for manufacturing overhead. (SO 3)

P20-2B   Juds Manufacturing Company produces one product, Kebo. Because of wide fluctuations in demand for Kebo, the Assembly Department experiences significant variations in monthly production levels.

The annual master manufacturing overhead budget is based on 300,000 direct labor hours. In July 27,500 labor hours were worked, and 27,500 hours were expected to be worked. The master manufacturing overhead budget for the year and the actual overhead costs incurred in July are as follows.

Overhead Costs	Master Budget (annual)	Actual in July
Variable		
Indirect labor	$ 360,000	$32,000
Indirect materials	210,000	17,000
Utilities	90,000	8,100
Maintenance	60,000	5,400
Fixed		
Supervision	192,000	16,000
Depreciation	120,000	10,000
Insurance and taxes	60,000	5,000
Total	$1,092,000	$93,500

Instructions

(a) Total costs:
*   22,500 DLH $85,000*

(b) Budget $97,000
*   Actual $93,500*

(a) Prepare a monthly flexible overhead budget for the year ending December 31, 2005, assuming monthly production levels range from 22,500 to 30,000 direct labor hours. Use increments of 2,500 direct labor hours.

(b) Prepare a budget performance report for the month of July 2005 comparing actual results with budget data based on the flexible budget.

(c) ▭▭▭▭▷ Were costs effectively controlled? Explain.

(d) State the formula for computing the total monthly budgeted costs in Juds Company.

(e) Prepare the flexible budget graph showing total budgeted costs at 25,000 and 27,500 direct labor hours. Use increments of 5,000 on the horizontal axis and increments of $10,000 on the vertical axis.

P20-3B Lorch Company uses budgets in controlling costs. The May 2005 budget report for the company's Packaging Department is as follows.

State total budgeted cost formula, and prepare flexible budget reports for 2 time periods.
(SO 2, 3)

LORCH COMPANY
Budget Report
Packaging Department
For the Month Ended May 31, 2005

Manufacturing Costs	Budget	Actual	Difference Favorable F Unfavorable U
Variable costs			
Direct materials	$ 30,000	$ 32,000	$2,000 U
Direct labor	50,000	53,000	3,000 U
Indirect materials	15,000	15,200	200 U
Indirect labor	12,500	13,000	500 U
Utilities	7,500	7,100	400 F
Maintenance	5,000	5,200	200 U
Total variable	120,000	125,500	5,500 U
Fixed costs			
Rent	9,000	9,000	–0–
Supervision	9,000	9,000	–0–
Depreciation	5,000	5,000	–0–
Total fixed	23,000	23,000	–0–
Total costs	$143,000	$148,500	$5,500 U

The budget amounts in the report were on the master budget for the year, which assumed that 600,000 units would be produced. (*Hint:* The budget amounts above are one-twelfth of the master budget for the year.)

   The company president was displeased with the department manager's performance. The department manager, who thought he had done a good job, could not understand the unfavorable results. In May, 55,000 units were produced.

Instructions
   (a) State the total budgeted cost formula.
   (b) Prepare a budget report for May using flexible budget data. Why does this report provide a better basis for evaluating performance than the report based on static budget data? Assume 57,000 units were expected to be produced in the Packaging Department.
   (c) In June, 40,000 units were produced when 39,000 were expected. Prepare the budget report using flexible budget data, assuming (1) each variable cost was 20% less in June than its actual cost in May, and (2) fixed costs were the same in the month of June as in May.

(b) Budget $155,000

(c) Budget $119,000
    Actual $123,400

P20-4B Peters Manufacturing Inc. operates the Home Appliance Division as a profit center. Operating data for this division for the year ended December 31, 2005, are as follows.

Prepare responsibility report for a profit center.
(SO 6)

	Budget	Difference from Budget
Sales	$2,400,000	$100,000 U
Cost of goods sold		
Variable	1,200,000	57,000 U
Controllable fixed	200,000	10,000 F
Selling and administrative		
Variable	240,000	8,000 F
Controllable fixed	60,000	6,000 U
Noncontrollable fixed costs	50,000	2,000 U

In addition, Peters Manufacturing incurs $150,000 of indirect fixed costs that were budgeted at $155,000. Twenty percent (20%) of these costs are allocated to the Home Appliance Division. None of these costs are controllable by the division manager.

(a) Contribution
   margin $149,000 U
Controllable
   margin $145,000 U

Instructions

(a) Prepare a responsibility report for the Home Appliance Division (a profit center) for the year.

(b) ▭▭▭▭▷ Comment on the manager's performance in controlling revenues and costs.

(c) Identify any costs excluded from the responsibility report and explain why they were excluded.

Prepare responsibility report for an investment center, and compute ROI.
(SO 7)

P20-5B Ridder Manufacturing Company manufactures a variety of garden and lawn equipment. The company operates through three divisions. Each division is an investment center. Operating data for the Lawnmower Division for the year ended December 31, 2005, and relevant budget data are as follows.

	Actual	**Comparison with Budget**
Sales	$2,800,000	$200,000 unfavorable
Variable cost of goods sold	1,400,000	$150,000 unfavorable
Variable selling and administrative expenses	300,000	$ 50,000 favorable
Controllable fixed cost of goods sold	270,000	On target
Controllable fixed selling and administrative expenses	130,000	On target

Average operating assets for the year for the Lawnmower Division were $4,000,000 which was also the budgeted amount.

Instructions

(a) Controllable margin:
   Budget $1,000
   Actual $ 700

(a) Prepare a responsibility report (in thousands of dollars) for the Lawnmower Division.

(b) Evaluate the manager's performance. Which items will likely be investigated by top management?

(c) Compute the expected ROI in 2006 for the Lawnmower Division, assuming the following changes.

(c) (2) 21.9%

   (1) Variable cost of goods sold is decreased by 15%.
   (2) Average operating assets are decreased by 20%.
   (3) Sales are increased by $500,000 and this increase is expected to increase contribution margin by $200,000.

▶ BROADENING YOUR PERSPECTIVE

Group Decision Case

BYP20-1 Green Pastures is a 400-acre farm on the outskirts of the Kentucky Bluegrass, specializing in the boarding of broodmares and their foals. A recent economic downturn in the thoroughbred industry has led to a decline in breeding activities, and it has made the boarding business extremely competitive. To meet the competition, Green Pastures planned in 2005 to entertain clients, advertise more extensively, and absorb expenses formerly paid by clients such as veterinary and blacksmith fees.

The budget report for 2005 is presented on the next page. As shown, the static income statement budget for the year is based on an expected 21,900 boarding days at $25 per mare. The variable expenses per mare per day were budgeted: Feed $5, Veterinary fees $3, Blacksmith fees $0.30, and Supplies $0.40. All other budgeted expenses were either semifixed or fixed.

During the year, management decided not to replace a worker who quit in March, but it did issue a new advertising brochure and did more entertaining of clients.[2]

GREEN PASTURES
Static Budget Income Statement
Year Ended December 31, 2006

	Actual	Master Budget	Difference
Number of mares	52	60	8*
Number of boarding days	18,980	21,900	2,920*
Sales	$379,600	$547,500	$167,900*
Less variable expenses:			
Feed	104,390	109,500	5,110
Veterinary fees	58,838	65,700	6,862
Blacksmith fees	6,074	6,570	496
Supplies	7,402	8,760	1,358
Total variable expenses	176,704	190,530	13,826
Contribution margin	202,896	356,970	154,074*
Less fixed expenses:			
Depreciation	40,000	40,000	–0–
Insurance	11,000	11,000	–0–
Utilities	12,000	14,000	2,000
Repairs and maintenance	10,000	11,000	1,000
Labor	88,000	96,000	8,000
Advertisement	12,000	8,000	4,000*
Entertainment	7,000	5,000	2,000*
Total fixed expense	180,000	185,000	5,000
Net income	$ 22,896	$171,970	$149,074*

*Unfavorable.

Instructions
With the class divided into groups, answer the following.
(a) Based on the static budget report:
   (1) What was the primary cause(s) of the loss in net income?
   (2) Did management do a good, average, or poor job of controlling expenses?
   (3) Were management's decisions to stay competitive sound?

(b) Prepare a flexible budget report for the year.
(c) Based on the flexible budget report, answer the three questions in part (a) above.
(d) What course of action do you recommend for the management of Green Pastures?

Managerial Analysis

BYP20-2 Lakenvelder Dutch manufactures expensive watch cases sold as souvenirs. Three of its sales departments are: Retail Sales, Wholesale Sales, and Outlet Sales. The Retail Sales Department is a profit center. The Wholesale Sales Department is a cost center. Its managers merely take orders from customers who purchase through the company's wholesale catalog. The Outlet Sales Department is an investment center, because each manager is given full responsibility for an outlet store location. The manager can hire and discharge employees, purchase, maintain, and sell equipment, and in general is fairly independent of company control.

---

[2]Data for this case are based on Hans Sprohge and John Talbott, "New Applications for Variance Analysis," *Journal of Accountancy* (AICPA, New York), April 1989, pp. 137–141.

Rena Worthington is a manager in the Retail Sales Department. Winston Hillhouse manages the Wholesale Sales Department. Oscar Hadley manages the Golden Gate Club outlet store in San Francisco. The following are the budget responsibility reports for each of the three departments.

Budget

	Retail Sales	Wholesale Sales	Outlet Sales
Sales	$ 750,000	$ 400,000	$200,000
Variable costs			
Cost of goods sold	150,000	100,000	25,000
Advertising	100,000	30,000	5,000
Sales salaries	75,000	15,000	3,000
Printing	10,000	20,000	5,000
Travel	20,000	30,000	2,000
Fixed costs			
Rent	50,000	30,000	10,000
Insurance	5,000	2,000	1,000
Depreciation	75,000	100,000	40,000
Investment in assets	$1,000,000	$1,200,000	$800,000

Actual Results

	Retail Sales	Wholesale Sales	Outlet Sales
Sales	$ 750,000	$ 400,000	$200,000
Variable costs			
Cost of goods sold	195,000	120,000	26,250
Advertising	100,000	30,000	5,000
Sales salaries	75,000	15,000	3,000
Printing	10,000	20,000	5,000
Travel	15,000	20,000	1,500
Fixed costs			
Rent	40,000	50,000	12,000
Insurance	5,000	2,000	1,000
Depreciation	80,000	90,000	60,000
Investment in assets	$1,000,000	$1,200,000	$800,000

Instructions

(a) Determine which of the items should be included in the responsibility report for each of the three managers.

(b) Compare the budgeted measures with the actual results. Decide which results should be called to the attention of each manager.

Real-World Focus

BYP20-3   Computer Associates International, Inc., delivers the software that manages e-business. CA's world-class solutions address all aspects of e-business process management, information management, and infrastructure management. Founded in 1976, CA serves organizations in more than 100 countries, including 99 percent of the *Fortune* 500 companies.

Presented on the next page is information from the company's annual report.

| COMPUTER ASSOCIATES INTERNATIONAL |
| Management Discussion |

The Company has experienced a pattern of business whereby revenue for its third and fourth fiscal quarters reflects an increase over first- and second-quarter revenue. The Company attributes this increase to clients' increased spending at the end of their calendar year budgetary periods and the culmination of its annual sales plan. Since the Company's costs do not increase proportionately with the third- and fourth-quarters' increase in revenue, the higher revenue in these quarters results in greater profit margins and income. Fourth-quarter profitability is traditionally affected by significant new hirings, training, and education expenditures for the succeeding year.

Instructions
(a) Why don't the company's costs increase proportionately as the revenues increase in the third and fourth quarters?
(b) What type of budgeting seems appropriate for the Computer Associates situation?

Exploring the Web

BYP20-4   Genelle and Doug have recorded the story of their wedding planning. They are on a strict budget and need help in preparing what they call "a somewhat flexible budget."

Address: **www.wednet.com/inspire/wedstory/story1.htm**
(or go to **www.wiley.com/college/kimmel**)

Steps
1. Go to Genelle and Doug's Web site, and read about their trials and tribulations in planning a wedding.
2. Review the **Planning and Budgeting** section in "Part 1" of their story. They mention that this is a "somewhat flexible budget" for 250 guests, totalling $7,150. They would like to reduce their total costs to $7,000, if at all possible.

Instructions
Recast Genelle and Doug's budget into a truly flexible budget so that they can see the effects on their total costs of reducing the number of invited guests to 225 or 200.

Communication Activity

BYP20-5   The manufacturing overhead budget for Carthage Corporation contains the following items.

Variable factory expenses		Fixed factory expenses	
Indirect materials	$ 75,000	Supervision	$ 51,000
Indirect labor	36,000	Inspection costs	3,000
Maintenance expenses	30,000	Insurance expenses	6,000
Manufacturing supplies	18,000	Depreciation	45,000
Total variable	$159,000	Total fixed	$105,000

The budget was based on an estimated 6,000 units being produced. During November 2005, 4,500 units were produced, and the following costs incurred.

Variable factory expenses		Fixed factory expenses	
Indirect materials	$ 75,600	Supervision	$ 57,900
Indirect labor	40,500	Inspection costs	3,600
Maintenance expenses	24,600	Insurance expenses	6,600
Manufacturing supplies	15,300	Depreciation	44,100
Total variable	$156,000	Total fixed	$112,200

Instructions

(a) Determine which items would be controllable by B. Sherrick, the production manager.
(b) How much should have been spent to manufacture 4,500 units?
(c) Prepare a flexible manufacturing overhead budget report for Ms. Sherrick.
(d) Prepare a responsibility report. Include only the costs that would have been controllable by Ms. Sherrick. In an attached memo, describe clearly for Ms. Sherrick the areas in which her performance needs to be improved.

Research Case

BYP20-6   The February 2000 issue of the *Journal of Accountancy* contains an article by Russ Banham entitled "Better Budgets."

Instructions

Read the article and answer the following questions.

(a) Why have some companies decided not to do major overhauls of their budgeting systems after some initial investigations into the possibility? What percentage of companies that attempt overhauls give up before finishing?
(b) What is the "new planning paradigm"?
(c) What does the author argue is the "final link" necessary for successful budgeting and planning?

Ethics Case

BYP20-7   In order to meet competition and achieve its profit goals, NP Corporation has chosen the decentralized form of organization. Each manager of a decentralized investment center is measured on the basis of profit contribution, market penetration, and return on investment. Failure to meet the objectives established by corporate management for these measures has not been acceptable and usually has resulted in demotion or dismissal of an investment center manager.

An anonymous survey of managers in the company revealed that the managers feel the pressure to compromise their personal ethical standards to achieve the corporate objectives. For example, at certain plant locations there was pressure to reduce quality control to a level which could not assure that all unsafe products would be rejected. Also, sales personnel were encouraged to use questionable sales tactics, including gifts and other incentives to purchasing agents, to obtain orders.

The chief executive officer is disturbed by the survey findings. In his opinion such behavior cannot be condoned by the company.

Instructions

(a) Who are the stakeholders (the affected parties) in the situation?
(b) Identify the ethical implications, conflicts, or dilemmas in the above situation.
(c) What might the company do to reduce the pressures on managers and decrease the ethical conflicts?

(CMA adapted)

Answers to Self-Study Questions

1. c   2. b   3. a   4. d   5. a   6. d   7. d   8. b   9. b   10. d   *11. c

Remember to go back to the Navigator box on the chapter-opening page and check off your completed work.

Performance Evaluation Through Standard Costs

STUDY OBJECTIVES

After studying this chapter,
you should be able to:

1 Distinguish between a standard and a budget.

2 Identify the advantages of standard costs.

3 Describe how standards are set.

4 State the formulas for determining direct materials and direct labor variances.

5 State the formulas for determining manufacturing overhead variances.

6 Discuss the reporting of variances.

7 Prepare an income statement for management under a standard costing system.

THE NAVIGATOR ✔

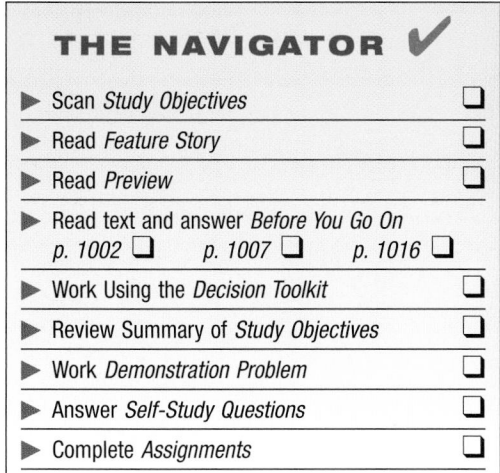

- ▶ Scan *Study Objectives* ☐
- ▶ Read *Feature Story* ☐
- ▶ Read *Preview* ☐
- ▶ Read text and answer *Before You Go On*
  p. 1002 ☐   p. 1007 ☐   p. 1016 ☐
- ▶ Work Using the *Decision Toolkit* ☐
- ▶ Review Summary of *Study Objectives* ☐
- ▶ Work *Demonstration Problem* ☐
- ▶ Answer *Self-Study Questions* ☐
- ▶ Complete *Assignments* ☐

FEATURE STORY

Highlighting Performance Efficiency

There's a very good chance that the highlighter you're holding in your hand was made by **Sanford**, a maker of permanent markers and other writing instruments. Sanford, headquartered in Illinois, annually sells hundreds of millions of dollars' worth of ACCENT highlighters, fine-point pens, Sharpie permanent markers, Expo dry-erase markers for overhead projectors, and other writing instruments.

Since Sanford makes literally billions of writing utensils per year, the company must keep tight control over manufacturing costs. A very important part of Sanford's manufacturing process is determining how much direct materials, labor, and overhead should cost. These costs are then compared to actual costs to assess performance efficiency. Raw materials for Sanford's markers include a barrel, plug, cap, ink reservoir, and a nib (tip). These parts are assembled by machine to produce thousands of units per hour. A major component of manufacturing overhead is machine maintenance—some fixed, some variable.

"Labor costs are associated with material handling and equipment maintenance functions. Although the assembly process is highly automated, labor is still required to move raw materials to the machine and to package the finished product. In addition, highly skilled technicians are required to service and maintain each piece of equipment," says Mike Orr, vice president, operations.

Labor rates are predictable because the hourly workers are covered by a union contract. The story is the same with the fringe benefits and some supervisory salaries. Even volume levels are fairly predictable—demand for the product is high—so fixed overhead is efficiently absorbed. Raw material standard costs are based on the previous year's actual prices plus any anticipated inflation. Lately, though, inflation has been so low that the company is considering any price increase in raw material to be unfavorable because its standards will remain unchanged.

www.sanfordcorp.com

Standards are a fact of life. You met the admission standards for the school you are attending. The vehicle that you drive had to meet certain governmental emissions standards. The hamburgers and salads you eat in a restaurant have to meet certain health and nutritional standards before they can be sold. And, as described in our Feature Story, **Sanford Corp.** develops standards for the costs of its materials, labor, and overhead which it compares with its actual costs. The reason for standards in these cases is very simple: They help to ensure that overall product quality is high. Without standards, quality control is lost.

In this chapter we continue the study of controlling costs. You will learn how to develop standard costs that permit the evaluation of performance.

The content and organization of Chapter 21 are as follows.

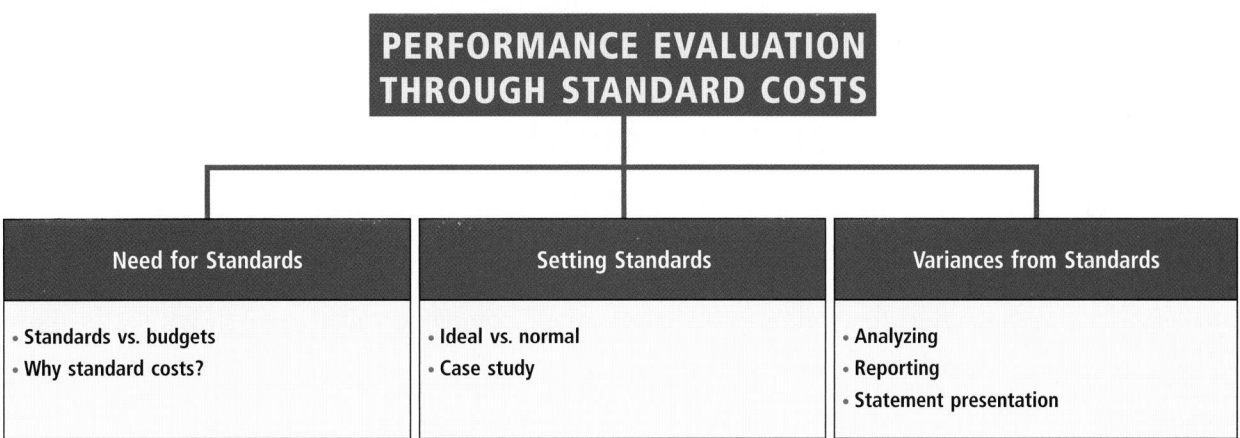

PERFORMANCE EVALUATION THROUGH STANDARD COSTS

Need for Standards	Setting Standards	Variances from Standards
• Standards vs. budgets • Why standard costs?	• Ideal vs. normal • Case study	• Analyzing • Reporting • Statement presentation

☑ THE NAVIGATOR

The Need for Standards

Standards are common in business. Those imposed by government agencies are often called **regulations**. They include the Fair Labor Standards Act, the Equal Employment Opportunity Act, and a multitude of environmental standards. Standards established internally by a company may extend to personnel matters, such as employee absenteeism and ethical codes of conduct, quality control standards for products, and standard costs for goods and services. In managerial accounting, standard costs are predetermined unit costs, which are used as measures of performance.

We will focus on manufacturing operations in the remainder of this chapter. But you should also recognize that standard costs also apply to many types of service businesses as well. For example, a fast-food restaurant such as **McDonald's** knows the price it should pay for pickles, beef, buns, and other ingredients. It also knows how much time it should take an employee to flip hamburgers. If too much is paid for pickles or too much time is taken to prepare Big Macs, the deviations are noticed and corrective action is taken. Standard costs also may be used in not-for-profit enterprises such as universities, charitable organizations, and governmental agencies.

DISTINGUISHING BETWEEN STANDARDS AND BUDGETS

In concept, **standards** and **budgets** are essentially the same. Both are predetermined costs, and both contribute to management planning and control. There is a difference, however, in the way the terms are expressed. A standard is a **unit** amount. A budget is a **total** amount. Thus, it is customary to state that the standard cost of direct labor for a unit of product is $10. If 5,000 units of the product are produced, the $50,000 of direct labor is the **budgeted** labor cost. A standard is the budgeted cost per unit of product. A standard is therefore concerned with each individual cost component that makes up the entire budget.

There are important accounting differences between budgets and standards. Except in the application of manufacturing overhead to jobs and processes, budget data are not journalized in cost accounting systems. In contrast, as will be illustrated in the appendix to this chapter, standard costs may be incorporated into cost accounting systems. Also, a company may report its inventories at standard cost in its financial statements, but it would not report inventories at budgeted costs.

WHY STANDARD COSTS?

Standard costs offer a number of advantages to an organization, as shown in Illustration 21-1. These advantages will be realized only when standard costs are carefully established and prudently used. Using standards solely as a means of placing blame can have a negative effect on managers and employees. In an effort to minimize this effect, many companies offer wage incentives to those who meet their standards.

Illustration 21-1
Advantages of standard costs

Advantages of standard costs

Facilitate management planning

Promote greater economy by making employees more "cost-conscious"

Useful in setting selling prices

Contribute to management control by providing basis for evaluation of cost control

Useful in highlighting variances in management by exception

Simplify costing of inventories and reduce clerical costs

Setting Standard Costs—A Difficult Task

The setting of standard costs to produce a unit of product is a difficult task. It requires input from all persons who have responsibility for costs and quantities. To determine the standard cost of direct materials, management may have to consult purchasing agents, product managers, quality control engineers, and production supervisors. In setting the cost standard for direct labor, pay rate data are obtained from the payroll department, and the labor time requirements may be determined by industrial engineers. The managerial accountant provides important input to management into the standards-setting process by accumulating historical cost data and by knowing how costs respond to changes in activity levels.

STUDY OBJECTIVE
3
Describe how standards are set.

To be effective in controlling costs, standard costs need to be current at all times. Thus, standards should be under continuous review. They should be changed whenever it is determined that the existing standard is not a good measure of performance. Circumstances that may warrant revision of a standard include changed wage rates resulting from a new union contract, a change in product specifications, or the implementation of a new manufacturing method.

IDEAL VERSUS NORMAL STANDARDS

Standards may be set at one of two levels: ideal or normal. Ideal standards represent optimum levels of performance under perfect operating conditions. Normal standards represent efficient levels of performance that are attainable under expected operating conditions.

Some managers believe ideal standards will stimulate workers to ever-increasing improvement. However, most managers believe that ideal standards lower the morale of the entire workforce because they are so difficult, if not impossible, to meet. Very few companies use ideal standards.

Most companies that use standards set them at a normal level. Properly set, normal standards should be **rigorous but attainable**. Normal standards allow for rest periods, machine breakdowns, and other "normal" contingencies in the production process. It will be assumed in the remainder of this chapter that standard costs are set at a normal level.

Helpful Hint When standards are set too high, employees sometimes feel pressure to consider unethical practices to meet these standards.

A CASE STUDY

To establish the standard cost of producing a product, it is necessary to establish standards for each manufacturing cost element—direct materials, direct labor, and manufacturing overhead. The standard for each element is derived from the standard price to be paid and the standard quantity to be used. To illustrate, we will look at a case study of how standard costs are set. In this extended example, we will assume that Xonic, Inc. wishes to use standard costs to measure performance in filling an order for 1,000 gallons of Weed-O, a liquid weed killer.

Direct Materials

The direct materials price standard is the cost per unit of direct materials that should be incurred. This standard should be based on the purchasing department's best estimate of the **cost of raw materials**. This is frequently based on current purchase prices. The price standard should also include an amount for related costs such as receiving, storing, and handling. The materials price standard per pound of material for Xonic's weed killer is:

Illustration 21-2 Setting direct materials price standard

Item	Price
Purchase price, net of discounts	$2.70
Freight	0.20
Receiving and handling	0.10
Standard direct materials price per pound	**$3.00**

The **direct materials quantity standard** is the quantity of direct materials that should be used per unit of finished goods. This standard is expressed as a physical measure, such as pounds, barrels, or board feet. In setting the standard, management should consider both the quality and quantity of materials required to manufacture the product. The standard should include allowances for unavoidable waste and normal spoilage. The standard quantity per unit for Xonic, Inc. is as follows.

Illustration 21-3 Setting direct materials quantity standard

Item	Quantity (Pounds)
Required materials	3.5
Allowance for waste	0.4
Allowance for spoilage	0.1
Standard direct materials quantity per unit	**4.0**

The standard direct materials cost per unit is the standard direct materials price times the standard direct materials quantity. For Xonic, Inc., the standard direct materials cost per gallon of Weed-O is $12.00 ($3.00 × 4.0 pounds).

Direct Labor

Alternative Terminology
The direct labor price standard is also called the *direct labor rate standard.*

The **direct labor price standard** is the rate per hour that should be incurred for direct labor. This standard is based on current wage rates, adjusted for anticipated changes such as cost of living adjustments (COLAs). The price standard also generally includes employer payroll taxes and fringe benefits, such as paid holidays and vacations. For Xonic, Inc., the direct labor price standard is as follows.

Illustration 21-4 Setting direct labor price standard

Item	Price
Hourly wage rate	$ 7.50
COLA	0.25
Payroll taxes	0.75
Fringe benefits	1.50
Standard direct labor rate per hour	**$10.00**

Alternative Terminology
The direct labor quantity standard is also called the *direct labor efficiency standard.*

The **direct labor quantity standard** is the time that should be required to make one unit of the product. This standard is especially critical in labor-intensive companies. Allowances should be made in this standard for rest periods, cleanup, machine setup, and machine downtime. For Xonic, Inc., the direct labor quantity standard is as follows.

Item	Quantity (Hours)
Actual production time	1.5
Rest periods and cleanup	0.2
Setup and downtime	0.3
Standard direct labor hours per unit	**2.0**

Illustration 21-5 Setting direct labor quantity standard

The standard direct labor cost per unit is the standard direct labor rate times the standard direct labor hours. For Xonic, Inc., the standard direct labor cost per gallon of Weed-O is $20 ($10.00 × 2.0 hours).

Manufacturing Overhead

For manufacturing overhead, a **standard predetermined overhead rate** is used in setting the standard. This overhead rate is determined by dividing budgeted overhead costs by an expected standard activity index. For example, the index may be standard direct labor hours or standard machine hours.

As discussed in Chapter 17, many companies employ activity-based costing (ABC) to allocate overhead costs. Because ABC uses multiple activity indices to allocate overhead costs, it results in a better correlation between activities and costs incurred. As a result, the use of ABC can significantly improve the usefulness of a standard costing system for management decision making.

Xonic, Inc. uses standard direct labor hours as the activity index. The company expects to produce 13,200 gallons of Weed-O during the year at normal capacity. Since it takes 2 direct labor hours for each gallon, total standard direct labor hours are 26,400 (13,200 × 2). At this level of activity, overhead costs are budgeted to be $132,000. Of that amount, $79,200 are variable and $52,800 are fixed. The standard predetermined overhead rates are computed as shown in Illustration 21-6.

Calculating the overhead rate

Overhead ÷ Standard activity index

Budgeted Overhead Costs	Amount	÷	Standard Direct Labor Hours	=	Overhead Rate per Direct Labor Hour
Variable	$ 79,200		26,400		$3.00
Fixed	52,800		26,400		2.00
Total	$132,000		26,400		$5.00

Illustration 21-6 Computing predetermined overhead rates

The standard manufacturing overhead rate per unit is the predetermined overhead rate times the activity index quantity standard. For Xonic, Inc., which uses direct labor hours as its activity index, the standard manufacturing overhead rate per gallon of Weed-O is $10 ($5 × 2 hours).

Total Standard Cost per Unit

Now that the standard quantity and price have been established per unit of product, the total standard cost can be determined. The total standard cost per unit is the sum of the standard costs of direct materials, direct labor, and manufacturing overhead. For Xonic, Inc., the total standard cost per gallon of Weed-O is $42, as shown on the standard cost card in Illustration 21-7 (page 1002).

Illustration 21-7 Standard cost per gallon of Weed-O

Product: Weed-O			Unit Measure: Gallon	
Manufacturing Cost Elements	Standard Quantity	×	Standard Price =	Standard Cost
Direct materials	4 pounds		$ 3.00	$12.00
Direct labor	2 hours		$10.00	$20.00
Manufacturing overhead	2 hours		$ 5.00	$10.00
				$42.00

A standard cost card is prepared for each product. This card provides the basis for determining variances from standards.

Business Insight
MANAGEMENT PERSPECTIVE

Setting standards can be difficult. Consider **Susan's Chili Factory**, which manufactures and sells chili. The cost of manufacturing Susan's chili consists of the costs of raw materials, labor to convert the basic ingredients to chili, and overhead. We will use materials cost as an example. Three standards need to be developed: (1) What should be the formula (mix) of ingredients for one gallon of chili? (2) What should be the normal wastage (or shrinkage) for the individual ingredients? (3) What should be the standard cost for the individual ingredients that go into the chili?

Susan's Chili Factory also illustrates how standard costs can be used by management in controlling costs. Suppose that summer droughts have reduced crop yields. As a result, prices have doubled for beans, onions, and peppers. In this case, actual costs will be significantly higher than standard costs, which will cause management to evaluate the situation. Management might decide to increase the price charged for a gallon of chili. It might reexamine the product mix to see if other types of ingredients can be used. Or it might curtail production until ingredients can be purchased at or near standard costs. Similarly, assume that poor maintenance caused the onion-dicing blades to become dull. As a result, usage of onions to make a gallon of chili tripled. Because this deviation is quickly highlighted through standard costs, corrective action can be promptly taken.

SOURCE: Adapted from David R. Beran, "Cost Reduction Through Control Reporting," *Management Accounting*, April 1982, pp. 29–33.

BEFORE YOU GO ON . . .

▶ Review It

1. How do standards differ from budgets?
2. What are the advantages of standard costs to an organization?
3. Distinguish between normal standards and ideal standards. Which standard is more widely used? Why?

Do It

The management of Arapahoe Company has decided to use standard costs. Management asks you to explain the components used in setting the standard cost per unit for direct materials, direct labor, and manufacturing overhead.

Action Plan

• Differentiate between the two components of each standard: price and quantity.

Solution

The standard direct materials cost per unit is the standard direct materials price times the standard direct materials quantity. The standard direct labor cost per unit is the standard direct labor rate times the standard direct labor hours. The standard manufacturing overhead rate per unit is the standard predetermined overhead rate times the activity index quantity standard.

Related exercise material: BE21-2, BE21-3, and E21-1.

Variances from Standards

One of the major management uses of standard costs is to identify variances from standards. **Variances** are the differences between total actual costs and total standard costs. To illustrate, we will assume that in producing 1,000 gallons of Weed-O in the month of June, Xonic, Inc. incurred the following costs.

Alternative Terminology
In business, the term *variance* is also used to indicate differences between total budgeted and total actual costs.

Illustration 21-8 Actual production costs

Direct materials	$13,020
Direct labor	20,580
Variable overhead	6,500
Fixed overhead	4,400
Total actual costs	$44,500

Total standard costs are determined by multiplying the units produced by the standard cost per unit. The total standard cost of Weed-O is $42,000 (1,000 gallons × $42). Thus, the total variance is $2,500, as shown below.

Illustration 21-9 Computation of total variance

Actual costs	$44,500
Standard costs	42,000
Total variance	**$ 2,500**

Note that the variance is expressed in total dollars and not on a per unit basis.

When actual costs exceed standard costs, the variance is **unfavorable**. The $2,500 variance in June for Weed-O is unfavorable. An unfavorable variance has a negative connotation. It suggests that too much was paid for one or more of the manufacturing cost elements or that the elements were used inefficiently.

If actual costs are less than standard costs, the variance is **favorable**. A favorable variance has a positive connotation. It suggests efficiencies in incurring manufacturing costs and in using direct materials, direct labor, and manufacturing overhead. However, be careful: A favorable variance could be obtained by using inferior materials. In printing wedding invitations, for example, a favorable variance could result from using an inferior grade of paper. Or, a favorable variance might be achieved in installing tires on an automobile assembly line by tightening only half of the lug bolts. The point should be obvious: A variance is not favorable if quality control standards have been sacrificed.

ANALYZING VARIANCES

To interpret properly the significance of a variance, you must analyze it to determine the underlying factors. Analyzing variances begins by determining the cost elements that comprise the variance. **For each manufacturing cost element, a total dollar variance is computed. Then this variance is analyzed into a price variance and a quantity variance.** The relationships are shown graphically as follows.

Illustration 21-10
Variance relationships

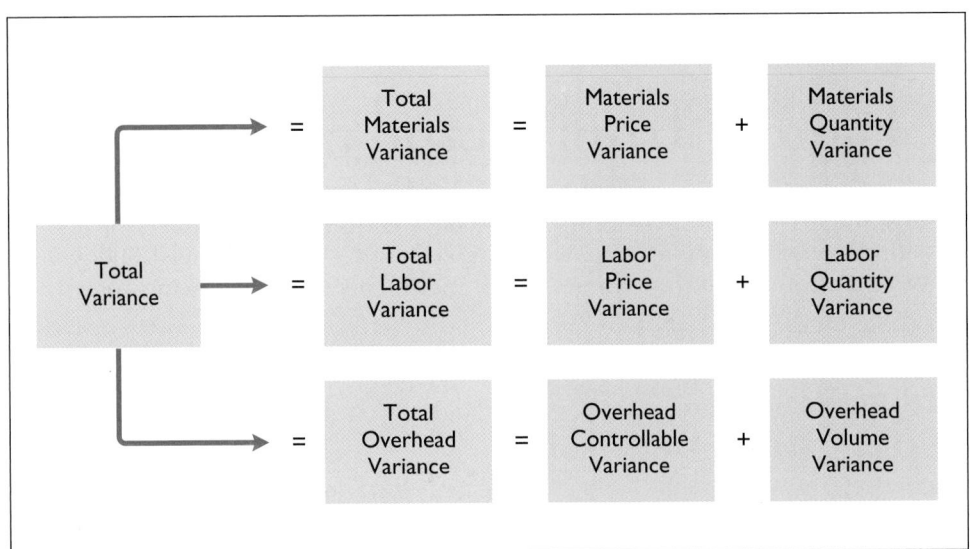

Each of the variances is explained below.

STUDY OBJECTIVE
4
State the formulas for determining direct materials and direct labor variances.

Direct Materials Variances

In completing the order for 1,000 gallons of Weed-O, Xonic used 4,200 pounds of direct materials. These were purchased at a cost of $3.10 per unit. The **total materials variance** is computed from the following formula.

Illustration 21-11 Formula for total materials variance

Actual Quantity × Actual Price (AQ) × (AP)	−	Standard Quantity × Standard Price (SQ) × (SP)	=	Total Materials Variance (TMV)

For Xonic, Inc., the total materials variance is $1,020 ($13,020 − $12,000) unfavorable as shown below.

$$(4,200 \times \$3.10) - (4,000 \times \$3.00) = \$1,020 \text{ U}$$

Next, the total variance is analyzed to determine the amount attributable to price (costs) and to quantity (use). The **materials price variance** is computed from the following formula.[1]

Actual Quantity × Actual Price (AQ) × (AP)	−	Actual Quantity × Standard Price (AQ) × (SP)	=	Materials Price Variance (MPV)

Illustration 21-12
Formula for materials price variance

For Xonic, Inc., the materials price variance is $420 ($13,020 − $12,600) unfavorable as shown below.

$$(4,200 \times \$3.10) - (4,200 \times \$3.00) = \$420 \text{ U}$$

The price variance can also be computed by multiplying the actual quantity purchased by the difference between the actual and standard price per unit. The computation in this case is $4,200 \times (\$3.10 - \$3.00) = \$420$ U.

The **materials quantity variance** is determined from the following formula.

Helpful Hint The alternative formula is:

$$\boxed{AQ} \times \boxed{AP - SP} = \boxed{MPV}$$

Actual Quantity × Standard Price (AQ) × (SP)	−	Standard Quantity × Standard Price (SQ) × (SP)	=	Materials Quantity Variance (MQV)

Illustration 21-13 Formula for materials quantity variance

For Xonic, Inc., the materials quantity variance is $600 ($12,600 − $12,000) unfavorable, as shown below.

$$(4,200 \times \$3.00) - (4,000 \times \$3.00) = \$600 \text{ U}$$

This variance can also be computed by applying the standard price to the difference between actual and standard quantities used. The computation in this example is $\$3.00 \times (4,200 - 4,000) = \$600$ U.

The total materials variance of $1,020(U), therefore, consists of the following.

Helpful Hint The alternative formula is:

$$\boxed{SP} \times \boxed{AQ - SQ} = \boxed{MQV}$$

Materials price variance	$ 420 U
Materials quantity variance	600 U
Total materials variance	**$1,020** U

Illustration 21-14
Summary of materials variances

A matrix is sometimes used to analyze a variance. **When the matrix is used, the formulas for each cost element are computed first and then the variances.** The completed matrix for the direct materials variance for Xonic, Inc. is

---

[1]We will assume that all materials purchased during the period are used in production and that no units remain in inventory at the end of the period.

shown in Illustration 21-15. The matrix provides a convenient structure for determining each variance.

Illustration 21-15 Matrix for direct materials variances

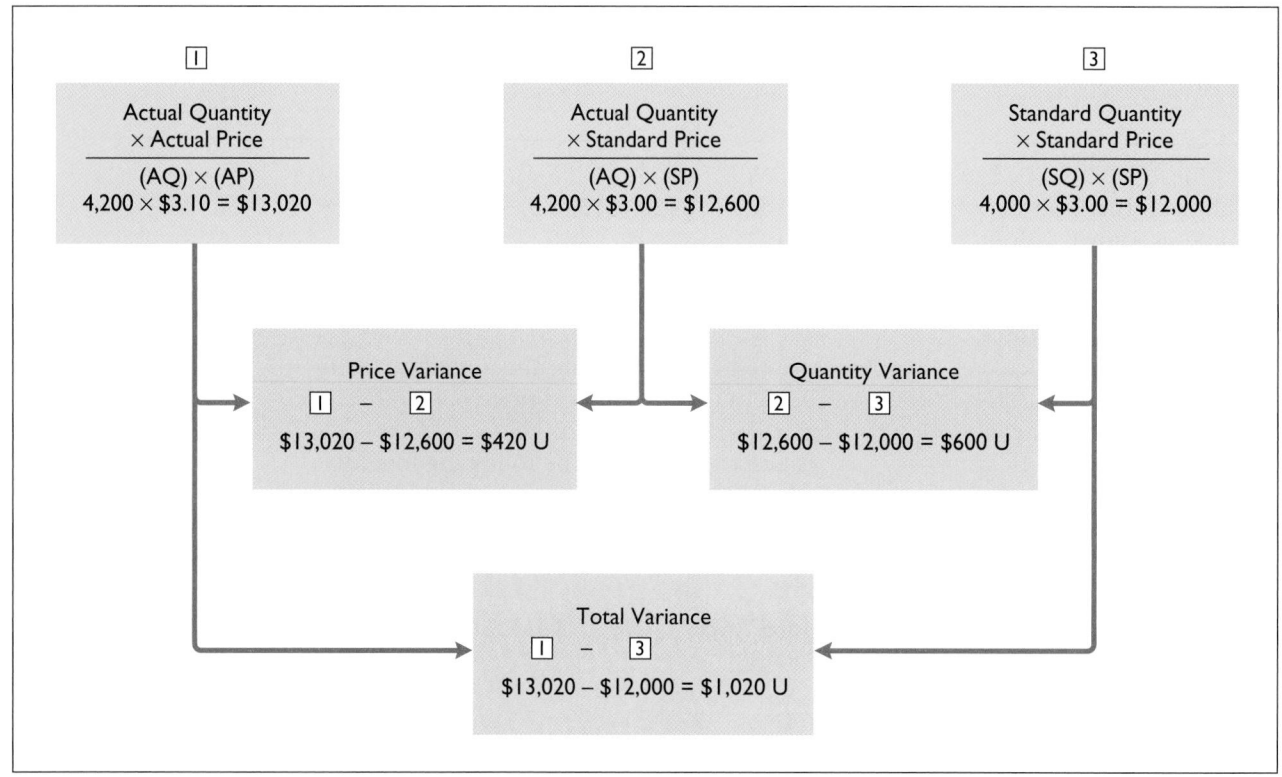

CAUSES OF MATERIALS VARIANCES. What are the causes of a variance? The causes may relate to both internal and external factors. **The investigation of a materials price variance usually begins in the purchasing department.** Many factors affect the price paid for raw materials. These include the delivery method used, availability of quantity and cash discounts, and the quality of the materials requested. To the extent that these factors have been considered in setting the price standard, the purchasing department should be responsible for any variances.

However, a variance may be beyond the control of the purchasing department. Sometimes, for example, prices may rise faster than expected. Moreover, actions by groups over which the company has no control, such as the OPEC nations' oil price increases, may cause an unfavorable variance. There are also times when a production department may be responsible for the price variance. This may occur when a rush order forces the company to pay a higher price for the materials.

The starting point for determining the cause(s) of an unfavorable **materials quantity variance** is in the **production department**. If the variances are due to inexperienced workers, faulty machinery, or carelessness, the production department would be responsible. However, if the materials obtained by the purchasing department were of inferior quality, then the purchasing department should be responsible.

Business Insight
MANAGEMENT PERSPECTIVE

If purchase price variances are used as a basis for measuring performance, purchasing departments often will continually search for the lowest-cost item. However, this basis can become counterproductive if it leads to late deliveries of the goods or the purchase of inferior-quality goods.

BEFORE YOU GO ON . . .

▶ **Review It**

1. What are the three main components of the total variance from standard cost?
2. What are the formulas for computing the total, price, and quantity variances for direct materials?

▶ **Do It**

The standard cost of Product XX includes two units of direct materials at $8.00 per unit. During July, 22,000 units of direct materials are purchased at $7.50 and used to produce 10,000 units. Compute the total, price, and quantity variances for materials.

Action Plan

Use the formulas for computing each of the materials variances:

- Total materials variance $= (AQ \times AP) - (SQ \times SP)$
- Materials price variance $= (AQ \times AP) - (AQ \times SP)$
- Materials quantity variance $= (AQ \times SP) - (SQ \times SP)$

Solution

Substituting amounts into the formulas, the variances are:

Total materials variance $= (22{,}000 \times \$7.50) - (20{,}000 \times \$8.00) = \$5{,}000$ unfavorable.

Materials price variance $= (22{,}000 \times \$7.50) - (22{,}000 \times \$8.00) = \$11{,}000$ favorable.

Materials quantity variance $= (22{,}000 \times \$8.00) - (20{,}000 \times \$8.00) = \$16{,}000$ unfavorable.

Related exercise material: BE21-4, BE21-5, BE21-6, BE21-7, BE21-8, E21-2, E21-3, E21-4, E21-6, E21-7, E21-8, E21-9, and E21-12.

☑ THE NAVIGATOR

DECISION TOOLKIT

Decision Checkpoints	Info Needed for Decision	Tool to Use for Decision	How to Evaluate Results
Has management accomplished its price and quantity objectives regarding materials?	Actual cost and standard cost of materials	Materials price and materials quantity variances	Positive (favorable) variances suggest that price and quantity objectives have been met.

Direct Labor Variances

The process of determining direct labor variances is the same as for determining the direct materials variances. In completing the Weed-O order, Xonic, Inc. incurred 2,100 direct labor hours at an average hourly rate of $9.80. The standard hours allowed for the units produced were 2,000 hours (1,000 units × 2 hours). The standard labor rate was $10 per hour. The **total labor variance** is obtained from the following formula.

Illustration 21-16 Formula for total labor variance

Actual Hours × Actual Rate (AH) × (AR)	−	**Standard Hours × Standard Rate (SH) × (SR)**	=	**Total Labor Variance (TLV)**

The total labor variance is $580 ($20,580 − $20,000) unfavorable, as shown below.

$$(2,100 \times \$9.80) - (2,000 \times \$10.00) = \$580 \text{ U}$$

The formula for the **labor price variance** is:

Illustration 21-17 Formula for labor price variance

Actual Hours × Actual Rate (AH) × (AR)	−	**Actual Hours × Standard Rate (AH) × (SR)**	=	**Labor Price Variance (LPV)**

For Xonic, Inc., the labor price variance is $420 ($20,580 − $21,000) favorable as shown below.

$$(2,100 \times \$9.80) - (2,100 \times \$10.00) = \$420 \text{ F}$$

Helpful Hint The alternative formula is:
$$\boxed{AH} \times \boxed{AR - SR} = \boxed{LPV}$$

This variance can also be computed by multiplying actual hours worked by the difference between the actual pay rate and the standard pay rate. The computation in this example is 2,100 × ($9.80 − $10.00) = $420 F.

The **labor quantity variance** is derived from the following formula.

Illustration 21-18 Formula for labor quantity variance

Actual Hours × Standard Rate (AH) × (SR)	−	**Standard Hours × Standard Rate (SH) × (SR)**	=	**Labor Quantity Variance (LQV)**

For Xonic, Inc., the labor quantity variance is $1,000 ($21,000 − $20,000) unfavorable:

$$(2,100 \times \$10.00) - (2,000 \times \$10.00) = \$1,000 \text{ U}$$

Helpful Hint The alternative formula is:
$$\boxed{SR} \times \boxed{AH - SH} = \boxed{LQV}$$

The same result can be obtained by multiplying the standard rate by the difference between actual hours worked and standard hours allowed. In this case the computation is $10.00 × (2,100 − 2,000) = $1,000 U.

The total direct labor variance of $580 U, therefore, consists of:

Labor price variance	$ 420 F
Labor quantity variance	1,000 U
Total direct labor variance	**$ 580 U**

Illustration 21-19
Summary of labor variances

These results can also be obtained from the matrix in Illustration 21-20.

Illustration 21-20 Matrix for direct labor variances

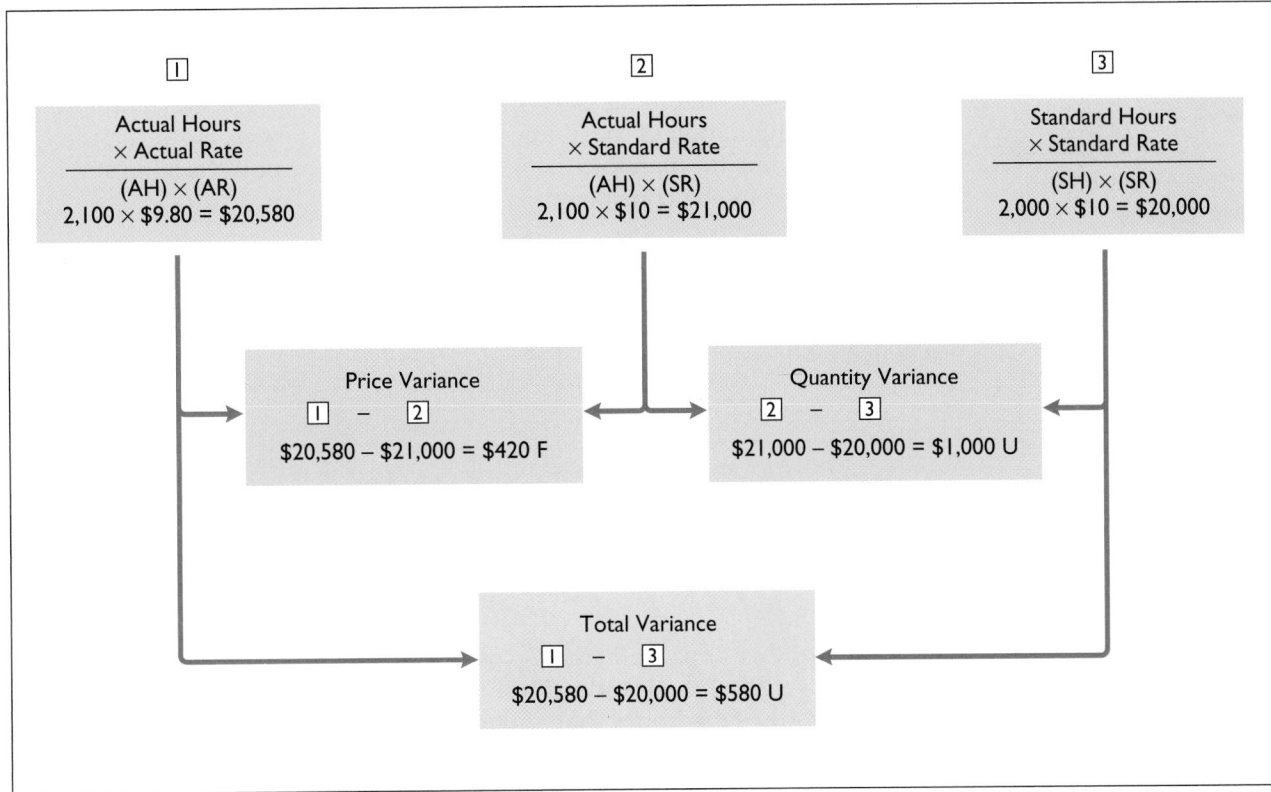

CAUSES OF LABOR VARIANCES.

Labor price variances usually result from two factors: (1) paying workers **higher wages than expected**, and (2) **misallocation of workers**. In companies where pay rates are determined by union contracts, labor price variances should be infrequent. When workers are not unionized, there is a much higher likelihood of such variances. The responsibility for these variances rests with the manager who authorized the wage increase.

Misallocation of the workforce refers to using skilled workers in place of unskilled workers and vice versa. The use of an inexperienced worker instead of an experienced one will result in a favorable price variance because of the lower pay rate of the unskilled worker. An unfavorable price variance would result if a skilled worker were substituted for an inexperienced one. The production department generally is responsible for labor price variances resulting from misallocation of the workforce.

Labor quantity variances relate to the **efficiency of workers**. The cause of a quantity variance generally can be traced to the production department. The causes of an unfavorable variance may be poor training, worker fatigue, faulty machinery, or carelessness. These causes are the responsibility of the **production department**. However, if the excess time is due to inferior materials, the responsibility falls outside the production department.

DECISION TOOLKIT

Decision Checkpoints	Info Needed for Decision	Tool to Use for Decision	How to Evaluate Results
Has management accomplished its price and quantity objectives regarding materials?	Actual cost and standard cost of labor	Labor price and labor quantity variances	Positive (favorable) variances suggest that price and quantity objectives have been met.

Manufacturing Overhead Variances

The computation of the manufacturing overhead variances is conceptually the same as the computation of the materials and labor variances. However, the task is more challenging for manufacturing overhead because both variable and fixed overhead costs must be considered.

TOTAL OVERHEAD VARIANCE. The **total overhead variance** is the difference between actual overhead costs and overhead costs applied to work done. As indicated earlier, manufacturing overhead costs incurred by Xonic were $10,900, as follows.

Illustration 21-21 Actual overhead costs

Variable overhead	$ 6,500
Fixed overhead	4,400
Total actual overhead	**$10,900**

With standard costs, manufacturing overhead costs are applied to work in process on the basis of the **standard hours allowed** for the work done. **Standard hours allowed** are the hours that should have been worked for the units produced. For the Weed-O order, the standard hours allowed are 2,000. The predetermined overhead rate is $5 per direct labor hour. Thus, overhead applied is $10,000 (2,000 × $5). Note that actual hours of direct labor (2,100) are not used in applying manufacturing overhead.

The formula for the total overhead variance is:

Illustration 21-22
Formula for total overhead variance

$$\text{Actual Overhead} - \text{Overhead Applied*} = \text{Total Overhead Variance}$$

*Based on standard hours allowed.

Thus, for Xonic, Inc., the total overhead variance is $900 unfavorable as shown below.

$$\$10,900 - \$10,000 = \$900 \text{ U}$$

The overhead variance is generally analyzed through a price variance and a quantity variance. The name usually given to the price variance is the **overhead controllable variance**, whereas the quantity variance is referred to as the **overhead volume variance**.

OVERHEAD CONTROLLABLE VARIANCE. The overhead controllable variance shows whether overhead costs were effectively controlled. To compute this variance, actual overhead costs incurred are compared with budgeted costs for the **standard hours allowed**. The bud-geted costs are determined from the flexible manufacturing overhead budget. The budget for Xonic, Inc. is as follows.

XONIC, INC. Flexible Manufacturing Overhead Budget				
Activity Index				
Standard direct labor hours	1,800	2,000	2,200	2,400
Costs				
Variable costs				
Indirect materials	$1,800	$ 2,000	$ 2,200	$ 2,400
Indirect labor	2,700	3,000	3,300	3,600
Utilities	900	1,000	1,100	1,200
Total variable	5,400	6,000	6,600	7,200
Fixed costs				
Supervision	3,000	3,000	3,000	3,000
Depreciation	1,400	1,400	1,400	1,400
Total fixed	4,400	4,400	4,400	4,400
Total costs	$9,800	$10,400	$11,000	$11,600

Illustration 21-23 Flexible budget using standard direct labor hours

As shown, the budgeted costs for 2,000 standard hours are $10,400 ($6,000 variable and $4,400 fixed).[2]

The formula for the overhead controllable variance is:

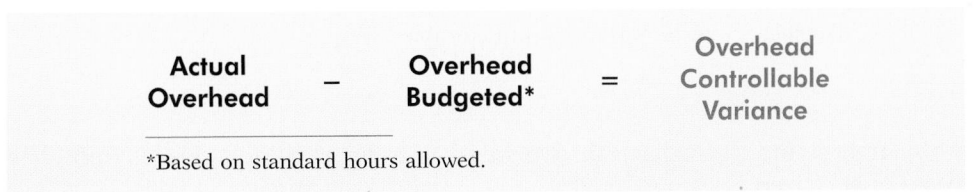

| Actual Overhead | − | Overhead Budgeted* | = | Overhead Controllable Variance |

*Based on standard hours allowed.

Illustration 21-24 Formula for overhead controllable variance

The overhead controllable variance for Xonic, Inc. is $500 unfavorable as shown below.

$$\$10,900 - \$10,400 = \$500 \text{ U}$$

Most controllable variances are associated with variable costs, which are controllable costs. Fixed costs are usually known at the time the budget is prepared. At Xonic, Inc., the variance is accounted for by comparing the actual variable overhead costs ($6,500) with the budgeted variable costs ($6,000).

Management can compare actual and budgeted overhead for each manufacturing overhead cost that contributes to the controllable variance. In addition, cost and quantity variances can be developed for each overhead cost, such as indirect materials and indirect labor.

---

[2]The flexible budget formula is: fixed costs $4,400 plus variable costs $3 per hour. Thus, total budgeted costs are $4,400 + ($3 × 2,000), or $10,400.

OVERHEAD VOLUME VARIANCE. The overhead volume variance indicates whether plant facilities were efficiently used. The formula for computing the volume variance is as follows.

Illustration 21-25 Formula for overhead volume variance

$$\text{Overhead Budgeted*} - \text{Overhead Applied*} = \text{Overhead Volume Variance}$$

*Based on standard hours allowed.

Both the factors in this formula have been explained above. The overhead budgeted is the same as the amount used in computing the controllable variance, or $10,400 in our example. Overhead applied of $10,000 is the amount used in determining the total overhead variance. For Xonic Inc. the overhead volume variance is $400 unfavorable as shown below.

$$\$10,400 - \$10,000 = \$400 \text{ U}$$

We can analyze the volume variance in even more detail. As shown in the flexible manufacturing overhead budget, the budgeted overhead of $10,400 consists of $6,000 variable and $4,400 fixed. As shown in Illustration 21-6 (page 1001), the predetermined overhead rate of $5 consists of $3 variable and $2 fixed. The detailed analysis, therefore, is:

Illustration 21-26 Detailed analysis of overhead volume variance

Overhead budgeted		
Variable costs	$6,000	
Fixed costs	4,400	$10,400
Overhead applied		
Variable costs (2,000 × $3)	6,000	
Fixed costs (2,000 × $2)	4,000	10,000
Overhead volume variance—unfavorable		$ 400

This analysis indicates that **the overhead volume variance relates solely to fixed costs** (fixed costs budgeted $4,400 − fixed costs applied $4,000). Thus, **the volume variance measures the amount that fixed overhead costs are under- or overapplied**.

We have already established that total fixed costs remain the same at every level of activity within the relevant range. A predetermined overhead rate based on normal capacity is used in applying overhead. **It follows that if the standard hours allowed are less than the standard hours at normal capacity, fixed overhead costs will be underapplied.** In contrast, **if production exceeds normal capacity, fixed overhead costs will be overapplied**.

An alternative formula for computing the overhead volume variance is shown in Illustration 21-27.

Illustration 21-27 Alternative formula for overhead volume variance

$$\text{Fixed Overhead Rate} \times (\text{Normal Capacity Hours} - \text{Standard Hours Allowed}) = \text{Overhead Volume Variance}$$

In Xonic, Inc. normal capacity is 26,400 hours for the year, or 2,200 hours for a month (26,400 ÷ 12). The fixed overhead rate is $2 per hour. Thus, the volume variance is $400 unfavorable as shown below.

$$\$2 \times (2{,}200 - 2{,}000) = \$400 \text{ U}$$

The total overhead variance of $900 unfavorable for Xonic, Inc., therefore, consists of the following.

Overhead controllable variance	$ 500 U
Overhead volume variance	400 U
Total overhead variance	**$900** U

Illustration 21-28
Summary of overhead variances

The results can also be obtained from the matrix in Illustration 21-29.

Illustration 21-29 Matrix for manufacturing overhead variances

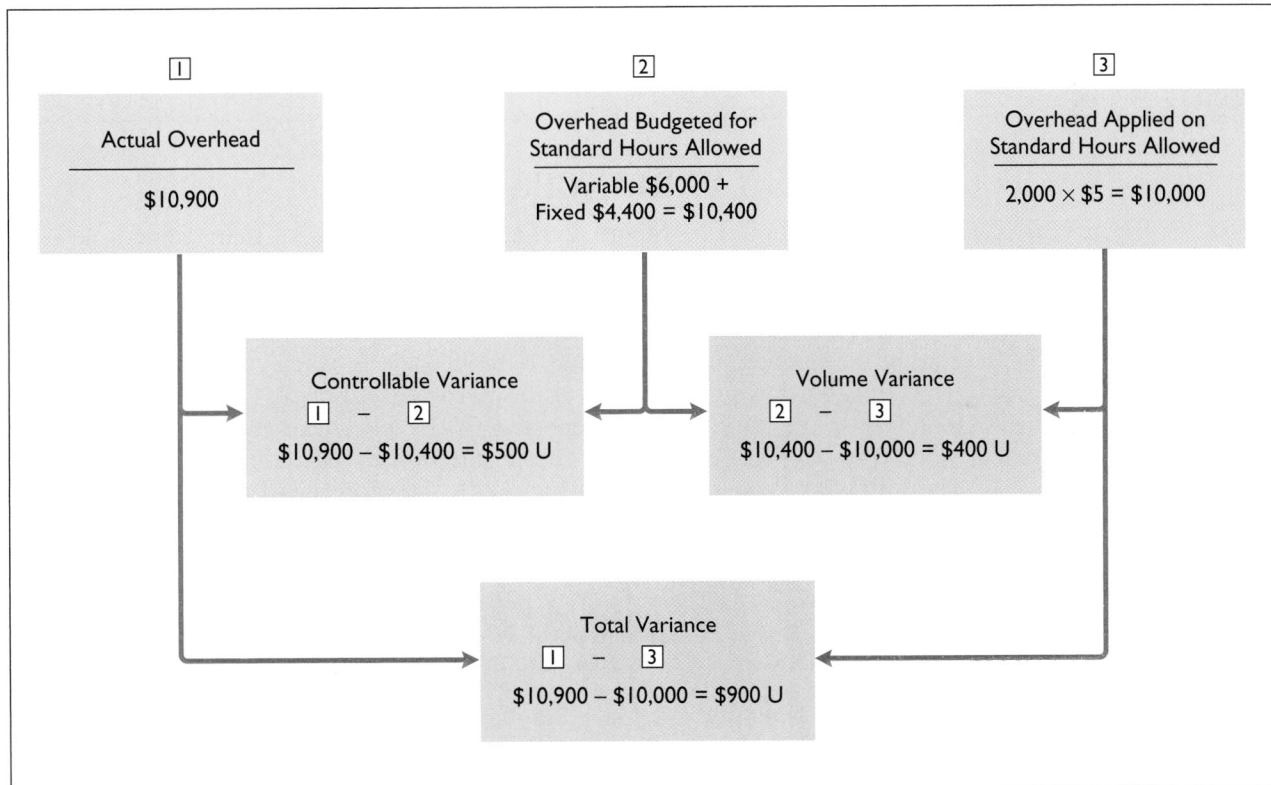

In computing the overhead variances, it is important to remember the following.

1. Standard hours allowed are used in each of the variances.
2. Budgeted costs for the controllable variance are derived from the flexible budget.
3. The controllable variance generally pertains to variable costs.
4. The volume variance pertains solely to fixed costs.

Controllable Variance

Production Dept.

Overhead Volume Variance

Production or Sales Dept.

CAUSES OF MANUFACTURING OVERHEAD VARIANCES. Since the **controllable variance** relates to variable manufacturing costs, the responsibility for the variance rests with the **production department**. The cause of an unfavorable variance may be: (1) **higher than expected use** of indirect materials, indirect labor, and factory supplies, or (2) **increases in indirect manufacturing costs**, such as fuel and maintenance costs.

The **overhead volume variance** is the responsibility of the **production department** if the cause is inefficient use of direct labor or machine breakdowns. When the cause is a **lack of sales orders**, the responsibility rests **outside** the production department.

DECISION TOOLKIT

Decision Checkpoints	Info Needed for Decision	Tool to Use for Decision	How to Evaluate Results
Has management accomplished its price and quantity objectives regarding overhead?	Actual cost and standard cost of overhead	Overhead controllable variance and overhead volume variance	Positive (favorable) variances suggest that price and quantity objectives have been met.

REPORTING VARIANCES

All variances should be reported to appropriate levels of management as soon as possible. The sooner management is informed, the sooner problems can be evaluated and corrective actions taken if necessary.

The form, content, and frequency of variance reports vary considerably among companies. One approach is to prepare a weekly report for each department that has primary responsibility for cost control. Under this approach, materials price variances are reported to the purchasing department, and all other variances are reported to the production department that did the work. The following report for Xonic, Inc., with the materials for the Weed-O order listed first, illustrates this approach.

STUDY OBJECTIVE
6
Discuss the reporting of variances.

Illustration 21-30
Materials price variance report

XONIC, INC.
Variance Report—Purchasing Department
For Week Ended June 8, 2005

Type of Materials	Quantity Purchased	Actual Price	Standard Price	Price Variance	Explanation
X 100	4,200 lbs.	$3.10	$3.00	$ 420 U	Rush order
X 142	1,200 units	2.75	2.80	60 F	Quantity discount
A 85	600 doz.	5.20	5.10	60 U	Regular supplier on strike
Total price variance				**$420 U**	

The explanation column is completed after consultation with the purchasing department manager.

Variance reports facilitate the principle of "management by exception" explained in Chapter 20. For example, the vice president of purchasing can use the report shown above to evaluate the effectiveness of the purchasing department manager. Or, the vice president of production can use production department variance reports to determine how well each production manager is controlling costs. In using variance reports, top management normally looks for **significant variances**. These may be judged on the basis of some quantitative measure, such as more than 10 percent of the standard or more than $1,000.

Business Insight
MANAGEMENT PERSPECTIVE

Computerized standard cost systems represent one of the most complex accounting systems to develop and maintain. The standard cost system must be fully integrated into the general ledger. It must allow for the creation and timely maintenance of the database of standard usage and costs for every product. It must perform variance computations. And it must also produce variance reports by product, department, or employee. With the increased use of automation and robotics, the computerized standard cost system may even be tied directly into these systems to gather variance information.

STATEMENT PRESENTATION OF VARIANCES

In income statements **prepared for management** under a standard cost accounting system, **cost of goods sold is stated at standard cost and the variances are separately disclosed**, as shown in Illustration 21-31. The statement shown is based entirely on the production and sale of Weed-O. It assumes selling and administrative costs of $3,000. Observe that each variance is shown, as well as the total net variance. In this example, variations from standard costs reduced net income by $2,500.

STUDY OBJECTIVE
7

Prepare an income statement for management under a standard costing system.

Illustration 21-31
Variances in income statement for management

XONIC, INC. Income Statement For the Month Ended June 30, 2005		
Sales		$60,000
Cost of goods sold (at standard)		42,000
Gross profit (at standard)		18,000
Variances		
Materials price	$ 420	
Materials quantity	600	
Labor price	(420)	
Labor quantity	1,000	
Overhead controllable	500	
Overhead volume	400	
Total variance unfavorable		2,500
Gross profit (actual)		15,500
Selling and administrative expenses		3,000
Net income		$12,500

In financial statements prepared for stockholders and other external users, standard costs may be used. The costing of inventories at standard costs is in accordance with generally accepted accounting principles when there are no significant differences between actual costs and standard costs. **Hewlett-Packard** and **Jostens, Inc.**, for example, report their inventories at standard costs. However, if there are significant differences between actual and standard costs, inventories and cost of goods sold must be reported at actual costs.

It is also possible to show the variances in an income statement prepared in the contribution margin format. To do so, it is necessary to analyze the overhead variances into variable and fixed components. This type of analysis is explained in cost accounting textbooks.

BEFORE YOU GO ON . . .

▶ **Review It**

1. What are the formulas for computing the total, price, and quantity variances for direct labor?

2. What are the formulas for computing the total, controllable, and volume variances for manufacturing overhead?

3. How are standard costs and variances reported in income statements prepared for management?

Using the Decision Toolkit

Assume that during the past month **Sanford** produced 10,000 cartons of Liquid ACCENT® highlighters. Liquid ACCENT® offers a translucent barrel and cap with a visible ink supply for see-through color. The special fluorescent ink is fade- and water-resistant. Each carton contains 100 boxes of markers, and each box contains five markers. The markers come in boxes of one of five fluorescent colors—orange, blue, yellow, green, and pink—and in a five-color set.

Assume the following additional facts: The standard cost for one carton of 500 markers is as follows.

Manufacturing Cost Elements	Standard Quantity	×	Price	=	Cost
Direct materials					
Tips (boxes of 500)	500	×	$ 0.03	=	$ 15.00
Translucent barrels and caps (boxes of 500)	500	×	$ 0.09	=	45.00
Fluorescent ink (100 oz. containers)	100 oz.	×	$ 0.32	=	32.00
Total direct materials					92.00
Direct labor	0.25 hours	×	$ 9.00	=	2.25
Overhead	0.25 hours	×	$48.00	=	12.00
					$106.25

During the month, the following transactions occurred in manufacturing the 10,000 cartons of highlighters.

1. Purchased 10,000 boxes of tips for $148,000 ($14.80 per 500 tips); purchased 10,200 boxes of translucent barrels and caps for $453,900 ($44.50 per 500 barrels and caps); and purchased 9,900 containers of fluorescent ink for $328,185 ($33.15 per 100 ounces).

2. All materials purchased during the period were used to make markers during the period.

3. 2,300 direct labor hours were worked at a total labor cost of $20,240 (an average hourly rate of $8.80).

4. Variable manufacturing overhead incurred was $34,600, and fixed overhead incurred was $84,000.

The manufacturing overhead rate of $48.00 is based on a normal capacity of 2,600 direct labor hours. The total budget at this capacity is $83,980 fixed and $40,820 variable.

Instructions

Determine whether Sanford met its price and quantity objectives relative to materials, labor, and overhead.

Solution

To determine whether Sanford met its price and quantity objectives, compute the total variance and the variances for each of the manufacturing cost elements.

Total Variance

Actual cost incurred:		
Direct materials		
Tips	$148,000	
Translucent barrels and caps	453,900	
Fluorescent ink	328,185	
Total direct materials		$ 930,085
Direct labor		20,240
Overhead		118,600
Total actual costs		1,068,925
Standard cost (10,000 × $106.25)		1,062,500
Total variance		$ 6,425 U

Direct Materials Variances

Total	=	$930,085	−	$920,000	=	$10,085 U
				(10,000 × $92)		
Price (Tips)	=	$148,000	−	$150,000	=	$ 2,000 F
		(10,000 × $14.80)		(10,000 × $15.00)		
Price (Barrels and caps)	=	$453,900	−	$459,000	=	$ 5,100 F
		(10,200 × $44.50)		(10,200 × $45.00)		
Price (Ink)	=	$328,185	−	$316,800	=	$11,385 U
		(9,900 × $33.15)		(9,900 × $32.00)		
Quantity (Tips)	=	$150,000	−	$150,000	=	$ 0
		(10,000 × $15.00)		(10,000 × $15.00)		
Quantity (Barrels and caps)	=	$459,000	−	$450,000	=	$ 9,000 U
		(10,200 × $45.00)		(10,000 × $45.00)		
Quantity (Ink)	=	$316,800	−	$320,000	=	$ 3,200 F
		(9,900 × $32.00)		(10,000 × $32.00)		

Direct Labor Variances

Total	=	$20,240	−	$22,500	=	$ 2,260 F
		(2,300 × $8.80)		(2,500 × $9.00)		
Price	=	$20,240	−	$20,700	=	$ 460 F
		(2,300 × $8.80)		(2,300 × $9.00)		
Quantity	=	$20,700	−	$22,500	=	$ 1,800 F
		(2,300 × $9.00)		(2,500 × $9.00)		

Overhead Variances

Total	=	$118,600	−	$120,000	=	$1,400 F
		($84,000 + $34,600)		(2,500 × $48)		
Controllable	=	$118,600	−	$123,230	=	$4,630 F
		($84,000 + $34,600)		[(2,500 × $15.70*) + $83,980]		
Volume	=	$123,230	−	$120,000	=	$3,230 U
		[(2,500 × $15.70*) + $83,980] − (2,500 × $48)				

---

*40,820 ÷ 2,600 = $15.70

Sanford's total variance was an unfavorable $6,425. The unfavorable materials variance outweighed the favorable labor and overhead variances. The primary determinants were an unfavorable price variance for ink and an unfavorable quantity variance for barrels and caps.

Summary of Study Objectives

1 *Distinguish between a standard and a budget.* Both standards and budgets are predetermined costs. The primary difference is that a standard is a unit amount, whereas a budget is a total amount. A standard may be regarded as the budgeted cost per unit of product.

2 *Identify the advantages of standard costs.* Standard costs offer a number of advantages. They (a) facilitate management planning, (b) promote greater economy and efficiency, (c) are useful in setting selling prices, (d) contribute to management control, (e) permit "management by exception," and (f) simplify the costing of inventories and reduce clerical costs.

3 *Describe how standards are set.* The direct materials price standard should be based on the delivered cost of raw materials plus an allowance for receiving and handling. The direct materials quantity standard should establish the required quantity plus an allowance for waste and spoilage.

The direct labor price standard should be based on current wage rates and anticipated adjustments such as COLAs. It also generally includes payroll taxes and fringe benefits. Direct labor quantity standards should be based on required production time plus an allowance for rest periods, cleanup, machine setup, and machine downtime.

For manufacturing overhead, a standard predetermined overhead rate is used. It is based on an expected standard activity index such as standard direct labor hours or standard direct labor cost.

4 *State the formulas for determining direct materials and direct labor variances.* The formulas for the direct materials variances are:

$$\begin{pmatrix} \text{Actual quantity} \\ \times \text{Actual price} \end{pmatrix} - \begin{pmatrix} \text{Standard quantity} \\ \times \text{Standard price} \end{pmatrix} = \begin{matrix} \text{Total} \\ \text{materials} \\ \text{variance} \end{matrix}$$

$$\begin{pmatrix} \text{Actual quantity} \\ \times \text{Actual price} \end{pmatrix} - \begin{pmatrix} \text{Actual quantity} \\ \times \text{Standard price} \end{pmatrix} = \begin{matrix} \text{Materials} \\ \text{price} \\ \text{variance} \end{matrix}$$

$$\begin{pmatrix} \text{Actual quantity} \\ \times \text{Standard price} \end{pmatrix} - \begin{pmatrix} \text{Standard quantity} \\ \times \text{Standard price} \end{pmatrix} = \begin{matrix} \text{Materials} \\ \text{quantity} \\ \text{variance} \end{matrix}$$

The formulas for the direct labor variances are:

$$\begin{pmatrix} \text{Actual hours} \\ \times \text{Actual rate} \end{pmatrix} - \begin{pmatrix} \text{Standard hours} \\ \times \text{Standard rate} \end{pmatrix} = \begin{matrix} \text{Total} \\ \text{labor} \\ \text{variance} \end{matrix}$$

$$\begin{pmatrix} \text{Actual hours} \\ \times \text{Actual rate} \end{pmatrix} - \begin{pmatrix} \text{Actual hours} \\ \times \text{Standard rate} \end{pmatrix} = \begin{matrix} \text{Labor} \\ \text{price} \\ \text{variance} \end{matrix}$$

$$\begin{pmatrix} \text{Actual hours} \\ \times \text{Standard rate} \end{pmatrix} - \begin{pmatrix} \text{Standard hours} \\ \times \text{Standard rate} \end{pmatrix} = \begin{matrix} \text{Labor} \\ \text{quantity} \\ \text{variance} \end{matrix}$$

5 *State the formulas for determining manufacturing overhead variances.* The formulas for the manufacturing overhead variances are:

$$\begin{matrix} \text{Actual} \\ \text{overhead} \end{matrix} - \begin{matrix} \text{Overhead} \\ \text{applied} \end{matrix} = \begin{matrix} \text{Total overhead} \\ \text{variance} \end{matrix}$$

$$\begin{matrix} \text{Actual} \\ \text{overhead} \end{matrix} - \begin{matrix} \text{Overhead} \\ \text{budgeted} \end{matrix} = \begin{matrix} \text{Overhead control-} \\ \text{lable variance} \end{matrix}$$

$$\begin{matrix} \text{Overhead} \\ \text{budgeted} \end{matrix} - \begin{matrix} \text{Overhead} \\ \text{applied} \end{matrix} = \begin{matrix} \text{Overhead volume} \\ \text{variance} \end{matrix}$$

6 *Discuss the reporting of variances.* Variances are reported to management in variance reports. The reports facilitate management by exception by highlighting significant differences.

7 *Prepare an income statement for management under a standard costing system.* Under a standard costing system, an income statement prepared for management will report cost of goods sold at standard cost and then disclose each variance separately.

DECISION TOOLKIT—A SUMMARY

Decision Checkpoints	Info Needed for Decision	Tool to Use for Decision	How to Evaluate Results
Has management accomplished its price and quantity objectives regarding materials?	Actual cost and standard cost of materials	Materials price and materials quantity variances	Positive (favorable) variances suggest that price and quantity objectives have been met.
Has management accomplished its price and quantity objectives regarding labor?	Actual cost and standard cost of labor	Labor price and labor quantity variances	Positive (favorable) variances suggest that price and quantity objectives have been met.
Has management accomplished its price and quantity objectives regarding overhead?	Actual cost and standard cost of overhead	Overhead controllable variance and overhead volume variance	Positive (favorable) variances suggest that price and quantity objectives have been met.

APPENDIX
STANDARD COST ACCOUNTING SYSTEM

A **standard cost accounting system** is a double-entry system of accounting. In this system, standard costs are used in making entries, and variances are formally recognized in the accounts. A standard cost system may be used with either job order or process costing. At this point, we will explain and illustrate a **standard cost**, **job order cost accounting system**. The system is based on two important assumptions: (1) Variances from standards are recognized at the earliest opportunity. (2) The Work in Process account is maintained exclusively on the basis of standard costs. In practice, there are many variations among standard cost systems. The system described here should prepare you for systems you see in the "real world."

> **STUDY OBJECTIVE 8**
>
> Identify the features of a standard cost accounting system.

Journal Entries

We will use the transactions of Xonic, Inc. to illustrate the journal entries. Note as you study the entries that the major difference between the entries here and those for the job order cost accounting system in Chapter 16 is the **variance accounts**.

1. Purchase raw materials on account for $13,020 when the standard cost is $12,600.

Raw Materials Inventory	12,600	
Materials Price Variance	420	
Accounts Payable		13,020
(To record purchase of materials)		

The inventory account is debited for actual quantities at standard cost. This enables the perpetual materials records to show actual quantities. The price variance, which is unfavorable, is debited to Materials Price Variance.

2. Incur direct labor costs of $20,580 when the standard labor cost is $21,000.

Factory Labor	21,000	
Labor Price Variance		420
Wages Payable		20,580
(To record direct labor costs)		

Like the raw materials inventory account, Factory Labor is debited for actual hours worked at the standard hourly rate of pay. In this case, the labor variance is favorable. Thus, Labor Price Variance is credited.

3. Incur actual manufacturing overhead costs of $10,900.

Manufacturing Overhead	10,900	
Accounts Payable/Cash/Acc. Depreciation		10,900
(To record overhead incurred)		

The controllable overhead variance is not recorded at this time. It depends on standard hours applied to work in process. This amount is not known at the time overhead is incurred.

4. Issue raw materials for production at a cost of $12,600 when the standard cost is $12,000.

Work in Process Inventory	12,000	
Materials Quantity Variance	600	
Raw Materials Inventory		12,600
(To record issuance of raw materials)		

Work in Process Inventory is debited for standard materials quantities used at standard prices. The variance account is debited because the variance is unfavorable. Raw Materials Inventory is credited for actual quantities at standard prices.

5. Assign factory labor to production at a cost of $21,000 when standard cost is $20,000.

Work in Process Inventory	20,000	
Labor Quantity Variance	1,000	
Factory Labor		21,000
(To assign factory labor to jobs)		

Work in Process Inventory is debited for standard labor hours at standard rates. The unfavorable variance is debited to Labor Quantity Variance. The credit to Factory Labor produces a zero balance in this account.

6. Applying manufacturing overhead to production $10,000.

Work in Process Inventory	10,000	
Manufacturing Overhead		10,000
(To assign overhead to jobs)		

Work in Process Inventory is debited for standard hours allowed multiplied by the standard overhead rate.

7. Transfer completed work to finished goods $42,000.

Finished Goods Inventory	42,000	
Work in Process Inventory		42,000
(To record transfer of completed work to finished goods)		

In this example, both inventory accounts are at standard cost.

8. The 1,000 gallons of Weed-O are sold for $60,000.

Accounts Receivable	60,000	
Cost of Goods Sold	42,000	
Sales		60,000
Finished Goods Inventory		42,000
(To record sale of finished goods and the cost of goods sold)		

Cost of Goods Sold is debited at standard cost. Gross profit, in turn, is the difference between sales and the standard cost of goods sold.

9. Recognize unfavorable overhead variances: controllable, $500; volume, $400.

Overhead Controllable Variance	500	
Overhead Volume Variance	400	
Manufacturing Overhead		900
(To recognize overhead variances)		

Prior to this entry, a debit balance of $900 existed in Manufacturing Overhead. This entry therefore produces a zero balance in the Manufacturing Overhead account. The information needed for this entry is often not available until the end of the accounting period.

Ledger Accounts

The cost accounts for Xonic, Inc., after posting the entries, are shown in Illustration 21A-1. Note that six variance accounts are included in the ledger. The remaining accounts are the same as those illustrated for a job order cost system in Chapter 16, in which only actual costs were used.

Illustration 21A-1 Cost accounts with variances

Helpful Hint All debit balances in variance accounts indicate unfavorable variances; all credit balances indicate favorable variances.

Summary of Study Objective for Appendix

8 *Identify the features of a standard cost accounting system.* In a standard cost accounting system, standard costs are journalized and posted, and separate variance accounts are maintained in the ledger.

When differences between actual costs and standard costs do not differ significantly, inventories may be reported at standard costs.

Glossary

Direct labor price standard The rate per hour that should be incurred for direct labor. (p. 1000)

Direct labor quantity standard The time that should be required to make one unit of product. (p. 1000)

Direct materials price standard The cost per unit of direct materials that should be incurred. (p. 999)

Direct materials quantity standard The quantity of direct materials that should be used per unit of finished goods. (p. 1000)

Ideal standards Standards based on the optimum level of performance under perfect operating conditions. (p. 999)

Labor price variance The difference between the actual hours times the actual rate and the actual hours times the standard rate for labor. (p. 1008)

Labor quantity variance The difference between actual hours times the standard rate and standard hours times the standard rate for labor. (p. 1008)

Materials price variance The difference between the actual quantity times the actual price and the actual quantity times the standard price for materials. (p. 1005)

Materials quantity variance The difference between the actual quantity times the standard price and the standard quantity times the standard price for materials. (p. 1005)

Normal standards Standards based on an efficient level of performance that are attainable under expected operating conditions. (p. 999)

Overhead controllable variance The difference between actual overhead incurred and overhead budgeted for the standard hours allowed. (p. 1011)

Overhead volume variance The difference between overhead budgeted for the standard hours allowed and the overhead applied. (p. 1012)

Standard cost accounting system A double-entry system of accounting in which standard costs are used in making entries and variances are recognized in the accounts. (p. 1019)

Standard costs Predetermined unit costs which are used as measures of performance. (p. 997)

Standard hours allowed The hours that should have been worked for the units produced. (p. 1110)

Standard predetermined overhead rate An overhead rate determined by dividing budgeted overhead costs by an expected standard activity index. (p. 1001)

Total labor variance The difference between actual hours times the actual rate and standard hours times the standard rate for labor. (p. 1008)

Total materials variance The difference between the actual quantity times the actual price and the standard quantity times the standard price of materials. (p. 1004)

Total overhead variance The difference between actual overhead costs and overhead costs applied to work done. (p. 1010)

Variances The difference between total actual costs and total standard costs. (p. 1003)

Demonstration Problem

Manlow Company makes a cologne called Allure. The standard cost for one bottle of Allure is as follows.

Manufacturing Cost Elements	Quantity	×	Price	=	Cost
Direct materials	6 oz.	×	$ 0.90	=	$ 5.40
Direct labor	0.5 hrs.	×	$12.00	=	6.00
Manufacturing overhead	0.5 hrs.	×	$ 4.80	=	2.40
					$13.80

During the month, the following transactions occurred in manufacturing 10,000 bottles of Allure.

1. 58,000 ounces of materials were purchased at $1.00 per ounce.
2. All the materials purchased were used to produce the 10,000 bottles of Allure.
3. 4,900 direct labor hours were worked at a total labor cost of $56,350.
4. Variable manufacturing overhead incurred was $15,000 and fixed overhead incurred was $10,400.

The manufacturing overhead rate of $4.80 is based on a normal capacity of 5,200 direct labor hours. The total budget at this capacity is $10,400 fixed and $14,560 variable.

Instructions

Compute the total variance and the variances for each of the manufacturing cost elements.

Solution to Demonstration Problem

Total Variance

Actual costs incurred		
Direct materials	$ 58,000	
Direct labor	56,350	
Manufacturing overhead	25,400	
	139,750	
Standard cost (10,000 × $13.80)	138,000	
Total variance	$ 1,750 (U)	

Direct Materials Variances

Total	=	$58,000	−	$54,000	=	$4,000 U
		(58,000 × $1.00)		(60,000 × $0.90)		
Price	=	$58,000	−	$52,200	=	$5,800 U
		(58,000 × $1.00)		(58,000 × $0.90)		
Quantity	=	$52,200	−	$54,000	=	$1,800 F
		(58,000 × $0.90)		(60,000 × $0.90)		

Direct Labor Variances

Total	=	$56,350	−	$60,000	=	$3,650 F
		(4,900 × $11.50)		(5,000 × $12.00)		
Price	=	$56,350	−	$58,800	=	$2,450 F
		(4,900 × $11.50)		(4,900 × $12.00)		
Quantity	=	$58,800	−	$60,000	=	$1,200 F
		(4,900 × $12.00)		(5,000 × $12.00)		

Overhead Variances

Total	=	$25,400	−	$24,000	=	$1,400 U
		($15,000 + $10,400)		(5,000 × $4.80)		
Controllable	=	$25,400	−	$24,400	=	$1,000 U
		($15,000 + $10,400)		($14,000 + $10,400)		
Volume	=	$24,400	−	$24,000	=	$ 400 U
		($14,000 + $10,400)		(5,000 × $4.80)		

Action Plan

- Check to make sure the total variance and the sum of the individual variances are equal.
- Find the price variance first, then the quantity variance.
- Base budgeted overhead costs on flexible budget data.
- Base overhead applied on standard hours allowed.
- Ignore actual hours worked in computing overhead variances.
- Relate the overhead volume variance solely to fixed costs.

☑ THE NAVIGATOR

Note: All asterisked Questions, Exercises, and Problems relate to material in the appendix to the chapter.

Self-Study Questions

Self-Study/Self-Test

Answers are at the end of the chapter.

(SO 1)   1. Standards differ from budgets in that:
(a) budgets but not standards may be used in valuing inventories.
(b) budgets but not standards may be journalized and posted.
(c) budgets are a total amount and standards are a unit amount.
(d) only budgets contribute to management planning and control.

(SO 2)   2. The advantages of standard costs include all of the following *except:*
(a) management by exception may be used.
(b) management planning is facilitated.
(c) they may simplify the costing of inventories.
(d) management must use a static budget.

(SO 3)   3. The setting of standards is:
(a) a managerial accounting decision.
(b) a management decision.
(c) a worker decision.
(d) preferably set at the ideal level of performance.

(SO 4)   4. Each of the following formulas is correct *except*:
(a) Labor price variance = (Actual hours × Actual rate) − (Actual hours × Standard rate).
(b) Overhead controllable variance = Actual overhead − Overhead budgeted.
(c) Materials price variance = (Actual quantity × Actual cost) − (Standard quantity × Standard cost).
(d) Overhead volume variance = Overhead budgeted − Overhead applied.

(SO 4)   5. In producing product AA, 6,300 pounds of direct materials were used at a cost of $1.10 per pound. The standard was 6,000 pounds at $1 per pound. The direct materials quantity variance is:
(a) $330 unfavorable.
(b) $300 unfavorable.
(c) $600 unfavorable.
(d) $630 unfavorable.

(SO 4)   6. In producing product ZZ, 14,800 direct labor hours were used at a rate of $8.20 per hour. The standard was 15,000 hours at $8.00 per hour. Based on these data, the direct labor:
(a) quantity variance is $1,600 favorable.
(b) quantity variance is $1,600 unfavorable.
(c) price variance is $2,960 favorable.
(d) price variance is $3,000 unfavorable.

(SO 5)   7. Which of the following is *correct* about overhead variances?
(a) The controllable variance generally pertains to fixed overhead costs.
(b) The volume variance pertains solely to variable overhead costs.
(c) Standard hours actually worked are used in each variance.
(d) Budgeted overhead costs are based on the flexible overhead budget.

(SO 5)   8. The formula for computing the total overhead variance is:
(a) actual overhead less overhead applied.
(b) overhead budgeted less overhead applied.
(c) actual overhead less overhead budgeted.
(d) No correct answer given.

(SO 6)   9. Which of the following is *incorrect* about variance reports?
(a) They facilitate "management by exception."
(b) They should only be sent to the top level of management.
(c) They should be prepared as soon as possible.
(d) They may vary in form, content, and frequency among companies.

(SO 8) *10. Which of the following is *incorrect* about a standard cost accounting system?
(a) It is applicable to job order costing.
(b) It is applicable to process costing.
(c) It is a single-entry system.
(d) It keeps separate accounts for each variance.

Questions

1. (a) "Standard costs are the expected total cost of completing a job." Is this correct? Explain.
   (b) "A standard imposed by a governmental agency is known as a regulation." Do you agree? Explain.

2. (a) Explain the similarities and differences between standards and budgets.

   (b) Contrast the accounting for standards and budgets.

3. Standard costs facilitate management planning. What are the other advantages of standard costs?

4. Contrast the roles of the management accountant and management in setting standard costs.

5. Distinguish between an ideal standard and a normal standard.

6. What factors should be considered in setting (a) the materials price standard and (b) the materials quantity standard?

7. "The objective in setting the direct labor quantity standard is to determine the aggregate time required to make one unit of product." Do you agree? What allowances should be made in setting this standard?

8. How is the predetermined overhead rate determined when standard costs are used?

9. What is the difference between a favorable cost variance and an unfavorable cost variance?

10. In each of the following formulas, supply the words that should be inserted for each number in parentheses.
    (a) (Actual quantity × (1)) − (Standard quantity × (2)) = Total materials variance
    (b) ((3) × Actual price) − (Actual quantity × (4)) = Materials price variance
    (c) (Actual quantity × (5)) − ((6) × Standard price) = Materials quantity variance

11. In the direct labor variance matrix, there are three factors: (1) Actual hours × Actual rate, (2) Actual hours × Standard rate, and (3) Standard hours × Standard rate. Using the numbers, indicate the formulas for each of the direct labor variances.

12. Dant Company's standard predetermined overhead rate is $6.00 per direct labor hour. For the month of June, 26,000 actual hours were worked, and 27,500 standard hours were allowed. Normal capacity hours were 28,000. How much overhead was applied?

13. If the $6.00 per hour overhead rate in question 12 consists of $4.00 variable, and actual overhead costs

were $163,000, what is the overhead controllable variance for June? Is the variance favorable or unfavorable?

14. Using the data in questions 12 and 13, what is the overhead volume variance for June? Is the variance favorable or unfavorable?

15. What is the purpose of computing the overhead volume variance? What is the basic formula for this variance?

16. Ellen Landis does not understand why the overhead volume variance indicates that fixed overhead costs are under- or overapplied. Clarify this matter for Ellen.

17. Stan LaRue is attempting to outline the important points about overhead variances on a class examination. List four points that Stan should include in his outline.

18. How often should variances be reported to management? What principle may be used with variance reports?

19. What circumstances may cause the purchasing department to be responsible for both an unfavorable materials price variance and an unfavorable materials quantity variance?

20. (a) How are variances reported in income statements prepared for management? (b) May standard costs be used in preparing financial statements for stockholders? Explain.

*21. (a) Explain the basic features of a standard cost accounting system. (b) What type of balance will exist in the variance account when (1) the materials price variance is unfavorable and (2) the labor quantity variance is favorable?

Brief Exercises

BE21-1 Tumbo Company uses both standards and budgets. For the year, estimated production of Product X is 500,000 units. Total estimated costs for materials and labor are $1,200,000 and $1,600,000. Compute the estimates for (a) a standard cost and (b) a budgeted cost.

Distinguish between a standard and a budget.
(SO 1)

BE21-2 Nurmi Company accumulates the following data concerning raw materials in making one gallon of finished product: (1) Price—net purchase price $3.50, freight-in $0.20, and receiving and handling $0.10. (2) Quantity—required materials 2.6 pounds, allowance for waste and spoilage 0.4 pounds. Compute the following.
  (a) Standard direct materials price per gallon.
  (b) Standard direct materials quantity per gallon.
  (c) Total standard material cost per gallon.

Set direct materials standard.
(SO 3)

BE21-3 Labor data for making one gallon of finished product in Nurmi Company are as follows: (1) Price—hourly wage rate $10.00, payroll taxes $0.80, and fringe benefits $1.20. (2) Quantity—actual production time 1.6 hours, rest periods and clean up 0.25 hours, and setup and downtime 0.15 hours. Compute the following.
  (a) Standard direct labor rate per hour.
  (b) Standard direct labor hours per gallon.
  (c) Standard labor cost per gallon.

Set direct labor standard.
(SO 3)

Compute direct materials variances.
(SO 4)

BE21-4 Nadia Company's standard materials cost per unit of output is $8 (2 pounds × $4.00). During July, the company purchases and uses 3,300 pounds of materials costing $13,365 in making 1,500 units of finished product. Compute the total, price, and quantity materials variances.

Compute direct labor variances.
(SO 4)

BE21-5 Kimiko Company's standard labor cost per unit of output is $18 (2 hours × $9.00 per hour). During August, the company incurs 1,850 hours of direct labor at an hourly cost of $9.60 per hour in making 1,000 units of finished product. Compute the total, price, and quantity labor variances.

Compute total manufacturing overhead variance.
(SO 5)

BE21-6 In October, Hilo Company reports 21,000 actual direct labor hours, and it incurs $98,000 of manufacturing overhead costs. Standard hours allowed for the work done is 20,000 hours. The predetermined overhead rate is $5.00 per direct labor hour. Compute the total manufacturing overhead variance.

Compute the manufacturing overhead controllable variance.
(SO 5)

BE21-7 Some overhead data for Hilo Company are given in BE21-6. In addition, the flexible manufacturing overhead budget shows that budgeted variable costs are $4.00 per direct labor hour, and budgeted fixed costs are $25,000. Compute the manufacturing overhead controllable variance.

Compute overhead volume variance.
(SO 5)

BE21-8 Using the data in BE21-6 and BE21-7, compute the manufacturing overhead volume variance.

Journalize materials variances.
(SO 8)

*BE21-9 Journalize the following transactions for Nashua Manufacturing.
(a) Purchased 6,000 units of raw materials on account for $11,700. The standard cost was $12,000.
(b) Issued 5,600 units of raw materials for production. The standard units were 5,800.

Journalize labor variances.
(SO 8)

*BE21-10 Journalize the following transactions for Harlem Manufacturing.
(a) Incurred direct labor costs of $24,000 for 3,000 hours. The standard labor cost was $24,300.
(b) Assigned 3,000 direct labor hours costing $24,000 to production. Standard hours were 3,100.

Exercises

Compute standard materials costs.
(SO 3)

E21-1 Robin Ritz manufactures and sells homemade wine, and he wants to develop a standard cost per gallon. The following are required for production of a 50-gallon batch.

    3,000 ounces of grape concentrate at $0.05 per ounce

    54 pounds of granulated sugar at $0.30 per pound

    70 lemons at $0.60 each

    50 yeast tablets at $0.25 each

    50 nutrient tablets at $0.20 each

    2,500 ounces of water at $0.0043 per ounce

Robin estimates that 4% of the grape concentrate is wasted, 10% of the sugar is lost, and 20% of the lemons cannot be used.

Instructions
Compute the standard cost of the ingredients for one gallon of wine. (Carry computations to three decimal places.)

Compute materials price and quantity variances.
(SO 4)

E21-2 The standard cost of Product B manufactured by Lopez Company includes three units of direct materials at $5.00 per unit. During June, 30,000 units of direct materials are purchased at a cost of $4.80 per unit, and 27,200 units of direct materials are used to produce 9,000 units of Product B.

Instructions
(a) Compute the materials price and quantity variances.
(b) Repeat (a), assuming the purchase price is $5.10 and the quantity used is 26,400 units.

Compute labor price and quantity variances.
(SO 4)

E21-3 Napier Company's standard labor cost of producing one unit of Product DD is 3.9 hours at the rate of $12.00 per hour. During August, 40,800 hours of labor are incurred at a cost of $12.10 per hour to produce 10,000 units of Product DD.

Instructions

(a) Compute the labor price and quantity variances.

(b) Repeat (a), assuming the standard is 4.2 hours of direct labor at $12.20 per hour.

E21-4 Kayjay Inc., which produces a single product, has prepared the following standard cost sheet for one unit of the product.

Direct materials (8 pounds at $2.50 per pound) $20.00
Direct labor (3 hours at $12.00 per hour) $36.00

Compute materials and labor variances.
(SO 4)

During the month of April, the company manufactures 250 units and incurs the following actual costs.

Direct materials (1,900 pounds—purchased and used) $5,035
Direct labor (700 hours) $8,050

Instructions

Compute the total, price, and quantity variances for materials and labor.

E21-5 The following direct materials and direct labor data pertain to the operations of Juan Manufacturing Company for the month of August.

Compute the materials and labor variances and list reasons for unfavorable variances.
(SO 4, 6)

Costs		**Quantities**	
Actual labor rate	$13.00 per hour	Actual hours incurred and used	4,200 hours
Actual materials price	$128.00 per ton	Actual quantity of materials purchased and used	1,230 tons
Standard labor rate	$12.00 per hour	Standard hours used	4,300 hours
Standard materials price	$130.00 per ton	Standard quantity of materials used	1,200 tons

Instructions

(a) Compute the total, price, and quantity variances for materials and labor.

(b) ▯▭▭▭▷ Provide two possible explanations for each of the unfavorable variances calculated above, and suggest where responsibility for the unfavorable result might be placed.

E21-6 The following information was taken from the annual manufacturing overhead cost budget of SooTech Company.

Compute manufacturing overhead variances and interpret findings.
(SO 5)

Variable manufacturing overhead costs $33,000
Fixed manufacturing overhead costs $19,800
Normal production level in hours   16,500
Normal production level in units   4,125

During the year, 4,000 units were produced, 16,100 hours were worked, and the actual manufacturing overhead was $54,000. Actual fixed manufacturing overhead costs equaled budgeted fixed manufacturing overhead costs. Overhead is applied on the basis of direct labor hours.

Instructions

(a) Compute the total, fixed, and variable predetermined manufacturing overhead rates.

(b) Compute the total, controllable, and volume overhead variances.

(c) ▯▭▭▭▷ Briefly interpret the overhead controllable and volume variances computed in (b).

E21-7 Manufacturing overhead data for the production of Product H by Fierello Company are as follows.

Compute overhead variances, and journalize transactions and adjusting entry.
(SO 5, 8)

Overhead incurred for 51,000 actual direct labor hours worked $213,000
Overhead rate (variable $3.00; fixed $1.00) at normal capacity of 54,000
    direct labor hours $4.00
Standard hours allowed for work done   51,000

Instructions
 (a) Compute the total, controllable, and volume overhead variances.
 *(b) Journalize the incurrence of the overhead costs and the application of overhead to the job, assuming a standard cost accounting system is used.
 *(c) Prepare the adjusting entry for the overhead variances.

Prepare a variance report for direct labor.
(SO 4, 6)

E21-8 During March 2005, Tenza Tool & Die Company worked on four jobs. A review of direct labor costs reveals the following summary data.

| Job Number | Actual | | Standard | | Total Variance |
	Hours	Costs	Hours	Costs	
A257	220	$ 4,400	226	$4,520	$ 120 F
A258	450	10,350	430	8,600	1,750 U
A259	300	6,150	300	6,000	150 U
A260	116	2,088	110	2,200	112 F
Total variance					$1,668 U

Analysis reveals that Job A257 was a repeat job. Job A258 was a rush order that required overtime work at premium rates of pay. Job A259 required a more experienced replacement worker on one shift. Work on Job A260 was done for one day by a new trainee when a regular worker was absent.

Instructions
Prepare a report for the plant supervisor on direct labor cost variances for March. The report should have columns for (1) Job No., (2) Actual Hours, (3) Standard Hours, (4) Labor Quantity Variance, (5) Actual Rate, (6) Standard Rate, (7) Labor Price Variance, and (8) Explanations.

Prepare income statement for management.
(SO 7)

E21-9 Alvarez Company uses a standard cost accounting system. During January, the company reported the following manufacturing variances account balances.

Materials price variance	$1,250 debit	Labor quantity variance	$ 725 debit
Materials quantity variance	700 credit	Overhead controllable	200 credit
Labor price variance	525 debit	Overhead volume	1,000 debit

In addition, 6,000 units of product were sold at $8.00 per unit. Each unit sold had a standard cost of $5.00. Selling and administrative expenses were $9,000 for the month.

Instructions
Prepare an income statement for management for the month ending January 31, 2005.

Journalize entries for materials and labor variances.
(SO 8)

*E21-10 Data for Kayjay Inc. are given in E21-4.

Instructions
Journalize the entries to record the materials and labor variances.

Journalize entries in a standard cost accounting system.
(SO 8)

*E21-11 DeSoto Company installed a standard cost system on January 1. Selected transactions for the month of January are as follows.
 1. Purchased 18,000 units of raw materials on account at a cost of $4.50 per unit. Standard cost was $4.00 per unit.
 2. Issued 18,000 units of raw materials for jobs that required 17,600 standard units of raw materials.
 3. Incurred 15,200 actual hours of direct labor at an actual rate of $4.80 per hour. The standard rate is $5.00 per hour. (Credit Wages Payable)
 4. Performed 15,200 hours of direct labor on jobs when standard hours were 15,400.
 5. Applied overhead to jobs at the rate of 100% of direct labor cost for standard hours allowed.

Instructions
Journalize the January transactions.

Answer questions concerning missing entries and balances.
(SO 4, 5, 8)

*E21-12 Amand Company uses a standard cost accounting system. Some of the ledger accounts have been destroyed in a fire. The controller asks your help in reconstructing

some missing entries and balances. (*Note:* Assume that the amount of raw materials purchased was equal to the amount used.)

Instructions

Answer the following questions.

(a) Materials Price Variance shows a $3,000 favorable balance. Accounts Payable shows $126,000 of raw materials purchases. What was the amount debited to Raw Materials Inventory for raw materials purchased?

(b) Materials Quantity Variance shows a $3,000 unfavorable balance. Raw Materials Inventory shows a zero balance. What was the amount debited to Work in Process Inventory for direct materials used?

(c) Labor Price Variance shows a $1,500 unfavorable balance. Factory Labor shows a debit of $152,000 for wages incurred. What was the amount credited to Wages Payable?

(d) Factory Labor shows a credit of $152,000 for direct labor used. Labor Quantity Variance shows a $900 unfavorable balance. What was the amount debited to Work in Process for direct labor used?

(e) Overhead applied to Work in Process totaled $165,000. If the total overhead variance was $1,300 unfavorable, what was the amount of overhead costs debited to Manufacturing Overhead?

(f) Overhead Controllable Variance shows a debit balance of $1,500. What was the amount and type of balance (debit or credit) in Overhead Volume Variance?

Problems: Set A

P21-1A Moore Corporation manufactures a single product. The standard cost per unit of product is shown below.

Compute variances.
(SO 4, 5)

Direct materials—1 pound plastic at $7.00 per pound	$ 7.00
Direct labor—1.5 hours at $12.00 per hour	18.00
Variable manufacturing overhead	11.25
Fixed manufacturing overhead	3.75
Total standard cost per unit	$40.00

The predetermined manufacturing overhead rate is $10 per direct labor hour ($15.00 ÷ 1.5). This rate was computed from a master manufacturing overhead budget based on normal production of 90,000 direct labor hours (60,000 units) for the year. The master budget showed total variable costs of $675,000 and total fixed costs of $225,000. Actual costs for October in producing 5,000 units were as follows.

Direct materials (5,100 pounds)	$ 36,720
Direct labor (7,000 hours)	86,100
Variable overhead	56,170
Fixed overhead	19,680
Total manufacturing costs	$198,670

The purchasing department normally buys the quantities of raw materials that are expected to be used in production each month. Raw materials inventories, therefore, can be ignored.

Instructions

Compute all of the materials, labor, and overhead variances.

Materials price
  variance $1,020 U
Labor quantity
  variance $6,000 F

P21-2A Ellison Manufacturing Corporation accumulates the following data relative to jobs started and finished during the month of June 2005.

Compute variances, and
prepare income statement.
(SO 4, 5, 7)

Costs and Production Data	Actual	Standard
Raw materials purchases, 10,500 units	$ 23,100	$ 21,000
Raw materials units used	10,500	10,000
Direct labor payroll	$122,100	$120,000
Direct labor hours worked	14,800	15,000
Manufacturing overhead incurred	$182,500	
Manufacturing overhead applied		$184,500
Machine hours expected to be used at normal capacity		42,500
Budgeted fixed overhead for June		$46,750
Variable overhead rate per hour		$3.00

Overhead is applied on the basis of standard machine hours. Three hours of machine time are required for each direct labor hour. The jobs were sold for $400,000. Selling and administrative expenses were $40,000.

Instructions

(a) Laber price
variance $ 3,700 U

(b) Net income $32,300

(a) Compute all of the variances for direct materials, direct labor, and manufacturing overhead.

(b) Prepare an income statement for management. Ignore income taxes.

Compute variances, and identify significant variances.
(SO 4, 5, 6)

P21-3A Novall Clothiers is a small company that manufactures tall-men's suits. The company has used a standard cost accounting system. In May 2006, 11,300 suits were produced.

The following standard and actual cost data applied to the month of May when normal capacity was 14,000 direct labor hours.

Cost Element	Standard (per unit)	Actual
Direct materials	8 yards at $4.50 per yard	$375,150 for 91,500 yards ($4.10 per yard)
Direct labor	1.2 hours at $13.00 per hour	$204,450 for 14,500 hours ($14.10 per hour)
Overhead	1.2 hours at $6.00 per hour (fixed $3.50; variable $2.50)	$49,000 fixed overhead $36,000 variable overhead

Overhead is applied on the basis of direct labor hours. At normal capacity, budgeted fixed overhead costs were $49,000, and budgeted variable overhead was $35,000.

Instructions

(a) Materials quantity
variance $4,950

Overhead controllable
variance $2,100 U

(a) Compute the total, price, and quantity variances for (1) materials and (2) labor, and the total, controllable, and volume variances for manufacturing overhead.

(b) ▭▭▭▶ Which of the materials and labor variances should be investigated if management considers a variance of more than 7% from standard to be significant?

Answer questions about variances.
(SO 4, 5)

P21-4A Calpine Manufacturing Company uses a standard cost accounting system. In 2005, 32,000 units were produced. Each unit took several pounds of direct materials and $1\frac{1}{4}$ standard hours of direct labor at a standard hourly rate of $12.00. Normal capacity was 50,000 direct labor hours. During the year, 133,000 pounds of raw materials were purchased at $0.92 per pound. All pounds purchased were used during the year.

Instructions

(a) If the materials price variance was $3,990 favorable, what was the standard materials price per pound?

(b) If the materials quantity variance was $1,710 unfavorable, what was the standard materials quantity per unit?

(c) 40,000 hours

(c) What were the standard hours allowed for the units produced?

(d) If the labor quantity variance was $7,200 unfavorable, what were the actual direct labor hours worked?

(e) If the labor price variance was $6,090 favorable, what was the actual rate per hour?

(f) If total budgeted manufacturing overhead was $340,000 at normal capacity, what was the predetermined overhead rate?

(g) What was the standard cost per unit of product?

(h) $272,000

(h) How much overhead was applied to production during the year?

(i) If the fixed overhead rate was $2.00, what was the overhead volume variance?

(j) If the overhead controllable variance is $3,000 unfavorable, what were the total variable overhead costs incurred?

(k) Using one or more answers above, what were the total costs assigned to work in process?

Journalize and post standard cost entries, and prepare income statement. (SO 4, 5, 8)

*P21-5A Walton Corporation uses standard costs with its job order cost accounting system. In January, an order (Job No. 12) for 2,000 units of Product B was received. The standard cost of one unit of Product B is as follows.

Direct materials	3 pounds at $1.00 per pound	$ 3.00
Direct labor	1 hour at $8.00 per hour	8.00
Overhead	2 hours (variable $4.00 per machine hour; fixed $2.25 per machine hour)	12.50
Standard cost per unit		$23.50

Normal capacity for the month was 4,200 machine hours. During January, the following transactions applicable to Job No. 12 occurred.

1. Purchased 6,250 pounds of raw materials on account at $1.06 per pound.
2. Requisitioned 6,250 pounds of raw materials for Job No. 12.
3. Incurred 2,200 hours of direct labor at a rate of $7.80 per hour.
4. Worked 2,200 hours of direct labor on Job No. 12.
5. Incurred manufacturing overhead on account $25,800.
6. Applied overhead to Job No. 12 on basis of standard machine hours used.
7. Completed Job No. 12.
8. Billed customer for Job No. 12 at a selling price of $70,000.
9. Incurred selling and administrative expenses on account $2,000.

Instructions
(a) Journalize the transactions.
(b) Post to the job order cost accounts.
(c) Prepare the entry to recognize the overhead variances.
(d) Prepare the January 2006 income statement for management.

(c) Overhead volume
    variance $ 450 U
(d) Net income $18,415

Problems: Set B

Compute variances. (SO 4, 5)

P21-1B Flesch Corporation manufactures a single product. The standard cost per unit of product is as follows.

Direct materials—2 pounds of plastic at $5.00 per pound	$10.00
Direct labor—2 hours at $12.00 per hour	24.00
Variable manufacturing overhead	12.00
Fixed manufacturing overhead	6.00
Total standard cost per unit	$52.00

The master manufacturing overhead budget for the year based on normal productive capacity of 180,000 direct labor hours (90,000 units) shows total variable costs of $1,080,000 and total fixed costs of $540,000. Overhead is applied on the basis of direct labor hours. Actual costs for November in producing 7,700 units were as follows.

Direct materials (15,000 pounds)	$ 72,000
Direct labor (14,900 hours)	183,270
Variable overhead	88,990
Fixed overhead	44,000
Total manufacturing costs	$388,260

The purchasing department normally buys the quantities of raw materials that are expected to be used in production each month. Raw materials inventories, therefore, can be ignored.

Materials quantity
variance $2,000 F

*Compute variances, and
prepare income statement.*
(SO 4, 5, 7)

Instructions

Compute all of the materials, labor, and overhead variances.

P21-2B Onasis Manufacturing Company uses a standard cost accounting system. In July 2005, it accumulates the following data relative to jobs started and finished.

Cost and Production Data	Actual	Standard
Raw materials		
Units purchased	17,500	
Units used	17,500	18,000
Unit cost	$3.40	$3.00
Direct labor		
Hours worked	2,900	3,000
Hourly rate	$11.80	$12.00
Manufacturing overhead		
Incurred	$87,500	
Applied		$97,500

Manufacturing overhead was applied on the basis of direct labor hours. Normal capacity for the month was 2,800 direct labor hours. At normal capacity, budgeted overhead costs were: variable $56,000 and fixed $35,000.

Jobs finished during the month were sold for $240,000. Selling and administrative expenses were $25,000.

Instructions

(a) Labor quantity
variance $ 1,200 F
(b) Net income $ 33,780

(a) Compute all of the variances for direct materials, direct labor, and manufacturing overhead.

(b) Prepare an income statement for management. Ignore income taxes.

*Compute variances, and
identify significant variances.*
(SO 4, 5, 7)

P21-3B True-Value Clothiers manufactures women's business suits. The company uses a standard cost accounting system. In March 2005, 12,000 suits were made. The following standard and actual cost data applied to the month of March when normal capacity was 15,000 direct labor hours.

Cost Element	Standard (per unit)	Actual
Direct materials	5 yards at $7.00 per yard	$424,800 for 59,000 yards ($7.20 per yard)
Direct labor	1.0 hour at $12.00 per hour	$127,680 for 11,400 hours ($11.20 per hour)
Overhead	1.0 hour at $9.30 per hour (fixed $6.30; variable $3.00)	$90,000 fixed overhead $42,000 variable overhead

Overhead is applied on the basis of direct labor hours. At normal capacity, budgeted fixed overhead costs were $94,500, and budgeted variable overhead costs were $45,000.

Instructions

(a) Total materials
variance $4,800 U
Labor price
variance $ 9,120 F

(a) Compute the total, price, and quantity variances for (1) materials and (2) labor, and compute the total, controllable, and volume variances for manufacturing overhead.

(b) ▭▭▭▷ Which of the materials and labor variances should be investigated if management considers a variance of more than 6% from standard to be significant?

*Answer questions about
variances.*
(SO 4, 5)

P21-4B Oaks Manufacturing Company uses a standard cost accounting system. In 2005, 36,000 units were produced. Each unit took several pounds of direct materials and $1\frac{1}{4}$ standard hours of direct labor at a standard hourly rate of $12.00. Normal capacity was 42,000 direct labor hours. During the year, 132,000 pounds of raw materials were purchased at $0.90 per pound. All pounds purchased were used during the year.

Instructions

(a) If the materials price variance was $6,600 unfavorable, what was the standard materials price per pound?

(b) 3.75 pounds

(b) If the materials quantity variance was $2,550 favorable, what was the standard materials quantity per unit?

(c) What were the standard hours allowed for the units produced?

(d) If the labor quantity variance was $8,400 unfavorable, what were the actual direct labor hours worked?

(e) If the labor price variance was $9,140 favorable, what was the actual rate per hour?   (e) $11.80

(f) If total budgeted manufacturing overhead was $319,200 at normal capacity, what was the predetermined overhead rate?

(g) What was the standard cost per unit of product?

(h) How much overhead was applied to production during the year?

(i) If the fixed overhead rate was $2.50, what was the overhead volume variance?

(j) If the overhead controllable variance was $3,000 favorable, what were the total variable overhead costs incurred?   (j) $226,500

(k) Using selected answers above, what were the total costs assigned to work in process?

*P21-5B Pomona Manufacturing Company uses standard costs with its job order cost accounting system. In January, an order (Job 84) was received for 4,000 units of Product D. The standard cost of 1 unit of Product D is as follows.

Journalize and post standard cost entries, and prepare income statement.
(SO 4, 5, 8)

Direct materials—1.4 pounds at $4.00 per pound	$ 5.60
Direct labor—1 hour at $9.00 per hour	9.00
Overhead—1 hour (variable $7.40; fixed $10.00)	17.40
Standard cost per unit	$32.00

Overhead is applied on the basis of direct labor hours. Normal capacity for the month of January was 4,500 direct labor hours. During January, the following transactions applicable to Job No. 84 occurred.

1. Purchased 6,200 pounds of raw materials on account at $3.50 per pound.
2. Requisitioned 6,200 pounds of raw materials for production.
3. Incurred 3,900 hours of direct labor at $9.25 per hour.
4. Worked 3,900 hours of direct labor on Job No. 84.
5. Incurred $73,650 of manufacturing overhead on account.
6. Applied overhead to Job No. 84 on the basis of direct labor hours.
7. Transferred Job No. 84 to finished goods.
8. Billed customer for Job No. 84 at a selling price of $250,000.
9. Incurred selling and administrative expenses on account $61,000.

Instructions

(a) Journalize the transactions.

(b) Post to the job order cost accounts.

(c) Prepare the entry to recognize the overhead variances.

(d) Prepare the income statement for management for January 2005.

(a) Labor price
    variance $ 975 U

(d) Net income $57,575

▷ BROADENING YOUR PERSPECTIVE

Group Decision Case

BYP21-1 Gates Professionals, a management consulting firm, specializes in strategic planning for financial institutions. Bob Menard and Alice Chavez, partners in the firm, are assembling a new strategic planning model for use by clients. The model is designed for use on most microcomputers and replaces a rather lengthy manual model currently marketed by the firm. To market the new model Bob and Alice will need to provide clients with an estimate of the number of labor hours and computer time needed to operate the model. The model is currently being test marketed at five small financial institutions. These financial institutions are listed below, along with the number of combined computer/labor hours used by each institution to run the model one time.

Financial Institutions	Computer/Labor Hours Required
Midland National	25
First State	45
Financial Federal	40
Pacific America	30
Lakeview National	30
Total	170
Average	34

Any company that purchases the new model will need to purchase user manuals to access and operate the system. Also required are specialized computer forms that are sold only by Gates Professionals. User manuals will be sold to clients in cases of 20, at a cost of $400 per case. One manual must be used each time the model is run because each manual includes a nonreusable computer accessed password for operating the system. The specialized computer forms are sold in packages of 250, at a cost of $75 per package. One application of the model requires the use of 50 forms. This amount includes two forms that are generally wasted in each application due to printer alignment errors. The overall cost of the strategic planning model to user clients is $12,000. Most clients will use the model four times annually.

Gates Professionals must provide its clients with estimates of ongoing costs incurred in operating the new strategic planning model. They would like to provide this information in the form of standard costs.

Instructions

With the class divided into groups, answer the following.

(a) What factors should be considered in setting a standard for computer/labor hours?

(b) What alternatives for setting a standard for computer/labor hours might be used?

(c) What standard for computer/labor hours would you select? Justify your answer.

(d) Determine the standard materials cost associated with the user manuals and computer forms for each application of the strategic planning model.

Managerial Analysis

BYP21-2 Mo Vaughn and Associates is a medium-sized company located near a large metropolitan area in the Midwest. The company manufactures cabinets of mahogany, oak, and other fine woods for use in expensive homes, restaurants, and hotels. Although some of the work is custom, many of the cabinets are a standard size.

One such non-custom model is called Luxury Base Frame. Standard production is 1,000 units. Each unit has a direct labor hour standard of 5 hours. Overhead is applied to production based on standard direct labor hours. During the most recent month, only 900 units were produced; 4,500 direct labor hours were allowed for standard production, but only 4,000 hours were used. Standard and actual overhead costs were as follows.

	Standard (1,000 units)	Actual (900 units)
Indirect materials	$ 12,000	$ 12,300
Indirect labor	43,000	51,000
(Fixed) Manufacturing supervisors salaries	22,000	22,000
(Fixed) Manufacturing office employees salaries	13,000	11,500
(Fixed) Engineering costs	27,000	25,000
Computer costs	10,000	10,000
Electricity	2,500	2,500
(Fixed) Manufacturing building depreciation	8,000	8,000
(Fixed) Machinery depreciation	3,000	3,000
(Fixed) Trucks and forklift depreciation	1,500	1,500
Small tools	700	1,400
(Fixed) Insurance	500	500
(Fixed) Property taxes	300	300
Total	$143,500	$149,000

Instructions

(a) Determine the overhead application rate.

(b) Determine how much overhead was applied to production.

(c) Calculate the controllable overhead variance and the overhead volume variance.

(d) Decide which overhead variances should be investigated.

(e) Discuss causes of the overhead variances. What can management do to improve its performance next month?

Real-World Focus

BYP21-3 Glassmaster Co. was incorporated in 1946 as Koolvent Metal Awning Company. Its current name was adopted in 1982 to reflect the more general nature of its products. The company is organized as two divisions and one subsidiary. One division focuses on the manufacture of filaments such as fishing line and sewing thread; the other division manufactures antennas and specialty fiberglass products. Its subsidiary manufactures flexible steel wire controls and molded control panels.

The annual report of Glassmaster provides the following information.

GLASSMASTER COMPANY
Management Discussion

Gross profit margins for the year improved to 20.9% of sales compared to last year's 18.5%. All operations reported improved margins due in large part to improved operating efficiencies as a result of cost reduction measures implemented during the second and third quarters of the fiscal year and increased manufacturing throughout due to higher unit volume sales. Contributing to the improved margins was a favorable materials price variance due to competitive pricing by suppliers as a result of soft demand for petrochemical-based products. This favorable variance is temporary and will begin to reverse itself as stronger worldwide demand for commodity products improves in tandem with the economy. Partially offsetting these positive effects on profit margins were competitive pressures on sales prices of certain product lines. The company responded with pricing strategies designed to maintain and/or increase market share.

Instructions

(a) Is it apparent from the information whether Glassmaster utilizes standard costs?

(b) Do you think the price variance experienced should lead to changes in standard costs for the next fiscal year?

Exploring the Web

BYP21-4 The Caelus Management System (CMS) is a real-time, fully integrated decision support, operational control, and financial management system.

Address: **www.caelus.com** (or go to **www.wiley.com/college/kimmel**)

Steps

1. Choose **CMS Product Info** and answer part (a).

2. Choose **Standard Cost** and answer parts (b), (c), and (d).

Instructions

(a) List some of the modules that are familiar to you from either financial accounting topics or managerial accounting topics.

(b) What types of decisions does this module of the software support?

(c) Does this product distinguish between fixed and variable costs?

(d) The flexibility of this software allows managers to evaluate costs in a variety of different ways. Why is this important?

Communication Activity

BYP21-5 The setting of standards is critical to the effective use of standards in evaluating performance.

Instructions

Explain the following in a memo to your instructor.

(a) The comparative advantages and disadvantages of ideal versus normal standards.

(b) The factors that should be included in setting the price and quantity standards for direct materials, direct labor, and manufacturing overhead.

Research Case

BYP21-6 The December 1996 issue of *Accounting Horizons* contains an article by Carol B. Cheatham and Leo R. Cheatham entitled "Redesigning Cost Systems: Is Standard Costing Obsolete?"

Instructions

Read the article and answer the following questions.

(a) For what percent of U.S. manufacturing firms are standard cost systems still the cost system of choice?

(b) What are the major criticisms of standard cost systems?

(c) How does a standard cost system relate to activity-based costing (ABC)? And, how might activity-based costing (ABC) be used to enhance a company's costing system when standard costing is the primary system?

(d) What do the authors conclude from their study of standard cost systems?

Ethics Case

BYP21-7 At Lofton Manufacturing Company, production workers in the Painting Department are paid on the basis of productivity. The labor time standard for a unit of production is established through periodic time studies conducted by the Fisher Management Department. In a time study, the actual time required to complete a specific task by a worker is observed. Allowances are then made for preparation time, rest periods, and clean-up time. Dion Young is one of several veterans in the Painting Department.

Dion is informed by Fisher Management that he will be used in the time study for the painting of a new product. The findings will be the basis for establishing the labor time standard for the next 6 months. During the test, Dion deliberately slows his normal work pace in an effort to obtain a labor time standard that will be easy to meet. Because it is a new product, the Fisher Management representative who conducted the test is unaware that Dion did not give the test his best effort.

Instructions

(a) Who was benefited and who was harmed by Dion's actions?

(b) Was Dion ethical in the way he performed the time study test?

(c) What measure(s) might the company take to obtain valid data for setting the labor time standard?

Answers to Self-Study Questions

1. c   2. d   3. b   4. c   5. b   6. a   7. d   8. a   9. b   10. c

Remember to go back to the Navigator box on the chapter-opening page and check off your completed work.

Incremental Analysis and Capital Budgeting

STUDY OBJECTIVES

After studying this chapter,
you should be able to:

1 Identify the steps in management's decision-making process.

2 Describe the concept of incremental analysis.

3 Identify the relevant costs in accepting an order at a special price.

4 Identify the relevant costs in a make-or-buy decision.

5 Give the decision rule for whether to sell or process materials further.

6 Identify the factors to be considered in retaining or replacing equipment.

7 Explain the relevant factors in deciding whether to eliminate an unprofitable segment.

8 Determine which products to make and sell when resources are limited.

9 Contrast the annual rate of return and cash payback techniques in capital budgeting.

10 Distinguish between the net present value and internal rate of return methods.

 THE NAVIGATOR

THE NAVIGATOR ✔

▶ Scan *Study Objectives* ☐

▶ Read *Feature Story* ☐

▶ Read *Preview* ☐

▶ Read text and answer *Before You Go On*
   p. 1048 ☐   p. 1057 ☐

▶ Work Using the *Decision Toolkit* ☐

▶ Review Summary of *Study Objectives* ☐

▶ Work *Demonstration Problems 1 and 2* ☐

▶ Answer *Self-Study Questions* ☐

▶ Complete *Assignments* ☐

FEATURE STORY

Soup Is Good Food

When you hear the word *Campbell's,* what is the first thing that comes to mind? Soup. Campbell's *is* soup. It sells 38 percent of all the soup—including homemade—consumed in the United States. But can a company survive on soup alone? In an effort to expand its operations and to lessen its reliance on soup, **Campbell Soup Company** began searching for an additional line of business in 1990. Campbell's management believed it saw an opportunity in convenient meals that were low in fat, nutritionally rich, and had therapeutic value for heart patients and diabetics. This venture would require a huge investment—but the rewards were potentially tremendous.

The initial investment required building food labs, hiring nutritional scientists, researching prototype products, constructing new production facilities, and marketing the new products. Management predicted that with an initial investment of roughly $55 million, the company might generate sales of $200 million per year.

By 1994 the company had created 24 meals, and an extensive field-study revealed considerable health benefits from the products. Unfortunately, initial sales of the new product line, called Intelligent Quisine, were less than stellar. In 1997 a consulting firm was hired to evaluate whether the project should be continued. Product development of the new line was costing $20 million per year—a sum that some managers felt could be better spent developing new products in other divisions, or expanding overseas operations. In 1998 the project was discontinued.

Campbell's was not giving up on growth, but simply had decided to refocus its efforts on soup. The company's annual report stated management's philosophy: "Soup will be our growth engine." Campbell's is now selling off many of its non-soup businesses and in a recent year introduced twenty new soup products.

Source: Vanessa O'Connell, "Food for Thought: How Campbell Saw a Breakthrough Menu Turn into Leftovers," *Wall Street Journal* (October 6, 1998).

www.campbellsoup.com

An important purpose of management accounting is to provide relevant information for decision making. Examples of these decisions include the following: (1) **Campbell Soup**'s decision to produce "therapeutic meals" rather than some other food product. (2) **Boeing**'s strategic decisions to spend $5 billion to build a plane for the 21st century—the B-777—and to cancel development of a larger version of the B-747. (3) **The Coca-Cola Company**'s decision to spend $750 million to build twelve plants in Russia.

This chapter begins with an explanation of management's decision-making process. It then considers the topics of incremental analysis and capital budgeting.

The content and organization of Chapter 22 are as follows.

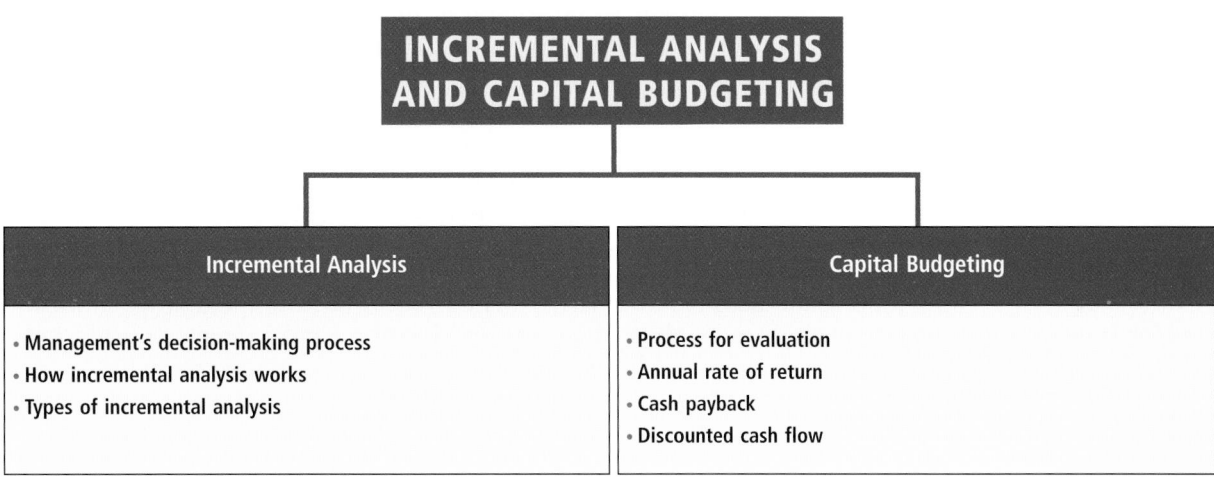

SECTION ONE
INCREMENTAL ANALYSIS

Management's Decision-Making Process

Making decisions is an important management function. Management's decision-making process does not always follow a set pattern, because decisions vary significantly in their scope, urgency, and importance. It is possible, though, to identify some steps that are frequently involved in the process. These steps are shown in Illustration 22-1 (page 1040).

Accounting's contribution to the decision-making process occurs primarily in Steps 2 and 4. In Step 2, for each possible course of action, relevant revenue and cost data are provided. These show the expected overall effect on net income. In Step 4, internal reports are prepared that review the actual impact of the decision.

In making business decisions, management ordinarily considers both financial and nonfinancial information. **Financial** information is related to revenues and costs and their effect on the company's overall profitability. **Nonfinancial**

STUDY OBJECTIVE
1
Identify the steps in management's decision-making process.

1. Identify the problem and assign responsibility ➔ 2. Determine and evaluate possible courses of action ➔ 3. Make a decision ➔ 4. Review results of the decision

Illustration 22-1
Management's decision-making process

information relates to such factors as the effect of the decision on employee turnover, the environment, or the overall image of the company in the community. Although the nonfinancial information can be as important as the financial information, we will focus primarily on financial information that is relevant to the decision.

Decisions involve a choice among alternative courses of action. Suppose that you were deciding whether to purchase or lease an IBM PC for use in doing your accounting homework. The financial data relate to the cost of leasing versus the cost of purchasing. For example, leasing would involve periodic lease payments; purchasing would require "up-front" payment of the purchase price. In other words, the financial data relevant to the decision are the data that would vary among the possible alternatives. The process used to identify the financial data that change under alternative courses of action is called **incremental analysis**. In some cases, you will find that when you use incremental analysis, both costs **and** revenues will change. In other cases, only costs **or** revenues will change.

Just as your decision to buy or lease a PC will affect your future, similar decisions—on a larger scale—will affect a company's future. Incremental analysis identifies the probable effects of those decisions on future earnings. Such analysis inevitably involves estimates and uncertainty. Gathering data for incremental analyses may involve market analysts, engineers, and accountants. In quantifying the data, the accountant is expected to produce the most reliable information available at the time the decision must be made.

STUDY OBJECTIVE 2

Describe the concept of incremental analysis.

Alternative Terminology
Incremental analysis is also called *differential analysis* because the analysis focuses on differences.

How Incremental Analysis Works

The basic approach in incremental analysis is illustrated in the following example.

Illustration 22-2 Basic approach in incremental analysis

	Alternative A	Alternative B	Net Income Increase (Decrease)
Revenues	$125,000	$110,000	$(15,000)
Costs	100,000	80,000	20,000
Net income	$ 25,000	$ 30,000	$ 5,000

In this example, alternative B is being compared with alternative A. The net income column shows the differences between the alternatives. In this case, incremental revenue will be $15,000 less under alternative B than under alternative A. But a $20,000 incremental cost saving will be realized.[1] Thus, alternative B will produce $5,000 more net income than alternative A.

---

[1] Although income taxes are sometimes important in incremental analysis, they are ignored in the chapter for simplicity's sake.

Incremental analysis sometimes involves changes that at first glance might seem contrary to your intuition. For example, sometimes variable costs **do not** change under the alternative courses of action. Also, sometimes fixed costs **do** change. For example, direct labor, normally a variable cost, is not an incremental cost in deciding between two new factory machines if each asset requires the same amount of direct labor. In contrast, rent expense, normally a fixed cost, is an incremental cost in a decision to continue occupancy of a building or to purchase or lease a new building.

Types of Incremental Analysis

A number of different types of decisions involve incremental analysis. The more common types of decisions are whether to:

1. Accept an order at a special price.

2. Make or buy.

3. Sell or process further.

4. Retain or replace equipment.

5. Eliminate an unprofitable business segment.

6. Allocate limited resources.

We will consider each of these types of analysis in the following pages.

ACCEPT AN ORDER AT A SPECIAL PRICE

Sometimes, a company may have an opportunity to obtain additional business if it is willing to make a major price concession to a specific customer. To illustrate, assume that Sunbelt Company produces 100,000 automatic blenders per month, which is 80 percent of plant capacity. Variable manufacturing costs are $8 per unit. Fixed manufacturing costs are $400,000, or $4 per unit. The blenders are normally sold directly to retailers at $20 each. Sunbelt has an offer from Mexico Co. (a foreign wholesaler) to purchase an additional 2,000 blenders at $11 per unit. Acceptance of the offer would not affect normal sales of the product, and the additional units can be manufactured without increasing plant capacity. What should management do?

If management makes its decision on the basis of the total cost per unit of $12 ($8 + $4), the order would be rejected, because costs ($12) would exceed revenues ($11) by $1 per unit. However, since the units can be produced within existing plant capacity, the special order **will not increase fixed costs**. The relevant data for the decision, therefore, are the variable manufacturing costs per unit of $8 and the expected revenue of $11 per unit. Thus, as shown in Illustration 22-3, Sunbelt will increase its net income by $6,000 by accepting this special order.

STUDY OBJECTIVE

3

Identify the relevant costs in accepting an order at a special price.

Helpful Hint This is a good example of different costs for different purposes. In the long-run all costs are relevant, but for this decision only costs that change are relevant.

	Reject Order	Accept Order	Net Income Increase (Decrease)
Revenues	$-0-	$22,000	$ 22,000
Costs	-0-	16,000	(16,000)
Net income	$-0-	$ 6,000	$ 6,000

Illustration 22-3
Incremental analysis—accepting an order at a special price

Two points should be emphasized: First, it is assumed that sales of the product in other markets would not be affected by this special order. If other sales were affected, then Sunbelt would have to consider the lost sales in making the decision. Second, if Sunbelt is operating at full capacity, it is likely that the special order would be rejected. Under such circumstances, the company would have to expand plant capacity. In that case, the special order would have to absorb these additional fixed manufacturing costs, as well as the variable manufacturing costs.

MAKE OR BUY

When a manufacturer assembles component parts in producing a finished product, management must decide whether to make or buy the components. For example, **General Motors Corporation** may either make or buy the batteries, tires, and radios used in its cars. Similarly, **Zenith Corporation** may make or buy the electronic circuitry, cabinets, and speakers for its television sets. The decision to make or buy components should be made on the basis of incremental analysis.

To illustrate the analysis, assume that Baron Company incurs the following annual costs in producing 25,000 ignition switches for motor scooters.

Illustration 22-4 **Annual product cost data**

Direct materials	$ 50,000
Direct labor	75,000
Variable manufacturing overhead	40,000
Fixed manufacturing overhead	60,000
Total manufacturing costs	$225,000
Total cost per unit ($225,000 ÷ 25,000)	$9.00

Or, Baron Company may purchase the ignition switches from Ignition, Inc. at a price of $8 per unit. The question again is, "What should management do?"

At first glance, it appears that management should purchase the ignition switches for $8, rather than make them at a cost of $9. However, a review of operations indicates that if the ignition switches are purchased from Ignition, Inc., all of Baron's variable costs but only $10,000 of its fixed manufacturing costs will be eliminated. Thus, $50,000 of the fixed manufacturing costs will remain if the ignition switches are purchased. The relevant costs for incremental analysis are as follows.

Illustration 22-5 Incremental analysis— make or buy

	Make	**Buy**	**Net Income Increase (Decrease)**
Direct materials	$ 50,000	$ –0–	$ 50,000
Direct labor	75,000	–0–	75,000
Variable manufacturing costs	40,000	–0–	40,000
Fixed manufacturing costs	60,000	50,000	10,000
Purchase price (25,000 × $8)	–0–	200,000	(200,000)
Total annual cost	$225,000	$250,000	$ (25,000)

This analysis indicates that Baron Company will incur $25,000 of additional cost by buying the ignition switches. Therefore, Baron should continue to make the ignition switches, even though the total manufacturing cost is $1 higher than the purchase price. The reason is that if the company purchases the ignition switches, it will still have fixed costs of $50,000 to absorb.

The foregoing analysis is complete only if the productive capacity used to make the ignition switches cannot be converted to another purpose. If there is an opportunity to use this productive capacity in some other manner, then this opportunity cost must be considered. **Opportunity cost** is the potential benefit that may be obtained by following an alternative course of action.

To illustrate, assume that through buying the switches, Baron Company can use the released productive capacity to generate additional income of $28,000. This lost income is an additional cost of continuing to make the switches in the make-or-buy decision. This opportunity cost therefore is added to the "Make" column, for comparison. As shown, it is now advantageous to buy the ignition switches.

	Make	Buy	Net Income Increase (Decrease)
Total annual cost	$225,000	$250,000	$(25,000)
Opportunity cost	28,000	–0–	28,000
Total cost	$253,000	$250,000	$ 3,000

Illustration 22-6
Incremental analysis—make or buy, with opportunity cost

The qualitative factors in this decision include the possible loss of jobs for employees who produce the ignition switches. In addition, management must assess how long the supplier will be able to satisfy the company's quality control standards at the quoted price per unit.

Business Insight
ACCOUNTING IN ACTION

In the bicycle industry, nearly all bikes of quality are made with **Shimano** parts. This dominance by a single supplier has made bikes a sort of commodity. That is, if all bikes are made from the same parts, then what does it matter what brand of bike you buy? As a consequence, the majority of profits go to Shimano, with bike manufacturers that use Shimano parts having to accept an increasingly small profit margin.

To break this trend, and increase its profit margins, **Cannondale Corporation** has decided to take "the approach that we manufacture the whole bicycle, not just taking a frame and putting somebody's parts on it." Similar steps are being taken by **Trek Bicycle Corporation** and **Specialized Bicycle Components Inc.** These companies recognize that they are taking a risk. In order to compete with Shimano, they will have to dramatically step up their research and development efforts and significantly increase their efficiency in the manufacture of parts. This will be difficult given Shimano's huge volume advantage.

SOURCE: Ross Kerber, "Bike Maker Faces a Tactical Shift," *Wall Street Journal* (October 12, 1998), p. B1.

SELL OR PROCESS FURTHER

Many manufacturers have the option of selling products at a given point in the production cycle or continuing to process with the expectation of selling them at a higher price. For example, a bicycle manufacturer such as **Schwinn** could sell its 10-speed bicycles to retailers either unassembled or assembled, and a furniture manufacturer such as **Ethan Allen** could sell its dining room sets to furniture stores either unfinished or finished. The sell-or-process further decision

STUDY OBJECTIVE
5
Give the decision rule for whether to sell or process materials further.

should be made on the basis of incremental analysis. The basic decision rule is: **Process further as long as the incremental revenue from such processing exceeds the incremental processing costs.**

Assume, for example, that Woodmasters Inc. makes tables. The cost to manufacture an unfinished table is $35, computed as follows.

Illustration 22-7 Per unit cost of unfinished table

Direct material	$15
Direct labor	10
Variable manufacturing overhead	6
Fixed manufacturing overhead	4
Manufacturing cost per unit	**$35**

The selling price per unfinished unit is $50. Woodmasters currently has unused productive capacity that is expected to continue indefinitely. Management concludes that some of this capacity can be used to finish the tables and sell them at $60 per unit. For a finished table, direct materials will increase $2 and direct labor costs will increase $4. Variable manufacturing overhead costs will increase by $2.40 (60% of direct labor). No increase is anticipated in fixed manufacturing overhead. The incremental analysis on a per unit basis is as follows.

Illustration 22-8 Incremental analysis—sell or process further

	Sell	Process Further	Net Income Increase (Decrease)
Sales per unit	$50.00	$60.00	$10.00
Cost per unit			
Direct materials	15.00	17.00	(2.00)
Direct labor	10.00	14.00	(4.00)
Variable manufacturing overhead	6.00	8.40	(2.40)
Fixed manufacturing overhead	4.00	4.00	–0–
Total	$35.00	$43.40	$(8.40)
Net income per unit	$15.00	$16.60	$ 1.60

Helpful Hint Current net income is known. Net income from processing further is an estimate. In making its decision, management could add a "risk" factor for the estimate.

It would be advantageous for Woodmaster to process the tables further. The incremental revenue of $10.00 from the additional processing is $1.60 higher than the incremental processing costs of $8.40.

RETAIN OR REPLACE EQUIPMENT

STUDY OBJECTIVE 6

Identify the factors to be considered in retaining or replacing equipment.

Management often has to decide whether to continue using an asset or replace it. To illustrate, assume that Jeffcoat Company has a factory machine with a book value of $40,000 and a remaining useful life of 4 years. A new machine is available that costs $120,000. It is expected to have zero salvage value at the end of its 4-year useful life. If the new machine is acquired, variable manufacturing costs are expected to decrease from $160,000 to $125,000 annually, and the old unit will be scrapped. The incremental analysis for the 4-year period is as follows.

Illustration 22-9
Incremental analysis—
retain or replace
equipment

	Retain Equipment	Replace Equipment	Net Income Increase (Decrease)
Variable manufacturing costs	$640,000^a	$500,000^b	$ 140,000
New machine cost		120,000	(120,000)
Total	$640,000	$620,000	$ 20,000

^{a}(4 years × $160,000)
^{b}(4 years × $125,000)

In this case, it would be to the company's advantage to replace the equipment. The lower variable manufacturing costs due to replacement more than offset the cost of the new equipment.

One other point should be mentioned regarding Jeffcoat's decision: **The book value of the old machine does not affect the decision.** Book value is a sunk cost, which is a cost that cannot be changed by any present or future decision. Sunk costs **are not relevant in incremental analysis.** In this example, if the asset is retained, book value will be depreciated over its remaining useful life. Or, if the new unit is acquired, book value will be recognized as a loss of the current period. Thus, the effect of book value on current and future earnings is the same regardless of the replacement decision. **Any trade-in allowance or cash disposal value of the existing asset**, **however**, **is relevant** to the decision, because this value will not be realized if the asset is continued in use.

ELIMINATE AN UNPROFITABLE SEGMENT

Management sometimes must decide whether to eliminate an unprofitable business segment. Again, the key is to focus on the data that change under the alternative courses of action. To illustrate, assume that Martina Company manufactures tennis racquets in three models: Pro, Master, and Champ. Pro and Master are profitable lines. Champ (highlighted in color in the table below) operates at a loss. Condensed income statement data are:

STUDY OBJECTIVE
7
Explain the relevant factors in deciding whether to eliminate an unprofitable segment.

Illustration 22-10
Segment income data

	Pro	Master	Champ	Total
Sales	$800,000	$300,000	$100,000	$1,200,000
Variable expenses	520,000	210,000	90,000	820,000
Contribution margin	280,000	90,000	10,000	380,000
Fixed expenses	80,000	50,000	30,000	160,000
Net income	$200,000	$ 40,000	$ (20,000)	$ 220,000

It might be expected that total net income will increase by $20,000 to $240,000 if the unprofitable line of racquets is eliminated. However, **net income may decrease if the Champ line is discontinued**. The reason is that the fixed expenses allocated to the Champ racquets will have to be absorbed by the other products. To illustrate, assume that the $30,000 of fixed costs applicable to the unprofitable segment are allocated ⅔ and ⅓ to the Pro and Master product lines, respectively. Fixed expenses will increase to $100,000 ($80,000 + $20,000) in the Pro line and to $60,000 ($50,000 + $10,000) in the Master line. The revised income statement is:

Helpful Hint A decision to discontinue a segment based solely on the bottom line—net loss—is inappropriate.

Illustration 22-11 Income data after eliminating unprofitable product line

	Pro	Master	Total
Sales	$800,000	$300,000	$1,100,000
Variable expenses	520,000	210,000	730,000
Contribution margin	280,000	90,000	370,000
Fixed expenses	**100,000**	**60,000**	160,000
Net income	$180,000	$ 30,000	$ 210,000

Total net income has decreased $10,000 ($220,000 − $210,000). This result is also obtained in the following incremental analysis of the Champ racquets.

Illustration 22-12 Incremental analysis—eliminating an unprofitable segment

	Continue	Eliminate	Net Income Increase (Decrease)
Sales	$100,000	$ –0–	$(100,000)
Variable expenses	90,000	–0–	90,000
Contribution margin	10,000	–0–	(10,000)
Fixed expenses	30,000	30,000	–0–
Net income	$ (20,000)	$(30,000)	$ (10,000)

The loss in net income is attributable to the contribution margin of $10,000 that will not be realized if the segment is discontinued.

In deciding on the future status of an unprofitable segment, management should consider the effect of elimination on related product lines. It may be possible for continuing product lines to obtain some or all of the sales lost by the discontinued product line. In some businesses, services or products may be linked—for example, free checking accounts at a bank, or coffee at a donut shop. In addition, management should consider the effect of eliminating the product line on employees who may have to be discharged or retrained.

Business Insight
ACCOUNTING IN ACTION

In 1994 **Quaker Oats** paid $1.7 billion for one of America's hottest new beverage companies. While some observers thought that Quaker Oats had overpaid, Quaker's management believed it was an exciting purchase because it would make a great strategic partner for Quaker Oats' famous sport drink—Gatorade. For a variety of reasons, the acquisition didn't work out. One of those reasons was that at about the same time, several other major beverage manufacturers decided to begin producing and selling competing fruit and tea drinks. Worse yet, the processing methods used by these other manufacturers appeared to allow them to produce their drinks much more inexpensively. Only a few years after purchasing the beverage company, Quaker Oats sold it and took a $1.4 billion loss. Management stated that by selling this division, the company could reduce its debt burden and focus on its cereal brands and Gatorade.

DECISION TOOLKIT

Decision Checkpoints	Info Needed for Decision	Tool to Use for Decision	How to Evaluate Results
Which alternative should the company choose?	All relevant costs and opportunity costs	Compare relevant cost of each alternative.	Choose the alternative that maximizes net income.

ALLOCATE LIMITED RESOURCES

Everyone's resources are limited. For a company, the limited resource may be floor space in a retail department store, or raw materials, direct labor hours, or machine capacity in a manufacturing company. When a company has limited resources, management must decide which products to make and sell in order to maximize net income.

STUDY OBJECTIVE
8
Determine which products to make and sell when resources are limited.

To illustrate, assume that Collins Company manufactures deluxe and standard pen and pencil sets. The limiting resource is machine capacity, which is 3,600 hours per month. Relevant data consist of the following.

Illustration 22-13
Contribution margin and machine hours

	Deluxe Sets	Standard Sets
Contribution margin per unit	$8	$6
Machine hours required	4	2

The deluxe sets may appear to be more profitable: they have a higher contribution margin ($8) than the standard sets ($6). However, note that the standard sets take fewer machine hours to produce than the deluxe sets. Therefore, it is necessary to find the **contribution margin per unit of limited resource**, in this case, contribution margin per machine hour. This is obtained by dividing the contribution margin per unit of each product by the number of units of the limited resource required for each product. The computation shows that the standard sets have a higher contribution margin per unit of limited resource.

Helpful Hint CM alone is not enough in this decision. The key factor is CM per limited resource.

Illustration 22-14
Contribution margin per unit of limited resource

	Deluxe Sets	Standard Sets
Contribution margin per unit (a)	$8	$6
Machine hours required (b)	4	2
Contribution margin per unit of limited resource [(a) ÷ (b)]	$2	$3

If Collins Company can increase machine capacity from 3,600 hours to 4,200 hours, the additional 600 hours could be used to produce either the standard or deluxe pen and pencil sets. The total contribution margin under each alternative is found by multiplying the machine hours by the contribution margin per unit of limited resource as shown below.

Illustration 22-15
Incremental analysis— computation of total contribution margin

	Produce Deluxe Sets	Produce Standard Sets
Machine hours (a)	600	600
Contribution margin per unit of limited resource (b)	$ 2	$ 3
Contribution margin [(a) × (b)]	$1,200	$1,800

From this analysis, we can see that to maximize net income, all of the increased capacity should be used to make and sell the standard sets.

DECISION TOOLKIT

Decision Checkpoints	Info Needed for Decision	Tool to Use for Decision	How to Evaluate Results
How many units of product A and B should we produce in light of a limited resource?	Contribution margin per unit, limited resource required per unit	$$\text{Contribution margin per unit of limited resource} = \frac{\text{Contribution margin per unit}}{\text{Limited resource per unit}}$$	Any additional capacity of limited resource should be applied toward the product with higher contribution margin per unit of limited resource.

BEFORE YOU GO ON . . .

▶ Review It

1. Give three examples of how incremental analysis might be used.
2. What is the decision rule in deciding to sell or process products further?
3. How may the elimination of an unprofitable segment decrease the overall net income of a company?
4. What is the critical factor in allocating limited resources?

▶ Do It

Cobb Company incurs a cost of $28 per unit, of which $18 is variable, to make a product that normally sells for $42. A foreign wholesaler offers to buy 5,000 units at $25 each. Cobb will incur shipping costs of $1 per unit. Compute the net income (loss) Cobb will realize by accepting the special order, assuming Cobb has excess operating capacity. Should Cobb Company accept the special order?

Action Plan

• Identify all revenues that will change as a result of accepting the order.
• Identify all costs that will change as a result of accepting the order, and net this amount against the change in revenues.

Solution

	Reject	Accept	Net Income Increase (Decrease)
Revenues	$–0–	$125,000	$125,000
Costs	–0–	95,000*	(95,000)
Net income	$–0–	$ 30,000	$ 30,000

*(5,000 × $18) + (5,000 × $1)

Given the result of the above analysis, Cobb Company should accept the special order.

Related exercise material: BE22-2, BE22-3, and E22-1.

 THE NAVIGATOR

SECTION TWO
CAPITAL BUDGETING

Individuals make capital expenditures when they buy a new home, car, or television set. Similarly, businesses make capital expenditures when they modernize plant facilities or expand operations. Companies like **Campbell Soup** must constantly determine how to invest their resources. Other examples: Hollywood studios recently built 25 new sound stage projects to allow for additional filming in future years. **Starwood Hotels and Resorts Worldwide, Inc.** committed a total of $1 billion in 1998 and 1999 to renovate its existing hotel properties, while at roughly the same time, the hotel industry canceled about $2 billion worth of *new* construction scheduled through the year 2000. And **Union Pacific Resources Group Inc.** announced that it would cut its 1998 capital budget by 19 percent in order to use the funds to reduce its outstanding debt.

In business, as for individuals, the amount of possible capital expenditures usually exceeds the funds available for such expenditures. Thus, the resources available must be allocated (budgeted) among the competing alternatives. The process of making capital expenditure decisions in business is known as capital budgeting. Capital budgeting involves choosing among various capital projects to find the one(s) that will maximize a company's return on investment.

Process for Evaluation

Many companies follow a standard process in capital budgeting. At least once a year, proposals for projects are requested from each department. The proposals are screened by a capital budgeting committee, which submits its findings to the officers of the company. The officers, in turn, select the projects they believe to be most worthy of funding. They submit this list to the board of directors. Ultimately, the directors approve the capital expenditure budget for the year.

The involvement of top management and the board of directors in the process demonstrates the importance of capital budgeting decisions. These decisions often have a significant impact on a company's future profitability. In fact, poor capital budgeting decisions have led to the bankruptcy of some companies. Accounting data are indispensable in assessing the probable effects of capital expenditures.

To provide management with relevant data for capital budgeting decisions, you should be familiar with the quantitative techniques that may be used. The three most common techniques are: (1) annual rate of return, (2) cash payback, and (3) discounted cash flow. To illustrate the three quantitative techniques, assume that Tappan Company is considering an investment of $130,000 in new equipment. The new equipment is expected to last 10 years. It will have zero salvage value at the end of its useful life. The straight-line method of depreciation is used for accounting purposes. The expected annual revenues and costs of the new product that will be produced from the investment are:

Sales		$200,000
Less: Costs and expenses		
Manufacturing costs (exclusive of depreciation)	$145,000	
Depreciation expenses ($130,000 ÷ 10)	13,000	
Selling and administrative expenses	22,000	180,000
Income before income taxes		20,000
Income tax expense		7,000
Net income		$ 13,000

Illustration 22-16
Estimated annual net income from capital expenditure

Annual Rate of Return

The annual rate of return technique is based directly on accounting data. It indicates **the profitability of a capital expenditure** by dividing expected annual net income by the average investment. The formula for computing annual rate of return is shown in Illustration 22-17.

STUDY OBJECTIVE
9
Contrast the annual rate of return and cash payback techniques in capital budgeting.

Expected Annual Net Income	÷	Average Investment	=	Annual Rate of Return

Illustration 22-17 Annual rate of return formula

Expected annual net income is obtained from the projected income statement. Tappan Company's expected annual net income is $13,000. Average investment is derived from the following formula.

Illustration 22-18 Formula for computing average investment

$$\text{Average Investment} = \frac{\text{Original Investment} + \text{Value at End of Useful Life}}{2}$$

The value at the end of useful life is equal to the asset's salvage value, if any. For Tappan Company, average investment is $65,000 [($130,000 + $0) ÷ 2]. The expected annual rate of return for Tappan Company's investment in new equipment is therefore 20 percent, computed as follows:

$$\$13,000 \div \$65,000 = 20\%$$

Management then compares this annual rate of return with its required minimum rate of return for investments of similar risk. The minimum rate of return (also called the **hurdle rate** or **cutoff rate**) is generally based on the company's **cost of capital**. The cost of capital is the rate of return that management expects to pay on all borrowed and equity funds. It does not relate to the cost of funding a specific project. The decision rule is: **A project is acceptable if its rate of return is greater than management's minimum rate of return. It is unacceptable when the reverse is true.** When the rate of return technique is used in deciding among several acceptable projects, **the higher the rate of return for a given risk**, **the more attractive the investment**.

The principal advantages of this technique are simplicity of calculation and management's familiarity with the accounting terms used in the computation. A major limitation of the annual rate of return approach is that it does not consider the time value of money. For example, no consideration is given as to whether cash inflows will occur early or late in the life of the investment. As explained in Appendix C, recognition of the time value of money can make a significant difference between the future value and the present value of an investment.

Helpful Hint A capital budgeting decision based on only one technique may be misleading. It is often wise to analyze the investment from a number of different perspectives.

Cash Payback

The **cash payback technique** identifies the time period required to recover the cost of the capital investment from the annual cash inflow produced by the investment. The formula for computing the cash payback period is:

Illustration 22-19 Cash payback formula

$$\text{Cost of Capital Investment} \div \text{Annual Cash Inflow} = \text{Cash Payback Period}$$

Helpful Hint Annual cash inflow can also be approximated by net cash provided by operating activities from the statement of cash flows.

Annual (or **net**) **cash inflow** is approximated by taking net income and adding back depreciation expense. Depreciation expense is added back because depreciation on the capital expenditure does not involve an annual outflow of cash. Accordingly, the depreciation deducted in determining net income must be added back to determine annual cash inflows. In the Tappan Company example, annual cash inflow is $26,000, as shown below.

Illustration 22-20 Computation of annual cash inflow

Net income	$ 13,000
Add: Depreciation expense	13,000
Annual cash inflow	**$26,000**

The cash payback period in this example is therefore 5 years, computed as follows.

$$\$130,000 \div \$26,000 = 5 \text{ years}$$

The evaluation of the payback period is often related to the expected useful life of the asset. For example, assume that at Tappan Company a project is unacceptable if the payback period is longer than 60 percent of the asset's expected useful life. The 5-year payback period in this case is 50 percent of the project's expected useful life. Thus, the project is acceptable. It follows that when the payback technique is used to decide among acceptable alternative projects, **the shorter the payback period, the more attractive the investment**. This is true for two reasons: (1) The earlier the investment is recovered, the sooner the cash funds can be used for other purposes. And (2) the risk of loss from obsolescence and changed economic conditions is less in a shorter payback period.

The computation of the cash payback period above assumes equal cash flows in each year of the investment's life. In many cases, this assumption is not valid. In the case of **uneven** cash flows, the cash payback period is determined when the cumulative cash flows from the investment equals the cost of the investment. To illustrate, assume that Chan Company proposes an investment in a new Web site which is estimated to cost $300,000. The proposed investment cost, annual cash inflows, cumulative cash inflows, and the cash payback period are shown in Illustration 22-21.

Illustration 22-21 Cash inflow schedule

Year	Investment	Annual Cash Inflow	Cumulative Cash Inflow
0	$300,000		
1		$ 60,000	$ 60,000
2		90,000	150,000
3		90,000	240,000
4		120,000	360,000
5		100,000	460,000
		Cash payback period = 3.5 years	

As indicated from Illustration 22-21, at the end of year 3, cumulative cash inflow of $240,000 is less than the investment cost of $300,000, but at the end of year 4 the cumulative cash inflow of $360,000 exceeds the investment cost. The cash inflow needed in year 4 to equal the investment cost is $60,000 ($300,000 − $240,000). Assuming the cash inflow occurred evenly during year 4, this amount is then divided by the annual cash inflow in year 4 ($120,000) to determine the point during the year the cash payback occurs. Thus, .50 ($60,000/$120,000) or half of the year is computed, and the cash payback period would be 3.5 years.

The cash payback technique may be useful as an initial screening tool. It also may be the most critical factor in the capital budgeting decision for a company that desires a fast turnaround of its investment because of a weak cash position. Like the annual rate of return, cash payback is relatively easy to compute and understand.

However, cash payback should not ordinarily be the only basis for the capital budgeting decision because it ignores the expected profitability of the project. To illustrate, assume that Projects A and B have the same payback period, but Project A's useful life is double the useful life of Project B's. Project A's earning power, therefore, is twice as long as Project B's. A further disadvantage of this technique is that it ignores the time value of money.

Discounted Cash Flow

STUDY OBJECTIVE
10
Distinguish between the net present value and internal rate of return methods.

The **discounted cash flow technique** is generally recognized as the best conceptual approach to making capital budgeting decisions. This technique considers both the estimated total cash inflows from the investment and the time value of money. The expected total cash inflow consists of the sum of the annual cash inflows plus the estimated liquidation proceeds when the asset is sold for salvage at the end of its useful life. But because liquidation proceeds are generally immaterial, they are ignored in subsequent discussions.

Two methods are used with the discounted cash flow technique: (1) net present value and (2) internal rate of return. Before we discuss the methods, we recommend that you examine Appendix C if you need a review of present value concepts.

NET PRESENT VALUE METHOD

Under the **net present value method**, cash inflows are discounted to their present value and then compared with the capital outlay required by the investment. The difference between these two amounts is referred to as **net present value**. The interest rate to be used in discounting the future cash inflows is the required minimum rate of return. The decision rule is this: **A proposal is acceptable when net present value is zero or positive.** This means that the rate of return on the investment equals or exceeds the required rate of return. When net present value is negative, the project is unacceptable. Illustration 22-22 shows the net present value decision criteria.

Illustration 22-22 Net present value decision criteria

*E*THICS NOTE
Discounted future cash flows may not take into account all of the important considerations needed to make an informed capital budgeting decision. Other issues, for example, could include worker safety, product quality, and environmental impact.

When making a selection among acceptable proposals, **the higher the positive net present value, the more attractive the investment**. The application of this method to two cases is described in the next two sections. In each case, we will assume that the investment has no salvage value.

Equal Annual Cash Flows

Tappan Company's annual cash inflows are $26,000. If we assume this amount **is uniform over the asset's useful life**, the present value of the annual cash inflows can be computed by using the present value of an annuity of 1 for 10 periods (in Table 2, Appendix C). The computations at rates of return of 12 percent and 15 percent, respectively, are:

	Present Values at Different Discount Rates	
	12%	**15%**
Discount factor for 10 periods	5.65022	5.01877
Present value of cash inflows:		
$26,000 × 5.65022	$146,906	
$26,000 × 5.01877		$130,488

Illustration 22-23 Present value of annual cash inflows

The analysis of the proposal by the net present value method is as follows:

	12%	**15%**
Present value of future cash inflows	$146,906	$130,488
Capital investment	130,000	130,000
Positive (negative) net present value	$ 16,906	$ 488

Illustration 22-24 Computations of net present value

The proposed capital expenditure is acceptable at a required rate of return of both 12 percent and 15 percent because the net present values are positive.

Unequal Annual Cash Inflows

When annual cash inflows are unequal, we cannot use annuity tables to calculate their present value. Instead, tables showing the **present value of a single future amount must be applied to each annual cash inflow**. To illustrate, assume that Tappan Company management expects the same aggregate annual cash inflow ($260,000) but a declining market demand for the new product over the life of the equipment. The present value of the annual cash flows is calculated as follows using Table 1 in Appendix C.

Year	**Assumed Annual Cash Inflows**	**Discount Factor**		**Present Value**	
		12%	**15%**	**12%**	**15%**
	(1)	(2)	(3)	(1) × (2)	(1) × (3)
1	$ 36,000	.89286	.86957	$ 32,143	$ 31,305
2	32,000	.79719	.75614	25,510	24,196
3	29,000	.71178	.65752	20,642	19,068
4	27,000	.63552	.57175	17,159	15,437
5	26,000	.56743	.49718	14,753	12,927
6	24,000	.50663	.43233	12,159	10,376
7	23,000	.45235	.37594	10,404	8,647
8	22,000	.40388	.32690	8,885	7,192
9	21,000	.36061	.28426	7,573	5,969
10	20,000	.32197	.24719	6,439	4,944
	$260,000			$155,667	$140,061

Illustration 22-25 Computing present value of unequal annual cash inflows

Therefore, the analysis of the proposal by the net present value method is as follows.

Illustration 22-26 Analysis of proposal using net present value method

	12%	15%
Present value of future cash inflows	$155,667	$140,061
Capital investment	130,000	130,000
Positive (negative) net present value	**$ 25,667**	**$ 10,061**

In this example, the present values of the cash inflows are greater than the $130,000 capital investment. Thus, the project is acceptable at both a 12 percent and 15 percent required rate of return. The difference between the present values using the 12 percent rate under equal cash inflows ($146,906) and unequal cash inflows ($155,667) is due to the pattern of the inflows.

Business Insight
ACCOUNTING IN ACTION

Inaccurate trend forecasting and market positioning are often more detrimental to a capital budget decision than using the wrong discount rate. **Ampex** patented the VCR, but failed to see its market potential. **Westinghouse** made the same mistake with flat-screen video display. More often, companies adopt projects or businesses but later discontinue them in response to market changes. **Texas Instruments** announced it would stop manufacturing computer chips, after investing to become one of the world's leading suppliers. The company has dropped out of some twelve business lines in recent years.

SOURCE: World Research Advisory Inc. (London, August 1998), page 4.

DECISION TOOLKIT

Decision Checkpoints	Info Needed for Decision	Tool to Use for Decision	How to Evaluate Results
Should the company invest in a proposed project?	Cash flow estimates, discount rate	Net present value = Present value of future cash flows less capital investment	The investment is financially acceptable if net present value is positive.

INTERNAL RATE OF RETURN METHOD

The **internal rate of return method** finds the **interest yield of the potential investment**. The **internal rate of return** is the rate that will cause the present value of the proposed capital expenditure to equal the present value of the expected annual cash inflows. The determination of the internal rate of return involves two steps.

Step 1. Compute the internal rate of return factor. The formula for this factor is:

Capital Investment	÷	Annual Cash Inflows	=	Internal Rate of Return Factor

Illustration 22-27 Formula for internal rate of return factor

The computation for the Tappan Company, assuming equal annual cash inflows[2] is:

$$\$130,000 \div \$26,000 = 5.0$$

Step 2. Use the factor and the present value of an annuity of 1 table to find the internal rate of return. Table 2 of Appendix C is used in this step. The internal rate of return is found by locating the discount factor that is closest to the internal rate of return factor for the time period covered by the annual cash flows.

In Tappan Company, the annual cash inflows are expected to continue for 10 years. Thus, it is necessary to read across the period-10 row in Table 2 to find the discount factor. Row 10 is reproduced below for your convenience.

TABLE 2
PRESENT VALUE OF AN ANNUITY OF 1

(*n*) Periods	5%	6%	8%	9%	10%	11%	12%	15%
10	7.72173	7.36009	6.71008	6.41766	6.14457	5.88923	5.65022	5.01877

In this case, the closest discount factor to 5.0 is 5.01877, which represents an interest rate of approximately 15 percent. The rate of return can be further determined by interpolation, but since we are using estimated annual cash flows such precision is seldom required.

The internal rate of return that has been determined is then compared to management's required minimum rate of return. The decision rule is: **Accept the project when the internal rate of return is equal to or greater than the required rate of return. Reject the project when the internal rate of return is less than the required rate.** These relationships are shown graphically in Illustration 22-28.

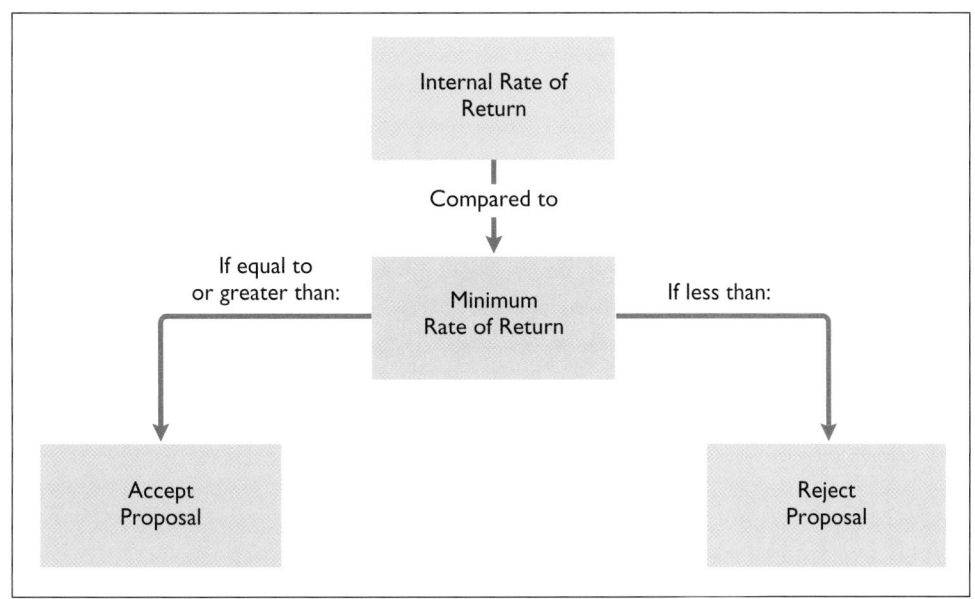

Illustration 22-28 Internal rate of return decision criteria

---

[2]When annual cash inflows are equal, the internal rate of return factor is the same as the cash payback period.

Assuming the minimum required rate of return is 10 percent for Tappan Company, the project is acceptable because the 15 percent internal rate of return is greater than the required rate.

The internal rate of return method is widely used in practice. Most managers find the internal rate of return easy to interpret.

DECISION TOOLKIT

Decision Checkpoints	Info Needed for Decision	Tool to Use for Decision	How to Evaluate Results
Should the company invest in a proposed project?	Estimated cash flows and the required rate of return (hurdle rate)	Internal rate of return = Interest rate that results in a net present value of zero	If the internal rate of return exceeds the specified discount rate (hurdle rate) for the project, then the project is financially acceptable.

Business Insight
ACCOUNTING IN ACTION

Which capital budgeting methods are used the most? One survey asked financial officers which method they used in considering expenditures for factory automation. Internal rate of return and cash payback were the most popular methods. Subjective evaluation—though not, strictly speaking, a capital budgeting method—also turned out to be popular with finance professionals.

Method	Primary Use*	Secondary Use*
Internal rate of return	55%	31%
Cash payback	29	48
Net present value	14	34
Annual rate of return	4	8
Subjective evaluation	9	49
Other	7	2

*The percentages in each column sum to more than 100% because some respondents indicated the use of more than one primary technique and many respondents use more than one secondary technique.

SOURCE: James A. Hendricks, "Applying Cost Accounting to Factory Automation," *Management Accounting*.

COMPARISON OF DISCOUNTED CASH FLOW METHODS

A comparison of the two discounted cash flow methods—net present value and internal rate of return—is presented in Illustration 22-29. When properly used, either method will provide management with relevant quantitative data for making capital budgeting decisions.

Item	Net Present Value	Internal Rate of Return
1. Objective	Compute net present value (a dollar amount).	Compute internal rate of return (a percentage).
2. Decision rule	If net present value is zero or positive, accept the proposal. If net present value is negative, reject the proposal.	If internal rate of return is equal to or greater than the minimum required rate of return, accept the proposal. If internal rate of return is less than the minimum rate, reject the proposal.

Illustration 22-29
Comparison of discounted cash flow methods

Business Insight
ACCOUNTING IN ACTION

One reason that e-business is changing the face of business so quickly is that the cost of the necessary hardware and software has fallen so rapidly. For example, an executive at **General Electric (GE)** reports that the company developed software for its own electronic-auction site for only $15,000. In discussing e-business related capital expenditures, a GE executive in Europe noted, "the incremental investment required is extraordinarily small compared with our overall investment. A $300 million investment for a company making $4 billion to $5 billion is [just a few] weeks of cash flow." He added that the cash payback period on these projects is a few months, rather than years. Thus, GE experienced almost "instant" productivity gains.

SOURCE: "E-Management: Inside the Machine," *The Economist* (November 11, 2000).

BEFORE YOU GO ON . . .

▶ **Review It**

1. What is the formula for and the decision rule in using the annual rate of return method?
2. What is the formula for the cash payback method?
3. When is a proposal acceptable under (a) the net present value method and (b) the internal rate of return method?

☑ THE NAVIGATOR

Using the Decision Toolkit

Suppose **Hewlett-Packard Company** must decide whether to make or buy some of its components from **Solectron Corp.** The cost of producing 50,000 electrical connectors for its printers is $110,000, broken down as follows.

Direct materials	$60,000	Variable overhead	$12,000
Direct labor	30,000	Fixed overhead	8,000

Instead of making the electrical connectors at an average cost per unit of $2.20 ($110,000 ÷ 50,000), the company has an opportunity to buy the connectors at $2.15 per unit. If the connectors are purchased, all variable costs and one-half of the fixed costs will be eliminated.

Instructions

(a) Prepare an incremental analysis showing whether the company should make or buy the electrical connectors.

(b) Will your answer be different if the released productive capacity resulting from the purchase of the connectors will generate additional income of $25,000?

Solution

(a)

	Make	Buy	Net Income Increase (Decrease)
Direct materials	$ 60,000	$ –0–	$ 60,000
Direct labor	30,000	–0–	30,000
Variable manufacturing costs	12,000	–0–	12,000
Fixed manufacturing costs	8,000	4,000	4,000
Purchase price	–0–	107,500	(107,500)
Total cost	$110,000	$111,500	$ (1,500)

This analysis indicates that Hewlett-Packard will incur $1,500 of additional costs if it buys the electrical connectors. H-P therefore would choose to make the connectors.

(b)

	Make	Buy	Net Income Increase (Decrease)
Total cost	$110,000	$111,500	$ (1,500)
Opportunity cost	25,000	–0–	25,000
Total cost	$135,000	$111,500	$23,500

Yes, the answer is different. The analysis shows that if additional capacity is released, net income will be increased by $23,500 if the electrical connectors are purchased. In this case, H-P would choose to purchase the connectors.

Summary of Study Objectives

1 *Identify the steps in management's decision-making process.* Management's decision-making process consists of (a) identifying the problem or opportunity, (b) determining possible courses of action, (c) making the decision, and (d) reviewing the results of the decision.

2 *Describe the concept of incremental analysis.* Incremental analysis is the process that is used to identify financial data that change under alternative courses of action. These data are relevant to the decision because they will vary in the future among the possible alternatives.

3 *Identify the relevant costs in accepting an order at a special price.* The relevant information in accepting an order at a special price is the difference between the variable manufacturing costs to produce the special order and expected revenues.

4 *Identify the relevant costs in a make-or-buy decision.* In a make-or-buy decision, the relevant costs are (a) the variable manufacturing costs that will be saved, (b) the purchase price, and (c) opportunity costs.

5 *Give the decision rule for whether to sell or process materials further.* The decision rule for whether to sell or process materials further is: Process further as long as the incremental revenue from processing exceeds the incremental processing costs.

6 *Identify the factors to be considered in retaining or replacing equipment.* The factors to be considered in determining whether equipment should be retained or replaced are the effects on variable costs and the cost of the new equipment. Also, any disposal value of the existing asset must be considered.

7 *Explain the relevant factors in deciding whether to eliminate an unprofitable segment.* In deciding whether to eliminate an unprofitable segment, it is necessary to determine the contribution margin, if any, produced by the segment and the disposition of the segment's fixed expenses.

8 *Determine which products to make and sell when resources are limited.* When a company has limited resources, it is necessary to find the contribution margin per unit of limited resource. Then multiply this amount by the units of limited resource to determine which product maximizes net income.

9 *Contrast the annual rate of return and cash payback techniques in capital budgeting.* The annual rate of return is obtained by dividing expected annual net income by the average investment. The higher the rate of return, the more attractive the investment. The cash payback technique identifies the time period to recover the cost of the investment. The formula is: Cost of capital expenditure divided by estimated annual cash inflow equals cash payback period. The shorter the payback period, the more attractive the investment.

10 *Distinguish between the net present value and internal rate of return methods.* Under the net present value method, the present value of future cash inflows is compared with the capital investment to determine net present value. The decision rule is: Accept the project if net present value is zero or positive. Reject the investment if net present value is negative.

Under the internal rate of return method, the objective is to find the interest yield of the potential investment. The decision rule is: Accept the project when the internal rate of return is equal to or greater than the required rate of return. Reject the project when the internal rate of return is less than the required rate.

DECISION TOOLKIT—A SUMMARY

Decision Checkpoints	Info Needed for Decision	Tool to Use for Decision	How to Evaluate Results
Which alternative should the company choose?	All relevant costs and opportunity costs	Compare relevant cost of each alternative.	Choose the alternative that maximizes net income.
How many units of product A and B should we produce in light of a limited resource?	Contribution margin per unit, limited resource required per unit	$\frac{\text{Contribution margin per unit of limited resource}}{} = \frac{\text{Contribution margin per unit}}{\text{Limited resource per unit}}$	Any additional capacity of limited resource should be applied toward the product with higher contribution margin per unit of limited resource.
Should the company invest in a proposed project?	Cash flow estimates, discount rate	$\text{Net present value} = \frac{\text{Present value of future cash flows}}{} \text{less capital investment}$	The investment is financially acceptable if net present value is positive.
Should the company invest in a proposed project?	Estimated cash flows and the required rate of return (hurdle rate)	Internal rate of return = Interest rate that results in a net present value of zero	If the internal rate of return exceeds the specified discount rate (hurdle rate) for the project, then the project is financially acceptable.

Glossary

Annual rate of return technique   The determination of the profitability of a capital expenditure by dividing expected annual net income by the average investment. (p. 1049).

Capital budgeting   The process of making capital expenditure decisions in business. (p. 1049).

Cash payback technique   A capital budgeting technique that identifies the time period required to recover the cost of a capital investment from the annual cash inflow produced by the investment. (p. 1050).

Cost of capital   The rate of return that management expects to pay on all borrowed and equity funds. (p. 1050).

Discounted cash flow technique   A capital budgeting technique that considers both the estimated total cash inflows from the investment and the time value of money. (p. 1052).

Incremental analysis   The process of identifying the financial data that change under alternative courses of action. (p. 1040).

Internal rate of return The rate that will cause the present value of the proposed capital expenditure to equal the present value of the expected annual cash inflows. (p. 1054).

Internal rate of return method A method used in capital budgeting that results in finding the interest yield of the potential investment. (p. 1054).

Net present value The difference that results when the original capital outlay is subtracted from the discounted cash inflows. (p. 1052).

Net present value method A method used in capital budgeting in which cash inflows are discounted to their present value and then compared to the capital outlay required by the investment. (p. 1052).

Opportunity cost The potential benefit that may be obtained from following an alternative course of action. (p. 1043).

Sunk cost A cost that cannot be changed by any present or future decision. (p. 1045).

Demonstration Problem 1

Juanita Company must decide whether to make or buy some of its components. The costs of producing 60,000 electrical cords for its floor lamps are as follows.

Direct materials	$65,000	Variable overhead	$15,000
Direct labor	30,000	Fixed overhed	10,000

Instead of making the electrical cords at an average cost per unit of $2.00 ($120,000 ÷ 60,000), the company has an opportunity to buy the cords at $1.90 per unit. If the cords are purchased, all variable costs and $2,000 of the fixed costs will be eliminated.

Instructions

(a) Prepare an incremental analysis showing whether the company should make or buy the electrical cords.

(b) Will your answer be different if the released productive capacity will generate additional income of $20,000?

Solution to Demonstration Problem 1

(a)

	Make	Buy	Net Income Increase (Decrease)
Direct materials	$ 65,000	$ –0–	$ 65,000
Direct labor	30,000	–0–	30,000
Variable manufacturing costs	15,000	–0–	15,000
Fixed manufacturing costs	10,000	8,000	2,000
Purchase price	–0–	114,000	(114,000)
Total cost	$120,000	$122,000	$ (2,000)

This analysis indicates that Juanita Company will incur $2,000 of additional costs if it buys the electrical cords.

(b)

	Make	Buy	Net Income Increase (Decrease)
Total cost	$120,000	$122,000	$ (2,000)
Opportunity cost	20,000		20,000
Total cost	$140,000	$122,000	$ 18,000

Yes, the answer is different because the analysis shows that net income will be increased by $18,000 if the electrical cords are purchased.

☑ THE NAVIGATOR

Demonstration Problem 2

Sierra Company is considering a long-term capital investment project called ZIP. The project will require an investment of $120,000, and it will have a useful life of 4 years. Annual net income for ZIP is expected to be: Year 1, $12,000; Year 2, $10,000; Year 3, $8,000; and Year 4, $6,000. Depreciation is computed by the straight-line method with no salvage value. The company's cost of capital is 12%.

Instructions

(Round all computations to two decimal places.)
(a) Compute the annual rate of return for the project.
(b) Compute the cash payback period for the project. (Round to two decimals.)
(c) Compute the net present value for the project. (Round to nearest dollar.)
(d) Should the project be accepted? Why?

Solution to Demonstration Problem 2

(a) $9,000 ($36,000 ÷ 4) ÷ $60,000 ($120,000 ÷ 2) = 15%
(b) Depreciation expense is $120,000 ÷ 4 years = 30,000. Annual cash inflows are:
   Year 1, $12,000 + $30,000 = $42,000
   Year 2, $10,000 + $30,000 = $40,000
   Year 3, $8,000 + $30,000 = $38,000
   Year 4, $6,000 + $30,000 = $36,000
   Cumulative cash inflows would be $82,000 ($42,000 + $40,000) at the end of year 2, and $120,000 ($42,000 + $40,000 + $38,000) at the end of year 3. Since the cumulative cash flows at the end of year 3 exactly equals the initial cash investment of $120,000, the cash payback period is 3 years.
(c)

Year	Discount Factor	Cash Inflow	Present Value
1	.89286	$42,000	$ 37,500
2	.79719	40,000	31,888
3	.71178	38,000	27,048
4	.63552	36,000	22,879
			119,315
		Capital investment	120,000
		Negative net present value	$ (685)

(d) The annual rate of return of 15% is good. However, the cash payback period is 75% of the project's useful life, and net present value is negative. The recommendation is to reject the project.

Action Plan
- To compute annual rate of return, divide expected annual net income by average investment.
- To compute cash payback, divide cost of the investment by annual cash inflows.
- Recall that annual cash inflow equals annual net income plus annual depreciation expense.
- Be careful to use the correct discount factor in using the net present value method.

☑ THE NAVIGATOR

Self-Study Questions

Self-Study/Self-Test

Answers are at the end of the chapter.

(SO 1) 1. Three of the steps in management's decision process are: (1) Review results of decision. (2) Determine and evaluate possible courses of action. (3) Make the decision. The steps are prepared in the following order.
   (a) (1), (2), (3).
   (b) (3), (2), (1).
   (c) (2), (1), (3).
   (d) (2), (3), (1).

2. Incremental analysis is the process of identify- (SO 2)
   ing the financial data that:
   (a) do not change under alternative courses of action.
   (b) change under alternative courses of action.
   (c) are mixed under alternative courses of action.
   (d) No correct answer is given.

(SO 3)   3. It costs a company $14 of variable costs and $6 of fixed costs to produce product A that sells for $30. A foreign buyer offers to purchase 3,000 units at $18 each. If the special offer is accepted and produced with unused capacity, net income will:
(a) decrease $6,000.
(b) increase $6,000.
(c) increase $12,000.
(d) increase $9,000.

(SO 4)   4. In a make-or-buy decision, relevant costs are:
(a) manufacturing costs that will be saved.
(b) the purchase price of the units.
(c) opportunity costs.
(d) all of the above.

(SO 5)   5. The decision rule in a sell-or-process-further decision is: Process further as long as the incremental revenue from processing exceeds:
(a) incremental processing costs.
(b) variable processing costs.
(c) fixed processing costs.
(d) No correct answer is given.

(SO 6)   6. In a decision to retain or replace equipment, the book value of the old equipment is a(n):
(a) opportunity cost.
(b) sunk cost.
(c) incremental cost.
(d) marginal cost.

(SO 7)   7. If an unprofitable segment is eliminated:
(a) net income will always increase.
(b) variable expenses of the eliminated segment will have to be absorbed by other segments.
(c) fixed expenses allocated to the eliminated segment will have to be absorbed by other segments.
(d) net income will always decrease.

8. If the contribution margin per unit is $15 and   (SO 8)
it takes 3.0 machine hours to produce the unit, the contribution margin per unit of limited resource is:
(a) $25.
(b) $5.
(c) $45.
(d) No correct answer is given.

9. Which of the following is *incorrect* about the an-   (SO 9)
nual rate of return technique?
(a) The calculation is simple.
(b) The accounting terms used are familiar to management.
(c) The timing of the cash inflows is not considered.
(d) The time value of money is considered.

10. A positive net present value means that the: (SO 10)
(a) project's rate of return is less than the cutoff rate.
(b) project's rate of return exceeds the required rate of return.
(c) project's rate of return equals the required rate of return.
(d) project is unacceptable.

Questions

Because of the decision-oriented aspect of the material in this chapter, all of the Questions in this chapter employ decision tools.

1. What steps are frequently involved in management's decision-making process?

2. Your roommate, Terry Duffy, contends that accounting contributes to most of the steps in management's decision-making process. Is your roommate correct? Explain.

3. "Incremental analysis involves the accumulation of information concerning a single course of action. "Do you agree? Why?

4. Stan Free asks your help concerning the relevance of variable and fixed costs in incremental analysis. Help Stan with his problem.

5. What data are relevant in deciding whether to accept an order at a special price?

6. Mike Muzzillo Company has an opportunity to buy parts at $7 each that currently cost $10 to make. What manufacturing costs are relevant to this make-or-buy decision?

7. Define the term "opportunity cost." How may this cost be relevant in a make-or-buy decision?

8. What is the decision rule in deciding whether to sell a product or process it further?

9. Your roommate, Loren Foelske, is confused about sunk costs. Explain to your roommate the meaning of sunk costs and their relevance to a decision to retain or replace equipment.

10. Cindy Tisinai Inc. has one product line that is unprofitable. What circumstances may cause overall company net income to be lower if the unprofitable product line is eliminated?

11. How is the contribution margin per unit of limited resources computed?

12. Describe the process a company may use in screening and approving the capital expenditure budget.

13. Your classmate, Jana Kingston, is confused about the factors that are included in the annual rate of return technique. What is the formula for this technique?

14. Jose Trevino is trying to understand the term "cost of capital." Define the term, and indicate its relevance to the decision rule under the annual rate of return technique.

15. Charles Barth claims the formula for the cash payback technique is the same as the formula for the

annual rate of return technique. Is Charles correct? What is the formula for the cash payback technique?

16. What are the advantages and disadvantages of the cash payback technique?

17. Two types of present value tables may be used with the discounted cash flow technique. Identify the tables and the circumstance(s) when each table should be used.

18. What is the decision rule under the net present value method?

19. Identify the steps required in using the internal rate of return method.

20. Roger Holloway Company uses the internal rate of return method. What is the decision rule for this method?

Brief Exercises

All of the Brief Exercises in this chapter employ decision tools.

BE22-1 The steps in management's decision-making process are listed in random order below. Indicate the order in which the steps should be executed.

_____ Make a decision.
_____ Identify the problem and assign responsibility.
_____ Review results of the decision.
_____ Determine and evaluate possible courses of action.

Identify the steps in management's decision-making process.
(SO 1)

BE22-2 Diehl Company is considering two alternatives. Alternative A will have sales of $150,000 and costs of $100,000. Alternative B will have sales of $185,000 and costs of $125,000. Compare Alternative A to Alternative B showing incremental revenues, costs, and net income.

Determine incremental changes.
(SO 2)

BE22-3 In Armanda Company it costs $30 per unit ($20 variable and $10 fixed) to make a product that normally sells for $45. A foreign wholesaler offers to buy 4,000 units at $23 each. Armanda will incur special shipping costs of $1 per unit. Assuming that Armanda has excess operating capacity, indicate the net income (loss) Armanda would realize by accepting the special order.

Determine whether to accept a special order.
(SO 3)

BE22-4 Sparrow Manufacturing incurs unit costs of $8 ($5 variable and $3 fixed) in making a sub-assembly part for its finished product. A supplier offers to make 10,000 of the part at $6.00 per unit. If the offer is accepted, Sparrow will save all variable costs but no fixed costs. Prepare an analysis showing the total cost saving, if any, Sparrow will realize by buying the part.

Determine whether to make or buy a part.
(SO 4)

BE22-5 Kleckner Inc. makes unfinished bookcases that it sells for $60. Production costs are $30 variable and $10 fixed. Because it has unused capacity, Kleckner is considering finishing the bookcases and selling them for $70. Variable finishing costs are expected to be $6 per unit with no increase in fixed costs. Prepare an analysis on a per unit basis showing whether Kleckner should sell unfinished or finished bookcases.

Determine whether to sell or process further.
(SO 5)

BE22-6 Alice Company has a factory machine with a book value of $90,000 and a remaining useful life of 4 years. A new machine is available at a cost of $200,000. This machine will have a 4-year useful life with no salvage value. The new machine will lower annual variable manufacturing costs from $600,000 to $440,000. Prepare an analysis showing whether the old machine should be retained or replaced.

Determine whether to retain or replace equipment.
(SO 6)

BE22-7 Kansas, Inc. manufactures golf clubs in three models. For the year, the Eagle line has a net loss of $20,000 from sales $200,000, variable expenses $180,000, and fixed expenses $40,000. If the Eagle line is eliminated, $25,000 of fixed costs will remain. Prepare an analysis showing whether the Eagle line should be eliminated.

Determine whether to eliminate an unprofitable segment.
(SO 7)

BE22-8 In Seabee Company, data concerning two products are: Contribution margin per unit—Product A $9, Product B $12; machine hours required for one unit—Product A 2, Product B 3. Compute the contribution margin per unit of limited resource for each product.

Show allocation of limited resources.
(SO 8)

BE22-9 Satina Company is considering purchasing new equipment for $400,000. It is expected that the equipment will produce annual net income of $24,000 over its 10-year useful life. Annual depreciation will be $40,000. Compute the payback period.

Compute the cash payback period for a capital investment.
(SO 9)

BE22-10 Desi Company accumulates the following data concerning a proposed capital investment: cash cost $225,000, annual cash inflow $42,000, present value factor of cash inflows for 10 years 5.65 (rounded). Determine the net present value, and indicate whether the investment should be made.

Compute net present value of an investment.
(SO 10)

Exercises

All of the Exercises in this chapter employ decision tools.

Make incremental analysis for special order.
(SO 3)

E22-1 Cortez Company manufactures toasters. For the first 8 months of 2005, the company reported the following operating results while operating at 75% of plant capacity.

Sales (400,000 units)	$4,000,000
Cost of goods sold	2,400,000
Gross profit	1,600,000
Operating expenses	900,000
Net income	$ 700,000

Cost of goods sold was 70% variable and 30% fixed. Operating expenses were 60% variable and 40% fixed.

In September, Cortez Company receives a special order for 25,000 toasters at $6.00 each from Alazar Company of Mexico City. Acceptance of the order would result in $3,000 of shipping costs but no increase in fixed operating expenses.

Instructions
(a) Prepare an incremental analysis for the special order.
(b) Should Cortez Company accept the special order? Why or why not?

Make incremental analysis for make-or-buy decision.
(SO 4)

E22-2 Roland Inc. has been manufacturing its own shades for its table lamps. The company is currently operating at 100% of capacity. Variable manufacturing overhead is charged to production at the rate of 50% of direct labor cost. The direct materials and direct labor cost per unit to make the lamp shades are $4.00 and $6.00, respectively. Normal production is 40,000 table lamps per year.

A supplier offers to make the lamp shades at a price of $13.50 per unit. If Roland Inc. accepts the supplier's offer, all variable manufacturing costs will be eliminated, but the $40,000 of fixed manufacturing overhead currently being charged to the lamp shades will have to be absorbed by other products.

Instructions
(a) Prepare the incremental analysis for the decision to make or buy the lamp shades.
(b) Should Roland Inc. buy the lamp shades?
(c) Would your answer be different in (b) if the productive capacity released by not making the lamp shades could be used to produce income of $35,000?

Make incremental analysis for further processing of materials.
(SO 5)

E22-3 Sandy Santiago recently opened her own basketweaving studio. She sells finished baskets in addition to the raw materials needed by customers to weave baskets of their own. Sandy has put together a variety of raw material kits, each including materials at various stages of completion. Unfortunately, owing to space limitations, Sandy is unable to carry all varieties of kits originally assembled and must choose between two basic packages.

The basic introductory kit includes undyed, uncut reeds (with dye included) for weaving one basket. This basic package costs Sandy $12 and sells for $27. The second kit, called Stage 2, includes cut reeds that have already been dyed. With this kit the customer need only soak the reeds and weave the basket. Sandy is able to produce the second kit by using the basic materials included in the first kit and adding one hour of her own time, which she values at $18 per hour. Because she is more efficient at cutting and dying reeds than her average customer, Sandy is able to make two kits of the dyed reeds, in one hour, from one kit of undyed reeds. The kit of dyed and cut reeds sells for $34.

Instructions
Determine whether Sandy's basketweaving shop should carry the basic introductory kit with undyed and uncut reeds, or the Stage 2 kit with reeds already dyed and cut. Prepare an incremental analysis to support your answer.

Make incremental analysis for retaining or replacing equipment.
(SO 6)

E22-4 Cheng Enterprises uses a word processing computer to handle its sales invoices. Lately, business has been so good that it takes an extra 3 hours per night, plus every third Saturday, to keep up with the volume of sales invoices. Management is considering updating its computer with a faster model that would eliminate all of the overtime processing.

	Current Machine	New Machine
Original purchase cost	$ 15,000	$ 21,000
Accumulated depreciation	6,000	—
Estimated operating costs	20,000	16,000
Useful life	5 years	5 years

If sold now, the current machine would have a salvage value of $3,000. If operated for the remainder of its useful life, the current machine would have zero salvage value. The new machine is expected to have zero salvage value after 5 years.

Instructions
Should the current machine be replaced? (Ignore the time value of money.)

E22-5 Amy O'Neil, a recent graduate of Rolling's accounting program, evaluated the operating performance of Winser Company's six divisions. Amy made the following presentation to Winser's Board of Directors and suggested the Ketchum Division be eliminated. "If the Ketchum Division is eliminated," she said, "our total profits would increase by $16,870."

Make incremental analysis concerning elimination of division.
(SO 7)

	The Other Five Divisions	Ketchum Division	Total
Sales	$1,664,200	$ 98,200	$1,762,400
Cost of goods sold	978,520	76,470	1,054,990
Gross profit	685,680	21,730	707,410
Operating expenses	527,940	38,600	566,540
Net income	$ 157,740	$(16,870)	$ 140,870

In the Ketchum Division, cost of goods sold is $56,000 variable and $20,470 fixed, and operating expenses are $14,000 variable and $24,600 fixed. None of the Ketchum Division's fixed costs will be eliminated if the division is discontinued.

Instructions
Is Amy right about eliminating the Ketchum Division? Prepare a schedule to support your answer.

E22-6 Stein Company manufactures and sells three products. Relevant per unit data concerning each product are given below.

Compute contribution margin and determine the product to be manufactured.
(SO 8)

	Product		
	A	B	C
Selling price	$8	$12	$14
Variable costs and expenses	$4	$ 9	$12
Machine hours to produce	2	1	2

Instructions
(a) Compute the contribution margin per unit of the limited resource (machine hour) for each product.
(b) Assuming 3,000 additional machine hours are available, which product should be manufactured?
(c) Prepare an analysis showing the total contribution margin if the additional hours are (1) divided equally among the products, and (2) allocated entirely to the product identified in (b) above.

E22-7 Henning Service Center just purchased an automobile hoist for $11,000. The hoist has a 5-year life and an estimated salvage value of $960. Installation costs were $2,900, and freight charges were $660. Henning uses straight-line depreciation.

The new hoist will be used to replace mufflers and tires on automobiles. Henning estimates that the new hoist will enable his mechanics to replace four extra mufflers per week. Each muffler sells for $65 installed. The cost of a muffler is $35, and the labor cost to install a muffler is $10.

Compute cash payback period and annual rate of return.
(SO 9)

Instructions

(a) Compute the payback period for the new hoist.

(b) Compute the annual rate of return for the new hoist. (Round to one decimal.)

E22-8   Jimmy Castle Manufacturing Company is considering three new projects, each requiring an equipment investment of $23,000. Each project will last for 3 years and produce the following cash inflows.

Year	AA	BB	CC
1	$ 7,500	$ 9,500	$13,000
2	9,000	9,500	9,000
3	15,000	9,500	11,000
Total	$31,500	$28,500	$33,000

The equipment's salvage value is zero. Castle uses straight-line depreciation. Castle will not accept any project with a payback period over 2 years. Castle's minimum required rate of return is 15%.

Instructions

(a) Compute each project's payback period, indicating the most desirable project and the least desirable project using this method. (Round to two decimals.)

(b) Compute the net present value of each project. Does your evaluation change? (Round to nearest dollar.)

E22-9   Hinckley Company is considering a capital investment of $150,000 in additional productive facilities. The new machinery is expected to have a useful life of 5 years with no salvage value. Depreciation is by the straight-line method. During the life of the investment, annual net income and cash inflows are expected to be $12,000 and $42,000, respectively. Hinckley has a 15% cost of capital rate, which is the minimum acceptable rate of return on the investment.

Instructions

(Round to two decimals.)

(a) Compute (1) the annual rate of return and (2) the cash payback period on the proposed capital expenditure.

(b) Using the discounted cash flow technique, compute the net present value.

E22-10   Tucci Company is considering three capital expenditure projects. Relevant data for the projects are as follows.

Project	Investment	Annual Income	Life of Project
22A	$240,000	$15,000	6 years
23A	270,000	21,400	9 years
24A	288,000	20,000	8 years

Annual income is constant over the life of the project. Each project is expected to have zero salvage value at the end of the project. Tucci Company uses the straight-line method of depreciation.

Instructions

(a) Determine the internal rate of return for each project. Round the internal rate of return factor to three decimals.

(b) If Tucci Company's minimum required rate of return is 11%, which projects are acceptable?

Problems: Set A

🔧══C   All of the Problems in this chapter employ decision tools.

P22-1A   Ramos Company is currently producing 16,000 units per month, which is 80% of its production capacity. Variable manufacturing costs are currently $11.00 per unit. Fixed manufacturing costs are $48,000 per month. Ramos pays a 9% sales commission to its sales people, has $30,000 in fixed administrative expenses per month, and is averaging $320,000 in sales per month.

A special order received from a foreign company would enable Ramos Company to operate at 100% capacity. The foreign company offered to pay 75% of Ramos's current selling price per unit. If the order is accepted, Ramos will have to spend an extra $2.00 per unit to package the product for overseas shipping. Also, Ramos Company would need to lease a new stamping machine to imprint the foreign company's logo on the product, at a monthly cost of $2,500. The special order would require a sales commission of $3,000.

Instructions

(a) Compute the number of units involved in the special order and the foreign company's offered price per unit.

(b) What is the manufacturing cost of producing one unit of Ramos's product for regular customers?

(c) Prepare an incremental analysis of the special order. Should management accept the order?

(d) What is the lowest price that Ramos could accept for the special order to earn net income of $1.20 per unit?

(e) ▭▭▭➤ What nonfinancial factors should management consider in making its decision?

Unlike previous chapters, check figures are not shown in this chapter because most would be final, not intermediate, answers.

P22-2A The management of Mendez Manufacturing Company has asked for your assistance in deciding whether to continue manufacturing a part or to buy it from an outside supplier. The part, called Tropica, is a component of Mendez's finished product.

An analysis of the accounting records and the production data revealed the following information for the year ending December 31, 2005.

Make incremental analysis related to make or buy; consider opportunity cost, and identify nonfinancial factors.
(SO 4)

1. The Machinery Department produced 36,000 units of Tropica.
2. Each Tropica unit requires 10 minutes to produce. Three people in the Machinery Department work full time (2,000 hours per year) producing Tropica. Each person is paid $11.00 per hour.
3. The cost of materials per Tropica unit is $2.00.
4. Manufacturing overhead costs directly applicable to the production of Tropica are: indirect labor, $5,500; utilities, $1,300; depreciation, $1,600; property taxes and insurance, $1,000. All of the costs will be eliminated if Tropica is purchased.
5. The lowest price for a Tropica from an outside supplier is $3.70 per unit. Freight charges will be $0.30 per unit, and a part-time receiving clerk at $8,500 per year will be required.
6. If Tropica is purchased, the excess space will be used to store Mendez's finished product. Currently, Mendez rents storage space at approximately $0.60 per unit stored per year. Approximately 4,500 units per year are stored in the rented space.

Instructions

(a) Prepare an incremental analysis for the make-or-buy decision. Should Mendez make or buy the part? Why?

(b) Prepare an incremental analysis, assuming the released facilities can be used to produce $10,000 of net income in addition to the savings on the rental of storage space. What decision should now be made?

(c) ▭▭▭➤ What nonfinancial factors should be considered in the decision?

P22-3A Sorrento Manufacturing Company has four operating divisions. During the first quarter of 2005 the company reported total income from operations of $61,000 and the following results for the divisions.

Compute contribution margin, and prepare incremental analysis concerning elimination of divisions.
(SO 7)

	Division			
	Boston	**Miami**	**San Diego**	**Tacoma**
Sales	$450,000	$730,000	$920,000	$520,000
Cost of goods sold	380,000	480,000	576,000	430,000
Selling and administrative expenses	120,000	207,000	246,000	120,000
Income (loss) from operations	$ (50,000)	$ 43,000	$ 98,000	$ (30,000)

Analysis reveals the following percentages of variable costs in each division.

	Boston	**Miami**	**San Diego**	**Tacoma**
Cost of goods sold	95%	80%	90%	90%
Selling and administrative expenses	80	60	70	60

Discontinuance of any division would save 60% of the fixed costs and expenses for that division.

Top management is deeply concerned about the unprofitable divisions (Boston and Tacoma). The consensus is that one or both of the divisions should be eliminated.

Instructions
(a) Compute the contribution margin for the two unprofitable divisions.
(b) Prepare an incremental analysis concerning the possible elimination of (1) the Boston Division and (2) the Tacoma Division. What course of action do you recommend for each division?
(c) Prepare a columnar condensed income statement using the CVP format for Sorrento Manufacturing Company, assuming (1) the Boston Division is eliminated, and (2) the unavoidable fixed costs and expenses of the Boston Division are allocated 30% to Miami, 50% to San Diego, and 20% to Tacoma.
(d) Compare the total income from operations with the Boston Division ($61,000) to total income from operations without this division.

Compute rate of return, cash payback, and net present value.
(SO 9, 10)

P22-4A The Shmi Corporation is considering three long-term capital investment proposals. Relevant data on each project are as follows.

	Project		
	Brown	**Red**	**Yellow**
Capital investment	$160,000	$200,000	$250,000
Annual net income:			
Year 1	25,000	20,000	31,000
2	16,000	20,000	24,000
3	13,000	20,000	23,000
4	10,000	20,000	22,000
5	8,000	20,000	20,000
Total	$ 72,000	$100,000	$120,000

Salvage value is expected to be zero at the end of each project. Depreciation is computed by the straight-line method (5-year life). The company's minimum rate of return is the company's cost of capital which is 12%.

Instructions
(a) Compute the average annual rate of return for each project. (Round to two decimals.)
(b) Compute the cash payback period for each project. (Round to two decimals.)
(c) Compute the net present value for each project. (Round to nearest dollar.)
(d) Rank the projects on each of the foregoing bases. Which project do you recommend?

Compute annual rate of return, cash payback, and net present value.
(SO 9, 10)

P22-5A Tammy Schipper is managing director of the Village Day Care Center. Village is currently set up as a full-time child care facility for children between the ages of 12 months and 6 years. Tammy is trying to determine whether the center should expand its facilities to incorporate a newborn care room for infants between the ages of 6 weeks and 12 months. The necessary space already exists. An investment of $20,000 would be needed, however, to purchase cribs, high chairs, etc. The equipment purchased for the room would have a 5-year useful life with zero salvage value.

The newborn nursery would be staffed to handle 12 infants on a full-time basis. The parents of each infant would be charged $150 weekly, and the facility would operate 52 weeks of the year. Staffing the nursery would require two full-time specialists and five part-time assistants at an annual cost of $74,000. Food, diapers, and other miscellaneous supplies are expected to total $14,000 annually.

Instructions
(a) Determine (1) annual net income and (2) cash inflow for the new nursery.
(b) Compute (1) the annual rate of return and (2) the cash payback period for the new nursery. (Round to two decimals.)
(c) Assuming that Village can borrow the money needed for expansion at 12%, compute the net present value of the new room. (Round to the nearest dollar.)
(d) What should Tammy conclude from these computations?

Problems: Set B

P22-1B High-Five Inc. manufactures basketballs for the National Basketball Association (NBA). For the first 6 months of 2005, the company reported the following operating results while operating at 90% of plant capacity.

Make incremental analysis for special order, and identify nonfinancial factors in decision.
(SO 3)

	Amount	Per Unit
Sales	$4,500,000	$50.00
Cost of goods sold	3,600,000	40.00
Selling and administrative expenses	360,000	4.00
Net income	$ 540,000	$ 6.00

Fixed costs for the period were: Cost of goods sold $900,000, and selling and administrative expenses $180,000.

In July, normally a slack manufacturing month, High-Five receives a special order for 5,000 basketballs at $34 each from the Italian Basketball Association (IBA). Acceptance of the order would increase variable selling and administrative expenses $0.40 per unit because of shipping costs but would not increase fixed costs and expenses.

Instructions
(a) Prepare an incremental analysis for the special order.
(b) Should High-Five Inc. accept the special order?
(c) What is the minimum selling price on the special order to produce net income of $3.00 per ball?
(d) ✏️ What nonfinancial factors should management consider in making its decision?

P22-2B The management of Oswego Manufacturing Company is trying to decide whether to continue manufacturing a part or to buy it from an outside supplier. The part, called WISCO, is a component of the company's finished product.

Make incremental analysis related to make or buy; consider opportunity cost, and identify nonfinancial factors.
(SO 4)

The following information was collected from the accounting records and production data for the year ending December 31, 2005.
1. 7,000 units of WISCO were produced in the Machining Department.
2. Variable manufacturing costs applicable to the production of each WISCO unit were: direct materials $4.75, direct labor $4.80, indirect labor $0.45, utilities $0.35.
3. Fixed manufacturing costs applicable to the production of WISCO were:

Cost Item	Direct	Allocated
Depreciation	$1,600	$ 900
Property taxes	400	200
Insurance	900	600
	$2,900	$1,700

All variable manufacturing and direct fixed costs will be eliminated if WISCO is purchased. Allocated costs will have to be absorbed by other production departments.
4. The lowest quotation for 7,000 WISCO units from a supplier is $77,000.
5. If WISCO units are purchased, freight and inspection costs would be $0.30 per unit, and receiving costs totaling $750 per year would be incurred by the Machining Department.

Instructions
(a) Prepare an incremental analysis for WISCO. Your analysis should have columns for (1) Make WISCO, (2) Buy WISCO, and (3) Net Income Increase/Decrease.
(b) Based on your analysis, what decision should management make?
(c) Would the decision be different if Oswego Company has the opportunity to produce $5,000 of net income with the facilities currently being used to manufacture WISCO? Show computations.
(d) ✏️ What nonfinancial factors should management consider in making its decision?

Compute contribution margin, and prepare incremental analysis concerning elimination of divisions.
(SO 7)

P22-3B Steffan Manufacturing Company has four operating divisions. During the first quarter of 2005, the company reported aggregate income from operations of $165,000 and the following divisional results.

	Division			
	I	**II**	**III**	**IV**
Sales	$490,000	$410,000	$300,000	$200,000
Cost of goods sold	300,000	250,000	270,000	180,000
Selling and administrative expenses	60,000	80,000	35,000	60,000
Income (loss) from operations	$130,000	$ 80,000	$ (5,000)	$ (40,000)

Analysis reveals the following percentages of variable costs in each division.

	I	**II**	**III**	**IV**
Cost of goods sold	70%	80%	75%	90%
Selling and administrative expenses	40	50	60	70

Discontinuance of any division would save 50% of the fixed costs and expenses for that division.

Top management is very concerned about the unprofitable divisions (III and IV). Consensus is that one or both of the divisions should be discontinued.

Instructions
(a) Compute the contribution margin for Divisions III and IV.
(b) Prepare an incremental analysis concerning the possible discontinuance of (1) Division III and (2) Division IV. What course of action do you recommend for each division?
(c) Prepare a columnar condensed income statement for Steffan Manufacturing, assuming Division IV is eliminated. Use the CVP format. Division IV's unavoidable fixed costs are allocated equally to the continuing divisions.
(d) Reconcile the total income from operations ($165,000) with the total income from operations without Division IV.

Compute rate of return, cash payback, and net present value.
(SO 9, 10)

P22-4B The Oslo Corporation is considering three long-term capital investment proposals. Each investment has a useful life of 5 years. Relevant data on each project are as follows.

	Project Tic	**Project Tac**	**Project Toe**
Capital investment	$160,000	$180,000	$200,000
Annual net income:			
Year 1	13,000	18,000	27,000
2	13,000	17,000	22,000
3	13,000	16,000	21,000
4	13,000	12,000	18,000
5	13,000	9,000	12,000
Total	$ 65,000	$ 72,000	$100,000

Depreciation is computed by the straight-line method with no salvage value. The company's cost of capital is 15%.

Instructions
(a) Compute the annual rate of return for each project. (Round to two decimals.)
(b) Compute the cash payback period for each project. (Round to two decimals.)
(c) Compute the net present value for each project. (Round to nearest dollar.)
(d) Rank the projects on each of the foregoing bases. Which project do you recommend?

Compute annual rate of return, cash payback, and net present value.
(SO, 9, 10)

P22-5B Sara Donish is an accounting major at a midwestern state university located approximately 60 miles from a major city. Many of the students attending the university are from the metropolitan area and visit their homes regularly on the weekends. Sara, an entrepreneur at heart, realizes that few good commuting alternatives are available for students doing weekend travel. She believes that a weekend commuting service could be organized and run profitably from several suburban and downtown shopping mall locations. Sara has gathered the following investment information.

1. Six used vans would cost a total of $66,000 to purchase and would have a 3-year useful life with negligible salvage value. Sara plans to use straight-line depreciation.
2. Ten drivers would have to be employed at a total payroll expense of $50,000.
3. Other annual out of pocket expenses associated with running the commuter service would include Gasoline $12,000, Maintenance $2,800, Repairs $3,500, Insurance $3,200, Advertising $1,500. (Exclude interest expense.)
4. Sara has visited several financial institutions to discuss funding for her new venture. The best interest rate she has been able to negotiate is 12%. Use this rate for cost of capital.
5. Sara expects each van to make nine round trips weekly and carry an average of five students each trip. The service is expected to operate 30 weeks each years. Each student will be charged $12.00 for a round-trip ticket.

Instructions
(a) Determine the annual (1) net income, and (2) cash inflow for the commuter service.
(b) Compute (1) the annual rate of return, and (2) the cash payback period. (Round to two decimals.)
(c) Compute the net present value of the commuter service. (Round to the nearest dollar.)
(d) ☐▬▬▷ What should Sara conclude from these computations?

Comprehensive Problem: Chapters 15 to 22

You would like to start a business manufacturing a unique model of bicycle helmet. In preparation for an interview with the bank to discuss your financing needs, you develop answers to the following questions. A number of assumptions are required; clearly note all assumptions that you make.

Instructions
(a) Identify the types of costs that would likely be involved in making this product.
(b) Set up five columns as indicated.

	Product Costs			
Item	Direct Materials	Direct Labor	Manufacturing Overhead	Period Costs

Classify the costs you identified in (a) into the manufacturing cost classifications of product costs (direct materials, direct labor, and manufacturing overhead) and period costs.
(c) Assign hypothetical monthly dollar figures to the costs you identified in (a) and (b).
(d) Assume you have no raw materials or work in process beginning or ending inventories. Prepare a projected cost of goods manufactured schedule for the first month of operations.
(e) Project the number of helmets you expect to produce the first month of operations. Compute the cost to produce one bicycle helmet. Review the result to ensure it is reasonable; if not, return to part (c) and adjust the monthly dollar figures you assigned accordingly.
(f) What type of cost accounting system will you likely use—job order or process costing?
(g) Explain how you would assign costs in either the job order or process costing system you plan to use.

(h) Classify your costs as either variable or fixed costs. For simplicity, assign all costs to either variable or fixed, assuming there are no mixed costs, using the format shown.

Item	Variable Costs	Fixed Costs	Total Costs

(i) Compute the unit variable cost, using the production number you determined in (e).
(j) Project the number of helmets you anticipate selling the first month of operations. Set a unit selling price, and compute both the contribution margin per unit and the contribution margin ratio.
(k) Determine your break-even point in dollars and in units.
(l) Prepare projected operating budgets (sales, production, direct materials, direct labor, manufacturing overhead, selling and administrative expense, and income statement).

Assumptions will be required for each of the following:

Direct materials budget:	Quantity of direct materials required to produce one helmet; cost per unit of quantity; desired ending direct materials (assume none).
Direct labor budget:	Direct labor time required per helmet; direct labor cost per hour.
Budgeted income statement:	Income tax expense is 45% of income from operations.

(m) Prepare a cash budget for the month. Assume the percentage of sales that will be collected from customers is 75%, and the percentage of direct materials that will be paid in the current month is 75%.
(n) Determine a relevant range of activity, using the number of helmets produced as your activity index. Prepare a flexible total cost monthly budget for two additional activity levels.
(o) Identify one potential cause of materials, direct labor, and manufacturing overhead variances for your product.
(p) Assume that you wish to purchase production equipment that costs $720,000. Determine the cash payback period, utilizing the monthly cash flow that you computed in part (m) multiplied by 12 months (for simplicity).
(q) Identify any non-quantitative factors that should be considered before commencing your business venture.

▶ BROADENING YOUR PERSPECTIVE

Group Decision Case

BYP22-1   Barrister Company is considering the purchase of a new machine. The invoice price of the machine is $115,000, freight charges are estimated to be $4,000, and installation costs are expected to be $6,000. Salvage value of the new equipment is expected to be zero after a useful life of 4 years. Existing equipment could be retained and used for an additional 4 years if the new machine is not purchased. At that time, the salvage value of the equipment would be zero. If the new machine is purchased now, the existing machine would be scrapped. Barrister's accountant, Diane Gallup, has accumulated the following data regarding annual sales and expenses with and without the new machine.

1. Without the new machine, Barrister can sell 11,000 units of product annually at a per unit selling price of $100. If the new unit is purchased, the number of units produced and sold would increase by 20%. The selling price would remain the same.
2. The new machine is faster than the old machine, and it is more efficient in its usage of materials. With the old machine the gross profit rate will be 26.5% of sales. With the new machine the rate will be 28% of sales.
3. Annual selling expenses are $180,000 with the current equipment. Because the new equipment would produce a greater number of units to be sold, annual selling expenses are expected to increase by 10% if it is purchased.

4. Annual administrative expenses are expected to be $100,000 with the old machine and $113,000 with the new machine.

5. The current book value of the existing machine is $36,000. Barrister uses straight-line depreciation.

6. Barrister's management wants a minimum rate of return of 15% on its investment and a payback period of no more than 3 years.

Instructions

With the class divided into groups, answer the following. (Ignore income tax effects.)

(a) Prepare an incremental analysis for the 4 years showing whether Barrister should keep the existing machine or buy the new machine.

(b) Calculate the annual rate of return for the new machine. (Round to two decimals.)

(c) Compute the payback period for the new machine. (Round to two decimals.)

(d) Compute the net present value of the new machine. (Round to the nearest dollar.)

(e) On the basis of the foregoing data, would you recommend that Barrister buy the machine? Why?

Managerial Analysis

BYP22-2 Sanchez Company manufactures private-label small electronic products, such as alarm clocks, calculators, kitchen timers, stopwatches, and automatic pencil sharpeners. Some of the products are sold as sets, and others are sold individually. Products are studied as to their sales potential, and then cost estimates are made. The Engineering Department develops production plans, and then production begins. The company has generally had very successful product introduction. Only two products introduced by the company have been discontinued.

One of the products currently sold is a multi-alarm alarm clock. The clock has four alarms that can be programmed to sound at various times and for varying lengths of time. The company has experienced a great deal of difficulty in making the circuit boards for the clocks. The production process has never operated smoothly. The product is unprofitable at the present time, primarily because of warranty repairs and product recalls. Two models of the clocks were recalled, for example, because they sometimes caused an electric shock when the alarms were being shut off. The Engineering Department is attempting to revise the manufacturing process, but the revision will take another 6 months at least.

The clocks were very popular when they were introduced, and since they are private-label, the company has not suffered much from the recalls. Presently, the company has a very large order for several items from Kmart Stores. The order includes 5,000 of the multi-alarm clocks. When the company suggested that Kmart purchase the clocks from another manufacturer, Kmart threatened to rescind the entire order unless the clocks were included.

The company has therefore investigated the possibility of having another company make the clocks for them. The clocks were bid for the Kmart order, based on an estimated $5 cost to manufacture, as follows.

Circuit board, 1 each @ $1.00	$1.00
Plastic case, 1 each @ $0.50	0.50
Alarms, 4 @ $0.15 each	0.60
Labor, 15 minutes @ $10/hour	2.50
Overhead, $1.60 per labor hour	0.40

Sanchez could purchase clocks to fill the Kmart order for $9 from Silver Star, a Korean manufacturer with a very good quality record. Silver Star has offered to reduce the price to $7.50 after Sanchez has been a customer for 6 months, placing an order of at least 1,000 units per month. If Sanchez becomes a "preferred customer" by purchasing 15,000 units per year, the price would be reduced still further to $4.50.

Alpha Products, a local manufacturer, has also offered to make clocks for Sanchez. They have offered to sell 5,000 clocks for $3 each. However, Alpha Products has been in business for only 6 months. They have experienced significant turnover in their labor force, and the local media have reported that the owners may soon face tax evasion charges. The owner of Alpha Products is an electronic engineer, however, and the quality of the clocks is likely to be good.

If Sanchez decides to purchase the clocks from either Silver Star or Alpha, all the costs to manufacturer could be avoided, except a total of $5,000 in overhead costs for machine depreciation. The machinery is fairly new, and has no alternate use.

Instructions
(a) What is the difference in profit under each of the alternatives if the clocks are to be sold for $12.50 each to Kmart?
(b) What are the most important nonfinancial factors that Sanchez should consider when making this decision?
(c) What should Sanchez do in regard to the Kmart order? What should it do in regard to continuing to manufacture the multi-alarm alarm clocks? Be prepared to defend your answer.

Real-World Focus

BYP22-3 Founded in 1983, the Beverly Hills Fan Company is located in Woodland Hills, California. With 23 employees and sales of less than $10 million, the company is relatively small. Management feels that there is potential for growth in the upscale market for ceiling fans and lighting. They are particularly optimistic about growth in Mexican and Canadian markets.

Presented below is information from the president's letter in the company's annual report.

BEVERLY HILLS FAN COMPANY
President's Letter

An aggressive product development program was initiated during the past year resulting in new ceiling fan models planned for introduction in 1993. Award winning industrial designer Ron Rezek created several new fan models for the Beverly Hills Fan and L.A. Fan lines, including a new Showroom Collection, designed specifically for the architectural and designer markets. Each of these models has received critical acclaim, and order commitments for 1993 have been outstanding. Additionally, our Custom Color and special order fans continued to enjoy increasing popularity and sales gains as more and more customers desire fans that match their specific interior decors. Currently, Beverly Hills Fan Company offers a product line of over 100 models of contemporary, traditional, and transitional ceiling fans.

Instructions
(a) What points did the company management need to consider before deciding to offer the special-order fans to customers?
(b) How would incremental analysis be employed to assist in this decision?

Exploring the Web

BYP22-4 Campbell Soup Company is an international provider of soup products. Management is very interested in continuing to grow the company in its core business, while "spinning off" those businesses that are not part of its core operation.

Address: **www.campbellsoupcompany.com** (or go to **www.wiley.com/college/kimmel**)

Steps
1. Go to the home page of Campbell Soup Company at the address shown above.
2. Choose **Investor Center**.
3. Choose **Annual Report**.
4. Choose the 2002 annual report, or the current annual report if 2002 is no longer available.

Instructions

Review the financial statements and management's discussion and analysis, and answer the following questions.

  (a) What was the total amount reported as "Purchases of Plant Assets" in the 2002 statement of cash flows? How does this amount compare with the previous year?
  (b) What range of interest rates does the company report on its long-term liabilities in the notes to its financial statements?
  (c) Assume that this year's capital expenditures are expected to increase cash flows by $35 million. What is the expected internal rate of return (IRR) for these capital expenditures? (Assume a 10-year period for the cash flows.)

Communication Activity

BYP22-5 Refer back to Exercise 22-7 to address the following.

Instructions

Prepare a memo to Mary Ann Griffin, your supervisor. Show your calculations from E22-7, parts **(a)** and **(b)**. In one or two paragraphs, discuss important nonfinancial considerations. Make any assumptions you believe to be necessary. Make a recommendation, based on your analysis.

Research Cases

BYP22-6 The April 1998 issue of *Management Accounting* includes an article by Julie Hertenstein and Marjorie Platt entitled "Why Product Development Teams Need Management Accountants."

Instructions

Read the article and answer the following questions.

  (a) What percentage of a product's cost are determined at the design stage?
  (b) Why do the authors say that management accountants can provide a broader perspective on costs than purchasing managers?
  (c) What are some of the roles and responsibilities that management accountants can have on a design team?
  (d) What are some nonfinancial measures used to evaluate industrial design performance?

BYP22-7 The April 21, 1997, issue of *Forbes* includes an article by Toni Mack entitled "The Tiger Is on the Prowl."

Instructions

Read the article and answer the following questions.

  (a) What have been the relative capital spending practices of **Royal Dutch Shell** versus **Mobil Corp.** versus **Exxon**?
  (b) What has been "the religion" (business objective) of Exxon's headquarters since 1983?
  (c) What was Exxon's capital budget in 1994 and 1995? What is Exxon's capital budget expected to swell to in 2 or 3 years?
  (d) Did Exxon's capital spending strategy pay off during the past 15 years?

Ethics Case

BYP22-8 Bristle Brush Company operates in a state where corporate taxes and workmen's compensation insurance rates have recently doubled. Bristle's president has assigned you the task of preparing an economic analysis and making a recommendation about whether to move the company's entire operation to Missouri. The president is slightly in favor of such a move because Missouri is his boyhood home, and he also owns a fishing lodge there.

You have just completed building your dream house, moved in, and sodded the lawn. Your children are all doing well in school and sports and, along with your spouse, want no part of a move to Missouri. If the company does move, so will you because your town is a one-industry community, and you and your spouse will have to move to have employment. Moving when everyone else does will cause you to take a big loss on the sale of your house. The same hardships will be suffered by your coworkers, and the town will be devastated.

In compiling the costs of moving versus not moving, you have latitude in the assumptions you make, the estimates you compute, and the discount rates and time periods you project. You are in a position to influence the decision singlehandedly.

Instructions

(a) Who are the stakeholders in this situation?

(b) What are the ethical issues in this situation?

(c) What would you do in this situation?

Answers to Self-Study Questions

1. d   2. b   3. c   4. d   5. a   6. b   7. c   8. b   9. d   10. b

 Remember to go back to the Navigator box on the chapter-opening page and check off your completed work.

Specimen Financial Statements: Tootsie Roll Industries, Inc.

The Annual Report

Once each year a corporation communicates to its stockholders and other interested parties by issuing a complete set of audited financial statements. The annual report, as this communication is called, summarizes the financial results of the company's operations for the year and its plans for the future. Many annual reports are attractive, multicolored, glossy public relations pieces, containing pictures of corporate officers and directors as well as photos and descriptions of new products and new buildings. Yet the basic function of every annual report is to report financial information, almost all of which is a product of the corporation's accounting system.

Tootsie Roll Annual Report Walkthrough

The content and organization of corporate annual reports have become fairly standardized. Excluding the public relations part of the report (pictures, products, and propaganda), the following items are the traditional financial portions of the annual report:

Financial Highlights
Letter to the Stockholders
Management's Discussion and Analysis
Financial Statements
Notes to the Financial Statements
Auditor's Report
Supplementary Financial Information

In this appendix we illustrate current financial reporting with a comprehensive set of corporate financial statements that are prepared in accordance with generally accepted accounting principles and audited by an international independent certified public accounting firm. We are grateful for permission to use the actual financial statements and other accompanying financial information from the annual report of a large, publicly held company, **Tootsie Roll Industries, Inc.**

Financial Highlights

The financial highlights section is usually presented inside the front cover of the annual report or on its first two pages. This section generally reports the total or per share amounts for five to ten financial items for the current year and one or more previous years. Financial items from the income statement and the balance sheet that typically are presented are sales, income from continuing operations, net income, net income per share, dividends per common share, and the amount of capital expenditures. The financial highlights section from **Tootsie Roll Industries' Annual Report** is shown on page A-2. We have also included Tootsie Roll's discussion of its corporate principles and corporate profile.

The financial information herein is reprinted with permission from the Tootsie Roll Industries, Inc. 2002 Annual Report. The complete financial statements for Tootsie Roll Industries are also available on the book's companion Web site and on the CD that comes with the book.

Financial Highlights

	December 31,	
	2002	2001
	(in thousands except per share data)	
Net Sales	$393,185	$391,755
Net Earnings	66,388	65,687
Working Capital	161,852	188,250
Net Property, Plant and Equipment	128,869	132,575
Shareholders' Equity	526,740	508,461
Average Shares Outstanding*	51,553	51,947
Per Share Items*		
Net Earnings	$1.29	$1.26
Cash Dividends Paid	.28	.27

*Adjusted for stock dividends.

Corporate Profile

Tootsie Roll Industries, Inc. has been engaged in the manufacture and sale of candy for 106 years. Our products are primarily sold under the familiar brand names, Tootsie Roll, Tootsie Roll Pops, Caramel Apple Pops, Child's Play, Charms, Blow Pop, Blue Razz, Cella's chocolate covered cherries, Mason Dots, Mason Crows, Junior Mints, Charleston Chew, Sugar Daddy, Sugar Babies, Andes and Fluffy Stuff cotton candy.

Corporate Principles

We believe that the differences among companies are attributable to the caliber of their people, and therefore we strive to attract and retain superior people for each job.

We believe that an open family atmosphere at work combined with professional management fosters cooperation and enables each individual to maximize his or her contribution to the company and realize the corresponding rewards.

We do not jeopardize long-term growth for immediate, short-term results.

We maintain a conservative financial posture in the deployment and management of our assets.

We run a trim operation and continually strive to eliminate waste, minimize cost and implement performance improvements.

We invest in the latest and most productive equipment to deliver the best quality product to our customers at the lowest cost.

We seek to outsource functions where appropriate and to vertically integrate operations where it is financially advantageous to do so.

We view our well known brands as prized assets to be aggressively advertised and promoted to each new generation of consumers.

Melvin J. Gordon, Chairman and Chief Executive Officer and Ellen R. Gordon, President and Chief Operating Officer.

Letter to the Stockholders

Nearly every annual report contains a letter to the stockholders from the chairman of the board or the president, or both. This letter typically discusses the company's accomplishments during the past year and highlights significant events such as mergers and acquisitions, new products, operating achievements, business philosophy, changes in officers or directors, financing commitments, expansion plans, and future prospects. The letter to the stockholders signed by Melvin J. Gordon, Chairman of the Board and Chief Executive Officer, and Ellen R. Gordon, President and Chief Operating Officer, of **Tootsie Roll Industries** is shown below.

To Our Shareholders

Sales in 2002 were $393 million, compared to 2001 sales of $392 million. Sales in both years are now being reported net of certain consumer and trade promotion expenses as required under the new accounting rules.

We were encouraged by sales growth in many of our core brands and key markets during the year, but these gains were mitigated by generally weak domestic economic conditions, retail bankruptcies, overall competitive activity and lower Mexican sales.

Reported net earnings in 2002 were $66 million compared with prior year net earnings of $66 million. Earnings per share were $1.29 compared to $1.26 in 2001 reflecting the fewer shares outstanding in 2002.

In 2002, we adopted the new accounting rules that eliminated amortization of goodwill and intangibles. Without the favorable effect of this accounting change, and adjusting for the non-recurring items that occurred in 2001, earnings in 2002 would have declined by $0.05 per share, principally due to higher ingredient costs and lower investment income.

Other key financial highlights of 2002 include:

- Cash dividends were paid for the sixtieth consecutive year, and totaled $14 million.

- The thirty-eighth consecutive annual stock dividend was distributed in April.

- Capital projects totalling $14 million to increase efficiency, improve quality and to add capacity in support of growth items were approved, some of which will be expended in 2003.

- 948,600 of the company's common shares were repurchased on the open market for a total of $32 million.

The company's balance sheet strengthened during 2002 despite the considerable financial resources committed to these activities. Cash and investments in marketable securities grew by $16 million during the year. We remain fully prepared to respond to investment opportunities, such as product development, capital projects and suitable business acquisitions, as they may arise, and are actively pursuing all of these channels of opportunity.

Sales and Marketing

We have long recognized the competitive advantage of having strong brands. The backdrop of 2002 was a persistently slow domestic economy and large retailer bankruptcies. Such conditions, along with intense competition for retail space and the consumer's hard-earned dollars, increasingly highlighted the value and staying power of our core brands, most of which grew in 2002.

Our sales gains were the result of continued implementation of targeted promotional programs such as shippers, combo packs and bonus bags throughout the year. These programs are popular with both retailers and consumers and reinforce the attributes of quality and value that are so closely associated with our products.

In 2002, we experienced another strong Halloween sales period. Our bagged goods, including the popular Child's Play mixed product assortment, continued to sell well through the mass merchandise, drug and warehouse club classes of trade.

Our flagship brand, Tootsie Roll, continued to emphasize its branded value positioning both to the trade and to consumers. One offering that highlights this strategy is our Bonus Bag promotion, which features 15% more candy for free. Not only does this promotion attract consumer attention, but the trade is pleased with the rapid shelf turns it generates.

Tootsie Roll Midgee Bonus Bag

Line extensions represented another avenue of sales growth in 2002. Tootsie "Mini" Pops, a miniature replica of our famous

Tootsie Pop Miniatures

Tootsie Pop—right down to the chewy, chocolatey Tootsie Roll center—were introduced in large bags for Halloween. Building on the instant success of this item, seasonal offerings of Tootsie Pop Miniatures for Easter and Valentine were added to the line toward the end of 2002.

We extended the Andes line into the change-maker market by introducing a special piece size in an airtight, fin-sealed wrapper, suitable for individual retail sale. For Christmas, Andes mints were embossed with festive wreaths, Christmas trees and snowmen to create an exciting seasonal line extension. Both of these new Andes

Andes new changemaker

items retain the characteristic rectangular, multilayered appearance and delicious crème de menthe flavor that typify the brand.

Our traditional boxed "theater" line, consisting of Dots, Crows, Junior Mints, Sugar Babies and Charleston "Mini" Chews contributed to sales growth in 2002. This "top shelf" assortment of jumbo, reclosable boxes now features Dots in three delicious flavors: Original, Tropical and Wildberry.

The new "Big Box" of Junior Mints was another successful extension in

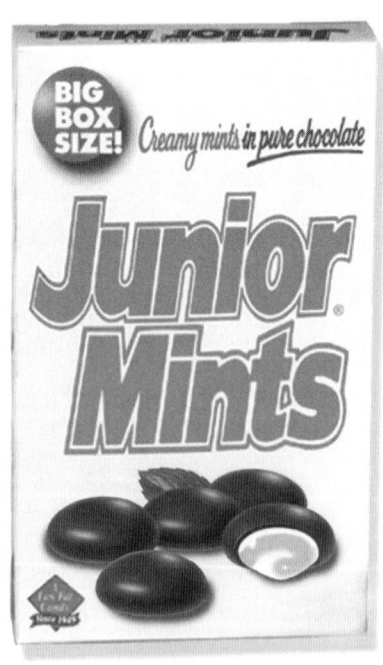

Junior Mints BIG BOX

the boxed category. This Big Box features vertically oriented graphics creating an exceptional consumer impression on the store shelf.

The newest addition to our Blow Pop line, Black Ice, was introduced in 2002. It features opaque crystalline hard candy surrounding a mysterious-looking black rasberry bubble gum center.

Black Ice Blow Pops

We also introduced Fluffy Stuff Cotton Candy Pops in 2002. They are traditional flat pops with flavor and package graphics that mirror our Fluffy Stuff cotton candy.

Fluffy Stuff Cotton Candy Pops

In response to rising packaging and ingredient costs, during the fourth quarter of 2002, we as well as others in the industry announced price increases that became effective in the first quarter of 2003. We believe that some of our fourth quarter sales growth was attributable to customer "buy-in" in anticipation of this increase.

U.S. Armed Forces

Our company has been honored by its long association with the military. Tootsie Rolls and Charms Squares have been included in military rations for many years, and in 2002 we had several new and gratifying contacts with the military.

In March, we took part in Operation Valentine, a morale-building mission for our soldiers in Afghanistan and elsewhere, by sending the troops more than 1 million pieces of candy.

Afghan child with Tootsie Rolls

The shipment was split between foot-long Tootsie Rolls, and limited edition Tootsie Roll Midgees, in patriotic red, white and blue wrappers. This gift, which brought our soldiers a nostalgic reminder of home, was in turn shared with local children in those war-torn lands.

In the fall of 2002, we were greatly honored by the Marine and Army survivors of the Korean War battle of the Chosin Reservoir. Temperatures during this famous battle fell to 36 degrees below zero, and the troops survived for many days on Tootsie Rolls and Charms Squares because their rations had frozen solid.

A Bosnian child receives a sweet gift

In recognition of the bond that this experience created between the company and these brave soldiers we were named honorary members of the "Chosin Few," the only civilians to have ever been so honored.

Advertising and Public Relations

Our products again received extensive cable television exposure on the Food Network's *Unwrapped,* program. New segments featuring Andes Candies and Charms Dead Head pops were added to the series along with previous shows about Tootsie Pops and Blow Pops in a lollipop segment, Dots and Junior Mints in a piece about "movie candy," and Charleston Chew and Sugar Babies in a look at "retro" candy.

Exposure on this highly rated program, including periodic replays,

Blow Pop Lollipop Shop

is helpful in generating positive awareness of our products.

Also in 2002, the Betty Crocker "Creepy Spider Cupcake Kit," featured Dots in a colorful and creative Halloween baking set, and the "Blow Pop Lollipop Shop" from Natural Science Industries, marketed a play set that enables a child to make their very own Blow Pop with a real bubble gum center!

Creepy Spider Cupcake Mix

Many articles and stories appeared in newspapers and magazines during the year commenting favorably on the company and its well-known products. Notably, Chief Executive Magazine ranked our Chairman and Chief Executive Officer as one of the best performing executives in the food, beverage and tobacco industries for the third consecutive year.

Manufacturing

Capital projects totalling $14 million were approved during the year to increase efficiency, improve quality and to support future growth. Most notably, during the year we commenced projects to significantly reengineer two major production lines. We view such ongoing investments in the company as being vital to maintaining our stature as one of the industry's most efficient producers.

We have stepped up our focus on the human element in our operations by providing targeted training to certain employee groups. This is designed to help them decrease costs and to eliminate unfavorable variances by modifying production activities to meet production needs more efficiently. We have also installed feedback systems to improve productivity and reduce or eliminate waste—a major priority within the company.

Purchasing

Although the Consumer Price Index only rose by 2.4% during the year, 2002 was a year of steady cost increases in many basic materials used by industry.

Of particular note in our industry, cocoa supplies from the Ivory Coast, the world's largest producer, were disrupted by civil war driving prices for this ingredient to a 17 year high.

Corn prices, and, in turn, corn syrup prices increased due to weather related crop reductions in the US. The domestic price of both raw and refined sugar increased due to USDA imposed marketing allotments.

In the area of packaging, printed film, which is made from plastic resins, rose during the year due to the rising price of oil. In addition the price of corrugated packaging increased as suppliers moved to cover their increased costs.

Although these cost increases affected our results in 2002, our hedging program shielded us from their full impact. We continue to use competitive bidding, hedging and forward purchase contracts to control costs and lock in prices at favorable levels when we feel it is prudent to do so.

Information Technology

The redevelopment of several core business applications was a major emphasis in 2002 and has neared completion. These new applications will give us state-of-the-art, web enabled tools which streamline current processes while they increase system flexibility to accommodate the ever-evolving requirements of our customers.

We also invested in additional processing and data storage hardware during the year. We view information technology as a key strategic tool, and are committed to deploying leading edge technology in this area.

International

Sales grew in Canada as volume gains more than offset devaluation of the Canadian dollar against the US dollar. Growth came from both expanded distribution of existing products and from new product introductions.

In Mexico, the focus in 2002 was on profitability rather than on volume. Accordingly, sales were lower but margins and operating income improved during the year.

Our export program through Tootsie Roll Worldwide continued to show growth during 2002. Our shipments increased during the year and actual in-market sales growth was encouraging.

New markets opened during the year have allowed us to expand our presence in untapped markets in Central America and the Middle East, while growth in some of our key Asian markets continued in 2002.

In Appreciation...

We wish to thank the many loyal employees, customers, suppliers, sales brokers and foreign distributors who have worked with us during these challenging times, as well as our shareholders who have been supportive through the many years.

We remain committed to growing our company in sales and in profitability and hope to extend the legacy of our famous brands to coming generations.

Melvin J. Gordon

Melvin J. Gordon
Chairman of the Board and
Chief Executive Officer

Ellen R. Gordon

Ellen R. Gordon
President and
Chief Operating Officer

Management Discussion and Analysis

The management discussion and analysis (MD&A) section covers three financial aspects of a company: its results of operations, its ability to pay near-term obli-gations, and its ability to fund operations and expansion. Management must highlight favorable or unfavorable trends and identify significant events and uncertainties that affect these three factors. This discussion obviously involves a number of subjective estimates and opinions. The MD&A section of **Tootsie Roll**'s annual report is presented on the next page.

Management's Discussion and Analysis of Financial Condition and Results of Operations

(in thousands except per share, percentage and ratio figures)

NET SALES
Millions of dollars

$360 — 98
$369 — 99
$397 — 00
$392 — 01
$393 — 02

NET EARNINGS
Per Share

$1.25 — 98
$1.34 — 99
$1.45 — 00
$1.26 — 01
$1.29 — 02

FINANCIAL REVIEW

This financial review discusses the company's financial condition, results of operations, liquidity and capital resources, market risks and critical accounting policies. It should be read in conjunction with the Consolidated Financial Statements and related footnotes that follow this discussion.

FINANCIAL CONDITION

Our financial condition remained strong in 2002, bolstered by our profitable operations during the year.

Shareholder equity increased to $526,740 from $508,461 in the prior year, reflecting net earnings of $66,388 partially offset by stock repurchases of $32,314 and cash dividends of $14,304. The company has paid cash dividends for sixty consecutive years.

Shareholders also received a 3% stock dividend in 2002, the thirty-eighth consecutive year that one has been distributed.

Working capital was $161,852 in 2002, $26,398 lower than in 2001 because the proceeds from maturing investments were used to purchase investments with maturities greater than one year, causing a shift from current to non-current assets. Total cash and investments grew to $262,745 from $246,292 in the prior year, an increase of $16,453.

The company continues to maintain a conservative financial posture. Aside from an immaterial amount of operating leases, the company has no off-balance sheet financing arrangements, and our simple financial structure does not utilize any "special purpose entities" or other obscure financing arrangements.

We have sufficient capital, generated principally from operations, to respond to investment opportunities as they may arise. Accordingly, we continue to seek appropriate acquisitions to complement our existing business.

RESULTS OF OPERATIONS

2002 vs. 2001

Net sales increased in 2002 to $393,185 from $391,755 in 2001. Many of our core brands showed growth throughout the year. However, these gains were partially offset by lower Mexican sales, retail bankruptcies, competitive pressure and weak economic conditions that dampened retail traffic.

Effective January 1, 2002, the company adopted the new accounting requirements that treat certain consumer and trade promotions as a reduction in net sales rather than as an operating expense. The effect of the above was to reduce both net sales and operating expenses by $29,990 and $31,741 in 2002 and 2001, respectively.

Sales remained at the highest level in the third quarter due to successful Halloween promotions, although sales through the first nine months of 2002 were lower than in 2001 due to factors cited above. Sales went ahead in the fourth quarter, although we believe that some of the sales increase in the fourth quarter can be attributed to customer "buy-in" in anticipation of a price increase that became effective in the first quarter of 2003.

Sales in our Canadian operation increased due to further gains in distribution and successful promotions, while sales in Mexico declined as a result of a concentration on margin improvement and local competitive pressure.

Cost of goods sold increased from 55.3% to 56.1% of sales. The increase in cost of goods sold is due to higher raw materials cost and product mix in 2002, partially offset by a non-recurring inventory write down of $1,100 pre-tax and a plant closing charge of $1,500 pre-tax in the third and fourth quarters, respectively, of 2001.

Due to the seasonal nature of our business and corresponding variations in product mix, gross

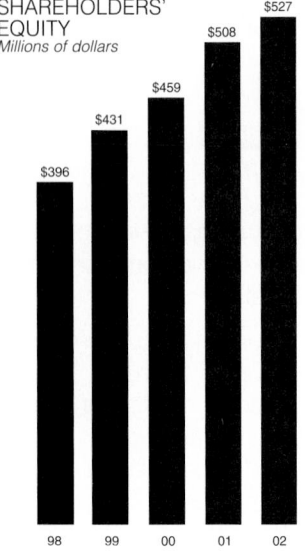

SHAREHOLDERS' EQUITY
Millions of dollars

$396 $431 $459 $508 $527
98   99   00   01   02

CASH DIVIDENDS
Per Share

$0.18 $0.22 $0.26 $0.27 $0.28
98   99   00   01   02

margins were lower in the second half of the year than in the first half.

Selling, marketing and administrative expense, declined as a percentage of sales to 19.3% in 2002 from 19.8% in 2001, due to cost containment measures and lower advertising expenditures. Both numbers are net of the reclassification of promotional expenses, which have been accounted for as a reduction of sales.

Effective January 1, 2002, the company adopted the new accounting rules pertaining to acquired goodwill and intangibles.

This had the effect of eliminating the amortization of such goodwill and intangibles, which was $3,778 in the prior year. Accordingly, earnings from operations increased from $93,944 to $96,669.

Other income, consisting primarily of interest income, net of interest expense, was $4,019 in 2002 versus $6,843 in 2001 due to lower interest rates in 2002 and an investment capital gain in 2001. The effective tax rate was 34.1% in 2002 as compared to 34.8% in 2001.

Consolidated net earnings were $66,388 and $65,687 and earnings per share were $1.29 and $1.26 in 2002 and 2001, respectively. Earnings per share increased by a greater percentage than did earnings due to share repurchases. Average shares outstanding were 51,553 and 51,947 in 2002 and 2001, respectively.

Comparative earnings per share were affected by the aforementioned investment capital gain of $962 or $.02 per share, net of income tax, and nonrecurring charges of $1,803 or $.03 per share, net of income tax, in 2001. Excluding the effects of these nonrecurring adjustments in 2001 and adjusting for the effects of goodwill amortization, net earnings per share for 2002 and 2001 were $1.29 and $1.34, respectively, a decrease of $.05 per share or 4%.

2001 vs. 2000

Sales in 2001 were $391,755 a decrease of 1% from the $396,816 sales of 2000. Halloween sales once again made the third quarter our highest selling period, although third quarter and nine month 2001 sales declined from the prior year periods due to unfavorable economic conditions and increased competitive pressures. These adverse factors were somewhat offset by successful marketing and promotional programs in certain trade classes, sales of new products

and by sales of brands acquired during 2000.

Cost of goods sold was $216,657 or 55.3% of sales in 2001 as compared to $207,100 or 52.2% of sales in 2000. The increase in cost of goods sold is due to product mix, lower profit margins of the brands acquired in 2000, and higher overhead costs from multiple plant locations, including increased energy costs.

In addition, the nonrecurring inventory adjustment of $1,100 and plant closing charge of $1,500 added to cost of goods sold in the third and fourth quarters, respectively. These charges, coupled with the seasonality nature of our business and product mix, caused gross margins for third and fourth quarters to fall below the 44.7% of sales averaged over the entire year.

Selling, marketing and administrative expense, as a percent of sales increased from 19.0% in 2000 to 19.8% in 2001 due to higher distribution and delivery expenses relating to higher fuel costs, and higher customer deductions.

Amortization of intangibles increased from $3,420 in 2000 to $3,778 in 2001, reflecting a full year of amortization associated with the brands acquired during 2000. As a result of the lower sales and higher costs discussed above, earnings from operations declined from $110,729 to $93,944.

Other income was $6,843 in 2001 versus $7,079 in 2000, due to lower interest rates, partially offset by the investment capital gain. The effective tax rate was 34.8% in 2001 versus 35.7% in 2000.

Consolidated net earnings were $65,687 and $75,737 and earnings per share were $1.26 and $1.45 in 2001 and 2000, respectively. Average shares outstanding declined to 51,947 from 52,394 due to share repurchases.

LIQUIDITY AND CAPITAL RESOURCES

Cash flows from operating activities were $71,203 in 2002, $78,584 in 2001 and $82,591 in 2000. The decline in 2002 versus 2001 is attributable to higher accounts receivable and inventories, partially offset by higher accounts payable and accrued liabilities. The decline in 2001 versus 2000 was due to lower net earnings partially offset by lower accounts receivable and higher depreciation and amortization.

Cash flows from investing activities in 2002 reflect capital expenditures of $10,308 and a net increase in marketable securities of $14,996. In 2001, capital expenditures were $14,148 and marketable securities increased by $2,686. In 2000, capital expenditures were $16,189, $74,293 was used for the purchase of Fluffy Stuff and Andes Candies, and marketable securities decreased by $26,305, which was used to help finance the acquisitions.

Cash flows from financing activities reflect share repurchases of $32,314, $1,932 and $32,945 in 2002, 2001 and 2000, respectively. In 2000 there were short-term borrowings of $43,625 related to the Andes acquisition, which were subsequently repaid.

Cash dividends of $14,610, $14,168 and $13,091 were paid in 2002, 2001 and 2000, respectively. 2002 was the sixtieth consecutive year in which we have paid cash dividends.

QUANTITATIVE AND QUALITATIVE DISCLOSURE OF MARKET RISK

The company is exposed to various market risks, including fluctuations in the prices of ingredients and packaging material. At December 31, 2002 the company had open contracts to purchase approximately half of its expected 2003 and 2004 sugar usage. We also invest in securities with maturities of generally up to four years, the majority of which are held to maturity, which limits the company's exposure to interest rate fluctuations. There was no material change in the company's market risk during 2002.

CRITICAL ACCOUNTING POLICIES

Preparation of the company's financial statements involves judgements due to uncertainties affecting the application of accounting policies, and the likelihood that different amounts would be reported under different conditions or using different assumptions. In the opinion of management, the company does not have any individual accounting policy that is "critical." However, following is a summary of the more significant accounting policies and methods used.

Revenue recognition, customer incentive programs, advertising and marketing

Revenue, net of applicable provisions for discounts, returns allowances, and certain advertising and promotional costs, is recognized upon delivery of products to customers. Provisions for bad debts are recorded as selling, marketing and administrative expense. Provisions for allowances are based upon the terms of programs offered to customers, historical trends of deductions and customer credit quality. Such provisions have not been significant to the company's financial position or results of operations.

Intangible assets

Effective January 1, 2002 the company adopted SFAS No. 142, whereby goodwill and other indefinite lived assets are not amortized, but are instead subjected to regular testing for impairment. The methodologies used to estimate fair value in such tests require the use of significant judgements and assumptions, including projected cash flows and discount rates. The company's intangible assets consist primarily of trademarks and goodwill, the values of which the company has determined are not impaired.

Investments

The company invests in certain high-quality debt securities primarily Aa or better rated municipal bonds. The accounting for such investments is outlined in Note 1. No credit losses have been incurred on these investments.

Guarantees

The Financial Accounting Standards Board issued Interpretation No. 45 "Guarantor's Accounting and Disclosure Requirements for Guarantees, Including Indirect Guarantees of Indebtedness to Others" relating to the accounting for and disclosure of certain types of guarantees. The disclosure provisions are effective for financial statements with years ending after December 15, 2002. No disclosures were required for the company as a result of adoption of this standard, as it has no such guarantees outstanding.

Other Matters

In the opinion of management, other than contracts for raw materials, principally commodity hedges entered into in the ordinary course of business, the company does not have any significant contractual obligations or future commitments, and is not involved in any significant transactions with related parties.

The company provides split dollar life insurance benefits to certain executive officers and records an asset equal to the cumulative insurance premiums paid on the related policies. The company will fully recover the premiums paid under the terms of the plan. The Sarbanes-Oxley Act (the Act) amended the Securities Exchange Act of 1934 to generally prohibit both direct and indirect corporate loans to certain executive officers and directors of publicly traded companies, but does not directly address split dollar life insurance premiums. Accordingly, the company has ceased making premium payments with respect to existing policies while it evaluates the potential impact of the Act on the split dollar life insurance benefit plan. The cessation in insurance premiums has no impact on the amount recoverable of the split dollar life insurance asset, which was $58,263 at December 31, 2002.

CONSOLIDATED STATEMENT OF

Financial Position

TOOTSIE ROLL INDUSTRIES, INC. AND SUBSIDIARIES   (in thousands)

Assets

December 31,

	2002	2001
CURRENT ASSETS:		
Cash and cash equivalents	$105,507	$106,532
Investments	40,737	68,629
Accounts receivable trade, less allowances of $2,005 and $2,037	22,686	20,403
Other receivables	4,073	3,329
Inventories:		
Finished goods and work-in-process	26,591	24,770
Raw materials and supplies	17,054	16,392
Prepaid expenses	3,819	4,269
Deferred income taxes	4,481	1,772
Total current assets	224,948	246,096
PROPERTY, PLANT AND EQUIPMENT, at cost:		
Land	8,297	8,354
Buildings	43,948	43,613
Machinery and equipment	196,706	189,528
	248,951	241,495
Less — Accumulated depreciation	120,082	108,920
	128,869	132,575
OTHER ASSETS:		
Goodwill	38,151	38,151
Trademarks	79,348	79,348
Investments	116,501	71,131
Split dollar officer life insurance	58,263	51,375
	292,263	240,005
	$646,080	$618,676

Financial Statements and Accompanying Notes

The standard set of financial statements consists of: (1) a comparative income statement for three years, (2) a comparative balance sheet for two years, (3) a comparative statement of cash flows for three years, (4) a statement of retained earnings (or stockholders' equity) for three years, and (5) a set of accompanying notes that are considered an integral part of the financial statements. The auditor's report, unless stated otherwise, covers the financial statements and the accompanying notes. The financial statements and accompanying notes plus some supplementary data and analyses for Tootsie Roll Industries follow.

(in thousands except per share data)

Liabilities and Shareholders' Equity   December 31,

	2002	2001
CURRENT LIABILITIES:		
Accounts payable	$ 12,505	$ 9,223
Dividends payable	3,579	3,536
Accrued liabilities	35,825	34,295
Income taxes payable	11,187	10,792
Total current liabilities	63,096	57,846
NONCURRENT LIABILITIES:		
Deferred income taxes	19,654	16,792
Postretirement health care and life insurance benefits	8,151	7,450
Industrial development bonds	7,500	7,500
Deferred compensation and other liabilities	20,939	20,627
Total noncurrent liabilities	56,244	52,369
SHAREHOLDERS' EQUITY:		
Common stock, $.69-4/9 par value—		
120,000 and 120,000 shares authorized—		
34,248 and 34,139, respectively, issued	23,783	23,708
Class B common stock, $.69-4/9 par value—		
40,000 and 40,000 shares authorized—		
16,759 and 16,319, respectively, issued	11,638	11,332
Capital in excess of par value	355,658	323,981
Retained earnings, per accompanying statement	148,705	161,345
Accumulated other comprehensive earnings (loss)	(11,052)	(9,913)
Treasury stock (at cost)—		
55 shares and 53 shares, respectively	(1,992)	(1,992)
	526,740	508,461
	$646,080	$618,676

CONSOLIDATED STATEMENT OF

Earnings, Comprehensive Earnings and Retained Earnings

TOOTSIE ROLL INDUSTRIES, INC. AND SUBSIDIARIES   (in thousands except per share data)

	For the year ended December 31,		
	2002	2001	2000
Net sales	$393,185	$391,755	$396,816
Cost of goods sold	220,765	216,657	207,100
Gross margin	172,420	175,098	189,716
Selling, marketing and administrative expenses	75,751	77,376	75,567
Amortization of intangible assets	—	3,778	3,420
Earnings from operations	96,669	93,944	110,729
Other income, net	4,019	6,843	7,079
Earnings before income taxes	100,688	100,787	117,808
Provision for income taxes	34,300	35,100	42,071
Net earnings	$ 66,388	$ 65,687	$ 75,737
Net earnings	$ 66,388	$ 65,687	$ 75,737
Other comprehensive earnings (loss)	(1,139)	277	(1,250)
Comprehensive earnings	$ 65,249	$ 65,964	$ 74,487
Retained earnings at beginning of year	$161,345	$180,123	$158,619
Net earnings	66,388	65,687	75,737
Cash dividends ($.28, $.27 and $.26 per share, respectively)	(14,304)	(14,021)	(13,350)
Stock dividends	(64,724)	(70,444)	(40,883)
Retained earnings at end of year	$148,705	$161,345	$180,123
Earnings per share	$ 1.29	$ 1.26	$ 1.45
Average common and class B common shares outstanding	51,553	51,947	52,394

(The accompanying notes are an integral part of these statements.)

CONSOLIDATED STATEMENT OF

Cash Flows

TOOTSIE ROLL INDUSTRIES, INC. AND SUBSIDIARIES   (in thousands)

For the year ended December 31,

	2002	2001	2000
CASH FLOWS FROM OPERATING ACTIVITIES:			
Net earnings	$ 66,388	$ 65,687	$ 75,737
Adjustments to reconcile net earnings to net cash provided by operating activities:			
Depreciation and amortization	12,354	16,700	13,314
Gain on retirement of fixed assets	—	—	(46)
Purchase of trading securities	(2,481)	(2,921)	(2,290)
Changes in operating assets and liabilities, excluding acquisitions:			
Accounts receivable	(2,887)	3,096	(4,460)
Other receivables	115	(2,100)	4,486
Inventories	(2,734)	910	(768)
Prepaid expenses and other assets	(6,902)	(8,857)	(7,903)
Accounts payable and accrued liabilities	5,049	(224)	(1,717)
Income taxes payable and deferred	485	4,402	5,691
Postretirement health care and life insurance benefits	700	494	399
Deferred compensation and other liabilities	312	1,206	337
Other	804	191	(189)
Net cash provided by operating activities	71,203	78,584	82,591
CASH FLOWS FROM INVESTING ACTIVITIES:			
Acquisitions of businesses, net of cash acquired	—	—	(74,293)
Capital expenditures	(10,308)	(14,148)	(16,189)
Purchase of held to maturity securities	(262,229)	(240,609)	(154,032)
Maturity of held to maturity securities	250,345	228,397	176,576
Purchase of available for sale securities	(35,217)	(64,640)	(78,993)
Sale and maturity of available for sale securities	32,105	74,166	82,754
Net cash used in investing activities	(25,304)	(16,834)	(64,177)
CASH FLOWS FROM FINANCING ACTIVITIES:			
Issuance of notes payable	—	—	43,625
Repayments of notes payable	—	—	(43,625)
Shares repurchased and retired	(32,314)	(1,932)	(32,945)
Dividends paid in cash	(14,610)	(14,168)	(13,091)
Net cash used in financing activities	(46,924)	(16,100)	(46,036)
Increase (decrease) in cash and cash equivalents	(1,025)	45,650	(27,622)
Cash and cash equivalents at beginning of year	106,532	60,882	88,504
Cash and cash equivalents at end of year	$105,507	$106,532	$ 60,882
Supplemental cash flow information:			
Income taxes paid	$ 34,099	$ 30,490	$ 35,750
Interest paid	$ 309	$ 356	$ 1,067

(The accompanying notes are an integral part of these statements.)

Notes to Consolidated Financial Statements

($ in thousands except per share data)

TOOTSIE ROLL INDUSTRIES, INC. AND SUBSIDIARIES

NOTE 1—SIGNIFICANT ACCOUNTING POLICIES:

Basis of consolidation:

The consolidated financial statements include the accounts of Tootsie Roll Industries, Inc. and its wholly-owned subsidiaries (the company), which are primarily engaged in the manufacture and sale of candy products. All significant intercompany transactions have been eliminated.

The preparation of financial statements in conformity with generally accepted accounting principles requires management to make estimates and assumptions that affect the reported amounts of assets and liabilities and disclosure of contingent assets and liabilities at the date of the financial statements and the reported amounts of revenues and expenses during the reporting period. Actual results could differ from those estimates.

Certain reclassifications have been made to the prior year financial statements to conform to the current year presentation.

Revenue recognition and other accounting pronouncements:

Revenues are recognized when products are shipped and delivered to customers. Shipping and handling costs of $28,579, $28,069, and $26,661 in 2002, 2001 and 2000, respectively, are included in selling, marketing and administrative expenses. Accounts receivable are unsecured. Revenues from a major customer aggregated approximately 19.6%, 16.9% and 17.8% of total net sales during the years ended December 31, 2002, 2001 and 2000, respectively.

Emerging Issues Task Force Issue No. 00-25, "Vendor Income Statement Characterization of Consideration Paid to a Reseller of the Vendor's Products" and Issue No. 00-14, "Accounting for Certain Sales Incentives" require that cooperative advertising and certain sales incentives costs traditionally reported as selling, marketing and administrative expense be reclassified as a reduction of net sales beginning January 1, 2002. Prior period consolidated statements of earnings have been reclassified to reflect this change. As a result, $31,741, $30,238 of such expenses were reclassified to a reduction of net sales for the years ended December 31, 2001 and 2000, respectively. These reclassifications will not affect the company's financial position, earnings from operations or net income.

Effective January 1, 2001, the company adopted SFAS 133 "Accounting for Derivative Instruments and Certain Hedging Activities" and the related SFAS 138 "Accounting for Certain Derivative Instruments and Certain Hedging Activities" with no material effect on the company's results of operations or financial position. These standards require that derivative instruments be recorded on the balance sheet at fair value, and that changes therein be recorded either in earnings or other comprehensive earnings, depending on whether the derivative is designated and effective as part of a hedge transaction and, if so, the type of hedge transaction. Gains and losses on derivative instruments reported in other comprehensive earnings are reclassified to earnings in the periods in which earnings are affected by the hedged item.

From time to time, the company enters into commodities futures contracts that are intended and effective as hedges of market price risks associated with the anticipated purchase of certain raw materials (primarily sugar). To qualify as a hedge, the company evaluates a variety of characteristics of these transactions, including the probability that the anticipated transaction will occur. If the anticipated transaction were not to occur, the gain or loss would then be recognized in current earnings.

To qualify for hedge accounting, financial instruments must maintain a high correlation with the item being hedged throughout the hedged period. The company does not engage in trading or other speculative use of derivative instruments. The company does assume the risk that counter parties may not be able to meet the terms of their contracts. The company does not expect any losses as a result of counter party defaults, and at December 31, 2002 had open contracts to purchase approximately half of its expected 2003 and 2004 sugar usage.

The Financial Accounting Standards Board issued Interpretation No. 45 "Guarantor's Accounting and Disclosure Requirements for Guarantees, Including Indirect Guarantees of Indebtedness to Others" relating to the accounting for and disclosure of certain types of guarantees. The disclosure provisions are effective for financial statements with years ending after December 15, 2002. No disclosures were required for the company as a result of adoption of this standard, as it has no such guarantees outstanding.

During 2002, the Financial Accounting Standards Board finalized SFAS No. 146 "Accounting for Costs Associated with Exit or Disposal Activities" for exit and disposal activities that are initiated after December 31, 2002. This statement requires that a liability for a cost associated with an exit or disposal activity be recognized when the liability is incurred. The company does not expect adoption of this standard to have a material impact on its 2003 consolidation financial statements.

Cash and cash equivalents:

The company considers temporary cash investments with an original maturity of three months or less to be cash equivalents.

Investments:

Investments consist of various marketable securities with maturities of generally up to four years. The company classifies debt and equity securities as either held to maturity, available for sale or trading. Held to maturity securities represent those securities that the company has both the positive intent and ability to hold to maturity and are carried at amortized cost. Available for sale securities represent those securities that do not meet the classification of held to maturity, are not actively traded and are carried at fair value. Unrealized gains and losses on these securities are excluded from earnings and are reported as a separate component of shareholders' equity, net of applicable taxes, until realized. Trading securities relate to deferred compensation arrangements and are carried at fair value.

Inventories:

Inventories are stated at cost, not in excess of market. The cost of domestic inventories ($40,064 and $35,982 at December 31, 2002 and 2001, respectively) has been determined by the last-in, first-out (LIFO) method. The excess of current cost over LIFO cost of inventories approximates $5,137 and $4,261 at December 31, 2002 and 2001, respectively. The cost of foreign inventories ($3,581 and $5,180 at December 31, 2002 and 2001, respectively) has been determined by the first-in, first-out (FIFO) method.

Property, plant and equipment:

Depreciation is computed for financial reporting purposes by use of the straight-line method based on useful lives of 20 to 35 years for buildings and 5 to 20 years for machinery and equipment. Depreciation expense was $12,354, $14,148 and $10,069 in 2002, 2001 and 2000, respectively, including $744 relating to equipment disposals and $1,275 of equipment that was written down related to a plant closing in 2002 and 2001 respectively.

Carrying value of long-lived assets:

Effective January 1, 2002, the company adopted SFAS No. 144, "Accounting for the Impairment or Disposal of Long-Lived Assets." This statement requires that long-lived assets be reviewed for impairment as events of changes in circumstances occur indicating that the amount of the asset reflected in the company's balance sheet may not be recoverable. An estimate of undiscounted cash flows produced by the asset, or the appropriate group of assets, is comred to the carrying value to determine whether impairment exists. An impairment charge would then be recorded to write the carrying value down to its fair value. The determination of fair value involves the use of estimates of future cash flows that involve considerable management judgment and are based upon assumptions about expected future operating performance. The actual cash flows could differ from management's estimates due to changes in business conditions, operating performance, and economic conditions. No significant impairment charges were recorded by the company during 2002.

Postretirement health care and life insurance benefits:

The company provides certain postretirement health care and life insurance benefits. The cost of these postretirement benefits is accrued during employees' working careers. The company also provides split dollar life insurance benefits to certain executive officers. The company records an asset equal to the cumulative insurance premiums that will be recovered upon the death of a covered employee(s) or earlier under the terms of the plan. The Sarbanes-Oxley Act (the Act) amended the Securities Exchange Act of 1934 to generally prohibit corporate loans to certain executive officers and directors of publicly traded companies. This prohibition applies to both direct and indirect loans. Because the Act does not directly address split dollar life insurance premiums, the impact of the Act on the company's split dollar life insurance plan is not currently known. The company has ceased making premium payments with respect to existing policies and is considering the potential impact of the Act on the split dollar life insurance benefit plan. The cessation of insurance premiums has no impact on the amount recoverable of the split dollar life insurance asset.

Intangible assets:

On January 1, 2002, the company adopted SFAS 142, "Goodwill and Other Intangible Assets." As a result of its adoption, the company has reclassified $79,348 and $38,151 from intangible assets to trademarks and goodwill, respectively. All trademarks have been assessed by management to have indefinite lives because they are expected to generate cash flows indefinitely. Thus, the company has ceased amortization expense on all trademarks and goodwill as of January 1, 2002.

The company has identified its reporting units related to goodwill and completed its goodwill impairment tests as of January 1, 2002 which require that management compare the fair value of the reporting unit with its carrying value. The reporting units were not considered to be impaired. The company also completed its impairment test of the indefinite lived trademarks which required management to compare the fair value of the trademarks to the carrying value. The trademarks were not considered to be impaired.

The impairment tests performed require that the company determine the fair market value of its reporting units for comparison to the carrying value of such net assets to assess whether an impairment exists. The methodologies used to estimate fair market value involve the use of estimates and assumptions, including projected revenues, earnings, cash flows and discount rates.

In addition, the company is required to conduct an annual review of its goodwill and trademarks for potential impairment. In 2002, this review was completed and no impairment was found.

Comprehensive earnings:

Comprehensive earnings includes net earnings, foreign currency translation adjustments and unrealized gains/ losses on commodity contracts and marketable securities.

Earnings per share:

A dual presentation of basic and diluted earnings per share is not required due to the lack of potentially dilutive securities under the company's simple capital structure. Therefore, all earnings per share amounts represent basic earnings per share.

NOTE 2—ACQUISITIONS:

During 2000, the company acquired the assets of two confectionery companies for $74,293 in cash, which was funded through existing cash and $38,800 of short term borrowings. The acquisition cost has been allocated to the assets acquired and liabilities assumed based on their respective appraised values as follows:

Current assets	$ 6,304
Property, plant and equipment	29,400
Intangible assets, primarily trademarks	39,546
Liabilities	(957)
Total purchase price	$74,293

The acquisitions were accounted for by the purchase method. Accordingly, the operating results of the acquired businesses have been included in the consolidated financial statements since the date of acquisition. The operating results of the acquired businesses did not have a material effect on the company's financial statements.

NOTE 3—ACCRUED LIABILITIES:

Accrued liabilities are comprised of the following:

	December 31, 2002	2001
Compensation	$11,211	$10,516
Other employee benefits	4,666	4,375
Taxes, other than income	2,542	2,549
Advertising and promotions	10,894	9,777
Other	6,512	7,078
	$35,825	$34,295

NOTE 4—INCOME TAXES:

The domestic and foreign components of pretax income are as follows:

	2002	2001	2000
Domestic	$ 98,978	$ 98,827	$115,823
Foreign	1,710	1,960	1,985
	$100,688	$100,787	$117,808

The provision for income taxes is comprised of the following:

	2002	2001	2000
Current:			
Federal	$32,303	$27,588	$33,908
Foreign	553	749	426
State	1,523	2,480	3,613
	34,379	30,817	37,947
Deferred:			
Federal	(286)	4,011	3,500
Foreign	176	52	346
State	31	220	278
	(79)	4,283	4,124
	$34,300	$35,100	$42,071

Deferred income taxes are comprised of the following:

	December 31, 2002	2001
Workers' compensation	$ —	$ 527
Reserve for uncollectible accounts	475	432
Other accrued expenses	3,629	1,199
VEBA funding	(469)	(450)
Other, net	846	64
Net current deferred income tax asset	$4,481	$1,772

	December 31, 2002	2001
Depreciation	$15,629	$15,309
Post retirement benefits	(2,885)	(2,570)
Deductible goodwill and trademarks	10,908	9,036
Deferred compensation	(7,205)	(6,595)
Accrued DISC commissions	2,602	2,377
Foreign subsidiary tax loss carryforward	(411)	(1,100)
Other, net	1,016	335
Net long-term deferred income tax liability	$19,654	$16,792

At December 31, 2002, gross deferred tax assets and gross deferred tax liabilities were $17,847 and $33,020, respectively. The deferred tax assets are shown net of valuation allowances of $2,014 and $1,897 at December 31, 2002 and December 31, 2001, respectively, relating to prepaid taxes in a foreign jurisdiction.

The effective income tax rate differs from the statutory rate as follows:

	2002	2001	2000
U.S. statutory rate	35.0%	35.0%	35.0%
State income taxes, net	1.0	1.8	2.2
Amortization of intangible assets	—	0.4	0.4
Exempt municipal bond interest	(1.8)	(2.0)	(1.8)
Other, net	(0.1)	(0.4)	(0.1)
Effective income tax rate	34.1%	34.8%	35.7%

The company has not provided for U.S. federal or foreign withholding taxes on $6,506 and $6,883 of foreign subsidiaries' undistributed earnings as of December 31, 2002 and December 31, 2001, respectively because such earnings are considered to be permanently reinvested. It is not practicable to determine the amount of income taxes that would be payable upon remittance of the undistributed earnings.

NOTE 5—GOODWILL AND OTHER INTANGIBLE ASSETS:

The company ceased amortizing its intangible assets in conjunction with the January 1, 2002 adoption of SFAS 142. The proforma effects of such adoption are as follows:

	2002	2001	2000
Reported net income	$66,388	$65,687	$75,737
Add back: goodwill amortization	—	1,473	1,423
Add back: trademark amortization	—	2,305	1,996
Tax effect	—	(927)	(793)
Adjusted net income	$66,388	$68,538	$78,363
Reported basic earnings per share	$ 1.29	$ 1.26	$ 1.45
Goodwill amortization	—	.03	.03
Trademark amortization	—	.05	.04
Tax effect	—	(.02)	(.02)
Adjusted basic earnings per share	$ 1.29	$ 1.32	$ 1.50

NOTE 6—SHARE CAPITAL AND CAPITAL IN EXCESS OF PAR VALUE:

	Common Stock		Class B Common Stock		Treasury Stock		Capital in excess of par value
	Shares	Amount	Shares	Amount	Shares	Amount	
	(000's)		(000's)		(000's)		
Balance at January 1, 2000	32,854	$22,815	15,707	$10,908	(50)	$(1,992)	$249,236
Issuance of 3% stock dividend	969	673	470	326	(2)	—	39,742
Conversion of Class B common shares to common shares	121	84	(121)	(84)	—	—	—
Purchase and retirement of common shares	(958)	(665)	—	—	—	—	(32,280)
Balance at December 31, 2000	32,986	22,907	16,056	11,150	(52)	(1,992)	256,698
Issuance of 3% stock dividend	986	685	480	333	(1)	—	69,180
Conversion of Class B common shares to common shares	217	151	(217)	(151)	—	—	—
Purchase and retirement of common shares	(50)	(35)	—	—	—	—	(1,897)
Balance at December 31, 2001	34,139	23,708	16,319	11,332	(53)	(1,992)	323,981
Issuance of 3% stock dividend	1,009	700	488	339	(2)	—	63,332
Conversion of Class B common shares to common shares	48	33	(48)	(33)	—	—	—
Purchase and retirement of common shares	(948)	(658)	—	—	—	—	(31,655)
Balance at December 31, 2002	34,248	$23,783	16,759	$11,638	(55)	$(1,992)	$355,658

The Class B Common Stock has essentially the same rights as Common Stock, except that each share of Class B Common Stock has ten votes per share (compared to one vote per share of Common Stock), is not traded on any exchange, is restricted as to transfer and is convertible on a share-for-share basis, at any time and at no cost to the holders, into shares of Common Stock which are traded on the New York Stock Exchange.

Average shares outstanding and all per share amounts included in the financial statements and notes thereto have been adjusted retroactively to reflect annual three percent stock dividends.

NOTE 7—INDUSTRIAL DEVELOPMENT BONDS:

Industrial development bonds are due in 2027. The average floating interest rate was 1.5% and 3.0% in 2002 and 2001, respectively.

NOTE 8—EMPLOYEE BENEFIT PLANS:

Pension plans:

The company sponsors defined contribution pension plans covering certain nonunion employees with over one year of credited service. The company's policy is to fund pension costs accrued based on compensation levels. Total pension expense for 2002, 2001 and 2000 approximated $2,867, $2,823 and $2,535, respectively. The company also maintains certain profit sharing and savings-investment plans. Company contributions in 2002, 2001 and 2000 to these plans were $709, $765 and $754, respectively.

The company also contributes to multi-employer defined benefit pension plans for its union employees. Such contributions aggregated $1,055, $859 and $787 in 2002, 2001 and 2000, respectively. The relative position of each employer associated with the multi-employer plans with respect to the actuarial present value of benefits and net plan assets is not determinable by the company.

Postretirement health care and life insurance benefit plans:

The company provides certain postretirement health care and life insurance benefits for corporate office and management employees. Employees become eligible for these benefits if they meet minimum age and service requirements and if they agree to contribute a portion of the cost. The company has the right to modify or terminate these benefits. The company does not fund postretirement health care and life insurance benefits in advance of payments for benefit claims.

The changes in the accumulated postretirement benefit obligation at December 31, 2002 and 2001 consist of the following:

	December 31,	
	2002	2001
Benefit obligation, beginning of year	$7,450	$6,956
Net periodic postretirement benefit cost	913	705
Benefits paid	(212)	(211)
Benefit obligation, end of year	$8,151	$7,450

Net periodic postretirement benefit cost included the following components:

	2002	2001	2000
Service cost—benefits attributed to service during the period	$462	$351	$286
Interest cost on the accumulated postretirement benefit obligation	481	422	341
Amortization of unrecognized net gain	(30)	(68)	(109)
Net periodic postretirement benefit cost	$913	$705	$518

For measurement purposes, a 10.0% annual rate of increase in the per capita cost of covered health care benefits was assumed for 2002; the rate was assumed to decrease gradually to 5.5% for 2011 and remain at that level thereafter. The health care cost trend rate assumption has a significant effect on the amounts reported. The weighted average discount rate used in determining the accumulated postretirement benefit obligation was 6.5% and 7.0% at December 31, 2002 and 2001, respectively.

Increasing or decreasing the health care trend rates by one percentage point in each year would have the following effect:

	1% Increase	1% Decrease
Effect on postretirement benefit obligation	$1,589	$(1,293)
Effect on total of service and interest cost components	$ 167	$ (133)

NOTE 9—OTHER INCOME, NET:

Other income (expense) is comprised of the following:

	2002	2001	2000
Interest income	$5,553	$6,556	$7,636
Interest expense	(309)	(356)	(866)
Dividend income	3	55	421
Foreign exchange losses	(206)	(177)	(42)
Royalty income	371	403	225
Miscellaneous, net	(1,393)	362	(295)
	$4,019	$6,843	$7,079

NOTE 10—COMMITMENTS:

Rental expense aggregated $941, $1,000 and $894 in 2002, 2001 and 2000, respectively.

Future operating lease commitments are not significant.

NOTE 11—COMPREHENSIVE INCOME:

Components of accumulated other comprehensive earnings (loss) are shown as follows:

	Foreign Currency	Unrealized Gains (Losses) on Securities	Unrealized Gains (Losses) on Derivatives	Accumulated Other Comprehensive Earnings/(Loss)
Balance at January 1, 2000	$(10,429)	$1,489	$ 0	$ (8,940)
Change during period	(394)	(856)	—	(1,250)
Balance at December 31, 2000	(10,823)	633	0	(10,190)
Change during period	846	(184)	(385)	277
Balance at December 31, 2001	(9,977)	449	(385)	(9,913)
Change during period	(1,533)	(465)	859	(1,139)
Balance at December 31, 2002	$(11,510)	$ (16)	$ 474	$(11,052)

The individual tax effects of each component of other comprehensive earnings (loss) for the year ended December 31, 2002 are shown as follows:

	Before Tax Amount	Tax (Expense) Benefit	Net-of-Tax Tax Amount
Foreign currency translation adjustment	$(1,533)	$—	$(1,533)
Unrealized gains (losses) on securities:			
Unrealized holding gains (losses) arising during 2002	(798)	294	(504)
Less: reclassification adjustment for gains (losses) realized in earnings	(60)	21	(39)
Net unrealized gains	(738)	273	(465)
Unrealized gains (losses) on derivatives:			
Unrealized holding gains (losses) arising during 2002	(65)	24	(41)
Less: reclassification adjustment for gains (losses) realized in earnings	(1,429)	529	(900)
Net unrealized gains	1,364	(505)	859
Other comprehensive earnings	$(907)	$(232)	$(1,139)

NOTE 12—DISCLOSURES ABOUT THE FAIR VALUE AND CARRYING AMOUNT OF FINANCIAL INSTRUMENTS:

The carrying amount approximates fair value of cash and cash equivalents because of the short maturity of those instruments. The fair values of investments are estimated based on quoted market prices. The fair value of the company's industrial development bonds approximates their carrying value because they have a floating interest rate. The carrying amount and estimated fair values of the company's financial instruments are as follows:

	2002		2001	
	Carrying Amount	Fair Value	Carrying Amount	Fair Value
Cash and cash equivalents	$105,507	$105,507	$106,532	$106,532
Investments held to maturity	119,730	121,541	102,585	103,543
Investments available for sale	22,226	22,226	22,253	22,253
Investments in trading securities	15,281	15,281	14,922	14,922
Industrial development bonds	7,500	7,500	7,500	7,500

A summary of the aggregate fair value, gross unrealized gains, gross unrealized losses and amortized cost basis of the company's investment portfolio by major security type is as follows:

| | December 31, 2002 | | | | December 31, 2001 | | | |
	Amortized Cost	Fair Value	Unrealized Gains	Unrealized Losses	Amortized Cost	Fair Value	Unrealized Gains	Unrealized Losses
Held to Maturity:								
Municipal bonds	$134,425	136,240	$1,815	—	$127,667	$128,631	964	—
Unit investment trusts of municipal bonds	505	502	—	(3)	918	910	—	(8)
	$134,930	$136,742	$1,815	$ (3)	$128,585	$129,541	$964	$ (8)
Available for Sale:								
Municipal bonds	$ 24,281	$ 24,275	—	$ (6)	$ 23,697	$ 23,665	$ —	$ (14)
Mutual funds	2,454	2,436	—	$(18)	2,454	3,179	725	—
	$ 26,735	$ 26,711	—	$(24)	$ 26,133	$ 26,844	$725	$ (14)

Held to maturity securities of $15,200 and $26,000 and available for sale securities of $4,485 and $4,591 were included in cash and cash equivalents at December 31, 2002 and 2001, respectively. There were no securities with maturities greater than four years and gross realized gains and losses on the sale of available for sale securities in 2002 and 2001 were not significant.

| | 2002 | | | 2001 | | | 2000 | | |
	United States	Mexico and Canada	Consoli-dated	United States	Mexico and Canada	Consoli-dated	United States	Mexico and Canada	Consoli-dated
Sales to unaffiliated customers	$365,920	$27,265	$393,185	$362,290	$29,465	$391,755	$366,213	$30,603	$396,816
Sales between geographic areas	4,978	2,892		3,649	2,731		3,626	3,343	
	$370,898	$30,157		$365,939	$32,196		$369,839	$33,946	
Net earnings	$ 65,413	$ 975	$ 66,388	$ 65,370	$ 317	$ 65,687	$ 73,929	$ 1,808	$ 75,737
Total assets	$627,436	$18,644	$646,080	$596,303	$22,373	$618,676	$540,697	$21,745	$562,442
Net assets	$511,743	$14,997	$526,740	$489,552	$18,909	$508,461	$439,685	$19,011	$458,696

Auditor's Report

All publicly held corporations, as well as many other enterprises and organizations (both profit and not-for-profit, large and small) engage the services of independent certified public accountants for the purpose of obtaining an objective, expert report on their financial statements. Based on a comprehensive examination of the company's accounting system, accounting records, and the financial statements, the outside CPA issues the auditor's report.

The standard auditor's report consists of three paragraphs: (1) an introductory paragraph, (2) a scope paragraph, and (3) the opinion paragraph. In the introductory paragraph, the auditor identifies who and what was audited and indicates the responsibilities of management and the auditor relative to the financial statements. In the scope paragraph the auditor states that the audit was conducted in accordance with generally accepted auditing standards and discusses the nature and limitations of the audit. In the opinion paragraph, the auditor expresses an informed opinion as to (1) the fairness of the financial statements and (2) their conformity with generally accepted accounting principles. The Report of PricewaterhouseCoopers LLP appearing in **Tootsie Roll**'s Annual Report is shown on the next page.

Report of Independent Accountants

To the Board of Directors and Shareholders of Tootsie Roll Industries, Inc:

In our opinion, the accompanying consolidated statements of financial position and the related consolidated statements of earnings, comprehensive earnings and retained earnings and of cash flows present fairly, in all material respects, the financial position of Tootsie Roll Industries, Inc. and its subsidiaries at December 31, 2002 and 2001, and the results of their operations and their cash flows for each of the three years in the period ended December 31, 2002 in conformity with accounting principles generally accepted in the United States of America. These financial statements are the responsibility of the company's management; our responsibility is to express an opinion on these financial statements based on our audits. We conducted our audits of these statements in accordance with auditing standards generally accepted in the United States of America, which require that we plan and perform the audit to obtain reasonable assurance about whether the financial statements are free of material misstatement. An audit includes examining, on a test basis, evidence supporting the amounts and disclosures in the financial statements, assessing the accounting principles used and significant estimates made by management, and evaluating the overall financial statement presentation. We believe that our audits provide a reasonable basis for our opinion.

Chicago, Illinois
February 10, 2003

Supplementary Financial Information

In addition to the financial statements and the accompanying notes, supplementary financial information is often presented. **Tootsie Roll** has provided quarterly financial data, stock performance information, and a five-year summary of earnings and financial highlights.

Quarterly Financial Data (Unaudited)

TOOTSIE ROLL INDUSTRIES, INC. AND SUBSIDIARIES

			(Thousands of dollars except per share data)		
2002	First	Second	Third	Fourth	Total
Net sales	$78,991	$77,131	$146,298	$90,765	$393,185
Gross margin	35,831	35,755	61,960	38,874	172,420
Net earnings	12,772	12,316	26,616	14,684	66,388
Net earnings per share	.25	.24	.51	.29	1.29
2001					
Net sales	$75,858	$79,987	$148,456	$87,454	$391,755
Gross margin	36,194	36,623	65,979	36,302	175,098
Net earnings	12,385	13,902	27,010	12,390	65,687
Net earnings per share	.24	.27	.52	.23	1.26
2000					
Net sales	$72,143	$83,506	$155,331	$85,836	$396,816
Gross margin	35,195	41,339	72,683	40,499	189,716
Net earnings	13,063	15,652	31,514	15,508	75,737
Net earnings per share	.25	.30	.60	.30	1.45

Net earnings per share is based upon average outstanding shares as adjusted for 3% stock dividends issued during the second quarter of each year. The sum of the per share amounts may not equal annual amounts due to rounding.

2002-2001 QUARTERLY SUMMARY OF TOOTSIE ROLL INDUSTRIES, INC. STOCK PRICE AND DIVIDENDS PER SHARE.

STOCK PRICES*

	2002		2001	
	High	Low	High	Low
1st Qtr	$45.99	$37.85	$51.10	$43.31
2nd Qtr	$47.97	$37.84	$48.89	$38.54
3rd Qtr	$38.97	$29.72	$40.55	$35.08
4th Qtr	$31.96	$29.51	$39.44	$36.35

*NYSE—Composite Quotations

Estimated Number of shareholders at December 31, 2002   25,000

DIVIDENDS

	2002	2001
1st Qtr	$.0680	$.0660
2nd Qtr	$.0700	$.0680
3rd Qtr	$.0700	$.0680
4th Qtr	$.0700	$.0680

NOTE: In addition to the above cash dividends, a 3% stock dividend was issued on April 17, 2002 and April 18, 2001. Cash dividends are restated to reflect 3% stock dividends.

Five Year Summary of Earnings and Financial Highlights

TOOTSIE ROLL INDUSTRIES, INC. AND SUBSIDIARIES

(Thousands of dollars except per share, percentage and ratio figures)

(See Management's Comments starting on page 6)

	2002	2001	2000	1999	1998
Sales and Earnings Data (2)					
Net sales	$393,185	$391,755	$396,816	$369,335	$360,165
Gross margin	172,420	175,098	189,716	176,774	172,548
Interest expense	309	356	866	453	756
Provision for income taxes	34,300	35,100	42,071	40,137	38,537
Net earnings	66,388	65,687	75,737	71,310	67,526
% of sales	16.9%	16.8%	19.1%	19.3%	18.7%
% of shareholders' equity	12.6%	12.9%	16.5%	16.6%	17.0%
Per Common Share Data (1)(2)					
Net earnings	1.29	1.26	1.45	1.34	1.25
Cash dividends declared	.28	.27	.26	.22	.18
Stock dividends	3%	3%	3%	3%	3%
Additional Financial Data					
Working capital	$161,852	$188,250	$145,765	$168,423	$175,155
Net cash provided by operating activities	71,203	78,584	82,591	72,935	77,735
Net cash used in investing activities	25,304	16,834	64,177	26,993	34,829
Net cash used in financing activities	46,924	16,100	46,036	38,182	22,595
Property, plant & equipment additions	10,308	14,148	16,189	20,283	14,878
Net property, plant & equipment	128,869	132,575	131,118	95,897	83,024
Total assets	646,080	618,676	562,442	529,416	487,423
Long term debt	7,500	7,500	7,500	7,500	7,500
Shareholders' equity	526,740	508,461	458,696	430,646	396,457
Average shares outstanding (1)	51,553	51,947	52,394	53,372	53,880

(1) Adjusted for annual 3% stock dividends and the 2-for-1 stock split effective July 13, 1998.

(2) Adjusted for the reclassification of certain selling, marketing and administrative expenses as a reduction of net sales.

Board of Directors

Melvin J. Gordon[1]	Chairman of the Board and Chief Executive Officer
Ellen R. Gordon[1]	President and Chief Operating Officer
Charles W. Seibert[2][3]	Retired Banker
Lana Jane Lewis-Brent[2][3]	President, Paul Brent Designer, Inc.
Richard P. Bergeman[2][3]	Retired Senior Vice President, Bestfoods

[1]Member of the Executive Committee

[2]Member of the Audit Committee

[3]Member of the Compensation Committee

Officers

Melvin J. Gordon	Chairman of the Board and Chief Executive Officer
Ellen R. Gordon	President and Chief Operating Officer
G. Howard Ember, Jr.	Vice President, Finance & Asst. Secy
John W. Newlin, Jr.	Vice President. Manufacturing
Thomas E. Corr	Vice President, Marketing & Sales
James M. Hunt	Vice President, Physical Distribution
Barry P. Bowen	Treasurer & Asst. Secy.
Daniel P. Drechney	Controller

Offices, Plants

Executive Offices	7401 S. Cicero Ave. Chicago, Illinois 60629 www.tootsie.com
Plants	Illinois Tennessee Massachusetts Wisconsin New York Mexico City
Foreign Sales Offices	Mexico City, Mexico Mississauga, Ontario

Subsidiaries

Andes Candies L.P.	Tootsie Roll of Canada Ltd.
Andes Manufacturing LLC	Tootsie Roll Central Europe Ltd.
Andes Services LLC	The Tootsie Roll Company, Inc.
C.C. L.P., Inc.	Tootsie Roll Management, Inc.
C.G.C. Corporation	Tootsie Roll Mfg., Inc.
C.G.P., Inc	Tootsie Rolls—Latin America, Inc.
Cambridge Brands, Inc.	Tootsie Roll Worldwide Ltd.
Cambridge Brands Mfg., Inc.	The Sweets Mix Company, Inc.
Cambridge Brands Services, Inc.	TRI de Latino America S.A. de C.V.
Cella's Confections, Inc.	TRI Finance, Inc.
Charms Company	TRI International Co.
Charms L.P.	TRI-Mass., Inc.
Charms Marketing Company	TRI Sales Co.
Henry Eisen Advertising Agency, Inc.	TRI Sales Finance LLC
J.T. Company, Inc.	Tutsi S.A. de C.V.
O'Tec Industries, Inc.	World Trade & Marketing Ltd.

Other Information

Stock Exchange	New York Stock Exchange, Inc. (Since 1922)
Stock Identification	Ticker Symbol: TR CUSIP No. 890516 10-7
Stock Transfer Agent and Stock Registrar	Mellon Investor Services LLC Overpeck Centre 85 Challenger Road Ridgefield Park, NJ 07660 1-800-851-9677 www.melloninvestor.com
Independent Accountants	PricewaterhouseCoopers LLP One North Wacker Chicago, Il 60606
General Counsel	Becker Ross Stone DeStefano & Klein 317 Madison Avenue New York, NY 10017
Annual Meeting	May 5, 2003 Mutual Building, Room 1200 909 East Main Street Richmond. VA 23219

Specimen Financial Statements: Hershey Foods Corporation

HERSHEY FOODS CORPORATION

CONSOLIDATED STATEMENTS OF INCOME

For the years ended December 31, In thousands of dollars except per share amounts	2002	2001	2000
Net Sales	**$4,120,317**	$4,137,217	$3,820,416
Costs and Expenses:			
Cost of sales	**2,561,052**	2,668,530	2,471,151
Selling, marketing and administrative	**833,426**	846,976	726,615
Business realignment and asset impairments	**27,552**	228,314	—
Gain on sale of business	**—**	(19,237)	—
Total costs and expenses	**3,422,030**	3,724,583	3,197,766
Income before Interest and Income Taxes	**698,287**	412,634	622,650
Interest expense, net	**60,722**	69,093	76,011
Income before Income Taxes	**637,565**	343,541	546,639
Provision for income taxes	**233,987**	136,385	212,096
Net Income	**$ 403,578**	$ 207,156	$ 334,543
Net Income Per Share—Basic	**$ 2.96**	$ 1.52	$ 2.44
Net Income Per Share—Diluted	**$ 2.93**	$ 1.50	$ 2.42
Cash Dividends Paid Per Share:			
Common Stock	**$ 1.260**	$ 1.165	$ 1.080
Class B Common Stock	**1.135**	1.050	.975

The notes to consolidated financial statements are an integral part of these statements.

HERSHEY FOODS CORPORATION

CONSOLIDATED BALANCE SHEETS

December 31,	2002	2001
In thousands of dollars		
ASSETS		
Current Assets:		
Cash and cash equivalents	$ 297,743	$ 134,147
Accounts receivable—trade	370,976	361,726
Inventories	503,291	512,134
Deferred income taxes	—	96,939
Prepaid expenses and other	91,608	62,595
Total current assets	1,263,618	1,167,541
Property, Plant and Equipment, Net	1,486,055	1,534,901
Goodwill	378,453	388,702
Other Intangibles	39,898	40,426
Other Assets	312,527	115,860
Total assets	$ 3,480,551	$ 3,247,430
LIABILITIES AND STOCKHOLDERS' EQUITY		
Current Liabilities:		
Accounts payable	$ 124,507	$ 133,049
Accrued liabilities	356,716	462,901
Accrued income taxes	12,731	2,568
Deferred income taxes	24,768	—
Short-term debt	11,135	7,005
Current portion of long-term debt	16,989	921
Total current liabilities	546,846	606,444
Long-term Debt	851,800	876,972
Other Long-term Liabilities	362,162	361,041
Deferred Income Taxes	348,040	255,769
Total liabilities	2,108,848	2,100,226
Stockholders' Equity:		
Preferred Stock, shares issued: none in 2002 and 2001	—	—
Common Stock, shares issued: 149,528,564 in 2002 and 149,517,064 in 2001	149,528	149,516
Class B Common Stock, shares issued: 30,422,308 in 2002 and 30,433,808 in 2001	30,422	30,434
Additional paid-in capital	593	3,263
Unearned ESOP compensation	(12,774)	(15,967)
Retained earnings	2,991,090	2,755,333
Treasury—Common Stock shares, at cost: 45,730,735 in 2002 and 44,311,870 in 2001	(1,808,227)	(1,689,243)
Accumulated other comprehensive income (loss)	21,071	(86,132)
Total stockholders' equity	1,371,703	1,147,204
Total liabilities and stockholders' equity	$ 3,480,551	$ 3,247,430

The notes to consolidated financial statements are an integral part of these balance sheets.

HERSHEY FOODS CORPORATION

CONSOLIDATED STATEMENTS OF CASH FLOWS

For the years ended December 31,	2002	2001	2000
In thousands of dollars			
Cash Flows Provided from (Used by)			
Operating Activities			
Net income	**$ 403,578**	$ 207,156	$ 334,543
Adjustments to reconcile net income to net cash provided from operations:			
Depreciation and amortization	**177,908**	190,494	175,964
Deferred income taxes	**137,817**	(49,342)	(16,400)
Gain on sale of business, net of tax of $18,134	**—**	(1,103)	—
Business realignment initiatives	**21,509**	171,852	—
Asset impairment write-downs	**—**	53,100	—
Changes in assets and liabilities, net of effects from business acquisitions and divestitures:			
Accounts receivable—trade	**(9,250)**	17,954	(26,930)
Inventories	**8,843**	94,405	28,029
Accounts payable	**(8,542)**	(16,183)	7,280
Other assets and liabilities	**(106,520)**	38,072	(90,277)
Net Cash Provided from Operating Activities	**625,343**	706,405	412,209
Cash Flows Provided from (Used by)			
Investing Activities			
Capital additions	**(132,736)**	(160,105)	(138,333)
Capitalized software additions	**(11,836)**	(9,845)	(4,686)
Business acquisitions	**—**	(17,079)	(135,000)
Proceeds from divestitures	**12,000**	59,900	—
Other, net	**—**	3,142	6,206
Net Cash (Used by) Investing Activities	**(132,572)**	(123,987)	(271,813)
Cash Flows Provided from (Used by)			
Financing Activities			
Net change in short-term borrowings	**4,130**	(250,589)	48,428
Long-term borrowings	**304**	379	187
Repayment of long-term debt	**(9,578)**	(826)	(2,815)
Cash dividends paid	**(167,821)**	(154,750)	(144,891)
Exercise of stock options	**86,491**	30,210	24,376
Incentive plan transactions	**(158,507)**	(64,342)	(51,859)
Repurchase of Common Stock	**(84,194)**	(40,322)	(99,931)
Net Cash (Used by) Financing Activities	**(329,175)**	(480,240)	(226,505)
Increase (Decrease) in Cash and Cash Equivalents	**163,596**	102,178	(86,109)
Cash and Cash Equivalents as of January 1	**134,147**	31,969	118,078
Cash and Cash Equivalents as of December 31	**$ 297,743**	$ 134,147	$ 31,969
Interest Paid	**$ 64,343**	$ 72,043	$ 81,465
Income Taxes Paid	**57,495**	171,362	299,104

The notes to consolidated financial statements are an integral part of these statements.

HERSHEY FOODS CORPORATION

CONSOLIDATED STATEMENTS OF STOCKHOLDERS' EQUITY

In thousands of dollars	Preferred Stock	Common Stock	Class B Common Stock	Additional Paid-in Capital	Unearned ESOP Compensation	Retained Earnings	Treasury Common Stock	Accumulated Other Comprehensive Income (Loss)	Total Stockholders' Equity
Balance as of January 1, 2000	$—	$149,507	$30,443	$30,079	$(22,354)	$2,513,275	$(1,552,708)	$(49,615)	$1,098,627
Net income						334,543			334,543
Other comprehensive (loss)								(7,101)	(7,101)
Comprehensive income									327,442
Dividends:									
Common Stock, $1.08 per share						(115,209)			(115,209)
Class B Common Stock, $.975 per share						(29,682)			(29,682)
Conversion of Class B Common Stock into Common Stock		1	(1)						
Incentive plan transactions				(426)					(426)
Exercise of stock options				(16,728)			7,551		(9,177)
Employee stock ownership trust/benefits transactions				199	3,193				3,392
Repurchase of Common Stock							(99,931)		(99,931)
Balance as of December 31, 2000	—	149,508	30,442	13,124	(19,161)	2,702,927	(1,645,088)	(56,716)	1,175,036
Net income						207,156			207,156
Other comprehensive (loss)								(29,416)	(29,416)
Comprehensive income									177,740
Dividends:									
Common Stock, $1.165 per share						(122,790)			(122,790)
Class B Common Stock, $1.05 per share						(31,960)			(31,960)
Conversion of Class B Common Stock into Common Stock		8	(8)						
Incentive plan transactions				1,062					1,062
Exercise of stock options				(11,863)			(3,833)		(15,696)
Employee stock ownership trust/benefits transactions				940	3,194				4,134
Repurchase of Common Stock							(40,322)		(40,322)
Balance as of December 31, 2001	—	149,516	30,434	3,263	(15,967)	2,755,333	(1,689,243)	(86,132)	1,147,204
Net income						403,578			403,578
Other comprehensive income								107,203	107,203
Comprehensive income									510,781
Dividends:									
Common Stock, $1.26 per share						(133,285)			(133,285)
Class B Common Stock, $1.135 per share						(34,536)			(34,536)
Conversion of Class B Common Stock into Common Stock		12	(12)						—
Incentive plan transactions				(298)					(298)
Exercise of stock options				(3,517)			(34,790)		(38,307)
Employee stock ownership trust/benefits transactions				1,145	3,193				4,338
Repurchase of Common Stock							(84,194)		(84,194)
Balance as of December 31, 2002	$—	$149,528	$30,422	$593	$(12,774)	$2,991,090	$(1,808,227)	$21,071	$1,371,703

The notes to consolidated financial statements are an integral part of these statements.

Time Value of Money

After studying this appendix,
you should be able to:

1 Distinguish between simple and compound interest.

2 Solve for future value of a single amount.

3 Solve for future value of an annuity.

4 Identify the variables fundamental to solving present value problems.

5 Solve for present value of a single amount.

6 Solve for present value of an annuity.

7 Compute the present value of notes and bonds.

Would you rather receive $1,000 today or a year from now? You should prefer to receive the $1,000 today because you can invest the $1,000 and earn interest on it. As a result, you will have more than $1,000 a year from now. What this example illustrates is the concept of the **time value of money**. Everyone prefers to receive money today rather than in the future because of the interest factor.

Nature of Interest

Interest is payment for the use of another person's money. It is the difference between the amount borrowed or invested (called the principal) and the amount repaid or collected. The amount of interest to be paid or collected is usually stated as a rate over a specific period of time. The rate of interest is generally stated as an annual rate.

The amount of interest involved in any financing transaction is based on three elements:

1. **Principal (p):** The original amount borrowed or invested.

2. **Interest Rate (i):** An annual percentage of the principal.

3. **Time (n):** The number of years that the principal is borrowed or invested.

SIMPLE INTEREST

Simple interest is computed on the principal amount only. It is the return on the principal for one period. Simple interest is usually expressed as shown in Illustration C-1 on the next page.

Illustration C-1
Interest computation

Interest	=	Principal _p_	×	Rate _i_	×	Time _n_

For example, if you borrowed $5,000 for 2 years at a simple interest rate of 12% annually, you would pay $1,200 in total interest computed as follows:

$$\text{Interest} = p \times i \times n$$
$$= \$5{,}000 \times .12 \times 2$$
$$= \$1{,}200$$

COMPOUND INTEREST

Compound interest is computed on principal **and** on any interest earned that has not been paid or withdrawn. It is the return on (or growth of) the principal for two or more time periods. Compounding computes interest not only on the principal but also on the interest earned to date on that principal, assuming the interest is left on deposit.

To illustrate the difference between simple and compound interest, assume that you deposit $1,000 in Bank Two, where it will earn simple interest of 9% per year, and you deposit another $1,000 in Citizens Bank, where it will earn compound interest of 9% per year compounded annually. Also assume that in both cases you will not withdraw any interest until 3 years from the date of deposit. The computation of interest to be received and the accumulated year-end balances are indicated in Illustration C-2.

Illustration C-2 Simple
versus compound interest

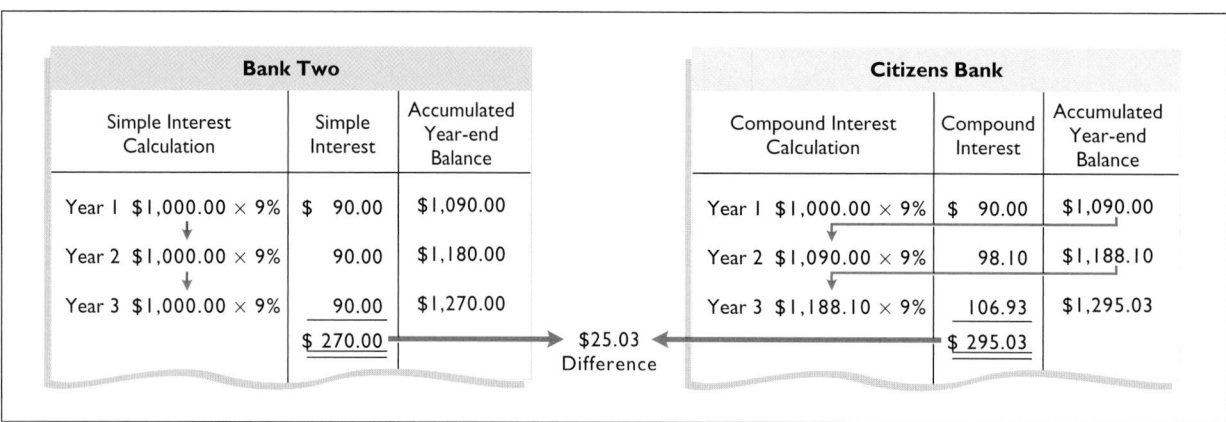

Note in Illustration C-2 that simple interest uses the initial principal of $1,000 to compute the interest in all 3 years. Compound interest uses the accumulated balance (principal plus interest to date) at each year-end to compute interest in the succeeding year—which explains why your compound interest account is larger.

Obviously, if you had a choice between investing your money at simple interest or at compound interest, you would choose compound interest, all other things—especially risk—being equal. In the example, compounding provides $25.03 of additional interest income. For practical purposes, compounding assumes that unpaid interest earned becomes a part of the principal, and the accumulated balance at the end of each year becomes the new principal on which interest is earned during the next year.

As can be seen in Illustration C-2, you should invest your money at Citizens Bank, which compounds interest annually. Compound interest is used in most business situations. Simple interest is generally applicable only to short-term situations of one year or less.

SECTION ONE
FUTURE VALUE CONCEPTS

Future Value of a Single Amount

STUDY OBJECTIVE
2
Solve for future value of a single amount.

The **future value of a single amount** is the value at a future date of a given amount invested, assuming compound interest. For example, in Illustration C-2, $1,295.03 is the future value of the $1,000 at the end of 3 years. The $1,295.03 could be determined more easily by using the following formula:

$$FV = p \times (1 + i)^n$$

Illustration C-3
Formula for future value

where:

FV = future value of a single amount
p = principal (or present value)
i = interest rate for one period
n = number of periods

The $1,295.03 is computed as follows:

$$
\begin{aligned}
FV &= p \times (1 + i)^n \\
&= \$1,000 \times (1 + i)^3 \\
&= \$1,000 \times 1.29503 \\
&= \$1,295.03
\end{aligned}
$$

The 1.29503 is computed by multiplying (1.09 × 1.09 × 1.09). The amounts in this example can be depicted in the time diagram shown in Illustration C-4.

Illustration C-4
Time diagram

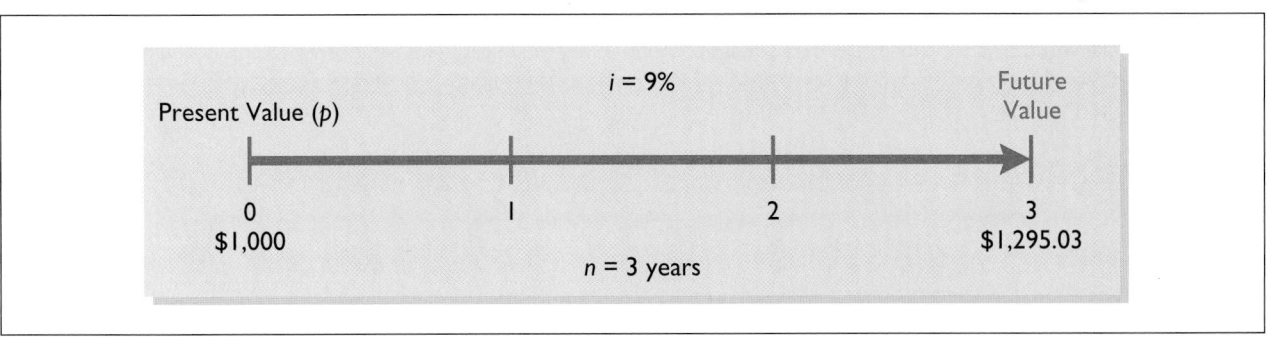

Another method that may be used to compute the future value of a single amount involves the use of a compound interest table. This table shows the future value of 1 for n periods. Table 1 on the next page is such a table.

TABLE 1 Future Value of 1

(n) Periods	4%	5%	6%	8%	9%	10%	11%	12%	15%
1	1.04000	1.05000	1.06000	1.08000	1.09000	1.10000	1.11000	1.12000	1.15000
2	1.08160	1.10250	1.12360	1.16640	1.18810	1.21000	1.23210	1.25440	1.32250
3	1.12486	1.15763	1.19102	1.25971	1.29503	1.33100	1.36763	1.40493	1.52088
4	1.16986	1.21551	1.26248	1.36049	1.41158	1.46410	1.51807	1.57352	1.74901
5	1.21665	1.27628	1.33823	1.46933	1.53862	1.61051	1.68506	1.76234	2.01136
6	1.26532	1.34010	1.41852	1.58687	1.67710	1.77156	1.87041	1.97382	2.31306
7	1.31593	1.40710	1.50363	1.71382	1.82804	1.94872	2.07616	2.21068	2.66002
8	1.36857	1.47746	1.59385	1.85093	1.99256	2.14359	2.30454	2.47596	3.05902
9	1.42331	1.55133	1.68948	1.99900	2.17189	2.35795	2.55803	2.77308	3.51788
10	1.48024	1.62889	1.79085	2.15892	2.36736	2.59374	2.83942	3.10585	4.04556
11	1.53945	1.71034	1.89830	2.33164	2.58043	2.85312	3.15176	3.47855	4.65239
12	1.60103	1.79586	2.01220	2.51817	2.81267	3.13843	3.49845	3.89598	5.35025
13	1.66507	1.88565	2.13293	2.71962	3.06581	3.45227	3.88328	4.36349	6.15279
14	1.73168	1.97993	2.26090	2.93719	3.34173	3.79750	4.31044	4.88711	7.07571
15	1.80094	2.07893	2.39656	3.17217	3.64248	4.17725	4.78459	5.47357	8.13706
16	1.87298	2.18287	2.54035	3.42594	3.97031	4.59497	5.31089	6.13039	9.35762
17	1.94790	2.29202	2.69277	3.70002	4.32763	5.05447	5.89509	6.86604	10.76126
18	2.02582	2.40662	2.85434	3.99602	4.71712	5.55992	6.54355	7.68997	12.37545
19	2.10685	2.52695	3.02560	4.31570	5.14166	6.11591	7.26334	8.61276	14.23177
20	2.19112	2.65330	3.20714	4.66096	5.60441	6.72750	8.06231	9.64629	16.36654

In Table 1, n is the number of compounding periods, the percentages are the periodic interest rates, and the 5-digit decimal numbers in the respective columns are the future value of 1 factors. In using Table 1, the principal amount is multiplied by the future value factor for the specified number of periods and interest rate. For example, the future value factor for 2 periods at 9% is 1.18810. Multiplying this factor by $1,000 equals $1,188.10—which is the accumulated balance at the end of year 2 in the Citizens Bank example in Illustration C-2. The $1,295.03 accumulated balance at the end of the third year can be calculated from Table 1 by multiplying the future value factor for 3 periods (1.29503) by the $1,000.

The demonstration problem in Illustration C-5 shows how to use Table 1.

Illustration C-5
Demonstration problem—
Using Table 1 for *FV* of 1

John and Mary Rich invested $20,000 in a savings account paying 6% interest at the time their son, Mike, was born. The money is to be used by Mike for his college education. On his 18th birthday, Mike withdraws the money from his savings account. How much did Mike withdraw from his account?

Present Value (*p*)   *i* = 6%   Future Value = ?

0   1   2   3   4   5   6   7   8   9   10   11   12   13   14   15   16   17   18
$20,000

n = 18 years

Answer: The future value factor from Table 1 is 2.85434 (18 periods at 6%). The future value of $20,000 earning 6% per year for 18 years is **$57,086.80** ($20,000 × 2.85434).

Future Value of an Annuity

The preceding discussion involved the accumulation of only a single principal sum. Individuals and businesses frequently encounter situations in which a **series** of equal dollar amounts are to be paid or received periodically, such as loans or lease (rental) contracts. Such payments or receipts of equal dollar amounts are referred to as **annuities**. The **future value of an annuity** is the sum of all the payments (receipts) plus the accumulated compound interest on them. In computing the future value of an annuity, it is necessary to know (1) the interest rate, (2) the number of compounding periods, and (3) the amount of the periodic payments or receipts.

STUDY OBJECTIVE
——— **3** ———
Solve for future value of an annuity.

To illustrate the computation of the future value of an annuity, assume that you invest $2,000 at the end of each year for 3 years at 5% interest compounded annually. This situation is depicted in the time diagram in Illustration C-6.

Illustration C-6 Time diagram for a 3-year annuity

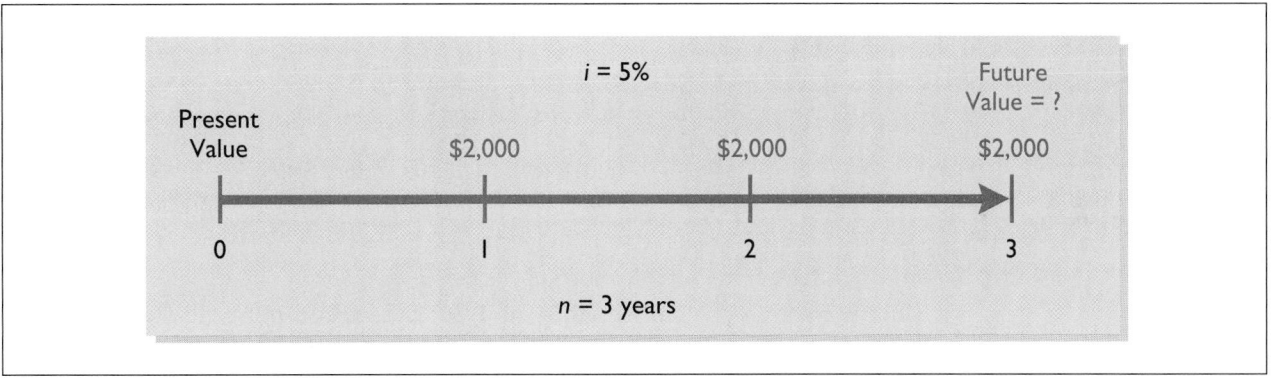

As can be seen from the preceding diagram, the $2,000 invested at the end of year 1 will earn interest for 2 years (years 2 and 3), and the $2,000 invested at the end of year 2 will earn interest for 1 year (year 3). However, the last $2,000 investment (made at the end of year 3) will not earn any interest. The future value of these periodic payments could be computed using the future value factors from Table 1, as shown in Illustration C-7.

Year Invested	Amount Invested	×	Future Value of 1 Factor at 5%	=	Future Value
1	$2,000	×	1.10250		$2,205
2	$2,000	×	1.05000		2,100
3	$2,000	×	1.00000		2,000
			3.15250		$6,305

Illustration C-7 Future value of periodic payment computation

The first $2,000 investment is multiplied by the future value factor for 2 periods (1.1025) because 2 years' interest will accumulate on it (in years 2 and 3). The second $2,000 investment will earn only 1 year's interest (in year 3) and therefore is multiplied by the future value factor for 1 year (1.0500). The final $2,000 investment is made at the end of the third year and will not earn any interest. Consequently, the future value of the last $2,000 invested is only $2,000 since it does not accumulate any interest.

Calculating the future value of each individual cash flow is required when the periodic payments or receipts are not equal in each period. However, when the periodic payments (receipts) are **the same in each period**, the future value can be computed by using a future value of an annuity of 1 table. Table 2 is such a table.

TABLE 2   Future Value of an Annuity of 1

(n) Periods	4%	5%	6%	8%	9%	10%	11%	12%	15%
1	1.00000	1.00000	1.00000	1.00000	1.00000	1.00000	1.00000	1.00000	1.00000
2	2.04000	2.05000	2.06000	2.08000	2.09000	2.10000	2.11000	2.12000	2.15000
3	3.12160	3.15250	3.18360	3.24640	3.27810	3.31000	3.34210	3.37440	3.47250
4	4.24646	4.31013	4.37462	4.50611	4.57313	4.64100	4.70973	4.77933	4.99338
5	5.41632	5.52563	5.63709	5.86660	5.98471	6.10510	6.22780	6.35285	6.74238
6	6.63298	6.80191	6.97532	7.33592	7.52334	7.71561	7.91286	8.11519	8.75374
7	7.89829	8.14201	8.39384	8.92280	9.20044	9.48717	9.78327	10.08901	11.06680
8	9.21423	9.54911	9.89747	10.63663	11.02847	11.43589	11.85943	12.29969	13.72682
9	10.58280	11.02656	11.49132	12.48756	13.02104	13.57948	14.16397	14.77566	16.78584
10	12.00611	12.57789	13.18079	14.48656	15.19293	15.93743	16.72201	17.54874	20.30372
11	13.48635	14.20679	14.97164	16.64549	17.56029	18.53117	19.56143	20.65458	24.34928
12	15.02581	15.91713	16.86994	18.97713	20.14072	21.38428	22.71319	24.13313	29.00167
13	16.62684	17.71298	18.88214	21.49530	22.95339	24.52271	26.21164	28.02911	34.35192
14	18.29191	19.59863	21.01507	24.21492	26.01919	27.97498	30.09492	32.39260	40.50471
15	20.02359	21.57856	23.27597	27.15211	29.36092	31.77248	34.40536	37.27972	47.58041
16	21.82453	23.65749	25.67253	30.32428	33.00340	35.94973	39.18995	42.75328	55.71747
17	23.69751	25.84037	28.21288	33.75023	36.97351	40.54470	44.50084	48.88367	65.07509
18	25.64541	28.13238	30.90565	37.45024	41.30134	45.59917	50.39593	55.74972	75.83636
19	27.67123	30.53900	33.75999	41.44626	46.01846	51.15909	56.93949	63.43968	88.21181
20	29.77808	33.06595	36.78559	45.76196	51.16012	57.27500	64.20283	72.05244	102.44358

Table 2 shows the future value of 1 to be received periodically for a given number of periods. From Table 2 it can be seen that the future value of an annuity of 1 factor for 3 periods at 5% is 3.15250. The future value factor is the total of the three individual future value factors as shown in Illustration C-7. Multiplying this amount by the annual investment of $2,000 produces a future value of $6,305.

The demonstration problem in Illustration C-8 shows how to use Table 2.

Illustration C-8
Demonstration problem—
Using Table 2 for *FV* of an annuity of 1

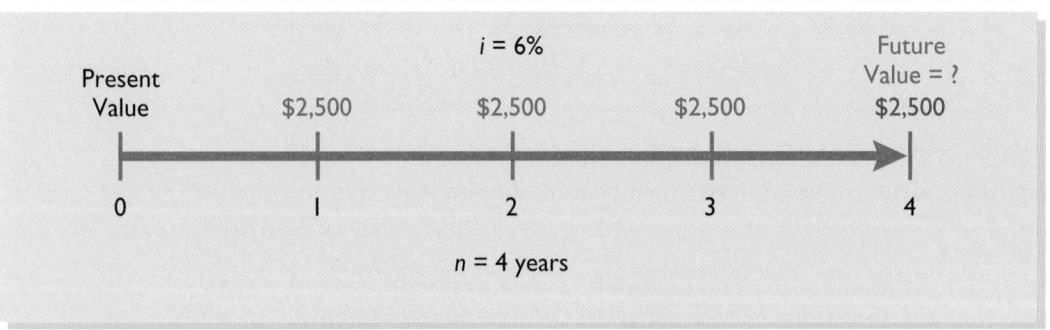

John and Char Lewis' daughter, Debra, has just started high school. They decide to start a college fund for her and will invest $2,500 in a savings account at the end of each year she is in high school (4 payments total). The account will earn 6% interest compounded annually. How much will be in the college fund at the time Debra graduates from high school?

i = 6%

Present Value $2,500 $2,500 $2,500   Future Value = ? $2,500

0   1   2   3   4

n = 4 years

Answer: The future value factor from Table 2 is 4.37462 (4 periods at 6%). The future value of $2,500 invested each year for 4 years at 6% interest is **$10,936.55** ($2,500 × 4.37462).

Present Value Variables

The **present value**, like the future value, is based on three variables: (1) the dollar amount to be received (future amount), (2) the length of time until the amount is received (number of periods), and (3) the interest rate (the discount rate). The process of determining the present value is referred to as **discounting the future amount**.

In this textbook, present value computations are used in measuring several items. For example, in Chapter 10, to determine the market price of a bond, the present value of the principal and interest payments is computed. In addition, the determination of the amount to be reported for notes payable and lease liability involves present value computations.

> **STUDY OBJECTIVE**
> **4**
> Identify the variables fundamental to solving present value problems.

Present Value of a Single Amount

To illustrate present value concepts, assume that you are willing to invest a sum of money that will yield $1,000 at the end of one year. In other words, what amount would you need to invest today to have $1,000 one year from now? If you want a 10% rate of return, the investment or present value is $909.09 ($1,000 ÷ 1.10). The formula for calculating present value is shown in Illustration C-9.

> **STUDY OBJECTIVE**
> **5**
> Solve for present value of a single amount.

Present Value = Future Value ÷ $(1 + i)^1$

Illustration C-9 Formula for present value

The computation of $1,000 discounted at 10% for one year is as follows:

$$PV = FV \div (1 + 10\%)^1$$
$$= \$1{,}000 \div 1.10$$
$$= \$909.09$$

The future amount ($1,000), the discount rate (10%), and the number of periods (1) are known. The variables in this situation can be depicted in the time diagram in Illustration C-10.

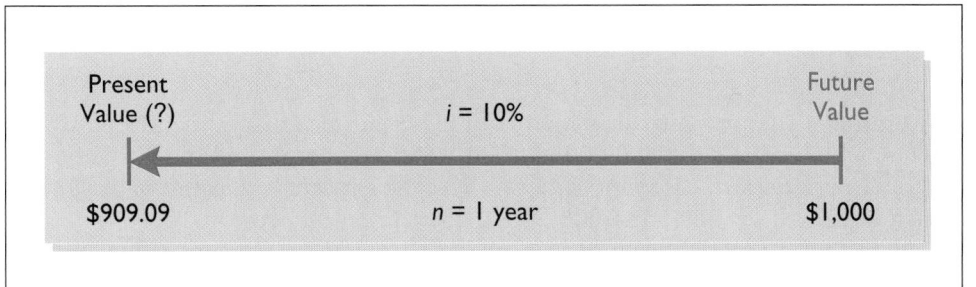

Illustration C-10
Finding present value if discounted for one period

If the single amount of $1,000 is to be received **in 2 years** and discounted at 10% $[PV = \$1{,}000 \div (1 + 10\%)^2]$, its present value is $826.45 [($1,000 ÷ 1.10) ÷ 1.10], depicted as shown in Illustration C-11 on the next page.

Illustration C-11
Finding present value if
discounted for two periods

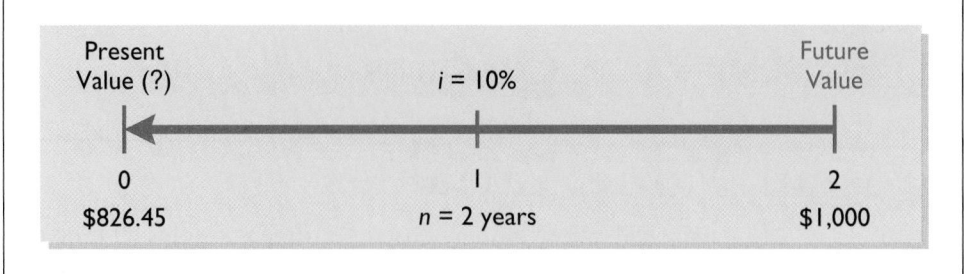

The present value of 1 may also be determined through tables that show the present value of 1 for *n* periods. In Table 3, *n* is the number of discounting periods involved. The percentages are the periodic interest rates or discount rates, and the 5-digit decimal numbers in the respective columns are the present value of 1 factors.

When Table 3 is used, the future value is multiplied by the present value factor specified at the intersection of the number of periods and the discount rate.

TABLE 3   Present Value of 1

(*n*) Periods	4%	5%	6%	8%	9%	10%	11%	12%	15%
1	.96154	.95238	.94340	.92593	.91743	.90909	.90090	.89286	.86957
2	.92456	.90703	.89000	.85734	.84168	.82645	.81162	.79719	.75614
3	.88900	.86384	.83962	.79383	.77218	.75132	.73119	.71178	.65752
4	.85480	.82270	.79209	.73503	.70843	.68301	.65873	.63552	.57175
5	.82193	.78353	.74726	.68058	.64993	.62092	.59345	.56743	.49718
6	.79031	.74622	.70496	.63017	.59627	.56447	.53464	.50663	.43233
7	.75992	.71068	.66506	.58349	.54703	.51316	.48166	.45235	.37594
8	.73069	.67684	.62741	.54027	.50187	.46651	.43393	.40388	.32690
9	.70259	.64461	.59190	.50025	.46043	.42410	.39092	.36061	.28426
10	.67556	.61391	.55839	.46319	.42241	.38554	.35218	.32197	.24719
11	.64958	.58468	.52679	.42888	.38753	.35049	.31728	.28748	.21494
12	.62460	.55684	.49697	.39711	.35554	.31863	.28584	.25668	.18691
13	.60057	.53032	.46884	.36770	.32618	.28966	.25751	.22917	.16253
14	.57748	.50507	.44230	.34046	.29925	.26333	.23199	.20462	.14133
15	.55526	.48102	.41727	.31524	.27454	.23939	.20900	.18270	.12289
16	.53391	.45811	.39365	.29189	.25187	.21763	.18829	.16312	.10687
17	.51337	.43630	.37136	.27027	.23107	.19785	.16963	.14564	.09293
18	.49363	.41552	.35034	.25025	.21199	.17986	.15282	.13004	.08081
19	.47464	.39573	.33051	.23171	.19449	.16351	.13768	.11611	.07027
20	.45639	.37689	.31180	.21455	.17843	.14864	.12403	.10367	.06110

For example, the present value factor for 1 period at a discount rate of 10% is .90909, which equals the $909.09 ($1,000 × .90909) computed in Illustration C-9. For 2 periods at a discount rate of 10%, the present value factor is .82645, which equals the $826.45 ($1,000 × .82645) computed previously.

Note that a higher discount rate produces a smaller present value. For example, using a 15% discount rate, the present value of $1,000 due one year from now is $869.57 versus $909.09 at 10%. Also note that the further removed from the present the future value is, the smaller the present value. For example, using the same discount rate of 10%, the present value of $1,000 due in **5 years** is $620.92 versus the present value of $1,000 due in **1 year**, which is $909.09.

The following two demonstration problems (Illustrations C-12, C-13) illustrate how to use Table 3.

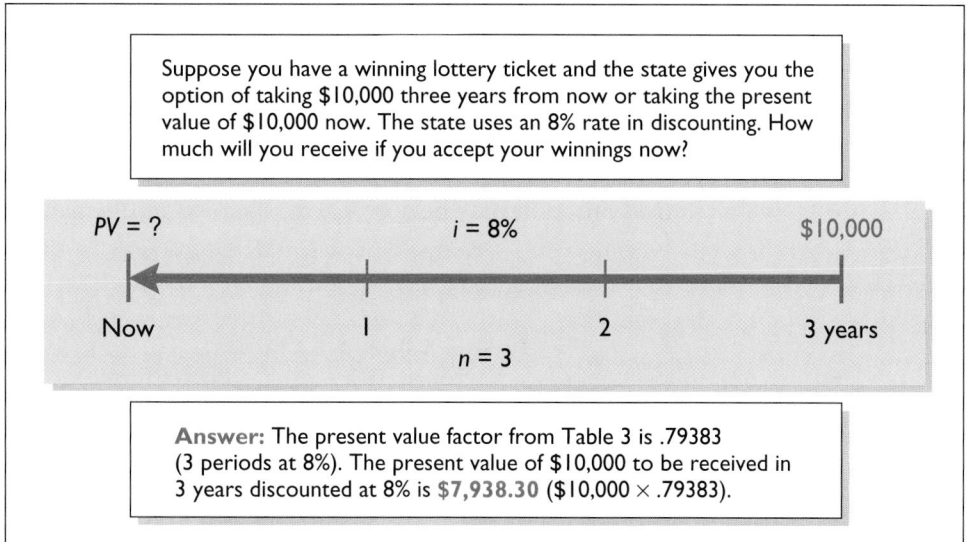

Illustration C-12
Demonstration problem—
Using Table 3 for *PV* of 1

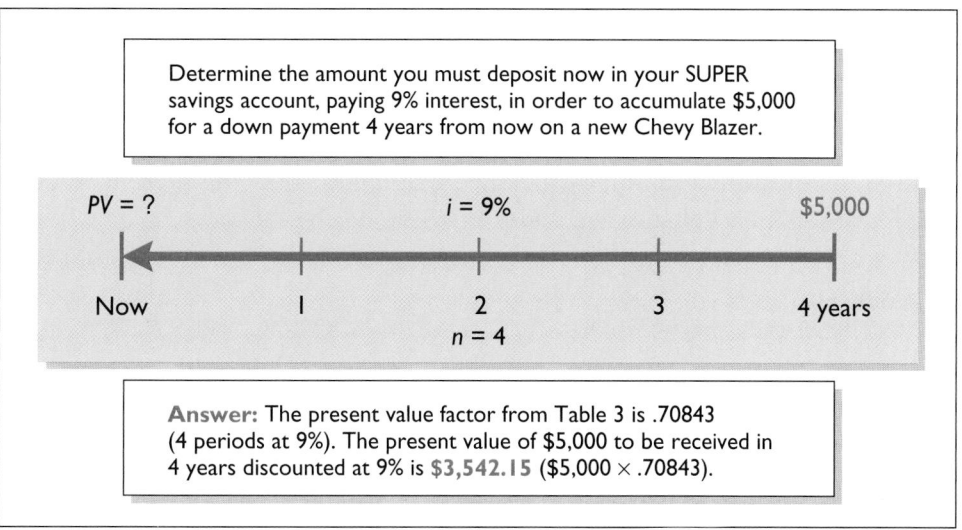

Illustration C-13
Demonstration problem—
Using Table 3 for *PV* of 1

Present Value of an Annuity

The preceding discussion involved the discounting of only a single future amount. Businesses and individuals frequently engage in transactions in which a series of equal dollar amounts are to be received or paid periodically. Examples of a series of periodic receipts or payments are loan agreements, installment sales, mortgage notes, lease (rental) contracts, and pension obligations. These series of periodic receipts or payments are called **annuities**.

In computing the present value of an annuity, it is necessary to know (1) the discount rate, (2) the number of discount periods, and (3) the amount of the periodic receipts or payments. To illustrate the computation of the present value of an annuity, assume that you will receive $1,000 cash annually for 3 years at a time when the discount rate is 10%. This situation is depicted in the time diagram in Illustration C-14 on the next page.

STUDY OBJECTIVE
6
Solve for present value of an annuity.

Illustration C-14 Time diagram for a 3-year annuity

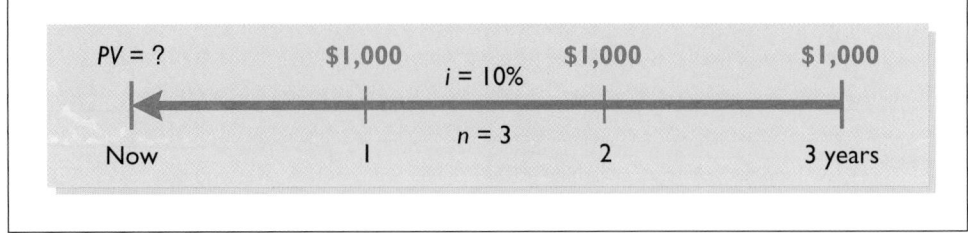

The present value in this situation may be computed as shown in Illustration C-15.

Illustration C-15 Present value of a series of future amounts computation

Future Amount	×	Present Value of 1 Factor at 10%	=	Present Value
$1,000 (one year away)		.90909		$ 909.09
1,000 (two years away)		.82645		826.45
1,000 (three years away)		.75132		751.32
		2.48686		**$2,486.86**

This method of calculation is required when the periodic cash flows are not uniform in each period. However, when the future receipts are the same in each period, there are two other ways to compute present value. First, the annual cash flow can be multiplied by the sum of the three present value factors. In the previous example, $1,000 × 2.48686 equals $2,486.86. Second, annuity tables may be used. As illustrated in Table 4 below, these tables show the present value of 1 to be received periodically for a given number of periods.

TABLE 4   Present Value of an Annuity of 1

(n) Periods	4%	5%	6%	8%	9%	10%	11%	12%	15%
1	.96154	.95238	.94340	.92593	.91743	.90909	.90090	.89286	.86957
2	1.88609	1.85941	1.83339	1.78326	1.75911	1.73554	1.71252	1.69005	1.62571
3	2.77509	2.72325	2.67301	2.57710	2.53130	2.48685	2.44371	2.40183	2.28323
4	3.62990	3.54595	3.46511	3.31213	3.23972	3.16986	3.10245	3.03735	2.85498
5	4.45182	4.32948	4.21236	3.99271	3.88965	3.79079	3.69590	3.60478	3.35216
6	5.24214	5.07569	4.91732	4.62288	4.48592	4.35526	4.23054	4.11141	3.78448
7	6.00205	5.78637	5.58238	5.20637	5.03295	4.86842	4.71220	4.56376	4.16042
8	6.73274	6.46321	6.20979	5.74664	5.53482	5.33493	5.14612	4.96764	4.48732
9	7.43533	7.10782	6.80169	6.24689	5.99525	5.75902	5.53705	5.32825	4.77158
10	8.11090	7.72173	7.36009	6.71008	6.41766	6.14457	5.88923	5.65022	5.01877
11	8.76048	8.30641	7.88687	7.13896	6.80519	6.49506	6.20652	5.93770	5.23371
12	9.38507	8.86325	8.38384	7.53608	7.16073	6.81369	6.49236	6.19437	5.42062
13	9.98565	9.39357	8.85268	7.90378	7.48690	7.10336	6.74987	6.42355	5.58315
14	10.56312	9.89864	9.29498	8.24424	7.78615	7.36669	6.98187	6.62817	5.72448
15	11.11839	10.37966	9.71225	8.55948	8.06069	7.60608	7.19087	6.81086	5.84737
16	11.65230	10.83777	10.10590	8.85137	8.31256	7.82371	7.37916	6.97399	5.95424
17	12.16567	11.27407	10.47726	9.12164	8.54363	8.02155	7.54879	7.11963	6.04716
18	12.65930	11.68959	10.82760	9.37189	8.75563	8.20141	7.70162	7.24967	6.12797
19	13.13394	12.08532	11.15812	9.60360	8.95012	8.36492	7.83929	7.36578	6.19823
20	13.59033	12.46221	11.46992	9.81815	9.12855	8.51356	7.96333	7.46944	6.25933

From Table 4 it can be seen that the present value of an annuity of 1 factor for three periods at 10% is 2.48685.[1] This present value factor is the total of the three individual present value factors, as shown in Illustration C-15. Applying this amount to the annual cash flow of $1,000 produces a present value of $2,486.85.

The following demonstration problem (Illustration C-16) illustrates how to use Table 4.

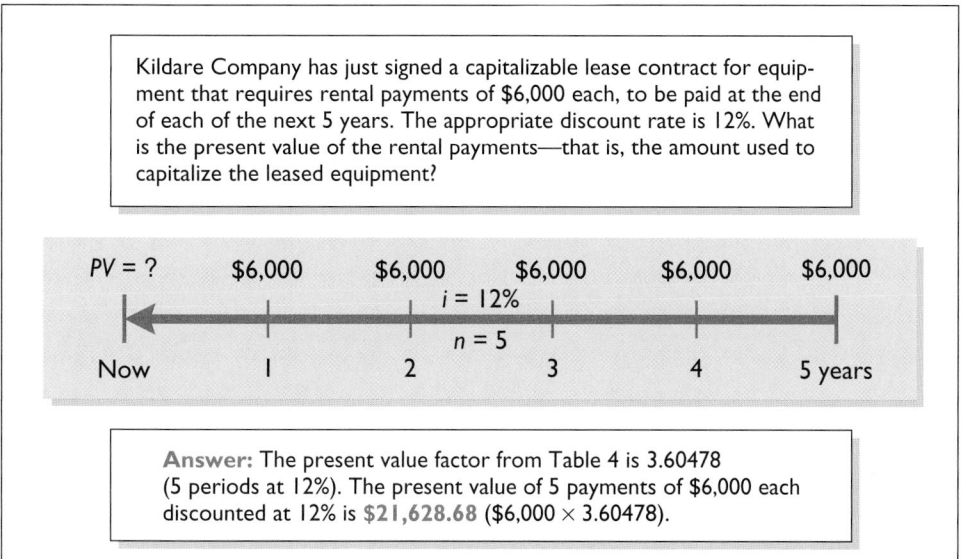

Illustration C-16
Demonstration problem—
Using Table 4 for *PV* of
an annuity of 1

Time Periods and Discounting

In the preceding calculations, the discounting has been done on an annual basis using an annual interest rate. Discounting may also be done over shorter periods of time such as monthly, quarterly, or semiannually.

When the time frame is less than one year, it is necessary to convert the annual interest rate to the applicable time frame. Assume, for example, that the investor in Illustration C-14 received $500 **semiannually** for 3 years instead of $1,000 annually. In this case, the number of periods becomes 6 (3 × 2), the discount rate is 5% (10% ÷ 2), the present value factor from Table 4 is 5.07569, and the present value of the future cash flows is $2,537.85 (5.07569 × $500). This amount is slightly higher than the $2,486.86 computed in Illustration C-15 because interest is computed twice during the same year; therefore interest is earned on the first half year's interest.

Computing the Present Value of a Long-Term Note or Bond

The present value (or market price) of a long-term note or bond is a function of three variables: (1) the payment amounts, (2) the length of time until the amounts are paid, and (3) the discount rate. Our illustration uses a 5-year bond issue.

STUDY OBJECTIVE

7

Compute the present value of notes and bonds.

---

[1] The difference of .00001 between 2.48686 and 2.48685 is due to rounding.

The first variable (dollars to be paid) is made up of two elements: (1) a series of interest payments (an annuity) and (2) the principal amount (a single sum). To compute the present value of the bond, both the interest payments and the principal amount must be discounted—two different computations. The time diagrams for a bond due in 5 years are shown in Illustration C-17.

Illustration C-17 Present value of a bond time diagram

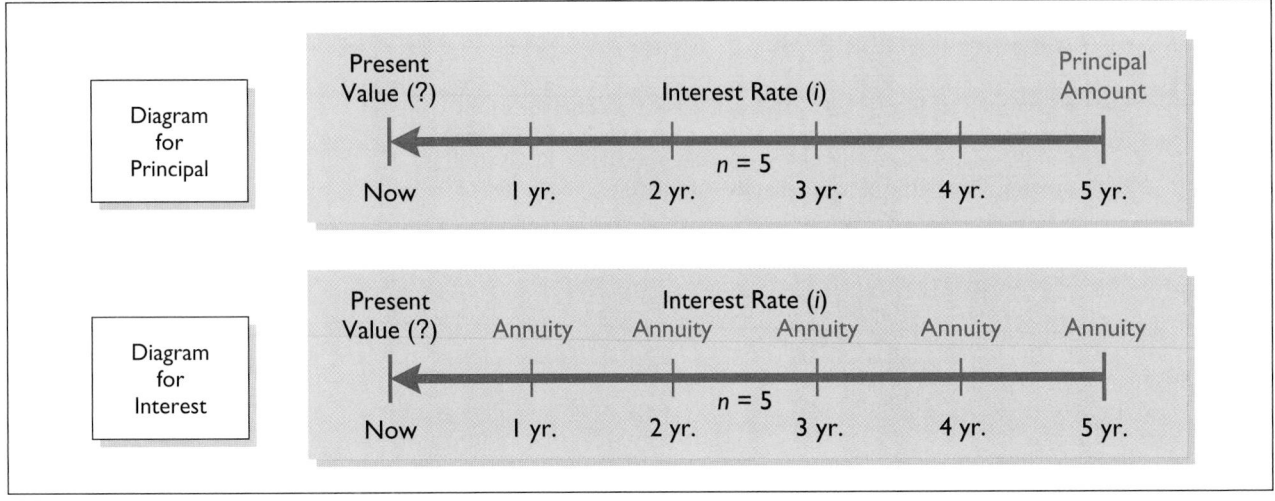

When the investor's market interest rate is equal to the bond's contractual interest rate, the present value of the bonds will equal the face value of the bonds. To illustrate, assume a bond issue of 10%, 5-year bonds with a face value of $100,000 with interest payable **semiannually** on January 1 and July 1. If the discount rate is the same as the contractual rate, the bonds will sell at face value. In this case, the investor will receive (1) $100,000 at maturity and (2) a series of ten $5,000 interest payments [($100,000 × 10%) ÷ 2] over the term of the bonds. The length of time is expressed in terms of interest periods—in this case—10, and the discount rate per interest period, 5%. The following time diagram (Illustration C-18) depicts the variables involved in this discounting situation.

Illustration C-18 Time diagram for present value of a 10%, 5-year bond paying interest semiannually

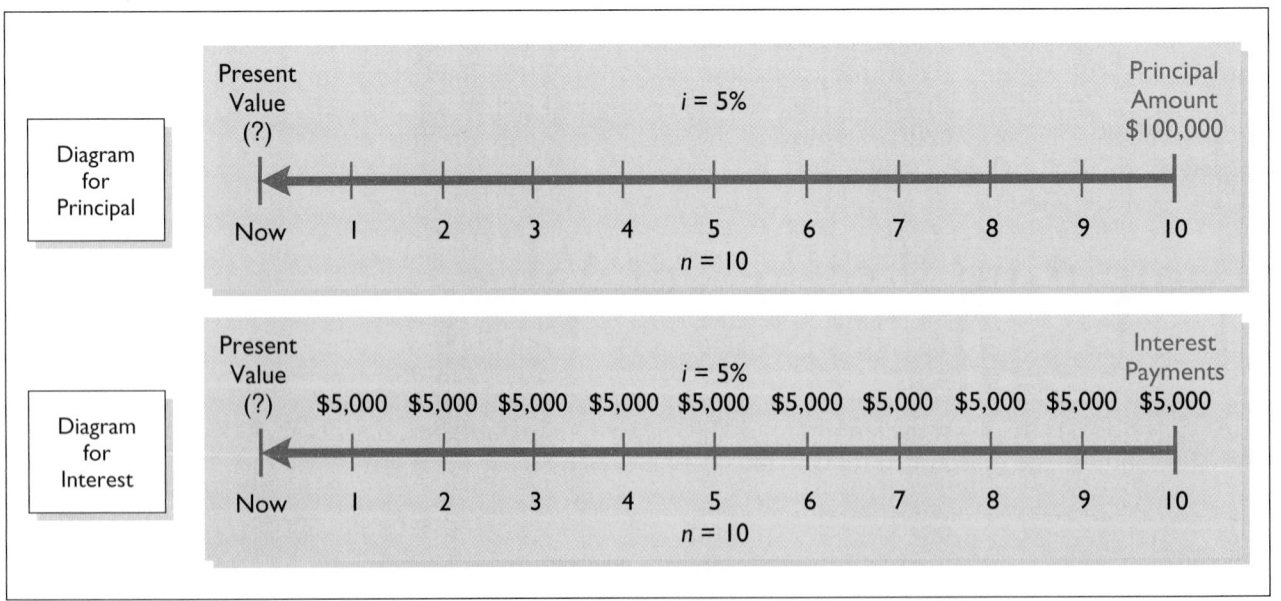

The computation of the present value of these bonds is shown in Illustration C-19.

10% Contractual Rate—10% Discount Rate

Present value of principal to be received at maturity
$100,000 × *PV* of 1 due in 10 periods at 5%
$100,000 × .61391 (Table 3) .... $ 61,391
Present value of interest to be received periodically over the term of the bonds
$5,000 × *PV* of 1 due periodically for 10 periods at 5%
$5,000 × 7.72173 (Table 4) 38,609*
Present value of bonds **$100,000**

---

*Rounded

Illustration C-19 Present value of principal and interest (face value)

Now assume that the investor's required rate of return is 12%, not 10%. The future amounts are again $100,000 and $5,000, respectively, but now a discount rate of 6% (12% ÷ 2) must be used. The present value of the bonds is $92,639, as computed in Illustration C-20.

10% Contractual Rate—12% Discount Rate

Present value of principal to be received at maturity
$100,000 × .55839 (Table 3) $55,839
Present value of interest to be received periodically over the term of the bonds
$5,000 × 7.36009 (Table 4) 36,800
Present value of bonds **$92,639**

Illustration C-20 Present value of principal and interest (discount)

Conversely, if the discount rate is 8% and the contractual rate is 10%, the present value of the bonds is $108,111, computed as shown in Illustration C-21.

10% Contractual Rate—8% Discount Rate

Present value of principal to be received at maturity
$100,000 × .67556 (Table 3) .... $ 67,556
Present value of interest to be received periodically over the term of the bonds
$5,000 × 8.11090 (Table 4) 40,555
Present value of bonds **$108,111**

Illustration C-21 Present value of principal and interest (premium)

The above discussion relied on present value tables in solving present value problems. Electronic hand-held calculators may also be used to compute present values without the use of these tables. Many calculators, especially the "business" calculators, have present value (*PV*) functions that allow you to calculate present values by merely inputting the proper amount, discount rate, periods, and pressing the PV key.

Summary of Study Objectives

1 *Distinguish between simple and compound interest.* Simple interest is computed on the principal only, while compound interest is computed on the principal and any interest earned that has not been withdrawn.

2 *Solve for future value of a single amount.* Prepare a time diagram of the problem. Identify the principal amount, the number of compounding periods, and the interest rate. Using the future value of 1 table, multiply the principal amount by the future value factor specified at the intersection of the number of periods and the interest rate.

3 *Solve for future value of an annuity.* Prepare a time diagram of the problem. Identify the amount of the periodic payments, the number of compounding periods, and the interest rate. Using the future value of an annuity of 1 table, multiply the amount of the payments by the future value factor specified at the intersection of the number of periods and the interest rate.

4 *Identify the variables fundamental to solving present value problems.* The following three variables are fundamental to solving present value problems: (1) the future amount, (2) the number of periods, and (3) the interest rate (the discount rate).

5 *Solve for present value of a single amount.* Prepare a time diagram of the problem. Identify the future amount, the number of discounting periods, and the discount (interest) rate. Using the present value of a single amount table, multiply the future amount by the present value factor specified at the intersection of the number of periods and the discount rate.

6 *Solve for present value of an annuity.* Prepare a time diagram of the problem. Identify the future amounts (annuities), the number of discounting periods, and the discount (interest) rate. Using the present value of an annuity of 1 table, multiply the amount of the annuity by the present value factor specified at the intersection of the number of periods and the interest rate.

7 *Compute the present value of notes and bonds.* Determine the present value of the principal amount: Multiply the principal amount (a single future amount) by the present value factor (from the present value of 1 table) intersecting at the number of periods (number of interest payments) and the discount rate. Determine the present value of the series of interest payments: Multiply the amount of the interest payment by the present value factor (from the present value of an annuity of 1 table) intersecting at the number of periods (number of interest payments) and the discount rate. Add the present value of the principal amount to the present value of the interest payments to arrive at the present value of the note or bond.

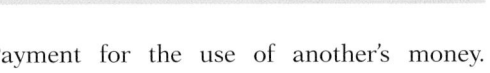

Glossary

Annuity A series of equal dollar amounts to be paid or received periodically. (p. C-5)

Compound interest The interest computed on the principal and any interest earned that has not been paid or withdrawn. (p. C-2)

Discounting the future amount(s) The process of determining present value. (p. C-7)

Future value of a single amount The value at a future date of a given amount invested assuming compound interest. (p. C-3)

Future value of an annuity The sum of all the payments or receipts plus the accumulated compound interest on them. (p. C-5)

Interest Payment for the use of another's money. (p. C-1)

Present value The value now of a given amount to be paid or received in the future assuming compound interest. (p. C-7)

Present value of an annuity The value now of a series of future receipts or payments discounted assuming compound interest. (p. C-9)

Principal The amount borrowed or invested. (p. C-1)

Simple interest The interest computed on the principal only. (p. C-1)

Brief Exercises (use tables to solve exercises)

Compute the future value of a single amount.
(SO 2)

BEC-1 Peter Gora invested $8,000 at 8% annual interest, and left the money invested without withdrawing any of the interest for 12 years. At the end of the 12 years, Peter withdrew the accumulated amount of money. (a) What amount did Peter withdraw, assuming the investment earns simple interest? (b) What amount did Peter withdraw, assuming the investment earns interest compounded annually?

BEC-2   For each of the following cases, indicate (a) to what interest rate columns and (b) to what number of periods you would refer in looking up the future value factor.

Use future value tables.
(SO 2, 3)

  (1) In Table 1 (future value of 1):

	Annual Rate	Number of Years Invested	Compounded
Case A	6%	3	Annually
Case B	5%	5	Semiannually

  (2) In Table 2 (future value of an annuity of 1):

	Annual Rate	Number of Years Invested	Compounded
Case A	5%	8	Annually
Case B	4%	3	Semiannually

BEC-3   Ferris Company signed a lease for an office building for a period of 12 years. Under the lease agreement, a security deposit of $10,000 is made. The deposit will be returned at the expiration of the lease with interest compounded at 6% per year. What amount will Ferris receive at the time the lease expires?

Compute the future value of a single amount.
(SO 2)

BEC-4   Humphrey Company issued $1,000,000, 10-year bonds and agreed to make annual sinking fund deposits of $75,000. The deposits are made at the end of each year into an account paying 5% annual interest. What amount will be in the sinking fund at the end of 10 years?

Compute the future value of an annuity.
(SO 3)

BEC-5   Paul and Chris Hoeft invested $7,000 in a savings account paying 6% annual interest when their daughter, Laurel, was born. They also deposited $1,000 on each of her birthdays until she was 18 (including her 18th birthday). How much was in the savings account on her 18th birthday (after the last deposit)?

Compute the future value of a single amount and of an annuity.
(SO 2, 3)

BEC-6   Matt Schram borrowed $15,000 on July 1, 2005. This amount plus accrued interest at 9% compounded annually is to be repaid on July 1, 2010. How much will Matt have to repay on July 1, 2010?

Compute the future value of a single amount.
(SO 2)

BEC-7   For each of the following cases, indicate (a) to what interest rate columns and (b) to what number of periods you would refer in looking up the discount rate.

Use present value tables.
(SO 5, 6)

  (1) In Table 3 (present value of 1):

	Annual Rate	Number of Years Involved	Discounts per Year
Case A	12%	6	Annually
Case B	10%	11	Annually
Case C	8%	10	Semiannually

  (2) In Table 4 (present value of an annuity of 1):

	Annual Rate	Number of Years Involved	Number of Payments Involved	Frequency of Payments
Case A	12%	20	20	Annually
Case B	10%	5	5	Annually
Case C	8%	4	8	Semiannually

BEC-8   **(a)** What is the present value of $10,000 due 9 periods from now, discounted at 10%?

  (b) What is the present value of $10,000 to be received at the end of each of 6 periods, discounted at 9%?

Determine present values.
(SO 5, 6)

BEC-9   Jacobsen Company is considering an investment which will return a lump sum of $500,000 five years from now. What amount should Jacobsen Company pay for this investment to earn an 11% return?

Compute the present value of a single amount investment.
(SO 5)

BEC-10   Candy Stick Company earns 12% on an investment that will return $875,000 eight years from now. What is the amount Candy Stick should invest now to earn this rate of return?

Compute the present value of a single amount investment.
(SO 5)

Compute the present value of an annuity investment.
(SO 6)

BEC-11 Welz Company is considering investing in an annuity contract that will return $25,000 annually at the end of each year for 15 years. What amount should Welz Company pay for this investment if it earns a 5% return?

Compute the present value of an annuity investment.
(SO 6)

BEC-12 Owens Enterprises earns 8% on an investment that pays back $110,000 at the end of each of the next 6 years. What is the amount Owens Enterprises invested to earn the 8% rate of return?

Compute the present value of bonds.
(SO 5, 6, 7)

BEC-13 Styer Railroad Co. is about to issue $100,000 of 10-year bonds paying an 10% interest rate, with interest payable semiannually. The discount rate for such securities is 8%. How much can Styer expect to receive for the sale of these bonds?

Compute the present value of bonds.
(SO 5, 6, 7)

BEC-14 Assume the same information as BEC-13 except that the discount rate was 12% instead of 8%. In this case, how much can Styer expect to receive from the sale of these bonds?

Compute the present value of a note.
(SO 5, 6, 7)

BEC-15 Cortez Taco Company receives a $50,000, 6-year note bearing interest of 8% (paid annually) from a customer at a time when the discount rate is 10%. What is the present value of the note received by Cortez?

Compute the present value of bonds.
(SO 5, 6, 7)

BEC-16 Irish Treasures Enterprises issued 9%, 8-year, $2,000,000 par value bonds that pay interest semiannually on October 1 and April 1. The bonds are dated April 1, 2005, and are issued on that date. The discount rate of interest for such bonds on April 1, 2005, is 12%. What cash proceeds did Irish Treasures receive from issuance of the bonds?

Compute the present value of a machine for purposes of making a purchase decision.
(SO 7)

BEC-17 Taylor Larson owns a garage and is contemplating purchasing a tire retreading machine for $16,100. After estimating costs and revenues, Taylor projects a net cash flow from the retreading machine of $2,690 annually for 8 years. Taylor hopes to earn a return of 12 percent on such investments. What is the present value of the retreading operation? Should Taylor purchase the retreading machine?

Compute the present value of a note.
(SO 5, 6)

BEC-18 Aaron Ford Company issues a 10%, 5-year mortgage note on January 1, 2005, to obtain financing for new equipment. Land is used as collateral for the note. The terms provide for semiannual installment payments of $112,825. What were the cash proceeds received from the issuance of the note?

Compute the maximum price to pay for a machine.
(SO 7)

BEC-19 Pearcy Company is considering purchasing equipment. The equipment will produce the following cash flows: Year 1, $35,000; Year 2, $45,000; Year 3, $55,000. Pearcy requires a minimum rate of return of 11%. What is the maximum price Pearcy should pay for this equipment?

Compute the interest rate on a single amount.
(SO 5)

BEC-20 If Heidi Hargarten invests $2,745.40 now and she will receive $10,000 at the end of 15 years, what annual rate of interest will Heidi earn on her investment? [*Hint:* Use Table 3.]

Compute the number of periods of a single amount.
(SO 5)

BEC-21 Natzke Cork has been offered the opportunity of investing $45,235 now. The investment will earn 12% per year and at the end of that time will return Natzke $100,000. How many years must Natzke wait to receive $100,000? [*Hint:* Use Table 3.]

Compute the interest rate on an annuity.
(SO 6)

BEC-22 Ruby Bielik made an investment of $7963.33. From this investment, she will receive $1,000 annually for the next 20 years starting one year from now. What rate of interest will Ruby's investment be earning for her? [*Hint:* Use Table 4.]

Compute the number of periods of an annuity.
(SO 6)

BEC-23 Shannon Lawton invests $7,536.08 now for a series of $1,000 annual returns beginning one year from now. Shannon will earn a return of 8% on the initial investment. How many annual payments of $1,000 will Shannon receive? [*Hint:* Use Table 4.]

Payroll Accounting

After studying this appendix,
you should be able to:

1 Discuss the objectives of internal control for payroll.

2 Compute and record the payroll for a pay period.

3 Describe and record employer payroll taxes.

Payroll and related fringe benefits often make up a large percentage of current liabilities. Employee compensation is often the most significant expense that a company incurs. For example, **General Motors** recently reported total employees of 386,000 and labor costs of $21.6 billion. Add to labor costs such fringe benefits as health insurance, life insurance, disability insurance, and so on, and you can see why proper accounting and control of payroll are so important.

Payroll accounting involves more than paying employees' wages. Companies are required by law to maintain payroll records for each employee, file and pay payroll taxes, and comply with numerous state and federal tax laws related to employee compensation. Accounting for payroll has become much more complex due to these regulations.

Payroll Defined

The term "payroll" pertains to both salaries and wages. Managerial, administrative, and sales personnel are generally paid **salaries**. Salaries are often expressed in terms of a specified amount per month or per year rather than an hourly rate. For example, the faculty and administrative personnel at the college or university you are attending are paid salaries. In contrast, store clerks, factory employees, and manual laborers are normally paid **wages**. Wages are based on a rate per hour or on a piecework basis (such as per unit of product). Frequently, the terms "salaries" and "wages" are used interchangeably.

The term "payroll" does not apply to payments made for services of professionals such as certified public accountants, attorneys, and architects. Such professionals are independent contractors rather than salaried employees. Payments to them are called **fees**, rather than salaries or wages. This distinction is important because government regulations relating to the payment and reporting of payroll taxes apply only to employees.

Internal Control of Payroll

Internal control was introduced in Chapter 7. As applied to payrolls, the objectives of internal control are (1) to safeguard company assets against unauthorized payments of payrolls, and (2) to ensure the accuracy and reliability of the accounting records pertaining to payrolls.

Irregularities often result if internal control is lax. Overstating hours, using unauthorized pay rates, adding fictitious employees to the payroll, continuing terminated employees on the payroll, and distributing duplicate payroll checks are all methods of stealing from a company. Moreover, inaccurate records will result in incorrect paychecks, financial statements, and payroll tax returns.

Payroll activities involve four functions: hiring employees, timekeeping, preparing the payroll, and paying the payroll. For effective internal control, these four functions should be assigned to different departments or individuals. To illustrate these functions, we will examine the case of Academy Company and one of its employees, Michael Jordan.

Hiring Employees

Human resources

Human Resources department documents and authorizes employment.

HIRING EMPLOYEES

The human resources (personnel) department is responsible for posting job openings, screening and interviewing applicants, and hiring employees. From a control standpoint, this department provides significant documentation and authorization. When an employee is hired, the human resources department prepares an authorization form. The one used by Academy Company for Michael Jordan is shown in Illustration D-1.

Illustration D-1
Authorization form prepared by the human resources department

ACADEMY COMPANY

Employee Name __Jordan,__ __Michael__   Starting Date __9/01/03__
     LAST   FIRST   MI

Classification __Skilled-Level 10__   Social Security No. __329-36-9547__

Department __Shipping__   Division __Entertainment__

NEW HIRE	Classification __Clerk__ Salary Grade __Level 10__ Trans. from Temp. ☐ Rate $ __10.00__ per __hour__ Bonus __N/A__ Non-exempt ☒ Exempt ☐
RATE CHANGE	New Rate $ __12.00__ Effective Date __9/1/05__ Present Rate $ __10.00__ Merit ☒ Promotion ☐ Decrease ☐ Other _____ Previous Increase Date __None__ Amount $ _____ per _____ Type _____
SEPARATION	Resignation ☐ Discharge ☐ Retirement ☐ Reason _____ Leave of absence ☐ From _____ to _____ Type _____ Last Day Worked _____
APPROVALS	__BEW__ __9/1/04__ __EMW__ __9-1-04__ BRANCH OR DEPT. MANAGER DATE DIVISION V.P. *James E. Speer* DATE PERSONNEL DEPARTMENT

The authorization form is sent to the payroll department, where it is used to place the new employee on the payroll. A chief concern of the human resources department is ensuring the accuracy of this form. The reason is quite simple: one of the most common types of payroll frauds is adding fictitious employees to the payroll.

The human resources department is also responsible for authorizing changes in employment status. Specifically, they must authorize (1) changes in pay rates and (2) terminations of employment. Every authorization should be in writing, and a copy of the change in status should be sent to the payroll department. Notice in Illustration D-1 that Jordan received a pay increase of $2 per hour.

TIMEKEEPING

Another area in which internal control is important is timekeeping. Hourly employees are usually required to record time worked by "punching" a time clock. Times of arrival and departure are automatically recorded by the employee by inserting a time card into the clock. Michael Jordan's time card is shown in Illustration D-2.

In large companies, time clock procedures are often monitored by a supervisor or security guard to make sure an employee punches only one card. At the end of the pay period, each employee's supervisor approves the hours shown by signing the time card. When overtime hours are involved, approval by a supervisor is usually mandatory. This guards against unauthorized overtime. The approved time cards are then sent to the payroll department. For salaried employees, a manually prepared weekly or monthly time report kept by a supervisor may be used to record time worked.

Timekeeping

Supervisors monitor hours worked through time cards and time reports.

Illustration D-2
Time card

Preparing the Payroll

Two (or more) employees verify payroll amounts; supervisor approves.

PREPARING THE PAYROLL

The payroll is prepared in the payroll department on the basis of two inputs: (1) human resources department authorizations and (2) approved time cards. Numerous calculations are involved in determining gross wages and payroll deductions. Therefore, a second payroll department employee, working independently, verifies all calculated amounts, and a payroll department supervisor then approves the payroll. The payroll department is also responsible for preparing (but not signing) payroll checks, maintaining payroll records, and preparing payroll tax returns.

PAYING THE PAYROLL

Paying the Payroll

Treasurer signs and distributes checks.

The payroll is paid by the treasurer's department. **Payment by check minimizes the risk of loss from theft, and the endorsed check provides proof of payment.** For good internal control, payroll checks should be prenumbered, and all checks should be accounted for. All checks must be signed by the treasurer (or a designated agent). Distribution of the payroll checks to employees should be controlled by the treasurer's department. Many employees have their pay credited electronically to their bank account. To control such disbursements, receipts detailing gross pay, deductions, and net pay are provided to employees.

Occasionally the payroll is paid in currency. In such cases it is customary to have a second person count the cash in each pay envelope. The paymaster should obtain a signed receipt from the employee upon payment.

Determining the Payroll

Determining the payroll involves computing three amounts: (1) gross earnings, (2) payroll deductions, and (3) net pay.

STUDY OBJECTIVE
2
Compute and record the payroll for a pay period.

GROSS EARNINGS

Gross earnings is the total compensation earned by an employee. It consists of wages or salaries, plus any bonuses and commissions.

Total **wages** for an employee are determined by multiplying the hours worked by the hourly rate of pay. In addition to the hourly pay rate, most companies are required by law to pay hourly workers a minimum of $1\frac{1}{2}$ times the regular hourly rate for overtime work in excess of 8 hours per day or 40 hours per week. In addition, many employers pay overtime rates for work done at night, on weekends, and on holidays.

Michael Jordan's time card (Illustration D-2) shows that he worked 44 hours for the weekly pay period ending January 14. The computation of his gross earnings (total wages) is shown in Illustration D-3.

Helpful Hint The law that governs pay rates is the Federal Fair Labor Standards Act. It applies to all companies involved in interstate commerce.

Illustration D-3
Computation of total wages

Type of Pay	Hours	×	Rate	=	Gross Earnings
Regular	40	×	$12.00	=	$ 480.00
Overtime	4	×	18.00	=	72.00
Total wages					**$552.00**

This computation assumes that Jordan receives $1\frac{1}{2}$ times his regular hourly rate ($12.00 × 1.5) for his overtime hours. Union contracts often require that overtime rates be as much as twice the regular rates.

The **salary** for an employee is generally based on a monthly or yearly rate. These rates are then prorated to the payroll periods used by the company. Most executive and administrative positions are salaried. Federal law does not require overtime pay for employees in such positions.

Many companies have bonus agreements for management personnel and other employees. A recent survey found that over 94% of the largest U.S. manufacturing companies offer annual bonuses to their key executives. Bonus arrangements may be based on such factors as increased sales or net income. Bonuses may be paid in cash and/or by granting executives and employees the opportunity to acquire shares of company stock at favorable prices (called stock option plans).

*E*THICS NOTE

Bonuses often reward outstanding individual performance; but successful corporations also need considerable teamwork. A challenge is to motivate individuals while preventing an unethical employee from taking another's idea for his or her own advantage.

PAYROLL DEDUCTIONS

As anyone who has received a paycheck knows, gross earnings are usually very different from the amount actually received. The difference is due to payroll deductions. Such deductions do not result in payroll tax expense to the employer. The employer is merely a collection agent, and subsequently transfers the amounts deducted to the government and designated recipients. Payroll deductions may be mandatory or voluntary. Mandatory deductions are required by law and consist of FICA taxes and income taxes. Voluntary deductions are at the option of the employee. Illustration D-4 summarizes the types of payroll deductions.

Illustration D-4 Payroll deductions

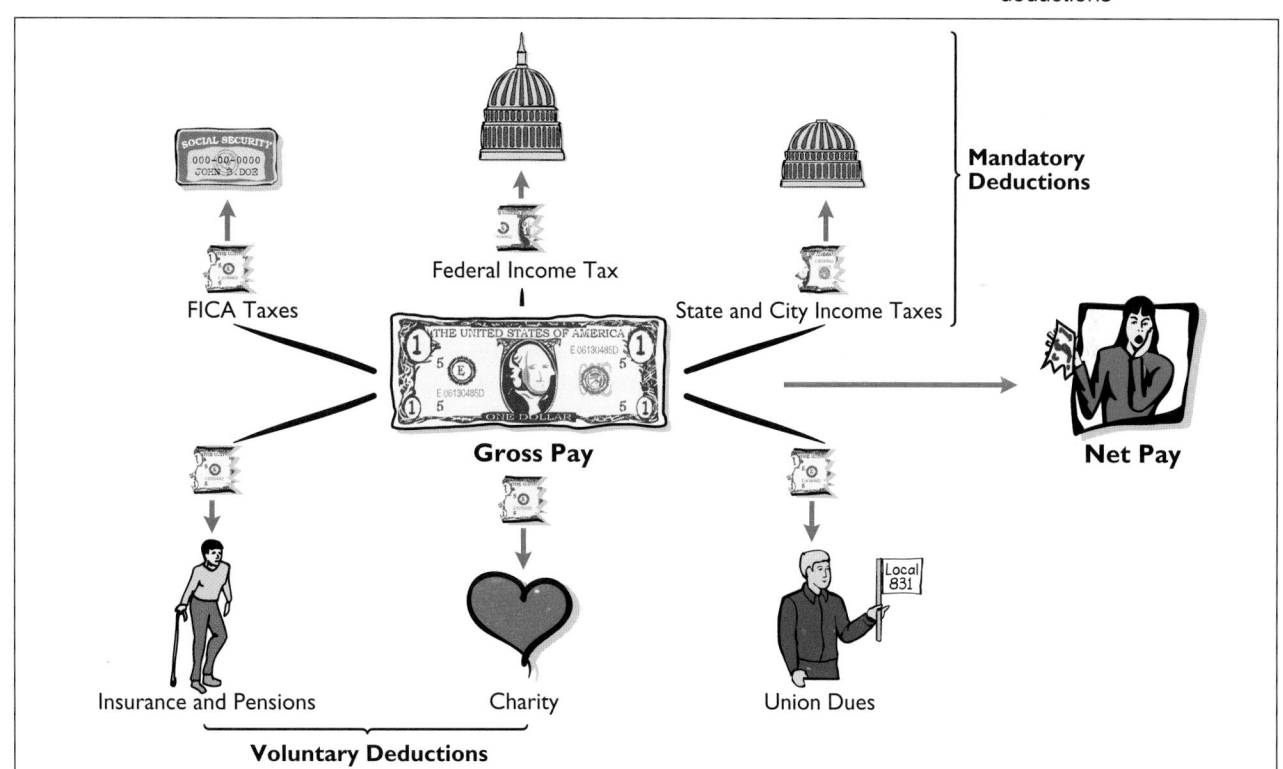

FICA Taxes

In 1937 Congress enacted the Federal Insurance Contribution Act (FICA). **FICA taxes are designed to provide workers with supplemental retirement, employment disability, and medical benefits.** In 1965, benefits were expanded to include Medicare for individuals over 65 years of age. The benefits are financed by a tax levied on employees' earnings. FICA taxes are commonly referred to as **Social Security taxes**.

The tax rate and the tax base for FICA taxes are set by Congress. When FICA taxes were first imposed, the rate was 1% on the first $3,000 of gross earnings, or a maximum of $30 per year. The rate and base have changed dramatically since that time! In 2002, the rate was 7.65% (6.2% Social Security plus 1.45% Medicare) on the first $87,000 of gross earnings for each employee.[1] For purpose of illustration in this appendix, we will assume a rate of 8% on the first $87,000 of gross earnings, or a maximum of $6,960. Using the 8% rate, the FICA withholding for Jordan for the weekly pay period ending January 14 is $44.16 ($552 × 8%).

Income Taxes

Under the U.S. pay-as-you-go system of federal income taxes, employers are required to withhold income taxes from employees each pay period. The amount to be withheld is determined by three variables: (1) the employee's gross earnings; (2) the number of allowances claimed by the employee; and (3) the length of the pay period. The number of allowances claimed typically includes the employee, his or her spouse, and other dependents. **To indicate to the Internal Revenue Service the number of allowances claimed, the employee must complete an Employee's Withholding Allowance Certificate (Form W-4).** As shown in Illustration D-5, Michael Jordan claims two allowances on his W-4.

Illustration D-5 W-4 form

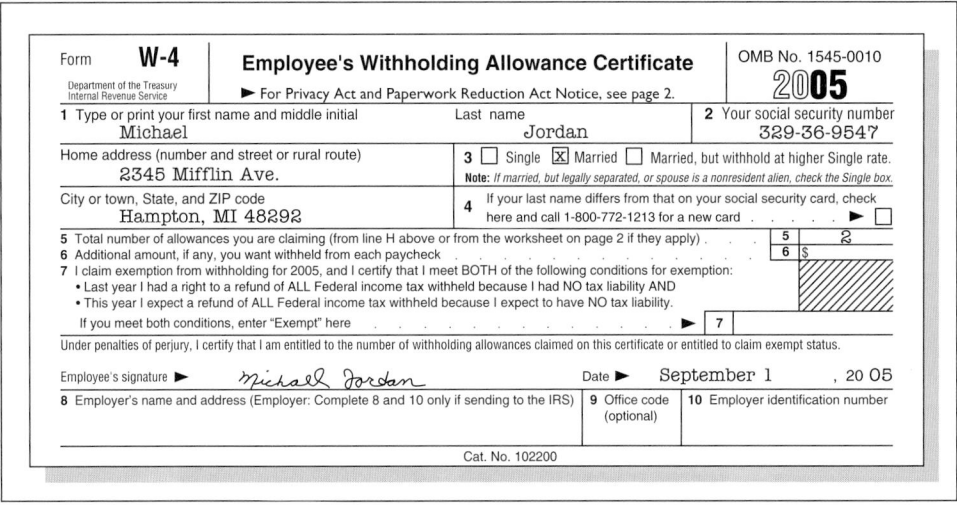

Withholding tables furnished by the Internal Revenue Service indicate the amount of income tax to be withheld. Withholding amounts are based on gross wages and the number of allowances claimed. Separate tables are provided for weekly, biweekly, semimonthly, and monthly pay periods. The withholding tax table for Michael Jordan (assuming he earns $552 per week) is shown in Illustration D-6 (next page). For a weekly salary of $552 with two allowances, the income tax to be withheld is $49.

Most states (and some cities) also require **employers** to withhold income taxes from employees' earnings. As a rule, the amounts withheld are a percentage (specified in the state revenue code) of the amount withheld for the federal

---

[1]The Medicare provision also includes a tax of 1.45% on gross earnings in excess of $87,000. In the interest of simplification, we ignore this 1.45% charge in our end-of-chapter assignment material. We assume zero FICA withholdings on gross earnings above $87,000.

MARRIED Persons — WEEKLY Payroll Period
(For Wages Paid in 2005)

If the wages are –		And the number of withholding allowances claimed is –										
At least	But less than	0	1	2	3	4	5	6	7	8	9	10
		The amount of income tax to be withheld is –										
490	500	56	48	40	32	24	17	9	1	0	0	0
500	510	57	49	42	34	26	18	10	3	0	0	0
510	520	59	51	43	35	27	20	12	4	0	0	0
520	530	60	52	45	37	29	21	13	6	0	0	0
530	540	62	54	46	38	30	23	15	7	0	0	0
540	550	63	55	48	40	32	24	16	9	1	0	0
550	560	65	57	49	41	33	26	18	10	2	0	0
560	570	66	58	51	43	35	27	19	12	4	0	0
570	580	68	60	52	44	36	29	21	13	5	0	0
580	590	69	61	54	46	38	30	22	15	7	0	0
590	600	71	63	55	47	39	32	24	16	8	1	0
600	610	72	64	57	49	41	33	25	18	10	2	0
610	620	74	66	58	50	42	35	27	19	11	4	0
620	630	75	67	60	52	44	36	28	21	13	5	0
630	640	77	69	61	53	45	38	30	22	14	7	0
640	650	78	70	63	55	47	39	31	24	16	8	0
650	660	80	72	64	56	48	41	33	25	17	10	2
660	670	81	73	66	58	50	42	34	27	19	11	3
670	680	83	75	67	59	51	44	36	28	20	13	5
680	690	84	76	69	61	53	45	37	30	22	14	6

income tax. Or they may be a specified percentage of the employee's earnings. For the sake of simplicity, we have assumed that Jordan's wages are subject to state income taxes of 2%, or $11.04 (2% × $552) per week.

There is no limit on the amount of gross earnings subject to income tax withholdings. In fact, the higher the earnings, the higher the amount of taxes withheld.

Other Deductions

Employees may voluntarily authorize withholdings for charitable, retirement, and other purposes. All voluntary deductions from gross earnings should be authorized in writing by the employee. The authorization(s) may be made individually or as part of a group plan. Deductions for charitable organizations, such as the United Fund, or for financial arrangements, such as U.S. savings bonds and repayment of loans from company credit unions, are made individually. Deductions for union dues, health and life insurance, and pension plans are often made on a group basis. We will assume that Jordan has weekly voluntary deductions of $10 for the United Fund and $5 for union dues.

NET PAY

Net pay is determined by subtracting payroll deductions from gross earnings. For Michael Jordan, net pay for the pay period is $432.80, computed as shown in Illustration D-7 (page D-8). Assuming that Michael Jordan's wages for each week during the year are $552, total wages for the year are $28,704 (52 × $552). Thus, all of Jordan's wages are subject to FICA tax during the year. Let's assume that Jordan's department head earns $1,350 per week, or $70,200 for the year. Since only the first $65,000 is subject to FICA taxes, the maximum FICA withholdings on the department head's earnings would be $5,200 ($65,000 × 8%).

Alternative Terminology
Net pay is also called *take-home pay*.

Illustration D-7
Computation of net pay

Gross earnings		$ 552.00
Payroll deductions:		
FICA taxes	$44.16	
Federal income taxes	49.00	
State income taxes	11.04	
United Fund	10.00	
Union dues	5.00	119.20
Net pay		**$432.80**

Recording the Payroll

Recording the payroll involves maintaining payroll department records, recognizing payroll expenses and liabilities, and recording payment of the payroll.

MAINTAINING PAYROLL DEPARTMENT RECORDS

To comply with state and federal laws, an employer must keep a cumulative record of each employee's gross earnings, deductions, and net pay during the year. The record that provides this information is the **employee earnings record**. Michael Jordan's employee earnings record is shown in Illustration D-8.

Illustration D-8
Employee earnings record

ACADEMY COMPANY
Employee Earnings Record
for the Year 2005

Name	Michael Jordan	Address	2345 Mifflin Ave.
Social Security Number	329-36-9547		Hampton, Michigan 48292
Date of Birth	December 24, 1967	Telephone	555-238-9051
Date Employed	September 1, 2003	Date Employment Ended	
Sex	Male	Exemptions	2
Single	Married X		

2005 Period Ending	Total Hours	Gross Earnings				Deductions						Payment	
		Regular	Overtime	Total	Cumulative	FICA	Fed. Inc. Tax	State Inc. Tax	United Fund	Union Dues	Total	Net Amount	Check No.
1/7	42	480.00	36.00	516.00	516.00	41.28	43.00	10.32	10.00	5.00	109.60	406.40	974
1/14	44	480.00	72.00	552.00	1,068.00	44.16	49.00	11.04	10.00	5.00	119.20	432.80	1028
1/21	43	480.00	54.00	534.00	1,602.00	42.72	46.00	10.68	10.00	5.00	114.40	419.60	1077
1/28	42	480.00	36.00	516.00	2,118.00	41.28	43.00	10.32	10.00	5.00	109.60	406.40	1133
Jan. Total		1,920.00	198.00	2,118.00		169.44	181.00	42.36	40.00	20.00	452.80	1,665.20	

A separate earnings record is kept for each employee. It is updated after each pay period. The cumulative payroll data on the earnings record are used by the employer to: (1) determine when an employee has earned the maximum earnings subject to FICA taxes, (2) file state and federal payroll tax returns (as explained later in the appendix), and (3) provide each employee with a statement of gross earnings and tax withholdings for the year. Illustration D-12 (on page D-13) shows this statement.

In addition to employee earnings records, many companies find it useful to prepare a **payroll register**. This record accumulates the gross earnings, deductions, and net pay by employee for each pay period. It provides the documentation for preparing a paycheck for each employee. Academy Company's payroll register is presented in Illustration D-9. It shows the data for Michael Jordan in the wages section. In this example, Academy Company's total weekly payroll is $17,210, as shown in the gross earnings column.

Illustration D-9 Payroll register

ACADEMY COMPANY
Payroll Register
for the Week Ending January 14, 2005

| Employee | Total Hours | Earnings | | | Deductions | | | | | | Paid | | Accounts Debited | |
		Regular	Over-time	Gross	FICA	Federal Income Tax	State Income Tax	United Fund	Union Dues	Total	Net Pay	Check No.	Office Salaries Expense	Wages Expense
Office Salaries														
Arnold, Patricia	40	580.00		580.00	46.40	61.00	11.60	15.00		134.00	446.00	998	580.00	
Canton, Matthew	40	590.00		590.00	47.20	63.00	11.80	20.00		142.00	448.00	999	590.00	
Mueller, William	40	530.00		530.00	42.40	54.00	10.60	11.00		118.00	412.0	1010	530.00	
Subtotal		5,200.00		5,200.00	416.00	1,090.00	104.00	120.00		1,730.00	3,470.00		5,200.00	
Wages														
Bennett, Robin	42	480.00	36.00	516.00	41.28	43.00	10.32	18.00	5.00	117.60	398.40	1025		516.00
Jordan, Michael	44	480.00	72.00	552.00	44.16	49.00	11.04	10.00	5.00	119.20	432.80	1028		552.00
Milroy, Lee	43	480.00	54.00	534.00	42.72	46.00	10.68	10.00	5.00	114.40	419.60	1040		534.00
Subtotal		11,000.00	1,010.00	12,010.00	960.80	2,400.00	240.20	301.50	115.00	4,017.50	7,992.50			12,010.00
Total		16,200.00	1,010.00	17,210.00	1,376.80	3,490.00	344.20	421.50	115.00	5,747.50	11,462.50		5,200.00	12,010.00

Note that this record is a listing of each employee's payroll data for the pay period. In some companies, a payroll register is a journal or book of original entry. Postings are made from it directly to ledger accounts. In other companies, the payroll register is a memorandum record that provides the data for a general journal entry and subsequent posting to the ledger accounts. At Academy Company, the latter procedure is followed.

RECOGNIZING PAYROLL EXPENSES AND LIABILITIES

From the payroll register in Illustration D-9, a journal entry is made to record the payroll. For the week ending January 14 the entry is:

Jan. 14	Office Salaries Expense	5,200.00	
	Wages Expense	12,010.00	
	FICA Taxes Payable		1,376.80
	Federal Income Taxes Payable		3,490.00
	State Income Taxes Payable		344.20
	United Fund Payable		421.50
	Union Dues Payable		115.00
	Salaries and Wages Payable		11,462.50
	(To record payroll for the week ending January 14)		

A = L + SE
+1,376.80 −5,200.00 Exp
+3,490.00 −12,010.00 Exp
+344.20
+421.50
+115.00
+11,462.50

Cash Flows
no effect

Specific liability accounts are credited for the mandatory and voluntary deductions made during the pay period. In the example, debits to Office Salaries and Wages Expense are used for gross earnings because office workers are on a salary and other employees are paid on an hourly rate. In other companies, there may be debits to other accounts such as Store Salaries or Sales Salaries. The amount credited to Salaries and Wages Payable is the sum of the individual checks the employees will receive.

RECORDING PAYMENT OF THE PAYROLL

Payment by check is made either from the employer's regular bank account or a payroll bank account. Each paycheck is usually accompanied by a detachable **statement of earnings** document. This shows the employee's gross earnings, payroll deductions, and net pay for the period and for the year-to-date. The Academy Company uses its regular bank account for payroll checks. The paycheck and statement of earnings for Michael Jordan are shown in Illustration D-10.

Illustration D-10
Paycheck and statement of earnings

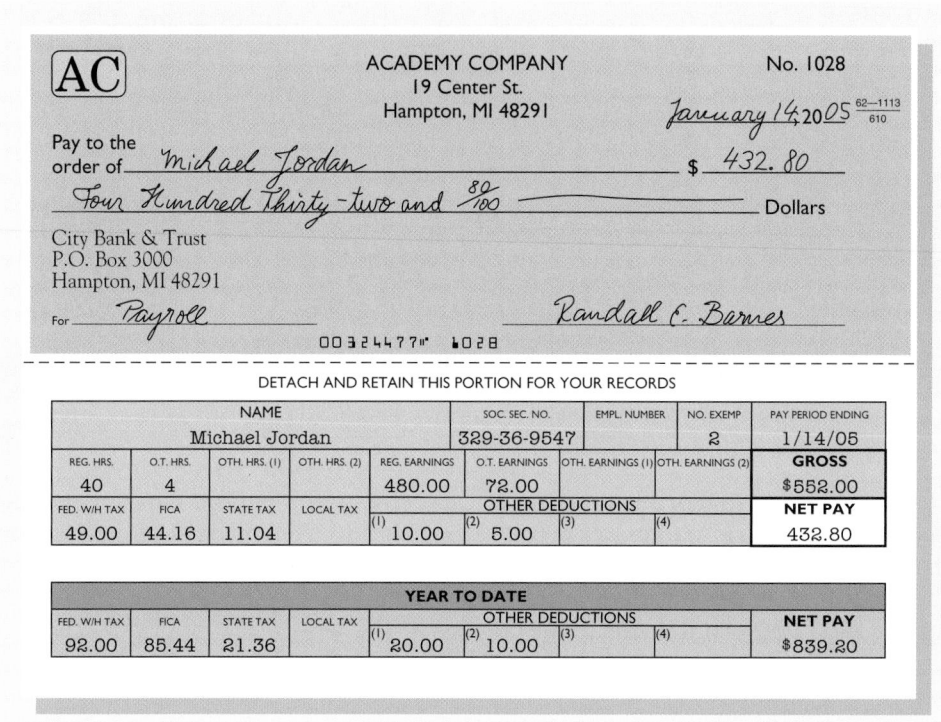

Helpful Hint Do any of the income tax liabilities result in payroll tax expense for the employer? Answer: No. The employer is acting only as a collection agent for the government.

Following payment of the payroll, the check numbers are entered in the payroll register. The entry to record payment of the payroll for Academy Company is as follows.

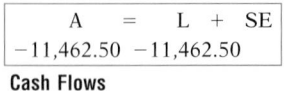

A	=	L	+	SE
−11,462.50		−11,462.50		

Cash Flows
−11,462.50

Jan. 14	Salaries and Wages Payable	11,462.50	
	Cash		11,462.50
	(To record payment of payroll)		

When currency is used in payment, one check is prepared for the payroll's total amount of net pay. This check is then cashed, and the coins and currency are inserted in individual pay envelopes for disbursement to individual employees.

Employer Payroll Taxes

STUDY OBJECTIVE
3
Describe and record employer payroll taxes.

Payroll tax expense for businesses results from three taxes **levied on employers** by governmental agencies. These taxes are: (1) FICA, (2) federal unemployment tax, and (3) state unemployment tax. These taxes plus such items as paid vacations and pensions are collectively referred to as **fringe benefits**. As indicated earlier, the cost of fringe benefits in many companies is substantial.

FICA TAXES

We have seen that each employee must pay FICA taxes. An employer must match each employee's FICA contribution. The matching contribution results in **payroll tax expense** to the employer. The employer's tax is subject to the same rate and maximum earnings applicable to the employee. The account, FICA Taxes Payable, is used for both the employee's and the employer's FICA contributions. For the January 14 payroll, Academy Company's FICA tax contribution is $1,376.80 ($17,210.00 × 8%).

FEDERAL UNEMPLOYMENT TAXES

The Federal Unemployment Tax Act (FUTA) is another feature of the federal Social Security program. **Federal unemployment taxes** provide benefits for a limited period of time to employees who lose their jobs through no fault of their own. Under provisions of the Act, the employer is required to pay a tax of 6.2% on the first $9,000 of gross wages paid to each employee during a calendar year. The law allows the employer a maximum credit of 5.4% on the federal rate for contributions to state unemployment taxes. Because of this provision, state unemployment tax laws generally provide for a 5.4% rate. The effective federal unemployment tax rate thus becomes 0.8% (6.2% − 5.4%). This tax is borne **entirely by the employer**. There is no deduction or withholding from employees.

> **Helpful Hint** FICA taxes are paid by both the employer and employee. Federal unemployment taxes and (in most states) the state unemployment taxes are borne entirely by the employer.

The account Federal Unemployment Taxes Payable is used to recognize this liability. The federal unemployment tax for Academy Company for the January 14 payroll is $137.68 ($17,210.00 × 0.8%).

STATE UNEMPLOYMENT TAXES

All states have unemployment compensation programs under state unemployment tax acts (SUTA). Like federal unemployment taxes, **state unemployment taxes** provide benefits to employees who lose their jobs. These taxes are levied on employers.[2] The basic rate is usually 5.4% on the first $9,000 of wages paid to an employee during the year. The basic rate is adjusted according to the employer's experience rating: Companies with a history of unstable employment may pay more than the basic rate. Companies with a history of stable employment may pay less than 5.4%. Regardless of the rate paid, the credit on the federal unemployment tax is still 5.4%.

The account State Unemployment Taxes Payable is used for this liability. The state unemployment tax for Academy Company for the January 14 payroll is $929.34 ($17,210.00 × 5.4%).

RECORDING EMPLOYER PAYROLL TAXES

Employer payroll taxes are usually recorded at the same time the payroll is journalized. The entire amount of gross pay ($17,210.00) shown in the payroll register in Illustration D-9 is subject to each of the three taxes mentioned above. Accordingly, the entry to record the payroll tax expense associated with the January 14 payroll is:

---

[2]In a few states, the employee is also required to make a contribution. In this textbook, including the homework, we will assume that the tax is only on the employer.

A	=	L	+	SE
		+1,376.80		−2,443.82 Exp
		+137.68		
		+929.34		

Cash Flows
no effect

Jan. 14	Payroll Tax Expense	2,443.82	
	FICA Taxes Payable		1,376.80
	Federal Unemployment Taxes Payable		137.68
	State Unemployment Taxes Payable		929.34
	(To record employer's payroll taxes on		
	January 14 payroll)		

Separate liability accounts are used instead of a single credit to Payroll Taxes Payable. Why? Because these liabilities are payable to different taxing authorities at different dates. The liability accounts are classified in the balance sheet as current liabilities since they will be paid within the next year. Payroll Tax Expense is classified on the income statement as an operating expense. Illustration D-11 summarizes the types of employer payroll taxes.

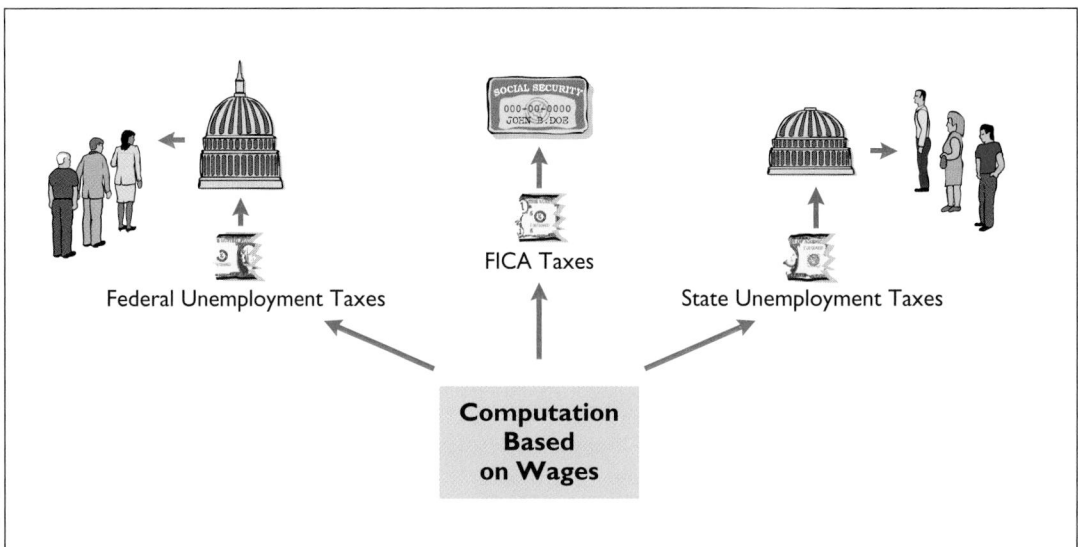

Illustration D-11
Employer payroll taxes

Filing and Remitting Payroll Taxes

Preparation of payroll tax returns is the responsibility of the payroll department. Payment of the taxes is made by the treasurer's department. Much of the information for the returns is obtained from employee earnings records.

For purposes of reporting and remitting to the IRS, FICA taxes and federal income taxes that were withheld are combined. **The taxes must be reported quarterly**, no later than one month following the close of each quarter. The remitting requirements depend on the amount of taxes withheld and the length of the pay period. Remittances are made through deposits in either a Federal Reserve bank or an authorized commercial bank.

Federal unemployment taxes are generally filed and remitted **annually** on or before January 31 of the subsequent year. Earlier payments are required when the tax exceeds a specified amount. State unemployment taxes usually must be filed and paid by the **end of the month following each quarter**. When payroll taxes are paid, payroll liability accounts are debited, and Cash is credited.

The employer is also required to provide each employee with a **Wage and Tax Statement (Form W-2)** by January 31 following the end of a calendar year. This statement shows gross earnings, FICA taxes withheld, and income taxes withheld for the year. The required W-2 form for Michael Jordan, using assumed annual data, is shown in Illustration D-12.

The employer must send a copy of each employee's Wage and Tax Statement (Form W-2) to the Social Security Administration. This agency subsequently furnishes the Internal Revenue Service with the income data required.

Form **W-2 Wage and Tax Statement**		Calendar Year **2005**

1 Control number

OMB No. 1545-0008

2 Employer's name, address and ZIP code

Academy Company
19 Center St.
Hampton, MI 48291

3 Employer's identification number
36-2167852

4 Employer's State number

5 Stat. employee   Deceased   Legal rep.   942 emp.   Subtotal   Void
☐   ☐   ☐   ☐   ☐   ☐

6 Allocated tips

7 Advance EIC payment

8 Employee's social security number
329-36-9547

9 Federal income tax withheld
$2,248.00

10 Wages, tips, other compensation
$26,300.00

11 Social security tax withheld
$2,104.00

12 Employee's name, address, and ZIP code

Michael Jordan
2345 Mifflin Ave.
Hampton, MI 48292

13 Social security wages
$26,300.00

14 Social security tips

16

17 State income tax
$526.00

18 State wages, tips, etc.

19 Name of State
Michigan

20 Local income tax

21 Local wages, tips, etc.

22 Name of locality

Summary of Study Objectives

1 *Discuss the objectives of internal control for payroll.* The objectives of internal control for payroll are (1) to safeguard company assets against unauthorized payments of payrolls, and (2) to ensure the accuracy of the accounting records pertaining to payrolls.

2 *Compute and record the payroll for a pay period.* The computation of the payroll involves gross earnings, payroll deductions, and net pay. In recording the payroll, Salaries (or Wages) Expense is debited for gross earnings, individual tax and other liability accounts are credited for payroll deductions, and Salaries (Wages) Payable is credited for net pay. When the payroll is paid, Salaries and Wages Payable is debited, and Cash is credited.

3 *Describe and record employer payroll taxes.* Employer payroll taxes consist of FICA, federal unemployment taxes, and state unemployment taxes. The taxes are usually accrued at the time the payroll is recorded by debiting Payroll Tax Expense and crediting separate liability accounts for each type of tax.

Glossary

Bonus Compensation to management personnel and other employees, based on factors such as increased sales or the amount of net income. (p. D-5)

Employee earnings record A cumulative record of each employee's gross earnings, deductions, and net pay during the year. (p. D-8)

Employee's Withholding Allowance Certificate (Form W-4) An Internal Revenue Service form on which the employee indicates the number of allowances claimed for withholding federal income taxes. (p. D-6)

Federal unemployment taxes Taxes imposed on the employer that provide benefits for a limited time period to employees who lose their jobs through no fault of their own. (p. D-11)

FICA taxes Taxes designed to provide workers with supplemental retirement, employment disability, and medical benefits. (p. D-5)

Gross earnings Total compensation earned by an employee. (p. D-4)

Net pay Gross earnings less payroll deductions. (p. D-7)

Payroll deductions Deductions from gross earnings to determine the amount of a paycheck. (p. D-5)

Payroll register A payroll record that accumulates the gross earnings, deductions, and net pay by employee for each pay period. (p. D-8)

Salaries Specified amount per month or per year paid to managers and administrative personnel. (p. D-1)

Statement of earnings   A document attached to a paycheck that indicates the employee's gross earnings, payroll deductions, and net pay. (p. D-10)

State unemployment taxes   Taxes imposed on the employer that provide benefits to employees who lose their jobs. (p. D-11)

Wage and Tax Statement (Form W-2)   A form showing gross earnings, FICA taxes withheld, and income taxes withheld which is prepared annually by an employer for each employee. (p. D-12)

Wages   Amounts paid to employees based on a rate per hour or on a piece-work basis. (p. D-1)

Questions

1. You are a newly hired accountant with Schindlebeck Company. On your first day, the controller asks you to identify the main internal control objectives related to payroll accounting. How would you respond?

2. What are the four functions associated with payroll activities?

3. What is the difference between gross pay and net pay? Which amount should a company record as wages or salaries expense?

4. Which payroll tax is levied on both employers and employees?

5. Are the federal and state income taxes withheld from employee paychecks a payroll tax expense for the employer? Explain your answer.

6. What do the following acronyms stand for: FICA, FUTA, and SUTA?

7. What information is shown on a W-4 statement? On a W-2 statement?

8. Distinguish between the two types of payroll deductions and give examples of each.

9. What are the primary uses of the employees earnings record?

10. (a) Identify the three types of employer payroll taxes.
    (b) How are tax liability accounts and Payroll Tax Expense classified in the financial statements?

Brief Exercises

Identify payroll functions.
(SO 1)

BED-1   Gutierrez Company has the following payroll procedures.
(a) Supervisor approves overtime work.
(b) The human resources department prepares hiring authorization forms for new hires.
(c) A second payroll department employee verifies payroll calculations.
(d) The treasurer's department pays employees.

Identify the payroll function to which each procedure pertains.

Compute gross earnings and net pay.
(SO 2)

BED-2   Becky Sherrick's regular hourly wage rate is $14, and she receives an hourly rate of $21 for work in excess of 40 hours. During a January pay period, Becky works 45 hours. Becky's federal income tax withholding is $95, and she has no voluntary deductions. Compute Becky Sherrick's gross earnings and net pay for the pay period.

Record a payroll and the payment of wages.
(SO 2)

BED-3   Data for Becky Sherrick are presented in BED-2. Prepare the journal entries to record (a) Becky's pay for the period and (b) the payment of Becky's wages. Use January 15 for the end of the pay period and the payment date.

Record employer payroll taxes.
(SO 3)

BED-4   In January, gross earnings in Bri Company totaled $70,000. All earnings are subject to 8% FICA taxes, 5.4% state unemployment taxes, and 0.8% federal unemployment taxes. Prepare the entry to record January payroll tax expense.

Exercises

Compute net pay and record pay for one employee.
(SO 2)

ED-1   Linda O'Neill's regular hourly wage rate is $16.00, and she receives a wage of 1½ times the regular hourly rate for work in excess of 40 hours. During a March weekly pay period Linda worked 42 hours. Her gross earnings prior to the current week were $8,000. Linda is married and claims three withholding allowances. Her only voluntary deduction is for group hospitalization insurance at $15.00 per week.

Instructions
   (a) Compute the following amounts for Linda's wages for the current week.

   (1) Gross earnings.
   (2) FICA taxes. (Assume an 8% rate on maximum of $87,000.)
   (3) Federal income taxes withheld. (Use the withholding table in the text, page D-7.)
   (4) State income taxes withheld. (Assume a 2.0% rate.)
   (5) Net pay.

   (b) Record Linda's pay, assuming she is an office computer operator.

ED-2   Employee earnings records for Borelias Company reveal the following gross earnings for four employees through the pay period of December 15.

Compute maximum FICA deductions.
(SO 2)

C. Mull	$83,500	D. Chambers	$86,100
L. Church	$85,600	T. Olejnik	$87,000

For the pay period ending December 31, each employee's gross earnings is $3,000. The FICA tax rate is 8% on gross earnings of $87,000.

Instructions
Compute the FICA withholdings that should be made for each employee for the December 31 pay period. (Show computations.)

ED-3   Martinez Company has the following data for the weekly payroll ending January 31.

Prepare payroll register and record payroll and payroll tax expense.
(SO 2, 3)

Employee	M	T	W	T	F	S	Hourly Rate	Federal Income Tax Withholding	Health Insurance
M. Miller	8	8	9	8	10	3	$10	$34	$10
E. Neupert	8	8	8	8	8	2	12	37	15
K. Mann	9	10	8	8	9	0	13	58	15

Employees are paid 1½ times the regular hourly rate for all hours worked in excess of 40 hours per week. FICA taxes are 8% on the first $87,000 of gross earnings. Martinez Company is subject to 5.4% state unemployment taxes and 0.8% federal unemployment taxes on the first $9,000 of gross earnings.

Instructions
   (a) Prepare the payroll register for the weekly payroll.
   (b) Prepare the journal entries to record the payroll and Martinez's payroll tax expense.

ED-4   Selected data from a February payroll register for Andrew Manion Company are presented below. Some amounts are intentionally omitted.

Compute missing payroll amounts and record payroll.
(SO 2)

Gross earnings:			
Regular	$8,900	State income taxes	$ (3)
Overtime	(1)	Union dues	100
Total	(2)	Total deductions	(4)
Deductions:		Net pay	$7,660
FICA taxes	$ 800	Accounts debited:	
Federal income taxes	1,140	Warehouse wages	(5)
		Store wages	$4,000

FICA taxes are 8%. State income taxes are 3% of gross earnings.

Instructions
   (a) Fill in the missing amounts.
   (b) Journalize the February payroll and the payment of the payroll.

ED-5   According to a payroll register summary of Parolini Company, the amount of employees' gross pay in December was $800,000, of which $70,000 was not subject to FICA tax and $760,000 was not subject to state and federal unemployment taxes.

Determine employer's payroll taxes and record payroll tax expense.
(SO 3)

Instructions
(a) Determine the employer's payroll tax expense for the month, using the following rates: FICA 8%, state unemployment 5.4%, federal unemployment 0.8%.
(b) Prepare the journal entry to record December payroll tax expense.

Problems

Identify internal control weaknesses and make recommendations for improvement.
(SO 1)

PD-1 Selected payroll procedures of Palmcopiolet Company are described below.
1. Department managers interview applicants and on the basis of the interview either hire or reject the applicants. When an applicant is hired, the applicant fills out a W-4 form (Employer's Withholding Exemption Certificate). One copy of the form is sent to the human resources department, and one copy is sent to the payroll department as notice that the individual has been hired. On the copy of the W-4 sent to payroll, the managers manually indicate the hourly pay rate for the new hire.
2. The payroll checks are manually signed by the chief accountant and given to the department managers for distribution to employees in their department. The managers are responsible for seeing that any absent employees receive their checks.
3. There are two clerks in the payroll department. The payroll is divided alphabetically; one clerk has employees A to L and the other has employees M to Z. Each clerk computes the gross earnings, deductions, and net pay for employees in the section and posts the data to the employee earning records.

Instructions
(a) Indicate the weaknesses in internal control.
(b) For each weakness, describe the control procedures that will provide effective internal control. Use the following format for your answer:

(a) Weaknesses   (b) Recommended Procedures

Prepare payroll register and payroll entries.
(SO 2, 3)

PD-2 Happy Hardware has four employees who are paid on an hourly basis plus time-and-a half for all hours worked in excess of 40 a week. Payroll data for the week ended March 15, 2005, are presented below.

Employee	Hours Worked	Hourly Rate	Federal Income Tax Withholdings	United Fund
Joe McKane	40	$14.00	$?	$5.00
Mary Miller	42	13.00	?	5.00
Andy Manion	44	13.00	60	8.00
Kim Cheng	46	13.00	51	5.00

McKane and Miller are married. They claim 0 and 4 withholding allowances, respectively. The following tax rates are applicable: FICA 8%, state income taxes 3%, state unemployment taxes 5.4%, and federal unemployment 0.8%. The first three employees are sales clerks (store wages expense). The fourth employee performs administrative duties (office wages expense).

Instructions
(a) Net pay $1,862.06
(a) Prepare a payroll register for the weekly payroll. (Use the wage-bracket withholding table in the text for federal income tax withholdings.)
(b) Journalize the payroll on March 15, 2005, and the accrual of employer payroll taxes.
(c) Journalize the payment of the payroll on March 16, 2005.
(d) Cash paid $ 586.64
(d) Journalize the deposit in a Federal Reserve bank on March 31, 2005, of the FICA and federal income taxes payable to the government.

Journalize payroll transactions and adjusting entries.
(SO 2, 3)

PD-3 The following payroll liability accounts are included in the ledger of Nam Viet Company on January 1, 2005.

Peachtree

FICA Taxes Payable	$ 760.00
Federal Income Taxes Payable	1,004.60
State Income Taxes Payable	108.95
Federal Unemployment Taxes Payable	288.95
State Unemployment Taxes Payable	1,954.40
Union Dues Payable	870.00
U.S. Savings Bonds Payable	360.00

In January, the following transactions occurred.

Jan. 10   Sent check for $870.00 to union treasurer for union dues.
   12   Deposited check for $1,764.60 in Federal Reserve bank for FICA taxes and federal income taxes withheld.
   15   Purchased U.S. Savings Bonds for employees by writing check for $360.00.
   17   Paid state income taxes withheld from employees.
   20   Paid federal and state unemployment taxes.
   31   Completed monthly payroll register, which shows office salaries $14,600, store wages $28,400, FICA taxes withheld $3,440, federal income taxes payable $1,684, state income taxes payable $360, union dues payable $400, United Fund contributions payable $1,888, and net pay $35,228.
   31   Prepared payroll checks for the net pay and distributed checks to employees.

At January 31, the company also makes the following accrued adjustments pertaining to employee compensation.
  1. Employer payroll taxes: FICA taxes 8%, federal unemployment taxes 0.8%, and state unemployment taxes 5.4%.
  2. Vacation pay: 6% of gross earnings.

Instructions
  (a) Journalize the January transactions.
  (b) Journalize the adjustments pertaining to employee compensation at January 31.

(b) Payroll tax expense $6,106.00; vacation benefits expense $2,580

PD-4 For the year ended December 31, 2005, Malaysia Electrical Repair Company reports the following summary payroll data.

Prepare entries for payroll and payroll taxes, and prepare W-2 data.
(SO 2, 3)

Gross earnings:	
Administrative salaries	$180,000
Electricians' wages	470,000
Total	$650,000
Deductions:	
FICA taxes	$ 45,200
Federal income taxes withheld	188,000
State income taxes withheld (2.6%)	16,900
United Fund contributions payable	32,500
Hospital insurance premiums	20,300
Total	$302,900

Malaysia Company's payroll taxes are: FICA 8%, state unemployment 2.5% (due to a stable employment record), and 0.8% federal unemployment. Gross earnings subject to FICA taxes total $565,000, and gross earnings subject to unemployment taxes total $145,000.

Instructions
  (a) Prepare a summary journal entry at December 31 for the full year's payroll.
  (b) Journalize the adjusting entry at December 31 to record the employer's payroll taxes.
  (c) The W-2 Wage and Tax Statement requires the following dollar data.

(a) Wages payable $347,100
(b) Payroll tax
*   expense $ 49,985*

Wages, Tips, Other Compensation	Federal Income Tax Withheld	State Income Tax Withheld	FICA Wages	FICA Tax Withheld

Complete the required data for the following employees.

Employee	Gross Earnings	Federal Income Tax Withheld
Anna Makarov	$59,000	$28,500
Sharon Livingston	28,000	10,800

Subsidiary Ledgers and Special Journals

SECTION ONE
EXPANDING THE LEDGER— SUBSIDIARY LEDGERS

Nature and Purpose of Subsidiary Ledgers

Imagine a business that has several thousand charge (credit) customers and shows the transactions with these customers in only one general ledger account— Accounts Receivable. It would be virtually impossible to determine the balance owed by an individual customer at any specific time. Similarly, the amount payable to one creditor would be difficult to locate quickly from a single Accounts Payable account in the general ledger.

Instead, companies use subsidiary ledgers to keep track of individual balances. A **subsidiary ledger** is a group of accounts with a common characteristic (for example, all accounts receivable). The subsidiary ledger frees the general ledger from the details of individual balances. A subsidiary ledger is an addition to, and an expansion of, the general ledger.

Two common subsidiary ledgers are:

1. The **accounts receivable** (or **customers'**) **subsidiary ledger**, which collects transaction data of individual customers.

2. The **accounts payable** (or **creditors'**) **subsidiary ledger**, which collects transaction data of individual creditors.

In each of these subsidiary ledgers, individual accounts are usually arranged in alphabetical order.

The detailed data from a subsidiary ledger are summarized in a general ledger account. For example, the detailed data from the accounts receivable subsidiary ledger are summarized in Accounts Receivable in the general ledger. The general ledger account that summarizes subsidiary ledger data is called a **control account**. An overview of the relationship of subsidiary ledgers to the general ledger is shown in Illustration E-1. The general ledger control accounts and subsidiary ledger accounts are shown in green color. Note that cash and stockholders' equity in this illustration are not control accounts because there are no subsidiary ledger accounts related to these accounts.

Illustration E-1
Relationship of general ledger and subsidiary ledgers

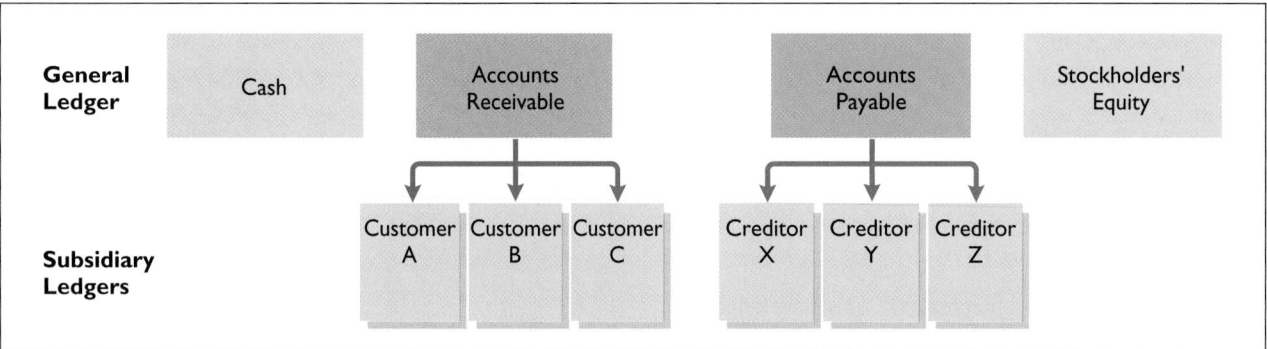

Each general ledger control account balance must equal the composite balance of the individual accounts in the related subsidiary ledger at the end of an accounting period. For example, the balance in Accounts Payable in Illustration E-1 must equal the total of the subsidiary balances of Creditors X + Y + Z.

EXAMPLE

An example of a control account and subsidiary ledger for Larson Enterprises is provided in Illustration E-2. (The explanation column in these accounts is not shown in this and subsequent illustrations due to space considerations.)

Illustration E-2
Relationship between general and subsidiary ledgers

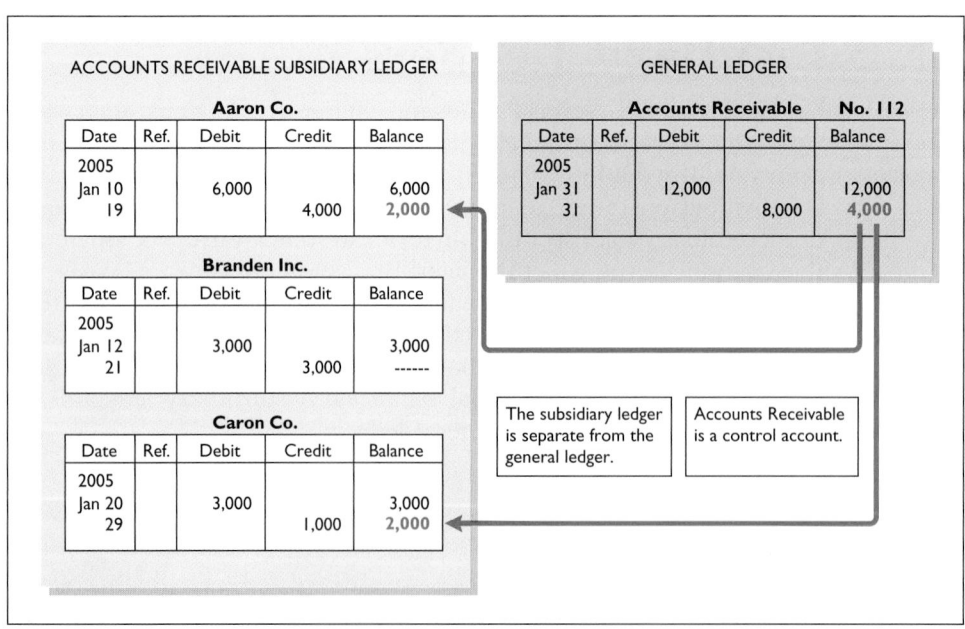

The example is based on the transactions listed below.

Credit Sales			Collections on Account		
Jan. 10	Aaron Co.	$ 6,000	Jan. 19	Aaron Co.	$4,000
12	Branden Inc.	3,000	21	Branden Inc.	3,000
20	Caron Co.	3,000	29	Caron Co.	1,000
		$12,000			$8,000

The total debits ($12,000) and credits ($8,000) in Accounts Receivable in the general ledger are reconcilable to the detailed debits and credits in the subsidiary accounts. Also, the balance of $4,000 in the control account agrees with the total of the balances in the individual accounts (Aaron Co. $2,000 + Branden Inc. $0 + Caron Co. $2,000) in the subsidiary ledger.

As shown, postings are made monthly to the control accounts in the general ledger. This practice allows monthly financial statements to be prepared. Postings to the individual accounts in the subsidiary ledger are made daily. Daily posting ensures that account information is current. This enables the company to monitor credit limits, bill customers, and answer inquiries from customers about their account balances.

Advantages of Subsidiary Ledgers

Subsidiary ledgers have several advantages. They:

1. **Show transactions affecting one customer or one creditor in a single account**, thus providing up-to-date information on specific account balances.
2. **Free the general ledger of excessive details.** As a result, a trial balance of the general ledger does not contain vast numbers of individual account balances.
3. **Help locate errors in individual accounts** by reducing the number of accounts in one ledger and by using control accounts.
4. **Make possible a division of labor** in posting. One employee can post to the general ledger while someone else posts to the subsidiary ledgers.

SECTION TWO
EXPANDING THE JOURNAL—SPECIAL JOURNALS

So far you have learned to journalize transactions in a two-column general journal and post each entry to the general ledger. This procedure is satisfactory in only the very smallest companies. To expedite journalizing and posting, most companies use special journals **in addition to the general journal**.

A **special journal** is used to record similar types of transactions. Examples would be all sales of merchandise on account, or all cash receipts. The special journals a company uses depends largely on the types of transactions that occur frequently. Most merchandising enterprises use the journals shown in Illustration E-4 (on the next page) to record transactions daily.

If a transaction cannot be recorded in a special journal, it is recorded in the general journal. For example, if you had special journals only for the four types of transactions shown in Illustration E-4, purchase returns and

Illustration E-4 Use of special journals and the general journal

allowances would be recorded in the general journal. So would sales returns and allowances. Similarly, **correcting**, **adjusting**, **and closing entries are recorded in the general journal**. Other types of special journals may sometimes be used in some situations. For example, when sales returns and allowances are frequent, special journals may be used to record these transactions.

Special journals **permit greater division of labor** because several people can record entries in different journals at the same time. For example, one employee may journalize all cash receipts, and another may journalize all credit sales. Also, the use of special journals **reduces the time needed to complete the posting process**. With special journals, some accounts may be posted monthly, instead of daily, as will be illustrated later in the chapter.

Sales Journal

The **sales journal** is used to record sales of merchandise on account. Cash sales of merchandise are entered in the cash receipts journal. Credit sales of assets other than merchandise are entered in the general journal.

JOURNALIZING CREDIT SALES

Helpful Hint Postings are also made daily to individual ledger accounts in the inventory subsidiary ledger to maintain a perpetual inventory.

Illustration E-5
Journalizing credit sales—perpetual inventory system

Karns Wholesale Supply uses a **perpetual inventory** system. Under this system, each entry in the sales journal results in one entry **at selling price**—a debit to Accounts Receivable (a control account) and a credit of equal amount to Sales—and another entry at cost. The entry **at cost** is a debit to Cost of Goods Sold and a credit of equal amount to Merchandise Inventory (a control account). The sales journal for Karns Wholesale Supply is shown in Illustration E-5. (It uses as-

KARNS WHOLESALE SUPPLY					
		Sales Journal			S1
Date	Account Debited	Invoice No.	Ref.	Accts. Receivable Dr. Sales Cr.	Cost of Goods Sold Dr. Merchandise Inventory Cr.
2005					
May 3	Abbot Sisters	101		10,600	6,360
7	Babson Co.	102		11,350	7,370
14	Carson Bros.	103		7,800	5,070
19	Deli Co.	104		9,300	6,510
21	Abbot Sisters	105		15,400	10,780
24	Deli Co.	106		21,210	15,900
27	Babson Co.	107		14,570	10,200
				90,230	62,190

sumed credit sales transactions for sales invoices 101–107.) A sales journal with two amount columns, like that in Illustration E-5, shows a transaction at both selling price and cost on a single line. The reference (Ref.) column is not used in journalizing. It is used in posting the sales journal, as explained in the next section. Also, note that, unlike the general journal, an explanation is not required for each entry in a special journal. Finally, note that each invoice is prenumbered to ensure that all invoices are journalized.

POSTING THE SALES JOURNAL

Postings from the sales journal are made **daily to the individual accounts receivable** in the subsidiary ledger. Posting **to the general ledger** is made **monthly**. Illustration E-6 shows both the daily and monthly postings.

Illustration E-6 Posting the sales journal

[1]The normal balance for Merchandise Inventory is a debit. But, because of the sequence in which we have posted the special journals, with the sales journals first, the credits to Merchandise Inventory are posted before the debits. This posting sequence explains the credit balance, in Merchandise Inventory, which exists only until the other journals are posted.

A check mark (✓) is inserted in the reference posting column to indicate that the daily posting to the customer's account has been made. A check mark (✓) is used in this illustration because the subsidiary ledger accounts are not numbered. At the end of the month, the column totals of the sales journal are posted to the general ledger. Here, the column totals are a debit of $90,230 to Accounts Receivable (account No. 112), a credit of $90,230 to Sales (account No. 401), a debit of $62,190 to Cost of Goods Sold (account No. 505), and a credit of $62,190 to Merchandise Inventory (account No. 120). Insertion of the account numbers below the column total indicates that the postings have been made. In both the general ledger and subsidiary ledger accounts, the reference **S1** indicates that the posting came from page 1 of the sales journal.

PROVING THE LEDGERS

The next step is to "prove" the ledgers. To do so, we must determine two things: (1) The total of the general ledger debit balances must equal the total of the general ledger credit balances. (2) The sum of the subsidiary ledger balances must equal the balance in the control account. The proof of the postings from the sales journal to the general and subsidiary ledger is shown in Illustration E-7.

Illustration E-7 Proving the equality of the postings from the sales journal

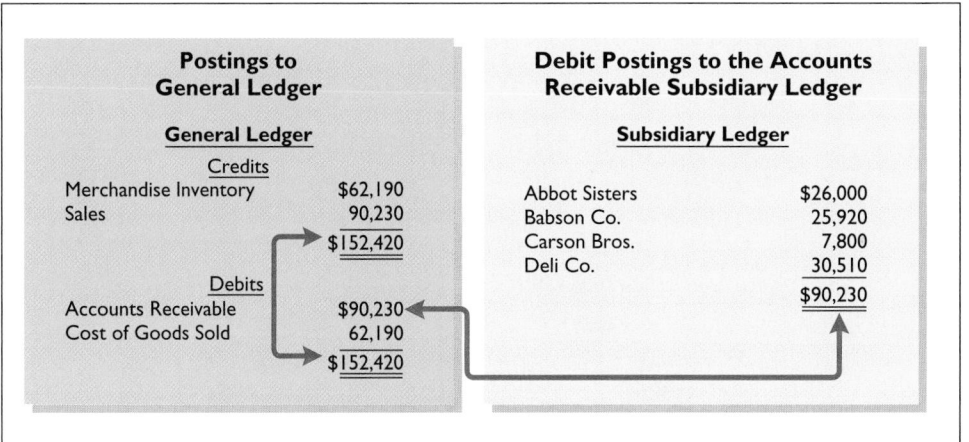

ADVANTAGES OF THE SALES JOURNAL

The use of a special journal to record sales on account has a number of advantages. First, the one-line entry for each sales transaction **saves time**. In the sales journal, it is not necessary to write out the four account titles for each transaction. Second, only totals, rather than individual entries, are posted to the general ledger. This **saves posting time and reduces the possibilities of errors in posting**. Finally, **a division of labor results**, because one individual can take responsibility for the sales journal.

Cash Receipts Journal

All receipts of cash are recorded in the **cash receipts journal**. The most common types of cash receipts are cash sales of merchandise and collections of accounts receivable. Many other possibilities exist, such as receipt of money from bank loans and cash proceeds from disposal of equipment. A one- or two-column cash receipts journal would not have space enough for all possible cash receipt transactions. Therefore, a multiple-column cash receipts journal is used.

Generally, a cash receipts journal includes the following columns: debit columns for cash and sales discounts; and credit columns for accounts receivable, sales, and "other" accounts. The Other Accounts category is used when the cash receipt does not involve a cash sale or a collection of accounts receivable. Under a perpetual inventory system, each sales entry is accompanied by another entry that debits Cost of Goods Sold and credits Merchandise Inventory for the cost of the merchandise sold. This entry may be recorded separately. A six-column cash receipts journal is shown in Illustration E-8 (on page E-8).

Additional credit columns may be used if they significantly reduce postings to a specific account. For example, a loan company, such as **Household International**, receives thousands of cash collections from customers. A significant saving in posting would result from using separate credit columns for Loans Receivable and Interest Revenue, rather than using the Other Accounts credit column. In contrast, a retailer that has only one interest collection a month would not find it useful to have a separate column for Interest Revenue.

JOURNALIZING CASH RECEIPTS TRANSACTIONS

To illustrate the journalizing of cash receipts transactions, we will continue with the May transactions of Karns Wholesale Supply. Collections from customers relate to the entries recorded in the sales journal in Illustration E-5. The entries in the cash receipts journal are based on the following cash receipts.

May	1	Stockholders invest $5,000 in the business in common stock.
	7	Cash sales of merchandise total $1,900 (cost, $1,240).
	10	A check for $10,388 is received from Abbot Sisters in payment of invoice No. 101 for $10,600 less a 2% discount.
	12	Cash sales of merchandise total $2,600 (cost, $1,690).
	17	A check for $11,123 is received from Babson Co. in payment of invoice No. 102 for $11,350 less a 2% discount.
	22	Cash is received by signing a note for $6,000.
	23	A check for $7,644 is received from Carson Bros. in full for invoice No. 103 for $7,800 less a 2% discount.
	28	A check for $9,114 is received from Deli Co. in full for invoice No. 104 for $9,300 less a 2% discount.

Further information about the columns in the cash receipts journal (see Illustration E-8) is listed below.

Debit Columns:

1. **Cash.** The amount of cash actually received in each transaction is entered in this column. The column total indicates the total cash receipts for the month.

2. **Sales Discounts.** Karns includes a Sales Discounts column in its cash receipts journal. By doing so, it is not necessary to enter sales discount items in the general journal. As a result, the collection of an account receivable within the discount period is expressed on one line in the appropriate columns of the cash receipts journal.

Credit Columns:

3. **Accounts Receivable.** The Accounts Receivable column is used to record cash collections on account. The amount entered here is the amount to be credited to the individual customer's account.

4. **Sales.** The Sales column records all cash sales of merchandise. Cash sales of other assets (plant assets, for example) are not reported in this column.

5. **Other Accounts.** The Other Accounts column is used whenever the credit is other than to Accounts Receivable or Sales. For example, in the first

Helpful Hint When is an account title entered in the "Account Credited" column of the cash receipts journal? Answer: A *subsidiary ledger* title is entered whenever the entry involves a collection of accounts receivable. A *general ledger* account title is entered whenever the entry involves an account that is not the subject of a special column (and an amount must be entered in the Other Accounts column). No account title is entered there if neither of the foregoing applies.

Illustration E-8
Journalizing and posting
the cash receipts journal

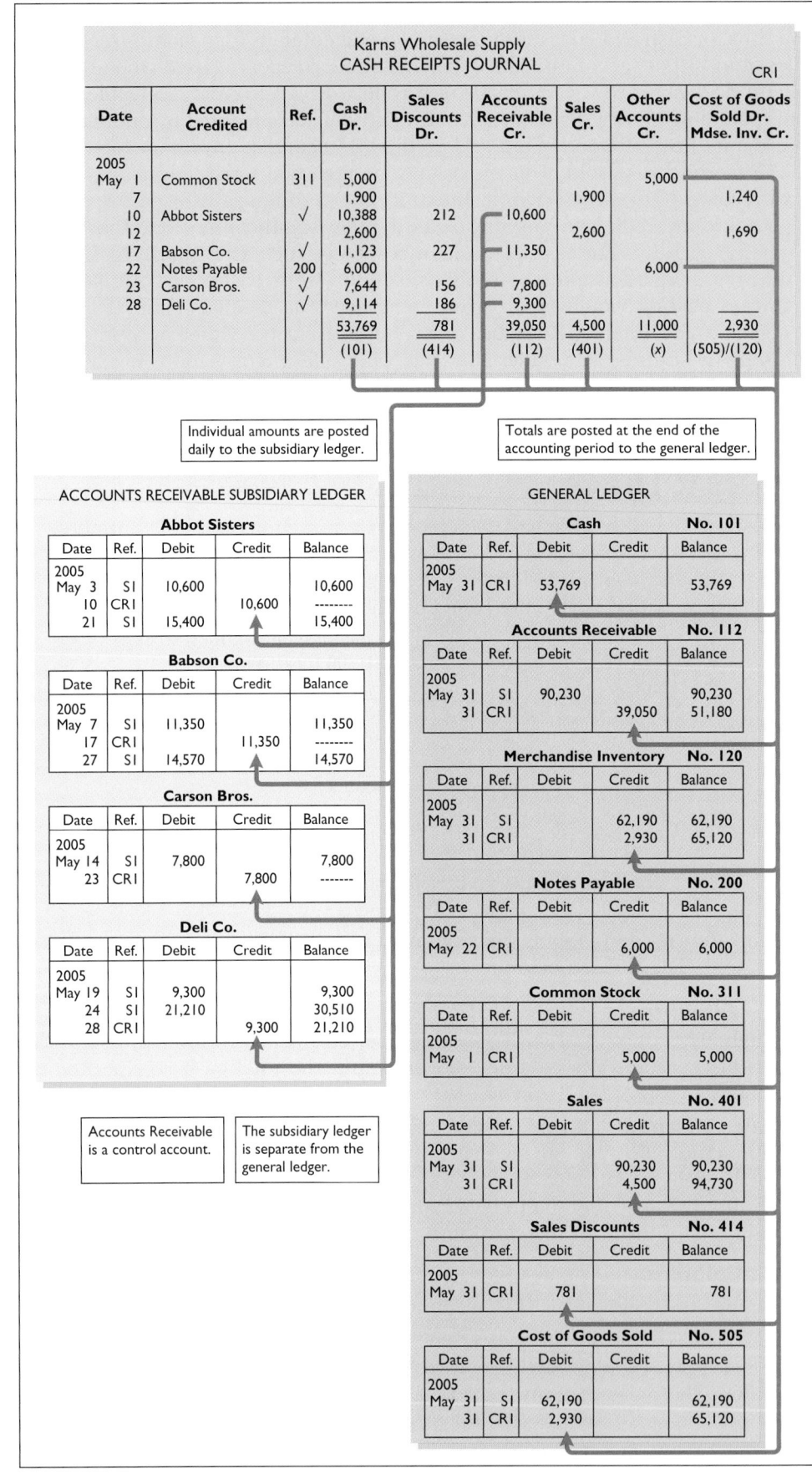

entry, $5,000 is entered as a credit to Common Stock. This column is often referred to as the **sundry accounts column**.

Debit and Credit Column:

6. **Cost of Goods Sold and Merchandise Inventory.** This column records debits to Cost of Goods Sold and credits to Merchandise Inventory.

In a multi-column journal, generally only one line is needed for each entry. Debit and credit amounts for each line must be equal. When the collection from Abbot Sisters on May 10 is journalized, for example, three amounts are indicated. Note also that the Account Credited column is used to identify both general ledger and subsidiary ledger account titles. General ledger accounts are illustrated in the May 1 and May 22 entries. A subsidiary account is illustrated in the May 10 entry for the collection from Abbot Sisters.

When the journalizing of a multi-column journal has been completed, the amount columns are totaled, and the totals are compared to prove the equality of debits and credits. The proof of the equality of Karns's cash receipts journal is shown in Illustration E-9. Totaling the columns of a journal and proving the equality of the totals is called **footing** and **cross-footing** a journal.

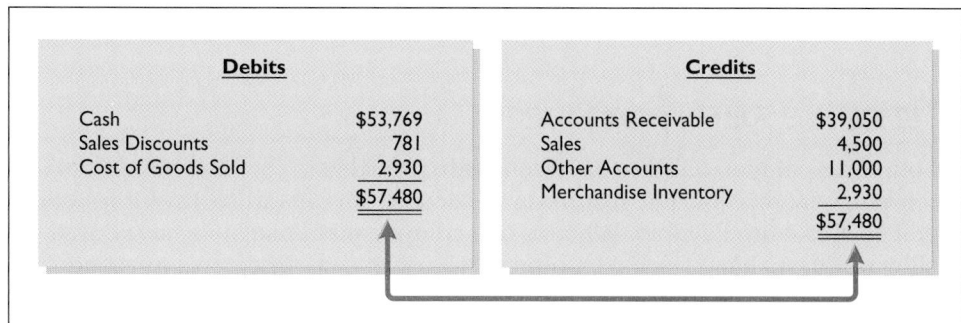

Illustration E-9 Proving the equality of the cash receipts journal

Debits		Credits	
Cash	$53,769	Accounts Receivable	$39,050
Sales Discounts	781	Sales	4,500
Cost of Goods Sold	2,930	Other Accounts	11,000
	$57,480	Merchandise Inventory	2,930
			$57,480

POSTING THE CASH RECEIPTS JOURNAL

Posting a multi-column journal involves the following steps.

1. All column totals except for the Other Accounts total are posted **once at the end of the month** to the account title(s) specified in the column heading (such as Cash or Accounts Receivable). Account numbers are entered below the column totals to show that they have been posted. Cash is posted to account No. 101, accounts receivable to account No. 112, merchandise inventory to account No. 120, sales to account No. 401, sales discounts to account No. 414, and cost of goods sold to account No. 505.

2. The **individual amounts comprising the Other Accounts total are posted separately** to the general ledger accounts specified in the Account Credited column. See, for example, the credit posting to Common Stock. The total amount of this column is not posted. The symbol (X) is inserted below the total to this column to indicate that the amount has not been posted.

3. The individual amounts in a column, posted in total to a control account (Accounts Receivable, in this case), are posted **daily to the subsidiary ledger** account specified in the Account Credited column. See, for example, the credit posting of $10,600 to Abbot Sisters.

The symbol **CR** is used in both the subsidiary and general ledgers to identify postings from the cash receipts journal.

STUDY OBJECTIVE
3
Indicate how a multi-column journal is posted.

PROVING THE LEDGERS

After posting of the cash receipts journal is completed, it is necessary to prove the ledgers. As shown in Illustration E-10, the general ledger totals are in agreement. Also, the sum of the subsidiary ledger balances equals the control account balance.

Illustration E-10 Proving the ledgers after posting the sales and the cash receipts journals

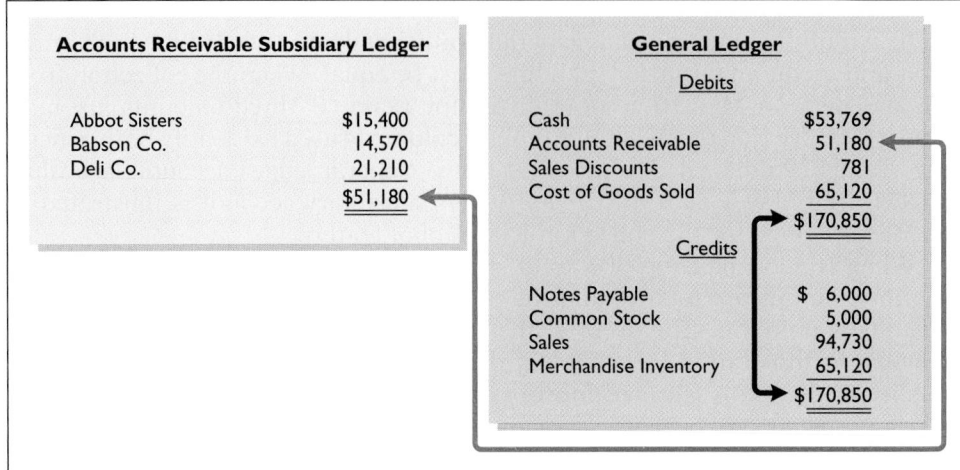

Purchases Journal

All purchases of merchandise on account are recorded in the **purchases journal**. Each entry in this journal results in a debit to Merchandise Inventory and a credit to Accounts Payable. When a one-column purchases journal is used (as in Illustration E-12, page E-11), other types of purchases on account and cash purchases cannot be journalized in it. For example, credit purchases of equipment or supplies must be recorded in the general journal. Likewise, all cash purchases are entered in the cash payments journal. As illustrated later, where credit purchases for items other than merchandise are numerous, the purchases journal is often expanded to a multi-column format.

JOURNALIZING CREDIT PURCHASES OF MERCHANDISE

Entries in the purchases journal are made from purchase invoices. The journalizing procedure is similar to that for a sales journal. In contrast to the sales journal, the purchases journal may not have an invoice number column, because invoices received from different suppliers will not be in numerical sequence. To assure that all purchase invoices are recorded, some companies consecutively number each invoice upon receipt and then use an internal document number column in the purchases journal.

Karns Wholesale Supply made the assumed credit purchases shown in Illustration E-11. The purchases journal for Karns Wholesale Supply is shown in Illustration E-12.

Illustration E-11 Credit purchases transactions

Date	Supplier	Amount
5/6	Jasper Manufacturing Inc.	$11,000
5/10	Eaton and Howe Inc.	7,200
5/14	Fabor and Son	6,900
5/19	Jasper Manufacturing Inc.	17,500
5/26	Fabor and Son	8,700
5/29	Eaton and Howe Inc.	12,600

Illustration E-12
Journalizing and posting
the purchases journal

Karns Wholesale Supply
PURCHASES JOURNAL
P1

Date	Account Credited	Terms	Ref.	Merchandise Inventory Dr. Accounts Payable Cr.
2005				
May 6	Jasper Manufacturing Inc.	2/10, n/30	√	11,000
10	Eaton and Howe Inc.	3/10, n/30	√	7,200
14	Fabor and Son	1/10, n/30	√	6,900
19	Jasper Manufacturing Inc.	2/10, n/30	√	17,500
26	Fabor and Son	1/10, n/30	√	8,700
29	Eaton and Howe Inc.	3/10, n/30	√	12,600
				63,900
				(120)/(201)

Helpful Hint A single-column purchases journal needs only to be footed to prove the equality of debits and credits.

Totals are posted at the end of the accounting period to the general ledger.

Individual amounts are posted daily to the subsidiary ledger.

ACCOUNTS PAYABLE SUBSIDIARY LEDGER

Eaton and Howe Inc.

Date	Ref.	Debit	Credit	Balance
2005				
May 10	P1		7,200	7,200
29	P1		12,600	19,800

Fabor and Son

Date	Ref.	Debit	Credit	Balance
2005				
May 14	P1		6,900	6,900
26	P1		8,700	15,600

Jasper Manufacturing Inc.

Date	Ref.	Debit	Credit	Balance
2005				
May 6	P1		11,000	11,000
19	P1		17,500	28,500

GENERAL LEDGER

Merchandise Inventory   No. 120

Date	Ref.	Debit	Credit	Balance
2005				
May 31	S1		62,190	62,190
31	CR1		2,930	65,120
31	P1	63,900		1,220

Accounts Payable   No. 201

Date	Ref.	Debit	Credit	Balance
2005				
May 31	P1		63,900	63,900

The subsidiary ledger is separate from the general ledger.

Accounts Payable is a control account.

POSTING THE PURCHASES JOURNAL

The procedures for posting the purchases journal are similar to those for the sales journal. In this case, postings are made **daily** to the **accounts payable ledger** and **monthly** to Merchandise Inventory and Accounts Payable in the general ledger. In both ledgers, P1 is used in the reference column to show that the postings are from page 1 of the purchases journal. Proof of the equality of the postings from the purchases journal to both ledgers is shown as follows.

Helpful Hint Postings to subsidiary ledger accounts are done daily because it is often necessary to know a current balance for the subsidiary accounts.

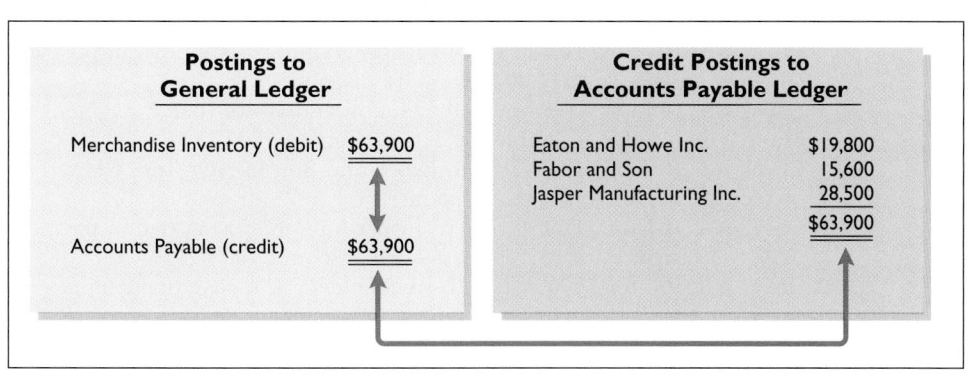

Postings to General Ledger		Credit Postings to Accounts Payable Ledger	
Merchandise Inventory (debit)	$63,900	Eaton and Howe Inc.	$19,800
		Fabor and Son	15,600
		Jasper Manufacturing Inc.	28,500
Accounts Payable (credit)	$63,900		$63,900

EXPANDING THE PURCHASES JOURNAL

Some companies expand the purchases journal to include all types of purchases on account. Instead of one column for merchandise inventory and accounts payable, they use a multiple-column format. The multi-column format usually includes a credit column for accounts payable and debit columns for purchases of merchandise, of office supplies, of store supplies, and other accounts. Illustration E-14 is an example of a multi-column purchases journal for Hanover Co. The posting procedures are similar to those illustrated earlier for posting the cash receipts journal.

Illustration E-14 Multi-column purchases journal

HANOVER CO.
Purchases Journal   P1

Date	Account Credited	Ref.	Accounts Payable Cr.	Merchandise Inventory Dr.	Office Supplies Dr.	Store Supplies Dr.	Other Accounts Dr. Account	Ref.	Amount
2005									
June 1	Signe Audio	✓	2,000		2,000				
3	Wright Co.	✓	1,500	1,500					
5	Orange Tree Co.	✓	2,600				Equipment	157	2,600
30	Sue's Business Forms	✓	800			800			
			56,600	43,000	7,500	1,200			4,900

Cash Payments Journal

All disbursements of cash are entered in a **cash payments journal**. Entries are made from prenumbered checks. Because cash payments are made for various purposes, the cash payments journal has multiple columns. A four-column journal is shown in Illustration E-15 (next page).

JOURNALIZING CASH PAYMENTS TRANSACTIONS

The procedures for journalizing transactions in this journal are similar to those described earlier for the cash receipts journal. Each transaction is entered on one line, and for each line there must be equal debit and credit amounts. The entries in the cash payments journal in Illustration E-15 are based on the following transactions for Karns Wholesale Supply.

May 1   Check No. 101 for $1,200 issued for the annual premium on a fire insurance policy.

     3   Check No. 102 for $100 issued in payment of freight when terms were FOB shipping point.

     8   Check No. 103 for $4,400 issued for the purchase of merchandise.

    10   Check No. 104 for $10,780 sent to Jasper Manufacturing Inc. in payment of May 6 invoice for $11,000 less a 2% discount.

    19   Check No. 105 for $6,984 mailed to Eaton and Howe Inc. in payment of May 10 invoice for $7,200 less a 3% discount.

    23   Check No. 106 for $6,831 sent to Fabor and Son in payment of May 14 invoice for $6,900 less a 1% discount.

    28   Check No. 107 for $17,150 sent to Jasper Manufacturing Inc. in payment of May 19 invoice for $17,500 less a 2% discount.

    30   Check No. 108 for $500 issued to stockholders as a cash dividend.

Note that whenever an amount is entered in the Other Accounts column, a specific general ledger account must be identified in the Account Debited column.

Illustration E-15
Journalizing and posting
the cash payments journal

Karns Wholesale Supply
CASH PAYMENTS JOURNAL

CP1

Date	Ck. No.	Account Debited	Ref.	Other Accounts Dr.	Accounts Payable Dr.	Merchandise Inventory Cr.	Cash Cr.
2005							
May 1	101	Prepaid Insurance	130	1,200			1,200
3	102	Mdse. Inventory	120	100			100
8	103	Mdse. Inventory	120	4,400			4,400
10	104	Jasper Manuf. Inc.	✓		11,000	220	10,780
19	105	Eaton & Howe Inc.	✓		7,200	216	6,984
23	106	Fabor and Son	✓		6,900	69	6,831
28	107	Jasper Manuf. Inc.	✓		17,500	350	17,150
30	108	Dividends	332	500			500
				6,200	42,600	855	47,945
				(x)	(201)	(120)	(101)

Individual amounts are posted daily to the subsidiary ledger.	Totals are posted at the end of the accounting period to the general ledger.

ACCOUNTS PAYABLE SUBSIDIARY LEDGER

Eaton and Howe Inc.

Date	Ref.	Debit	Credit	Balance
2005				
May 10	P1		7,200	7,200
19	CP1	7,200		-------
29	P1		12,600	12,600

Fabor and Son

Date	Ref.	Debit	Credit	Balance
2005				
May 14	P1		6,900	6,900
23	CP1	6,900		-------
26	P1		8,700	8,700

Jasper Manufacturing Inc.

Date	Ref.	Debit	Credit	Balance
2005				
May 6	P1		11,000	11,000
10	CP1	11,000		--------
19	P1		17,500	17,500
28	CP1	17,500		--------

Accounts Payable is a control account.	The subsidiary ledger is separate from the general ledger.

GENERAL LEDGER

Cash   No. 101

Date	Ref.	Debit	Credit	Balance
2005				
May 31	CR1	53,769		53,769
31	CP1		47,945	5,824

Merchandise Inventory   No. 120

Date	Ref.	Debit	Credit	Balance
2005				
May 3	CP1	100		100
8	CP1	4,400		4,500
31	S1		62,190	(57,690)
31	CR1		2,930	(60,620)
31	P1	63,900		3,280
31	CP1		855	2,425

Prepaid Insurance   No. 130

Date	Ref.	Debit	Credit	Balance
2005				
May 1	CP1	1,200		1,200

Accounts Payable   No. 201

Date	Ref.	Debit	Credit	Balance
2005				
May 31	P1		63,900	63,900
31	CP1	42,600		21,300

Dividends   No. 332

Date	Ref.	Debit	Credit	Balance
2005				
May 30	CP1	500		500

The entries for checks No. 101, 102, and 103 illustrate this situation. Similarly, a subsidiary account must be identified in the Account Debited column whenever an amount is entered in the Accounts Payable column. See, for example, the entry for check No. 104.

After the cash payments have been journalized, the columns are totaled. The totals are then balanced to prove the equality of debits and credits.

POSTING THE CASH PAYMENTS JOURNAL

The procedures for posting the cash payments journal are similar to those for the cash receipts journal. The amounts recorded in the Accounts Payable column are posted individually to the subsidiary ledger and in total to the control account. Merchandise Inventory and Cash are posted only in total at the end of the month. Transactions in the Other Accounts column are posted individually to the appropriate account(s) affected. No totals are posted for this column.

The posting of the cash payments journal is shown in Illustration E-15 (on the previous page). Note that the symbol **CP** is used as the posting reference. After postings are completed, the equality of the debit and credit balances in the general ledger should be determined. In addition, the control account balances should agree with the subsidiary ledger total balance. The agreement of these balances is shown in Illustration E-16.

Illustration E-16 Proving the ledgers after postings from the sales, cash receipts, purchases, and cash payments journals

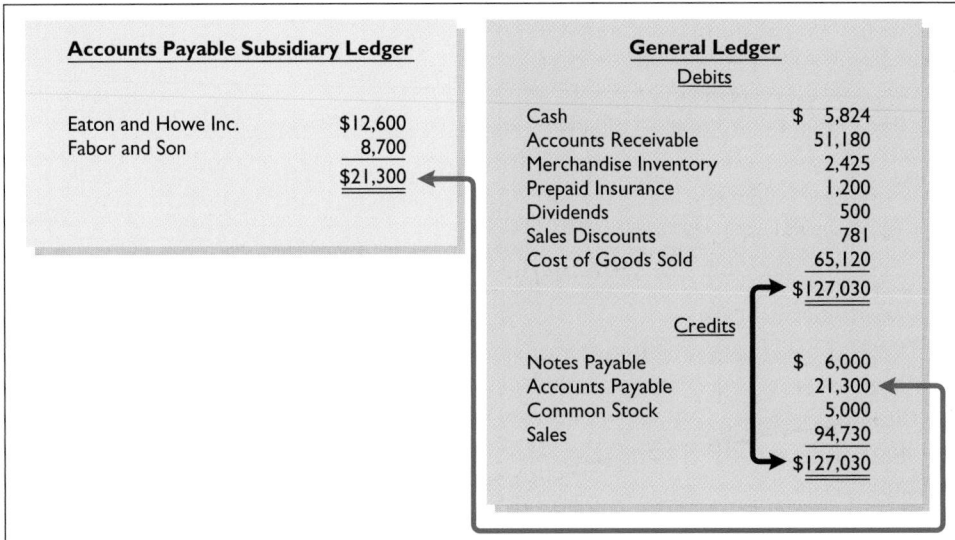

Accounts Payable Subsidiary Ledger	
Eaton and Howe Inc.	$12,600
Fabor and Son	8,700
	$21,300

General Ledger

Debits

Cash	$ 5,824
Accounts Receivable	51,180
Merchandise Inventory	2,425
Prepaid Insurance	1,200
Dividends	500
Sales Discounts	781
Cost of Goods Sold	65,120
	$127,030

Credits

Notes Payable	$ 6,000
Accounts Payable	21,300
Common Stock	5,000
Sales	94,730
	$127,030

Effects of Special Journals on General Journal

Special journals for sales, purchases, and cash substantially reduce the number of entries that are made in the general journal. **Only transactions that cannot be entered in a special journal are recorded in the general journal.** For example, the general journal may be used to record such transactions as granting of credit to a customer for a sales return or allowance, granting of credit from a supplier for purchases returned, acceptance of a note receivable from a customer, and purchase of equipment by issuing a note payable. Also, correcting, adjusting, and closing entries are made in the general journal.

The general journal has columns for date, account title and explanation, reference, and debit and credit amounts. When control and subsidiary accounts are not involved, the procedures for journalizing and posting of transactions are the same as those described in earlier chapters. When control and subsidiary accounts are involved, two changes from the earlier procedures are required:

1. In **journalizing**, both the control and the subsidiary accounts must be identified.

2. In **posting**, there must be a **dual posting**: once to the control account and once to the subsidiary account.

To illustrate, assume that on May 31, Karns Wholesale Supply returns $500 of merchandise for credit to Fabor and Son. The entry in the general journal and the posting of the entry are shown in Illustration E-17. Note that if cash is received instead of credit granted on this return, then the transaction is recorded in the cash receipts journal.

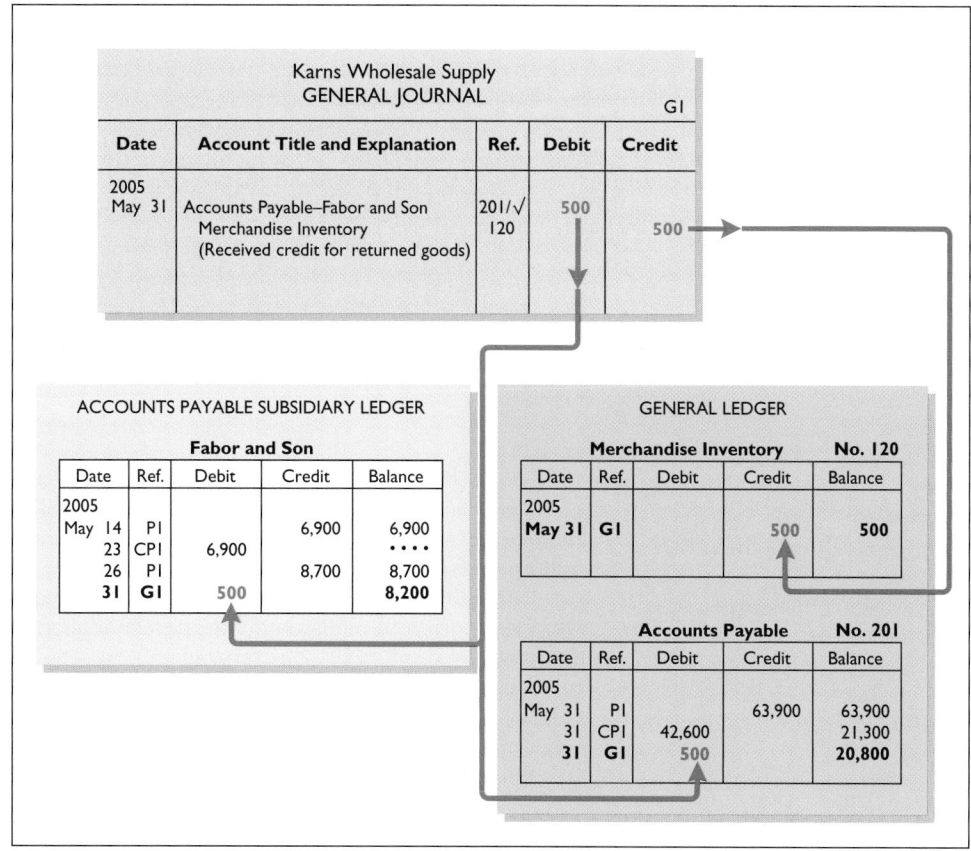

Illustration E-17
Journalizing and posting the general journal

Observe in the journal that two accounts are indicated for the debit, and two postings ("201/✓") are indicated in the reference column. One amount is posted to the control account and the other to the creditor's account in the subsidiary ledger.

Summary of Study Objectives

1 *Describe the nature and purpose of a subsidiary ledger.* A subsidiary ledger is a group of accounts with a common characteristic. It facilitates the recording process by freeing the general ledger from details of individual balances.

2 *Explain how special journals are used in journalizing.* A special journal is used to group similar types of transactions. In a special journal, generally only one line is used to record a complete transaction.

3 *Indicate how a multi-column journal is posted.* In posting a multi-column journal:
(a) All column totals except for the Other Accounts column are posted once at the end of the month

to the account title specified in the column heading.
(b) The total of the Other Accounts column is not posted. Instead, the individual amounts comprising the total are posted separately to the general ledger accounts specified in the Account Credited column.
(c) The individual amounts in a column posted in total to a control account are posted daily to the subsidiary ledger accounts specified in the Account Credited column.

Glossary

Accounts payable (creditors') subsidiary ledger A subsidiary ledger that collects transaction data of individual creditors. (p. E-1).

Accounts receivable (customers') subsidiary ledger A subsidiary ledger that collects transaction data of individual customers. (p. E-1).

Cash payments journal A special journal used to record all cash paid. (p. E-12).

Cash receipts journal A special journal used to record all cash received. (p. E-6).

Control account An account in the general ledger that summarizes a subsidiary ledger. (p. E-2).

Purchases journal A special journal used to record all purchases of merchandise on account. (p. E-10).

Sales journal A special journal used to record all sales of merchandise on account. (p. E-4).

Special journal A journal that is used to record similar types of transactions, such as all credit sales. (p. E-3).

Subsidiary ledger A group of accounts with a common characteristic. (p. E-1).

Questions

1. What are the advantages of using subsidiary ledgers?

2. (a) When are postings normally made to (1) the subsidiary accounts and (2) the general ledger control accounts? (b) Describe the relationship between a control account and a subsidiary ledger.

3. Identify and explain the four special journals discussed in the chapter. List an advantage of using each of these journals rather than using only a general journal.

4. A. Mega Company uses special journals. A sale made on account to K. Hansen for $435 was recorded in a sales journal. A few days later, K. Hansen returns $70 worth of merchandise for credit. Where should A. Mega Company record the sales return? Why?

5. A $500 purchase of merchandise on account from Julia Company was properly recorded in the purchases journal. When posted, however, the amount recorded in the subsidiary ledger was $50. How might this error be discovered?

6. Why would special journals used in different businesses not be identical in format? Can you think of a business that would maintain a cash receipts journal but not include a column for accounts receivable?

7. The cash and the accounts receivable columns in the cash receipts journal were mistakenly overadded by $4,000 at the end of the month. (a) Will the customers' ledger agree with the Accounts Receivable control account? (b) Assuming no other errors, will the trial balance totals be equal?

8. One column total of a special journal is posted at month-end to only two general ledger accounts. One of these two accounts is Accounts Receivable. What is the name of this special journal? What is the other general ledger account to which that same month-end total is posted?

9. In what journal would the following transactions be recorded? (Assume that a two-column sales journal and a single-column purchases journal are used.)
   (a) Recording of depreciation expense for the year.
   (b) Credit given to a customer for merchandise purchased on credit and returned.
   (c) Sales of merchandise for cash.
   (d) Sales of merchandise on account.
   (e) Collection of cash on account from a customer.
   (f) Purchase of office supplies on account.

10. In what journal would the following transactions be recorded? (Assume that a two-column sales journal and a single-column purchases journal are used.)
   (a) Cash received from signing a note payable.
   (b) Investment of cash by stockholders of the company.
   (c) Closing of the expense accounts at the end of the year.
   (d) Purchase of merchandise on account.
   (e) Credit received for merchandise purchased and returned to supplier.
   (f) Payment of cash on account due a supplier.

11. What transactions might be included in a multiple-column purchases journal that would not be included in a single-column purchases journal?

12. Give an example of a transaction in the general journal that causes an entry to be posted twice (i.e., to two accounts), one in the general ledger, the other in the subsidiary ledger. Does this affect the debit/credit equality of the general ledger?

13. Give some examples of appropriate general journal transactions for an organization using special journals.

Brief Exercises

BEE-1 Presented below is information related to Bradley Company for its first month of operations. Identify the balances that appear in the accounts receivable subsidiary ledger and the accounts receivable balance that appears in the general ledger at the end of January.

Credit Sales			**Cash Collections**		
Jan. 7	Avon Co.	$8,000	Jan. 17	Avon Co.	$7,000
15	Barto Co.	6,000	24	Barto Co.	5,000
23	Cecil Co.	9,000	29	Cecil Co.	9,000

BEE-2 Identify in what ledger (general or subsidiary) each of the following accounts is shown.
1. Rent Expense
2. Accounts Receivable—Olsen
3. Notes Payable
4. Accounts Payable—Kerns

BEE-3 Identify the journal in which each of the following transactions is recorded.
1. Cash sales
2. Payment of cash dividends
3. Cash purchase of land
4. Credit sales
5. Purchase of merchandise on account
6. Receipt of cash for services performed

BEE-4 Indicate whether each of the following debits and credits is included in the cash receipts journal. (Use "Yes" or "No" to answer this question.)
1. Debit to Sales
2. Credit to Merchandise Inventory
3. Credit to Accounts Receivable
4. Debit to Accounts Payable

BEE-5 Steering Computer Components Inc. uses a multi-column cash receipts journal. Indicate which column(s) is/are posted only in total, only daily, or both in total and daily.
1. Accounts Receivable
2. Sales Discounts
3. Cash
4. Other Accounts

BEE-6 Cohen Co. uses special journals and a general journal. Identify the journal in which each of the following transactions is recorded.
(a) Purchased equipment on account.
(b) Purchased merchandise on account.
(c) Paid utility expense in cash.
(d) Sold merchandise on account.

BEE-7 Identify the special journal(s) in which the following column headings appear.
1. Sales Discounts Dr.
2. Accounts Receivable Cr.
3. Cash Dr.
4. Sales Cr.
5. Merchandise Inventory Dr.

Exercises

EE-1 Yan Company uses both special journals and a general journal as described in this appendix. On June 30, after all monthly postings had been completed, the Accounts Receivable control account in the general ledger had a debit balance of $350,000; the Accounts Payable control account had a credit balance of $87,000.

The July transactions recorded in the special journals are summarized below. No entries affecting accounts receivable and accounts payable were recorded in the general journal for July.

Sales journal	Total sales $161,400
Purchases journal	Total purchases $54,360
Cash receipts journal	Accounts receivable column total $141,000
Cash payments journal	Accounts payable column total $47,500

Instructions
(a) What is the balance of the Accounts Receivable control account after the monthly postings on July 31?

(b) What is the balance of the Accounts Payable control account after the monthly postings on July 31?

(c) To what account(s) is the column total of $161,400 in the sales journal posted?

(d) To what account(s) is the accounts receivable column total of $141,000 in the cash receipts journal posted?

Explain postings to subsidiary ledger.
(SO 1)

EE-2 Presented below is the subsidiary accounts receivable account of Warren Moyer.

Date	Ref.	Debit	Credit	Balance
2002				
Sept. 2	S31	61,000		61,000
9	G4		14,000	47,000
27	CR8		47,000	—

Instructions

Write a memo that explains each transaction.

Post various journals to control and subsidiary accounts.
(SO 1, 2)

EE-3 On September 1 the balance of the Accounts Receivable control account in the general ledger of Odesto Company was $11,960. The customers' subsidiary ledger contained account balances as follows: Edmonds $2,440, Park $2,640, Roemer $2,060, Schulz $4,820. At the end of September the various journals contained the following information.

Sales journal: Sales to Schulz $800; to Edmonds $1,350; to Henry $1,030; to Roemer $1,100.

Cash receipts journal: Cash received from Roemer $1,310; from Schulz $2,300; from Henry $410; from Park $1,800; from Edmonds $1,240.

General journal: An allowance is granted to Schulz $220.

Instructions

(a) Set up control and subsidiary accounts and enter the beginning balances. Do not construct the journals.

(b) Post the various journals. Post the items as individual items or as totals, whichever would be the appropriate procedure. (No sales discounts given.)

(c) Prepare a list of customers and prove the agreement of the controlling account with the subsidiary ledger at September 30, 2005.

Record transactions in sales and purchases journals.
(SO 1, 2)

EE-4 Hurley Company uses special journals and a general journal. The following transactions occurred during September 2005.

Sept. 2 Sold merchandise on account to S. Rusch, invoice no. 101, $480, terms n/30. The cost of the merchandise sold was $300.

10 Purchased merchandise on account from L. Dayne $600, terms 2/10, n/30.

12 Purchased office equipment on account from B. Piazza $6,500.

21 Sold merchandise on account to L. Perez, invoice no. 102 for $800, terms 2/10, n/30. The cost of the merchandise sold was $480.

25 Purchased merchandise on account from F. Sage $900, terms n/30.

27 Sold merchandise to M. Deitrich for $700 cash. The cost of the merchandise sold was $420.

Instructions

(a) Draw a sales journal (see Illustration E-6) and a single-column purchase journal (see Illustration E-12). (Use page 1 for each journal.)

(b) Record the transaction(s) for September that should be journalized in the sales journal and the purchases journal.

Record transactions in cash receipts and cash payments journals.
(SO 1, 2)

EE-5 Pena Co. uses special journals and a general journal. The following transactions occurred during May 2005.

May 1 R. Pena invested $60,000 cash in the business in exchange for common stock.

2 Sold merchandise to J. Simon for $6,000 cash. The cost of the merchandise sold was $4,200.

3 Purchased merchandise for $9,000 from L. M. Farr using check no. 101.

14 Paid salary to S. Little $700 by issuing check no. 102.
16 Sold merchandise on account to B. Jones for $900, terms n/30. The cost of the merchandise sold was $630.
22 A check of $9,000 is received from R. Dusto in full for invoice 101; no discount given.

Instructions

(a) Draw a multiple-column cash receipts journal (see Illustration E-8) and a multiple-column cash payments journal (see Illustration E-15). (Use page 1 for each journal.)

(b) Record the transaction(s) for May that should be journalized in the cash receipts journal and cash payments journal.

EE-6 Abbott Company uses the columnar cash journals illustrated in the textbook. In April, the following selected cash transactions occurred.

Explain journalizing in cash journals.
(SO 2)

1. Made a refund to a customer for the return of damaged goods.
2. Received collection from customer within the 3% discount period.
3. Purchased merchandise for cash.
4. Paid a creditor within the 3% discount period.
5. Received collection from customer after the 3% discount period had expired.
6. Paid freight on merchandise purchased.
7. Paid cash for office equipment.
8. Received cash refund from supplier for merchandise returned.
9. Paid cash dividend to stockholders.
10. Made cash sales.

Instructions

Indicate (a) the journal, and (b) the columns in the journal that should be used in recording each transaction.

EE-7 Santiago Company has the following selected transactions during March.

Journalize transactions in general journal and post.
(SO 1, 2)

Mar. 2 Purchased equipment costing $6,000 from Briggs Company on account.
5 Received credit memorandum for $300 from Sanchez Company for merchandise damaged in shipment to Santiago.
7 Issued a credit memorandum for $400 to Sparks Company for merchandise the customer returned. The returned merchandise had a cost of $260.

Santiago Company uses a one-column purchases journal, a sales journal, the columnar cash journals used in the text, and a general journal.

Instructions

(a) Journalize the transactions in the general journal.

(b) ▭▬▶ In a brief memo to the president of Santiago Company, explain the postings to the control and subsidiary accounts.

EE-8 Below are some typical transactions incurred by Heide Company.

Indicate journalizing in special journals.
(SO 2)

1. Payment of creditors on account.
2. Return of merchandise sold for credit.
3. Collection on account from customers.
4. Sale of land for cash.
5. Sale of merchandise on account.
6. Sale of merchandise for cash.
7. Received credit for merchandise purchased on credit.
8. Sales discount taken on goods sold.
9. Payment of employee wages.
10. Paid a cash dividend to stockholders.
11. Depreciation on building.
12. Purchase of office supplies for cash.
13. Purchase of merchandise on account.

Instructions

For each transaction, indicate whether it would normally be recorded in a cash receipts journal, cash payments journal, sales journal, single-column purchases journal, or general journal.

Explain posting to control account and subsidiary ledger.
(SO 1, 3)

EE-9 The general ledger of Williams Company contained the following Accounts Payable control account (in T-account form). Also shown is the related subsidiary ledger.

GENERAL LEDGER

Accounts Payable

Feb. 15	General journal	1,400	Feb.	1	Balance	26,025	
28	?	?		5	General journal	265	
				11	General journal	550	
				28	Purchases	13,900	
			Feb.	28	Balance	9,840	

ACCOUNTS PAYABLE LEDGER

Sealy

Feb. 28 Bal. 4,600	

Wolcott

Feb. 28 Bal. ?	

Gates

Feb. 28 Bal. 2,000	

Instructions

(a) Indicate the missing posting reference and amount in the control account, and the missing ending balance in the subsidiary ledger.

(b) Indicate the amounts in the control account that were dual-posted (i.e., posted to the control account and the subsidiary accounts).

Prepare purchases and general journals.
(SO 1, 2)

EE-10   Selected accounts from the ledgers of Juan Perez Company at July 31 showed the following.

GENERAL LEDGER

Store Equipment   No. 153

Date	Explanation	Ref.	Debit	Credit	Balance
July 1		G1	3,600		3,600

Merchandise Inventory   No. 120

Date	Explanation	Ref.	Debit	Credit	Balance
July 15		G1	400		400
18		G1		100	300
25		G1		200	100
31		P1	8,400		8,500

Accounts Payable   No. 201

Date	Explanation	Ref.	Debit	Credit	Balance
July 1		G1		3,600	3,600
15		G1		400	4,000
18		G1	100		3,900
25		G1	200		3,700
31		P1		8,400	12,100

ACCOUNTS PAYABLE LEDGER

Alou Equipment Co.

Date	Explanation	Ref.	Debit	Credit	Balance
July 1		G1		3,600	3,600

Dunlap Co.

Date	Explanation	Ref.	Debit	Credit	Balance
July 14		P1		1,100	1,100
25		G1	200		900

Benton Co.

Date	Explanation	Ref.	Debit	Credit	Balance
July 3		P1		2,000	2,000
20		P1		700	2,700

Emerick Co.

Date	Explanation	Ref.	Debit	Credit	Balance
July 12		P1		500	500
21		P1		600	1,100

Comerica Materials

Date	Explanation	Ref.	Debit	Credit	Balance
July 17		P1		1,400	1,400
18		G1	100		1,300
29		P1		2,100	3,400

Galant Transit

Date	Explanation	Ref.	Debit	Credit	Balance
July 15		G1		400	400

Instructions

From the data, prepare:

(a) the single-column purchases journal for July.

(b) the general journal entries for July.

EE-11   Valdez Products uses both special journals and a general journal as described in this appendix. Valdez also posts customers' accounts in the accounts receivable subsidiary ledger. The postings for the most recent month are included in the subsidiary T accounts below.

Determine correct posting amount to control account. (SO 3)

Ellie		
Bal.	340	250
	200	

Rambo		
Bal.	150	150
	290	

Panos		
Bal.	–0–	145
	145	

Tenant		
Bal.	120	120
	190	
	170	

Instructions

Determine the correct amount of the end-of-month posting from the sales journal to the Accounts Receivable control account.

Problems

PE-1   Lemon Company's chart of accounts includes the following selected accounts.

Journalize transactions in cash receipts journal; post to control account and subsidiary ledger. (SO 1, 2, 3)

Peachtree

101 Cash	401 Sales
112 Accounts Receivable	414 Sales Discounts
120 Merchandise Inventory	505 Cost of Goods Sold
311 Common Stock	

On April 1 the accounts receivable ledger of Lemon Company showed the following balances: Horner $1,550, Harris $1,200, Northeast Co. $2,900, and Smith $1,700. The April transactions involving the receipt of cash were as follows.

Apr. 1   Stockholders invested additional cash in the business, $6,000, for common stock.

4   Received check for payment of account from Smith less 2% cash discount.

5   Received check for $620 in payment of invoice no. 307 from Northeast Co.

8   Made cash sales of merchandise totaling $7,245. The cost of the merchandise sold was $4,347.

10   Received check for $800 in payment of invoice no. 309 from Horner.

11   Received cash refund from a supplier for damaged merchandise $550.

23   Received check for $1,500 in payment of invoice no. 310 from Northeast Co.

29   Received check for payment of account from Harris.

Instructions

(a) Journalize the transactions above in a six-column cash receipts journal with columns for Cash Dr., Sales Discounts Dr., Accounts Receivable Cr., Sales Cr., Other Accounts Cr., and Cost of Goods Sold Dr./Merchandise Inventory Cr. Foot and crossfoot the journal.

(a) Balancing totals $19,615

(b) Insert the beginning balances in the Accounts Receivable control and subsidiary accounts, and post the April transactions to these accounts.

(c) Prove the agreement of the control account and subsidiary account balances.

(c) Accounts receivable $ 1,530

Journalize transactions in cash payments journal; post to control account and subsidiary ledgers.
(SO 1, 2, 3)

PE-2 Simpson Company's chart of accounts includes the following selected accounts.

101 Cash	201 Accounts Payable
120 Merchandise Inventory	332 Dividends
130 Prepaid Insurance	505 Cost of Goods Sold
157 Equipment	

On October 1 the accounts payable ledger of Simpson Company showed the following balances: Hester Company $1,700, Milo Co. $2,500, Ontario Co. $1,400, and Pagan Company $3,700. The October transactions involving the payment of cash were as follows.

Oct. 1 Purchased merchandise, check no. 63, $700.
3 Purchased equipment, check no. 64, $800.
5 Paid Hester Company balance due of $1,700, less 2% discount, check no. 65, $1,666.
10 Purchased merchandise, check no. 66, $2,250.
15 Paid Ontario Co. balance due of $1,400, check no. 67.
16 A cash dividend is paid in the amount of $400, check no. 68.
19 Paid Milo Co. in full for invoice no. 610, $1,400 less 2% cash discount, check no. 69, $1,372.
29 Paid Pagan Company in full for invoice no. 264, $2,600, check no. 70.

Instructions

(a) Balancing totals $11,250

(a) Journalize the transactions above in a four-column cash payments journal with columns for Other Accounts Dr., Accounts Payable Dr., Merchandise Inventory Cr., and Cash Cr. Foot and crossfoot the journal.

(b) Insert the beginning balances in the Accounts Payable control and subsidiary accounts, and post the October transactions to these accounts.

(c) Accounts payable $ 2,200

(c) Prove the agreement of the control account and the subsidiary account balances.

Journalize transactions in multi-column purchases journal; post to the general and subsidiary ledgers.
(SO 1, 2, 3)

Peachtree

PE-3 The chart of accounts of Hernandez Company includes the following selected accounts.

112 Accounts Receivable	401 Sales
120 Merchandise Inventory	412 Sales Returns and Allowances
126 Supplies	505 Cost of Goods Sold
157 Equipment	610 Advertising Expense
201 Accounts Payable	

In July the following selected transactions were completed. All purchases and sales were on account. The cost of all merchandise sold was 70% of the sales price.

July 1 Purchased merchandise from Denton Company $7,000.
2 Received freight bill from Johnson Shipping on Denton purchase $400.
3 Made sales to Lyons Company $1,300, and to Franklin Bros. $1,900.
5 Purchased merchandise from Grant Company $3,200.
8 Received credit on merchandise returned to Grant Company $300.
13 Purchased store supplies from Brent Supply $720.
15 Purchased merchandise from Denton Company $3,600 and from Ruiz Company $2,900.
16 Made sales to Martin Company $3,450 and to Franklin Bros. $1,570.
18 Received bill for advertising from Marlin Advertisements $600.
21 Made sales to Lyons Company $310 and to Randee Company $2,300.
22 Granted allowance to Lyons Company for merchandise damaged in shipment $40.
24 Purchased merchandise from Grant Company $3,000.
26 Purchased equipment from Brent Supply $600.
28 Received freight bill from Johnson Shipping on Grant purchase of July 24, $380.
30 Made sales to Martin Company $4,900.

Instructions

(a) Purchases journal:
  Accounts Payable $22,400
  Sales journal $15,730

(a) Journalize the transactions above in a purchases journal, a sales journal, and a general journal. The purchases journal should have the following column headings:

Date, Account Credited (Debited), Ref., Other Accounts Dr., and Merchandise Inventory Dr., Accounts Payable Cr.

(b) Post to both the general and subsidiary ledger accounts. (Assume that all accounts have zero beginning balances.)

(c) Prove the agreement of the control and subsidiary accounts.

(c) Accounts Receivable $15,690

PE-4 Selected accounts from the chart of accounts of Clark Company are shown below.

Journalize transactions in special journals.
(SO 1, 2, 3)

101 Cash	401 Sales
112 Accounts Receivable	412 Sales Returns and Allowances
120 Merchandise Inventory	414 Sales Discounts
126 Supplies	505 Cost of Goods Sold
157 Equipment	726 Salaries Expense
201 Accounts Payable	

The cost of all merchandise sold was 60% of the sales price. During January, Clark completed the following transactions.

Jan. 3 Purchased merchandise on account from Bell Co. $10,000.
4 Purchased supplies for cash $80.
4 Sold merchandise on account to Gilbert $7,250, invoice no. 371, terms 1/10, n/30.
5 Issued a debit memorandum to Bell Co. and returned $300 worth of damaged goods.
6 Made cash sales for the week totaling $3,150.
8 Purchased merchandise on account from Law Co. $4,500.
9 Sold merchandise on account to Mays Corp. $5,800, invoice no. 372, terms 1/10, n/30.
11 Purchased merchandise on account from Hoble Co. $3,700.
13 Paid in full Bell Co. on account less a 2% discount.
13 Made cash sales for the week totaling $5,340.
15 Received payment from Mays Corp. for invoice no. 372.
15 Paid semi-monthly salaries of $14,300 to employees.
17 Received payment from Gilbert for invoice no. 371.
17 Sold merchandise on account to Amber Co. $1,200, invoice no. 373, terms 1/10, n/30.
19 Purchased equipment on account from Johnson Corp. $5,500.
20 Made cash sales for the week totaling $3,200.
20 Paid in full Law Co. on account less a 2% discount.
23 Purchased merchandise on account from Bell Co. $7,800.
24 Purchased merchandise on account from Levine Corp. $4,690.
27 Made cash sales for the week totaling $3,730.
30 Received payment from Amber Co. for invoice no. 373.
31 Paid semi-monthly salaries of $13,200 to employees.
31 Sold merchandise on account to Gilbert $9,330, invoice no. 374, terms 1/10, n/30.

Clark Company uses the following journals.
1. Sales journal.
2. Single-column purchases journal.
3. Cash receipts journal with columns for Cash Dr., Sales Discounts Dr., Accounts Receivable Cr., Sales Cr., Other Accounts Cr., and Cost of Goods Sold Dr./Merchandise Inventory Cr.
4. Cash payments journal with columns for Other Accounts Dr., Accounts Payable Dr., Merchandise Inventory Cr., and Cash Cr.
5. General journal.

Instructions
Using the selected accounts provided:
(a) Record the January transactions in the appropriate journal noted.
(b) Foot and crossfoot all special journals.
(c) Show how postings would be made by placing ledger account numbers and check-marks as needed in the journals. (Actual posting to ledger accounts is not required.)

(a) Sales journal $23,580

Journalize in sales and cash receipts journals; post; prepare a trial balance; prove control to subsidiary; prepare adjusting entries; prepare an adjusted trial balance.
(SO 1, 2, 3)

Peachtree

PE-5 Presented below are the purchases and cash payments journals for Collins Co. for its first month of operations.

PURCHASES JOURNAL			**P1**

Date	Account Credited	Ref.	Merchandise Inventory Dr. Accounts Payable Cr.
July 4	J. Dixon		6,800
5	W. Engel		7,500
11	R. Gamble		3,920
13	M. Hill		15,300
20	D. Jacob		8,800
			42,320

CASH PAYMENTS JOURNAL						**CP1**

Date	Account Debited	Ref.	Other Accounts Dr.	Accounts Payable Dr.	Merchandise Inventory Cr.	Cash Cr.
July 4	Store Supplies		600			600
10	W. Engel			7,500	75	7,425
11	Prepaid Rent		6,000			6,000
15	J. Dixon			6,800		6,800
19	Dividends		2,500			2,500
21	M. Hill			15,300	153	15,147
			9,100	29,600	228	38,472

In addition, the following transactions have not been journalized for July. The cost of all merchandise sold was 65% of the sales price.

July 1	The founder, R. Collins, invests $80,000 in cash in exchange for common stock.
6	Sell merchandise on account to Hardy Co. $5,400 terms 1/10, n/30.
7	Make cash sales totaling $4,000.
8	Sell merchandise on account to D. Wasburn $3,600, terms 1/10, n/30.
10	Sell merchandise on account to L. Lemansky $4,900, terms 1/10, n/30.
13	Receive payment in full from D. Wasburn.
16	Receive payment in full from L. Lemansky.
20	Receive payment in full from Hardy Co.
21	Sell merchandise on account to S. Kane $4,000, terms 1/10, n/30.
29	Returned damaged goods to J. Dixon and received cash refund of $450.

Instructions
(a) Open the following accounts in the general ledger.

101 Cash	332 Dividends
112 Accounts Receivable	401 Sales
120 Merchandise Inventory	414 Sales Discounts
127 Store Supplies	505 Cost of Goods Sold
131 Prepaid Rent	631 Supplies Expense
201 Accounts Payable	729 Rent Expense
311 Common Stock	

(b) Cash receipts
  journal balancing
  totals $98,350

(b) Journalize the transactions that have not been journalized in the sales journal, the cash receipts journal (see Illustration E-8), and the general journal.
(c) Post to the accounts receivable and accounts payable subsidiary ledgers. Follow the sequence of transactions as shown in the problem.

(d) Post the individual entries and totals to the general ledger.

(e) Prepare a trial balance at July 31, 2005.

(f) Determine whether the subsidiary ledgers agree with the control accounts in the general ledger.

(g) The following adjustments at the end of July are necessary.

(1) A count of supplies indicates that $140 is still on hand.

(2) Recognize rent expense for July, $500.

Prepare the necessary entries in the general journal. Post the entries to the general ledger.

(h) Prepare an adjusted trial balance at July 31, 2005.

PE-6 The post-closing trial balance for Alomar Co. is as follows.

Journalize in special journals; post; prepare a trial balance.
(SO 1, 2, 3)

ALOMAR CO.
Post-Closing Trial Balance
December 31, 2005

	Debit	Credit
Cash	$ 41,500	
Accounts Receivable	15,000	
Notes Receivable	45,000	
Merchandise Inventory	23,000	
Equipment	6,450	
Accumulated Depreciation—Equipment		$ 1,500
Accounts Payable		43,000
Common Stock		86,450
	$130,950	$130,950

The subsidiary ledgers contain the following information: (1) accounts receivable—R. Barton $2,500, B. Cole $7,500, S. Devine $5,000; (2) accounts payable—S. Field $10,000, R. Grilson $18,000, and D. Harms $15,000. The cost of all merchandise sold was 65% of the sales price.

The transactions for January 2006 are as follows.

Jan. 3   Sell merchandise to B. Senton $4,000, terms 2/10, n/30.

     5   Purchase merchandise from S. Warren $2,500, terms 2/10, n/30.

     7   Receive a check from S. Devine $3,500.

   11   Pay freight on merchandise purchased $300.

   12   Pay rent of $1,000 for January.

   13   Receive payment in full from B. Senton.

   14   Post all entries to the subsidiary ledgers. Issue a credit memo to acknowledge receipt of damaged merchandise of $700 returned by R. Barton.

   15   Send D. Harms a check for $14,850 in full payment of account, discount $150.

   17   Purchase merchandise from D. Lapeska $1,600, terms 2/10, n/30.

   18   Pay sales salaries of $2,800 and office salaries $1,500.

   20   Give R. Grilson a 60-day note for $18,000 in full payment of account payable.

   23   Total cash sales amount to $8,600.

   24   Post all entries to the subsidiary ledgers. Sell merchandise on account to B. Cole $7,700, terms 1/10, n/30.

   27   Send S. Warren a check for $950.

   29   Receive payment on a note of $40,000 from S. Lava.

   30   Return merchandise of $500 to D. Lapeska for credit. Post all journals to the subsidiary ledger.

Instructions

(a) Open general and subsidiary ledger accounts for the following.

101 Cash	311 Common Stock
112 Accounts Receivable	401 Sales
115 Notes Receivable	412 Sales Returns and Allowances
120 Merchandise Inventory	414 Sales Discounts
157 Equipment	505 Cost of Goods Sold
158 Accumulated Depreciation—Equipment	726 Salaries Expense
200 Notes Payable	727 Office Salaries Expense
201 Accounts Payable	729 Rent Expense

(b) Record the January transactions in a sales journal, a single-column purchases journal, a cash receipts journal (see Illustration E-8), a cash payments journal (see Illustration E-15), and a general journal.

(c) Post the appropriate amounts to the general ledger.

(d) Prepare a trial balance at January 31, 2006.

(e) Determine whether the subsidiary ledgers agree with controlling accounts in the general ledger.

Accounting for Sole Proprietorships

STUDY OBJECTIVES

After studying this appendix,
you should be able to:

1 Identify the differences in equity accounts between a corporation and a sole proprietorship.

2 Understand what accounts increase and decrease owner's equity.

3 Describe the differences between a retained earnings statement and an owner's equity statement.

4 Explain the process of closing the books for a sole proprietorship.

Chapter 1 identified three forms of business organization. Two forms, the sole proprietorship and the partnership, were discussed only briefly. Emphasis was placed on the corporate form in Chapter 1 as well as in subsequent chapters.

The purpose of this appendix is to discuss and illustrate the accounting for the operations and financial condition of a sole proprietorship. **The primary difference between accounting and reporting for a sole proprietorship and a corporation involves accounting for equity transactions.** Because a sole proprietorship has a single owner rather than numerous stockholders, a sole proprietorship uses a permanent **owner's capital account**, such as "Sally Jones, Capital," instead of Common Stock and Retained Earnings. In a sole proprietorship there is no need to separate owner's investments from net income retained for dividends because the sole proprietor does not declare or receive dividends. Instead, withdrawals by the owner of cash or other assets from the business for personal use are recorded in a temporary **drawing** account. The different equity accounts are contrasted as shown in Illustration F-1.

STUDY OBJECTIVE
1
Identify the differences in equity accounts between a corporation and a sole proprietorship.

Corporation	Sole Proprietorship
Stockholders' equity	Owner's equity
Common stock	Owner's Name, Capital
Retained earnings	

Illustration F-1
Equity section of the balance sheet—corporation vs. proprietorship

For purposes of comparing the accounting for a corporation with a sole proprietorship, the illustrations in this Appendix F assume a sole proprietorship owned by R. Neal and named Sierra Company. **Except for equity transactions we use the same accounts, amounts, and transactions as those of Sierra Corporation presented in Chapters 1 through 4.**

Owner's Equity in a Sole Proprietorship

The ownership claim on total assets is known as **owner's equity**. It is equal to total assets minus total liabilities.

INCREASES IN OWNER'S EQUITY

In a proprietorship, owner's equity is increased by owner's investments and revenues.

Investments by Owner

Investments by owner are the assets the owner puts into the business. These investments increase owner's equity.

Revenues

Revenues are the gross increase in owner's equity resulting from business activities entered into for the purpose of earning income.

DECREASES IN OWNER'S EQUITY

In a proprietorship, owner's equity is decreased by owner's drawings and expenses.

Drawings

An owner may withdraw cash or other assets for personal use. These withdrawals could be recorded as a direct decrease of owner's equity. However, it is generally considered preferable to use a separate classification called **drawings** to determine the total withdrawals for each accounting period. **Drawings decrease owner's equity**.

Expenses

Expenses are the cost of assets consumed or services used in the process of earning revenue. They are **decreases in owner's equity that result from operating the business**.

In summary, owner's equity is increased by an owner's investments and by revenues from business operations. In contrast, owner's equity is decreased by an owner's withdrawals of assets and by expenses. These relationships are shown in Illustration F-2. **Net income** results when revenues exceed expenses. A **net loss** occurs when expenses exceed revenues.

Illustration F-2
Increases and decreases
in owner's equity

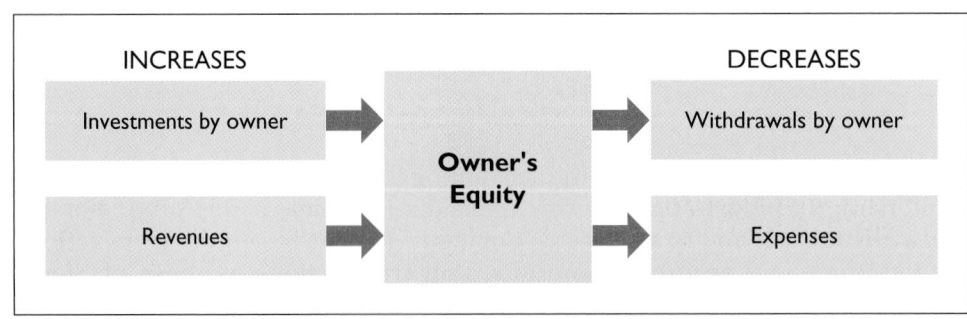

Recording Transactions of a Proprietorship

Chapter 3 described the basic steps employed in the accounting process as follows:

Analyze transactions.
Record transactions in the journal.
Post journal entries to the general ledger.
Prepare a trial balance.

These same steps apply to all forms of business. Illustration 3-2 (page 110) presented the impact of Sierra's transactions on its accounting equation. Illustration F-3 shows how the same transactions would have been recorded for a sole proprietor. The only differences are related to the accounts used to record equity transactions. Those differences are highlighted here in red.

Illustration F-3 Summary of transactions

	Assets				=	Liabilities			+	Owner's Equity	
	Cash	+ Supplies	+ Prepaid Insurance	+ Office Equipment	=	Notes Payable	+ Accounts Payable	+ Unearned Revenue	+	R. Neal, Capital	
(1)	+$10,000				=					+$10,000	Investment by owner
(2)	+5,000					+$5,000					
	15,000				=	5,000			+	10,000	
(3)	−5,000			+$5,000							
	10,000			+ 5,000	=	5,000			+	10,000	
(4)	+1,200							+$1,200			
	11,200			+ 5,000	=	5,000		+ 1,200	+	10,000	
(5)	+10,000									+10,000	Service Revenue
	21,200			+ 5,000	=	5,000		+ 1,200	+	20,000	
(6)	−900									−900	Rent Expense
	20,300			+ 5,000	=	5,000		+ 1,200	+	19,100	
(7)	−600		+$600								
	19,700	+ 600		+ 5,000	=	5,000		+ 1,200	+	19,100	
(8)		+$2,500					+$2,500				
	19,700 +	2,500 +	600	+ 5,000	=	5,000 +	2,500	+ 1,200	+	19,100	
(9)	−500	+								−500	Drawings
	19,200 +	2,500 +	600	+ 5,000	=	5,000 +	2,500	+ 1,200	+	18,600	
(10)	−4,000									−4,000	Salaries Expense
	$15,200 +	$2,500 +	$600	+ $5,000	=	$5,000 +	$2,500	+ $1,200	+	$14,600	

$23,300 $23,300

Financial Statements for a Proprietorship

Chapter 4 described accounting for adjusting entries. A sole proprietor makes the same types of adjustments as a corporation. After recording and posting all of the adjustments, an adjusted trial balance is prepared. Illustrations F-4 and F-5 on the following pages show how the adjusted trial balance is used to prepare a sole proprietor's financial statements.

The primary differences between these statements and those of a corporation (presented in Illustrations 4-23 and 4-24) relate to the way equity is reported. A sole proprietor prepares an **owner's equity statement** rather than a retained earnings statement and uses different titles for the equity items shown on the balance sheet.

STUDY OBJECTIVE
3
Describe the differences between a retained earnings statement and an owner's equity statement.

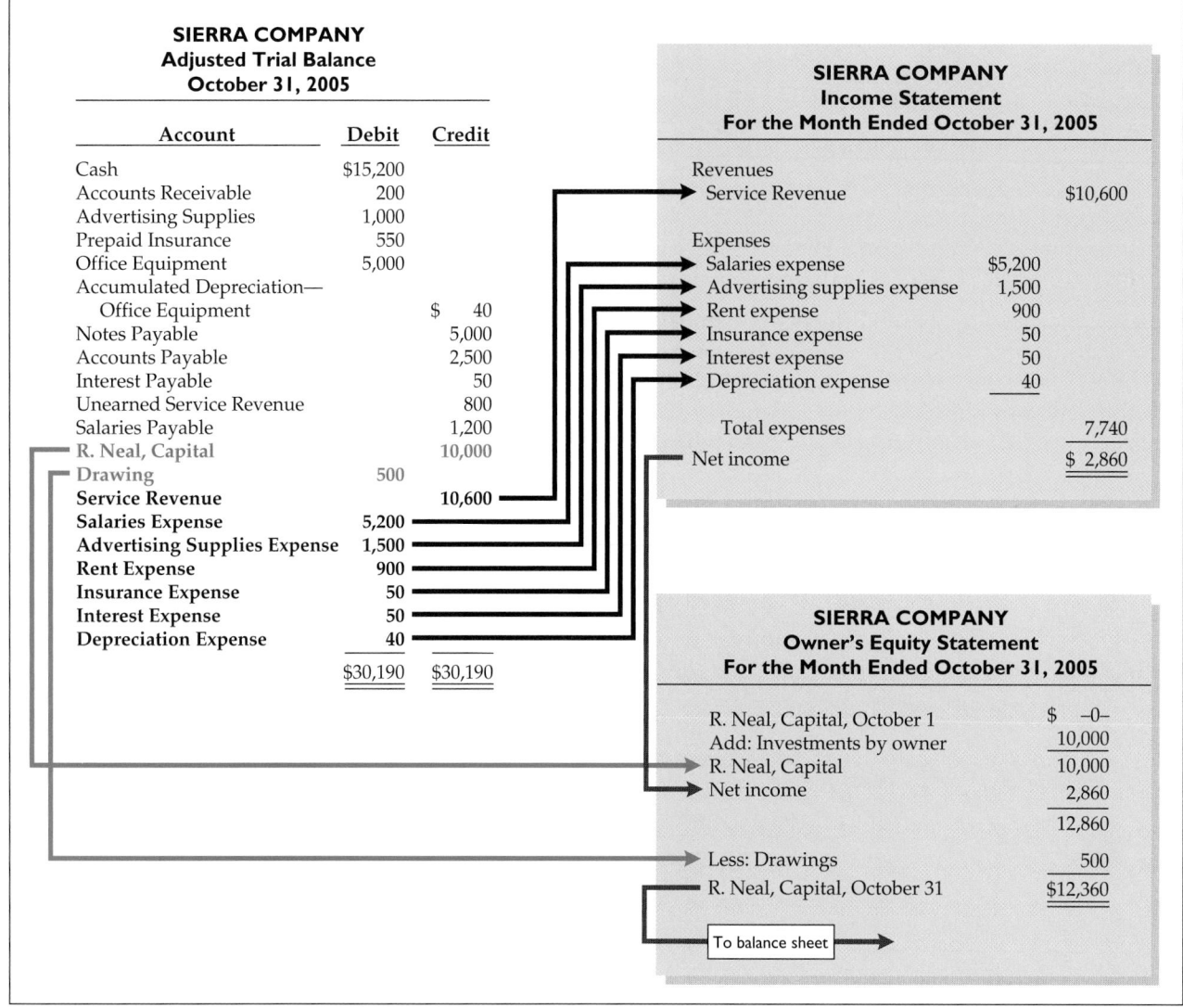

Illustration F-4
Preparation of the income
statement and owner's
equity statement from the
adjusted trial balance

Closing the Books of a Proprietorship

At the end of the accounting period, the temporary account balances are transferred to the permanent owner's equity account, Owner's Capital, through the preparation of closing entries. **Closing entries** for a proprietorship formally recognize in the ledger the transfer of net income (or net loss) and owner's drawing to owner's capital. The results of these entries are shown in the owner's equity statement.

Journalizing and posting closing entries is a required step in the accounting cycle. (See Illustration 4-27 on page 183 for Sierra Corporation.)

In preparing closing entries for a proprietorship, each income statement account could be closed directly to owner's capital. However, to do so would result in excessive detail in the permanent owner's capital account. Instead, the revenue and expense accounts are closed, in the same manner as for a corporation, to another temporary account, **Income Summary**. Only the net income or net loss is transferred from this account to Owner's Capital.

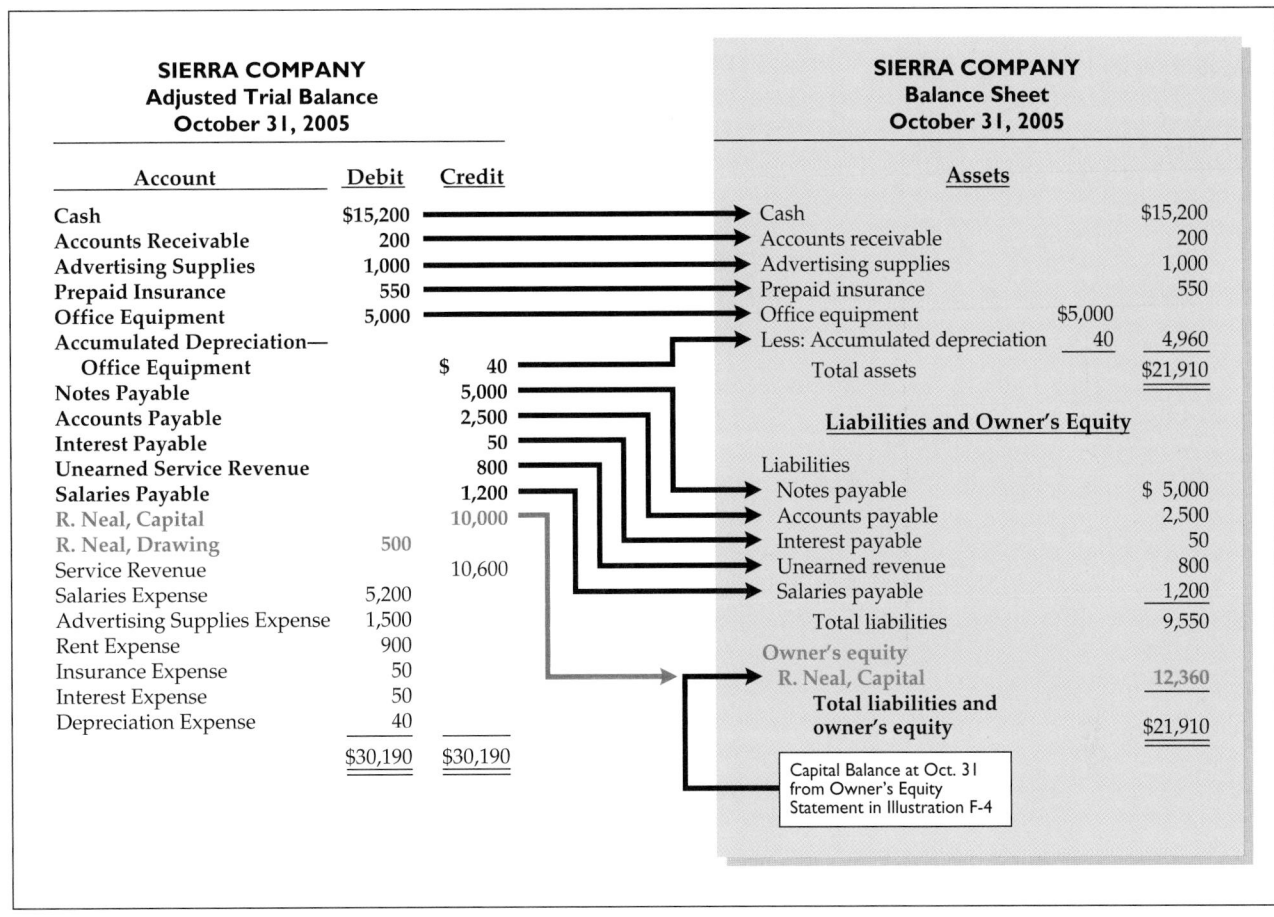

Closing entries for a proprietorship may be prepared directly from the adjusted balances in the ledger, from the income statement and balance sheet columns of the work sheet, or from the income and owner's equity statements. Separate closing entries could be prepared for each nominal account, but the following four entries accomplish the desired result more efficiently:

1. Debit each revenue account for its balance, and credit Income Summary for total revenues.

2. Debit Income Summary for total expenses, and credit each expense account for its balance.

3. Debit Income Summary and credit Owner's Capital for the amount of net income.

4. Debit Owner's Capital for the balance in the Owner's Drawing account, and credit Owner's Drawing for the same amount.

Helpful Hint Owner's Drawing is closed directly to Capital and *not* to Income Summary because Owner's Drawing is not an expense.

The four entries are referenced in the diagram of the closing process shown in Illustration F-6 and in the journal entries in Illustration F-7, both on page F-6. The posting of closing entries is shown in Illustration F-8 (page F-7).

If there were a net loss because expenses exceeded revenues, entry 3 in Illustration F-6 would be reversed: Credit Income Summary and debit Owner's Capital.

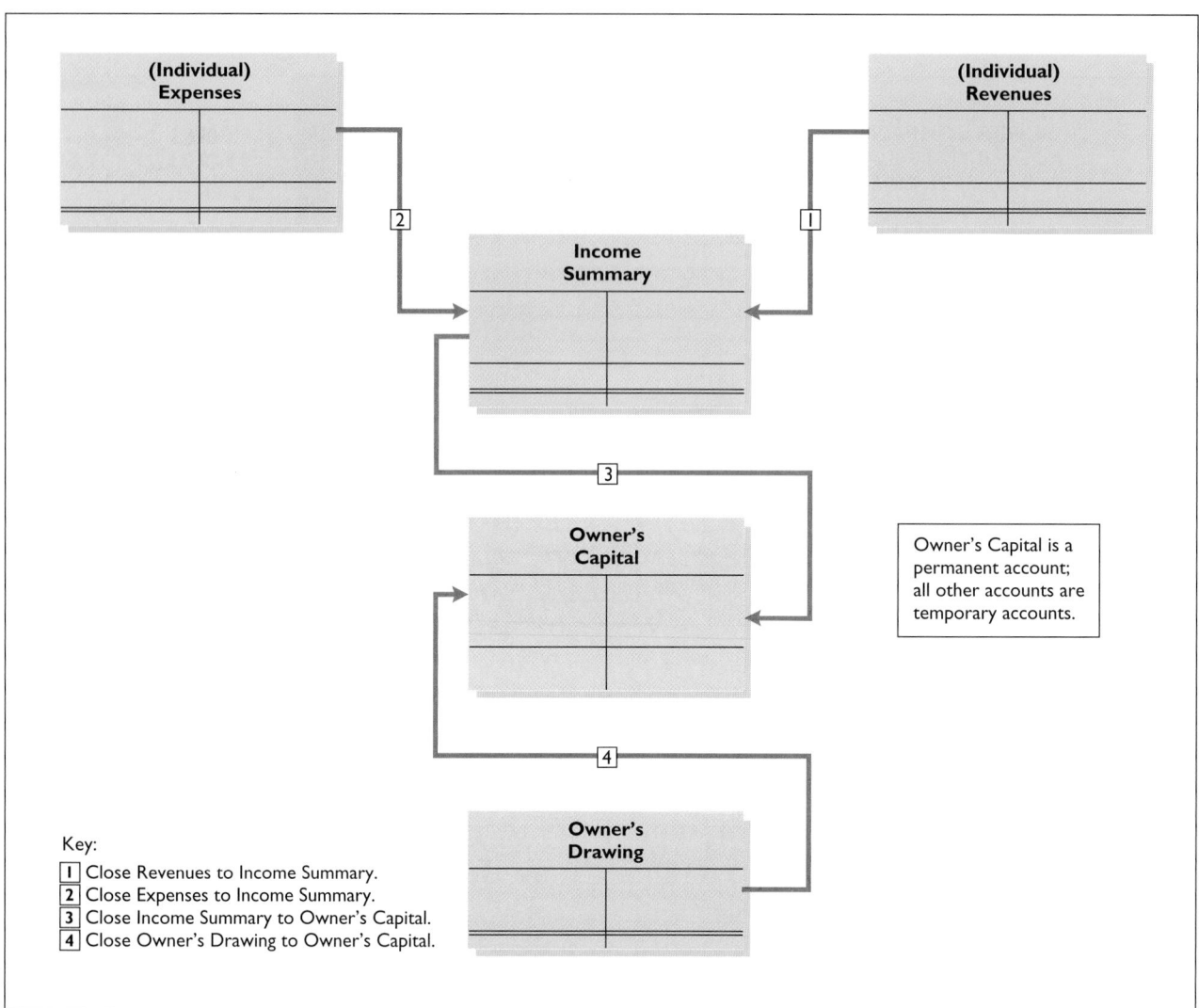

Illustration F-6
Diagram of closing process

Key:
1. Close Revenues to Income Summary.
2. Close Expenses to Income Summary.
3. Close Income Summary to Owner's Capital.
4. Close Owner's Drawing to Owner's Capital.

Owner's Capital is a permanent account; all other accounts are temporary accounts.

Illustration F-7
Closing entries journalized

Helpful Hint Income Summary is a very descriptive title: Total revenues are closed to Income Summary, total expenses are closed to Income Summary, and the balance in the Income Summary is a net income or net loss.

GENERAL JOURNAL

Date		Account Titles and Explanation	Debit	Credit
		Closing Entries		
2005		(1)		
Oct.	31	Service Revenue	10,600	
		Income Summary		10,600
		(To close revenue account)		
		(2)		
	31	Income Summary	7,740	
		Salaries Expense		5,200
		Advertising Supplies Expense		1,500
		Rent Expense		900
		Insurance Expense		50
		Interest Expense		50
		Depreciation Expense		40
		(To close expense accounts)		
		(3)		
	31	Income Summary	2,860	
		R. Neal, Capital		2,860
		(To close net income to owner's capital)		
		(4)		
	31	**R. Neal, Capital**	500	
		R. Neal, Drawing		500
		(To close drawings to owner's capital)		

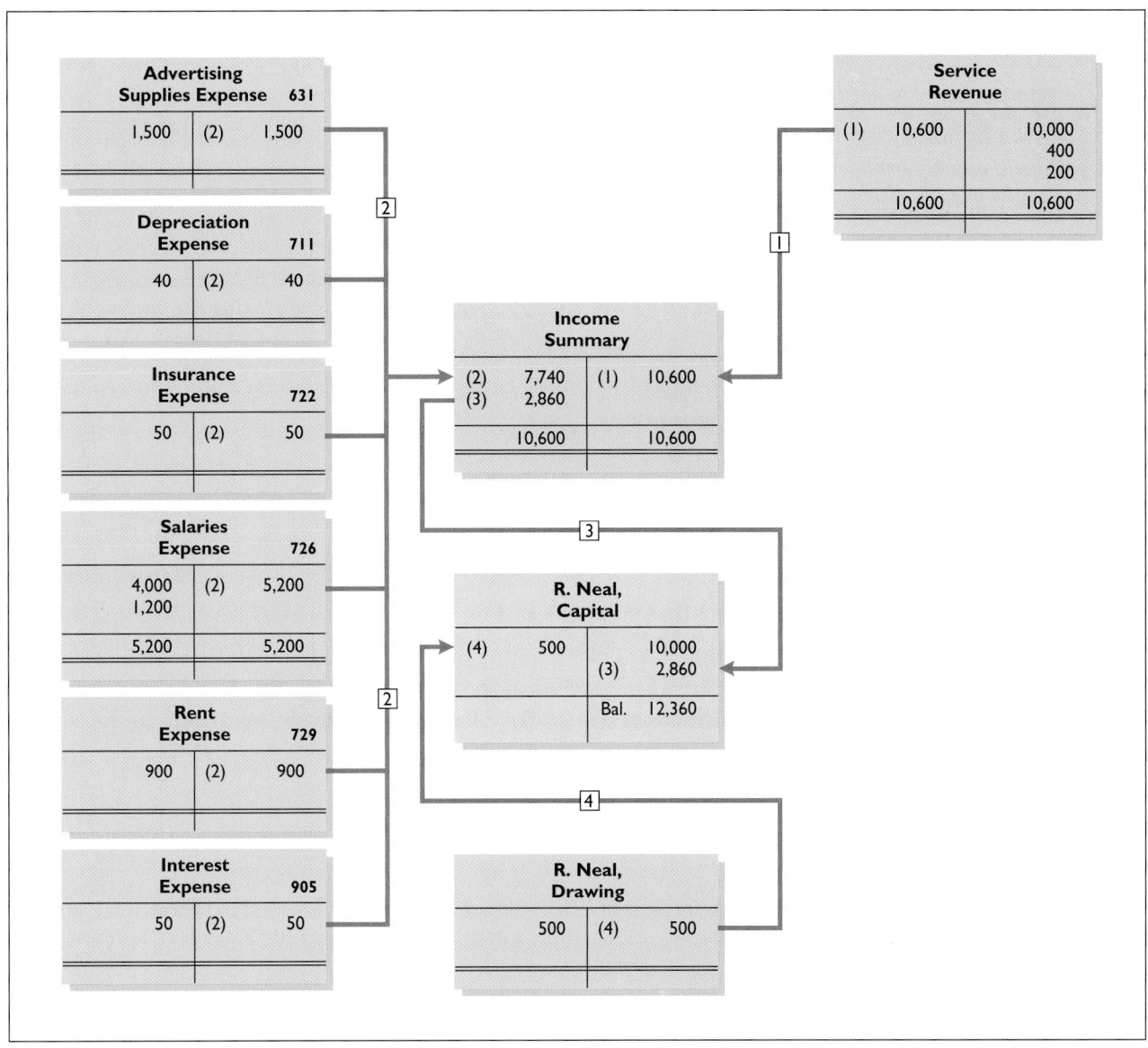

Illustration F-8
Posting of closing entries

Preparing a Post-Closing Trial Balance for a Proprietorship

After all closing entries are journalized and posted, the **post-closing trial balance** is prepared from the ledger. A post-closing trial balance is a list of all permanent accounts and their balances after closing entries are journalized and posted. As with a corporation, **the purpose of a proprietorship post-closing trial balance is to prove the equality of the permanent account balances that are carried forward into the next accounting period.** Since all temporary accounts will have zero balances, **the post-closing trial balance will contain only permanent—balance sheet—accounts.**

Summary of Study Objectives

1 *Identify the differences in equity accounts between a corporation and a sole proprietorship.* A sole proprietorship uses a permanent owner's equity Capital account instead of Common Stock and Retained Earnings. Withdrawals of cash or other assets by the owner for personal use are recorded in a temporary Drawing account.

2 *Understand what account transactions increase and decrease owner's equity.* Investments by the owner and revenue increase owner's equity. Owner's drawings and expenses decrease owner's equity.

3 *Describe the differences between a retained earnings statement and an owner's equity statement.* A sole proprietor prepares an owner's equity state-

ment rather than a retained earnings statement. The owner's equity statement shows the beginning balance in the owner's capital account (instead of retained earnings, as shown in the retained earnings statement), plus any investments made by the owner, less any drawings (in place of dividends, shown in the retained earnings statement).

4 *Explain the process of closing the books for a sole proprietorship.* In closing the books for a sole proprietorship, separate entries are made to close revenues and expenses to Income Summary, Income Summary to Owner's Capital, and Owner's Drawing to Owner's Capital.

Glossary

Drawings Withdrawal of cash or other assets from a sole proprietorship for the personal use of the owner. (p. F-2).

Investments by owner The assets put into the business by a sole proprietor. (p. F-2).

Owner's equity The ownership claim on the total assets of a sole proprietorship. (p. F-2).

Owner's equity statement The financial statement prepared for a sole proprietorship to summarize the changes in owner's equity for a specific period of time. (p. F-3).

Questions

1. What is the basic accounting equation for a sole proprietorship?

2. What are the differences in the equity accounts of a sole proprietorship versus those of a corporation?

3. What items affect owner's equity, and in what direction?

4. In February 2005, Joe Kirby invested an additional $10,000 in his business, Kirby's Pharmacy, which is

organized as a proprietorship. Kirby's accountant, Lance Jones, recorded this receipt as an increase in cash revenues. Is this treatment appropriate? Why or why not?

5. What are the steps in preparing an owner's equity statement?

6. Identify the account(s) debited and credited in each of the required closing entries for a sole proprietorship, assuming the company has net income for the year.

Brief Exercises

Determine effect of transactions on basic accounting equation.
(SO 2)

BEF-1 Presented below are three business transactions. On a sheet of paper, list the letters (a), (b), (c) with columns for assets, liabilities, and owner's equity. For each column, indicate whether the transactions increased (+), decreased (−), or had no effect (NE) on assets, liabilities, and owner's equity.

(a) Invested cash in the business.
(b) Withdrawal of cash by owner.
(c) Received cash from a customer who had previously been billed for services provided.

Determine effect of transactions on owner's equity.
(SO 2)

BEF-2 Presented below are three transactions. Mark each transaction as affecting owner's investment (I), owner's drawing (D), revenue (R), expense (E), or not affecting owner's equity (NOE).

_____ **(a)** Received cash for services performed
_____ **(b)** Paid cash to purchase equipment
_____ **(c)** Paid employee salaries

BEF-3 For each of the following accounts indicate the effects of (a) a debit and (b) a credit on the accounts and (c) the normal balance of the account.

Indicate debit and credit effects and normal balance. (SO 2)

1. Accounts Payable.
2. Advertising Expense.
3. Service Revenue.
4. Accounts Receivable.
5. B. C. Jardine, Capital.
6. B. C. Jardine, Drawing.

Exercises

EF-1 An analysis of the transactions made by Roberta Mendez & Co., a certified public accounting firm, for the month of August is shown below. Each increase and decrease in owner's equity is explained.

Analyze transactions and compute net income. (SO 2)

	Cash	+ Accounts Receivable	+ Supplies	+ Office Equipment	= Accounts Payable	+ Owner's Equity R. Mendez, Capital	
1.	+$12,000					+$12,000	Investment
2.	−2,000			+$5,000	+$3,000		
3.	−750		+$750				
4.	+2,600	+$3,700				+6,300	Service Revenue
5.	−1,500				−1,500		
6.	−2,000					−2,000	Drawings
7.	−650					−650	Rent Expense
8.	+450	−450					
9.	−2,900					−2,900	Salaries Expense
10.					+500	−500	Utilities Expense

Instructions

(a) ▭▶ Describe each transaction that occurred for the month.
(b) Determine how much owner's equity increased for the month.
(c) Compute the amount of net income for the month.

(b) Increase in O.E. $12,250
(c) Net income $2,250

EF-2 Presented below is information related to the sole proprietorship of Mark Garland, attorney.

Prepare an owner's equity statement. (SO 3)

Legal service revenue—2005	$360,000
Total expenses—2005	211,000
Assets, January 1, 2005	85,000
Liabilities, January 1, 2005	62,000
Assets, December 31, 2005	168,000
Liabilities, December 31, 2005	70,000
Drawings—2005	?

Instructions

Prepare the 2005 owner's equity statement for Mark Garland's legal practice.

Capital, Dec. 31 $98,000

EF-3 The adjusted trial balance of Mozart Company at the end of its fiscal year is:

Prepare income statement, owner's equity statement, and balance sheet. (SO 1, 2, 3, 4)

MOZART COMPANY
Adjusted Trial Balance
July 31, 2005

No.	Account Titles	Debits	Credits
101	Cash	$ 14,940	
112	Accounts Receivable	8,780	
157	Equipment	15,900	
167	Accumulated Depreciation		$ 5,400
201	Accounts Payable		4,220
208	Unearned Rent Revenue		1,800
301	W.A. Mozart, Capital		45,200
306	W.A. Mozart, Drawing	14,000	
404	Commission Revenue		65,100
429	Rent Revenue		6,500
711	Depreciation Expense	4,000	
720	Salaries Expense	55,700	
732	Utilities Expense	14,900	
		$128,220	$128,220

Instructions

(a) Net loss $ 3,000
(b) Total assets $34,220

(a) Prepare an income statement and an owner's equity statement for the year. Mozart did not make any capital investments during the year.
(b) Prepare a classified balance sheet at July 31.

Problems

Prepare income statement, owner's equity statement, and balance sheet.
(SO 1, 2, 3, 4)

PF-1 On May 1, Dennis Chambers started Skyline Flying School, a company that provides flying lessons, by investing $45,000 cash in the business. Following are the assets and liabilities of the company on May 31, 2005, and the revenues and expenses for the month of May.

Cash	$ 6,500	Notes Payable	$30,000
Accounts Receivable	7,200	Rent Expense	1,200
Equipment	64,000	Repair Expense	400
Lesson Revenue	8,600	Fuel Expense	2,500
Advertising Expense	500	Insurance Expense	400
		Accounts Payable	800

Dennis Chambers made no additional investment in May, but he withdrew $1,700 in cash for personal use.

Instructions

(a) Net income $ 3,600
Owner's equity $46,900
Total assets $77,700
(b) Net income $ 1,200
Owner's equity $44,500

(a) Prepare an income statement and owner's equity statement for the month of May and a balance sheet at May 31.
(b) Prepare an income statement and owner's equity statement for May assuming that the data above need to be adjusted for the following items: (1) $900 of revenue was earned and billed but not collected at May 31, and (2) $3,300 of fuel expense was incurred but not paid.

Prepare financial statements, closing entries, and post-closing trial balance.
(SO 1, 2, 3, 4)

Peachtree

PF-2 The adjusted trial balance columns of the work sheet for Shmi Skywalker Company is as follows.

SHMI SKYWALKER COMPANY
Adjusted Trial Balance
For the Year Ended December 31, 2005

Account No.	Account Titles	Dr.	Cr.
101	Cash	20,800	
112	Accounts Receivable	15,400	
126	Supplies	2,300	
130	Prepaid Insurance	4,800	
151	Office Equipment	44,000	
152	Accumulated Depreciation—Office Equipment		18,000
200	Notes Payable		20,000
201	Accounts Payable		8,000
212	Salaries Payable		3,000
230	Interest Payable		1,000
301	S. Skywalker, Capital		36,000
306	S. Skywalker, Drawing	12,000	
400	Service Revenue		79,000
610	Advertising Expense	12,000	
631	Supplies Expense	3,700	
711	Depreciation Expense	6,000	
722	Insurance Expense	4,000	
726	Salaries Expense	39,000	
905	Interest Expense	1,000	
	Totals	165,000	165,000

Instructions
(a) Prepare an income statement, owner's equity statement, and a classified balance sheet. $10,000 of the notes payable become due in 2006. S. Skywalker did not make any additional investments in the business during 2005.
(b) Prepare the closing entries.
(c) Post the closing entries. Use the three-column form of account. Income summary is No. 350.
(d) Prepare a post-closing trial balance.

(a) Net income $13,300
Current assets $43,300
Current liabilities $22,000

(d) Post-closing trial
balance $87,300

PF-3 The adjusted trial balance columns of the work sheet for Boss Nass Company, owned by Boss Nass, are as follows.

Prepare financial statements, closing entries, and post-closing trial balance. (SO 1, 2, 3, 4)

BOSS NASS COMPANY
Adjusted Trial Balance
For the Year Ended December 31, 2005

Account No.	Account Titles	Dr.	Cr.
101	Cash	13,600	
112	Accounts Receivable	15,400	
126	Supplies	1,500	
130	Prepaid Insurance	2,800	
151	Office Equipment	34,000	
152	Accumulated Depreciation—Office Equipment		8,000
200	Notes Payable		16,000
201	Accounts Payable		6,000
212	Salaries Payable		3,000
230	Interest Payable		500
301	Boss Nass, Capital		25,000
306	Boss Nass, Drawing	10,000	
400	Service Revenue		88,000
610	Advertising Expense	12,000	
631	Supplies Expense	5,700	
711	Depreciation Expense	4,000	
722	Insurance Expense	5,000	
726	Salaries Expense	42,000	
905	Interest Expense	500	
	Totals	146,500	146,500

Instructions
(a) Prepare an income statement, owner's equity statement, and a classified balance sheet (*Note:* $10,000 of the notes payable become due in 2006.) Boss Nass did not make any additional investments in the business during the year.
(b) Prepare the closing entries. Use J14 for the journal page.
(c) Post the closing entries. Use the three-column form of account. Income Summary is No. 350.
(d) Prepare a post-closing trial balance.

(a) Net income $18,800
Current assets $33,300
Current liabilities $19,500

(d) Post-closing trial
balance $67,300

Accounting for Partnerships

Partnership Form of Organization

The Uniform Partnership Act provides the basic rules for the formation and operation of partnerships in most states in the United States. This act defines a **partnership** as an association of two or more persons to carry on as co-owners of a business for profit. Partnerships are common in retail establishments and in small manufacturing companies. Also, accountants, lawyers, and doctors find it desirable to form partnerships with other professionals in their field. Professional partnerships vary in size from a medical partnership of 3 to 5 doctors, to 150 to 200 partners in a large law firm, to more than 2,000 partners in an international accounting firm.

CHARACTERISTICS OF PARTNERSHIPS

Partnerships are fairly easy to form. They can be formed simply by a verbal agreement or, more formally, by putting in writing the rights and obligations of the partners. Partners who have not put their agreement in writing sometimes have found that the characteristics of partnerships can lead to later difficulties. The principal characteristics of the partnership form of business organization are shown in Illustration G-1 (page G-2) and explained in the following sections.

Association of Individuals

The voluntary association of two or more individuals in a partnership may be based on as simple an act as a handshake. However, it is preferable to state

Illustration G-1
Partnership characteristics

the agreement in writing. Under the Uniform Partnership Act, a partnership is a legal entity for certain purposes. For instance, property (land, buildings, equipment) can be owned in the name of the partnership, and the firm can sue or be sued. **A partnership also is an accounting entity for financial reporting purposes.** Thus, the purely personal assets, liabilities, and transactions of the partners are excluded from the accounting records of the partnership.

The net income of a partnership is not taxed as a separate entity. But, a partnership must file an information tax return showing partnership net income and each partner's share of that net income. Each partner's share is taxable at personal tax rates, regardless of the amount of net income withdrawn from the business during the year.

Mutual Agency

Helpful Hint Because of mutual agency, an individual should be extremely cautious in selecting partners.

Mutual agency means that each partner acts on behalf of the partnership when engaging in partnership business. The act of any partner is binding on all other partners. This is true even when partners act beyond the scope of their authority, so long as the act appears to be appropriate for the partnership. For example, a partner of a grocery store who purchases a delivery truck creates a binding contract in the name of the partnership, even if the partnership agreement denies this authority. On the other hand, if a partner in a law firm purchased a snowmobile for the partnership, such an act would not be binding on the partnership. The purchase is clearly outside the scope of partnership business.

Limited Life

A partnership does not have unlimited life. It may be ended voluntarily at any time through the acceptance of a new partner or the withdrawal of a partner. A partnership may be ended involuntarily by the death or incapacity of a partner. Thus the life of a partnership is indefinite. Partnership dissolution occurs whenever a partner withdraws or a new partner is admitted. Dissolution of a partnership does not necessarily mean that the business ends. If the continuing partners agree, operations can continue without interruption by forming a new partnership.

Unlimited Liability

Each partner is **personally and individually liable** for all partnership liabilities. Creditors' claims attach first to partnership assets. If these are insufficient, the claims then attach to the personal resources of any partner, irrespective of that partner's equity in the partnership. Because each partner is responsible for all the debts of the partnership, each partner is said to have **unlimited liability**.

Co-Ownership of Property

Partnership assets are owned jointly by the partners. If the partnership is dissolved, the assets do not legally revert to the original contributor. Each partner has a claim on total assets equal to the balance in his or her respective capital account. This claim does not attach to specific assets that an individual partner contributed to the firm. Similarly, if a partner invests a building in the partnership valued at $100,000 and the building is later sold at a gain of $20,000, that partner does not personally receive the entire gain.

Partnership net income (or net loss) is also co-owned. **If the partnership contract does not specify to the contrary, all net income or net loss is shared equally by the partners.** As you will see later, though, partners may agree to unequal sharing of net income or net loss.

ORGANIZATIONS WITH PARTNERSHIP CHARACTERISTICS

With surprising speed, states are creating special forms of business organizations that have partnership characteristics. These new organizations are being adopted by many small companies. These special forms are: limited partnerships, limited liability partnerships, limited liability companies, and "S" corporations.

Limited Partnerships

In a limited partnership, one or more partners have **unlimited liability** and one or more partners have **limited liability** for the debts of the firm. Those with unlimited liability are called general partners. Those with limited liability are called limited partners. Limited partners are responsible for the debts of the partnership up to the limit of their investment in the firm. This organization is identified in its name with the words "Limited Partnership," or "Ltd.," or "LP." For the privilege of limited liability, the limited partner usually accepts less compensation than a general partner and exercises less influence in the affairs of the firm.

Limited Liability Partnership

Most states allow professionals such as lawyers, doctors, and accountants to form a limited liability partnership or "LLP." The LLP is designed to protect innocent partners from malpractice or negligence claims resulting from the acts of another partner. LLPs generally carry large insurance policies in case the partnership is guilty of malpractice.

Limited Liability Companies

A new, hybrid form of business organization with certain features like a corporation and others like a limited partnership is the limited liability company, or "LLC" (or "LC"). An LLC usually has a limited life. The owners, called **members**, have limited liability like owners of a corporation. Whereas limited partners do not actively participate in the management of a limited partnership (LP), the members of a limited liability company (LLC) can assume an active management role. For income tax purposes, the IRS usually classifies an LLC as a partnership.

"S" Corporations

An "S" corporation is a corporation that is taxed in the same way that a partnership is taxed. To qualify as an "S" corporation, the company must have 75 or fewer stockholders, all of whom must be citizens or residents of the United States. The advantage of an "S" corporation (also called a Sub-Chapter "S" corporation) is that, like a partnership and unlike a corporation, it does not pay income taxes.

ADVANTAGES AND DISADVANTAGES OF PARTNERSHIPS

Why do people choose partnerships? One major advantage of a partnership is that the **skills and resources of two or more individuals can be combined**. For example, a large public accounting firm such as Ernst & Young must have expertise in auditing, taxation, and management consulting. In addition, a partnership is **easily formed and is relatively free from governmental regulations and restrictions**. A partnership does not have to contend with the "red tape" that a corporation must face. Also, decisions can be made quickly on substantive matters affecting the firm; there is no board of directors that must be consulted.

On the other hand, partnerships also have some major disadvantages: **mutual agency**, **limited life**, and **unlimited liability**. Unlimited liability is particularly troublesome. Many individuals fear they may lose not only their initial investment but also their personal assets, if those assets are needed to pay partnership creditors. As a result, partnerships often find it difficult to obtain large amounts of investment capital. That is one reason why the largest business enterprises in the United States are corporations, not partnerships.

The advantages and disadvantages of the partnership form of business organization are summarized in Illustration G-2.

Illustration G-2
Advantages and
disadvantages of a
partnership

Advantages	Disadvantages
Combining skills and resources of two or more individuals	Mutual agency
Ease of formation	Limited life
Freedom from governmental regulations and restrictions	Unlimited liability
Ease of decision making	

THE PARTNERSHIP AGREEMENT

Ideally, the agreement of two or more individuals to form a partnership should be expressed in writing. This written contract is often called the partnership agreement or **articles of co-partnership**. The partnership agreement contains such basic information as the name and principal location of the firm, the purpose of the business, and date of inception. In addition, relationships among the partners should be specified, such as:

1. Names and capital contributions of partners.
2. Rights and duties of partners.
3. Basis for sharing net income or net loss.
4. Provision for withdrawals of assets.
5. Procedures for submitting disputes to arbitration.
6. Procedures for the withdrawal or addition of a partner.
7. Rights and duties of surviving partners in the event of a partner's death.

We cannot overemphasize the importance of a written contract. The agreement should be drawn with care and should attempt to anticipate all possible situations, contingencies, and disagreements. The help of a lawyer is highly desirable in preparing the agreement.

Basic Partnership Accounting

We now turn to the basic accounting for partnerships. The major accounting issues relate to forming the partnership, dividing income or loss, and preparing financial statements.

FORMING A PARTNERSHIP

Each partner's initial investment in a partnership is entered in the partnership records. These investments should be recorded at the **fair market value of the assets at the date of their transfer to the partnership**. The values assigned must be agreed to by all of the partners.

> **STUDY OBJECTIVE**
> **2**
> Explain the accounting entries for the formation of a partnership.

To illustrate, assume that A. Rolfe and T. Shea combine their proprietorships to start a partnership named U.S. Software. The firm will specialize in developing financial modeling software packages. Rolfe and Shea have the following assets prior to the formation of the partnership.

	Book Value		Market Value	
	A. Rolfe	**T. Shea**	**A. Rolfe**	**T. Shea**
Cash	$ 8,000	$ 9,000	$ 8,000	$ 9,000
Office equipment	5,000		4,000	
Accumulated depreciation	(2,000)			
Accounts receivable		4,000		4,000
Allowance for doubtful accounts		(700)		(1,000)
	$11,000	$12,300	$12,000	$12,000

Illustration G-3 Book and market values of assets invested

The entries to record the investments are:

Investment of A. Rolfe

Cash	8,000	
Office Equipment	4,000	
A. Rolfe, Capital		12,000
(To record investment of Rolfe)		

A	=	L	+	OE
+8,000				+12,000
+4,000				

Cash Flows
+8,000

Investment of T. Shea

Cash	9,000	
Accounts Receivable	4,000	
Allowance for Doubtful Accounts		1,000
T. Shea, Capital		12,000
(To record investment of Shea)		

A	=	L	+	OE
+9,000				+12,000
+4,000				
−1,000				

Cash Flows
+9,000

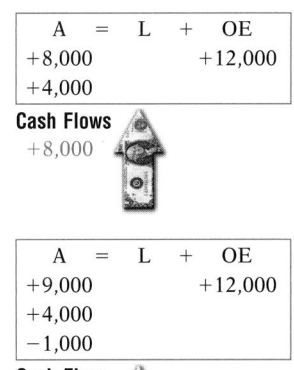

Note that neither the original cost of the office equipment ($5,000) nor its book value ($5,000 − $2,000) is recorded by the partnership. The equipment is recorded at its fair market value, $4,000. Because the equipment has not been used by the partnership, there is no accumulated depreciation.

In contrast, the gross claims on customers ($4,000) are carried forward to the partnership. The allowance for doubtful accounts is adjusted to $1,000 to arrive at a cash (net) realizable value of $3,000. A partnership may start with an allowance for doubtful accounts because it will continue to collect existing accounts receivable, some of which are expected to be uncollectible. In addition, this procedure maintains the control and subsidiary relationship between Accounts Receivable and the accounts receivable subsidiary ledger.

After the partnership has been formed, the accounting for transactions is similar to any other type of business organization. For example, all transactions with outside parties, such as the purchase or sale of merchandise inventory and the payment or receipt of cash, should be recorded the same for a partnership as for a corporation.

The steps in the accounting cycle described in Chapter 4 also apply to a partnership. For example, the partnership prepares a trial balance and journalizes and posts adjusting entries. A work sheet may be used. There are minor differences in journalizing and posting closing entries and in preparing financial statements, as explained in the following sections.

DIVIDING NET INCOME OR NET LOSS

Partnership net income or net loss is shared equally unless the partnership contract indicates otherwise. The same basis of division usually applies to both net income and net loss. It is customary to refer to this basis as the **income ratio**, the **income and loss ratio**, or the **profit and loss (P&L) ratio**. Because of its wide acceptance, we will use the term income ratio to identify the basis for dividing net income and net loss. A partner's share of net income or net loss is recognized in the capital accounts through closing entries.

Closing Entries

Four entries are required in preparing closing entries for a partnership. The entries are:

1. Debit each revenue account for its balance, and credit Income Summary for total revenues.

2. Debit Income Summary for total expenses, and credit each expense account for its balance.

3. Debit Income Summary for its balance, and credit each partner's Capital account for his or her share of net income. Or, credit Income Summary, and debit each partner's Capital account for his or her share of net loss.

4. Debit each partner's Capital account for the balance in that partner's drawing account, and credit each partner's drawing account for the same amount.

The first two entries are the same as in a corporation. The last two entries are different because (1) there are two or more owners' capital and drawing accounts, and (2) it is necessary to divide net income (or net loss) among the partners.

To illustrate the last two closing entries, assume that AB Company has net income of $32,000 for 2005. The partners, L. Arbor and D. Barnett, share net income and net loss equally. Drawings for the year were Arbor $8,000 and Barnett $6,000. The last two closing entries are:

Dec. 31	Income Summary	32,000	
	L. Arbor, Capital ($32,000 × 50%)		16,000
	D. Barnett, Capital ($32,000 × 50%)		16,000
	(To transfer net income to partners' capital accounts)		
31	L. Arbor, Capital	8,000	
	D. Barnett, Capital	6,000	
	L. Arbor, Drawing		8,000
	D. Barnett, Drawing		6,000
	(To close drawing accounts to capital accounts)		

Assume that the beginning capital balance is $47,000 for Arbor and $36,000 for Barnett. The capital and drawing accounts will show the following after posting the closing entries.

L. Arbor, Capital			
12/31 **Clos.** 8,000	1/1 Bal. 47,000		
	12/31 **Clos.** 16,000		
	12/31 Bal. 55,000		

D. Barnett, Capital			
12/31 **Clos.** 6,000	1/1 Bal. 36,000		
	12/31 **Clos.** 16,000		
	12/31 Bal. 46,000		

L. Arbor, Drawing	
12/31 Bal. 8,000	12/31 **Clos.** 8,000

D. Barnett, Drawing	
12/31 Bal. 6,000	12/31 **Clos.** 6,000

The partners' capital accounts are permanent accounts; their drawing accounts are temporary accounts. Normally, the capital accounts will have credit balances and the drawing accounts will have debit balances. Drawing accounts are debited when partners withdraw cash or other assets from the partnership for personal use.

Income Ratios

As noted earlier, the partnership agreement should specify the basis for sharing net income or net loss. The following are typical income ratios.

1. A fixed ratio, expressed as a proportion (6:4), a percentage (70% and 30%), or a fraction (2/3 and 1/3).
2. A ratio based either on capital balances at the beginning of the year or on average capital balances during the year.
3. Salaries to partners and the remainder on a fixed ratio.
4. Interest on partners' capital balances and the remainder on a fixed ratio.
5. Salaries to partners, interest on partners' capital, and the remainder on a fixed ratio.

The objective is to settle on a basis that will equitably reflect the partners' capital investment and service to the partnership.

A fixed ratio is easy to apply, and it may be an equitable basis in some circumstances. Assume, for example, that Hughes and Lane are partners. Each contributes the same amount of capital, but Hughes expects to work full-time in the partnership and Lane expects to work only half-time. Accordingly, the partners agree to a fixed ratio of 2/3 to Hughes and 1/3 to Lane.

A ratio based on capital balances may be appropriate when the funds invested in the partnership are considered the critical factor. Capital ratios may also be equitable when a manager is hired to run the business and the partners do not plan to take an active role in daily operations.

The three remaining ratios (items 3, 4, and 5) give specific recognition to differences among partners. These ratios provide salary allowances for time worked and interest allowances for capital invested. Then, any remaining net income or net loss is allocated on a fixed ratio. Some caution needs to be exercised in working with these types of income ratios. These ratios pertain exclusively to **the computations that are required in dividing net income or net loss** among the partners.

Salaries to partners and interest on partners' capital are not expenses of the partnership. Therefore, these items do not enter into the matching

of expenses with revenues and the determination of net income or net loss. For a partnership, as for other entities, salaries expense pertains to the cost of services performed by employees. Likewise, interest expense relates to the cost of borrowing from creditors. But partners, as owners, are not considered either **employees** or **creditors**. Therefore, when the income ratio includes a salary allowance for partners, some partnership agreements permit the partner to make monthly withdrawals of cash based on their "salary." Such withdrawals are debited to the partner's drawing account.

Salaries, Interest, and Remainder on a Fixed Ratio

Under income ratio (5) in the list above, the provisions for salaries and interest must be applied **before** the remainder is allocated on the specified fixed ratio. **This is true even if the provisions exceed net income. It is also true even if the partnership has suffered a net loss for the year.** Detailed information concerning the division of net income or net loss should be shown below net income on the income statement.

To illustrate this income ratio, assume that Sara King and Ray Lee are co-partners in the Kingslee Company. The partnership agreement provides for: (1) salary allowances of $8,400 to King and $6,000 to Lee, (2) interest allowances of 10% on capital balances at the beginning of the year, and (3) the remainder equally. Capital balances on January 1 were King $28,000, and Lee $24,000. In 2005, partnership net income is $22,000. The division of net income is as follows.

Illustration G-5 Income statement with division of net income

KINGSLEE COMPANY Income Statement (partial) For the Year Ended December 31, 2005			
Sales		$200,000	
Net income		$ 22,000	
Division of Net Income			
	Sara King	Ray Lee	Total
Salary allowance	$ 8,400	$ 6,000	$ 14,400
Interest allowance on partners' capital			
Sara King ($28,000 × 10%)	2,800		
Ray Lee ($24,000 × 10%)		2,400	
Total interest allowance			5,200
Total salaries and interest	11,200	8,400	19,600
Remaining income, $2,400			
($22,000 − $19,600)			
Sara King ($2,400 × 50%)	1,200		
Ray Lee ($2,400 × 50%)		1,200	
Total remainder			2,400
Total division of net income	$12,400	$9,600	$22,000

The entry to record the division of net income is:

A	=	L	+	OE
				−22,000
				+12,400
				+9,600

Cash Flows

no effect

Dec. 31	Income Summary	22,000	
	Sara King, Capital		12,400
	Ray Lee, Capital		9,600
	(To close net income to partners' capital)		

Now let's look at a situation in which the salary and interest allowances exceed net income. Assume that Kingslee Company's net income is only $18,000. In this case, the salary and interest allowances will create a deficiency of $1,600 ($19,600 − $18,000). The computations of the allowances are the same as those in the preceding example. Beginning with total salaries and interest, we complete the division of net income as follows.

	Sara King	Ray Lee	Total
Total salaries and interest	$ 11,200	$ 8,400	$ 19,600
Remaining deficiency ($1,600)			
($18,000 − $19,600)			
Sara King ($1,600 × 50%)	(800)		
Ray Lee ($1,600 × 50%)		(800)	
Total remainder			(1,600)
Total division	**$10,400**	**$7,600**	**$18,000**

Illustration G-6 Division of net income—income deficiency

PARTNERSHIP FINANCIAL STATEMENTS

The financial statements of a partnership are similar to those of a corporation. The income statement for a partnership is identical to the income statement for a corporation except for the additional section that reports the division of net income, as shown earlier.

The owners' equity statement for a partnership is called the **partners' capital statement**. Its function is to explain the changes in each partner's capital account and in total partnership capital during the year. The partners' capital statement for Kingslee Company is shown below. It is based on the division of $22,000 of net income in Illustration G-5. The statement includes assumed data for the additional investment and drawings.

STUDY OBJECTIVE 4

Describe the form and content of partnership financial statements.

KINGSLEE COMPANY Partners' Capital Statement For the Year Ended December 31, 2005			
	Sara King	Ray Lee	Total
Capital, January 1	$ 28,000	$ 24,000	$ 52,000
Add: Additional investment	2,000		2,000
Net income	12,400	9,600	22,000
	42,400	33,600	76,000
Less: Drawings	7,000	5,000	12,000
Capital, December 31	**$35,400**	**$28,600**	**$64,000**

Illustration G-7 Partners' capital statement

Helpful Hint Partners' capital may change due to (1) additional investment, (2) drawings, and (3) net income or net loss.

The partners' capital statement is prepared from the income statement and the partners' capital and drawing accounts.

The balance sheet for a partnership is the same as for a corporation except for the owner's equity section. In a partnership, the capital balances of each partner are shown in the balance sheet. The owners' equity section for Kingslee Company is shown in Illustration G-8 (page G-10).

Illustration G-8 Owners'
equity section of a
partnership balance sheet

KINGSLEE COMPANY Balance Sheet (partial) December 31, 2005		
Total liabilities (assumed amount)		$115,000
Owners' equity		
Sara King, Capital	$35,400	
Ray Lee, Capital	28,600	
Total owners' equity		64,000
Total liabilities and owners' equity		$179,000

Admission and Withdrawal of Partners

We have seen how the basic accounting for a partnership works. Another issue relates to the accounting for the addition or withdrawal of a partner. From an economic standpoint, the admission or withdrawal of a partner is often of minor significance in the continuity of the business. For example, in large public accounting or law firms, partners are added or dropped without any change in operating policies. Because the accounting for the admission or withdrawal of a partner is complex, it is discussed in more advanced accounting courses.

Liquidation of a Partnership

STUDY OBJECTIVE
5

Explain the effects of the entries to record the liquidation of a partnership.

The liquidation of a partnership terminates the business. It involves selling the assets of the firm, paying liabilities, and distributing any remaining assets to the partners. Liquidation may result from the sale of the business by mutual agreement of the partners, from the death of a partner, or from bankruptcy. In contrast to partnership dissolution, **partnership liquidation** ends both the legal and economic life of the entity.

From an accounting standpoint, liquidation should be preceded by completing the accounting cycle for the final operating period. This includes preparing adjusting entries and financial statements. It also involves preparing closing entries and a post-closing trial balance. Thus, only balance sheet accounts should be open as the liquidation process begins.

In liquidation, the sale of noncash assets for cash is called **realization**. Any difference between book value and the cash proceeds is called the **gain or loss on realization**. To liquidate a partnership, it is necessary to:

1. Sell noncash assets for cash and recognize a gain or loss on realization.
2. Allocate gain/loss on realization to the partners based on their income ratios.
3. Pay partnership liabilities in cash.
4. Distribute remaining cash to partners on the basis of their **capital balances**.

Each of the steps must be performed in sequence. Creditors must be paid **before** partners receive any cash distributions. Each step also must be recorded by an accounting entry.

When a partnership is liquidated, all partners may have credit balances in their capital accounts. This situation is called **no capital deficiency**. Or, at least one partner's capital account may have a debit balance. This situation is termed a **capital deficiency**. To illustrate each of these conditions, assume that the Ace Company is liquidated when its ledger shows the assets, liabilities, and owners' equity accounts listed in Illustration G-9.

Assets		Liabilities and Owners' Equity	
Cash	$ 5,000	Notes payable	$15,000
Accounts receivable	15,000	Accounts payable	16,000
Inventory	18,000	R. Arnet, Capital	15,000
Equipment	35,000	P. Carey, Capital	17,800
Accum. depr.—equipment	(8,000)	W. Eaton, Capital	1,200
	$65,000		$65,000

Illustration G-9 Account balances prior to liquidation

NO CAPITAL DEFICIENCY

The partners of Ace Company agree to liquidate the partnership on the following terms: (1) The noncash assets of the partnership will be sold to Jackson Enterprises for $75,000 cash. And (2) the partnership will pay its partnership liabilities. The income ratios of the partners are 3:2:1, respectively. The steps in the liquidation process are as follows.

1. The noncash assets (accounts receivable, inventory, and equipment) are sold for $75,000. The book value of these assets is $60,000 ($15,000 + $18,000 + $35,000 − $8,000). Thus a gain of $15,000 is realized on the sale. The entry is:

(1)

Cash	75,000	
Accumulated Depreciation—Equipment	8,000	
Accounts Receivable		15,000
Inventory		18,000
Equipment		35,000
Gain on Realization		15,000
(To record realization of noncash assets)		

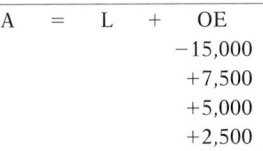

```
   A     =   L   +   OE
+75,000            +15,000
 +8,000
−15,000
−18,000
−35,000
```
Cash Flows
+75,000

2. The gain on realization of $15,000 is allocated to the partners on their income ratios, which are 3:2:1. The entry is:

(2)

Gain on Realization	15,000	
R. Arnet, Capital ($15,000 × 3/6)		7,500
P. Carey, Capital ($15,000 × 2/6)		5,000
W. Eaton, Capital ($15,000 × 1/6)		2,500
(To allocate gain to partners' capital accounts)		

```
 A   =   L   +   OE
            −15,000
             +7,500
             +5,000
             +2,500
```
Cash Flows
no effect

3. Partnership liabilities consist of Notes Payable $15,000 and Accounts Payable $16,000. Creditors are paid in full by a cash payment of $31,000. The entry is:

(3)

Notes Payable	15,000	
Accounts Payable	16,000	
Cash		31,000
(To record payment of partnership liabilities)		

```
   A     =    L    +  OE
−31,000   −15,000
          −16,000
```
Cash Flows
−31,000

4. The remaining cash is distributed to the partners on the basis of **their capital balances**. After the entries in the first three steps are posted, all partnership accounts, including Gain on Realization, will have zero balances except for four accounts: Cash $49,000; R. Arnet, Capital $22,500; P. Carey, Capital $22,800; and W. Eaton, Capital $3,700, as shown in Illustration G-10 (page G-12).

Cash		R. Arnet, Capital	P. Carey, Capital	W. Eaton, Capital
Bal. 5,000	(3) 31,000	Bal. 15,000	Bal. 17,800	Bal. 1,200
(1) 75,000		(2) 7,500	(2) 5,000	(2) 2,500
Bal. 49,000		Bal. 22,500	Bal. 22,800	Bal. 3,700

Illustration G-10
Ledger balances before
distribution of cash

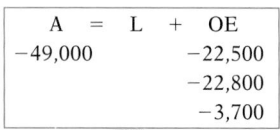

A = L + OE
−49,000   −22,500
             −22,800
             −3,700

Cash Flows

−49,000

Helpful Hint Zero balances
after posting is a quick proof
of the accuracy of the cash
distribution entry.

The entry to record the distribution of cash is as follows.

(4)

R. Arnet, Capital	22,500	
P. Carey, Capital	22,800	
W. Eaton, Capital	3,700	
Cash		49,000
(To record distribution of cash to partners)		

After this entry is posted, all partnership accounts will have zero balances.

A word of caution: **Cash should not be distributed to partners on the basis of their income-sharing ratios.** On this basis, Arnet would receive three-sixths, or $24,500, which would produce an erroneous debit balance of $2,000. The income ratio is the proper basis for allocating net income or loss. **It is not a proper basis for making the final distribution of cash to the partners.**

Schedule of Cash Payments

Some accountants prepare a cash payments schedule to determine the distribution of cash to the partners in the liquidation of a partnership. The **schedule of cash payments** is organized around the basic accounting equation. The schedule for the Ace Company is shown in Illustration G-11. The numbers in parentheses refer to the four required steps in the liquidation of a partnership. They also identify the accounting entries that must be made. The cash payments schedule is especially useful when the liquidation process extends over a period of time.

Illustration G-11
Schedule of cash
payments, no capital
deficiency

ACE COMPANY Schedule of Cash Payments												
Item		Cash	+	Noncash Assets	=	Liabilities	+	R. Arnet Capital	+	P. Carey Capital	+	W. Eaton Capital
Balances before liquidation		5,000	+	60,000	=	31,000	+	15,000	+	17,800	+	1,200
Sales of noncash assets and allocation of gain	(1)&(2)	75,000	+	(60,000)	=			7,500	+	5,000	+	2,500
New balances		80,000	+	–0–	=	31,000	+	22,500	+	22,800	+	3,700
Pay liabilities	(3)	(31,000)			=	(31,000)						
New balances		49,000	+	–0–	=	–0–	+	22,500	+	22,800	+	3,700
Cash distribution to partners	(4)	(49,000)			=			(22,500)	+	(22,800)	+	(3,700)
Final balances		–0–		–0–		–0–		–0–		–0–		–0–

CAPITAL DEFICIENCY

A capital deficiency may be caused by recurring net losses, excessive drawings, or losses from realization suffered during liquidation. To illustrate, assume that Ace Company is on the brink of bankruptcy. The partners decide to liquidate by having a "going-out-of-business" sale. Merchandise is sold at substantial discounts, and the equipment is sold at auction. Cash proceeds from these sales and collections from customers total only $42,000. Thus, the loss from liquidation is $18,000 ($60,000 − $42,000). The steps in the liquidation process are as follows.

1. The entry for the realization of noncash assets is:

(1)

Cash	42,000	
Accumulated Depreciation—Equipment	8,000	
Loss on Realization	18,000	
Accounts Receivable		15,000
Inventory		18,000
Equipment		35,000
(To record realization of noncash assets)		

A = L + OE
+42,000 −18,000
+8,000
−15,000
−18,000
−35,000
Cash Flows
+42,000

2. The loss on realization is allocated to the partners on the basis of their income ratios. The entry is:

(2)

R. Arnet, Capital ($18,000 × 3/6)	9,000	
P. Carey, Capital ($18,000 × 2/6)	6,000	
W. Eaton, Capital ($18,000 × 1/6)	3,000	
Loss on Realization		18,000
(To allocate loss on realization to partners)		

A = L + OE
−9,000
−6,000
−3,000
+18,000
Cash Flows
no effect

3. Partnership liabilities are paid. This entry is the same as in the previous example.

(3)

Notes Payable	15,000	
Accounts Payable	16,000	
Cash		31,000
(To record payment of partnership liabilities)		

A = L + OE
−31,000 −15,000
−16,000
Cash Flows
−31,000

4. After posting the three entries, two accounts will have debit balances—Cash $16,000, and W. Eaton, Capital $1,800. Two accounts will have credit balances—R. Arnet, Capital $6,000, and P. Carey, Capital $11,800. All four accounts are shown below.

Illustration G-12 Ledger balances before distribution of cash

Cash		R. Arnet, Capital		P. Carey, Capital		W. Eaton, Capital	
Bal. 5,000	(3) 31,000	(2) 9,000	Bal. 15,000	(2) 6,000	Bal. 17,800	(2) 3,000	Bal. 1,200
(1) 42,000			Bal. 6,000		Bal. 11,800	Bal. 1,800	
Bal. 16,000							

Eaton has a capital deficiency of $1,800, and thus owes the partnership $1,800. Arnet and Carey have a legally enforceable claim for that amount against Eaton's personal assets. The distribution of cash is still made on the basis of capital balances. But the amount will vary depending on how Eaton's deficiency is settled. Two alternatives are presented below.

Payment of Deficiency

If the partner with the capital deficiency pays the amount owed the partnership, the deficiency is eliminated. To illustrate, assume that Eaton pays $1,800 to the partnership. The entry is:

(a)

Cash	1,800	
W. Eaton, Capital		1,800
(To record payment of capital deficiency by Eaton)		

A = L + OE
+1,800   +1,800

Cash Flows
+1,800

After posting this entry, account balances are as follows.

Cash				R. Arnet, Capital				P. Carey, Capital				W. Eaton, Capital			
Bal. 5,000	(3) 31,000			(2) 9,000	Bal. 15,000			(2) 6,000	Bal. 17,800			(2) 3,000	Bal. 1,200		
(1) 42,000													(a) 1,800		
(a) 1,800					Bal. 6,000				Bal. 11,800						
Bal. 17,800													Bal. –0–		

Illustration G-13 Ledger balances after paying capital deficiency

The cash balance of $17,800 is now equal to the credit balances in the capital accounts (Arnet $6,000 + Carey $11,800). Cash now is distributed on the basis of these balances. The entry is:

A = L + OE
−17,800   −6,000
             −11,800

Cash Flows
−17,800

R. Arnet, Capital	6,000	
P. Carey, Capital	11,800	
Cash		17,800
(To record distribution of cash to the partners)		

After this entry is posted, all accounts will have zero balances.

Nonpayment of Deficiency

If a partner with a capital deficiency is unable to pay the amount owed to the partnership, the partners with credit balances must absorb the loss. The loss is allocated on the basis of the income ratios that exist between the partners with credit balances.

For example, the income ratios of Arnet and Carey are 3:2, or 3/5 and 2/5, respectively. Thus, the following entry would be made to remove Eaton's capital deficiency.

(a)

A = L + OE
      −1,080
      −720
      +1,800

R. Arnet, Capital ($1,800 × 3/5)	1,080	
P. Carey, Capital ($1,800 × 2/5)	720	
W. Eaton, Capital		1,800
(To record write-off of capital deficiency)		

Illustration G-14 Ledger balances after nonpayment of capital deficiency

After posting this entry, the cash and capital accounts will have the following balances.

Cash				R. Arnet, Capital				P. Carey, Capital				W. Eaton, Capital			
Bal. 5,000	(3) 31,000			(2) 9,000	Bal. 15,000			(2) 6,000	Bal. 17,800			(2) 3,000	Bal. 1,200		
(1) 42,000				(a) 1,080				(a) 720					(a) 1,800		
Bal. 16,000					Bal. 4,920				Bal. 11,080				Bal. –0–		

The cash balance of $16,000 now equals the sum of the credit balances in the capital accounts (Arnet $4,920 + Carey $11,080). The entry to record the distribution of cash is:

R. Arnet, Capital	4,920	
P. Carey, Capital	11,080	
Cash		16,000
(To record distribution of cash to the partners)		

A	=	L	+	OE
−16,000				−4,920
				−11,080

Cash Flows
−16,000

After this entry is posted, all accounts will have zero balances.

Summary of Study Objectives

1 *Identify the characteristics of the partnership form of business organization.* The principal characteristics of a partnership are: (a) association of individuals, (b) mutual agency, (c) limited life, (d) unlimited liability, and (e) co-ownership of property.

2 *Explain the accounting entries for the formation of a partnership.* When a partnership is formed, each partner's initial investment should be recorded at the fair market value of the assets at the date of their transfer to the partnership.

3 *Identify the bases for dividing net income or net loss.* Net income or net loss is divided on the basis of the income ratio, which may be (a) a fixed ratio, (b) a ratio based on beginning or average capital balances, (c) salaries to partners and the remainder on a fixed ratio, (d) interest on partners' capital and the remainder on a fixed ratio, and (e) salaries to part-

ners, interest on partners' capital, and the remainder on a fixed ratio.

4 *Describe the form and content of partnership financial statements.* The financial statements of a partnership are similar to those of a corporation. The principal differences are: (a) the division of net income is shown on the income statement, (b) the owners' equity statement is called a partners' capital statement, and (c) each partner's capital is reported on the balance sheet.

5 *Explain the effects of the entries to record the liquidation of a partnership.* When a partnership is liquidated, it is necessary to record the (a) sale of noncash assets, (b) allocation of the gain or loss on realization, (c) payment of partnership liabilities, and (d) distribution of cash to the partners on the basis of their capital balances.

Glossary

Capital deficiency A debit balance in a partner's capital account after allocation of gain or loss. (p. G-10).

General partner A partner who has unlimited liability for the debts of the firm. (p. G-3).

Income ratio The basis for dividing net income and net loss in a partnership. (p. G-6).

Limited liability company A form of business organization, usually classified as a partnership and usually with limited life, in which partners, who are called *members*, have limited liability. (p. G-3).

Limited liability partnership A partnership of professionals in which partners are given limited liability and the public is protected from malpractice by insurance carried by the partnership. (p. G-3).

Limited partner A partner who has limited liability for the debts of the firm. (p. G-3).

Limited partnership A partnership in which one or more general partners have unlimited liability and one or more partners have limited liability for the obligations of the firm. (p. G-3).

No capital deficiency All partners have credit balances after allocation of gain or loss. (p. G-3).

Partners' capital statement The owners' equity statement for a partnership which shows the changes in each partner's capital balance and in total partnership capital during the year. (p. G-9).

Partnership An association of two or more persons to carry on as co-owners of a business for profit. (p. G-1).

Partnership agreement A written contract expressing the voluntary agreement of two or more individuals in a partnership. (p. G-4).

Partnership dissolution A change in partners due to withdrawal or admission, which does not necessarily terminate the business. (p. G-1).

Partnership liquidation An event that ends both the legal and economic life of a partnership. (p. G-10).

"S" corporation Corporation, with 75 or fewer stockholders, that is taxed like a partnership. (p. G-4).

Schedule of cash payments A schedule showing the distribution of cash to the partners in a partnership liquidation. (p. G-12).

Questions

1. The characteristics of a partnership include the following: (a) association of individuals, (b) limited life, and (c) co-ownership of property. Explain each of these terms.

2. Vera Cruz is confused about the partnership characteristics of (a) mutual agency and (b) unlimited liability. Explain these two characteristics for Vera.

3. Swen Varberg and Egor Karlstad are considering a business venture. They ask you to explain the advantages and disadvantages of the partnership form of organization.

4. Ginny Brown and Dorothy Fleming form a partnership. Brown contributes land with a book value of $50,000 and a fair market value of $75,000. Brown also contributes equipment with a book value of $52,000 and a fair market value of $57,000. The partnership assumes a $20,000 mortgage on the land. What should be the balance in Brown's capital account upon formation of the partnership?

5. Roy Orbison, S. Innis, and David Bowie have a partnership called Depeche Mode. A dispute has arisen among the partners. Orbison has invested twice as much in assets as the other two partners, and he believes net income and net losses should be shared in accordance with the capital ratios. The partnership agreement does not specify the division of profits and losses. How will net income and net loss be divided?

6. Leon Redbone and Elvis Costello are discussing how income and losses should be divided in a partnership they plan to form. What factors should be considered in determining the division of net income or net loss?

7. Doreen Shaffer and Quincy Jones have partnership capital balances of $40,000 and $80,000, respectively. The partnership agreement indicates that net income or net loss should be shared equally. If net income for the partnership is $24,000, how should the net income be divided?

8. Robben Ford and Gregg Allman share net income and net loss equally. (a) Which account(s) is (are) debited and credited to record the division of net income between the partners? (b) If Robben Ford withdraws $30,000 in cash for personal use in lieu of salary, which account is debited and which is credited?

9. Partners Reba McEntire and B. Zander are provided salary allowances of $30,000 and $25,000, respectively. They divide the remainder of the partnership income in a ratio of 60:40. If partnership net income is $50,000, how much is allocated to McEntire and Zander?

10. Are the financial statements of a partnership similar to those of a corporation? Discuss.

11. Phil Collins and Herb Alpert are discussing the liquidation of a partnership. Phil maintains that all cash should be distributed to partners on the basis of their income ratios. Is he correct? Explain.

12. In continuing their discussion, Herb says that even in the case of a capital deficiency, all cash should still be distributed on the basis of capital balances. Is Herb correct? Explain.

13. Erin, Cole, and Morgan have income ratios of 5:3:2 and capital balances of $34,000, $31,000, and $28,000, respectively. Noncash assets are sold at a gain. After creditors are paid, $119,000 of cash is available for distribution to the partners. How much cash should be paid to Cole?

14. Before the final distribution of cash, account balances are: Cash $25,000; B. Springsteen, Capital $19,000 (Cr.); L. Hamilton, Capital $12,000 (Cr.); and T. Zaret, Capital $6,000 (Dr.). Zaret is unable to pay any of the capital deficiency. If the income-sharing ratios are 5:3:2, respectively, how much cash should be paid to L. Hamilton?

Brief Exercises

Journalize entries in forming a partnership.
(SO 2)

BEG-1   Britney Spears and Pablo Cruise decide to organize the ALL-Star partnership. Britney Spears invests $15,000 cash, and Cruise contributes $10,000 cash and equipment having a book value of $3,500. Prepare the entry to record Cruise's investment in the partnership, assuming the equipment has a fair market value of $7,000.

Prepare portion of opening balance sheet for partnership.
(SO 2)

BEG-2   H. Tylo and R. Moss decide to merge their proprietorships into a partnership called Tylomoss Company. The balance sheet of Moss Co. shows:

Accounts receivable	$16,000	
Less: Allowance for doubtful accounts	1,200	$14,800
Equipment	20,000	
Less: Accumulated depreciation	8,000	12,000

The partners agree that the net realizable value of the receivables is $12,500 and that the fair market value of the equipment is $10,000. Indicate how the four accounts should appear in the opening balance sheet of the partnership.

BEG-3   Led Zeppelin Co. reports net income of $70,000. The income ratios are Led 60% and Zeppelin 40%. Indicate the division of net income to each partner, and prepare the entry to distribute the net income.

Journalize the division of net income using fixed income ratios.
(SO 3)

BEG-4   MET Co. reports net income of $65,000. Partner salary allowances are Moses $20,000, Evelyn $5,000, and Tom $5,000. Indicate the division of net income to each partner, assuming the income ratio is 50:30:20, respectively.

Compute division of net income with a salary allowance and fixed ratios.
(SO 3)

BEG-5   Bill&Til Co. reports net income of $24,000. Interest allowances are Bill $6,000 and Til $5,000; salary allowances are Bill $15,000 and Til $10,000; the remainder is shared equally. Show the distribution of income on the income statement.

Show division of net income when allowances exceed net income.
(SO 3)

BEG-6   After liquidating noncash assets and paying creditors, account balances in the Missouri Co. are Cash $21,000, A Capital (Cr.) $9,000, R Capital (Cr.) $7,000, and B Capital (Cr.) $5,000. The partners share income equally. Journalize the final distribution of cash to the partners.

Journalize final cash distribution in liquidation.
(SO 5)

Exercises

EG-1   Frank Voris has owned and operated a proprietorship for several years. On January 1, he decides to terminate this business and become a partner in the firm of Payne and Voris. Voris's investment in the partnership consists of $15,000 in cash, and the following assets of the proprietorship: accounts receivable $14,000 less allowance for doubtful accounts of $2,000, and equipment $20,000 less accumulated depreciation of $4,000. It is agreed that the allowance for doubtful accounts should be $3,000 for the partnership. The fair market value of the equipment is $17,500.

Journalize entry for formation of a partnership.
(SO 2)

Instructions
Journalize Voris's admission to the firm of Payne and Voris.

EG-2   B. Manilow and O. Newton have capital balances on January 1 of $50,000 and $40,000, respectively. The partnership income-sharing agreement provides for (1) annual salaries of $20,000 for Manilow and $12,000 for Newton, (2) interest at 10% on beginning capital balances, and (3) remaining income or loss to be shared 70% by Manilow and 30% by Newton.

Prepare schedule showing distribution of net income and closing entry.
(SO 3)

Instructions
(a) Prepare a schedule showing the distribution of net income, assuming net income is
   (1) $55,000 and (2) $30,000.
(b) Journalize the allocation of net income in each of the situations above.

EG-3   In Fleetwood Mac Co., beginning capital balances on January 1, 2005, are Ken Tucki $20,000 and Chris Cross $18,000. During the year, drawings were Tucki $8,000 and Cross $3,000. Net income was $32,000, and the partners share income equally.

Prepare partners' capital statement and partial balance sheet.
(SO 4)

Instructions
(a) Prepare the partners' capital statement for the year.
(b) Prepare the owners' equity section of the balance sheet at December 31, 2005.

EG-4   The Pips Company at December 31 has cash $20,000, noncash assets $100,000, liabilities $55,000, and the following capital balances: Agnes $45,000 and Mildred $20,000. The firm is liquidated, and $120,000 in cash is received for the noncash assets. Agnes and Mildred income ratios are 55% and 45%, respectively.

Prepare cash distribution schedule.
(SO 5)

Instructions
Prepare a cash distribution schedule.

EG-5   Data for The Pips partnership are presented in EG-4.

Journalize transactions in a liquidation.
(SO 5)

Instructions
Prepare the entries to record:
(a) The sale of noncash assets.
(b) The allocation of the gain or loss on liquidation to the partners.
(c) Payment of creditors.
(d) Distribution of cash to the partners.

Journalize transactions with a capital deficiency.
(SO 5)

EG-6 Prior to the distribution of cash to the partners, the accounts in the MEL Company are: Cash $30,000, Maureen Capital (Cr.) $18,000, Ellen Capital (Cr.) $14,000, and Lou Capital (Dr.) $2000. The income ratios are 5:3:2, respectively.

Instructions
(a) Prepare the entry to record (1) Lou's payment of $2,000 in cash to the partnership and (2) the distribution of cash to the partners with credit balances.
(b) Prepare the entry to record (1) the absorption of Lou's capital deficiency by the other partners and (2) the distribution of cash to the partners with credit balances.

Problems

Prepare entries for formation of a partnership and a balance sheet.
(SO 2, 4)

Peachtree

PG-1 The post-closing trial balances of two proprietorships on January 1, 2005, are presented below.

	Mel Company		Gibson Company	
	Dr.	**Cr.**	**Dr.**	**Cr.**
Cash	$ 14,000		$13,000	
Accounts receivable	17,500		26,000	
Allowance for doubtful accounts		$ 3,000		$ 4,400
Merchandise inventory	26,500		18,400	
Equipment	45,000		28,000	
Accumulated depreciation—equipment		24,000		12,000
Notes payable		20,000		15,000
Accounts payable		20,000		31,000
Mel, Capital		36,000		
Gibson, Capital				23,000
	$103,000	$103,000	$85,400	$85,400

Mel and Gibson decide to form a partnership, Mel Gibson Company, with the following agreed upon valuations for noncash assets.

	Mel Company	Gibson Company
Accounts receivable	$17,500	$26,000
Allowance for doubtful accounts	4,500	4,000
Merchandise inventory	30,000	20,000
Equipment	25,000	18,000

All cash will be transferred to the partnership, and the partnership will assume all the liabilities of the two proprietorships. Further, it is agreed that Mel will invest $3,000 in cash, and Gibson will invest $18,000 in cash.

Instructions

(a) Mel, Capital $ 42,000
     Gibson, Capital $ 27,000

(c) Total assets $176,000

(a) Prepare separate journal entries to record the transfer of each proprietorship's assets and liabilities to the partnership.
(b) Journalize the additional cash investment by each partner.
(c) Prepare a balance sheet for the partnership on January 1, 2005.

Journalize divisions of net income and prepare a partners' capital statement.
(SO 3, 4)

PG-2 At the end of its first year of operations on December 31, 2005, MTC Company's accounts show the following.

Partner	Drawings	Capital
Teena Marie	$23,000	$48,000
Robin Tower	14,000	30,000
George Clinton	10,000	25,000

The capital balance represents each partner's initial capital investment. Therefore, net income or net loss for 2005 has not been closed to the partners' capital accounts.

Instructions

(a) Journalize the entry to record the division of net income for the year 2005 under each of the following independent assumptions.

(1) Net income is $28,000. Income is shared 6:3:1.

(2) Net income is $34,000. Marie and Tower are given salary allowances of $18,000 and $10,000, respectively. The remainder is shared equally.

(3) Net income is $22,000. Each partner is allowed interest of 10% on beginning capital balances. Marie is given a $15,000 salary allowance. The remainder is shared equally.

(b) Prepare a schedule showing the division of net income under assumption (3) above.

(c) Prepare a partners' capital statement for the year under assumption (3) above.

(a) (1) Marie $16,800
(2) Marie $20,000
(3) Marie $18,700

(c) Marie $43,700

PG-3 The partners in Wilkowski Company decide to liquidate the firm when the balance sheet shows the following.

Prepare entries with a capital deficiency in liquidation of a partnership.
(SO 5)

Peachtree

WILKOWSKI COMPANY
Balance Sheet
May 31, 2005

Assets		Liabilities and Owners' Equity	
Cash	$ 27,500	Notes payable	$ 13,500
Accounts receivable	25,000	Accounts payable	27,000
Allowance for doubtful accounts	(1,000)	Wages payable	3,800
Merchandise inventory	34,500	S. Wilkowski, Capital	36,000
Equipment	21,000	J. Harkins, Capital	20,000
Accumulated depreciation—equipment	(5,500)	Mick Jagger, Capital	1,200
Total	$101,500	Total	$101,500

The partners share income and loss 5:3:2. During the process of liquidation, the following transactions were completed in the following sequence.

1. A total of $53,000 was received from converting noncash assets into cash.
2. Liabilities were paid in full.
3. Mick Jagger paid his capital deficiency.
4. Cash was paid to the partners with credit balances.

Instructions

(a) Prepare the entries to record the transactions.

(b) Post to the cash and capital accounts.

(c) Assume that Jagger is unable to pay the capital deficiency.

(1) Prepare the entry to allocate Jagger's debit balance to Wilkowski and Harkins.

(2) Prepare the entry to record the final distribution of cash.

PHOTO CREDITS

Chapter 1 Opener: Photo by Andy Washnik with permission from Tootsie Roll Industries, Inc. Page 6: David McNew/Newsmaker/Getty Images News and Sport Services. Page 8: PhotoDisc, Inc./Getty Images. Pages 15, 18, 19, 20, 21, 22: Courtesy Tootsie Roll Industries Inc. Page 23: Hai Wen China Tourism Press/The Image Bank/Getty Images. Pages 26, 27 & 28: Courtesy Hershey Foods Corporation. Pages 45, 46 & 50: Tootsie Roll Industries Inc. Page 47: Courtesy of Nestlé S.A.

Chapter 2 Opener: ©Jeanne Strongin. Page 54: Artville, Inc./Getty Images. Page 55: SUPERSTOCK. Page 59: Courtesy The Coca-Cola Company. Page 60 (top): Reproduced with permission of Yahoo! Inc. ©1999 by Yahoo! Inc. YAHOO! and the YAHOO! logo are trademarks of YAHOO! Inc. Page 60 (center): Corbis Digital Stock. Page 60 (bottom): EyeWire, Inc./Getty Images. Page 61 (top): Jonathan Elderfield/Liaison Agency, Inc./Getty Images. Page 61 (bottom): Courtesy Northwest Airlines, Inc. Page 64 (top): James Schnepf/Liaison Agency, Inc./Getty Images. Page 64 (bottom): 2000 Artville, Inc/Getty Images. Page 66: Andy Caulfield/The Image Bank/Getty Images. Pages 67 & 68: James Schnepf/Liaison Agency, Inc./Getty Images. Page 71: Vladimir Pcholkin/FPG International/Getty Images. Page 72: James Schnepf/Liaison Agency, Inc./Getty Images. Page 75: Courtesy Tweeter Home Entertainment Group. Page 80: Courtesy of Circuit City. Page 187: Courtesy Humana.

Chapter 3 Opener: Chris Bell/Taxi/Getty Images. Page 109: Courtesy Rhino Foods. Page 113: Vera R Storman/Stone/Getty Images. Page 115: AFP/Corbis Images.

Chapter 4 Opener: Gary Buss/Taxi/Getty Images. Page 161: ©AP/Wide World Photos. Page 163: SUPERSTOCK. Page 166: Courtesy PepsiCo, Inc. Page 170: Illustration Works/Getty Images. Page 185: Courtesy Wal-Mart Stores, Inc. Page 186: John Bleck/Lori Nowicki & Associates. Pages 187 & 188: Humana Inc.

Chapter 5 Opener: Digital Vision/Getty Images. Page 222: Courtesy Morrow Snowboards Inc. Page 227: Grant V. Faint/The Image Bank/Getty Images. Pages 229 & 230: Courtesy Wal-Mart Stores, Inc. Page 232: Dennis Galante/Stone/Getty Images. Page 236: Amy Etra/PhotoEdit. Page 238: Bonnie Kamin/ PhotoEdit.

Chapter 6 Opener: VCG/FPG International/Getty Images. Page 268: Jim Bastardo/The Image Bank/Getty Images. Page 269: L.D. Gordon/The Image Bank/Getty Images. Page 278: Bob Krist/Stone/Getty Images. Page 279: PhotoDisc, Inc./Getty Images. Page 280: Jose Luis Pelaez, Inc./Corbis Images. Page 282: Courtesy Caterpillar Inc. Page 284: Courtesy of the Manitowoc Company. Page 307: Courtesy Morrow Snowboards Inc. Page 309 (top): "Fujifilm" is a trademark of Fuji Photo Film Co., Ltd. Page 309 (bottom): Courtesy Eastman Kodak Company.

Chapter 7 Opener: Abrams/Lacagnina/The Image Bank/Getty Images. Page 318: Gianni Dagli Orti/Corbis Images. Page 321: SUPERSTOCK. Page 323: Clint Eley/The Image Bank/Getty Images. Page 326: PhotoDisc, Inc./Getty Images.

Page 327: J.W. Burkey/Stone/Getty Images. Page 332: Courtesy of Rent-A-Wreck of America, Inc. Page 361: PhotoDisc, Inc./Getty Images. Page 362: Oracle is a registered trademark of the Oracle Corporation and/or its affiliates.

Chapter 8 Opener: William Whitehurst/Corbis Stock Market. Page 368: PhotoDisc/Getty Images. Page 369: Dennis Galante/Stone/Getty Images. Page 373: PhotoDisc, Inc./Getty Images. Page 379: Mark Harwood/Stone/Getty Images. Page 380: Patrick Bennett/Stone/Getty Images. Page 381: EyeWire, Inc./Getty Images. Page 382: Courtesy McKesson Corporation. Page 384: Dennis Nett/Syracuse Newspapers/The Image Works. Page 389: Dennis Galante/Stone/Getty Images. Page 407: ®The Scotts Company.

Chapter 9 Opener: Mike Eller/Courtesy Southwest Airlines Co. Page 415: AFP/Corbis Images. Page 418: Etienne de Malgaive/Liaison Agency, Inc./Getty Images. Page 421: John M. Roberts/Corbis Stock Market. Page 425: Courtesy Southwest Airlines. Page 426: Courtesy AirTran Airways, Inc. Page 428: Peter Poulides/Stone/Getty Images. Page 437: David McNew/Getty Images News and Sport Services. Page 439: Courtesy The Coca Cola Company.

Chapter 10 Opener: Courtesy Chrysler Corporation. Page 467: Pamela Hamilton/The Image Bank/Getty Images. Page 470: Dominique Sarraute/The Image Bank/Getty Images. Page 472: Digital Vision/Getty Images. Page 481: AKG Photo, London/Archiv/Photo Researchers. Page 483: Courtesy General Motors Corporation. Page 489: Scott Mills/Alamy Images. Pages 499, 500 & 501: PhotoDisc, Inc. Getty Images.

Chapter 11 Opener: Paul Severn/Allsport/Getty Images News and Sport Services. Page 530: Reuters NewMedia Inc./Corbis Images. Page 531: Darren Robb/Stone/Getty Images. Page 535: Courtesy Nike, Inc. Page 538: Alex Fevzer/Corbis Images. Page 543: Atsushi Tsunoda/Imagina/Alamy Images. Page 545: Frank White/Liaison Agency, Inc./Getty Images. Page 547 (top): Courtesy of Amazon.com, Inc. Page 547 (bottom): Information courtesy of Tektronix, Inc. Page 549 (top): Courtesy Kmart Corporation. Page 549 (bottom): 2003 Sara Lee Corporation.

Chapter 12 Opener: Newline Cinema/Photofest. Page 582: Jonathan Kirn/Stone/Getty Images.

Chapter 13 Opener: Rudi Von Briel/PhotoEdit. Page 620: Darren McCollester/Getty Images News and Sport Services. Page 625: William Whitehurst/Corbis Images. Page 645: PhotoDisc, Inc./Getty Images. Page 646: D. Redfearn/The Image Bank/ Getty Images. Page 649: Index Stock. Page 650: Courtesy Intel. Page 650: Intel Corporation/OR. Page 650: Courtesy Intel. Page 674: Courtesy Elan Corporation.

Chapter 14 Opener: Hugh Burden/Taxi/Getty Images. Page 682: Steven Bronstein/The Image Bank/Getty Images. Page 702: SUPERSTOCK. Page 703: Courtesy JC Penney. Page 712: Courtesy Toys "R" Us. Pages 688, 689, 690, 691, 697: Courtesy Kellogg Company.

Chapter 15   Opener: Artville, Inc./Getty Images. Page 742: Premium Stock/CORBIS. Page 743: Paul A. Souders/Corbis. Page 750: Eric Kamp/Index Stock. Page 752: Andrew Sacks/ Stone/Getty Images. Page 753: Shaun Egan/Stone/Getty Images.

Chapter 16   Opener: PhotoDisc, Inc./Getty Images. Page 781: David Frazier/Stone. Page 785: PhotoDisc, Inc./Getty Images. Page 789: Ed Honowitz/Stone/Getty Images. Page 795: Robert Tinney/Corbis Stock Market. Page 797: Richard Pasley/ Stock, Boston/PNI. Page 816: Information was provided by Parlex Corporation.

Chapter 17   Opener: Foodfolio/Alamy Images. Page 826: John Wilkinson/ Corbis Images. Page 835: James Leynse/Corbis SABA. Page 839: Jennie Oppenheimer/Stock Illustration Source/ Images.com. Page 840: Herrmann/Starke/Corbis Stock Market. Page 863: Courtesy General Microwave.

Chapter 18   Opener: Dave Crosier/Stone/Getty Images. Page 869: Martin Schreiber/Stone/Getty Images. Page 878: Royalty-Free/Corbis Images. Page 880: Cyberimage/Stone/Getty Images. Page 882: Yael/Retna. Page 885: Micheal Simpson/Taxi/ Getty Images.

Chapter 19   Opener: Artville, Inc./Getty Images. Page 909: Gary Conner/Index Stock. Page 913: Peter Zeray/Photonica. Page 916: Ralph Mercer/Stone/Getty Images. Page 924: Mark Wiens/Stone/Getty Images. Page 941: Courtesy Network Computing Devices Inc.

Chapter 20   Opener: EyeWire/Getty Images. Page 959: Artville/Getty Images. Page 962: EyeWire/Getty Images. Page 993: Courtesy Computer Associates.

Chapter 21   Opener: Dick Luria/Taxi/Getty Images. Page 1002: John Syoboda/Foodpix. Page 1007: Michel Tchervkoff/ The Image Bank/Getty Images. Page 1015: Garry Gay/ The Image Bank/Getty Images. Page 1035: Courtesy Glassmaster Company, Lexington, S.C.

Chapter 22   Opener: Royalty-Free/Corbis Images. Page 1043: Ed Eckstein/Corbis Images. Page 1046: William Tautic/ Corbis Stock Market. Page 1054: Tim Jonke/The Image Bank/ Getty Images. Page 1057: Ken Ross/Liaison Agency, Inc./Getty Images.

PLANT ASSETS (Chapter 9)

Computation of Annual Depreciation Expense

Straight-line	$\dfrac{\text{Cost} - \text{Salvage value}}{\text{Useful life (in years)}}$
*Units-of-activity	$\dfrac{\text{Depreciable cost}}{\text{Useful life (in units)}} \times$ Units of activity during year
*Declining-balance	Book value at beginning of year $\times$ Declining balance rate* *Declining-balance rate = 1 ÷ Useful life (in years)

Note: If depreciation is calculated for partial periods, the straight-line and declining-balance methods must be adjusted for the relevant proportion of the year. Multiply the annual depreciation expense by the number of months expired in the year divided by 12 months.

BONDS (Chapter 10)

Premium	Market interest rate < Contractual interest rate
Face Value	Market interest rate = Contractual interest rate
Discount	Market interest rate > Contractual interest rate

Computation of Annual Bond Interest Expense

Interest expense = Interest paid (payable) + Amortization of discount
(OR − Amortization of premium)

*Straight-line amortization	$\dfrac{\text{Bond discount (premium)}}{\text{Number of interest periods}}$
*Effective-interest amortization (preferred method)	Bond interest expense − Bond interest paid $\left(\begin{array}{c}\text{Carrying value of bonds} \\ \text{at beginning of period} \times \\ \text{Effective interest rate}\end{array}\right) - \left(\begin{array}{c}\text{Face amount of bonds} \times \\ \text{Contractual interest rate}\end{array}\right)$

STOCKHOLDERS' EQUITY (Chapter 11)

No-Par Value vs. Par Value Stock Journal Entries

No-Par Value	Par Value

Cash
  Common Stock
	Cash
	  Common Stock (par value)
	  Paid-in Capital in Excess of Par Value

Comparison of Dividend Effects

	Cash	Common Stock	Retained Earnings
Cash dividend	↓	No effect	↓
Stock dividend	No effect	↑	↓
Stock split	No effect	No effect	No effect

INVESTMENTS (Chapter 12)

Comparison of Long-Term Bond Investment and Liability Journal Entries

Event	Investor	Investee

Purchase / issue of bonds	Debt Investments
	  Cash
		Cash
		  Bonds Payable

Interest receipt / payment	Cash
	  Interest Revenue
		Interest Expense
		  Cash

Comparison of Cost and Equity Methods of Accounting for Long-Term Stock Investments

Event	Cost	Equity

Acquisition	Stock Investments
	  Cash
		Stock Investments
		  Cash

Investee reports earnings	No entry	Stock Investments Investment Revenue

Investee pays dividends	Cash
	  Dividend Revenue
		Cash
		  Stock Investments

STATEMENT OF CASH FLOWS (Chapter 13)

Cash flows from operating activities (**indirect method**)

Net income			$X
Add:	Decreases in current assets	$ X	
	Increases in current liabilities	X	
	Amortization and depreciation	X	
	Losses on disposals of assets	X	
Deduct:	Increases in current assets	(X)	
	Decreases in current liabilities	(X)	
	Gains on disposals of assets	(X)	X
Cash provided (used) by operating activities			$X

Cash flows from operating activities (**direct method**)

Cash receipts
  (Examples: from sales of goods and services to customers, from receipts
  of interest and dividends on loans and investments) $ X
Cash payments
  (Examples: to suppliers, for operating expenses, for interest, for taxes)   (X)
Cash provided (used) by operating activities $X

FINANCIAL STATEMENT ANALYSIS (Chapter 14)

Presentation of Irregular Items

Discontinued operations	Income statement (presented separately after "Income before irregular items")
Extraordinary items	Income statement (presented separately after "Discontinued operations")
Changes in accounting principle	Income statement (cumulative effect adjustment presented just above "Net income")

Income Statement and Comprehensive Income

Sales	$XX
Cost of goods sold	XX
Gross profit	XX
Operating expenses	XX
Income from operations	XX
Other revenues (expenses) and gains (losses)	XX
Income before income taxes	XX
Income tax expense	XX
Income before irregular items	XX
Irregular items	XX
Net income	XX
Other comprehensive income items	XX
Comprehensive income	$XX

*Items with asterisk are covered in appendix.

MANAGERIAL ACCOUNTING (Chapter 15)

Characteristics of Managerial Accounting

Primary Users	Internal users
Reports	Internal reports issued as needed
Purpose	Special purpose for a particular user
Content	Pertains to subunits, may be detailed, use of relevant data
Verification	No independent audits

Types of Manufacturing Costs

Direct materials	Raw materials directly associated with finished product
Direct labor	Work of employees directly associated with turning raw materials into finished product
Manufacturing overhead	Costs indirectly associated with manufacture of finished product

JOB ORDER AND PROCESS COSTING (Chapters 16 and 17)

Types of Accounting Systems

Job order	Costs are assigned to each unit or each batch of goods
Process cost	Costs are applied to similar products that are mass-produced in a continuous fashion

Job Order and Process Cost Flow

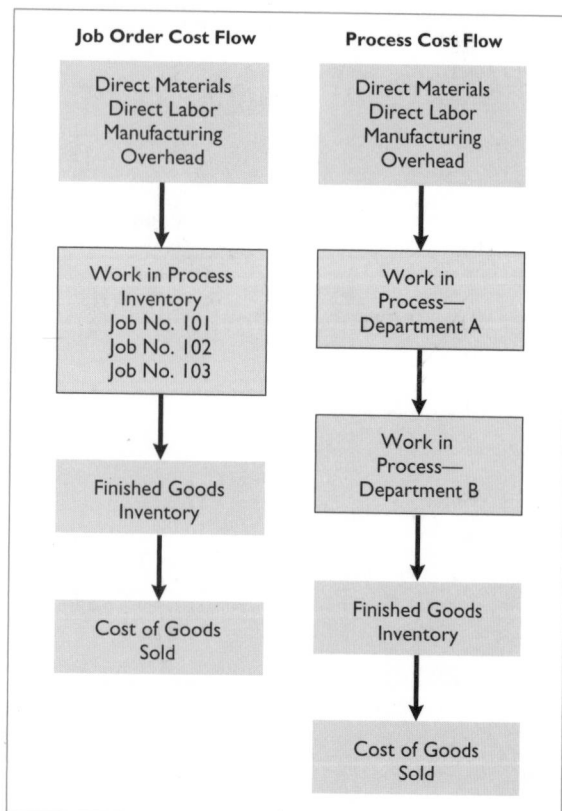

COST-VOLUME-PROFIT (Chapter 18)

Types of Costs

Variable costs	Vary in total directly and proportionately with changes in activity level
Fixed costs	Remain the same in total regardless of change in activity level
Mixed costs	Contain both a fixed and a variable element

CVP Income Statement Format

	Total	Per Unit
Sales	$XX	$XX
Variable costs	XX	XX
Contribution margin	XX	XX
Fixed costs	XX	
Net income	$XX	

Breakeven Point

$$\text{Break-even point in units} = \text{Fixed costs} \div \text{Contribution margin per unit}$$

Target Net Income

$$\text{Required sales in units} = \left(\text{Fixed costs} + \text{Target net income} \right) \div \text{Contribution margin per unit}$$

BUDGETS (Chapter 19)

Components of the Master Budget

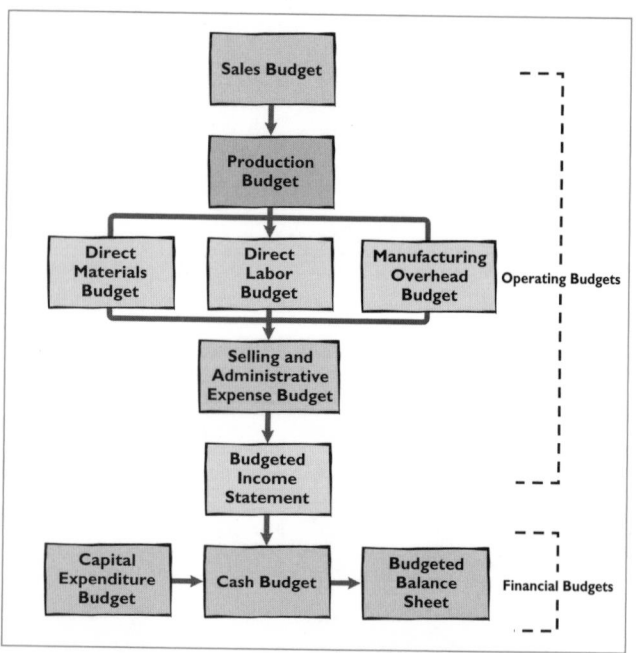